# NEW PRACTICAL DICTIONARY FOR CROSS WORD PUZZLES

# NEW PRACTICAL
# DICTIONARY
## FOR CROSS WORD
## PUZZLES

Compiled by

### FRANK EATON NEWMAN

REVISED, ENLARGED EDITION
MORE THAN 70,000 ANSWERS TO DEFINITIONS

DOUBLEDAY & COMPANY, INC.

Garden City, New York

# FOREWORD

A new, 24-page supplement of up-to-date words has been added to this newly revised edition. It will be found on page 301.

This dictionary is equipped with many of the latest and most suitable words for the cross word puzzle solver.

The listing of words in this revised and enlarged *New Practical Dictionary for Cross Word Puzzles* enables the novice as well as the expert to apply this short-cut method in locating the word desired.

Definitions are listed in light type and answers in bold capital letters.

The purpose of this book, as conceived by the compiler, is not to attempt to explain the meaning of the words included, but to present them in an easy-to-find manner for use in solving the problem.

While the primary aim of the work is to aid the puzzle solver, the fund of facts concerning various subjects and other research information make it a useful addition to any library as a reference book.

The welcome accorded the previous editions of my *Dictionary*, as evidenced by the sale of the book, encouraged me to compile and publish this enlarged work.

To those who have so generously contributed to this book and to the memory of my beloved wife and the devotees of this fascinating and educational pastime, this book is dedicated.

FRANK EATON NEWMAN

# ABBREVIATIONS

abb(r). ..................... abbreviated
Abys. ...................... Abyssinian
Af. ........................... Africa
Afr. ........................... African
A., Am. .................... America
Amer. ...................... American
anc. ......................... ancient
Ang-Sax. ................. Anglo-Saxon
Ar. .......................... Arabia
Arab. ....................... Arabian
arc. ......................... archaic
arch. ...................... architecture
assoc. ..................... associated
Assyr. ...................... Assyrian
astron. ..................... astronomy
Aus. ....................... Austria(n)
Austral. ................. Australia(n)
Babyl. ..................... Babylonia(n)
Ber. ......................... Bermuda
Bib. ......................... Biblical
biol. ........................ biology
bot. ......................... botany
Braz. ....................... Brazilian
Cal. ......................... California
Can. ........................ Canadian
Cen. ........................ Central
char. ...................... character
charac. ................... characteristic
Chin. ....................... Chinese
col. ......................... colloquial
collec. ..................... collective
comb. ...................... combining
comp. ...................... compound
compo. ..................... composition
Const. ..................... Constantinople
deriv. ...................... derivative
dial. ........................ dialect
E., Ea. ..................... east
Eccl. ....................... ecclesiastical
Egypt. ...................... Egyptian
Eng. ........................ England
Ethiop. .................... Ethiopian
Eur. ........................ European
exclam. .................... exclamation
fig. ......................... figuratively
Fr. .......................... France, French
geomet. .................... geometrical
Ger. ........................ Germany
Gr. ......................... Greece, Greek
Hawai. ..................... Hawalian
Heb. ........................ Hebrew
her. ......................... heraldry
Hung. ...................... Hungarian

Ind. ......................... Indian
inflam. ..................... inflammation
inst(r). .................... instrument
isl. .......................... island(s)
It., Ital. .................. Italian
Jap. ......................... Japanese
lang. ....................... language
Lat. ......................... Latin
leg. ......................... legendary
math. ....................... mathematical
meas. ....................... measure
med. ........................ medicinal
Medit. ..................... Mediterranean
memb. ...................... member
Mex. ........................ Mexican
miscel. ..................... miscellaneous
mix. ........................ mixture
Moham. .................... Mohammedan
mon. ........................ monetary
mus. ........................ musical
myth. ...................... mythology
naut. ....................... nautical
N. Z. ....................... New Zealand
N., No. .................... north, number
obs. ......................... obsolete
per(t). ..................... pertaining
penin. ...................... peninsula
peren. ...................... perennial
Peruv. ...................... Peruvian
Phil. I. .................... Philippine Is.
pl. .......................... plural
poet. ....................... poetical
Poly. ....................... Polynesian
prov. ....................... provincial
Rom. ........................ Roman
Rus(s). ..................... Russian
Scand. ..................... Scandinavian
Scot. ....................... Scottish
Script. ..................... Scripture
Shak. ....................... Shakspere
Skr. ......................... Sanskrit
S., So. ..................... south
Sp., Span. ................. Spanish
sub. ........................ substance
Tag. ........................ Tagalog
ter. ......................... territorial
Test. ....................... Testament
Teu(t). .................... Teutonic
trop. ....................... tropical
U. S. ....................... United States
var. ........................ variable, variant
W. .......................... west
zool. ....................... zoological

# A

A, letter ........................... AY
A.F.L. head .................... MEANY
A.R.C. first pres. ............ BARTON
"a faithful friend" .......... ACHATES
aa; Hawaii ..................... LAVA
aard-vark .............. ANTEATER
Aaron's death mount ............ HOR
Aaron's rod ................. MULLEIN
Aaron's son ................... ABIHU
ab; prefix ..................... AWAY
abaca .......................... HEMP
Abaddan ........ SATAN, APOLLYON
abalona; Eng. ................ ORMER,
    ASSEIR, SEA EAR, SNAIL
abandon ........ ABDICATE, WAIVE,
    MAROON
abandoned ................. DERELICT
abatement ...... DECREASE, LETUP,
    MIOSIS
abbe ........................... MONK
abbess; Gr. ................... AMMA
abbot; Celtic ................... COARB
abbot, dignity of an ...... ABBACY
Abbot hero ................. ROLLO
abderite, the ......... DEMOCRITUS
abdicate ............ REMIT, RESIGN,
    RETIRE
abdominal limb ............ PLEOPOD
Abelard's lady love ........... ELOISE
abet .... EGG, FOMENT, INCITE, AID
    HELP, INSTIGATE
abhor ....DETEST, HATE, LOATHE
abhorrence .... AVERSION, ODIUM,
    WLATE
abide ......... DWELL, LIVE, STAY
abies .............. FIRS, CONIFERS
abigail ........................ MAID
Abijah's son ..................... ASA
ability .... CALIBER, CAN, FACULTY
abject person .. MISERABLE, HELOT
abjure ........ RECANT, REPUDIATE
ablution .... BATHING, CLEANSING
Abner char. ..................... LIL
abnormal desire .........ONIOMANIA
abode   HABITAT, INN, RESET, WON
abode of dead; Babyl. ARALU, AARU
abode of dead of hades ...... ORCUS
abode of human beings; myth MIGARD
abode, oriental ................. DAR
abolish   ANNUL, CANCEL, REPEAL
abolitionist; Am. ......... STEVENS
abomination ... PLAGUE, AVERSION
aboriginal ......... NATAL, FIRST
aborigines ...... SAVAGES, NATIVES
abound .... SWARM, FLEET, TEEM,
    SNEE
abounding; suffix ...... FUL, ULANT

about .............. ANENST, CIRCA,
    CONCERNING
above ... OVER, ATOP, ABUNE, OER,
    PAST, ALOFT, HIGHER
above zero ..................... PLUS
abraded ........ SMOOTH, ERASED,
    SCRAPED, RAW, FLAT, LEVEL
Abraham's birthplace ............ UR
Abraham's father ............ TERAH
Abraham's grandfather .... NAHOR
Abraham's nephew .............. LOT
Abraham's son .... MEDAN, SHUAH
Abraham's wife   KETURAH, SARAH
abramis .............. BREAM, CARP
Abram's brother .... HARAN, NAHOR
Abram's wife ................. SARAI
abrasive ........ EMERY, QUARTZ,
    ERODENT, SAND
abraxas ...... CHARM, GEM, STONE
abridge   REWRITE, CURTAIL, LASK,
    RAZEE, DIMINISH
abridgement .... COMPEND, EPITOME
abrogate (see abolish)
abrogating, act of ...... CASSATION,
    RESCISSION
abrupt STEEP, RUDE, HASTY, CURT,
    CRAGGY, BRUSQUE, ICTIC
Absalom's captain of the host . AMASA
Absalom's slayer ................. JOAB
abscond .. FLEE, DECAMP, ELOINE,
    DESERT, ESCAPE, ELOPE
absence of blood poison .. ASEPSIS
absence of hair .......... ACOMIA
absence of taste ............ AGEUSIA
absentee; Austral. ........ CONVICT
absinthe ...................... GENIPI
absolute .. DEAD, VERY, PLENARY,
    UTTER, TOTAL
absolute independence ........ ALOD
absolute superlative . PURE, ELATIVE
absolve .. ACQUIT, REMIT, PARDON
absolved FREED, CLEARED, SHROVE
absorb ENGULF, SUCK, DRINK, SOAK
absorbed ........ RAPT, ENGROSSED
abstain ..... CEASE, DENY, DISUSE,
    SPARE, WAIVE
abstained .... REFRAINED, FORBORE
abstract .... STEAL, ENS, ENTIA,
    EPITOME, BRIEF, COMPEND
abstract (rare) .............. PRECIS
abstruse ...... HIDDEN, ESOTERIC,
    ACROATIC, DEEP, RECONDITE
abundance . EXUBERANCE, GALORE,
    RIFE, PLENTY, UBERTY
abuse .. REVILE, RAIL, SNASH, VAIN
abyss ...... GULF, PIT, DEPTH, POT,
    VORAGO

1

abyss; Babyl. myth .............. APSU
Abyssinia ......... AXUM, ETHIOPIA
Abyssinian banana ........ ENSETE
   " coin ................ TALARI
   " district ...... HARAR, LASTA
   " division ........ SHOA, TIGRE
   " drink .......... BOUSA, MESE
   " emperor .............. NEGUS
   " fly ....................... ZIMB
   " governor .................. RAS
   " herbaceous plant ........ TEFF
   " lake ...... DEMBEA, TZANA
   " language .. AMHARIC, AGOW
   " language of the religion GEEZ
   " oxen .................. GALLA
   " primate .............. ABUNA
   " prince ................... RAS
Abyssinian river MOFER, ABAI, GASH,
                 MAREB
   " tribe .................... AFAR
acacia .... BABUL, LOCUST, ARABIC
academic .... SCHOLASTIC, CLASSIC
acadian, Fr. .. DESCENDANT, CAJUN
acarus; genus .................. MITE
acaudel ........ TAILLESS, ANUROUS
accelerate .. FAVOR, SPEED, HASTEN
accent ...... MARK, ICTUS, STRESS
accenting syllable .... ARSIS, UPBEAT
accept ADMIT, ALLOW, FANG, WILN
accept as equal ...... NOSTRIFICATE
accepted standard . PAR, NORM, TYPE
access ....... ENTREE, ENTRY, FIT
accessory APPURTENANT, ABETTOR
acclaim ...... ECLAT, LAUD, PRAISE
acclamation SHOUT, VOTE, PLAUDIT,
                 CRY
acclivity ...... SLOPE, HILL, TALUS
accolade .... AWARD, HONOR, OSCAR
accomplice .. ABETTOR, PAL, LOUKE,
     ALLY, BUDDY, CHUM, SNILL
accomplish .... DO, ENACT, EFFECT
accord CONCERT, UNITY, UNANIME
according to ....... ALLA, PURSUANT
accouter .... ARRAY, EQUIP, CIRD
account .. TAB, WORTH, SAKE, TAIL,
                TALE
accredit . DEPUTE, ALLOT, APPOINT
accrue .... RESULT, ENSUE, ISSUE
accumulate ........ COLLECT, FUND,
      HOARD, STORE, AMASS
accuse . IMPLEAD, APPEAL, DELATE
accustom TOUGHEN, ENURE, HABIT
accustom to .......... WONT, HABIT
ace ...... ONE, TIB, UNIT, JOT, PIP
ace of clubs; Sp. .............. BASTO
ace-queen comb. ............ TENACE
acerb BITTER, HARSH, SHARP, TART
acetaldehyde .............. ETHANAL
acetic acid .. VINEGAR, ESTER, SOUR
acetone .................... KEYTONE
acetose ...... ACID, SOUR, ACETOUS
acetylene deriv. .... TOLANE, TOLAN
ache .................. PAIN, THROB
achene, one celled ........ UTRICLE
achieve ATTAIN, REALIZE, DO, WIN
Achilles' father .............. PELEUS

Achilles, slayer of ........... PARIS
achiote ........ ANNATTO, ARNATTO
achira ........................ CANNA
achsa ........................ ANKLET
acid . NITRIC, OLEATE, TART, YAR
acid removing ........ EDULCORANT
acidity ............ ACERBITY, ACOR
acids AMIC, AMINO, SELANIC, ULMIC
acknowledge .. OWN, SIGN, THANK,
                 AVOW
acme HEYDAY, CLIMAX, APEX, CAP
acolyte .. HELPER, PATENER, BOY
acomia .................... BALDNESS
acorn ........................ CAMATA
acorn barnacle ...... SCUTA, VALVES
acorn-shaped .............. BALANOID
acorns .............. OVEST, MAST
acoustic bronze vases ........ ECHEA
acquaint .. APPRISE, TELL, POSSESS
acquiesce .. ACCEDE, AGREE, CHIME
acquire .. EARN, LEARN, GET, REAP
acquit ...... EXCULPATE, EXCUSE,
             CLEAR, FREE
acre, ¼ of .............. ROOD, SNOOD
acre, ½ plot; S. Afr. .......... ERVEN
acrid .. SHARP, ARUM, BASK, SOUR
acrimonious . CAUSTIC, ACID, SNELL
Acrisius' daughter .......... DANAE
acroamatic .. ABSTRUSE, ESOTERIC,
                 ORAL
acrobat of India .................. NAT
acrolith ........ CARYATID, STATUE
acropolis .. CADMEA, LARISSA, HILL
across ATHWART, OVER, TRAVERSE
across; prefix ........ TRAN, DIA
act .. DEED, COME, DO, SHIFT, SLIM,
                EMOTE
act fussily; col. .................. PRISS
act of ceremonious leave taking CONGE
act of loyalty .... HOMAGE, FEALTY
act of ruling .................. REGLE
acting by turns ............. ALTERN
action .. BEFOOT, VENUE, AGENCY,
            PRAXIS, DEED
action, field of ...... ARENA, STAGE
action to recover ............ TROVER
active ........ AGILE, BRISK, SPRY
activity .. STIR, ACTION, OPERATION
      MIME, MUM, THESPIAN, SERIO
actor, poor .. BARNSTORMER, HAM
actors in a play ................ CAST
actor's part ...... ROLE, FUNCTION
actress ............ INGENUE, STAR
actual .. VERITABLE, ESSE, POSIT,
                REAL
acuate .......... ROUSE, MOVE, EGG,
     INCITE, INSTIGATE, SHARPEN
acuity .................... EDGE, WIT
acute angle, crossing at .. CHIASMA
ad lib ...... IMPROVISE, OFFHAND
ad patres ...................... DEAD
adage PROVERB, DICT, MAXIM, SAW
Adam and Eve ........ PUTTYROOT
Adam; Norse .................... ASK
"Adam Bede"; author of ....... ELIOT

2

adamant .. HARD, STONY, SOLIDITY
Adam's grandson .............. ENOS
Adam's needle ............... YUCCA
Adam's other wife ........... LILITH
Adam's rib ..................... EVE
Adam's son .... ABEL, CAIN, SETH
add up ............ SUM, TOT, FOOT
adda ................ LIZARD, SKINK
Addams; writer ................ JANE
added to ......... AND, EKED, PLUS
adder; arc .. SNAKE, VIPER, WHORL
addiction ........ HABIT, DISPOSED,
PRONE, WAY, WONT
Addison; Brit. poet ........ JOSEPH
Addison, poet, name of CLIO, ATTICUS
addition .. ADDEND, AUGEND, EKE,
EIK, ELL
ALSO, AND, ELSE, TOO
addition; contract ............ RIDER
addition of sound to end of word .....
PARACOGE
additional stipend to heirs ...... ANN
additions; math. .......... ADDENDS
addled .. ASEA, MUDDLED, PUTRID
address .... GREET, CALL, ACCOST,
TACT, TULK
adduce .. ADVANCE, ASSIGN, CITE,
QUOTE
adequate EQUAL, DUE, ABLE, DIGNE
Adhem, Ben ................... ABOU
adhere, cause to .. GLUE, ACCRETE,
CLING, CLEG
adherent ....... DISCIPLE, VOTARY
adherents .. ISTS, ITES, SEQUELAE
adhibit .. APPLY, AFFIX, ATTACH,
ADMIT
adipose ....... FAT, PURSY, SQUAB
adit .. ENTRANCE, ACCESS, STULM
adjacent CONTIGUOUS, NEGH, ABUT
adjectival ............... ADNOMINAL
adjective ................. ADNOUN
adjourn .. DEFER, PROROGUE, RISE
adjoust; obs. ........ SUGGEST, ADD
adjudge ........ DEEM, AWARD, TRY
adjudicate ........ ACT, TRY, HEAR
adjument; obs. .... SUPPORT, HELP
adjure .... BESEECH, CRAVE, ETHE
adjust TRIM, SQUARE, ATTUNE, FIT
adjutant .... HELPER, STORK, ALLY
admeasure ..................... METE
Admetus' wife ............ ALCESTIS
administer .... HUSBAND, MANAGE
administration .... SWAY REGIMEN
admission .. ACCESS, ADIT, ENTREE
admit ALLOW, PROFESS, RECEIVE,
ADHIBIT
admixture .......... ALLOY, BLEND
admonish .. CHIDE, ADVISE, WARN
ado BUSTLE, FUSS, POTHER, STIR
adobe .......... BRICK, CLAY, SILT
adolescence..NONAGE, YOUTH, LAD
adorn ............ DRESS, GARNISH,
DECORATE, ENRICH, ROUGE
adorn, to ... DIGHT, GRACE, PINK,
TRAP
Adriatic, island in ........ LAGOSTA

adrift ..... DERELICT, LOST, ASEA,
LIGAN
adroit ...... CLEVER, DEFT, NEAT,
HABILE, TIGHT
adroite; Fr. .......... ON, RIGHT, TO
adulterate ...... DEBESE, DEACON,
SOPHISTICATE, DEFILE
adult insect ................... IMAGO
adult pike ..................... LUCE
adust ........... SALLOW, GLOOMY
advance ........ MARCH, NOSE, RISE
advance by degrees ... CREEP, INCH
advantage .... BOTE, SAKE, BUNCE,
START, STEAD, PROFIT, USE
adventitious .... CASUAL, EPISODIC
adventure ..... QUEST, GEST, SEEK
adventuress DEMIREP, GOLDDIGGER
advice ........... AVIS, LORE, REDE
advice, contain ........ MENTORIAL
advise ............ ACQUAINT, TELL
adviser ......... MONITOR, NESTOR
advisory ...... URGING, HORTATIVE
advocate ............ ABETTOR, PRO
PARACLETE, APOLOGIST
advocate of the novel .......... NED
adytum ....... SANCTUARY, SHRINE
Aegean Is., anc. inhab. .... SAMIOTE,
LELEGE
Aegean Sea, arm of ............ SAROS
Aegean Sea, isl. in .. IOS, NIO, SAMOS
Aegeon, wife of ............ AEMILIA
aeger .. SICK, AEGROTAT, EXCUSE
Aegir, wife of ..................... RAN
Aeneas' father ............ ANCHISES
Aneas, follower of ........ ACHATES
Aeneas' great grandson ........ BRUT
Aeneas' wife ................. CREUSA
Aeolian lyric representative SAPPHO
Aeolus' daughter ........ HALCYONE
aeonian ...... ETERNAL, INFINITE
aerial cable car ............ TELPHER
aerolite ................. METEORITE
aeroplane (see 'airplane')
aeropleustic .......... AERONAUTIC
aerose; rare ...... COPPER, BRASSY
aerostat ................... BALLOON
aerugo ......... RUST, VERTEGRIS
Aehter, father of ............ EREBUS
afar .. AWAY, OFF, HAMITE, AT, TO
Afar, one of the ................ SAHO
affected FEIGNED, POSEY, FALLAL
affeeror ............ AMERCER, AMI
afferent ............ BEAR, ESODOIC
affiance BETROTH, PLEDGE, PLIGHT
affiliate ... JOIN, CONNECT, ADOPT
affinity ...... RELATION, RAPPORT
affirm .... ASSERT, AVER, SWEAR,
VOUCH, STATE
affirmation .......... PONENT, VOW
affirmative .... AMEN, OATH, ATEN,
AVERMENT
affirmative reply by opposition LITOTES
affix . PEN, SEAL, STAMP, SUBJOIN
afflatus ................. BREATHING
affliction ... SCOURGE, TRAY, WOE

3

afford GIVE, GRANT, LEND, THOLE  
affray .. MELEE, BATTLE, COMBAT  
affright ........ CONFUSE, ALARM, DAUNT, AGRISE  
affy .. BETROTH, ESPOUSE, TRUST  
Afghan .................... DURANI  
Afghan Ameer ............. SHERE  
Afghan coin ................ ANANIA  
Afghan lang. .... PASHTO, PUSHTO  
Afghan prince ...... AMEER, AMIR  
Afghan stock ............. SEMITIC  
Afghan tribe ................. ULUS  
afloat .... FLOORED, BUOY, ASEA  
aforesaid ............ PRIOR, DITTO, ANTECEDENT  
aforethought ............. PREPENSE, DELIBERATE  
afounde; obs. ................. PERISH  
afraid; obs. ........ ADRAD, WROTHE  
afreet; Arab. myth .. JINNEE, AFRIT  
afret; obs. ................... DEVOUR  
Africa, anc. name ............. LIBYA  
Africa, town in ................. ISA  
African: [also South (S) African]  
   " antelope, BISA, ELAND,  
   " GEMSBOK, KOB, KOODOO,  
   " ORIBI, KUDU, NAGOR, TOPI,  
   " RIETBOK(C)  
   " base (N) ............ TUNTS  
   " bird ............. TURAKOO  
   " boss (S) ................ BASS  
   " bowstring hemp ........ IFE  
   " burrowing animal (S)  
       SURICATE  
   " bustard; (S) ........ PAAUW  
   " cape ..................... RAS  
   " capital ............... DAKAR  
   " carnivore (S) ........ RATEL, SERVAL  
   " cat fish ................ SHAL  
   " charm .............. GRIGRI  
   " chief's residence ...... TATA  
   " civet .............. NANDINE  
   " city ........... ORAN, TUNIS  
   " coin ......... PESA, TOQUE  
   " colonist; (S) .......... BOER  
   " colony .... ALGERIA, KENYA  
   " cony .. DAS, DAMAN, DASSY  
   " corn, ear of; (S) .... MEALIE  
   " council; (S) .......... RAAD  
   " desert ...... SAHARA, ERG  
   " dialect; (S) ............ TAAL  
   " district ............ RUANDA  
   " drink .............. OMEIRES  
   " family ...... BANTU, TSHI  
   " fetish .................. JUJU  
African fly .......... KIVU, TSETSE  
   " fox; obs. .......... FENNEC  
   " fox; (S) .... ASSE, CAAMA  
   " French colony .... ALGERIA  
   " garment ............ KAROSS  
   " gazelle ................. ARIEL  
   " general in Boer war .. BOTHA  
   " giant; Gr. ........ ANTAEUS  
   " giraffe-like animal .... OKAPI  
   " gold bearing ridge .... RAND  
   " grass .............. ESPARTO  
   " grassy country; (S) .. VELD  

   " gulf ................. GUINEA  
   " harp .................. NANGA  
   " headland ................ RAS  
   " hill; (S) .................. KOP  
   " hornbill ................ TOCK  
   " horse disease ........ SURRA  
   " hunt .................... SAFARI  
   " hut .................... KRAAL  
   " jackal ................... DIEB  
   " king ................. NUMIDIA  
   " lake .................. NYASSA  
   " language .... TAAL, BANTU  
   " monkey .. MONA, COLOBUS, GRIVET  
   " mountain pass; (S) ...... NEK  
   " mount. range .......... ATLAS  
   " native ..... ASHA, ASHANTI, DAMARA, FULA (H)  
   " native; (S) .... ZULU, BOER  
   " negro ............. TIBU, JUR  
   " ostrich ................. RHEA  
   " palm trees; genus .. RAPHIA  
   " peasant ................. KOPI  
   " pigmy .... HOTTENTOT, ITA  
   " plant; (S) ............... IXIA  
   " plateau; (S) KAROO, NIARE  
   " protected camp; (S) ... BOMA, LAAGER  
   " protectorate ...... ZANZIBAR  
   " race .................. SOMALI  
   " rawhide strap; (S) .... RIEM  
   " region ................ SUDAN  
   " religious sect ...... ABELITE  
   " residence .............. TATA  
   " river CONGO, BENIN, GABUM  
   " river; (S) .. SENEGAL, VAAL  
   " rug ................. KAROSS  
   " soldier ...... ASKARI, SPAHI  
   " sorcery ..................... OBI  
   " stockade; (S) BOMA, KRAAL  
   " stork; (S) .................. FE  
   " Topi ................. TIANG  
   " town .......... ELAT, STAD  
   " tree ...... ARTAR, BAOBAB, BITO, SHEA  
   " tree; genus ........... OLAX  
   " tree; (S) .... COLA, ASSAGAI  
   " tribe .......... BONI, BANTU  
   " valley; (S) .. DAAL, LAAGTE, WADI  
   " village; (S) .. STAD, KRAAL  
   " wheat .. IMPHEE, SORGHUM  
   " wild sheep .......... AOUDAD  
   " wild wolf .............. AARD  
   " wood ................. TEAK  
   " worm .................... LOA  
Afrikaans ................... TAAL  
aft ................. ABAFT, ASTERN  
after the style of ............... ALA  
aftermath ...... ARRISH, EAGRASS, EDDISH, ROWEN  
afterpiece .......... EPODE, EXODE  
afterthought ........... REGRET, RUE  
afterward ............ LATER, THEN  
Agag, slayer of ............. SAMUEL  
again . ANEW, EFT, ENCORE, MORE  
against ... ANTI, VERSUS, CON, GAIN  
Aga's son ....................... ALI  

4

agalite .......................... TALC
agallochum .... AGAL, AGAR, ALOE
agama ............. LIZARD, GUANA
Agamemnon's brother ... MENELAUS
    "    daughter .... IPHIGENIA,
                     ELECTRA
    "    father ........... ATREUS
    "    son ............ ORESTES
    "    wife ... CLYTEMNESTRA
agar-agar, found in ........ GELOSE
agaric ....... TOUCHWOOD, FUNGUS
agate .... MARBLE, ONYX, QUARTZ,
                      RUBY
agave AGAUE, AMOLE, ALOE, DATIL
agave fiber ...... ISTLE, PITA, SISAL
age RIPEN, AEON, EON, ERA, YEARS
" , abb., Lat. ................... AET
" , an .......... DAY, TIME, OLAM
" , at the same ............. COEVAL
" of moon on June first ..... EPACT
" , old .................... SENESCE
" , parentage ...... ELD, PARAGE
" , per. to an ........ ERAL, EVAL
" , per. to old .... GERATIC, SENILE
" , of reptiles ............ MONTANA
aged ... OLDEN, NESTORIAN, ANILE
agency .. HAND, MEANS, OPA, TASS
Agency; headed by Johnson ...... ESA
agendum .......... LITURGY, RITUAL
Agenor's daughter ........... EUROPA
Agenor's father ............. ANTENOR
agent .. DOER, GENE, IST, PROCTOR,
    SPY, ENVOY, FACTOR, SCALPER
agent native, employed by foreign firm
                COMPRADOR
Aggeus ....................... HAGGAI
agglomerate .... MASS, SLAG, LUMP,
                  HEAP
aggrandize ........ ADVANCE, EXALT
aggravate .. ENHANCE, NAG, TWIT
aggregate fruit of strawberry ETAERIO
agialid ........................... BITO
agile LISH, LISSOME, SPRINGE, SPRY
agitate ALARM, CHURN, SEEK, STIR,
       WEY, FRET, ROUSE
aglet .. LACE, SPANGLE, STUD, TAG
agnail ....... HANGNAIL, WHITLOW
agnate .. AKIN, COGNATE, KINDRED
agnomen .... EPITHET, NICKNAME,
       SURNAME, ALAS, NAME
agnus .................. DEL, LAMB
ago ...... ERST, GONE, PAST, SENS
agog .......... EAGER, EXPECTANT,
               WONDER
agonic; arc. .................... AGO
agonize .. RACK, STRAIN, TORTURE
agony GRIPE, PAIN, PANIC, THROE
agouti .............. PACA, RODENT
agree ...... CONCUR, GRANT, JIBE,
             MATCH, TALLY
agree to .. CHIME, PLACEBO, TOADY
agreeable ........ DULCET, SUAVE,
       AMENE, CONSONANT, LIEF
agreement TREATY, CARTEL, MISE,
    ACCORD, DEAL, FIT, PACT,
            UNISON, TAIL
agrestic .......... RURAL, RUSTIC

agricultural overseer ..... AGRONOME
Agrippina's son ................ NERO
agua ............................. TOAD
aguacate; Sp. .............. AVOCADA
Ahab's daughter .......... ATHALIE
Ahab's wife ................. JEZEBEL
Aherne, T.V. star ............. BRIAN
Ahira, father of ............... ENAN
Ahiram, angel of; var. ........... DIV
ai ............................... SLOTH
aid ............ ABET, HELP, SUCCOR
Aida, lover of .............. RADAMES
Aida's rival .............. AMNERIS
aide .... SUBALTERN, ASSISTANT
aiglet .......... POINT, AGLET, TAG
aim .. INTENT, BUTT, GOAL, SCOPE,
              END, POINT
Aintab coin ..................... IKLIK
air .......... MIEN, TUNE, ASPECT,
              BEARING
air-base; U.S. ..... GUAM, IDLEWILD
Airdefense Comm. .......... CHIDLAW
air, comb. form for ........ AER, AERI
air-tight . HERMETICAL, EREMETIC
" component ................. ARGON
" dry ........................ SCOTCH
" , foul ...................... SEPTON
" gauge .............. AEROMETER
" , in the open ........ ALFRESCO
" navigation officer .... AVIGATOR
" , per. to the ............... AURAL
" port; part of .............. APRON
" race marker ............ PYLON
" route bet. Montana and Moscow
              ALSIB
" , spirit of the ............. ARIEL
" vesicle in algae ...... AEROCYST
" warm ...................... OAM
airman, non-flying ............. KIWI
airplane .. HELICOPTER, AIRCRAFT,
              PLANE
airplane car ................. GONDOLA
airplane, bombing .. STORK, AVION,
              TAUB
" cockpit .............. CABIN
" , device .............. RADAR
" , part ............. LONGERON
" tail part .... EMPENNAGE
" throttle ............... GUN
" type .. BOMBER, FIGHTER
" , type of .... GIRO, GLIDER,
              SPAD
" wing support .... CABANE
" wing tip .......... AILERON
airport; Eng. ............. AERODROME
air-raid shelter ................ ABRI
airs, given to lofty .. PRISSY, NICE,
           PRECISE, PRIM
airvesicle in algae ...... AEROCYST
airy ...... AERIAL, JAUNTY, GAY
aisle ........ NAVE, ALLEY, LANE
ait ........ EYOT, HOLM, ISLET
Ajax the Less, father of .. TELAMON
ajenjo; Sp. ................ ABSINTH
ajutage ........................ TUBE
akin AGNATE, AIM, GERMANE, SIB
Akmolinsk, Sib. capital of ...... OMSK

Alabama, city in..ANNISTON, SELMA
Alabama county ............. LAMAR
alamandite .................. GARNET
alameda ...... PROMENADE, WALK
alamo .......... MISSION, POPLAR
alan, or aland .................. DOG
alange ... DREARY, DISMAL, DULL
alantin ...................... INULIN
alar . WINGED, PTERIC, AXILLARY
alarm .... TOCSIN, DISMAY, FEAR,
PANIC
alas .... OHONE, OIME, HEU, OCH
alas; Gr. ................... OTOTOTOI
alas; Lat. ...................... VAE
Alaska, capital of .......... JUNEAU
Alaska, former cap. of ........ SITKA
Alaskan city .. NOME, ANCHORAGE
Alaskan, Ind. liquor .... HOOCHINOO
Alaskan outer garment ...... PARKA
Albania, bronze coin of .. QUINTAR
Albania, capital of .......... TIRANA
Albanian dialect ............... TOSK
Albanian king ................... ZOG
Albanian river . ARTA, DRIN, MATIA
Albanian seaport ........ SCUTARI
albatross, the sooty ........ NELLY
Albeniz, composer .......... ISAAC
albite, variety of ......PERICLINE
albuminoid substance ... ALEURONE
Alcinous' daughter ..... NAUSICAA
Alcinous, famous gardens of SCHERIA
alcohol, contained in . VINIC, ETHYL,
AMYL,
alcohol, crystalline ........ TALITOL
alcohol from idose ......... IDITE
alcohol from orange blossom . NEROL
alcohol anon. .......... DIPSOMANIA
alcoholic beverage ... MEAD, NEGUS
alcoholic content, increase in NEEDLE
alcoholic sugar ............. TROSSE
alcoid bird ..................... AUK
alcove .......... BAY, NOOK, ORIEL
aldehyde deriv. ............. ACETAL
alder, yellow ............ SAGEROSE
ale, a kind of FLIP, PURL, ALEGAR,
MUM
alee, opposed to ............ STOSS
alembic ...... CUP, RETORT, STILL,
VESSEL
Alencon product .................LACE
Aleppo, modern name ...... BEREA
alert, mentally .... PEART, AWARE
Aleut ...................... UNUNGUN
Aleutian isle .......... ATTU, ATKA
alewife ...... WALLEYE, HERRING
Alex. Hamilton's birthday .... NEVIS
Alexander the Great, country won by .
PARTHIA
Alexandria; patriarch ......... PAPA
Alexandrian theologian ...... ARIUS
alfalfa .......... LUCERNE, GRASS
alfresco .................... OUTSIDE
alga ............... DEMID, DIATOM
algae; genus ...... ALARIA, DASYA
algaroba ..................... CAROB
Algeria, Roman name for .. POMARIA
Algerian ruler ............ BEY, DEY

Algerian ½ bushel ............ TARRI
Algerian seaport ...... BONA, ORAN
Algerian soldier .. SEPOY, SPAHEE,
SPAHI
Algerian tirailleur ............ TURCO
Algerian weight .............. ROTL
algesis ................ ACHE, PAIN
Algonquin Ind. .... OTTAWA, ALGIC
Ali Baba's brother .......... CASSIM
alias .... EPITHET, (PEN) NAME,
OTHER, TITLE, ELSE
alidade ..................... DIOPTER
alien .......... FOREIGN, REMOTE,
ADVERSE, METIC, PERIGRENE
alien raider .............. INVADER
alien resident; Heb. ............ GER
alienate ...... DEMISE, ESTRANGE,
WEAN
alike; comb. form ............... ISO
alike in stupidity ...... UNASINOUS
aliment .. FOOD, PABLUM, MANNA
alined .............. AROW, JOINED
alkali .... SALTWORT, SODA, LYE,
SALT
alkaline ............. LIME, OXIDE
alkaloid ........ ARABINE, ARICIN,
CICUTIN, SOLANINE, EMETINE,
ESERINE
alkaloid, an amorphous .... DITAMIN
alkaloid, crys. .. CODEINE, KAIRINE
alkaloid, mustard seed .... SINAPIN
alkaloid poison ............ CURARE
alkaloid, poison hemlock ...... CONIN
all ...... EVERY, TOTAL, WHOLE
all, comb. form ................. PAN
all; mus. ...................... TUTTI
all, prefix ...................... OMNI
allan ........................... GULL
allanite ...................... ORTHITE
allasch; Rus. ...........KUMMEL
Allatu; Babyl. myth .......... ARALU
allay .... ALEGGE, COOL, AGATE,
EASE
alleged force .... OU, OD, ODYLE, OG
allegory ...... PARABLE, EMBLEM
Allen, Mr. ................... ETHAN
allergy IMMUNITY, SENSITIVENESS
alleviate .............. ALLAY, EASE
alley ............ LANE, BLIND, MIG
allied .. KINDRED, AGNATE, AKIN,
SIMILAR, KIN, COGNATE
alligator CAYMAN, NIGER, JACARE,
YACARE
alligator, kind of LAGARTO, LIZARD
alligator pear AGUACATE, AVOCADO
allocating ...... METING, SHARE
allot ......... CAVEL, CAST, METE
allowance .... LEAVE, ARRAS, SIZE,
TARE, TRET
allowed ...... ENDURE, LET, LOW
allowing that ........ IF, PROVIDED
alloy .......... ASEM, KONEL, LAY
" , black metal .......... NIELLO
" , Chinese ............ PAKTONG
" , copper and zinc ...... BRASS,
TOMBAC
" in cheap jewelry ..... OROIDE
" , iron and carbon ....... STEEL

6

" like German silver ...... ALBATA
" nickel and steel .......... INVAR
" , pewter-like ................ BIDRI
" rich in zinc .......... TUTENAG
" , tin and copper ...... PEWTER
" , tin and lead PEWTER, TERNE
" used to line tea chests; Fr. CALIN
alloyed ............ SPURIOUS, BASE
all-seed herb; genus ........ RADIOLA
allure ...... BAIT, SEDUCE, DECOY
alluring .... ALLICIENT, CHARMING
allusion INSTANCE, INKLING, HINT
allusive METAPHORICAL, PUNNING
alluvial clay ................ ADOBE
alluvial deposit .. MUD, SILT, PLACER
alluvial fan .................. DELTA
alluvial matter ................ GEEST
ally .. LEAGUE, UNION, PAL, JOIN
allylene .................... PROPINE
almain .......... GERMAN, DANCE
almandine ................. SPINEL
almond .................. AMYGDALA
almond flavored liquor .... RATAFIA
almond furnace ............... ALMAN
almond, Malay ............ KANARI
almond oil; Fr. ............... AMARIN
almond; Persia ............. BADAM
alms .... HANDOUT, CORBAN, DOLE,
CHARITY, PASSADE
alms chest ...... RELIQUARY, ARCA
alms distributor ............ ALMONER
alnus ........................ ALDER
aloe; Am. ...... AGAVE, TAMBAC
alone .. SOLO, SINGLE, SOLITARY
alone, stage direction ........ SOLUS
aloof .... ABACK, ADRIGH, FROSTY
alpaca ................ (L)LAMA, PACO
alpaca-like ...... GUANACO, VICENA
Alpha ...... CHIEF, DENEB, FIRST
alphabet ........ CROSSROW, PRIMER
" character .. OGAM, OGHAM,
RUNE
" Kashmir .......... SARADA
" teacher of .. ABECEDARIAN
Alpine dress ................ DIRNDL
Alpine dwelling .............. CHALET
Alpine herdsman ................ SENN
Alpine primrose .......... AURICULA
Alpine wild goat .. STEINBOK, IBEX
Alpine wind .................. FOEHN
Alps, highest peak of ........ BLANC
Alps; Ital. .............. DOLOMITES
Alps pass .... CENIS, COL, SIMPLON
Alps peak .................. BERNINA
alsike ...................... CLOVER
also .... AND, EKE, TOO, BESIDES
altar ................ ARA, CHANCEL
altar carpet ............... PEDALE
altar cloth .... DOSSAL, HAPLOMA,
PALLA
altar offerings ............ ALTERAGE
altar, part of an .. APSE, PREDELLA
altar rail .................... SEPTUM
altar, rel. to an .... PISCINA, PYX
altar screen .............. REREDOS
altar shelf ...... GRADIN, RETABLE
altar, top of .... MENSA, FRONTAL

alter ........ VARY, MUTATE, WEND
alter ego ............. FRIEND, SELF
alterant .... REMEDY, AID, HELP
alternate ...... ELSE, OTHER, VARY
althorn ............ ATTO, SAXHORN
although ........ EEN, EVEN, THAT
altiloquence ...... BOMBAST, LOFTY
altitude barometer ...... OROMETER
aluminous pyroxene ........ AUGITE
aluminum comp. ........ WAVELLITE,
THERMITE
aluminum hydroxide ...... BAUXITE
aluminum pistachio color .. EPIDOTE
alveary ............ BEEHIVE, HIVE
alveolate .. HONEYCOMBED, PITTED
alveus ................ CHANNEL, BED
always AY, AYE, EER, EVER, SIMLE
Aly's father ...................... AGA
ama ................. VESSEL, AMULA
amalgamate BLEND, MERGE, UNITE,
COMBINE
amalgamating pan .............. TINA
amanuensis .............. SCRIVENER
amaryllis, kind of MISTRESS, AGAVE
amass .............. GATHER, HEAP
amateur DABBLER, TYRO, NOVICE,
DILETTANTE
amateur, non ....... PRO, SKILLED
amative AMOROUS, EROTIC, LOVING
amatory .......... EROTIC, LOVING
amaze STAGGER, STUN, ASTONISH
Amazon estuary ................ PARA
Amazon rise .................. ANDES
Amazon river, named by ORELLAWA
ambages ........ DEVIOUS, SPEECH
ambassador .... ENVOY, MINISTER,
AGENT, DIPLOMAT, LEGATE
ambassador, lady ...... LUCE, MESTA
amber ...... YELLOW, ELECTRUM
ambergris .............. PERFUMERY
ambiguity .. PARADOX, OBSCURITY
ambitious .......... ASPIRE, ETTLE,
EMULOUS
ambry .. CUPBOARD, CLOSET, DA,
PANTRY
ambulate . MOVE, WALK, GAD, HIKE
ambush ..... BUSSE, TRAP, SHOMA,
COVER
"Amelia," char. in Fielding's BATH
ameliorate ...... BETTER, REFORM,
EMEND
amend ............ BETTER, BEETE
amends, make .. EXPIATE, REDRESS,
ATONE
ament ...... CATTAIL, CATKIN, JUL
amerce ...... TREAT, FINE, MULCT
America, myth, discoverer of VOTAN
America, reputed discov. of .... ERIC
American: [also South (S) Amer.]
" archbishop ........ RIORDAN
" (S) arid ground .... ESPINAL
" author ...... ADAMIC, ASCH
" authoress .............. FERN
" balsam ................ TOLU
" bird; (see 'birds')
" blight ................ APHIS
" cartoonist .............. NAST

7

" century plant .......... ALOE
" chemist ................ UREY
" China root .... GREENBRIAR
" columbo ............. GENTIAN
" composer ............. NEVIN
" deal ................... PINE
" desolate region; (S) .. PUNA
" divine ............. RANDALL
" dye; (S) ............... LANA
" edible tuber; (S) .......... OCA
" educator .............. KERR
" elders ............. SAMBUCUS
" elk ..................... WAPITI
" elm ................... ULMUS
" engineer ............... EADS
" finch .................. JUNCO
" fir; genus .... ABIES, PICEA
" flea; (S) ... CHIGOE, CHIGRE
" guinea pig ............. PACA
" herdsman; (S) .... LLANERO
" humming bird; (S) WARRIOR
" humorist .. ADE, COBB, NYE
" Indian (see also 'Indian, Am.')
" Indian, of the .. AMERINDIC
" Indian of the pampas; (S) ....
                            PAMPERO
" inventor of colored photog. ...
                            IVES
" jurist (1824-8) ...... COOLEY
" jute .............. MALLOW
" lawyer and senator ..... FRYE
" linguist stock; (S) ...... ONA
" lion ........ COUGAR, PUMA
" mammal; (S) ........ GRISON
" mezereon .. LEATHERWOOD
" monkey; (S) .. TEETEE, TITI
" Montaigne ...... EMERSON
" naturalist .... BAIRD, SETON
" nature writer ........ BEEBE
" nightshade ..... POKEWEED,
                            SOLANUM
" nutmeg .......... CALABASH
" painter .. SARGENT, HOMER,
                    RYDER, SLOANE
" palm; (S) ................ ITA
" party, (1653) abb. ........ KNS
" patriot .... REVERE, ALLEN,
                    HALE, OTIS
" philanthropist ...... BARTON
" physician ............. MINOT
" pioneer .............. BOONE
" plain; (S) .......... PAMPAS
" plant cutter; genus .........
                            PHYTOTOMA
" plants; (see 'plants and
            shrubs')
" poet ...... LANIER, TOWNE,
        AGEE, BENET, AIKEN
" portrait painter ...... PEALE
" powerful feline animal ........
                            JAGUAR
" quadruped .......... BADGER
" raccoon; (S) .......... COATI
" Red Cross organizer BARTON
" river; (S) ....... INCA, SINU
American rodent; (S) .......... PACA
" rodent, largest; (S) CAPYBARA

" ruminant; (S) ...... LLAMA
" serpent; (S) ........ ABOMA
" socialist ................ DEBS
" Socrates ........ FRANKLIN
" staghorn ............. SUMAC
" stake driver ...... BITTERN
" stock .................... YUMA
" suffrage leader ........ CATT
" tick; (S) .......... CARAPATO
" tiger ................ JAGUAR
" toad; (S) .............. AGUA
" toad; genus ............ BUFO
" treeless plain; (S) .. LLANO
" trumpeter; (S) ...... AGAMI
" ungulate; (S) .......... TAPIR
" vine .................. GUACO
" weapon; (S) .......... BOLAS
" weasel-like animal .. TAIRA,
                            TAYR
" wild cat; (S) .......... EYRA
" wind; (S) ........ PAMPERO
" wood sorrel; (S) ........ OCA
" writer of fables .......... ADE
" yew .............. HEMLOCK
Amerind .... UTE, CREE, REDSKIN
Amerind symbol .............. XAT
Amerindian OKI, CHEROKEE, SQUAW
Ametu, wife of ............. ACESTIS
amice ........ CAPE, HOOD, EPHOD
Amici's microscope .... ENGYSCOPE
amide, an ................. ANILIDE
amidic .......................... AMIC
amidine ................... STARCH
Amina, mother of .......... TERESA
amino acid ................... LEUCINE
aminobenzene ................. ANILIN
ammonia comp. .. DIAMINE, AMIDE,
                            AMINE
ammoniac plant .............. OSHAC
ammunition holder ............ TRAY
amoeba, an ........ PROTEUS, OLM
amole ............ AGAVE, NAHUATL
among .. AMID(ST), IN, MID, IMELLE
Amon's wife .................... MUT
amor ...... LOVER, EROS, AMOROSO
amorc, one of ....... ROSICRUCIAN
amorous .... LOVING, EROTIC, JOLLY
amorphous .. CHAOTIC, FORMLESS
amount on which rates are assessed
                            RATAL
ampersand .............. AND, ALSO
amphibia; genus ................ RANA
amphibian .... ANURA, FROG, OLM,
        TOAD, CAUDATE, AIRPLANE
amphibian, immature ...... TADPOLE
amphibole .................. EDENITE
amphibole, dark green ...... URALITE
amphitheatre ........ ARENA, CAVEA
amphora ................ URN, VASE
ample ...... ENOUGH, PROLIX, FULL
amplify .... DILATE, EXTEND, PAD
amt; Sp. .......................... TIA
amula ............................ AMA
amulet CHARM, PERIAPT, TALISMAN
amusing . DIVERTING, METICULOUS,
            DROLL, FARCICAL, RISIBLE
amygdala ........ ALMOND, TONSIL

8

Amy's sisters ..... MEG, BETH, JO
an octave; mus. ............ EIGHTH
ana ........ MEMORABILIA, EVENTS
anaconda ................ ABOMA, BOA
Anacreon's birthplace .......... TEOS
anaesthetic GAS, SEDATIVE, OPIATE
anagram .............. REBUS, GAME
analgesic .......... CODEINE, OPIUM
analogy .. SIMILARITY, AGREEMENT
analyze .. DISSECT, DECOMPOUND,
                         ASSAY, PARSE
Anam tribes ................... MOIS
Anamese boat .............. GAYYOU
Anamese weight ................... TA
Ananias's wife ............ SAPPHIRA
anaqua ...................... ANAMA
anarchist .... NIHILIST, TERRORIST,
                                   RED
anarchy . DISORDER, LICENSE, RIOT
anathematize .......... CURSE, BAN
Anatolian goddess ................ MA
anatomy . SKELETON, STRUCTURE,
                                  BODY
anatomy of animals ..... ZOOTOMY
Anaximander's first principle ........
                              APEIRONA
ancestor ELDER, APETUS, FORBEAR,
                  FAMILY, STOCK, SIRE
ancestor, remote ... ATAVUS, ATAVIC
ancestral .... AVAL, AVITAL, LARES
ancestry .... LINEAL, ATHEL, RACE
anchor .... KEDGE, KILLICK, MOOR
anchor, bill of ..................... PEE
anchor, lift ........................ CAT
anchor-lifting appar. ....... CAPSTAN
anchor, part of .......... PALM, ARM
anchor ring ............ TORE, TOROID
anchor, small .............. GRAPNEL
anchor, timber ............ GROUSER
anchorage .. MOORAGE, ROADSTEAD
anchoret ........ ASCETIC, EREMITE
anchorite ........... MONK, STYLITE
anchovy .............. ALICE, SPRAT
ancient ELD, OLD, AGED, PRIMEVAL,
                           GRANDEVAL
anc. Celtic divinity ..............ESUS
" country ...................... ELIS
" country, per. to ............. EOLIC
" dance; var. ............... CORANT
" dog ................. AURORA, EOS
" Greek weight ................. OBOL
" Irish frock .................. INAR
" sword ...................... ESTOC
" tribe; Bib. ................... ICENI
and ............. AMPERSAND, ALSO
and; Fr. .................... ET. ETAL
and not .............. NOR, NEITHER
and so forth ............ (ETC) ETERA
Andalusia, province in .......... JAEN
Andean deer .................. PUDU
Andean tableland .. PARAMOS, PUNA
Andean tribe ................... ANTI
Anderson, Eddie ........ ROCHESTER
Anderson; singer .......... MARIAN
andiron ......... FIREDOG, HESSIAN
andrenid .......................... BEE
android ...................... ROBOT

anecdotage ............. SENILE, ANA
anemic ................... LOW, WAN
anele .............. ANOINT, SHRIVE
anent ........ ABOUT, WITH, ON, RE
anesthetic ............ ETHYLIDENE
angel .. EGREGOR, CHERUB, DULIA,
                                 SERAPH
angel, apostate ................ EBLIS
angel in "Paradise Lost" ...... URIEL
angel of death .. SAMUEL, AZRAEL,
                                 DANITE
angel of the planet Jupiter . ZADKIEL
angel of music; Koran ...... ISRAFIL
angel, Spanish for ............ SERAF
Angel; T.V. star .......... HEATHER
angel who ruled the air .... RUCHIEL
Angeli; actress ................... PIER
angels .... SAINTS, SERAPHIM, (PL)
anger BILE, RILE, FUME, IRE, TEEN,
                            TIFF, RAGE
angle .... RAVELIN, ANCON, ARRIS,
                      HADE, INTRIGUE
angle, at an acute .......... AKIMBO
angle, keel and bowsprit .... STEEVE
angle of a trench ................. ZIG
angle of pipe ...................... TEE
angle of ramification ............ AXIL
angle, to .............. FISH, SCHEME
Anglian kingdom .............. DEIRA
Anglo-Ind. empire, founder of . CLIVE
Anglo-Ind. gatehouse ...... CERAME
Anglo-Ind. native nurse ...... AYAH
Anglo-Ind. pageant ....... TAMASHA
Anglo-Ind. revenue official DESSAYES
Anglo-Ind. weight ........ TOLA, SER
Anglo-Saxon armor ...... HAUBERK
"        "    assembly GEMOT, MOOT
"        "    bard ........ BEOWULF
"        "    council .... HEPTARCHY
"        "    court ............ GEMOT
"        "    fine for manslaughter ....
                             WEREGILD
"        "    freeman ........ THANE
"        "    god ............ WODEN
"        "    goddess ....... EOSTRE
"        "    infantry .......... FYRD
"        "    king ........ EDGAR, INE
"        "    letter ........ EDH, ETH
"        "    one of king's council ....
                                WITAN
"        "    sheriff ............ REEVE
"        "    writer .......... AELFRIC
angry ...... IRATE, LACONIC, HUFF,
              CROSS, ARACUND, IREFUL,
                            MOVE, MAD
anguillid .......................... EEL
anguish ..... AGONY, DOLOR, PANG,
              MISERY, REMORSE, THROE,
angular ... SCRAWNY, BONY, GAUNT
angular meas.; unit of ............ MIL
anhydrous ........................ DRY
aniline dye .... BENZOLE, MAGENTA
animal anatomy ......... ZOOTOMY
"     and plant life ... BIOTA, BIOS
"     , burrowing ........ WOMBAT
"     , cat tribe ............ OUNCE
"     , coat of ............ PELAGE

9

" , Egypt ................. ADDA
" food, caused by .... CREATIC
" , footless ................ APOD
" form ............ TELEOZOON
" , imaginary ............ SNARK
" , lean ................ RICKLE
" life, simple form of .. AMEBA
" life, study of ...... ZOOLOGY
" of Madagascar ....... TENREC
" , pet .......... CADE, COSSET
" , small; Fr. ............. TOTO
" , spotted .. DAPPLE, PIEBALD
" starch ........... GLYCOGEN
" with legs used as oars .......
REMIPED
" , ten-footed ........ DECAPOD
" with longbody .... ANNELID
animal's body .................. SOMA
animals carrying young . MARSUPIAL
animal's intrea food ........ COYPU
animals molt .............. EXUVIAE
animals; Scot ................. MERES
animals with no nervous system .....
ACRITA
animate ...... ACT, ENSOUL, FIRE
animated ...... ALIVE, BRISK, GAY
anion, opposed to .......... CATION
anise ......... DILL, ANET, CUMIN
ankle . CUIT, TARSUS, COOT, TALUS
ankle bone .. TARSAL, ASTRAGALUS
ankle iron .................... BASIL
ankles; per. to .............. TALARIC
anlage .................... PROTON
Ann; wife of Henry VIII .. BOLEYN
anna, ¼ of an .................. PICE
anna .............. COIN, HOACTZIN
Annamese measure .. TA, GON, MAU
annatto ...... ARCHIOTE, ORELLIN
Anne Oakley .................. PASS
anneal .... FUSE, TEMPER, SMELT
annealing chamber ............ LEER
annex .................... ADD. JOIN
annotation ........ GLOSS, APOSTIL,
COMMENT, NOTE, REFERENCE
annotator ...................... NOTER
announcement ................. BLURB
annoy IRK, BAIT, BORE, DEVIL, NAG,
HARASS, VEX
annoyance, expression of ........ TUT
annoyer .. TRIER, HARRIER, NOIER
annual dedicatory service of certain
churches ................ ENCAENIA
annual ...... ETESIAN, OCRA, OKRA
annual income .............. RENTES
annuity .......... INCOME, TONTINE
annul BLANK, CASS, CANCEL, UNDO
annular reinforcement .......... SPUT
annunciator .. INDICATOR, TELLER
anodyne ...... SEDATIVE, OPIATE
anoint .. ALYNE, ANELE, FAT, OIL,
SMEAR
anoint, as a priest ... ANOIL, SHRIVE
anomalous .......... ODD, ABNORMAL
anon ........ ONCE, SOON, THENCE
another FURTHER, SECOND, ALIAS
ant ...... PISMIRE, ANAY, EMMET,
MYRMICID, TERMITE, MIRE

ant, queen .............. MICROGYNE
ant, worker ...... QUEEN, ERGATE,
NEUTER
antagonist .. RIVAL, FOE, FOEMAN
antagonistic ................. INIMICAL
Antarctic explorer ...... BYRD, ROSS
anteater ........ PANGOLIN, MANIS,
AARDVARK
anteater; Amer. ........ TAMANDUA
anteater, Tasmanian ....... ECHIDNA
antedate .............. PREMUNDANE
ant-nest ................. FORMICARY
ants, genus of .. FORMICA, ECITON,
TERMES
antelope  GAZEL, GAZELLE, TAKIN,
YAKIN
" , African .... HARTEBEEST,
KOB, KONZE, KUDU,
QUREBI, ORIBI, ORYX,
WANTO STEINBOK
" , African (N) TORA, ADDAX,
BONGO
antelope, African (S) .... BLESBOK,
BONTE-BOK, ELAND,
GEMSBOK, GNU, GUEVI,
ORIBI, PALLAH,
SPRING-BOK
" , Afr. (S) striped .. KOODOO,
KUDU
" , ancient .............. PYGARG
" , Chinese ............ DZEREN
" , E. Indian NILGAI, NYLGAU
" , Egypt ............... BUBALIS
" , European .......... CHAMOIS
" , genus .... BUBAL, BUBALIS
" , goat .................. SEROW
" , Himalayan .. CHIRU, GORAL,
KEMAS
" , Indian .... CHICARA, NYL,
SASIN
" , red buck ............ PALLAH
" , reddish-brown, W. Afr. .....
NAGOR
" , Siberian ............... SAIGA
" , Somaliland ............ BEIRA
" , So. Amer. ........ BLESBOK,
SASSABY
" , striped ............. OTEROP
" , Thibetan .... CHIRU, GOA
antelope-like ................. BOVID
antenna .......... FEELER, AERIAL
antenna, insect; end of ...... CLAVA
anterior PRIOR, BEFORE, PREVIOUS
anthelion HALO, AUREOLE, NIMBUS
anthem SONG, MOTET, ANTIPHONY
anther ....... STAMEN, TIP, POLLEN
anthesis .......... BLOOM, BLOSSOM
anthocyanin ................... DENIN
anthologize ................. COMPILE
anthology .... ANA, COLLECTANEA
anthozoan ........... CORYL, POLYP
anthrax ............... CARBUNCLE
anthropoid ................. APE, LAR
antic DIDO, PRANK, CAPER, DROLL
anti-aircraft ........ ACKACK, FLAK
anticlimax .... BATHOS, DECREASE
anti-cyclone .. HIGH, CALM, DEAD

10

antidote SMILE, SODA, CORRECTIVE
antidote to madness .... CHRYSOLITE
Antigone's sister ............. ISMENE
antimony ...... SB, KOHL, STIBIUM
antimony for eyelids; Ind. ..... SURMA
antiquity .. PALEOLOGY, AGO, ELD,
            ANCIENT, PAST, YORE
antiseptic AMADOL, EUSOL, IATROL,
            EGOL, IODIN, IODOL, SALOL
antiseptic acid .. BORIC, TEREBENE
antiseptic astringent ARGENTAMINE
antiseptic surgery, father of .. LISTER
antitoxin lymph ....... SERA, SERUM
antler, branch of . PRONG, BAY, BEZ,
                                BROW
antler branches .... BEAMS, TYNES
antler, unbranched ..... SPIKE, DAG,
                        HORN, DAGUE
antlia ........................... PUMP
Antonio ...................... MORENO
Antony and Cleopatra char..... IRAS
Anu's consort ................... ANAT
anvil .......... STITHY, TEEST, JAW
anvil bone ..................... INCUS
Anvil City .................... NOME
anvil, horn of .................. BEAK
anvil striker .................. SMITH
anxiety .... CARE, CONCERN, HOW
any .......... ONI, ALL, ARY, SOME
any of various stars ......... DENEB
anything ....... ANYWISE, AUGHT
anything high flown .............. ELA
anything of least value ...... PLACK
anything remote, per. to ..... FORANE
aorist .............. TENSE, ACTION
Apache chief, Ind. ........ GERONIMO
Apache jacket ................. BIETLE
apart ........ ASIDE, SOLUS, SPLIT
apart, places ......... ALOOF, ALONE,
                                ENISLES
apartment ...................... SUITE
apartheid; expres. for ........ MALAN
ape ........ CHIMPANZEE, GIBBON,
            GORILLA, PRIMATE, KRA,
            ORANG, OURANG
ape, anthropod TROGLODYTE, SOKO,
                                LAR
ape, gibbon of Sumatra ..... SIAMONG
ape, to . PORTRAY, COPY, PARROT,
                        SIMULATE, MIME
apeman ...................... ALALUS
aperture ...... VENT, ORIFICE, RIMA
aperture, narrow ...... STOMA, SLOT
apes; genus .................... SIMIA
apex ...... ACME, CACUMEN, NOON,
                                ZENITH
apex covering .................... EPI
apex, having a rounded ...... RETUSE
apex of elbow ................ ANCON
aphis .... APHID, LOUSE, PUCERON
aphorism . ADAGE, AXIOM, DICTUM,
            MAXIM, PROVERBIAL, SAW
aphoristic ....... TRUTH, GNOMICAL
Aphrodite ......... URANIA, VENUS
Aphrodite's mother ............ DIONE
Aphrodite's sweetheart ........ ARES
Aphrodite's temple site ...... PAPHOS

apiaceous herb ................ NONDO
apician ..... EPICUREAN, GLUTTON
apidae genus ................. BOMBUS
apiece ...... EACH, PER, SERATIM
aplomb ASSURANCE, POISE, SURETY
apocarpus fruit; as a strawberry ......
                                ETAERIO
apocopate ......... ELIDE, SHORTEN
apocryphal book .... TOBIT, ESDRA
apograph . COPY, ECTYPE, REPLICA
apoidea ......................... APINA
Apollo and Artemis .......... DELIAN
Apollo, birthplace of .......... DELOS
Apollo, mother of .... LATONA, LETO
Apollo, priest of ............... ABARIS
Apollo, seat of .................. ABAE
Apollo's festival .............. DELIA
Apollo's son .............. ION, IAMUS
Apollo's twin ...... ARTEMIS, DIANA
apollyon ...................... DEVIL
apologue .... FABLE, MYTH, STORY
apoplexy, plant .................. ESCA
apostate ..... DISLOYAL, PERVERT
                                DESERTER
apostate, an ...... RAT, RENEGADE,
                                SECEDER
apostle of Rome .... SCHOLAR, NERI
apostle of the Franks .......... REMI
apostle of the Goths ........ ULFILAS
apothegm AXIOM, ADAGE, DICTUM,
            APHORISM, SAYING
appangage ............ STATE, LAND
apparatus ............ GEAR, RIGGING
apparatus for depositing concrete under
water ...................... TREMIE
apparatus, sound determining ..........
                                EOPHONE
apparent OVERT, PATENT, VISIBLE
apparition .... GHOST, REVENANT,
            PHANTOM, SPECTER, SHADE,
                        EIDOLON, WRAITH
appealing .. BESEECHING, CATCHY
appear ... EMERGE, LOOM, ARRIVE,
                                SEEM
appearance ........ AIR, GUISE, MIEN,
            RESEMBLANCE, OSTENT, PHASE
appease ............ CALM, PLACATE
appellation ........ EPITHET, TITLE,
                                NAME
append ADD, ADJOIN, AFFIX, HANG,
                                ANNEX
appendage .. TAB, AWN, PENDICLE
appetite APPETENCE, ZEST, OREXIS
appetite, huge ...... GARGANTUAN
appetitive ORECTIC, HUNGER, WANT
appetizer .. CANAPE, RELEVE, ZEST
applaud .. EXTOL, LAUD, PRAISE
applauders .... CLAQUE, CLAPPERS
applause BRAVO, ECLAT, ENCORE,
                                HAND
apple ........ GOLDEN, ROSE, SORB,
            COSTARD, QUEENING, CRAB,
            RUSSET, SPY
   "    , Austral. .......... EMEU, EMU
   "    blight ................... APHID
   "    , crushed .............. POMACE

11

" disease ................ STIPPEN
" , emu; Austral. ...... COLANE
" , immature ............ CODLING
" , love ................. TOMATO
" , Persian ............... PEACH
" seed ...................... PIP
" seller; Eng. ............ COSTER
" soursop or custard ...... ANONA
apple-like ............ BEL, TOMATO
apple-like fruit .............. QUINCE
apple-shaped ............ POMIFORM
applethorne .................. EPIGENE
apple-worm .................. MOTH
apples, per. to .................. MALIC
applied decoration, form of .. GESSO
apply ....... EMPLOY, UTILIZE, USE
appoggiatura ........... GRACENOTE
appointment .... SET, TRYST, DATE
apportion .............. ALLOT, METE
appraise .. ASSAY, EVALUE, LOVE
apprehend DREAD, REAR, ARREST,
           BELIEVE, NAB, SEIZE
apprehended ... FEARED, SENSATE
apprehension .... CAPTURE, ALARM
apprentice .................. TRAINEE
approach .... ADIT, COME, STALK
approbation ...... FAVOR, PLAUDIT
appropriate .. PROPER, FIT, USURP,
                    DUE, APT
apricot cordial ............ PERSICO
apricot, oriental ................ UME
apron TAYO, BRAT, BOOT, HOOVER,
                    TOUSER
apron, child's ........ BISHOP, TIER
apropos ....... POINT, HAPPY, PAT
apt .. ASPERT, CLEVER, DEFT, FIT,
                    PAT
apteryx .................... MOA, KIWI
aptitude . ELAIR, TALENT, LEANING,
                    SHILL
aqua; Lat. ................... WATER
aquamarine BERYL, BLUE, PIGMENT
aquarium ...... GLOBE, POND, TANK
aquatic performer .............. SEAL
"     salamander .......... TRITON
"     switchback .......... CHUTE
aqueduct .... CONDUIT, SERVITUDE,
                    CANAL
aqueduct of Sylvius ............ ITER
aqueous solution .............. JAVEL
aquila; Lat. .................. EAGLE
Ara. constellation ............ ALTAR
Arab .... SARACEN, GAMIN, TATAR,
                    SEMITE
Arab faction in Medina ........ AUS
Arab yeoman ................. YEMEN
Arabia ......................... SAUDI
Arabia (Felix) ............... YEMEN
Arabia, gazelle of ............. CORA
Arabian ancestor; myth .... KAHTAN
"     abode ................... DAR
"     beverage ............. LEBAN
"     chieftain; AMIR, EMIR, REIS,
                    SHEIK
"     city ...... CHAFRA, DAMAR,
                    MEDINA, SANA

" "City of Pillars," anc. .. IREM
" coin   CARAT, KABIK, PEISA
" date, kind of ......... KHOLA
" demon ........ EBLIS, GENIE
" desert ... DAHNA, PETRAEA
" devils, prince of ....... EBLIS
" district .................. ASIR
" dromedary BELOOL, HEJEEN
" evil spirit .. AFREET, AFRIT
" fair, animal ............ AKAD
" garment, loose .......... ABA
" garment, outer ......... HAIK
" geographical district .. HEJAZ
" grain measure ....... TOMAN
" gum tree ............. KAFAL
" head gear, part of ...... AGAL
" headkerchief cord ...... AGAL
" judge .................. CADI
" kingdom ........ HIRA, IRAK
" larch .................. ITHEL
" leader ............... KOLEYB
" letter ........ ALIF, TA, KAF
" measure ............. COVIDO
" measure, unit ........ ARDEB
" monarchy, oldest .... YEMEN
"Arabian Nights," char. in .... AGIB,
                    AMINA, SINBAD
"Arabian Nights" Illustrator .. DULAC
Arabian nomad .... SARACEN, SLEB
" oasis ......... DOUMA, JOWF
" panther ............... FAHD
" poison wind ......... SIMOOM
" porridge deriv. ........ SAMH
" romance, an ........... ANTAR
" ruler .......... EMEER, EMIR
" "Sacred Territory" .. HARAM
" seaport ...... ADEN, MOCHA
" seashore ......... TEHAMAH
" shrub .................... KAT
" spirit; myth. AFREET, JINN
" state ................. OMAN
" sultanate .............. OMAN
" tamarisk .............. TALH
" teachers ............. ULEMA
" tent village .......... DOUAR
Arabian thorny bush ......... MESAA
"     town, extinct ........ MAREB
"     tribe .... ASIR, AUS, KEDAR
"     Utopia ........... KAIF, KEF
"     wagon ............. ARABA
"     weight ...... NEVAT, CHEKI
                    DIRHEM, KELLA
Arabic acid .................... ARABIN
Arabic for father ........ ABOU, ABU
Arabic for river .............. BAHR
Arabic letter .. BA, THA, JIM, KHA,
       DAL, LAM, MIM, NUN, DAD, YA
Arabic mirage ................. SERAB
Arabic scripture ........... ALCORAN
araceae family .......... ARUM, TARO
araceous ...................... AROID
araceous plant CABBAGE, LILY, TARO,
                    ARUM
arachida, the .................. ACERA
arachnid SPIDER, MITE, SCORPION,
                    TICK

12

arachnoid trap .................. WEB
arado ........................... LAND
Arafura Sea Islands ............. ARU
Arakanese ...................... MAGHI
Aramaic dialect ............... SYRIAC
Aramean deity ............... RIMMON
Arawakan Ind. tribe; Brazil .. GUANA
arbinose; rel. to ............. ARABAN
arbiter . REFEREE, JUDGE, UMPIRE
arbitrary ........ DESPOTIC, THETIC
arbitrary dictum .. DOGMA, FIGMENT
arbitrator ...... REFEREE, MUNSIF
arbor   BOWER, PERGOLA, TRELLIS
arboreal animal; ........AI, DASYURE,
                    SLOTH, UNAU
arborescent ................. DENROID
arc, chord of ..................... SINE
arc, 1/100 of ............... CENTARE
arcade . ARCATURE, PORTICO, ORB
Arcadian ......... BUCOLIC, RUSTIC,
                    SHEPHERD
Arcadian god ................ LADON
Arcadian princess ............ AUGE
arcanum ...... SECRET, MYSTERY
arch FORNIX, ARC, CHIEF, HANCE,
                    PEN
arch fiend .......... DEVIL, SATAN
arch, pointed .................. OGIVE
arch trick ...... ROGUISH, WAGGISH
archaic exclamation .............. POX
archangel SATAN, MICHAEL, URIEL
archbishop ......... METROPOLITAN,
                    PRIMATE, ABP
Archbishop of Mentz; leg. .... HATTO
archbishopric .................... SEE
arched ........ .... VAULTED, COPED,
              CAMBERED, CAMERATED
archery target, center ........ CLOUT
archetypal ........ ORIGINAL, IDEAL
archetype IDEA, EXAMPLE, MODEL
architectural pier ............. ANTA
arcograph ............. CYCLOGRAPH
arctic ........... NORTHERN, POLAR
Arctic exploration base ........ ETAH
Arctic explorer ERIC, KANE, PEARY
Arctic hooded jacket ....... ANORAK
arcubalist ................ CROSSBOW
Arden, Miss ..................... EVE
ardent ...... AFICIONADOS, EAGER,
                    RETHE, WARM
ardent, become .......... ENTHUSE
ardor ZEAL, ELAN, SPLEEN, VERVE
ardor; Fr. ........ FOUGUE, ARDEUR
area at base of bird's bill ...... CERE
area, small .. CLOSE, AREOLA, TREF
areca palm .................... BETEL
areceae family ................. ARAL
arefy ............................. DRY
arena FIELD, RING, HIPPODROME,
              SPACE, SPHERE, RINK
arenose ....................... SANDY
areola SPOT, CELL, ARMLET, RING
Ares ............................. MARS
Ares, parents of HERA, ZEUS, ENYA
Ares, sister of ................. ERIS
argali, bearded ............. AOUDAD

Argentina's first lady .......... EVITA
Argentine, a president of ...... ROSAS
Argentine city ...... SALTA, LANUS
Argentine river port ....... ROSARIO
Argentine town ................ AZUL
Argentine treeless plain .... PAMPAS
Argentine writing ............ PAMPA
argillaceous ........ SLATY, CLAYEY,
              DOUGHY, SPONGY, CLEDGY
argo ....................... BOAT, SHIP
Argolis, vale of ............... NEMEA
Argonaut, the .................. JASON
Argos, princess of ............ OANAE
argot CANT, FLASH, SLANG, LINGO
argue MOOT, RATIOCINATE, WORD
argument ...... DEBATE, POLEMIC
argumentative .. ERISTIC, FORENSIC
Arias; It. .......................... SOLI
arid LEAN, DRY, JEJUNE, STERILE
Aries ............................. RAM
arikara .......................... REE
arista .. BEARD, APPENDAGE, AWN
aristocrat ...... LORD, PARVENU
Aristotle's birthplace ........ STAGIRA
Arius, disciple of .............. ARIAN
Arizona county ................ PINAL
Arizona, river in ................. GILA
Arizona State flower ........ SAGUARO
arm bone HUMERUS, ULNA, RADIUS
arm hole, sleeve ................ SCYE
arm, per. to .... BRACHIAL, ELBOW
arm (Swahili) ................ MKONO
arm, to walk arm in .......... OXTER
armadillo, genus .............. TATU
   "      , giant, of Argentina PELUDO
   "      , giant, of Brazil .... TATOU
   "      , S. Amer. .. POYOU, PEBA,
                    TATOUAY
   "      , three banded ....... APAR,
                    MATACO
armadillo-like extinct animal ..........
                    GLYPTODON
armament works; Ger. ........ SKODA
armed band . POSSE, ASKARI, HOST
armed galley; Norse ............ AESC
armed with a noose .. LAQUEARIAN
Armen singer .................... KAY
Armenian mtn. .............. ARARAT
Armenia's capital ............ ERIVAN
armhole, garment ....... MAIL, SCYE
armistice ............ PEACE, TRUCE
armor MAIL, PLATE, EGIS, GRAITH,
                    AVENTAIL, TACE
   "      , arm REREBRACE, BRASSART
   "      for head .............. SCONCE
   "      for a horse .......... BARDES
   "      for horse's head .... TESTIERE
   "      for the thigh ......... CUISH
   "      for the throat ......... GORGET
   "      , parts of . CUIRASS, GREAVE,
                    TASSE, JERYNE, TASSET
   "      , protective . PANOPLY, AEGIS
   "      , shoulder ........... AILETTE
   "      , thigh ................ CUISSE
armored vehicle .......... TANK, CAR
armory material; col. .............. OD

13

arm-pit ... CHELIDON, ALA, AXILLA
arms, having eight ........ OCTOPOD
Armstrong, Louis ...... TRUMPETER
army ...... HORDE, HOST, MILITIA
   "    brown color .......... ROSARIO
   "    chaplain ............... PADRE
   "    engineer ............. SAPPER
   "    follower ............... SUTLER
arnot .................... EARTHNUT
aroids; (see 'plants') .. TANIA, TARO
aroma ................. NIDOR, SAVOR
aromatic PUNGENT, BALMY, SPICY,
            SAVORY, REDOLENT
aromatic fruit ............... NUTMEG
aromatic gum ............... MYRRH
aromatic herb CLARY, NONDO, MINT
aromatic med. leaves ....... BUCHU
aromatic seed ............... ANISE
aromatic spice ....... CLOVE, MACE
aromatic tree ............... BALSAM
arose ............... SPRANG, STOOD
arouse .. ACCITE, SUMMON, EVOKE,
      ANIMATE, EXCITE, REVIVE
arracacha ......................... APIO
arraign ...... CITE, INDITE, PEACH
arrange ALINE, ETTLE, PLAT, RAIL
arrange in battle formation . DEPLOY
arrange in layers STRATOSE, TIERS
arrange in piles .... COCK, STACKS
arrange, side by side ..... APPOSE
arranged in threes ........ TERNATE
arranged on a landing ..... YARDED
arrangement .......... COLLOCATION
arras ........ TAPESTRY, DRAPERY
array .. MARSHAL, DECK, MUSTER,
    ADORN, DRESS, PAREL, ROBE
arrest; col. .. DWARF, STUNT, NAB,
    HALT, RESTRAIN, STOP, SIST
arrish ......................... STUBBLE
arrival time (aviation) .......... ETA
arrogant CAVALIER, JOLLY, PROUD,
                       HIGH
arrive ................. FLOW, COME
arrow .......... DART, REED, SHAFT
   "    , feathered ............... VIRE
   "    , fit to string of bow ... NOCK
   "    handle ................. STELE
   "    maker . BOWYER, FLETCHER
   "    points, obsidian used in making
                    IZTLE
   "    poison; S. Afr. .... ECHUGIN
   "    , poisoned ............. SUMPIT
   "    poisons .... ANTIAR, CURARE,
    INEE, UPAS, URALI, WOORALI
   "    , short .................. SPRITE
arrow-root ........ CANNA, ARARAO
arrow-root; Brazil .......... TAPIOCA
arrow-root, source of ...... MARANTA,
                    TACCA
arrow-shaped ............... BELOID
arrow-smith ............... ARTISAN
arrow-worm ............... SAGITTA
arroya ............. HONDU, HONSHU
arse ............. BUTTOCKS, RUMP
arsenate of copper .......... ERINITE
arsenic sulphide ......... REALGAR

arsenides, mixture of ......... SPEISS
arsis ........................... ICTUS
arson .. BURNING, CAUTERY, FIRE
arsonist ......................... PYRO
art; obs. .......... ARS, SCELE, WIT
art in general ..... TECHNIC, SKILL
art, realistic .................. GENRE
art school ....................... DADA
Artagus' country ............... SPAIN
Artemis; Gr. ...................... UPIS
artery, large ...... STREET, AORTA
artery of neck .............. CAROTID
artery, pulse of ............... ICTUS
artful .... POLITIC, PRACTIC, WILY
arthritis ......................... GOUT
arthropoda .... TRILOBITA, PHYLA
arthrotome ................. SCALPEL
Arthur, Chester ................. ALAN
Arthur (King), lance of .......... RON
Arthurian king .................. BORS
Arthurian lady ............... ELAINE
Arthurian legend, Geraint's wife ENID
Arthurian legends, town of ASTOLAT
Arthur's (K.) final resting place ........
                    AVALON
artichoke, a kind of BUR, CANADA,
                    CYNARA
artichoke, Chinese ........ CHOROGI
artichoke, leafstalk of ....... CHARD
article; Fr. .......... LA, LE, LES, UN
article; Span. ...................... LAS
artifice TRICK, CRAFT, GUILE, RUSE,
                     WILE
artifice, subtle FINESSE, STRATAGEM
artificial butter .... ANATTO, OLEO
artificial fiber ................ ARALAC
artificial language ESPERANTO, RO,
                    IDO
artificial unit of tone ............... NIL
artillery discharge . RAFALE, SALVO
artisan ........ CRAFTSMAN, FEVER
artist, young; Fr. .............. RAPIN
artist's medium .............. TEMPERA
artless ........ NAIF, NAIVE, CANDID
artlessness .. NAIVETE, INNOCENCE
arts, the three liberal ...... TRIVIUM
arum plants; genus TARO, ARIODES
arum water .................... CALLA
Aryan ................... MEDE, SLAV
Aryan deity ................ ORMUZD
Aryan god of fire ............... AGNI
Aryan of India ................ HINDU
as ...... WHILE, SIMILAR, SUPPOSE
as; Sp. ........................ COMO
as it is written; mus. .............. STA
as usual; mus. ................. SOLITO
asafetida .. LASER, FERULA, HING
Asa's father .................... ABIA
asbestos AMIANTHUS, AMPHIBOLE
ascend .. ARISE, UPGO, STAIR, STY
ascendency . MASTERY, AFFLUENCE
ascending ..... MOUNTING, ANODAL
ascent, steep STIPE, INCLINE, SLOPE
ascetic .. ESSENE, HERMIT, STOIC,
      RECLUSE, SOLITARY, YOGA
ascription of praise .......... GLORIA

aseptic .... STERILE, UNFRUITFUL
Asgard, bridge to; myth .... BIFROST
ash .......... EMBER, CORPSE, ASE
ash, fruit of .......... KEY, SAMARA
ash, mountain; Am. ........... RONE
ash, prickly; Afr. ............. ARTAR
ash tree .............. ROWAN, SORB
"ash tree," the mighty .. YGDRASYL
Ash Wednesday, first day of .. LENT
ashweed ................ GOUTWEED
ashen .... PALE, LIVID, CINEROUS,
GRAY, WAN
Asher, son of ........ ISUI, JIMNAH
Asherite, an ................... AMAL
Asher's daughter .. SERAH, BERIAH
ashes, of ................. CINERARY
ashes, the ................ FRAXINUS
ashkokos ............ CONY, DAMAN
ashy WAXEN, CERACEOUS, CERAL
Asia, central oasis in .......... MERV
"   , desert in ................... GOBI
"   , former kingdom ........ KOREA
"   , independent kingdom .. NEPAL
"   Minor, city of ..... MYRA, TROY,
USHAK, ISSUS
"   Minor, Greek term ... ANATOLIA
"   Minor, mountain in .......... IDA
"   Minor province; Rom. .. GALATIA
"   Minor, river in . CAICUS, HALYS
IRIS
"   Minor, woodless region . AXYLUS
Asian (Central) nomad .... KIPCHAK
Asian feline ................... OUNCE
Asian French protectorate .... ANAM
Asian open grassy tract .... MAIDAN
Asian tongue, (Central) ......PAMIF
Asiatic country KOREA, IRAK, IRAN,
SIAM
"   coins (see 'coin')
"   goat antelope ........ SEROW
"   imamate .............. YEMEN
"   kingdom ........ ELAM, IRAQ
"   lake .... BAIKAL, BALKASH
"   mammal ............... PANDA
"   measures (see 'measure')
"   medicine man ...... SHAMAN
"   millet .................. DARI
"   mountain .... ALTA, KALKA,
URAL
"   native ........ INNUIT, YUIT
"   nomad, per. to ..... TATARIC
"   people.. HUNS, SERES, SERIC
"   plague ............ CHOLERA
"   plant ...... SESAME, RAMIE
"   revolving storm ... TYPHOON
"   river MENKONG, AMUR, ILI,
OB, YALU
"   rodent ...... MARMOT, PIKA
"   sea .............. ARAL, AZOL
"   seaport ............. SINOPE
"   snow storm ......... BURAN
"   timber, hard ........ NARRA
"   trade wind ........ MONSOON
"   tree ........ ASAK, MEDLAR
"   tribe ... TAI, TURKI, UZBEG
"   tropical shrubs; genus . THEA

"   weapon .............. ADAGA
"   weight (see 'weight')
Asiatics ................... ANAMESE
aside .. AWAY, GONE, OFF, HENCE,
PRIVATE, WHISPER, APART
asinine ..... IDIOTIC, INEPT, SILLY,
ASS, OBTUSE, NUTTY, STUPID
ask; var. ................ SPER, SPUR
askew ASKANT, AGEE, AMISS, AWRY
asleep ....... DORMANT, UNARISEN
asp ............... COBRA, URAEUS
aspect PHASE, SHAPE, AIR, GUISE,
MIEN, SITUATION, STATE
aspect, general .............. FACIES
aspect of two planets in relation to the
zodiac ....................... DECIL
aspen QUAKING, POPLAR, TREMBLE
asperse .... VILIFY, LIBEL, REVILE,
SLUR
asphyxia ................. ACROTISM
asphyxiant ............... APNOEA(L)
aspic ASP, GALANTINE, LAVENDER
aspiration ............ DESIRE, HOPE
ass ..... DONKEY, JACKASS, DOLT
ass; comb. form ................. ONO
ass, wild ......... ONAGER, QUAGGA
assa ........................... CAAMA
Assam mongoloid ............... GARO
Assam shrub ................... TEA
Assam silk worm ........ ERIA, ERI
Assamese dialect ........ AO, LHOTA
Assamese hill tribesman AHOM, AKA
Assam's capital .......... SHILLONG
assart ............ CLEARING, GRUB
assault ............ CHARGE, ONSET
assassin ... SICARIAN, CAIN, THUG
assay .. DOCIMASY, PROSULT, TRY
assayer ...... TESTER, EXPLORER,
TRIER
assaying vessel ........ CUPEL, CUP
assemble ......... MASS, POD, SAMN,
MUSTER
assembled ....... MET, RECRUITED
assembly ...... BEVY, DIET, SYNOD
assembly hall, Pueblo .......... KIVA
assembly place; Gr. .......... AGORA
assent ACCEDE, AMEN, GRANT, NOD
assert . ALLEGE, AVER, POSE, SAY,
STATE, VOICE
assert as real ................... POSIT
assess EXTENT, LEVY, MISE, RATE
assess for repairs . BOTE, MEASURE
assess or tax ..... SCOT, ASK, CESS
assess re. rates ..... RATAL, WORTH
assessment; Old Eng. law SCUTAGE,
TAC
assessor ... JUDGE, RATER, JURAT
asseverate .... VOW, OATH, SWEAR
assign ..... ALLOT, FIX, SEAL, SET
assimilated ...... ONED, IMITATED
assish ............ ASININE, STUPID
assist . ABET, AVAIL, SPEED, HELP
assist for compensation .. LOGROLL
assistance ........ ALMS, DOLE, GIFT
assistant .. AID, ALLY, POSTULATE
assistants .. AIDES, STAFF, MATES

15

assize, an COURT, OYER, TRIBUNAL
associate . CHUM, CRONY, HOBNOB,
ALLY, BUDDY
association football ........... SOCCER
association of merchants .... HANSE
assonance ........ PARAGRAM, PUN
assuasive ................. LENATIVE
assume ............ PREMISE, INFER,
ARROGATE, USURP, DON, FEIGN
assured .......... YEA, CERTAINTY
assuredly; arc .. CERTES, SURE(LY)
Assyria ........................ ASSHUR
Assyria, anc. capital of; .... ANTIOCH,
NINEVEH
Assyrian ....... AMORITE, SHEMITE
"  city . ARBELA, HARA, OPIS
"  city; anc. ........... AKKAD
"  god (see also 'God')
"  god ... ASHUR, ASUR, IRA,
NABO, NINIB, NUSKU,
SIN, ZU
"  goddess (see also 'Goddess')
"  goddess .. ALLATU, FURY,
ISHTAR, ISTAR, NANA,
SARPANIT, ZIRBANIT
"  juniper-like shrub .. RETEM
"  mountain ........... ZAGROS
"  queen .......... SEMIRAMIS
Assyrian river ........ ADHIAN, ZAB
"  sun god ............. HADAD
"  weight ................ COLA
astacus CRAB, CRAWFISH, LOBSTER
Astaire's partner ................ RITA
Astaire's sister ............... ADELE
astatic needle inv. ........... AMPERE
asteism ........ RAILLERY, CLEVER,
GENTEEL
asterisk mark ................... STAR
astern ........ ABAFT, AFT, REAR,
OCCIPUT
asteroid; first discovered ....... CERES
asteroid nearest Earth .......... EROD
asthmatic .. PURSY, OBESE, PUFFY
astir ...... EAGER, VIGILANT, AGOG
Astolat's lily maid ............ ELAINE
astound .. AMAZE, STAGGER, STUN
astrakhan ................. KARAKUL
astral .. STARRY, STELLAR, LAMP
astral fluid ............ OD, ODYL(E)
astray, go ... ASTRIDE, ERR, MANG,
DEVIATE, SIN, WRY
astringent HAREM, SALUMIN, COTO,
SHRUNK, ALUM
astringent gum ................. KINO
astrolabe . PLANISPHERE, ALIDAD
astrologer JOSHI, MERLIN, SHAMAN
astrological belief .......... SIDERISM
astronomical ................. URANIC
astronomical cycle ............. SAROS
astronomical inst. .... ABA, ARMIL,
ORRERY, SECTOR
astronomical meas. ............. APSIS
astronomy, muse of ........ URANIA
astute .... KEEN, SHREWD, CANNY
asunder ........... ATWAIN, APART

asylum .. RETREAT, ALTAR, JAIL,
HOME, HAVEN
at ............ CASH, ALS, ATTEN
at all EVER, ANYWAY, ANY, AUGHT,
AVA
at home ................... HERE, IN
at last ULTIMATELY, EXTREMELY
at long last ........... FINALLY, END
at present; Sp. ............... AHORA
at right angles to the keel .. ABEAM
at the same time .... COETANEOUS,
COEVAL
ataman .......... HETMAN, COSSACK
atap ............................. NIPA
ateles paniscus .............. COAITA
athanor, type of ............ FURNACE
Athena, form of .............. ERGANE
Athena; per to .......... PALLADIAN
Athena Promachos; poet. .. PALLAS
Athenian architect ............ ATTIC,
ICTINUS
"  astronomer ........ METON
"  clan ................... OBE
"  courtesan ........ THAIS
"  general .. NICIAS, PHOCION
"  hill ........ NYMPH, PNYX
"  juryman ............ DICAST
"  law giver ............ SOLON
"  law maker .......... DRACO
"  magistrate ........ ARCHON
"  market place ...... AGORA
"  room .. ADYTUM, ATRIUM,
CELLA
"  sculptor ........... PHIDIAS
"  temple ........ NIKE, ZEUS
"  title ................... ALEA
"  tribunal ...... AREOPAGUS
Athens, anc. assembly ....... BOULE
Athens, magistrate of ........ DRACO
athirst ...... AVID, DRY, PARCHED
athletic ............ LUSTY, BRAWNY,
STALWART
athletic prize ................... AGON
athwart ........ TRAVERSE, ACROSS
Atlantic flier CORRIGAN, LINDBERGH
atlas ..... MAINSTAY, SATIN, MAPS
Atlas' daughter ............. CALYPSO
Atlas' mother .............. CLYMENE
Atli's wife ................. GUDRUN
atloid .................... ATLANTAL
atmosphere ................... AURA
atmospheric gas ..... ARGON, XENON
atoll ............... TARAWA, BIKINI
atom CORPUSCLE, BIT, ION, IOTA,
MONAD
atom bomb test ........ ENIWETOK,
KWAJALEIN
atomic ....... MOLECULAR, MINUTE
atomy ........ MOTE, PIGMY, PYGMY
atone for ......... AMEND, EXPIATE
atonic sound ...... SURD, UNHEARD
atramental ............ INKY, BLACK
Atreus, brother of ........THYESTES
Atridae, father of the ...... ATREUS
atrous ............... BLACK, EBON

attach .. SEIZE, ANNEX, APPEND, JOIN, LOVE, INSET
attached ......... ADNATE, AFFIXED
attached by base ............ SESSILE
attack ........ ICTUS, AFFRET, FIT, BESET, BLITZ, OFFENSE, AGGRESS, OPPUGN, YOKE
attain WIN, EARN, END, GAIN, GET, ACHIEVE, REACH, PROVE
attainment ........ AVOWED, SKILL
attar ...................... PERFUME
attempt ... EFFORT, SEEK, ESSAY, TRY, SAY
attend EAR, SERVE, HARK, HO, HOA, AID, FOLLOW, TEND
attendants SUITE, RETINUE, TRAIN
attended ................... MINDED
attending ones ........ ENTOURAGE
attention ...... EAR, LISTEN, HIST
attentive ALERT, EARED, INTEND, WARY
attenuate ........ THIN, DECREASE, RAREFY
attest .. SEAL, ADJURE, AFFIRM
attic . CLASSICAL, COCKLOFT, LOFT
attic bird ............ NIGHTINGALE
attic muse ............... XENOPHON
Attica, sub-division of ........ DEME
Attica valley ................. LCARIA
Attila (king of Huns) ........ ETZEL
attire ARRAY, GARB, ADIGHT, GUISE, LIVERY, REGALIA
attired in armor ........ PANOPLIED
attitudinize .. POSE, MINCE, SIMPER
Attorney Gen. ......... BROWNELL
attract ALLURE, BAIT, DRAW, PULL, TOLE, ENTICE
attracted and repelled .. AMBIVALENT
attribute QUALITY, ASCRIBE, OWE, PLACE, POWER
attribute mark ............. SYMBOL
attrition .... ABRASION, FRICTION, MASSAGE, RUBBING, WEAR
Atwell; T.V. star ............. LIONEL
au fait; Fr. ................... EXPERT
Auber; opera by .............. MASON
auction .. PORTSALE, ROUP, SALE, DISPOSAL, VENDUE
audacious . BRAZEN, SAUCY, BOLD
audacity ........ TEMERITY, CRUST, COURAGE
Auden; poet; Brit. ......... WYSTAN
audibertia, synonym of ..... RAMONA
audience EAR, ASSEMBLY, PUBLIC
audition .. HEARING, HEA, TRYOUT
auditor HEARER, APPOSER, CENSOR
auditory . OTIC, AURAL, AURICULAR
auger . GIMLET, WIMBLE, BORER, TERRIER
auger's cutting edge .............. LIP
augment ...... SWELL, ADD, EKE, EXPAND
augur .... PORTEND, BODE, OMEN, PRESAGE
August, first day of; Eng. . LAMMAS
auk ALCA, MURRE, ROTCH, ARRIE

auk family ...... ALCIDINE, ALCINE
auks; genus ............ ALLE, ALCA
aula ........................ EMBLICK
"Auld Hornie," Scot. .......... DEVIL
aunt; Fr. ...................... TANTE
aunt; Sp. ......................... TIA
aura ............... BUZZARD, CROW
aural ............. AURICULAR, OTIC
aurelia ................... CHRYSALIS
aureola ...... GLORIA, LIGHT, HALO
au revoir ............ GOODBY, ADIEU
auricle ..... PINNA, TRUMPET, EAR
auriferous .................... GOLDEN
Auriga, star in ............. CAPELLA
auroch ........... BISON, TUR, URUS
aurora; Gr. myth. ................. EOS
auroral EASTERN, DAWN, ROSEATE, EOAN
aurum ........................... GOLD
auspices CHARGE, OMEN, EGIS, AID, SIGN, FAVOR
Austen, J.; novel by ........... EMMA
Austen; writer .................. JANE
austere . ASCETIC, HARSH, STERN
Australia, settlers of .. BASS, COOK
Australia, native of .. MYALL, MAORI
Australian acacia ............. MYALL
"    arboreal animal ... DASYURE, KOALA
"    beef-wood .............. BELAR
"    clover fern ........... NARDOO
"    conversation ......... YABBER
"    cry ................... CODER
"    food fish . MADO, TREVALLY
"    gale .................. BUSTER
"    gum tree .... TUART, KARRI
"    hawk .................. KAHU
"    horse ................ WALER
"    island .............. NEPTUNE
"    lake ......... EYRE, FROME
"    lizard ............... GOANNA
"    mahogany ......... GUNNING
"    manna ................. LAAP
"    marsupial ...... KOALA, TAIT
"    measure of capacity .... ARNA
"    mountain ............... BLUE
"    native's cry ......... COOEE
"    ostrich ................... EMU
"    parakeet ........... ROSELLA
"    petrel .................... TITI
"    plant .............. WARATAN
"    seaport .............. SYDNEY
"    sheep shearing floor . BOARD
"    shrub .............. CORREA
"    shrubs; genus ....... OLEARIA
"    soldier ............... ANZAC
"    spotted cat ........ DASYURE
Australian throwing stick WOMERAH ..WOMMALA
"    tree ........ TUART, BELAR
"    water mole ........ PLATYPUS
"    wild dog .............. DINGO
"    zone (arid), per. to SONORAN
Austria, cave amphibian of .... OLM
Austrian coin ...... HELLER, DUCAT
"    measure .............. SEIDEL

17

" pheasant .............. LEIPOA
" psychiatrist .......... ADLER
" rifleman ................ JAGER
" river ... DRAVE, MUR, ENNS,
ISER
" ruler, former .......... KAISER
" shrub ................... URY
authentic ..... ORIGINAL, CERTAIN,
TRUE
author ....... PARENT, PROJECTOR
author of "Carmen" ....... MERIMEE
author of "Joseph and His Brother"
MANN
author of Sanskrit novels ..... PILPAI
author of "The Raven" .......... POE
author remarque ............... ERICH
authoritative letter .... WRIT, BREVE
authors; Amer. ....... ALGER, RANA
auto, type of ...... BERLIN, SEDAN
autochthon, an . NATIVE, INDIGENE
auto court ..................... MOTEL
autocrat ...... DESPOT, MONOCRAT
MOGUL, TORSE, TSAR
automaton ....... ANDROID, GOLEM,
FIGURE, PUPPET, ROBOT
automobile part .... STATOR, CHOKE
autopsy ................... NECROPSY
autumn flower ................. ASTER
auxiliary .......... SUB, ALAR, ALLY,
HELPER, COADJUTOR
avail, be of ...... SERVICE, USE, SIT
available, be .. ENURE, FREE, OPEN
avarice .......... GREED, CUPIDITY,
AVIDITY
ave ............................. HAIL
avellane ........... FILBERT, HAZEL
avenaceous ..................... OATY
avenger .... NEMESIS, VINDICATOR
avenging spirit .... FURY, KER, ATE,
MAGAERA
avenue GATE, ARTERY, PIKE, ROAD
avens .......................... GEUM
average ...... PAR, MEAN, MEDIAL,
NORMAL, MEDIOCRE
averred ...... ASSERTED, STATED
averse ......... LOATH, RELUCTANT
aversion to society .... ANTHROPO-
PHOBIA
avert .. DETER, THWART, PARRY,
CHECK, RETARD, SHIELD
aviator ........ ACE, ICARUS, PILOT
avid .. EAGER, GREEDY, DESIROUS
avifauna .............. ORNIS, BIRD
avocada .................. AGUACATE
avocet ........... BARKER, GODWIT
avoid . ELUDE, ESCHEW, EVITATE,
AVERT, EVITE, SHUN
avoidance .......... SHIRKING, GOBY
avowal .. OATH, DEPONE, SWEAR
await ...... BIDE, PROFIT, SUFFICE
award .. ACCOLADE, ALLOT, MEED,
PRIZE, MEDAL(LION), OSCAR
away ... OUT, ASIDE, FRO, ADRIGH,
OFF, VIA
aware HEP, CONSCIOUS, MINDFUL,
RECK

away from the mouth ...... ABORAL
away; prefix ................. APO, DE
aweather, opposed to ............ ALEE
aweigh ......................... ATRIP
awkward ......... LOUTISH, GALOOT,
GAUCHE, INAPT
awl ........... BROACH, TAP, ELSEN
awn .. AVEL, ARISTA, BARB, BEARD,
BULLEN
awning ... SHELTER, TILT, CANOPY
awning; Rom. ............. VELARIUM
awns, remove the ................ AVEL
A.W.O.L. worker ............ STRIKER
awry ....... ASQUINT, AGEE, AMISS,
EVIL, OBLIQUE, ASKEW
ax ..... ADZ, AXE, HACHE, POLEAX
axil ................. ALA, STEM, WING
axilla ...................... ARMPIT
axis of a vertebrate ............ AXON
axle ....... SKENE, ARBOR, BAR, PIN
axle, in the ..................... ALAR
axle, near center .............. AXILE
aye ...... EVER, PRO, AY, YEA, YES
aye-aye ........................ LEMUR
Ayers; movie star ................ LEW
Azores, port of ................ HORTA
azote .............. AZOT, NITROGEN
Aztec, god of winds .......... EECATL
Aztec hero ...................... NATA
Aztec language ............. NAHUATL
Aztec temple .... TEOCALLI, TEOPAN
Aztecs, country of ........... AZTLAN
azure .. CERULEAN, BICE, CELESTE
azygous ............... ODD, SINGLE
azym; Heb. .................... BREAD
azym, opposed to ........... ENZYME
azymous .............. UNLEAVENED


# B

B, letter ...................... BE, BEE
baa ............................ BLEAT
babble .... PRATTLE, BLAT, PRATE,
PURL
Baba ............................. ALI
Babel ........ CLANG, DIN, DISCORD,
JARGON
bable; Scot. .................. BAWBEE
Babism, creed of ............ BAHAISM
baboon .............. PAPA, CHACMA
babul; Afr. ................. ATTALEH
babul, the ..................... ACACIA
baby airplane ................. STORK
baby carriage ...... PERAMBULATOR
GOCART
baby food ........................ PAP
Babylon ....................... SHINOR
"      , abode of dead .........ARALU
"      , anc. kingdom near ..... ELAM
"      , division of ..... ELAM, NITUK
Babylonian canal .............. JESUF
"      dead language ...... ACCAD
"      deity (see 'Deity')
"      Earth Mother ...... ISHTAR

18

"   god .............. OANNES
"   god (see 'God')
"   goddess (see 'Goddess')
"   hell ................. ALALU
"   hero; myth ........ ETANA
"   monarch, early .. ALOROS
                        DUNGY
"   numeral ... CYCLE, SAROS
"   palace, anc. ......... KASR
"   people ...... SUMERIAN(S)
"   river .............. TIGRIS
"   temple ........ BEL, ISTAR
"   tower ............ ZIGURAT
Babylonian weight, anc. ...... MINA
baby's complete outfit .... LAYETTE
bac ............................. VAT
baccarat term ............... BANCO
baccate ...................... PULPY
Bacchanal, cry of ............. EVOE
bacchante, a .............. MAENAD
Bacchus, cry of joy for .... IACCHUS
bachelor .... AGAMIST, CELIBATE,
        MISOGAMIST, COELEBS
bachelor's button ...... KNAPWEED
back ........ SUPPORT, FRO, REAR
back, go ........ RETURN, REGRESS
"   of insects ...... NOTUM, NOTA
"   out, col. ................ FUNK
"   , per. to the . DORSAL, TERGAL
"   ; prefix ............ RE, RETRO
backbite .... MALIGN, VILIFY, SASS,
                        ASPERSE
backbone ...................... RIDGE
backbone, animal's .. CHINE, SPINE
backbone of a fish ......... GRATE
backgammon term ............ BLOT
backward .. SLACK, AVERSE, HIND,
        TARDY, RETRORSE, FRO
backwater ...... BAYOU, THROTTLE
bacteria ........ AEROBIA, AEROBE
bacteria destroyer ............ LYSIN
bacteria, exclusion of .. ANTISEPSIS
bacterium ... SARCENA, BACILLUS,
                        FUNGUS
bacterium culture .......... ALINITE
bad .... BASE, WANTON, EVIL, ILL
bad custom ............ CACOETHES
Bad-Land Mountain ......... BUTTE
bad legislation .......... DYSNOMY,
                        ASYNOMY
bad luck .. AMBSACE, DEUCE, EVIL
badmannered ................. GOOP
bad; Sp. ...................... MALO
badge EMBLEM, ENSIGN, PIN, STAR
badger .. HECKLE, PATE, BAUSON
"   , cape ................. HYRAX
"   , Dutch .................... DAS
"   , English ............ HAWKER
"   , European ............ BROCK
"   , genus ............... MELES
"   , honey ............... RATEL
"   of Java ............. TELEDU
"   State ............ WISCONSIN
"   , to FRET, HARRY, HECKLE,
                        TEASE, BAIT
baffle .... COD, POT, BALK, EVADE,
    DEFEAT, FOIL, HINDER, ENOSE
baffling ........ ELUSIVE, EVASIVE

bag ...... ASCUS, ETUI, POKE, SAC,
        STEAL, CYST, SACHET
baggage effects .......... DUNNAGE
bagnio ................ BAG, PRISON
bagpipe, flute pipe of .... CHANTER,
                        DRONE
bagpipe music ............ PIBROCH
bagpipe, small SOURDELINE, DRUM,
                        MUSETTE
bagpipe music ............. PIBROCH
bags ...... SNARES, BAITS, TRAPS
bagworm ............. CATERPILLAR
bah ........ ROT, PAH, FIDDLEDEE
Bahama Island ............... ABACO
Bahama Is. capital ......... NASSAU
Bahamas, fabulous, Is. of .... BIMINI
baikie ........................... STICK
bail . ANDI, BOND, LADE, BESTOW,
                        DEAL
Baile, father of; Irish myth. .. BUAN
bailey; Eng. .................. PRISON
bailiff; Scot. .................. REEVE
bait .. DECOY, LURE, BRIBE, TRAP
bait, to drop ............... DAP, DIB
baked apple ......... CLOUDBERRY
baker ROASTER, OVEN, VICTUALER
Baker workshop ............... YALE
baker's dozen INBREAD, THIRTEEN
baker's itch .............. PSORIASIS
baker's itch caused by yeast .. RASH
baker's kneading trough .... BRAKE
baker's shovel ................. PEEL
bakie ........................... PEAT
baking dish ............... RAMEKIN
Bakongo god ................ DEISOS
Bakongo goddess ........... NZAMBI
balance OFFSET, EVEN, POISE, REST
balance of sails ................ ATRY
balance weight ............... RIDER
Balas ruby ................... SPINEL
balata gum ................... CHICLE
balcony ...... BRATTICE, GARRET,
                        SOLLAR
bald .... MERE, POLLED, EPILOSE,
            BARE, PLAIN, MAOL
Balder, giant who caused death of LOKI
balderdash ........ NONSENSE, ROT
Balder's wife, Norse myth. .. NANNA
baldicoot .............. MONK, COOT
baldness ....... ALOPECIA, ACOMIA
baldric BAIT, GIRDLE, ZODIAC, BELT
bale; arc. .................. LADE, DIP
bale of figs; Sp. ... SEROON, SERON
Balearic Is. ................. MINORCA
Balearic Is. lang. ............ CATALAN
baleen ......... BOIS, WHALEBONE
baleful .. NOISOME, SAD, WOEFUL
baleise ......................... FLOG
baler ...................... BUNDLER
Balibago ......................... HAU
balk, in fishing ................ COND
balker ........... HUER, ALARMER
Balkis was queen of ......... SHEBA
ball .... PELLET, CONGLOBE, ORB,
    IVORY, GLOBE, SPHERE, DANCE
ball of rice or meat .......... PINDA
ball of wood .................. KNUR
ballad SONNET, DERRY, LAY, SONG

19

ballarag ..................... BULLY
ballet DANSEUSE, BEZANT, DRAMA,
        MASQUE, CHOREOGRAPH
ball-game .. FUNGO, KENO, TRIGON
ball-game;*Eng. .. BOWL, CRICKET,
        RUGBY
ball-game; Sp. ............. PELOTA
ball-game 'stretch' inning ......... '7'
balloon MONTGOLFIER, AEROSTAT,
        BAG
balloon framework ........ NACELLE
ballot ... SUFFRAGE, ELECT, VOTE
balm ANODYNE, BALSAM, UNGUENT
balmy ............ MOONY, DREAMY
balneation ..................... BATH
balsam, gum resin .......... STORAX,
        BDELLIUM
balsam; S. Am. .... TOLU, COPAIBA
balsam; Swiss ................... RIGA
Baltic island .. ALSEN, DAGO, OSEL
Baltic seaport ........ REVAL, RIGA
Baluch tribesman .............. MARI
Baluchistan, British capital of QUETTA
    "       , capital of ....... KELAT
    "       coarse grain ..... JOWAR
    "       , division of ......... LUS
    "       , dominant race of ........
        BRAHOES
    "       mountain ......... HALA,
        KOHISTAN
Baluchistan river ...... BOLAN, GAJ,
        MOOLA
    "       ruler .... KAHN, SIRDAR
    "       town .... BAGH, BEYLA,
        DADUR
balustrade .. BALCONET, BANISTER
Balzac ..................... HONORE
Balzac heroine ........ ANTOINETTE
bam ..... HOAX, TRICK, WHEEDLE
Bambi ......................... DEER
bamboo, sacred ............. NANDIN
ban TABU, CURSE, TABOO, EXCLUDE
ban, office .................... BANAT
Bana, daughter of ............. USHA
banal ... CORNY, PLATITUDINOUS,
    CLICHE, FLAT, STALE, TRITE
banana: Abys. .............. ENSETE
banana bunch .. ...... STEM, HAND
banana plant .. MUSA, PESANG
banana-like .............. PLANTAIN
Bana's daughter .............. USHA
band; arc. .................... TENIA
band in the brain ........... LIGULA
band leaders .............. CHORAGI
band, narrow .................. TAPE
band of teeth .............. RADULA
band to fasten garments; Fr. . PATTE
band wheel .................. RIGGER
bandage .. TRUSS, FILLET, LIGATE,
        SPICA, SWATHE
bandage for nose ........ ACCIPITER
bandit FOOTPAD, THIEF, LADRONE
bandmaster ................... SOUSA
bandoline ................... POMADE
bane ....... PEST, POISON, VENOM
baneful, something ...... UPAS, VILE
bang .. CUDGEL, RAP, SLAM, CLAP,
    BEAT, IMPEL, SOUND, SLAK

Bani, son of .................... UEL
banish .. DEPORT, DISPEL, EXILE,
    PUNISH, EJECT, EXPATRIATE
Banister, Dr. ................. ROGER
banjo, Jap. ................ SAMISEN
bank .. BRAE, DUN, WOUGH, SAND
bankrupt ..... INSOLVENT, BREAK,
    FAILURE, SMASH, QUISBY
banquet .. DIFFA, FEAST, JUNKET
bant ............ DIET, BANTINGISM
banteng ................... TSINE, OX
banter .... JOSH, ASTEISM, BORAK,
    CHAFF, JEST, ERSIFLAGE
Bantu family, one of . DUALA, ZULU,
        VIRA, YAKU
Bantu language .... SUTO, VILI, ILA
Bantu tribe, Fr. Congo ... BAKALAI
banxring; Sumatra .. TANA, TUPAIA
boabab tree, leaves of ......... LALO
baptismal ........ FONTAL, SPRING
baptizing font ..... LAVER, PISCINA
baquet ................. ROD, WAND
bar ..... BETTY, FID, ROD, DETER
bar, door .............. RISP, STANG
bar legally ......... ESTOP, HINDER
        PREVENT
bar, soap frame ................ SESS
Bara, Miss .................... THEDA
barb ...... FLUE, JAG, SPINE, NAG
barb of a feather .... RAMUS, HARL,
        PINNULA
Barbarian .. VANDAL, GOTH, HUN,
        SAVAGE
barbarian; N. Afr. .......... BERBER
barbarians who pay tribute . LAETAE
barbarity ........ FERITY, BRUTAL
barbarous ............ CRUEL, FELL
Barbary ape ....... SIMIAN, MAGOT
Barbary States MOROCCO, ALGIERS,
        TUNIS, TRIPOLI
barbed UNCINATE, BENT, HOOKED
barbed wire obstacle ........ ABATIS
barber ............ FIGARO, TONSOR
bard . POET, DRUID, RUNER, SCOP,
        VATES, MINSTREL
bard's river .................... AVON
bards in anc. Wales .......... OVATE
bare MERE, NUDE, STRIP, SCARRY
bare (boundary) ...... MEER, MERE
barely ...... MERELY, FAINT, JIMP
bargain ..... PACT, PACTION, PRIG
barge ...... HOY, PRAAM, TENDER,
        FLOAT
barium sulphate ............ BARITE
barium; symbol for ............... BA
bark ................ CORTEX, RIND
    "   , a kind of .. BARGE, PINNACE
    "   , animal's .... BAY, YAP, YELP
    "   cloth; (mulberry) .........TAPA
    "   , having ......... CORTICATED
    "   , inner .......... BAST, LIBER
    "   of a tree; E. Ind. ........ NIEPA
    "   of the paper mulberry .... TAPA
    "   , strip of .................. ROSS
    "   tonic; W. Ind. ....... CANELLA
    "   trees ...................... REND
    "   yielding yercum ......... MUDAR
barker; slang PISTOL, TOUT, SPIELER

barking iron ...................... SPUD
bark-louse ........................ APHIS
barley, four rowed ................ BIGG
barley, parched ............... TSAMBA
barley, six rowed ................. BERE
barley, steeped ................... MALT
barley water; Lat. ............ PTISANA
barm ................. YEAST, LEAVEN
barn ......... BYRE, MEW, SKIPPER
"Barnaby Rudge," char. in .. VARDEN
Barnaby's Mr. O'Malley LEPRECHAUN
barnacle; her. ...... CIRRIPED, BREY
barnacles; col. Eng. ..... SPECTACLES
barometer, a kind of GLASS, ANEROID
barometer gauge ....... MANOMETER
barometric line ................ ISOBAR
baron ..... FREEMAN, NOBLE, PEER
"Baron Munchauson" .......... PEARL
baron; old law ............... HUSBAND
baronet ....................... SIR, BART
barrack .............. CASERN, CAMP
barracuda ........... SENNET, SPET
barrel ... KNAG, KEG, TIERCE, BUTT
barrel of herring ......... CADE, CRAN
barrel, small ............. KILDERKIN
barrel-maker .................. COOPER
barren ..... DULL, STERILE, EFFETE
barricade .. ABATIS, BAR, OBSTACLE
barrier .. SCREEN, ALP, DAM, FENCE
barrister ... ATTORNEY, COUNSELOR
barrow .. MOUND, TUMULUS, GRAVE
Barrymore ...................... LIONEL
bartender TAPSTER, BISTRO, MIXER
barter .. PERMUTE, SWAP, TRAFFIC,
                COMMERCE, TRADE
bartizan ....................... TURRET
Baruch; statesman ......... BERNARD
bas blue .............. BLUESTOCKING
basal lobes in leaves of mosses ... ALA
basanite ................ TOUCHSTONE
base ....... CLAM, MEAN, LOW, SITE
  " , Attic; Gr. ......... SOPHOCLES
  " , coal tar .............. ANILINE
  " hit; slang ................ BINGLE
  " of bird's bill ................ CERE
  " of column ..... DADO, PATTEN,
                              PLINTH
  " , root ..................... RADIX
baseball club ........ SOX, DODGERS,
                GIANTS, YANKEES
baseball team ..................... NINE
baseball's comm. ................. FRICK
baseball's preacher ................. ROE
basement .................... HYPOGEA
bases of number sys. ......... RADICES
bash; col. ... BAT, MASH, LAM, WHAP
Bashan, king of ..................... OG
bashful .......... SHEEPY, MODEST,
  BLUSHING, TIMID, VERECUND,
                              COY
basic part ........................ ROOT
basilica .. CANOPY, SHRINE, TEMPLE
basin LAVER, CHAFER, FONT, PAN,
                STOUP, DOCK, VESSEL
basin of the brain ............ CAVITY
basin, ornamental ........... CUVETTE
bask ........ REVEL, APRICATE, SUN

basket .... SCUTTLE, DOSSER, BIN,
  HAMPER, MAUND, GABION
  " , fish .. CAWL, CRAIL, CREEL,
                              KREEL
  " , flat, for figs ........... CABAS
  " for figs, rush .......... TAPNET
  " for fruit .... POTTLE, PUNNET
  " , hop-picker's ................. BIN
  " , kind of ..... CAUL, TUMBRIL
  " suspended from balloon ... CAR,
                              NACELLE
  " to carry coal in mine ..... CORF
  " used in "pelota" ........ CESTA
  " weaving, filling in ... SLEWING
  " , wicker BASSINET, HANAPER
  " , willow ................. OSIER
basket, watertight ........... WATTAPE
basket work ........ SLARTH, SLATH
basketball; forward ........... CAGER
basketball; col. ..................... RIM
basketball team ................... FIVE
basking shark .............. SAILFISH
Basque ancestor ............. IBERIAN
Basque cap ..................... BERET
Basque numeral .............. BI, SEI
Basque province ...... ALVA, BISCAY
bassoon ................ OBOE, FAGOT
bassoon, mouthpiece of ........ TUDEL
bast ......... BARK, RAMIE, PHLOEM
basta; mus. ......... ENOUGH, STOP
baste CUDGEL, THRASH, SEW, LARD
bat .......... BACKE, REREMOUSE
  " , as the ................ ALIPED
  " , Eur. .... SEROTINE, NOCTULE
  " flying; order ........ CHIROPTERA
  " , mining .................. SHALE
  " , S. Amer. .............. VAMPIRE
  " , species of ........ PIPISTRELLE
  " , wingfooted .............. ALIPED
Bataan bay ..................... SUBIC
Bataan capital .............. BALANGA
bath house ......... BAGNIO, CABANA
bath tub; Sp. .................... TINA
bathe SUFFUSE, BASK, LAVE, STEW
baton .. WAND, SCEPTRE, SUPPORT
baton race ...................... RELAY
batrachian reptile ................ TOAD
batter FRUSH, PASTE, RAM, SLOPE
batter cake .................. WAFFLE
battery, floating .. PRAM, ARTILLERY
battery plate ...................... GRID
battle area ........ ARENA, TERRAIN
battle array .. ACIES, HERSE, ORDER
battle cry ............... AUX-ARMES
battle of Bataan ....... CORREGIDOR
battle trophy ................... SCALP
battlefield .... ARMAGEDDON, CHAMP
battlement ......... CRENEL, PINION,
        EMBRASURE, RAMPART
battologize ....... ITERATE, REPEAT
batty; sl. .............. CRAZY, SILLY
bauble .. GEWGAW, CIPHER, TRIVIA
Bavarian river .................... ISAR
baw-bee; Scot. ............... BILLION
bawl ....BARK, BOOHOO, CRY, YELL
bay ........ BIGHT, COO, VOE, GULF
bay color ........................ ROAN
bay fruit comp. ............... LAURIN

21

bay of the sea ........ INLET, SINUS
Bay State: abb. ................ MASS.
bay, the sweet ............ BREWSTER
Bayard's master ............ RINALDO
Baylor Univ. site ............... WACO
bazaar ... AGORA, EXPOSITION, FAIR
be .........ARE, EXIST, LIE, WHOLE
be equal ..... EVEN, PAR, COMPARE
be gone ..... HISS, SCAT, ABROGATE
be officially engaged ............... SIT
be undecided ......... PEND, DURING
beach ....... PRAYA, PLAYA, SANDS,
        COAST, STRAND, SHILLA
beacon ..... SIGN, FANAL, PHAROS,
    COCK, FLAG, VANE, SEAMARK
beacon light ... LANTERN, CRESSET
beacon on a summit ............. PIKE
Beaconsfield ................. DISRAELI
bead, elongated glass ......... BUGLE
beadle .... OFFICER, POKER, MACER
bead-roll ...................... ROSARY
beads, string of .. ROSARY, CHAPLET
beadsman ....... PRECULAR, CLERGY
beady ..................... GLOBULAR
beagle ..... HOUND, SHARK, BRUTE
beak ............. LORA, NEB, TUTEL
beak of ship .... BOW, RAM, SPERON
beak, trim with ............... PREEN
beaked ................... EROSTRATE
beaker .. BOCAL, CUP, GLASS, TASS
beakless ................. EROSTRATE
beam .... RAY, SILE, SHINE, CABER
beaming .. BRIGHT, RADIANT, ROSY
beamy ........... JOYOUS, MIRTHFUL
bean ........ URD, LENTIL, ADSUKI,
        CALABAR, SOYA, TONKA
bean, buck ......... MENYANTHES
    "   calabar ........ ESERINE, ISERE
    "   , Eng. ................ MAZAGAN
    "   fly ...................... MIDAS
    "   , kidney ............. HARICOT
    "   , lima; Sp. ................. HABA
    "   , locust ................. CAROB
    "   , Mex. ........ FREJOL, FRIJOL
    "   plant ............ LOCO, SENNA
    "   , ripe seeds of LENTIL, HARICOT
    "   , per. to eye of ......... HILAR
    "   , the yam ...............KAMAS
    "   weevil ................. HARIA
bear CARRY, ENDURE, TOTE, WEAR
bear; astron. .................... URSA
bear, Austral. ................. KOALA
bear, brown .................. URSUS
bear; Hindu .................. BHALU
bear; honey .............. MELURSUS
bear, Syrian .................. DUBB
bear, wooly .................. WOOBUT
bearcat, red .................... PANDA
beard AVEL, AWN, ARISTA, GOATEE
beard, hair-like ............... CRINITE
beard; obs. ...................... ANE
bearded ARISTATE, AWNY, BARBATE
bearing ....... AIM, AIR, PORT, MIEN,
                    ORIENT
bearing the writer's name . ONYMOUS
beast .... ANIMAL, BRUTE, BURPO,
                    PARD
beast, colossal MONSTER, BEHEMOTH

beat .... PULSE, DRUB, LACE, WAP,
                    WHAP
beat; col. POMMEL, LARRUP, SLAT,
                BASTINADO, TAN
beat into plate ............ MALLEATE
beat; naut. ...................... TACK
beat, to; Scot. ................. TOWEN
beau ........ BLADE, FLAME, SWAIN
beaut ................. MOUCHE, LULU
beautifier .................. MASCARA
beautiful ...... BONNY, FAIR, MERE,
                    TEMPEAN
beautiful eyes .................. TULIPS
beauty ..... HOURI, NINON, GRACES,
            HEBE, HELEN, VENUS
beauty, reigning ............... BELLE
beaver ............ KERSEY, CASTOR
beaver skin .................... PLEW
bebeeru ............... GREENHEART
because INASMUCH, SINCE, FOR, AS
because; Sp. ................... PORQUE
Bechuanaland tribe ........... NARON
Becker; opera by ....... FRAUENLOB
becloud ......... DIM, OBSCURE, HIDE
become dull ... HEBETATE, APATHY
bed .. BUNK, LAIR, LITTER, BILLET
bed frame ............. STEAD, STOCK
bed; slang ............... DOSS, SLEEP
bed; small .. BASSINET, COT, PALET
bedbug .............. CHINCH, CIMEX
bede, in mining .... FLANG, PICKAXE
bedeck PRINK, ADORN, TRAP, TRIM
Bedouin ........ ARAB, NOMAD, RIFF
bedroom ..... CABIN, CUBICLE, FLAT
bedstone in a porcelain mill ... PAVER
bee .......................... APIS, DOR
    "   , Eng.; obs. .................... FLY
    "   family ................... APIDAE
    "   , girl named for ......... MELISSA
    "   glue .................... PROPOLIS
    "   keeper ..... APIARIST, SKEPPIST
    "   , male .................... DRONE
    "   martin ................. KINGBIRD
    "   , nest building ............ CARDER
    "   , part of a ................. LORUM
    "   plant ..................... BALM
    "   , pollen brush of ............ SCOPA
beech nuts ...................... MAST
beef, dried ................... BUCCAN
beef, in onions ............... MIROTON
beef, lean ...................... LIRE
beehive .... APIARY, ALVEARY, SKEP
beehive covering ............... SUPER
beehive State ................... UTAH
beekeeper ...... APIARIST, SKEPPIST
Beer; author ................. THOMAS
beer jug ................... MUG, TOBY
beer king; myth. .......... GAMBRINUS
beer, malt ................... PORTER
beer, moistening wood with ... CISSING
beer mug ..... SEIDEL, STEIN
beer shop ...................... FARO
beer, spiced ................... FLIP
beer-plant ............. BEERY, HOPS
beery ...................... MAUDLIN
bees; genus ...................... APIS
beeswax, per. to .. CERESIN, CEROTIC
beet, a kind of ............ CHARD, ASA

22

beet; genus ...................... BETA
beet sugar ................... SUCROSE
Beethoven; opera by ......... FIDELIO
Beethoven; comp. ......................
Beethoven's opus 27 .......... SONATA
beetle .... AMARA, BORDER, MELOE,
 WEEVIL
 " , any snout .......... CURCULO
 " , click .... DOR, ELATER, TORA
 " , downy ................... BUZZ
beetle, early stage ............. LARVA
 " , gaudy .............. LADYBUG
 " , grapevine .............. THRIP
 " , horny substance of .... CHITIN
 " , order .......... COLEOPTERA
 " , pepper ................... ITMO
beetle-like insect ............ EARWIG
beetle-like talisman .......... SCARAB
beetles; family ......... ELATERIDAE
beetles, ground; genus AMARA, FIDIA
beetle's wing cover ............ SHARD
beetle's wings, upper ........ ELYTRA
befell ............ CAME, HAP, TIDED
before CORAM, AVANT, ERE, FORNE,
 DAWN, PRECESSION, YER
before; prefix ............. PRE, PRAE
before this time ....... GONE, OVER,
 ERENOW, PRIOR, SAID, FORMER
beg ....... BESEECH, IMPLORE, SUE,
 CADGE, ASK, CRAVE, ENTREAT,
 MAUND, PLEAD, PRAY
beg; Scot. ........................ SORN
began ....... ENTERED, AROSE, CON
beget ....... PROCREATE, KEN, KIND
begetters PARENTS, PATERS, SIRES
beggar ...... MENDICANT, TINKARD,
 IDLER, POOR, LAZAR
beggarly .. PEGRALL, PETTY, MEAN
begin ................... OPEN, START
beginner ..... DEBUTANT, ENTRANT,
 CLERK, LEAD, PUPIL, TYRO
beginning ... ONSET, ALPHA, ORIGIN
beginning to exist .... EGG, NASCENT
begone ..... OUT, AROINT, AVAUNT,
 GET, WHISK, SCAT, VIA
begrime ........................... SOIL
beguile .. COZEN, LURE, WISE, VAMP
Beh, son of ......................... IRI
behalf .. SIDE, BENISON, WINDFALL
behalf .. DEPORT, LET, ACT, BEAR
beheld ............................. SEEN
behemoth ............. BEAST, HIPPO
behest ...... BID, MANDATE, ORDER
behind .... (AB)AFT, LATE, TARDY,
 HIDDEN, AFTER
behold .............. ECCE, LO, VOILA
beige ........... ECRU, HOPI, GREGE
being ............. TROLL, ONTOLOGY
being, actual; Lat. .............. ESSE
being, have ...... ENTITY, EXIST, AM
being in front ................ ANTEAL
being, simple ........ MONAD, HUMAN
being, spirit of ........... ENS, ENTIA
Beja ........................... HAMITE
Bela's son ........................... IRI
belaying cleat KEVEL, BOLLARD, BIT
beldam FURY, ALECTO, TISIPHONE,
 CRONE

beleaguerment ......... BESET, SIEGE
Belgian ........ FLEMING, WALLOON
 " battle (1746) ........ ROCOURT
 " block layer ............ PAVER
 " canal ................... YSER
 " commune .... ATH, TAMINES,
 ANS
 " currency unit ........ BELGA
 " dialect .............. WALLOON
 " ex-premier .......... PIERLOT
 " Fr. battle-ground ARDENNES
 " Gaul, tribe of ... NERVU, REMI
 " king, former ......... ALBERT
 " lowland ............... POLDER
 " marble ................ RANCE
 " professor ............ AGREGE
Belgian river .. LESSE, MEUSE, YSER
 " spring .. HUY, TONGRES, SPA
 " town .. ALOST, ATH, GHENT,
 NAMUR, OSTENDE, MONS,
 YPRES
 " violinist ............... YSAYE
Belgian-Congo ruminant ....... OKAPI
Belial ............................ DEVIL
belief ... CREDO, CREED, SECT, FAY,
 DOGMA, MIND, VIEW, TENET
believer in all religions ....... OMNIST
believer in God ...... DEIST, THEIST
believer in reality of matter ..........
 CARTESIAN
believers ......................... ISTS
bell ..... CODON, CAMPANA, KNELL,
 CARILLON, GONG, TOCSIN
bell town ..................... ADANO
belladonna .................. MANICON
belladonna derivative ........ ATROPIN
belles-lettres ............ LITERATURE
bellicose ....... MILITANT, WARLIKE
Bellini; opera by ............... NORMA
Bellini's "sleepwalker" ........ AMINA
bell-mouthed; Fr. .............. EVASE
bellowing .. AROAR, YAWPING, WAIL
belly PENETRALIA, BULGE, PAUNCH
belly-god ... SYBARITE, CORMORANT
belong ........ APPERTAIN, INHERE
belonging to a particular people ........
 ENDEMIC
belongings ......... CHATTEL, TRAPS
beloved one ............ INAMORATA
below .... FLAT, NEATH, SOTTO(lt.)
belt ... CINGLE, BALDRICK, CESTUS,
 CORDON, RING, ZONE, GIRDLE
belt conveyor ................... APRON
belt; Jewish ................... ZONAR
bema ....... CHANCEL, SANCTUARY
bemoan ....... DEPLORE, WAIL, SOB
bemuse .......... DISTRACT, ADDLE
bench EXEDRA, BERMA, PEW, SIEGE
bench-hook .................... CRAMP
bend CROOK, FLEX, INFLEX, KINK,
 SAG, CROUCH, NID, WARP, PLEACH
bend back ........ RECURVE, BULGE
bend, form a .................... COPE
bend (up) in timber ............... SNY
bending .... LITHE, PLIANT, SUPPLE
benedict ............... BRIDEGROOM
benefactor ..... PROMOTER, DONOR,
 FREE, LARGE, OPEN, PATRON

benefice, first fruit of ......... ANNAT
benefit ...... HELP, AVAIL, BEHOOF,
INTEREST, PROW, SAKE
Benet; Amer. poet ......... STEPHEN
Bengal ant thrush .......... NURANG
Bengal bison ................... GAUR
Bengal boat ................... BATEL
Bengal City ........... DACCA, PATNA
Bengal cotton ................... ADATI
Bengal, district in .............. NADIA
Bengal governor .............. CASEY
Bengal groom ........... SAICE, SYCE
Bengal native ......... KOL, BANIAN
Bengal quince ............ BAEL, BEL
Benin negro ................... EBOE
benjamin ................... BENZOIN
benne seeds ................ SESAMES
bent SWAYED, CRANK, BIAS, TASTE
benthos ....................... FAUNA
benumb .... HEBETATE, NIP, SCRAM
benzine hydrocarbon ........ XYLENE
benzoin, gum .............. BENJAMIN
"Beowulf" ....................... EPIC
bequest ................... LEGACY
berate .. SCOLD, CENSURE, UPBRAID
Berber dialect .............. TUAREG
Berea-grit ............. SANDSTONE
bereave .... DEPRIVE, DIVEST, STRIP
Berber HARATIN, HAMITE, KABYLE
beret ................. BIRETTA, TAM
berg ..... BARROW, MOUNTAIN, ICE
beri-beri ................... DROPSY
Berkshire race course .......... ASCOT
beri-beri; Jap ................ KAKKE
berm ....................... TERRACE
Bermuda grass ................... DOOB
Bernard De ................... VOTO
Bernecia, founder of .............. IDA
Berra ........................... YOGI
berry ....... CURRANT, BACCA, HAW,
ALLSPICE, SALAL
berry; slang ................... DOLLAR
berry smoked in cigarettes .... CUBEB
berry-like ................... BACCATE
berserk .. BRAVO, PIRATE, WARRIOR
Bert; comedian ................ LAHR
Bert; T.V. star ............... PARKS
bertha ..... CAPE, CANNON, COLLAR
beseech ........ OBTEST, OBSECRATE
beseeching ............... PRECATIVE
beset HARRY, OBSESS, SIT, ATTACK
beshrew .......... CURSE, EXECRATE
besides..... THEN, ALSO, OVER, TOO
besiege ........ BESET, GIRD, OBSIDE
besieged camp .... ......... LEAGUER
besmear SLAKE, SMOTTER, BEBLOT,
DAUB
besom ........ BROOM, MOP, STRIGIL
bespangle ...... STUD, STAR, ADORN
bespeak .. ADDRESS, ORDER, SHOW
bespoil .. FLEECE, STRIP, PLUNDER
best .. UTMOST, VANQUISH, OUTWIT
best; comb. form .............. ARISTO
bestial name AGEE, EPICURIST, HOG
bestow GRANT, ADD, GIVE, RENDER
bet ..... HEDGE, GO, STAKE, WAGER
bet, in roulette ................... BAS
betake oneself      REPAIR, JOURNEY

Betelgeuse ...................... STAR
betelnut seed ............... CATECHU
betelnut tree ................... ARECA
Bethlemite, rich ................... BOAZ
betimes ........ EARLY, SOON, ANON
betoken DENOTE, PRESAGE, AUGUR
betray ...... BEGUILE, PEACH, SELL
betrayer SEDUCER, TRAITOR, JUDAS
betroth ........ AFFY, EARL, TOKEN
better ....... EMEND, TOP, IMPROVE
betting system ............... PARLAY
between ........... AMELL, AVERAGE
between; law ................ MESNE
bevel ........ EDGE, ASLANT, SNAPE
bevel out ........................ REAM
beveled edge .......... BEARD, WANE
beverage ALE, CIDER, GROG, NEGUS,
TEA
beverage; Arab. ................. LEBAN
beverage, delicious ..... POP, MORAT,
NECTAR
beverage, oriental ...... RAKEE, RAKI,
ARRACK
beverage; Poly. ................... KAVA
beverage; S. Am. ................ MATE
beverage stand ............... CELLARET
bevy ......... COVEY, FLOCK, HERD
bewail ............. GRIEVE, LAMENT
bewildered ........ ASEA, CONFUSED
bewilderment ..... AGAPE, DAZE, ATE
bewitch ............ CHARM, ENAMOR,
ENSORCEL
bewitching HEXING, MAGICAL, SIREN
bewray ........ DISCLOSE, REVEAL
beyond YONSIDE, BY, PAST, YONDER
beyond; prefix ................... META
bezel ...... TEMPLATE, FACET, RIM
bhang ........................... HEMP
bhang, product of ............ MAJOON
bias ..... CLINAMEN, PARTIAL, PLY,
POISE, SLOPE, TENDENCY,
SLANT
Bible, books of the ..... MACCABEES
Bible, line of ................... STICH
"    , of Luther's translation in .......
WARTBURG
"    , Syrian version of .... PESHITO
"    , version of ........... VULGATE
"    , Zoan of the ............ TANIS
Biblical Amalek king .......... AGAG
"    ascetic order ......... ESSENE
"    character ................... GOG
"    city GOLM, RESEN, AVEN, UR
"    coin ........... MITE, TALENT
"    fortress ............. DATHEMA
"    horned wild animal ..... REEM
"    king ...... BERA, OMRI, SAUL
"    kingdom ................. ELAM
"    lion ........................ ARI
"    merchant .............. TUBAL
"    mountain ..... ARARAT, HOR,
ABLA, SINAI, HOREB, NEBO
"    name .......... ANAK, ANANI,
ARAM, AROD, AROM, EBAL,
EBED, ER, EZEL, GADDI,
HELI, IRA, IRAD, ISHMAEL,
IVAH, JAEL, MAGOG,
MERAB, MESHACH, NER,

NOB, ON, OSEE, REBA, SEMEL, UCAL, UR, VASHTI
" ornament .. URIM, THUMMIM
" place ................. ENDOR
" priest ................... ELI
" prophet .... ASAHIAH, AMOS, ELIAS
" timber cut edgewise .... ASIEL
" tower ......... BABEL, EDAR
" well ............... ESEC, ESEK
" , worthless ............. RACA
bibliotheca ................ LIBRARY
bibulous one ............ DRUNK, SOT
bicker ARGUE, DISPUTE, PETTIFOG
bicycle for two .............. TANDEM
bid .. ENJOIN, OVERTURE, TENDER
biddy ...................... CHICKEN
bier .. PYRE, CATAFALQUE, LITTER
bifurcation ........ BRANCHED, WYE
big shot; sl. ................... VIP
big toe ..................... HALLUX
bighorn; Am. ................ ARGALI
bight ..... LOOP, BAY, NOOSE, GULF
bilingual ........ DIGLOT, POLYGLOT
bilk .... GYP, HOAX, TRICK, CHEAT
bill .... BEAK, LIST, TAB, TICKET
bill of an anchor .................. PEE
bill of fare ............ CARTE, MENU
bill of ......................... RIGHTS
bill, protuberance at ...... NEB, CERE
bill stroke ....................... PECK
billhook ........... KNIFE, SNAGGER
billiard shot ......... CAROM, MASSE
billingsgate, arguing with ... ABUSIVE, FOUL
billionaire ..................... NABOB
billow .. EAGRE, BORE, WAVE, SEA, SURGE
billy .......... CAN, CLUB, CUDGEL, COMRADE
bin for fish ...................... KENCH
binate ........... DOUBLE, TWOFOLD
bind ...................... GIRD, ROPE
bind to secrecy .......... FRAP, TILE
bind with fetters ... GYVE, TIE, IRON
binding, limp .................... YAPP
binding machine ............... BALER
binding together ....... COLLIGATION
bindle-stiff .................... TRAMP
binge ............. HIT, SOAK, SPREE
bingo ....... LOTTO, TANGO, BEANO
bingo, forerunner of ............. TAP
binnacle .... PYX, COMPASS, NEEDLE
binomics ........ ECOLOGY, BIOLOGY
biography LIFE, MEMOIR, RECOUNT
biological decadence ....... PARACME
biological factor ................. GENE
biological fissure ............... RIMA
biological division ........... GENERA
biology .................... GENETICS
bion, opposed to ........... MORPHON
bipennis ............... AX, WEAPON
biplane ........... SPAD, AIRPLANE
birch ....... BETULA, FLOG, STICK
bird, adjutant ...... STORK, ARGALA, MARABOU
" , African ... COLY, LORY, LOURI

" Arctic ............... LONGSPUR
" ajaja, genus ........ SPOONBILL
" , albatross, black ........ NELLY
" , Andean, large ........ CONDOR
" apteryx ...... IAO, KIWI, OWENI
" , area from bill to eye of a LORE
" , Asian ............. MYNA, PITTA
" , auk family; genus .....PUFFIN, ALCA
" , Austral. .......... EMEW, EMU, PARDALOTE
" , Austral.; genus ........ LEIPOA
" beak ........ CERAL, LORA, NEB, ROSTRA
" , blackbird RAVEN, ANI, MERL, MERLE
" , blackbird, Eur. AMSEL, OUSEL, OUZEL
" , bluebird; genus ......... IRENA
" , bobolink .............. ORTOLAN
" , bob-white ....... COLIN, QUAIL
" , Braz. ..... CARIAMA, SERIEMA
" , Braz. fruit eating ..... TOUCAN
" , brilliant tropical ..... JACAMAR, TROGON
" brood ..................... COVEY
" , butcher ................. SHRIKE
" , carrion crow URUBU, VULTURE
" catcher .................. FOWLER
" , chatterer ................... JAY
" , class of ..................... AVES
" , cockatoo ................. ARARA
" , corvine .. CROW, DAW, RAVEN
" , courlan .. JACAMAR, TINAMON
" , crocodile . SICSAC, TROCHILUS
" , cuckoo black-bird .... ANI, ANO
" , cuckoo, of E. Indies ...... KOEL
" , cuculoid ..................... ANI
" , crow, cry of ................. CAW
" , crow-like CORVINE, PIE, ROOK
" , Cuban ... TOCORORO, TROGON
" , dabchick . GREBE, GALLINULE
" , diving .... AUK, GREBE, LOON
" dog .......... POINTER, SETTER
" , duck family ...... MERGANSER, SMEW
" , dunlin ..................... STIB
" , eagle; Bib. ................. GIER
" , eagle, sea; Eur. .... ERN, ERNE
" , eagle, nest of .... AERIE, EYRIE
" , E. Ind. song ............. SHAMA
" , Egypt. sacred ............. IBIS
" , emu-like ........ CASSOWARY
" , Eur. wren ....... REED, SEDGE
" , extinct AUK, DODO, MOA, ROC
bird, falcon ......... MERLIN, SAKER, TERCEL
" , finch ......... TOWHEE, MORO,
" , falcon, E. Ind. ...... BESRA, PEREGRINE, SHAHIN REDPOOL
" , finch, yellow ............. SERIN
" , finchlike ........... GROSBEAK, CHEWINK
" , fish hawk ............. OSPREY
" , flightless .. DODO, EMU, MOA, OSTRICH, PENGUIN

25

" , flightless; genus .... APTERYX, NOTORNIS
" , flycatcher .... OSCINE, PEWEE
" , food ..................... CAPON
" , frigate ...................... IWA
" , fulmar, giant ............ NELLY
" , gallinaceous, order of RASORES
" , game .............. PTARMIGAN
" , gluttonous ....... CORMORANT
" , guan; genus .......... ORTALIS
" , gull, per. to ............ LARINE
" , gull, sea .... MAA, MEW, TERN
" , gull-like TERN, JAEGER, SKUA
" , Hawaiian ... MAMO, IWA, IIWI, OOAA
" , hawk ............... CARACARA
" , hawk, E. Ind. ....... GOSHAWK, SHIKRA
" , hawk, small .......EYAS, KITE
" , hawk-like .............. OSPREY
" , heron ................... EGRET
" , heron family ... IBIS, BITTERN
" , honey-eating .... TUI, MANUAO
" house ............ NEST, AVIARY
" , humming COLIBRI, TROCHILUS
" , humming; S. Am. ....... SYLPH
" , humming, topaz ............ AVE
" , iao .................... MANUAO
" , ibis ............ STORK, GUARA
" , Ind. ...... AMADAVIT, SHAMA
" , insectivorous ........... VIREO
" , jackdaw ...... COE, KAE, DAW
" jaw, part of ............... MALA
" , jay-like .................... PIET
" , keel bill .................... ANI
" , killing of ............. AVACIDE
" , kite; Eur. .............. GLEDE
" , large EMU, GUAN, KITE, MOA
" , large, wading ........... JABIRU
" , Latin for ................. AVIS
" life ....................... ORNIS
" , limicoline ............. AVOCET
" , long legged ............. WADER
" , long neck ............... SWAN
" , loon-like ............... GREBE
" , lyre .................... MENURA
" , macaw; Austral. .. ARA, ARARA
" , magpie ............. MAG, PIET
" , marsh, long leg .......... STILT
" , martin; Eur. ........ MARTLET
" , meadow lark .......... ACORN
" , mound .... LEIPOA, MEGAPOD
" , New Zeal. LOWAN, KIWI, MOA, TUI
" , non-passerine .. HOOPOE, TODY
" of India .................... AVIS
bird of Jove ................... EAGLE
" of June ............... PEACOCK
" of petrel family ........ FULMAR
" of prey BUZZARD, (GOS)HAWK, EAGLE, OWL, _LANT
" of prey; Eur. ... KITE, KESTREL
" of prey; order ........ RAPTORES
" of Savanas; Brazil ..... SERIEMA
" of the crow family ..... CHOUGH
" of the rail family ......... CRAKE
" of the snipe family .... GODWIT
" , oldest known ARCHAEOPTERY

" , one year old ........ ANNOTINE
" , oriole ................... PIROL
" , oscine ...... CROW, TANAGER, VIREO
" , osprey ............. ERN, ERNE
" , ostrich-like ................ EMU
" , owl; Samoan ............. LULU
" , parrot . KAKA, KAKAPOS, KEA
" , parson ................. POE, TUI
" , partridge ............. SEESEE
" , partridge-like ....... TINAMOU, TINAMIDA
" , passerine .... SPARROW, PITA, STARLING
" , pelican-like ............. SOLAN
" pepper ................. CAPSICUM
" , per. to ........ AVIAN, AVINE, ORNITHIC
" , petrel; N. Z. ................ TITI
" , pewee ................. PHOEBE
" , pheasant's nest ........... NIDE
" , pigeons; genus .......... GOURA
" , pigeons; type of ........... NUN
" , plover-like .......... LAPWING
" , quail-like .. TINAMOU, TURNIX
" , rail ..... CRAKE, MOHO, SORA, WEKAS
" , rain, migratory ....... PLOVER
" , ratital order of ..... EMU, MOA, OSTRICH
" , raven; Hawaii ......... ALALA
" , reed ................. BOBOLINK
" , ring dove ...............CUSHAT
" , ruff ............... SANDPIPER
" , ruff, female ............ REEVE
" , Samoan ..................... IAO
" , sandpiper, female ....... REEVE
" , sandpiper, Old World .. DUNLIN, TEREK
" , sea ......... GANNET, MURRE, PETREL, SULA
" , sea, auk family ........ PUFFIN
" , shore .. AVOCET, SORA, STILT, WILLET
" , short tailed .............. BREVE
" , Sinbad's .................... ROC
" , small ........ TIT, WREN, TODY
" , small singing ............. PIPIT
" , snake ................ ANHINGA
" , snipe .. CURLEY DOWITCHER
" , S. Amer. ..... GUAN, TOUCAN, WARRIOR
" , song; Ind. .............. SHAMA
" , song, organ of ......... SYRINX
" , sorrel, wood ................ OCA
" , starling .......... MINO, MYNA, STARNEL
" , stib .................... DUNLIN
bird, stitch-bird ................... IHI
" , stork; Afr. .......... MARABOU
" , stork-like wading ......... IBIS
" , swallow; Eur. .......MARTLET
" , swallow-like ...... HIRUNDINE, MARTIN, TERN, SWIFT
" , swimming ...... GREBE, SWAN
" , talking .... MINA, MINO, MYNA
" , Tasmanian ....... PARDALOTE
" , three toed .............. STILT

26

"  , thrush; Eur. ............. OUSEL
"  , thrush family ........... SHAMA
"  , thrush, golden ......... ORIOLE
"  , thrush, Wilson's ........ VEERY
"  , thrush, song .......... MAVIS
"  , toucan, black .............. TOCO
"  , towhee bunting ..... CHEWINK
"  , trop. Am. ............ MANAKIN
"  , tropical, wading ....... JACANA
"  , trumpeter ............... AGAMI
"  , turkey-like ...... CURASSOW,
        LEIPOA
"  , unfledged; obs. .......... QUAB
"  , unmusical ............ TANAGER
"  , vestment ............. GREMIAL
"  , vulture, black ........... URUBU
"  , wading COOT, CURLEW, HERN,
        HERON, IBIS, JACANA, RAIL,
        SORA, TERN, UMBRETTE,
        STORK
"  , warbler ..... PIPIT, REDSTART
"  , waxwing; Am. ...........CEDAR
"  , weaver; genus ........ MUNIA
"  , weaver; S. Amer. ........ TAHA
"  , West Ind. ............ ANI, TODY
"  , woman ................ AVIATRIX
"  , yellow hammer .......... FINCH,
        FLICKER
"  , yellow billed .......... CUCKOO
"  , young ............. FLEDGLING
bird's foot, adapted for perching
        ENSESSO
birds; genus ICTERUS, ANSER, OTIS,
        PITTA
bird's head, side of .............. LORU
birds, long billed .......... CREEPER,
        NUTHATCH
birds of given region .......... ORNIS
birds, of the ........... AVIAN, AVINE
birds, per. to singing ......... OSCINE
birds, scientific study of ...... OOLOGY
birds, seedeater ......... CHICKADEE,
        GROSBEAK, JUNCO
birds, the ....................... AVES
birl .......................... ROTATE
birth ... GENESIS, NEE, BEGINNING
birth, before .............. PRENATAL
birth rate ................. NATALITY
birth-root ................. TRILLIUM
birthday poem .......... GENETHLIAC
birthmark ........... NAEVUS, BLAIN
birthplace of Alexander the Great
        PELLA
birthright HERITAGE, INHERITANCE
birthstone ............. SUPERSTITION
"      for Jan'y ......... GARNET
"      for Feb. ....... AMETHYST
"      for Mar. ..... BLOODSTONE
"      for Apr. ........ DIAMOND
"      for May ......... EMERALD
"      for June ............ AGATE
"      for July ....... CORNELIAN
"      for Aug. ....... SARDONYX
"      for Sep. ..... CHRYSOLITE
"      for Oct. .............. OPAL
"      for Nov. ............ TOPAZ
"      for Dec. ....... TURQUOISE

bis ........ AGAIN, ENCORE, TWICE,
        REPEAT
Biscay, language of .......... BASQUE
biscuit ........ WAFER, BUN, PANAL,
        RATAFEE, RUSK, SCONE, SNAP,
        PANTILE, CRACKER
bishop, chess ..................... ALFIN
"   , in education ........... TUTOR
"   of Alexandria ............ ARIUS
"   , first year revenue ..... ANNAT
"   of Rome ................... POPE
bishop weed .............. AMMI, GOUT
bishopric ............... DIOCESE, SEE
bishopric, raise to .............. MITRE
bishop's cap ..................... HURA
"   cap, plant; genus HURA
"   seat .......... APSE, BEMA,
        CATHEDRA
"   staff ................. CROSIER
"   staff of office ......... CROOK
"   title ... PRIMATE, PRELATE,
        ABBA
"   upper robe ........ CHIMERE
"   vestment ... COPE, GREMIAL,
        ROCHET
bisk; var. ........................ SOUP
bism; Scot. ....................... GULF
bismerian ....................... MOCK
bison .. BOVINE, BUFFALO, AUROCH
bissyn .................... FLAX, LINEN
bistort .................. SNAKEWEED
bistro ...... BAR(TENDER), TAVERN
bisulcate ..................... CLOVEN
bit ..... ACE, IOTA, JOT, MOTE, POD,
        ATOM, WHIT, MORSEL, SNAFFLE
bite ...... STING, NIP, WHEAL, EAT
bite impatiently ............... CHAMP
biting of nails ...... PHANEROMANIA
bito .......................... AGIALID
bitter ACID, AMARA, ACERB, ACRID,
        IRATE
bitter crystalline substance . AMARINE
bitter sentiment ... ACRIMONY, HATE
bitter substance .. ALUM, PICROMEL,
        ALOIN
bitter vetch ......................... ERS
bitterness ....... ACOR, RUE, ATTER,
        ACHE, PAIN, SMART, MARAH
bitters; Fr. ............. AMER, AIGRE
bitumen ..... ASPHALT, TAR, PITCH
bituminous shale .................. BAT
bivalve ........ PANDORA, MOLLUSK
bivalves, fresh water; genus ..... UNIO
bivouac .... ENCAMP, ETAPE, CAMP
bizarre ... GROTESQUE, ODD, ANTIC,
        EXOTIC, QUAINT, QUEER
bizarre; Fr. ........... DEDAL, OUTRE
Bizet; opera by ............... CARMEN
Bjoerling, Jussi ................. TENOR
Bjornson hero ................... ARNE
black ..... JET, EBON, INKY, NEGRO,
        RAVEN, NIGRINE, SMOOCH
"   alloy .................... NIELLO
"   and blue .. ECCHYMOSIS, LIVID
"   art ............ EVIL, MAGIC
"   beer ................. DANTZIC
"   bird; Assyr. ................... ZU
"   ; Celtic ....................DHU

27

" , coal .................. ATROUS
" , comb. form ...... ATER, ATRO
" crys. mineral .......... KNOPITE
" diamond ................... COAL
" garnet .............. MELANITE
" gram, ...................... URD
" gum ................. TUPELO
" hematite ........ PSILOMELANE
" mineral .... URANINITE, IRIDE
" pigment of eye ......... MELANIN
" rhinoceros .............. BORELE
Black Plague ................. BUBONIC
Black Sea, old name for ...... EUXINE
Black Sea, per to ............ PONTIC
Black Sea port ................ ODESSA
black silver .............. STEPHANITE
blackamoor ..................... NEGRO
blackball ..... PILL, PIP, OSTRACIZE
black-beetle .............. COCKROACH
black-bird .... MERLE, RAVEN, ANI,
                                OUZEL
blackboard ................... SLATE
blacken ................... JAPAN, INK
blackened ................... SOOTED
black-eyed nymph (damsel) .... HOURI
black-fin snapper ................. SESI
black-fish ................... TAUTOG
black-foot ........... MATCHMAKER
blackguard ........... GAMIN, KNAVE
black-hand of Naples ...... CAMORRA
black-heart ................. CHERRY
black-hole .................. DUNGEON
blackfish ..................... SWART
black-jack . CARAMEL, SPHALERITE
black-jack, mining .......... BLENDE
black-leg ..................... CHEAT
blackmailing; law ......... CHANTAGE
black-martin .................. SWIFT
black-saltwort .................. GLAUX
blacksmith ...... FARRIER, STRIKER
blacksmith's shop ............. STITHY
black-snake ........ RACER, COLUBER
black-tellurium ........... NAGYAGITE
blackthorn ......................... SLOE
blackthorn, fruit of .............. HAW
black-vulture; C. Amer. ........ URUBU
black-water ................. PYROSIS
black-weed ................. RAGWEED
black-widow .................. SPIDER
black-wort ................. COMFREY
bladder kelp ................ SEAWEED
blade .. BIT, TOLEDO, GRAIN, LEAF,
                                SPIRE
blaeberry ................. VACCINIUM
blague ...................... BRAG, LIE
blah .......... NONSENSE, RUBBISH
blain ........ BLISTER, BULLA, SORE
Blaine, Miss ................... VIVIAN
blait of a market ................ DULL
blame . CENSURE, REPROACH, CALL,
             OBLOQUY, ODIUM, SHEND
blanch .. ARGENT, ETIOLATE, LEAD
bland ....... AFFABLE, MILD, SOFT,
             AMENITY, GENTLE, SUAVE
blandation ................. FLATTERY
blander ........... BEGUILE, CAJOLE
blanket .... AFGHAN, BROT, COTTA,
             QUILT, MANTA, STROUD

blanket, small ................. THROW
blare of a trumpet ......... TANTARA,
                                FANFARE
blast furnace, section of ......... BOSH
blasted .. RUINED, BLIGHTED, SERE
blastie; Scot. .................. DWARF
blastomere forming endoderm ......
                                ENTOMERE
blat .................... BLEAT, BLURT
blatant ...... COARSE, GIORY, NOISY
blaubok ......................... ETAAC
blaver; Scot. ................... VIOLET
blaze ...... FLAME, FLARE, MARK
blaze star ...................... NOVA
blazer .................... JACKET
bleach . BLANCH, ETIOLATE, PATCH
bleaching vat ..................... KEIR
bleak, (a fish) ........ SPRAT, ABLEN,
                                ABLET
"Bleak House" heroine ............ ADA
blear, of the eye ........... DIM, SORE
bleared ..... RHEUMY, DUSKY, INKY
bleater ..................... SHEEP
bleb ... BULLA, BLISTER, PUSTULE
bleffert; Scot. .................. SQUALL
bleib; Scot. ................... BLISTER
blemish BLOT, MACULE, MAR, SCAR,
             FLAW, INJURY, SLUR, TACHE
blemish in cloth .. DEFECT, AMPER,
                                SULLY
blench ...... FLINCH, PALE, QUAIL
blend .... MERGE, FUSE, GRADATE,
             TINCTURE, TINGE, MIX, SEEL
blend colors . RUN, FONDU, SCUMBLE
bless ...... CONSECRATE, HALLOW,
                                MACARIZE
blessed; Fr. ................... SACRE
blessing ....... BENISON, BOON, SAIN
blight .... BLAST, RUIN, SEER, SMUT
blind alley ................... IMPASSE
blind flower girl .................. NIDIA
blind impulse ..................... ATE
blind; Sp. ...................... CIEGO
blind staggers ..................... GID
blind worm ..................... ORVET
blindfolder .................. HOODMAN
blindness ....... ANOPSIA, ABLEPSIA
blinds, as a hawk ............... SEELS
bliss ......... FELICITY, RAPTURE
blissful ............. ECSTATIC, SEELY
blister ........ BLEB, BLAIN, BLURE
blithe ............. AIRY, GAY, MERRY
blizzard, Alaska ................. PURGA
bloated ........ TUMEFIED, TURGID,
                                CONVEX
blob ........ MARK, SPLOTCH, BLOT,
             BUBBLE, WEN, DROP
block .... DAM, NOG, HINDER, MASS,
                                STYMIE
" , falconry ............... PERCH
" , flat; Arch. ........... MUTULE
" , hawser ................... BITT
" house ...................... FORT
" , ice ...................... SERAC
" , iron stamp .............. VOL
" , mechanical .......... PULLEY
" , nautical ............ DEADEYE
" of type metal ............. QUAT

28

" of wood .. BESET, BUST, CUBE, LOON
" , pedestal plinth .... SOCLE, DIE
" , small ............... TESSERA
blockhead .... DUNCE, NINNY, DOLT, ASS, FOOL, IDIOT, OAF
blockhead board ................. DOLL
block-like ...................... STUPID
blood . GORE, BLADE, SPARK, FLUID
" bank deposit ............... PINT
" , boltered ............. CLOTTED
" , charac. of ............. HEMIC
" color ............... SANGUINE
" , coloring matter of ..... CRUOR
" disease .............. LEUKEMIA
" emulsion ................. CHYLE
" feud ................ VENDETTA
" fluid; comb. form ......... SERO
" fluid part .............. PLASMA
" , letting ......... PHLEBOTOMY
" lineage .......... SIB, DESCENT, PROGENY
" of the gods ............. ICHOR
" poisoning ............ PYAEMIA
" ; prefix .......... HEMA, HEMO
" , red .................. VENOUS
" slackening ............... STASIS
" , stagnation of .. CLOT, CRUOR, GRUME, GORE
" vessel .... VAS, ARTERY, VEIN
bloodless ........ ANAEMIC, ATONY, LANGUOR
bloodlike HEMATOID, BURKE, GORE
blood-money ...................... CRO
bloodsucker ...... VAMPIRE, LEECH
bloody ......... GORY, SANGUINARY, CRUENT
bloom . BLOW, FUZZ, HEYDAY, DEW, FLOWER, YOUTH, DOWN
bloomer ........ TROUSER, MISTAKE
bloomery ........... HEARTH, FORGE
blossom ....... BELL, BLOOM, BLOW
blossom keels ................. CARINAE
blot .. BLUR, SULLY, SMEAR, ERROR
blot out .......... DELETE, EFFACE, EXPUNGE, DELE, DESTROY
blotch .... MOTTLE, MACULA, BLEB, BULLA
blotch of color ..... GOUT, LIPSTICK
blotter .................... BLAD, PAD
blouse ....... SMOCK, TUNIC, WAIST
blow .... DINT, PANT, SLOG, CLOUT, THWACK, BUFFET, PLUMP
blow cement on sculpture ..... KIBOSH
blow; col. ...... ONER, RANT, VAUNT
blow in gusts ....... WHIFFLE, FLAN
blow up ........ INFLATE, ENLARGE
blow with cudgel ......... LAMBSKIN, CONK(ER)
blowing out; Skt. ............ NIRVANA
blowzed .... RUDDY, FLUSHED, RED
blubber ............ FAT, WEEP, CRY
blubber, cut ............... FLENSED
bludgeon ........ CUDGEL, MACE, BAT, SHILLALAH, CLUB
blue, azure-like ................... BICE
" back ........ TROUT, HERRING
" ball .................... NILGAU

" cap .............. SCOT, TOMTIT
" ; col. ................. PEDANTIC
" , dark ..................... PERSE
" dye ... CYANINE, ANIL, WOAD
" Eagle Agency ................NRA
" fin ............ HERRING, TUNA
" gill .................... SUNFISH
" fish ...................... TAILER
" grass ........................ POA
" jeans ...................... LEVIS
" penciler ................. EDITOR
" pigment .. BICE, SMALT, INDIGO
" print ................. DIAGRAM
" , shade of .... AZURE, COBALT
" vitriol .............. BLUESTONE
blue and lemon ............. BELTON
Bluebeard's wife ............. FATIMA
bluebottle, the ........ CORNFLOWER
blues .. DISMALS, DUMPS, MEGRIMS
bluff . BANK, CLIFF, CRUSTY, RUDE
bluish-gray ................... CESIOUS
bluish green-blue ......... CALAMINE
blunder ... BULL, ERR, SLIP, BONER, ERROR, FAILURE, MISDO
blunt ... ASSUAGE, BLATE, OBTUND
blunt in emotivity ......... HEBETATE
blur ...... BLOB, MACKLE, MACULE
blurb .. AD, RAVE, ANNOUNCEMENT
blush ..... COLOR, MANTLE, FLUSH
blushingly . ERUBESCENTLY, ROSILY
bluster ....... ROAR, BOUNCE, RANT, THREATEN, RODOMONTADE
Blyth, actress .................... ANN
boa, ringed .................... ABOMA
boar ..... APER, BARROW, HOG, SUS
boar; Hindu ................. VARAHA
boar, wild, per. to ............ APRINE
boar, young ................... HOGGET
board, fixed size ............... DEAL
board, spring .. ALCALDE, FLEXIBLE
boards ...... KEEPS, STAGE, FEEDS
boar's head ...................... HURE
boast ... BRAG, GAB, VAPOR, VAUNT
boaster ............. BRAVADO, JINGO
boastful ............. THRASONICAL
boastful speech ......... KOMPOLOGY
boasting ................... GASCONADE
boat .. GIG, ARK, BUSS, CAT, COBUL, TROW
" , African slave ........... DHOW
" , anc. Britons' ........ CORACLE
" , Bolivian ............... BALSA
" brace ................. THWART
" captain in the East ......... RAIS
" , Chinese .............. SAMPAN
" , dispatch ....... OOLAK, AVISO
" , Dutch ................. PRAAM, TRECKSCHUYT
" , Dutch, small ........ HOOKER
" , Eskimo .... OOMIAC, OOMISK
" , E. Ind. ... DINGEY, DINGHEY, DONI
" , flat bottom DORY, BAC, PUNT, SCOW, BATEAU
" , flat bottom fishing ..... BARIS, COBLE
" , freight, of Nile ......... BARIS
" , French .............. CARAVEL

29

"  , half-decked ......... WHERRY
"  , heavy decked ....... CANALER
"  , India ................ MASOOLA
"  , Indian River ........ ALMADIA
"  , Italian .............. GONDOLA
"  , kind of raft ........... BARGE,
                              CATAMARAN
"  , large merchant .......ARGOSY
"  , large; W. Ind. ......... MOSES
"  light, used in Bosporus .. COIQUE
"  , man of war's ....... PINNACE
"  , Malayan ......... TOUP, PROA
"  , name of Jason's ......... ARGO
"  propelled by three rowers .......
                              RANDAN
"  shaped ............. NAVICULAR
"  , ships .................... YAWL
"  , small ..... SHALLOP, SKULL,
                              SKIFF
"  , small fishing ... COG, COGGLE
"  , small flat bottom . DORY, PUNT
"  , state, Venetian .. BUCENTAUR
"  , steam ...................... TUG
"  tender ....................... HOY
"  used by Britons ....... CORACLE
"  , W. Ind. merchant .. DROGHER
boatman; Gr. .................. PHAON
boat-shape vessel ........ NAVICELLA
boat-shaped ornament ........... NEF
boats, collection of ............... TOW
boatswain of a Lascar crew .. SERANG
boatswain's whistle ............. PIPE
boat timber ..................... KEEL
Boaz, son of ..................... OBED
Boaz, wife of .................... RUTH
bob .. PENDANT, BAB, FLOAT, DOCK
bob cat .......................... LYNX
bobbin SPOOL, PIRN, REEL, SPINDLE
bobization syllable .................. NI
bobolink ..................... ORTOLAN
bobtail; Scot. ................. STRUNT
bocaccio; Cal. ..................... COD
Boccaccio classic ......... DECAMERON
bode AUGUR, PORTEND, FORETELL
bodega; Sp. .............. WINESHOP
bodice ............... BASQUE, WAIST
bodkin .... AWL, PONIARD, DAGGER
body, anterior part of ....... PROSOMA
"  cavity ................. COELOM
"  , injury of . MAYHEM, TRAUMA
"  joint .... ELBOW, LIMB, WRIST
"  , main ....... PHYSIQUE, UNIT,
                              CORSE
"  of a vehicle ......... BED, BOX
body, per. to ........ TRUNK, TORSE,
                              SOMAL
"  small ................... NANOID
"  stimulant ............ HORMONE
"  twist ................ FLOUNCE
Boer dialect .................... TAAL
Boer general ................... BOTHA
boeuf; Fr. ...................... BEEF
bog ...... FEN, MARSH, MOOR, OOZE
bog manganese ................... WAD
bog peat ................. CESS, MOSS
bog plant ..................... ABAMA
bogey .. BUGABOO, BUGBEAR, BOGY
boggy ............. MIRY, SOFT, WET

bogle ...... ALARM, GOBLIN, SCARE
bohea ................................ TEA
Bohemia, district in ............ EGER
Bohemian ..... PICARD, HUS, ARTY,
                              GYPSY
"  character .............. MIMI
"  city .................. PRAHA
"  dance ... REDOWA, TALIAN
"  garnet .............. PYROPE
"  mountain range ......... ERZ
"  vesuviante ......... EGERAN
boidae; chief genera ...... BOA, ERYZ,
                              PYTHON
boil .... ANTHRAX, SEETHE, STEW,
                       ANGER, BUBBLE, STY
boiled ...................... ESTUATED
boiler ...... YET, CALDRON, COPPER
boiler, a .. ALEMBIC, RETORT, TANK
boiler reinforcer ................ SPUT
boiler-tube scaler ............. SOOTER
bokardo ............ DOKAMO, PRISON
bold ...... BRAZEN, EPILOSE, PERT,
                              FORWARD
bold style of type ....... TEXT, DARK
bole .. CRYPT, DOSE, STEM, TRUNK
bolero ..... JACKET, DANCE, WAIST
bolide .............. MISSILE, METEOR
Bolivia, dept. in ................ ORURO
Bolivian coin .................. TOMINE
boll .......... GROW, PERICARP, POD
bolo .............. KNIFE, MACHETE
Bologna, anc. It. name .... BONONIA,
                              FELSINA
Bolshevik secret police .......... OGPU
bolt .. DREDGE, SIFT, PAWL, RIVET,
                CLOSE, FASTEN, RUN, GULP
bolt, a .. TOGGLE, NAB, PIN, PINTLE
bolter ............. SIEVE, DESERTER
bolthead ........ MATRASS, ALEMBIC
bolus; Lat. ................ CLOD, LUMP
bom ................................. BOA
bomb .. GRENADE, MARMITE, BLARE
bombardment CANNONADE, STRAFE,
                              RAFALE
bombardon .. BASSOON, OBOE, TUBA
bombast ...... FUSTIAN, GAS, RAGE,
                       BOASTING, RANT
bombastic .... INFLATED, OROTUND,
                       TURGID, GRANDIOSE
Bombay town ................. MIRAJ
bomber ....... AIRRAIDER, CORSAIR,
                FURY, HAVOC, MARAUDER
bomber-PBM .............. MARINER
bombinate ................ BOOM, HUM
bombing plane; Fr. ............ AVION
bombproof chamber ..... ABRI, CASE-
                              MATE
bomb-pump ................. STIRRUP
bombyx ..................... ERI, ERIA
bonasus ......... AUROCH, BISON, OX
bond ...... DUTY, LINK, NEXUS, TIE,
                COMPACT, RELATION, VOW
bond; Fr. ...................... RENTE
bondage .. SERVITUDE, THRALDOM,
                              YOKE
bondland ................. COPYHOLD
bondman .............. CHURL, ESNE

bondsman ... SURETY, SERF, SLAVE, HELOT, STOOGE, VILLEIN
bone .... OCCIPITAL, OS, RIB, TIBIA
" , breast .... RATITE, STERNUM
" , cavities ................... ANTRA
" , cheek ................. MALAR
" ; comb. form ............. OSTEO
" curvature ........... LORDOSIS
" decay ........... OSITE, CARIES
" disease .... RACHITIS, RICKETS
" , face ................ MAXILLA
" , flank .................... ILIA
" in finger ........ PHALANGE
" , inflamed ............. OSTEITIS
" , inflammatory disease of CARIES
" in fore arm ............... ULNA
" of a fish ............... OPERCLE
" of wrist ............... CARPALE
" oil ........... LANOSE, OLANIN
" oil compound .......... LANOSE
" , process of temporal .. MASTOID
" , plowshare ....... PYGOSTYLE, VOMER
" , small .... OSSELET, OSSICLE
" tarsus ................. BALISTA
" , thigh ................... FEMUR
bone-anvil ...................... INCUS
bone-black .................... ABAISER
boneless ................... OXOSSEOUS
boner ............. ERROR, BLUNDER
bones ................................OSSA
boneset ......... FEVERWORT, SAGE, THOROUGHWORT
bongo; Afr. ................ ANTELOPE
boniro ......................... COBIA
boniata ......................... YAM
bonita ......................... ATU
"Bon Homme Richard"; opponent ..... SERAPIS
bonnet ............ CHAPEAU, TOQUE, CORONET
bonnet, resembling a ........ MITRATE
bonnet string ................... BRIDE
Bonneville dam site .......... OREGON
bons mot; Fr. .................... QUIP
bony tissue ........... OSSEIN, SCRAG
boo, like a cow ............. LOW, MOO
boob ........ DUNCE, FOOL, NITWIT
booed .......................... HOOTED
boojum ......................... SNARK
book, announcement of a new .. BLURB
" awarded to undergraduate at Harvard .................... DETUR
" , back of a ............... SPINE
" , handsomely printed .. ALDINE
" , introduction to ...... ISAGOGE
" of devotions ............. MISSAL
" of hours .................. HORA
" of nobility ............ PEERAGE
" of psalms ............. PSALTER
" of rubrics ................. ORDO
" palm .......... TALIERA, TARA
" , shape and size ........ FORMAT
" sheath ................... FOREL
" selection ............. PERICOPE
" seller ............. BIBLIOPOLE
books ...... MOS, REGISTERS, TOMES
boom RESOUND, ROAR, SPAR, SPRIT

boomerang ....... RESILE, RICOCHET
boon ...... GAY, JOVIAL, JIB, BENE, FAVOR
boor .. LOUT, CARLOT, CHURL, CAD, OAF, CARL, CLOWN, TIKE
boorish .. GAWKY, RUDE, UNCOUTH
boot, Eskimo ................... KAMIK
bootlegger's wares .......... POTEEN
boot of a bird ................... OCREA
boot, stout . PAC, BALMORAL, STOGY
bootlick ........................ FAWN
bootlicker .................... YESMAN
booth STALL, LOGE, CRAME
boots, wearing ......... OCHREATED
booty ... PREY, GAIN, LOOT, SWAG, GRAFT, PRIZE, SPOIL, PELF
borax, crude ................... TINCAL
border TIP, ABUT, EDGE, RAND, RIM, SKIRT, FRONTIER
border, make a raised ............ MILL
border on stamps ......... TRESSURE
bordered ....... FLANKED, LIMBATE, VERGED
bore .. PROSER, IRK, STOOD, AUGER, DIAMETER, PLAGUE, TEWEL
bore, in a river ........ EAGRE, TIDE
bore; mus. ................... CALIBRE
bore, to pierce .. HOLE, TEREBRATE
Boreas .................... NORTHER
boredom ......... ENNUYE, TEDIUM, ANNOY, ENNUI
Borge, Victor .................... DANE
boring tool ............. BIT, WIMBLE
borings ........................ CHIPS
Boris Godunoff, char. ......... DIMITRI
born, by birth ...................... NEE
born, well ........... EUGENIC, FREE
borne, was ......... CARRIED, RODE
Borneo, aborigine of ..... IBAN, DYAK
Borneo ape ................... ORANG
Borneo, capital of ............. BRUNAI
Borneo, river in .............. BARAM
Borodin; opera by ................ IGOR
Borodin opera hero .............. IGOR
borrower .. LOANEE, DEBTOR, OWER
Borscht base ................... BEETS
bos .............. BEEF, COW, NEAT
bos, a yearling ................... CALF
bosh; rare ......... SKETCH, TRIVIA
bosh; slang .. ROT, SPOIL, END, JOKE
bosine ...................... TRUMPET
Bosnia, slavic native of ....... CROAT
boss .. DIRECTOR, FOREMAN, OVERMAN, DEAN, JEHU, STRAW
boss, a .. STUD, KNOB, KNOP, UMBO
bot .................... BOTT, LARVA
botanical angle ................... AXIL
botanical cell ...... SPORE, ENERGID
botanical change ....... CRATICULAR, PELORIA
botanical depression ......... VARIOLE
botanist ...... BROWN, RAY, THOME
botany ...................... PHYTOLOGY
botch ... BUNGLE, COBBLE, FIASCO, FAIL, MUX, MESS
botfly larvae ..................... BOTS
botfly-like ...................... BRIZE

31

bother ...... AIL, BUSTLE, HARASS, PESTER
bothy; Scot. ........... COTTAGE, HUT
bottle .. VIAL, COSTREL, KIT, PHIAL,
CARBOY, PIG
bottom .. BED, LEES, NADIR, PLAYA,
BASE
bottom facet of a brilliant .... CULET
bottom, marshy .................. SIKE
bounce; col. ............. FIRE, DISMISS
bound ... LEAP, CONFINE, DELIMIT,
SECURED
boundary ....... LINE, AMBIT, MERE,
VERGE, BOURNE, LIMIT
boundary, common ... CONTERMINAL
bounded ............. LEAPT, SPRANG
bounder .... CAD, GENT, SNOB, CUB
bounty . BONUS, REWARD, LARGESS
bouquet ...... AROMA, ODOR, POSEY,
NOSEGAY
Bourbon, capital of ......... REUNION
bourgeois, Fr. ................. CITIZEN
bourne ............. AIM, LIMIT, GOAL
bouse .... DRINK, HAUL, LIFT, TOPE
bout .... ESSAY, GO, ROUND, SETTO,
MATCH, TURN
bovine ......... BULL, OX, TAURINE
bovine; Asiatic ..................... YAK
bovine hybrid ................ CATALO
bovine mammal .................. ZEBU
bow ...... KNEE, ARC, CONGE, NOD,
SALAAM
bow low ...... BINGE, SALAM, STOOP
bow; naut. .............. BEAK, PROW
bow (ship's), fullest part ....... LOOF
bowdlerize ............... EXPURGATE
bowed .......... ARCATE, ARCUATED
bowel .. COMPASSION, PITY, COLON
bower .. RETREAT, ANCHOR, ARBOR
bowery; Dutch .................. FARM
bowfin ............... AMIA, LAWYER
bowl ........ CRATER, KITTY, BASIN,
MAZER, PATINA
bowler ..................... TRUNDLE
bowling ...................... TENPINS
bowling green .................... RINK
bowling pin .................. NINEPIN
bows ............................. KNITS
bowsprit, lateral stay ........ SHROUD
bowsprit, part of . BEE, CHOCK, HEEL
bowsprit rests .......... APRON, STEM
box . COFFURE, CAR, CASE, DORINE,
CARTON, MOUNT, LOGE
box, alms ......................... ARCA
box elder; genus ................ ACER
box for tea ................. CANISTER
box of tools ............... CHEST, KIT
boxer ............. CHINESE, SPARER
boxers, (prize); .. BAER, BRADDOCK,
CARNERA, CORBETT, DEMPSEY,
FITZSIMMONS, JEFFRIES, JOHN-
SON, LOUIS, SHARKEY, SCHME-
LING, SULLIVAN, TUNNEY, WIL-
LARD
boxing commis. of N.Y. ...............
CHRISTENBERRY
boxing match . SPARRING, GO, SETTO
box-shaped tomb .................. CIST

boxwood tree .................. SERON
boy ........ SHAVER, LAD, TAD, TOT
boy; Sp. ......................... NINO
'Boy Scout' founder BADEN-POWELL
brace ...... LEG, STRUT, PAIR, TWO
brace and a half ...... LEASH, THREE
bracelet ............. ARMIL, SANKHA
brachyuran ................... DORIPPE
bracing .......... QUICK, TONIC, AIR
bracket .. CONSOLE, CORBEL, STRUT
bract ..... SPATHE, GLUME, PALEA,
PALET
brad ................. NAIL, PIN, SPRIG
Bradley, Gen. ................... OMAR
brag ... ANCON, CROW, GASCONADE,
VAPOR, BOAST, VAUNT
Brahma .......... CREATOR, HINDOO
Brahman ...................... ARYAN
Brahman "deity" .. AGNI, AP, DYAUS,
NADI
Brahman, learned ............ PUNDIT
Brahman precept .. SUTRA, NETINETI
Brahman title .................... AYA
braid .... CUE, LACET, PLAIT, TRESS
brain box ......................... PAN
" canal ...................... ITER
" , external membrane ..... DURA
" grooves .................. SULCI
" matter .................... ALBA
" membrane .................. TELA
" orifice .................... LURA
" , per. to ...... CEREBELLAR,
CEREBRAL, ENCEPHALIC
" stone .............. MEANDRINA
" tissue .................. AREOLAR
" tumor .................. GLIOMA
brake ........ CURB, FERN, THICKET
brake, part of a .................. SHOE
bramble ..... THORN, BLACKBERRY,
BRIER
brambly .. PRICKLY, SPINY, DUMAL
bran, inferior ................... TREET
branch FORK, RAME, RICE, STOLON,
VIMEN
" , angle formed ............ AXIL
" , local .................... COURT
" of a nerve .............. RAMUS
" of ethics that discusses happiness
EUDEMONICS
" , per. to ...... COMAL, RAMAL
branched ........ RAMAL, CLADOSE,
RAMOSE
branches ..................... RAMAGE
branches, three ............. TRISKELE
branchiae ...................... GILLS
brand ...... EMBER, MARK, STAMP,
STIGMA, LABEL
brand of Smyrna figs .......... ELEME
brandish .............. SHAKE, SWING
branding ......... STIGMATIZATION
brandling ....... EARTHWORM, PARR
brandy .................... COGNAC
" , a content of ............ ETHER
" and soda .................... PEG
" cordial ................. ROSOLIO
" , French ................... MARC
" mastic .................... RAKI
brank ............ BRIDLE, PILLORY

32

brant ......... CHEN, GOOSE, QUINK
brass, to imitate gold ........ ORMOLU
brassica ... CABBAGE, COLE, KALE
brasslike alloy .... PLATEN, LATTEN
brassy ...... BRAZEN, BOLD, REEDY
brat ...... BAIRN, ELF, IMP, MINOR
brave, be ...... HEROIC, MANLY, BE-
DARE, UNTIMOROUS
Braves' owner ................ PERINI
bravo ......... BANDIT, GOOD, HEAR
brawl; .. FRACAS, FRAY, RIOT, ROW,
SHINDY
bray ..... HEEHAW, CRUSH, GRIND
brazen faced ......... PERT, DISPLAY
Brazil, first sighted by ....... CABRAL
" flycatcher ............ YETAPAS
" , land crab of ....... HORSEMAN
" , medicine plant of . JABORANDI
" nut ...................... PARA
" palm .... BABASSU, CARNAUBA
" president ................ VARGAS
" rubber region ................. ICA
" rubber tree ................ HEVEA
" , seaport of ..... BAHIA, CEARA
Brazil, state in ...... CEARA, PARANA
" town ................... MANAOS
" , wild Indian of .... AMIRANHA,
TAPUYA
" wood; Fr. ................ BRASIL
Brazilian aborigine ............. CARIB
" club moss ......... PILLIGAN
" dance ................ MAXIXE
" drink ................... ASSAI
" ipecac ................ EVEA
" long legged bird .... SERIEMA
" money .......... MILREI, REI
" parrot ARA, MACAW, TIRIBA
" plant ................... CAROA
" tree .... SATINE, ANDA, APA
" Venice ............... RECIFE
breach ...... CLEFT, GAP, RENT
breach of etiquette ......... SOLECISM
bread ... LOAF, PONE, RUSK, LOAVE
bread, boiled and seasoned ...... CUSH
bread crumbs ................. PANADA
bread crust .......... CAROB, RIND
bread, leavened; Afr. ........... KISRA
bread of Passover ............. AZYM
bread pudding ...... RANDA
bread soaked in broth ...... BREWIS
bread spread ......... BUTTER, OLEO
bread, toasted ................ SIPPET
break, gap . HIATUS, RUIN, RUPTURE
break molten glass in water DRAGADE
break out ............. ERUPT, RASH
breakable ........ SHELLY, BRITTLE
break-bone fever ............ DENGUE
breaker ...................... COMBER
breaking down, a ......... CATACLASM
breakstones ................. CALCULI
breakwater .... JETTY, DIKE, MOLE,
OBSTRUCTION, REFUGE, PIER
bream ...................... BROOM
bream; Jap. ...................... TAI
bream, young sea ............... CHAD
breast ... AMASTY, CHEST, THORAX,
STEM

breastband, substitute for .... COLLAR
breastbone .................. STERNUM
breastbone, flat .............. RATITE
breastpin ....... BROOCH, PECTORAL
breastplate, object in ...... THUMMIN
URIM
breastplate; obs. ... LORICA, POITREL
breastwork ........ BRAYE, PARAPET
breath ........... ANDE, PANT, PECH,
PNEUMA
breath, to catch the ............. GULP
breathe .... PANT, PUFF, ASPIRATE,
RESPIRE
breathe out ........ SNORT, SUSPIRE
breathe, to .......... HALITUS, PNEO
breathing . GASP, PNEUMA, WHEEZE
breathing orifice ............ SPIRACLE
breathing, painful ......... DYSPNOEA
breathing, smooth ............... LENE
breathing sound ................. RALE
breech .... BUTTOCKS, DOWP, TIGE
breech site .................... HAUSSE
breeches, riding ............ JODHPURS
breeching .......... HARNESS, ROPE
breeding place ................. NIDUS
breeze fly .................... WHAME
breeze, gentle . ZEPHYR, PIRR, AURA,
ZEPHYREAN
breezy day on Lake Geneva .... REBAT
bressumer ........................ BEAM
breve .......... WRIT, MINIM, ORDER
breviary ....... COMPEND, EPITOME
brew ...... ALE, CONCOCT, FOMENT,
COOK, CURE, HATCH, PLOT
brewer's grain MALT, BARLEY, CORN
brewer's yeast ...... LEAVEN, BARM
brewery refuse ....... DRAFF, DREGS
brewing, amount of one ......... GYLE
bribe; slang . SUBORN, BOODLE, SOP
bric-a-brack CURIO, VIRTU, BIBELOT
brick, air .................... GRATING
" fire holes .................... KILN
" of wood .................... DOOK
" , part of a .................. BAT
" refuse ......... SAMEL, SANDAL
" , unburnt and dried ..... ADOBE
" , vitrified .................. BURR
bricks, best class of ........... STOCK
bride .... ANEMONE, BAR, TIE, HENS
"bride of the sea" ............. VENUS
bridegroom's gift to bride ... HANDSEL
bridesmaid bonnet .......... CORONET
bridewell ....... GAOL, JAIL, PRISON
bridge ....... PONTOON, PONS, SPAN
bridge holding ............... TENACE
bridge of a bow inst. .... PONTICELLO
bridge of a musical inst. ...... MAGAS
bridge term .... TENACE, NIL, BOOK,
SLAM
bridle ...... SCRATCH, BIT, LORAIN
brief SHORT, TERSE, EPITOME, FEW,
COMPACT, CURT, SPAN, PITHY
briery .... SPINY, AWN, BUR, SHARP
brigand ......... BANDIT, CATERAN,
BEDOUIN, PIRATE, PICAROON
bright .. APT, NITID, NAIF, SUNNY,
BLAZE, HALO, LUSTRE, SLEEK
bright colored ............. SERRANO

bright, make ........ BURN, FURBISH
brighten ENGILD, SMARTEN, CHEER
brightness ............ NITOR, SHEEN
brilliancy .......... GLITTER, ECLAT
brilliant . EMINENT, SIGNAL, STONE
brilliant coterie ............... GALAXY
brilliant shade ............... PATINA
brim .. POKE, BRINK, EDGE, MARGE
brimming ........ BUMPERED, FULL
brine ....... PICKLE, TEARS, BRACK
brine pit ........................ WYCH
brine-shrimp ................ ARTEMIA
bring forth ....... CAUSE, RISE, EAN
bring into court ....... SIST, ARREST,
                                  AMEND
bring near, to ............... APPOSE
bring out for exhibition .......... TROT
brink ...... EDGE, BORDER, MARGE,
         DITCH, FOSS(E), RIM, VERGE
brioche .......... CUSHION, SAVARIN
brisk ... SPRY, PERK, ALIVE, YARE,
         ACTIVE, PROMPT, KEDGE
Bristed, Chas., pen name .... BENSON
bristle ..... CHAETA, HAIR, PALPUS
bristle-like appendage .... AWN, SETA
bristle, surgical ................ SETON
bristled ...... ECHINATE, HORRENT
bristle-like tip ................ ARISTA
bristly .. SCOPATE, HISPID, SETOSE
Britain, anc. people of ...... SILURES
Britain, myth. king of .......... BRUT,
                                 ARTEGAL
Britain, old name for ........ ALBION
British ...................... ASHANTI
  "      administrator ......... ELLIOT
British author ........... MEE, SHUTE
  "      cavalry ........... YEOMANRY
  "      channel ............... SOLENT
  "      chief; anc. ...... PENDRAGON
  "      colony ADEN, MALDA, KENYA
  "      E. Afr. tribe ............ BARI
  "      financier ................ BEIT
  "      Firth of Clyde ........... BUTE
  "      General .......... BRADDOCK
  "      gum ................ DEXTRIN
  "      gun .......... ENFIELD, STEN
  "      India, city in ............. AGRA
  "      India coin ............ RUPEE
  "      India, district in .. FAIZABAD
  "      India, division of ........ OUDH
  "      India, founder of ........ IVAN
  "      India, province ........ ASSAM,
                             BURMA, ORISSA
  "      Is. village ............. ARAWE
  "      kings, legendary ........ BRUT,
                             ARTHUR, LUD
  "      legislator ......... COMMONER
  "      naturalist .............. SLOANE
  "      novelist .. ARTHUR, MACHEN
  "      orator ........ WILLIAM, PITT
  "      order ................. GARTER
  "      parish official ........ BEADLE
  "      Parl. record ........ HANSARD
  "      poet AUDEN, HUGH, WYSTAN
  "      possession in Malay P. ........
                                  DINDINGS
  "      possession in S. Afr. .. NATAL
  "      Prime Minister .......... EDEN

  "      Prime Min.; ex. ...... ATTLEE,
                                  CHURCHILL
  "      protectorate in Borneo BRUNEI
  "      protectorate in E. Afr. UGANDA
  "      pudding ................. SUET
  "      race; anc. ......... DICT, ICENI
  "      Royal Guard officer ...... EXON
  "      saint ................... ALBAN
  "      seaport ................ COWES
  "      seaport, Malay P. . SINGAPORE
  "      soldier; abr. ........... ATKINS
  "      S. Afr. native of ...... BASUTO
  "      statesman .. HOARE, SAMUEL
  "      tea, a kind of ............ ELM
  "      theorist ................. LASKI
  "      VIP ..................... EDEN
  "      W. Afr. .. GAMBIA, NIGERIA
  "      writer .............. TENNENT
Britons; anc. ICENI, ANGLES, JUTES,
                              PICTS, SCOTS
Brittany, per. to ............ ARMORIC
brittle substance CRISP, FRIABLE, AA
broach AWL, REAMER, PIERCE, TAP,
             BEGIN, PUBLISH, SHED
broad and flat .............. TABULATE
broad expanded lip ............ ALATE
broadbill; E. Ind. ...... RAYA, GAPER
broadcast ................ RADIO, T.V.
broaden ENNOBLE, EXPAND, DILATE
broadminded . TOLERANT, CATHOLIC
broadsword ....... BILL, CLAYMORE,
          CUTLASS, CIMETER, KRIS,
                                 FERRARA
Brobdingnagian ................. GIANT
brocade ...... BAUDEKIN, BROCHE
brocard ETHICS, GIBE, MAXIM, RULE
brocket ........ PITA, DEER, SPITTER
brogan ....... BROGUE, SHOE, BOOT
Brogi's wife ....................... IDUN
broil .... GRILLADE, BRAISE, GRILL,
             FRACAS, SCORCH
broken in back ............... CHINED
broken paper .................. CASSE
broken pottery ................. SHERD
broken wind .................. HEAVES
broker .. AGENT, FACTOR, CHANGER
brokerage business ........ AGIOTAGE
broncho buck .............. ESTRAPADE
Brontë .......... EMILY, CHARLOTTE
bronze ........ BROWN, ALLOY, TAN
bronze, colored like ......... AENEOUS
bronze, gilded ................ ORMOLU
bronze, Roman ................... AES
bronze, variety of .. PATINA, LATTEN
brooch PIN, CLASP, OUCH, ARMILLA,
       FIBULA, TIARA, PECTORAL,
                                  CAMEO
brood .. FRY, HATCH, SIT, COGITATE
brood buds on thallus of lichens ........
                                  SOREDIA
brood of pheasants .......... NID, NYE
brook RUN, BECK, RILLET, RUNNEL,
          BEAR, ABIDE, SUFFER, SIKE
broom .. WHISK, BESOM, MOP, SWAB
broom plant .................... SPART
broth .... IMRICH, IMRIGH, POTTAGE
brothel, a ........ KIP, BAGNIO, BATH

34

brother OBLATE, MONK, BILLY, FRA,
MALE, FRATER, FELLOW, PEER
brought up by hand ... BRED, CADE
Brown; actress ............. VANESSA
brown and white ............. ROAN
  " coal ................. LIGNITE
  " , dark ....... BURNET, PUCE
  " , dark reddish .. CUBA, BAY,
SEPIA, KHAKI
  " hematite .......... LIMONITE
  " , light ........ TENNE, BEIGE
  " papers ............... KRAFTS
  " pigment .... BISTER, UMBER
  " thrasher ............ THRUSH
  " , to turn .... TOAST, AUGUST
brownie ....... ELF, KOBOLD, NIS,
CAMERA, GOBLIN, PIXIE
Brownian movem't ........ PEDESES
Browning's home ............. ASOLO
browse ...... BRUT, CROP, NIBBLE
Broz. ........................... TITO
Bruce; actor ................. NIGEL
Brubeck, Mr. .................. DAVE
bruise .... MAWL, CONTUSE, FRAY
bruised ............ HUMBLE, LIVID
bruit ........ RUMOR, NOISE, TELL,
REPORT
brumal storm ...... SLEET, HIEMAL
brume .......... FOG, VAPOR, MIST
brush GRAZING, THICKET, LOCUST
brush, a small ................ FITCH
brush; Fr. ................... BROSSE
brushwood TEENET, COPPICE, RICE,
SCROG, BOSCAGE, SCRUB
brushy . HIRSUTE, HAIRY, SHAGGY
brusque ..... GRUFF, BLUNT, CURT
brutag MAD, CARNAL, INSENSATE,
CADDISH
bryophyte, place for cultivating ......
MOSSERIE
bryozoa ..... RETEPORE, POLYZOA
bubal; Afr. .............. ANTELOPE
bubble .. SEED, BEAD, BLEB, BOIL,
NIL, NULLITY, CHEAT
bubble breaking sound ........ BLOB
bubble up .... TUMOR, INTUMESCE
buccal; per. to CHEEK, MOUTH, ORAL
buccaneer ....... CORSAIR, VIKING
buccaneer CORSAIR, VIKING, PIRATE,
RIFLER, SPOILER, MAROONER
Bucephalus ..... STEED, CHARGER
buck ..... NEGRO, STAG, PRICKET
buck, blue ................... ETAAC
buck, India black ............. SASIN
Buck; novelist ................ PEARL
buck, red ................... PALLAH
bucket . PAIL, BOWK, SKEEL, STOP
buckle ..... DISTORT, TACHE, TIE
buckler ................. RONDELLE
buck's antler ............ ADVANCER
bucks in fourth year ........ SORES
buckthorn, bark of ....... CASCARA
bucolic AGRESTIC, ECLOGUE, RURAL
bud .. GEMMA, BULB, CION, GERM,
BOURGEON, SPROUT, KNOP
bud, blighted ................ BLAST
Buddha ......... GAUTAMA, SAKYA

Buddha, mother of the ........ MAYA
Buddhism, cause of finite existence ...
NIDANA
Buddhism, center of .......... LASSA
Buddhism, founder of ...... GOTAMA
Buddhism, the nexus ........ KARMA
Buddhism, will to live ....... TANHA
Buddhist angel ............... DEVA
  " church ............... TERA
  " column ................ LAT
  " evil spirit ............ MARA
  " fate ................. KARMA
  " festival ................ BON
  " final liberation .. NIRVANA
  " gateway ............ TORAN
  " hell ............... NARAKA
  " monastery ...... TERA, LA
  " monk ...... BO, TALAPOIN
  " pagoda ................. TEE
  " priest .. LAMA, MAHATMA
  " priest, or Fohist ... BONZE
  " relic mound ........ STUPA
  " sacred language ..... PALI
  " sect in Japan ......... LEN
  " shrine .... DAGOBA, TOPE
  " stupa ........ AMARAVATI
  " temple ............ VIHARA
  " title of respect . MAHATMA
budget, family .... BUNCH, PACKET
buds, send forth ....... BURGEON
buffalo ........ CARIBOU, TIMARAU,
ZAMOUSE
  " ; Eur. .................. BISON
  " ; hybrid ............. CATALO
  " meat; Afr. .......... BILTONG
  " , S. Afr. ............ NAIRE
  " , water; Phil. I. ... CARABAO
  " , wild, of Ind. . ARNA, ARNEE
  " , wild ox; Celebes ...... ANOA
buffet .... SLAP, STOOL, BAR, TOSS
buffoon ANDREW, CLOWN, MIMER,
ACTOR, HUMORIST, ZANY
buffoonery .... JAPERY, DROLLERY
bufo; Lat. ..................... TOAD
bug; Lat. ..................... CIMEX
bugaboo ............ JUMBO, MUMBO
buggy ............ INFESTED, SHAY
bugbear .. BOGEY, OGRE, BUGABOO
bugle call .... RETREAT, TANTARA
bugle note ........ REVEILLE, TAPS
bugle, strain on ..... TIRALEE, MOT
bugle weed ................. INDIGO
bugle, yellow ................... IVA
bugs, genus .................. EMESA
build .. REAR, CONSTRUCT, FORM,
RAISE, STATURE
build a nest .................. NIDIFY
builder .... CARPENTER, ERECTOR
builder of airfields .......... SEABEE
builder of Cretan labyrinth DAEDALUS
bulb, glass ............... AMPOULE
bulblike ............... ONION, CORM
bulbule .................... BULBLET
Bulgaria ...................... TUNA
Bulgarian capital ............. SOFIA
  " coast town ........ VARNA
  " coin .......... LEV, LEW
  " commis. ........ SISTOUA

"     early ruler .......... ASEN
"     mongrel race .. GAGAOUS
"     mountain ...... RHODOPE
"     Tsar ................ BORIS
bulge . BLOAT, SWELL, BUG, KNOB
bulging . TUMID, CONVEX, GIBBOUS
bulk ....... MAJORITY, MASS, SIZE,
     VOLUME, ALL, TOTAL, WHOLE
bull ... MINATOUR, TAURUS, ZEBU,
     TORO
bull-doze ..................... RAM
bull fighter ............... MATODOR
bull fighter on foot .......... TORERO
bull, like a ................ TAURINE
bull, sacred, of Egypt .......... APIS
Bull; violinist .................. OLE
bull, young; Scot. ............. STOT
bullet ....... TRACER, SHOT, SLUG
bulletproof shelter ABRI, MANTELET
bullfinch ..... ALP, OLF, OLP, NOPE
bullion, uncoined gold .. BAR, INGOT,
     BILLOT, MASS
bullock .............. STEER, STIRX
bully ... HECTOR, MAJOR, SHANNY
bully tree ................... BALATA
bumble ......... BITTERN, BULRUSH
bulrush ............ SCIRPUS, TULE
bulwark . BAIL, RAMPART, SCONCE
Bulwer Lytton's Eng. schoolmaster ...
     ARAM
bumkin ....... SWAB, BOOR, LOUT,
     YOKEL, CLOD, RUBE, GAWK
bumper CARANGOID, FACER, TOAST
bun ...................... ROLL, WIG
bunch . FAGOT, LOT, SET, BUDGET
bunch, small ........... TUFT, WISP
bund ............ DAM, DIKE, QUAY
bundle BINDLE, BOLT, HANK, SHEAF
bundle, large .......... SHOOK, BALE
bundle of twigs .............. FAGOT
bung .............. MAUL, STOPPER
bungle in hunting ............ TAILOR
bunk ...... HOKUM, SLEEP, ABIDE,
     DWELL
bunker ..... BIN, SANDHOLE, CRIB
bunko .......... CHEAT, SWINDLE
bunting ETAMINE, ORTOLAN, PAPE
bunyip ......................... SHAM
buoy .... DAN, DEADHEAD, LIGAN,
     FLOAT, HOPE, NUN, RAISER
buoyant .... LEVITATE, CHEERFUL
burbot ... EELPOUT, LING, MARIA,
     LOTE
burbots; genus ................. LOTA
burd ..... LADY, MAIDEN, WOMAN
burden . BIRN, CUMBER, ONUS, TAX
burden bearer; Bib. .. AMASA, AMOS
burdock ..... LAPPA, HURR, CLITE
bureau .. DESK, DRESSER, OFFICE
burfish ...................... ATINGA
burganet ........ HELMET, MORION
burgeen ..... BUD, SHOOT, SPROUT
burglar ........ CRACKSMAN, YEGG
Burgoyne's nickname .......... BRAG
burial INTERMENT, PYRE, INHUME,
     INURN, SEPULTURE
burial case . CASKET, COFFIN, BIER
burial mound ...... LOW, TUMULUS,
     GRAVE, BARROW

burial, one who wraps for .... CERER
burial pile ...................... PYRE
burin ................. GRAVER, ROD
burke LYNCH, MURDER, SLAY, KILL
burl ............. LUMP, KNOT, ROE
burlesque .. FUN, OVERDO, PARODY
burletta; mus. ...... FARCE, OPERA
burley ...................... TOBACCO
burly .......... FAT, OBESE, STOUT
Burma, city in ............. RANGOON
Burma, district in ........ TOUNGOO
Burma, divisions of .. YEU, ARAKAN,
     PEGU
Burma, former capital of ....... AVA
Burmese dagger .......... DOW, DAH
"     gibbon ................. LAR
"     girl .................... MIMA
Burmese hill ......... CHIN, KACHIN
"     measure ............... DHA
"     mus. inst. .......... TORAN
"     native ...... LAI, PEGUAN
"     peasant ................. TAO
"     plateau ............... SHAN
"     river ............. IRAWADI
"     spirit or demon ........ NAT
"     robber ............. DACOIT
"     shelter ............. ZAYAT
"     shrimp ............. NAPEE
"     stock breeder .... CHOLIAR
"     tribe ...... TAI, SHAN
"     weight ..... RUAY, TICAL,
     KYAT, VIS
burn CENSE, CHAR, SCALD, SEAR,
     SERE
burn, as of wood ............ BRAND
burn, mark caused by .... ENCAUMA
burn, surface .................. SINGE
burn the midnight oil .. LUCUBRATE
burned .......... USTULATE, ADUST
burning ...... ARSON, EAGER, FIRE,
     AFIRE, CAUTERY
burnisher AGATE, POLISHER, TOOL
burnsides ...... BEARD, WHISKERS
burnt in ...................... INUST
burnt sugar ............... CARAMEL
burr CIRCLE, HALO, WHETSTONE,
     POD
burr plant ................... TEASEL
burrock ......................... DAM
burrow .. HOLE, MOIL, MINE, ROOT
burrowing animal .... MOLE, ARMA-
     DILLO
burrowing mammal; Cape Col. ........
     SURICATE
bursar ................. TREASURER
burst forth . REAVE, REND, ERUPT
bury ...... INTER, INHUME, INURN
bury, to hide . CACHE, CLOAK, VEIL
bury vegetables ................ CAMP
bush ...... BOSCAGE, TOD, SHRUB
bush, burning ............... WAHOO
bush of hair ................... SHAG
bushels, forty ................... WEY
bushing ............ ABRID, LINING
bushy ........... DUMAL, DUMOSE
bushy heap ..................... TOD
bushy shrub, holly family .... YAPON

36

bushwacker ............... GUERILLA
business CRAFT, GEAR, OFFICE, INC.
business memo. .............. AGENDA
business, per. to ........... PRAGMATIC
business trust ....... CARTEL, TRADE
buskin .. TRAGIC, BRODEKIN, SHOE
buss .... DECK, DRESS, SMACK, KISS
busse ........................ AMBUSH
bustard; genus ................... OTIS
bustard, large; Lat. ........... TARDA
bustard, little; Lat. ........... TETRAX
bustards ...................... OTIDAE
bustle POTHER, TUMULT, STIR, ADO
busybody ... PRAGMATIC, QUIDNUNC
but . SED, HENCE, SAVE, WITHOUT,
MERE
but, in music .......................MA
butcher bird .................. SHRIKE
butcher's hook ............ GAMBREL
butler ......... CELLARER, SPENCER
butt ........ BUCK, RAM, TUP, CASK,
PUSH
butt of joke ......................... IT
butt, one-third of ... TERCE, TIERCE
butte ..HILL, DUNE, MOUND, KNOLL
butter and eggs RAMSTED, TOADFLAX
butter, connected with ..... BUTYRIC,
CAPRICA
butter coloring .. ANATTO, ARNOTTO
buttercup; Eng. ............. CROWTOE
butter-cup, fruit of; var ...... AKENE
butter-like ..... CACAO, MARGARINE,
BUTYROUS
butter, semi-fluid ................. GHEE
butter substitute ....... OLEO, SUINE
butterflies .............. LEPIDOPTERA
butterfly ..... FRITILLARY, VANESSA
butterfly fish .................... PARU
butterfly, peacock .................... IO
butterfly, small ................... BLUE
butterwort .............. STEEPWEED
buttery .. PANTRY, SPENCE, LARDER
button KNOP, STUD, BUCKLE, HOOK
buttons; col. ....................... PAGE
Buttons, Mr. ........... RED, SKATER
button-hole stitch; Fr. ........ FESTON
buttress ...... STAY, SUPPORT, PROP
buttress against a mole wall .... PILA
buzzard . AURA, BEETLE, DOR, FLY,
GLEDE
buzzard; Amer. ................. BUTEO
buzzard, bald ................. OSPREY
buzzard, honey .... BEEHAWK, PERN
buzzard, moor ................. HARPY
buzzard, turkey ................. JOHN
by ... ASIDE, WITH, AGO, AT, PAST,
PER, NEAR
by and by ..... ANON, IMMEDIATELY
by heart ................. MEMORITER
by reason of this .......... HEREAT
byway ........ LANE, ALLEY, PATH
by word of mouth ..... PAROL, ORAL
byword PROVERB, PHRASE, SAYING
bygone .... OLDEN, ELAPSED, PAST
Byronian hero ................... LARA
byway ......... LANE, ALLEY, PATH

# C

C, letter ........................... CEE
caama .......................... ASSE
cabal ......... PARTY, PLOT, JUNTO
cabbage .. CHOU, WORT, CAUL, COLE
"       a kind of . COLZA, KOHLRABI
"       broth .... BORECOLE, KALE
"       , any white ...... COLEWORT
"       ; genus ................... COS
"       salad ........ KRAUT, SLAW
"       tree ...................... HAT
"       , variety of ........... SAVOY
"       worm ................ LOOPER
caber .................... BEAM, POLE
cabin ... COACH, HUT, SHED, SHACK
cabinet .... ALMIRAH, BAHUT, BUHL
cabinet, open shelved ..... ETAGERE
cable; per. to ............. COAX(I)AL
cabling ...... RUDENTURE, MOLDING
cabochon ...................... STONE
caboose, ship's ................ GALLEY
cacao-seed powder ............ BROMA
cacao-shell extract .......... MARTOL
cachalot ........ PHYSETER, WHALE
cache ...... CONCEAL, STORE, HIDE
cachet ....... WAFER, SEAL, STAMP
cachexy ................ ILL, MORBID
cacholong ........................ OPAL
cackle .... LAUGH, CHATTER, CANK,
CHAT, GOSSIP, TALK, KEAK
cactus; (see "plant")
cad BOUNDER, HEEL, HICK, YOKEL
cadaver ......... CORPSE, SKELETON
caddish ...................... ILLBRED
cadence . MODULATION, TONE, LILT
cade ........................ JUNIPER
cadet ... SON, YOUTH, JUNIOR, PLEB
cadent ....................... FALLING
cadge ........ BEG, MOOCH, SPONGE
Cadmus' daughter ......INO, SEMELE
Cadmus' father .............. AGENOR
Cadmus' sister .............. EUROPA
Cadmus' wife ............. HARMONIA
Caducci; Ital. poet ......... GIOSUE
caduceus ........... WAND, SCEPTER
caduceus group ............ AMA, AMC
caen-stone ............... LIMESTONE
Caesar, colleague of ......... BIBULUS
Caesar, death scene of .......... NOLA
Caesar weed fiber .......... ARAMINA
Caesar's mother ............. AURELIA
Caesar's sister .................... ATIA
Caesium, associated with .. RUBIDIUM
Caesura ....... BREAK, PAUSE, REST
caffeine ........ THEINE, DIURETIC
cafila; Arab. ............... CARAVAN
cage for hauling .................. MEW
cahoots, in; slang ........... LEAGUE,
PARTNERS
Cain's son ..................... ENOCH
cairngorm, brown ............ QUARTZ
caisson BOX, CHEST, WAGON, CASE
caisson disease ................ BENDS
caitiff .... BASE, DESPICABLE, VILE

cajole ......... PALP, CHEAT, COAX, WHEELDE
cake ... BANNOCK, BATTY, CIMBAL, CONCRETE, HARDEN, SCONE
cake, corn ...................... PONE
cake, flat ................... PLACENT
cake, rounded .. CHARLOTTE, TORT, NUT
cake, seed ........................ WIG
cake, thin ... FARL, JUMBLE, WAFER
cake walk ........... MARCH, STRUT
calaber bean ..................... ISERE
calaboose ........ GAOL, JAIL, PRISON
calamitous ....... BLOW, EVIL, DIRE
calamity .... BLOW, BALE, HYDRA, DISASTER, REVERSE, WRACK
calash; Phil. Is. .............. CALESA
calcar .......................... SPUR
calcareous ...... SPAR, TRAVERTINE, CORAL
calcareous deposit ...... STALAGMITE
calced .......................... SHOD
calcium carbonate, kind of ....... TUFA
calcium oxide ................... LIME
calcium phosphate .......... APATITE
calcium sulphate .... GYPSUM, HEPAR
calculate .... COUNT, AIM, AVERAGE
calculator ...... ABACUS, TABLE
calculous ............. GRITTY, STONY
Calcutta weight ................ PANK
calderite, variety of ........... GARNET
caldron ....... BOILER, KETTLE, VAT
Caleb's daughter .............. ACHSAH
Caleb's son ................... IRU, HUR
calefy ........ CAUMA, WARM, HEAT
calendar, church .. ORDO, MASS, ROW
calenture ...................... FEVER
calf, motherless .. MAVERICK, DOGIE
calf of leg, per. to.............. SURAL
calf, skin of ...................... KIP
calf's cry ....................... BLAT
Caliban, deity of ............ SETEBOS
Caliban's witch mother ..... SYCORAX
caliber .. BORE, DEGREE, DIAMETER
calico; E. Ind. ................. SALLOO
calico machine blanket ...... LAPPING
calico printing of star colors .... TEER
calico steam dye process .... TOPICAL
California bay ...... MONTEREY
California city ...... PALOMAR, NAPA, CHINO
"        evergreen shrub .... SALAL, KUMQUAT
"        Pass ............... SONORA
"        rockfish ...... REINA, RENA
"        spot (big) ............... SUR
caliph .............. ALI, IMAM, OMAR
calisthenics system ........ DELSARTE
calk .... CHINSE, OCCLUDE, CLOSE, COPY, SNUG
calker ........................ STAVER
call ... CA, BAN, CLEPE, DUB, TERM
call out ........ INVOKE, EPE, EVOKE
call together ..... CONVOKE, MUSTER
callant; Scot. ................. BOY, LAD
called ... YCLEPT, NAMED, DUBBED
calligrapher ...... COPYIST, PENMAN

calling .. ART, EVOCATION, METIER, PURSUIT, TRADE, NAME
callous, render HARDEN, HORN, SEAR
Calloway, Mr. ...................... CAB
calm .. BALMY, MILD, ABATE, DILL, LULL, QUIET, PACATE
calming, act of ............. SEDATION
calorie, per. to ................. THERM
calumet ........................... PIPE
calumniate BELIE, LIBEL, SLANDER
calumniator, a; Gr. ........ THERSITES
calumny ............ SLUR, LAMPOON
calyx ....... COVERING, HUSK, CUP
calyx, division of ............... SEPAL
calyx of flower ............ PERIANTH
cam ..... LOBE, COG, WIPER, CATCH
camail ...... HOOD, GUARD, TIPPET
camalig; Phil. I. ................... HUT
camarilla ........... CABAL, CLIQUE
Camarines Norte, capitol ....... DAET
camass, the death .......... LOBELIA
Cambodia, anc. capitol ...... ANGKOR
Cambodia great river ........ MEKONG
Cambodia, native of .......... KHMER
Cambodia seaport .......... KAMPOT
cambrai, swan of .......... FENELON
Cambria ...................... WALES
Cambria, zone of .......... OLENUS
Cambridge boat race ........... LENT
"        honor exam ........ TRIPOS
"        student .... SIZAR, OPTIME
came down ........ DESCENDED, LIT
camel ..... DROMEDARY, MAHARIK, DELOUL
camel, female ................... NAGA
camel, two-humped ........ BACTRIAN
camel's hair cloth ...... CAMLET, ABA
camel's keeper ................... OBIL
camel's thorn ................ ALHAGI
cameloid; S. Am. ........... LLAMA
cameo ANAGLYPH, ONYX, RELIEVO
camera, dark ................. OBSCURA
camera, light ................. LUCIDA
camera, part of ............... FINDER
camera, revolving ......... PANORAM
camera shot .................... STILL
Cameroon people, one of ......... SARA
camorra .................... BLOUSE
camp ..... BIVOUAC, ETAPE, TABOR
camp, besieged ............. LEAGUER
campaign ................... CRUSADE
campanula ................ HAREBELL
camphor ........... BORNEOL, LEVO
camphor, a kind of ........... ALANT
campion, the; genus .......... SILENE
camps, of ............ CASTRENSIAN
camps P.X. ................ CANTEEN
campus ................ QUAD, FIELD
cam-wheel projec. ............... LOBE
can .... CONSERVE, MAY, MUN, TIN
Canaan, city of ............ AI, HAZOR
Canaanite calendar (see Hebrew)
Canaan's son; Bib. ............. SIDON
Canadian airport ............ GANDER
"        crookneck ......... CUSHAW
"        cabin sleeping berth . BAULK
"        canal ............ WELLAND

38

"   cattlepen .......... CORRAL
"   free-grant district MUSKOKO
"   goose; genus ...... BRANTA
"   grape ............. ISABELLA
"   Indian DENE, HARES, CREE,
                  SIOUX
"   land measure ...... ARPENT
"   lynx .................. PISHU
"   national park ....... JASPER
"   pea .................. VETCH
"   penalty; law ......... DEDIT
"   peninsula ............. GASPE
"   physician ............ OSLER
"   policeman ........ MOUNTIE
"   province; abbr. ........ ALTA
"   river .... NELSON, OTTOWA
"   snake root ......... GINGER
"   squaw ............. MAHALA
"   turpentine ......... BALSAM
canaille ... RABBLE, MOB, RIFFRAFF
canal ........ DUCT, SUEZ, PANAMA,
        RACEWAY, MEATUS
canal, bank of a .................. BERM
canal, broad ...................... SHAT
canal slack water .............. LODE
canal, spiral of cochlea ........ SCALA
canard ..... CHEAT, DUCK, HUMBUG,
      AIRPLANE, RUMOR, HOAX
canary seed ..................... ALPIST
canasta play ................... MELD
cancel, ...... ANNUL, ERASE, DELE,
      QUASH, RESCIND, REVOKE
cancer .......... CARCINOMA, CRAB
candent ........ FIG, GLOWING, HOT
Candia .......................... CRETE
candid ..... FRANK, OPEN, HONEST,
                PURE
Candiot ....................... CRETAN
candle .......... CIERGE, DIP, SERGE
candle holder ................. SCONCE
candle, melt and run down ..... SWEAL
candle, wax ......... TAPER, BOUGIE
candlenut tree ............ AMA, KUKU
candlestick ........ CRUSIE, LAMPAD
candlestick, branched .... GIRANDOLE
"   , many branched ...... JESSE
"   , ornamental ...... PRICKET,
                LUSTRE
"   , three-branched . TRICERIUM
candy .... PRALINE, LOLLY, COMFIT,
            FONDANT
candytuffs, the ................. IBERIS
cane ..... STEM, RATTAN, SCOURGE
cane sugar .................. SUCROSE
cangue; Chin. .............. PILLORY
canine ......... CUR, FICE, PUP, TIKE
canine tooth ................. LANIARY
cankerworm .................... RUCUL
cannele ....... , .................. REP
cannibalism .............. EXOPHAGY
cannikin ........................... CUP
cannon MORTAR, HOWITZER, CRACK
"   ball ........ MISSILE, PELLET
"   , knob at breech end CASCABEL
"   old time ........ ASPIC, SAKER
"   , part of a .. CHASE, RIMBASE
"   , per. to a .... BORE, BREECH
"   platform ........ TERREPLEIN

"   , projecting boss of TRUNNION
cannon, small; obs. MINION, ROBINET
"   , used for firing .... LINSTOCK
cannot be cut ......... INTRENCHANT
cannular ..................... TUBULAR
cannulated ................... HOLLOW
canoe, Afr. .................. ALMADIA
"   , Arctic tribal .......... KAYAK
"   , Cen. Amer. ............ PITPAN
"   dugout ... PIRAGUA, PIROGUE
"   Eskimo ....... OOMIAK, UMIAK
"   , flying; Malay ........... PROA
"   , kind of large ......... BUNGO
"   , Malabar .............. TONEE
"   , skin covered ........... BIDAR
canon ...... CRITERION, LAW, RULE
canon, enigmatical ............. NODUS
canonical hours ......... NONE, SEXT,
                VESPERS
canonicals ROBE, ALB, COPE, COWL,
                STOLE
canonize ........................ SAINT
canopy ........... CECLE, CIEL, COPE
canopy, over a bed or tomb ... TESTER
canopy, over an altar .... BALDACHIN
canorous ........ MELODIOUS, CLEAR
cant JARGON, ARGOT, LINGO, SLANG
canted position ....... ALIST, HIELD,
                ATILT
Canterbury Archb. ............. LANG
Canterbury gallop ............. AUBIN
canthook ................... PEAV(E)Y
canticle ...... SONG, ODE, BRAVURA
canto .. FIT, PACE, PASSUS, STANZA
Canton flannel ................... NAP
Cantor's wife ..................... IDA
canvas covering ................. TILT
canvas-like fabric ............ WIGAN
canyon of the comics ......... STEVE
canyon wall .................... DALLE
canzonet .. SONG, CENTO, MADRIGAL
caoutchouc, source of .... CEARA, ULE
cap ......... ETON, BOINA, CORNET,
      CLOCHE, KEFFIEH, TAM
"   , child's hood ............. BIGGIN
"   , close ............. COIF, TOQUE
"   , flat eccl. ...... BARRET, BERET
"   , Jewish headdress ........ MITRE
"   , knitted ............... THRUM
"   , military ... HAVELOCK, SHAKO,
                KEPI
"   , military; Eng. ............. BUSBY
"   , night .................... MUTCH
"   , oriental ....... CALPAC(K), FEZ,
              TURBAN
"   , Roman ................... PILEUS
"   , Scotch ........ BALMORAL, TAM
"   , shaped ............... PILEATE
"   sheepskin ................ CALPAC
"   , skull PILEUS, CALLOT, HOUVE
"   , square eccl. ............ BIRETTA
"   , steel .............. CERVELIERE
capable ABLE, CAN, EFFICIENT, APT
capable of listening to reason ..........
              PERVIOUS
capcious ............... AMPLE, MUCH
cape .. RAS, AMICE, FICHU, TALMA,
          TANG, MANTLE

" , a; obs. .......... SAGUM, GAPE
" , acute angled ............ POINT
" elk ......................... ELAND
" , Jap. ...................... MINO
" , kind of large ....... PELERINE, TALMA
" of land ..................... NESS
" pigeon ...... PETREL, PINTADO
Cape Colony plateau ........... KAROO
Cape of Good Hope, discoverer of DIAZ
Cape Verde Island ................. SAL
Cape Verde Is. native . SERER, BRAVA
Capek (Karel); play ............. RUR
capel .......... HORSE, NAG, WALL
caper SKIP, ANTIC, CURLYCUE, DIDO, PRANCE
capibara ....... CAVY, HOG, RODENT
capillary .. HAIRLIKE, MINUTE, FINE
capital letter, anc. ....... MAJUSCULE
capote .... BONNET, MANTLE, HOOD
caprate, a ............ RUTATE, SALT
caprice WHIM, VAGARY, TOY, FREAK
Capricorn ........................ GOAT
capriole . CAPER, HEADDRESS, LEAP
capripedes ..................... SATYRS
caprylate, a ................. OCTOATE
capsheaf ...................... CROWN
capstan bar ................... LEVER
capsule . PILL, DETONATOR, THECA, WAFER
captain, allowance paid to ... PRIMAGE
captain to the host; Bib. ........ JOAB
captain's boat ..................... GIG
caption ............. LEGEND, TITLE
captious CRITICAL, CAVILING, CARP
captivate ................. ENAMO(U)R
capture .. NAB, RAVEN, BAG, PREY, COP
captured, a thing ........ PRIS, PRIZE
capuche .............. COWEL, HOOD
caput .... DOOMED, HEAD, CITIZEN
carabao ..................... BUFFALO
caracal; Asian .................. LYNX
caracara, S. Amer. ............. HAWK
caracole SNAIL, WHEEL, STAIRCASE
carapace ........ CARAPAX, LORICA, SHELL, SHIELD, TEST
carapato; S. Amer. ............... TICK
caravan, Arab. ................ CAFILA
caravansary ... HOTEL, IMARET, INN, SERAI, HOSTEL
caravel ... NINA(H), PINTA, BEETLE
caraway cooky .......... SEED CAKE
carbine .. MUSKET, RIFLE, ESCOPET
carbohydrate ................. STARCH
carbolic acid ................. PHENOL
carbon . LEAD, SOOT, COKE, CRAYON
carbonate of potash ....... PEARLASH
carborundum .................... EMERY
carboy ............ BOTTLE, FLAGON
carcajou .... GLUTTON, WOLVERINE
card ............... ACE, TEN, DEUCE
card, as wool or flax ... COMB, TEASE, TUM

card game ..... BACCARAT, BASSET, BEZIQUE, BUNKO, CRIBBAGE, ECARTE, FARO, GLEEK, HOC, LOO, MONTE, NAP, OMBRE, PAM, PIQUET, ROUNCE, SKAT, WHIST, SOLITAIRE, STUSS, TAROT, MACAO, SPOILFIVE, KENO
card game (rare) ........... CAYENNE
card, playing term .. CAT, HARRY, PIC
card slam ...................... VOLE
cardinal, office of a .......... DATARIA
cardinal's rank ..................... HAT
cards, spare hand in .............. CAT
care for .... ATTEND, BACH, FORCE, FANCY, LOVE, YEARN, RECK
careen .............. HEEL, LIST, TIP
caress ... FONDLE, CULLY, DANDLE
Carew's lady-love ................ CELIA
cargo .... FREIGHT, LOAD, LADING, GOODS, MAILS, LAST
cargo from wrecked ship .... FLOTSAM
Caribbean Sea bight ........ DARIEN
caribe .......... PARANHA, PIRAYA
caricature ....... CARTOON, PARODY
carina, without a .......... RATITE
cark ........ HARASS, WORRY, VEX
carl .. CHURL, RUSTIC, HEMP, MAN
Carmichael, Mr. .............. HOAGY
carnage, place of ........ SHAMBLES
carnation ......... PINK, PICKERAL
carnelian, chalcedony .......... SARD
Carney, Mr. ...................... ART
carnivora; genus ........... URSUS
carnivora BEAR, CAT, DOG, FELIDAE, GENET, HYENA, OTTER, PEKAN, PUMA, RATEL, SEAL, SERVAL, TIGER, MEERKAT
carnivorous guana-like reptile ......... TUATARA
carnotite .................... URANIUM
carob ...................... ALGAROBA
carol ...... TRILL, WARBLE, YODEL
carol, Christmas ................. NOEL
Caroline (Pac.) base ......... PELELIU
carousal ....... BINGE, FEAST, ORGY, REVEL, WASSAIL
carouse ....... BIRLE, BOUSE, SPREE
'carousel' inspiration ......... LILIOM
carp ..... CAVIL, CENSURE, NIBBLE
carpel .... CORE, PISTIL, ACHENIUM
carpels, mass of .............. SOREMA
carpenter ......... WRIGHT, JOINER
carpenter bee .............. XYLOCOPA
carper ...................... CAVILER
carpet KALI, MAT, TAPETE, CLOTH
carplike fish ...................... IDE
carpus ...................... WRIST
carrack ..................... GALLEON
carrageen ....................... MOSS
carrelage ...................... TILING
carriage CALASH, SURREY, MANNER, MIEN, CHAISE
" , baby ...... GOCART, PRAM, CLARENCE
" , four-wheeled .. DEARBORN, LANDAU
" , kind of GIG, JINGLE, SADO

40

"    , one horse ...... TRAP, FLY, CARIOLE
"    , part of a ........ HORNBAR
"    , Russian .......... KIBITKA, TARANTAS
"    shackle ................... BAR
"    , two-wheeled ....... CISIUM, STANHOPE
Carroll, Lewis; char. ........... ALICE
Carroll; T.V. star ................ JEAN
carrot ................ DAUCUS, DRIAS
carrots; genus ................. CARUM
carrow; Irish ............. GAMESTER
carry ... SCENT, BEAR, TOTE, WAFT
carry an effigy ..................... GUY
carry away, as property ....... ELOIN
carry on ........ WAGE, AGYE, RANT
cart ......... WAIN, DRAY, CARETTA, LORRIE, TONGA
"    , a rough ................ TUMBRIL
"    , end of a ..................... TIB
"    ladder ............. RACK, ZAVE
"    , milkman's .................. PRAM
"    , oriental ................. ARABA
cartel .......... DEFY, PACT, PAPER
Carthage .. CARTAGO, POENI, PUNICI
"    citadel ........ BOZRA, BYRSA
"    district ................. MARA
"    division .............. TAENIA
"    emblem ................... PALM
"    , foe of ................. CATO
"    fort ................. GOLETTA
"    , founder of ........... DIDO
"    official head of government .... SUFFETE
"    queen .................... DIDO
"    , suburb of ......... MEGARA
Carthage, subjects of ....... LIBYANS, NOMADS
Carthaginian cap.; anc. ...... CARALIS
"    god .... MOLOCH, VAAL
"    moon goddess .... TANIT
"    warrior ........... MAGO
Carthusian ......... EREMITE, MONK
"    chronicler ........ FERRARI
"    monastery ....... CERTOSA
"    , noted .............. HUGH
"    superior of convent .. PRIOR
cartograph ...... PLAT, CHART, MAP
cartoonist ............ (PETER) ARNO
cartridge holder ................... CLIP
carucate .................... ARABLE
caruncle ...... GILL, WATTLE, COMB, PROTUBERANCE
carve .... ENGRAVE, CHISEL, INCISE
carve pheasant ................... ALAY
carving .. SCULPTURE, ANAGLYPHY
carving in stone ................ CAMEO
casaba ................. MUSKMELON
cascara ................. BUCKTHORN
case ..... CRATEAPSE, EVENT, INRO
case for holding a book ......... FOREL
case for liquor bottles ..... CELLARET
case, small ...... TYE, ETWEE, ETUI, TROUSSE
casein ........... LEGUMIN, PROTOID
cases ...................... MATTERS

cash; slang ... EXCHEQUER, DARBY, DUST
cash note ...................... MELT
cashew fruit ............... ANACARD
cashew nut oil ............... CARDOL
cashier . TELLER, BURSAR, PURSER
casing ......... COVER, SHEATHING
cask ... KEG, BARECA, BUTT, CADE, TUN
cask, bulge of ................... BILGE
cask rim ....................... CHIMB
cask stave ....................... LAG
cask support ................. STILLAGE
cask, wine ..................... TIERCE
casket ..... ACERRA, CIST, PYX, TYE
casket for the relics of a saint CHASSE
Cassandra .................... SERESS
Cassandra's father ............. PRIAM
cassava product ............. MANIOC
casserole .. STEW, RAGOUT, VESSEL
cassia ......... CINNAMON, LAXATIVE
cassia; genus .................... SENNA
cassimere ............. KERSEYMERE
Cassiopeia's daughter ... ANDROMEDA
cassock ...... GOWN, GIPE, SOUTANE
cassowary ............... EMU, RATITE
cast coverings of animals ... EXUVIAE
cast down ........... ABASE, DEJECT
cast off ....... MOLT, SLOUGH, SPEW
cast underhand ........ HURL, HEAVE
castanea ................... CHESTNUT
castaway ....... DERELICT, PARIAH, OUTCAST, USELESS, NOMIC
caste, Hindu ......... SUDRA, VARNA
caste, minor Hindu ....... GATI, KULA
caster ........ CLOAK, CRUET, VIAL
castigatory ..................... PENAL
Castile, northern ............... VIEJA
Castile, province ........ AVILA, SORIA
Castile river .. DOURO, EBRO, XUCAR
Castile, southern ............. NUEVA
casting mold ..... MATRIX, MATRICE
castle ... CHATEAU, DONJON, KEEP, ROOK
castle-building ............... ADREAM
castle on the coast of Cornwall ........ TINTAGIL
castor ............. BEAVER, CRUET
Castor and Pollux . GEMINI, DIOSCURI
castor bean poison ............. RICIN
Castor, mother of ............... LEDA
castor silk .......... SUMS, ERI, ERIA
Castor's slayer ................... IDAS
casts up .................. ADDS, TOTS
casual ... CHANCE, RANDOM, STRAY
cat .... FELID, FELINE, GIB, MANX, MALTESE, FELIS, TIGER
"    ; Amer. ...... ANGORA, MARGAY, OCELOT
"    ; Amer. (South) ............. EYRA
"    cry MEW, MEOW, MIAOU, WAUL
"    , house-working ......... MOUSER
"    Medit. river ............... GENET
"    , old female ......... GRIMALKIN
"    , wild .... BALU, PUMA, JAGUAR, OCELOT, MANUL, CIVET, PANTHER, SERVAL

41

catacomb ........... CRYPT, GROTTO
catacomb burial niche ....... LOCULE
catafalque ........................ BIER
catalan ............ SHARPER, THIEF
catamaran ............. BALSA, RAFT
catamaran; S. Amer. ....... JANGADA
cataplasm ............ PAP, POULTICE
catapult .......... ONAGER, BALISTA,
   ROBINET, SLINGSHOT, SCORPION
cataract ...... CASCADE, FALL, LINN
catarrh .............. COLD, RHEUM
catch-all ........ BAG, BASKET, ETC.
catchfly, the plant ............ SILENE
catchword .............. SLOGAN, CUE
catechu, yellow .............. GAMBIER
catechumen ................... PUPIL
category ... CLASS, GENRE, SPECIES,
                              STATE
cater .. PROVIDE, PANDER, PURVEY
caterpillar .. ERUCA, HOCK, WOOBUT,
                       OUBIT, CANKER
caterpillar hair ................... SETA
caterpillar; N. Z. ...... AWETO, WERI
caterwaul ...................... MIAUL
catfish ..... TANDAN, HASSAR, POUT
catfish, electric ................... RAAD
catgut ........ VIOLIN, CORD, ROPP,
                              THARM
cation ............................ ION
catkin .................. AMENT, RAG
cat-like animal of India ....... ZIBET
catmint ..................... NIP, NEP
catnip .......... NIP, CATARIA, NEP
catnip and ground ivy ........ NEPETA
cat-o-nine-tails ................. WHIP
cats-eye ............ CHRYSOBERYL,
                         CHATOYANT
cats-paw TOOL, CULLY, DUPE, GULL
cats-tail ....................... CLOUD
cat's whisker .............. SMELLER
cattail ... TOTORA, DODD, MATREED
cattail, narrow-leaved ......... REREE
cattle BOVINE, KINE, TAURUS, ZOBO,
                          GUERNSEY
   "   , black .................. KERRY
   "   , dwarf ........ DEVON, NIATA
   "   feed for hire ............ AGIST
   "   genus ...................... BOS
   "   , long haired ......... DISHLEY
   "   pen .. BARTH, BAWN, KRALL,
                              REEVE
   "   plague, Fr. ............. MURIE
   "   raik ........ RANGE, PASTURE
   "   stealer .. ABACTOR, RUSTLER
Caucasian, dialect ............. KARTLI
   "   family ................ ARYAN
   "   goat ...................... TUR
   "   language .. UDI, ANDI, AVAR,
                            SEMITIC
   "   milk liquor ............ KEFIR
   "   mountaineer ............ LAK
   "   race .. SEMITE, IRAN, OSSET
Caucasus peak .... ELBRUZ, KAZBEK
caucho tree ...................... ULE
caucuses .... PRIMARIES, MEETINGS
caudal appendage .............. TAIL
caul, an infant's ............. HOUVE

cauldron .... COPPER, POT, KETTLE,
                               VAT
Caulfield, Miss .................. JOAN
cauma ................... WARM, HEAT
cause; med. ............... AETIOLOGY
cause to arch ................... ROACH
cause to buy high and sell low ........
                            WHIPSAW
causerie CONVERSE, PARLEY, CHAT
causes, science of ......... ETIOLOGY
causeuse ......................... SOFA
caustic ....... SNAPPISH, MORDANT,
               BURNING, PYROTIC, TART
caustic agent ................ ERODENT
caustic solution .................... LYE
cauterize CHAR, SINGE, BURN, SEAR,
                               INUST
cautious ... CHARY, CANNY, FABIAN,
                  CIRCUMSPECT, WARE
cavalcade ........ PAGEANT, PARADE
cavalryman ..... DRAGOON, HUSSAR,
                            TROOPER
cavalryman; Algerian ........... SPAHI
cave .... ANTRE, CRYPT, DEN, GROT
cave dwellers .. TAURI, TROGLODYTE
cavern . CAVE, LAIR, ANTRE, CROFT
caves, inhabiting ........ SPEL(A)EAN
caves, scien. study of ... SPELEOLOGY
caviar ............ OVA, RELISH, ROE
caviar, fish yielding ........ STERLET,
                            STURGEON
cavil .............. CARP, HAFT, MARL
cavities .... ANTRA, AULAE, CARIES
cavity LUMEN, CLOACA, PIT, SINUS,
                         CAVA, VUG
cavity, body ...... COELOM, COELUM
cavity, crystal lined; per. to .. GEODIC
cavity of skull ................. FOSSA
cavity, per. to heart ........... ATRIUM
cavort .......... CAPER, DIDO, PRANK
cavy ......... PACA, CAPIBARA, PIG,
                            RODENT
caw ................... KAAK, QUARK
cayenne-pepper ............ CAPSICUM
cease .. PRETERMIT, PETER, STINT,
                 REFRAIN, STOP, WONDE
ceased ... DESISTED, DEAD, KILLED
Cecrop's daughter ............. HERSE
cedar, Austral. ........ TOON, TOONA
cedar, N. Am. .... SAVIN, WAXWING
cede .. GRANT, YIELD, SURRENDER
ceiling, division in ............ TRAVE
ceiling mine .................... ASTEL
ceilings, paneled ........ LACUNARIA
celebrating victory ......... EPINICIAN
celerity .......... DISPATCH, HASTE
celery, wild ........ SMALLAGE, ACHE
celestial ........ CHINAMAN, URANIC
celestial being ..... ANGEL, CHERUB,
                              SERAPH
celestial elev. of mind ...... ANAGOGE
Celeus' daughter ........ ANDROMEDA
cell ...... EGG, KIL, GERM, CYTODE,
                            NEURONE
cell division; bot. ........... SPIREME
cell division, direct .. AMITOSIS, LININ
cell in Egypt. tomb ......... SERDAB
cell structure, study of .... CYTOLOGY

42

cell, a; Rom. ........... NAOS, CELLA
cellaret ................... TANTALUS
cells .................. LAURA, LOCULI
cells, honeycomb ............ ALVEOLI

cellular .... ALVEOLATE, AREOLAR,
                             FAVIFORM
celluloid ................... XYLONITE
celosia, feathered .... HEATHERDELL
celt ......... GAEL, EOLITH, CHISEL
Celt, legendary ................... ITH
Celtic ............................ ERSE
Celtic abbot .................... COARB
Celtic land holder ............ TANIST
Celtic word for mountain ........ BEN
cement .. PUTTY, GLUE, JOIN, LUTE
cement, hydraulic ..... PAAR, ROMAN
cemetery ...... MORTUARY, LITTEN,
              NECROPOLIS, BONEYARD
cenobite .. ESSENE, MONK, RECLUSE
cenoby .. ABBEY, PRIORY, CLOISTER
censer ..... INCENSORY, THURIBLE
censure ..... FLAY, CHIDE, SLATING,
              BLAME, TARGE, IMPEACH
cent ................... COIN, PENNY
center ...... CORE, FOCUS, NUCLEUS
center, away from ............ DISTAL
center line, along ............ AXIATE
center line of a verse .......... CESURA
centerpiece ................. EPERGNE
centipede ....... MYRIAPOD, EARWIG
central ............................ MID
centrifugal; bot. ................. CYME
centuries, ten ............... CHILIAD
century plant ... ADE, AGAVE, ALOE,
                          MAGUEY
ceorl ................. CHURL, THANE
cepa ............................. ONION
cephalopod . INK, OCTOPUS, CUTTLE
ceral ............................. WAXY
ceramic sieve ................... LAUN
ceramist ..................... POTTER
cerate .................. WAX, SALVE
ceratose ........................ HORNY
cerberus ................... HELLDOG
cereal, coarse part of ........... BRAN
cereal food ............ RICE, HOMINY
cereal grass . OAT, RAGI, GRAIN, RYE
cerebro spinal axis ............ NEURA
ceremonial fuss ........ PANJANDRUM
ceremonious leave taking ....... CONGE
ceremony ...... FORM, RITE, RITUAL
cerinus group ................ YTTRIUM
cerium ........................ CEROUS
cero fish ...................... CAVALLA
certain ..... AMEN, ONE, YEA, TRUE
certainly; prov. Eng. ............ WAT
certify .... VOUCH, ASSURE, ATTEST
cerulean ................ AZURE, BLUE
cervine ................ CERVID, DEER
cespitose ....................... TUFTS
cessation of being .... DESITION, END,
                             LETUP
cetacean ........... SUSU, APOD, INIA
cetacean of the dolphin family ..........
                             NARWHAL
cetic acid, salt of ............. CETATE
cetyl oily compound ......... CETENE

Ceylon ...................... SINHALA
" aborigines ........... VEDDAHS
" grass ........ CHENA, PATANA
" language .......... PALI, TAMIL
" lotus ................. NELUMBO
" moss ........ AGAR, GULAMAN,
                            JAFFNA
" palm ................. TALIPOT
" rice in the husk ........ PADDY
" seaport .................. GALLE
Ceylon town ............ KANDY, UVA
Ceylonese ................. TAMIL, TODA
" garment .......... SARONG
" measure .......... PARAH
" native ......... CINGALESE
" sea sands ............. PAAR
Ceylonite ...................... SPINEL
chabouk ................. HORSEWHIP
chack; Scot. ................... SNACK
chacma, S. Afr. .............. BABOON
chaeta ...... SETA, STALK, BRISTLE
chafe ............. FRET, RAGE, RUB
chaff ...... BANTER, STUFF, TRASH
chaffer .............. HIGGLE, DICKER
chaffinch . SHELLY, ROBINET, SPINK
chaffy ...... WORTHLESS, PALEATE,
             ACEROSE, PALACEOUS
chafing ....................... GALLING
chain TORC, TORQUE, GYVE, RANGE
chain of quotations ... CATENA, FILE
chair, litterlike ................... KAGO
chair, portable ................. SEDAN
chair-back, part of ............. SPLAT
chalcedon, green .............. JASPER
chalcedony ..... AGATE, ONYX, SARD
chalcolite ............... TORBERNITE
Chaldean city ....................... UR
Chaldean time cycle ............ SAROS
chalice AMA, CUP, GRAIL, BLOSSOM
chalice flower ............... DAFFODIL
chalice, pall of ............. ANIMETTA
chalk sponge ................... ASCON
challenge . DEFY, CALL, DARE, GAGE
challenge to duel .............. CARTEL
chalybite ................... SIDERITE
chamber ... KIVA, ROOM, LOCULUS
chamber; judge's ..... INNS, CAMERA
chambers, two legislative BICAMERAL
chambray ................... GINGHAM
chamois; Old Test. ........... AOUDAD
champion .. ESPOUSE, DEFEND, ACE,
                           HERO
champion, knight ............ PALADIN
chance .. LOT, GO, HAP, ODDS, TIDE,
                          HAPLY
chance; comb. form ........... TYCHO
chancel, part of ................. BEMA
chancel seats ................. SEDILIA
Chaney, Mr. ...................... LON
change .... AMEND, SHIFT, MODIFY,
              COINS, MART, MUTATE
change; mus. ..................... MUTA
changeable ... MOBILE, CHAMELEON,
                       PROTEAN
changeling ................. DOLT, OAF
channel ...... DIKE, KENNEL, SINUS,
                          STRIA
" bone ................. COLLAR

" British ....... LEAT, SLEEVE, SOLENT
" , iron ................... HOOK
" of a river .. FLUME, ALVEUS
" , sea ................. TROUGH
" to inland ................. GAT
" , water ................. GURT
channeled ................... VOLUTED
chanson ...... LYRIC, SONG, BALLAD
chant ............... INTONE, INTROIT
chanticleer ................. ROOSTER
chaos ABYSS, CHASM, GULF, BABEL,
       MESS, IMBROGLIO, PI, PIE
chaos, primeval fluid of ............. NU
Chaos' son .................... EREBUS
Chaos' wife ................. NOX, NYX
chaotic ............. MUDDLE, SNAFU
chap BOY, LAD, CHINK, KIBE, SPRAY
chape, a ..................... CRAMPET
chapel . ALTAR, BETHEL, ORATORY,
            CHANTRY, SISTINE
chapel or porch ............... GALILEE
chapler ...................... ANADEM
Chaplin, Mrs. ................... OONA
chaps ......... CHOPS, JAWS, FLEWS
chapped ............ HUMBLE, KIBED
chapter, per. to a ......... CAPITULAR
character QUALITY, TRAIT, REPUTE,
          ETHOLOGY, STRIPE, ROLE
"    giver ................. TONER
"    in anc. Irish alphabet OGHAM
"    of a community ...... ETHOS
"    , Teutonic alphabet ... RUNE
"    , to indicate relative pitch ...
                        NEUME
characteristic .......... DEPICT, COST,
                  SYMPTOMATIC
characterize ................. ENTITLE
characterizing ability to use tools ......
                        CHRESTIC
charcoal ........... FUSAIN, LIGNITE
charcoal ingredient .............. PEAT
charge .......... INDICT, ONUS, TAX
charger .......... STEED, WARHORSE
charge in combat ...... ONSET, REAM
chariot; anc. .. CURRE, ESSED, RATH
chariot; poet. ................... WAIN
chariot to carry statue of a god . RATH
chariot, top ................... CALASH
chariot, two horse ................. BIGA
chariot, two wheeled .......... ESSEDA
charioteer; astron. ............ AURIGA
charioteer, famous ................. HUR
charity ......... LOVE, ALMS, DOLE,
          BOUNTY, PITY, LARGESS
charlatan .......... EMPIRIC, QUACK
Charlemagne, knight of ..... PALADIN,
                        GANO
Charlemagne's brother ... CARLOMAN
"       court, hero of ROLAND
"       father .......... PEPIN
"       so-called nephew
                      ORLANDO
Charles Dickens' pen name ........ BOZ
Charles's Wain ....... DIPPER, BEAR
charlock .......... KRAUT, MUSTARD
charm ..... SPELL, GRACE, AMULET,
    PERIAPT, FETICH, TALISMAN

charm; Afr. ........................ OBI
charm, jewel ........... BRIMBORION,
                        BRELOQUE
charm, to .. ALLAY, ENAMOR, TAKE
charmer ...... MAGICIAN, SORCERER,
          EXORCIST, MAGI, SIREN
charnel house ............... OSSUARY
Charpentier; opera by ........ LOUISE
chars .................. BURNS, COALS
chart ............. GRAPH, MAP, PLAT
chase ..... PURSUE, CHEVY, TRACK
Chase; authoress ................. ILKA
chastened ........ PUNISHED, SMOTE
chastise ..... SPANK, TRIM, SWINGE,
        BLAME, SLAP, TAUNT, WHIP
chat .. PRATE, CONFAB, COZE, TOVE
chat; Fr. ................. CAUSERIE
chatelaine .. ETUI, BROOCH, TORQUE
chatter ... BABBLE, PRATE, GIBBER,
          CLACK, JABBER, TATTLE
chatterer ............. MAG, JAY, PIET
chattle, to recover ........... DETINUE
Chaucer's pilgrim .............. REEVE
Chaucer's title .................... DAN
cheap; Sp. .................... BARATO
cheat .. COZEN, FLEECE, BAM, DISH,
                            GYP
cheat by trick ........... THIMBLERIG
cheater; slang ..... TOPPER, BILKER,
                            GULL
check ...... NIP, REIN, BIT, DETENT,
          NAB, TAB, SNUB, STEM
checker ...... TESSELLATE, FREAK
checkered ................ VAIR, PLAID
checkers ................... DRAUGHTS
checkerwood inlay ............ MOSAIC
checkerwork . ................. TESSEL
checkmate ........ BAFFLE, DEFEAT,
        GAIN, LICK, STOP, STYMIE
checks by rein ............. SACCADES
Cheddar ...................... CHEESE
cheder; Jewish ............... SCHOOL
cheek ..... TEMERITY, GENA, GLEG,
          NERVE, SAUCE, JOWL
cheek muscle ............ BUCCINATOR
cheek; per. to ........ GENAL, MALAR,
                        BUCCAL
cheek of spearhead .............. JAMB
cheeks distended ........... BUCCATE
cheep ........ CHIRP, SQUEAK, PEEP,
                            PULE
cheer ........ ELATE, ROOT, MIRTH,
                        REPAST
cheerword ...................... RAH
cheerful ... GLADSOME, ROSY, GLEG,
        JOCUND, SUNNY, PEART
cheese, cement .................... GLUE
"    dish ...... FONDUE, OMELET
"    , French ...... LIVAROOT
"    , inferior ............... DICK
"    , Italian ........... PARMESAN
"    knife ................ SPATULA
"    magot ............... SKIPPER
"    , main constituent of . CASEIN
"    , soft ................... BRIE
"    , Swiss .... COTTAGE, EDAM,
                        SAPSAGO
"    toaster; slang .......... SWORD

44

"  , whole milk ........ DUNLOP
cheesy ........ SKIPPERY, CASEOUS
cheetah ...................... YOUSE
chelonian ................. TORTOISE
chemical cleansant ....... KRYPTON
"       compound; AMIDE, AMIN,
         AZINE, AZO, BORIDE,
         CERIA, INOSITE, IODIDE,
         ISOMER, LEUCINE, META-
         MER, STEARATE, TOU-
         LENE, XANTHINE, YIT-
         TERBIA, AZOLE, ELATE-
         RIN
"       element ARGON, HALOGEN
"       radical .... TOLYL, BUTYL
"       salt ........ SAL, SINIGRIN
"       substance .. IRIDOL, LININ
"       suffix . YL, AN, ANE, OLIC
"       telephone operator .. MOTO-
                            GRAPH
"       unit ................. TITER
chemise SHIFT, LINGERIE, UNDIES
chemist ...... ANALYST, DRUGGIST
cherish AID, ADORE, PET, FOSTER,
         NURSE, LOVE, PRIZE, WOO
cherry CAPULIN, RUDDY, MORELLO
"       gum, part of ....... CERASIN
"       red .................... CERISE
"       , sour .. AMARELLE, EGRIOT
"       , sweet ............ LAMBERT
"       , variety of MOREL, OXHEART
"       , wild .... MAZZARD, GEAN,
                            MARASCA
cherub .. EUDEMON, SPIRIT, SERA-
            PHIM, SAINT, STAR
chess, opening in .... MOVE, DEBUT,
            CHASSE, GAMBIT
chess problems ............... DUALS
chess term ................... FIDATE
chessmen ........ BISHOP, CASTLE,
         KNIGHT, MEN, PAWN, ROOK
chest .. ARCA, ARK, CIST, LOCKER
"       , animal ............. BRISKET
"       for supplies .......... WANIGAN
"       human ................. THORAX
"       per. to the ............ MIDRIFF
"       , Scot. for ................. KIST
"       sound .................... RALE
Chester, Eng.; rel. to .... CESTRIAN
chestnut colored ........... MARRON,
                        CASTANEOUS
chestnut, Poly ................ RATA
chestnut, rel. to .... BURR, ESCULIC
chestnut, water ...... STRIPE, LING
chevron shape ................... VEE
chevrotain ........ DEERLET, NAPU
chew .............. CHAMP, MUNCH,
            MANDICATE, CHAVEL
chew, inability to ........ AMOSESIS
chewing gum ingredient ... CHICKLE
chewy confection ................. GUM
Chian turpentine . ALK, TEREBINTH
Chiang-Kai-shek's wife .. MEI, LING,
                            SOONG
Chicago play district ,.......... LOOP
chicanery .. TRICKERY, SOPHISTRY
chick-a-dee .............. TITMOUSE

chickaree ................. SQUIRREL
chicken lava ...................... AA
chicken, young .... FRAYER, POULT
chickle ........................... GUM
chick-pea; E. Ind. ............. GRAM
chick-pea; genus ............. CICER
chickweeds; genus ........... ALSINE
chicory ..................... ENDIVE
chide ........ BLAME, NOISE, RATE
chief .... STAPLE, ARCH, CAPTAIN,
            HEAD, MAIN, RAIS, REIS
chief deity of Panapolis ......... MIN
chief excellence .............. FORTE
chief magistrate ............. SYNDIC
chief of the Seminoles .... OSCEOLA
chief, oriental ....... KAHN, SIRDAR
chigoe ......................... FLEA
chikara; Bengal ......... ANTELOPE
chilblain, ulcerated .......... KIBE
child .... BAIRN, BATA, CHIT, TAD,
                        TIKE, TOT
child, comb. form of .. . PAEDO, PED
child dedicated to monastic life;
                        OBLATUS
child of light and day .......... EROS
child of mixed blood ...... MESTEE
child of noble birth .......... CHILDE
child psychologist ................ ILG
child, small . BABE, BRAT, PEEWEE
child, spirit of a; Gaelic ...... TARAN
child; Tag. .................... ANAC
childish ...... IMMATURE, PUERILE
childlike adult .............. MORON
                        ASTER
children; dial. Eng. ....... PROGENY
children of heaven and earth TITANS
children's patron saint ....... SANTA
Chile, aborigines ............... INCAS
"    , capital of ......... SANTIAGO
"    , coastal winds of ...... SURES
"    , meaning of ............ SNOW
Chile mountain peak ........ JUNCAL
"    , province in ........ ATACAMA,
            ARAUCO, MAULE, TACNA
"    , rivers in .... BIOBIO, BUENO,
                        ITATA, LOA
Chilean bamboo-like tree ..... COLEU
"       fort .................... MAIPU
"       mineral bath . COLINA, TORO
"       shrub poison .......... LITHI
"       tree, large .......... ALERCE
"       seaport ................ LOTA
chili con ..................... CARNE
chill .. COLD, ICE, RIGOR, SHIVER,
                        AGUE, ALGOR
chill night air .............. SNELLY
chilly . BLEAK, RAW, ALGID, LASH
chime ......... CYMBAL, EDGE, RIM
chime of nine bells, changes on ......
                        CATERS
chimerical .... AIRBUILT, UTOPIAN,
                        ROMANTIC
chimney ............... LUM, TEWEL
chimney-piece ....... PAREL, INGLE
chimpanzee ................. NCHEGA
chin .............. MENTUM, MENTA
chin; comb. form ............. GENIO
China, anc. SERIES, SINOE, CATAIA

45

| | | |
|---|---|---|
| " | , anc. state of ............ TSAO | |
| " | , dynasty of ............... HSIA | |
| " | , foreign establishment in HONG | |
| " | , mediaeval ... CATHAY, KITAI | |
| " | , prefecture in .............. FU | |
| china | ........ DRESDEN, PORCELAIN | |
| chine | ............. FISSURE, RAVINE | |
| Chinese | ...... SINIC, SERES, SERIAN, | |
| | SINAEAN | |
| " | aromatic root ......... GINSENG | |
| " | barbarians ................ ESIN | |
| " | black tea ............... OOLONG | |
| " | boat .......... JUNK, SAMPAN | |
| " | buttress, kind of ......... WUTA | |
| " | city ........... TSINING, AMOY | |
| " | civet ..................... RASSE | |
| " | cloth ............ MOXA, PULO | |
| " | , comb. form for ........ SINICO | |
| " | commissioner ............... LIN | |
| " | condiment .............. NAPEE | |
| " | court ................. UEMEN | |
| " | deer ............... ELAPHURE | |
| " | department ..................FU | |
| " | dependency ............. TIBET | |
| " | dish ................. AME, LING | |
| " | district ................. HSIEN | |
| " | dog ............... CHOW, PEKE | |
| " | duck eggs, preserved .... PIDAN | |
| " | divinity .................... JOSS | |
| " | early race ........... KHITANS | |
| " | dynasty ... CHOW, HAN, KIN, LAN, HEH, LIAO, MING, SHANG, SUNG, TANG, TSIN | |
| " | dynasty, first .............. HSIA | |
| " | early race ........... KHITANS | |
| " | , enemy of the ....... TATARS | |
| " | exchange ............... SYCEE | |
| " | extra tax ............. SQUEEZE | |
| " | fabric, silk ................. SHA | |
| " | fish ................... TREPANG | |
| " | flute, old ........... CHE, TCHE | |
| " | food ................. TREPANG | |
| " | gateway ............... PAILOU | |
| " | general .................... MA | |
| " | gentry .............. LITERATI | |
| " | glue ...................... AGAR | |
| " | gong ................. TAMTAM | |
| Chinese god | ....... SHEN, JOSS, TAO | |
| " | grand secretariat ....... NEIKO | |
| " | grass ................. RAMEE | |
| " | guild ................... TONG | |
| " | harbor ............... CHEFOO | |
| " | idol ............. JOSS, PAGOD | |
| " | illustrious sovereign .. KUBLAI | |
| " | immigrant ............ HAKKA | |
| " | indigo ................. ISATIS | |
| " | inventor ............... TSAE | |
| " | jade ..................... YU | |
| " | knock-head ............ COTOW | |
| " | language ................ SHAN | |
| " | language rel. to SINOLOGICAL | |
| " | licentiates degree ..... SIUTSAI | |
| " | limestone ............. SINIAN | |
| " | mandarin's residence .. YAMEN | |
| " | measures ..... CHANG, CHIH, FUN, TSUN, TU | |
| " | merchant's corporation .. HONG | |

| | | |
|---|---|---|
| " | military organiztaion ... MAN-CHU | |
| " | money ..... PU, MACE, TAEL, TIAO | |
| " | Mongol dynasty ......... YUAN | |
| " | monkey ................. DOUC | |
| " | mountain ...... LUNG, TAE | |
| " | musical instrument ........ KIN | |
| " | name of Buddha ............ FO | |
| " | name of Gobi desert ... SHAMO | |
| " | nest of boxes ............ INRO | |
| " | noodles ................. MEIN | |
| " | numeral, hundred .......... PIH | |
| " | numeral, ten thousand ... WAN | |
| " | numeral, thousand ..... TSEEN | |
| " | numerals, 1 to 10 ... YIH, URH, SAN, SZE, WOO, LUH, TSIEH, PA, KEW, SHIH | |
| " | nurse .................... AMAH | |
| " | official ............... TAOYAN | |
| " | oil tree ................. TUNG | |
| " | orange ............ MANDARIN | |
| " | ounce .................... TAEL | |
| " | pagoda .................... TAA | |
| " | , per. to ......... SINESIAN | |
| " | philosopher ........... LATOSE | |
| " | plant ....... GINSENG, RAMIE | |
| " | poet ..................... LIPO | |
| " | pound .................. CATTY | |
| " | president ................. SEN | |
| " | province ..... CHIHLI, HWEL, SHANSI, KIANGSI | |
| " | race; anc. ........ DARD, SINIC | |
| " | red ...... CHROME, SCARLET | |
| " | religion, a ............. TAOISM | |
| " | rich earth ............. LOESS | |
| " | river .. HAN, ILI, TARIM, WEI | |
| " | roller ............. SIRGANG | |
| " | rood ...................... LI | |
| " | rooster's strut ............ LAK | |
| " | root (dried) ........ GALANGA | |
| " | sauce ...................... SOY | |
| " | seaport ...... CANTON, AMOY | |
| " | secret society ...... TONG | |
| " | sect ...................... TAOU | |
| " | sedge ............. MATI, KALI | |
| " | servant ................. AMAH | |
| " | shrub ......... TEA, REA, TAA | |
| " | silk ..................... TASAR | |
| " | silkworm ................ SINA | |
| " | silver, uncoined ........ SYCEE | |
| Chinese skiff | ................. SAMPAN | |
| " | society .... HUI, HOEY, TONG | |
| " | sovereigns; anc. .. KEE, YAOU | |
| " | tax ....................... LIKIN | |
| " | tea ....................... CHA | |
| " | temple ......... TAA, PAGODA | |
| " | territorial division ..... HSIEN | |
| " | toy ................. TANGRAM | |
| " | treaty port .. AMOY, ICHANG | |
| " | U.N. delegate ......... CHANG | |
| " | vegetable ................. UDO | |
| " | wax insects .............. PELA | |
| " | weight .. CHEE, LIANG, YIN, CATTY, PICUL, HAO | |
| " | weight, ounce ........... TAEL | |
| " | weight; var. ............. TSIEN | |
| " | wind inst. ............. CHENG | |

**46**

Chinese-white .................... ZINC
chink ... CRACK, INTERSTICE, BORE
chink; cok ................ CASH, COIN
chinks, full of ........ RIFTY, RIMOSE
Chinook powwow ............... WAWA
Chinook chief .................... TYEE
chinquapin ............... RATTLENUT
chinse ................... CLOSE, CALK
chin-whelk ................. SYCOSIS
Chios inhab. ..................... SCIOT
chip ..... GALLET, SCRAP, BONNET
chipped, not polished .. PALEOLITHIC
chipper ............... CHIRP, LIVELY
chip's stone ....................... NIG
Chips, Mr. .................... DONAT
chiro ......... FRANCESCA, SEERING
chiropter ................ ALIPED, BAT
chirp .................... CHEEP, PUE
chirrup ................ PEEP, TWEET
chiru .................... SAIGA, SUS
chisel ......... CUT, GOUGE, BURIN
chisel, broad .................... DROVE
chisel, mason's .............. POMMEL
chisel, paring ................... SLICK
chisel, stone; Irish ............... CELT
chiseled appearance; Fr. ...... CISELE
chit .......... NOTE, CHILD, SHOOT
chiton .... LIMPET, MOLLUSK, ROBE
chive ........ GARLIC, ONION, CHIP
chivy ............. CHASE, NAG, RUN
chlamys, military ............. CLOAK
chlorine family BROMINE, FLUORINE,
                              IODINE
chlorophosphate ............. APATITE
chlorophyl .... ETIOLIN, LEAFGREEN
chock ................ CLEAT, WEDGE
chocolate, powder for ........ PINOLA
chocolate trees; genus ...... (CACAOS),
                              COLA
chod-chod .......................... GEM
choice .... OPTION, SELECT, CHARY,
           RARE, DESIRE, MIND, WILL
choice; in a lottery ................. GIG
choice; make a ................... OPT
choicest part .......... ELITE, BEST
choir vestments ................ COTTA
choke ... BURKE, GOB, ENOSE, GAG,
          CLOSE, STIFLE, WORRY
choler ... IRE, ANGER, RAGE, FOAM
choleric .... IRATE, IRACUND, TESTY
choose ....... ELECT, OPTATE, CULL,
         LIST, OPT, PREFER, SELECT
choose jointly .................... COOPT
chop ..... HEW, JOWL, MINCE, DICE
Chopin's country ... FRANCE, POLAND
chopping instrument .............. SAX
chord, a common ............... TRIAD
chortle ............ CHUCKLE, SNORT
chorus ............ ACCORD, UNISON
chorus girl ................... CHORINE
Chosen .......................... KOREA
chough ................. CROW, CHOW
chowchow ........................ OLIO
Christ stopped at ............... EBOLI
Christian church ................ ORANT
Christian, oriental .............. UNIAT
Christian State ............... ARMENIA
Christian unity ............... IRENICS

Christianity .............. XTY, XNTY
Christmas ......... YULE, YULETIDE
"   carol ...... NOEL, NOWEL
"   food; Dutch ............... EEL
"   mummer .............. GUISER
"   oriental ................. UNIAT
"   rose ............ HELLEBORE
Christopher; abb. ............... XPER
chromosome ................... IDANT
chronicle ACCOUNT, ANNAL, DIARY
chronology error ........... PROLEPSIS
chrysalis, early stage ........... PUPA
chrysalis, insect .... AURELIA, KELL
chrysolite, mineral . OLIVIN, PERIDOT
chub; Eur. ...................... POLL
chuck; slang .................... FOOD
chuckle .. CHORTLE, CLUCK, LAUGH
chum ........... CAD, CRONY, PAL
chunky person JUNT, STOUT, THICK
church FANE, TEMPLE, CATHEDRAL
"   , a cathedral ........ MINSTER
"   altar offerings .... ALTARAGE
"   and state ........... ERASTIAN
"   calendar ................. ORDO
"   chapel ............. ORATORY
"   council ................. SYNOD
"   dignitary . PRIMATE, BISHOP,
                              DEAN
"   dissenter ........... SECTARY
"   district .............. PARISH
"   , division in a ........ SCHISM
"   doorkeeper .......... OSTIARY
"   episcopacy .......... PRELACY
"   judicatory ............ CLASSIS
"   , land belonging to a ... GLEBE
"   leader ............. HIERARCH
"   , middle body of a ....... NAVE
"   officer; beadle .... PRESBYTER
"   official .... SACRIST, VERGER,
                              BEADLE
"   , one of a millenial .. SHAKER
"   papal court ............... SEE
"   , part of a BEMA, TRANSEPT
"   peace device ....... IRENICON
"   reading desk AMBO, LECTERN
"   reliquary ................. APSE
"   revenue ............ BENEFICE
"   rite .................. LAVABO
"   , Roman ............ BASILICA
"   , Scotch ................ KIRK
"   , seaman's ............ BETHEL
"   stipend granted .... PREBEND
"   traffic in anything sacred ......
                              SIMONY
"   vault .................... CRYPT
"   warden .... TRUSTEE, STRAW
"   warden's assistant . SIDESMAN
Churchill's daughter ............ SARAH
Churchill's forte .............. PROSE
"   Order ............... GARTER
"   son-in-law .......... SOAMES
"   trade-mark .......... CIGAR
churl .... BOOR, HIND, KNAVE, OAF,
          CARL, CEORL, VILLEIN,
churlish ............. RUSTIC, SORDID
cibol ............... ONION, SHALLOT
ciborium ........................ PYX
cicatrice ....................... SCAR

47

cicatrization ................... ULOSIS
cicatrize ............ HEAL, RESTORE
cicely ......................... MYRRH
Cicero, target of ............. CATILINE
cicerone ......... CONDUCTOR, PILOT,
    GUIDE, COURIER, DRAGOMAN
cichlid food dish ... BOLTI, SUNFISH
Cid .......... POEM, CHIEF, LEADER
Cid's sword ................. COLADA
cide; Lat. .................... KILLING
ci-devant ............. FORMER, LATE
cierge ...... CANDLE, CERGE, SERGE
cigar, crude .. CULEBRA, CHEROOT
cigar, inferior ................... TOBY
cigar, long thin .. PANETELA, STOGIE
cigar, mild ..................... CLARO
cigar, Sp. ....................... ROPO
cigarette ...... CUBEB, FAG, GASPER
cilium ....................... EYELASH
Cimmerian ..................... BLACK
cinches; sl. ..................... PIPES
cinchona, yield from ......... QUININE
cincture GIRDLE, BALDRIC, CESTUS
cinder .....SLAG, ASH(ES), CLINKER
cinerarium ................ MORTUARY
cinerator ......... ASHERY, FURNACE
cinnamon ............ CANEL, CASSIA
cinnamon stone . GARNET, ESSONITE
cinquefoil ......... FRASIER, CLOVER
cipango ............... NIPPON, JAPAN
cipher .. AUGHT, CODE, MONOGRAM,
    ZERO, OE, NIL, NOBODY
cipo ........................... LIANA
Circe ....................... TEMPTER
Circe's Island .................. AEAEA
Circe's brother ............... AEETES
circle .. EDDY, CAROL, ORB, RHOMB,
    RIGOL, LOOP, CLASS, RING, SET
circle of celestial sphere ..... COLURE
circuit .. AMBIT, BOUT, GYRE, ZONE
circuit of judges ................ EYRE
circular ...... CINGULAR, BILL, ORB
    "    enclosure ........... LIS, LISS
    "    letter .......... ENCYCLICAL
    "    ornament ........... PATERA
    "    , per. to .......... ARC, GYRE
    "    sinus ........... CORONARY
    "    tread .................... VOLT
circulate SPREAD, TROIL, DIFFUSE,
    PASS
circumference . AMBIT, AUGE, GIRTH
circumlocution ... AMBAGE, WINDING
circumspect WARY, CAREFUL, CHARY
circumstance .......... EVENT, STATE
circus rider ............... DESULTOR
cistern RAINTUB, BAC, BACOR, URN,
    VAT, IMPLUVIUM
citadel .... TOWER, ALAMO, CASTLE,
    FORT
cital ......... SUMMONS, CALL, CITE
citified, col. ........ APING, FASHION
citizen ... DENIZEN, DWELLER, CIT
citron-like .. LEMON, LIME, CEDRAT
citrus drink ...................... ADE
citrus fruit ..... CITRANGE, CITRON,
    GRAPE, SHADDOCK, LEMON,
    ORANGE
cittern head, obs. .............. DUNCE

city, cathedral ...... LINCOLN, YORK
    "   court ............... MUNICIPAL
    "   of a bishop, Eng. ............ SEE
    "   of masts ................ LONDON
    "   of Palm Trees, Bib. .... JERICHO
city, of the .................... URBAN
    "   of the Dead ...... NECROPOLIS
    "   of the Gods ......... ASGARD
    "   of the Kings ............... LIRA
    "   of the Straits ......... DETROIT
    "   of the Sun ............. BALBEC
    "   of the Violet Crown .... ATHENS
    "   of Victory ................. CAIRO
    "   ward ............... WATCHMAN
civet ........... NANDINE, PERFUME
    "   , palm ......... PARADOXURE
    "   , palm, E. Ind. ........ MUSANG
    "   , tree-climbing ........... RASSE
civet-cat, flg. ............ DANDY, FOP
civet-like ..................... GENET
civic, per. to ........ OPPIDAN, URBAN
civil .. DECENT, POLITICAL, HENDE
civil wrong ...................... TORT
civilian dress ................... MUFTI
clad .............. ATTIRED, ROBED
claim . LIEN, TITLE, ASSERT, RIGHT
claim presumptuously ..... ARROGATE
Clair; director .................. RENE
Claire, Miss ........................ INA
clairvoyant .... SEER, PROPHET, SEE
clam .......... BAND, CLOG, SMEAR
clam killing snail ............. WINKLE
clam, long ....................... MYA
clam, razor ..................... SOLEN
clam, round ................... QUAHOG
clam shell opening .............. GAPE
clam-like .......... CHAMA, COCKLE
clamor ... BUNK, DIN, VOCAL, BERE,
    CRY, WAIL, ROAR, NOISE
clamp .. CLOTHESPIN, GLAND, VISE
clamp; to ..... NIP, CLASP, NAIL, TIE
clan .. TRIBE, RACE, CLIQUE, GENS,
    SEPT, FAMILY, PARTY
clan, head of a; obs. ........... ALDER
clandestine ..... SECRET, SLY, PRIVY
clang ........ DING, JANGLE, SHILL
clangor ... HUBBUB, UPROAR, DIN
clannish .......... TRIBAL, PRESTIGE
clarify DEFECATE, PURIFY, SERENE
clarionet ................. BEAN, REED
clarionet mouthpiece, socket .... BIRN
clasp .. DALK, HASP, MORSE, OUCH,
    BELT, STICK, TACHE
class .. CASTE, GENUS, CATEGORIZE,
    ILK, ORDER, RANK
class of Cymrl ................. AILLT
classical ..... CHASTE, PURE, ATTIC
classification .......... SORT, GENUS,
    TAXONOMY, ANALYSIS, TAXIS
classify ...... TICKET, LIST, DIGEST,
    CATALOGUE, REGISTER, TYPE
clavis .............. GLOSSARY, KEY
claw .. NAIL, TALON, UNGUIS, UNCE
claw-hammer coat .............. DRESS
claw of crustacean ............. CHELA
clay, baked .... ADOBE, BRICK, TILE,
    TASCO
    "   beds; Eng. ................. GAULT

" box ...................... SAGGER
" calcium carbonate ......... MARL
" composition .................. LUTE
" , constituent of ........ ALUMINA
" deposit ...................... LOESS
" , fine tryable .............. PRYAN
" , fine yellow ...... EAGLESTONE,
OCHRE
" manure ............. MALM, MARL
" pigeon .................. TARGET
" , polishing ................. RABAT
clay, potter's ..... ARGIL, PETUNTSE
" , prepare for pottery .. PUG, BOTT
" tropical ................ LATERITE
clayey ...... LUTOSE, MALM, BOLAR
clean; Heb. .................. KOSHER
cleaner ............. SOAP, SWEEPER
clean ship's bottom ............. BREAM
cleaning agent ................. BORAX
cleanse .... ABSTERGE, DEPURATE,
PURGE, DETERGE, RINSE
cleansing .................... ABULENT
clear .. LUCULENT, LUCID, NET, RID
clear, to shine through .. DIAPHANOUS
clearer ........... CLARIFIER, PURER
cleat ....... BATTEN, STRIP, KEVEL
cleat, make fast around ........ BELAY
cleave .. SPLIT, REND, CLING, POR-
FEND, COHERE, RIVE, DISPART
cleaver ...... FROE, FROW, BILLHOOK
clecho; her. ...................... URDE
cleft .... CHAPPY, GAP, REFT, RIMA
Clemens, (S) pen name ...... (MARK)
TWAIN
clement .............. MILD, LENIENT
Cleopatra's attendant ............. IRAS
Cleopatra's downfall ............. ASP
Cleopatra's river, of ........ NILOTIC
Cleo's lover ................ ANTONY
clepe .. BID, CALL, CHRISTEN, NAME
clepsydra .. CLOCK, DIAL, HORLOGE
clergy .. CLOTH, CLERICALS, PULPIT
clergyman's residence .......... MANSE
cleric ........... DEAN, CLERGYMAN
cleric, non ........................ LAIC
clerical .... SCRIBAL, MINISTERIAL
clerical profession .. DESK, PRIORSHIP
clerical vestment ........ AMICE, ALB,
FANON, ORALE, CLOTH
clericis laicos .................... BULL
clerk; Scot. ...................... WRITE
clever ........ ADROIT, DEFT, SMART
clevis .................. CATCH, HOOK
clew .............. GLOME, KEY, TINT
cliche .................. BANAL, TRITE
click ................. PAWL, RATCHET
click; slang ..................... AGREE
cliff ......... ARETE, CLEVE, SHORE
cliff, channel between ............. GAT
cliff, rough ........................ COL
cliff; So. Africa .................... KLIP
climax ........... ACME, APOGEE, EPI
climb ... GAD, GRIMP, SHIN, SPEEL
climbing ....... SCALING, SCANDENT
"       , adapted for .... SCANSORIAL
"       fern ...................... NITO
"       vine .. BINE, CUPSEED, HOP,
BRYONY, LIANA

clime ....... REALM, REGION, ZONE
clinch .. CLUTCH, SEIZE, GRIP, NAIL
clingfish; W. Ind .............. TESTAR
clink .... PRISON, RIME, SLAP, TING
clinquant ...................... TINSEL
clip ....... BARB, SHEAR, LIP, SNIP,
TRIM
clips; obs. .............. NOTS, NOTTS
clique ......... RING, COTERIE, SET
Cloaca Maxima of Rome ...... SEWER
cloak .... DOLMAN, GREGO, MANTO,
PALL
cloak, anc. Irish .................. INAR
cloak, hooded ...... CAPOTE, CAMAIL
cloak, loose .... ABOLLA, PALETOT,
PONCHO, PELISSE
cloak; Span. .................... MANTA
clock ......... KNOCK, NEF, TIME
clock, anc. water ........ CLEPSYDRA
clock, astronomical ........ SIDEREAL
clock weight ..................... PEISE
clod . DOLT, EARTH, LOAM, GROUND
clod-pate ... FOOL, IMBECILE, INEPT
clog .... CHOPINE, HAMPER, SABOT,
PATTEN
clog with mud ................. DAGGLE
cloister NUNNERY, ABBEY, FRIARY,
STOA
cloistress ......... NUN, RELIGIEUSE
clophony ........................ ROSIN
close FINALE, STIVY, END, OCCLUDE,
SEAL, AREA, DENSE, SHUT, YARD
close; poet. ..................... ANEAR
close the eyes .................... SEEL
closed condition of opening .. ATRESIA
close-grained wood of Guiana ... LANA
closely . ALMOST, BARELY, NEARLY,
JUST
closet ..... AMBRY, EWRY, AMBUSH
closing measure of a composition CODA
clot ...... COAGULATE, LUMP, MASS
cloth ...... NANKEEN, LIRE, PELLE
"       , a blister in ................ YAW
"       chalice .................... BURSE
"       , checkered .............. PLAID
"       , chrisom .................. CODE
"       , coarse hemp ............ GUNNY
"       , coarse linen .......... DOWLAS
"       , dealer in ....... DRAPER, COG-
MAN
"       finisher ............... BEETLER
"       , flaw in .................. BRACK
"       , goat's hair .............. TIBET
"       , insertion of cord ........ SHIRR
"       , linen; Fr. ................. BRIN
"       , linen; Sp. ................. CREA
"       measure ............. ELL, NAIL
"       , milled woolen ........ BEAVER
"       , modern ............. ACETATE
"       , mulberry bark ............ TAPA
"       , muslin .................. ADATI
"       of camel's hair .............. ABA
"       , selvage ....... LISTING, ROON
"       , soft .................. RUGENE
"       , Tibet ................. CAMLET
"       , twilled .. JANE, JEAN, SERGE
"       , twilled cotton .......... DENIM
"       used as a dressing ....... STUPE

49

" used for straining ..... TAMIS
" , weather proof ......... TARRY
" , woolen ...... KELT, TARTAN
clothe .. DRAPE, GARB, GIRD, ROBE
clothe, to INVEST, VESTURE, ENDUE
clothes ATTIRE, REGALIA, RIG, TOGS
clothes; Fr. ................... DRAP
clothes moth .................. TINEA
clothing ......... RAIMENT, BUREL,
FRIPPERY
clothing spy; slang ............ KEEK
cloud, filmy ......... NUBIA, CIRRUS
" , groups of stars ...... NEBULA
" masses ....... STRATA, RACKS
" , to ....................... SULLY
" , to bewilder ...... OBFUSCATE
cloudberry ........... BAKEDAPPLE
clouds, in round wooly masses CUMULI
" , luminous ................ NIMBI
clouds, nebulous envelope around nucleus of comet ........ COMA
" , per. to ......... NEPHOLOGY
" , the producing of NUBIFEROUS
" , vapory ................... RACK
cloudy . FILMY, DIM, MURKY, HAZY
clout .................. BUMP, PIECE
cloven . CLEFT, SPLIT, BISULCATE
clovenhoofed .. DEVILISH, SATANIC
clover LUXURY, MELILOT, ALSIKE,
TREFOIL
clover, a kind of LUCERNE, LADINO
MEDIC
clown . LOUT, MIME, YAHOO, ZANY
clown; col. .................... HODGE
clown, boastful ....... SCARAMOUCH
clown in "Twelfth Night" .... FESTE
clownish ..... CHURLISH, LOUTISH,
GAWKY
cloy .............. GUT, PALL, SATE
cloyed ..... AMPLE, GORGED, FULL
club . MACE, POLT, THUMP, BILLY
club, Maori .................... MERE
club service ............... KIWANIS
club shaped ............... CLAVATE
club, social ...... COTERIE, FRIARS
club, woman's .............. SOROSIS
clubfoot .................... TALIPES
clue HINT, INTIMATION, KEY, TIP
clump ................. TUFT, MOTTE
clumsy ... INAPT, UNCOUTH, MAL-
ADROIT, GAUCHE, UGLY, UNFIT
clumsy thing .. BIG, INAPE, JUMBO
Cluny, product of .............. LACE
clupeid ..... HERRING, LILE, SHAD
cluster . CYME, CLUMP, FASCICLE,
TUFT
" , flower .. RACEME, PANICLE
" , of fibres ................. NEP
" of seven stars ........ PLEIAD
clustered ACINIFORM, GLOMERATE
clustered grains ........ GRUMMOSE
clusters, grown in ....... ACERVATE
clutch lifting device ...... CRAMPON
Clypeus .................... NASSUS
clyster ......... ENEMA, INJECTION
Clytemnestra's mother ......... LEDA
cnemis ................. SHIN, TIBIA
coach . DILIGENCE, PRIME, STAGE,
TRAIN

coach, hackney .............. JARVEY
coach-dog .............. DALMATIAN
coach-man ............ WHIP, JEHU
coagulate CAKE, CLOT, CURD, GEL,
POSSET
coagulent, a ................. RENNET
coal . BASS, BRAT, EMBER, CARBON
" , bad, soft ......... SWAD, SMUT
" bin ..................... BUNKER
" carrying box ................ DAN
" deposit, lateral face ........ BORD
" derivative ............... CRESOL
" , immature form of ..... LIGNITE
" tar, derivative of .......... PITCH
" tar, distillate .......... TOLUENE
" tar, paraffine series .... DECANE
" tar, product of ............ LYSOL
" , volcanic ................. SCORIA
" wagon ..... CORB, CORF, TRAM
coal, waste of COOM(B), CULM, GOAF
coalesce ............ MERGE, UNITE
coalescence ...... FUSION, LEAGUE,
UNION
coal-fish, young ......... SEY, PARR
coal-like substance ............... JET
coal-miner ................. COLLIER
coalminer's consumption ..............
ANTHRACOSIS
coarse ...... DANK, RIBALD, RUDE
coarse grass ......... QUITCH, REED
coarse hominy ......... SAMP, CORN
coarse, obtuse .. FAT, GROSS, CRASS
coarse tow, flax ............ CODILLA
coast ..... SEASIDE, BEACH, CLEVE
coast dweller .............. ORARIAN
coast guard .................... SPAR
coat, anc. Rom. ................. TOGA
" , an outer .... JOSEPH, COATEE
" , coarse ................ CAPOTE
" , Eskimo ...................... TE
" long ............... REDINGOTE
" , long sleeved .......... CAFTAN
" , loose ........ PALETOT, SACK
" , man's close fitting ... SURTOUT
" of a mammal ......... PELAGE
" of mail .... ARMOR, HAUBERK,
HABERGEON
" with an alloy ............. TERNE
coati-like ....... NARCIA, RACCOON
coating, copper and bronze .. PATINA
coating for wounds ..... COLLODION
coating on inside of boiler ....... FUR
coats ........................ GLAZES
coats, brown; Mex. .......... NARICA
coax ............. CANT, CAJOLE, COG
cob LEADER, HORSE, AXIS, CHIEF
cob, black-backed .............. GULL
cobalt bloom ............ ERYTHRITE
cobalt symbol ..................... CO
cobaltiferous arsenopyrite . DANAITE
cobble DARN, MEND, PATCH, PAVE
cobbler .. SOUTER, SUTOR, CRISPIN
cobbler's wax .................. ROZET
Cobham .......... (JNO)OLDCASTLE
cobia .................... BONITO
cobra ... ASP, SNAKE, VIPER, NAJA
cobweb ....... NET, FICTION, TRAP
cobwebby ARACHNOID, ARANEOUS

cocaine source ................... COCA
Cochin-China capital ......... SAIGON
Cochin-China inhabitant ... ANAMESE
cochineal, assoc. with ... ACID, NOPAL
cochleate ..................... SPIRAL
cockade ............. KNOT, ROSETTE
cock and bull story .......... CANARD
cockatoo .............. ARARA, GALAH
cockatrice ................... BASILISK
cocker SPANIEL, PAMPER, CODDLE,
PET
cockle .... GITH, KILN, OAST, SHELL
cockpit ........ ARENA, CABIN, WELL
cockpit of Europe ............ BELGIUM
cock-spur ...................... THORN
cocktail ........ SIDECAR, MARTINI
cocky ........ SMART, PERT, SAUCY
cocoa ............. THEOBROMINE
cocoa, oilless ................... BROMA
cocoanut husk fibre ............... COIR
cocoanut, meat of dried ......... COPRA
cocoa-plum; Lat. ................ ICACO
cocoon .......... KELL, CLEW, POD
cocoon thread; Fr. ............... BAVE
coct .... BAKE, COOK, DIGEST, BOIL
cocus-wood ..................... EBONY
cod . BURBOT, COR, CULTUS, SCROD
coddle .. HUMOR, PAMPER, PARBOIL
code CANON, LAW, CODEX, PILLOW,
SALIC
coded message ......... CRYPTOGRAM
codfish .................. CUSK, TORSK
codfish; genus .................. GADUS
codfish ready for cooking .... SCRODE
codger ...... MEAN, FELLOW, MISER
codicil ... DIPLOMA, RIDER, SEQUEL
codify ................. CODE, DIGEST
codling .......... COD, HAKE, APPLE
coe-horn ..................... MORTAR
Coelebs; Lat. ............. BACHELOR,
BATCHELER
coelum; arch. .................. SOFFIT
coerce ... COMPEL, CURB, DRAGOON
coercion ................. CONSTRAINT
coffee ........... JAVA, MOCHA, RIO
coffee berry, exterior of .......... PULP
coffee cup holder ................. ZARF
coffee, extract from ........ CAFFEINE
coffee house ............... CAFE, INN
coffee pot ...................... BIGGIN
coffee, root used with ........ CHICORY
coffer ......... CHEST, ARK, CAISSON
coffin cloth .............. CLOAK, PALL
coffin, pre-historic ...... CIST, CHEST
cog ..... GEAR, CAM, CATCH, TOOTH
cog-foist ...................... CHEAT
cogitate ...... MULL, MUSE, PONDER
cognate .. RELATIVE, ALLIED, AKIN
cognizance ... AWAKE, KEN, AWARE
cognize ............ KNOW, PERCEIVE
cognomen ..PATRONYMIC, SURNAME,
TITLE, YCLEPT
coheir ............. PARCENER, JOINT
cohere ADHERE, GLUTINATE, STICK
coil .... CURL, ANSA, MESH, QUERL,
TOIL, TWINE
coil into ball ....... CONVOLVE, CLUE
coiled . TWIRLED, TORTILE, EILOID

coin, (see also 'gold coin')
coin ................. MINT, TALENT
" , Abyssinia ............... TALARI
" , agola .................. MACUTA
" , Amer. early ............... ROSA
" , Anglo-Indian ....... LAC, LAKH
" , Anglo-Saxon ..... SCEATT, ORA
" , Arabia ........ CARAT, KABIK,
TALLARI
" , Argentine .... CENTAVO, PESO
" , Australia ................... DUMP
" , Austria ...... DUCAT, HELLER,
GULDEN, KRONE
" , Brazil ... CONTO, MILREI, REE,
REI
" , British-India ........... RUPEE
" , Bulgaria ............. LEV, LEW
" , Chile ESCUDO, CENTAVO, PESO
" , China ... LIANG, MACE, TAEL,
TIAO
" , Colombia ................... PESO
" , copper ............ BATZ, CENT
" , debased .................... RAP
" , Denmark .......... ORE, KRONE
" , Dutch ...................... DOIT
" , E. African ........ RUPIE, PESA
" , East Indian ..... ANNA, RUPEE
" , Ecuador ................. SUCRE
" , Egypt .. FODDAH, KEES, PARA
" , English GROAT, GUINEA, ORA,
CAROLUS, PENCE, RYAL
" , Ethiopia ............... TALARI
" , European, old DUCAT, PISTOLE
" , French ....... ECU, OBOLE, SOU
" , French gold ........ LOUIS, RIAL
coin, front of ............... OBVERSE
" , German ........ KRONE, MARK,
THALER
" , Greek ....... DIOBOL, LEPTON,
OBOLUS, DRACHMA
" , Greek; anc. ............. DUCAT
" , Holland ... FLORIN, GUILDER
" , Hungary ................. PENGO
" , India ANNA, PICE, PIE, RUPEE,
LAK
" , Indo-China ............... SAPEK
" , Ireland ..................... RAP
" , Italy ........... JULIO, LIRA
" , Italy, anc RUSPO, SOLDO, TARI,
TESTONE
" , Japan ...... BU, MO, RIN, SEN,
TEMPO, YEN
" , Jewish ................... GERAH
" , Mediaeval ............... BANCO
" , Mex. . CENTAVO, PESO, TLACO
" , Mexico; old ............ CUARTO
" , metallic ................ SPECIE
" , Morocco MITKAL, OKIA, OUNCE
" , Nepal ................... MOHAR
" , Norway ........ KRONE, ORE
" , Oriental ................ DINAR
" , Persia ... ABASSI, ASAR, BISTI,
DARIC, DINAR, KRAN, PUL,
TOMAN
" , Peru ....... CENTAVO, DINERO,
LIBRA, PESETA, SOL
" , Poland .... KREUTZER, ZLOTY
" , Portugal . DOBRA, MILREI, REI

" , roll of .............. ROULEAU
" , Roman gold ......... SOLIDUS
" , Rome .......... AS, AES, SEMIS,
          SESTERCE
" , Roumania ..... BAN, LEU, LEY
" , Russia ....... ABASSI, COPECK
" , Scandinavia ......... KRONAR
" , Servia ............ DINAR, PARA
" , shekel 1/20 of .......... GERAH
" , Siam .. AT, ATT, BAT, CATTY,
          FUANG, LOT, TICAL
" , silver amalgam .. TESTER, PINA
" , Spain DOBLA, DURA, PESETA,
          PESO, REAL
" , Sweden .......... KRONA, ORE
" , Switzerland ...... BATZ, FRANC,
          RAPPE
" , trifling .................... DOIT
" , Tripoli .............. PIASTRE
" , Turkey ...... ALTILIK, ASPER,
          ONLUK, PARA
" , United States BIT, CENT, DIME,
          DOLLAR, EAGLE, NICKEL
" , Venezuela ................. PESO
" , Venice OSELE, DUCAT, GAZET
coiner ...... NEOLOGIST, NEOTERIST
coins ............................. ORI
coins, per. to ........... NUMISMATICS
coke; sl. ..................... COCAINE
col ....................... NECK, NEK
cold ...... BLEAK, FRIGID, ICY, NIP
" , a ......... CATARRH, RHEUM
" , biting .................... ALGID
" chap ........................ KIBE
" , intensely ................. GELID
cold mist; Scot. ................. DROW
" , per. to ........ FRIGORIC, ICY
" , Spanish for ............... FRIO
" steel ........ BAYONET, SWORD
" , wind; S. Eur. ............ BISE
cold-blooded ..... POIKILOTHERMAL
Cole; singer .......... (NAT) PORTER
colewort ......................... KALE
colic ........ ENTERALGIA, TORMINA
collar ........................... ETON
" bone ................ CLAVICLE
" , clerical ............... RABAT
" , frilled .................. RUFF
" , jeweled ........... CARCANET
" , plaited ............... RUCHE
" , turned down ........ RABATO
" , twisted ............. TORQUE
collect .... PRAYER, COMPILE, LEVY,
          AMASS, TAX, BAG, SHEAVE
collection ...... REPERTOIRE, HEAP,
          ROSARY
collection, a .. SET, LEVIES, SORITES
collection of detail papers .... CORPUS,
          DOSSIER
collection of facts .. ANALECTA, ANA
collec. of proper names ONOMASTICON
collection of small implements .........
          TROUSSE
collector of bird eggs ...... OOLOGIST
colleen ................... GIRL, MAID
college girl ....................... COED
" graduate ........... ALUMNUS

" grounds ........ QUAD, LAWN,
          CAMPUS
" half year .......... SEMESTER
" hall .............. AULA, DORM
" in Garden City, L.I. .. ADELPHI
" in N. J. ........ SETON (HALL)
" license for absence ..... EXEAT
" , mid-western .............. COE
" mode of training ... DRESSURE
" officer ................ PROCTOR
" professor; Eng. ............ DON
" servant .................... GYP
" treasurer ............. BURSAR
" tree ........................ ELM
collide ...... CLASH, CRASH, HURTLE
collided ..................... SMUDGED
collier .......................... MINER
collodion, a ........ GUNCOTTON, SOL
colloquy ...... CHAT, PARLEY, TALK
Cologne, one of the three kings of ......
          GASPAR
Colman, Mr. ................... RONNIE
Colombian, per. to .............. TYPE
Colombian town ......... CALI, PASTO
coloni; Lat. ...................... LITI
colonist, Austral. .......... STERLING
colonizer ... ANT, OECIST, PLANTER
colophonite .................... GARNET
colophony ...................... ROSIN
color .... TINT, GAMP, LAKE, BLUSH
" , auburn ................. TITIAN
" bark .................... MOCHA
" , bay ................. MALABAR
" , beige ................... ECRU
" , bitter-sweet ......... LOBSTER
" , black .................... EBON
" blister ..................... BLOB
" blotch ..................... GOUT
" , blue ..................... PERSE
" , blue, grayish AZURINE, MERLE
" , green blue ............. EMAIL
" , blue, greenish .. BERYL, CYAN
" , blue, greenish-green MESANGE
" , blue, marine ............ NAVY
" , blue, pearl ............ METAL
" , blue shade ......... RUSSIAN
color, bluish-green .......... GOBELIN
" , brown purple ........... PUCE
" , brown, rustic ........ ESKIMO
" , brown shade .... SEDGE, TAN,
          VERONA
" , gray green ........... RESEDA
" , gray, pale yellowish .. PONGEE
" , grayish blue ......... AZURINE
" , green blue ............. EMAIL
" , green gray ........... RESEDA
" , green shade ... PARIS, PARROT
" , green, willow ... MIGNONETTE
" , green woodbine ...... PERIDOT
" , greenish-green blue . MESANGE
" , hue between green and blue ....
          CYAN
" , indigo, dye ................ NIL
" mark, indistinct .. NEBULATION
" , markings ........ RIVULATIONS
" , maroon ............. MARONE
" , nude ................. SEASAN
" , oakwood ............... MESA

"     , purple brown ............ PUCE
"     , red brazil ............... ROZET
"     , red, dull ...RUFOUS, TAWNY
"     , red, fiery ............. MINIUM
"     , red shade .. SCARLET, CERISE
"     , reddish-blue; ..... ANEMONE,
                                    MAGENTA
"     , reddish-yellow .......... LAMA
"     spectrum ............. VIBGYOR
"     , streak of ............... FLECK
"     , tan .................... ORIOLE
"     , to DYE, HUE, STAIN, TINGE,
                                      TINT
"     , to paint ............... IMPASTE
"     vehicle ................. MEGILP
"     , white ........ ERMINE, SNOW
"     , willow green .......... RESEDA
"     , woodbine green ...... PERIDOT
"     , yellow-brownish-red ..... DEER
"     , yellow, brownish-reddish-red ...
                                       BOLE
"     , yellow, citron ......... MIMOSA
"     , yellow, reddish ACORN, ALOMA
"     , yellow, reddish-red .... TOTEM
"     , yellowish gray (pale) . PONGEE
Colorado city .................. LAMAR
Colorado, county in LARIMER, OTERO
Colorado Indian ........... ARAPAHOE
Colorado mountain ...... RATON, OSO
Colorado peak ... ESTES, PTARMIGAN
Colorado river .................... GILA
colored, highly .............. PRISMAL
colorless gas ...... KETENE, STIBINE
colorless liquid comp. ......... PYRROL
colorless liquid in alcohol ..... ACETAL
colors, blending of in calico print ......
                                       FONDU
colors, spectrum ....... BLUE, GREEN,
            INDIGO, ORANGE, RED,
                    VIOLET, YELLOW
colors, the ....................... FLAG
colors, to blend .. SOFTEN, SCUMBLE
colossal beast ............. BEHEMOTH
colt, female ...................... FILLY
columbate ................... NIOBATE
Columbia Univ. symbol ........... LION
columbium ................... NIOBIUM
Columbus' birthplace .......... GENOA
Columbus' port of embarkation PALOS
column ....................... PILLAR
"     base ................... PLINTH
"     , Buddhist ................. LAT
"     figure, female ..... CARYATID
"     figure, male ........ TELAMON
"     , kind of a ............... ANTA
"     , outward form of .. ENTASIS,
                                     GALBE
"     , ring of an annulated BAGUE
"     , shaft of FUST, TIGE, SCAPE
"     , small ................. STELE
"     , square engaged ....... ANTA,
                                  PILASTER
"     support ................ SOCLE
columnar; rare ... TERETE, STELENE
columns, sub-base of .... STYLOBATE
coma .. CARUS, SLEEP, CATALEPSY
comate ...... INSENSIBILITY, HAIRY

comb .... CARD, CARUNCLE, CREST,
                                    TEASE
comb, shaped like a...... PECTINATE
combat .... ACTION, CHAPLE, COPE,
                                    JOUST
combat, challenge to single ... CARTEL
combine ............... AMALGAMATE
combining form for equal ......... ISO
"     form for far ............ TELE
"     form for hundred .... HECTO
"     form for private ....... IDIO
"     form for tooth ..... ODONTO
"     form for weight ...... BARO
"     power of an element .........
                                  VALENCE
combustion residue .............. ASTA
come before ................. PREVENE
come down ................... ALIGHT
come out .......... EMERGE, SPRING
come under ................. SUBVENE
comedian ....................... BUFF
comedy SLAPSTICK, COMIC, DRAMA
comestibles MANNA, VICTUALS, FOOD
comet, envelope of ............... COMA
comet's tail ............... STREAMER
comfit . CONFECT, PRALINE, CANDY
comfort EASE, NEPENTHE, SOLACE
comfort, means of ....... EUDEMONIC
comic afterpiece ............... EXODE
comic char. ............. LULU, NEMO
comic strip PENNY, CAPP, FAGO, MIK
comic strip (Steve) .......... CANYON
comical .... CUTUP, DROLL, RISIBLE
comity ..................... URBANITY
command ...... BECK, BEHEST, BID,
            MANDATE, STEVEN, FIAT
command; arc. ................... HEST
command market ............. CORNER
command, to ................. ENJOIN
commander .............. CID, CHIEF
"     of 1st army ...... HODGES
"     of 3rd army ...... PATTON
"     of 7th army ........ PATCH
"     of 9th army ...... SIMPSON
"     of 12th army ... BRADLEY
"     of USAAF ......... SPAATZ
"     ; Turk. ................ AGA
commandments ............ PRECEPTS
commandments, the ten . DECALOGUE
commence .... ARISE, OPEN, SPRING
commenced ................ INCHOATE
commencement . NOVITIATE, SOURCE
commend . COMMIT, PRAISE, EXTOL,
                                      KEN
commensurate ......... EQUAL, EVEN
comment ........ POSTIL, ANNOTATE,
                                  DESCANT
commentary ...... REMARKS, GLOSS
commentator ............. GLOSSATOR
commingle ........... INMIX, BLEND
comminute .... MILL, CRUSH, GRIND
comminuted ...... FINE, PULVERIZED
commiseration ......... RUTH, PITY
commissioned ALLOTTED, BREVETED
commissure ... SEAM, JOINT, MITRE
committee of the U.S.S.R. ....... TSIK
commodity .................... WARE

common ....... GENERAL, AVERAGE, ORNERY, PLEBEIAN
common gannet ................ SOLAN
common people; Sp. ............ GENTE
common sort ................... RUCK
common to both sexes ....... EPICENE
commonalty ............. VARLETRY, PLEB(EIAN)
commonly accepted ......... VULGATE
commonplace ....HUMDRUM, BANAL, TRITE, STALE, DAILY, USUAL
commons ... FOOD, KEEP, PABULUM
commonwealth .... REPUBLIC, STATE
commotion .............. FLARE, RIOT
commune CONVERSE, SHARE, AREA, REALM, SOIL, IMPART
commune in France ............. USSEL
commune in Siberia ............... STIP
commune in the Netherlands ..... EDE
communion ...... EUCHARIST, HOST, VIATICUM
communion plate .... WAFER, PATEN
Communist Council ............ SOVIET
community; Russ. ................. MIR
Comoro Is. ................... MOHELI
comose ....... HAIRY, BRUSH, TUFT
compact ETUI, PRESS, FAST, DENSE, TERSE, SOLID, TRIG, TREATY
companion .. MATEY, ALLY, CRONY, MATE
companion, an equal ....... COMPEER
companion, constant ......... SHADOW
companion, faithful ......... ACHATES
companion; Fr. ................... FERE
companion, Sp. for ............. AMIGO
company BAND, BEVY, TEAM, TROOP
company of soldiers ......... PHALANX
compare . COLLATE, EVEN, SEMBLE, LIKEN
comparison ....... PARABLE, SIMILE
compartment .. BIN, CELL, CELLULE
compass ..... REACH, SWEEP, GYRO
compass beam ............. TRAMMEL
compass point ....... AIRT, AZIMUTH, RHUMB
compass sight ................... VANE
compass suspender ............ GIMBAL
compassion .............. PITY, RUTH
compel ....... DRIVE, DONE, PRESS, COERCE, DRAGOON
compellative ... NAME, APPELATIVE
compendium ...... DIGEST, EPITOME, REPARATION
compensation .. SOLATIA, HIRE, PAY
compete .. EMULATE, COPE, MATCH, CONTEND, STRIVE, VIE
competent ...SMART, CAPAX, ABLE, APT, FIT
competition ........ RIVALRY, STRIFE
competitor .................... RIVAL
Compiegne's river ........ AISNE, OISE
compilation ........... NODE, DIGEST
complain .. CROAK, REPINE, TWANK
complain peevishly .. MOAN, YAMMER
complaisant BONER, KIND, LENIENT
complete ... FULL, PLENARY, SOLE, END, STARK, MATURE, UTTER
complexion ............. BLEE, TINGE

complicate ......... INTORT, TANGLE
complication ........... NODE, SNARL
comply ............... ASSENT, YIELD
component ... ELEMENT, INTEGRAL
comport .. ACCORD, ACT, TOLERANT
composed WOVE, WROTE, ENTENTE
composer of "Aida" ............ VERDI
"       of "Carmen" .......... BIZET
"       of "Ernani" .......... VERDI
"       of "Oberon" ......... WEBER
"       of "The Merry Widow" LEHAR
composition ... OPUS, PIECE, THEME
"       for nine instruments NONET
"       of ivory dust ....... EBURIN
"       , per. to a ....... SYNTHESIS
"       premise of ........... LEMMA
"       of select works ....... CENTO
compound ..... MIX, FARRAGO, OLIO
"       , bitter crystalline .... ALION
"       , chem. ................ PYRAN
"       in assarabacca root ASARONE
"       in fleshy fruits ....... PECTIN
"       in incandescent mantles CERIA
"       of iron and sulphur .. PYRITE
"       , yellow .............. ANISIL
comprehend ........... GRASP, SENSE, TRAMMEL, FATHOM, SEE, REALIZE
compress ....... CLING, CROWD, FIRM
compulsion ...... COACTION, DURESS
compulsory service; Rom. .... ANGARY
compunction ... PENITENCE, QUALM, REMORSE, REGRET, RUE
comrade .... FRATER, BUDDY, PAL, PEER, ALLY, MATE
con READ, SQUIRREL, STEER, ANTI
con over ..... SCAN, PERUSE, STUDY
conative state .................. NISUS
concatenation ....... CHAIN, LINKED, STRING
concave mirrors ............. SPECULA
concave moulding ........... SCOTIA
conceal CLOAK, FEIGN, PALM, WRY
conceal; as goods ............ ELOI(G)N
concealed .. CLANDESTINE, LATENT, VEILED, DOGGO, PERDUE
concealed by mask ......... LARVATE
concede ............... ADMIT, AGREE
conceit FLAM, IDEA, PRIDE, VAGARY, WHIM, TEMPANY, EGO
conceited ........... PRIGGISM, VAIN
conceive .... THINK, BRAIN, IDEATE
conception .... IDEA, NOTION, IMAGE
concern ....... AFFAIR, CARE, SAKE, EVENT, GRIEF, WEIGHT
concerning ... ABOUT, ANENST, FOR, ANENT, ON, RE
concert hall LYCEUM, ODEON, ODEUM
conch ................. APSE, COCKLE
conciliate .. APPEASE, EASE, PACIFY
conciliatory ......... IRENIC, ASSENT
concise.... CURT, PITHY, SUCCINCT, PRECIS
conclude CLOSE, END, INFER, REST
concluded.......... FINIS, ILLATION, EPILOG(UE)

conclusive answer .... SOCKDOLAGER
concoct ........... COOK, BREW, MIX
concordant ................ UNISONAL
concordat ...... UNISONAL, TREATY
concrete; Fr. ................... BETON
concretion ............. CLOT, PEARL
concur ...... ACCORD, CHIME, HAND
concurrent SYNDROME, SYNERGETIC
concuss ................. JAR, SHAKE
condemn . BAN, DECRY, DOOM, FILE
condense .............. DECOCT, MIX
condescend ........... DEIGN, STOOP
condign .. JUST, DESERVED, FITTING
condiment .... SAUCE, CURRY, MACE,
                                  SAGE
condition .. IF, ESTATE, COVIN, FOG,
                            TERM, HAZE
condition of stupor .......... NARCOSE
condone . ABSOLVE, REMIT, PARDON
conduce .... ADVANCE, LEND, TEND
conduct ACTION, CONVEY, DEMEAN,
                                   RUN
conductor ... CICERONE, GUIDE, CAD
conductor by which an electric current
   leaves ...................... CATHODE
conduit .... MAIN, PIPE, DUCT, RACE
cone ....................... STROBILE
cone, retorting .................... PINA
cone tree FIR, LARCH, PINE, SPRUCE
Conestoga wagon ......... FREIGHTER
coney .............. DAMAN, RABBIT
confection ......... CIMBAL, NOUGAT,
                                PRALINE
confection, soft molded ....... DULCE,
                                FONDANT
confederate ......... ALLY, ABETTOR,
                          LEAGUE, STALL
confer knighthood upon ........... DUB
conferring respect ........ HONORIFIC
confess .... ADMIT, REVEAL, AVOW,
          OWN, RUE, REGRET, REPENT
confession ........... CREED, SHRIFT
confessional .... CREEDAL, LECTERN
confetti ........... BONBONS, CANDY
confetti, egg shell filled with CASCARON
confidential ...... ESOTERIC, SECRET
confine CAGE, DAM, IMMURE, LIMIT,
                               STRAITEN
confined ................ BOUND, PENT
confined to the initiated .... ESOTERIC
confirm .... ASSURE, PROVE, RATIFY
confirmed .. INVETERATE, RATIFIED
confiscate ............. USURP, SEIZE
conflict .......... BOUT, FRAY, WAR,
                               DISCORD
confront .. COMPARE, FACE, OPPOSE
confuse ......... ABASH, BEFUDDLE,
                              DERANGE
confused . CHAGRINED, FLUSTERED,
                        MUSSY, RATTLED
confusion .. ADO, MOIL, CHAOS, DIN,
                    PIE, BABEL, WELTER
congeal .. ICE, PECTIZE, SET, DENSE
congealed, capable of being . GELABLE
congenital .......... INBORN, INNATE
congenitally attached ........ ADNATE
conger trap ................. EELPOT
conglobation .................... BALL

congo ........... EEL, SALAMANDER
congo snake ...... AMPHIUMA, SIREN
Congo, capital ................... BOMA
Congo, cool season ........... CACIMBO
Congo, discoverer of .............. CAM
Congo, dry season .......... BANGALA
Congo river ..................... ZAIRE
Congo, wet season ........... KUNDEY
Congoese beer ................. GARAPA
Congoese common tongue ...... FIOTE
Congoese councillor ......... MACOTA
Congoese plant ................ MANIOC
cogou; China ...................... TEA
congratulate .... MACARIZE, SALUTE
congregate ASSEMBLE, HERD, TROOP
congruous .. FIT, MEET, CONSONANT
conical mass of coiled threads .... COP
conies, the ................ HYRACES
coniferous .. TORREY, CEDAR, PINE,
                           YEW, PINALE
coniuni ..................... HEMLOCK
conjecture ..... AIM, ETTLE, GUESS,
              SUPPOSAL, CONJOIN, MEET
conjoined parts ............... ADNEXA
conjugal felic.; symbol ... SARDONYX
connected with a purpose TELIC, MET
connecting bar of vehicle ...... SLIDER
connection ENLINKED, HANG, NEXUS
connective ................. SYNDETIC
connive at OVERLOOK, WINK, BLINK
conquered ......... BESTED, FAILURE
conquistador ................. CORTEZ
consanguineous ....... KINSHIP, AKIN
conscience ..... CASUISTRY, ERINYS,
                        INWIT, CRICKET
consciousness in experimental psychology
                                   LIMEN
consecrate ANOINT, BLESS, HALLOW,
                                    SAIN
consecrated oil ................ CHRISM
consecrated, some thing ...... SACRUM
consent .... ACCEDE, AGREE, GRANT
consentient AMENITOUS, UNANIMOUS
consequence ... END, ISSUE, WEIGHT
conservative . PRESERVATIVE, TORY,
                                DIEHARD
conserve, grape ................. UVATE
consider .... AIM, EAR, HEED, RATE,
                                  WISEN
considering .................... SINCE, IF
consignee ........ AWARDEE, FACTOR
consisting of names ...... ONOMASTIC
consisting of one word ...... MONEPIC
consolation ..................... SOLACE
console . COMFORT, CHEER, SOLACE
consolidate . KNIT, COMBINE, MERGE
consonant DENTAL, LENIS, SPIRANT
   "      aspirated ............. SURD
   "      , per. to a....... FRICATIVE,
                                 PALATAL
   "      producing a hissing sound ...
                               SIBILANT
   "      , voiceless ... ATONIC, LENE
consort ....... MATE, MINGLE, WIFE
consort of Siva ................... DEVI
conspicuous ........ FLARE, SALIENT,
                       SIGNAL, LIONIZED

55

conspiracy . INTRIGUE, CABAL, PLOT
conspire . PLOT, COLLUDE, CONCUR
constable ....... TIPSTAFF, BAILIFF,
    BEADLE, COP, POLICE
constancy; symb. ............ GARNET
constant . GRAVITY, STILL, WEIGHT
constant, interseptal .... PARAMETER
Constantinople, caravansary .. IMARET
  "  , foreign quarter ....... PERA
  "  , schools ............ MAHALEH
  "  , Turkish name . ISTAMBOUL
  "  , valley ................. LYCUS
constellation ........... ANSER, URSA
  "  , Halley's ...... APUS, GRUS,
    MUSCA, PHOENIX
constellation, Hevelius' ... ANTINOUS,
    CERBERUS, LACERTA,
    LYNX
  "  in the Zodiac ARIES, CANCER,
    GEMINI, LEO, LIBRA,
    TAURUS, VIRGO
  "  , long winding .... ERIDANUS
  "  , Northern AURIGA, BOOTES,
    CYGNUS, DRACO, LYRA,
    PERSEUS, SAGITTA,
    ANDROMEDAE
  "  , peacock ............... PAVO
  "  , Southern ....... ARA, ARGO,
    CANIS, CETUS, HYDRA,
    LEPUS, LUPUS, ORION,
    PISCIS, ALTAR ORION
constellation's brightest star ...... COR
"Constitution" .......... "IRONSIDES"
constitutional temperament ... CRASIS
constraint ... FORCE, BOND, DURESS
constrict ....... ASTRINGE, NARROW
constrictor .......... BOA, SPHINCTER
construe PARSE, RENDER, EXPLAIN
consuetude . CUSTOM, USAGE, HABIT
consuetudinary ................. RITUAL
consume . BURN, EAT, FRET, SPEND,
    USE
consumed ; Hawaii ................. PAU
consummate . ACHIEVE, IDEAL, END
consumption ....... PHTHISIS, WASTE
contact ......... IMPACT, TANGENCY,
    SYZYGY, ARRIVE, DO, MEET
contagion ...... MIASMA, POX, VIRUS
contagion, warding off .. ALEXITERIC
container ...... PAIL, TEACUP, CAN,
    CARTON, BAG, COMPACT,
    POUCH
container, large glass ......... CARBOY
containing tin ............... STANNIC
contaminate . DEFILE, SULLY, TAINT
contemn . . DESPISE, HATE, REJECT
contemporaneous ............. COEVAL
contempt .... DISDAIN, GECK, SCORN,
    BAH
contempt; Sp. .............. FICO, FIGO
contemptible fellow .... SCRUB, SKATE
contend ..... COPE, WAR, BATE, VIE,
    WAGE
contender ...... BATTLER, STICKLER
contest ..... TOURNEY, AGON, BOUT,
    COPE, SUE
contest in law ... DEFEND, LITIGATE
continent, hypothetical ..... CASCADIA

contingency . CASE, CHANCE, EVENT
contingent EVENTUATE, PROVISORY
continually AY, AYE, EVER, ETERNAL
continue to last ............ PERDURE
continued .... PROTRACTED, SERIAL
continuous ....... CHRONIC, LASTING
contort ................ TWIST, GNARL
contorted ..... COILED, PERVERTED,
    (A)WRY
contour .. LINEAMENT, PERIPHERY,
    PROFILE, OUTLINE
contour of deformation ...... ISOBASE
contract .... INCUR, HALE, SHRIVEL,
    STRAITEN, INDENTURE
contract, a ...... OBLIGATION, PACT
contracting muscle .......... AGONIST
contraction ... ELISION, STRICTURE,
    SPASM, COUP, FIST, TIS
contraction, per. to SYSTOLIC, TYPIST
contradict .. BELIE, IMPUGN, REBUT
contradiction ................. PARADOX
contralto, famous .............. HOMER
contravene OPPOSE, VIOLATE, DENY,
    HINDER, THWART
contribution .. ARTICLE, BOON, GIFT
contribution, form of  TAX, TIP, PAY
contrite, was ........... RUED, SORRY
contrivance ................... DEVICE
control .. MANAGE, REGIMEN, REIN,
    POWER, RULE, SWAY, WIELD
controversial ..... POLEMIC, ERISTIC
controversial area ................ SAAR
controvert .. DISCUSS, MOOT, ARGUE
contumely ..................... SCORN
contuse .............. BLOW, BRUISE
convalescent .............. ANASTATIC
convened.. SAT, CAME, MET, UNITED
conventional NOMIC, FORMAL, USAGE
conversation CAUSERIE, CHAT, TALK
conversation of three ........ TRIALOG
converse lovingly .... COMMUNE, COO
convert .... ALINE, DECODE, ELECT,
    THEIST, PROSELYTE
convex ........... BOMBED, GIBBOUS
convex moulding ...... OVOLO, TORUS
convexity of the shaft of a column ......
    ENTASIS
convey .. DEED, CEDE, GRANT, PASS
convey beyond jurisdiction ...... ELOIN
conveyance .... LOAD, LATION, TAXI,
    CAR, NORIMON, TRAILER, VAN
conveyance; Law .. CESSION, DEMISE
convict .. TERMER, TRUSTY, FELON,
    LIFER, CONDEMN
convincing .......... COGENT, PROOF
convivial ....... BOON, FESTAL, GAY
convocation DIET, SYNOD, COUNCIL
convolution of the brain ....... GYRUS
convulsion SHRUG, SPASTIC, THROE
cony ....... DAS, FUR, PIKA, RABBIT
cony; Lat. ..................... LAPUS
cony; Script.; .... ASHKOKO, DAMAN,
    GANAM, HYRAX
coo ......... CHIRR, CHOUGH, CURR,
    MURMUR
cook . STEAM, FRY, GRILL, SEETHE,
    STEW
cook, chief .............. CHEF, HEAD

cook lightly ......... BRAISE, SAUTE
cook room .......... CUDDY, GALLEY
cooking, the art of ......... MAGIRICS
cooking vessel . SPIDER, AUTOCLAVE
cool ........ NERVY, FAN, CHILL, ICE
Coolidge's vice pres. ........... DAWES
coon, (raccoon) ............. MAPACH
coon-tie ................ ARROWROOT
coop ...... COTE, HUTCH, MEW, PEN
Cooper; Mr. ..................... GARY
cooper's plane ................. HOWEL
coordinate (in radio) ........ SYNTONY
coot .. SCOTER, FOOL, DOLT, SMYTH
copal .................. RESIN, ANIME
copestone ..... COMPLETION, CROWN
coping of scrap wall ......... CORDON
copious ............. AMPLE, PLENTY
Copland; composer ............. AARON
copper ...... CAULDRON, SEN, CENT
"     alloy ...... RHEOTAN, BRASS,
                                OROIDE
"     brass ................. CHALCO
"     cup ...................... DOP
"     engraving variety of ...........
                            MEZZOTINT
"     green phosphate ...... EHLITE
"     , Latin for .......... CUPRUM
"     , Roman    .         AES
"     sulphate............. VITRIOL
"     symbol .................... CU
coprosterol .................. SEROLIN
copse ........ BOSCAGE, BOSK, HOLT
copy of original ... ECTYPE, REPLICA
copy, true ...... EXTRACT, ESTREAT
copyist ........ APER, MIME, ARTIST
coquito .......................... PALM
coracoid ............. BONE, HOOKED
corah .............. UNDYED, PLAIN
coral ........... MADREPORA, PEARL
coral branch ................. RAMICLE
coral island ...... KEY, ATOLL, REEF
coral septa ....................... PALI
coral snakes; genus ............. ELAPS
coral with porous walls ....... PORITE
corb ...... CREEL, DOSSER, BASKET
corbel ..... STRUT, CONSOLE, ANCON
corbel, per. to ............... PANNIER
corbie .................. CROW, RAVEN
cord, drapery ............... TORSADE
cord of goats' hair .............. AGAL
cordage fiber .... SISAL, HEMP, PITA,
                                 ERUC
corded ................ REPPED, TIED
cordelle ....................... TASSEL
cordial, a ......... SHRUB, PERISCOT
cordiality ... EMPRESSMENT, ARDOR
cord-like structure ......... FUNICULE
cordon ....... ENSIGN, STAR, BADGE,
                      INCLOSURE, COPING
core ...... AME, HEART, NAVE, GIST
core of a mold ...... MATRIX, NOWEL
core of ear of maize .............. COB
corf ............ BASKET, CORB, SKIP
corin; rare .................. GAZELLE
corium .............. ARMOUR, DERM
cork ......... PLUG, SHIVE, STOPPLE
cork, noise of drawing .......... CLOOP
cork tissue .................... SUBER

cork, wax in .................... CERIN
corking ... EXCELLENT, FINE, WHIT
corkwood ..................... BALSA
cormorant, the NORIE, SCART, SHAG,
                                 URILE
cormorant-like ........... SNAKEBIRD
corn .......... CLAVUS, MAIZE, SALT
corn-crib ........................ BIN
"   flag .................. GLADIOLUS
"   , hulled .................. HOMINY
"   , Indian ..... MAIZE, ZEA, SAMP
"   juice ................... WHISKEY
"   knife ................... MACHETE
"   lily ......................... IXIA
"   meal ....................... MASA
"   meal bread ................. PONE
"   meal, fried ........... HOECAKE
"   meal mush ............... ATOLE
cornea, related to ................. EYE
corned ................ SALE, SALTED
corneine ................... APHANYTE
corner ....... CANT, COIGNE, INGLE,
                          QUOIN, NOOK
corner, to ............... POSE, TREE
corners ..... HERNES, NICHES, INNS
cornerstone .............. CURBSTONE
corner-stones ................ DIATONI
cornice ............. ASTRAGAL, DRIP
Cornish diamond .............. QUARTZ
Cornwall mine ................... BAL
corolla; her. .................... GALEA
corolla leaf ..................... UNIE
corolla, part of ... PERIANTH, PETAL
corollary, a ...... PORISM, ADJUNCT
corona ........ AUREOLE, SCYPHUS
coronal ... BAYS, ROSARY, GARLAND
coronet . DIADEM, ANADEM, CROWN,
                                 TIARA
corporal .......................... NCO
corporate; law UNITED, ALLEGATION
corporate town ................... BURG
corporeal . HYLIC, BODILY, SOMATIC
corpse ... CADAVER, COIL, CARCASS
corpulent ......... FAT, OBESE, SUG
corpuscles, lack of red ....... ANEMIA
corral POUND, STOCKADE, STY, PEN
correct .... CHASTEN, EDIT, EMEND,
                DUE, INFORM, PUNISH, ORDER
correct; abb. ......... O.K., RT., OKAY
correlative ...... MUTUAL, NOR, OR
correspond ...... FIT, EQUAL, TALLY
correspondence ........... HOMOLOGY
correspondent ........ CONFORMABLE
corresponding in sound ........ RIMIC
corresponding part ........... ISOMERE
corroborative .......... ADMINICULAR
corrode ........ RUST, CANKER, EAT,
                      BURN, ERODE, GNAW
corrosive ............. ACID, ERODINE
corrugated ...... CRIMPED, RUGATE
corrugation ..... CREASE, WRINKLE,
                                 PUCKER
corrupt .. ATTAINT, POISON, POURY,
                      ROT, AUGEAN, BRIBE,
                                 DEBASE
corsair ... FREEBOOTER, PICAROON,
                                 PIRATE
corselet ......... ALLECRET, BODICE

57

corselet, body ........ ARMOR, COVER
corset strip ............. STAY, BUSK
Corsican seaport ............... BASTIA
cortex ................... BARK, RIND
corundum .... SAND, CHAFE, EMERY
corundum, variety of............. RUBY,
SAPPHIRE
coryza sign ............ COLD, SNEEZE
cosmetic .... HENNA, PAINT, ROUGE,
MASCARA
cosmetic, medicated .......... LOTION
cosmetic, white lead .......... CERUSE
cosmic, opposed to ....... ACRONYCAL
cosmos . ... REALM, EARTH, GLOBE,
HARMONY, ORDER, WORLD
Cossack .......................... RUSS
"    , chief .. ATAMAN, HETMAN
"    district ............... VOISKO
"    elder ............... ATAMAN
"    organization unit . STANITSA
"    squadron ... SOTNA, SOTNIA
"    whip ................. KNOUT
Cossack's mount ........... CHARGER
cosset .......... FONDLE, LAMB, PET
cost ........... CHARGE, LOSS, PRICE
costa ...................... RIB, VEIN
costard ................. HEAD, APPLE
costume, odd ............. RIG, TOG
cot; Anglo-Ind. ............. CHARPOY
coterie ....... CIRCLE, CLIQUE, SET,
CAMARILLA
cotton, a dye for ........... SULPHIDE
"    clearer ................ GIN
"    cloth .. DORIA, KHAKI, SURAT
"    cloth, blemish in ........... NIT
"    drilling ................ DENIM
"    fabric ....... GALATEA, LENO,
PERCALE, SCRIM, TERRY,
WIGAN, SILESIA, DIMITY,
NANKIN
"    fiber............. LINT, LINTER
"    fiber for glazing ...... VISCOSE
"    gauze .................... LENO
"    gin attachment ........ MOTER
"    lawn ................ BATISTE
"    machine ................. MULE
cotton material .... MALABAR, MOXA,
JACONET
"    seed vessel ........ BOLE, BOLL
"    thread ................... LISLE
"    tree; E. Ind. ............. SIMAL
"    , twilled .................. JEAN
cotton-tail .......... HARE, LEVERET
cotton-warp cloth ........... SATINET
cotton-wood ................... ALAMO
couch . DIVAN, SOFA, LAIR, CANAPE
couch, per. to ................. SOFANE
— coue; Fr. .................... EMILE
cougar ............. PUMA, PANTHER
cough, caused by a .......... TUSSIVE
cough, rel. to a ................ BECHIC
council ..... CABAL, JUNTA, SENATE
council chamber ......... CAMARILLA
council, church ................ SYNOD
council, national ................ DIET
council, rel. to a ............ CAMERAL
council table cover ............. TAPIS
counsel, ill ................. ABOULIA

counsel; Scot. .................... REDE
counselor, woman ........... EGERIA
count of Mayence, a ............. GAN
Count of Monte Cristo ....... DANTES
Count of Rousillon .......... BERTRAM
count, per. to ...... TALLY, COMITAL
count, to; Eng. .................... TOT
countenance ... ABET, FACE, VISAGE
counterfeit .. FALSE, FORGE, QUEER,
SHAM, BOGUS, SIMULAR,
BASE
counter-irritant ........ MOXA, SETON
countermand ..... ABOLISH, CANCEL
counterpart .. COPY, IMAGE, DOUBLE
counters ....... MEN, IVORY, TOKEN
counting frame ................ ABACUS
country . VALE, PAIS, LAND, WEALD
"    , ancient ........ ELIS, GAUL
"    bumpkin ...... CARL, CHURL,
CLOD, YAHOO, YOKEL
"    gallant ................. SWAIN
"    , per. to ........... AGRESTIC
"    , rel. to ... PREDIAL, URBAN
"    , Rom. ........... CAMPAGNA
"    ways ........ LANES, PATHS
countryman ................. PATRIOT
county ....... DOMAIN, SHIRE, SEAT
coup ................. SCOOP, STROKE
couple BRACE, DYAD, SPAN, TWAIN,
TWO, PAIR, TEAM
coupled ............. GEMINI, GEMEL
couples, growing in ........... BINATE
couplet ...... PAIR, DISTICH, BRACE
courage GRIT, HEART, METAL, SAND,
NERVE, VALOR
courage; symb. ......... BLOODSTONE
courageous HARDY, SPARTAN, GAME
courier ESTAFET, DRAGOMAN, GUIDE
course PATH, CURRY, ROTE, SERIES,
HEAT, RUN, ROUTE
court .. PARVIS, AREA, BAR, SPARK,
WOO
"    assistant ............... ELISOR
"    crier ................... BEADLE
"    , criminal .............. ASSIZE
"    , English ............ SOC, LEET
"    exemption .............. ESSOIN
"    hearing ................... OYER
"    , local; Eng. ............. GEMOT
"    minutes .................. ACTA
"    of circuit judges .......... EYRE
"    of justice; Rom. ......... CURIA
court of the Mikado ............ DAIRI
"    , open; Rom. ............. ATRIA
"    , open; Sp. ............. PATIO
"    , royal, per. to ............ AULIC
"    Turkish ................... GATE
courteous ...... DEBONAIR, URBANE
courtly .... ELEGANT, HEND, AULIC
courts, belonging to public . FORENSIC
courtship .. ROMANCE, SUIT, PLIGHT
court-writ ... SUBPOENA, SUMMONS
courtyard .... CORTILE, CURTILAGE,
TRANCE, AREA, QUADRANGLE,
PATIO
couteau; Fr. .................... KNIFE
cove . FELLOW, NOOK, BIGHT, SUMP
covenant ........ AGREEMENT, PACT

cover CEIL, TOP, CAP, LID, THATCH, HIDE, LAP, COSY
cover scatteringly ............. STREW
cover with horny plates .... SCUTATE
cover with silky down ...... SERICATE
covered by vines .............. LINAED
   "   meat with bacon .... LARDED
   "   with small figures; her. SEME
covering .. PELAGE, TEGUMEN, TILT
covering all continents ...... EPEIRIC
covering, decorative ...... CAPARISON
covers a bet ..................... FADES
covert ...... SECRET, DEN, LAIR, LIE
covet ......... ASPIRE, ENVY, YISSE
covetous GREEDY, MISERLY, FRUGAL
cow DAUNT, BOVINE, BROCK, VACH, INTIMIDATE, THREATEN
   " barn ..................... BYRE
   " , English beef ............. SUSSEX
   " ; genus ...................... BOS
   " , hornless .......... MOIL, MULET
   " , Irish breed .............. KERRY
   " , lowing of a ................. MOO
   " , milk yielding ............. MILCH
   " , mother ............... CALVER
   " , order of sea .......... SIRENIA
   " pen .................... VACHERY
   " , Scotch breed ANGUS, AYRSHIRE
   " , sea .................. MANATEE
   " , unbranded .......... MAVERICK
   " , young .. STIRK, CALF, HEIFER
cowardly .... CRAVEN, NIDGET, SHY
cowboy; Sp. .. LLANERO, VAQUERO
cowboy's breeches CHAPS, JODHPURS
cowes . DAUNTS, OVERAWES, AWES
cows ...................... KEE, KINE
Cox, Wally ................. PEEPER(S)
coxcomb ........ DANDY, DUDE, FOP
coy ........... DEMURE, ARCH, SHY, BASHFUL, MODEST, PAT
coyote, hunting .............. WOLFING
coypu; S. Amer. .............. RODENT
coypu fur ..................... NUTRIA
coze ..................... CHAT, TALK
cozen .... BEGUILE, CHEAT, TRICK
cozy ........ SNUG, COVERING, QUILT
cozy retreat ...... NUCK, DEN, NEST, INGLE
crab ... FIDDLER, MAIAN, MOLLUSK
crab, king ................... LIMULUS
crab, middle portion of ....... METOPE
crabapple; Scot. ................ SCROG
crabs .. BRACHYURA, CANCER, UCA
crab's claw .................... CHELA
crabs; genus ................ OCYPODE
crack ...... CHAP, KIBE, RIFT, RIME
crackle ... CREPITATE, CRINK, SNAP
cracksman .......... BURGLAR, YEGG
crack-up; slang ......... EXTOL, LAUD
cradle .... CUNABULA, SLEE, SOLEN
cradle, a child's ................ CADRE
craft ........... ART, TRADE, POLICE
crafty ........ SLY, TOD, WILY, WISE
crag ......... ARETE, BRACK, CLIFF
Craig, Isabel; pen name ........... ISA
crake ... RAIL, CROW, RAVEN, SORA
crakow ................... BOOT, SHOE
cram ...................... BONE

crane fly ..................... TIPULA
crane; Malayan ................ SARUS
crane, ship's ................... DAVIT
crane, the ...................... GRUS
crane, traveling ....... TITAN, JENNY
crane's arm ........................ JIB
craniometrical point INION, STENION, PTERION
cranium ....... SKULL, CEREBRUM
crank ....... WINCH, FANATIC, WIT
crape .. CLERGY, CRIMP, FRIZ, CURL
crass ........ CRUDE, DENSE, THICK, COARSE
crate .. CRADLE, ENCASE, HAMPER
crater ............. CALDERA, MAAR
cravat ... TIE, ASCOT, STOCK, TECK
crave ........ BEG, HANKER, YEARN
craven ........ POLTROON, COWARD
craw ...................... CROP, MAW
crawfish; Austral. ............. YABBY
crawl .... CRINGE, FAWN, GROVEL, CREEP, INCH, SHUG
crawler ..................... REPTILE
crayon ..... PENCIL, PASTEL, CHALK
craze .. FUROR, FAD, MANIA, MAZE
crazy ...... AMOK, LOCO, REE, MAD
   " , slightly ...... POTTY, WACKY
cream .......... ELITE, REAM, BEST
cream mixed wtih wine ... SILLABUB
cream of tartar ................ ARGOL
creation .... WRINKLE, FOLD, RUCK
creation . MAKING, COSMOS, WORLD
creator of the world ...... DEMIURGE
credit IMPUTE, FAITH, TICK, TRUST, BELIEF, HONOR
creditor, greedy ..... SHYLOCK, DUN
creek .. ESTERO, RIO, SPRUIT, WICK
creel ........ TRAP, BANK, BASKET
creep away meanly .. SKULK, STEAL, SLINK
creephole ............... SUBTERFUGE
creeping .. REPTANT, SYCOPHANTIC
creese ....... SWORD, KRIS, WEAPON CRENA
Cremona .............. AMATI, VIOLIN
crenate .................. SCALLOPED
crenoid ................ ROUGHEDGED
Creole and Indian .......... MESTIZO
Creole State ............... LOUISIANA
crepitate ...... CRACKLE, SNAP
crescent .............. (SEMI)LUNAR
crescent, per. to a..... BICORN, HORN
crescent shaped ...... LUNATE, LUNE
crespie ........................ WHALE
cresset ........ FLAMBEAU, TORCH
crest ... COMB, COP, COPPLE, RIDGE
Crest College ................... CEDAR
crest, sharp ..................... ARETE
crested .... CORONATED, CRISTATE, PILEATE
crested dogstail grass ...... TRANEEN
Cretan earth spirits ........ CURETES
Cretan monster ........... MINATOUR
Crete, legendary king of ....... MINOS
Crete, man of brass who guarded TALOS
cretin ........... IDIOT, MYXEDEMA
cretism .... FALSEHOOD, LYING, LIE

cretose ...................... CHALKY
crib. BUNKER, PONY, RACK, STEAL,
BIN, CRATCH, MANGER
cribbage points ........... NOBS, PEG
cricket, a (see also locust) ...... GRIG
cricket; genus ............... ACHETA
"     , high pitched sound ..........
STRIDULATE
"     , position in . SNICK, MIDOFF
"     , run scored in ........... BYE
"     , term in ............... OVER
"     , Yorker in ............. TICE
crime of trafficking in a benefice ........
SIMONY
Crimea, river of the ............. ALMA
Crimea, tribe in the ....... INKERMAN
Crimean Sea ..................... AZOF
criminal . CONVICT, FELON, NOCENT
criminal intent ........ DOLE, DOLOSE
crimp ...... CURL, FRIZZ, CRINKLE,
NOTCH, WRINKLE
crimson . LAC, RED, CARMINE, PINK
crine ...... HAIR, SHRINK, SHRIVEL
crined ........................... MANED
cringe QUAIL, BINGE, FAWN, KNEE,
SUBMIT, TRUCKLE
cringle EYELET, CIRCLE, DISK, ORB
crinite ................. FOSSIL, HAIRY
crinkle ...... CURL, KINK, WRINKLE
crinkled ........ CONTORTUPLICATE
cripple, Scottish ............. LAMITER
cripple, to .... HOCK, LAME, SCOTCH
crisis, having no ........... ACRITICAL
crisp ... FRIABLE, BRITTLE, CHEEP,
FRANGIBLE, RUMPLED, SPALT
crispin ................... SHOEMAKER
cristate ...................... CRESTED
criteria ...................... METRICS
criterion .... CANON, MODEL, NORM,
STANDARD, TYPE, TEST
critic .... BOASTER, NOMUS, ZOILUS,
BOOER, LITERATOR
critic, a contemptible .. CRITICASTER
critical .............. EDGY, ZOILEAN
critical mark ...... OBELISK, OBELUS
criticism .............. CAVIL, REVIEW
criticize CENSURE, ROAST, SCARIFY,
ANIMADVERT
critics, severe .... SLATERS, CENSORS
croaked ... KILLED, CAWED, CRIED
croaking ..................... RAUCOUS
Croat tribe SCLAV, WENDISH, SLAV
Croatian city ........ AGRAM, FIUME
Croatian mountain ........... KAPELA
Croatian river ............... BEDNYA
Croatian territory ............ BANAT
crock ....... SOIL, EWE, SMUT, SOOT
Crockett; Texan ............... DAVID
Crockett's Chapel .............. ALAMO
crocodile, Amer. .............. ACUTUS
"     bird ................. PLOVER
"     bird; Lat. ....... TROCHILOS
"     , common MUGGER, NILOTIC
"     like ......... GAVIAL, NAKO
"     , marsh ................ GOA
"     of the Nile ....... VULGARIS
croft ..... COTTAGE, FARM, BOTTLE
cromlech ................... DOLMEN

crone .... BELDAME, HAG, VETERAN
Cronyn; actor .................. HUME
crook, bishop's ............... CROSIER
crook or bend ................ AKIMBO
crooked ... RENT, ASKEW, WRY, ZAG
crop ............. REAP, CRAW, MAW
crop, hunting ................... WHIP
crop of a fowl ................. GEBBIE
crop, out ..................... BASSET
crop, to cut ................ CLIP, LOP
crops for cattle only ......... SOILAGE
Crosby; singer ................... BING
cross .... CORSE, CELTIC, GO, ROOD,
TRACE
cross barred ......... TRABECULATE
cross guard ................... CHAPE
cross, tau ...... ANKH, CRUX, TACE
crossbeam, a ................... TRAVE
crosspiece ........ BUCK, YOKE, SPAR
crossquestion ...... EXAMINE, TARGE
cross-roads of the world ...... LISBON
crossrow ................... ALPHABET
cross-shaped ............... CRUCIAL
cross-word puzzle ......... SEMANTIC,
ANAGRAM
crotchet ....... FAD, VAGARY, WHIM
croton bug ............... COCKROACH
crouch ...... FAW, SQUAT, TRUCKLE
croup CYNANCHE, CATARRH, CROAK
crouse ......... BOLD, BRISK, COCKY
crouton ................... BIT, SIPPET
crow ........ ROOK, AGA, CAW, DAW,
CORVINE
crow, Cornish .................. AYLET
crow, to ...... BRAG, VAPOR, VAUNT
crowd, the ...... BIKE, POSSE, RUCK,
SWARM, DROVE, HORDE
crowded ........ ELBOWED, SERRIED
crown ... DIADEM, CORONA, MITIER,
PATE, TIAR
crown prince ....... ATHELING, HEIR
crown, to ............ CORONATE, CAP
crown wheel ................ CONTRATE
crowned ...... CRESTED, CRISTATED
crucial .............. SEVERE, FINAL
cruciation ..... TORTURE, CROSSING
crucible ........ ETNA, POT, RETORT
crucifix .......... PAX, ROOD, CROSS
crude .......... CRASS, ROUGH, RAW
cruel ...... SAVAGE, BRUTAL, FELL,
TYRANNIC
cruet ...... AMA, AMPULLA, CASTOR
crumbly ........... BRASHY, FRIABLE
crumple .. WRINKLE, RAFFLE, RUCK
crunch .... CHAMP, CRUMP, MUNCH
cruor ................. BLOOD, GORE
crural joint ....................... KNEE
"Crusade in Europe"; by ...............
EISENHOWER
crusader ........ TEMPLAR, PILGRIM
crusader's foe .. SALADIN, SARACEN
crusader's port ................... ACRE
crush .......... CROWD, PRESS, SINK
crush room ................... FOYER
crushed sugar cone ......... BAGASSE
crustacean LOBSTER, CRAB, PRAWN
"     feeler ............. ANTENNA
"     , footless ............... APUS

"  , fossil ............ TRILOBITE
"  ; genus ...... ERYON, HIPPA
"  , king crab .......... LIMULUS
"  larva form .............. ALIMA
"  , limb of ............. PODITE
"  , small .. COPEPODA, ISOPOD
crustaceous .................. SHELLY
crux ....... PUZZLE, RIDDLE, ANKH,
CROSS
cry PISH, AVAST, HEP, WEEP, PULE,
YELP, HUE, SOB, TEST, TRIAL
"  , a party . SHIBBOLETH, SLOGAN
"  as a child ........... MEWL, PULE
"  for cattle ..................... HOY
"  , mystic ..................... OM
"  , to ................. IMPLORE
cry to urge on ....... TANTIVY, YOICK
cry up .......................... EXTOL
crying .... PULING, WAIL, CLAMANT
cryptocerate bug .............. CORIXA
cryptogram .. CODE, ACROGEN, FERN
cryptogrammic ............. AGAMOUS
crystal gazing, do ................ SCRY
crystal, twin .................. MACLE
crystalline ................ PELLUCID
"  alkaloid poison .... ATROPINE,
AMARINE, DATURINE, JERVINE
"  base ................. ALANINE
"  compound .... SERINE, OSCIN,
HAEMIN, ACICULITE, AIKINITE
"  globulin ............. VITELLIN
"  hollow nodule ......... GEODE
"  mineral ............. APHTITE
"  pine tar .............. RETENE
"  rock ..... DIORITE, GREISEN
"  salt ................... BORAX
"  structure ............. SPARRY
"  substance . ALBAN, AMARINE,
UREA
"  substance, colorless ... ORCINE
"  substance, sugar-like . DULCIN
crystallite ............... WHINSTONE
crystals, dewy with ........... DRUSY
ctenophora ........... BEROE, CESTUS
cub ........ CODLIN, FRY, PUP, EAM,
LIONET
Cuban coin ............ GOURDE, PESO
"  dance ................... RUMBA
"  ex-president ........ MACHADO
"  fortification .......... TROCHA
"  municipality ......... PALMIRA
"  port ..................... DUABI
"  tempest .............. BAYAMO
"  tobacco ........ CAPA, VUELTA
"  town ................... GUINES
"  ward .................. BARRIO
cubic body .................. DICE, DIE
cubic decimeter ................. LITRE
cubic measure .................. CORD
cubic meter ..................... STERE
cubicle ............. CELL, BEDROOM
cubitus ......................... ULNA
Cuchullin's wife ....... EMER, EIMER
cuckoo, allied to the ............... ANI
"  , Amer.; Lat. ...... COCCYZUS
"  bees; genus ......... NOMADA
"  family ............ CUCULIDAE
"  , Indian; genus .......... KOEL

"  pint ..................... ARUM
"  vulgate ................. LARUS
cuckoo's mate ............. WRYNECK
cuckoo-spits; genus ......... CERCOPIS
cucullate ........ COWELED, HOODED
cucumber PEPO, CONGER, GHERKIN
cucumber, sea ............... PEDATA
cucumber; Sp. ................ PEPINO
cucurbit ........................ GOURD
cud ...... MERYCISM, QUID, RUMEN
cuddle SNUGGLE, HUG, NESTLE, PET
cudgel .. STAFF, SHILLALAH, STAVE
cudgel, to BASTE, DRUB, FUSTIGATE
cudgeled, one who is .......... BEATEE
cue ........... HIT, ROD, TAIL, TIP
cue of hair ................... TAIL, PIG
cuerpo ......... TORSO, HULK, BODY
cuerpo, in .......... SOMATIC, NAKED
cuestra .......................... RIDGE
cuff ...................... BOX, CLOUT
cuif .... COOF, DOLT, LOUT, NINNY
cuirass ARMOR, MAIL, LORIC, LORICA
cull .... DUPE, GULL, PIKE, SELECT
culmination .... ACME, AUGE, NOON
cultivate .... EAR, FARM, TILL, TEEL
cultivated .. HOED, TILLED, URBAN
culture .. AGAR, ART, POLICY, TILTH
cumin, sweet ................... ANISE
culver ................ DOVE, PIGEON
cummerbund ................... SASH
cumshaw . GRATUITY, PRESENT, TIP
cunabula ...................... CRADLE
cuneiform ....... SPHENOID, WEDGY
cunning .... ARTFUL, CRAFT(Y), SLY,
WILY
cunningly formed ............. DAEDAL
cup bearer ............ PINCERN, SAKI
"  , drinking .. TOSS, GODET, TIG,
TASS
"  , earthenware .............. MUG
"  for assaying metals .... BEAKER,
CUPEL
"  , large drinking .. GRAIL, JORUM
"  of a flower ............... CALYX
"  of Olympus ................ HEBE
"  , Russian ................ CHARK
"  , small ..... CRUSE, CANNIKIN,
NOGGIN
"  , small; obs. ........ CALICULAR,
NIPPERKIN
"  to hold precious stones while cutting
DOP
cupboard.... ARMOIRE, AMBRY, KAS
cupboard; Sp. ............. APARADOR
cupel ................... REFINE, TEST
Cupid .......... AMOR, EROS, LOVE
Cupid's sweetheart ........... PSYCHE
cupidity .... AVARICE, GREED, LUST
cupidity demon ........... MAMMON
cup-like .................... CALICULAR
cup-like stone ................. GEODE
cup-like vessel .................. ZARF
cupola ............. LANTERN, DOME
cur ........... MUT, MONGREL, TIKE
cur, a ........................... FICE
curare; obs., var. ............... URARI
curassow ......... CRAX, MITU, BIRD
curate ..... DOMINIE, PRIEST, ABBE

curative ................. REMEDIAL
curb .... BIT, CHECK, REIN, STRAIN
curch .................... KERCHIEF
curd ........... CRUD, CASEIN, OAST
curdle .... EARN, LOP, POSSET, SAM
cure ...... CORN, REEST, THERAPY
cure by change of atmospheric conditions
APEUTICS, CLIMATOTHER
cure-all ........... ELIXIR, PANACEA
"Curfew Shall Not Ring Tonight" author
THORPE
Curie, Miss ...................... EVE
curious ...... UNUSUAL, ODD, RARE
curl ......... KINK, TOUPET, TRESS
curled .. SPIRY, CRIMPED, TWISTED
curlew ...... GODWIT, FUTE, SNIPE,
WHAUP
curlew; Old World MARLIN, BUSTARD
curlew; Tahiti .................. KIOEA
curling mark ..................... TEE
curls, formed into.............. CRISPS
curly ........ KINKY, WAVY, OUNDY
curlycue ........ FLOURISH, PARAPH,
CAPER, ESS
curmudgeon ............. CRAB, MISER
curn; Scot .................... GRAIN
currant, substance in .......... ALITE
currants; genus ................ RIBES
current .... GOING, INSTANT, RAPID,
FLOW, HABIT, USUAL, RIFE
curse ...... BANE, ANATHEMA, BAN
cursed ........ ODIOUS, EXECRABLE
curt ......... BLUFF, BRIEF, SHORT
curtail ......... LOP, PARE, REDUCE
curtilage ...... AREA, (COURT) YARD
curvature ...... LORDOSIS, CYRTOSIS
curve .... ARC, BEND, CROOK, TURN,
ESS, OGEE
curve, double point of ........ ACNODE
curve, convex side up . ANTICLINICAL
curve, cusp of a .............. SPINODE
curve invented by Diocles .... CISSOID
curve, outer of arch ...... EXTRADOS
curve parallel to an ellipse .... TOROID
curved ......... ARCIFORM, ARCUATE
curved, as a bill .............. ADUNC
curved processes ................ HAMI
curved wedge .................... CAM
curves, winds ................ CROOKS
curvet ...... CAPER, FRISK, GAMBOL
curvet, half turn ........... CARACOLE
cuscuta; genus .............. DODDER
cushat ................ DOVE, PIGEON
cushion ..... DASHPOT, BOTT, PAD
cushion-like organ on insects' foot ......
PLANTULA
cusk ................ BURBOT, FISH
cusp ...... CANTLE, APEX, CORNER,
END, PARACONE
custard-apple tree PAWPAW, ANONA
custard tart ..................... FLAN
custodianship ............ NEOCORATE
custody ..... CHARGE, TRUST, SAFE
custom URE, ASAL, THAEW, USAGE,
WONT, USE, MORE, RITE
custom with the force of law ..... MOS
cut ........ LOB, LOP, MOW, CARVE,
NOTCH, SNEE(D), SCISSEL

cut a random ........ MOW, SEVER,
(BE)SLASH, SERRATE
cut, capable of being ......... SECTILE
cut down vertically .... SLICE, SCARP
"   in half ................. DIMIDIATE
"   in squares .................... DICE
"   of an axe .... HACK, GASH, KERF
"   off BOB, SNICK, SCIND, SHORN,
TAIL
"   off, as a horse's mane...... ROACH
"   off little by little .... EXCISE, DRIB
"   off wool ....................... DOD
"   open; Fr. ................... FENDU
"   , or pare off .............. RESECT
"   out ............. EXCIDE, EXCISE
"   short .................... POLLED
"   up ....... GRIEVE, DICE, HARRY
"   with geometric surfaces FACETED
"   with shears ................ SHIRL
cutaneous .................... DERMAL
cuticle ...... EPIDERMIS, SCARFSKIN
cuticle blister .......... BLEB, BULLA
cutis .................... DERMA, SKIN
cutlass; anc. Ger. .. DUSACK, TESACK
cutter .... FACER, INCISOR, SLEIGH,
SLICER, SLOOP
cutting .. TART, CARF, SCION, SLIP,
TWIG, TRENCHANT, SNEEING
cutting into two parts ........ SECANT
cutting off last letter of word APOCOPE
cutting, rel. to .............. SECTILE
cuttle-bone ................. OSSELET
cuttle fish .... SEPIA, SQUID, SOUND
cuttle fish fluid .................. INK
cuvette .. BUCKET, CUNETTE, POT,
TRENCH, TUB, BASIN
cyanite ........... BLUE, DISTHENE
Cyclades . IOS, KEA, MILOS, NAXOS,
PAROS, TINOS
cycle .. SAROS, AGE, EON, WHEEL
cyclograph .............. ARCOGRAPH
cyclone .................... TORNADO
Cyclops ........................ GIANT
cyclostome ................ LAMPREY
cygnet ........................ SWAN
cylinder GABION, ROLLER, PLATEN
cylinder of a printing machine INKER
cylindrical saw .............. CROWN
"    transverse section .. TERETE
cyma reversa Lat. .............. OGEE
cymba; Lat. .................... BOAT
cymbal, oriental ............ TAL, ZEL
cymbalo ................ DULCIMER
Cymbeline's daughter ........ IMOGEN
cymosa inflorescence .... ANTHELA
Cymric ..................... WELSH
Cymric bard ..... ANEURIN, MERLIN
Cymric god ...... DYLAN, GWYDION
Cymric god of dead .......... PWYLL
Cymric god of Sun ........... LLEU
cynic .......... DOGLIKE, SNARLER,
TIMON, ASCETIC, EGOTIST,
MOROSE
cynosure .. LOADSTAR, POLESTAR
Cynthia ............... LUNA, MOON
cypress, mock ......... BELVEDERE

cyprinoid fish ...... IDE, SENTOREE, SUNDOREE, DACE
Cyrenaic ...................... HEDONIC
Cyrenaica meas. .................. DRA
Cyrus ............................ SUN
Cyrus, daughter of .......... ATOSSA
Cytherea ...................... VENUS
cyst ........ BAG, POUCH, SAC, WEN
Cyzicum, bishop of ....... EUNOMIUS
czar ..................... TSAR, TZAR
Czech ........................ SLOVAK
Czech capital .... PRAGUE, PRAHA
Czech leader .... (EDUARD), BENES
Czech munition plant ........ SKODA
Czech river ..................... ISER
Czecho-Slovakia, city of .... PILSEN, BRNO

# D

D. letter ........................... DE
dabbler ... DILETTANTE, SCIOLIST
dabblingly ........ SUPERFICIALLY, CURSORILY
dabchick ...... GALLINULE, GREBE
Dacian, early .................. AVAR
dacoit of India .............. BANDIT
dactyl ........................ ADONIC
dactylic hexameter .............. EPOS
daddle ... TODDLE, WADDLE, WALK
daddy long legs .. SPINNER, TIPULID
dado ......... DIE, BASE, WAINSCOT
daedal ...... INGENIOUS, SKILLFUL
Daedalus, slain by ............ TALOS
Daedalus' son; Gr. ........... ICARIUS
daer; Irish ..................... SAER
daff ..................... DALLY, PLAY
Dagda's son ................... ANGUS
dagger ........ BAYONET, PANADE, SKEAN, BODKIN, PONIARD, SNEE
   "   , broad ...... ANLACE, DIESIS
   "   handle .................... HILT
   "   , Malay . CREESE, CRIS, KRIS
   "   , Philippine .............. ITAC
   "   , Scotch .................. DIRK
   "   , sharp ............ STILETTO
   "   , short .............. KATAR
   "   stroke ...... STAB, STOCCADO
daggle-tailed .................... DIRTY
daily ADAY, DIURNAL, QUOTIDIAN
dainties ...... CATES, ESTE, TIDBIT
dairy .......... LACTARIUM, TAMBO
dais ESTRADE, PLATFORM, TABLE
daisy ........... GERBERA, GOWAN, MORGAN
daisy, oxeye .................. SHASTA
dale .. DELL, DINGLE, GLEN, VALE
dale, a kind of ................ DENE
dale, as of water ............. SPOUT
dally DAWDLE, PINGLE, TOY, BIDE, LOITER, TRIFLE
Dalmatia ...................... SOLTA
Dalmatian .................... SERB

dam ... GIRTH, BURROCK, POUND, OBSTRUCT, RESTRAIN, WEIR
dam; N. Amer. .. BOULDER, COULEE
damage .... LOSS, NOXAL, SCATHE, HURT, IMPAIR, MAR, STRAFE
daman ................ HYRAX, LAMB
Damascus, river of ......... ABANA
damask ........ ROSE, CLOTH, PINK
damp . HUMID, MOIST, DANK, WET
damp, become .................... EVE
dance . POLONAISE, BALL, BALLET, TOE, FARANDOLA(E), HOP
   "   , an old ALLEMANDE, VOLTA
   "   , ancient ............ CORANTO
   "   , Bohemian .......... REDOWA
   "   clumsily .............. BALTER
   "   , Cuban ................ RUMBA
   "   , English .. ALTHEA, MORRIS
   "   , folk, Eur. .... TARANTELLA, KOLO
   "   , formal, old PAVAN, FARANDO
   "   , French BOREE, GAVOT, BAL
   "   , Italian COURANTE, CALATA
   "   , gay RIGADOON, GALLIARD
   "   , mirthful ... GALOP, CONGA, CAPER
   "   , modern ...... SHAG, TANGO
   "   motion, per. to ........ GESTIC
   "   , New Zealand .......... HAKA
   "   , old fashioned ... HORNPIPE, LOURE
   "   , rel. to a NAUTCH, BIJESTIC
   "   , school .................. PROM
   "   , Spanish ........ CABALLERO
   "   , Sp. Gipsy .............. POLO
   "   step ... CHASSE, COUPE, PAS
   "   term ..................... PLIE
   "   , weird ............ MACABRE
dancer ..... ALMEH, DEGAS, ALMA, CHORINE
dancer's pole .................... POY
dancing, art of ............ ORCHESIS, CHOREOGRAPHY
dancing girls ............ DEVADASIS, GEISHAS, GESTICS
dancing, muse of .... TERPSICHORE
dancing partner ............ GIGOLO
dancing, rel. to .. GESTIC, SALTANT
dandelion .............. TARAXACUM
dandify ......... ADONIZE, SPRUCE
dandle .. NURSE, PAT, PET, CARESS
dandruff ........ DANDRIFF, SCURF
dandy .... FOP, TOFF, BEAN, DUDE
dangerous DIRE, CRITICAL, FERAL, INSECURE, OMINOUS, PARLOUS
dangle .. DROOP, LOLL, LOP, HANG
Danish anatomist .............. STENO
   "   Alice .................... ELSE
   "   artist .................. BLOCH
   "   astronomer .......... BRAHE
   "   cottar freeholder .... JUNSTER
   "   dependency ............ FAROE
   "   early ruler .... KLAK, SWEYN
   "   fjord ...................... ISE
   "   king .................. CANUTE
   "   measure ALEN, ANKER, FOD, LAST

```
"       monetary unit  ESER, KRONE,        day-spring ................... DAWN
                                   ORE      day's march .................. ETAPE
"       parliament ......... RIGSDAG        day's work; Scot. .............. DARG
"       physician ........... FINSEN        days-of-yore .............. HASBEEN
"       prince ............. HAVELOK        daze . ASEA, BEMUSE, FOG, MAZE,
"       ter. division  RIBE, ALT, AMT                                    STUN
"       weight ....... CENTNER, LOD         dazzling ..................... GARISH
Danish W. Indies; (see 'Virgin Isl's')     De Becque, M. .................. EZIO
danseuse .. BALLERINA, CORYPHEE             deacon's stole .............. ORARION
Dantean verse form ........ SESTINA         dead .. CEASE, FEY, NAPOO, OBIT
Dante's love ............... BEATRICE       dead-head ............ BUOY, SPRUE
Dantes, Ed. (Fr.) ............ COMTE        dead-house ............ OSSUARIUM
Danube fish .................... HUCH       dead, rose from the ...... RESURGED
Daphne's father ............. LADON         Dead Sea, country near ....... MOAB
Daphnis, lover of ........... CHLOE         dead tree ...... RAMPICK, RAMPIKE
dapple BEDIP, FLECK, SPOT, ROAN             deaden ....... DAMP, OPIATE, MUTE
dappled .... . SPOTTED, PIEBALD,            dead, rose from the ..... RESURGED
                                SORREL      deadly ...... FATAL, INTERNECINE,
dare OSSE, RISK, BRAVE, FASHION                   KILLING, SIN, LETHAL, MORT
dark MELANIC, OCCULT, STYGIAN,              deaf and dumb ........ SURDOMUTE
        BLACK, DIM, JOYLESS, WAN            deaf, to make ............... ADEAVE
dark hue .. SOMBRE, SWART, DUSKY            deafness AMUSIA, ADDER, SURDITY
darken ..... OBFUSCATE, BECLOUD,            deal .. TRADE, SALE, PINE, ALLOT
                                SADDEN      dealer in drugs . PHARMACOPOLIST
darkish area on moon .......... MARE        dean ...... DELL, DOYEN, VALLEY
darkness TENEBRES, MURK, SHADE,             dean; per. to a ............. DECANAL
                                EREBUS      dearth .. FAMINE, WANT, PAUCITY
darling ... CHERI, JO, LIEVE, PET           death EVANISHMENT, OBIT, MORT
darling; Irish ............ ACUSHLA,        death, bringing ............. FUNEST
                           MAVOURNEEN       death, mercy .......... EUTHANASIA
darnel .............. COCKLE, TARE          deathlessness ........... ATHANASIA
dart .. ELANCE, FLIT, JACULATE,             debar .. ESTOP, SECLUDE, HINDER
               MISSILE, SCOOT, LICK         debase .. ABASE, CORRUPT, ALLOY
das ........................ BADGER         debased .......... VITIATED, VILE,
dash . PLASH, ARDOR, ELAN, LACE                                     LOWERED
dashes ........................ OBELI       debate .. ARGUE, CANVASS, MOOT,
dashing, as a wave .... PLANGENT                     REASON, TALK, PLEAD
dashing style BRAVURA, GAY, BLADE           debate, per. to ....... QUODLIBET,
dastard CRAVEN, CAD, POLTROON                              FORENSIC, CLOSURE
datary ................... CARDINAL         debauch ...... BOUT, ORGIE, SPLORE
date clause in writing ........ TESTE       debauchee .... RAKE, ROUE, SATYR
date-on-line, coin .......... EXERGUE       debilitate .. WEAKEN, UNMAN, SAP
date plum .................. SAPOTE         debility ........ INFIRMITY, ATONY
daub .... PLASTER, GAUM, SMEAR,             debization . LA, BE, CE, DE, ME, FL,
         BLOB, SOIL, SULLY, TEER                                         GE
daunt ... FAZE, AMATE, AWE, COW             deblaterate ..................... GAB
daut; Scot. ........ CARESS, FONDLE         debonair SUAVE, URBANE, BUOYANT
dauphin, rel. to .......... DELPHINE        debris ......... SCREEN, DRIBLETS,
David; actor .................. NIVEN                               ODDMENTS
David Copperfield, "child wife" in DORA     debris of abandoned coal mine THURST
David's general ...... IGAL, ABIGAIL,       debt ........ LIABILITY, DUE, POST
        ABNER, REI, SHAMMAH                 debt, per. to ............ GARNISHEE
Davis ........ (RICHARD) HARDING            debts ............ ARREARS, DELINA
Davis; actress ................ BETTE       debutante .. BUD, DEB, SOPHMORE
davit .................. CRANE, SPAR        decade ......... DECENNIUM, TEN
dawdle . IDLE, LAG, POTTER, POKE            decamp .... FLEE, ABSQUATULATE,
dawn ...... DEW, SUNUP, AURORA,                      ABSCOND, MOVE, VAMOSE
                                UPRISE      decanter .. CARAFE, CROFT, EWER
dawn, per. to ...... EO, EOAN, EOS          decapod ..... CRAB, PRAWN, SQUID
day .............. AGE, EPOCH, ERA          decapod crustacea; genus HOMARUS
day-blindness ........ NYCTALOPIA           decayed ..... DEAF, CARIOUS, DOTY
day-dream ........ REVERY, FANCY,           decayed spot in fruit ......... BLET
                                REVERIE     decease . LATE, DEMISE, FAIL, OBIT
day, lasting for one ........... DIARY      deceased DECEDENT, LATE, DEAD
day nursery; Fr. ............ CRECHE        deceit .. GUILE, COVIN, COZENAGE
day scholar ................ EXTERN         deceitful .... GNATHONIC, ARTFUL,
day-sight ............ HEMERALOPIA                                       WILY
```

64

deceive SILE, HOCUS, ABUSE, FLAM, GULL, ILLUDE, DUPE
deceiver .... BETRAYER, TRAPAN, TRICKSTER, GAY
deception .... ILLUSION, LIE, JAPE, WILE
deceptive ...... SIRENIC, HOLLOW, VAGUE
decibles, ten ...................... BEL
decide upon .. ELECT, ADOPT, VOTE
decimal ................ TEN, TENTH
decimal, circulating .... REPETEND
decimate BURK, SLAUGHTER, SLAY, FEW, SUBTRACT, KILL
decipher ........ DECODE, UNRAVEL
decision .. DOOM, METTLE, NERVE
decision, a ........ REDE, VERDICT
decision; law .................. ARRET
decisive .. FINAL, CRITICAL, END
deck, lower .................... ORLOP
deck, raised border ........ COAMING
deck out .. ARRAY, ADORN, DIZEN, ENRICH, GILD, TIFF
declaim .. ORATE, SPOUT, BLEEZE, BLAZON, HERALD, MOUTH, PERORATE
declaimer .................. RANTER
declare .... ALLEGE, AVER, AVOW, PUBLISH, SPREAD, MELD, SAY, STATE
decline . ABATE, TABES, DIP, EBB, REFUSE, REJECT, WANE, SLUMP
declivity .......... DESCENT, SCARP
decoction . TISANE, APOZEM, SAPE, CREMOR
decompose and melt ............. FRIT
decor .... DECORATION, SCENERY
decorate ................ SCRIMSHAW
decorate with letters ........ MINIATE
decorate garishly .......... BEDIZEN
decorate with raised pattern BROCADE
decorated ...... NIELLED, ADORNED
decorated, as pottery .... SIGILLATE
decorated initial letter ............. FAC
decoration, form of mineral ........ SGRAFFITO
decoration, metallic .......... PURFLE
decoration, per. to ........ MEDALLIC
decorative metal ware .......... TOLE
decorticate .... STRIP, BARK, PARE, PEEL
decoy LURE, STOOLPIGEON, TOLE, CALLER
decoy for gamblers ........... CAPPER
decrease ............ ABATE, DECESS
decree ...... NISI, ACT, EDICT, EMIT
decree, authoritative . CANON, ARET, ARRET
decree, imperial ........ FIAT, IRADE
decree, papal .................... BULL
decree, Russ. ................. UKASE
decrees ........... ENACTS, WILLS
decrepit ........ OLD, RAMSHACKLE
decrier ............ CROAKER, WEAK
decry ...... BELITTLE, DISCREDIT
decussation ........ INTERSECTION, CHIASMA

deduct .......... BATE, FAIK, TAKE, RETRENCH
deed ... ACT, FEAT, GEST, RECORD
deed, one who grants by .. REMISER
deem .. CONSIDER, JUDGE, OPINE
deep dish, fruit .............. COBBLER
deep lethargic sleep .......... SOPOR
deep orange tint .............. TENNE
deep sound ...................... BONG
deer ................ CERVIDAE, ELK
" , Amer. .... CARIBOU, WAPITI
" , antler of ... DAG, TRESTINE
" , female of the DOE, HIND, ROE
" , grass ................ RHEXIA
" , hog of India .. ATLAS, PARA
" , horns of a .......... BALCON
" , large Amer. .......... MOOSE
" , like the fallow ...... DAMINE
" , male of the ............. BUCK
" of India . AXIS, KAKAR, RUSA
" , Persian .............. MARAL
" pigmy; Malay ........ PLANDOK
deer, red, male . HART, OLEN, STAG
" , rusine ........... AXIS, RING
" , short tail of ............ SCUT
" , small ... MUNTJAC, RATWA, ROE
" , S. Amer. ...... PITA, GUEMAL
" , three year old ........ SOREL
" , track of a .............. SLOT
" , two year old BROCK, BROCKET
" , young ..... FAWN, SPITTER
deerlet ........ CHEVROTAIN, NAPU
deer-like giraffe ................. OKAPI
deer's cry ...................... BELL
deer's unbranched antler ........ DAG
deface .. MAR, MUTILATE, INJURE
defame .. SPATTER, LIBEL, VILIFY
default .... DEFICIT, LACK, WANT, MORA, LOSS
defeat .. REVERSE, BEST, MASTER, CONFUTE, FACER, WORST
defeating .. ANATREPTIC, FAILURE
defecate .......... PURIFY, REFINE
defect in cloth .................... YAW
defect in timber .......... LAG, SHAN
defend ...... GUARD, SHEND, WARD
defendant; law ............ REUS
defender of the people .... TRIBUNE
defense .. SEPIMENT, ALIBI, PLEA
defense, making a salient angle ...... RAVELIN
defense, means of .......... ABATIS
defensive dike .......... ESTACADE
defensive slope ................. GLACIS
deference ........ FEALTY, HOMAGE
deficiency .... SHORTAGE, ULLAGE
defile TAINT, POLLUTE, MOIL, PASS, SULLY
Defoe character .............. FRIDAY
Defoe; essayist .............. DANIEL
deform . CRIPPLE, DISFIGURE, MAR
deformed imbecile ........... CRETIN
deformity of the foot TALIPES, VARUS
defraud ...... GULL, ROB, SWINDLE, CHEAT, BILK, COZEN

deft .. ADROIT, CLEVER, EXPERT, APT, FIT, MEET, PAT
defy ...... BEARD, CARTEL, DARE, BRAVE
degage; Fr. ...... UNCONSTRAINED, EASY
degraded DEBASED, LOW, SHAMED, DEMOTED
degree STEP, RANK, RATE, CLASS, HONOUR, TERM, STAIR
d'Herblay ..................... ARAMS
deification .............. APOTHEOSIS
deify ........ APOTHEOSIZE, EXALT, BEGOD
deiform .......... DIVINE, GODLIKE
Deity .......... BAAL, NUMEN, GOD
  " , Assyrian; ASHUR, ASUR, EL, NEBO, NERGAL, NINIB, SHAMASH, SIRAS
  " at Ephesus .............. DIANA
  " , avenging (Gr.); .... ALASTOR, ANTEROS
  " , Babyl. .... ANU, BEL, DAGAN, ALALU, EA, HEA
  " , Babyl. tutelary ... MERODACH
  " , Bohemian ................ BYSS
  " , Celtic; .. ARAWN, BELI, ESUS, TARANIS
  " , classic woodland ........ FAUN
  " , Egypt.; .. AMEN, AMON, BES, MENT, HERSHEF, MIN, NU, OSIRIS, PASHT, PAKHT, SEB, SET, SERAPIS
  " Germanic ................ DONAR
Deity, Greek; ..... ATHENA, CHAOS, CYBELE, INO, MORS, SATYR, ZEUS
  " , Hindu ...... KRISHNA, MANU, RAMA, DEVA, SIVA, VARUNA, SISHNU
  " holidays .................. FERIA
  " , Icelandic .................. TIVI
  " , Italian .... CONSUS, FAUNUS, FLORA
  " , Japanese ......... EBISU, SHA
  " , Latin for ................ DEUS
  " , lesser ................ BUNENE
  " , Norse ............. THOR, VAN
  " , Melanesian ................ QAT
  " of averting evils ............. BES
  " of human sacrifice .... MOLOCH
  " of mockery .............. MOMUS
  " of music ............... APOLLO
  " of underworld ...... DIS, GWYN, OSIRIS
  " of woodland .............. SATYR
  " Phrygian ......... ATTIS, ATYS
  " , Roman; FAUN, JUNO, MORS, PALES, JANUS, PICUS, VACUNA
  " , Sanskrit ADITI, MANU, DEVI, UMA
  " , Scythian ................ ONGA
  " , sylvan .................... PAN
  " , Welsh ................. DYLAN
dejected ... DROOPY, AMORT, DAMP
delate ......... ACCUSE, DENOUNCE

delay ...... RETARD, CUNCTATION, FUTURE, LATEN, DALLY, LAG
delay, unjustifiable ............ MORA
dele .... DELETE, ERASE, REMOVE
delegate ......... DEPUTE, LEGATE
delete . EFFACE, EXPUNGE, DELE, ERASE
deletion of last letter of word ......... APOCOPE
deletion, restore a .............. STET
delibate ........ CULL, SIP, PLUCK
deliberate PREPENSE, COOL, THINK
Delibes; opera by ............. LAKME
deliberate ....................... PEEL
delicacy .... CATE, TIDBIT, KNACK
delicate ........ DAINTY, NICE, SLY, MINIKIN
delicious .... NECTAREOUS, TASTY
delight .. BLISS, GLEE, JOY, MIRTH
delineate ... DEPICT, PAINT, LIMN, MAP, OUTLINE, SHOW
deliquesce ........ DISSOLVE, MELT
delirium tremens ........ HORRORS, OENOMANIA
delitescent .................. LATENT
deliver .. HIT, COUGH, RID, UTTER
deliver of an evil spirit .. EXORCISE
dell .. DENE, SLADE, VALE, DALE, DINGLE, RAVINE
Delmar, Miss. .................... VINA
Delphi, modern name of ...... KASTRI
Delphi, priestess of .......... PYTHIA
delude .. DUPE, FLAM, JIG, DECEIVE
delusion MIRAGE, RUSE, MOCKERY, PHANTASM
delusions of grandeur MEGALOMANIA
delve ...... DIG, MINE, TILL, SPADE
demagogue .. OCHLOCRAT, STATIST
demand .... DUN, CRY, ELICIT, ASK
demeanor .......... CARRIAGE, MIEN
demented ...... LOONY, LUNY, MAD
demi-god HERO, MOBOCRAT, SATYR
demiurgic .................. OMNIFIC
demolish ........ RAZE, RUIN, UNDO
demon .... ATUA, DEUCE, FIEND
  " , cunning OGRE, IMP, DAEDAL
  " , female ........ LAMIA, MARA
  " , Hindu ................. ASURA
  " , Maori .................. ATUA
  " , Moham ............... EBLIG
  " , of vanity; Heb. ... ASMODEUS
  " , rel. to a ........... EXORCIST
  " , wood .................... NAT
  " worship ...... DEMONOLATRY
demons, assembly of ........ SABBAT
demons in Arabian legends . AFREETS
demonstrate .................. EVINCE
demonstrative ...... GUSHING, THAT
demos .......... DISTRICT, PEOPLE
demure ... STAID, COY, GRAVE, MIM
den, wild animals Rom. ....... CAVEA, LAIR
den, wild animals; Rom. ...... CAVEA
denary .......................... TEN
denaturant ................ PYRIDINE
dendroid ARBORESCENT, TREELIKE
dendrophilous .............. ARBOREAL
denies, one who ............. NEGANT

denizen .... INHABITANT, CITIZEN, CIT, FREEMAN, HELLION
Denmark, anc. name of ....... THULE
" , city of ELSINORE, AARHUS
" , coin of ...... KRONE, ORE
" , county in ............ SORO
" , dry wind of ........... SKAI
" , first great composer of ...... WEYSE
" , first king of ........ GORM
" , island of .. ALS, FALSTER, FUNEN, MOEN
" , oil seed of ........... RAPE
" , peninsula of .... JUTLAND
" , port of ............ KORSOR
" , powerful ruler of . CANUTE
" , prince of . OGIER, HAMLET
" , sand ridge of ....... SCAW, SKAGEN
" , ter. division of .. ALT, AMT
" , wild animal BOAR, UROCH
dennet ........................... GIG
denominate .... STYLE, CALL, DUB, TERM
denomination PARTY, SCHOOL, SECT
denoting customary action USITATIVE
denoting final end ............ TELK
denounce .......... ASSAIL, SCATHE
de novo .... ANEW, AFRESH, AGAIN
dense .. POPULOUS, CRASS, DEWY, GROSS
dent ............... DINGE, HOLLOW
dental drill ............... CAVITRON
dentate ....... SERRATE, TOOTHED
dentine ........................ IVORY
denture ....................... TEETH
denude ............ STRIP, UNROBE
deny .. NEGATE, ABJURE, DEBAR, WARN
deny, to; Lat. .................. NEGO
depart .. EGRESS, MOSEY, VAMOSE
departed .... NAPOO, OFFED, DEAD
depend HINGE, RELY, HANG, LEAN, LOP
dependency .. APPANAGE, COLONY
dependency, Hindu ........... TALUK
dependent .... ADJECTIVE, CLIENT, SPONGER
dependent .................. SERVILE
depending upon an uncertain contingency ................... ALETORY
depict .... DELINEATE, HUE, LIMN, PAINT, PORTRAY
depilate .............. HUSK, SHAVE
depilatory .................... RUSMA
deplore .... BEWAIL, REGRET, RUE
deportment; obs. ............. GESTE
depose ... AVER, TESTIFY, UNSEAT
deposit . BED, MARL, OOZE, PLACE
deposit box for coins ... PYX, METER
deposit containing gold ..... PLACER
deposit, loan .................. LOESS
deposit of black tissues . MELANOSIS
deposit of ore .................. GULF
depot; Fr. ...................... GARE
depraved ..... EVIL, SHREWD, VILE
depreciated ..... SHRUNK, FALLEN

depredate ... PILLAGE, RASE, ROB, SPOIL
depress ... ABATE, DAMPEN, DENT
depressed .. AREOLA, EXANIMOUS, DIRE, DISMAL, SAD
depression .... TROUGH, COL, DENT, FOSSA, PIT, VAPORS
deprive ... DEMENT, MULCT, TAKE
deprived . AMERCED, REFT, SHORN
depth . ABYSS, EXTENT, ACUMEN, GULF, OCEAN, SEA, HOLL
deputies, sheriff ............... POSSE
deputy ............... AGENT, VICAR
derelict ...... ABANDONED, TRAMP, WRECK, CASTAWAY
deride . FLEER, JEER, JIBE, MOCK, SCOFF
deriv. of name of a race .. EPONYMY
derive .. DRAW, DESUME, EVOLVE, CONCLUDE, EDUCE, INFER
derived, to be ............. DESCAND
dermal filament ................ HAIR
derogate . DECRY, REPEAL, ANNUL
derrick ....... CRANE, RIG, STEEVE
derrick for execution .... HANGMAN
derrick, part of a .. BOOM, GIN, LEG
dervish .... FAKIR, HERMIT, MONK
descant ..... EXPATIATE, SOPRANO
descendants POSTERITY, PROGENY, BREED, LITTER, SCION
descended ... ALIT, STOOPED, FELL
descended from same ancestor ........ CONSANGUINEOUS
descended, source ..... ROOT, STIRP
descent ............. BIRTH, ORIGIN
describe DEPICT, DEPENCIL, POINT, NAME, STATE
description . VERSION, CLASS, SORT
descry KEN, SIGHT, ESPY, DETECT, SEE
Desdemona, husband of ... OTHELLO
desert . RENEGE, ERG, DUE, MEED, EMPTY, RAT, MERIT
desert in Africa ...... SAHARA, REG
desert in Asia ................... GOBI
desert in Egypt .................. TIH
desert in Russia ............ TUNDRA
desert, per. to EREMIC, OASIS, SERE
desert plant ........ ALHAGI, CACTI
desert, sandy; Sp.-Am. ... HORNADA
deserter ......... ABANDONER, RAT RENEGADE
deserve .............. EARN, MERIT
desiccated ........ ARID, DRY, SERE
desiccation ............... XERANSIS
design ..... DESTINE, FORM, PLAN
design; Scot ................... ETTLE
designate .. MARK, ENTITLE, CALL
designating an appendage of the brain PINEAL
desipience ........ FOLLY, CONCEIT, TRIFLING
desire ... COVET, EYE, CARE, YEN, HEART, CRAVE
demanthus .................... ACUAN
desolate ...... BLEAK, LORN, SACK, ALONE

despoil ... FLEECE, REAVE, DIVEST, INJURE, RIP, ROB
despot .. AUTOCRAT, TSAR, TYRANT
despumate ...................... SCUM
dessert .. COURSE, MOUSSE, SNACK
destinies ............ FATES, FURIES
destiny .... DOOM, EURE, FATE, LOT
destiny, oriental ............. KISMET
destiny; Romany term ......... BAHI
destitute ........ NAIS, NEEDY, VOID
destroy .. ROOT, RAZE, RUIN, SACK, MARPLOT, UNDO
destroyed ........ ATE, INEXISTENT
destroyer ........ HUN, ICONOCLAST
"Destroy. Angel" Fungus .. AMANITA
"Destroying Angel," Mormon . DANITE
destruction ..... HAVOC, PERDITION, HOLOCAUST, TALA, STRY
destruction of species .... GENOCIDE
destructive ................. ANERETIC
destructive insect . LOCUST, TERMITE
destructor .. FURNACE, ICE, WINTER
detach ............. ISOLATE, SEVER
detachment ....... DISUNION, PARTY
detail .... NARRATE, ITEM, STATUE
detains; law ................ DETINET
detection ..... SCENT, ESPIAL, SPOT
detective .... BEAGLE, SLEUTH, SPY, TEC, SPOTTER, TAILER
detective story charac. ..... CORONER
detent ...... CLICK, TONGUE, PAWL
detergent . ANNITE, SAPONIN, SOAP, CLEANER
deteriorate ...... CORRUPT, WORSEN
determine ... CONTRIVE, END, FIRM, FIT, DIJUDICATE
detersion .... ABLUTION, WASHING
detest .. EXECRATE, HATE, ABHOR, LOATHE
detour .... WINDING, DIVERT, TURN
detract .......... DECRY, DEROGATE
d'etre raison; Fr. ........ EXISTENCE
detriment ...... HURT, INJURY, LOSS
detritus ............... DEBRIS, TUFF
devastate ....... RAPE, SACK, STRIP
devastation ........ HAVOC, RAVAGE
develop . EDUCATE, EVOLVE, RIPEN
developing early ............. PRECOX
development, incomplete .... APLASIA
development of plants ........ EOSERE
development, per. to ........ GENETIC
Devi, beneficent ................ GAURI
Devi, light ....................... UMA
Devi, malignant ............... DURGA
Devi, parent of ............. HIMAVAT
deviate ...... YAW, ERR, MISS, RUN, STRAY, DIGRESS
deviate from vertical ........... HADE
deviate suddenly ............ MUTATE
device for cutting gem facets .......... GENIOSTAT
devil ..... SATAN, AZAZEL, BELIAL, BELZEBUB, DULE, DEUCE, DICKENS, IMP, LUCIFER, BWANA
" , female ............ DEMONESS
" fish .... MANTA, OCTOPUS, RAY
" , rel. to VELIDIS, YEZIDI, IZEDI

" of the bottomless pit APOLLYON
devil-dog ...................... MARINE
devilkin .......................... IMP
devil-may-care .............. DEFIANT
devilry ..... ART, MAGIC, DEVILTRY
devil's bones ...................... DICE
devil's godmother ............... BABA
devils, principal AMAYON, AHRIMAN, ORMAZD
deviltry DIABLERIE, FIENDISHNESS
devious ..... ERRING, SINFUL, MAZY
devious way ..................... RUSE
Devis ................. CHANDI, KALI
Devi's consort .................... SIVA
devise ....... FRAME, ARRAY, AIM, EXCOGITATE, INVENT, SCHEME
devised, not .............. INTESTATE
deviser of intelligence test ..... BINET
devotee of beauty .. (A)ESTHETE, IST
devotion .... ADORATION, PIETISM, CULT, ZEAL, WORSHIP
devotional exercise .............. AVES
devotional period ............ NOVENA
devour ravenously WOLF, GLUTTONY
devouring; her. .............. VORANT
Dev's land ...................... EIRE
De Witt .................... CLINTON
dewlap; bot. ................... PALEA
dewy .... RORAL, RORIC, ROY, EVE
dexterity FINESSE, MAGIC, SLEIGHT
dexterous APT, ADROIT, DEFT, YARE, ADEPT
dextrosazone ............... OSAZONE
dextrose ....................... SUGAR
dey; Scot. ................. DAIRYMAID
diabetic remedy ............. INSULIN
diacope ........................ TMESIS
diacritic ......... DIAERESIS, MARK
diacritic, in printing .. BREVE, TILDE
diadem ..... RIGOL, TIARA, CROWN
diagnostic ........ SYMPTOM, EXACT
diagram; Fr. ................... EPURE
diagram, illustrative ............. ICON
diagraph ......................... EA
dialect ........ LOGIC, IDIOM, LINGO
dialect of Asia Minor ......... AFOLIC
dialing ..................... GNOMONICS
diameter .... CALIBER, MODULE, PI, BREADTH, BORE, WIDTH
diametric ........ AVERSE, UTMOST
diametrically ............. DIRECTLY
diametrically opposite .. ANTIPODAL
diamond ............ GEM, ADAMANT
" , blue white .......... HOPE
" crystal ............. GLASSIE
" , cup for cutting ........ DOP
" , cuts a .............. FACET
" , famous .. MOGUL, ORLOFF, PITT
" , geometrical ..... LOZENGE, RHOMB
" , having true lustre of a NAIF
" , inferior .............. BORT
" , native ............. CARBON
" , rough ............. BRAIT
" , small splinter-like .... ROSE
" , wheels ............. SKIVES
diamonds; sl. ..................... ICE

Diana ...................... DELIA
Diana's parents . JUPITER, LATONA
diaphanous .. SHEER, THIN, LUCID
diary .. LOG, RECORD, CHRONICLE
diaskeuast ......... EDITOR, CRITIC
diaspora; Heb. ............... GOLAH
diatonic, opposed to .... CHROMATIC
diatonic run ................. TIRADE
diatonic scale ............... GAMUT
diatribe ....... PHILIPPIC, TIRADE,
SCREED
dib ......... BOB, DIP, MONEY, DAP
dibber ...................... DIPPLE
dice ..... BONES, CRAP, CUBE, DIE
dice game naturals .......... SEVENS
dice, number six in ....... SISE, SICE
dice, cheat in throwing .......... COG
diced .......................... RICED
Dickens, char. .......... TIM, FAGIN
Dickens, Chas., pseudonym ...... BOZ
dicker .... BARTER, DAKIR, TRADE
dickey .. COLLAR, SEAT, PANTLET
dictionary ..... LEXICON, CALEPIN,
ONOMASTICON, GRADUS
dictionary, like a ...... THESAURUS,
LEXICAL
dictum ............. MAXIM, SAYING
didactic .. TEACHING, MENTORIAL
diddle ........... CHEAT, SWINDLE
dido ANTIC, CAPER, TRICK, PRANK
Dido's sister .................. ANNA
Dido's wooer ............... AENEAS
die DADO, DICE, DOD, SICCA, STAMP
die, highest number on .......... SISE
"Die Lorelei," author of ...... HEINE
"Die-hard" ................... TORY
"Dies—" Latin hymn ........... IRAE
diet, course of .. RATION, REGIMEN
difference ..... DISPARAIL, NUANCE
different ....... OTHER, SUNDRY
difficulty ...... CAVIL, KNOT, RUB,
SCRAPE
difficulty, per. to ...... CRUX, SPINY
diffident .................... COY, SHY
diffuse SNED, PERVADE, NERVOUS
diffusion thru membrane .. OSMOSIS,
MIX
diffusive .......... AMPLE, OSMOTIC
dig ........... DELVE, JAB, MYLGE,
EXCAVATE
dig, as a pioneer ........ PION, MINE
digest ABSTRACT, CODE, PANDECT
digestion ........ EUPEPSIA, PEPSIS
digestion, having good ... EUPEPTIC
digestion, per. to .. CHYLE, CHYME
digestive ....... AGENT, MAGNESIA
digestive tract ............. ENTERON
digger, soldier ............... SAPPER
digging, adapted for ..... FOSSORIAL
digging, fitted for .......... FODIENT
digging tool ............. LOY, SPADE
digit . FINGER, TOE, UNIT, CIPHER
digit, entity ................. INTEGER
digit, manual ................. THUMB
digit on a dog's foot ..... DEWCLAW
digit, shield for ...... FINGERSTALL
digitus ........ DACTYLUS, TARSUS
diglot .................... BILINGUAL
dignified ..... ELEVATED, AUGUST,

DECOROUS, STATELY, TOGATED
dignities; Lat. ............... DECORA
digression ...... ECBOLE, EPISODE,
LOOP
dike .... DITCH, LEVEE, GAP, GULF
dike, military .. ESTACADE, MOUND
dike rock ..................... ODINITE
diked land ................... POLDER
dilapidate .. HAVOC, RUIN, WRECK
dilation of a hollow organ .. ECTASIS
dilemma .... NODE, BRIKE, SNARE,
POLEMICS, SORITES, TRAP
dilettante ... AMATEUR, DABBLER,
ESTHETE
diligence . SEDULITY, STAGECOACH
diligent .......... OPEROSE, ACTIVE
dill seed ................ ANISE, ANET
dilute, as wine .......... LENGTHEN
diluted ......... ATTENUATED, OUT
dim .. BLEAR, CALIGINOUS, FAINT,
OBSCURE, DULL, ECLIPSE
diminish PLOY, BATE, PETER, TAIL,
CURTAIL, TAPER, WANE
diminution ............ DECREMENT
diminutive .. RUNTY, PETITE, WEE
"      breed of fowl ... BANTAM,
BANTY
diminutive; suffix ............... ULE
dim-sighted ........... MOONBLIND,
PURBLIND
diners, group of ............... MESS
dingle .. DALE, DELL, GLEN, VALE
dingy DUSKY, GRIMY, COLD, OURIE
dining-room ..... CENACLE, SALON
dinner, per. to ............ PRANDIAL
dinosaurs, per. to .... SAUROPODUS,
MESOZOIC
Dinsmore, Miss ................ ELSIE
dint ........ NICK, NOTCH, STROKE
diocese ............ BISHOPRIC, SEE
Dione ........................ VENUS
Dionysus ................... BACCHUS
Dionysus, mother of ........ SEMELE
Dionysus' surname ........ ZAGREUS
diopter ........... ALIDADE, LEVEL
Dioscuri, the .............. CASTORES
dip . SOP, BAIL, DAP, DOUSE, LADE
dip in liquid ................... MERSE
diphthong ...................... AE, OE
diploma ...... DEGREE, SHEEPSKIN
dipper . GRAB, PIET, SCOOP, PIGGIN
diplomatic ....... CRAFTY, POLITIC,
TACTFUL, ARTFUL
diplomatic corps, head of; Fr. DOYEN
dipody ...................... SYZYGY
dipsomaniac ....... DRUNKARD, SOT
diptera ................... FLY, GNAT
diptora, lobe of wing ......... ALULA
dire FUNEST, BANEFUL, FEARFUL
direct BOSS, MARSHAL, AIM, LEAD,
STEER, MANAGE
direct a squadron of planes AVIGATE
direct lines of descent in a group .....
PHYLA
direction in chorus ............. SOLI
direction, without fixed .... ASTATIC
directly ........ FLAT, SPANG, SOON
directrix ................... DIRIGENT
directs ... CONS, HEADS, TEACHES

dirge ........ CORONACH, HEARSE, THRENODY
dirge, a .... LAMENT, GRIEF, SONG
dirge, requiem masses ........ KEEN, TRENTAL
dirigible . SHENANDOAH, BALLOON
dirigible, framework ...... NACELLE
dirk ..... DAGGER, SNEE, OBELISK
dirty .......... FOUL, SORDID, VILE
dis, prefix for ................. TWICE
disable .. CRIPPLE, MAIME, GRUEL
disagreeable ......... CROSS, NASTY, FULSOME
disagreement between nations ....... DETENTE
disappear ...................... PASS
disapproval ............... BOO, HISS
disburse . EXPEND, SPEND, WASTE
disc ...... MEDALLION, DIAL, MAN, MEDAL
disc, as a plate .............. PATEN
discarded ........ SCRAPPED, SHED, CASTOFF, SLUFFED
discarded place ..... LIMBO, ABODE
discern . READ, DESCRY, KEN, SEE
discerner ....... ESPIER, WATCHER
discerning ........... ASTUTE, NICE
discernment ...... SAGACITY, TACT
discharge ... QUIETUS, EMIT, FIRE, BLAST, SALVO, VOLLEY, SPEED
discharge from office ...... QUIETUS
disciple .... ADHERENT, SCHOLAR
disciple; suffix ................... ITE
disciplinarian ............ MARTINET
discipline ......... TRAIN, CHASTEN
discolored, as if burned .. USTULATE
discomfited ........... CHEAP, ROUT
discomfort . MISEASE, AGONY, PAIN
discord ... CACOPHONY, VARIANCE
discordant music ........ SCORDATO, CHARIVARI
Discordia ...................... ERIS
discourage ...... DETER, OPPOSE
discourse .... DESCANT, PRELECT, SCREED, SERMON, DISSERT
discover ...................... LEARN
discoverer of Amer. ..... COLUMBUS ERIC (?)
discoverer of N. Pole ........ PEARY
discovery ..... DETECTION, ESPIAL
discredit ......... ASPERSE, REVILE
discretion ....... PRUDENCE, WILL
discriminate ...... DIFFERENTIATE, RECOGNIZE, SECERN
discrimination .... ACUMEN, TASTE
discus ... DISK, QUOIT, TRENCHER
discus thrower ........ DISCOBOLUS
discuss DISSERT, CANVASS, MOOT, SIFT
disdain ......... CONTEMPT, SCORN
disease; abbr. ...................... TB
"  , animal ... HOOSE, NAGANA
"  , cause of .............. GERM
"  , declining stage of ............. CATABASIS
"  , fatal .......... PEST, LYSSA
"  , investigator of ETIOLOGIST
"  , jumping ......... LATA, TIC
"  , malignant ........ PLAGUE
"  , nervous ... PELLAGRA, TIC

"  , of apple .......... STIPPEN
"  , of chickens ...... ROUP, PIP
"  , of hock of horses ... SPAVIN
"  , origin of ........ ETIOLOGY
"  , per. to ..... CLINIC, LOIMIC
"  , rel. to a ...... ENDEMIC
"  , S. Afr. ............... NENTA
"  , suffix .................... ITIS
diseased ............ MORBID, SICKLY
disembark ......... DETRAIN, LAND
disembowel ..... EVISCERATE, GUT, HULK
disencumber ......... RELEASE, RID
disenfranchisement; Gr. ...... ATIMY
disentangle .... UNRAVEL, SLEAVE, TEASE
disfigure ..... SCAR, MAR, MANGLE
disgrace ATTAINT, ODIUM, SHEND, ABASE, OBLOQUY, SULLY
disgrace, public, in Greece .... ATIMY
disguise CAMOUFLAGE, MET, MUMM
disguised ...... COVERT, CLOAKED
dish ..... BOAT, CHARGER, CRUSE, PATINA
dishearten AMATE, DEJECT, UNMAN
dishevel ......... TOUSE, DERANGE
dishonest lawyer ..... PETTIFOGGER
disinfectant ........ IODIN, PHENOL
disinherit ........ DEPRIVE, UNGET
disintegrate, as by water .... ERODE, CORRADE
disinter ......... EXHUME, UNBURY
disinvest; rare ............... DIVEST
disk ......... ATEN, SEQUIN, DIAL, HARROW, MEDAL
disk for securing letters .... WAFER
dislike ...... ANTIPATHY, ODIUM
dislike of children ..... MISOPAEDIA
disliked, delusion of being MISOMANIA
dislocate ............... SPLAY, LUX
dislocation ..... FAULT, LUXATION
dislodge ............... MOVE, STIR
dismal ............ DREAR, JOYLESS
dismay APPAL(L), DAUNT, TERRIFY
dismiss ....... AMAND, RELEGATE, REMUE, CASHIER, GATE, SHELVE
dismissal; Fr. ................. CONGE
dismounted ..... ALIT, DESCENDED
disobedient .... UNBAIN, UNREADY
disorder ...... DERAY, SNARL
disorderly ...... CHAOTIC, TUMBLY, MESSY
disparage ............. DECRY, SLUR
disparaging ............. DECAYING, DEFAMATORY, UNFAVORABLE
"  , immplying evil ............. PEJORATIVE
dispatch .. POST, KILL, SEND, SLAY
dispensation .. ECONOMY, SCHEME, ERA
dispenser of alms ...... ALMONER
display ......... SCENE, AIR, SHOW, SPLURGE, FLAUNT, UNCASE
displease .... OFFEND, PIQUE, MIFF
disposed favorable ....... PROPEND
disposition ..... BENT, BIAS, MOOD, ANIMUS, MORALE, NATURE
disposition toward work ... ERGASIA
dispossess ... DIVEST, EVICT, OUST
disprove ........ CONFUTE, REFUTE

disputant ....... ARGUER, DEBATER
disputation .................. POLEMIC
disputatious ...... ARGUMENTATIVE,
ERISTIC
dispute . DISSENT, BICKER, HIGGLE,
SPAR
disputer ..................... MOOTER
Disraeli, nickname of .......... DIZZY
disruptive explosive ....... MELINITE
dissection of glands .... ADENOTOMY
disseize ...... OUST, EVICT, DEPOSE
disseminate . EFFUSE, SPREAD, SOW
dissenter .... HERETIC, RECUSANT,
SECTARY
dissertation ... THESIS, DISCOURSE,
TRACT
dissociate ...................... SEVER
dissipate ......... DISPEL, SCATTER
dissolute .......... ABANDONED, LAX
dissolved substance ......... SOLUTE
distal angle ..................... AXIL
distance ... SHAVE, MILEAGE, STEP
distance, at a; poet. ............ YOND
distance, inst. for determining .........
TELEMETER
distant .... FOREIGN, AFAR, ALOOF,
COLD, REMOTE, UTMOST
distended .... PATULOUS, BLOATED
distich ...................... COUPLET
distil(1) DROP, TRICKLE, EXTRACT
distillation .................. CATARRH
distilled extract of bitter orange ......
NEROLI
distilling device ............ ALEMBIC
distinctive mark ... BADGE, CACHET
distort ..... DEFORM, TWIST, WARP
distorted; mus. .............. RUBATO
distortion of head to one side .. LOXIA
distracted ... FRANTIC, CRAZY, MAD
distraught ...... AGITATED, CRAZED
distress ..... AGONY, AIL, DISTRAIN
distribute .... DOLE, ASSIGN, METE
district . CANTON, DEMESNE, PALE,
REALM, REGION, WICK
district, local ... AREA, SLUM, WARD
disturb .............. MOLEST, ROUST
disunite UNTEAM, UNYOKE, DISCERP
disyllabic foot .............. TROCHEE
ditch ...... DIKE, FOSS, MOAT, SAP,
TRENCH, ACEQUIA
ditch, part of a ........... GRAFFAGE
ditch, slope of a ............... SCARP
dithyramb ..... HYMN, POETRY, ODE
diurnal ............ DAILY, JOURNAL
diurnal bird of prey ... HAWK, EAGLE
divagare .......... DIGRESS, STRAY
divan; Fr. . SETTEE, SOFA, CANAPE
divergence ... RADIATION, FORKING
diversify . MODIFY, VARY, VARIATE
diver's instrument .. RESPIROMETER
diver's gear .............. FLIPPERS
diversion .......... DISPORT, SPORT
divert ...... AMUSE, AVERT, PARRY,
DISTRACT
divest .... DOFF, REFT, STRIP, TIRL
divide . SEPARATE, CLEAVE, FORK,
LOT, SEVER, SHARE
divide into feet .................. SCAN

divide into four parts ........... RALY
divide into number of parts ............
MULTISECT
divided ............... SPLIT, ZONED
divided by a linear sinus ........ BIFID
divided into sections ....... PARTIAL
divided nearly to base ...... PARTITE
dividend .............. BONUS, SHARE
dividing walls ................. SEPTA
divination . AUGURY, CAPNOMANCY
"      by dreams . ONEIROMANCY
"      by figures .... GEOMANCY
"      by forehead METOPOMANCY
"      by means of burning straws .
SIDEROMANCY
"      by rods .. RHABDOMANCY
"      by sword .....................
MACHAIROMANCY
"Divine Comedy"; author ..... DANTE
divine communication ........ ORACLE
divine spirit ................... NUMEN
divine word .......... GRACE, LOGOS
divine work, a ............. THEURGY
divinely inspired ........... ENTHEAL
diving bell ................. NAUTILUS
divining rod ................. DOWSER
divinity . THEOLOGUMENON, DEITY,
IDOL
divinity; Heb. ADONAI, ELOHIM, JAH
divinity of fate; myth. .......... NORN
divisible ................... PARTIBLE
division .............. PART, SCHISM
"      , as in a ceiling ...... TRAVE
"      , many ............. EOGAEA
"      of a leaf ................. LOBE
"      of land ............. CANTON
"      of shield; her. . PALY, ARGOL
"      of the Koran .......... SURA
"      , restricted .... MEER, MERE
divorce law ................... TALAK
divot ............. SOD, TURF, CLOD
divulge .............. CONFIDE, TELL
dizziness ......... VERTIGO, WHIRL
do it again; Lat. ................. ITERA
dobby .............. GOBLIN, SPRITE
dock . JETTY, PIER, WHARF, BANG,
BASIN
dock post ................... BOLLARD
doctor's assistant ............ INTERN
doctrine LOGIC, DOGMA, ISM, LORE,
TENET, CABALA
doctrine, secret ... ESOTERIC, ISHMA
doctrine, single princ. ........ HENISM
document, provisional .......... SCRIP
document, true copy ........ ESTREAT
documents, place for ..... ARCHIVES,
CARTULARY
dod; Gael. ................... FIT, SULK
dodder ............ SHAKE, CUSCUTA
doddering .......... FOOLISH, INANE
dodge ...... PALTER, PARRY, DUCK,
ELUDE, JOUK, TRIFLE
Dodger pitcher ............... LABINE
Dodgson, Chas. ............ CARROLL
doff ............ DIVEST, STRIP, VAIL
dog ... SHADOW, SYRE, CUR, DANE,
WHELP, ALCO, CHOW, FEIST

71

" , Buster Brown's ........... TIGE
" coach .............. DALMATIAN
" , duck hunting ........... TOLER
" , extinct breed of ........ TALBOT
" family; genus ........... CANIS
" , fierce ...... KOLSUN, BANDOG
" , F.D.R.'s ......... FALA, FALLA
dog genus ....................... CANIS
" guarding the portals of the under-
    world ............. CERBERUS
" house .. KENNEL, LAIR, BOXER
" , howling of a . ULULATION, ARR
" , hunting . BASSET, RETRIEVER,
    TALBOT, TREER
" , hunting; Eur. ........ GRIFFON
" , hyena-like ............... SIMIR
" in "Punch and Judy's show"; Eng.
    TOBY
" in "The Thin Man" ........ ASTA
" , nondescript ....... MALEMUTE,
    POOCH
" of India, fierce . BUANSU, DHOLE
" rose ..................... CANKER
" rose, fruit of the ........ HEP, HIP
" Russ. ................... SAMOYED
" salmon ................... KETA
" salmon, humpback ........ HOLIA
" , Scottish ............ SEALYHAM
" , short-eared ............... ALAN
" , short-legged ........... BEAGLE
" , small ...... FEIST, TIKE, ALCO,
    SCHIPPERKE
" star ............... ASTA, SIRIUS
" star; Gr. ................... SOTHIS
" star; var. .................... SOPT
" , swift ................. WHIPPET
" two-headed ............. ORTHRUS
" whelk ...................... NASSA
" , wild, of Austral. .......... DINGO
" , wild, of Japan ......... TANATE
" , wild, of S. Amer. ..... AGOUARA
dogbane fruit ................... ABOLI
dogdays ................... CANICULE
dogear; arch. .......... ACROTERIUM
dog-fennel ................. HOGWEED
doggerel ..... MEAN, TRIVIAL, RIME
dogie ............. CALF, MAVERICK
dog-like animal ............... JACKAL
dogma, affected .............. CANT
dogmas ....... DOCTRINES, TENETS
dogmatic saying ... DICTUM, LEVITIC
"Dogpatch" depicter ............ CAPP
dogwood . CORNUS, OSIER, CORNEL,
    NUS, SUMAC
doing .......... ADO, BUSY, HUSTLE
doldrum ............. CALM, TEDIUM
dole ...... ALMS, PITTANCE, METE,
    GRIEF, SORROW
doleful ......... DISMAL, DREE, SAD
doleman; Alger ............... SENAM
doll, rag . PUPPET, TOY, MOP, MAMA
dolly; Indian ..................... TRAY
dolphin ...... BOUTO, DORADO, INIA
dolt DUNCE, ASS, CLODPATE, LOON,
    OAF
domain ............. EMPIRE, REALM
"Dombey and Son," char. in . CUTTLE

domestic ...... DOMAL, ENCHORIAL,
    INTESTINE, TAME
domestic establishment ..... MENAGE
dominate ... OVERTOP, RULE, SWAY
domineer .... BOSS, BLUSTER, LORD
dominion by 10,000 ..... MYRIARCHY
domino ...... CLOAK, AMICE, MASK,
    IVORY
domino, spot on .................... PIP
domite .................... TRACHITE
"Don Juan," Gr. girl in Byron's ........
    HAIDEE
Don Quixote; doctor in ........ PEDRO
Don Quixote's steed ..... ROSINANTE
Donet's area; capital ........ STALINO
donkey ............ ANE, ASS, BURRO
donkey; Eng. ......... MOKE, NEDDY
doohickey .................... DINGUS
Dooley, Mr.; creator of ...... DUNNE
doomed DEATH, FATED, FEY, GONER
doomsday; Norse ........ RAGNAROK
Doone .......................... LORNA
door knocker bar ................. RISP
door; Lat. .................... JANUA
door, part of a ... JAMB, RAIL, STILE
door, Persian ...................... DAR
door-keeper HASP, OSTIARY, TYLER
Dore, Miss ...................... ANNE
doric capital, part of ......... ABACUS
doric fillet at bottom of frieze TAENIA
doric frieze, space between triglyphs ..
    METOPE
dormancy ....... LATENCE, TORPOR
dormant .. ASLEEP, TORPID, INERT,
    LATENT
dormouse ........ LEROT, LOIR, MUR
dormouse; Scot. ....... LERION, MOY
dorsal .. NEURAL, NOTAL, TERGAL,
    BACK
dorsal, opposed to ......... VENTRAL
dorsal, per. to ..... NEURAL, NOTAL,
    TERGAL
dose; med. .......... BOLUS, POTION
dosseret .......... ABACUS, PULVINO
dossil ................... SPIGOT, TENT
dot PERIOD, POINT, DOWRY, SPECK
dotted ............. PIEBALD, PINTO
dotterel .................... DUPE, GULL
dotterel, the ............... MORINEL
dots, cover with ............ STIPPLE
double .... BINATE, DUPLEX, TWIN,
    BREVE
double course for foot races; Gr. .......
    DIAULOS
double dagger .................. DIESIS
double faced .............. ANCIPITAL
double ring .................... GEMEL
double-ripper ....... SLED, BOBSLED
doubletree .................. EVENER
doubloon ........................ ONZA
doubt ................. PYRRHONISM
dough .... NOODLE, DUFF, LEAVEN,
    PASTE, SPUD
doughnut; sl. ................. SINKER
Douglas is its cap. (is of) ........ MAN
dove ..... INCA, NUN, COO, CULVER,
    TUMBLER
dove; genus ................. COLUMBA

dovekie ........ ALLE, AUK, ROTCHE
dovekie, black .......... GUILLEMOT
dowel .......... COAK, PIN, PINTLE
dower BEQUEST, GRANT, DOTATION
down .... NAP, DOWL, FLOOR, FUZZ,
            BELOW, DUNE, LEA
down, comb. form . CAT, CATA, CATH
down; Fr. .......................... BAS
down feather .............. PLUMULE
down quilt ................... DUVET
downfall RUIN, DESCENT, REVERSE
downright .... BLUNT, FLAT, STARK,
            ARRANT
downy .. FLOCCULENT, PUBESCENT
downy with soft hairs PILAR, VILLOUS
dowry ............ GIFT, MONEY, DOT
doxy ............ DOCTRINE, OPINION
doyen ........................... DEAN
doze ...... CATNAP, DROWSE, NAP
drachma, 1/20 of a ............. OBOL
draft .......... PROTOCOL, SKETCH,
            CONSCRIPT
Draeseke; opera by ......... HERRAT
drag ........ HAUL, HALE, LUG, TOW
drag deer .............. TOLL, TUMP
dragoman .............. INTERPRETER
dragon ................... DRAKE, ORC
dragon flies, order of ....... ODONATA
dragon; Gr. .................... LADON
dragon of darkness ........... RAHAB
dragon; Poly ..................... ATI
dragon tail; Hindu ............. KETU
drain DITCH, EMPTY, GAW, LEACH,
            SAP, TRENCH
drake ................. DUCK, DRAGON
dram ...................... NIP, SLUG
drama ..... PLAY, DIORAMA, OPERA
drama, introduction of a .. PROTASIS
drama, main action ........ EPITASIS
drama, sudden reverse in a ...........
            PERIPETEIA
dramatic .... SCENIC, STAGY, VIVID
dramatic, per to .......... HISTRIONIC
dramatize ..................... ENACT
drapery on bedstead ........... PAND
drapery, rel. to ............. CASTING
drastic .. RADICAL, SEVERE, STERN
draught .. DENOMEL, DOSE, POTION
draught; arch . PLAN, COPY, DESIGN
draught, full sized ............. EPURE
draughts .................. CHECKERS
Dravidian ...................... CROAT
Dravidian tongue .............. TAMIL
draw .... DRAFT, TIE, ETCH, TOLE,
            TOW, TUG
draw away ........ ABDUCE, DIVERT
draw close ...... ATEAL, APPROACH,
            NEAR
draw out .... PROTRACT, CONTINUE
draw tight; rare .............. THRAP
draw together .......... COUL, FRAP,
            ASSEMBLE
drawback . WINCE, RESILE, DEFECT,
            OUT
drawer TILL, ARTIST, RECEPTACLE
drawing back ............. RETRAHENT
drawn .. ETIOLATED, HOVE, TEIND
draws or paints, one who ..... LIMNER

dread ............ AWE, FEAR, GRISE
dreadful .............. DIRE, UNGAIN
dreamer ......... FANTAST, METER,
            MADMAN
dreamy tranquility ... REVERIE, KEF
dreams . VISIONS, MUSE, VAGARIES
dreams, interpretation of ONEIROLOGY
dreary .... DISMAL, DULL, ALANGE,
            ALONE, INSULAR, OURIE
dredge ...... TRAIN, SIFT, DRAGUE,
            RAISE
dredger, in milling ........... DUSTER
dregs SORDOR, SILT, DRAFF, LEES,
            DIRT, REFUSE, SLUDGE
dregs, soft pulpy . RESIDUE, MAGMA
drench DOUSE, IMBUE, HOSE, SOAK,
            SATURATE
drenched ......................... ASOP
dress .. ATTIRE, DECK, DIGHT, RIG,
            TOGS
"  a wound ................. PANSE
"  as stone ...........  NIDGE, NIG
"  , external ................. GARB
"  flax .......................... TED
"  gaudily ..... BEDIZEN, PRANK
"  leather .... CURRY, TAW, TEW
"  , looped part .............. POUF
"  material ....... VOILE, FAILLE
"  , riding ................... HABIT
"  stone ........ NIDGE, NIG, RAY
"  up ............... ARRAY, PRIG
"  worn by pilgrims to Mecca IHRAM
dressed up ............... TITIVATED
dresser ....... LEVANTER, BUREAU,
            TABLE
dress-maker MODISTE, SEAMSTRESS
Drew's co-star ................ REHAN
dressmaking term ............ GODET
Dreyfus; champion of ......... EMILE
dribble .... TRICKLE, GUSH, SPOUT
dried and cured meat .... PEMMICAN,
            BILTONG
dried tubers of orchids ........ SALEP
drier .... DESICCATOR, EXSICCANT
drift .. TENOR, CRESCENT, INTENT,
            TREAT, AIM, PILE, TREND
drill ......... BORE, PIERCE, TRAIN,
            AUGER, EXERCISE
drilling TRAINING, NURTURE, DENIM
drink ...... ADE, ALE, NIPA, PANAL,
            SILLABUB
"  , ancient ................. MORAT
"  , Arabian ................. BOZA
"  , brandy (spiced) ... SANGAREE
"  , fermented .... MEAD, PTISAN
"  , gruel-like ............ CAUDLE
"  habitually ....... TIPPLE, TOPE
"  made of gin or rum ...... GROG,
            BUMBO
"  of the gods ............ NECTAR
"  of the Tatars .......... KUMISS
"  , Oriental ................ SAKE
"  , plant juice; E. Ind. ...... SOMA
"  , Russian ............... VODKA
"  , small intoxicating DRAM, TOT,
            NIP
"  , soft .................. ADE, POP
"  , S. Sea Island ............. AVA

" , spirituous ..... TODDY, DRAM, RATAFIA
" , sweetened .. JULEP, ORGEAT, POSSET
" , wine, water and sugar NEGUS
" with the lips ........... SIP, SUP
drinker SOAKER, POTER, TOPER, SOT
drinking bout POTATION, CARNALITY
drinking bowl ................. MAZER
drinking cup ......... CYLIX, FACER, JOLLYBOYS
drinking horn ............... RHYTON
drinking, pledge in .......... PROPINE
drip .............. LEAK, SILE, SEEP
drive ...... CAA, CALL, ROUST, SLOG
drivel ... DOTE, DROOL, SONK, MAD
driveler ...... FOOL, IDIOT, DOTARD
driver .... JEHU, WHIP, MOTORIST
driver, camel ................. SARWAN
drizzle MISLE, MIST, MIZZLE, SMUR
droll ..... BUFFOON, JESTER, ZANY
droll saying ..... GIBE, TAUNT, QUIP
dromedary .......... DELUL, CAMEL
dromedary-like ........... BACTRIAN
drone ........... SNAIL, HUM, IDLER
drool ............. DRIVEL, SLABBER
droop PINE, LOP, FADE, SAG, WILT
droop or nod ................. NUTATE
drooping on one side ........... ALOP
drop ..... BLOB, FALL, GOUT, OMIT, REMIT
drop, a single .. BLUB, DREPE, MINIM
drop by drop ................. GUTTAT
drop gently ............... DAP, PLOP
drop, serene ............. AMAUROSIS
drop, sudden ................. HANCE
dropping glass ....... STACTOMETER
dropsical ..................... EDEMIC
dropsy .............. EDEMA, TUMOR
dross SCORIA, SCUM, SCOBS, SPRUE, SLAG
dross of iron ................. SINTER
drought plant ........... XEROPHYTE
droughty; Scot. ................. WAT
drove CROWD, FLOCK, HERD, RODE
drowning .... NOYADE, DEMERSION
drowse . SLEEP, DOZE, DOVER, NOD
drowsiness . LETHARGY, OSCITANCE
drudge .. HACK, PLOD, SLAVE, FAG, LABOR, LABOUR, MOIL
drug .. ATROPIA, COCAINE, TONGA
drug, active principle of ........ ALOIN
drug, hypnotic .. TRIONAL, VERENOL
drug, nux vomica ........... TETANIC
drugget ......................... MAT
drugs ............. DOPE, NARCOTIC
Druid priestess of opera ...... NORMA
drum ............ BEAT, HILL, RIDGE
drum call ...... RAPPEL, RATAPLAN, TATTOO
" , hand ...... TABOR, TIMBREL
" , Indian ............... NAGARA
" , low beat of a ..... DUB, RUFF
" , Moorish ............ ATABAL
" , Oriental . ANACARA, TOMTOM
" roll at sunrise ............. DIAN
" , string ................. SNARE
" , tighten a ................ FRAP

drum-like TABRET, BARREL, NAKER
drunk; bot. ... RAD, REDE, DARNEL
drunkard ...... DIPSOMANIAC, SOT, TOSSPOT
drunken bout ..... RAT, ORGY, BOUSE
drupelet .. TRYMA, ACINUS, NUTLET
drupetum ................... ETAERIO
drunt ................... DRAWL, PET
dry SECO, ARID, ESSENE, SICCATE, XEROTIC, AERIFY, WIPE
" , as a narrative .......... JEJUNE
" , comb. form for ............ XERO
" , French for .................... SEC
" , to ........ BLOT, SERE, AREFY
dryad ................. DEITY, NYMPH
drying ............ KILN, SICCATIVE
drying frame ............ AIRER, SESS
drying machine ............... TEDDER
drying, spread for ............... TED
dryness of skin ... XEROSIS, ARIDITY
dryness, period of DROUTH, DROUGHT
dry-stone diker ................. COWAN
Du Maurier, Miss ........... DAPHNE
duad ........... DUAL, DYAD, TWO
dub .. CALL, NAME, POKE, THRUST, STYLE, TITLE
dubious .... SHADY, SEAMY, VAGUE
duck, Amer. ............... REDHEAD
" , common Eur. ... SHELDRAKE
" fabric .................... CLOTH
" ; genus ......... ANAS, ANSER
" , Hawaiian ........ NENE, NENI
" hawk .................. FALCON
" , large ............... MUSCOVY
" , litter of small ........... TEAM
" , long-tailed ........... HARLED
" , N. Sea ................ SCOTER
" , per. to .............. ANATINE
" , pintail QUERQUEDULE, SMEE
" , river .................... TEAL
" , sea ............ EIDER, SCAUP
" , small .................... SMEW
" , to; rare .............. MERSE
" , to; slang DODGE, DIP, SOUSE
" , wild ............... MALLARD
" , with bill swollen at base ....... SCOTER
duckbill; Aus. ............. PLATYPUS
duck-like .............. COOT, DECOY
duckweed ..................... LEMNA
ducks; genus AYTHYA, NYROCA, AIX
ducks, flock of .................... SORD
duct .... CANAL, PIPE, TUBE, RACE
duct; Lat. ......................... VAS
ductile ........... TENSILE, ELASTIC
ductless gland ............. THYMUS
ductless gland on upper surface of midbrain .................. PINEAL
dude ..... JOHNNIE, COXCOMB, FOP
due ............. DEBT, DUTY, RIGHT
duel ............ MONOMACHIA, TILT
dugong ................. HALICORE
dugout; Fr. .................... ABRI
dugout canoe ............... PIROGUE
dulcet .. ARIOSE, SWEET, TUNEFUL
dulcimer .................. PSALTERY
dulcimer, kind of .... CITOLE, SITAR, SITOL

dulcimer, Oriental .. CANUN, SANTIR
dull .. INERT, PALLING, DIM, DRAB,
   BLUNT, JEJUNE, OBTUND, VAPID
dull and heavy ..... STODGY, LEADY
dull finish .............. MATTE, MAT
dull, of cloth .................. STARY
dull statement .......... PLATITUDE
dullard .......... DUNCE, MOPE, OAF
dullness ....... COLDNESS, PHLEGM
dulse ...................... SEAWEED
Dumas char. .................. ATHOS
dumb ............. MUTE, APHONY
dummy ... PEL, SHAM, SUBSTITUTE
dummy, whist .................. MORT
dump .... PLUMP, TUNE, TIP, THUD
dun .............. ASK, FAVEL, TAN
dun color ............ BROWN, GREY
dunce ..... COOT, DOLT, OAF, GONY,
               FOOL HOBBIL
dunk ............ DIP, SOP, SOUSE
dunlin ... SANDPIPER, STIB, PURRE
Dunne, Miss .................... IRENE
dupe ..... CHEAT, DELUDE, TRICK,
               BILK, FRAUD
dupe, a TOOL, FOX, CATSPAW, CULL
dupe, nutlike fruit ............ TRYMA
duplicate ....... BIS, DUPLEX, COPY,
            REPLICATE, TWIN
duplicity ............. FRAUD, GUILE
durable ....... FIRM, TOUGH, STOUT
Durante byword ........ CALABASH
duration .... SPACE, ELDEST, DATE,
     PERIOD, SPAN, TIME, TRICE
D'Urberville girl ................ TESS
Durocher, Mr. .............. LIP, LEO
durra ............ MILLET, SORGHUM
dusky ....... DARK, DIM, SWARTHY,
    MURKY, UMBRA, TAWNY
dust COOM(B), BRISS, PILM, STIVE,
     MONEY, TRASH, STOUR
dust, reduce to .................. MULL
Dutch aborigines ............. CELTS
"   badger ...................... DAS
"   bailiff ................. BALJEW
"   botanist ............... VRIES
"   coin ......... DOIT, DAALDER
"   colonist ................. BOER
"   commune .......... EDE, EPE
"   dependency in Sumatra ACHIN
"   dialect ..... DIETSCH, TAAL
"   family of printers .... ELZEVIR
"   "good meadow" ....... BETAW
"   Guiana ............. SURINAM
"   island ARU, CELEBES, TEXEL
"   judge ................. SCHOUT
"   liquid meas. . AAM, DUIM, EL,
                  KAN
"   merchant vessel .... GALLIOT
"   military commander ..... ALVA
"   militia .......... SCHUTTERY
"   name of an early ruler ... DIRK
"   news agency ........... ANETA
Dutch painter ................... HALS
"   poet ............... DACOSTA
"   political party .... COD, HOEK,
                 HOOK
"   promoter ..... PATROON, TAK
"   radio station; Eng. ... ORANGE

"   ruler, William II, died at BREDA
"   scholar ............. ERASMUS
"   statesman ........... KUYPER,
              THORBECKE
"   town .............. TIEL, EDE
"   uncle .............. EME, OOM
"   village .......... OEST, ZALK
"   weight ......... LOOD, POND
"   writer .... BEKKER, VONDEL
Dutchman .................... HOGEN
duty ...... LASTAGE, EXCISE, FEU,
   OFFICE, TAX, TOLL, IMPOST
duty, arduous ....... DEVOIR, ONUS,
               TASK
duty; Hindu ................ DHARMA
Dvorak; compo. ................ ANTON
dwarf ELF, GNOME, MANIKIN, RUNT
"  , "all powerful king" ALBERICH
"  animal ................... RUNT
"  ; archaic ......... DANDIPRAT
"  cattle; S. Am. ......... NIATA
"  , fabled ...... PIGMY, PYGMY
"  , fifth avatar of Vishnu VAMAN
"  , fish shaped ....... ANDVARE
"  , kind of . ATROPHY, CONJON,
     TROLL, CRILE, CRUT,
      DURGAN, GRIG
"  , Scottish ...... DROICH, URF
"  , Sigurd's foster father . REGIN
"  , to .................... STUNT
dwarfishness ................. NANISM
dwarfs, "the Seven" . BASHFUL, DOC,
    DOPEY, GRUMPY, HAPPY,
    SLEEPY, SNEEZY
dwell ............ BIDE, LIVE, LODGE
dwelling .... RESIDENT, DAR, HEFT,
     QUARTER, WEEM, FLAT
dwelling-house complete . MESSUAGE
dwelling in the fields ... ARVICOLINE
dwelling in groves ..... NEMORICOLE
dwindle .... SHRINK, LESSEN, PINE
dwindling ................... AWASTE
dyak, at sea .................... IBAN
Dyak blowgun ............ SUMPITAN
dye ...... KINO, LIT, COLOR, IMBUE,
              STAIN
"  , coal tar ....... EOSIN, AZARINE
"  component .......... AZO, DIAZO
"  cosmetic, oriental . RED, HENNA
"  , crimson ............... RELBUN
"  , delicate ............... TINGE
"  , flavin ............ QUERCITRON
"  for silk .............. LUTEOLIN
"  , indigo ................... ANIL
"  , morindin ................... AL
"  plant ............ CHAY, SUMAC
"  plant ................. ALKANET
"  preparation of soot ........ KOHL
"  , red ........ CERISE, AAL, ALT,
              EOSINE
"  , red poison ............. AURINE
"  , reddish-brown .......... ERIKA
"  root pigment ............ MADDER
"  , rose red ............ RHODAMIN
"  , source of purple ........ MUREX
dye stuff, ground mineral .. ORPIMENT
"  stuff, reddish .. ISATIN, MADDER
"  , substance in .......... MORDANT

" used by Hindu women ....... **ALTA**
" , violet ....... **ORSELLE, ARCHIL**
" , yellowish pulp **ANATO, ANATTO**
dyeing apparatus ................. **AGER**
" chamber ................. **OVEN**
" to produce marble effects **BATIK**
dyer's furze ................. **DYEWEED**
dyer's grape .............. **POKEWEED**
dyes, basis of ............... **ANILINE**
dyestuff, indigo-like ............ **WOAD**
dyestuff obtained from anthracine .....
................................... **ALIZARIN**
dyestuff, red **MAGENTA, CHAY, EOSIN**
dyeweed ............... **WOADWAXEN**
dying, a ........................ **LAST**
dyke ..... **DAM, DIKE, HAHA, WALL**
dynamics ............. **IMPEL, START**
dynamite, a kind of ........... **HECLA**
dynamite, inventor of .......... **NOBEL**
dynamite projectile ........... **DUALIN**
dynamo .................. **GENERATOR**
dynamo, inventor of ......... **FARADAY**
dynamo, part of ...... **LIMB, STATOR,**
**YOKE**
dynasty ...................... **LORDSHIP**
dynasty, Chin. . **FO, HAN, ISIN, MING,**
**SUNG, TANG, YIN**
dynasty of E. Caliphs, member **AMMIAD**
dysphoria ................... **ANXIETY**
Dzhugashvili .................. **STALIN**

# E

E, letter ............................ **EA**
each ..... **PER, ALL, EVERY, APIECE**
eager **AGASP, AGOG, APT, AVID,**
**THIRST, ARDENT**
eagle.. **N.R.A., ERNE, BERGUT, ERN,**
**GIER**
eagle; genus ..................... **AQUILA**
eagle, male ..................... **TERCEL**
eagle ray ...................... **OBISPO**
eagle, rel. to ............. **HARPY, JOVE**
eagles, brood of............... **AERIE**
eagle's nest .... **AERIE, EYRIE, EYRY**
eaglestone ...................... **ETITE**
eagre .................... **BORE, HYGRE**
ear, anvil of the ................. **INCUS**
" , auricle of .................. **PINNA**
" bone .......... **STAPES, STIRRUP**
" cavity .................. **COCHLEA**
" , elongated depression ... **SCAPHA**
" , external ................ **AURICLE**
" hammer ................. **MALLEU**
" , inflammation of .......... **OTITIS**
" , lobe of the ........ **EARLAP, LUG**
" , membrane of the ... **TECTORIUM**
" of corn; S. Afr. ............ **MEALIE**
" of grain .................... **SPIKE**
" , outer .................. **CONCHA**
" , parts of ............ **LOBE, TRAGI**
" , per. to **LOBAR, PAROTIC, OTIC,**
**AURAL**
" , per. to interior of...... **ENTOTIC**
ear, science of the .......... **OTOLOGY**
" shell .................... **ABALONE**

" specialist .................. **AURIST**
" , thin plate of bone over inner ......
**TEGMEN**
ear-ache .......... **OTALGY, OTALGIA**
ear-cockle .................... **PURPLES**
ear-pick ................... **AURISCALP**
ear-ring ....... **PENDLE, GIRANDOLE**
ears, ringing in the ......... **SYRIGMUS**
ear-shaped gastropod ......... **ORMER,**
**ABALONE**
ear-stone ..................... **OTOLITE**
ear-trumpet, double ..... **TOPOPHONE**
ear-wax ..................... **CERUMEN**
Earldom, Sussex ............ **ARUNDEL**
earl ...... **NOBLEMAN, NEEDLEFISH**
earliest ....... **FIRST, ALERT, CHIEF**
early .. **MATUTINAL, BETIME, SOON**
early Greek colonists ......... **OECISTS**
early origin ................. **ANCIENT**
early; poet. ......... **RATH, RATHE**
earn .... **GAIN, WIN, ADDLE, ETTLE,**
**MERIT**
earnest ..... **SOBER, INCRE, PLEDGE**
earnest money .... **ARLES, HANDSEL,**
**TOKEN**
earnestness ......... **STUDY, UNCTION**
earth .. **CLAY, DIRT, GLOBE, TERRA,**
**WORLD**
" born . **TERRIGENOUS, MORTAL**
" , center of ... **CENTROSPHERE**
" , comb. form .............. **GEO**
" deposit .... **SOIL, MARL, MOLD**
" goddess . **TARI, DEMETER, GE,**
**SEMELE**
" layers; mining .......... **SLOAM**
" , lump of ................ **CLOD**
" metal ...... **ERBIUM, PROTORE**
" , occur at surface of .. **EPIGENE**
" , of the .................. **GEAL**
" , per. to the **SESMIC, TERRENE**
" , the; poet. ................ **VALE**
" , volcanic .............. **TRASS**
earth-born ............. **LOW, VULGAR**
Earth deified ..................... **SEB**
earth-drake ................. **DRAGON**
earthen jar ...................... **OLLA**
earthenware ......... **DELFT, JASPER,**
**PORCELAIN**
earthenware vases ............. **ECHEA**
earthflax .................. **AMIANTHUS**
earthiness ................. **TERROSITY**
earthkin .................... **TERELLA**
earthling ................. **TELLURIST**
earthnut ...... **CHUFA, POD, ARNOT,**
**PEANUT**
earthquake ......... **SEISM, TEMBLOR**
earthquake; Tag. .............. **LINDOL**
Earth's axis ..................... **HINGE**
Earth's crust tract ............. **HORST**
earths; Scot. .................. **EARDS**
earth's surface above center of an earthquake .................. **EPICENTER**
earth-star; genus .......... **GEASTER**
earth-work, an ........ **AGGER, TUMP**
earthworm ....... **DEWWORM, EASSE,**
**ESS**
earthy ............................ **PACO**
earthy metallic oxide ............ **ACHER**
ease .. **MOLLIFY, RELIEVE, SOOTHE**

easiest; Shak. ............... EFTEST
easily DEXTEROUSLY, EATH, SLEEK
east .... ORIENT, LEVANT, SUNRISE
E. Africa, Brit. protectorate in KENYA
E. African native house ....... TEMBE
E. African negro tribe ............ BARI
E. African slave vessel .......... DHOW
E. African sultanate ...... ZANZIBAR
E. African tree ................... MOLI
E. India, discoverer of ........... GAMA
E. India, founder of British ..... CLIVE
E. India, glorious .................. SRI
E. Indian aborigines ......... ARYANS,
                                         BENGALI
"      antelope .... CHIRU, NILGAI
"      army servant ....... LASCAR
"      beetle .............. BLISTER
"      beetle, species of ............
                                         CANTHARIS
"      berry-like fruit .... LANSEH,
                                         LANSA
"      bison ................... GAUR
"      bison, sacred GAYAL, TSINE
"      black buck ... BEZORATICA
"      blue cow ............ NILGAI
"      broad bill bird ........ RAYA
"      cashmere ............ ULWAN
"      chamois ............. SARAU
"      chief DATO, RANA, SIRDAR
"      city ........ AGRA, BENGAL,
                                         SURAT
"      coin .. ANNA, PICE, RUPEE
"      deer ....... CHITAL, GERAU
"      disease ............... LANAS
"      dodder ................ AMIL
"      drink .................. NIPA
"      drinking pot ......... LOTAH
"      early tribe . DASAS, DASYUS
"      embanked road ...... PRAYA
"      fabaceous tree ....... DHAK
"      fabric; var. ......... ROMAL
"      falcon ............... BESRA
"      fan ................. PUNKAH
"      farmer ................ RYOT
"      fiber plant OADAL, NILGIRI
"      fruit ..................... BEL
"      fruit pigeon ........ TRERON
"      fruit tree ............ PAPAW
"      garment ............... SARI
"      goat, wild MARKHOR, TAHR
"      groom ................. SYCE
"      gum tree, deriv. of .... KINO
"      harvest ............... RABO
"      herb ... ROSELLE, SESAME
"      hog, wild ............ PIGMY
"      Islands; (Dutch) . ADI, LETI,
                         JAVA, SUMATRA
"      kingdom ............. NEPAL
"      lace ................... GOTA
"      mail ................... DAK
"      mammal ............ TARSIER
"      money of account ..... ANNA
"      mountain ............. GHAT
"      mus. inst. .... BINA, SAROD,
                                         VINA
"      muslin .......... JAMDANEE
"      nation; anc. .......... TAMIL
"      Nilgiri, one of ..... BADAGA
"      nurse ................ AMAH

"      nut ..................... BEN
"      panda .................. WAH
E. Indian peasant ............... RYOT
"      plant ... CHAY, SILA, SUNN
"      plant, fiber of ......... JUTE
"      poison .......... BISH, BIKH
"      race ................... SWAT
"      race or caste ......... VARNA
"      rat ............. BANDICOOT
"      region ............. MALABAR
"      religious body ....... SARAS
"      root ........... ATEES, ATIS
"      ruler ............... AKBAR
"      ruminant ............. ZEBU
"      sacred city ........ BENARES
"      screen .............. TATTIE
"      seaman .............. LASCAR
"      sect ............ JAIN, JAINA
"      servant ............... MATY
"      sheep, wild ... SNA, SHAPU,
                                         URIAL
"      shrub ....... MUDAR, ODAL
"      snuff ............... RAPEE
"      soldier ............... SEPOY
"      sugar, coarse ... GUR, RAAB
"      swine ............. BABIRUSA
"      timber tree ..... SAL, TOON
"      title .................. RAJA
"      title for master ...... SAHIB
"      town .............. HOOGHLY
"      tree ...... ALUS, AMPAC,
                     BANYAN, ENG, SISSOO,
                     ENGELG, MARGOSA
"      tree bark ............. NIEPA
"      tribe ...... KADERS, MARIS,
                                   PULIARS
"      vessel ............ PATAMAR
"      vine ................... ODAL
"      viol .................. RUANA
"      warrior .............. SINGH
"      water vessel .......... LOTA
"      weight CATTY, RATTI, SER,
                                       TOLA
"      wild cattle ............ GAUR
"      xylophone ............ SARON
E. Indies, island of .............. BALI
east wind ....................... EURUS
Easter ............ EED, PAAS, PACE
Easter, feast of ................. PASCH
Easter festival .................. PAAS
Easter, per. to ............... PASCHAL
eastern ORIENTAL, ASIATIC, ORTIVE
eastern palace ................... SERAI
eastern people ........ SERES, AVARS
eastern ruler ............ EHEER, EMIR
easy .............. EATH, FACILE, GLIB
eat .. SMOOTH, FEED, MANAGE, SUP
"  away ....... CANKER, CORRODE,
                                   ERODE, FRET
"   between meals ............. BEVER
"   greedily .. GAMP, GORGE, RAVEN
"   heartily ...................... THORN
"   immoderately ................. GLUT
"   in gulps ....................... LAB
eatable ................... ESCULENT
eater of raw flesh ....... OMOPHAGIST
eating .................. BIT, CANKER
eating, excessive ............ EDACITY
eating hall ....................... MESS

"	place ............... AUTOMAT
eavesdrop .................. STILLICIDE
Eban, diplomat ................... ABBA
ebb ....... NEAP, RECEDE, REFLUX,
WANE
ebb and flow ........... TIDE, AESTUS
Ebers' son ..................... PELEG
ebullate ............. BOIL, BUBBLE
eccentric ...... ERRATIC, ODD, TIKE
eccentric piece ................... CAM
ecclesiastic, an English ........ ORMIN
ecclesiastical attendant .... ACOLYTE
"	banner ............ LABARUM
"	benefice ............... GLEBE
"	cape ................. CAPPA
"	council ............. SYNOD
"	court ... CLASSIS, ROTA
"	hood ................. AMICE
"	office for a widow VIDUATE
"	seat .... DEANERY, SEDILE
"	skull cap BIRETTA, CALLOTE
"	surplus .............. COTTA
"	vestment ... AMICE, STOLE,
VAGAS
echidna .................. ANTEATER
echinate .......... BRISTLY, SPINY
echoing .................. ITERANT
echoing back .............. RESONANT
echimyine rodent .............. HUTIA
eclat .... GLORY, RENOWN, PRAISE
eclipse . OBSCURE, SURPASS, STAIN
eclipse, part. .............. PENUMBRA
ecology .................... BIGNOMICS
economics .............. PLUTOLOGY
economize ......... SCRIMP, STINT,
HUSBAND, SAVE, RETRENCH
ecru ........ BEIGE, TAN, YELLOW
ecstasy ......... TRANCE, RAPTURE
ectad, opposed to ............. ENTAD
ecu .................... COIN, SHIELD
Ecuador, capital of ............. QUITO
Ecuador, province in ............. ORO
ecumenical council ........... TRENT
eczema .......... HERPES, TETTER
edacity ............ AVARICE, GREED
edaphic .................. LOCAL, SOIL
eddish ...... ARRISH, AFTERMATH,
PARK, PASTURE, EDGREW
eddy ....... SWIRL, GULF, VORTEX,
WREATHE, WHIRLPOOL, BORE
edema ............... DROPSY, TUMOR
Eden . GLORY, HEAVEN, PARADISE
edentare .................... AL, SLOTH
edentare, 3 toed ...... ADVENTURINE
Ederle, Miss ........... GERTRUDE
edge .. LABRUM, BRIM, HEM, RAND,
RIM, MARGIN, SELVEDGE
edge, keen ............... ZEST, ARRIS
edge, to ......................... SIDLE
edged irregularly ............... EROSE
edges of a vessel ................. LIPS
edging ........... RUCHE, TATTING
edible .... COMESTIBLE, ESCULENT
edible fungus ................ MOREL
edible mud worm ................ IPO
edible nut .................... CASHEW
edible seed .... BEAN, PEA, PEANUT
edible tuber . TARO, UVA, YAM, OCA

edict ASSIZE, ARRET, ACT, DECREE,
UKASE, ESCRIPT, MANDATE
edict, Pope's ..................... BULL
"Edinburgh Magazine" ......... MAGA
Edinburgh, part of ............. LEITH
Edinburgh, poet. name ........ EDINA
edit, to ........... REVISE, REWORD,
ARRANGE
edition in six texts ........ HEXAPLA
editor ........ REVISER, REDACTOR
editorial ......... ARTICLE, LEADER
Edom, land of ..... IDUMEA, TEMAN
Edomite chieftain ............... IRAM
educated ...... ERUDITE, LITERATE
education ...... LITERACY, TUITION
educational authority .......... BINET
educe ...... DRAW, EVOLVE, ELICIT
Edwards; showman ............... GUS
edwit ................. BLAME, TAUNT
eel, bright colored ............. MORAY
eel, conger ................... ELVER
eel, marine .................... CONGER
eel, sand ............. CRIG, LAUNCE
eel-fish .................... TANDAN
eel-like ......... TUNA, LANT, OPAH
eelpout ... BURBOT, LING, WEASEL
eels, fish for ............... SNIGGLE
eels, migration of .......... EELFARE
eel-spear ..................... ELGER
eelware ................... CROWFOOT
eelworm .......... NEMA, NEMATODE
eerie ............. UNCANNY, WEIRD
efface ...... EXPUNGE, ERASE, ODIC
effect . COMPASS, SEQUEL, ACHIEVE
effeminate ..... COCKNEY, EPICENE
effervesce ...... BUBBLE, HISS, BOIL
effervescent, make .......... AERATE
effete .......... BAREN, IDLE, SERE
efficacy .. ...... POTENCY, POWER
effigy ....... ICON, GUY, FACSIMILE
effluvium .... AURA, REEK, FLATUS
effluxion ...... EMANATION, LAPSE,
STREAM
effort ..... BURST, CONATUS, JUMP,
TUG, STRAIN, NISUS, PES
effrontery ..................... BRASS
effulgence ......... GLORY, LUSTER,
AGLOW, RUTILANT, SPLENDOR
effusive, be . GUSH, DRIBBLE, RANT
eft ........ LIZARD, NEWT, TRITON
eftsoon ........ AGAIN, FORTHWITH
egad .... ECOD, EXPLETIVE, OATH
egest ............. DISCHARGE, VOID
egg capsule .................... OVISAC
egg; comb. form ............. OO, OVI
egg, fertilized ............... OOSPERM
egg; Fr. .......................... OVE
egg, large ............. BLOCKBUSTER
egg, part of LATEBRA, YELK, YOLK
egg shaped .... OVUM, OOID, OVATE,
OVOID
egg shell .................... SHARD
egg, small ............... OVULE, NIT
egg, white of ................. GLAIR
eggs ................. BOMBS, URGES
eggs, fish ............... BERRY, ROE
eggs pres., Chin. ............. PIDAN
eggs, tester of ............. CANDLER

78

eggshell color ................. ECRU
Egil, brother of ............. VOLUND
ego ........ JIVATMA, ATMAN, SELF
egress .......... OUTLET, ISSUANCE
egret ........................... HERON
Egypt, anc. Christians of ..... COPTS
" , capital of upper ..... ASYOOT
" city of; anc. ..... NO, ABYDOS
" , in Hebrew ......... MIZRAIM
" , in hieroglyphics ......... KEM
" , lower division of ..... MAZOR
" sunset god ................ TEM
" , the soul .............. BA, KA
" , upper division of . PATHROS
Egyptian ............ NILOT, GYPSY
" antique coin .. ESHREEN, NU
" ape, myth. ................ AANI
" astral body .................. KA
" bull, myth. ...... APIS, BACTS
" celebrated ruler ............ ALI
" Christian ................ COPT
" City of the Sun ........ AN, ON
" commander-in-chief .. SIRDAR
" conqueror ........ AMR, AMRU
" cosmetic powder ........ KOHL
" currency ...... FODDA, KEES,
                              PURSE
" dancing girl ALMA, GHAWAZI
Egyptian deity (see "Deity")
" Diana ...... PAKHT, SEKHET
" divinity .......... HOR, PTAH
" dog, anc. breed ....... SALUKI
" dye plant .... HENNA, HINNA
" fabled monster ........ SPHINX
" falcon-headed deity ... HORUS
" festival .................... ISIS
" , for "father" ........... ATEF
" fruit of the cactus ......... FIG
" god (see 'God') ........ ANUBIS
" goddess (see 'Goddess') .. APET
" goddess of life ............ ISIS
" governor ................. BEY
" grass, course ........ HALFEH
" hare-like mammal .... HYRAX
" hawk-headed man .......... RA
" healer ................. ARABI
" island ........ ELEPHANTINE,
                               RODA
" jar ................... CANOPIC
" jinee, myth. .... AMSET, HAPI
" judge of dead .......... OSIRIS
" lake ................... MOERIS
" khedive's estate ........ DAIRA
" king ................. PTOLEMY
" land ................. FEDDAN
" leaping mouse ........ JERBOA
" light-house ........... PHAROS
" lizard ................... ADDA
" lotus ............... NYMPHOEA
" measure ...... ARDEB, CUBIT,
              KELEH, KHET, PIK
" monarch ............ RAMESES
" mountain ............... UEKIA
" mus. performer, female ALMEH
" peasant .............. FELLAH
" pebble ............... JASPER
" Pharaoh's hen ...... VULTURE
" plain ................. ASASEFF

" port ................... BOOLAK
" pound ..................... ROTL
" privet ........ HENNA, HINNA
" province; anc. ......... NOME
" queen ........... CLEOPATRA,
                            KHAZNEH
" queen of the gods ........ SATI
" rattle ................. SISTRUM
" reed ..... BYBLUS, PAPYRUS
" royal symbol; anc. ........ ASP
" ruler ............... KHEDIVE
" scribe ..................... ANI
" serpent; myth .......... APEPI
" solar disk .............. ATEN
" soul; myth. ......... BA, SAHU
" sultan ................ SALADIN
" symbol ................. ANKH
" symbol of fertility ... SERAPIS
" symbol of sovereignty URAEUS
" symbolic eye .............. UTA
" temple ........ EDOON, OSIRIS
" temple; anc. .......... THOTH
" temple, site of ...... KARNAK
" thief; shak. .............. DOXY
" thorn ................. BABUL
" title .......... CALIPH, PASHA
" tomb, cell in .......... SERDAB
" town . SYENE, ASWAN, SAIS
" unit of capac. ......... ARDEB
" unit of currency ...... GERSH,
                            PIASTRE
Egyptian vegetable . VETCH, LENTIL,
                                LUPIN
" viceroy .............. KHEDIVE
" village .... ABYDOS, ABOUKIR,
                      ADFOO, EDFU
" water bottle ......... DORUCK
" water raising device .. SAKIEH,
                      SHADOOF, TABUT
" weasel-like animal ICHNEUMON
" weight .. KET, KANTAR, KAT,
        OCHA, OKIEH, OKE, UCKIA
" wind ..... KAMSIN, KHAMSIN
eider .................... DOWN, WAMP
eidolon ........ IMAGE, APPARITION,
                            PHANTOM
eight fold ............ OCTO, OCTUPLE
eight in number; P.I. ............ UALO
eight performers ............ OCTETTE
eight, series of ...... OGDOAD, OCTAD
eight; Sp. ....................... OCHO
eight tones ........ DIATONIC, UNCAE
eighteen inch meas. ............ CUBIT
Eire, president of .............. HYDE
Eisenhower, Gen. ................. IKE
      " , Mamie .. (NEE) DOWD
either member of a board .. DUUMVIR
eject .. EMIT, EXPEL, EVICT, OUST,
                      DISLODGE, VOID
eke ............ ADD, ETCH, IMP, TAB
Elam capital ...................... SUSA
elan ....... ARDOR, DASH, SPIRIT
elapse .. DIE, GO, PASS, LAPSE, RUN
elasticity DUCTILITY, GIVE, SPRING
elasticity, science in solids ELATERICS
elasticize .......... STENT, STRETCH
elated ..... GLEEFUL, PERKED, RAD
Elbe, tributary of ........ EGER, ISFR

79

elbow ............. SQUEEZE, ANCON
elbow, per. to the ............. ULNAR
elbow, touch with the ........ NUDGE
Elcesaites, founder of the ...... ELKAI
elder MORMON, OLDER, SIRE, EBUL,
             IVA
elder statesman; Jap. .......... GENRO
elderly ........ GRAY, OLD, VETERAN
eldest; law .................... EIGNE
eldritch ................. EERIE, WILD
elect .. CHOOSE, NAME, ELITE, ORT
electioneer .................... STUMP
elector .............. ELISOR, VOTER
Electra's brother ............ ORESTES
electric particle ................... ION
electrical appliance SPARKER, STEPUP
" atmosphere .............. AURA
" atom ................ ELECTRON
" circuit regulator ..... BOOSTER
" coil ..................... TELSA
" constituent ............... ANION
" current; per. to .......... AUDIO
" measure ........... MEGADYNE
" odic force ................ ELOD
" particle ................ CATION
" pressure detector .. TASIMETER
" terminal .......... ELECTRODE
" unit (see also 'unit')
" unit ... VOLT, HENRY, JOULE,
           WATT
" unit of capacity ......... FARAD
" unit of pressure ........ BARAD
" unit of quantity ..... COULOMB
" unit of reluctance .. OERSTED,
           REL
electricity, unit of .... AMPERE, MHO,
          OHM
electromagnet, disc. of ...... OERSTED
electronic detect. ............. RADAR
electrum ....................... AMBER
eleemosynary ................. DONEE
elegiac ............ FUNEREAL, POEM
elegance ...... GRACE, LUX, BEAUTY
elegant ..... GENT, RICH, COURTLY
elegy, funeral ...... LAMENT, DIRGE,
        NENIA, REQUIEM
element ...... COMPONENT, METAL,
        SILICON, NEON
" , even ................. ARTIAD
" , inert gas ..... NEON, XENON
" , non-volatile ......... BARIUM
" of air .................... ARGON
" of plan .................... RAY
" of the earth group .... ERBIUM
" , poisonous ........... ARSENIC
" , rare metallic ........ IRIDIUM,
         YTTRIUM
" , rare white ............. INDIUM
" similar to another with different
    atomic weight .... ISOTOPE
" , very rare .......... HAFNIUM
elemental spirit ................ GENIE
elementary .... INCHOATE, PRIMARY
elemi .............. RESIN, ELEMINE
elephant apple tree .......... FERONIA
" boy ................... SABU
" cry ..................... BARR
" , extinct .......... MASTODON
" , keeper of .......... MAHOUT

" pen ................... KRALL
" , per. to the .... PACHYDERM
" seat, protected ..... HOWDAH
" staff for goading ....... ANKUS
" tusk ..... IVORY, SCRIVELLO
" , young of ............... CALF
elephant's ear .................... TARO
elevate ..... RISE, EXALT, PROMOTE
elevated summer house .. BELVEDERE
elevating muscle ............. LEVATOR
elevation of mind .......... ANAGOGE
elevator car .................... CAGE
elf .... NIX, FAY, GNOME, IMP, OAF,
      OUPH(E), SPRITE
elf; Persian ...................... PERI
elfkin shelter ............. TOADSTOOL
elfish sprite; myth. .............. DRAC
elicit .. EDUCE, EXTRACT, STRETCH
eligible APT, MEET, COMPETENT, FIT
eliminate ...... ERASE, RID, DETACH
Elijah; Ital. ...................... ELIA
Elinor ——, poet ............... WYLIE
Eliot, novel; hero ............. MARNER
Eliot, heroine .................. ROMOLA
Eli's son ..................... HOPHNI
Elisha's servant ............... GENAZI
elision .... SYNCOPE, ABRIDGEMENT
elite assemblage ..... GALAXY, STARS
Elizabeth's mother ........... BOLEYN
elk .... MOOSE, ALCE, ELAND, LOSH,
        SAMBUR
elk bark ............. BAY, MAGNOLIA
Elkanah's son ................. SAMUEL
Elkanah's wife ............... HANNAH
elke ................. GOOSE, SWAN
ellipse ................... CURVE, OVAL
elm borer .................... LAMIID
elm, fruit of the .............. SAMARA
elm, genus .................... ULMUS
Elmo's fire .............. CORPOSANT
elongated . LANK, LINEAR, PROLATE
eloquent . CICERONIAN, ORATORICAL
else .............. ESNE, OTHERWISE
elude SHUN, AVOID, DOUBLE, EVADE
elusive EQUIVOCAL, EVASIVE, EELY
elutheria bark, yield of . CASCARILLA
elution, washings from ... ELULATE
eluxate; rare ............. DISLOCATE
elven BROWNIE, FAY, PIXY, NIX, ELF
elver .................. CONGER, EEL
elytrin ......................... CHITIN
elytrum of a beetle ............ SHARD
em, half of ....................... EN
emaciation; Lat. .............. TABES
emanate ....... ISSUE, SPRING, RISE
emanation .... NITON, AURA, VAPOR
emancipate ........ FREE, MANUMIT
emancipator ....... FREER, LINCOLN
embalm ............. PERFUME, CERE
embankment .......... DIKE, LEVEE
embankment hole .............. GIME
embankment in rice fields .... PILAPIL
embattled ................ CRENELED
embellish .... DRESS, ADORN, GILD,
      GARNISH, ROUGE,
          BEDECK
ember .. COAL, ASH, CINDER, IZLE,
       PERIOD, GLEED
embitter .... ACERBATE, ENVENOM

emblem ........ BEE, BADGE, TYPE
emblem of a clan ............ TOTEM
emblem of authority ......... MACE
emblic ......................... AULA
embodiment .... AVATAR, MATTER,
EPITOME
embodiment of Ptah ............. APIS
embolism .......... INTERCALATION
embrace .... CARESS, HUG, ACCOLL,
CLASP
embroider .. TAT, DECORATE, PURL
embroidery frame ........ TABOURET
emend .. CORRECT, RECTIFY, EDIT,
RIGHT
emerald ............. BERYL, GREEN
emerald; obs. .............. SMARAGD
emerge .......... ISSUE, PEND, RISE
emery ..... CORUNDUM, ABRADANT
emesis ..................... VOMITING
Emile Zola; book by ............ NANA
eminence .. DIGNITY, HILL, RIDEAU
eminent ...... HIGH, LOFTY, SHINE
emir, jurisdiction of an .... EMIRATE
emissary ...... AGENT, SCOUT, SPY
emit ...... EMANATE, PLUFF, SHED,
UTTER, ERUCT, EXHALE
emmet ................. ANT, PISMIRE
emolument ................ FEE, GAIN
Emory Univ. site .......... ATLANTA
emotion ...... IRE, PATHOS, ONDE,
TREMOR, CHERISH
emotionless ............ APATHETIC,
UNFEELING
emperor .. CZAR, IMPERATOR, INCA
emphasize .................... STRESS
empiric ........ CHARLATAN, QUACK
employer ...... HIRER, BLOKE, USER
emptiness ................ INANITION
empty .. IDLE, INANE, VOID, TOOM,
VACUOUS, CLEAR, VACANT
empyreal ...... AERIAL, CELESTIAL
empyrean .............. ETHER, SKY
emu wren ................. STIPITURE
emyd ......................... TURTLE
emulate ...... COMPETE, RIVAL, VIE
enact .... ORDAIN, DECREE, ENJOIN
enactment . CANON, DECREE, EDICT,
LAW, ORDINANCE, USAGE,
VETO
encamp .... BIVOUAC, TENT, SIEGE
enchain ....... ENCIRCLE, FETTER,
LODGE, FASTEN, PIN
enchant ...... BEWITCH, ENSORCEL
enchantment ........ CHARM, SPELL
enchantress .. CIRCE, SIREN, WITCH
encircle ...... ENVIRON, GIRD, ORB,
INORB, ENFOLD, ZONE
enclose .. CORRAL, ENCLAVE, HEM
enclosed area .................. SEPT
enclosing .................. AMBIENT
enclosure STOCKADE, YARD, BAWN,
PEN, CAGE
encomium ........ TRIBUTE, ELOGE,
PANEGYRIC
encore .... AGAIN, BIS, ECHO, OVER
"  , anti .... BOO, CATCALL, HISS
encourage .... ABET, RALLY, BOOST
Encratites, founder of ...... TATIAN

encroach on ...... TRENCH, INVADE
encumber .... LOAD, SADDLE, CLOG
encyclic ...... PANDECT, TREATISE,
LETTER
encyclopedic learning .. POLYHISTOR
end .. AIM, CEASE, CLOSE, OMEGA,
TOE, LIMIT, TAIL
end, boundary .... BOURN, ABUTTAL
end of a character .......... TENON
endeavor SEEK, AIM, STRIVE, ESSAY,
VIE, EFFORT, ETTLE
endine thermo .............. CALORIC
ending .... CONCLUSION, DESINENT
endless ............... ANATA, ETERN
endow .. VEST, BESTOW, DOTE, DUE
endowment .... APPANAGE, DOWER,
GRANT, GIFT, TALENT
endue .... DIGEST, DOWER, INVEST
endure .. BEAR, LAST, LIVE, BROOK,
DREE, ABIDE, UNDERGO
Eneas; Fr. ........................ ENEE
enemy ...... HATER, FRENNE, FOE,
RIVAL
energize .. BRACE, FORTIFY, NERVE
energy ...... PEP, STHENIA, BENT,
ACTINIC, ERG
energy, potential .............. ERGAL
energy, want of .. ATONY, ANEURIA,
INERTIA
enervate .... DRAIN, EXHAUST, SAP
enfilade ............ BARRAGE, RAKE
engage ... BIND, PLIGHT, PROMISE
engender ............ BEGET, BREED
engine .... MOTOR, CORVY, MOGUL,
GIN
engine of warfare .......... ONAGER,
CATAPULT, RAM
England, anc. name .......... ALBION
"  , district of York .... ILKLEY
"  , early conqueror of .. HORSA
"  , early name of .... EGBERT
"  , forest in .......... ARDEN
"  , headland of .......... NAZE
"  , most southerly port of ......
LIZARD
"  , north-west; anc. .. ARGYLE
"  , per. to ...... ANGLOPHOBE
"  , symbol of ............ BULL
English .......... SILURES, ANGLE,
ANGLICAN
"  actor ........ MAUDE, TREE
"  address to queen .... MAAM
"  Antarctic explorer .... SCOTT
"  archbishop ............ LAUD
"  author .. ROLLE, LANDOR,
OPIE
"  authoress .......... BRONTE
"  authoritative ruler; anc. ......
BRETWALDA
"  aviators; Fr. slang for .. RAFS
"  bailiff ................. REEVE
"  canal laborer ........ NAVVY
English cascade ............ LADORE
"  castle site ........ ARUNDEL
"  circuit court .......... EYRE
"  city ................. LEEDS
"  clergyman .... INGE, NEALE,
WESLEY

" coin GEORGE, GUINEA, ORA
" coin; anc. .. CAROLUS, RIAL
" coin, silver, old ...... GROAT
" comedian ............. TOOLE
" commander ........... HAIG
" composer .... ELGAR, ARNE,
DELIUS
" conservative party .... TORY
" conspirator ........ FAWKES
" country festival ........ ALE
" county ESSEX, KENT, YORK
" county division; anc. ........
WAPENTAKE
" county hundreds .. LATHES,
RAPES
" court .. EYRE, SOC, GEMOT,
LEET
" dandy; slang ...........TOFF
" diarist ............... PEPYS
" diplomat ............. EDEN
" district court, per. to .. SAKE,
SOC
" divine ................ PALEY
" domain .............. MANOR
" dramatist .. TOBIN, PINERO,
READE
" editor ................. MEE
" elm ........... CAMPESTRIS
" episcopal diocese ...... SEE
" essayist ........ LANG, ELIA,
STEELE
" etcher ............... HADEN
" executioner .......... KETCH
" festival ................. ALP
" financier ......... GRESHAM
" forest .............. ARDEN
" fortified town; obs. .... BERG
" founder of Northumberland ..
DEIRA
" franchise ............... SOC
" free tenant .......... DRENG
" freeman .... CEORL, THANE
" freemen .. CHURLS, LOETS
" hamlet ............... DORP
" headland ......... BOLERIUM
" heathen ruler; anc. .. PENDA
" historian .... GROTE, BEDE,
GIBBON
" hog .................. ESSEX
" honor exam .......... TRIPOS
" hymnodist ........... NEALE
" impresario .......... CARTE
" horse dealer .......... COPER
" king .... INE, HAL, HAROLD
" king, 946 ............ EDRED
" king of Northumberland ....
EADGAR
" kingdom, early ...... DEIRA
" landed proprietor .... SQUIRE
" lawn billiards ........ TROCO
" lapwing ............. TEWIT
" legendary king .... ARTHUR
" legislature ... PARLIAMENT
" letter ..................... AR
" liberal party .......... WHIG
" limestone ........... OOLITE
" measure of coal ........ CORF
English mendicant orders .... FRIARS

" mine wagon ........ ROLLEY
" minister of state ...... PEEL,
PITT, WALPOLE
" monk .................. BEDE
" mountain peak .... CHEVIOT,
WYDDVA
" musician .............. ARNE
" name of rifle ........ SNIDER
" navigator .... DRAKE, ROSS
" ninth C. Statute ...... DANE
" nobility . THEGNS, EARL(S)
" northern tribe; anc. .. PICTS
" novelist .... (HALL), CAINE
" painter .... PAYNTER, OPIE
" pamphleteer . DEFOE, SWIFT
" patron saint ........ GEORGE
" poet .. GRAY, KEATS, LANG,
CAREW, POPE, SHELLEY
" poet, earliest ..... CAEDMON
" poet laureate ......... CIBBER
" political philosopher . BURKE
" pot herb .............. CLARY
" pottery ............. SPODE
" printer ............ CAXTON
" prose writer . AELFRIC, ORM
" prose writer, first .... BEDA,
BEDE, BAEDA
" race-course .......... ASCOT
" reformer, 1750-1814 . SPENCE
" remade woolen cloth SHODDY
" revolution song .. LILLIBUL-
LERO
" river AVON, ESK, EXE, NEN,
EDEN, OUSE, CAM, URE, TEES,
TRENT, TYNE, YARE
" rock strata ........ PERMIAN
" ruler, early ........... OFFA
" school ................ ETON
" schoolboy ......... ETONIAN
" schoolmaster .......... ARAM
" scientist . CONNEL, DARWIN
" serf ................. THRALL
" settlement, group ......... GA
" settlers, early ........ JUTES
" ship money .......... PREST
" slave ................. ESNE
" slice of bread ........ CANCH
" , sobriquent given to .. BONO
" socialist ........... FABIAN
" statesman .......... BURKE,
CRANMER, PITT
" stone monument CROMLECH
" surgeon .... HADEN, PAGET
" tax .......... EXCISE, GELD
" tax, army service money ....
PREST
" textile . FLAX, HEMP, JUTE
" thicket ............ SPINNEY
" traveler and author .. LIGON
" treaty of ............ TROYES
" village ............... BOURG
" wager of battle .... ORNEST
" warrior and king CNUT, KNUD
" women's army corps, one of ..
WAAC
" writer PAGET, DORAN, FOX,
HENTY
Englishman .. SASSENACH, GODDAM

Englishman's gift to bride ...... DOS
engrave ....... CHISEL, CUT, INFIX
engraver's tool ................ BURIN
engraving ......... CHASING, PRINT
    "    , act of ........ CELATURE
    "    by dots ........... STIPPLE
    "    coin; anc. ........ CAROLUS
engraving on wood ..... XYLOGRAPH
    "    stone ............ INTAGLIO
engrossed BUSY, EMPLOYED, RAPT
enhance . ENARM, INCREASE, WAX
enigma REBUS, CHARADE, GRAPH,
        RIDDLE, MYSTERY, WHY
enigmatic ..................... MYSTIC
enisled . ALONE, APART, ISOLATED
enjoin ..... BID, DECREE, DIRECT,
                            ORDER
enjoying ..... FRUITION, FRUITIVE
enkerchief ..................... DRAPE
enlarged .......... DILATED, HIRED
enlarged mass in nose .... ADENOID
enlarging grad. ................ EVASE
enlightened person .... ILLUMINATO
enliven ........ ANIMATE, REFRESH
enmesh .. INSNARE, KNOT, SNARL
enmity . HATRED, RANCOR, ANDE,
            FEUD, COLD, DISCORD
ennead .......................... NINE
ennui .. FATIGUE, LANGUOR, BORE
enormous ... HUGE, VAST, TITANIC
Enos' grandmother .............. EVE
Enos' uncle .................... ABEL
enough .... FULLY, QUITE, ANOGH,
                        BUS, BASTA
enough; ital. .................. BASTA
enraged .......... ANGERED, IRATE
enraptured ..... ECSTATIC, BEATIC
enrich .. ENDOW, INCREASE, LARD
enroll ............ ENTER, IMPANEL,
                    MATRICULATE
ens .................. BEING, ENTITY
ensiform ........... XIPHISTERNUM,
                            XIPHOID
ensign bearer .......... ORIFLAMME,
                            ANCIENT
ensign of Othello ................ IAGO
ensign, papel ............. GONFALON
ensigns of sovereignty ..... REGALIA
ensilage .......... SILAGE, FODDER
ensiled ......................... SILOED
ensnare . SNIGGLE, BENET, NOOSE,
        WEB, BITE, TRAP, TRICK
ensorcel ..... BEWITCH, ENCHANT
entablature ........... TRABEATION
entad, opposed to ............ ECTAD
entangle ...... WEB, MAT, RAFFLE,
        TRAMMEL, RAVEL, MESH
entanglement . LIMING, IMBROGLIO,
                            SNARE
enter . RECORD, BORE, EAT, INCUR
entertain ........ DIVERT, REGALE,
                    AMUSE, TREAT
entertain ........ GLEE, ENTRACTE
entertainment of strangers ..........
                        XENODOCHY
enthusiasm . ARDOR, ENVY, ESTRO,
        VERVE, MANIA, ZEAL
enthusiast ......... RIGOT, ZEALOT,
                    ACTIVE, FAN

enthymeme ARGUMENT, THOUGHT
entice .... INVEIGH, TEMPT, LURE,
                            TOLE
enticer ....... SEDUCER, DECOYER
entitles .... NAMES, DUBS, CALLS
entity ........... SOUL, ENS, BEING,
        EXISTENCE, THING, UNIT
entomb ............. BURY, HEARSE
entourage .......... ATTENDANTS,
                    ENVIRONMENT
entrance ... PORTAL, ADIT, INLET,
        POSTERN, GATE, INGRESS, WAY
entranced ..................... RAPT
entreat ADJURE, BESEECH, HALSE,
            SOLICIT, IMPLORE
entree .. ADMISSION, ACCESS, DISH
entrepot .... DEPOT, WAREHOUSE
entresol ................ MEZZANINE
entry . MINUTE, HALL, ITEM, POST
entwine ......... ENLACE, WEAVE
enumeration .. TALE, CENSUS, LIST
enunciate ....... DECLARE, UTTER
envelop ............ SHROUD, WRAP
envelope ... BURR, CASE, SHROUD,
                        VESICLE
envenom ........... TAINT, POISON
environ HEM, OUTSKIRT, PURLIEU
environment ...... TERRAIN, AREA,
                        MILIEU
envoy . (AB)LEGATE, POSTSCRIPT
envy .... RANKLE, COVET, EVEST
enzyme .. ASE, DIASTASE, PEPSIN,
        PTYALIN, LACCASE, OLEASE
enzyme, leather making .. TANNASE
enzyme, opposed to ............ AZYM
eolith ................ CELT, AX(E)
eon .............. ERA, AGE, CYCLE
eonic .......................... ERAL
ephah, tenth of ............... OMER
epic ............. POEM, EPOS, SAGA
epic poem ...... EPOPEE, ENEID
epic; Span. ...................... CID
epicarp ......................... HUSK
Epictetus was one ........... STOIC
epicure ........ FRIAND, GOURMET,
        GLUTTON, SYBARITE
epicurean .. APICIAN, LUXURIOUS
epicurism ........... GASTRONOMY,
                        HEDONISM
epidemic ...... FLU, PEST, PLAGUE
epidermal tissue .......... KERATIN
epidermis .......... BARK, CUTICLE
epigram . ADAGE, POSY, QUIP, MOT
epigram couplet ............ DISTICH
epilepsy .......... CATALEPSY, FIT
epileptic, to be ......... MIRYACHIT
epimetheus' wife ........ PANDORA
epimyth ..................... MORAL
epinephrin ............ ADRENALIN
Epirus, native of ......... EPIROTE
Epirus, town in; anc. .... DODONA
epistle . LETTER, MISSIVE, FAVOR,
            NOTE, BILLET, POST
epithet .... AGNOMEN, (BY)NAME
epithet for Jupiter .... THUNDERER
epitome .. BRIEF, DIGEST, CONCISE
epoch . EON, AGE, DAY, ERA, TIME
epoptic ..................... MYSTIC

83

Epsom, rel. to; Eng. ........ DERBY
equable ...... EEN, EVEN, STEADY
equal ..... BOTH, EVEN, FERE, TIE,
   COORDINATE, RIVAL, SAME
equal, an .... MATCH, MEET, PAR
equal angled figure ........ ISOGON
equal, comb. form ........ ISO, PARI
equal quantity ...... IDENTIC, ANA
equal to three short syllables TRISEME
equality . IDENTITY, JUSTICE, PAR
equality; Fr. .............. EGALITE
equality of civil rights ... ISONOMY
equatorial .................. TORRID
equestrian .... HORSEMAN, RIDER
equestrian; Amer. ........ REVERE
equilateral parallelogram .... RHOMB
equilibrist .............. BALANCER
equilibrium, want of ...... ASTASIA
equine cry ....... NEIGH, WHINNY
equine disease .............. FARCY
equip ...... RIG, FEAT, GIRD, IMP
equipoise ....... BALANCE, EQUAL
equitable .... HONEST, FAIR, JUST
equitable; Rom. law .. BONITARIAN
equivocal AMPHIBOLIC, ENIGMATIC
equivocate TERGIVERSATE, FENCE,
               PALTER
era AGE, CYCLE, DATE, EON, TIME
eradicate EPILATE, ANNUL, LEVEL,
                ROOT
erase .... DELE, DELETE, EFFACE
ere ........ PRIOR, RATHER, YER
Erebus ...................... HADES
Erebus' brother ......... NOX, NYX
Erebus' father .............. CHAOS
Erebus, children of ........ AETHER,
              HEMERA
erect . MURE, REAR, STAY, RAISE
eretrian ..................... ELIAN
erewhile ................ FORMERLY
ergo ........................ HENCE
ergon .................. WORK, ERG
Eric, the ...................... RED
erica ..................... HEATH(S)
Eridani, star in .............. KEID
Erin ARYAN, HIBERNIA, IRELAND
Erin, deriv. of .......... EIRE, ERIE
erinaceous ............. HEDGEHOG
ermine ......... ERMALIN, STOAT
eroded ...... EATEN, EROSE, ATE
Eros .................. CUPID, AMOR
erotic AMATIVE, AMOROUS, LOVING
errai ........................ CEPHEI
erratic ........ ROGUE, VAGRANT,
         NOMADIC, WHACKY
erring ......... ASTRAY, SINNING,
             PECCABLE
error .. ERRATA, LAPSE, SIN, SLIP,
   WOGH, BONER, MISCUE
ersatz ................ SUBSTITUTE
Erse ........ CELT, GAEL, GAELIC
erstwhile popular song CUCARACHA
erudition WISDOM, LETTERS, LORE
eruption ....... EXANTHEMA, RASH
Erwin; comedian .............. STU
erysipelas ..................... ROSE
erythrina, tree of; genus ... DADAP
Esau, descendant of ...... EDOMITE
Esau, later name of ......... EDOM

escape .... ELOPE, EVADE, FLEE,
   INNER, JAYSTIC, SECRET,
   AVOID, LAM
escargot ...................... SNAIL
escarpment .......... SLOPE, STEEP
Escaut .................... SCHELDT
eschalot .................. SHALLOT
eschew ... ABSTAIN, AVOID, SHUN
escolar, the ................... PALU
escorted ......... GUARDED, PAID
escorts ATTENDS, BEAUX, USHERS,
              SEES
escrow ................. BOND, DEED
escuage .................. SCUTAGE
esculent .... COMESTIBLE, EDIBLE
escutcheon .......... ARMS, CREST
escutcheon, voided ............ ORLE
Esdras ................ APOCRYPHA
eskar-like ................... OSCAR
esker .......... EISCIR, OS, RIDGE
Eskimo ........ ALASKIAN, ALEUT,
        INNUIT, YUIT, ITA
  descent .......... TURANIAN
  dog ... HUSKY, MALEMUTE
  fur coat ............ TEMIAK
  garment ............. PARKA
  hood ................ AMOWT
  house ................ TOPEK
  knife .................... ULU
  male attire, per. to . LABRET
  memorial post ......... XAT
  of Asia ........ TUSKI, YUIT
  open-skin boat ...... UMIAK
  settlement ............ ETAH
  skin-covered canoe . BAIDAR,
              KAYAK
  skin house .......... TOPEK
  snow house .... IGLOO, IGLU
esodic ................... AFFERENT
esophagus ............ MERI, GULA
esoteric doctrine .......... CABALA,
             ABSTRUSE
esoteric knowledge ......... GNOSIS
espalier .................... TRELLIS
espionage ................ ESPY, SPY
esplanade LEVEL, WALKS, GLACIS,
              ROAD
esprit de corps ...... MORALE, WIT,
             SPIRIT
esquire SHIELDBEARER, ARMORER
ess ................ CURVE, SIGMOID
essay ................ CHRIA, TRIAL
essays of ..................... ELIA
essay, short ........ THESIS, TRACT
essence ........ ATTAR, GIST, ENS,
         MARROW, PITH
essential ...... METAL, INHERENT,
  GREAT, ENTRINSIC, MORTAL
essential ingredient of horny tissue ..
             KERATIN
establish .. FOUND, RADICATE, FIX
establishment, domestic .. MENAGE
estate .. ASSETS, MANOR, MISTER
  BESTOW, CONFER, ENDOW, RANK
estate, per. to an PRESS, DEMESNE
estate which is absolute property of
  owner ..................... ALOD
esteem .... ADMIRE, ADORE, AIM,
   HONOR, PRIDE, VALUE

ester, an ...... TROPATE, SILICATE, STEARIN
Esther's husband .......... XERXES
estimate AIM, AUDIT, METE, RANK, RATE, ADJUDGE, MEASURE
estivate .................... SUMMER
Estonian island ................. OESEL
Estonian meas. ................... LIIN
Estonian ox-cart .............. KULAK
Estonia's capital; anc. ........ REVAL
estrange .. ALIENATE, WEAN, PART
estray .......................... WAIF
estuary ......... BAY, FIRTH, FRITH
estuary of Amazon .............. PARA
esurient .......... GREEDY, HUNGRY
et al ......... ELSEWHERE, OTHERS
Etanin .................... DRACONIS
etch .......... BITE, CUT, CORRODE, AFTERMATH, ENGRAVE
eternal .......... AGELESS, EONIAN
eternity ... AEON, EON, TIME, OLAM
Eternity; Lat. .................. AEVO
etesian ..... PERIODICAL, ANNUAL, SEASONAL
etheostomoid ................. DARTER
ether ................ AIR, SKY, SPACE
ether compound ..... ANISOL, ESTER
ethereal fluid .......... AERY, ICHOR
ether-making residue ..... ETHERIN
ethical .. VIRTUOUS, MORAL, RIGHT
Ethiopia, anc. capital of ...... MEROE
Ethiopia, queen of ......... CANDACE
Ethiopia, southern ........... MEROE
Ethiopia, title of ex-ruler ..... NEGUS
Ethiopian ape ............... GELADA
    "    banana ............ ENSETE
    "    battleground ....... APOWA
    "    breed of cattle ....... SANGA
    "    city .............. NAPATA
    "    coins .............. TALARI
    "    dialect ............... GEEZ
    "    ibex ............... WALIE
    "    king ..... NEGUS, MEMNON
    "    lake ............... TSANA
    "    native ...... DOKO, NEGRO
    "    prince ................. RAS
    "    river ................... OMO
ethyl cyanide ......... PROPIONITRIL
ethyl derivative .. ALCOHOL, ETHER
ethyl hydride ................. ETHANE
ethyl oxide ..................... ETHER
ethyl, symbol of .................. ETH
Etonian holiday .................. VAC
Etruscan title ..................... LAR
ettle ........ AIM, INTENT, SUPPOSE
etui ................... CASE, TROUSSE
etymon ...... RADICAL, RADIX, ROOT
Etzel ......................... ATTILA
eucalypt; Austral. .... MALLEE, YATE
eucharist box ................. PIX, PYX
eucharist vessel PATEN, AMA, AMULA
eucharistic plate ............. PATINA
eucharistic wine .............. KRAMA
euchite ..................... SATANIST
Euclid's origin .............. MEGARA
eugenic aid .................. EUGENOL
Eugubium, Ital. ................ GUBBIO
eulachon ............... CANDLEFISH

eulogistic ........................ ELOGE
eulogize ...... EXTOL, LAUD, BOOST
eulogy .... ENCOMIUM, PANEGYRIC
euphonium ...................... TUBA
euphony ......... MELODY, METER
Euphrates tributary ......... TIGRIS
Eurasia, region in ............. TATARY
Eurasian range ............... URAL(S)
eureka ........... AHA, TRIUMPH
Euripides drama hero ............. ION
Euripides; play by ............ HELENA
euripus ............... FLOW, STRAIT
Europe and Africa ......... EURAFRIC
Europe and Asia EURASIAN, SCYTHIA
Europe, as a field of operation .... ETO
European LAPP, DANE, FINN, LETT, SLAV
    "    battlefield ............ MARNE
    "    blackbird ............. MERLE
    "    burbots ................ LOTE
    "    coal basin ............. SAAR
    "    dormouse ............... LOIR
    "    fresh water fish .... BARBEL, RUDD
    "    ground squirrel SISEL, SUSLIK
    "    health resort .......... BADEN
    "    hunting dog ....... GRIFFON
    "    kite ................... GLEDE
    "    linden ................. TEIL
    "    people, a .............. BALTS
    "    plover ........... DOTTEREL
    "    pole cat .............. FERRET
    "    porgy ................. PARGO
    "    province; anc. ......... DACIA
    "    race, member of ... SLOVENE
    "    river .................... ISAR
    "    root, ash ............... SORB
    "    shad .................. ALOSE
    "    shad; var. ............. ALLIS
    "    shrew ................... ERD
    "    shallow ........... MARTLET
    "    tree ........... TEREBINTH
    "    water crowfoot ... EELWARE
eutectic .................... FUSIBILITY
Eurytus' daughter ............... IOLE
evade BILK, SHIRK, ILLUDE, SHUNT, AVOID
evaded ............ GEED, EXEMPTED
evaluate ..... APPRAISE, ESTIMATE, RATE, ASSESS
evanesce ............... FADE, VANISH
Evans, Mary Ann, pen name ... ELIOT
evaporate, to .......... DRY, EXHALE
eve ............. DAMPEN, WET, IVA
even ....... EQUABLE, PLANE, TIED, LEVEL
evened .................... SMOOTHED
even if ......... THO, SPITE, THOUGH
evening ....... SOIREE, DEN, SHADES
evening; Ger. .................. ABEND
evening; Heb. ................... EREB
evening star .... HESPER, MERCURY, VENUS, MOON, PLANET
eventide . VESPER, DUSK, TWILIGHT
eventually ...... CASE, LASTLY, YET
eventuate ............ RESULT, TURN
ever .............. EER, ONCE, ANON
Everest Mtn. peak ............ LHOTSE

85

evergreen ........ BARETTA, SPRUCE,
   ABELMOSK, TARATA, PINE
evergreen, cedar-like ........ DEODAR
evergreen shrub .. OLEANDER, SAVIN
evergreens OLAX, TARAIRE, CAROB,
                         TOYON
everlasting .... AGELONG, ETERNAL,
                     ETERNE
everted (Med.) ................ ECTOPIC
every .......... EACH, ILK, ANY, RUN
everything ......... ALL, TOTAL, SUM
evict EJECT, EXPEL, OUST, REMOVE
evidence ........ PROBATE, DEPONE
evil child   IMP, DEEV, NIS, NIX(IE)
evil deed SIN, HARM, HURT, INJURE
" doer ........ CHEAT, MISCREANT
" omen ...................... KNELL
" , per. to ......... BELIAL, DEVIL
" spirit ..... BUGAN, CACODEMON,
                     TROW
" spirit, a chief ........... AMAIMON
" spirit; Heb. myth. .... ASMODEUS
" spirit; Iroquois ................. OKI
" spirit of blame; Gr. ........ MOMUS
" spirit supposed to prey on corpses ..
                    GHOUL
evils .............. ILLS, MALA, ERRS
evoke .......... EDUCE, CALL, VOICE
evolute ........................ UNROLL
evolution, doctrine of ....... BIOGENY,
                   COSMISM
evolve ............ DEDUCE, UNFOLD
ewe ................... KEB, THEAVE
ewe, old ....................... CRONE
ewer ......... SUBLIME, CROCK, URN
exact .... LITERAL, ESTREAT, JUST,
              MINUTE, STRICT
ex libris; Lat. ............ BOOKPLATE
exaggerated .. OUTRE, EXCEPTIONAL
exalt .............. ELEVATE, EXTOL
exalted ............. ELATED, SHEEN
examine . TRY, APPOSE, LAIT, PORE,
        TEST, PERUSE, EXPLORE
examiner ..... REGARDER, CONNER,
                  CENSOR
example .. PINK, BYSEN, PARADIGM,
                     SUM
exam taker .................... TESTEE
exanimo; Lat. ............. SINCERELY
exasperate ......... GALL, INCENSE,
                 ENRAGE
excavate .................. DIG, SCOOP
excavated .. CAVED, EXHUMED, DUG
excavation ...... MINE, MUCK, PIT
excavation for ore ............. STOPE
excavation, surface ........ OPENCAST
exceedingly ............ VERY, MANY
excel .......... BEST, DING, PRECEL
excellence DESERT, MERIT, PROBITY
excellent .... ATHEL, BRAVO, AONE
excelse ... ........ EMINENT, LOFTY
except ... BESIDES, BUT, BAR, SAVE
exception, take ..... DEMUR, DOUBT,
         QUALIFY, RESENT
excerpt .............. CHOICE, SCRAP
excess .... SURPLUS, NIMIETY, TOO,
              OVER, PLUS
excessive ......... EXTREME, UNDUE
excessive development of twigs . PLICA

excessively .. ENORM, TOO, UNDULY
exchange .... BANDY, BOURSE, RAP,
                    SWAP
exchequer ......................... FISC
excise ........... TOLL, TAX, IMPOST
excite ... BESTIR, AGITATE, ELATE,
                    ROIL
excited .. AROUSED, AGOG, BLEEZY,
                  HOOPLA
exclaimed .......... CRIED, SHOUTED
exclamation . AH, AHA, AHEM, ALAS,
    BAH, EGAD, FIE, HIP, OHO,
    OW, PAH, PHEW, PHO, TUT,
    HAH, HEY, EVOE, YAH
exclamation; col. .......... ....... DRAT
exclamation pledging a toast .. SKOAL
exclude .......... EJECT, OMIT, BAR
exclusively ......... LIMITED, ALONE
excommunicate ........... UNCHURCH
excoriate ...... ABRADE, GALL, FLAY
excrescence BOSS, STUD, LUMP, KNOB
excursion .. JAUNT, TOUR, OUTLOPE,
        SALLY, CIRCUIT, TREK
excuse .. ALIBI, CONDONE, PRETEXT
excuse for non-appearance ...... PLEA,
                 ESSOIN
excuse of sickness ............. AEGER
execrate DETEST, ABOMINATE, HATE
execute .. HANG, SPEED, ACT, VEST
exegete .......... ADVISER, LEADER
exemplar ......... MODEL, PATTERN
exempt . .. IMMUNE, EXPERT, FREE,
         APART, REMOVED
exempt, an; Eng. ................ EXON
exemption ..................... ESSOIN
exequies .. FUNERAL, DIRGE, WAKE
exercise ........... PRAXIS, URE, USE
Exeter, per. to .................... EXON
exfoliation .................... SCALING
exhalation .... STEAM, AURA, FUME,
                  REEK
exhaust .... JADE, EMIT, FAG, MATE,
        SAP, DRAIN, DEPLETE
exhausted . TIRED, PETERED, DONE,
                 SPENT
exhibit STAGE, SHOW, AIR, EVINCE,
                 STATE
exhibiting ................. OSTENSIVE
exhibition rm. .......... PANOPTICON
exhilarate BUOY, ELATE, TITILLATE
exhilaration ............. JOYOUS, GAY
exhilaration, exclamation of .... EVOE
exhort .............. PREACH, URGE
exhume .......... DELVE, DISINTER
exigency .. ESSENTIAL, NEED, URGE,
                PRESSURE
exiguous ............ SMALL, STERILE
exile BANISH, DEPORT, EXPATRIATE
exist ......... ALIVE, AM, ARE, BE, IS
existence; Lat. ................. ESSE
existent, an ................. ENTITY
exit ....... EGRESS, ISSUE, OUTLET
exodus .... GOING, HEGIRA, FLIGHT
exonerate ACQUIT, CLEAR, RELEASE
exorcism ......... EXPULSION, SPELL
exordium ........ PROEM, OVERTURE
exotic ALIEN, FOREIGN, PEREGRINE
expand ...... SPLAY, DILATE, FLAN,
                 RETCH

expand to form pods ............... KID
expanding bullet .............. DUMDUM
expanse ....... SEA, OCEAN, REACH,
                      SPREAD, STRETCH
expatiate ...... ENLARGE, DESCANT
expect .......... DEEM, WAIT, HOPE
expecting ......................... ATIP
expedient; Fr. ............. RESSORT
expedient, temp. ............. STOPGAP
expedite .......... EASY, HIE, SPEED
expedition CRUSADE, DRAVE, SAFARI
expel ..... EXILE, EJECT, EXTRUDE,
            OUTRAY, SPURT, VOID
experiment PROOF, TEST, TRIAL, TRY
experimental trial ......... OVERRULE
expert ACE, ADROIT, GAIN, ADEPT,
                              MASTER
expiate ..... ATONE, PURGE, SHRIVE
expiation ................... PIACULAR
expire .. DIE, ELAPSE, PERISH, END
explain ......... SPEED, CLEAR, WISE
explanation, marginal notes . SCHOLIA
explanation of a passage ... EXEGESIS
explanatory inscrip. .......... TITULUS
expletive ..... THERE, OATH, CURSE,
                              VOILA
explode .... POP, DETONATE, BURST
exploding meteor ............... BOLIDE
exploding sun .................... NOVA
exploit .. ACT, BLEED, MILK, FEAT,
      GEST(E), DARE, DEED, HEROISM
explorer ... ERIC, RAE, BYRD, GAMA,
                                 OSA
explorer's hiding place for supplies .....
                              CACHET
explosion ... OUTBURST, POP, BLAST
explosive .......... AMATOL, CERIA,
      DYNAMITE, MINE, ROMITE,
                                 TNT
   "       , high . CORDITE, POWDER,
                              TONITE
   "       isometric mineral . THORITE
   "       , per. to an ............ FUSE
   "       picric acid ......... LYDDITE
   "       produced by lightning .........
                           FULGURITE
explosive sound ........ CHUG, PLUFF
exponent ... INDEX, NOTE, SYMPTON
expose ... BARE, PROPINE, UNMASK
exposed to donger ...... PERICLITATE
expository .......... EXEGETIC, ORAL
expressing desire .... WOULD, FANCY
expression ....... LOCUTION, ASPECT
expunge ... DELE, DELETE, EFFACE,
                              ERASE
expurgate .. CENSOR, PURGE, BATHE
exquisite .......... DELICATE, RARE
exscind ... EXCISE, EXTIRPATE, CUT
exsiccate ......... DRY, ARID, PARCH
extend ........ EKE, JUT, PROTRACT,
                        RENEW, SPAN
extent .............. DITTO, SEIZURE
exterior .......... ECTAL, EXTRINSIC
exterior, toward the .......... ECTAD
external .......... OUTER, CORTICAL
external world ............... NONEGO

extinct flying reptile ..... PTEROSAUR
extirpate ........ DELE, ROOT, STUB
extol GLORY, KUDOS, PRAISE, LAUD
extort .. WRING, COMPEL, EXTRACT
extortioner .. BLACKMAILER, HARPY
extract ...... CITE, ELICIT, ESTREAT
extract forcibly .............. EVULSE
extract from a book ........ PERICOPE
extract, S. Am. balsam ..... TOLUENE
extraction LINEAGE, ORIGIN, BIRTH
extraneous .......... EXOTIC, OUTER
extraordinary ..... UNCO, BIG, GREAT
extravagant; Fr. .. BAROQUE, OUTRE
extreme ..... RADICAL, LAST, SORE,
                        ULTRA, END
extremely ................ VERY, MANY
extremities ................ POLES, TIPS
exudation ....... SUDOR, EMANATION
exude .... EMIT, FLOW, OOZE, REEK
exultant ......... OVANT, SANGUINE
exults ..... CROWS, ELATES, LEAPS,
                              PRIDES
eye OPTIC, ORB, EE, OGLE, SEE, UTA
  "    , a black ........ SHINER, MOUSE,
                           HYPOPYON
  "    , cavity of the .............. ORBIT
  "    , colored portion of ............ IRIS
  "    disease ................. GLAUCOMA
  "    doctor, noted Am. ........ PERERA
  "    dropper ................. PIPETTE
  "    flap ... VISOR, BLINKER, PATCH,
                           BLINDER
eye, Gaelic for .................. EEN
  "    , German for ................ AUGE
  "    glass LORGNON, MONOCLE, LENS
  "    , inner coat of ........... RETINA
  "    magic ...................... RADAR
  "    , opening in the ........... PUPIL
  "    , part of IRIDE, STRALE, UVEA
  "    , per. to the ................ IRIAN
  "    shield ...................... PATCH
  "    , slang for ................... GLIM
  "    strings ................... TENDONS
  "    thread worm .................. LOA
eyeball ....................... GLENE
eyeball, anterior portion of . CORNEA
eyebrow ...... SUPERCILIUM, BREE
eyelash dye ................. MASCARA
eyelashes ....................... CILIA
eyelet ....... GROMMET, CRINGLE
eyelid darkener ................. KOHL
eyelid, incision of ....... TARSOTOMY
eyelid, paralytic droop of upper PTOSIS
eyelid, per. to the ...... PALPEBRAL
  " -like .... OCELLATED, OCELLUS
eyes, close the .................. SEEL
eyes, films in the ........... NEBULAE
eyes, furnished with ....... OCULATE
eyes of beans .................... HILA
eyesore .......... BLEMISH, DEFECT
eyewash .... EXCUSE, APPLESAUCE
eyewater ...... COLLYRIUM, BORIC
                           (ACID)
eyot .............................. AIT
eyrie ............................. NEST
Ezrahite ...................... HEMAN

# F

F, letter ........................... EF
F.D.R.'s mother ................ SARA
Fabian policy .... INERTIA, LEEWAY
fable ..... LEGEND, LIE, APOLOGUE
fable; poet. .................... MYTH
fable writer ................... AESOP
fabled being .................. TROLL
fables, teller of ......... PARABOLIST
Fabray, Miss ............... NANETTE
fabric .... FELT, WEB, ATLAS, RAS, FAILLE, LANSDOWNE
   " , coarse .. CRASH, MAT, CADIS, PUTTO, RATINE
   " , cotton and worsted ............ PARAMATTA
   " , crinkled ...... CREPE, CRAPE
   " design with wax coating BATIK
   " , figured ............... MOREEN
   " , heavy ..... BROCADE, DENIM
   " , hempen ............. BURLAP
   " , lace ................. ALLOVER
   " , light worsted ....... ETAMINE
   " , linen ................... SCRIM
   " , Moorish; anc. .......... TIRAZ
   " , of waste fabrics ..... MUNGO
   " , printed .. PERCALE CHALLIS
   " , ribbed ........... REP, TWILL
   " shiny ................. SATEEN
   " , silk . ALCAHA, SURAH, GROS
   " , silk and gold .. ACCA, SAMITE
   " , striped ............. GALATEA
   " , textile ............. DELAINE
   " , velvet-like ... TERRY, PANNE
   " , watered silk .......... MOIRE
   " , woolen .. PRUNELLA, BEIGE, TABINET
fabric, woven silk TRICOT, SARSENET, PIQUET
fabricate ....... MAKE, COIN, MINT, SCHEME, FALSIFY
fabrication . ROMANCE, LIE, TISSUE, WEB, COGGERY, DECEIT, GUILE
fabricator ...... FORGER, INVENTER
fabrico, method of ornamenting ...... FAGOTING
fabrics, dealer in ............ MERCER
fabulist ............ AESOP, FABLER
fabulous animal ......... ROSMARINE, UNICORN, BASALISK
fabulous being ............. CENTAUR
fabulous serpent ........... BASILISK
facade; arch. .. FRONT, REAR, FACIA
face ... MEET, ANSWER, GRIMACE, MOUE, SNOOT
face downward .......... LIE, PRONE, OUTSTARE
face guard ................... BEAVER
face with masonry ... BATCH, REVET
facer ........ POSER, SOCKDOLOGER
faces with twelve planes .............. DODECAHEDRAL
facet ........ BEZEL, CULET, FACE
facetious . COMICAL, DROLL, WITTY
facile ...... EASY, PLIABLE, READY
facilitate ...... FURTHER, QUICKEN

facility ......... ART, MEANS, EASE
facing direction of glacier cones STOSS
facsimile .. COPY, MATCH, REPLICA
fact .. FIAT, DATUM, DEED, FEAT, TRUTH, KEYNOTE
fact, state as a ................. POSIT
faction . BLOC, CABAL, JUNTO, SIDE
factious . TURBULENT, DEMAGOGIC
factitious ....... ARTIFICIAL, MADE
——facto ......................... IPSO
factor ..... AGENT, BROKER, GENE
factotum ......... SERVANT, AGENT
faculties ..... TALENTS, COGNITION
faddish ................. ISM, ISMAL
faddist ......... NEO, MONOMANIAC
fade ... DAVER, DOW, PETER, WILT
faded ... DIM, DULL, FAINT, PASSE
fadge .............. AGREE, FIT, SUIT
Fadiman; writer ............ CLIFTON
fading .................... FUGITIVE
fads ................. FONDLE, RAGE
"Faery Queen," char. in ... AMORET, ATE, UNA
"Faery Queen," witch in ... ACRASIA
Fafnir's brother ............... REGIN
Fafnir, slayer of; Norse myth. SIGURD
fag .. HACK, SLAVE, TIRE, DRUDGE
fag end ........................ RUCK
fail ..... PETER, DEFECT, EBB, PES
fail to follow suit .. RENIG, RENEGE
failing .... BLOT, FOIBLE, CADENT
failure ............. DUD, FOIL, LACK
faineant; Fr. .................. OTIOSE
faint .......... DIM, SWELT, SWOON
fainting ......... SYNCOPE, TALME
"Fair Maid of Brabant" .... ADELAIS
"Fair Maid of Kent" ......... JOANNA
fair, per. to a ............. NUNDINAL
fairies, queen of the ............. MAB
fairness ......... BEAUTY, CANDOR
fairy ELVE, ELFKIN, ELF, FAY, PERI, PIXY
   " , air ..................... SYLPH
   " fort .................. SHEE, LIS
   " ghost ................... SPRITE
   " king ................... OBERON
   " queen ......... TITANIA, UNA
   " shoemaker ...... LEPRECHAUN
   " spirit of death ....... BANSHEE
fairy story .. ALLEGORY, NARRATIVE
   " , tricky .................... PUCK
faith ........ BELIEF, CREED, TROTH
faithful FAST, LEAL, LIEGE, SWEER
faithful friend . ACHATES, OBEDIENT
fake; slang .......... CHEAT, TRICK
fakes of a cable ................ TIERS
fakir ..... MENDICANT, MONK, YOGI
falcon ........... SORAGE, KESTREL
   " , Arctic ................... GYR
   " , desert .............. LANNER
   " , English ............. HOBBY
   " , English epithet for ......... ... PEREGRINE
   " , European ............. SAKER
   " , male ................. TERCEL
   " , N. Amer. ............. ANATUM
   " of India ... LAGGAR, LUGGER, SHAHIN

" , rapacious; genus .. RAPTORES
" , rel. to the ......... ACCIPITER
" , ribbon to secure ........ JESS
" , small ...... BESRA, MERLIN
falconry, bait in .................. LURE
falconry, earliest recorders of ...........
MARTIAL, PLINY
falconry, implement used in .... HOOD
falconry, to recover in ........ REBATE
fall ........ DROP, PLOP, RUIN, SIN,
RELAPSE
Fall guy; slang ................. PATSY
fallacy .. IDOLUM, SOPHISM, ERROR
fallal .............. GEWGAW, FINERY
falling ......................... CADENT
falling sickness ........... EPILEPSY
false ... UNRELIABLE, TALE, LUKE,
PSEUDO, SHAM, SOPHISTRY
false form of thinking ........... IDOLA
false friend ........ TRAITOR, JUDAS
false hair ....... TETE, TOPEE, TOPI
false items .................... SPURIA
false, show to be ............. DEBUNK
false swearing .. SLANDER, PERJURY
false wing ...................... ALULA
falsehood CANARD, FLAM, LIE, TALE,
FRAUD, PERJURY
falsify .... FORGE, PERVERT, BELIE,
GARBLE, DISTORT
falter ..... TREMBLE, GLIR, WAVER
fame CRY, NOTE, PRICE, RENOWN,
GLORY, REPUTE
fame; colloq. .................... KUDOS
famed ........ EMINENT, NOTORIOUS
familiar saying .... SAW, ADAGE, MOT
family .... LINE, GENS, ILK, STIRPS,
TRIBE
family, famous Italian ........... ESTE
family name ................ SURNAME
family of plants ........... RANAL(ES)
family, per. to ... LINEAGE, NEPOTIC
famous . NAMED, NOTED, EMINENT,
CASTE, MERE
famous cardinal ............. NEWMAN
famous murderer ........ ARAM, CAIN
fan ........ COOL, FOMENT, WINNOW
"Fanfan the ——" ............. TULIP
fan form .......... ROOTER, PLICATE
fan-light .................... TRANSOM
fan, oriental swinging .. OGI, PUNKAH
fan, sticks of a .... .. BRIN, PANACHE
fanatic ...... BIGOT, LUNATIC, MAD,
ZEALOT, PHRENETIC
fanatical ....... ENERGUMEN, RABID
fancied ........ IMAGINED, WEENED,
IDEATED
fancy ... DREAM, FAD, BRAIN, IDEA,
MEGRIM
fandango ............. DANCE, BALL
fane ... TEMPLE, BASILICA, SHRINE
fanfare ..... CALL, SHOW, TANTARA
fanfaron .................. BRAGGERY
fang ... FALK, CLAW, TALON, TINE,
TUSK
fangle CUT, FASHION, STYLE, VOGUE
fanion; Fr. ................... BANNER
fanning device PUNKA(H), EJECTOR
fanon .. MANIPLE, PHANON, ORALE,
VANE

fantastic imitation ......... PARODY,
TRAVESTY
fantastic style .... OUTRE, BAROQUE,
ROCOCO
fantasy ...... FANCY, IDEA, IMAGINE
fantoccini ................... PUPPETS
fanwort ................. WATERLILY
fantod; slang ...... FUSS, PET, SULKS
far; comb. form ................. TELE
far East news service .. ANETA, TASS
far, prefix ......................... TEL
farceur ........ JOKER, WAG, CLOWN
farcical .......... ATELLAN, RIBALD
fare ........ FOOD, DIET, RATE, TRY,
INELUCTABLE, PAY
farewell . ADIOS, AVE, CONGE, VALE
farinaceous drink .............. PTISAN
farinaceous meal ........ SAGO, SALEP
farm ...... COTLAND, CROFT, MAINS
" complete .............. GRANGE
" fee ...................... MANOR
" out buildings .......... STEDING
" , Spanish ............. HACIENDA
" tenant ................... COTTER
farmer .... PLANTER, COCKY, RYOT
farmer, migratory; slang ........ OKIE
farmer; S. Afr. .................. BOER
farmhouse, a single; Eng. ... ONSTEAD
farming .. HUSBANDRY, FRUGALITY
farmstead ............... FARM, BYRE
farmyard; Eng. ............... BARTON
faro, combination of cards in . CATHOP
faro, form of .......... MONTE, STUSS
Faroe Is. colonizer ........... KAMBAN
" " duck ....... EIDER, PUFFIN
" " fish .................... CHARR
" " sheep ................... FAAR
" " whirlwind .................. OE
Faroe Islands ....... BORDO, OSTERO,
SANDO, STROMO, VAAG
farrow .......... DRAPE, LITTER, PIG
far-sighted person ....... PRESBYOPE
fascia ................. BAND, FILLET
fascicle ........... CLUSTER, BUNDLE
fascinating ..... SIREN, BEWITCHING
Fascist theory, founder of .... PARETO
fashion RAGE, CRAZE, MODE, VOGUE
fashion, rel. to . GUISE, TIMBER, TON
fashionable gathering ...... ALAMODE,
SALON
fashionable; Span. .......... OPUESTO
fast ........ APACE, CHEAP, ASLEEP
fasten ...... TACK, NAIL, LACE, PIN,
CHAIN, ROPE, THRAP, RIVET
fastener ...... PEG, CLAMP, HALTER
fastening, comb. form ......... DESMO
fastidious ......... CRITICAL, DAINTY
fastigiate ........... CONICAL, POINTER
fastness CELERITY, CITADEL, FORT
fat ...... OILY, ESTER, LIPA, OBESE,
SAIM, SUET, PINGUID
fat, animal ........ ADIPOSE, ADEPS,
GREASE
fat; comb. form ................ STEAT
fat, constituent of ........... STEARIN
fat, deriv. of . OLEO, SEBACIC, SEBIC
fat in butter ............ CAPRIN, OLEO
fat, liquid part of ...... ELAIN, OLEIN
fat of geese .................. AXUNGE

fat, swine ...................... LARD
fat, wool ............ SUINT, LANOLIN
fat-yielding tree of Afr. ......... SHEA
fate . DOOM, DESTINY, KISMET, LOT
fate who measures the thread of life ...
                    LACHESIS
fate; Buddhist ................. KARMA
fated .. DOOMED, FEY, FINAL, LAST
fates; myth. ..... ATROPOS, CLOTHO,
       MOIRA, DECUMA, MORTA,
       NONA, PARCA
fates, the three collec.; Gr. .... MOIRAI
fates, the three collec.; Rom. . PARCAE
father ABBA, ABU, AMA, DAD, PERE,
       SIRE, PAPA
   "  , a wise ............... MENTOR
   "  of Agamemnon ........ ATREUS
   "  of English learning ....... BEDE
"Father of Mankind" ......... IAPETUS
"Father of the Gods" .. AMEN, AMON
   "  , rel. to ..... PADRE, AGNATE
fatherless ...... ORBATE, PRIVATION
father's brother ................ EME
fathom .. DELVE, PROBE, TEST, TRY,
       PLUMMET, PLUMB, SOUND
fatigue ... WEARY, BORE, FAG, JADE
Fatima, descendant of ... SAYID, SEID
Fatima's step-brother ............. ALI
fatten ........... BATTEN, PINGUEFY
fatty acid ........... ADIPIC, VALERIC
fatty substance from wool of sheep .....
                 SUINT
fatty tumor .................... LIPOMA
fatuous .... IDIOTIC, INANE, VACANT
faucet ...... COCK, HORSE, PEG, TAP,
       ROBINET
faujasite ...................... ZEOLITE
fault CAVIL, CULPA, FOIBLE, LAPSE
fault, find .......... CARP, CENSURE
fault in mining .. HADE, LEAP, LODE
faultily ............ AMISS, WRONGLY
faultless ... IMPECCABLE, PERFECT,
       PARAGON, RIGHT
faun .................... SATYR, DEITY
Fauntleroy's mother ........ DEAREST
Faunus' son ...................... ACIS
faux pas ............ ERROR, MISSTEP
favor ......... GRACE, LETTER, ORE,
       RESEMBLE
favorite DEAR, MINION, NINGLE, PET
favoritism ................... NEPOTISM
fawn ............ CRINGE, BUCK, DOE
fawning ..... SERVILE, OBSEQUIOUS
fay .............. ELF, FAIRY, SPRITE
faze ............... DAUNT, DISTURB
feal .............. FAITHFUL, LOYAL
fealty .... HOMAGE, DUTY, RESPECT
fear ..... AWE, PHOBIA, UG, DREAD
   "  of being burned alive .............
       TAPHEPHOBIA
   "  of crossing road . DROMOPHOBIA
   "  of darkness ...... NYCTOPHOBIA
   "  of drafts .......... AEROPHOBIA
   "  of fire ............. PYROPHOBIA
   "  of lightning ...... TROPHOBIA
   "  of number 13 .....................
       TRIAKAIDEKAPHOBIA
   "  of open spaces ... AGORAPHOBIA
   "  of pain ............ ALGOPHOBIA

   "  of poisons .......... TOXIPHOBIA
   "  ; law .................... METUS
fearful . OVERAWED, CRAVEN, DIRE,
       PAVID
fearlessly ............... IMPAVIDLY
feast ...... JUNKET, PICNIC, REVEL
feast, funeral ................... ARVAL
Feast of Lots .................. PURIM
feast of St. Martin ..... MARTINMAS
feast, to ......... GRATIFY, REGALE
feat ....... STUNT, DEED, EXPLOIT
feather .... PENNA, PINNA, TONGUE
   "  , as an arrow ........ FLETCH
       FLEDGE
   "  , barb ...... HARL, PINNULA
   "  filament ................. DOWL
   "  , key ................... SPLINE
   "  , large strong .......... QUILL
   "  quill ................... REMEX
   "  , rel. to a .............. PINION
   "  , shaft of .............. SCAPE
   "  star; genus ....... ANTEDON
   "  to repair a ................. IMP
feathered, full PENNATED, FLEDGED,
       PLUMED
feathered keys ................... FINS
feathering ................... ENDYSIS
featherless ................. CALLOW
feathers ................. DOWN, SLEY
   "  , adorn with ...... IMPLUNE
   "  , adjust the ......... PLUME
   "  at base of bird's wing ALULA
   "  , quill ... AIGRET, COVERTS,
       PANACHE
   "  , short ................. CAPE
   "  , yellow .............. HULU
featly ............... FITLY, NEATLY
feature, principal ..... MOTIF, TRAIT
feaze ... UNRAVEL, UNTWIST
February 12-March 2 ....... RENTOSE
feculent ............ ROILY, TURBID
fee .... FIEF, HONORARIUM, BRIBE,
       TIP, RETAINER, WAGE
feeble . DOTTY, INFIRM, PUNY, LOT,
       TIP
feed or pasture cattle ......... AGIST
feeding, forced ............... GAVAGE
feel .... PALP, AIL, SENSE, SUFFER
feel fear ............................ UG
feeler ....... ANTENNA, TENTACLE,
       PALPUS
feelers ...................... PALPI
feeling, capable of ........ SENTIENT
feeling, show ................ EMOTE
fees from official patronage; col. . PAP
feet, combing two metric ..... DIPODY
feet, having ................. PEDATE
feet, number of ............ FOOTAGE
feet, per. to the ................ PODAL
feet, without ................. APOD
feign .. SHAM, ACT, MINT, GARBLE
feign sickness ............ MALINGER
feint .. PRETENSE, BLIND, FETCH
feint in fencing ............... APPEL
feist ............................ DOG
feldspar LEELITE, ALBITE, KAOLIN,
       ODINITE
felicitate ......... BLESS, MACARIZE

felicity ........... BLISS, HAPPINESS
feline JAGUAR, OUNCE, CAT, TIGER, TOM, MOUSER
fell ... BRUTAL, CRUEL, NOLP, CUT, FIERCE, PELT
fellow, a; Scot. .................... WAT
fellow; arch. .................. SIRRAH
fellow, base; Scot. ............. DRING
fellow, brutish ............... YAHOO
fellow, queer old .. MOONY, GEEZER
fellow, worthless ... SPALPEEN, CAD, LOSER
fellow, young .... YOUNKER, BLADE, CALLANT, CHAP
fellowship ................. SODALITY
felly .... CRAFTILY, FIERCELY, RIM
felon, a kind of WHITLOW, OUTCAST, BUM
felony .......... BURGLARY, CRIME
felt-like .................... PANNOSE
felwort ........ GENTIAN, MULLEIN
female ... GORGON, PEDANT, MORT
female figurine ................. ORANT
female fox .................... VIXEN
female of red deer ............. HIND
female warrior ............. AMAZON
feminine name ..... IRMA, ISA, NITA, SERENA
feminine suffix ................. ETTE
femme fatale ............... LORELEI
femur ..................... THIGH
fen .. MORASS, BOG, SUMP, SWAMP
fen water ...................... SUDS
fence ............. FAGIN, PALISADE
"   , interwoven ........... RADDLE
"   , movable .... STILE, GLANCE, HURDLE
"   , picket of a ............. PALE
"   ; slang ................. RASPER
"   , sunk ........... AHA, HAHA
"   , to .... SCRIME, SWORDPLAY
fencing breastplate ...... PLASTROM
"   , foot tap in .......... APPEL
"   , hit in ............... PUNTO
"   , parrying position in SECONDE
"   posture ........ CARTE, PEL, SEPTIME
"   , redoubling of an attack in .. REPRISE
"   stroke ........ BUTT, APPEL
"   sword .................. EPEE
"   sword, early Eng. .. SPATHOE
"   sword, modern ...... RAPIER, TUCKE
"   sword, small ............ FOIL
"   term ... QUARTE, RIPOSTE, TIERCE, PALING
"   thrust ...... FOIBLE, FORTE, PUNTO, REMISE
fend ....... AVERT, PARRY, WARD, SHIFT
fenestra, a .... FORAMEN, WINDOW
fennel . ANIS, AZOREAN, MAYWEED
fennel flowers; genus ....... NIGELLA
feral ...... DEADLY, WILD, FERINE
Ferdinand II, sobriquet given to BOMBA
fere ..... EQUAL, MATE, PEER, PAL
feretory ........... CHAPEL, SHRINE

ferment . SEETHE, YEAST, LEAVEN, BARM, FRET, BREW
ferment, active principle of a ENZYME
fermenting, stop from .. STUM, MUST
fern .. NARDOO, BRAKE, BRACKEN, TARA
"   , flowering ............. OSMUND
"   ; genus ...... TODEA, ANEMIA, POLYPODY
"   leaf ...................... FROND
"   , owl ................. NIGHTJAR
"   patches ..................... SORI
"   seeds ................... SPORES
fern-like plant . PETROID, ACROGEN
ferocious .... CRUEL, FELL, FERAL, TRUCULENT
ferret, female ..................... JILL
ferret, male ....................... HOB
ferric oxide powder ............. ROUGE
ferrotype ..................... TINTYPE
ferry ..... PONT, TRAJECT, WHERRY
fertilizer ... COMPOST, GUANO, MARL
fertilizer for cereals ........... ALINIT
ferule ......... FENNEL, ROD, RULER
fervid ........ FIERY, HOT, EXCITED
fervor ........... ARDOR, ZEAL, LOVE
fester ........... ABSCESS, RANKLE
festival FEIS, BEE, ALE, EED, FEAST, FETE, GALA
festival ball; Fr. ................... BAL
festival day, last .......... APODOSIS
festival in Holland ............. KERMIS
festival of Apollo ............... DELIA
festival procession; It. ......... CORSO
festivity ................... JOY, REVEL
festoon ....... GARLAND, SWAG, LAI
fetch .... CHEAT, RETRIEVE, BRING
fetial ...................... HERALDIC
fetich .............. IDOL, OBI, TOTEM
fetid ......... NOISOME, OLID, FUSTY
fetish ...... JUJU, MASCOT, AVATAR
fetter CHAIN, HOPPLE, BOND, GYVE
fetter, to unite .. SHACKLE, THRALL
feud ... QUARREL, FIEF, VENDETTA
feudal; Fr. ........................ FEOD
"   jurisdiction FEOFF, SOC, SOKE
"   , opposed to ....... ALLODIAL
"   service, per. to ........ BANAL
"   tax ...... TALLAGE, TAILAGE
"   tenant ............... SOCAGER
"   tenant; anc. ............ LEUDE
"   tenant's payment .......... TAC
"   tribute ................ HERIOT
fever ......... AGUE, ARDOR, ENECIA
fever, affected with ......... PYRETIC
fever, intermittent .......... QUARTAN
fever, kind of .. ELODES, OCTAN, TAP
fever reducer ....... DEFERVESCENT
fever spots ................ PETECHIAE
fever, tropical ................ DENGUE
feverish ......... FEBRILE, EXCITED
few; Span. ........................ POCOS
fey ............ DYING, SPELL, TIMID
fez .. CAP, TURBAN, BERET, BUSBY, CAFTAN, SHAKO, TARBOOSH
flat SANCTION, EDICT, ACT, ORDER
fiber cordage ............ HEMP, ERUC
"   , kind of ....... FILASSE, SISAL
"   knots in cotton ............. NEP

" of century plant ..... CLUSTERS, PITA
" of E. Ind. plant ......... RAMIE
" of wool ................... PILE
" palm .......... AGAVE, RAFFIA
" plant . ROSSELE, PITA, RAMEE
" plant, E. Ind. ......... AMBARRY
" , Tampico ................ ISTLE
" wood ............ ARALAC, BAST
" wool ..... KEMP, STAPLE, NEP
fibril .............. HAIRS, FILAMENT
fibroin ...................... COBWEB
fibroin, decomposed ......... ALANINE
fibula ....... BROOCH, CLASP, OUCH
fickle .... VEER, VOLATILE, ERRATIC
fickle girl ....... JILT, DECOY, FRAUD
fico ............... SNAP, FIG, TRIFLE
fictile ............ MOLDED, PLASTIC
fictitious .. FALSE, POETIC, CHIMERA
fictive ................. IMAGINARY
fiddle VIOLIN, CROWD, KIT, SCRAPE
fiddler, unskilled ...... TWEEDLEDEE
fidelity ................. HOLD, TROTH
fidelity; symb. ................ TOPAZ
fidget, slang ....... FANTOD, FUSSER
fidgety ........ DYSPHORIA, RESTIVE
field ...... ACRE, GLEBE, LEA, GRID
" ; Biblical .......... ANER, AGER
" duck ................... BUSTARD
" , extensive .......... SAVANNA(H)
" glass .... BINOCLE, TELESCOPE
" , inclosed ...... AGER, CROFT
" madder, deriv. of ...... RUBIACIN
" mouse; Amer. ............... VOLE
" of work ................. METIER
" , per. to a level .... CAMPESTRAL
" , stubble ................ ROWEN
"Field of Blood" ......... ACELDAMA
fields, of the ................... AGRAL
fiend; Shak. ............... AMAIMON
fiendish ......... AVERNAL, FENDEN
fiery      METTLESOME, ARDENT, ANGRY, HOT, IGNEOUS
fiery cross ................. CRANTARA
fiesta .......... FESTIVAL, HOLIDAY
fife .... FLUTE, ARRAY, BIT, TRIFLE
fig basket .............. CABAS, SERON
" , Italian for ................. FICO
" , kind of dried .......... CARICA
" , not to care a ...... FILLIP, SNAP
" , Smyrna ................ ELEME
fight .... BATTLE, MELEE, BARNEY, ROW, STRIFE, WARFARE
fight, desire to ...... ANIMUS, ENIMIE
"Fighting Bob"; USA .......... EVANS
fig-like ....... CARICOUS, SYCONIUM
figs, bales of ................. SEROON
figs, one cured by; Bib. .... HEZEKIAH
figuration ..... TROPICAL, ADORNING
figure SYMBOL, BOSH, DIGIT, DOLL, FORM, TYPE, ENTAIL
" , arch. .. CARYATID, TELAMON
" , equal angled ISAGON, ISOGEN
" of speech .......... ECPHONESIS, LITOTES, (EPI) TROPE
" of the earth .............. GEOID
" , pagan .................. IMAGE
" , part of human .. BUST, TORSO, TRUNK

" , to cut a; slang ........ DASH
figured; Fr. ................. FACONNE
figurine ..... TANAGRA, STATUETTE
figwort ....... MULLEIN, FOXGLOVE
Fiji Islands ........................ VITI
" " , capital of ......... SUVA
" " feudal service tenure LALA
" " group ............. LAU, RA
" " , some of the. KORO, ONO
filament ...... STRAND, DOWL, HAIR, HARL
filbert ...................... HAZEL
filch ...... NIM, ROB, PILFER, STEAL
file .............. ENTER, RAPE, ROW
" , a flat .................. QUANNET
" , comb makers ............ CARLET
" finisher ................... ENDER
" fish ................. TRIGGERFISH
" , half round ................. GRAIL
" of six soldiers ................. ROT
" , rough ..................... RASP
filibeg ................... KILT, SKIRT
filigree ............. FILIGRANA, LACE
filing ..................... LIMATURE
Filipino ............. ..... TAGAL, ATTA
" food staple ............... TARO
" governor general .......... IDE
" knife .................... BOLO
" native .................... MORO
" native language .... TAGALOG
Filipino, one of tribe ............... ATA
" peasant ........... LAO, TAO
" soldier ............. LADRONE
fill .... CHOKE, THILL, PAD, STUFF
fillet ............ IRLO, SOLA, RIBBON
fillet at bottom of frieze ..... REGULA, TAEINA
fillet for the hair ....... SNOOD, BAND
fillet, jeweled ......... DIADEM, TIARA
fillet, narrow . ANADEM, ORLE, STRIA
fillip .............. EXCITE, STIMULUS
filly ...... COLT, FOAL, GIRL, MARE
film, green ................. PATINATE
film, thin ............ BRAT, PELLICLE
fils; Fr. ............................ SON
filter PERCOLATE, COLATURE, OOZE, RAPE, CLEAN
filth . SQUALOR, FEN, MUCK, LUCRE
fimbriate .... HEM, FRINGED, HAIRY
fin-footed animal .......... PINNIPED
fin, spinous ................. ACANTHA
fin, under ................... VENTRAL
final . DERNIER, BEALL, END, TELIC
finale .... CODA, END, COMPLETION, SWAN SONG
finances PURSE, ACCOUNTS, FUNDS
finch SPINK, FRINGILLA, REDPOOL, SISKIN
" , Amer. ..... CHEWINK, JUNCO, TOWHEE
" , canary-like .............. SERIN
" , copper ............ CHAFFINX
" falcon; E. Ind. ......... HIERAX
" , gold ............ DRAWBIRD
" grass; genus, Aus. ... POEPHILA
" , house; Amer. LINNET, BURION
" , N. Afr. ................. MORO
" , yellow; Eur. ... SERIN, TARIN
finch-like bird ... TANAGER, CANARY

92

find faults ....... BEEF, CARP, MOTE
find out DETECT, SOLVE, UNRIDDLE
finding, a .............. SERENDIPITY
fine ......... LEGER, AMERCE, SCOT
" for a misdemeanor ....... MULCT
" , India ................... ABWAB
" , in law ............ AMAND, CRO
" line of a letter .............. SERIF
" muslin or silk ............. SHELA
" wool for shawls . PASHM, PUSHM
finery ......... GEEGAWS, GAUD(Y),
FRIPPERY
fine-spun ......... HAIR, VISIONARY
fingan stand ..................... ZARF
finger ................. DACTYL, DIGIT
" , fore                    INDEX
" , little ......... AURICULARIS,
MINIMUS, PINKIE
" , middle ............... MEDIUS
" , per. to .. ANNULAR, DIGITAL
" , ring ............ ANNULARIS
" stall ....................... COT
fingerling .......................... PARR
fingernail, mark at base of ... LUNULE
fingerprint mark ... LUNULE, WHORL
finial ........................ EPI, TEE
finical ..... PRUDISH, NICE, SPRUCE,
FASTIDIOUS, FUSSY
finish .... ELABORATE, CHARE, END
finished ........... FINE, OVER, RIPE
fink .......... SPY, STRIKEBREAKER
Finnish ambassador ..     PROCOPE
Finnish coinage ..... MARKKA, PENNI
" dialect ................ KAREL
" government ............... ABO
" harp ................ KANTELE
" island ................... SKAR
Finnish lake ................ ENARA
" poem ................... RUNE
" seaport ......... ABO, TURKU
finnikin ...................... PIGEON
finnimbrun ...................... TRIFLE
Finno-Ugric language, per. to URALIAN
Finns ................... SUOMI, VOD
fire KINDLE, IGNIS, FLAME, IGNITE
" , artillery ,.......... BARRAGE
" back .................... REREDOS
" basket ........ CRESSET, GRATE
" clay .................... TASKOS
" cracker ................. PETARD
" damp .......... METHANE, GAS
" drill ...................... CHARK
" , having power over IGNIPOTENT
" , miss ...................... SNAP
" opal ................. GIRASOLE
" worshipper . PARSI, PYROLATER
firearm; sl. ...................... GAT
firecrackers, box for ....... MARROON
fireman ............. STOKER, VAMP
fireplace; Scot. ................ INGLE
fireplace ledge ......... HOB, SHELF
fireplace; Span. ............... FOGON
fireworks .. GIRANDOLE, SERPENTS,
RIPRAP
fireworks, hissing .... GERB, FIZGIGS
firmament .. HEAVEN, SKY, VAULT
firmly set ........ PLANT, ROOTED
firmness, want of .. LAXITY, LOOSE
firn ............... ICE, SNOW, NEVE

firs, the ....................... ABIES
first .. NIEVE, PRIMUS, CHIEF, NEW,
MAIDEN
" born ..................... HEIR
" brass coin; Rom. ..... SESTERCE
" day of Roman month .. CALENDS
" globe circler ........ MAGELLAN
" installment EARNEST, HANDSEL
" letter of the Arabic alphabet ALIF
" mate ...................... EVE
" rate .. OK, OKAY, OKEH, SUPER
" year's revenue; Eccl. .... ANNAT
first third of an epic ........ INFERNO
first-year man at West Point ... PLEB
firth .......... FRITH, KYLE, ARM
fish, Amer. fresh water ..... DARTER
" , Amer. hyodon; genus MOONEYE
" , any of the teuthidae ..... SQUID
" , aquatic mammal .... MANATEE
" , Arctic ...................... BIB
" , bait ...................... KILLY
" , barracuda ...... SPET, SENNET
" bin for salting ........... KENCH
" , bivalve ................ SCALLOP
" , bleak ...................... BLAY
" , bonito ................ SKIPJACK
" , broken-bellied .......... THOKE
" , brook trout ...... CHAR, CHARR
" , burbot ......... EELPOT, LOTA
" , butter ................ GUNNEL
" , butterfly ................. BENNIE
" , carangoid .... CHAD, RUNNER,
SCAD
" , caribe ................... PIRAYA
" , carp family .. CHUB, IDE, RUD,
LOACH
" , cat, electric ............... RAAD
" , catch of ................ SHACK
" , cephaloptera ............. MANTA
" , chopped ................... CHUM
" , cigar ...................... SCAD
" , climbing ... ANABAS, SKIPPER
" , coal ...................... PARR
" , cobia ............... SERGEANT
fish, cod, the ..... BACALAO, TORSK
" , cod-like . CUSK, GADOID, LING
" condiment ............... PASTE
" , cow ................. MANATEE
" , crab and fiddler .......... UCA
" , Cuban ...... ESCOLAR, PALU
" , cuttle; genus ... SEPIA, SQUID
" , cyprinoid ... BARBEL, BREAM,
CHI, DACE, ID, IDE,
TENCH, UIT
" , devil ............. MANTA, RAY
" , dog ...... HOUND, SCYLLIUM
" , dolphin ........ COWFISH, INIA
" , E. Ind. .... ARCHER, DARTER,
DORAB, GOURAMI
" , edible .... COD, ID, HADDOCK,
LOACH, TAUTOG, TILE,
WEEVER, WRASSE
" , eel, bright colored OPAH, MORAY
" , eel, conger ............ ELVER
" , eel, marine ......... CONGER,
LAMPREY, LING
" , eel-like ........... APOD, LANT
" eggs ........................ ROE

" , elasmobranch ....... SAWFISH
" , Eur. BARREL, BOCES, DOREE, DORY, PICAREL, TENCH TIRU
" , Eur. food .. MAIGRE, MEAGRE
" , Eur. shad ............... ALOSE
" , Eur. spine ............. LYRIE
" , Eur. white LAVARET, MARENA
" (fabled) upholding world .... MAH
" female ..................... RAUN
" fence ...................... WEIR
" , flat ... DAB, TURBOT, SKATE, SOLE, PLAICE
" , flying ................. SAURY
" , flying; genus ..... EXOCOETUS
" , food ...... BAYA, CARP, CERO, GROOPER, HAKE, MEAGRE, MULLET, PLAICE, POMPANO, SARDINE, SCUP, SESELE, SHAD, TROUT, TUNA, SMELT
" , fresh water ANABAS, CRAPPIE, DURBOT, LOACH, DARTER, REDEYE
" , fresh water; genus ..... ESOX
" , frog ................... ANGLER
" , game ..... MARLIN, SALMON, SWORD, TARPON
" , ganoid, large .... GAR, DIPNOI, STURGEON
" ; genus . MOLA, PERCA, ELOPS
" ; genus, N. Am. ........... AMIA
" gig ...................... SPEAR
" , globe .................. DIODON
" , gobioid ................ LOTER
" , gobylike .......... DRAGONET
" , grampus .................. ORC
" , grouper, red .......... MERO
" , grunt ...... CROAKER, RONCO
" , half beak ................. IHI
" hawk ................... OSPREY
" , herring .... ALEWIFE, ALOSA, SPRAT
" , herring, barrel for ....... CADE
" , herring family .... PILCHARD
" , herring-like ANCHOVY, CISCO
" , herring measure ......... CRAN
fish, herring pond ............... OCEAN
" , herring, young ............ BRIT
" hook ............ GAFF, SPROAT
" , hound ................. GARFISH
" , imperfect ...... BARB, THOKE
" , Japanese ........... TAI, FUGU
" , jelly ....... MEDUSA, ACALEPH
" , jew ......... MERO, TARPON
" , kind of ..... ORFE, ORF, ROCK, THOSSE
" , king, ocean ...... BARB, OPAH
" ladder ...................... DAM
" , lake ................... LAKER
" , land traveling ........ ANABAS
" , largest fresh water . ARAPAIMA
" line, short ................. SNELL
" line, with series of hooks .. TROT
" , little ..... MINNOW, SARDINE, SMELT
" , mackerel, horse TONNY, TUNNY
" , mackerel-like .. BONITO, CERO, ESCOLAR

" , marine SCUP, BLENNY, CUSK, LING, GRUNT, CHOPA, MENHADEN, TARPUM
" , marine, of W. Indies .. ROBALO
" , maskanonge ............. LONGE
" , Medit. ............. ACO, SARGO
" , meter ............... INSPECTOR
" , milk .. ANGED, AWA, SABALO
" , mollusk, giant OCTOPUS, SQUID
" , mutton; Porto Rico ....... SAMA
" net ... SAGENE, SEINE, TRAWL
" net, bagging of a ........... BUNT
" net support ............... METER
" , New Zealand ............... IHI
" of the Nile ........ BICHIR, SAIDE
" , olive green BLENNY, SHANNY
" , ornamental ......... PARADISE
" , oyster ............... TAUTOG
" , parrot .... LANIA, LORO, SCAR
" , per. to certain ....... TELEOST
" , pen for .................. CRAWL
" , perch-like ............. DARTER
" , perch-like; genus ..... ANABAS
" , Philip. .............. LANGARAY
" , pike ........ DORE, GED, LUCE
" , pike-like ..... ARAPAIMA, GAR, LUCE, ROBALO
" , place for ............... WARREN
" pond ...................... BREAM
" , porgy ..................... SCUP
" , porgy; Jap. ................ TAI
" , pork ...................... SISI
" , Polynesian tagalog ....... ISDA
" , porpoise ..... DOLPHIN, INIA
" , poison; Jap. ............... FUGU
" , ray ... DOM, MANTA, SEPHEN, SKATE
" , red .......... CLEE, FATHEAD
" , redmouth ............. GRUNT
" , remora ................ PEGA
" -rice dish ............ KEDGEREE
" , river ascending ...... ANADROM
" , rock; Cal. ........ RENA, REINA
" , sail ..................... BOOHOO
" , sailor's choice ........... PORGY
" , salmon, adult ......... GILLING
" , salmon; Jap. ............. MASU
" , salmon, second year ..... SPROD
fish, salmon, young ... ALEVIN, PARR
" , salmonoid ..... POWAN, TROUT
" , salt water .... HAKE, TOMCOD, TUNA
" , sandshark ............ BONEDOG
" , sardine; Ind. ............ LILE
" sauce .... ALEC, ANCHOVY, SOY
" , scabbard .................. PARA
" scale ...................... GANOID
" , scallop ................. CRENA
" , sea ...................... TUNA
" , serranoid ............... LATES
" , shad; Eur. .............. ALOSE
" , shad-like ............ ALEWIFE
" , shark .............. MAKO, TOPE
" , shark family ........... ANGEL
" , shark's pilot .......... REMORA
" , sheat ...................... SOM
" , shell ..... ABALONE, LIMPET, SCALLOP
" , shiner ................... ROACH

94

" , shiny, enamel-like ..... GANOID
" , silvery; Samoan ........ SESELE
" , slender . SAURIES, GAR, SAURY
" , small loach ........... SMERLIN
" , smelt family ........ CAPELIN
" , snapper, black fin ......... SESI
" , soap .................... JABON
" , S. Amer. ...... ACARA, CARIBE
" , spade .................. PORGY
" , Spanish ................. RONCO
" , sparoid ... NAPA, PORGY, SAR,
                        TAI, SARGO
" spear .......................... GIG
" , spotted trout ........... MALMA
" , squirrel ............... MARIAN
" , sturgeon ............. STERLET
" , sub class of bony ... TELESOTE
" , sucking ............... REMORA
" , surf ................... ALFIONA
" , surgeon ................. TANG
" , synodontoid .............. TIRU
" , tarpon family; genus ... ELOPS
" , teleost ............ APODA, EEL
" , tench .................... TINCA
" , terrapins; genus EMYDEA, EMYS
" , threadfin ............. BARBUDO
" , to ............ ANGLE, TROLL
" , trap ...................... FYKE
" , toad ...................... SAPO
" tropical BARRACUDA, CHROMID,
        TYNOSA, PACO, ROBALO
" , tropical; genus ......... GERRES
" , trout family .. OQUASSA, CHAR
" upholding universe ......... MAH
" , voracious ..... CARIBE, SHARK
" , W. Indian ................... SESI
" , whale or sturgeon ...... BELUGA
" , whales, order of ......... CETE
" with gaff through ice ....... CHUG
" , whiting . LAVARET, GWYNIAD
" with spear-like snout ........ GAR
" , wolf ...................... LUPIN
" , young .... ALEVIN, FRY, PARR
fisher ......................... WEJACK
fisher, the PEKAN, (IZAAK) WALTON
fisher-like ................ WEASEL
fisherman, a kind of . EELER, SQUAM,
                        TOTY, SEINER
fish-hook .... ANGLE, BARB, SPROAT
fish-hook attached to snell ... GANGE
fish-hook, feathered ........ HACKLE
fish-hook leader .............. SNELL
fishing ... ... SNELLING, SPILLET
"     basket .... SLARTH, CREEL,
                        SLATH
"     bob ...................... BAB
"     fly .................... SEDGE
"     , living by ....... PISCATORY
"     , per. to ......... HALIEUTIC
"     smack .............. DOGGER
fish-like .. ............. ICHTHYIC
fish-line, part of ........ BOB, SNOOD
fishman ..................... MORMAN
fishpond ...................... PISCINA
fishwife ........................... FAG
fissle ............... HISS, WHISTLE
fissure .......... RIFT, RENT, CLEFT,
        RIMA, CHINK, LEAK, SLIT,
        CREVICE, CRACK, SPLIT

fist of hand .... NEIF, NIEVE, NEAF
fisticuffs ............. BOUT, COMBAT
fistula ...... CAVITY, SINUS, ULCER
fit .. APPOSITE, COMPETENT, DUE,
        ELIGIBLE, GEE, MEET, PAT
fit an arrow on the string ...... NOCK
fit or join closely FAY, GEAR, ADAPT
fitchew ..................... POLECAT
fitly ............ DULY, RIGHT, RITE
fitness .................. CONGRUITY
fitted ...... GIFTED, CLEVER, ABLE
fitted for digging ........... FODIENT
fitting APT, MEET, HEME, JUST, PAT
Fitzgerald, Miss ............... ELLA
five books of Moses .. PENTATEUCH
five finger ..................... OXLIP
five fold .................. QUINTUPLE
five lines of nonsense ..... LIMERICK
five of trumps at cinch ....... PEDRO
five per-cent of Earth's crust ... IRON
five year period . LUSTRUM, PENTAD
fix  AMEND, DILEMMA, POSED, SET
fixed time .. ERA, DATE, FAST, RUT
fjordlike passage ................. GAT
flaccid .................. LIMP, WEAK
flag . GONFALON, BUNTING, FLOOR,
                        SIGN, WEAK, FANE
" , flower ...................... IRIS
" , little . PENNANT, BANDEROLE
" , military ..... FANION, GUIDON
" , National ................. ENSIGN
" , Navy's swallow-tailed . BURGEE
" , pirate .................... ROGER
" , signal .................... CORNET
" , sweet ................. CALAMUS
" used by merchant vessels BURGEE
flagellant, 14th Cen. ............. ALBI
flageolet ...................... LARIGOD
flageolet; Hindu ............... BASAREE
flagon ...... JUG, EWER, DEMIJOHN,
        CANTEEN, CARAFE, STOUR
flagpole bracket ........ BRACCIALE
flagrant ARDENT, SCARLET, GREAT
flagstone ............... SHALE, SLAB
flail ............. SWINGLE, THRESH
flail, part of a ... CAPLING, SWIPLE
flair ...... TALENT, BRAINS, WITS
flake . CHIP, FLOC, LAMINA, SLATE
flaky ........... SQUAMOUS, SCALY
flambeau ......... CRESSET, TORCH
flame.... ARC, BEAM, LEYE, STEEM
flame, burst into ......... IGNESCENT
flamelet .................. FLAMMULE
flaneur ....... LOITERER, STROLLER
flannel, coarse ............... DOMETT
flap ......... LAPPET, BANGLE, TAB
flap, furnished with ........... LOBED
flap, membranous ................. LOMA
flap violently ..................... SLAT
flappera, a ................... SNICKET
flare ..... BLAZE, FLICKER, GLARE,
        FUSEE, FLECK, FLASH
flaring ............. BELLING, EVASE
flashing .... METEORIC, FLAUNTING
flashings .... COVER, FLOOR, METAL
flask .... CANTEEN, BETTY, CRUSE,
        OLPE, CARAFE, EWER, FLAGON
flask, glass .................. MATRASS

95

flask-shaped ............ LAGENIFORM
flat BANAL, PLANE, PRONE, STALE,
    LOW, SHOAL, SIMPLE, VAPID
" , a ........................... SUITE
" boat ........................... PUNT
" bodied ray ................ SKATE
" canopy ................... TESTER
" , in music ....... BEMOL, MOLLE
" part of wine ................ VAP
" roof ..................... TERROST
" surface AREA, PAGINA, TABULAR
flatiron ...................... SADIRON
flat-nosed ..................... SIMOUS
flattened at poles ............. OBLATE
flattened out ............. APPLANATE
flatter .... PALP, ADULATE, BLAND,
    BYE, OIL, EVENER, PLEASE
flatterer ........ COURTIER, FLUNKY,
    GLOZE, PARASITE, JENKINS
flattering ................ GNATHONIC,
    CEREMONIAL
flattery ......... BLARNEY, PHRASE,
    PALAVER, TAFFY
flat-worm .............. TREMATODE
flaunt TRAPSE, BOSH, BOAST, STOUT
Flavian amphitheatre .... COLOSSEUM
flavor SAUCE, AROMA, GUST, SAPOR,
    TACK, SAMPHIRE
flavor, as a relish ........ TANG, ZEST
flavored ................ RACY, TINCT
flaw ...... FAULT, MAR, RASE, WEM
flax ..................... LINEN, LINT
" bundle ..................... HEAD
" capsule ..................... BOLL
" cloth ............ STUPA, STUPE
" , coarse tow of ......... CODILLA
" , comb ......... CARD, HATCHEL
" , dust from ............... POUCE
" , earth ............... AMIANTHUS
" , fibrous part of ............ TOW
" filament ................... HARL
" , French for .................. LIN
" ; genus .................. LINUM
" , place for process .... RETTERY
" , refuse of . HARDS, HURDS, POB
" seed ................... LINSEED
" , soak ...................... RET
flax-weed ................... TOADFLY
flay . EXCORIATE, SCARIFY, TYRNE
flea .... PULEX, CHIGOE, CYCLOPS
fleche .......... FIELDWORK, SPIRE
flee .... ELOPE, AVOID, RUN, SHUN
fleece .... NAP, PILE, SKIN, MULCT
fleece, inferior part of ............ ABB
fleece, matted ......... WOOL, KET
fleer .......... GIBE, MOCK, SNEER
fleet .......... RAPID, NAVY, TRIDE
Fleet prison in London ........ FLETA
fleet; Span. ................. ARMADA
Flemish painter ............ RUBENS
flesh eating ............ SARCOPHAGY
flesh, like ................ CARNOSE
flesh; per to ............... SARCOUS
fleshy ...... ADIPOSE, FAT, OBESE
fleshy fruit .. PEAR, BACCA, DRUPE,
    POME
Fletcher's drama, hero ...... AMORET
fleur-de-lis ........ LUCE, LUCY, IRIS
flex ...... BEND, CURVE, DEFLECT

flexible .. LIMBER, LISSOME, LUTHE
flexible sheepskin .............. ROAN
flexion of a limb ........ ANACLASIS
flexure ........ GENU, CROOK, FOLD
flick .... FLIP, FLIRT, JERK, WHIP
flicker ...... YUCCA, BLAZE, GLARE
flickering ................ LAMBENT
flight .... EXODUS, FUGE, HEGIRA,
    VOLITATION, ABSCOND
flight ranges ..................... RADII
flightless .................... RATITE
flighty ...... BARMY, FICKLE, MAD
flim-flam .......... HOCUS, TRICK
flinch .... QUAIL, BLENCH, WINCE,
    WONDE, FEAR, SWERVE
fling about .... AGITATE, BETOSS
flint ......... CLINT, CHERT, SILEX
flippant ...... GLIB, CHATTY, PERT
flirt FIKE, JILL, JILT, COQUET(TE)
flit ......... ...... FLICKER, HOVER
flitter-mouse ..................... BAT
float .. BUOY, LURE, QUILL, RAFT,
    WATCH, CORK, SELL, WAFT
floating ............ AWASH, NATANT
floating plant .............. FROGBIT
flock COVEY, SKEIN, BEVY, DROVE,
    HIRSEL, HERD
flock, of a . RAFT, GAGGLE, GREGAL
flock of herons ...... SEDGE, SEIGE
flog .... LARRUP, WALE, CAT, TAN,
    WELT, YANK, BALEISE
flogging; Eng. sl. .............. TOKO
flood CATARACT, CATACLYSM, SEA,
    SPATE
flood gate .... CLOW, GOOL, SLUICE
flood-lights ..................... KLIEG
flood, tidal ..................... EAGRE
floor ...... PAYA, PAVE, OVERTHROW
floor, raised border ........ COAMING
floor-leader ..................... WHIP
Flopsy ...... COTTONTAIL, RABBIT
flooring slab ................... DALLE
flora and fauna ................ BIOTA
floral leaves .............. PERIANTH
floret bract ................... PALEA
florid ........ ORNATE, RED, RUDDY,
    RUBICUND
florid style .. MELISMATIC, ROCOCO
Florida city ...... OCALA, PALATKA
Florida plant ................ COONTIE
Florida river fish ............ TETARD
floss .... RUSHES, SLEAVE, STREAM
flote grass ................... FOXTAIL
Flotow; opera by ......... MARTHA
flotter, Scot. ............ FLOAT, WET
flounder PLAICE, TURBOT, WELTER,
    DAB, FAIL, TOSS
flour and butter mix ............ ROUX
flour in bread for diabetics
    ALEURONAT
flour pudding ..................... DUFF
flourish BRANDISH, PARAPH, WAVE
flout .. JIBE, JEER, SCOFF, FLEER,
    TRUSS
flow .... ISSUE, OOZE, SPOUT, WELL
flow of the tide .. EBB, FLUX, NEAP
flow out .............. EXUDE, ISSUE
flower algae; genus ......... NOSTOC

" , anemone, sea ......... CRASSE
" , apetalus; genus ....... TREMA
flower, aromatic .......... CAMOMILE
" , August ................ POPPY
" , avens, yellow ........ BENNET
" , buckwheat, fragrant ..... TITI
" bud ....................... KNOT
" , burry ................ TEASEL
" , butterfly lily ...... MARIPOSA
" , cardinal ............. LOBELIA
" center ...................... EYE
" cluster ................. UMBEL
" cluster, elongated .... RACEME
" cluster, flat top ....... CYME
" cluster, leaf in a ........ BRACT
" clusters, arranged in .............
                        PANICULATE
" , cormus ............... CROCUS
" , delicate pink ...... RHODORA
" , dogrose, fruit of .......... HIP
" , dry .................. AZALEA
" , Egypt, sacred .......... LOTUS
" envelope ............. PERIANTH
" , erica; genus ......... HEATH
" extract .......... ATTAR, OTTO
" , felwort ............. GENTIAN
" , field .................. GOWAN
" , fragrant ............. JASMINE
" , full bloom .......... ANTHESIS
" , garden .............. FREESIA
" garden .............. GREENERY
" ; genus ROSA, ADONIS, VIOLA
" growing in meadows .. PRATAL
" having leaves in sets of three ....
                        TRILLIUM
" head ...... PANICLE, TEASEL
" , heath ................ AZALEA
" , hibiscus; E. Ind. .... ROSEBLE
" , honeysuckle ........... ELDER
" , hyacinth, wild ........ CAMAS
" , in ........................ BELL
" , indigo .................... ANIL
" , iris ........................ ORRIS
" , Japanese ................... UDO
" , jasmine; Arab. .......... BELA
" , large white ........ BARTONIA
" leaf ...................... BRACT
" , lily .... ARUM, LOTUS, SEGO
" , lily, butterfly ...... MARIPOSA
" , lily, corn .................. IXIA
" , lily, palm .................... TI
" , marigold ............ COWSLIP
" , meadow ................ BLUET
" , New York State ........ ROSE
" , nightshade ........ TRILLIUM
" , of India ................. LARIA
" , Oklahoma ........ MISTLETOE
" of forgetfulness ......... LOTUS
" of kings .............. ARTHUR
" of poets .............. CHAUCER
" , orchid; N. Am. ... ARETHUSA
" , pansy ................... PENSE
" , part of .... ANTHER, BRACT,
            PISTIL, SEPAL, STAMEN
" , passion ............. MAYPOP
" , pinks, the ............ SILENE
" pistil ..................... CARPEL
" plat ........................ BED

" , ragwort, purple ...... JACOBY
" , reseda ......... MIGNONETTE
" rootstock ................... TARO
" , rose of Sharon ........ LOTUS
flower, rose, Persian ............. GUL
" , rose, wild ...... SWEETBRIAR
" , seed, a ...... OVULE, HERB
" , sheath of a ......... SPATHE
" , showy, peren. ........ AZALEA,
                ORCHID, CAMELLIA
" sifter ................... BOLTER
" spicule, star shaped ..... ASTER
" spike ........ AMENT, SPADIX
" , spring .......... HYACINTH
" stalk ...... PEDUNCLE, KEMP,
                        PETIOLE
" stand ................. EPERGNE
" , starwort ............... ASTER
" , summit of stamen .. ANTHER
" , Swiss ............. EDELWEISS
" , Syrian .................. RETEM
" , syringa; genus ........ LILAC
" , the ...................... ELITE
" , turban .................. TULIP
" , unfading ......... AMARANTH
" , water lily .............. LOTUS
" , white weed ............ DAISY
" , willow, bed .......... OSIERIE
" , wind ............... ANEMONE
" , wood sorrel .......... OXALIS
" , yellow, medicinal ......... RUE
flowering grasses; genus ...... STIPA
flowerless plant .... ACROGEN, FERN,
                        LICHEN
flower-like .................. ANTHOID
"Flower of My Heart" ...... ADELINE
flowers, bunch of ................ POSY
flower-shaped ............. FLEURON
flowing .......... AFFLUX, CURSIVE,
                    EMANANT, FLUX
flowing again ......... REMONTANT
flowing veil of Middle Ages .... VOLET
fluent ............ GLIDING, SOLUTE,
                        INTEGRAL
fluffy .. FLOSS, LINTY, FEATHERY
fluid .. AIR, FLUX, STEAM, GLUME,
                    SAP, GORSE
fluid, milk ................. PLASMA
fluid, thin; myth. ............. ICHOR
fluidity; genus .................... RHE
fluke ... CLEEX, COTTREL, BLADE,
                    HOOK, FLOUNDER
flunk .... FAIL, FLINCH, MISS, SLIP
flunkey ................ SNOB, TOADY
flurry .. FRET, AGITATION, HURRY
flushed AGLOW, FLORID, RED, RUBY
fluster ...... POTHER, MOVE, EXITE
flute, nose; Hindu ............. PUNGI
flute of bagpipe ............. CHANTER
flute player ...... TOOTLER, AULETE
flute stop .................. VENTAGE
flute, transverse ................ FIFE
fluting; arch. ...... STRIX, GADROON
flutter ...... AGITATE, FLIT, WAVE
flutteringly ................. PITAPAT
fluvial, per. to ........ AURA, RIVERS
flux .................. FLOW, PURGE

97

fly .. AVIATE, SOAR, WHIR, WHEW, WING
" , Afr. ........ ZIMB, ZEBUB, MAU, TSETSE
" , artificial ........ SEDGE, CLARET
" , as clouds .................... SCUD
" block ...................... PULLEY
" case ...................... ELYTRA
" catcher ....... PEEWEE, PHOEBE, KINGBIRD, TODY
" , golden-eyed .......... LACEWING
" , to .......... ALATE, FLIT, WING
" , very small ........ GNAT, MIDGE
flyaway .......................... GIDDY
flybane; genus ................. SILENE
flyblow ......................... LARVA
flying ...... VOLANT, AWING, BRIEF
flying condition ............... YARAK
"Flying Down to Rio," dance CARIOCA
"Flying Finn" ................. NURMI
flying machine ODTHOPTER, PLANE
flying signal ................... ROGER
fly-wheel ..................... WHORL
Flynn, Mr. .................... ERROL
foam SCUM, BARM, FROTH, SPUME, SUDS, BOIL, RAGE
foams .......... YEASTS, FERMENTS
fob .......... CHEAT, SHAM, TRICK
Foch; actress .................... NINA
fodder ........... ENSILAGE, SILAGE
fodder, rel. to ...... FORAGE, VETCH
fodder straw ................. STOVER
fodgel; Scot. .. FAT, PLUMP, STOUT
fodient ......... BURROWER, MOLE
fog AEROSOL, SMOG, BRUME, HAAR, ROKE, VAPOR
fog horn ....................... SIREN
fogdog ......................... STUBB
foggy .......... CLOUDY, NUBILOUS
fogy FOGRAM, HUNKER, MOSSBACK
foil .... ARC, BALK, EPEE, STOOGE
foist .......... INTERPOLATE, PALM
fold PLEAT, CRIMP, LAP, PLY, RUGA, WRAP, CLASP, PLICATURE
fold, a .. DRAPE, REEF, WELT, PEN, SINUS, CREASE
folded, fan ................... PLICATE
folded, not ................. EPLICATE
foliage, mass of .... SPRAY, BOQUET
foliated ........ TRACERY, SPATHIC
folio ........ PAGE, BOOK, NUMBER
folklore LEGENDS, NANCY, THRENE
folk song .. BLUES, FADO, LULLABY
folkway ..... ........ HUMAN, MORE
follicle ......... ARIL, CRYPT, CYST
follow .... HEED, DOG, ENSUE, TAG, TRACE, IMITATE, OBEY, TRAIL
follower COPIER, SEQUENT, VOLARY
follower of ism ..................... ITE
following . TRADE, RETINUE, NEXT, SECT, SINCE
folly ........ DESIPIENCE, SOTSHIP
foment . BREW, ABET, SPUR, STUPE
fond ........... DOTE, PARENTAL
fond of, foolishly .......... UXORIOUS
fondle ........ COSSET, INGLE, PET
fondling ... CARESSANT, PET, WAIF, NINNY

fondness ........ GRA, LOVE, DESIRE
fontanel .......... SETON, OPENING
food .. PEMMICAN, ALIMENT, DIET, FARE, ORT, PAP, POI, VIANDS
" , cocoa preparation ........ BROMA
" , daily ..................... TUCKER
" , diet .................... REGIMEN
" , lacking a desire for ...... ASITIA
" , miracle .................. MANNA
" of the gods ............. AMBROSIA
" , per. to ........ CHYLE, REFETE
" plant ......................... TARO
" room ....................... SPENCE
" , Scot. ...................... SCAFF
" , semi digested ............ CHYME
" (slang) .................... SCRAN
fool .... IDIOT, CLOWN, DUPE, NIZY, ZANY, DOTARD, RIDICULE
fool hen ...................... GROUSE
fool sage ...................... JESTER
foolhardy RASH, RECKLESS, ICARIAN
foolish HARISH, INEPT, MAD, RACA, DESIPIENT, ASININE, PUERILE
foolish fancy .... CHIMERA, IDIOTIC
fool's bauble .............. MAROTTE
fool's gold ..................... PYRITE
fool's stitch .................. TRICOT
foose; Scot. ............ HOUSELEEK
foot ........ PAW, GOER, SOLE, TOT
" , of three morae ........ TRISEME
" , part of a .................... INCH
" , per. to a .......... PEDI, PODAL
" , per. to sole of .......... PLANTAR
" , poetic ...... ANAPEST, DACTYL
" , study of .............. PODIATRY
" , two syllable ............ IAMBUS
foot-and-mouth disease .... MURRAIN
football ....................... ELEVEN
football field .................... GRID
football pass .............. LATERAL
footed, large ............. MEGAPOD
footings .............. BASIS, TERMS
footless .... APOD, FREE, NOMADIC
foot-like part .......... PEDATE, PES
foot-pad ..... THUG, HIGHWAYMAN
footprint mold ........... MOULAGE
foot-race double course .... DIAULOS
foots ............ SETTLINGS, DREGS
footstalk ................... PEDICEL
footway in air-ship ........ CATWALK
fop DUDE, NOB, ADON, BUCK, PUPPY
for .......... BECAUSE, PRO, SPITE
for aye ............ ALWAYS, EVER
for example; Lat. ................. VIDE
for fear that ..................... LEST
for instance ........................ EG
for shame ........ FIE, SHOCKED
for this reason ........ HENCE, ERGO
forage ...... FOOD, PLUNDER, RAID
foramina ...................... PORES
foray ............ INCURSION, RAID
foray; Scot. ..................... RADE
forbear .. ANCESTOR, SPARE, STOP
forbearance .. MERCY, PLACABILITY
forbearing ........ TOLERANT, PITY
forbid ........ TABOO, BAN, INHIBIT
forbidden city ................. LHASA

forbidding .... GRIM, PLAIN, STERN, UGLY
force ............ COMPEL, DINT, VIS
", alleged .. OD, ODYLE, OG, ELOD
", brief and sudden ........ BRUNT
" by ........................ AMAIN
" down ................... DETRUDE
", Latin for ................... VIS
", organized .................. ARMY
", unit of ........... STAFF, DYNE
forced feeding ............... GAVAGE
forcemeat .................... FARCE
forcing substance ........ CATALYST
Ford's (Henry) son ........... EDSEL
Fordham's team ................ RAMS
forearm ........... ANTEBRACHIUM
forearm, per. to ............. ULNAR
foreboding ...... MENACE, AUGURY, CROAK
forecaster .... SEER, NOSTRADAMUS
forefather .............. PROGENITOR
forefoot ......................... PAW
forefront .......... VANGUARD, VAN
foregoing .... ABOVE, PAST, PREFIX
forehead .......... BROW, SINCIPUT
forehead, of the ............ METOPIC, METOPOMANCY
foreign ...... ECDEMIC, PEREGRINE, EPIGENE, FORANE
foreign quarter ............ ENCLAVE
foreign quarter of Constantinople PARA
foreigner ........... ALIEN, GRINGO, TRAMONTANE
foreordain .... DESTINE, PREDICATE
forepart of horse's hoof .......... TOE
forerun ........ ANTECEDE, HERALD
foreshadow . ADUMBRATE, PRESAGE
foreshank ......................... SHIN
forest fire locator .......... ALIDADE
forest glade .................. CAMASS
forest keeper ................ RANGER
forest, love of .......... HEMOPHILY
forest, open space in ...... CLEARING, GLADE
forest, per. to a . NEMORAL, SYLVAN
forest road ...................... RIDE
forest, treeless ................ WOLD
forest trees, the ............. SYLVA
forestland for tillage ...... THWAITE
foretell ...... READ, AUGUR, BODE, FATIDIC, SPAE, VATICINATE
foretoken ........ OMEN, AUGUR(Y)
forever .. AKE, ETERNE, CONINUAL
forewarning ...... OMEN, PORTENT
forfeit in solo; Fr. .............. BETE
forfeit to God ........... DEODAND
forfeiture FINE, DEDIT, LOSS, TORT
forge ...... MINT, STITHY, IMITATE
forge, wrought iron ...... BLOOMERY
forget ...... OBLITE, REMIT, LAPSE
forgetfulness .... MANASSEH, LETHE
forgiven ........ EXCUSED, VENIAL
forgo .. NEGLECT, RESIGN, WAIVE
fork .......... GRAIP, PRONG, TINE
fork, to .. BIFURCATE, DIVARICATE
form . CAST, CHIC, CONTOUR, MOLD
form of government .......... POLITY

form, per. to .... RITE, HUE, MODAL, TAILLE
form, (philosophy) ............. EIDOS
formal entrance .............. DEBUT
formal warning .... ALARM, CAVEAT
formation, battle .............. HERSE
formed like a twisted chain ............. TORQUATED
former ...... ALDER, ERST, PASSED
former days ........ ELD, OLD, YORE
formerly . ERST, NEE, ONCE, THEN
formicid ........................... ANT
formless; theos .... ANIDIAN, ARUPA
formula CREED, LAW, RULE, LURRY, RITUAL, MAXIM
forsaken .......... LORN, REJECTED
Forester; opera by ............. LORLE
Fort Worth Inst. ................ T.C.U.
Forsyte ........................... SAGA
fortification, Old Fr. ........ BASTILE
fort ...... ABATIS, DUN, BULWARK
fort, sloping bank of .......... GLACIS
forthwith ........ BENDENE, AGAIN, EFTSOON
fortification ... PARADOS, RAVELIN, BASTION, REDOUBT, REDAN
fortified ........ CASTLED, ESCHEAT
fortify GIRD, EMBATTLE, ARM, MAN, STANK
fortress ALCAZAR, CITADEL, KAME, KEEP, BASTILE, DONJON
fortress, outwork of a ....... TENAIL
fortuitous ............. CHANCE, HAP
fortunate ..... DEXTER, EDI, FAUST
fortune ....... ESTATE, LOT, STARS
fortune teller . SIBYL, ORACLE, SEER
fortune tellers ... SPAEMEN, SPYNE
forty-five deg. angle ......... OCTANT
forty-two gal. cask ............ TERCE
forty-winks ...................... NAP
forward ..... PERT, FRONT, AHEAD, ACTIVE, VAIN, EAGER
forward, moving .............. PROAL
fosse ....... DITCH, MOAT, TRENCH
fossil ......... STONE, BALANITE
" , egg ................. OVULITE
" , footprint ........... ICHNITE
" resin .................... AMBER
" shell .................... DOLITE
" , toothlike ......... CONODONT
" , tubular structure ... SCIOLITE
" worm track .......... NEREITE
foster REAR, FOOD, BREED, NURSE
foster child STEPSON, DALT, NURRY
foul smelling ........... FETID, OLID
found, be ...................... EXIST
found on surface of earth .. EPIGENE
found, something ............ TROVE
foundation, forming BEDROCK, BASAL
founder of sisters of charity ... SETON
fountain WELL, AQUA, FONT, HEAD, GENESIS, SPRING, SPA, SYKE
fountain, nymph .. NAIDAD, EGERIA
fountain of youth ............. BIMINI
four footed ............... TETRAPOD
four bagger ................. HOMER
four-in-hand ......... ASCOT, SCARF
fourchette ................... FURCULA

fourgon; Fr. ......... TUMBRIL, VAN
four sided sail .............. LUGSAIL
fourpence ...... GROAT, FLAG, JOEY
foursome ...................... TETRAD
14 pounds ....................... STONE
fourth caliph ........................ ALI
4th Century Saint ............ BLAISE
fourth estate .................... PRESS
fourth gate, founding ............. GIT
fourth row ...................... DEE
foveate ........................ PITTED
fowl ... CAPON, POULT, COCK, HEN
fowl, a heavy ................ DORKIN
fowl, domestic . LEGHORN, MINORCA
fox ........................... CUB, TOD
fox, Afr. ............... ASSE, FENNEC
 " , Asiatic .................... ADIVE
 " glove leaves ........... DIGITALIS
 " hunter's hazard ............ OXER
 " killer ................ VULPECIDE
 " , paw of, per. to .............. PAD
 " ; Russ. ..... CORSAK, KARAGAN
"Fox Goose," star in the ...... ANSER
foxes, troop of ................ SKULK
foxtail ............. BRUSH, GRASSES
fracture ..... BREAK, CRACK, REND
fracture of skull ............ PILATION
fragile FRAIL, FROUGH, SLATTERY
fragment SNIP, ORT, SCRAP, SHARD,
                        SHRED, SIPPET
fragments ...... FLINDER, FARDEL,
                        GROTS, PASH
fragrance ......... AROMA, INCENSE
fragrant BALMY, OLENT, REDOLENT
fragrant ointment VALERIAN, NARD
fragrant wood ...... MIMOSA, ALOE,
                        CEDAR
frail ...... FLIMSY, SEELY, FEEBLE
frailty ..... ADAM, FAULT, DEFECT
framboesia ..................... YAWS
frame ..... BIN, CARCASS, CHASSIS,
                        RACK
 " , bar of soap ............. SESS
 " , cloth stretching .... TENTER
 " , counting ............ ABACUS
 " for fish line ............ CADER
 " in glass making ..... DROSSER
 " on ships table ......... FIDDLE
 " , per. to human ...... ...BENT
 " , skin drying .......... HERSE
 " torch ............... CRESSET
framework CRADLE, CADRE, SHELL
framework of certain pods .. PEPLUM
framework used in bleaching STILLAGE
France, (see also 'French')
 " , anc. name ... GALLIA, GAUL
 " , city in ... AGEN, CASTRES,
                        ARLES, LILLE
 " , department of; GERS, NORD,
                        SENS
 " , dialect in ........... PATOIS
 " , early conqueror of . CLOVIS
 " , edict in; law ......... ARRET
 " , patron saint of ...... DENIS
 " , Southern ............... MIDI
 " , symbol of ............. COCK
Francescan mission ........... ALAMO
franchise ......... RIGHT, LICENSE

franchise, Old Eng. VOTE, SOC, SOKE
Franciscan ................ MINORITE
francolin; Afr. ................. TITAR
frank ........... FREE, MARK, OPEN
frankincense OLIBANUM, THUS, TUS
Frankish dynasty .... MEROVINGIAN
Frankish king ................ CLOVIS
Frankish vassal ................ LEUD
Franklin sobriquet ............... BEN
Franks, per. to tribe of ......... SALIC
frantic, become ..... MANG, CRAZED,
                        FRENETIC
fraud DECEIT, IMPOSTURE, COVIN
fraudulency SUBREPTION, KNAVISH
fraught ............. FILLED, LADEN
fray ....... RAG, RUCTION, TIFFLE
                        HASSLE
freak ....... CAPRICE, FLAM, WHIM
freckle ..... SPOT, TACHE, LENTIGO
freckles, remover ........... ADARCE
free ABSOLVE, LAX, FRANK, LIBRE,
                RID, MANUMIT, RELEASE
freebooter ...... CATERAN, PIRATE,
                        SOTE
free from restraint ............. UNTIE
freedman .............. TIRO, THANE
freedom from doubt ..... CERTITUDE
freedom from infec. ......... ASEPSIS
freehold .................. LAND, ODAL
freeholder ................... YEOMAN
Freeman, Miss ................ MONA
freemason ................. TEMPLAR
freeze ......... BEICE, ICE, STEEVE,
                        CONGEAL
fremd .......... FOREIGN, STRANGE
French, (see also 'French')
 " Afr. possession ..... DAHOMEY
 " airplane ......... SPAD, AVION
 " alb ...................... AUBE
 " annuity .................. RENTE
 " artillery officer ..... DREYFUS
 " artist ........ RAPIN, MANET
 " author RENAN, DUMAS, HUGO,
                        LOTI, GIDE
 " author of self-mastery . COUE
 " bay ..................... BISCAY
 " bean ................... PHASEL
 " beauty .................. NINON
 " bonds ....... RENAN, RENTES
 " botanist .......... AUDIBERT
 " café noir ............. COFFEE
 " cake ................ DARIOLE
 " cardinal ............. MAZARIN
 " champagne ................. AY
 " chanteuse ............... PIAF
 " chemist HOLBACH, PASTEUR
 " city ......... RIOM, TARARE,
                CANNES, NIMES, PARIS
 " cleric .................... ABBE
 " , cloud in ................. NUE
 " coach ................ FIACRE
 " coin, former ............ LIARD
 " coin, old ........ OBOLE, ECU
 " coin, old gold ............ RIAL
 " coin, old silver ........... GROS
 " comedy, early ......... SOTIE
French commerce ............... AGEN

100

" commune .... NERAC, CENON,
      ANCRE, TARARE, USSEL
" composer .. RAVEL, HALEVY,
      LALO, INDY
" corn, mixed .......... MESLIN
" couturier ............... DIOR
" craze for imitating ............
      GALLOMANIA
" dance ................. GAVOT
" department ... ARLES, ORNE,
      EURE, GARD, ARIEGE
" departmental head . PREFECT
" diplomat ...... GENET, SEGUR
" dramatist .... DUMAS, HARDY
" duchy ........... AQUITAINE,
      LUXEMBURG
" dynasty ...... CAPET, VALOIS
" empress ............. EUGENIE
" enamel ware .......... LIMOGE
" engraver ............. PASTRE
" fabric ...... GROS, LAME, RAS
" financier ............. NECKER
" for wall ................... MUR
" fortification ......... PARADOS
" government grant ..... OCTROI
" hacking coach ....... FIACRE
" historian ... GUIZOT, RENAN,
      THIERS
" inn ................... HOSTEL
" island CORSICA, ILE, OLERON
" islands in Africa ..... COMORO
" journalist, first name of a LEON
" lace ..................... CLUNY
" lampoon ............... GESTE
" laugh ..................... RIS
" length unit ........... ARPENT
" legislature ............. SENAT
" liquer ................. COGNAC
" lyric ................. DESCORT
" lyric form, fourteen line .......
      RONDEL
" mandate ................. SYRIE
" marshal . FOCH, MURAT, NEY,
      SAXE
" matin lay ............ AUBADE
" measure; anc. .... AUNE, ELL,
      TOISE, VELTE
" merry ..................... GAI
" metaphysician ... DESCARTES
" method of fighting .... SAVATE
" military leader .......... FOCH
" misdemeanor ........... DELIT
" mode of cooking ....... SAUTE
" , morning ............. MATIN
" mountain ............. VOSGES
" mountain peak BLANC, CENIS
" musical theorist ....... CHEVE
" naval base ........... LORIENT
" navigator .......... FREYCINET
" navy minister ........ DABLAN
" novelist ...... DAUDET, LOTI,
      BENDA
      PROUST, SAND
" nursemaid ............. BONNE
" painter .. MANET, DAUBIGNY,
      DEGAS, COROT, LEMOINE,
      MILLET, RENOIR
" pancake ................ CREPE

" pastry .................. BABA
" paving brick .......... DALLE
" philosopher .. BAYLE, NAUDE
" physicist ............. AMPERE
" plane ................... SPAD
" poem; anc. ............... DIT
" political club ........ JACOBIN
" porcelain .............. SEVRES
" port .......... BREST, CAEN
" post in Africa ........... TUNIS
" president ... GREVY, LOUBET
" promissory note ... ASSIGNAT
French pronoun ......... IL, MOI, TU,
      ELLE
" prose writer .. AMYOT, MAROT
" protectorate .. ANNAM, LAOS
" psychologist ............ BINET
" racecourse .......... AUTEUIL
" recruit .................. BLEU
" refugee ............. EMIGRE
" Republic ........... ANDORRA
" resort .. ANTIBES, MENTONE,
      PAU
" revolutionist DANTON, MARAT
" river ... AIRE, AUBE, ISERE,
      LOIRE, LYS, VESLE, SOMME,
      MARNE, SISAI, MEUSE,
      RANCE, ORNE
" ruler ................. PIPPIN
" scholar ............. ABELARD
" school of painting . BARBIZON
" school, secondary ...... LYCEE
" sculptor ..... BARYE, RODIN,
      ETEX
" shield (old) ........... TARGE
" shooting match ............. TIR
" silk center ............. LYON
" silk, stout ................ GROS
" smoking room ... ESTAMINET
" soldier ....... POILU, ZOUAVE
" specialty ............. PERWOD
" square measure .......... ARE,
      CENTARE, HECTARE
" stable ................. ECURIE
" statesman . MORNY, CARNOT
" stoneware .............. GRES
" storm .................. ORAGE
" street .................... RUE
" surgery, father of ....... PARE
" Territory, Free .......... CHAD
" town .. AGEN, CRECY, LOOS,
      NESLE, NERAC, RIOM,
      SETE, PAU, SENS
" trade tax .............. PATENTE
" "Upper House" ........ SENAT
" weight, (see 'weight')
" woodland .............. FORET
" workman ............. BLOUSE
" world ................. MONDE
" writer .... RENAN, CABORIAU,
      STAEL, VOLTAIRE, HEINE,
      VILLON, AMAR, FEUILLET
Frenchman PICARD, GAUL, PARISIAN
frenzied ENRAGED, AMOK, FRANTIC
frequent .......... HAUNT, GO, OFT
fresh ........ CALLER, NEW, LUSH
fresh water algae ........... DESMID
freshet .... TIDE, SPATE, TORRENT

freshman; Eng. slang ..... JIB, COMP
fret FUME, ABRADE, NAG, ORP, VEX
fret, skin ......... HERPES, WHELK
Freudian term ............. EGO, ID(S)
friable .... BRITTLE, CRISP, SHORT,
      MEALY, FRAGIBLE, FRAIL
friar ....... LISTER, MINOR, ABBOT
friar bird ..................... PIMLICO
friar, black .............. DOMINICIAN
friar, gray .............. FRANCISCAN
friar, white ............... CARMELITE
fricative ... HISS, SPIRANT, CRONY,
      PAL
friction .............. ERASURE, RUB
frictional ..................... EROSIVE
friend .. AMI, ALLY, FOLK, QUAKER
friend; fem. Fr. ................... AMIE
friend; Span. ..................... AMIGO
friendly ..... AMICABLE, KIND, REL
friendly relations .. AMITY, AFFABLE
friendly understanding .... ENTENTE
Fresian .... ......... SYLT, FRIESE
frigate bird ....................... IWA
Frigga; Norse ................. FRIDAY
Frigg's husband ................. ODIN
Frigg's maid ................... FULLA
Frigg's messenger .............. GNAS
fright .... GUY, OGRE, PANIC, FRAY,
     ALARM, FEAR, TERROR, GAST
frighten . BOH, DAUNT, GHOST, RAD,
      SCARE
frijol; Mex. ...................... BEAN
frill .. RUSCHE, JABOT, FURBELOW
fringe ......... FAS, LOMA, THRUM
fringed ......... FIMBRIATE, LACED
fringing reef ................. CORAL
fritted ......... EATEN, LESSENED
fritter .. DALLY, DAWDLE, BANGLE
frizzed ........... CRAPED, CRIMPED
fro ........... BACK, FROM, HITHER
frock GOWN, SOUTANE, JAM, COAT,
      KIRTLE
frog . POLLYWOG, ANURAN, RONCO
froggeries ................... RANARIA
frog-like ...................... RANINE
frogs; genus ................... RANA
frolic FUN, LARK, MARLOCK, PRANK,
    BINGE, CAPER, FRISK, SPREE
from beginning to end .... OVER, ALL
from head to foot; Fr. ...... CAPAPIE
from, prefix ............. FRO, APO, DE
front .. FACADE, OBVERSE, FORNE,
     VAN
frontier boundary ...... LIMTROPHE
frontlet ....................... TIARA
frost-covered ........... ICED, RIMED
frost-fish KOKOPU, PARA, SCABBARD
frosty .. HOARY, RIMY, HUNCH, ICY
froth . SUDS, FOAM, SPUME, YEAST
frothy ................. GUISE, SPUMY
frou-frou .............. RUSTLE, STIR
frow ..................... SLATTERN
frown ........ IOUR, LOWER, GLOOM
frozen ...... CHILLY, GLACE, GELID
frozen dessert ......... ICE, MOUSSE,
      SHERBET
frozen vapor ........... FROST, RIME
frugal . ECONOMIC, CHARY, SPARE

fruit ........ AZAROLE, ATES, CROP
" , a kind of dry .......... REGMA
" , an aggregate ........ ETAERIO
" bat ......................... PECA
" cordial ......... RATAFIA, ADE
" , decay in .................. BLET
" , deriv. of .......... PHLORIZIN
" dots ......................... SORI
" dried ...................... PASA
" , firm centered ...... PULPLESS
" flesh, part of ............. PULP
" , goddess of; Rom. .... POMONA
" , hybrid ................... POMA
" jar, air tight seal ........ LUTE
" of a rose bush .............. HIP
" of an Amer. tree ....... SAPOTA
" of elm; arc. ............. SAMARA
" of gourd family ........... PEPO
" of gourd plants ....... SETON
" , outer covering of ........ RIND
" , over-ripe .............. DRUPE
" , per. to .............. POMONIC
" preserve .............. COMPOTE
" pulp ........................ PAP
" pulpy ....................... UVA
" , refuse to ............... MURC
fruit, science of the structure of .........
      CARPOLOGY
" skin ..................... EPICARP
" , small one seed DRUPE, ACHENE
" , small red ................. HAW
" , tapioca-like ............ SALEP
" , tomato-like ............ POMATO
" , tropical ........... INCA, MANGO
fruiterer ...................... COSTER
fruitless ...................... STERILE
fruits, maple ............... SAMARAS
frustrate ....... DASH, FOIL, ANIENT
frustration ............ BALK, DEFEAT
fry lightly ...................... SAUTE
frying-pan ......... SKILLET, SPIDER
fuddy-duddies ................. DODOES
Fuegian ......................... ONA
fuel . COMBUSTIBLES, ELDIN, PEAT,
      COAL, GAS, OIL
fugitive ............ EXILE, FLEEING
fugue ............ DIATONIC, TONAL,
     THEMES, RICERCARE
fugue, special passage in a .. STRETTA
fulcrum.. PROP, SHORE, STAY, BAIT,
      THOLE
fuliginous ....................... SOOTY
fulfillment .. FRUITION, FLOWERING
full and flowing .. ROTUND, PLENARY
full cloth ....................... WALK
full house .......... HAND, SRO
full of cracks ................. RIMOSE
full of; suffix ............. ITOUS, OSE
full of twigs ......... RODDY, RUDDY
full size draft; arch. ........... EPURE
fullers earth .................... BOLE
fuller's herb ................... TEASEL
fullness .......... SATIETY, SURFEIT,
    PLEROLA, MUCH, REPLETION
Fulton's folly ............. CLERMONT
fumarole, S. Am. ............ HORNITO
fume . STEAM, VAPOR, RAGE,
     ANGER, REEK
fumigator ...... AERATOR, SULPHUR

fuming ............. AREEK, RAGING
fun CHAFF, GIG, SPORT, JOKE, PLAY
function OFFICE, PARTY, RITE, USE
fundamental ....... BASAL, BASILAR,
       RADICAL, ORIGINAL
funeral ..... EXEQUIES, OBSEQUIES
  "   attendant ............... MUTE
  "   music, per. to .. THRENODIAL
  "   oration ................. ELOGE
  "   pile ...................... PYRE
  "   pyre .......... PILE, SUTTEE
  "   song . DIRGE, ELEGY, NENIA,
       REQUIEM, THRENODY
funereal ............. EXEQUIAL, SAD
funest .......................... DIRE
fungal .................... FUNG(O)US
fungi ...... BOLETUS, SPORE, YEAST
fungi; genus ..... ERYSIBE, AMANITA
fungi, parasitic ..... ERGOTS, AWETO
fungoid growth, minute ......... MOLD
fungoid tissue ................. TRAMA
fungous ..................... SPONGY
fungus .... MILDEW, MOLD, AGARIC,
       TUBER, AMADOU
  "   cells or sacs .............. ASCI
  "   dots ...................... TELIA
  "   , edible ....... CEPA, MOREL,
       TRUFFLE
  "   , edible purple ....... BLEWIT
  "   growing on rye ....... ERGOT
  "   , mushroom ........ AMANITA
fungus plant .................. UREDO
  "   , poisonous ...... AMANITINE
funicle ................. FIBER, STALK
funk ........ FEAR, FRIGHT, TERROR
fur PLATINA, FITCH, PELAGE, VAIR
fur bearing animal . MARTEN, GENET
fur; collec. .................... PELTRY
fur, 14th Century .... MINIVER, VAIR
fur, per. to ........ PELISSE, STOLE
furies .......................... DIRAE
furies, avenging ............... ERINYS
furies, gracious ......... EUMENIDES
furies, the three . ALECTO, MEGAERO,
       TISIPHONE
furl .............. BUNDLE, INROLL
furlined tippet ................. AMICE
furlong ........... STADE, STADIUM
furnace . SMELTER, KILN, CRESSET,
       ETNA, CALDRON, FORGE
furnace, part of ...... BOSH, HOWELL
furnace, tuyere of ........... TEWEL
furnace, upper stage in ...... HOWELL
furnish ...... CATER, LEND, ENDOW
furnish a person with wings ....... IMP
furnish with another point ...... RETIC
furniture .... ADAM, GOODS, GRAITH
furniture, parts of ............. SHOOK
furor ..... FLURRY, MANIA, TUMULT
furrow .... INTRENCH, HENT, PLOW,
       STITCH
furrow in a plank .... DAWK, RABBET
furrow, minute ................. STRIA
furrowed ..................... SULCATE
furrowing mark; Brit. .......... FEERE
furrows, having ............. GUTTERY
furrows, notch ................. SCORE
furry cover of a mammal ..... PELAGE
furry tail ...................... SCUT

furs, treating of ........ CARROTTAGE
furseal .......................... URSAL
further ........ AID, AND, MORE, YET
furtherance HELP, RELIEF, SUCCOR,
       AID
furtive . ARCH, COVERT, WARY, SLY,
       SKULKING
furze ............. GORSE, WHIN
furze; genus .................... ULEX
fusain ..................... CHARCOAL
fuse ...... SOLDER, ANNEAL, SMELT
fuse partially ................... FRIT
fusee .......................... FLARE
fusion, promoting mineral ...... SPALT
fuss ..... ADO, FIKE, PREEN, FUME
fussily, work .................. NIGGLE
fuster .......................... ZANTE
fustian ...... BOMBAST, RANT, MARL
fustic coloring matter .......... MORIN
fustigation ................. WHIPPING
fusty .............. MOLAX, STUFFY
futile ............ IDLE, OTIOSE, VAIN
future ............ STILL, YET, TO-BE


# G

G, letter ......................... GEE
G.I. address .................... A.P.O.
G.I. jewelry ................. DOGTAG
G.I. Joe ....................... PRIVATE
G.I. rifle ..................... GARAND
G.men ..................... FBI, FED
gabelle ................. EXCISE, TAX
gabion ......... BASKET, CYLINDER
gable ......... AILERON, PINION
gaby ........................... FOOL
gad TRAIP, ROVE, GOAD, GALLIVANT
Gad, son of ....................... ERI
Gad, tribe of ................... ERITES
Gad, Syrian deity ........... FORTUNE
Gaddan ..................... MALAY
gadfly ......... BRIMS, CLEG, STOUT,
       BREEZE
gadget THINGUMAJIG, THINGUMBOB
Gadhelic ...... GAELIC, IRISH, MANX
gadwall .......................... DUCK
"Gadzooks" .................... EGAD
Gaelic ............ ERSE, SCOTCH
Gaelic form of John ............... IAN
Gaelic hero ................... OSSIAN
Gaelic spirit ................ BANSHEE
Gaelic warrior ................ DAGDA
gaff ... SPAR, GAMBLE, HOOK, SPUR
gag .. CHOKE, RETCH, SCOB, HOAX,
       JOKE
Gahlee, native of ........... GALILEAN
gain ... REALIZE, LUCRE, GET, WIN,
       ATTAIN, APPROACH, REAP
gainsay .... DENY, IMPUGN, OPPOSE
gait . SHAMBLE, LOPE, RACK, STEP,
       WALK, PACE, STRIDE
gaiters ... PUTTEES, SPATS, STRAD
gala ........ FESTAL, FIESTA, POMP
galam .......................... SHEA
Galicia river ............... STYR, SAN
Galician, a ................. GALLEGO

Galilean ................. GAULONITE
galilee; arch. ....... PORCH, PORTICO
gallipot .............. BARRAS, RESIN
gall ..... BILE, SPITE, CHAFE, FELL,
SOW, VEX
Gallagher's partner ............ SHEAN
gallant ..... CICISBEO, HERO, SPARK
galled .... RAW, SENSITIVE, SORE
galleon ............. CARACK, ARGOSY
gallery ........ MUSEUM, LOFT, POY
galley ........ COIN, POOF, KITCHEN
galley, a light .................. FOIST
galley, armed       AESC, DROMOND
galley of retorts ............. MUFFLE
galley, Rom. ...... BIREME, TRIREME
galley, work on .................. EDIT
Gallic chariot ................... ESSED
gallimaufries .................... OLIOS
gallinae .. GROUSE, QUAIL, TURKEY,
PEAFOWL, RASORES
gallinule .................. HEN, RAIL
galloping .......... LOPING, TANTIVY
"Galloping dominoes" .......... DICE
gally ..... FLURRY, GALLOW, SCARE
Galway Is. ....................... ARAN
gam .......... HERD, SCHOOL, VISIT
gambler .... GAMER, DICER, PUNTER
gambler's accomplice ........... SHILL
gambling, per. to ......... ALEATORY
gambol CAPER, CURVET, PIG, ROMP
game ............. FUN, LAME, PLOY
"      , a BADMINTON, BENO, BINGO,
CRICKET, GOLF, POLO, LUDO,
DIBS, HALMA, TAROT
"    bird; Scot. .............. GROUSE
"    game bird; S. Am. ........ GUAN
"    digit; anc. ............... MORA
"    , gambling .............. BOULE
"    , Greek ................... AGON
"    like Napoleon ............. PAM
"    like tennis ............... FIVES
"    like ninepins .......... SKITTLES
"    , marbles ................... TAW
"    of chance ......... FARO, KENO
"    of skill ......... DARTS, CHESS
"    , oriental ......... HEI, FANTAN
"    , parlor ................. LOTTO
"    ragout ................. SALMI
"    , raisin ......... SNAPDRAGON
"    , Scottish ............... SHINTY
"    , Spanish ............... OMBER
gamecock, young ............... STAG
gamin ARAB, TAD, SERF, MUDLARK
gaming, possession of goods by finding ..
TROVER
gammon ......... HAM, BACON, BOSH
gamut ... ... RANGE, SCALE, SOLFA
gander ...... GANNET, GOOSE, STEG
gang ... CREW, SET, BAND, NUMBER
"Gangbusters," prod. of ......... LORD
Ganges Valley, salty efflorescence on ...
REH
gangling ....... LANKY, SPINDLING
gangrene ..... SPHACELUS, MORTIFY
gangrenous condition ....... NECROSIS
gannet ......... GOOSE, SOLAN, SULA
gannet; Can. ................. MARGOT
gap ...... CHASM, HIATUS, LACUNA,
FAULT, SPLIT, SHARD

gap in a hedge ................ MEUSE
gape .. DEHISCE, BILGE, OPE, YAWN
gapes, the .................... RICTUS
gapeseed ........................ SIGHT
gaping .......... RINGENT, CHAPPY
gaping of a plant capsule DEHISCENCE
garab tree ...................... BAHAN
Garapan Is. capital ............ SAIPAN
garble .......... MUTILATE, FALSIFY
Garbo, Miss ..................... GRETA
garden ........... PATCH, VERGER
garden of gold apples .. HESPERIDES
garden, spacious ......... PLEASANCE
garden-city of Amer. ........ CHICAGO
garden-city of Eng. ............. KENT
garden-city of Italy ............ SICILY
gardener's plague ......... CUTWORM
Gardner, Stanley ................ ERLE
gare; Span. ................. ENTRADA
Gardner, Miss .................... AVA
Gargantua's son ....... PANTAGRUEL
garfish ......................... SNOOK
Gargantua's wife ........... BABEBEC
garland .......... ROSARY, ANADEM,
FESTOON, LEI
garlic root .......... MOLY, RAMSON
garment, clergyman's ........ CASSOCK
"      , close fitting ....... COATEE
"      , Irish ................. INAR
"      like a tunic; Eng. .. TABARD
"      , Malay .. KABAYA, SARONG
"      , outer ..... HAORI, SMOCK,
COAT, PALETOT
"      , outer; Arab. .......... ABA
"      , outer, made of skins PARKA
"      , S. Amer. ......... KAROSS
"      , under ............... SHIFT
Garner, John ................... NANCE
garnet ...... APLOME, PYROPE, RED,
(H)ESSONITE
garnet, berry ............... CURRANT
garnet, clew; naut. ............. ROPE
garnet, common red ..... ALMANDITE
garnet, green .. OLIVINE, UVAROVITE
garret .... ATTIC, COCKLOFT, SOLER
garrot .......... DUCK, GOLDENEYE
garvie .......................... SPRAT
gas, a ....... NEON, RADON, ARGON,
BUTANE, DAMP
"    , an inert ................ ACTION
"    charger ................. AERATOR
"    , colorless ... KETENE, ETHENE,
OXANE
"    ; comb. form .......... AER, AERO
"    for synthetic rubber .. BUTADIENE
"    from hot springs .......... XENON
"    , marsh ................. METHANE
"    , nitrogen and carbon CYANOGEN
"    , non-inflammable ....... HELIUM
gaseous ............. TENUOUS, THIN
gaseous element ...... RADON, NEON,
XENON
gash .... CUT, SLASH, DAWK, INCISE
gasolene ....................... PETROL
gasp .......... HIATUS, PANT, YAWN
gastropod .. MOLLUSK, SLUG, SNAIL,
YET
"      , genus ...... HARPA, NERITE
"      , marine ..... ACERA, MUREX

104

" , per. to a ............ DIOECIA
gate ......... SPRUE, BAB, DAR, GIT,
PORTAL, START, HERSE
gate, rear .................... POSTERN
gateau; Fr. ..................... CAKE
gateway to Buddhist shrine .... TORAN
gather . REAP, BREW, FULL, SHIRR,
FOLD, ACQUIRE, PUCKER
gather and compare ......... COLLATE
gathered .......................... MET
gathering .... MEET, HALL, PARTY,
SUM
" , social ................... BEE
Gaucho knife ..................... BOLO
Gaucho tree ........................ USE
Gaucho weapon ............ MACHETE
gaud ................. ADORN, FINERY
gauge .... ESTIMATE, RATE, VALUE,
FEE, MODEL, NORM,
RULE, TYPE
" pointer ...................... ARM
Gaul, anc. people of ...... REMI, CELT
Gaul, tribe of ................... AEDUI
gaulin; W. Indies .... EGRET, HERON
Gaulish divinity TEUTATES, TARANIS
gaum, daub; dial. .................. GOM
gaunt ........... BONY, LEAN, UGLY
gauntlet ................. GLOVE, CUFF
gauze ..... MARLI, BAREGE, CREPE,
LENO, LISSE, HAZE
gauzy film in wine ....... BEESWING
gavial ................... CROCODILIAN
gawk ....... BOOBY, CUCKOO, FOOL
gay .......... DIBATAG, BOON, AIRY,
HOLIDAY, RORTY
gay, state of being . GENIAL, RIANCY
gaze .. GAPE, PORE, REGARD, CON,
LOOK, SCAN
gazebo ...................... PAVILION
gazelle (see also "antelope")
gazelle .... CORINNE, KEVEL, KUDU,
MOHR
" , Afr. ..... ADMI, CORA, ORYX
" , Arabian ................. ARIEL
" Cen. Asian ............... AHU
" , Clarke's ............. DIBATAG
" , four-horned ........ CHIKARA
" of the Sudan .......... DAMA
" Senegambian ............. KORIN
" S. African ........ SPRINGBOK
" Tibetan ............ GOA, DGOBA
gear ......... CAM, BAGGAGE, TOOLS
gecko ............. LIZARD, TARENTE
geese fat ...................... AXUNGE
geese, flock of wild .... RAFT, GAGGLE
geese; genus ........... ANSER, CHEN
geiger tree ................. SEBESTEN
gelatin ......... JELLY, AGAR, COLLIN
gelatin, plate ...................... BAT
gelatin, silk .................... SERIGIN
gelatin used as a cement ......... GLUE
gelid ............ ICY, COLD, FROZEN
gem ............. ATOS, JEWEL, OPAL
" , carnelian-like ............. SARD
" , Egyptian ............... SCARAB
" , flat facet of a ............. CULET
" for inlaying ............... CRUSTA
" , kind of .......... AQUAMARINE,
ALAMANDINE

" , modern ...... LIGURE, JACINTH
gem, relief ..................... CAMEO
" , rose ...................... BALAS
" of conjugal happiness . SARDONYX
" " friendship ............... TOPAZ
" " good luck ......... MOONSTONE
" " health ............... AGATE
" " immortality ......... EMERALD
" " lasting peace ......... DIAMOND
" " love ............... AMETHYST
" " purity .................... PEARL
" , State ...................... IDAHO
" that warns of danger ... CATSEYE
" of truth ............... SAPPHIRE
" " youth .................... BERYL
gemmation .................. BUDDING
gemsbok ............ CHAMOIS, ORYX
gendarme ......... POLICE, TROOPER
gender ......... BEGET, BREED, SEX
gender common to both ..... EPICENE
genealogical ..................... ORDER
genealogy ........... PEERAGE, TREE
genefe ....................... KNIFE
genera; Lat. ................... GENUS
general .. USUAL, VAGUE, COMMON,
GROSS
general aspect ................ FACIES
general effect ............. ENSEMBLE
generation, spontaneous ABIOGENESIS
genesis .. NASCENCY, ORIGIN, BIRTH
genial, become more ... WARM, THAW
geniculate ...................... KNEEL
genipap dye .................... LANA
genos; Gr. ..................... RACE
genouillere .................. KNEELET
genre .. CATEGORY, SPECIES, KIND,
GENUS, SORT, STYLE
gentiles, per. to ............... ETHNIC
gentle; mus. .................. AMABILE
gentle slope .................. GLACIS
gentleman .. SIR, KNIGHT, YOUNKER
"Gentlemen Prefer Blondes"; author ...
LOOS
gentry; dial. Eng. .............. NOBLE
genu ........ REND, KNEE, FLEXURE
genuflect ............. CURTSY, KNEEL
genuine ................... SIMONPURE
genus ......... CLASS, ORDER, SORT,
GENERAL
genus of birds ..... EOS, UNSER, TODI
" " birds, the gennet ....... SULA
" " bivalve mollusk ...... ANOMIA
" " bulbous herbs ....... TULIPA
" " burbots ................. LOTA
" " bustards ................ OTIS
" " carnivorous animals .. URSUS
" " cat .................... FELIS
" " climbing shrubs ..... TECOMA
" " crowned pigeons ...... GOURA
" " ducks ..... ANAS, HARELDA
" " fabaceous herbs .. PSORALEA
" " feather stars ...... ANTEDON
" " flowering shrubs .... FUCHSIA
" " fungi ................. AMAITA
" " fungi, fleshy ...... BOLETUS
" " gastropods .......... NERITE
" " gastropods, per. to ..... OLIVA
" " geese ................ ANSER
" " goose barnacles ....... LEPAS

105

"	" grasses . AVENA, POA, STIPA
"	" herbs ....... ACARUM, ARUM,
INULA, SESEL
"	" herbs; Amer. ...... LINARIA,
HEDEOMA
"	" hogs ..................... SUS
genus of lichens ............. EVERNIA
"	" lily family ......... BESSERA
"	" mollusks ............. NERITA
"	" morays .......... MURAENA
"	" nettles ............... URTICA
"	" N. Amer. perennials ...... IVA
"	" olives .................. OLEA
"	" oysters ............... OSTREA
"	" palm trees .......... BACABA
"	" perennial herbs ...... IMULA
"	" plants ..... NAIAS, NOLANA,
LOBELIA, GRINDELIA
"	" poisonous plants .. CERBERA
"	" pond tortoise ............ EMYS
"	" rats ........... SPALAX, MUS
"	" sand snakes ............. ERYX
"	" sheep ................... BOS
"	" shrubs SABIA, TREMA, RHUS
"	" shrubs; Austral. ... ALSTONIA
"	" spider monkeys ..... ATELES
"	" spiders ............. AGALENA
"	" squirrel ............. SCIURUS
"	" swans ................. OLOR
"	" swine ................... SUS
"	" tailless amphibians ..... RANA
"	" tarpon fish family ..... ELOPS
"	" terns ................ STERNA
"	" thistle plants ....... CARLINA
"	" tick ................... IXODES
"	" trees ....... MABA, STYRAX,
TREMA
"	" trop. Am. bulbs ..... TARIRI
"	" tropical herbs ....... TACCA,
URENA, ACUAN
"	" tropical shrubs ..... PISONIA,
IXORA
"	" whales .................. INIA
genus of woody vines ........ HEDERA
geode .......................... DRUSE
geography, per. to EXCLAVE, INCLAVE
geological age . PLIOCENE, CENOZOIC
"	division ..... EON, ERA, LIAS,
TRIAS
"	epoch ......... CHAZY, DRIFT,
EOCENE
"	epoch of S. Afr. ......... ECCA
"	formation ... TERRANE, IONE,
TRIASSIC
"	group ....... BALA, CARADOC
"	oldest period ..... ARCHAEAN
"	period ...... NEOCENE, LIAS,
EO, MIOCENE
"	subdivision ... TROPIC, GAULT
"	substance ............. ATANE
geologist, famous ............ HUXLEY
geologist of antiquity ......... STRABO
geometric poles ............ PERPOLES
geometrical body ....... LUNE, PRISM
"	point relating to curve ACNODE
"	premise .......... POSTULATE
"	study ................. CONICS
"	term ......... SINE, TANGENT
geometry coordinate ....... ABSCISSAS

geometry, figure in ...... ELLIPSOID
"	, proponent of EUCLID, PASCAL
"	, proportion in .......... PORISM
geoponic .......................... RURAL
George Eliot's true name ........ EVANS
Georgia, county in .... RABUN, TROUP
"Georgia peach" ................ TYRUS
Georgian ........................ SVAN
georgic ................. RURAL, POEM
Geraint's wife ................... ENID
geranial ........ CITRAL, ALDEHYDE
Geranium Lake ............. NACARAT
gerard ................ DEMON, FIEND
gerefa .. REEVE, BAILIFF, SHERIFF
gerfaunt .................... GIRAFFE
germ ............. BUD, SEED, SPORE
germ elements; per. to ......... GENIC
germ, fermenting ............... ZYME
germ of decay ................... TAINT
germ seed ........................ CHIT
German ....... JERRY, ALMAN, HUN,
TEUTON
"	admiral .................... SPEE
"	archbishop of Cologne .... ANNO
"	article ..................... DAS
"	artist ................... DURER
"	astronomer ........... KEPLER
"	bomber ................. STUKO
"	cake .................... TORTE
"	canal ..................... KIEL
"	cathedral town ......... ESSEN
"	city .. BONN, GOTHA, HALLE,
ULM, WESEL, ESSEN
"	coal region ................ SAAR
"	coin ......... MARK, THALER
"	composer ................ HASSE
"	district ..................... GAU
"	dam ...................... EDER
"	drinking salutation .... PROSIT
"	exclamation ................ ACH
"	general ............... MOLTKE
"	geologist ................ HEYNE
"	glass mfg. city ........... JENA
"	gold coin, former ...... KRONE
"	hall, students ........... BURSA
"	halls .................... AULAE
"	historian .. NEANDER, DAHN,
MOSER
"	in Italian ............. TEDESCO
"	inventor ............... BUNSEN
"	island ................. ALSEN
"	knight .................. RITTER
"	kobold ............. HODEKEN
"	letter .................... RUNE
"	lyric poems ............ LIEDER
"	manufacturing town ..... GERA
"	mathematician ...... LIEBNITZ
"	measles ............... RUBELLA
"	measure, chain .......... KETTE
"	measure; var. ........... EIMER
"	monoplane .............. TAUBE
"	mountain ................. HARZ
"	naturalist .............. HUGEL
"	naval base ....... EMDEN, KIEL
"	nobleman ............. BILLUNG
"	outer garment .......... SOMAR
"	painter ................. BEGAS
"	people .. JUTE, SUEVI, QUADI,
UBII

106

" philologist ... BENEKE, GRIMM
" philosopher .............. KANT
" physicist ..... DOPPLER, OHM
" pietist .... FRANCKE, SPENER
" president, first ........ EBERT
" rifleman ........ JAGER, YAGER
" river .... RUHR, EGER, ELBE,
    HUNTE, ELISTER, SAALE,
    WERRA, ISER, ODER, AAR
" ruler, early ............. OTHO
" scholar .......... ELZE, HEGEL
" seaport ................ EMDEN
" silver .................. ALBATA
" silver plate ......... ELECTRUM
" society ................ VEREIN
German soldier ................ KRAUT
" state .................... BADEN
" theologian ...... BAUER, ECK
" title of respect .. GRAFF, HERR
" watering place ............. EMS
" white wine ................ HOCK
" song ................. LIEDER
" sub ..................... UBOAT
Gershwin; compo. ...... GEORGE, IRA
gesso .............. CHALK, GYPSUM
get aboard ................... BERIDE
get along ................ MAKE OUT
get around ........ CAJOLE, OUTWIT
get away; sl. ..................... LAM
Ghandi's title .............. MAHATMA
germane .................... AKIN
germicide ...................... IODINE
Gertrude Atherton's pen name .... LIN
gesture .............. MOTION, SANNA
geum; genus .................... AVENS
geyser, mouth of .............. CRATER
gewgaw ............. BAUBLE, GAUD
Ghandi, place of confine ........ POONA
ghastly CADAVEROUS, PALE, LURID
ghost ...... EIDOLON, KER, LARVA,
    LEMUR, SPOOK, WRAITH, SHADE
ghost fish ........................ CHIRO
ghost plant ........... TUMBLEWEED
ghost spectre ............. REVENANT
ghoulish ............. VAMPIRIC, EERIE
giant .. TROLL, ANAK, ETEN, OGRE,
    THURSE, OTT
" , Asterius' father (Gr.) ... ANAX
" , deformed (Celt.) ..... FOMORS
" , evil (Norse) .............. LOKI
" , frost (Norse) ............ HRYM
" , Gerd's father (Norse) .. GYMER
" god; (Norse) ............. MIMIR
" , Greek myth. .......... COTTUS,
    CYCLOPS
" , handsome (Gr.) ........ ORION
" , Hindu myth. ............. BANA
" , hundred eyes (Gr.) ..... ARGUS
" , hundred hands (Gr.) ... GYGES
" , Moab. myth. .... EMIM, ZUZIM
" mentor ...................... LEO
" , Norse myth. . JOTUN, UTGARD
" , Oisin's father (Irish) ... FIONN
" , one eyed ... ARGES, BRONTES
" , Philistine .... ...... GOLIATH
" , primeval (Norse) . YMER, YMIR
" sea demon (Teut.) ........ WADE
" , shepherd (Gr.) ......... ARGES
" strong (Gr.) ............. TITAN

" , Vulcan's son (Gr.) ..... CACUS
giantess, Celt. myth. ........... DOMNU
" , Norse myth. ... GROA, NATT,
    NORN
" , Scand. myth.; SKULD, URTH,
    WYRD
giants, Moab .......... EMIM, ZUZIM
giants, one eyed .................. ALEC
gib ............... GUT, SALMON, CAT
gibber ...................... GALLOWS
gibbon ....................... APE, LAR
gibe HECKLE, SNEER, FLIRT, QUIP,
    SCOFF
Gibson group ...................... ANC
giddy woman ...... FLIBBERTIGIBBIT
gift .. FLEER, ALMS, ENAM, GRANT,
    TALENT, LAGNIAPPE, LEGACY
gift or bounty DOW, LARGESS, DOLE,
    FEE
gigantic . TITAN, COLOSSEAN, HUGE
giggle SNIGGER, CHUCKLE, TITTER
gila monster ................... LIZARD
gild ..... ADORN, AUREATE, TEMPT
Gileadite judge .................... JAIR
gill .......... CHOLLER, WATTLE
gimcrack ............. SHOWY, GAUDY
gimmer ................. CLASP, HINGE
gimp ......... JAG, NOTCH, ORRIS
gin ......... IF, SNARE, TOILS, TRAP
gin, liquor .......... SCHNAPPS, SLOE
ginger .............. MIOGA, PEP
" ; genus ............... ZINGIBER
" , pine ................... CEDAR
" root ............. COLTSFOOT
" , wild ................. ASARUM
gingerbread .................... PARKIN
gingerbread tree ................. DOOM
ginseng; genus ................. ARALIA
gipsy ........................ NOMAD
" , Dutch ...... APTAL, BAZIGAR,
    HEIDENEN
" , French ............. BOHEMIAN
" gentleman ............ ROM, RYE
" , German ............. ZIGEUNER
" , Hindu ............. KARACHEE
" horse ......................... GRI
" , Italian ............... ZINGABI
" language ............... ROMANY
" , Persian ............... SISECH
" pocketbook .................... LIL
" sea tribe, one of ...... SELUNG
" , Spanish .... GITANO, ZINCALO
"Gipsy Rose ——" .................. LEE
giraffe ............... CAMELOPARD
giraffe; Arab. .............. XIRAPHA
giraffe-like animal ............. OKAPI
girasol ......................... OPAL
gird ... ENCIRCLE, EQUIP, GORDEN
girdle .. RING, OBI, CEST, CINCTURE,
    SASH, CINGLE
girdle; Rom. .................. CESTUS
girdle, sash; Ind. ..... CUMMERBUND
girl ......... MISS, LASS, MINX, SIS
girl, Anglo-Irish ............ COLLEEN
girl, graceful .................... NYMPH
girl, lively ......... FILLY, GIGLOT
girth ENCIRCLE, GIRDLE, STRAP
gist .. ESSENCE, CORE, CHAT, CRUX,
    NUB, PITH

107

give ......... IMPART, GIE, DONATE, (EN)DOW
give back .. REMISE, REMIT, RECOUR
" forth ...... EMIT, EXHALE, EDIT, BLAZE
" sparingly ...... INCH, LOTH, SHY
" up . DEVOTE, CEDE, DOLE, FAIL
given by word of mouth ....... PAROL
gizz ............................... WIG
gizzard trout ............... GILLAROO
glabrous ............. BALD, SMOOTH
glacial ............................. ICY
" deposit ..... MORAINE, PLACER
" fragment ................. SERAC
" ice ................. FIRN, NEVE
" laminated structure . CIPOLLINO
" ridge ........ ESKAR, KAME, OS, OSAR
" waste deposit ........ DILUVIUM
glaciarium ........................ RINK
glacier, facing direction of ...... STOSS
" , rel. to a ............... CIRQUE
glacier-mill ................... MOULIN
glad ......... ELATED, FAIN, MERRY
glad tidings EVANGEL, GOSPEL, JOY
glade .. LAUND, DELL, GAP, VALLEY
glade; comb. form ............... NEMO
gladiator ......... FENCER, LANISTA
gladiators, anc. name for .. BUSTUARII
gladiators, school for ............ LUDI
gladly .......... FREELY, FAIN, LIEF, READILY
Gladsheim ..................... ASGARD
glance .. EYE, LEER, OGLE, GLEAM
glance-coal ............. ANTHRACITE
gland ........................ CAROTID
gland, salivary ............. PAROTID
gland secretion ............ HORMONE
gland-like .................. ADENOID
glands, inflam. of the ...... ADENITIS
glands, throat ................. CHOKE
glandular disease ............ ADENIA
glary ..... SLICK, SMOOTH, FROSTY
glashan; Scot. ................ CODFISH
glass, artificial gems ......... STRASS
" , Bohemian ......... SCHMELZE
" French for ............. VERRE
" , gall .................. ANATRON
" handling rod ............. PUNTY
" in mosaic ............. TESSERA
" jar ......... BOCAL, TALLBOY
" , make into sheets ... PLATTEN
" material ................... FRIT
" , molten ............... PARISON
" of volcanic origin ..... OBSIDIAN
" , piece of ................ PANE
" pond for plants ...... AQUARIUM
" scum ............. CALX, GALL
" showcase ............. VITRINE
glass tube for blowpipe .... MATRASS
glass-maker's oven .... TISAR, LEER
glassware oven ............... ALEER
glasswort ......... KALI, SALTWORT
glassy ......... CRYSTAL, SANIDINE, VITRIC
glassy sea ................... HYALINE
glassy substance ......... FELDSPAR, ENAMEL

glaster ...................... BAWL
Glaucus' father ............ SISYPHUS
Glaucus' wife ................... IONE
glaze .... COAT, ENAMEL, VENEER
glaze on Chinese porcelain . EELSKIN
glaze; slang .... ENAMEL, WINDOW
glazier's diamond ............ EMERIL
glazing machine .......... CALENDER
glead ......................... COAL
gleam . GLINT, CORUSCATE, GLOZE, FLAKE
glean ......................... REAP
glebe ..... CLOD, LUMP, SOIL, TURF
gleety ..................... ICHOROUS
glen ... DALE, DEN, DINGLE, VALE
gliadin ....................... GLUTIN
glib ... BLAND, FLUENT, VOLUBLE, OILY
glide ............. SKID, SKIP, SLIDE
gliding over .................. LABILE
glimmer ..... BLINK, SHEEN, LEAM
glimmering .................. INKLING
glimmering, false ............. GHOST
glioma ....................... TUMOR
glitter ................... CORUSCATE
globe . EARTH, MOON, ORB, SPHERE
globule  TEAR, BLOB, MINIM, DROP, PILL
glockenspiel ................... LYRA
gloomy DIM, EERIE, DREAR, TERNE, WAN, LURID, SAD, DOLESOME, TENEBRIFIC, ADUST, MURKY
"Gloomy Dean," the ............. INGE
gloriale ................... AUREOLA
glorify ... ADORE, BLESS, WORSHIP
glorious ....... ECSTATIC, ELATED, MERE
glory .... KUDOS, AUREOLA, FAME, HALO, TIR, HONOR
glory, bursting forth of ....... ECLAT
glory, cloud of ............... NIMBUS
gloss over ..... PALLIATE, EXCUSE, BLINK, WINK, FARD
glossy ...... SHEENY, GLACE, NITID
glossy compound ............ ENAMEL
glove .. CESTUS, GANT, CUFF, MIT, SUEDE, GAUNTLET
glove fabric ..... KID, LISLE, SUEDE
glove leather .................... NAPA
glove skins, to prepare .......... TAW
glower ....... GLARE, GAZE, GLOVE, STARE
glowing ........ ARDENT, LAMBENT, ASHINE, FLUSHED, WARM
Gluck; opera by ............. ARMIDA
Gluck; soprano ................ ALMA
glucose .......... RUTIN, DEXTROSE
glucose, rel. to ............... GULOSE
glucoside, sweet ... ESTEVIN, RUTIN, SALICIN
glue ................ CEMENT, PASTE
glut SURFEIT, SATE, CLOY, PAUNCH, FEED
glutin .......... GELATIN, GLIADIN
glutinous .......... SIZY, VISCID
glutton .. GOURMAND, CORMORANT
gluttony ....... VORACITY, EDACITY
glycerose, rel. to .......... FRUCTOSE

glycol ..................... PINACOL
glycolaldehyde ................ DIOSE
gnarl .............. GROWL, KNOT
gnash ........ GRATE, BITE, GRIND
gnawed, appear as ........... EROSE
gnawing ........... RODENT, PAIN
gnede ...................... MISERLY
gnome ....... IMP, DWARF, GOBLIN,
      BOGIE, DEEV, NIS, MAXIM
gnome in Ger. folk lore ..... KOBOLD
gnome, N. Amer. ............... OWL
gnomic .................... DIDACTIC
gnomon of a sundial ..... PIN, STYLE
gnostic representation ..... ABRASAX,
                            ABRAXAS
gnostic, second century .... SETHITE
gnu .......... ANTELOPE, KOKOON
go ....... GAE, GANG, SALLY, WEND,
                        WORK, FARE
go back ......... REGRESS, REVERT
go away .............. SCAT, SCRAM
go by plane .............. FLY, AERO
go; Lat. ................. VA, VADE
go about; naut. ........ TACK, WEAR
goa ...................... GAZELLE
goa powder ............... ARAROBA
goad ..... PROD, EGG, GAD, PRICK,
                              PROG
goal .... BOURNE, META, AIM, END,
            HOME, FATE, OBJECT
goal, distant ........ THULE, REACH
goanna ........... IGUANA, GUANO
goat antelope ................ SEROW
  " , Bezoar ................. PASAN
  " , Caucasian .......... TUR, ZAC
  " , female ................ CAPRA
  " , fish; genus ......... UPENEUS
  " , get one's ............... RILE
  " , Himalayan . GORAL, JEMLAN,
                              TAHR
  " , jaal ................... BEDEN
  " kind of ........... SHA, SCAPE
  " , male .................. BUCK
  " , Norse .............. HEIDRUN
  " sucker ............. DORHAWK
  " , wild . MARKHOR, IBEX, TAHR
goatish ......... CAPRINE, HIRCINE
goats; genus ................. CAPRA
goats-hair cloth ..... CAMLET, TIBET
goat's hair cord ............... AGAL
gob ... CHOKE, GOAF, MOUTH, TAR
Gobi Desert lake ............... HARA
Gobi Desert, part of ...... ALASHAN
gobioid fish ................. LOTER
goblet, a .. GLASS, BOCAL, HANAP,
                    TASS, CUP, SKULL
goblet, Eucharist .......... CHALICE
goblin ELF, BOGIE, TROW, GNOME,
                        OUPHE, BHUT
goblin, cave ................ KOBOLD
goblin; Scand. .................. NIS
goby ......................... MAPO
god, car to carry image of ...... RATH
God, anc. (Babyl.) .... UTU, ANSHAR
  " , anc. (Egypt.) . CHNEMU, PTAH,
                            ANUBIS
  " , anc. (Gr..) ............. CHAOS
  " , anc. (Ital.) .... PICUS, SATURN
  " , answer of a ............ ORACLE
  " , Asgard (Norse) ........ AS, ASA
  " , chief (Assyr. Babyl.) ..... NINIB
  " , chief (Babyl.) .. BEL, MARDUK
  " , chief (Celt.) .......... HAFGAN
  " , chief (Chinese) ............ JOSS
  " , chief (Gr.) ...... HADES, PTAH,
                              ZEUS
  " , chief (Irish) ........... DAGDA
  " , chief (Norse) .... FENIR, ODIN,
                    VALI, VANIR, YMIR
  " , dream (Gr.) ........... ONIROS
  " , earth (Babyl.) .......... DAGAN
  " , earth (Egypt.) ............. GEB
  " , Etruscan .. TINIA, TURMS, UNI
  " , evil (Babyl.) .................. ZU
  " , fish ..................... DAGON
  " , Gaelic ............. LER, MIDER
  " , goat .......................... PAN
  " hawk-headed (Egypt.) ...... HOR
  " , healer of sick (Babyl.) ...... EA
  " , Hebrew name ......... ELOHIM
  " , house (Rom.) ..... LAR, LARES
  " , incarnate (Egypt.) ..... MNEVIS
  " , Italian for ................... DIO
  " , jackal .................. ANUBIS
  " , Latin for ................... DEO
  " , Medit. (Persian) ..... MITHRAS
  " , moon (Assyr. Babyl.) ....... SIN
  " , moon (Egypt.) KHENSU, THOTH
  " Odin (Ger.) ............. WODAN
  " , patron (Rom.) ...... MERCURY
  " , principal (Egypt.) .......... MIN
  " , red ...................... MARS
  " , Saturday's ............. SAETER
  " , sea (Hindu) .......... VARUNA
  " , sea (Irish) .................... LER
  " , Semetic household ... STERAPH
  " , supreme (Babyl.) ANU, BEL, EA,
                              EAR
  " , supreme (Gr.) ...... ZEUS
  " , supreme (Scand.) ..... ALFADIR
  " , supreme (Tahitian) .... TAAROA
  " , thunderer (Babyl.) ...... LARES
  " , Thursday's .............. THOR
  " , tutelary (Rom.) ......... LARES
  " , unknown (Hindu) ........... KA
  " Vanir (Norse) .. FREY, NJORTH
  " wise (Teut.) ............. BALDER
God of agriculture .. FAUNUS, NEBO,
            NINGIRSU, OSIRIS, PISUS,
                        THOR
  " of battle (Norse) ........... ODIN
  " of beauty (Celt.) ........ AENGUS
  " of beauty (Gr.) APOLLO, HELIOS
  " of chase (Teut.) ............. ULL
  " of clouds (Norse) .......... YMIR
  " of darkness .. FORMORIAN, SET,
                              SIN
  " of dawn (Vedic) ASVINS, DYAUS
  " of day ..... HOR, HORUS, JANUS
  " of dead ANUBIS, ORCUS, OSIRIS,
            THANATOS, PWYLL, YAMA
  " of discord (Norse) .......... LOKI
  " of dreams MORPHEUS, SERAPIS
  " of Earth .... DAGAN, GEB, KEB,
                              SEB

" of evil ... GIRRU, NERGAL, SET, VARUNA
" of faith ........... SET, SANCUS
" of fertility . DAGAN, FREY, ING, OSIRIS
" of fire .... AGNI, DYAUS, GIRRU, LOGE, NUSKU, VULCAN
" of fish ........ DAGAN, PRIAPUS
" of force ...... MENT, PTAH, SHU
" of ghosts (Babyl.) ........ ENLIL
" of Hades (Gr.) ......... HERMES
" of Hades (Rom.) ...... DIS, PLUT
" of health ........... BELI, OSIRIS
" of hearth, (Etruscan) ........ LAR
" of heathen (Norse) ........ AESIR
" of Heavens (Babyl.) ......... ANU
" of Heavens (Egypt.) ......... NUT
" of herds (Rom.) .............. PAN
" of house (Rom.) .......... LARES
" of joy (Gr.) .............. COMUS
" of justice .. FORSETI, RAMMAN
" of law (Gr.) .............. ZEUS
" of light .... LUG, MITRA, OSIRIS, SHU
" of lightning (Hindu) ........ AGNI
" of love AENGUS, AMOR, BHAGA, CUPID, EROS, KAMA, POTHOS
" of marriage (Gr.) ........ HYMEN
" of medicine (Babyl.) NINGISHZIDA
" of mischief (Norse) ........ LOKI
" of Moon (Babyl.) .. NANNAR, SIN
" of mountains; ATLAS, OLYMPUS, TMOLUS
" of music .......... APOLLO, BES
" of night (Rom.) ........ SOMNUS
" of noontime (Egypt.) .......... RA
" of peace BALDER, EIR, FORSETE, FRET
" of pleasure (Egypt.) .......... BES
" of poetry (Norse) .. BRAGE, ODIN
" of rain ...... AGNI, ESUS, FREY, INDRA, ING, JUPITER
" of science (Egypt.) ........ THOTH
" of scribes, patron (Babyl.) .. NABU
" of seas . AEGER, ATLAS, DYLAN, LER, NEPTUNE, NEREUS, PONTUS, YMIR
" of sky ...... ANU, COEL, DYAUS, JUPITER, TYR, YMIR
" of solar disc (Egypt.) ...... ATEN
God of storms (Babyl.) ..... ADAD, ZU
" of Sun ...... AGNI, AMEN, AMON, BAAL, BELI, FREY, HELIOS, HORUS, ING, CHEPERA, MITHRAS, NERGAL, NINIB, RA, SHAMASH, SOL, TEM, UTU
" of thunder; .... DONAR, JUPITER, TARANIS, THOR, ZEUS
" of trade; (Norse) .......... VANIR
" of underworld (Rom.) DIS, HADES, ORCUS, PLUTO
" of vegetation .. ATTIS, BACCHUS, ESUS
" of victory ............ ODIN, ZEUS
" of war .... COEL, ER, IRA, MARS, MENT, ARES, NERGAL, THOR, TIU, TYR, WODEN
" of war; (Gaelic) ........... DAGDA

" of waters ..... EA, EAR, FONTUS, HEA, NEPTUNE, VARUNA
" of wealth ................... PLUTUS
" of winds .......... ADAD, AEOLUS, BOREAS, EURUS, KAARE, NJORD, VAYU
" of wine (Gr. Rom.) ..... BACCHUS
" of wisdom ..... EA, EAR, GANESA, NEBO, ODIN, SABU, SIN, TAT, THOTH
Godavari (B.I.) capital ...... ELLORE
Goddess .................... DEA
"       , avenging ............... FURY
"       , Babylonian ............ ERUA
"       , Carthaginian ......... TANIT
"       , catheaded (Egypt.) ... BAST, PACHT
"       , Etruscan MENFRA, TURAN, UNI
"       , hippo-headed; Egypt. .. APET
"       , Panopolis; (Egypt.) ..... MIN
"       of abundance .............. SRI
"       of actors ............ MINERVA
"       of agriculture ... BAU, CERES, ISIS, OPS
"       of air (Gr.) ..... AURA, HERA
"       of arts (Gr.) ......... ATHENA
"       of beauty (Norse) ..... FREYA
"       of beauty (Rom.) ...... VENUS
"       of betrothal (Norse) ....... VOR
"       of birth (Rom.) ........ PARCA
"       of captured arms .......... LUA
"       of Carthage ............. TANIT
"       of chance (Gr.) ........ TYCHE
"       of chase .... ARTEMIS, DIANE
"       of corn ................. CERES
"       of crops ................... OPS
"       of cross-roads (Gr.) .. HECATE
"       of cross-roads (Rom.) . TRIVIA
"       of dawn ....... EOS, MATUTA
"       of dawn (Hindu) ....... USHAS
"       of dawn (Rom.) ...... AURORA
"       of death ... DANU, HEL, HELA
"       of deep (Babyl.) .. NANA, NINA
"       of destiny (Gr.) ....... MOERA
"       of destiny (Norse) ...... NORN
"       of destruction (Gr.) ...... ARA
"       of destruction (Hindu) ... KALI
"       of discord (Gr.) .......... ERIS
"       of doom (Norse) URTH, WYRD
Goddess of Earth, mother (Babyl.) .... ARURU, ISHTAR
"       of Earth TARI, CERES, GAEA, GE, ERDA, HERTHA, LUA, OPS, SEB, SIF
"       of fate ................... NORN
"       of fields (Rom.) ....... LARES, TELLUS
"       of fire (Gr.) ........... HESTIA
"       of fire (Hawai.) ......... PELE
"       of fire (Rom.) ......... VESTA
"       of flowers (Gr.) ..... CHLORIS
"       of flowers (Rom.) ...... FLORA
"       of fortune ............. TYCHE
"       of ghosts (Gr.) ....... HECATE
"       of goblins (Gr.) ..... ARTEMIS
"       of harvest (Rom.) ......... OPS
"       of healing (Babyl.) BAU, GULA
"       of healing (Norse) ......... EIR

110

" of health (Gr.) DAMIA, HYGEA
" of health (Rom.) ...... SALUS
" of hearth (Gr.) ....... HESTIA, VESTA
" of Heavens (Egypt.) ...... NUT
" of history (Norse) ...... SAGA
" of hope ................... SPES
" of horses (Rom.) ...... EPONA
" of hunting (Rom.) .... DIANA, VACUNA
" of infatuation ............. ATE
" of joy (Egypt.) ...... HATHOR
" of justice .... ASTRAEA, DICE, MAAT
" of learning (Egypt.) .. SESHAT
" of light (Rom.) ....... LUCINA
" of love .... ASTARTE, ATHOR, FREYA, ISHTAR, VENUS
" of luck (Hindu) .... LAKSHMI, SHRI
" of marriage . GAEA, GE, HERA
" of Memphis (Egypt.) ..... DOR
" of mischief (Gr.) .......... ATE
" of Moon BENDIS, DIANA, ISIS, LUCINA, LUNA, ORTHIA, PHOEBE, SELENE
" of night ........... LETO, NOX
" of oceans (Babyl.) ....... NINA
" of order .. DICE, DIKE, IRENE
" of ovens ............. FORNAX
" of peace ..... EIR, IRENE, PAX
" of plenty (Rom.) .......... OPS
" of rainbows (Egypt.) ...... IRIS
" of retribution (Gr.) ....... ARA
" of seas (Gr.) ...... DORIS, INO
" of seas (Norse) .......... RANA
" of seasons (pl.) ....... HORAE
" of sky (Egypt.) .......... NUT
" of speech (Hindu) ......... VAC
" of state (Rom.) ........ VESTA
" of storms .............. HARPY
" of trees (fruit) ....... POMONA
" of truth (Egypt.) ....... MAAT
" of underworld ....... ALLATU, FERONIA, FURY, GAEA, HECATE, HEL, LARUNA
" of vegetation (Gr.) ..... COTYS
" of vegetation (Rom.) .. CERES, FLORA
" of vengeance (Gr.) ....... ARA
Goddess of victory (Gr.) .......... NIKE
" of virtue (Rom.) ........ FIDES
" of war .... ANAHITA, ANATU, ATHENA, BELLONA, ENYO, ISHTAR, VACUNA
" of waters (Babyl.) ...... ERUA
" of wealth (Hindu) ......... SRI
" of weaving (Gr.) ..... ERGANE
" of wedlock (Norse) ........ SIF
" of wisdom (Gr.) ...... PALLAS
" of womanhood (Egypt.) .. SATI
" of womanhood (Theban) .. MUT
" of youth (Gr.) .......... HEBE
" of Zealand (Teut.) . MERTHUS
godfather .................... SPONSOR
Godfrey's sister ............... KATHY
Gods, messenger of the ....... HERMES
gods, "bright land" of the ..... DELOS
godwit; Eng. .................... PRINE

Goethe's hero ................. FAUST
Goethe's home ............... WEIMAR
goggle ...................... STARE
goggler ...... CICHARRA, SCAD
goggler; Hawai. ............... AKULE
going ................... EXIT, ULTRA
going back on .............. APOSTASY
going in ................... INEUNT
Gold Coast colony TOGO, TOGOLAND, ASHANTI
Gold Coast language .............. TSHI
Gold Coast seaport ................ APAM
gold ....... GILT, ORO, AURUM, AUR
" braid ..................... ORRIS
" , cast mass of ............. INGOT
" coin (see also 'coin')
" coin of Austria .. DUCAT, KRONE
" coin of Egypt ......... BEDIDLIK
" coin of England ......... GUINEA
" coin of Eng., old .. ANGEL, RYAL
" coin of France ...... LOUIS, LUIS
" coin of France; obs. ....... SCUTE
" coin of Germany ......... KRONE
" coin of India .............. MOHUR
" coin of Italy .............. SCUDO
" coin of Italy, anc. Rom. AUREUS
" coin of Japan, obs. ...... ITZEBU, OBANG
" coin of Persia . ASHRAFI, TOMAN
" coin of Persia; obs. . ASAR, DARIC
" coin of Rome; anc. ........ SEMIS
" coin of Russia ......... IMPERIAL
" coin of Scotland ............. LION
" coin of Spain CENTEN. PISTOLE
" coin of Spain; obs. ...... DOBLON
" coin of Trukey .... LIRA, YUZLUK
" coin of United States ..... EAGLE
" colored fish ............. AURATA
" , containing .............. DORE
" discoverer of ............. SUTTER
" field ...................... OPHIR
" , fineness of ............... CARAT
" , imitation .............. ORMOLU
" lace ........... FILIGREE, ORRIS
" , like ...................AURATE
" , magic hord of ..... RHEINGOLD
" , seeker of ........... ARGONAUT
" sheet ........................ FOIL
" , symbol for .............. AU, OR
" , thin plate of ........... LATTEN
" vein .......................... LODE
" vessel ..................... CUPEL
" washing pan .............. BATEA
golden .. YELLOW, AUREATE, AURIC
"Golden Boy"; author .......... ODETS
golden age ............... SATURNIAN
" bough ............. MISTLETOE
" bug ................. LADYBIRD
" fleece ship ................. ARGO
"Golden King" ................. MIDAS
goldenrod ................. SOLIDAGO
goldfinch .... REDCAP, YELLOWBIRD
gold-like alloy ....... ASEM, ORMOLU, OROIDE
goldsmith's crucible CREVET, CRUSET
goldy-locks ............. BUTTERCUP
golem ................ DUNCE, BOOBY

111

golf club **BRASSIE, DRIVER, CLEEK, IRONS, MASHIE, PUTTER, SPOON, MIDIRON**
golf club head, end of .............. **TOE**
golf cup; U.S.; Gr. Br. ........ **RYDER**
"golf, Mr." .................. **NELSON**
golf term .... **TRAP, DIVOT, SCLAFF, BAFF, CHIP, PAR, PUTT, TEE, SLICE**
golfer .................. **JONES, SNEAD**
golfer, poor .................. **DUBBER**
Goliath's home town ............ **GATH**
gombeen man, Irish ........... **USURER**
Gomer, husband of ............ **HOSEA**
gomuti; Malay ................... **EJOO**
gomuti palm ................... **ARENG**
gone ... **PAST, AGO, OFF, YOT, LOST**
gone for good; slang .......... **NAPOO**
"Gone with the Wind," char. in ........ **MELANIE**
Goneril's sister ................ **REGAN**
goober ........................ **PEANUT**
good .... **MORAL, BEAU, BON, WEAL, UP**
good arrangement; Gr. ...... **EUTAXIA**
good bye .............. **ADIEU, TATA**
"Good Bye," composer of ...... **TOSTI**
good fellow; col. ...... **BRICK, TRUMP**
good for nothing .... **ADDLE, MEAN, SHOTTEN, CARRION, KET**
Good-King-Henry ............. **BLITE**
good news tidings **EVANGEL, GOSPEL**
good working order .......... **KILTER**
goodly ............. **READILY, WINNE**
goods ......... **FEE, WARES, WRACK**
"  , admit of taking .... **AVOWRY**
"  , cast overboard ........ **JETSAM**
"  , movable ........... **CHATTEL**
"  , covered by hides ...... **SEROON**
"  , stolen ............ **CRONK**
"  sunk with buoy markers **LIGAN**
goon .................... **ROUGH, THUG**
goosander ................ **JACKSAW**
goose **GREYLAG, BERNICLE, BRANT, SOLON**
"  , a pygmy ............. **GOSLET**
"  barnacle; genus ..... **ANATIFA, LEPAS**
"  , col. term ........ **DUPE, GULL**
"  , cry of a .... **CACKLE, HONK**
"  , fen ................ **GRAYLING**
"  foot herbs ............ **BLITES**
"  , footless, beakless ... **GANNET**
"  grease ................ **AXUNGE**
"  , Hawaiian ........ **NENE, NENI**
"  , male ................ **GANDER**
"  , rel. to ............ **ANSERINE**
"  , snow ........ **WAVEY, BRANT**
"  , wild **BERNICLE, BRANT, ELK, GANZA**
gooseberries; Scot. .......... **THAPES**
gooseberry; genus ............. **RIBES**
gopher, Mex. pocket .......... **TUCAN**
gopher; slang ............. **BURGLAR**
gopher State ............ **MINNESOTA**
gore . **PIERCE, STAB, CRUOR, NURT**
gore, as of cloth ............. **GUSSET**
gorel .............................. **PIG**

gorge . **SATE, CANYON, BOLT, GLUT, POUCH, STRID**
gorge; Hindu ................. **NULLAH**
"Gorgeous George" ........... **SISLER**
gorgerin .................... **NECKING**
Gorgon; Bib. ................. **JEZEBEL**
Gorgons ...... **EURYALE, MEDUSA, STHENO**
Gorgons, watchers for the ... **GRAEAE**
gorilla ............................. **APE**
gorilla, native name .......... **NGINA**
gormaw ................ **CORMORANT**
Gorme; songstress ............ **EYDIE**
gorrean ........................ **YOKE**
gorse ........... **FURZE, JUNIPER**
gorse hatcher; Eng. .... **WHEATEAR**
gory ...... **IMBRUED, BLOODY, RED**
Gosden, Freeman ............... **AMOS**
gosling ................. **GOOSE, GULL**
gospel ............ **EVANGEL, SPELL**
gospels, comb. of four **DIATESSARON**
gossamery ... **DIAPHANOUS, GAUZY, THIN, COBWEBBY**
gossip .. **EME, CAT, CHAT, CLAVER, ONDIT, NORATE, QUIDNUNC, TALEBEARER, TALK, TATTLE**
gossip; India .................... **GUP**
gossip, tattling .................... **PIE**
gossoon .......................... **LAD**
got down ........................ **ALIT**
Gothic bard .................. **RUNER**
gouge .... **CHEAT, CHISEL, FRAUD, BENT**
goulash; Hung. .............. **RAGOUT**
Gounod; opera by ............ **FAUST**
goupha ........................ **KUPHAR**
gourd .. **MELON, CALABASH, PEPO, CUCURBI, FLASK**
gourmand .. **GLUTTON, WOLVERINE**
gourmet ........ **TASTER, EPICURE**
gout . **ARTHRITIS, DROP, PODAGRA**
goutweed ............... **ASHWEED**
govern **REIGN, BRIDLE, LEAD, RUN, REGULATE**
governess; Sp. ........ **AYA, DUENNA**
government agency .............. **ECA**
government **REGIMEN, SWAY, POLITY**
government by ten ...... **DECARCHY**
government lands; Ind. ...... **AMANI**
government, no .............. **ACRACY**
governor . **DYNAST, REGENT, PILOT, VICEROY**
governor; Burma .............. **WOON**
governors, 1 of 10 .......... **DECARCH**
gowan; Scot. .................. **DAISY**
gown . **FROCK, SOUTANE, SULTANE**
gown; Middle Ages . **CYCLAS, CHITON**
gown, negligee ............ **MATINEE**
grabble ................ **GROPE, FEEL**
grace **FAVOR, ADORN, ESTE, GARB, ENHANCE, HONOR**
graceful **EASY, FEAT, GENT, SYLPH**
Graces, mother of ............ **AEGLE**
Graces, one of the . **THALIA, AGLAIA**
gracious **BENIGN, EDMOD, URBANE**
grackle .......................... **DAW**
gradation . **ABLAUT, NUANCE, STEP**
grade .......... **CLASS, RANK, SORT**

graduate .. ALUMNUS, GRADE, PASS
Graeae, the watchers for the Gorgons ..
    DEINO, NEYO, PEPHREDO
graft .......... IMP, CLAVE, INARCH
graft taker .................... BRIBEE
grafted; her. .................... ENTE
grafting method ............ CUTTAGE
grail ........ SANGREAL, SANGRAAL
grain CORN, OAT, ATOM, IOTA, WHIT
"   beard ............ AWN, ARISTA
"   , black ..................... URD
"   cradle ..................... CADRE
"   , deriv. of ................. MALT
"   disease ..................... SMUT
grain exchange .................... PIT
"   husk .......... GLUME, BRAN
"   measure of ........ GRIST, MOY
"   of pulpy fruit ...... DRUPELET
"   of wood .................. BATE
"   , 1/20 of a ................ MITE
"   , per. to ................ GROATS
"   , refuse of .................. PUG
"   , Russ. .................... EMMER
"   , sacrificial ................ ADOR
"   , shelter ................. HUTCH
"   , shock of .................. COP
"   , unbound bundle of .. GRAVEL
gram, molecular weight ........ MOLE
gramercy .................... THANKS
Grammann, opera by ........ INGRID
grammar, logic and rhetoric .. TRIVIA
grammarian .............. PROSODIST
grammatical arrangement .... TAXIS
grammatical case ............ DATIVE
grammatical construction, a SYNESIS
grammatical term .......... GENDER
grammatite ............. TREMOLITE
grample ................... CRABFISH
grampus .................... ORC, ORCA
granary .. SILO, ELEVATOR, LATHE,
    STOREHOUSE
grand .... HOMERIC, AUGUST, EPIC
grandchild ..................... OY, OYE
grandchild, great .............. IEROE
grandeur ,......... GLORY, MAJESTY
grandeval ............ AGED, ATAVUS
grandfather ...... AIEL, PATRIARCH
grandfather, per. to .. AVITAL, AVAL
grandfather's grandfather TRESAYLE
grandiose HOMERIC, EPIC, TURGID
grandmother ......... BELDAM, AVIA,
    GRANDAM
grandparent, per. to ............ AVAL
grandson .................... NEPOTE
grange . GRANARY, FARM, HEARTH
granilla ................... COCHINEAL
granite, constituent of .... FELSPAR,
    MICA, QUARTZ
"   , decomposed ........ GOWAN
"   , fine grained ...... HARLITE,
    APLITE
"   porphyry ............. ELVAN
"   , principal constituent of ......
    ORTHOCLASE
"   , variety of ...... ALASKITE,
    BIOTITE, MUSCOVITE

grant CEDE, APPANAGE, APPEASE,
    ADMIT, CONFER, LOAN,
    PERMIT, ENAM
granulate ...... GRAIN, CORN, KERN
granuloma ................ BIASTOMA
grape ...... DELAWARE, CONCORD,
    ISABELLA
"   body .................... CORESE
"   conserve ................ UVATE
"   culture .......... VITICULTURE
"   , deriv. of .............. ARGOL
grape disease ................ COLEUR
"   juice DIBS, MUST, STUM, SAPA
"   juice deposit .......... TARTAR
"   juice, rel. to .......... RACEMIC
"   , kind of . MALAGA, CATAWBA
"   parasite .............. PROCRIS
"   , pomace of .............. RAPE
"   rufuse BAGASSE, MARC, MURC
"   seeds ..................... ACINI
"   sugar .. MALTOSE, DEXTROSE
"   sun dried .................. PASA
"   vine disease .......... ERINOSE
"   vine, wild ................ CARO
"   , white ................ NIAGARA
grapefruit .... POMELO, SHADDOCK
grape-like .................. POKE, UVA
grapes, bunch of .................. BOB
"Grapes of Wrath," family in .. JOAD
grapeseed, a .................... ACINUS
graph, per. to ........ CHART, LOCUS
graphic ................ CLEAR, VIVID
graphite .. LEAD, PLUMBAGO, SOOT
grapple ........ WRESTLE, ATTACK,
    FASTEN, KNIT, BIND
    CLUTCH, LOCK
grapple for oysters ............ TONG
grappling iron ............ GRAPNEL
grasp HENT, EREPT, GRIPE, RICHE,
    GOUPEN
grasping .. CLAM, CLOSE, MISERLY
grasping, adapted for . PREHENSIVE
grass .................. SPART, HERB
"   , Amer. .. BOUTELOUA, GAMA
    RYE
    SESAME
"   , arrow .............. ESPARTO
"   , Asiatic .................... COIX
"   , Austrian beach ...... MARRAM
"   , bamboo-like ............ REED
"   , barn ................... ANKEE
"   beach ..................... MAT
"   , Bengal ............... MILLET
"   , Bermuda ............... DOOB
"   , blade of; Anglo-Ir. . TRANEEN
"   , blue June ................ POA
"   , bull .................... GAMA
"   , Burden's ............ REDTOP
"   , cant-like ............ SORGUM
"   carpet .................... SMUT
"   , cat-tail ............ TIMOTHY
"   , cereal .. RICE, MILLET, OAT,
    RYE
"   cloth-plant ............. RAMIE
"   , coarse Amer. .......... GAMA
"   corn ............ SEDGE, KAFIR
"   couch .................... BROME
"   country .................... VELD

" , creeping beard ...... FESCUE
" , crested dogs-tail .. TRANEEN
" , darnel ................... TARE
" , devil's ................. COUCH
" ditch ................... ENALID
" , dried ..................... HAY
" , edibles of .............. GRAIN
" , esparto ................. ALFA
" feather .................. STIPA
" , flyaway ................. BENT
" for hay .............. TIMOTHY
" , forage .... MILLET, REDTOP
" , fringed brome ........ CHESS
" for thatch .............. ALANG
" gama ................. SESAME
grass, goose ...... LOVEMAN, SPEAR
" , grapevine ......... MESQUITE
" , Guatemala ........ TEOSINTE
" , hunger .............. FOXTAIL
" husk ..................... GLUME
" , Indian cereal .......... RAGEE
" , jointed stem ............ CULM
" , Kentucky blue ............ POA
" , kind of .... BARLEY, BROME,
          EEL, TAPE, GAMA, NARD
" , kind of millet .......... PANIC
" , leaf ................... BLADE
" , lemon ............. COCKSPUR
" , Louisiana ............. BENA
" lyme ................. HASSOCK
" , marsh ................. SPART
" , mesquite ... GRAMA, NEEDLE
" , Mexican .. TEOSINTE, OTATE
" , Mexican whisk .......... DEER
" moor .................... HEATH
" , oat .................... AVENA
" , Philippine ............ COGON
" , poison rye .......... DARNEL
" , purple beard ........ NEEDLE
" , quaking ................ BRIZA
" , quitch ................ COUCH
" , reedy, Algerian .......... DISS
" rug ......................... MAT
" , rye .................. MARCITE
" , salt ................... ALKALI
" scale .................... PALEA
" , sedge ................. BROOM
" , seneca .............. VANILLA
" silt ..................... KNOT
" , So. Afr. country ...... VELDT
" , Spanish ............. ESPARTO
" , stiff or wiry ............ BENT
" , swamp ................. SEDGE
" , trampled by a stag ABATURE
" , tuft of .............. TUSSOCK
" used in paper manufacture ALFA
" , Virginia lyme ...... TERRELL
" , wiry .............. BENT, POA
grasses, chaffy scales in ...... GLUME
"          , genus of ARUNDO, STIPA,
          POA, SETARIA, AVENA
"     , imported; genus . SORGHUM
"     , meadow ................ POA
grassland ..................... SWARD
grassy plain ..................... LEA
grate . RASP, CHARK, RUB, SCRAPE
gratify .. ARRIDE, CONTENT, LUST
gratinate ........................ COOK

grating .... HARSH, HOARSE, GRID,
    HACK, RASPY, GRILLE, LATTICE
gratuitous ........ FREE, HAZARDED
gratuity ...... TIP, FEE, DOLE, GIFT,
          LAGNIAPPE, VAIL
gravamen .... CHARGE, GRIEVANCE
grave ........ FOSSE, SUANT, TOMB
grave cloth .............. CEREMENT
grave, rel. to ........ BARROW, URN
grave wax ............ ADIPOCERE
gravel .. CALCULI, BEACH, PUZZLE
gravel, alluvial ................ GEEST
gravelly beach ........... AIR, AYR
graver .. SCULPTOR, BURIN, STYLE
gravestone ........ MARKER, STELE
gravitate .... DROP, TUMBLE, FALL
gravure, rel. to .................. ROTO
gray ...... ACIER, ASHEN, TAUPE
gray, comb. form .............. POLIO
gray; Fr. ........................ GRIS
gray matter .......... BRAIN, OBEX
grayish metal . STEEL, MANGANESE
grayish rock ............. ANDESITE
grayling .......... HERRING, UMBER
graze .. NICK, BRUSH, RUB, SHAVE
graze cattle ...... PASTURE, AGIST
grease LARD, AXUNGE, FAT, MORT,
          SAIM, OIL
greasewood ........ ORACHE, CHICO
greasy YOLKY, OILY, PORKY, SLASY
great ........ NOBLE, SUBLIME, BIG,
          HUGE, TITANIC, PLENARY,
          HERCULANEAN
Great Barrier Is. ................. OTEA
great grandchild .................. IER
Great Lakes .......... ERIE, HURON,
          MICHIGAN, ONTARIO,
          SUPERIOR
great many; Ind. ................ LAC
great number ........... LAC, LAKH,
    LEGIONARY, GALAXY, HEAP,
          HOST
great spirit; Am. Ind. ...... MANITO
greater ............ LARGER, MAJOR
grebe ............. DABCHICK, LOON
Grecian ghost ................... KERE
Greco-Egypt. deity .......... SERAPIS
Greece, anc. bronze coin of .. LEPTON
" anc. ................... ATTICA
" , anc. division of .... ACHAEA
" , anc. name .......... HELLAS
" , Brit. commander .... SCOBIE
" , cape in ........... MATAPAN
" , city in; anc. ...... CHALCIS,
          ERETRIA, EUBOEA
" , father of the church of ......
          ORIGEN
" , headland in ........ ACTIUM
" , island of .. PELION, NAXOS
" , mountain in ........ ATHOS
" , nome of ................ ELIS
" , premier;(ex) ...... PAPAGOS
" , province of ........... NOME
" , seaport of ........... ENOS
" , subdivision of ...... PHYLE
" , town of; anc. ........ SERES
" , valley of ........... TEMPE
greed AVARICE, DESIRE, GLUTTONY

114

greediness .... EDACITY, CUPIDITY
greedy .. ESURIENT, OMNIVOROUS,
AVID
Greek, a CRETE, ARGIVE, HELLENE
" abbess ................ AMMA
" aurora ................... EOS
" avenging spirit ERINYS, KER,
ATE
" base; arch. ........... ATTIC
" castanets .......... CROTALA
" charioteer; myth. . PHAETON
" choral dance movement ......
STROPHE
" church, reserved sections .....
BEMATA
" citadel .......... ACROPOLIS
" city ....... BARCA, SPARTA,
LARISSA
" city; myth. .......... ARGOS
" clan, subdivision ........ OBE
" coin ......... OBOL, OBOLUS,
DRACHMA
" coin, small .......... LEPTON
" coin, standard ...... STATER,
NOMAS
" colonist .............. OECIST
" colony ......... ELEA, IONIA
Greek commander ........ NAVARCH
" commonality .......... DEMOS
" commune, modern ..... DEME
" counsellor .......... NESTOR
" courtesan ............. THAIS
" cup or bowl .......... DEPAS
" cupid ................... EROS
" dance .............. PYRRHIC
" deity, supreme ...... CRONUS
" demon of illness ... PYTHON
" dialect AEOLIC, DORIC, IONIC
" dirge; anc. ............. LINOS
" dramatist .......... THESPIS
" drinking cup ........ COTYLE
" enchantress .. CIRCE, MEDEA
" entertainer; anc. .. HETAIRA
" evil spirit ............ MOMUS
" fabulist ............... AESOP
" faction ................. ELAS
" Father .............. ORIGEN
" feast, religious ...... TONEA
" female worshipper .... ORANT
" festival ........ DELIA, AGON
" fire hero; myth. .... VULCAN
" foot race course ..... DIAULI
" foot soldier ........ HOPLITE
" garment ........... PEPLOS,
FUSTANELLA
" ghost .................... KER
" gifts ................... XENIA
" god (see also 'God')
" " of Aegean Sea .. NEREUS
" " of darkness ... ACRISIUS,
LAIUS
" " of flocks ............. PAN
" " of hurricane ........ OTUS
" " of love .. EROS, POTHOS
" " of rain ............. ZEUS
" " of rivers AXIUS, SELINUS,
SIMOIS
" " of sky .... ARGUS, ZEUS

" " of the heavens .. URANUS,
ZEUS
" " of the sea ....... AEGUS
NEREUS
" " of the setting sun ........
ENDYMION
" " of the sun ...... APOLLO,
HELIOS, MENTU, PHOEBUS
" " of the underworld PYTHON
" " of the winds .... AEOLUS,
EURUS
" " of vegetation . DIONYSUS
" " of war ARES, ENYALIUS
" " of youth ........ APOLLO
" goddess (see also 'Goddess')
" " of agriculture . ARTEMIS,
DEMETER
" " of beauty ... APHRODITE
" " of chance ........ TYCHE
" " of chastisement NEMESIS
" " of dark night ....... LETO
" " of dawn ...... ALCMENE,
ARIADNE, EOS
" " of destiny, or fate MOERA
" " of discord .......... ERIS
" " of earth ...... GAEA, GE
" " of fire ......... HESTIA
" " of halcyon days ALCYONE
" " of love ..... APHRODITE
Greek goddess of malicious mischief ..
ATE
" " of marriage .. DEMETER,
GAEA, GE, HERA
" " of memory MNEMOSYNE
" " of mist ....... NEPHELE
" " of nature, wild . ARTEMIS
" " of night HECATE, LETO,
NYX
" " of peace ...... IRENE
" " of pure air ..... AETHER,
HERA, HERE
" " of the chase .. ARTEMIS
" " of the clouds ..... NIOBE
" " of the heavens; HECATE,
HERA
" " of the moon; .. ARTEMIS,
ASTARTE, DIANA,
IO, SELENE
" " of the night; .. ARTEMIS,
LEDA, LETO
" " of the plains; ..... MAIA,
MAJESTA
" " of the sea ........... INO
" " of the sky ........ HERA
" " of the violet colored clouds
IOLE, JOCASTA
" " of twilight ...... HELEN,
PHAEDRA
" " of vengeance .. NEMESIS
" " of victory .......... NIKE
" " of wisdom .... MINERVA,
PALLAS
" " of youth ........... HEBE
" " queen of the heavens HERA
" " , triple .......... HECATE
" gods of the subterranean fire ..
TITANS
" giant .............. ANTAEUS

115

" governor ............. EPARCH
" gravestone .............. STELE
" guerilla ............... ANDART
" gymnasium ................. XYST
" hero ..... NESTOR, THESEUS
" historian .......... XENOPHON
" house, apartment in . ANDRON,
THALAMOS
Greek huntress ........... ATALANTA
" immigrant; anc. ........ METIC
" island .. CHIOS, CRETE, ELIS,
KOS, IONIAN, MILO,
NIO, SAMOS, SCIO
" island; myth. .......... NAXOS
" laver ................. LOUTER
" lawmaker .............. MINOS
" legendary hero ..... ALCINOUS
" legendary river god ERIDANUS
" letter .... ALPHA, BETA, CHI,
DELTA, ETA, EPSILON,
GAMMA, IOTA, KAPPA,
PHI, LAMBDA, MU, NU,
OMICRON, PSI, RHO,
SIGMA, TAU, THETA,
UPSILON, XI, ZETA,
OMEGA
" letter, discontinued . DIGAMMA
" letter, primitive .......... SAN
" love feast ............... AGAPE
" lyric poet ............. PINDAR
" magristrate .......... ARCHON
Greek magristrate, chief .. NOMARCH
" market place ........... AGORA
" marriage song ........ HYMEN
" measure ........ BEMA, POUS,
STADIUM
" monster of drought; myth .....
SPHINX
" mountain ... PARNASSUS, IDA,
OSSA, OITE, ACTIUM
" musical note; anc. ...... NETE
" musician ............... ARION
" note; mus. .............. NETE
" novelist ................ XENOS
" numismatist ......... LAMBROS
" overseer ................ EPHOR
" painter .................. GRECO
" parliament .............. BOULE
" patriarch .............. ARIUS
" peninsula .............. MOREA
" , per. to land ........... AGROS
" philologist ............ ASOPIOS
" philosopher; PLATO, THALES,
ZENO, GALEN, ELEA
" physician ............... GALEN
" pilaster ................. ANTA
" pillar ................... STELE
" platform .... LOGEION, BEMA
" poet; ... ARION, HOMER, ION,
PINDAR
" poetess ............... ERINNA
" populace .............. DEMOS
" portico ........... STOA, XYST
" priest, parish ......... PAPAS
" province .... NOME, BOEOTIA
" public disgrace ......... ATIMY
" river .................... ARTA
" root, for mimic ......... MIMO

" sacred inclosure .... TEMENOS,
SEKOS
" sage ................... THALES
" school, per. to a philosophy in ..
ELEATIC
" sculptor .............. PHIDIAS
" secret precinct ...... TEMENOS
" serf ................... PENEST
" slab .................... STELE
" slave, female . BAUBE, IAMBE
" solar hero; myth. . MELEAGER
" soldier; anc. ......... HOPLITE
" song .......... MELOS, OICOS
" soothsayer .......... CALCHAS
" sorceress .............. CIRCE
" spirit ......... KER, PNEUMA
" statesman ........ ARISTIDES,
PERICLES
" storm wind ............ LELAPS
" stronghold ................ SULI
" superintendent of public works .
EPH
" symbol ................. ORANT
" symbol; mus. . NETE, NEUME
" temple, parts of CELLA, NAOS
" tense of the verb ...... AORIST
" theatre ................. ODEON
" tongue ................. ROMAIC
" town ..... ELIS, SERES, ARTA
" township ................ DEME
" tragedy ............... RHESUS
" tunic .................. CHITON
" valley in Argolis ...... NEMEA
" vessels like wine skins .... ASCI
" war cry; anc. .......... ALALA
" warrior ............... ACAMAS
Greek warrior's belt ......... ZOUAVE
" weight ............ OBOL, MNA
" wooden statue ........ XOANON
" writer ...... LUCIAN, AELIAN,
AESOR
Greeks ...................... ARGIVES
Greeks; anc. ................ EOLIANS
green ........ CALLOW, FRESH, RAW,
VERDANT, CHLORINE,
UNRIPE
" arrow ................ YARROW
" color ...... JADE, VERT, MOSS
" , comb. form .......... PRASEO
" copper arsenate ...... ERENITE
" eyed ................ JEALOUS
" , grayish ............. RESEDA
" kind of . KELLY, CYAN, NILE,
VIRID, TERREVERTE
" , pale sea .......... CELADON
" sand ..................... MARL
" tea .................... HYSON
green-back herring ............. CISCO
Green; famous .............. GRETNA
greenbacks ..................... TENS
greenery ................... VERDURE
green-gage ..................... PLUM
greenheart .......... BEBEERU, TREE
greenhorn JAY, GULL, TYRO, YAHOO
greening ...................... APPLE
greenish yellow ..... OLIVE, CITRINE
Greenland, base in .............. ETAH
Greenland, discoverer of ......... ERIC

116

Greenland, series of .......... ATANE
Greenlander ...................... ITA
"Green Mansions," heroine .... RIMA
green-room ................... FOYER
green-sickness .............CHLOROSIS
green-tail fly .............. GRANNOM
greet ........ HALSE, ACCOST, HAIL
greeting HOW, SALUTE, AVE, ACCOIL
grego .............. CLOAK, JACKET
Gregorian lesser doxology, trope of ...
                               EUOUAE
grenade ...................... SHELL
grenade bag; Fr. ........... GIBERNE
grenadier (fish) ............ RATTAIL
Gretna Green visitor ........ ELOPER
grew to be ........ BECAME, WAXED
Grey; author ................... ZANE
grief ... DOLOR, RUE, TEEN, TRIAL,
                                  WOE
Grieg; compo. .............. EDVARD
Grieg's dancer .............. ANITRA
grieve LAMENT, MOURN, ERME, ERN,
                        CRY, COMPLAIN
grievous ........ ATTRITE, HEINOUS
griffe ...................... MULATTO
griffin ................. EAGLE, LION
grifter's henchman ............ SHILL
grig ................... CRICKET, EEL
grilse ...................... SALMON
grimace ... MOE, MOP, MOW, SHAM
grimalkin .......... CAT, MOLL, TOM
grime wave ..................... SOOT
grind MASTICATE, BRAY, DIG, MULL
grinders ...................... MOLARS
grinding stone ... METATE, MULLER
grinding substance EMERY, ABRASIVE
grindstone for grain ........... MANO
gringo .................... FOREIGNER
gripping device .......... DOG, VICE
grit .......... NERVE, SAND, PLUCK
gritty part of wheat ...... SEMOLINA
grivet monkey .................. TOTA
grizzly bear, hunter's name for ........
                              EPHRAIM
groat, half a ............ DANDIPRAT
grog .................... RUM, RUMBO
grommet ......... EYELET, RING
gromwell, common ...... STONESEED
groom STRAP, BRUSH, CURRY, TIDY
groove .. CHASE, EXERATE, FLUTE,
                                   RUT
groove cut in barrel RIFLING, CROZE
groove cut in masonry ...... RAGLET,
                               RAGGLE
groove, minute .................. STRIA
grooved .. CANALICULAR, STRIATE,
                               SULCATE
grooves . SCORES, SPLINES, LIRATE
grope ........ GRUBBLE, FEEL, TAY
grosbeak .............. FINCH, MORO
gross .. ENTIRE, AGGREGATE, SUM
grotesque ........ BIZARRE, CLOWN,
       BAROQUE, FREAK, ODD, UNIQUE
grotesque figure; Chin. ........ MAGOT
grotto .. CATACOMB, CAVE, VAULT
ground ...... CLOD, CLAY, GRITTED
ground, parcel of .............. SOLUM
ground, piece of rising ........ HURST

ground-hog; Am. ........... MARMOT
ground-hog day ........ CANDLEMAS
groundless fancy ........... CHIMERA
ground-nut; Afr. .............. GOBBE
grounds .... LEES, RESIDUE, DREGS
ground-squirrel CHIPMUNK, HACKEE
group of crustacea ........... CARIDEA
group of five ............... PENTAD
group of invertebrates ...... APTERA
group of nine ................ ENNEAD
group of seven .............. HEPTAD
grouped together ......... AGMINATE
groups of species ........... GENERA
grouse ................ PTARMIGAN
grouse courtship ................... LAK
grouse, Pallas sand ........ ATAAGEN
grouse, red; genus ......... LAGOPUS
grouse; slang .............. COMPLAIN
grouse, species of . BONASA, CANACE
grove, inhab. a ........... NEMORAL
grove of mango trees ........... TOPE
grove of pines .............. PINETUM
grove, sacred to Diana ......... NEMUS
grovel ..... CRAWL, CRINGE, FAWN,
                         WELTER, CREEP
grow ......... ACCRUE, RAISE, WAX
growing in couples .......... BINATE
growing in fields ...... CAMPESTRAL
growing in swamps ...... ULIGINOSE
growing in waste places ... RUDERAL
growing out ................... ENATE
growing together .......... ACCRETE
growing wild in fields .... AGRESTIAL
growl .. GIRN, GNAR, ROME, SNARL
grown, full MATURE, GILD, SEEDED
grows molars ............... TEETHES
growth ........ ACCRETION, SHOOT
growth, process of ........ NACENCY
growth, retarding of .... PARATONIC
grub ..... LARVA, MAGGOT, MATHE
grub axe .................. MATTOCK
grub clear of trees ........... ASSART
grub, to .. SLAVE, BOB, MOIL, SPUD
grubber .................... LADYFISH
grubble .......... FEEL, GROPE, TRY
grudge ...... HATRED, ENVY, SPITE
grue ............ SHIVER, ICE, SNOW
gruel of maize meal .......... ATOLE
gruesome ........ GRISLY, MACABRE
gruff RUDE, SURLY, CLUMSE, SNORE
grum .............. GIUM, LOW, SOUR
grumble . FRET, MAUNDER, CROAK,
              HONE, REPINE, MUTTER
grumous .............. ROOTY, THICK
Grus constellation ............ CRANE
guacharo ..................... OILBIRD
Guam, an idol in .............. ANITO
Guam, capital of ............. AGANA
Guam, hard wood tree .......... IPIL
Guam, port of ............ APRA, PITA
guan; genus ................ ORTALIS
Guana ................... ARAWAKAN
guana; Austral. .............. LIZARD
guanaco ...................... LLAMA
guano; N. Z. .............. TUATARA
guarantor ... WARRANTOR, SURETY
guarapucu .................... WAHOO

117

guard . FENDER, BANTAY, PATROL, PICKET
guard, freemason's ............. TILER
guardhouse, Navy ............... BRIG
guardian ...... TRUSTEE, TUTELAR, WARDEN, ANGEL, HELPER
guardian, watchful ARGUS, CERBERUS
guardian of church relics ............... MYSTAGOGUE
Guatemala monetary unit . QUETZAL
Guatemalan fruit ............... ANAY
gudgeon ................ DUPE, GULL
Gudrun's brother ............ GUNNAR
guava ........... ARACA, GUAMA
Gudrun's husband ............... ATLI
guenon ...................... MONKEY
guerdon .......... CROWN, PRIZE
Guiana (Fr.) tribesman ......... BONI
Guiana, hut in ............... BENAB
guide . PILOT, CLEW, KEY, MARON, STEER, COURIER, TEACH
guide book ............... BAEDEKER
guiding .................... DIRIGENT
guiding star .............. LODESTAR
guidon ....................... FLAG
Guido's scale, first note in ........ UT
Guido's scale, high note in ...... ALT
Guido's scale, highest note in ... ELA
Guido's scale, note in ......... ELAMI
Guild hall statue, London GOG, MAGOG
guile ...... FRAUD, TRAIN, DECEIT
guileless ARTLESS, SINCERE, NAIVE
guillemot ...... AUK, MURRE, AWK, MURSE, QUET
guillotine, wagon to ...... TUMBREL
guilt ...... CULP, SAKE, SCOUT, SIN
guimpe .............. CHEMISETTE
Guinea, bight in ............... BENIN
guinea corn ......... DURRA, MILLET
guinea fowl ......... KEET, PINTADO
guinea fowl; genus ......... GUTTERA
guinea pig; genus ...... CAVIA, CAVY
guinea pig, male ............... BOAR
guinea pig, S. Am. ............. PACA
Guinea, small tree of ........... AKEE
guise ... CLOAK, GARB, MIEN, WAY
guitar, half step raise of pitch . DITAL
guitar; India .................... VINA
guitar, oriental ............... SITAR
guitar, small .................... UKE
guitar-like inst. ... BANDORE, ROTE, SAMISE
gula ......... CYMA, GULLET, OGEE
gules .................... NECKPIECE
gulf .... ABYSS, BAY, CHASM, SINE
gulf, per. to ................. VORTEX
gulf weed ................. SARGASSO
gull LARID, PIRR, SEEDBIRD, SKUA, TEASER, XEME
gull, Eur. ............ PEWEE, PEWIT
gull; genus ................... LARUS
gull, Jaeger .................... ALLAN
gull, sea .......... COB, MEW, SKUA
gull, to ... CULLY, DUPE, GUDGEON
gull with small hind toe . KITTIWAKE
Gulliver, human met by ...... YAHOO
Gulliver's flying island ........ LAPUTA
gulls; genus ......... LARIDAE, XEMA

gully ..... ARROYO, WADI, COULOIR, GUT
gum .... CONIMA, AMRA, ASA, RESIN
" , a solid white ......... CAMPHOR
" , animal ................. GALAGO
" , arabic ........ ACACIA, ACACIN
" , arabic tree ............... KIKAR
" , catechu-like ... KINO, CHICKLE
" plant .......................... ULE
" resin . GALBAN, ELEMI, LOBAN, MYRRH
" resin narcotic .......... HASHISH
" tree .. XYLAN, HYAWA, TUART, BALATA
" tree, black ..... NYSSA, TUPELO
" , white substance used as ......... DEXTRIN
" with vanilla odor ........ STORAX
gumbo .................... OCRA, OKRA
gumboil ...................... PARULIS
gums, of the ...... GINGIVAL, ULETIC
gums, the ...................... ULA
gun ....... ROD, BAZOOKA, MORTAR, KRUPP
" , Afr. ......................... ROER
" , caliber of ................... BORE
" chamber ................ GOMER
" leather case ............... HOLSTER
" pointer device ... SIGHT, DOTTER
" sight ....................... BEAD
" , swiveled ............. AMUSETTE
gun-boat, light ................ TINCLAD
gun-catch ...................... SEAR
gun-cock ...................... NAB
gun-cotton ................ PYROXYLIN
gunlock, tumbler of ............. NUT
gunnysack ................ BAG, TAT
guns ...... ARMOR, WEAPONS, ARMS
gunstock corner ................. TOE
gunwale ...................... PORTOISE
guppy ........................ MINNOW
gurgling sound ....... CROOL, GUGGLE
Gurion, David ..................... BEN
gurnard ............... CUR, ROCHET
gurnet; genus ................ TRIGLA
Gurth; "Ivanhoe" ............. VASSAL
gush .... POUR, RAIL, SPIRT, STOUR
gusset .......................... GORE
gust .. BLAST, SAPOR, TANG, TASTE
gusto .......... ELAN, RELISH, ZEST
Guthrie, pen name ........... ANESTY
gutta .......................... DROP
gutter ........ CULLIS, EAVES, RONE, DITCH
gutter-snipe ............ ARAB, GAMIN
gutteral DRY, HUSKY, BURR, VELAR, THROATY
guy ......... BAFFLE, FOOL, EFFIGY
guy, a SHORE, STAY, VANG, FELLOW
guzzler .............. TOPER, GLUTTON
guzzles .............. DRINKS, TUNS
gypsum ..... SELENITE, ALABASTER
gypsy (see 'gipsy')
gypsy winch ...................... CRAB
gyrate ....... ROTATE, SPIN, TWIRL
gyrator ................... TOP, PILOT
gyre .................... CIRCLE, RING
gyves .... IRONS, FETTER, SHACKLE

# H

H, letter ....................... AITCH
H-shaped ....................... ZYGAL
H, sound of ............... ASPIRATE
habile ........ APT, DEXTEROUS, FIT
habit, riding .................. JOSEPH
habitat ......................... ABODE
habitat plant ..................... ECAD
habitual ........ ORDERLY, WONTED
habituate ...... ADDICT, INURE, USE
hachure ................. MARK, SHADE
hacienda ... FARM, CROFT, GRANGE,
PLANTATION
hack, literary .. DEVIL, GARRETEER,
WRITER
hackle ... COMB, HATCHEL, HAGGLE
hackneyed ... THREADBARE, BANAL,
TRITE, COMMONPLACE,
SAW, CLICHE
hades .... ABADDON, ARALU, ORCUS,
ABYSS, PIT
Hades, rel. to ......... LIMBO, SHEOL,
TARTARUS
Hades river ACHERON, LETHE, STYX
Hadley, Mr. ........... REED, GOLFER
haemostatic ............ ADRENALINE
haft ..... DUDGEON, HANDLE, BAIL
hafted ....................... ANSATED
hag ..... CRONE, HARRIDAN, VIXEN
hag, a ......... BELDAME, JEZEBEL
hag, one of three avenging deities FURY
Hagan; actress ..................... UTA
hagfish ............... BORER, MYXINE
haggle .... CHAFFER, PALTER, PRIG
hail .... GREET, SLEET, AHOY, AVE,
SIGNAL
hail, soft ................... GRAUPEL
hail-storm, device to prevent ...........
PARAGRELE
hair, a molting ............. ECDYSIS
"        braid ........................ CUE
"        , coarse rigid . CERDA, SETULA,
SETA
"        , comb. form .............. PILO
"        dresser; Fr. ........... FRISEUR
"        dressing ............... POMADE
"        dye ...................... HENNA
"        false .. PERUKE, FRONT, TETE
"        feeler .......... PALP, PALPUS
"        , fillet for the ........... SNOOD
"        , head of ........... CRINE, MOP
"        , like a tuft of .. SHAG, COMOID,
TUZZ
"        , like curly ........... CIRROSE
"        , lock of .... LOVELOCK, TRESS
"        , neck ..................... MANE
"        net ................. LINT, SNOOD
"        on end .................... STARE
"        pad ........................ RAT
"        , part in ..................... LIST
"        , per. to . LINUS, NOIL, CRINAL,
PILAR
"        plant ............ PILUS, PUBES
"        , remove ............. EPILATE
"        removing .......... DECALVANT
"        , roll at back of neck .. CHIGNON
"        shirt .................... CILICE

"        , strips of .......... EPILATES,
DEPILITATES
"        wave .................. MARCEL
"        , weak ................. CRINITE
"        , wisp of ................... TATE
"        , wooly .................. SHAG
"        worm ................. GORDIUS
haircloth ....................... CILICE
hair-do ...... BANG, BRAID, POODLE
hairiness ................... VILLOSITY
hairless .......... GLABROUS, PELON
hairlike processes ............ CILIATE
hairs, beset with ........... BARBATE
hairs on plants .................. VILLI
hairy .. PILOSE, COMATE, HIRSUTE,
PILAR
Haitian liberator .......... TOUSSAINT
Haitian sweet potato ......... BATATA
hakim; Moham. ........... PHYSICIAN
halberd ......... AX, FRAME, GLAIVE
halberd-shaped .. HASTATE, GISARME
halcyon ......... KINGFISHER, CALM,
TRANQUIL
Halcyone, father of ........... AEOLUS
Halcyone's husband ............. CEYX
hale HEARTY, WELL, ROBUST, PULL,
TRAIL, TUG, DRAG
Halevy; opera by ............... JUIVE
half HEMI, EN, DEMI, SEMI, MOIETY
half boot ............... BUSKIN, PAC
half breed ....... METIS, MESTEE
half breed; Span. ............ MESTIZO
half man, half horse ........ CENTAUR
half-nelson .................... HOLD
half turn ................. CARACOL(E)
half witted ......... IMBECILE, SILLY
half year's stipend ............ ANNAT
halibut ...................... FLATFISH
Halicarnassus, of .......... DIONYSIUS
halicore ...................... DUGONG
Halifax, Lord ................. SAVILE
halite ...................... SALT, SAL
halitus ................ AURA, BREATH
hall ATRIUM, AULA, FOYER, ODEON,
SALA, ENTRY, LYCEUM
hall for athletes ............. GYM, XYST
hall of Odin; Norse myth. . VALHALLA
hallow ....... SANCTIFY, VENERATE,
BLESS
hallowed spot ......... HOLY, BETHEL
hallucination ......... ALUSIA, ERROR,
FANTASY, CHIMERA
halo . AURA, BRUGH, NIMB, NIMBUS,
AUREOLE, GLORY, LIGHT
halogen ....... BROMINE, CHLORINE,
FLUORINE, IODINE
halt ....... CRIPPLED, END, MAIMED
halter .................. HANG, NOOSE
halved ...... BISECTED, DIMIDIATED
ham; sl. ....... AMATEUR, OVERACT
Hambletonian gait ............... TROT
hamfatter ...................... ACTOR
Hamite; N. Afr. ............. BERBER
Hamitic ......... KABYLE, SHILAH
Hamitic Negro; Afr. ........... MASAIS
Hamitic race, one of ........... SOMAL
Hamitic religion ............. MOSLEM
Hamito-Negro; S. Afr. ......... MASAI

119

hamlet ...... CASALE, ALDEE, DORP, THORP
Hamlet, scene of ........... ELSINORE
Hamlet's girl ................. OPHELIA
Hammarskjold, Mr. ............. DAG
hammer . MARGE, BEETLE, PLEXOR, MAUL
"      blow ....... POUND, MARTEL
"      end or head .... PEIN, PEEN, POLL
"      , half round set ..... FULLER
"      , large .... SLEDGE, BULLY, KEVEL
"      , operator of trip .... TILTER
"      , pavoir's ................ REEL
"      , presiding officer's ... GAVEL
"      , to .............. MALLEATE
"      , trip .................. OLIVER
hamper ... TRAMMEL, HOPPLE, PED, BASKET, MAUND, SEROON, HALT, IMPEDE
hampers ...... FETTERS, SHACKLES, STRAIT, IRONS
Ham's eldest son ................ CUSH
hamstring ...... HOUGH, HOX, LAME, MAIM
hanaper ........... BASKET, HAMPER
hand ..... FIST, MANUS, PAW, TILL
hand bag ETUI, RETICULE, SATCHEL
hand ball ............ FIVES, PELOTA
hand, palm of ........ LOOF, THENAR
hand, palm of ....... LOOF, THENAR, GOUPEN
hand, per. to the .............. CHIRAL
hand used in writing Arabic .... NESKI
handbill ........................ DODGER
hand-book .. MANUAL, CODEX, TOME
hand-cuffs BRACELETS, MANACLES, DARBY
Handel; compo. by ............. LARGO
handful ........... GRIP, KIRN, WISP
handicap ..... LAW, LISP, EQUALIZE
hand-jar ........................ KNIFE
handkerchief ................. MALABAR
handle . HEFT, HELVE, ANSA, HANK, HAFT
"      awkwardly ...... PAW, THUMB
"      , cross .................. POTENT
"      of a pail .................. BAIL
"      of plane ......... TOAT, TOTE
"      of spade ................ TILLER
"      , printing press ....... ROUNCE
"      , scythe ......... SNATH, SNED
"      , to ........... WIELD, TREAT
handled ...................... PALMED
hand-length ...................... SPAN
hand-mill ...................... QUERN
handometer .................. ODOGRAPH
hand-picked, as figs ......... ELEME
hands off .. TABOO, INTERDICT, QUIT
hands, without ............. AMANOUS
handsel EARNEST, GIFT, TEST, USE, TOKEN
hand-stamp .................... DATER
handstone ...................... MANO
handy ....... DEXTEROUS, ADROIT, DEFT, READY, HEPPEN
hang PEND, DANGLE, DRAPE, SWAG
"      down ......... LAVE, PERPEND

"      loosely .......... BANGLE, LOP
"      on ................. BUR, SHEEP
"      over .................... IMPEND
hang-dog .......... MEAN, SNEAKING
hanger on ..... TOADEATER, TOADY
hanging . DOSSAL, DORSAL, SESSILE
hangings .. ARRAS, DOSSER, DRAPES
hangman's noose, per. to .... HEMPEN
hangnail ......... AGNAIL, WHITLOW
hank of twine ............. RAN, SKEIN
hanker ....... CRAVE, LONG, YEARN
hanky-panky ................... TRICKY
Hannibal's father ......... HAMILCAR
"Hans Castorp," by ............. MANN
Hans Hauge follower .......... LESER
Hanseatic League ............ HANSA
haphazard ....... RANDOM, CHANCE
happen ...... EVENE, BEFALL, FARE, OCCUR
happening ....... SPORADIC, TIDING
happy .. BLEST, COSH, FAUST, GLAD
harageous ....... CRUEL, FIERCE
harakeke, N.Z. .................... FLAX
harangue ..... TIRADE, NAG, ORATE, SCREED, RANT, SPOUT
Haran's daughter ............. MILCAH
Haran's father ................. TERAH
haras .......................... STUD
harass . CHASE, BAIT, BESET, HASE, RATTEN, TEASE, HAGRIDE
Haratin ...................... BERBERS
harbinger .. USHER, HERALD, OMEN, INFORMANT, PRECURSOR
harbor RESET, COTHON, PIER, PORT
harbor master ............. HAVENER
hard STEELY, STONY, DOUR, STERN, TOR
hard coal .............. ANTHRACITE
hard shell ..................... LORICA
hard tough heartwood ........... DURA
hard wood; E. Ind. ........ ENG, TEAK
harden .. GEL, INURE, KERN, SEAR, STEELE, OSSIFY
hard-wood tree of Florida ........ MABI
hardy SET, HALE, LUSTY, SPARTAN
Hardy character .................. TESS
hare ....... CONY, RODENT, SCUT
"      , a young .............. LEVERET
"      , female ..................... DOE
"      ; genus ................. LEPUS
"      ; "Little Chief" .... CONY, PIKA
"      , male ................... BUCK
"      , ragout of .......... CIVET
"      ; S. Amer. .............. TAPETI
"      , tail of ................... SCUT
"      , track of .......... FILE, SLOT
hare-like ... ... LEPORINE, TURATT
hare-like animal ............... AGOUTI
harem .......... SERAGLIO, SERAI
harem, female slave in .... ODALISQUE
harem, rel. to ..... ODALISK, ZENANA
harem, room in ........ ADA, IDA, ODA
harlequin ................... CLOWNISH
harlequin duck .................... LADY
harm ........... DERE, MAR, SCATH
harmful .... MALEFICENT, NOCENT, BANEFUL, NOXIOUS, NOISOME
harmful influence ............... UPAS
harmless ................. INNOCUOUS

120

harmonious .. SPHERAL, CONSONANT
harmony TONE, CHIME, CHORD, KEY,
UNION, CONSONANCE
harness ..... ARMOR, GEAR, GRAITH
harness, part of HAME, TERRET, TUG
Harold the Saxon's wife ....... EDITH
harp ITERATE, KOTO, LYRE, NANGA,
TRUMP, PLECTRUM
harp-guitar key ................ DITAL
harpoon ............... IRON, SPEAR
harpsichord ...... CLAVECIN, SPINET
harpy ................ AELLO, EAGLE
harquebus fork ................... CROC
harquebusier ............... CARABIN
harridan .... HAG, JEZEBEL, VIRAGO
harrier ...................... HOUND
harrier, marsh ... HARPY, PUTTOCK
harrow . HERSE, GRACE, TILL, CHIP,
TEAR, SPADER
harrow, rest ................... WHIN
harsh STERN, GRIM, ACERB, DURE,
VENOM, ASPER, CRUEL, RASPY
harshness .......... RAUCITY, RIGOR
hart ............ DEER, SPADE, STAG
Harte, Francis; author .......... BRET
hartebeest ..... ASSE, CAAMA, TORA
harte-beest; Abr. ........ ANTELOPE,
BONTEBOK, KONZE
hartebeest-like .. BLESBOK, SASSABY
hartshorn, spirits of ........ AMMONIA
hartwort ...................... SESELI
haruspex ............. SOOTHSAYER
Harvard College book prize .... DETUR
harvest .. CROP, FRUIT, REAP, YIELD
harvest home ........ HOCKEY, KIRN
harvest in India ................. RABI
harvest tick ................. ACARID
"Harvey," actor in ......... STEWART
has not ........................... NAS
hashish drug ...... BHANG, NARCOTIC
hassle ...... FRAY, BRAWL, MELEE
Hasso; actress .................. SIGNE
hassock .... BASS, DOSS, FOOTSTOOL
hasten .. AMAIN, SCUD, APACE, HIE,
SCAMP
hastened ................... RAN, SPED
hasty ...... CURSORY, EAGER, RASH
hasty pudding ................... MUSH
hat .... TOQUE, BERET, FELT, TAM,
TOPPER, CHAPEAU
"   , broad rimmed .......... SHOVEL
"   , ecclesiastic ............ BIRETTA
"   , fur used in .............. CONEY
"   , hunter's ................... TERAI
"   , opera ...................... GIBUS
"   , pith .............. TOPEE, TOPI
"   plant; E. Ind. ................. SOLA
"   , Roman; anc. ............ PETASUS
"   , silk ........................ TILE
"   , slang for ................... DICER
"   , soft ..................... FEDORA
"   soldier's ................... SHAKO
"   , three cornered ......... TRICORN
hate .............. DETEST, LOATHE
hate, comb. form ................ MISO
hateful ........ EXECRABLE, ODIOUS
hater of sights .......... MISOSCOPIST
hauberk ...................... ARMOR
haughty .......... CAVALIER, PROUD

haul .... BOUSE, DRAW, HALE, LUG,
TREK
hauled up ...... TRICED, ARRESTED,
ROPED
haulm .................. STALK, STEM
haunch .......... HANCE, HIP, HUCK
haunt ..... NEST, OBSESS, DEN, LIE,
RESORT
hautboy ......................... OBOE
hauteur . ARROGANCE, CONTUMELY,
PRIDE
have effect ............ RESULT, TAKE
have; Scot ......................... HAE
have thought of ............... IDEATE
haven ... REFUGE, ASYLUM, HITHE,
PORT, HARBOR
havier ........................... DEER
having a pointed end ........ CUSPATE
having margin irregularly notched .....
EROSE
having no angles ............... AGONIC
having one end closed CAECAL, DEAD
having patches on surface SOREDIATE
having rank .................. GENETIC
having same ending ... CONTERMINAL
haw ......... CLOSE, EYELID, SLOE
hawk-headed god ................ HORUS
haws ........................... HUMS
Hawaii ....................... OWYHEE
Hawaiian breech cloth .......... MALO
"   bush .................. OLONA
"   canoe ............... WAAPA
"   canoe stripe ........... IAKUS
"   coffee .................... KONA
"   crater .............. KILAUEA
"   dance ................... HULA
"   drink .................... KAVA
"   fish ... AWA, LANIA, PALANI
"   fish bait ................ HOLA
"   flower .................... DEC
"   flower decoration .......... LEI
"   food ........ KALO, POI, TARO
"   food fish .......... LANIA, UKU
"   fruit .................... POHA
"   goddess of fire ........... PELE
"   goose ................... NENE
"   harbor .................. PEARL
"   honey eater ................ OO
Hawaiian island ...... KAUAI, LANAI,
OAHU
"   Is. precipice .............. PALI
"   Islands .......... SANDWICH
"   Islands, discoverer of GAETANO
"   lava ........................ AA
"   line ................. CREANCE
"   liquor ......... AWA KAWA
"   majagua ................. HAU
"   member of the royal family ....
ALII
"   mountain .......... KEA, LOA
"   mulberry, bark of the ... KAPA
"   musical inst. ........ UKULELE
"   native ................ KNAKA
"   neck piece ........... LAI, LEI
"   octopus .................. HEE
"   partnership ............... HUI
"   pit, baking ............... IMU
"   plant .......... OLONA, KALO
"   porch .......... LANA, LANAI

121

" president ................. DOLE
" puffin ........................ AO
" raven .................. ALALA
" salutation ............ ALOHA
" seaweed .................. LIMU
" shampoo .......... LOMILOMI
" shrub ............ AKIA, POHA
" silky fiber ............... PULU
" song ...................... MELE
" starchroot ................. PIA
" system of religion ..... TABOO
" thrush ....... OLOMAO, OMAO
" timber tree ................ KOA
" town ..................... HILO
" tree fern ................ AMAU
" vine in basket work ..... IE, IO
" volcano .............. KILAUEA
" worsted cloth ............ TAPA
" wreath .................... LEI
hawk . ASTUR, CARACARA, COOPERI
" , Anglo-Saxon .......... HAFOC
" , Austral. ..... KAHU, KESTREL
" fly, species of ............ ASILUS
" ; genus ............... ACCIPITER
" , European PUTTOCK, FALCON
" , male ................... TERCEL
" moth ....... SPHINGID, SPHINX
" of India ................ BADIUS
" , small ............. EYAS, KITE
" , sparrow ................ NISUS
hawked .......................... SOLD
hawker .......... PEDDLER, CADGER,
        CHAPMAN, FALCONER
hawking leash ........... JESS, LUNE
hawk-like ........ OSPREY, SURN, IO
hawk's bill ..................... PAWL
hawk's nest .................... AERIE
hawk's stomach ............. PANNEL
hawkshaw ................ DETECTIVE
hawkweed ..................... DINDLE
hawser frame .................... BITT
hawser iron . ............. CALKING
hawser post ................. BOLLARD
hawthorn ....... MAY, MAYFLOWER
hawthorn, fruit of ............... HAW
hay bird; Eur. ............. BLACKCAP
" fever ......................... ROSE
" fodder plant ............. SAINFOIN
" , kind of ............... TIMOTHY
" rabbit trap .................... NET
" , second growth .......... ROWEN
" spreader .................. TEDDER
haycock .... RACK, COB, COIL, RICK,
        PIKE
Hayes; comedian ............... GABBY
hayfork, dial. Eng. .............. PIKEL
Hayworth, Miss ................ RITA
hazard .... PERIL, JUMP, LOT, PAWN
hazardous CHANCY, JUMPY, QUEASY
haze .. FILM, FOG, MIST, SMOG,
        VAPOR
haze at sea ...................... GLIN
hazelnut .......... FILBERT, NIT
hazelnut, cultivated ........... COBNUT
he; Lat. ............................ IPSI
he remains, stage direction .... MANET
head ..... PATE, NOB, CAPUT, TETE
" , back part of .. OCCIPUT, POLL
" bandage .................. GALFA

" bandages .................. GAKA
" gear ... BERET, WIMPLE, CAP,
        HAT
" on the Aegis of Athena MEDUSA
" pence ......................... TAX
" , rel. to the .......... PARIETAL
" , to shave the ......... TONSURE
headache ............. CEPHALALGIA
headache, one side .......... MEGRIM
headdress ALMICE, CUPEE, PINNER,
        CAPELINE, WIG, TIARA
headdress, gauze ................. POUF
headdress, military ... SHAKO, BUSBY
headdress, sacerdotal ....... BIRETTA,
        MITER
headdress, steeple ............ HENNIN
headdress, widow's ......... BANDORE
headhunter; Malay .......... ITALONE
headland .... CAPE, KOP, NESS, RAS
headless ..... STUPID, ACEPHALOUS,
        ETETE
headless animal ............ ACEPHAL
headline .......... BANNER, DISPLAY
headshaped ................ CAPITATE
headsman .... EXECUTIONER, VIDAN
heal CURE, MEND, PACIFY, REMEDY
headwater ................... UPRIVER
healdick fur ...................... PEAN
healer ............................ ASA
healing ..................... CURATIVE
healing agent ............ LENIROBIN,
        CICATRIZER, SPA
healing, science of ........ IATROLOGY
heals .............. RESTORES, SAINS
health; comb. form ............... SANI
health and long life; symb. ..... PANSY
heap ... SORITE, STACK, COP, PILE,
        TUMP, AMASS
heap, per. to ................. ACERVAL
hearer ..................... AUDIENT
hearing ............. OVER, TRAIL
hearing, defective ............. OTOSIS
hearing, of ............. AURAL, OTIC
hearsay .... REPORT, RUMOR, TALK,
        BRUIT, GOSSIP
hearse .......... FRAME, RAKE, BIER
heart .......... CARDIA, COR
" action, too active ...... STHENIC
" ailment ................. ANGINA
" bleeding ............. DICENTRA
" cavities .................. ATRIA
" contraction ............ SYSTOLE
" , Egyptian ............ AB, HATI
" , innermost ................ CORE
" , per. to the .... CARDIAC, PITH
heartburn ..................... PYROSIS
heart-burning ................... ENVY
hearth, chamber of the ...... CAMERA
heart-shaped ................. CORDATE
heart-wood of a tree ...... DURAMEN
hearty ...... HALE, LUSTY, ROBUST,
        SINCERE
hearty stimulant ........ QUINIDINE,
        THIALDINE
heat ..... CALOR(IC), ARDOR, FIRE,
        ZEAL
heat, gentle .................... TEPOR
heat, great .................... CAUMA
heat, per. to .................. CALEFY

122

heat unit ..................... THERM
heater .................. ETNA, TISAR
heater, powder ........... SINTERER
heath .... MOOR, BENT, GRIG, PLAIN
heath-berry ................ BILBERRY
heath-bird ..................... GROUSE
heath; genus ................... ERICA
heathen ........... GENTILE, PAGAN,
PAYNIM, GODLESS
heathen, non-Jewish ......... ETHNIC
heathen, non-Moham. ........ INFIDEL
heather .. CROWBERRY, ERICA, LING
heaths, composed of ....... ERICETAL
heating vessel ................. RETORT
heave SCEND, THROW, FLING, HURL
heaven ... ETHER, ARCADIA, EDEN,
ELYSIUM, CIEL, SKY
heaven; comb. form ........... URANO
heaven; Scand. myth. ..... VALHALLA
heavenly ...... SUPERNAL, URANIAN
" being; Egypt. myth. ...... AFA
" body; .. COMET, MOON, STAR,
SUN
" path ................... ORBIT
heavens, per. to .... ORRERY, URANIC
heavier than aircraft ... HELICOPTER
heavy LEADEN, GLOOMY, HARD, SAD
hebdomad ............. SEVEN, WEEK
Hebraic anecdotal history .... ELOHIST
Hebrew ........... ZION, AB, SEMITE
" alien resident ............ GER
" allies ................ HABIRI
" alphabet ...... ALEPH (ALEF),
BETH, GIMEL, DALETH, HE,
VAU (WAW), ZAYIN, CHETH,
TETH, JOD (YOD, YODH),
CAPH (KAPH). LAMED
(LAMEDH), MEM, NUN,
SAMEKH, AIN (AYIN), PE,
SADHE, KOPH, RESH, SIN
(SHIN), TAV (TAW)
" ancestor ................ EBER
" brother-hood ......... ESSENE
" canonical law book .. TALMUD
" doctrine ANAMISM, KARAISM
" dry measure (see 'measure')
" ear of corn .............. ABIB
" excommun. ............. HEREM
" festival ........ PURIM, SEDER
" flute .............. NEHILOTH
" food inspector ........ SHOMER
" for hades .............. SHEOL
" healer ...................... ASA
" hen trader ...... BANIAN, YAN
" herdsman ................ AMOS
" high priest AARON, ELI, EZRA
" king of demons .... ASMODEUS
" "Law of Moses" TORA, TORAH
Hebrew marriage custom .. LEVIRATE
" measure . KES, OMER, EPHAH
" month .... TISHRI, HESHVAN
(BUL), KISLEV, TEBET,
SHEBAT (SEBAT), ADAR,
VEADAR, NISAN (ABIB),
IYAR(ZIV), SIVAN, TAMMUZ,
AB, ELUL
" name for God ........ ADONAI,
ELOHIM

" name (place) of Old Testament .
MISPEH, MIZPAH
" , next of kin ............. GOEL
" order ............... ESSENE
" passover month .......... ABIB
" psalms of praise ..... HALLEL
" priest ................ LEVITE
" prophet DANIEL, AMOS, NASI
" prophet, suppositious MALACHI
" prophetess .......... DEBORAH
" proselyte ................... GER
" quarter .............. GHETTO
" rain ...................... BUL
" scarf ....... ABNET, TALLITH
" scholar ............... SABORA
" seer . BALAAM, ISAAC, MOSES
" , unclean ................. TREF
" songs of praise ...... HALLEL
" stringed inst. .............. ASOR
" sun god ................... BAAL
" teacher ................... RAB
" tribe ............ DAN, LEVITES
" universe ................ OLAM
" vowel point ..... SEGO, TSERE
" weight .................. GERAH
" word .................... SELAH
" word for city ......... KIRJATH
Hebrides Is. IONA, RUM, SKYE, UISY
hecatomb .......... SACRIFICE, NUMBER
Hector's father . SLAUGHTER, PRIAM
Hector's wife ......... ANDROMACHE
Hecuba's husband .............. PRIAM
heddle of a loom ................. CAAM
heddles, a leaf of ............... GEAR
hedge .. BOMA, HAW, HAY, RADDLE
hedge trimmer .. PLASHER, TOPIARY
hedgehog ......... ECHINUS, ERICIUS
hedgehog, col. ................. URCHIN
hedgehog-like animal ........ TENREC
Hedin; explorer ................... SVEN
heed .. NOTE, GOME, LISTEN, MIND,
RECK, CARE, NOTICE
heedful .......... VIGILANT, ATTENT
heel .................. BOUNDER, CAD
heel bone .. CALCANEUM, FIBULA(R)
heel of the boot ................... DUCE
heeling .......................... ALIST
Heflin; actor ..................... VAN
heft .. BULK, FASCICULUS, WEIGHT
hegira .... EXODUS, FLIGHT, HEJIRA
heifer .................. COW, STIRK
height ... ALT, APEX, TOP, SUMMIT,
STATURE
height of action in a drama .............
CATASTASIS
heir ........... LEGATEE, HERITOR,
PARCENER, SCION, POSTERITY
heir; Scot. ...................... TEIND
Hejaz, holy city in .. MECCA, MEDINA
held; mus. .................. TENUTO
Helen of Troy, mother of ........ LEDA
Helen of Troy's son ............. DORUS
Helen of Troy's suitor .......... AJAX
Helena's husband, Shak. ... BERTRAM
helical ........................ SPIRAL
helicid, edible .................. SNAIL
Heliopolis ................ MATARIYA
Heliopolis, Bib. name .............. ON
Helios ................. SOL, APOLLO

123

heliotrope .................... GIRASOL
Hellene ....................... GREEK
hellbender ...... DEBAUCH, TWEEG,
                    SALAMANDER
Helles' mother ............. NEPHELE
helix simple .............. UNISPIRAL
Hellespont, anc. city on ..... ABYDOS
Heloise; husband of ......... ABELARD
helm .............. RUDDER, TEMON
helmet .... ARMET, GALEA, MORION
  " , adjustable flap of .. VENTAIL
  " , Anglo-Saxon ..... BEOWULF
  " bird ................. TURACOU
  " flower .... ACONITE, ORCHID
  " , French ............. HEAUME
  " , Italian ............... ELME
  " , light ............... SALLET
  " , lower part of ...... BEAVER
  " , nose guard of ........ NASAL
  " opening ................... VUE
  " perforation ...... OCULARIUM
  " , pith (sun) ..... TOPI, TOPEE
  " shaped .... GALEA, GALEATE
  " , type of .. BASINET, CASQUE
  " , upper part of . VISOR, VIZOR
helminth ....................... WORM
helmsman ........... CONNER, PILOT
helot .......... ESNE, SERF, SLAVE
help ..... STEAD, ABET, AID, CURE,
                     SUCCOR
help, a ........... BOTE, ADMINICLE
helper .......... ANSAR, TEAMMATE
helpless ........... LIMP, SPINELESS
Hel's watchdog; myth. ........ GARM
helve .............. HANDLE, SHAFT
hem in ................ BESET, FENCE
hematite ............ LIMONITE, ORE
Hemingway; author ......... ERNEST
hemlock . ABIES, TSUGA, KEX, YEW
hemorrhage ........... HEMOPHELIA
hemp ....... CORDILLA, PITA, TOW
hemp; Afr. ........ IFE, LHIAMBA
  " as a narcotic ......... HASHISH
  " , Bengal ................. SUNN
  " dried leaves ........ KEF, KIEF,
                     BHANG
  " fabric ................. BURLAP
  " fibre ............ AGAVE, SISAL
  " , flowering heads of ..... GANJA
  " , Hindustan .... SABZI, SIDDHI
  " , Indian ............... BHANG
  " , loose ................. OAKUM
  " , Manila ................. ABACA
  " , oil of; Ind. ...... CANNABENE
  " , Persian; var. ........... BANG
  " plant ...... BENG, CARL, SUNN
  " resin ................... CHARAS
  " , Russian .... RINE, KONOPEL
  " turbid drink ........ SUBDSCHI
hemuse ...................... ROEBUCK
hen, clam; genus ........... MACTRA
hen; extinct ................. HEATH
hen, Goethe's ............. PARTLET
hen harrier ................... HAWK
hen hawk .................. REDTAIL
hen, large water ......... GALLINULE
hen, mud ...................... RAIL
hen roost .............. PERCH, EVE

henbane content ............ HYOSCIN
henbit; genus .............. LAMIUM
hence; Lat. .................. ERGO
henchman ... GROOM, PAGE, SQUIRE
Hengest ..................... GELDING
Hengest's brother ............. HORSA
henna ........ ALCANA, ORCHANET
henotic ...................... IRENIC
henpeck ......................... NAG
Henry .......................... HAL
Henry II, wife of ......... ELEANOR
Henry IV, birthplace of ......... PAU
Henry VIII; wives .... ANNE, CATH-
                 ARINE, JANE
Henry VIII's widow ............. PARR
hen's bill ................. SAINFOIN
hent; obs. ............ GRASP, SEIZE
heofene ...................... HEAVEN
hepa ......................... SORITE
Hera, husband of ............... ZEUS
Hera, mother of ............... RHEA
Hera's rival ................... LETO
herald ......... MESSENGER, CRIER,
            PRECURSE, BLAZON
herald, coat of ............... TABARD
heraldic design .............. RUSTRE
  " fillet ...................... ORLE
  " shield, border in a; ...... ORLE,
                    BORDURE
  " shield, boss in a ......... UMBO
  " shield, broad vertical stripe in;
                    PALE
  " shield, concealed half of; .......
                   SINISTER
  " shield, division of ....... ENTE
  " shield, horizontal band across;
                    FESS
  " shield, rectangular division of ..
                   CANTON
  " , shield shaped ...... PELTATE
  " shield, two circular segments at
      sides ............... FLANCH
  " shield, upper third of .. CHIEF
  " shield, vertical position of PALY
  " shields, series of small .. VAIR
  " term ...... FRACTED, PATTE,
               SEME, URDE
  " wreath ................... TORSE
heraldry, an ordinary in ....... BEND
  " , back to back ... ADDORSED
  " , balls or plates .... ROUNDEL
  " , barnacle ............... BREY
  " , bastardy mark ....... BATON
  " , beakless and footless bird in..
                  MARTLET
  " , bear .................. GRISE
  " bearing .... TRESSURE, ORLE
  " , bearing of two curved lines;
                    GORE
  " , beast partly visible . ISSUANT
  " bend, small ............ COTISE
  " , blind .................. SEEL
  " , black ................. SABLE
  " , blue ................. AZURE
  " , body bent or folded ..........
                  DEBRUISED
  " , broken .............. ROMPU
  " , chaplet ................ ORLE

" , checkered ... VAIR, CHECKY
" , cherub ............. SERAPH
" , cross ...... NOWY, SALTIRE
" , cross-like CLECHE, PATONCE
heraldry, depicting animal's head .....
        CABOSHED
" , diapered with a kind of vair ..
        PAPILLONE
" , divided by bars ...... BARRY
" , divided into squares COMPONY
" duck, footless and beakless; ...
        CANNET
" either of two barrulets GEMEL
" , facing each other AFFRONTE
" , factor ................. GENE
" , figure like Y ........... PALL
" , fillet .................... ORLE
" , five ..................... PEAN
" , fore-leg of a beast ..... GAMB
" , fountain ............... SYKE
" , fur .. PEAN, POTENT, VAIR
" , gold in ............... AU, OR
" , grafted ................ ENTE
" , green .................... VERT
" , hairy ............... COMATE
" , head of dart or javelin bearing
        PHEON
" , headless ............. ETETE
" , horizontal band . BAR, FESS,
        FILL
" indented obliq. .......... RASE
" , large shield ....... PAVESSE,
        PAVIS
" , left side .......... SINISTER
" , lozenge (voided) .... MASCLE
" , metal end of a sheath ........
        BOTEROL
" , notched ............. RAGULY
" , one of the honorable ordinaries
        CHEVRON
" , ordinary ........... SALTIRE
" , ornament of headpiece CREST
" , ornamental clamp ............
        ESCARBUNCLE
" , overlapping plates TEGULATE
" , partly swallowed ENGOULED
" , pointed ............... URDE
" , purple ............. PURPURE
" , red tincture ......... GULES
" , running, as of a beast; ......
        COURANT
" , scattered ............. SEME
" , sheaf of grain ......... GARB
" , sitting, as a lion ... SEJANT
" , sitting down .......... ASSIS
" , sky blue ............. AZURE
" , snake ................. BISSE
" , springing up ....... JESSANT
" , squirrel skin ........... VAIR
" , standing position . STATANT
" Strewing .............. SEME
" , swimming ........... NAIANT
" , symbol of the Am. savage; ...
        TATTOO
" , symbol of the Danes . RAVEN
" , symbol of the tribe of Judah;
        LION
" , tincture, bright brown TENNE

" , to describe a coat-of-arms; ...
        BLAZON
" , triangular form ...... GYRON
heraldry, turned to show the back; ...
        AVERSANT
" , turning head toward spectator
        GARDANT, GAZE
" , vertical division ...... PALY
" , wavy .. ENTE, ONDE, UNDE
" , wickerwork trap ...... WEEL
" , winged ................. AILE
" , wreath ....... ORLE, TORSE
" , yellow ..................... OR
herb .. CARAWAY, PARSLEY, SAGE,
        THYME, TELLIMA, SEDGE
" , African .......... OKRA, YAMP
" , aromatic ANET, ANISE, BASIL,
        DILL
" , Asiatic .................. HEMP
" , bitter GENTIAN, ALOE, RUE,
        TANSY
" buckwheat family ...... SORREL
" , climbing .................. LENS
" , coarse weedy ... ERYNGO, IVA
" , dill ........................ ANET
" , coarse weedy .... ERYNGO, IVA
" dish ...................... SALAD
" edible ................. PARSNIP
" , Eurasian weedy ..... GOSMORE
" , European .. RUTA, TARRAGON
" eve .......................... IVA
" fabulous ................... MOLY
" flowering; genus ..... HEPATICA
" , fragrant ................ BALM
" , ginger ................ ALPINIA
" , kind of ......... WORT, BLITE,
        COMFRAY, NEP
" , large coarse; Eur. ELECAMPANE
" , Malayalam ........... ENTADA
" , medicinal ........ CORIANDER,
        SENNA, BONESET, TANSY
" , mint family ..... BALM, BASIL,
        HYSSOP
" , nightshade family . HENBANE
" of grace .................... RUE
" of the goosefoot order . QUINOA
" , onion-like .............. CHIVE
" , parsley family ... CICELY,
        FENNEL, ERYNGO
" , parsley family, Old World; ......
        CHERVIL
" , perennial . BALM, DIGITALIS,
        PIA, SEGO
" , perennial rocaceous; genus .....
        GEUM
" , poisonous hemlock .... CONIUM
" , pot ........ CYCLAMEN, WORT
" , small tropical LUFFA, LOOFAH
" , sweet aromatic ........ CICELY
" tonic ................... BONESET
" yielding starch .............. PIA
herbaceous plant, order of . EBULUS,
        RANAL, INULA
herbage .... TURF, PASTURE, GRASS
herbs, Asiatic; genus . APIOS, CICER
" Brazil; genus .......... NOLANA,
        MANIHOT

" ; genus ......... ARUM, RULAC, TOVARIA
" small Amer.; genus; HEDEOMA, SAGINA
Hercules' captor ................. IOLE
Hercules, mother of ........ ALCMENE
Hercules, wife of .. DEIANIRA, HEBE
herd DROVE, GREGAL, FLOTE, MOB, RAG, RABBLE
herdsman ........... SENN, VACHER, VAQUERO
herdsman, any ........... DAMOETAS
here; Fr. ........................... ICI
here and there ...... ABOUT, THINLY
here and there; Lat. ........... PASSIM
here-to-fore ................. ERENOW
hereditary ....... ANCESTRAL, LINEAL
heredity ............. ATAVISM, GENE
heritable land ..................... ODAL
heritage ........... CLERONOMY, LOT
hermeneutic .......... INTERPRETIVE
Hermes ................... MERCURY
"   deriv.; Skr. ....... SARAMEIAS
"   , father of ................ ZEUS
"   footgear ............ TALARIA
"   , mother of ............... MAIA
"   , personification .......... WIND
"   , son of ................... PAN
hermetic ................... HERMANIC
hermit ...... RECLUSE, ANCHORITE, EREMITE
hermit, rel. to ... ASCETIC, CENOBITE
Hernando de ..................... SOTO
hero .. IDOL, STAR, DEMIGOD, EREC
"   , Babyl. myth. ............ ETANA
"   in Persian legend ..... RUSTUM
"   , legendary ... AMADIS, PALADIN
"   lover ............ LEANDER
"   of Euripides' play ............ ION
"   of Romantic legend .... TRISTAN
"   of Russian epic poem ........ IGOR
"   of the first crusade ... TANERED
heroic .. BOLD, BRAVE, VIKING, EPIC
heroic events, series of .......... EPOS
heroic poem ................. EPOPEE
Herodia's daughter ............ SALOME
heroine, d'Urberville ............. TESS
heroine of "Last Days of Pompeii" ....
IONE
Herold; opera by .............. ZAMPA
heron ...... AIGRET, HERLE, ALBA, EGRET, HERN
"   family .. SHITESPOKE, ARDEA, CRANE
"   , flock of ................. SEDGE
"   , green ................... POKE
"   , N. Amer. ............... EXILIS
"   , night .... QUA, QUAWK, SOCO
"   , rare ................. BOATBILL
"   , small ................. BITTERN
heroner ........................ HAWK
herpes ..................... SHINGLES
herpetic ................. REPTILIAN
herring ........ RAUN, SPRAT
"   , a; slang ............. ALEWIFE
"   ; genus ................. ALOSA
"   , lake ................. CISCO
"   measure; Scot. ............ CRAN
"   pond ................. OCEAN

"   sauce ..................... ALEC
"   tub ..................... CADE
"   , young ... MATIE, BRIT, COB, SILE
herring-like ........ ANCHOVY, CISCO, LILE
hersum ......................... OBEY
Hertha .............. ERDA, NERTHUS
hesitate ......... DEMUR, HAW, HEM, SCOTCH, ERS
hesperian ............... BUTTERFLY
Hesperides ............... ATLANTIDES
Hesperus' daughter ........ ERYTHEA
hessonite ..................... GARNET
Hestia's mother .................. RHEA
hetaera ...................... LAIS
hetero; comb. form ............ OTHER
heterodoxy .................. HERESY
Hetman ................... ATAMAN
hex .. BEWITCH, JINX, HAG, SPELL
hexad, group of six .......... SESTET
hexadecane ................... CETANE
hexapod ..................... INSECT
hexastich ....... STANZA, STROPHE
heyday ........ MAY, JOY, WILDNESS
hiatus .. COL, GAP, LACUNA, BREAK, FISSURE, PAUSE
hibernate ........... SHACK, WINTER
Hibernia .............. ERIN, IRELAND
hibertia; Aus. .............. ROCKROSE
hickory; N. Am. ................ PECAN
hickory-nut ...... KISKATOM, PECAN
hickory wattle ................ ACACIA
hidden . LATENT, ARCANE, COVERT, CRYPTIC
hidden; Fr. ........... PERDU, SECRE
hide . HOOD, WRAP, CACHE, SKULK, ENSCONCE
hide, a ...................... KIP, PELT
hideous ............. GRIM, SCABROUS
hides ................... HIDATION
hides, to remove hair from ..... MOON, SLATE
hiding, in ............. PERDU, LOST
hiding place ... LATEBROUS, CACHE, MEW, LATIBULUM
hie ......... URGE, SCUD, GO, SPEED
hieroglyphics, key to ....... ROSETTA
higgle ........... CHAFFER, STICKLE
high .. ALOFT, GAMY, LOFTY, TALL, AERIE, SERENE, ELA, ALT
high-flown diction ......... EUPHUISM
high mountain .................... ALP
high-strung ............ TAUT, TENSE
highest; comb. form ..... BEST, ACRO
highest number of a die .......... SISE
highest point ... NOONTIDE, APOGEE
highfalutin .... HAUGHTY, POMPOUS
Highland of Cent. Asia ........ PAMIR
Highlander ................. TARTAN
Highlander mountain peak .... KAMET
highlander's furry pouch ... SPORRAN
highway ......... ITER, PIKE, TOBY
hilarity ....... GLEE, GAIETY, MIRTH
hill, cone shaped BRAE, COPPLE, LAW
"   , fortified ................. RATH
"   in S. Afr. ..................... KOP
"   in west U. S. ...... LOMA, LOMITA
"   , isolated .................. BUTTE

126

" myna ................ STARLING
" , round; Sp. ............. MORRO
" , short ................. KAME
" , small .......... DOWN, DUNE
" , top of a .... PAHA, COP, TOR
hillock ...... HURST, KNOLL, COPSE,
                              TERTRE
hills, chain of ......... AAS, RIDGE
hills, steep-rocky ............ SCARS
hillside; Scot. ............... BRAE
hilum of an organ ............. PORTA
hilum, per. to the ........... HILAR
him; dial ...... MUN, PIKAS, YAK, HE
Himalayan animal ... KAIL, MARMOT,
                              OUNCE
Himalayan antelope .......... GORAL
"       bearcat ........... PANDA
"       bird ............... CHOUGH
"       dweller ......... NEPALESE
"       forest ............ BHABAR
"       goat .. KRAS, GORAL, TAHR
"       grassy tract ......... TARAI
"       peak .... API, AKU, NEPAL,
              SIKIM, EVEREST, HUMP
"       pheasant ........... MONAL
"       sheep ............. NAHOOR
"       sub-ranges ....... SIWALIKS
"       tableland ............ TIBET
"       tea plant .......... AUCUBA
"       trees .. DEODAR, SAL, TOON
"       valley ........... DUN, MARI
"       walnut ........... CORYLUS
himself; Lat. ................. IPSE
Himyarite ...... AXUMITE, SABAEAN
hind ....... ROE, HEARST, PEASANT
hind bow of saddle ........... CANTLE
hind, red ...... CABRILLA, GROUPER
hinder ..... BACK, CRAMP, CUMBER,
              DETER, EMBAR, REAR
hindrance .......... RUB, CLOG, LET
Hindu ..... KOLI, SER, TAMIL, SIKH
"       acrobat ................. NAT
"       age of world ........... YUGA
"       , Anglicized ........... BABU
"       ascetic .......... YATI, YOGI
"       atheist ............ NASTIKA
"       bandit ............... DECAIT
"       barber ............... NADIT
"       barren land ............ USAR
"       bird ................ MUNIA
"       blacksmith ......... LOHAR
"       call to prayer .......... AZAN
"       caravansary ...... CHOULTRY
"       carpet for prayer ....... ASAN
"       carriage .... GHARRI, GHARRY
"       caste, lowest ......... SUDRA
"       caste, member of a .. JAT, MAL
"       caste, member of a low ... TELI
"       cavalry troop ........ RISALA
"       ceremonial gift . KHILAT, LEPA
"       city, any ............. ABAD
"       city, holy ... BENARES, MECCA
"       class ................. TELI
"       class member ......... MAL
"       congregation ......... SAMAJ
"       convent ............. MATH
"       court officer ......... AMALA
"       custom; obs. .......... SUTEE

" custom of incremating widows ...
                              SATI
" cymbals ................. TAL
" dancing girl; var. .. BAYADEER
" deity ..... DEVA, KAMA, SIVA,
                      VISHNU, MANU
" deity, 8th avatar of Vishnu ......
                          KRISHNA
" demon ................. ASURA
" dependency .......... TALUK
" deposit; law ............ ADHI
" dewey ................. SISIRA
" discount .............. BATTA
" doctrine ............ DHARMA
" drinking pot ........... LOTA
" dye, morindin ... AL, AAL, AWL
" ejaculation or manrra ...... OM
" elephant-headed god GANESHA
Hindu evil spirit; myth. ASURA, MARA
" fabled mountain ........ MERU
" fair ..................... MELA
" farmer ............... HAMAL
" female slave ........... DASI
" festival . DASAHARA, DEWALI,
                              HOLI
" festive day ............ PHAG
" flying beings; myth. . GARUDAS
" frosty .............. HEMANTA
" garment for female ....... SARI
" gentleman ...... BABOO, BABU
" gentleman, woman's ... SAREE,
                              SARI
" god (see also 'God')
" god ..... DEVI, BRAHMA, SIVA
" god of fire .............. AGNI
" god of love ............ KAMA
" god of nature ........... DEVA
" god of the dead ......... YAMA
" god of the sky ......... DYAUS
" god of the Triad ......... SIVA
" god of waters ........ VARUNA
" god of wisdom ....... GANESA
" goddess (see also 'Goddess')
" goddess UMA, DEVI, SHRI, VAC
" goddess of destruction .... KALI
" godling ............... DEVATA
" goldsmith ............. SONAR
" grant of land .... ENAM, INAM,
                              SASAN
" groom ................. SYCE
" guitar ................ SITAR
" hill-billy .............. BHIL
" holy books .... SASTRA, VEDA
" idol .......... PAGODA, SWAMI
" ignorance, philosophy of TAMAS
" incarnation .......... AVATAR
" jackal ................. KOLA
" kala .................. BULBUL
" kneeling mat ............ ASAN
" Kush mountain pass .... DORA,
                              IRAK
" lady ................... DEVI
" land grant ............. INAM
" language; anc. ...... SANSKRIT
" law books ............. MANU
" leader ........ GANDHI, SIRDAR
" lease ......... PATTA, POTTAH
" lease holder ......... IJARADAR
" life principle .. PRANA, ATMAN

127

" literature, sacred SRUTI, VEDA
" loin cloth ............... DHOTI
" lord .................... SWAMI
" lord of the world JAGANNATHA
" low-caste ......... KOLI, MAL
" margosa ................. NEEM
" master .......... SAHIB, MIAN
" meal ..................... ATA
" measure .......... HATH, KOS
" mendicant ................ NAGA
" merchant ...... BANIAN, TELI
" military .................... SIK
" money of account ........ ANNA
" month BAISAKH, JETH, ASARH,
SAWAN (SARAWAN), BHADON,
ASIN (KUAR), KATIK
(KARTIK), AGHAN, PUS, MAGH,
PHAGUN (PHALGUN), CHAIT
" mountain pass ......... GHAUT
Hindu musical inst. .. SAROD, SITAR,
VINA
" nobleman ............. RAJAH
" of Aryan speech ......... SWAT
" olympus ................. MERU
" , one of a gardener cast . MALI
" patriarch ................ PITRI
" peasant .................. RYOT
" philosophy; anc. ......... YOGA
" pottery ................. UDA
" prayer rug ............. ASANI
" prince .... MAHARAJ, RAJAH,
RANA
" princess . MAHARANI, RANEE,
RANI
" principle of existence . PRANA,
TATTVA
" private apartment .... MAHAL
" queen ........... RANEE, RANI
" rainy ................ VARSHA
" reign ..................... RAJ
" religion ... JAINISM, SIVAISM
" religious ascetic ......... MUNI
" " book ......... SASTRA
" " cymbals .......... TAL
" " devotee ......... MUNI
" " fair ............. MELA
" " formula .... MANTRA
" " rite ........ SRADDHA
" " sect, unorthodox JAINA
" " teacher ... GURU, PIR
" robe ..................... JAMA
" rule ...................... RAJ
" sacred literature, collection of ..
VEDA
" sage .. GAUTAMA, MAHATMA
" scarf ................... SAREE
" school of philosophy .MIMANSA
" school, Skt. ............... TOL
" scriptures .. TANTRA, SASTRA
" scriptures, per. to .... AGAMA,
TANTRIC
" sect, one of a ............. SADH
" serpent ................. NAGA
" soldier ................. SEPOY
" soul .................... ATMA
" spirit of evil ............ MARA
" spiritual darkness ...... TAMAS
" spring ............. VASANTA

" stele ...................... LAT
" store room .............. GOLA
" supreme eery ......... VISHNU
" swan; myth. ........... HANSA
" temple tower ....... SIKHORA,
SIKHRA, VIMANA
" title .... MIR, SIDI, RAO, NAIK
" title for a Europ. gentleman ....
SAHIB
" title of respect .... MIAN, SRI,
SWAMY, SREE
" trader .......... BANIAN, YAN
" trinity ........ BRAHMA, SIVA,
VISHNU
" trinity, the ........ TRIMURTI
" tribe, one of a ............. JAT
" , twenty (score) ........ CORGE
" veranda ................. PYAL
" village .................. ABADI
" viol ........ RUANA, SARINDA
" water nymph ............. APAS
" weaver ................. TANTI
" weight ................ MAUND
" widow ......... SATI, SUTTEE
" worshipper of Siva ...... SAIVA
Hindu worst of the four ages ... KALI
" writer ................ SIRCAR
Hinduism ................... ANIMISM
Hinduism, essence ............ ATMAN
Hinduize Nepalese ......... MURMIS
Hindustan Dravidian ........... TODA
Hindustan rice crop ..... AGHANEE
Hindustani ............. HINDI, URDU
Hindustani poet ........ SIRAJ, WALI
hinge joint ............. PIVOT, KNEE
hinny ........................... MULE
hint ALLUDE, EYEWINK, GLANCE,
CUE, MINT, REFER
hip .......... COXA, HUCK, HUCKLE
hip bones .............. ILIA, HUGGIN
hip muscle ................ ILIOPSOAS
hip, per. to the .............. SCIATIC
hippo., Bib. ............... BEHEMOTH
hippo, thong of hide ...... CHICOTTE
Hiram ........................ GRANT
hired . CHARTERED, HACK, SIGNED,
TICCA
hireling .... ALLOWE, ESNE, VENAL
hirsute ........................ HAIRY
hispid ........ STRIGOSE, STRIGOUS
hissing TST, FIZZ, SIBILANT, SHISH
historian ..... ANNALIST, ACTOR
historian, an ...... RALEIGH, TAINE
historical character ........... JUMEL
history DRAMA, ERA, PAST, MEMOIR
history, muse of ................. CLIO
history of individual development ......
ONTOGENY
"History of Fondling," character in ....
BLIFIL
hit ...... BOP, SLOG, BUFFET, ACE,
BUNT, FLICK, SRO, STRIKE
hits LAM, LARRUP, SWATS, SINGLES
hive .... STORE, SWARM, BOX, GUM
hives, nettle ................. UREDO
hoactzin ...................... ANNA
hoard .... AMASS, GARNER, SUPPLY
hoarder ...................... MISER

128

hoar frost ............... RAG, RIME
hoarseness .......... QUACK, HUSKY
hoary .... GRAY, OLD, CANESCENT
hoax ... BAM, BILK, CANARD, COD
hobbled ...... PASTERNED, LIMPED
hobby ........ BICYCLE, FAD, DOLLY
hobgoblin .. ELF, BOGEY, IMP, PUG,
SCRAT
hock ............. HAM, HOX, PAWN
hockey ............ HURLEY, SHINDY
hockey ball ...... NUR, ORR, PUCK
hockey cup ................ STANLEY
hockey goal ..................... CAGE
hockey stick; Irish ............. CAMAN
hockey team ...... SEVEN, SEXTET
hocus ..... DRUG, DECEIVE, FRAUD,
CHEAT
hodge-podge MESS, CENTO, MEDLEY,
OLIO, GALLIMAUFRY, MELANGE
Hodgins; author ................. ERIC
hoe; Scot. ..................... PADLE
hog food ...................... MAST
  "   , ground ................. MARMOT
  "   , salted side of .......... FLITCH
  "   shears ................. SNOUTER
  "   , S. Amer. ............... TAPIR
  "   weed ................. AMBROSIA
  "   , wild; N. Z. ............... BENE
  "   , young .......... SHOAT, SHOTE
hogfish ...................... CAPITAN
hoggerel ...................... SHEEP
hogget ........................ BOAR
hognut ......... EARTHNUT, OUABE
hog-peanut .............. EARTHPEA
hogs; genus ..................... SUS
hogshead .......... CASK, MEASURE
hogshead, 12b wine gal. ........ PIPE
hoi polloi ..................... MASSES
holden ........ ROMP, RUDE, TOMBOY
hoist ........ HEAVE, LIFT, REAR
hoisted up, as sails ............ ATRIP
hoisting device .... GIN, PARBUCKLE,
CAPSTAN, DAVIT
hoity-toity .......... ROMP, SNOOTY
hokum ............. BUNK, NONSENSE
hold back .............. DAM, INHIBIT
hold for nails .................... NOG
hold in a mold ................. SPRUE
hold; naut. .......... AVAST, HOWE
hold off .......... AVERT, REFRAIN
holder .... OWNER, TENANT, PAYEE
holding .............. TENURE, SEAT
holds a sprit .............. SNOTTER
hole ...... SLOT, DEN, GOURD, LILL
hole for ship's cable .......... HAWSE
hole in tracery .......... OILET, OYLE
holed up ...................... LAIRD
holes in garment for sleeves ... SCYES
holia ......................... SALMON
holiday ...... FERIA, FERIE, FIESTA
holiday, take ..................... LAKE
holla .................. CEASE, STOP
Holland ....................... DUTCH
  "   , city in . ARNHEIM, HAGUE,
LEYDEN
  "   clay ................. ZEKLEI
  "   commune ................. EPE

  "   dialect FRANKISH, FRISIAN,
SAXON
  "   early political party ... CODS,
HOEKS
  "   gin .............. SCHNAPPS
  "   marsh plant ........ DERRIE
  "   merchants' league ... HANSE
  "   , oldest inhabitants of . CELTS
  "   , painter of ............ EYCK
  "   pile worm NAVALIS, TEREDO
  "   province .......... DRENTHE,
ZEELAND
  "   river EMS, LEK, SCHELDT,
YSSEL
  "   river gravel ..... HEIBANEN
  "   rushes .............. DERRIE
  "   turf .............. PLAGGEN
  "   , village in .............. EDE
  "   writer ............ CATS, VOS
hollands, kind of ................... GIN
hollies, the ..................... ILEX
hollow CAVERNOUS, CAVAL, FALSE,
GORE, CAPSULAR
  "   , circular .. CORREI, CORRIE
  "   in tile ................... KEY
  "   , narrow ............ DINGLE
  "   spindle ............ TRIBLET
hollows, form ............ SCOOP, PIT
holly ... HULL, HOLM, ILEX, OPACA
  "   , European .............. ACEBO
  "   genus ................ OLEARIA
  "   , Indian tea ............. YAPON
  "   , per. to ................. ILICIC
  "   , sea ................ ERYNGIUM
hollyhocks ................. ALTHAEA
Hollywood prize ................. OSCAR
Hollywood star ....... LUNT, GABLE
holm ...... AIT, EYOT, ISLET, ILEX
holm thrush; Eng. ............ MISSEL
Holmes's word ....... ELEMENTARY
holt .................. COPSE, WOODS
holy ......... CHASTE, NUN, VESTAL
Holy Grail .................. SANGREAL
Holy Grail, achiever of .... GALAHAD
holy oil ....................... CHRISM
holy water font ...... CRUET, STOUP
homaloidal .... EVEN, FLAT, OMAL
hombre; Sp. ....................... MAN
homburg ............... FELT, HAT
home NEST, ASTRE, HABITAT, KERN
home base ..................... PLATE
home of Gods ............. OLYMPUS
home of the gods; Scand. .... ASGARD
home of Golden Fleece ...... COLCHIS
homely .... PLAIN, RUDE, SIMPLE
Homeric ......................... EPIC
Homeric saga .................. ILIAD
homeland; myth ............ HAVAIKI
Homer; artist .............. WINSLOW
Homer's birthplace ............ CYME
Homer's burial place .............. IOS
Homer's instrument ............ LYRE
Homer's legendary parent .... MELES
Homer's "Odyssey," singer in PHEMIUS
homesickness ........... NOSTALGIA
homespun ...................... RUSSET
homestead GARTH, FARMERY, TREF
homestead, of a single farm ONSTEAD

129

homestead out buildings .. STEADING
homestead site .......... TOFT, TREF
homicide; Teu. ............... MORTH
homily ........ SERMON, CONVERSE
hominy ......................... SAMP
homo; comb. form .......... COMMON
homo; Lat. ...................... MAN
homo sapiens ................... MAN
hone ...... GRUMBLE, PINE, STROP,
                                         SHARPEN
honey and mulberry juice .... MORAT
  " bear ... KINKAJOU, MELURSUS
  " bee ........ DESERET, DINGAR
  " buzzard ............ KITE, PERN
  " eater ................. IAO, MOHO
  " , fermented drink ........ MEAD
  " , Latin for ................... MEL
  " med. preparation ..... MELLITE
  " , per. to ............. MELISSIC
  " plant ..... CLEOME, FIGWORT
  " , source of ........... NECTAR
  " tube ................. NECTARY
  " weasel or badger ........ RATEL
honeycombed . ALVEOLATE, FAVOSE
honeydew ........ MELIGO, NECTAR
honeyed ........ MELLIFLUOUS
honeyed drink .................... MAAD
honeysuckle, swamp ........ AZALEA
Honolulu, cliff in ................. PALI
Honolulu suburb ................. EWA
honor .. TIP, ATHEL, EXALT, PROW
honor, hungering for ...... ESURIENT
honoria .................... DOUCEURS
honors ... DIGNITIES, GREE, TITLES
honors, an embrace ...... ACCOLADE
hood, clergyman's ........... AMICE
hood, cloak .... BURNOOSE, CAPOTE
hood, monk's .... AMICE, CAPOUCH,
                                    COWL
hood, part of a .............. CAMAIL
hood, Russian ............ BASHLYK
hooded .................... CUCULLATE
hooded seal ......... BLADDERNOSE
hoodwink .... BLEAR, DUPE, COSEN,
                     CHEAT, SEEL, WILE
hoof ...... PASTERN, CLEE, CLUVE
hoof paring tool .......... BUTTERIS
hoof print .................... PIST(E)
hoof-shaped .............. UNGULATE
hook .... HAMULE, CROCK, DECOY,
                     SNARE, TRAP
hook dagger .................. CHAPE
hook, large .......... GAFF, HANGLE
hook money ...................... LARI
hook, stretcher ............. TENTER
hookah ............ PIPE, NARGHILE
hooked . ADUNC, HAMATE, HAMOSE
hooked, as a fish .......... CLEEKED
hooked, as of elbow ...... ANCONAL
hooked prong .................... PEW
hooked-shaped .......... HAMULATE
hook-like FALCATE, SARP, UNCINAL
hooks .......................... HAMI
hook-shaped iron ...... CROC, KILP
hoop ........ BAIL, EMBRACE, RING
hoop skirt .............. CRINOLINE,
                 FARTHINGALE
hooper .............. SWAN, COOPER

hoosegow; slang JAIL, PRISON, CLINK
Hoosier State ............... INDIANA
hoot ...... BOO, WHOO, CRY, HONK
hoot, an owl .............. ULULATE
hop .. CAPER, FRISK, GAMBOL, HIP,
                              TRIP
hop bush ........................ AKE
hop disease ...................... FEN
hop flea .................... HALTICA
hop kiln .................. OAST, OST
hop marjoram ............... DITTANY
hop trees; genus ............ PTELEA
hop vine stem .................. BINE
hope ...... SPES, ASPIRE, OPTIMISM
hope; symb. ...................... OPAL
hoped for .................... SPERATE
hopeless ...... SARDONIC, FORLORN
hop-o-my-thumb ............. DWARF
hops alkaloid ............... LUPULIN
hops kiln ....................... OAST
hops between 2 and 4 years old .. OLDS
hops, narcotic in .......... HUMULIN
hopscotch stone ............ PEEVER
horde ................. TRIBE, TROOP
hordeolum ........................ STY
horizon ......... SEARIM, LIMIT
horizon, appear above ........... RISE
horizon, arc of the .......... AZIMUTH
horizon glass ................ SEXTANT
horizontally .... ACROSS, ATHWART
horn, blare of FANFARE, TANTARA
  " , crooked ............. BUCCINA
  " , drinking ............. RHYTON
  " , Jewish ............. SHOPHAR
  " , kind of ...... CROCKET, ZAIN
  " mouthpiece ............... BOCAL
  " of a crescent ............. CUSP
  " of an insect ......... ANTENNA
  " on beak of a bird .. EPITHEMA
  " on deer's antler ...... CROCHE
  " , pierce with a ........... GORE
  " , stag's ................ ANTLER
  " , unbranched ............... DAG
hornbill; Afr. .................... TOCK
Horne; entertainer ............. LENA
horn-like .... KERA, CERES, CORNU
horned animal ..................... GNU
horned animal, fabled ...... UNICORN
horned viper ........ ASP, CERASTES
hornet Lat. ................... CRABRO
hornless ........ POLLED, ACEROUS,
                 DODDED, POLEY
hornless cow ...... MULEY, MULLEY
hornpipe-like ............ MATELOTE
horns of a deer .............. BALCON
horny' scale .......... NAIL, SCUTE
horny tissue ................ CERATIN
horrible ................ DIRE, GRIM
Horsa, brother of ............ HENGIS
horse ...... CANUCK, BIDET, ARAB,
    BEAST, BLOCK, PACER, STEED
  " , ankle of a .............. HOCK
  " , Austral. WARRAGAL, WALER
  " , Barbary .................. BARB
  " blanket ................. MANTA
  " , British; slang .......... PRAD
  " buyer .............. KNACKER
  " , check back of ...... SACCADE

" chestnut ............. BUCKEYE
" , color of a PIED, PINTO, ROAN
" ; comb. form ............ HIPPO
" dealer; Eng. ............. COPER
" disease ....... SPAVIN, SURRA,
LAMPAS
" , easy-paced .............. PAD
" eyelid inflammation ...... HAW
" family ............ ASS, ZEBRA
" , female .................. MARE
" fennel .................. SESELI
" ; genus ................. EQUUS
" , giant; Norse ....... GOLDFAX
" , guide rope for ........ LONGE
" , half wild .......... MUSTANG
" , leap of a ............ CURVET
" mackerel SCAD, ATULE, TUNNY
" , male .. GELDING, STALLION
" of different colors CREAM, TAN,
PALOMINO
" , old PLUG, AVER, ROSINANTE
" , position of a ...... PESANTE
" prehistoric; Am. TIT, EOHIPPUS
" race board ................ TOTE
" , race (inferior) ...... PLATER
" , rearing of a .......... PESADE
" , resembling ........... EQUOID
" round up ............... RODEO
" shoe, calk on ........ CALTROP
" , small BRONCO, GENET, NAG,
TIT
" , spirited .. STEED, COURSER
" , swift ................ PACOLET
" track slope ............ CALADE
" training place .......... LONGE
" , trotting ...... COB, MORGAN
" , wheel ................. POLER
" , work; British ....... GARRAN
" , worthless .... JAPE, CROCK,
SHACK
Horse Mesa dam river ......... SALT
horsehide pellet .......... BASEBALL
horsemanship, art of ........ MANEGE
horse-radish tree ...... BEHEN, BEN
horsewhip ......... CHABOOK, FLOG
horse's cry .. NEIGH, NIE, WHINNY
horses, famous English ...... HEROD,
MATCHEM, ECLIPSE
horse's forehead .......... CHANFRIN
horse's hoof, part of ........ PASTERN
horse's leg, part of FETLOCK, INSTEP
horses, per. to .......... CABALLINE
Horus; Egypt. ..................... RA
Horus' father .................. OSIRIS
hospice, oriental ... MARET, IMARET
hospital(obs.) ............. MALADERY
hospitality to strangers XENODOCHY
host .... SERVER, ARMY, PYX, SUM
host receptacle .................. PAX
hostel ..... INN, MANSION, TAVERN,
MOTEL
hostler ...................... GROOM
hostilities . FEUD, ANIMUS, ENMITY,
WAR
hostility .... ANIMUS, ENMITY, WAR
hot; Span. .................... CALIDO
hot tempered .... IRACUND, BRETH
hotel TAVERN, FONDA, HOSTEL, INN

hotel keeper .............. BONIFACE
hothouse ...................... STOVE
hott; dial. Eng. .............. BASKET
Hottentot .......... NAMA, QUAQUA
" aborigine ........ NAMAQUA
" cloak ................ KAROSS
" encampment ......... KRAAL
" musical inst. ........ GORAH,
RAMKEE
" tobacco ............ DACCHA
" tribe ..... NAMA, OERLAAM
hough .......... HAMSTRING, HAWK
hound .. CERBERUS, OTTER, TREER
hound, hunting .. HARRIER, SETTER
hound, per. to a ............ SKIRTER
hound, small ...... BASSET, BEAGLE
hound, to ..................... BEDOG
hound, wolf ..................... ALAN
hour book ..................... HORAE
hour; Lat. ...................... HORA
houri ........................... NYMPH
hourly .......... FREQUENT, HORAL
house .... COTE, CASINO, GRANGE,
PENT
house, comb. form for ........... ECO
house, oriental ...... TEMBE, SERAI
house, per. to a .............. DOMAL
house, ranch ...... CASITA, CASA,
HACIENDA
house, Russ. log ................ IZBA
house, stately ................ PALACE
house, summer .... GAZEBO, RANCH,
VILLA
house, timber and plaster CALAMANCO
housewarming ................. INFARE
household .................... MENAGE
household fairy ................. PUCK
household tutelaries LARES, PENATES
housel ................... EUCHARIST
houses, buyer of old ...... KNACKER
Houshi Is.; Jap., town in ...... KURE
housing ......................... PAD
Houston College ................ RICE
hovel .. HOOD, HUT, SHACK, STACK,
CABIN, DEN, DUGOUT, HUTCH
Howard, S; play ..... "ALIEN CORN"
SHANTY
Howe; inventor ................. ELIAS
however .......... FAR, MUCH, YET
howitzer .............. GUN, SKODA
howler monkey; S. Am. ...... ARABA
hoyden ..................... TOMBOY
Hoyle; Eng. writer .......... EDMUND
Hreidmar's son; myth. ...... REGINN
hub ........ HUMMOCK, NAVE, HUT
hubble-bubble .................. PIPE
huckle .............. HAUNCH, HIP
"Hudibras"; author .......... BUTLER
huge .............. TITANIC, VAST
hugger-mugger .................. SLY
huisache, the ..... ACACIA, POPINAC
hum WHIZZ, DRONE, CROON, TUNE,
BOMBINATE
human .... HOMO, ADAMITE, MAN,
MORTAL
human frailty .................. ADAM
humanities ............. ADAMHOODS

131

humble ABASE, CHASTISE, DEMIT, LOW, MEEK
humboltine ................. OXALINE
humbug PAH, BOSH, CHEAT, FLAM, HOAX
humdinger ..................... ONER
humid ........ DAMP, MOIST, DANK
humiliate .. SHAME, ABASH, NITHER
humility ................... MODESTY
hummeling mach. ............ AWNER
humming bird AVA, COLIBRI, COSTA, BLUET, RUFOUS, SAPPHO, STAR, SYLPH, RACKETTAIL
humor CAPRICE, QUIRK, MOOD, CUE, WIT, WHIM, CATER
humor, ill ................. TID, TIFF
humus .......... MULCH, MOLD, SOIL
hun .............. GERMAN, VANDAL
Hun leader ........... ATLI, ATTILA
Hun race ............ AVAR, TARTAR
Hunan river .................... YUEN
hundred; comb. form ......... HECTO
hundred, one ................. CRORE
hundredfold ............... CENTUPLE
hundred-weight . CENTNER, CENTAL
"Hundred Years War" battle CRESSY
hundredth of a right angle ...... GRAD
Hungar; composer ........... LEHAR
Hungarian .......... DEAK, MAGYAR
   "   canal ................. BEGA
   "   cavern ........ OKNO, VODI
   "   county ................ ARVA
   "   dynasty ............... ARPAD
   "   monetary unit .... GULDEN, PENGO
   "   mountain .... ALPS, TATRA, VERTES
   "   river . RAAB, UNA, DRAVE, THEISS
   "   seaport ............... FIUME
   "   wine .................. TOKAY
   "   wine measure ITCZE, ANTAL,
hunger-bane ........... STARVATION
hunger, causing ........... ESURINE
hungry .... AVID, BARREN, ACORIA, EAGER, YAP
hungry horse .................... DAM
hunky; slang .. EVEN, RIGHT, WELL
Huns, conquerors of the ...... AVARS
Huns, king of the ............. ETZEL
hunt .... DIG, CHASE, SEEK, SCOUR
Hunt, Miss ................... MARSHA
hunter, a ACTAEON, JAGER, NIMROD, ORION, TRAPPER
hunting coyote ............. WOLFING
   "   dog ...... BASSET, BEAGLE
   "   expedition SHIKAR, SAFARI
   "   , fond of ........... VENATIC
   "   ; French ........... CHASSE
   "   leopard of Ind. ... CHEETAH
   "   weasel ............. FERRET
   "   with ........... CYNEGETIC
huntress; Gr. ...... ATLANTA, DIANA
hurdy-gurdy ... ROTA, LIRA, ORGAN
hurled ............. HURTLED, SENT
hurly ........ CONFUSION, UPROAR
hurly-burly .................. TUMULT
hurrah ........................... VIVA

hurried; mus. ............... AGITATO
hurry .. CHASE, SESSA, SPEED, HIE
hurry; shak. ................... SESSA
hurt .......... DERE, HARM, HARRY
hurtful MALEFIC, NOCENT, NOISOME
hurtle ........ CLASH, FLING, DASH
husbanded .................... STORED
husbandman ............... GRANGER
husbandry ...... THRIFTY, FARMER, TILLAGE
husband's brother ............. LEVIR
hush ALLAY, APPEASE, STILL, CLAM
Husing, Mr. ...................... TED
husk . SHOOD, BRAN, LEAM, SHUCK
Huss; martyr .................. JOHN
hussy ..................... BAG, CASE
hut ........ ISBA, COT, COTE, SHACK
hut, a mean HOVEL, HUMPY, SHANTY
hut, fisherman's ................. SKEO
hut, lean to ..................... SHED
hut of S. West ................ JACAL
hutch ........ PEN, COOP, WARREN
Huxley; essayist ............. ALDOUS
hyacinth ............... MUSK, STONE
hyacinth gem ................. ZIRCON
hyacinth, wild ................. CAMAS
Hyades, in the ......... ALDEBARAN
hyawa gum .......... CONIMA, RESIN
hybrid ...... CATALO, CROSS, MULE
hybrid animal ................. HINNY
hybrid, as a dog ........ MONGREL
hybrid citrus tree .......... TANGELO
hybrid equine ................. ZEBEC
hybrid growth .......... METEROSIS
hydra ............. POLYP, SERPENT
Hydra Is. (Gr.) mountain on .... ERE
Hydra Is., port of ............... MOLO
Hydra Is., Turkish name for .......... TCHAMLIZA
hydrargyrum ........... MERCURY
hydrate, ethyl .............. ALCOHOL
hydraulic brake .......... CATARACT
hydraulic device ............. TRÉMIE
hydrazide ..................... AMIDE
hydrazoate, a ................. AZID
hydriad; myth. ............... NYMPH
hydrocarbon, aromatic ...... CARANE, CHRYSENE
   "   coal tar ........... PYRENE
   "   , ethyl .............. CETANE
   "   , gaseous ........ FLUORINE
   "   inflammable ........ BUTANE
   "   , liquid .. CUMOL, NONANE, TOLUOL
   "   , oily . ETHERIN, VIRIDINEI
   "   radical ....... AMYL, XEXYL
   "   solid .............. CRYSENE
   "   solvent ............ XYLENE
   "   , unsaturated ...... OLEFINE
   "   , volatile .. BENZO, TETROL
   "   , white crystalline . DITOLYL, RETENE, TOLANE
hydrogen atoms, having two BIBASIC
hydrogenase ............. REDUCTASE
hydrohematite .............. TURGITE
hydroid family ......... SERTULARIA
hydromel ....................... MEAD
hydrophobia ........ LYSSA, RABIES

132

hydrophyllia .................. BRACTS
hydrous silicate ... STEATITE, TALC
hydrous sodium carbonate ... TRONA,
     URAO
hydrous wool fat .......... LANOLIN
hyena-like animal ....... AARDWOLF
hymenopter ........ BEE, WASP, ANT
hymn book ..... PSALTER, HYMNAL
hymn, non-metrical ....... CANTICLE
hymn or ode ....... EPINICION, SONG
hymn, sacred ANTHEM, TRISAGION,
     ODE
hymn, sung in unison ..... CHORALE
hyperbole, excessive ........... BLAH
hyperboles, utmost ............. ELAS
hyperbolic func. ................. COSH
Hyperion's daughter ............. EOS
hyphen ...................... DASH
hyphen, without a .............. SOLID
Hypipyle's father .............. THOAS
hypnotic ECTENIC, SLEEPY, ALDOL
hypnotic condition ..... ENDORMED,
     TRANCE
hypnotism, founder of ....... MESMER
hypnotize ......... CHARM, ENDORM
hypochondriac, mad .... NOSOMANIA
hypocrisy ............. PHARISAISM
hypothecate .................. PLEDGE
hypothesis ............. THEORY, ISM
hypothetical force ....... IDANT, OD
hyrax .......... CONY, DAMAN, DAS
hyrax of the Bible ......... SHAPHAN
hyrax-like .................. BADGER
hyson, of China .................... TEA
hyssop; Eur. .................... MINT
hysteria .......... FITFUL, NERVES


# I

I, letter .......................... EYE
I, excessive use of letter ... IOTACISM
I love; Lat. ...................... AMO
I have found .............. EUREKA
Iago, wife of .................. EMILIA
Iambic trimeter ........... SENARIUS
Iasi, coin of .................... LEU
Iberia .......................... SPAIN
Iberian ......................... PICT
ibex .......... SAKEEN, BOUQUETIN
ibex; Ethiop. .......... SAOL, WALIE
ibex; Siberian .................... TEK
ibid ............................. SAME
ibid, large; Phil. I. ......... MONITOR
ibn-Rushd; Arabic ........ AVERROES
ibn-Sina; Arabic .......... AVICENNA
Ibsen character ........... ASE, NORA
Ibsen's native land .......... NORWAY
Icarus' daughter ........... ERIGONE
ice floe SCONCE, PACK, PAN, QUERN
ice, glacial ............. SISH, SERAC
ice, mass of . GLACIER, BERG, CALF
ice, thin ....................... GRUE
iceberg, small ............. GROWLER
Iceland, bronze coin of ........ EYRIR

Icelandic chief gods . AESIR, BALDER,
    FORSETI, ODIN (WODEN),
    HEIMDALL, LOKI, THOR
    (DONAR), TYR (TIU)
Icelandic language ............. NORSE
Icelandic literature ..... EDDA, SAGA
Icelandic measure . FET, LINA, ALEN
Icelandic musician and poet .. SKALD
icteric .................... JAUNDICED
icy ......... COLD, GLACIAL, GELID
id ........................ ORFE, IDEM
Idaho; capital .................. BOISE
idant ................. CHROMOSOME
idea; comb. form ... WRINKLE, IDEO
ideal ........ FAULTLESS, UNREAL,
    UTOPIAN, COMPLETE, LIMIT
ideal, remote ................... THULE
ideate .......... CONCEIVE, THINK
identical ALIKE, SAME, VERY, REAL
ideologies ........ ISMS, VISIONARIES
Ides, ninth day before the .... NONES
idiocy AMENTIA, ANOESIA, FATUITY
idiom ............. DICTION, PHRASE
idiot .. MORON, CRETIN, NATURAL,
    OAF
idle . SORN, DRONE, LOAF, OTIOSE,
    TIFFLE, LAZY, MOON, VAIN,
    INERT
idleness .......... FANIENTE, SLOTH
idle, to ...................... GAMMER
idler DRONE, LOUNGER, DAWDLER
idling .......... MOONING, OTIOSE
idocrase .............. VESUVIANITE
idol, Antillean ............. GOD, ZEMI
idol; Saxon .... EIKON, ICON, AFGOD
idol, social ...................... LEON
idolator .......... BAALITE, PAGAN,
    HEATHEN
Idonesian ......................... ATA
idose ........................... IDITE
ids ............................ IDANT
Idumean .................... EDOMITE
Idun; Scand. myth ......... ISTHUNN
Idyls . IMAGES, POEMS, PASTORALS
"Idyls of the King," lady in . ETTARE
i.e. ............................ IDEST
if ever .................... AND, ONCE
if not; law ...................... NISI
iffy; col. .................. DOUBTFUL
Igdrasil; Scand. ........... YGDRASIL
igneous rock ......... DACITE, BOSS,
    DIABASE
ignoble .............. HUMBLE, LOW
ignited ...................... LIT, LIVE
ignoramus .. DOLT, DUNCE, NITWIT,
    SCIOLIST
ignorance .... INERUDITION, TAMAS
ignorant .......... INGRA, NESCIENT
ignore .... ELIDE, CUT, OMIT, SNUB,
    OVERLOOK
Igorots, division of a town ........ ATO
iguana; Austral. .. GOANNA, LIZARD
"Il Trovatore," gypsy in .. ACUZENA,
    MANERICO
ileus ......................... COLIC
ilex .................. HOLLY, OAK
Iliad, herald in the ......... STENTOR
Iliad, hero ......... ACHILLES, AJAX

ill ........ AILING, BAD, SICK, EVIL
ill-being ...................... ILLTH
ill counsel ................... ABULIA
ill temper ......... SPLEEN, ANIMUS
ill, feel ................. AIL, TOUT
ill, prefix ....................... MAL
illative ............... INFERENTIAL
illegal CONTRABAND, FOUL, ILLICIT
illegal toll, Eng. .......... MALTOLTE,
MALETOLT
Illinois, county in .............. KANE
Illinois, native of ............ SUCKER
illiterate ...... UNREAD, INERUDITE
ill-smelling plant ................ RUE
illuminate ...... IMBLAZE, MINIATE,
MYSTIC, CHEER, RALLY
illumination in eclipse .. PENUMBRA
illumination; unit of ...... PHOT, LUX
illumine ...... BLAZE, LIGHT, LIMN,
GLOSS
illustrate .......... CITE, ELUCIDATE,
PICTURE
illustration ... INSTANCE, EXAMPLE,
SIMILE
illustrious ........ EMINENT, CASTE,
FAMOUS
ill-will . GRUDGE, MALICE, ENMITY
image .... EIKON, GOD, ICON, IDOL,
PORTURE
image, mental ... EIDOLON, RECEPT
imagination ..... DREAM, FANTASY
imaginative ............... POETICAL
imagine, to .... CONCEIVE, IDEATE,
WEEN, FANCY, OPINE
imalm, an ...................... ALIM
imbar ............. FORTIFY, GUARD
imbecile .. WITLET, ANILE, MORON
imbecile, deformed ........... CRETIN
imbecility ...... FATUITY, ANOESIA,
MORIA, AMENTIA, IDIOCY
imbedded ................. ENFONCED
imbricate ............ BENT, SCALED
imbroglio . CABAL, INTRIGUE, PLOT
imbrue .. MACERATE, SOAK, STEEP
imbue ........ TINCT, DYE, INGRAIN,
LEAVEN, SATURATE
Imeritian ...................... IMER
imidogen comp. .............. AMID(E)
imitate ... MIMIC, APE, MIME, COPY
imitation ........ MIMESIS, PARODY,
APISM
imitation pearl .............. OLIVET
imitative in color or form . APATETIC
immature YOUNG, CRUDE, CALLOW,
RAW, GREEN, UNRIPE
immaturity ................... NONAGE
immemorial ...................... OLD
immense ...... FINE, VAST, ENORM,
VASTY, INFINITE, TITANIC
immerse ..... DOUSE, ENGROSS, DIP
immobile ......... FIXED, SET, FIRM
immoderate ................. UNDUE
immortal ... UNDYING, AMBROSIAL,
AMRITA, GLORIOUS, PERPETUAL
immortality .... ATHANASIA, FAME
immune body .............. DESMON
immune, render ............ VASTATE
immunity ....... ALLERGY, LICENSE

immure ........... CONFINE, WALL,
ENTOMB
immutable ...... ETERNAL, STABLE
imp FAIRY, FAY, SPRITE, BRAT, ELF
impact ....... FORCE, BINGO, CRAM,
STROKE, CEMENT, CONTACT
impair ......... MAR, RUIN, VITIATE
impaired, as of nerve . ANERETHISIA
impale . GORE, PIERCE, SPIT, STING
impalpable ...... FINE, INTANGIBLE
impartial ........ EQUITABLE, FAIR,
JUST
imparting motion ........... KINETIC
impasse . CUL-DE-SAC, STALEMATE
impatient ........ EAGER, RESTIVE,
ITCHING
impeach ACCUSE, ARRAIGN, INDICT
impede BLOCK, CLOG, LET, RETARD
impede, legally ESTOP, BAR, DEBAR
impediment ........ BARRIER, HITCH
impel ............ DRIVE, URGE, PUT
impelling forces; Lat. ..... MOMENTA
imperfect ......... FALLIBLE, FRAIL,
ERRABLE
imperfect goods ................ FENT
imperfect hand ............ ATELES
imperfect, prefix for ............. MAL
imperial officer ............. PALATINE
imperial structure ........... EMPIRE
impersonal .................... MANA
impersonate ....... PERSONIFY, ACT
imperturbability .......... ATARAXIA
impetus ..... BENSEL, BIRR, EAGER
impetuses ... MOMENTA, COLLISION
imphee .................... SORGHUM
impious ........ GODLESS, PROFANE
impish ........ ELVAN, MALIGNANT
implant ............. ENROOT, INFIX
implement ...... DATER, KIT, TOOL
"     , early flint ....... EOLITH
"     , kind of ........ PUPPET
"     of warfare; anc. ..... CROC
"     , to deprive of an RATTEN
"     used in hand printing ......
BRAYER
implements GEAR, GRAITH, TACKLE
implements, wood for handles of; ....
COCOBOLA
implied ....... INFERENTIAL, TACIT
implored ASKED, BEGGED, PRAYED,
PLED
imply ... SUPPOSE, ARGUE, INDUCE,
CONNOTE
impolite ........................ RUDE
imporous .... CLOSE, SOLID, DENSE,
import ..... DRIFT, VALUE, INTENT,
SENSE, TOUR
impose .. INFLICT, SUFFER, ENTAIL
impose upon FOB, DUPE, HUM, PALM
imposing ... REGAL, AUGUST, NOBLE
impost . TASK, TAX, TOLL, TRIBUTE
impost; India ................ ABWAB
imprecation ........... CURSE, OATH
impregnate .... TINCT, FECUNDATE
impresa .. DEVICE, EMBLEM, MOTTO
impresario ......... ENTREPRENEUR
impress ...... PRINT, DENT, STEAD
impression ..... IDEA, MARK, STAMP

134

imprison ..... CAGE, BOND, IMMURE
imprisonment ........ BAND, DURESS
impromptu ....... AUTOSCHEDIASTIC
improper AMISS, PAW, EVIL, WRONG
improve ............ AMEND, BETTER
improvise ...... PONG, VAMP, ADLIB,
        FLASH, HUNCH, EXTEMPORE
impudent MALAPERT, BRASSY, PERT,
            AIRS, CHEEKY, SAUCY
impugn .... ASPERSE, BLAME, DENY
impulse ESTRO, FORCE, ATE, RUSH
impunity .... EXEMPTION, FREEDOM
impure form of flint ............. CHERT
impure metallic product ....... ALLOY,
                                MATTE
impure ore ..................... SPEISS
impute .... ARET, ASCRIBE, CHARGE
in ............... INTO, AT, AT HOME
in a body ..................... UTTERLY
in a line ......................... AROW
in a row ........ SERIAL, ALINE
in a straight line .......... EREGIONE
in abundance ................. GALORE
in accordance with ........ PURSUANT
in addition ...... ALSO, FURTHERTOO
in-as-much as .. SINCE, SEEING, FOR
in case of .................. LEST, INRE
in cricket, the posts to batter's left ONS
in good time .... EARLY, PREMATURE
in music, muted ................. SORDA
in place of ......................... FOR
in position of a thrust ......... ATILT
in respect to ................... ANENT
in spite of ..................... MAUGRE
in the hole ......................... ACE
in the same place; Lat. .. IBID, IBIDEM
in the presence of; Lat. ........ CORAM
in what way; Lat. ......... QUOMODO
Ina; actress ................... CLAIRE
inability to chew .......... AMASESIS
inability to execute purposed movements
                              APRAXIA
inability to read aloud ........ ALEXIA
inability to stand erect ...... ASTASIA
Inachus, daughter of; Gr. ........... IO
inaction ........ ABEYANT, INERTIA,
                              TORPOR
inane .. INEPT, PUERILE, FATUOUS,
            SILLY, TRIVIAL, VOID
inapt .......... INEPT, UNSUITABLE
inarticulate .. DUMB, APHONY, MUTE
inattention .. SUPINE, DREAM, LOST
inaugurate ....... AUSPICATE, OMEN
inaugurate fortunately ..... HANDSEL
inauspicious ..... ADVERSE, MALIGN,
            UNTIMELY, HOSTILE
inborn ...... CONNATURAL, INNATE
inborn desire ............... CONATUS
inburst ..................... IRRUPTION
incase in a setting ......... ENCHASE
incarnation . EMBODIMENT, AVATAR
incarnation of Vishnu ........... RAMA
incense ........ MYRRH, TACAMAHAC
incense, the burning of ...... THURIFY
incense tree; genus .. BURSERA, ICICA
incensed .... ANGRY, WROTH, FIRED,
                        IRATE, STUNG
incentive MOTIVE, STIMULUS, BROD,
            CALL, GROUND, SPUR

inch, 12 seconds ................ PRIME
inch, part of an ............ LINE, MIL
inches, nine ...................... SPAN
inchoation ...... BEGINNING, ORIGIN
incident ............ EPISODE, EVENT
incidental .. BYE, EPISODIC, CASUAL
incidentally; Lat. ............. OBITER
incinerator CREMATORIUM, FURNACE
incipient . INCHOATE, INITIAL, SEAT
incision ............ CUT, GASH, SLIT
incite .. EGG, AGITATE, SPUR, ABET,
            BUZZ, STING, SUBORN
inclination .. GRADE, NOD, CONATUS,
            TASTE, SLANT, VERSANT
incline ... TEND, LEAN, RAKE, RAMP
incline, to .............. SLANT, CANT
inclined ... PROPENSE, APT, LEANT,
            PRONE, PRONATE
inclined to eat ................ ESURIEN
inclining .... DISPOSED, ALIST, BENT
inclose ........ EMBAR, ENCAVE, PIN
inclosed field ..................... AGER
inclosure . SEPIMENT, CORRAL, SEPT
including, not . BESIDES, ELSE, SAVE
inclusion ................... COMPRISAL
incognito ......... FEIGNED, VEILED
income ................ PORT, USANCE
income, rel. to .. TONTINE, ANNUITY
incommode ............. MOLEST, VEX
incomplete ........ CRUDE, INCHOATE
incongruous ........ ALIEN, ENTECHE
incorrect BASE, SOLECISTIC, WRONG
incorrect naming of objects ...........
                              PARANOMIA
incrassare ...... THICKEN, SWOLLEN
increase . AUGMENT, ACCRETE, EKE,
            WAX, ASCENT, RISE
incredulity, cry of ........... WALKER
increment ................... ACCRUAL
incubate BREED, HATCH, CLOCK, SIT
incubus ........ DEMON, NIGHTMARE
incult ..................... RUDE, WILD
incumbrance .. CLAIM, LIEN, BURDEN
incurable ................. INSANABLE
incursion ...... FORAY, RAID, INFLUX
incus ............... ANVIL, HAMMER
indecisive ....... SEESAW, TEETERY
indeclinable noun ............. APTOTE
indeed; Anglo-Irish ................ ARU
indefatigable .... SEDULOUS, ACTIVE
indefinite ....... AMBIGUOUS, VAGUE
indehiscent fruit ...... SAMARA, PEPO
indehiscent legume ........... LOMENT
indentation DINGE, CRENELET, JAB,
            NOTCH, BOWED, HOLLOW
indentation on a blade ......... CHOIL
indented ............. EROSE, RASEE
indeterminate, the .......... APEIRON
index, as of faith ............ GNOMON
index on a card ........... PIP, TABLE
indeyne ........................ WROTH
India ............. URDU, HINDUSTAN
    "    , air conditioner ......... TATTY
    "    , alcoholic drink of .... ARRACK
    "    , anc. emperor of ........ ASOKA
    "    , bean of ................... URD
    "    , British state in . INDORE, IDAR
    "    Brit. settlement ......... SURAT
    "    , bronze coin of ............. PICE

" , city in ....... AGRA, BARODA
" , coin of ...... ANNA, PICE, PIE,
RUPEE
" , coin of Travancore ..... FANAM
" , covered litter of ...... DOOLEE,
DOLY
" , epic of ............ RAMAYANA
" , European in ............ SAHIB
" , former provincial capital of ....
AGRA
" , gold pieces tied around bride's
neck in ................ TALIS
" , inland mail of ............ DAK
" , native state of ........ ALWAR,
BARODA, MANIPUR,
KASHMIR, POONCH
" , 100 lakhs ................ CRORE
India, people of N. West ......... JATS
" , region of ... ASSAM, MALABAR
" , religious community in PARSEE
" , river in ..... IDAWADI, INDUS,
RAPTI
" , robber of ............. DACOIT
" , sacred city of .......... NASIK
" , shrine in .... DEWAL, DAGOBA
" silk ..................... CABECA
" , 16 annas ............... RUPEE
" , spinning wheel of .... CHARKA
" , state ceremony in .... DURBAR
" , Sudra caste, one of ........ MAL
" , summer capital of ...... SIMLA
" , tower of .............. MINAR
" , wild dog of ........... DHOLE
" , wild sheep of ........ NAROOR,
OORIAL, SHA, SHABO
Indian; anc. .................... MAYA
" antelope ............... SASIN
" army officer; var. .. TANADAR
" assembly hall ........... KIVA
" astringent fruit ......... BHEL
" attendant, female ....... AYAH
" bed of a stream .... NULLAH
" bill of exchange ....... HUNDI
" bird, small song ... AMADAVIT
" bird, song ..... SHAMA, KOEL
" buffalo ......... ARNA, ARNEE
" bulbul (black) .......... KALA
" bush .................. KANHER
" butter .................. GHEE
" carpet .................. AGRA
" carriage ... RATH, GHARRY
" caste . LOHANA, RAJPUT, TAI
" caste, gardener .......... MALI
" caste, one of an agricultural ....
MEO
" caste mark .............. TILKA
" charm .................... OBI
" chief .......... RAJA, SIRDAR
" cigarette .................. BIRI
" city .. BENARES, SIBI, SURAT
" civet cat ...... ZIBET, ZIBETH
" coin .... ANNA, PICE, PI, PIE,
RUPEE, FANAM, MOHUR
" , comb. form ............ INDO
" corn ...... MAIZE, SAMP, ZEA
" cow ............... GAEKWAR
" cuckoo .................... KOEL
" dancing entertainment .........
NAUTCH

" deer ...................... AXIS
" deer; genus . CERVUS, CHITAL
" , designating an ...... KUSAN
" dialect .... PRAKRIT, PUSHTU
" dill ....................... SOYA
" disciple ................. CHELA
" district ................... AGRA
" dog ................... KOLSUN
" drama ................ NATAKA
" drink ..................... SOMA
" drug .................... BHANG
" dust storm .......... PEESASH
" dye stuff .............. AAL, AL
" elephant ............... HATHI
" elk .................. SAMBAR
" Empire, capital of ...... DELHI
" estate ................. TALUK
" executive .. NEHRU, PRASAD
" fan .................... PUNKAH
" festival .............. DEWALI
" (East) fibre plant .... AMBARY
" fig tree .................. PIPAL
" foot-print ................. PUG
" fruit ...................... BEL
Indian gateway ................ TORAN
" gazelle .............. CHIKARA
" , glorious ........... SHRI, SRI
" government estates .... AMANI
" groom ........... OBOLI, SYCE
" harem ....... SERAI, ZENANA
" harvest, spring ......... RABI
" head man of a village .. PATEL
" hog-deer ............... ATLAS
" hunting expedition .... SHIKAR
" jacket .................... KOLA
" king ............ RAJA, RAJAH
" king; myth. ............. NALA
" king of serpents; myth. SESHA
" kingdom ................ NEPAL
" laborer ................. PALLI
" land grant ............. SASAN
" language; anc. ..... SANSKRIT
" leader ................. NEHRU
" levee ................. DURBAR
" licorice, poison ......... ABRIN
" lieutenant governor ...... NAIB
" low class .............. BHAT
" macaque .............. RHESUS
" madder .............. AAL, AL
" mahogany ................ TOON
" mail ...................... DAK
" master ................. SAHIB
" matting ................. TATTA
" meal .............. ATA, ATTA
" measure . KOS, ADOULIE, GUZ
" medicinal nut ...... MALABAR
" medicine man ....... SHAMAN
" millet ........ DHOOR, DURRA
" mine laborers, chosen by lot ....
MITA
" minor native official .. AMEEN,
AMIN
" monetary unit ... CRORE, LAC,
LAKH
" mountain pass .......... GHAT
" mountains ... ABIL, VINDHYA
" mulberry ...... AAL, ACH, AL
" muslin ... GURRAH, DOREA
" narcotic .............. BHANG

136

"	narcotic, hemp ...... HASHISH
"	Nation; anc. ............ TAMIL
"	native cavalryman .... SOWAR
"	Nilgiri, one of tribe .. BADAGA
"	nurse .......... AMAH, AYAH
"	of Alaska ............ TLINGIT
"	officer ..... DEDAN, JEMADAR
"	palanquin ............. PALKEE
"	peasant ................. RYOT
"	pepper, climbing ...... BETEL
"	philosopher ............... YOGI
"	pillar ..................... LAT
"	police station ........... THANA
"	powder .................. ABIR
"	priest ................. SHAMAN
"	priest's garment ........ DHOTI
"	prime minister ........ DEWAN
"	prince ................... RANA
"	princess ................. RANI
"	queen ........... BEGUM, RANI
"	race; anc. ............... TAMIL
"	religious sect ........... SAMAJ
"	resort for invalids ABU, SIMLA
"	rice ...................... BORO
"	rich black loam ....&... REGUR
"	rifle pit .............. SANGAR
Indian river Sutlej, old name ............
	HYDASPES
"	rope dancer ............... NAT
"	ruler NAWAB, NABOB, RANA,
	RANEE, RAO
"	ruler, military ......... NIZAM
"	ruminant ................. ZEBU
"	sacred city ......... BENARES
"	sacred word ............... OM
"	sacrificial victim ....... TRAGA
"	sailor .................. LASCAR
"	sect ...................... BALI
"	servant ......... AMAH, MATY
"	servant, male ............. PAR
"	shed ................. PANDAL
"	sheep ........... OORIAL, SHA
"	shrine ................ DAGOBA
"	silk, finest ........... CABECA
"	skipper of a small boat SERANG
"	snake ...... KRAIT, BONGAR,
	KATUKA
"	soldier .......... PEON, SEPOY
"	state ....... GWALIOR, JAORA
"	state revenue lands .... AMANI
"	stone .................. LINGAM
"	sugar, crude ............. GUR
"	tax district ........... TAHSIL
"	tax-free land ........... ENAM
"	term of address ........ SAHIB
"	timber tree ........ DAR, SAL
"	title NAWAB, SAHIB, RAJA(H)
"	title of respect ..... MIAN, SRI
"	tree ..... BEL, ENG, GORAN,
	PIPAL
"	tree, hard wood .. POON, TEAK
"	trophy .................. SCALP
"	turbin ................ PUGREE
"	twilled cotton .. SALOO, SALU
"	viceroy ...... NABOB, NAWAB
"	village .................. ABADI
"	warrior ................ SINGH
"	water carrier ..... BHEESTEE
"	weapon .......... TOMAHAWK

"	weight .... CHITTAK, MASHA,
	MAUND, PICE, RATTI, RATI,
	SER, SEER, TANK, TOLA,
	VIS, VISS
"	weight; obs. ...... MANGELIN
"	(East) weight ......... CATTY
"	window screen ......... TATTY
"	(Amer.) .. CHIPPEWA, CREE,
	SAC, UTE, INCA, MIRANHA,
	LULE, PONCA
"	, Aht confederacy, one of ......
	NOOTKA
"	, Alabama ............. CREEK
"	, Alaska ............... ALEUT
"	, Algonquin . ARAPAHO, CREE,
	MOHICAN, NIANTIC, SAC,
	SAUK, WEA
"	(Amer.) bread .... TUCKAHOE
"	, Arizona .... APACHE, HOPI,
	PIMA, YUMA
"	blanket ................ STROUD
"	, bloodthirsty ......... KIOWA
"	, Bolivian .... CHARCA, ITEN,
	MOXO
"	, Caddoan ... REES, ARIKARA
"	, Cal. .. YUKI, PERICUI, SERI,
	YUROK
"	ceremonial pipe .... CALUMET
Indian chief LOGAN, SACHEM, TYEE,
	SAGAMORE, SANNUP
"	chief of Seminoles .. OSCEOLA
"	, chitchan ........... TUNEBO
"	, Creek ............ ALABAMA
"	, Dakota ................ SIOUX
"	, Dakota (N.) .... ARIKAREE,
	REE
"	, Delaware .......... LENAPE
"	, Ecuadorian ......... CANELO
"	, female of the ...... MAHALY
"	, Florida ......... SEMINOLE
"	, Georgia .............. CREEK
"	great spirit ........ MANITOU
"	group of So. Amer. ........ GES
"	, Guatemala ............ XINCA
"	hamlet .......... RANCHERIA
"	handkerchief ...... MALABAR
"	, Iroquois ..... ONEIDA, ERIE,
	HURON, SENECA
"	, Kansas .... PANI, PAWNEE
"	linguistic group ...... TINNEY
"	linguistic stock .... SASTEAN
"	marauder ........... GAUCHO
"	matting ................ TATTA
"	memorial post .. TOTEM, XAT
"	, mestizo . GRIFFE, LADINOS
"	, Mexican ...... SERI, YAQUI,
	AZTEC
"	Miami tribe .............. WEA
"	, Miss. river ........ MANDAN,
	TONIKAN
"	money ........ IOQUA, PEAG,
	SE(A)WAN, WAMPUM
"	, Nebraska .. OMAHA, PONCA
"	, New Mexico; ..... PUEBLO,
	ZUNI, TANO
"	, New York ....... IROQUOIS,
	SENECA
"	nomad ............... APACHE

137

"        of mixed blood ...... METISSE
"        of the Iroquois tribe .. MINGO
"        of the Pacific ...... CHINOOK,
            NOOTKA
"        , Oklahoma ...... ARAPAHOE
"        , Oregon ............. YANAN
"        ornament ........... RUNTEE
"        people ................ POMOS
"        , Peru ... BORO, INCA, CANA
"        pole .................. TOTEM
"        ponies ............... TINDER
"        pony ................. CAYUSE
"        pueblo ........... HOPI, ZUNI
"        Salishan ........... TULALIP
"        , Seowan SIOUAN, OTO, OTOE
"        Shoshone dial. ......... MOQUI
"        , Shoshonean ........ BANAK,
            BANNOCK, PIUTE, UTE
"        , Sioux . KAW, OTOE, OSAGE,
            TETON
"        , So. Amer. ... AYMARA, GES,
            ONA
"        , Sonorian ............... SERI
"        Tanoan ............... ISLETA
"        unit of money ........ PIMAN
"        village ............... PUEBLO
"        wampum ............ SEAWAN
"        , Washington or Vancouver ...
            AHT
Indian, western ..... HOPI, OTO, UTE
"        wigwam .............. TEPEE
Indiana model city ............. GARY
Indiana river ................ MAUMEE
Indiana, state nickname .... HOOSIER
Indiana, town in ....... PAOLI, GARY
Indians (miscellaneous)
"        , Aleutian Is. ....... AKKHAS
"        , Antilles ............... CARIB
"        , Arikara ............... REES
"        , Athapascan ........... DENE
"        , Bolivia ... MAROPA, MOXO,
            OTUKE
"        , Brazil; ..... ARAUA, CARIB.
            GUARANI, INCA, ACROA,
            TUPI
"        , British Colombia ...... NASS
"        , Canada ...... DENE, HAIDA
"        , Chili ............... ARAUCA
"        , Eskimo .......... AMERIND
"        Haida memorial post ... XYST
"        , Keresan ................ SIA
"        , Manitoba ............. CREE
"        , Mayan tribe ........ QUICHE
"        , Mexico ...... AZTEC, CORA,
            OPATA, OTOMI
"        , Panama ................ CUNA
"        , Peru ..... CANA, CHANGOS,
            PANO
"        , Rio Janeiro, female .. PURIS
"        , salishan ............ TULALIP
"        , S. Amer.; . ANETO, CARIB,
            ONA, OTA, TUPI
"        , S. Amer. group ......... GES
"        , Tapuyan ......... SEER, SER
"        , Tierra del Fuego . FUEGIAN,
            ONA
"        , Uruguay ............. YARO
"        , Venezuela .......... TIMOTE

"        , Vera Cruz ........ TOTONAC
"        , Wakashan ............. AHT
"        , Yucatan .............. MAYA
Indian's (Am.) "Yes" ............ UGH
indicate .. SIGNIFY, BETOKEN, CITE
indicator .. ANNUNCIATOR, ARROW,
            DIAL, VANE
indices ........ TABLES, INDEX(pl.)
indict .. ARRAIGN, ACCUSE, PANEL,
            CHARGE, (IM)PEACH
indifferent ........ BLASE, NEUTRAL
indigence ............... NEED, WANT
indigenous ...... ENDEMIC, INNATE,
            EDAPHIC, NATIVE
indigent ........ FREE, POOR, VOID,
            DESTITUTE, NEEDY
indigestion ... DYSPEPSIA, PHTHISIS
indignant ...... ANGRY, HOT, IRATE
indignation ................ BASE, IRE
indignity ...... DUDGEON, AFFRONT
indigo ................. BLUE, ANIL
"        and zinc ................ INDOL
"        , bale of ............... SEROON
"        berry ................. RANDIA
"        , Chinese .............. ISATIS
"        , commercial ...... INDIGOTIN
"        deriv. ................. KETOLE
"        ; genera ................. WOAD
"        , source of ...... ANIL, ISATIN
"        , wild ............. BAPTISIA
indisposition ............... MALAISE,
            AVERSENESS
indisputable ............. APODEICTIC
indite ................... PEN, WRITE
indistinct ....... VAGUE, DIM, HAZY
individual ............. SINGLE, SOLE
individual, comb. form ........... IDIO
individual compound ............ ZOON
individual, physiological ........ BION
individuality . EGOHOOD, ETHOLOGY,
            LONE, UNITS, NATURE
individuality, an; rare ......... SEITY
Indo-Arabic numerical system, rel. to ..
            ABACUS
Indo-Aryan ....................... JAT
Indo-China, Fr. possession .. ANNAM,
            LAOS
Indo-Chinese aborigines; . HOS, KHAS,
            MEOS, TAI, YAOS
"        "        alligator; genus CAYMAN
"        "        bull ............... ZEBU
"        "        council ........ COMBAT
"        "        delta .......... MEKONG
"        "        kingdom ........ NEPAL
"        "        native rock ... TRIASSIC
"        "        tongue ... AO, AKA, TAI,
            OBBARACH
"        "        tongue ... AO, AKA, TAI,
            WA
"        "        wood ............. TEAK
indoctrinate ......... COACH, EDIFY,
            INSTRUCT
Indo-Eur. .... ARYAN, CROAT, LETT
indolence .......... INERTIA, SLOTH
indolent .......... IRK, OTIOSE, IDLE
Indo-Malayan ............ MONGOLIAN
Indonesian tribe .... ATA, BATAVIAN

138

Indo-Persian meas. .............. GUZ
indorse ................ ATTEST, VISA
indubitable .. EVIDENT, FACT, SURE
inductance of circuit ......... HENRY
indulge ............. PAMPER, YIELD
indurate ........ SCLERAL, HARDEN
Indus tribesman ................ GOR
industrial magnate SHOGUN, TYCOON
industrious ..... DEEDY, ASSIDUOUS
indweller ...... DENIZEN, INDIGENE
inebriate .. DRUNKARD, SOT, TOPER
ineluctable .............. DOOM, FATE
inept ...... PUERILE, SILLY, UNFIT
inert ...... LATENT, TORPID, DOLD,
                                    SUPINE
inevitable ............ DUE, NEMESIS
infamy ...... OPPROBRIUM, SHAME
infant ....... MINOR, WEAN, BABY,
                                    CHILD
infantry ............ PEDAILE, UNIT
infatuate . CHARM, ENAMOR, BESOT
infatuation ..... ATE, MAD, FOOLISH
infeasibility RIGOR, IMPRACTICABLE
infected ... IMPURE, TAINTED, SMIT
infer ... PRESUME, DERIVE, FETCH
inference ... COROLLARY, ILLATION
inferiae; Rom. ........... SACRIFICES
inferior ...... LOWER, POOR, DICKY,
            SUBALTERN, LESS, MENIAL,
            MINOR, PETTY
inferior lawyer ......... LEGULEIAN,
                                PETTIFOGGER
inferior, said of judges ........ PUISNE
infernal . TARTAREAN, MALIGNANT
inferno ............... ABYSS, HADES
   "    , Biblical .......... GEHENNA
   "    , Buddhist .......... NARAKA
   "    , ferry to the ........... STYX
   "    , Hebrew .......... SHEOL
   "    in poetry ......... AVERNUS
   "    , rel. to .............. LIMBO
infested ...... HAUNTED, OVERRAN
infidel .. ATHEIST, DEIST, SARACEN
infirm person ........ ANILE, SENILE,
            DODDERER, DECREPIT, GREY
inflammable . ACCENDIBLE, PICEOUS
inflammable gas ............. ETHANE
inflammable liquid ......... ACETONE
inflammable substance ....... TINDER
inflammation of iris .. IRITIS, UVEITIS
inflammation of bone ........ OSTEITIS
inflated ....... BOLLEN, DISTENDED,
                        TURGID, BOMBASTIC
inflexible ........ IRON, RIGID, STIFF
inflict . IMPOSE, ADD, DEAL, WREAK
inflorescence, axial circle of ... WHORL
inflorescence, cluster . CYME, RACEME
inflorescence, per. to ........... WAVE
influence ..... PULL, IMPEL, IMPORT,
                    SWAY, INFLUX, WIN
influenza ............... GRIP, GRIPPE
influx ...... ILLAPSE, TIDE, IMPORT
inform ....................... APPRISE
information NEWS, AIR, AVISO, LORE
informative ........... VIVIFY, DATA
informer ..... AFFIRMER, DELATOR,
                                    NARK
infringement of a copyright ... PIRACY

infundibulum, contracted orifice of ....
                                    LURA
infusible white substance ...... CERIA
infusion .... TEA, DECOCTION, OLIO
infusion of malt ................. WORT
infusoria ....... CILIA, VORTICELLA
infusoria, group of ......... ACINETAE
Inge play ...................... PICNIC
ingenious .............. DEDAL, FINE
ingenuous ............ FRANK, NAIVE,
                                INVENTIVE
ingest .. EAT, SWALLOW, CONSUME
ingot ............... SYCEE, GAD, PIG
ingot workers ................ BARMEN
ingress .... ENTRY, ACCESS, PORTAL
inhabitant ... CIT, DENIZEN, CITIZEN
inhabitants of different sides of the
   equator, who cast shadows in opposite
   directions ................ ANTISCII
inhabiting an island ......... NESIOTE
inhab. the ground ....... TERRICOLE
inhale ..... RESPIRE, SNIFF, SMELL
inharmonious relationship ........ OUTS
inhere .... CLEAVE, CONSIST, LODGE
inherence .............. IMMANENCE
inherent .. OUR, INBORN, INTRINSIC,
                                    INNATE
inheritance; anc. law ............ SALIC
inheritor ...... HEIR, LEGATEE, DUE
inhibit ........ RESTRAIN, PROHIBIT
inhuman ..... BESTIAL, CRUEL, FELL
inimical ....... ADVERSE, HOSTILE
inimical, not ....................... FED
iniquity .............. EVIL, SIN, VICE
initial ornamental letter ..... PARAPH,
                                    FAC
initiated ...... OPEN, BEGAN, EPOPT
inject ........................... IMMIT
injection ............ CLYSTER, ENEMA
injunction ................ ADO, ORDER
injure ... GRIEVE, MAR, TEEN, LAME
injure by scorching ........... SCATHE
injurious ........... NOXIOUS, NUSANT
injury ...... DAMAGE, EVIL, LESION,
   DERE, HARM, WOUND, TRAUMA
injury, causing ............. MALEFIC
injury, sense of ............. UMBRAGE
ink ....................... BLACK, DAUB
ink bag ............................ SAC
ink berry ............. HOLLY, INDIGO
ink fish ....................... CUTTLE
ink spreader, in printing ..... BRAYER
inker ............................... PAD
inking pad in lithography ... DABBER,
                                TOMPION
inkle ..................... TAPE, YARN
inky .................... ATRAMENTAL
inky fluid ..................... MELENA
inlaid work ...................... BUHL
in-law, between two periods ... MESNE
inlay, metallic; Ital. . TARSIA, NIELLO
in-league ........... ALLY, CAHOOTS,
                                PARTNERS
inlet .. PORE, ARM, FIORD, RAE, RIA,
                                    SUMP
inlet, coast line ...... STRAIT, BIGHT
inlet in south U. S. ............. BAYOU
inlet in the Orkney Is. ............. VOE

139

inn ...... ABODE, TAVERN, FONDA, CABARET, HOTEL, MOTEL, HOSTEL
inn; Ital. ........ LOCANDO, OSTERIA
inn keeper ......... HOTE, BONIFACE, PUBLICAN
inn, near east ....... SERAI, IMARET, KAHN
innate ........... NATIVE, NATURAL
inner ... ESOTERIC, INTAL, OBSCURE
inner, comb. form .............. ENTO
inner sole ......................... RAND
innermost lining of a lymphatic INTIMA
Innisfail ...... EIRE, ERIN, IRELAND
in-no-way ........ NOT, NEVER, NOR
innocence; symb. ........... DIAMOND
innocent ......... FREE, PURE, SELY
innovation ............ CHANGE, NEW
inopportune .......... CONTRETEMPS
inordinate ....... FABULOUS, UNDUE
inquest ............. ASSIZE, SEARCH
inquiry ............. QUERY, EXAMEN
inquisitive .. PEERIE, PRYING, NOSY
insane ...... BATTY, FRANTIC, MAD, CRAZY, RAMMIST
insane asylum BEDLAM, MADHOUSE
insane excessive loquacity ... LERESIS
insane, to make DEMENT, DEMONIZE
insanity AMENTIA, VESANIA, MANIA
inscribe ....... DEPENCIL, ENGRAVE
inscription at end of book COLOPHON
inscrutable ABSTRUSE, MYSTERIOUS
insect NIT, TREMEX, APHID, LERP, SPIDER, ANTLION, ERI
" , an order of ACARID, DIPTERA
" antenna, end of .......... CLAVA
" back of ................. NOTUM
" , dipterous .......... MOSQUITO
" , eyes of an ............. OCELLI
" , four winged .......... BEETLE
" ; genus ........ CICADA, NEPA, TERMES, EMESA, CICALA, THRIPS
" , hard covering of ..... CHITINE
" , immature .............. LARVA
" larva ........... GRUB, MAGGOT
" leg ................... PROLEG
" , lepidopterous ............ MOTH
" like .................. ENTOMOID
" , mature ............... IMAGO
" , middle division of .... THORAX
" , migratory .............. LOCUST
" , molting of ........... ECDYSIS
" , order of ...... DOR, CRICKET, LOCUST
" , parisitic; Mex. ..... TURICATA
insect, per. to the eye of ..... STEMMA
" powder ........... PYRETHRUM
" resin ......................... LAC
" , slender grotesque ...... EMESA, MANTIS
" , small ............. BUG, APHID
" , social ................. ANT, BEE
" sound .................. STRIDOR
" stage in life ..... INSTAR, PUPA
" sting .................... ICTUS
" stinging ................. GADFLY
" wing spot .................. ISLE
" , winged ............... WASP
" , wingless .............. APTERA

" with tail forceps ....... EARWIG
insectivorous mammal ... HEDGEHOG, DESMAN
insect's feeler ................... PALP
insects, genus of aquatic ... RANATRA
insects, morbid excrescence of plants caused by ..................... GALL
insects; per. to .............. ENTOMIC
insects, plant feeding ......... THRIPS
insecure .. RICKETY, ASEA, DUBIOUS
inseminate ............ IMPLANT, SOW
insensibility .... ANALGESIA, CARUS, COMA SIRENE
insert ..... PANEL, IMMIT, INGRAFT
insert wrongly .................. FOIST
insertion of a letter in a word ........... EPENTHESIS, INSET
insertion of cords in cloth ...... SHIRR
inset .................. PANEL, INFLUX
inside out, turn ................ EVERT
insight ... ACUMEN, DISCERNMENT, KEN
insignia ...... BAR, REGALIA, BADGE
insignificant ... PETIT, PUNY, MINOR
insinuate HINT, INTIMATE, SUGGEST
insipid .. DRY, FLAT, STALE, VAPID
insist .......... (AF)FIRM, MAINTAIN
inspect .......... PRY, AGER, CONNER
inspiration ...... AFFLATUS, SPRITE
inspire ........... ANIMATE, INHALE
inspissate .................... THICKEN
instability ........ MUTABILITY, FAIL
install .............. INDUCT, ORDAIN
instance ...... EXAMPLE, REQUEST, MOTIVE, CASE
instant ... TIME, POP, POINT, TRICE, MOMENT
instead of .... ELSE, PLACE, STEAD, LIEU
instigate ....... ABET, INCITE, SPUR, SUBORN, STIMULATE
instruction ......... TUITION, LORE, TUTORAGE, NURTURE
instruction, art of ....... PAIDEUTICS
instructive ................. DIDACTIC, PROPAEDEUTIC
instrument .................... AGENT
" , astronomical; anc. ..... ARMIL
" , boring .............. JUMPER
" , comb. form ............ LABE
" for copying .... PANTOGRAPH
" for expanding a thing DILATER
" for finding latitude ........ ABA
" for measuring eggs . OOMETER
" for measuring electric current .. RHEOMETER
" for measuring sound waves; ....
instrument for measuring time ........ CHRONOSCOPE
" for striking grain .. STRICKLE
" , hooked .................. BILL
" of knowledge ....... ORGANON
" , sharp ................ STYLUS
" , stringed ................ WIRE
instrumental introduction .. INTRADA
" opus .................. SONATA
" performance .............. DUO
insular .......... NARROW, NESIOTE

140

insulate ..... SEGREGATE, ISOLATE, ISLE
insulating material ........... KERITE, OKONITE
insult ... CAG, FIG, FLOUT, RUFFLE, SLUR
insurance, applicant for ......... RISK
insurgent ... MUTINEER, REVOLTER, REBEL
intaglio DIAGLYPH, MATRIX, MOULD
integer, odd ................. GNOMEN
integral .. ALL, SUM, INNER, WHOLE
integrity ........ ENTIRETY, VIRTUE
integument ...... ARIL, TESTA, COAT, DERM, SKIN
intellect ... MIND, INWIT, NOEMICS, NOUS, MENTALITY
intellectual . SOPHIC, IDEAL, PALATE
intelligence NEWS, ACUMEN, AVYS, CAPACITY, MIND
intelligence only .............. NOESIS
intelligent ... APT, BRIGHT, ASTUTE, GASH
intelligent animal .............. CHIMP
intemperance ......... DEBAUCHERY, EXCESS, BOOZE, BIBACITY
intensity ........... DEEPEN, DEPTH, VEHEMENCE
intention .. AIM, END, MINT, RESIGN
inter ..... BURY, ENTOMB, INHUME, INURN
inter—— ..................... ALIA
intercalary .............. BISSEXTILE
intercalary month; Heb. ..... VEADAR
intercalate .. INSERT, INTERPOLATE
intercessor ...... BISHOP, MEDIATOR
interclavicle ............ EPISTEYNOM
intercolumniation ........... SYSTYLE
interdiction ........ BAN, TABU, VETO
interest .. BEHALF, SHARE, USURY, WEAL, SAVOR
interfere CLASH, MOLEST, CONFLICT
interfermometer rod ......... ETALON
interim ....... DIASTEM, INTERVAL, MEANTIME
interjection ...... DAM, CRIMINY, EH, EGAD, AW, OUTCRY
interlude ................... OVERTURE
interlude, short .. VERSICLE, VERSET
intermission ...... ENTRACTE, PAUSE
intermediate ................... MESNE
intermitter ................... RESTER
internal ........... ESOTERIC, INNER
international business comb. . CARTEL
international language, proposed; IDO, OD, ESPERANTO, RO, VOLAPUK
interpolate ......... FARSE, CORRUPT, FOIST
interpose ...... MEDIATE, DISAFFECT
interpret ......... OPEN, SCAN, REDE, RENDER, CONSTRUE
interpretation; Bib. ........ EXEGESIS
interpretation, twofold ... DITTOLOGY
interpretative ........ HERMENEUTIC
interpreter .. DRAGOMAN, EXEGETE, LATINER
interpreters of Koran .......... ULEMA
interrogation mark ........ EROTEME
interrogator .... PUMPER, INQUIRER

interred ................. INEARTHED
intersect ................. DECUSSATE
intersection; rel. to NODAL, SECANT
interstice . PORE, CRACK, CREVICE
interstice, per. to ......... AREOLAR
interstices ...... CHINKY, CLEFTED, RIMOSE
interval ....... GAP, INTERIM, REST, LAPSE, PITCH
intervening . INTERJACENT, MESNE
intervolve .............. ROLL, WIND
interweave . PLASH, PLAT, RADDLE, SPLICE
interwoven ...... NETTED, RETIARY
interwoven fabric ............ TISSUE
interwoven rods, as a hurdle WATTLE
intestine ......... COLON, DOMESTIC
intestine coating ................ CAUL
intestine part; comb. form ...... ILEO
intestine, part of the small .... ILEUM
intestine, per. to ............ ENTERIC
intimate .. SECRET, CHIEF, CRONY, PACK, SIB
intimate, to ... IMPLY, REFER, HINT
intimation .. CUE, HINT, ANNOUNCE
intimidate ... DAUNT, ABASH, COW, OVERAWE
into ................... AMONG, UNTIL
intolerance ... BIGOTRY, DOGMATISM
intonation ................. SONANCE
intone .... CHANT, CROON, INTROIT
intort ................... CURL, TWIST
intoxicant .. SOMA, GIN, WHISK(E)Y
intoxicated . SOT, SOSH, HEADY, LIT
intoxicating liquor, any ......... GROG
intractable ....... UNRULY, SULLEN
intrepidity ........... NERVE, VALOR
intricate; ......... DAEDAL, DEDAL, GORDIAN, MAZY
intrigue . AMOUR, BRIGUE, CABAL, PLOT
intrinsic ......... REAL, IMMANENT, INHERENT
introduce ... IMMIT, INFUSE, USHER
introducing new word ...... NEOLOGY
introduction ..... PREFACE, PROEM
introduction to treatise ..... ISAGOGE
introductory cry ........ HEAR, OYEZ
intromit ........ ADMIT, INTRODUCE
intrust ......... BEKEN, DELEGATE, COMMIT
intuit ................. KNOW, SENSE
intuitive ........... SEEING, NOETIC, PERCEIVING
inulase ..................... ENZYME
inulic acid, salt of .......... INULATE
inulin ....................... ALANTIN
inuncate ........................ HOOK
inundate ..... CATACLYSM, DELUGE
inundation ........ FRESHET, FLOOD
inure ........... BENEFIT, HARDEN, TOUGHEN
inurn ...... BURY, ENTOMB, INTER
invade . RAID, TRESPASS, INTRUDE
invalid ... NULL, VOID, SICK, WEAK
invalidate .......... QUASH, VITIATE
invariants, sifting ......... TAMISAGE
invasion ...... BREACH, IRRUPTION

141

invasion, military term ...... FORAY, INROAD, RAID
invective . CURSE, ABUSE, INVEIGH
inveigh .. CENSURE, ASSAIL, CHIDE
inveigle ...... SNARE, WIN, SEDUCE, WHEEDLE
invention .................... FIGMENT
inventor of dynamite .......... NOBEL
inventor of harp; Bib. ......... JUBAL
inventor of safety lamp ......... DAVY
inventory ........ CATALOG(UE), LIST
inversely ovate ............. OBOVATE
invertebrate ...... INSECT, MOLLUSK
invest ..... ENDUE, SPEND, CORRAL
invest with ... CLOTHE, FEOFF, DON
investigate INDAGATE, SIFT, WASH, PROBE
investigation .. ZETETIC, HEURISTIC
investment SEEGE, SIEGE, GARMENT
investor ..................... ENDURER
inveterate ................... CHRONIC
invigorate RENEW, BRACE, FORTIFY
invisible Empire ................. KLAN
invite .. BEG, SUE, TRY, ASK, ORDER
invocation of evil ........... MALISON
invoke ........ BEG, PRAY, IMPLORE
involucre ...................... WHORL
involve ENTAIL, LAP, WRAP, EVINCE
inward .......................... ENTAD
inwards, in general .......... INMEATS, UMBLES
inwick .......................... INRING
inwrap ... ABSORB, ENVELOP, ROLL
iodic poisoning ................ IODISM
iodide, tetra .................. SIOMINE
iodine antiseptic ...... IATROL, EIGON
iolite ...................... CORDIERITE
ion, negative .................... ANION
ion, rel. to ...................... CATION
ios; anc. .......................... NIO
iota ......... ACE, JOT, WHIT, ATOM
Iowa college ...................... COE
Iowa college town ............... AMES
ipecacs; genus .................... EVEA
iracund .................... CHOLERIC
Iran .......................... PERSIA
Iran, anc. people of ........ TAT, MADA
Iran, capital of ............ TEHERAN
Iran, city in .................... AMOL
Iranian ............. IRANIC, TUDAH
Iranian chief ..................... MIR
Iranian coin .............. RIAL, LARI
Iranian language ............... ARYAN
Iranian poet ..................... OMAR
Iran's ambass. to U.S. ...... ENTEZAM
Iraq, seaport of ................ BASRA
irascibility ............. CHOLER, IRE
irascible . BRASH, TESTY, ANGERED
irate .......... ANGRY, HOT, WROTH
Ireland .. IERNE, EIRE, ERIN, ERSE, HIBERNIA
"    , a lake or loch in ....... LOUGH
"    , anc. alphabet of ........ OGAM
"    , county in ... CLARE, KERRY, MAYO
"    , Danish settlers in .... OSTMEN
"    , island group off ......... ARAN
"    , lake in .................. ERNE

"    , one of a revolution association; FENIAN
"    , people of ............. IRISHRY
"    personified .............. IRENA
"    , poetical name ... INVERNIA, INNISFAIL
"    , river in .... SHANNON, ERNE
"    , song of .................. RANN
"    , symb. for ........... DEIRDRE
"    , system of land holding ........ RUNDALE
"    , town ... TARA, CORK, COBH, KILKENNY, SLIGO
Ireland's saint ............... PATRICK
irenic ....................... HENOTIC
iridescent .... OPALINE, NACREOUS, RIBALD
iridic acid, salt of ............ IRIDATE
iris ............ IXIA, ORRIS, RAINBOW
"    , any ......................... IRID
"    ; comb. form ................ IRIDO
"    , inflammation of pigment of ...... UVEITIS
"    , layer of .................... UVEA
"    , plant .......... TILEROOT, FLAG
"    , species of ................... SEG
Irish anc. musical inst. ........... CRUT
"    artist in metals ............. CERD
"    bard ........ ECNA, FERGUS
"    castle ....................... TARA
"    clan ................. SEPT, SIOL
"    clansman ................. AIRE
"    cloak; anc. ................. INAR
"    county ................. CLARE
"    cow-tribute .............. BOROIM
"    dialect .................... OGHAM
"    doctor .................... OLLAM
"    double edged dagger ..... SKENE
"    early kingdom ........ MUNSTER
"    ecclesiastics, early . ERENACHES
"    endearment term ..... ALANNAH
"    exclamation ...... ARRA, ARRAH
"    foot soldier ................. KERN
"    fortification ................. LIS
"    Free State, county in ....... LEIX
"    freebooter ............ RAPPAREE
"    freeman .................... AIRE
"    frock; anc. ......... LENN, INAR
"    general .................... SHEA
"    girdle ...................... CRISS
"    girl .................... COLLEEN
"    goblin ........... LEPRECHAUN
"    groggery .............. SHEBEEN
"    hood .................. COCHULL
"    island .. ACHILL, BEAR, CLEAR
"    island group ................ ARAN
"    king ............... ENNA, AED
"    laborers, class of ............ AIRE
"    legislature ................. DAIL
"    letter; anc. ................. OGAM
"    lighthouse rock ........ FASTNET
"    limestone ................... CALP
"    love ......................... GRA
"    militia ................ FENIAN
"    mineral springs ... CHALYBEATE
"    mode of speech; anc. .... OGHAM, OGAM
"    monk's cell ................... KIL
"    moss .............. CARRAGEEN

| | | |
|---|---|---|
| " mountain | OX |
| " mountain peak | ERRIGAL |
| " mus. festival | FEIS |
| " musical inst. | CRUT, LYRF, TIMPAN |
| " novelist | ASHE, REID, SHAW |
| " patriot | EMMET |
| " peasant | KERNE |
| " poet | YEATS |
| " princess | ISEULT |
| " proprietor; law | TANIST |
| " protestant | SASSENAGH |
| " rock | TRIASSIC |
| " saint | AIDAN |
| " sea god | LER |
| " shield, oblong | SCIATH |
| " shillaly | LAH |
| " society | FEINN |
| " soldier | ASHE, GALLOGLASS |
| " song | RANN |
| Irish steward | ERENACH |
| " strong chisel; anc. | CELT |
| " surgeon | COLLES |
| " tenant | FUIDHIR, SAER |
| " tribe | CINEL |
| " verse | RANN |
| " violin-like inst. | CROWD |
| " wandering harvester | SPALPEEN |
| " whiskey | POTEEN |
| Irishman | MILESIAN, PADDY, PAT, TEAGUE, AIRE, EIREANNACH, CELT |
| irk | BORE, NETTLE, VEX |
| iron | MITIS, MANGLE, PRESS |
| " block in stamp battery | VOL |
| " for closing staves | HORSE |
| " lamp | CRESSET |
| " moulder's tool | LIFTER |
| " ore | FERRIC, HEMATITE |
| " ore sand | ISERINE |
| " pin used in game of quoits | HOB |
| " protector for heel of boot | SHOD |
| " ready for rolling | LARGET |
| " sheet | ACICUL, TERNE |
| " , symbol for | FE |
| " weed; genus | VERNONIA |
| " wood | ACLE, HELC |
| iron-clad, an | MONITOR |
| irons | GYVE |
| irons, meteoric | SIDERITE |
| irons, native | ORE |
| ironstone | EAGLESTONE |
| irony | LAMPOON, SATIRE |
| irrational number | SURD |
| irregular | ANOMALOUS, ATACTIC, ATYPIC |
| irregular standard | ABERRANT |
| irregularly toothed | EROSE |
| irreligion | IMPIETY, APATHY, LAXITY |
| iirreligious | GODLESS, PAGAN |
| irrepressible, as laughter | HOMERIC |
| irrevocable | FINAL, END, STABLE |
| irritability; med. | ERETHISM |
| irritable | IRACUND, FIERY, SPLEENY, TECHY |
| irritable one | TARTAR |

| | | |
|---|---|---|
| irritant | POISON, PTOMAINE, VENOM |
| irritant, counter | SETON |
| irritants, susceptible to | ALLERGIC |
| irritate | RILE, CHAFE, EXACERBATE, IRE, VEX, GALL, PEEVE, NEEDLE |
| irritated | SMARTFUL, AFRET, NETTLED, GRATED, RANKLED |
| irruption | INVASION, INROAD |
| Irving Berlin's wife | ELLIN |
| is | EXISTS, DAY, HOUR, NOW, NONCE |
| is not | ISNT, NYS, NIS |
| Isaac's son | ESAU, GAD |
| Ishmael, mother of | HAGAR |
| Ishmael's son | KEDAR |
| Isinay | IGORROTE |
| isinglass | AGAR, CARLOCK, HUSO, MICA |
| Iris, brother and husband of | OSIRIS |
| Isis, shrine of | ISEUM |
| Isis; son of | SEPT |
| Islam convert | ANSAR, MURED |
| Islamic teacher | MULLAH, ALIM, AGA |
| Islamite | MOSLEM |
| island, Alaskan | ATTU, PRIBILOF, ALEUT |
| " , Aegean Sea | LEROS, SCID |
| " , Algerian | IOS |
| " , Baltic Sea | OSSEL |
| " , Caroline; N. Pac. | YAP |
| " , coral | ATOLL |
| " , Cycladean | MELOS, NAXIA |
| " , Danish | AERO, OE |
| " , enchanted | BALI |
| " , Dutch E. Indies | NIAS |
| " , fabulous; Ind. | ZANGBAR |
| " , Grecian | SAMOS |
| " group in S. W. Pac. | SAMOA |
| " group in N. Pac. | KURIL |
| " in New York harbor | ELLIS |
| " , inhabiting an | NESIOTE |
| " , Italian | ELBA |
| " , Leeward | BARBUDA |
| " , low | KEY |
| " , Mediterranean | CAPRI, CRETE, MALTA |
| " of an; prefix | NESO |
| " of Odysseus | ITHACA |
| " of Scotland | SHETLAND, ARRAN |
| " of the Nile | RODA |
| " of the Pacific | BONIN, GUAM |
| " off Jutland coast | ALS |
| " off N. Norway | SEILAND |
| " on Gulf of Riga | OSEL |
| " , Philippine | PANAY |
| " , small | AIT, CAY, KEY, OE, QUAY |
| " , small, near a larger | CALF |
| " , small river | EYOT, HOLM |
| " , Society group | TAHITI |
| " S. E. of Celebes | MUNA |
| " , South Sea | ATOLL |
| " , Tongo | ONO |
| " , W. Indies; Brit. | NEVIS |
| " west of Dutch New Guinea | ARU |

islands in Pacific .. ELLICE, SAMOAN,
QUEMOY
" , Ind. and Pacific Ocean .......
OCEANIA
" off coast of Asia Minor IONIAN
Isle of Man, old division of ... TREEN
Isle of Man officer ........ DEEMSTER
islet ........................ CAY, KEY
ism ....... BELIEF, DOGMA, TENET
ism, follower of .................. ITE
isolated .. QUARANTINED, ENISLED
isomer .................... METAMER
isomeric hydrocarbon ...... OCTANE,
TERPENE
isometric .. CUBIC, REGULAR, CUBE
isonomic ........................ SAME
isopiestic line ................ ISOBAR
Israel ........................... JACOB
Israel desert ................... NEGEV
Israel parliament ............ KNESSET
Israel, plain of .............. SHARON
Israeli diplomat ................ EBAN
Israelite .................. JEW, SION
Israelite scribe ................. EZRA
issue .. EMANATE, EMIT, ERISTIC,
END, TERM, ARISE, EDITION,
EMERGE
Istanbul, foreign quarter ........ PERA
Istanbul, Gr. quarter ........ FANAR
isthmus ...... BALK, LAND, STRAIT
isthmus, Malay and Siam ........ KRA
isurus; genus ................. SHARK
Isvara; Hindu myth. ............ SIVA
it is silent; mus. .............. TACET
it is so; Lat. ..................... SIC
ita ......................... NEGRITO
itac; Phil. Is. ................... KNIFE
Itala ....................... VULGATE
Italian actress ................. DUSE
" airplane, giant .......... CAPRONI
" ; anc. ...... ROMAN, PICENE,
SABINE
" astronomer ............. AMICI
" author .. DANTE, PETRARCH
Italian bandit .................. CACO
" bowl ................... TAZZA
" breed of cattle; ...... MODICA,
PADOLIAN
" cheese .... GRANA, GRUYERE
" city ...... ASTI, NOVI, TRENT,
UDINE, ROME, PISA, SPEZIA,
PARMA
" coins; abb. ............... FLRS
" colony ...... ERITREA, LIBIA
" commune .... ATESSA, DEGO,
MASSA, NOLA, ATRI, ASOLA,
ALBA, MEDA, URBINO
" composer ............. ROSSINI
" condiment ............ TAMARA
" country ............ CAMPAGNA
" culture, 14 C. ...... TRECENTO
" dairies .............. CASELLI
" dessert .............. SPUMONI
" dramatist ............ ALFIERA
" explorer ............ ABRUZZI
" faction .. BIANCHI, RAS, NERI
" family; .......... ASTI, CENCI,
COLONNA, ESTE

" festival .............. RIDOTTO
" for dear .................. CARO
" god .. FEBRUS, JANUS, PICUS,
TIBER
" god (see also 'God')
" goddess; ...... CERES, DIANA,
MINERVA, OPS, POMONA,
VENUS
" goddess (see also 'Goddess')
" goddess of welfare ...... SALUS
" guessing game .......... MORA
" hamlet ...... BORGO, CASALE
" health resort ........ AGNONE
" historian ................ CANTU
" house .................... CASA
" inlay .................. TARSIA
" innkeeper ........... PADRONE
" island off east coast .. PIANOSA
" lady ........ DONNA, SIGNORA
" lake ........... AVERNO, VICO
" language .... TUSCAN, OSCAN
" magistrate ........... PODESTA
" magistrate, chief ...... SYNDIC
" marble ................ CIPOLIN
" measure .............. BRACCIO
" mountain .. ALBANITA, CAVO,
CENIS
" meat balls ............ RAVIOLI
" musician, famous ....... GUIDO,
ROSINI
" name .................... ESTE
" naval base ........... TARANTO
" noblewoman ...... MARCHESA
" opera house ............ SCALA
" paste for soups ...... LASAGNE
" painter ........ RENI, CRESPI
" patriot ............. FOSCOLO
" peasant ........... CONTADINO
" people; anc. .. OSCAN, VOLSCI,
SABINES
" philosopher ....... VERA, DION
" physicist ........ ROSSI, VOLTA
" plague ............. PELLAGRA
" playing card, old ...... TAROT
" poet ............. REDI, TASSO
" polemical writer .... GIOBERTI
" police officer .......... SBIRRO
" political writer ........ GIUSTI
" porridge ............. POLENTA
" port ............ BARI, GENOA
" pottery ............. FAENZA
" , pre-Latin ............. OSCAN
" prima-donna ............. DIVA
" province ...... CUNEO, ESTE,
UDINE
" public entertainment . RIDOTTO
" race; anc. .......... SENONES,
PLASGIC
Italian resort ..................... LIDO
" river .. PIAVE, ADIGE, DORA,
ORCO, PO, ADDA, TIBER
" rue grass ............ MARCITE
" ruler, barbarian .... ODOACER
" ruler, early ........... ASTOLF
" satirist .............. ARETINO
.. " sausage ............... TALAME
" sculptor ........ LEONI, DUPRE
" seaport FIUME, POLA, TRANI

144

" secret society ......... MAFIA, CAMORRA
" sheep ................ MERINO
" ship ................ POLACCA
" spa ................ AGNONE
" title ............. CONTE, SER
" town .... ATRI, MEDA, ESTE, ELEA, ITRI, ASTI, POLA
" under, in ................ SOTTO
" university city ........... PISA
" valley ................... SACCO
" watering place ......... ABANO
" weight ........ LIBRA, ONCIA
" wind, hot .... SIROC, SIROCCO
" winds ... ANDAR, ORA, SOVER
" wine meas. ...... ORNA, ORNE
" writer .............. MANZONI
Italy, anc. country of .... TUSCANY, ETRURIA
Italy, anc. name of ........ AUSONIA
Italy, Celt of ............. SENONE
Italy, Gr. colony in ........... ELEA
Italy, marshy land in .... MAREMMA
itch .. PRURITUS, PSORA, SCABIES, RIFF
itch, barbers' ................ SYCOSIS
itch, salt rheum ............ ECZEMA
item .... ASSET, AGENDUM, ENTRY, ARTICLE, DETAIL
itimalic acid; rel. to .... PARACONIC
itineration EYRE, JOURNEY, ROVING
"Ivanhoe," author of ......... SCOTT
"Ivanhoe," char. in BOEUF, CEDRIC, ROWENA, ULRICA
ives ............................ BURL
ivorine ........................ WHITE
ivory, bone black .......... ABAISER
ivory carving, art of .... TOREUTICS
ivory dust and cement ..... EBURITE, EBURIN
ivory; Lat. ...................... EBUR
ivory-like .......... DENTINE, TUSK, EBURNEAN
ivory nut ........ TAGUA, ANTA
ivory, synthetic ............ IVORIDE
ivy, ground .................. HOVE(A)
ivy, per. to ................ HEDERAL
ivy, poison; genus .............. RHUS
I.W.W. emblem .............. SABCAT
ixtle ................... ISTLE, PITA
Izmir; Turk. name ........... SMYRNA

# J

J, letter ...................... JA, JAY
jaal goat .............. BEDEN, IBEX
jab .. PUNCH, THRUST, DIG, POKE
jabber .. BABBLE, GABBLE, PRATE
jabberwocky .. BRILLIG, RIGMAROLE
jabiru; Braz. ................... STORK
jacinth ........ ZIRCON, HYACINTH
jack ...... JUG, TANKARD, CLOWN, KNAVE
Jackson ......................... JAY
Jack-in-the pulpit .............. ARAD

jack of clubs in five-card loo .... PAM
"Jack Pudding" ... BUFFOON, ZANY
jack-a-daw ........... COE, DAWISH
jackal; Ind. ..................... KOLA
jackal god; myth. ............. APUAT
jackass .... DONKEY, DOLT, FOOL, WITLING, ONO
jacket .... BIETLE, ETON, REEFER
" , Arctic hooded ...... ANORAK
" , Eskimo .............. TEMIAK
" , knitted .... JERSEY, SONTAG
" , light, loose .. BLOUSE, JUMP
" , Scottish .......... CLEADING
" , short .... JERKIN, SPENCER
" , sleeveless .. VEST, BOLERO, PENELOPE
" , steel plated .......... ACTON, AKETOUN
" with short flaps ...... COATEE
" woman's ........ JUPE, JUPON
" worn in the Levant .... GREGO
jack-in-the-pulpit ..... WAKEROBIN
jacket-like ................ CAMISOLE
jacket; Sp. .............. CHAQUETA
Jack-Ketch ................ HANGMAN
jack-snipe .............. SANDPIPER
jackstays .................... HORSES
Jacob's brother ........ EDOM, ESAU
Jacob's daughter ........... DINAH
Jacob's eldest son .......... REUBEN
Jacob's father-in-law ........ LABAN
Jacob's ladder ................ PHLOX
Jacob's son .. JUDAH, ASHER, DAN, GAD, LEVI
Jacob's wife ........ LEAH, RACHEL
jaconet ..................... NAINSOOK
jade HUSSY, TIT, TIRE, NEPHRITE, YU, NAG, PLUG
jade-like stone ............... MURRA
jaeger ........ ALLAN, SHOOI, SKUA
jag .. BARB, CLEFT, LOAD, NOTCH
Jagannath, home of the ......... PURI
jagged .. CLEFT, EROSE, SERRATED
jaguar .. PANTHER, OUNCE, TIGER
Jah; Heb. ....................... GOD
jai-alai ....................... PELOTA
jai-alai, player of ........ PELOTARI
jai-alai racquet ............... CESTA
jail .. COOLER, BRIDEWELL, LIMBO
jail fever ................... TYPHUS
jam ...... BLOCK, BRUISE, CRAM
Jamaica bitter wood ........ QUASSAI
Jamaica cobnut .............. QUABE
jambee ....................... CANE
Jamshid, realm of ........... PERIS
jangling ........ CLASHING, HARSH
janitor ........... PORTER, SEXTON
Janizarian chief ................. DEY
japan .......... ENAMEL, LACQUER
Japan, largest city of ........ OSAKA
Japan, largest island ........ HONSHU
Japan, province in ................ UGO
Japanese aborigine ...... AINO, AINU
" ancient capital ........ NARA
" apricot ................... UME
" art of self defence .. JUJITSU
" badge of nobility ....... MON
" battle cry .......... BANZAI

145

" bay ............. ISE, YEDO
" boxes, set of .......... INRO
" bream .................... TAI
Japanese Buddha ...... AMIDA, APIS
" capital, eastern ..... TOKIO
" capital, western ..... SAIKIO
" carriage .............. SADOS
" case ................... INRO
" church ................. TERA
" city SENDAI, NARA, KOBE,
YEDO
" clan ............... GEN, HEI
" coin MO, RIN, SEN, TEMPO,
YEN
" commoner .......... HEIMIN
" commune ............. DESSA
" conveyance ........... KAGO
" councillor ............. KARO
" court .................. DAIRI
" crest ................... MON
" dancing girl ........ GEISHA
" deer .................... SIKA
" departments ........... KORI
" diplomat .......... TANAKA
" dog, wild .......... TANATE
" door ................... SIKA
" drama ................... NO
" emperor .......... MIKADO
" Empire, former name .. EDO
" family crest ........... MON
" fan ...................... OGI
" festival ................. BON
" fetish .................. OBE
" fish, poisonous ....... FUGU
" gateway .............. TORII
" gentry ........... SHIZOKU
" glue, rice paste ....... AME
" gold coin ............. OBAN
" gold fish ............. FUNA
" "great ruler" ...... TAIKUN
" herb .................... UDO
" lake ......... BIWA, SUWA
" language .............. AINU
" legislature ........... DIET
" litter, covered .. NORIMONO
" lute ................... BIWA
" measure, (see 'measure')
" mile ..................... RI
" military governor .. SHOGUN
" monastery ........... TERA
" money, 1/10 rin ......... MO
" musical inst. BIWA, SAMISEN
" naval base ........... KURE
" news service ....... DOMEI
" nobility, lesser .... SAMURAI
" ornament on costume ........
NETSUKE
" outcast ......... ' ETA, RONIN
" overcoat, straw ........ MINO
" pagoda ................. TAA
" palanquin . KAGO, NORIMON
" parasitic wasps; genus TIPHIA
" people, of north ...... AINUS
" petty nobility .. HATAMOTO
" pine ................. MATSU
" pottery, Delft-like ... AWATA
" prefecture KEN, MINO, OITA,
OWARI

" province ............... KUNI
" province; suffix ........ SHIU
" radish .............. DAIKON
" rain coat, straw ........ MINO
Japanese receptacle ............. INRO
" religion, early ....... SHINTO
" religious dance ......... NO
" revolving storm .. TYPHOON
" rice drink .............. SAKE
" rice glucose or paste .. AME
" river .......... TONEGAWA
" robe, outer .......... KIMONO
" rose ................... AINO
" salad plant ............. UDO
" salt water fish .......... AYU
" sash ...................... OBI
" sauce ................... UDO
" sea-port ...... SAKATA, TSU
" seaweed ................ NORI
" ship .................... ARGO
" shrub ................. GOUMI
" sock ................... TABO
" soldier's pay ........... SEN
" song ................... UTA
" statesman GENRO, MORI, ITO
" stomach cutting .. HARAKIRI
" style of painting ...... KANO
" suicide .......... SEPPUKU
" sun tree ............ HINOKI
" territorial nobles .... DAIMO
" town .................... TOI
" vegetable .............. UDO
" vine ................. KUDZU
" volcano, extinct .... ASOSAN
" weight ....... FUN, MO, RIN
" wind ............. MONSOON
" wooden shoes .......... GETA
" writing ................ KANA
" yeoman .............. GOSHI
Japan's Pittsburgh ......... YAWATA
Japetus; astron. .......... SATURN
Japheth, son of ... MESHECH, JAVAN
japonica; Jap. ................ QUINCE
" , clay or stone ........... STEEN
jar, coarse earthenware .... TERRINE,
CROCK
" , long necked water; .... GOGLET,
GURGLET
" , Spanish .................... OLLA
" , two handled .......... AMPHORA
" , very large .... CADUS, DOLIUM
jardiniere ........ POT, SOUP, VASE
jargon LINGO. CANT, RANE, ZIRCON,
ABRACADABRA
jargon; slang FLASH, ARGOT, DRIVEL
jarl; Scand. Chieftain, .......... EARL
jar-ring ....................... LUTE
jars ..... DOLIA, GRATES, RATTLES
jasmine ............ BELA, JESSAMY
Jason, lady deserted by ...... MEDEA
Jason's father ................. AESON
Jason's ship .................... ARGO
jasper ..... BIOTITE, MICA, MURRA
jaundice ................... ICTERUS
jaunty AIRY, PERKY, FINE, SHANTY
Java carriage ................... SADO
Java, island east of ............ BALI
Java pepper .................... CUBEB

146

Javanese badger ... RATEL, TELEDU
" carriage .............. SADOO
" climbing civet ........ RASSE
" dumb show .......... TOPENG
" mountain ............. AMAT
" squirrel .......... JELERANG
" tree ................... UPAS
" village community .... DESSA
" weight . TALI, AMAT, POND
javelin LANCE, DART, ASSAGAI, PILE
javelin; Persian ................ JERID
"Javert," creator of .......... HUGO
jaw .. MAW, CHAP, CHOKE, GONIA,
WANG
jaw; comb. form ........... GNATHO
jaw, lower ................. MANDIBLE
jaw, muscle of ............ MASSETER
jaw; per. to ................ GNATHIC
jaw, upper ................. MAXILLA
jawless .................... AGNATHIC
Jeanne; actress ........... CRAIN
jayhawker ..... GUERILLA, KANSAN
jeans ........ OVERALLS, TROUSERS
jeer . TAUNT, DERIDE, JAPE, JIBE,
MOB
Jeeter Lester's favorite vegetable .....
TURNIP
jeeves, play ................. BUTTLE
Jefferson's home ...... MONTICELLO
Jehoahaz's mother ....... HAMUTAL
Jejune MEAGER, ARID, BANAL, DRY,
STALE
jelly, animal .............. GELATINE
jelly fish ACALEPH, MEDUSA, QUARL
jelly-fish, comb. of ............ CTENE
" , stinging .......... SEANETTLE
" , umbrella of a ........... PILEUS
jelly, grape; Fr. ................ SAPA
jelly, meat .................... ASPIC
jelly, vegetable ............... PECTIN
jelly-like ... GELATINOUS, COLLOID,
GEL
jena glass objective ........... UNAR
jennet ........ ASS, DONKEY, HORSE
Jenny; "Swedish Nightingale" .. LINL
jeopardy .... HAZARD, PERIL, RISK
jeremiad ...... TALE, LAMENT, WOE
jerk . TWITCH, NIDGE, TIC, TWEAK
jerked beef ................. CHARQUI
Jerry ......................... KRAUT
jersey livelong ........... ENAEAA
Jerusalem; anc. name ....... SALEM
Jerusalem thorn ............. DETAMA
Jespersen's language ........... IDO
jess .......... RIBBON, STRAP
jessur .............. DABOIA, SNAKE
jest JAPE, MOT, QUIP, TRIFLE, WIT
jester .. CLOWN, MIME, WAG, ZANY
jester, roving student ...... GOLIARD
Jesuit saint ................... REGIS
jet .. SPURT, COAL, EBONY, SPRAY,
STREAM
jetty ........ MOLE, PIER, WHARF
jewel .. BRILLIANT, GEM, JOY, NAIF
jewel setting .. BEZEL, OUCH, DOP,
PAVE
jeweler's magnify. glass ...... LOUPE
jeweler's weight .............. KARAT

jewelry . LOGIES, BIJOUTRY, QUOIN
jewelry alloy .................. OROIDE
jewels, set of ............... PARURE
jewelry, cheap ................ PASTE
jewelweed .............. CELANDINE
"jewels of the Madonna;" char. .......
STELLA
Jewett; writer ...... (SARAH), ORNE
Jewish, (see 'Hebrew')
Jewish organiz. .................... ITO
Jewish priest's girdle ......... ABNET
Jewish skullcap ............ YAMILKE
Jews, dispersion of ........ DIASPORA
Jewsharp ..... CREMBALUM, TRUMP
Jezebel .... GORGON, FURY, VIRAGO
jib CHORE, SINECURE, BALK, BOOM
jib of a derrick .................. SPAR
jibe AGREE, HARMONIZE, FIT, FLING
jiffy ..... INSTANT, SECOND, TRICE
jiggle ............... DANCE, SHAKE
jimmy ..... BAR, BETTY, CROWBAR
'Jimmy Valentine' ......... BURGLAR
Jimson weed DATURA, STRAMONIUM
jingle ................ CLINK, TINGLE
jinn .............................. EBLIS
jinni ............... GENIE, DEMON
jinni, female ............... JENNIYEH
jitters ........... DITHERS, NERVES
jittery ............. EDGY, JUMPY
jiujutsu ................... JUJITSU
jivatma ................. ATMAN, EGO
"Jo and Beth"; sister, of ......... AMI
Joan of Arc, name for ..... PUCELLE
Joan's spouse ................ DARBY
job . TASK, CHORE, STINT, CHARE
jockey ............. CAVALIER, DISC
jocose MERRY, DROLL, DRY, LEPID
jocular .. JESTING, LOCO, WAGGISH
"Joey" ........................... PAL
jog .. REMIND, DUNCH, TROT, MOG
"John Brown's Body," author of BENET
John Payne ................... ACTOR
'johnnie' .................. LOTHARIO
johnny-cake ......... HOECAKE, PONE
Johnson (Mrs.), the former ....... OSA
Johnstron; senator .............. OLIN
join LOCK, ADD, COALESCE, MEET,
SOLDER, PIN
joint .. TENON, HIP, HINGE, SEAM,
ELBOW
" , cavity .................. BURSA
" in stem ................... NODE
" lubricator ............. SYNOVIA
" , make tight ............. STEM
" of plant stem ...... PHYTOMER,
PHYTON
" , right angle ........ ELL, KNEE
" , to put out of .......... LUXATE
jointed stem of grass ........... CULM
joke ..... GAG, QUIP, SALLY, JAPE,
JEST
joked; sl. .................... JOSHED
joker . MISTIGRIS, CARD, DOR, WAG
jolly ..... BUXOM, CHEER, CROUSE
jolly boat ...................... YAWL
Joloano ......................... SULU
Jolson, Al. ....................... ASA
jolt ..... SHAKE, JAR, JOUNCE, JUT

147

Jonah; slang .................... JINX
jonquil .................... NARCISSUS
Joppolo's title ..................... MAS
Jordan, part of ................. MOAB
Jose——; dancer .............. GRECO
"Joseph Andrews," char. in Fielding's .
............................... ADAMS
Joseph's wife .............. ASENATH
josh; sl. ............. BANTER, KID
Joshua's burial place .......... GAASH
Joshua's father .................. NUN
Josip Broz ........................ TITO
jostle ....... ELBOW, RUSH, SHOCK
joss ......... CROWD, MASTER, IDOL
jot .. ITEM, ACE, BIT, IOTA, MINIM,
ATOM, MITE, POINT, TITTLE, WHIT
jotting ....... MEMO, ENTRY, NOTE
joule, part of a .................... ERG
journal RECORD, DIARY, REGISTER,
............................... PAPER
journey .. TREK, FARE, RUN, TOUR,
............................... WEND
journey in circuit .............. EYRE
journey, per. to a ...... ITINERANCY,
............................... VIATIC
journey up ................. ANABASIS
joust .. COMBAT, TILT, BOUT, SPAR
Jove ........................ JUPITER
jowl ... CHAP, HEAD, JAW, CHEEK
joy .......... BLISS, ECSTASY, GLEE
joyous .... MERRY, BAUD, ELATED,
............................... VESTAL
Judah, anc. city of ............. AMAM
Judah, first born of ............... ER
Judah's son .................. SHELAH
Judaism, convert to ............. GER
Judas ......... BETRAYER, TRAITOR
Judean king ............. ASA, HEROD
judge ...... DEEM, EDILE, KEEPER,
............................... OPINE, TRIER
judge, Isle of Man ....... DEEMSTER
judge's aide ............... ASSESSOR
judge's chamber, per. to .. CAMERAL
judges entry after verdict ... POSTEA
judges, said of ............... PUISNE
judge's seat ..................... BANC
judgment ........... DOOM, OPINION
judicious  WISE, POLITIC, PRUDENT
judo ......................... JUJITSU
jug .......... BUIRE, CRUSE, EWER,
............ FLAGON, OLPE, TOBY
Juggernaut; Hindu ......... KRISHNA
jugs, room for ................. EWRY
jujube ......... BER, ELB, LOZENGE
Jules Verne's Captain of the "Nautilus"
............................... NEMO
Juliana's house .............. ORANGE
Juliet's father .............. CAPULET
jumble ....... MEDLEY, MIX, PI, PIE,
............ RAFF, ROG, BLEND, HASH
jump .... HOP, LEAP, START, LOWP
jump, in Greek game ....... HALMA
jumping ..................... SALTANT
jumping rodent ............. JERBOA
jumping stick .................. POGO
junco ............ FINCH, SNOWBIRD
juncture ...... CRISIS, PASS, STRAIT
June bug ........................ DOR

junior ...... CADET, PUISNE, PUNY
juniper ..... CEDAR, RETEM, SAVIN,
............................... CADE
junk .. CABLE, ROPE, SOMA, TRASH
junker; Ger. ................... SQUIRE
junket ..... BANQUET, FEAST, DISH
Juno ........................ UNI, HERA
Juno, messenger of .............,..... IRIS
junta; Sp. ...... COUNCIL, MEETING
junto ... CLIQUE, FACTION, CABAL
Jupiter, consort of .............. JUNO
Jupiter, son of ................. ARCAS
Jupiter's daughter ......... MINERVA
jural ............... LEGAL, RIGHTS
Jurassic division ................. LIAS
jurema ....................... ACACIA
jurisdiction SOKE, SEE, SOC, VENUE
jurisdiction of an emir ..... EMIRATE
jury ...... VENIRE, ASSIZE, PANEL
juryman ........... ASSIZER, JUROR
juryman, anc. Athenian ...... DICAST
jus; law ........................... IUS
just clear of ground ........ AWEIGH
justice ...... DOOM, EQUITY, RIGHT
justice of the peace .......... SQUIRE
justices, supreme court ....... CHASE,
ELLSWORTH, FULLER, HUGHES,
JAY, MARSHALL, RUTLEDGE,
TAFT, TAITE, TANEY, STONE
justification ............... DEFENSE,
............................... VINDICATION
justify . EXCUSE, CLEAR, WARRANT
justle ..... BUMP, BOLT, COG, JOLT
jut out .............. ABUT, BEETLE
jute cloth .... BURLAP, GUNNY, TAT
jutes ........................... DESIS
Jutlander ...................... DANE
jutting rock ...... TOR, BRAE, CRAG
jutty ............ JETTY, PIER, MOLE
Juventas, personified ........... HEBE
juxtaposition . CONTIGUITY, TOUCH


# K

K, letter .................... CA, CAY
kaddish; Heb. ............. DOXOLOGY
Kaffir ......................... INFIDEL
Kaffir corn; Afr. ............... MILLET
Kaffir language ................... XOSA
Kaffir warriors ................... IMPI
Kafir, rel. to ............. MATABELE
kago; Jap. ............... PALANQUIN
kaiak, Eskimo .................. CANOE
kaka; N. Z. ................... PARROT
kale ........ BORECOLE, BROCCOLI,
............................... COLLARD
kale, sea; Eng. .................... COLE
kali ....................... GLASSWORT
kalinite ........................ ALUM
kalmuck ...................... ELEUT
kanae; N. Z. ................... MULLET
Kanarese sect ................... BALI
kanari; Java ................. ALMOND
Kandh ........................ KHOND
kangaroo ... MACROPODIAN, JEROBA
"    , female .......... DOE, GIN

"  , male; Aus. BILBI, BOOMER
"  , rat ................ POTOROO
"  , young ................ JOEY
Kansas, city in .......... IOLA, PAOLA
kapok tree ...................... CEIBA
kaput ................ DOOMED, RUINED
Karachi is its capital .......... SIND
Karaism, believer in ......... ANANITE
karakul ................ LAMA, SHEEP
Karelian Lake ..................... SEG
Karenina, Miss ................... ANNA
Karloff; actor ................... BORIS
karma ............... DESTINY, FATE
Kartvelian ...................... SVANE
karyotin ................ CHROMATIN
kat shrub ...................... KAFTA
katchung ...................... PEANUT
kava ................................ AVA
Kay ——, writer ................ BOYLE
Keats; poem by .................. LAMIA
Kazan; film direc. ................ ELIA
kea; N. Z. .................... PARROT
keck RETCH, BELCH, SPUE, VOMIT
ked ................................ TICK
keel over .............. CAPSIZE, KEEL
keel, part of .................... SKEG
keel, without a ............... RATITE
keel-like ...... CARINAL, CARINATED
keen ....... ASTUTE, BITTER, GARE,
              SNELL, TART, SHARP
keen; Irish ..................... CAOINE
keenness .. EDGE, ACIES, PUNGENCY
keep CASE, SAVE, DONJON, RETAIN
keep out ... EXCEPT, EXCLUDE, BAR
keep under .................. MORTIFY
keeper of a door lock ... RISP, STANG,
                          TILER, NAB
keeper of the golden apple; Norse myth.
                               ITHUN
keeper of the marches .... MARGRAVE
keeper of the royal park ...... RANGER
—— keepers .................. FINDERS
keeping ...... HOLDING, TUTELAGE,
          CONGRUITY, UNION, BOARD
keeps a course; naut. ........... CAPES
keepsake RELIC, TOKEN, SOUVENIR
keeve ............... KIER, TUB, VAT
Kefauver, Mr. ................... ESTES
keg CADE, CASK, FIRKIN, TUN, VAT
keg, open a ................... UNHEAD
Keith; actor ...................... IAN
Kelly, Mr. ....................... GENE
kelp .. VARIC, WRACK, WARE, ASH,
                             SEAWEED
kelter ........... CONDITION, ORDER
ken ... LORE, PRESCIENCE, DESCRY
Kent district; Eng. ............ ERITH
Kentuckian .......... CORNCRACKER
Kenba's capital ............... NAIROBI
Keos native .................... CEAN
kerb ....................... CURB, SLIT
kerchief ....................... CURCH
Keresan Indian ...................... SIA
kernel ..... GIST, SEED, NUT, GRAIN,
           CAUSE, CORE, HEART, PITH
kernel, having a ........... NUCLEATE
ketch .............. SAIC, JACK, SHIP
kethib .............. KERE, KRI
ketone ........ ACETONE, BUTYRONE

Kett, Miss ...................... ETTA
kettle used in the south ........ SIROP
kettle-drum ...... NAKER, TIMPANO
kettle-drum, cavalry ........ ANACARA
kettle-drum; Span. ........... ATABAL
key . COTTER, ISLET, CLAVIS, CLEW
"  , a crib ........................ PONY
"  false ........................ GLUT
"  filler ........................ ULLER
"  fruit ........................ SAMARA
"  , in music; It. ............... TASTO
"  , locksmithing .............. WARD
"  of instrument ........... MANUAL
"  , per. to ................... TONAL
"  , telegraph ............... TAPPER
keyboard .... DIGITORIUM, CLAVIER
keyboard inst. ................ CELESTA
keyed up ............ AGOG, EAGER
keynote sign; mus. .............. ISON
Keyserling, Mr. ................... LEON
keystone SAGITTA, SUPPORT, WEDGE
Keystone State, founder of ...... PENN
khan ........................ INN, ALY
khan keeper ............... KHANJEE
kiang ........................ ONAGER
kibblings ........................ BAIT
kibe ...................... CHILBLAIN
kibitzer .................... SPECTATOR
kick .... BOOT, CALCITRATE, FUNK,
                               KEVEL
kicking ......................... WINCH
kickshaw ...... BAUBLE, TOY, FOOD
kid; sl. ................. BANTER, JOSH
kid, undressed ................. SUEDE
kiddy; slang ......... OUTWIT, HOAX
kidnap ...... ABDUCT, SEIZE, TAKE,
                               STEAL
kidney bean; Fr. .............. PHASEL
kidney stone ...... JADE, NEPHRITE
kidneys, the ................... RENAL
kidney-shaped ............. RENIFORM
Kienzel; opera by ............. URVASI
Kilauea, goddess of the crater of PELE
kill . BLAST, BURKE, OCCIDE, SLAY
kill by stoning ............ LAPIDATE
killer ....................... CETACEAN
killer whale; genus .............. ORCA
killing .. CARNAGE, FATAL, GAROTE
killing of a wolf ............. LUPICIDE
killing of old men .......... SENICIDE
Kilmer poem ................... TREES
kiln ........ OAST, OST, OVEN, TILER
kiloliter .......................... STERE
kilt, a little ...... FILIBEG, PHILIBEG
kin, near akin ..... GERMANE, FOLKS
kind .... CLASS, STRAIN, SORT, ILK,
             GENUS, TRIBE, SEELY
"  of feldspar ................. GABRO
"  of grass .......... BROME, NARD
"  of match .................. FUSEE
"  of monk hood ............... ATEE
"  of spaniel ............. SPRINGER
"  of stone ................. PERIDOT
"  of syllogism ...... EPICHEIREMA
"  of tea ......... CEYLON, OOLONG
kindle ........... BURN, FIRE, ROUSE
kindly .............. BENIGN, BLITHE
kindred .. COGNATE, ALLIED, AKIN,
            BLOOD, KITH, TIE, SIB

kindred species .......... COGENERIC
kinds ....................... NATURES
kine .......... CATTLE, COW, BEAST
kinematograph, form of TACHYSCOPE
king ... SOVEREIGN, ROI, REGULES,
        AUTHORITY, RANK, REX
king, Albanian ..................... ZOG
king, French for ................... ROI
King Arthur, death place of . CAMLAN
"    " , father of ......... UTHER
"    " , foster brother of .... KAY
"    " , knights of ... GALAHAD,
                GARETH
"    " , resting place of . AVALON
"    " , wife of ..... GUENEVER
King Arthur's capital ...... CAMELOT
"    " clown ......... DAGONET
King Arthur's court, lady in ..... ENID
"    " fairy sister ..................
              MORGANLEFAY
"    " father-in-law . LEOGADAN
"    " lance ......... RON, RONE
"    " magic sword . EXCALIBUR
"    " mother IGRAINE, YGERNE
"    " nephew ......... GAWAIN,
              MODRED
"    " seneschal ... KEN, LREUX
"    " shield, name of. PRIDWIN
King Canute's consort ........... EMMA
King Cole ......................... NAT
King David's cave ......... ADULLAM
King David's faithful friend .... ITTAI
King David's father ............ JESSE
King David's son . ABSALOM, AMNON
King Gath ..................... ACHISH
King Lear's daughter . GONERIL, MOL
"    " dog ................. TRAY
"    " favorite daughter .........
              CORDELIA
"    " second daughter .. REGAN
king, legendary ................. MIDAS
king, Midian .............. EVI, REBA
king of Amalek ................. AGAG
" of Arcadia; Gr. leg. ...... LYCAON
" of Assyria ..................... PUL
" of Bashan ..................... OG
" of beggars; Eng. ......... CAREW
" of birds ................... EAGLE
" of Britain; leg. ........ ARTEGAL,
  BLADUD, BELINUS, ELIDURE,
  LEAR, LUD
" of Bulgaria ............. BORIS
" of Corinth; Gr. ......... POLYBUS
" of Damascus ............. ARETUS
" of Egypt; (present) ....... FUAD,
              FAROUK
" of England ............. STEPHEN
" of England and Denmark .. KNUT
" of fairies ................ OBERON
" of Gerar ............. ABIMELECH
" of Hamath ............... TOI, TOU
" of Hazor .................. JABIN
" of herrings ............... OPAH
" of Huns; myth. .............. ATLI
" of Iran .................. XERXES
" of Iraq ................... FEISAL
" of Israel AHAB, BAASHA, ELAH,
          OMRI, PEKAH
" of Israel, last ........... HOSHEA

" of Judah . ABIJAH, AHAZ, AMON,
              ASA
" of Judea ............ ASA, HEROD
" of Langobards ........... ALBOIN
" of Moab ......... MALAK, EGLON
" of Naples, 19th cent. ...... MURAT
" of Norway .......... OLAF, OLAV
" of Persia ...... CYRUS, XERXES
" of Phrygia; myth. ......... MIDAS
" of Pylus; anc. Gr. ........ NESTOR
" of serpent race ............. SESHA
" of Sodom .................... BERA
" of Spain ...................... REY
" of Sussex ................... ELLA
" of Syria ...... HAZAEL, REZIN
" of the Ammonites ........ HANUN
" of the Amorites ............ SIHON
" of the Devas .............. INDRA
" of the fairies ............ OBERON
" of the Fomors ............. BALOR
" of the Lapithae; myth. ..... IXION
" of the mullets ............... BASS
" of the sea breams ........ BRAISE
" of the Zulus .......... CETEWAYO
king of Thebes, wife of ......... DIRCE
" of Troy, in the "Aeneid" ... PRIAM
" of Tyre .................... HIRAM
" of waters ................ AMAZON
" of Wessex ................... INE
" of Zobah ............. HADADZER
" , petty ................. REGULUS
" , Scottish ...... ROBERT, BRUCE
" , Spanish .................... RAY
" , Spartan ............ MENELAUS
" , steward to a ......... DAPIFER
" , the greedy ............... MIDAS
" , third of India ................ ASA
" , Volsunga saga ............ ATLI
king-crab .................. LIMULUS
kingdom .. REALM, EMPIRE, ESTATE
"Kingdom by the sea" dweller .........
              ANNABEL
kingdom near Babylon .......... ELAM
kingdom, N. Ind. .............. NEPAL
kingdom of Nimrod ............ BABEL
king-fish ............. BARB, OPAH
king-geld ................... ESCUAGE
kinglet .......... LIONET, WREN
kingly ... LEONINE, AUGUST, REGAL
king's body guard .............. THANE
king's chamber ............ CAMARILLA
kings-clover ................. MELILOT
king's-evil ................. SCROFULA
king's servant .............. DAPIFER
king-ship ................... ROYALTY
king's-letter .................. BRIEF
king-snake ............. OPHIBOLUS
king-tyrant ................. KINGBIRD
kink .. KNOT, TWIST, SNARL, WHIM
kink in thread ................. BURL
kinkajou, the ................... POTTO
kinship, in Moham. law ........ NASAB
kinsman ..... RELATIVE, SIB, MALE
kiosk ...................... PAVILION
Kipling's "Shere Khan" ........ TIGER
kirtle .......... SKIRT, COAT, TUNIC
kismet ....... DESTINY, FATE, DOOM
kiss ......................... OSCULATE
kiss; in Italy ................... BACIO

kiss of peace    PAX, CALUMET, PIPE
kiss, playful ............. SMACK, BUSS
"Kiss"; sculptor of ............. RODIN
kissing, science of . PHILEMATOLOGY
kitchen garden ................ OLITORY
kitchen, naut. .................. GALLEY
kite ........ MILAN, ELANET, GLEDE
kite; genus ................... ELANET
kitty .............. CAT, ANTE, POOL
kiwi ...................... ROA, MOA
kiwi; genus ................. APTERYX
Klamath sucker ................... YEN
kleptomaniac ........ THIEF, FILCHER
klieg eyes ...................... EDEMA
knack .... HANG, MOCK, SKILL, ART,
FEAT, EASE
knarl . GNARL, KNAG, KNURL, NODE
knave . RAUTENER, ROGUE, LOREL,
LOSEL
knave in cribbage ................ NOB
knave of clubs ................... PAM
knead to softness .. ELT, MALAXATE
knee bone .......................... DIB
" flexure ...................... GENU
" , inflammation of the .... GONITIS
" joint ...................... HOCK
" , rel. to the .................. HAM
" , to bend the ....... GENUFLECT
kneecap ..................... PATELLA
kneecap-like ................. ROTULAT
kneeling desk ............. PRIEDIEU
knapsack .......... BAG, KIT, POUCH
knew ......... KENNED, WOT, WIST
knickknack ...... GIMCRACK, TRIFLE
knife, Burmese ................... DAH
" , comb. form ............... DORI
" , curved Hindu ............ KUKRI
" , Irish .................... SKEAN
" , large; Phil ................ ITAC
" , large pocket ...... BOLO, SNEE
" , Malay ................. CREESE
" , Maori ................... PATU
" , Moro .................. BARONG
" , one bladed ........... BARLOW
" , plaster and paint .... SPATULA
" , Spanish ............... MACHETE
knife-like dagger ................. DIRK
knight ..... SIR, GALLANT, EQUITE,
EQUES, LOVER, TEMPLAR
knight errant ................. PALADIN
knight of the Red Eagle ........... KRE
knight of the "Round Table" BOHORT,
YWAINE
knight, one next in order .... ARMIGER
knighthood ........ CHIVALRY, HOST,
ACCOLADE
knightly's bride ................. EMMA
knight's cloak ................. TABARD
knight's fight .................. JOUST
knit . COUPLE, JOIN, ICNUTE, SEAM
knitting UNION, BROCADE, CROCHET
knitting, stitch in ................ PURL
knitting machine guide .......... SLEY
knob ......... KNURL, NODE, UMBO
" in wood ..................... NUR
" , medicinal ........... TUBERCLE
" , ornamental BOSS, KNOB, STUD
" , per. to a ................. ORLET
" , pointed ................. FINIAL

knobby ...... NODOSE, HARD, LUMPS
knobkerrie ......................... KIRI
knob-like ...................... NOPAL
knobstick ................ RAT, SNOB
knock out of shape .............. BASH
knocking, sharp ................ RATTAT
knock-knee ............. INKNEE, XLEG
knoll HILLOCK, MOUND, KNAP, TOLL
knot SNAG, JOINT, NODE, TIE, TUFT
" , fibrous ...................... NEP
" in wood .... KNAR, NURL, BURL,
KNAG
" of hair or silk .............. NOIL
" , running ................... NOOSE
" , tree ............... GNARL, NUR
" weed ................. ALLSEEDS
knots, free from ... ENODATE, ENODE
knotted ..................... NODATED
know . REGARD, REVEAL, KEN, WIS,
WOT
knowall ...... WISEACRE, QUIDNUNC
knowing HEP, SCIENT, EPISTOMONIC
knowledge KEN, KITH, LORE, OLOGY,
SCIENTIA
knowledge, an object of ...... SCIBILE
knowledge, means to ........ ORGANON
knowledge, superficial ....... SCIOLIST
knowledge, univer. ...... PANTOLOGY
knowledge, without ....... ATECHNIC
known ............... BEKEN, COUTH
knuckle ............. SUBMIT, YIELD
knuckle bone ...................... DIB
knurl ................... MILL, RIDGE
kobold ......... GNOME, HOBGOBLIN,
BROWNIE, NIS
koel; Ind. ..................... CUCKOO
kohinoor .................. DIAMOND
kokama .................. GEMSBOK
koklass .................... PUCRAS
kokoon .......................... GNU
kola ....................... JACKAL
kookoom ....................... ORYX
koprosterin ................. SEROLIN
Koran, division of ... ALCORAN, SURA,
SURO
Koran scholar ................. ULEMA
Koran, teacher of ........... ALFAQUI
Korea ...................... CHOSEN
Korea, capital of ...... SEOUL, KEIJO
Korea, city in ................. FUSAN
Korean leader (first family) .... RHEE
Korean meet. place ...... KAESONG
Korean port. ........ GENSAN, PUSAN
Korean river ................... YALU
Korean soldier .................... ROK
Korean stockade ................ KOJE
Korean weight .................... KON
Korea's regent .................... ITO
kosher ........................ CLEAN
kosher meat, maker of ....... PORGER
kosher, opposed to ............. TREF
krall ................... ENCLOSURE
Kretschmer; opera by ..... FOLKUNGS
krimmer ................. LAMBSKIN
Ku Klux Klan; It. ......... CAMORRA,
SHEETED
kulak; Russ. ..................... FIST
kulanapan ...................... POMO
kumiss; Afr. .................. OMEIRIS

151

kumiss-like .................. KEFIRIC
Kuomintang dept. .............. YUANS
Kurab ——, Delhi .............. MINAR
Kurile Is. ...................... ITURUP
kust .............................. NODE
kust in cotton fibre ............. NEP
Kwantung seaport .......... DAIREN
Kyushu base .................. SASEBO
Kyushu Is. volcano ................ ASO

# L

L, letter ...................... EL, ELL
labellum .......................... LIP
labile ........................ UNSTABLE
"La Boheme" heroine ........... MIMI
labor . WORK, TASK, TRAVAIL, MOIL
labored .......... OPEROSE, STIFF
laborer ....... FELLAH, PEON, TOTY
laborer, inferior .............. SEGGON
laborer on canals ............. NAVVY
laborer, oriental .............. COOLIE
labyrinth ............. MAZE, DAEDAL
Lacania sect. ..................... OBE
lace ....... GIN, NET, NOOSE, SNARE
"   cape .................. MANTILLA
"   , frilled .................... RUCHE
"   , fringed work of ....... CREPINE
"   front ...................... JABOT
"   , gold or silver .......... ORRIS
"   , heavy ..... TATTING, GUIPURE
"   , kind of . POTLACE, FILET, VAL
"   , kind of point ......... ALENCON
"   , make ...................... TAT
"   Mechlin .................. MALINE
"   , metal tag on ............. AGLET
"   opening ................... EYELET
"   string ..................... THONG
"   , to ....... ENTWINE, WEAVE
"   weave-cushion .............. BOTT
lacerate ...... RIP, CUT, REND, TEAR
lacerated ................. RENT, TORN
lachrymose ................. TEARFUL
lacing .................... THRASHING
lack ........ REQUIRE, WANT, NEED
lack of tone ................... ATONY
lackey .. FOOTMAN, FLUNKY, TOADY
lacking ................. DEVOID, SHY
lacking cross guard ..... CHAPULESS
Laconian subdivision ............ OBE
laconic ... CONCISE, TERSE, BRIEF
lacquer ENAMEL, VARNISH, JAPAN
ladder ... RUN, STEE, STY, SCALADO
ladder, attack with ....... ESCALADE
ladder, part of ................. RUNG
ladder-like ................... SCALAR
lading of ships ............. CARGOES
ladle ............. DIP, BOWL, SCOOP
ladle, spout of ................. GEAT
ladrone .... ROGUE, THIEF, ROBBER
Ladrone Island ...... GUAJAN, GUAM
lady ...... BURD, FEMALE, WOMAN
lady; Ital. ................... DONNA
"Lady of Lyons," heroine of PAULINE
"Lady of the Lake" .. ELLEN, VIVIAN
lady; Span. .......... DONA, SENORA

ladybird ......... BEETLE, VEDALIA
ladyfish ...................... PUDANO
lady-like ...................... SHEIK
ladylove ........................ DELIA
lady's silk habit .............. PELISSE
lady's slipper ................ ORCHID
lady's thumb .......... PEACHWORT
lady's work-basket .............. CABA
lag ........ DELAY, IDYE, LOITER
La Gioconda ............. MONA LISA
La Gioconda char. ............. LAURA
lagomorah .... HARE, PIKA, RABBIT
Lahr; comedian ................ BERT
laic ... CIVIL, SECULAR, TEMPORAL
lair CAVE, CAVERN, DEN, LIE, TRAP
laity ...... LAYMEN, PEOPLE, FOLD
Laius, son of ............... OEDIPUS
lake .................. ERIE, MEER
"   , African ............... NYASSA
"   at Geneva ............... LEMAN
"   Garda day breeze ............ ORA
"   Geneva day breeze ...... REBAT
"   George, fanciful name   HORICON
"   in California .............. TAHOE
"   in Finland ................ ENARA
"   in Panama ............... GATUN
"   in the Sudan ...... CHAD, TSAD
"   in Wales ................. BALA
"   man made ................. MEAD
"   of Hades ............... AVERNUS
"Lake of the Cat" .............. ERIE
lake, outlet of a ................ BAYOU
"   , per. to a ......... LACUSTRAL
"   , shallow ................ LAGOON
"   , small mountain .......... TARN
Lake's mother .................. NAAL
lama, Tibet .......... MONK, PRIEST
lamb ................ EANLING, YEAN
"   , a pet .......... CADE, COSSET
"   , as a symbol ............ AGNUS
"   , bore young ............. EANED
"   , breast of ............... CARRE
"   , bring forth .............. YEAN
"   , grown female ............. EWE
Lamb, Chas., pen name ........ ELIA
lambent .................... GLOWING
lame . BILT, CRIPPLE, HALT, MAIM
lame; Span. .................... COJO
Lamech's wife .................. ADAH
lamella ............... PLATE, SCALE
lament .... HONE, MOAN, PLANGOR,
     REPINE, ELEGIZE, RUE, WEX
lamentation . SIGH, ELEGIAC, GROT,
     TEARS
lamina of gray matter in brain .. OBEX
laminated ...... SPATHIC, TABULAR
laminated rock ...... SHAUL, SHALE,
     FISSILE
laminiplantar ............. CALIGATED
lamp ...... CRUSIE, ETNA, LUCERN,
     LUCIGEN
lamp condensing ring ............ CRIC
lamp, miner's ................... DAVY
lamp, safety ............... GEORDIE
lamp waving in image worship ARATI
lamplighter .................... SPILL
lampoon .... IAMBIC, LIBEL, SATIRE
lampoon, brief ......... SQUIB, SKIT

Lancashire, Eng., section of . ECCLES
Lancaster, Mr. ................. BURT
lance  JAVELIN, SPEAR, DART, CUT
lance head .................... MORNE
lance sergeant ............ CORPORAL
Lancelot's love .............. ELAINE
lancer . UHLAN, HUSSAR, TROOPER
Lanchester, Miss ................ ELSA
lancinate .. STAB, LACERATE, TEAR
lancet, point of .................. NEB
land, a cleared ..... FIELD, ASSART,
                                     ACRE
"  , a close ................. GARTH
"  , barren .................... GALL
"  , border of .............. RAND
"  connection NEK, REACH, NECK
"  , cultivated . ARADO, TILLAGE,
                                 TILTH
"  , ecclesiastical benefice .. GLEBE
"  , equitable division of ...........
                  AGRARIANISM
"  , fallow ...................... LEA
"  grant tenant; Ind. ... ENAMDAR
"  held in fee simple . ALOD, ODAL,
                            UDAL
"  in return for service ...... FEOFF
"  left fallow .............. ARDER
"  , low stream ............. HOLM
"  mark, west U.S. .......... SENAL
"  , meadow .................. LEA
"Land o' Cakes" ......... SCOTLAND
land, per. to ..... GEOPONIC, AGROS
"  piled up ................. CAIRN
"  , plowed ...... ARADA, ARADO
"  , point of low .............. SPIT
"  , prepare, for seed ........ TILL
"  , reverting to state .. ESCHEAT
"  , Scottish ................... ERD
"  , small triangle of ........ GORE
"  , snow covered ..... SAVANNA
"  , strip of; Eng. dial. ....... RAP
"  tenure ............ LEASEHOLD
"  , to ................... DEBARK
"  , tongue of; Ind. ........ DOAB
"  , triangular piece of ..... DELTA
"  valued for taxes .... CADASTRE
landed .......... TITHES, PRAEDIAL
landing place .............. AIRPORT
landlord . HOST, OWNER, BONIFACE
landmark BOUNDARY, COPA, SENAL
Landowska; mus. ............ MANDA
landscape ........ DEPICT, PAYSAGE
land-scurvy ................ PURPURA
landslide .............. EBOULEMENT
landtag ........ DIET, LEGISLATURE
language ........ DIET, LIP, TONGUE
"  , artificial ... ESPARANTO,
        VOLAPUK, IDO, OD, RO
"  , Buddhist .............. PALI
"  , French; slang ..... ARGOT
"  , of 63 down .......... TAAL
"  of the Caucas ......... ANDI
language, ordinary ............ PROSE
"  , Oriental .............. TAI
"  , thieves ............. ARGOT
languages, know all ... PANTOGLOT
languet ............. PROCESS, REED
languish ...... DROOP, WASTE, PINE

languishingly .............. APHONY
languor, .... LASSITUDE, KEF, KIEF
lanner; Eup. ................. FALCQN
lantern light ................. GLIM
lanterns, feast of ................ BON
lanuginose ................... DOWNY
lanyard ...... THONG, WAPP, CORD,
                                 ROPE
Lanza, Mario ................ TENOR
Laodamia, father of ....... ACASTUS
Laomedon, son of ........ TITHONUS
laos, Chinese tribesman .......... YUN
lap-dog ..................... PET, POM
lapel .... REVERS, FACING, REVERE
lapidation, act of  PELTING, STONING
lapin ....................... RABBIT
lapis lazuli ............... SAPPHIRUS
Lapithae, king of the .......... IXION
lappet ....... LOBE, WATTLE, FLAP
lappet on dress .................... PAN
lapse . ERROR, ERR, MISSTEP, SLIP,
                             TARDY
lapwing . PLOVER, HOOPOE, PEWIT,
                             TUIT
lapwing; S. Amer. ........ TREUTERO
larboard ................ ELSE, PORT
larch .................... TAMARACK
larch; genus .................... LARIX
lard and wax ............... CERATES
lard, animal ................. AXUNGE
lard, as in cooking .......... ENARM
lard, rel. to .......... FLARE, FLECK
larder  BUTTERY, PANTRY, SPENCE
large letters of old manuscript UNCIAL
largest fresh water fish ... ARAPAIMA
lariat  NOOSE, LASSO, REATA, ROPE
lark ......... ADVENTURE, PRANK
lark; Can. ................. ALOUETTE
lark-like bird .................... PIPIT
larva, early stage ...... PUPA, REDIA
"  , final stage of .... CHRYSALIS
"  , footless .............. MAGGOT
"  of a beetle ................. GRUB
"  of eye ........................ LOA
"  of horse fly ................. BOT
"  , wingless ............. CREEPER
larve .................. GHOST, MASK
lascar boatswain; E. Ind. .... SERANG
lash ... QUIRT, SMITE, SPLICE, TIE,
           RATE, SCOLD, SCOURGE
lashed ........... FLOGGED, TRICED
lasket ................... LATCH(ING)
lassie; Irish ................ COLLEEN
lasso . LARIAT, CABESTRO, REATA,
           LASH, ROPE, NOOSE
last ..... LOWEST, UTMOST, OMEGA
last, but one ................. PENULT
last, but two .. ANTEPENULTIMATE
"Last Days of Pompeii," char. in IONE
Last of the Goths ......... RODERICK
Last of the Mohicans ......... UNCAS
last person in a contest ........ MELL
"Last Supper," picture of ... CENA(S)
last syllable of a word ....... ULTIMA
latch . SNECK, BELAY, HOOK, LOCK
latchet on a shoe ................. TAP
late . RECENT, TARDY, DEEP, NEW
late at school .................. SERO

153

late; comb. form ............... NEO
later .. POSTERIOR, AFTER, PUISNE
lateral seme ................... RAPHE
laterite ....................... CABOOK
latex of a plant ............... MILK
lathe, kind of .... MONITOR, TURRET
lathe, primitive ................ POLE
lathe, watchmaker's ...... MANDREL
lathe, wood turning .... BLANCHARD
lather ......... FOAM, FROTH, SOAP
Latin ............. ROMANIC, ROMAN
" deities ........................ DI
" goddess ..................... DEA
" historian ............... JUSTIN
" holidays ................ FERIA
" noun case ............. DATIVE
" poet .................. HORACE
" pronoun ...................... TE
" Version of Bible ......... ITALA
latria ................ (HYPER)DULIA
"Latter day Saint" .......... MORMON,
                                IRVINGITE
lattice GRILLE, TRELLIS, CANCELLI
lattice work ............... ESPALIER
lattice-like ............. CLATHRATE
Latvian .......................... LETT
Latvian capital .............. RIGA
Latvian monetary unit ... LATU, LAT
laud .......... SING, EXTOL, PRAISE
laudation .................. PANEGYRIC
laugh ......... CHORTLE, CHUCKLE
laugh in a coarse manner ... DERIDE,
                    FLEER, GUFFAW, ROAR
laughable .. COMIC, DROLL, RISIBLE
laughing ............. MERRY, RIANT
"Laughing Boy" tribesmen . NAVAJOS
laughing stock ............... HYENAS
laughs, one who never .... AGELAST
laughter; Lat. .................. RISUS
laughter, provoking ..... GELOGENIC
launch .... HURL, START, DESCANT,
                        LANCE, BEGIN
laurel ........ BAY, DAPHNE, IVY
laurel bay ............... MAGNOLIA
laurel, fresh water .......... SALMON
laurel; genera ............... KALMIA
laurel; Mex. ................. MADRONA
laurel wreath ................ IRESINE
lava .... AA, ASH, LATITE, TAXITE
" , cinder .................. SCORIA
" field; Mex. .......... PEDREGAL
" , fragment of ......... LAPILLOS
" , round lump of ........... BOMB
" , solidified ............. COULEE
lavaliere .................... PENDANT
lave ............. ABSTERGE, BATHE
lavender, the great; Eur. ....... ASPIC
lavish ...... FREE, PRODIGAL, GIVE,
                    LUSH, FEE, TIP
law CANON, CODE, DROIT, STATUTE
" , a stranger in Hebrew ...... GER
" breaker ........ FELON, SINNER
" , bring a suit .......... IMPLEAD
" , decree ............. NISI, EDICT
" , degree ................... LLB
" , fictitious name in ......... DOE
" for fourth offenders .... BAUMES
" , German ................. SALIC

" , Latin ......... IUS, LEGE, LEX
" , like for like ............ TALION
" , Mosaic ............... TORA(H),
                            PENTATEUCH
" officer of a city ...... POLICETOR
" , opposing ............ ANTINOMY
" , per. to ............... FORENSIC
" , points in .............. LIS, RES
" , points of ................. GONIA
" student ............... STAGIARY
" term TROVER, CONSTAT, IVISI,
                            NISI
law usance ..................... USAGE
" volume ................... CODEX
" , within the ............ ENNOMIC
lawful .. LEGITIMATE, LEGAL, LICIT
lawlessness ..... ANARCHY, LICENSE,
                    MUTINY, VICIOUS, RIOT
lawmaker ...... LEGISLATOR, SOLON
Lawrence, Miss ........... GERTRUDE
laws of Manu .................. SUTRA
lawsuit . ACTION, LITIGATION, CASE,
                            LEGE
lawyer BARRISTER, JURIST, LEGIST
lawyer; Amer. .................. HIRST
lawyer; Span. ............... ABOGADA
lawyers' patron saint ............ IVES
laxative ..... APERIENT, PURGATIVE
lay ....... DITTY, PAVE, PUT, PLACE
lay up .......... HEAP, REST, STORE
layer COAT, STRATA, LAMINA, TIER
layer, to ..................... PROVINE
layers of stone ................. DESS
layman .. LAIC, AMATEUR, GAUCHE
lazar .......... LOATHSOME, LEPER
lazy fellow ..... BUM, DRONE, IDLER,
                            LUSK
"Lazy Susan" .......... TURNTABLE
lea ............ LAY, MEAD, MEADOW
leach ...................... LAXIVIATE
lead, black .. GRAPHITE, PLUMBAGO,
                            WAD
" astray ................. MANG
" glass for gemmaking .... STRASS
" , mock .... BLENDE, PLUMMET
" monoxide ............. LITHARGE
" ore; (sulphide) ......... GALENA
" , quality of ............... BING
" telluride ............... ALTAITE
" , white ................. CERUSE
leader ... ETHNARCH, COCK, CHIEF,
                            DUX
leader; Bib. .................... MOSES
leader, chorus . CANTOR, CORYPHEUS
" of Caledonian boar hunt; ......
                            MELEAGER
" of race or nation ETHNAGOGUE
" of the Argonauts ....... JASON
" of thieves ................. ALI
" , sheep .......... SHEPHERD,
                            BELLWETHER
leading .................. CHIEF, MAIN
leading military unit .............. VAN
leaf bud ........................ GEMMA
" , curvature of a ....... EPINASTY
" disease .................. ERINEA
" , hinged .................... FLAP
" , large .................... FROND
" manna .................... LERP

154

" defense .................... ALIBI
" delay ..................... MORA
" hearing ........ OYER, JURIDIC
" offense ................. DELICT
" plea ..................... ABATER
" possession .............. SEIZIN
" preposition ......... SUR, RE(S)
" process ..... CAVEAT, DETINET
" record .................. ESTREAT
" site ...................... VENUE
" summons ........... SUBPOENA
" warning ............... CAVEAT
" wrong ......... TORT, MALUM
legally competent .............. CAPAX
legend . EDDA, FABLE, TALE, MYTH,
               SAGA, CAPTION
legendary slave woman BAUBO, IAMBE
legendary water sprite ........ UNDINE
leger ... FINE, BOOK, LEDGER, SLAB
legging, furnished with a ... OCREATE
leggings COGGERS, GAMBADE, STRAD
legislative ............. DIET, SENATE
legislative assembly ........... ASSIZE
legislature, both branches BICAMERAL
legitimate .. LAWFUL, LICIT, LEGAL
legume ... POD, BEAN, CASEIN, PEA,
               UVA
legumin from lupines ..... CONGLUTIN
leguminous seeds .. LOMENTS, PULSE
Lehar; composer .............. FRANZ
lehm .............................. LOAM
Lehman was its head .......... UNRRA
Leigh, Miss ................... VIVIEN
leiocome ...................... DEXTRIN
leipoa .............. LOWAN, MALLEE
leister .......................... SPEAR
leisure .. EASE, TIME, OTIOSE, TOOM
leisure; Lat. ..................... OTIUM
Lemkin, Dr.; Pole ............ RAPHAEL
lemniscus ..................... OBELUS
lemon .......................... CITRUS
lemon grass ................. RUSA, SIRI
lemon, product of the .......... CIRRIC
lemon-like fruit .................. LIME
lemur . AYEAYE, MONKEY, SEMIAPE
lemur; Asia ..................... LORIS
lemur, flying ....... COLUGO, GALAGO
lemur, Madagascan .............. INDRI,
               MONGOOSE
lemur, ruffed .. MACACO, MAKI, VARI
lemuroid ........................ POTTO
lene ........ SMOOTH, UNASPIRATED
length; prefix ..................... LONGI
length unit ... DHA, MICRON, PARSEC
lengthy ........... PROLIX, VERBOSE
lenis; Lat. ..................... GENTLE
lenitive ........................... MILD
lens, inflam. of the crystalline ........
               GLENITIS
lens, telo-photic .................. ADON
lens, type of MENISCUS, UNAR, TORIC
Lent ................. QUADRAGESIMA
Lenten season; Fr. ........... CAREME
lenticular .................... PHACOID
lentigo ...................... FRECKLE
lentil meal .............. REVALENTA
l'envoi POSTSCRIPT, STANZA, VERSE
Leoncavallo; opera by ..... PAGLIACCI
leopard ..... OCELOT, PARD, JAGUAR

leopard, hunting ............ CHEETAH
leopard, snow .................. OUNCE
lepadidae; family ......... BARNACLE
lepadidae; genus .............. LEPAS
leper ...... LEPROSY, LAZAR, LEPRA
lepidopter ........................ MOTH
lepidosiren ........................ DOKO
Lepotine Alp .................. LEONE
leprechaun ..... ELF, GOBLIN, PIGMY,
               SPRITE
leprous ...................... UNCLEAN
lepus ............................ HARE
"Les Miserables"; char. in .. FANTINE
less ............ MINOR, FEW, MINUS
lessees, body of ........... TENANTRY
lessen .. ABATE, PALLIATE, MINCE,
               WANE, MINIFY
let . ALLOW, LEASE, PERMIT, RENT
let go ......................... UNHAND
let it be given ................... DETUR
let it stand ...................... STET
let it stand; mus. ................... STA
let up ........................... CEASE
lethargic .... COMA, INERT, TORPID,
               COMATOSE
lethargic sleep ................. SOPOR
lethargy ........ LETHARGY, STUPOR
lethe .... OBLIVION, DEATH, ABYSS
Leto ............................ LATONA
Leto, son of ...... APOLLO, ARTEMIS
letter; law ................... DEMISED
letter, a ...... CHAIN, ELL, ESS, TEE,
               BREVE
" , cross stroke of ........ SERIF
" , cut off last ........ APOCOPE
" , designating stars ...... BETA
" , early Teutonic ........ RUNE
" , English ........... EFF, ZED
" , for letter ........ LITERATIM
" , from the Pope ......... BULL
" initial ...................... FAC
" of challenge .......... CARTEL
" , official ................. BULL
" opener ................ CENSOR
" , short ...... MISSIVE, CHIT,
               CHITTY
lettering, 17 Cen. ................ FAC
letters, illuminate with .... MINIATE
letters, man of .......... LITERATUS
lettuce .... MINION, COS, ROMAINE
lettuce; genus .............. LACTUCA
lettuce, sea .... LAVER, ULVA, ALGA
leucite ......................... LENAD
levant, madder of the ...... ALIZARI
levantine garment .......... CAFTAN
levantine ketch XEBEC, SAIC, SETTEE
levantine valley ................ WADI
levee ........ DIKE, DURBAR, QUAY,
               CHEER
level .. RASE, EVEN, GRADE, RAZE
level; comb. form ............. PLANI
level plot .... PARTERRE, TERRACE
level sandy ridge ............. LANDE
level, to sight along ............. BONE
lever CRANK, TAPPET, PEAVY, BAR,
               PRISE, PRY
lever for crossbow .......... GARROT
lever in lumbering .......... SAMSON

156

leveret .......................... HARE
leviathan .. WHALE, HUGE, TITANIC
levin FLASH, LIGHTEN, LIGHTNING
levin brand ......... THUNDERBOLT
Levi's son ...... GERSHOM, MERARI
levitate ................. FLOAT, RISE
Levite mus. composer ........ ASAPH
levy .... COLLECT, ESTREAT, TAX
Lewis Carroll; char. .. MADHATTER
Lewis' Gantry ................ ELMER
Lewis, Miss .................. MONICA
Lexicographer ............. ONOMASTIC
Leyte capital ............. TACLOBAN
Leyte, town in ................ DULAG
liability OBLIGATION, DEBT, DUTY
liability, halting of ........... CESSER
liable ....... APT, BOUND, SUBJECT
liana .......................... CIPO
liang ................... TAEL, TALE
liar ... CHEAT, FIBBER, ANANIAS,
WERNARD
lias system, exponent of .. JURASSIC
libel ........ LAMPOON, ROORBACK
liberal ECLECTIC, FRANK, AMPLE
liberate .. FREE, REDEEM, RANSOM
Liberian tribe ..................... GI
library .... AGENCY, BIBLIOTHECA
libretto ...... BOOK, TEXT, WORDS
Libyan port ................... DARNA
Libyan queen loved by Zeus .. LAMIA
license ....... RIGHT, APPROBATE,
BANDON, LAXITY
lichen ................... PARELLA
lichen, deriv. of ...... MOSS, LITMUS
lichen used for dyeing .... RATMARA
lichens; genus ... EVERNIA, USNEA
Lichtenstein monetary unit .. RAPPEN
licit .. LAWFUL, LEGAL, DUE, JUST
licorice .......... ABRIN, JEQUIRITY
licorice, seed of .............. GOONCH
lid CAP, CASE, ROOF, BRED, COVER,
TILT
lid-like part ............ OPERCULUM
lie .. LIGE, FIB, MENDACITY, REST
lies face down ............. PRONATE
lieu .................. PLACE, STEAD
life ................. HOURS, VIE, DAYS
life, past middle ........ AUTUMNAL
life; prefix ......................... BIO
life principle ........ ATMAN, PRANA
life, prolonger of ............. ELIXER
life, rel. to ............ BIOTIC, BIOTA
"Life with Father," author ...... DAY
"Life with Mother," family in ... DAY
life, without .................... AZOIC
lifebelt filling ................ KAPOK
lifetime ......... AGE, DAYS, WORLD
lift ....... AID, HELP, PERK, RAISE
lifting muscle .. ERECTOR, LEVATOR
ligament, comb. form ......... DESMO
ligamentum of back of neck . NUCHA
ligan, rel. to ..... FLOTSAM, JETSAM
ligature ................. TAENIA, TIE
lige ........................... FIB, LIE
light .. LUME, FINE, LAMP, LEGER,
SLEAZY, ILLUMINE
"    , a burning .. TORCH, CRESSET
"    , act of making ... LEVITATION

"    anchor, used in warping . KEDGE
"    , beacon ................. FANAL
"    , celestial ........... LUMINARY
"    , circle of ..... AUREOLA, HALO
"    , cloud of ................ NIMBUS
"    , comb. form .............. PHOT
"    dress fabric ....... PARAMATTA
"    , faint ..................... GLIM
"    flux ..................... HEFNER
"    flux, unit of ............. LUMEN
"    handed .................... DEFT
"    headed .............. BEEHEAD
"    image .................. SPECTRA
"    river boat ........... SHALLOP
"    , spirit of; Persia ....... ORMAZD
"    , standard of ............ CARCEL
"    , type of ............... KLIEG
"    unit .................. LUX, RAD
"    , without ............. APHOTIC
lighter ........ SCOW, BARGE, BOAT
"Lighthorse Harry" .............. LEE
lighthouse PHARE, FANAL, PHAROS
lightning ................. LAIT, LEVIN
lightning rod ............. ARRESTER
ligneous ............... WOODY, XYLOID
"lights out" ..................... TAPS
ligulate ............ LORATE, THONG
like ..... SIMILAR, AS, COPY, EQUAL
like a kneecap ............. ROTULAT
like a sealion .............. OTARIINE
like a travesty .............. PRODIC
like, allied ................. COGNATE
like millet seed ............. MILIARY
like; suffix ................. INE, OID
likely ...... COMELY, SEEMLY, APT
likeness ...... EFFIGY, ICON, IMAGE,
GUISE
likewise ..... ALSO, DITTO, EKE, TOO
likewise not ...................... NOR
Lilith's successor .................. EVE
lilliputian ............ MIDGET, TINY
Lilli's husband .................... REX
lily ....... WOKAS, ALOE, IXIA, LIS,
LOTUS
"    , butterfly .... MARIPOSA, SEGO
"    daffodil; genus ...... NARCISSUS
"    encrinite ................ PALEON
lily family; ALOE, BESSERA, CAMAS,
SQUILL
"    , gold banded; Jap ... AURATUM
"    , palm ......................... TI
"    , sand ................ SOAPROOT
"    , shaped like a ....... CRINOID
"    , "The Turk's Cap" .. MARTAGON
"    , water ....... LOTUS, CASTALIA,
NYMPHAEA
"Lily-Maid of Astolat" ...... ELAINE
lily-of-the-valley bud ............. PIP
limacine ............... SLUG, SNAIL
limax ............................. SLUG
limb ......... BRANCH, LEG, BOUGH
limb adapted for swimming NECTOPOD
limb, anthropoid ............. PODIUM
limbec .......... STILL, LIMBECK
limber .............. PLIANT, AGILE
limbo ...... HELL, JAIL, PRISON
limbs, destitute of AMELIA, ACOLOUS
limbs, to fetter ................. GYVE

157

lime .......... CALX, CATCH, LEASH
" bush ...................... SNARE
" , deriv. of .... APATITE, CALCIC
" hound ...................... LYAM
" , per. to ...... CALCIFY, SLACK
" powder ....... CONITE, KONITE
" , thick dark ..... RAUPENLEIM
" tree ....... BASS, LINDEN, TEIL
limen ................... THRESHOLD
limestone, blue or gray . MALM, LIAS
limestone, crystalline ....... MARBLE
limestone, green ............. OOLITE
limestone; Irish ............... CALP
limestone, var. of ..... CAEN, LEITH
lime-wort ............... DIANTHUS
limit .... FIX, BOURN, MERE, SPAN,
TERM, PALE
limit, comb. form ................. ORI
limited ....... FEW, FINITE, LOCAL,
SCANT, TOPICAL
limited to a certain area ..............
TOPOPOLITAN
limn ....... DEPICT, DRAW, PAINT
limp ..... FLABBY, FLACCID, HALT,
FAIL, HOP, SOFT, LAX
limpid .......... CLEAR, PELLUCID
Lincoln, portrayer of ....... MASSEY
Lincoln's Secy of war ...... STANTON
Lind; singer ................. JENNY
linden; genus ....... LIN, TIEL, TILIA
line .... ROUTE, CORD, GRY, TOME,
(A)ROW
" , as a ball of thread ...... CLEW
" for fastening sail ........ EARING
" , hair . LEGER, CERIPH, SERIF
" , human ................... CUE
" in trigonometry . SECANT, SINE
" joining barometric points ISOBAR
" not meeting curve . ASYMPLOTE
" of color .................. STREAK
" of junction ................ SEAM
" of no magnetic declination AGONIC
" of similar temp. ...... ISOTHERE
" of soldiers ...... CORDON, FILE,
RANK
" that cuts a curve ...... SECANT
" the inside ................... CEIL
" , the root of a ............. CEIL
" with bricks .............. REVET
lineage BLOOD, LINE, RACE, STOCK,
STRAIN, KINDRED, TRENE
lineament ......... FEATURE, MARK,
OUTLINE
linen ..... GULIX, BARRAS, CRASH,
DOWLAS, LINGERIE
" cloth; Span. ............... CREA
" coarse ................ LOCKRAM
" fabric .................... SCRIM
" , fine ...... CAMBRIC, DAMASK,
LAWN
" for window shades ... HOLLAND
" , officer in charge of . NAPERER
" room .................... EWERY
" , sail ..................... DUCK
" , scraped ...... LANGATE, LINT
" tape ...................... INKLE
" , table ................. NAPERY
" vestment ... ALB, AMICE, AMIT

" weaver; Bib. ................ HURI
liner ..................... SHIP, SHIM
lines, winding ............. MEANDER
ling ...... BURBOT, HEATHER
linger DELAY, DWELL, HOVER, LAG,
LENG
lingo ..... CANT, JARGON, DATTER,
PATOIS
lingua; Lat. ................. TONGUE
linguae of some insects .... GLOSSAE
linguist .................. POLYGLOT,
CLASSICIST
link .... NEXUS, RIK, TORCH, YOKE
linking ................. ANNECTENT
links, connect in series .. CATENATE
lint .. TENT, FLAX, FLUFF, HEMP,
NAP
lion; Lat. ........................ LEO
lion, mountain ...... PUMA, COUGAR
lion, rel. to ................... GRIFFIN
lion whelp ...................... LIONET
lion-headed consort of Ra ........ MUT
lip in a casting ladle .......... GEAT
lip, or edge ................. LABRUM
lip ornament ...... PELELE, LABRET
lip, swollen ............... BLOBBER
lip, tumid upper ............. CHILOMA
lip, under .......................... JIB
lip-formed .......... EDGED, LABIAL
lipide ............ CERIDE, STERIDE
lipoma ...................... TUMOR
lipped, rel. to ............... HARLED
lips ........................... GAM
lips, combo. form ............. LABIO
liquefied by heat .............. FUSILE
liquefy ........ FUSE, MELT, THAW
liqueur MARC, RATAFIA, CURACAO,
COGNAC
liqueur, add flavoring to ........ TUN
liqueur, aromatic ........ ABSINTHE
liqueur, of anise and caraway seeds ..
KUMMEL
liquid, clear ...... ACETONE, ALDOL
" fatty oil . ELAIN, FURFURAL,
OLEIN
" , having no .......... ANEROID
" , light colorless .. TRIDECANE
" , thick .. DOPE, GRAITH, TAR
" , weak .................. BLASH
liquidate ................... AMORTIZE
liquor .. RUM, RYE, TIPPLE, ELIXIR
" bottle case ......... CELLARET
" from must ............. ARROPE
" , fruit .......... RATAFIA, GIN
" , intoxicating .... LUSH, TAPE
" , malt ............ STOUT, ALE
" , oriental ............. ARRACK
" rice ...................... SAKE
" taken to remove taste of coffee
CHASSE
liripipe .............. SCARF, TIPPET
lissom .... LITHE, LIMBER, SUPPLE,
AGILE
list ....... NAME, HEEL, CANT, TIP,
CAREEN
" , as a council ...... ROTA
" of candidates ...... LEET, SLATE
" of officers ................ ROSTER

" , writing .................... SCRIP
listen .... EAVESDROP, HARK, EAR,
LEST
listening ..................... AUDIENT
listening post ................ ECOUTE
listing .. EDGE, SELVAGE, STRIPS
listlessness .. ACEDIA, ENNUI, ENUF
lists .. ARENA, RECORDS, PLEASE,
ROLL
Liszt; pianist ................... FRANZ
lit ........ DYESTUFF, DYE, STAIN
litany ........... EKTENE, ORISON,
ROGATION, COLLECT
life; dial. Eng. .................. FEW
literary . LETTERED, VERSED, BLUE
"      criticism .......... EPICRISIS
"      effort ........ LUCUBRATION
"      fragments .. ANA, ANALECTA
"      hack ..................... GRUB
"      laws ..................... BLUE
"      productions ............ OPERA
"      style .... PEDANTIC, PROSE
"      style, affectation in .. PURISM
lithe AGILE, SLIM, LISSOME, BAIN,
SVELTE
Lithuania, capital of ......... KAUNAS,
KOVNO
Lithuanian .... AESTII, BALT, LETT
Lithuanian coin .......... LITAS, LIT
Lithuanian seaport .......... MEMEL
litter ........ BIER, CABIN, COFFIN,
DOOLEE, JUMBLE, MESS
litter of pigs ........ FAR, FARROW
litter, to ............ STREW, MULCH
little PUNY, TINY, WEE, DARLING
little by little ........ LITLUM, POCO
little flag .............. BANDEROLE
"Little Henry" ................... HAL
little ring ................... ANNULET
little toe .................... MINIMUS
littoral .............. REGION, SHORE
lituate ....................... FORKED
litura ........................... BLUR
liturgy ... CONSUETUDINARY, RITE,
RITUAL
livaite ....................... YENITE
live .... LEEVE, BREATHE, DWELL,
EXIST
live by shift and stratagem .... SHARK
live by sponging CADGE, SYCOPHANT
live through ................... TRADE
liveliness ..... ACTIVITY, VIVACITY,
LILT, BRISK, RAPID
lively SPRY, AGILE, GAY, GRIG, VIF,
CADENCE, SWING, YARE, TITTUPY
lively air ...................... LILT
lively; mus. ................. ANIMATO
liven ............... CHEER, ROUSE
liver, disease of the ...... CIRRHOSIS
liver, per. to the HEPATIC, VISCERA
liverwort ...... AGRIMONY, HEPATICA
liverwort lettuce ............ PYROLA
liverworts; genus ............ RICCIA
living BEING, LIFE, QUICK, EXTANT
"      again .............. REDIVIVUS
"      , capable of ........... VIABLE
"      , characterized by independence;
BION

"      dead ..................... ZOMBI
"      , ecclesiastical ...... BENEFICE
living in currents .............. LOTIC
"      in deep sea ...... BATHYBIC
"      in seclusion ...... EREMITISM
"      in tents .............. SCENITE
Livistona palm .................. FAN
lixiviate ......... ALKALI, LEACH
lixivium ........................ LYE
liza ......................... MULLET
lizard ...... NEWT, EFT, MONITOR,
SAURIAN, MOLOCH, SALAMANDER
"      , beaded .................. GILA
"      , climbing; Cen. Am. . IGUANA
"      , Egyptian .............. ADDA
"      , fabulous winged .... DRAGON
"      , insectivorous .. CHAMELEON
"      , kind of ANOLI, NERT, URAN
"      ; Mex.; genus ....... BASILISK
"      , monitor ...... URAN, VARAN
"      , Old World; genus .... AGAMA
"      , Philippine .............. IBID
"      , sand .......... ADDA, SKINK
"      , serpent ................. SEPS
"      , spiny ................... DABB
"      , stellion .............. HARDIM
"      , veranoid ............ WARAN
"      , wall ...... TARENTE, GECKO
lizards; genus .......... AGAMA, UTA
llama, domestic . ALPACA, KECHUA
llama, wild ..... GUANACO, VICUNA
llano .......................... PLAIN
lo ............. ECCE, SEE, BEHOLD
loach; genus ................ COBITIS
load FREIGHT, DOPE, CARK, ONUS,
JAG, CARGO, ONERATE
load, to ..................... ONERATE
loader of vessels ...... STEVEDORE
loads .. INCUBUS, LADES, CHARGES
loaf ................... IDLE, LOUNGE
loam, calcareous .............. LOESS
loam, constituent of .. CHALK, CLAY,
SOIL, LIME
loam, Indiana black .......... REGUR
loan-in .......................... LANE
loath ........... AVERSE, HOSTILE
loathe ...... ABHOR, DETEST, HATE
loathsome .... CLOYING, FOUL, VILE
lob ............. COP, BOX, LOP, TILL
lobby .. TRANCE, CORRIDOR, HALL
lobe of the wing, posterior .. ALULAR
lobes .......................... TESTES
loblolly .......................... PINE
lobster claw ........ NIPPER, CHELA
"      eggs .............. CORAL, ROE
"      floating trap ...... POT, CORF,
CREEL
"      , last somite of ...... TELSON
"      , part of a .......... THORAX
"      , rel. to; .. BARNACLE, CRAB,
SHRIMP
"      , small .......... JOE, PAWK
local EDAPHIC, EPICHORIC, SQUAT
local court .................... GEMOT
local irritant ................. ARNICA
locale ...... IDIOM, SCENE, VENUE
locality AREA, PLACE, SITUS, SPOT
locality, particular ........ ENDEMIC

159

loch LINCTURE, LIN, LAKE, NESS, POND
lock .... HASP, DETENT, COTTER, STECKLE
lock of hair ... BERGER, CURL, DAG, TRESS
locker for bow and arrow .. ASCHAM
lockjaw ........ TETANUS, TRISMUS
lock-stepper; slang ......... CONVICT
lock-up; slang CALABOOSE, LIMBO, JUG
locks-man ................... WARDEN
locomotive cow catcher ....... PILOT
locomotive, heavy ............ MOGUL
Locrine's daughter ......... SABRINA
locus ......... AREA, AXODE, RANK
locust ...... WETA, CICADA, CICALA
locust creak ............. STRIDULATE
locust tree ........... ACACIA, CAROB
locust tree; Am. .. CLAMMY, HONEY
locust-like insect ............ MANTIS
lode, mining .................... VUG
lodge, enter surreptitiously .. COWAN
lodges .. ROOMS, STOWS, ENCAMPS, HARBORS, ROOSTS
lodging cars ................ DOLLIES
lodging place; Fr. ............. GITE
lofty ... AERIE, ANDEAN, EMINENT, EYRY, ALPINE, TALL
log measure ................ SCALAGE
log, split ................. PUNCHEON
logarithm inventor ............ NAPIER
logarithmic unit ................. BEL
logger's felt boots .............. PACS
logging, evade work in .......... SNIB
logging rock, a ............... LOGGAN
logging sled ........ TODE, TRAVOIS
logging wheels, a pair of .. KATYDID
logic, a premise of IDOLUM, LEMMA
logic, Aristotelian .......... FORMAL, ORGANON
logic, Baconian .......... INDUCTIVE
logic, fallacy in ............ ODOLUM
logic, to affirm in ............ PONENT
logical outcome ................. END
logion .............. MAXIM, SAYING
logograph ...... ANAGRAM, RIDDLE
log roller ..................... DECKER
logs, implement for skidding .... TODE
logs, men who nose ........ SNIPERS
logs, revolve floating ............ BIRL
loin cloth ...................... MARO
loin of mutton ........ CHUMP, RACK
loins ........................... REINS
Loire, city on ............... ORLEANS
Loire (river), old name ........ LIGER
Loire tributary ................ INDRE
loiterer .............. LAGGER, IDLER
Loki, daughter of ........ HEL, HELA
Loki, son of .................... NARE
Loki, wife of ................. SIGYN
lomboy; Java ................... PLUM
lomilomi; Hawai. ...... PRESS, RUB
London, anc. Rom. name .... AGUSTA
London art gallery ............. TATE
London Club ................. KITCAT
London hawker ........ COSTER, MUN
London prison ............ NEWGATE

London suburb .............. EALING
London subway ................. TUBE
London, West End .............. SOHO
Londoner ................... COCKNEY
Lone Ranger's companion .... TONTO
"Lone Star" state ............ TEXAS
lonely .. DESOLATE, DREARY, LORN
long ........ HONE, WORDY, YEARN, PROLIX
" decorative scarf ............ SARI
" discourse .............. DESCANT
" fagot .................... ESCINE
" flexible shoot ............ RIMER
" for .... HANKER, PINE, CRAVE
" jump; Gr. ................. HALMO
" legged bird ................ STILT
long legged bug .............. EMESA
" life ................. LONGEVITY
" limbed .................. RANGY
" since ........................ YORE
" spear ....................... LANCE
" story .............. RIGMAROLE
" tailed monkey ............. KAHA
longing; slang ..................... YEN
longshoreman DOCKER, STEVEDORE, STOWER
loo .................................. PAM
look .. BODE, CON, KEN, PORE, PRY
look obliquely ................... SKEW
look pryingly .... PEEK, KEEK, PEEP
look slyly ...... GLANCE, GLY, LEER, OGLE
look steadily ............. GAZE, SCAN
looked for ................... SOUGHT
lookout on ship .............. CONNER
loom .. APPEAR, SEEM, AIR, MIEN
loom bar ....................... EASER
loom harness ................... LEAF
loom, heddles of a ............ CAAM
loom, lower level of a ............ LAM
loom reed ....................... SLEY
loon ........ DIVER, GREBE, WABBY
loop .... TAB, ANSA, BRIDE, TERRY
loop in lace .................... PICOT
loop in lariat ................. HONDOO
loop of a rope ................. BIGHT
loop of steel; Ind. .... OOLLY, WOOTZ
loop, running ................. NOOSE
loophole ...... MEUSE, PLEA, OILET
loose ends DAGS, TAGRAGS, SLACK
loose jointed ................. LANKY
loose robe for women ...... PEIGNOIR, SIMAR
loose woolen shirt; Ind. ...... BANIAN
loosen ................ PRIED, RELAX
loot ...... PLUNDER, SACK, SPOILS
lop off ........... SNIP, OCHE, SNED
loquacious, be ................ PRATE
loquacity .... GARRULITY, LERESIS
lord GRANLEE, LIEGE, PEER, EARL
lord of a sanjak ................... BEY
lord, wife of a .................. LADY
Lord's Prayer, The .. PATERNOSTER
lordly ........... DESPOTIC, UPPISH
lore .... WISDOM, ERUDITION, LEAR
Lorelei ........................ SIREN
loris ........................... LEMUR
lorlea .......... CORSELET, CUIRASS

Lortzing; opera by .......... UNDINE
lose LEESE, MISS, FORFEIT, AMIT,
 SPILL, ESTRANGE
loss ............ FORFEITURE, LEAK
loss of eyelashes ........ MADAROSIS
loss of feeling ........ ANAESTHESIA
 " of hair ................ ALOPECIA
 " of memory ............ AMNESIA
 " of reason .............. AMENTIA
 " of sense of smell ...... ANOSMIA
 " of speech ...... APHASIA, MUTE,
 ALALIA
 " of voice ................ APHONIA
 " of will power ............ ABULIA
lost .. MISLAID, GONE, LORN, ASEA
lost color ............ FADED, PALED
lot .... SCAD, SHARE, DOOM, FATE,
 MUCH
Lot, father of ................ HARAN
Lot's sister .................. MILCAH
lotica ........................... LUTE
lots, divination by ...... SORTILEGE
lottery . CHANCE, PRIZES, RAFFLE,
 TERN, BINGO
lotus ...... CHINQUAPIN, NELUMBO
lotus tree ............ JUJUBE, SADR
loudmouthed .......... THERSITICAL
Louis Viaud, pen name .......... LOTI
Louise de la Rame, pen name . OUIDA
Louisiana .................. PELICAN
Louisiana acc't book .......... BILAN
louse, immature .......... NIT, APHID
lout ...... BEND, BOW, GAWK, HIT,
 LOOBY, LURK
love .... WOO, AMO, AGRE, FANCY,
 GRA
 " affair .................... AMOUR
 " feast, early Christian .... AGAPE
 " , full of .......... EROTIC, DOTE,
 AMATIVE
 " ; Gr. ...................... MINNE
 " , god of ........ AMOR, BHAGA,
 CUPID, EROS, KAMA
 " , goddess of ... ATHOR, FREYA,
 VENUS
 " knot .................... AMORET
 " of fine arts ................ VIRTU
 " , parental ................ STORGE
 " potion .................. PHILTER
love-bird .................... PARROT
lover ....... BEAU, MINION, ROMEO
Lovers' Leap promontory; Gr. LUCATE
"Lovelace," heroine of ..... LUCASTA
"Love's Labor Lost"; clown COSTARD
loving ......... AMOROUS, AMATIVE,
 EROTIC, ARDENT, FOND
loving, comb. form ............. PHILE
loving cup, kind of ................ TIG
low ...... SNEAKY, BAS, MOO, ORRA
low dividing wall in Roman circus .....
 SPINA
Iowan ............ LEIPOA, MALLEE
lower ... DIP, DIM, DEMIT, RESIGN,
 NETHER, DEMOTE
lower, as the topsail ............ VAIL
lowest class of animal life .... MOEBA
lowest point .. NADIR, NETHERMOST

lowest point in a planet's orbit ........
 PERIGEE
lowest ranked peer ........... BARON
lowland .... HILM, SPIT, MOLEHILL
low-lived .............. BASE, MEAN
loxia ...................... WRYNECK
loyal ........ LEAL, STANCH, TRUE,
 LIEGE
loyalty ......... FIDELITY, FEALTY,
 HOMAGE
lozenge ......... PASTILLE, TROCHE
lubber ........ BOOR, CHURL, GAWK
lubricator ............ OILER, DOPER
Lucco, saint of ............ ANSELMO
lucerne ......... FODDER, ALFALFA
lucid ........ BRIGHT, SANE, CLEAR,
 VIVID
lucidity ........... SANITY, CLARITY
lucifer ...... LEVIL, MATCH, SATAN,
 VENUS
luck .. SWASTIKA, FORTUITY, HAP
luck, bad ........ ACE, CESS, DEUCE
lucky ................ CANNY, WITCH
lucky-stone ............ ALECTORIAN
lucrative .............. FAT, PAYING
lucre . PELF, EMOLUMENT, PROFIT
ludicrous ......... JESTING, RISIBLE
Ludolphian number ................ PI
lull HUSH, STILL, ROCK, MITIGATE
lug .................... EAR, LOOP
lug, to ... PULL, TUG, HALE, HAUL,
 TOTE, DRAG
lugs .............. CONCEITED, AIRS
lug-worm ............ ANNELID, LOB
luke-warm, to make ......... TEPIFY
lumberman tree marker ..... SCORER
lumberman's shoe .... LARIGAN, PAC
lumberman's sled . WYNN, TRAVOIS
luminary ..... RADIANT, STAR, SUN
luminous impression ... PHOSPHENE
lummox ....... BOOR, LOUT, YAHOO
lump ... CLOT, MASS, LOB, NODULE
lump of clay ............. CLOD, CLAG
lumpish ...... DULL, STOLID, INERT
lumpy jaw ......... ACTINOMYCOSIS
lunacy ... MADNESS, MANIA, MOON
lunatic asylum ........ BETHLEHEM
lunch room ............ CAFE, DINER
luncheon ....... NUNCHEON, TIFFIN
lung ailment ............ CHALICOSIS
lung sound .......... RATTLE, RALE
lungs .............. LIGHTS, POMON
Lupino, Miss ..................... IDA
lurch ..... ROLL, SWAG, BILK, JOLT,
 CAREEN
lure ....... BAIT, DECOY, ATTRACT
lurer ............... ENTICER, SIREN
lurid ............... RED, DIM, DARK
lurk ...... SKULK, SNEAK, LATENT
lush .... DRINK, JUICY, SUCCULENT
luster ........ NAIF, GLASS, SHEEN,
 GLORY
luster, bronze-like ........ SCHILLER
lusterless ................. DULL, MAT
lustrous .. BRIGHT, NITID, ORIENT,
 RISING, SILKY
lustrous, naturally ...... NAIF, NITID
lusty .............. ROBUST, STURDY

161

lute ........... CEMENT, CLAY, TAR
lute; mus. ....... ASOR, PANDORE,
THEORBO, GUITAR, UKULELE
lutjanoid fish .................... SESI
luxuriant RANK, FERTILE, UBERTY
luxury, lover of ............ SYBARITE
Luzon hardwood .............. NARRA
Luzon mountain ........... PAGSAN
Luzon native . ITANEGA, TINGUIANE
Luzon negrito ........... AETA, ATTA
Luzon, people of . TAGALAS, ABACAS
Luzon savage ATA, IGOROT, IGALOT
luzonite; var. of .......... ENARGITE
Lyaeus .......................... WINE
lyam; her. ..................... LEASH
lyard ........................... GRAY
Lydia, anc. capital ........... SARDIS
Lydian ................. EFFEMINATE
Lydian, a ................. BASANITE
Lydian king ....... CROESUS, GYGES
lye ................. LIXIVIUM, BUCK
lying .......... DECUMBENT, FALSE
lying hid .............. DELITESCENT
lying prone ....... PASSIVE, SUPINE
lying talker, a ................. FUDGE
lymph ............. CASEIN, SERUM
lymphatic ....... PLASMIC, AQUATIC
lynx ... CARACAL, LOSSE, LUCERN
lynx-eyed .................... OXYOPIA
lynxlike .................... WILDCAT
lyre ........... ASOR, HARP, SHELL
lyre-bird .................... MENURA
lyre or harp ................. TRIGON
lyrelike instrument ........ CITHARA,
SACKBUT
lyre-shaped ................. LYRATE
lyric ode ...................... EPODE
lyric poem .................... MELIC
lyric poem of 13 lines ..... RONDEAU
lyric poet .................... ODIST
Lytton; novelist .............. BULWER
Lytell; actor .................. BERT

# M

M, letter ......................... EM
mabolo; Phil. Is. .................. PLUM
macabre ..... GHASTLY, GRIM, LURID
macaco ............ LEMUR, MONKEY
Macao, coin of ..................... AVO
MacArthur .................... ARTHUR
macaque ............... KRA, RHESUS
Macaulay; novelist .............. ROSE
macaw ... ARARAUNA, ARA, ARARA,
MARACAN
macaws, per. to ................ ARINE
mace .. GAVEL, CROC, STAFF, STICK
mace bearer ........ BEADLE, MACER
mace of a nutmeg .............. ARIL
mace, reed ....................... DOD
mace, royal .................. SCEPTRE
Macedonia, city in .............. BEREA
macerate ......... RET, SOAK, STEEP
Machen; novelist: Brit. ....... ARTHUR
machete ................. KNIFE, BOLO
Machiavellian ...... DECEIT, CRAFTY

machinate ... PLOT, CABAL, SCHEME
machination ....... DESIGN, SCHEME
machine ...... AUTOMATON, SYSTEM
"    for glazing ........ CALENDER
"    for maturing cloth ....... AGER
"    for separating ore .... VANNER
"    for shaping objects by pressure
EXTRUDER
"    for softening clay MALAXATOR
"    gun; . GATLING, HOTCHKISS,
MAXIM
"    gun party, hidden ....... NEST
"    , pile driving .............. GIN
"    , political ............. SYSTEM
macilent ..... LEAN, THIN, MARCOR
Mackenzie, Miss ............... GISELE
mackerel, chub ............... TINKER
mackerel; genus ............ SCOMBER
mackerel, horse .... JUREL, SAUREL,
TUNNY
mackerel, large .......... CERO, PETO
mackerel net ................. SPILLER
mackerel; Sp. .................. SIERRA
mackerel, young ............... SPIKE
mackerel-like ......... SCAD, BONITO
mackle ............... BLUR, MACULE
macula ............. BLOTCH, SPOT
mad MANIACAL, FRENETIC, INSANE,
WILD, RABID
"Mad Anthony" ............... WAYNE
Madagascar fiber palm ....... RAFFIA
"    , insect of ............ TENREC
"    lemur ................... INDRIS
"    mammal .... TENREC, TEMEE
"    , tribe of ........ BARA, HOVA,
MALAGASY
madam ...... HUSSY, SENORA, FRAU
Madam Chiang's maiden name SOONG
Madam Gynt .................... ASE
Madame Butterfly ..... CHOCHO(SAN)
madcap .... BLOOD, HOTSPUR, RASH
madden ... INCENSE, CRAZE, VEX
madder family, natural name .... AAL
madder; genus ............... RUBIA
madder, Indian ........... AAL, AL
madder root pigment, inferior ... MULL
made public .... DELATED, ACCUSED
Madeira Is., dry wind of ....... LESTE
Madeira wine ................. TINTA
mad-house ... BEDLAM, CHAOS, ROW
madness IRE, WEDE, FRENZY, RAGE
Madras, town in ................ ADONI
Madras weight .............. POLLAM
madre pore .................... CORAL
Madrid, public park ............ PRADO
madrigal GLEE, POEM, ODE, VERSES
Mae West .................... LIFEBELT
magazine ..... EPHEMERIS, TABLOID
magazine messenger ........ PACOLET
magazine rifle ................ MAUSER
—— majesty .................... LESE
maggot .... GENTLE, GRUB, MATHE,
MAWK
Magi, the .... BALTHASAR, CASPAR,
MELCHIOR
magic ..... ART, FAIRY, RUNE, SHOW
"    , act of ......... CONJURATION
"    cube ...................... NASIK
"    ejaculation .................. OM

162

"    , goddess of ............. CIRCE
"    lant. color. glass ........ TINTER
"    seals ................... SIGILLA
"    symbol ... PENTACLE, CARACT
"    wand; Gr. myth. .... CADUCEUS
"    white ...... THEURGY, TURGY
magical ........ CHARMING, GOETIC
magician ... MAGE, THAUMATURGE,
                    WIZARD, SORCERER
magician, a great ....... ARCHIMAGE,
                    MANDRAKE, MERLIN
magician's assistant ........ FAMULUS
magistrate ........ EPHOR, ALCALDE,
                    BAILIE, SYNDIC, PUISNE
magistrate, chief ...... DOGE, JUDGE
magistrate of anc. Athens ... ARCHON
Maglie, Mr. ....................... SAL
Magnani; Ital. actress ........... ANNA
magnate .... BARON, LORD, BIGWIG
magnate, Pasha ............. BASHAW
magnesium fluorid ......... SELLAITE
magnesium silicate ............. TALC
magnesium sulphate ........ ESOMITE,
                    LOWEITE
magnesium, symbol for ........... MG
magnet .. LOADSTONE, LODESTONE
magnet, electro ............. SOLENOID
magnet, per. to a ... ARMATURE, RED
magnet, type of ................... BAR
magnetized steel sphere .... TERELLA
magnets .................. STYLENOIDS
magnific ..................... POMPOUS
magnolia; Chin. ................. YULAN
magnum opus .................. WORK
magpie MADGE, PICA, PIET, TALKER,
                    PIANET
magpie diver ..................... SMEW
magpie shrike ............. TANAGER
Magyar ................. HUNGARIAN
mahogany ........ RATTEEN, RATON
mahogany; Ind. ...... TOON, TOTARA
mahogany, streak in ............. ROE
Mahomet, Old Eng. form ....... MACON
Mahomet; (see 'Mohammed')
Mahomet's tomb, location ... MEDINA
Mahomet's uncle .............. ABBAS
maid, a lady's ............... ABIGAIL
"Maid of Athens" ............. MACRI
maiden changed into a heifer ...... IO
maiden turned into a spider ARACHNE
mail .. DAK, DAWK, POST, CONSIGN
mail boat ..................... PACKET
mail, coat of ........ ARMOR, BRINIE,
                    HAUBERK
maiming of body .. MAYHEM, MAIHEM
main .... SEA, CHIEF, OCEAN, PRIME
main action of a drama .... EPITASIS
main beam ................. WALKING
main point ................. GIST, JET
Maine, city in ........ SACO, BANGOR
Maine, promontory in .......... KINEO
Maine's symbol .................. PINE
Maine university town ......... ORONO
maintainable ................ TENABLE
maintenance ..... ALIMONY, UPKEEP
maize; genus .................... ZEA
maize, Indian .................... CORN
maize; S. Afr. ............... MEALIES
majagua, a .................. GUANA

major domo SENESCHAL, STEWARD
major; mus. ........... DUR, DITONES
majorana; Mex. ............ LANTANA
majority ..... AGE, MOST, SENIORITY
make choice; rare ................ OPT
"    colored ware .......... SPATTLE
"    famous ................ ETERNIZE
"    ill ......................... AIL
"    level .............. EVEN, TRUE
"    over ..... ALIENATE, REVAMP,
                    REDO
"    public ..... AIR, BRUIT, NOISE,
                    DELATE
"    resistance .. MUTINY, REVOLT,
                    REBEL
"    smooth .......... SLEEK, SLICK
make-believe .... FEINT, PRETENSE,
                    SHAM
makeshift ................... STOPGAP
makes calm ................ SERENES
makes even ................ SQUARES
makes fast ................. BELAYS
makes fun of ..................... RIBS
makes pretentious ......... BUCKRAM
makua ............................ KUA
malachite green .................. BICE
malady, nerve .. MORB, PESTILENCE,
                    AMOK
malapert ................. BOLD, SAUCY
malaria ...... MIASMA, ANOPHELES,
                    MIASM
Malay, Christianized ... AGUE, ABACA,
                    MORO, ILOKANO
"    coin ........... TAMPANG, TRA
"    convulsive tic ............ LATA
"    crane ................... SALUS
"    dagger ......... CREESE, KRIS
"    dress ................... SARONG
"    feather palm ............ ARENG
"    fiber tree .............. TERAP
"    gibbon ..................... LAR
"    Island .................. BORNEO
"    jacket ..................... BAJU
"    knife ..................... KRISS
"    law ...................... ADAT
"    malady, to kill ........... AMOK
"    measure ................... PAU
"    negrito ............. ATA, ATTA
"    neuralgia ................. LATA
"    of Luzon ............ ITALONE
"    race, one of . TAGAL, VISAYAN
"    sea coast town ....... MALACCA
"    state ...... KEDAH, PERAK
"    title of respect .......... TUAN
"    tree of the mallow order .........
                    DURIAN
"    tribe ............ ARIPAS, ATA
Malay Is. tree ..................... UPAS
Malay; 'sir' in .................... TUAN
Malayan wild ox ........... BANTENG
malcontent .. FENIAN, REB, UNEASY
male ........ STAMINAL, HE, MANLY,
                    VIRILE
male being with 100 eyes ........ ARGUS
male bird ..................... TOM
male figure supporting column .........
                    TELAMON
male, gelded ..................... GALT
male plant ...................... MAS

163

malediction .... ANATHEMA, CURSE, BAN, THREAT, MALISON
malefactor ........ CRIMINAL, FELON
malevolent ENVIOUS, EVIL, HATING, GRUDGE, SPITE, ILL
malice ....... ENVY, RANCOR, SPITE
malign .. DEFAME, VILIFY, ASPERSE
malign creatures ........... HARPIES
malignant ILL, EVIL, FALON, VICIOUS
malignity ......... VENOM, VIOLENCE
malison ........... CURSE, TORMENT
malkin .. SLATTERN, DOWDY, DRAB
mallard; genus ..................... ANAS
malleable iron proc. ............. MITIS
mallee bird ........... LEIPO, LOWAN
mallet, a kind of .. TUP, MACE, MAUL
"  , hatter's .............. BEATER
"  , leaden ................. MADGE
"  , presiding officer's ..... GAVEL
"  , wooden ................ BEETLE
mallow .. SIDA, ALTEA, HOCK, MAW
malmsey ............. MADEIRA, WINE
malodorous ..................... FETID
malt froth ....................... BARM
malt infusion ................... WORT
malt mixture ... MALTATE, ZYTHUM
malt, tasting of ................. CORNY
malt vinegar ......... ALEGAR, WORT
maltese ................. CROSS, GRAY
malty ............................ ALISH
mameluke ...................... SLAVE
Mamie's town ...... BOONE, DENVER
mammal ....... RHYTHM, APE, MAN, BEAR, ECHIDNA, PRIMATE, LORI
"  , aquatic ........... DUGONG, MANATEE
"  , Australian ..... KANGAROO
"  , carnivorous ........ PANDA
"  , cat-like ........ MONGOOSE, OCELOT
"  , cetacean DOLPHIN, WHALE
"  , class name, deriv. of; Lat. ... TEAT
"  , flight .................. BAT
"  , gnawing ...... MOUSE, RAT
"  , Indian ...... OUNCE, ZEBU
"  , insectivorous ........ BAT
"  , lower order of . MARSUPIAL
"  , marine, large ...... SHARK, WALRUS
"  , marsupial; Am. .. OPOSSUM
"  , nocturnal .. LEMUR, RATEL
"  of Palestine .......... DAMAN
"  of swine family .... PECORA, PECCARY
"  , order of marine . CETACEA, CETE
"  , So. Amer. ...... TAYRA, AI, COATI, TAPIR
mammals, gnawing order of RODENTIA
mammock SCRAP, FRAGMENT, HILL
man . FORTIFY, PERSON, SOMEONE, VIR, WER
"  , a brazen ................. TALOS
"  bound to single life ... CELIBATE
"  , elderly ... SIRE, AGED, SENILE
"  , Iron .................... TALUS
"  , Latin for ................ HOMO
man, newly married ....... BENEDICT

"  of all work ........... FACTOTUM
"  of letters .. LITERATUS, SAVANT
"Man of Ross" ................. KYRLE
man, sea ..... MERMAN, SAILOR, TAR
"Man Without a Country," author ..... HALE
man-like ..................... ANDROID
manage TEND, DIGHT, MAN, WIELD
manageable ........... DOCILE, YARE
managed ........................... RAN
management .... GESTION, CONDUCT
manager ......... DIRECTOR, GRIEVE, OPERATOR
manager of business ........ GERENT, ENTREPRENEUR
manakin .... DWARF, MODEL, PIPRA
manana; Span. ........... TOMORROW
manas ..................... EGO, MIND
manciple ......... SLAVE, STEWARD
mandarin's residence ......... YAMEN
mandate ... EDICT, ORDER, BEHEST
mandatory DIRECTORY, PRECEPTIVE
mandible ....... BEAK, JAW, CHOPS
mandrake ..... MANDRAGORA, POPPY
mandrel .... ARBOR, LATHE, BOBBIN
mandrel, miner's ................. PICK
mandrill ....................... BABOON
manducate ...................... CHEW
mane .. JUBA, ROACH, BRUSH, SHAG
maneuver .. ARTIFICE, RUSE, TRICK
mange ...... ......... FODDER, ITCH
mange, cause of ....... ACARID, MITE
mange, sheep ...................... SCAB
manger .. BIN, CRIB, BUNKER, RACK
mangle .... MAGG, MAR, CALENDER
mango ........................... BAUNO
mango bird; Ind. .............. ORIOLE
mango fruit ............ AMINI, DRUPE
mango grove ...................... TOPE
mangrove; Ind. ................ GORAN
mangrove pole; E. Afr. ....... BORITY
mangy ..... RONION, SCURVY, MEAN
maniacal ............ DEMONIAC, MAD
manifest .... OPEN, OVERT, PATENT, LIST, PUBLIC
manifest one's self ... SHOW, VISIBLE
manifestation; eccl. ........... AVATAR
manifested ... TOKENED, DISCLOSED
manifesto ......... EDICT, RESCRIPT
manikin PHANTOM, DWARF, MODEL
Manila airfield .................. CLARK
Manila bayboat .............. BILALO
Manila Bay hero .............. DEWEY
maniple ............. FANON, ORALE
manipulate ......... HANDLE, RIG, USE
mankind .. HUMANITY, ADAM, FOLK
manna ........... LAAP, LERP, FOOD
manner .... AIR, MIEN, SORT, STYLE
manner of making something FACTURE
Mann's (Tho.) daughter ....... ERICA
manor .. HALL, MANSION, DEMESNE, ESTATE
manred ....... HOMAGE, VASSALAGE
mantel, incandescent ..... FILAMENT
mantelet ........ SHELTER, BLINDAGE
mantis crab .................. SQUILLA
mantle .... CAPE, CLOAK, PALLIUM, FOAM, ROBE, SPREAD
mantle, kind of . PALL, COPE, OCREA

"Mantuan Swan" .............. VIRGIL
manual; mus. ............... CLAVIER
manual training ....... SLOYD, CRAFT
manumission ............... FREEING
manumit FREE, LIBERATE, RELEASE
manuscript ........... FOLIO, CODEX
manuscript marks, old . DORSO, OBELI
manuscripts, unpublished .... INEDITA
Manxman ........................ CELT
Maori Adam ...................... TIKI
 "  canoe ...................... WAKA
 "  clan .... RINGATU, ATI, HAPU
 "  fuel tree ................ MAPAU
 "  hand weapon .............. PATU
 "  parrot bird .................. TUI
 "  raft ........... MOGUEY, MOKI
 "  rootstock .................... ROI
 "  storage pit ................. RUA
 "  wages ...................... UTU
 "  war club .................. MERE
Maorian hero .................... MAUI
map CHART, PLAT, CARTE, SKETCH
maple cup ...................... MAZER
maple, flowering .......... ABUTILON
maple seed .................... SAMARA
maple sugar spout .............. SPILE
maple tree; genus .... ACER, ASARUM
mar ....... BLEMISH, DEFACE, SCAR
marabou ............ ARGALA, STORK
maranatha .................... CURSE
marasca ...................... CHERRY
marasmus ......... PASS, WASTING
maraud .. PLUNDER, ROB, PILLAGE
marauder; Scot. ............ CATERAN
marble AGATE, BASALT, DOLOMITE,
           MIB, MIG
 "  , Belgian .............. RANCE
 "  game ...................... TAW
 "  , in a literary sense BROCATEL
 "  , variety of ........... CIPOLIN
"Marble Faun," char. in ....... HILDA
Marcel .......................... MIME
march ... FILE, IDES, PARADE, HIKE
March sisters ... AMY, MEG, BETH, JO
Marco Polo's title ............ MESSER
Mardi Gras king .................. REX
mare ... JADD, MEARE, YAUD, HORSE
mare's tail .............. ARKS, CLOUD
Margaret of Anjou's father ...... RENE
margarin ........................ OLEO
marge .......................... SHORE
Margery; "Mother Goose" char. .. DAW
margin . FRINGE, BRIM, EDGE, RIM,
        SIDE, BRINK
marginal note .. APOSTIL, SCHOLIUM
marginal reading; Hebrew ......... KRI
Mariana base ................. SAIPAN
marigold .. ASTER, CAPER, COWSLIP
marigold; genus .............. TAGETES
marikina .................... TAMARIN
marinal ...................... SALINE
marine ............ NAVAL, OCEANIC
 "  , American ................ TAR
 "  animal ..... ACALEPH, SALPA
 "  animals, per. to ...... PELAGIC
 "  benthonic plant ...... ENALID
 "  calcareous skeleton .... CORAL
 "  crustacean ........ BARNACLE
 "  English ................. JOLLY

 "  gastropod .. APLYSIA, MUREX
 "  individuals ...... MERPEOPLE
 "  plant group ......... BENTHOS
 "  vertebrate, lowest order ......
          LANCELET
 "  whale food ............... BRIT
mariner . JACKY, SALT, WATERMAN,
       SAILOR, SEAMAN
mariner's compass card ......... ROSE
mariner's compass, points of RHUMBS
marjoram ............ MINT, ORIGAN
mark . TRAIT, BRAND, DOT, LABEL,
         TARGET
 "  , critical ................ OBELUS
 "  , diacritic BREVE, TILDE, TSERE
 "  , distinctive ...... SIGN, STAMP,
         CATCHET
 "  for identification ....... DAGGER,
         EARMARK
 "  for omission ................ DELE
 "  in curling ................... TEE
 "  of disgrace ............. STIGMA
 "  of omission ............. CARET
 "  over a vowel .......... MACRON
 "  , printer's .... DIESIS, OBELISK
 "  with a pointed instrument SCRIVE
 "  with scars ............. ENSEAM
Mark Twain ............... CLEMENS
marked with rounded sables .........
         PELLETED
marker, air-race .............. PYLON
market MART, FORA, RIALTO, SALE
market place ... AGORA, EMPORIUM,
         PLAZA
marksman .................... SNIPER
marl ...... MARLITE, GREENSAND,
         MALM
marlinspike ...................... FID
Marlowe; actress ............. JULIA
marmalade .. CONFECTION, SAPOTE
marmalade tree; genus ..... ACHRAS
marmoset ......... SAGOIN, MONKEY
marmoset, black tailed .......... MICO
marmoset, suirrel-like ..... TAMARIN
marmot ............ BOBAC, RODENT
marmot, Himalayan .............. PIA
marmota ................. ARCTOMYS
maroon ABANDON, SLAVE, ISOLATE
Marpessa's abductor ............. IDAS
marque; naut. .............. LICENSE
marquee ........... SHELTER, TENT
marquetry material ........... NACRE
marriage broker ........ SCHATCHEN
marriage, hater of ...... MISOGAMIST
marriage notice ................. BANS
marriage, non-recognition of . AGAMY
marriage outside the tribe . EXOGAMY
marriage rate ......... NUPTIALITY
marriage, second ... DEUTEROGAMY,
       DIGAMY, DIGAMUS
marrow MEDULLA, PITH, ESSENCE
marrow bones ............... KNEES
marrow sap; Scot. ............. KEEST
Mars ........................... ARES
Mars, green belt on ............ LIBYA
Mars, per. to ..... AREAN, MARTIAN
Mars, priests of ................. SALII
Mars, red ..... COLCOTHAR, TOTEM

Mars, spot on ................. OASIS
Marseillaise, author of ...... ROUGET
                                (LISLE)
marseilles soap .............. CASTILE
marsh ... LERNA, QUAG, BOG, FEN,
                        .MORASS, MIRE
   "   bird ..... SORA, STILT, SNIPE
   "   crocodile ................... GOA
   "   drained .................... DAM
   "   fever TRAIDENUM, HELODES
   "   gas .. FIREDAMP, METHANE
   "   grass ................... SEDGE
marsh harrier ................. HARPY
   "   hawk ................. HARRIER
   "   plant . BULRUSH, IVA, TULE
   "   rosemary ......... MOORWORT
marshal ... GUIDE, RANGE, USHER,
                   ALINE, ARRAY
marshal of France ..... MORAI, NEY
marshes, inhabiting . LIMNOPHILOUS
marshmallow ................... ALTEA
marshy ...... BOGGY, FENNY, WET,
                   PALUDINE
marshy land; Ital. .......... PONTINE,
                   MAREMMA
marshy place ......... SWALE, SLEW
marsupial .... TAPOATAEA, KOALA,
      OPOSSUM, DIPROTODON
Marta, of movies ............. TOREN
marten .............. FISHER, SABLE
martyr, saint wife of a pagan .........
                   ANASTASIA
marvel ......... PRODIGY, WONDER
Maryland county ... ANNE-ARUNDEL
Marx .............. CHICO, GROUCHO
masculine ...... MALE, MAS, VIRILE
masculine name ................. IVOR
Masefield poem ............ CARGOES
mask VISOR, CLOAK, DOMINO, VEIL
mask, crest on tragic ......... ONKOS
masked ......... HIDDEN, LARVATE
masked comedy; It. ......... SCAPINO
masker ..................... MUMMER
masonic door keeper ........... TILER
mason's mixing rod .............. RAB
masquerade DISGUISE, REVEL, MUMM
mass ................ CLOTURE, LUMP
mass book ..................... MISSAL
mass, confused ................... COT
mass directory ................. ORDO
mass of coal ...................... JUD
mass, per. to a ............... MOLAR
Mass. state flower ......... ARBUTUS
mass vestment ................. AMICE
massacre ......... CARNAGE, HAVOC,
        POGROM, DECIMATE
massage ............... KNEAD, RUB
massager, woman ........ MASSEUSE
Massenet; opera by MANON, SAPPHO,
                   THAIS
Massy, Miss .................... ILONA
mast STUFF, ACORNS, NUTS, SPAR
mast platform ............. MANITOP
mast supports ................. STEPS
master ......... MAN, CHIEF, LORD
      MIAN, PALRONE, RAB, RABBI
master of cer. ............ MC, EMCEE
master of Syracuse ............. DION

master stroke .................. COUP
master, to ....... CONQUER, SUBDUE,
                   SUBJECT
mastery ... SKILL, VICTORY, GREE,
         SWAY, ASCENDANCY
mastic ............ ASA, GAM, VISCID
mastic, a kind of ...... TUM, RESIN
mastodon ............ GIANT, MAMMUT
mat, to .. SNARL, TWIST, BOLSTER
mata hari ......................... SPY
Mataco .............. APAR, INDIAN
matador's garment ............. CAPE
matador's staff ............. MULETA
matador's sword ........... ESTOQUE
match .. CAP, TALLY, COPY, MATE,
    LUCIFER, FUSEE, PEER, PIT,
                   VESTA
match in politics ......... LOCOFOCO
match or class ......... SORT, EQUAL
matchless ....... ALONE, PEERLESS
match-lock ....................... GUN
mate .......... PAIR, FERE, MARRY,
                   MARINER
materia medica ............ ACOLOGY
material .. HYLIC, PLASMA, STUFF,
                   SWATCH
material for embroidery . ARRASENE
material of which glass is made FRIT
material, silk ...... TULLE, FAILLE,
                   SATIN
material, upholstery SCRIM, LAMPAS
maternal relationship ...... ENATION
matgrass ........... MARRAM, NARD
math ....................... MOWING
mathe ............... GRUB, MAGGOT
mathematical arbitray number RADIX
   "     constant ...... PARAMETER
   "     diagram ............. GRAPH
   "     function .......... (CO)SINE
   "     inst. NABLA, QUATERNION,
                   VERNIER
   "     irrational number ..... SURD
   "     line ................. VECTOR
   "     motion, after the fashion of ..
                  REPTARY
   "     pure number ....... SCALAR
   "     surface .............. NAPPE
   "     symbol ... DIGIT, FACIEND,
                 ..OPERAND
   "     term .................. COSH
mathematician; Gr. .......... EUCLID
matinee ... LEVEE, SALON, SOIREE,
                   PARTY
matras of a crossbow .......... BOLT
matrass .. BOTTLE, FLASK, CARAFE
matrass, a kind of ...... BOLTHEAD
matriculate ENROL, ENTER, ADMIT
matrix .. BED, MOULD, CAST, FORM
matrix ores, bed in ......... GANGUE
matter .... BODY, COPY, PITH, PUS,
      GEAR, ELEMENTS, ATOMS
matthiola ...................... STOCK
mattock-like .... ADZ, AXE, PICKAX
mature ... PERFECT, AGE, DIGEST,
      RIPE(N), SEASON, COMPLETE
maturing ................... RATHRIPE
maty; Ind. .................. SERVANT
mau ......................... TSETSE

Mau Mau land ................. KENYA
maud ............ RUG, SHAWL, HAG
maudlin ............... BEERY, TIPSY
maudlin state  TEARFUL, FUDDLED
Maugham heroine ............. SADIE
Maugham play .................... RAIN
maul ..... BEETLE, MALLET, MOTH
maul, mason's ................. GAVEL
Mauna—— ........................ LOA
maund .......... BASKET, HAMPER
mauve ............ VIOLET, MALLOW
maverick ............. CALF, DOGIE
maw ....... CRAW, CROP, STOMACH
mawkish .... SICKLY, STALE, VAPID
maxilla ................... JAW(BONE)
maxim MOTTO, GNOME, RULE, SAW,
                                    AXIOM
maxim, concise . ADAGE, APHORISM
maxims ........ LOGIA, MORALISMS
Maxwell, Miss .................... ELSA
may apple ............... MANDRAKE
May first ..................... BELTAN
May fly ......... DUN, EPHEMERID
May tree ................. HAWTHORN
Mayan Indian of Mex. ........... MAM
Mayence, count of ................ GAN
mayfish .................... KILLFISH
mayflower ARBUTUS, HAWTHORNE
mazed .......... MEANDERED, LOST
"Mazo de la Roche" by ........ JALNA
McCambridge, Miss ...... MERCEDES
mead ...... HYDROMEL, METHEGLIN
McConnell; 'Smilin' ............... ED
McLaglen's role .......... INFORMER
meadow SWALE, BAAN, LEA, MEAD
meadow mice ............. ARVICOLA
meadow mouse ................. VOLE
meadow sweet; genus ....... SPIRAEA
meager . ARID, BARE, SCANT, SLIM
Meadows, Miss ................ JAYNE
meal ...... MESS, POWDER, REPAST,
                        RATION, TIFFIN
meal, coarse ................... GROUT
mealy ........ FARINACEOUS, PALE
mean .. SNIDE, MEDIAL, AVERAGE,
        MILDLE, BASE, SENSE, SMALL
meaning, without ............. NULL
meaningless refrain .......... DERRY
means of flight .. ALAE, (AIR)PLANE
meantime .... INTERVAL, INTERIM
measles ...... MORBILLI, RUBEOLA
measure LITER, HAIR, METE, ROTL,
                            TIME, STEP
    "    , Anam .... SAO, TAC, MAU
    "    , Argentine ............. SINO
    "    , Biblical ...... CAB, CUBIT,
                EPHAH, HIN, HOMER,
                MANHEH, SPAN
    "    , Brazil ................... PE
    "    , Chinese .... CHANG, CHIH,
                            TSUN, TU
    "    , Chinese, rood ............ LI
    "    , cloth of length ........ ELL
    "    , Cuban ...... TAREA
    "    , dry; Arab. ............. ARK
    "    , dry; Egypt. ........ ARDES
    "    , dry; Heb. . CAB, EPHA(H),
                            OMER, KOR
    "    , dry; Tunistan ... SAA, SAH
    "    , Dutch ....... AAM, ANKER
    "    , Dutch E. Ind. DEPA, PARAH
    "    , Eng. land ........ MANENT
    "    , European .......... ANKER
    "    , foot ............. ANAPEST
    "    for plant growth ..............
                            AUXANOMETER
    "    for vibrations ....... SIRENE
    "    , French (old) MINOT, TOISE
    "    , herring; British ...... CRAN
    "    , Indian ..... ADOULIE, GUZ
    "    , Indo-Persian .... GAZ, GUZ
    "    , Japanese . MO, RI, RIN, SE,
                                    SHO
    "    , Javanese ........... PALEN
    "    , land . RI, ACRE, AR, ARE,
                                    MILE
    "    , land; Swiss ...... IMI, IMMI
    "    , Libyan ................. DRA
    "    , liquid .... CARGA, TIERCE
    "    , liquid; Bib. DRAM, HIN, LOG
    "    , liquid; Phil. T. .... APATAN
    "    , Malacca .............. ASTA
    "    , medicinal ......... HEMINA
    "    , metric ...... ARE, MICRON
    "    , metric cube ........ STERE
    "    , music ................. CODA
    "    , nautical ............. KNOT
    "    , Netherlands KAN, STREEP,
                                    EL
    "    of capacity .... CASK, CRAN,
                                ORNA
    "    of distance; Ind. var. ... COSS,
                                    KOS
    "    of Earth .......... GEODESY
    "    of length .. CUBIT, MIKRON,
                PACE, METER, ROD, PERCH
measure of length; anc. ........ TOISE
    "    of length; Russian ... VERST
    "    of length; Turkey . DRA, PIK
    "    of length, ¾ of an inch DIGIT
    "    of length, 2¼ inches .. NAILS
    "    of magnetism ........ GAUSS
    "    of Paraguay ............ SINO
    "    of Rangoon ............. LAN
    "    of sounds ............. DECIBEL
    "    of two mterical feet . DIPODY
    "    of weight . GRAM, METAGE,
                                    BALE
    "    of wine in cask ........ BUTT
    "    160 square perches ..... ACRE
    "    oriental .................... RI
    "    , outlaw ............. RONIN
    "    , Persian ........ PARASANG
    "    , Scandinavian ........ ALEN
    "    , Siamese ............ SESTI
    "    , Spanish .... VARA, LINEA
    "    , Tunisian ....... SAA, SAAH
    "    , Turkish . ALMUD, DJERIB,
                                    OKA
    "    , wire .................... MIL
"Mease for Measure;" char. ... LUCIO
measurement  METAGE, SUBSTANCE
measuring instrument ...... ALIDADE,
                                    STADIA
measuring rod .............. CALIPER

meat .............. MORSEL, ATTA
" balls .................. RAVIOLI
" , cut of ...... FILET, BRISKET,
ICEBONE
" , dried and cured HAM, BILTONG
" eater ............... CARNIVORA
" , fat ..................... SPECK
" jelly, (savory) ........ ASPIC
" , minced .. SANDERS, RISSOLE
" pie ........... RISSOLE, PASTY
" , piece of COLP, COLLOP, RAND
" preserve ................... CORN
" , ragout of ........... HARICOT
" roasted on a stick ....... CABOB
meatless .......... MAIGRE, LENTEN
meatus CANAL, OPENING, PASSAGE
Mecca, pilgramage to .......... HADJ
Mecca, pilgrims' dress ........ IHRAM
Mecca, shrine at ............. KAABA
Meccan governor .......... SHEREEF
mechanical .......... INVOLUNTARY,
DOOMED
mechanical man .............. ROBOT
mechanism RIGGING, TACKLE, GEAR
medal BADGE, MEDALLION, PLAQUE
medallion ... TABLET, COIN, CAMEO
meddle .. TAMPER, OBTRUDE, FUSS
meddlesome ........ PRAGMATICAL,
CURIOUS
Medea's father ............... AERTES
medial ............. MIDDLE, MEAN
median ......... MESNE, AVERAGE
Median prince ................. REBA
median line of a valve ........ RAPHE
median plane ................ MESON
mediant; mus. ................. THIRD
mediant, rel. to ................ MODE
mediate ...... CHEW, OPINE, HALVE
mediator ... MUSER, INTERCESSOR,
ARBITER
medic; sl. ......................... DOC
medical ......... CURATIVE, IATRIC
" air chief ................ EAKER
" compound .............. HEPAR
medical drug .................... SENNA
" group ..................... AMA
" monster ............... TERAS
" officer ............. CORONER
" science, division of . THERAPY
" , suffix ..................... ITIS
" treatment; comb. form IATRIA,
IATRY
" weed ................. SPURGE
medicated fluid .............. LOTION
medicinal herb BONESET, CHIRETTA
" plant COHOSH, RUE, SPURGE
" plant leaf ............ SENNA
" remedy .......... ANTIDOTE
" root . JENA, JALAP, ARTAR
" tea .................. TISANE
" unit .................. HEPAR
medicine administrator ....... DOSER
" , kind of mild ....... TISANE
" man ...... PRIEST, SHAMAN
" , of equal parts in ...... ANA
" quack ............ NOSTRUM
" , science of ........ PHYSICS,
IATRO

" , universal ........ PANACEA
" , watery ............ PTISAN
medicine-like ............... PILULAR
mediety; law ................ MOIETY
medieval galley ...... AESC, BIREME,
GALIOT
" helmet .............. ARMET
" hooked weapon ....... ONCIN
" monster ........ WEREWOLF
" prayer book ........ PORTASS
" preparation of dandelion .....
TARAXACUM
" receptacle ........... BAHUT
" shield ................... ECU
" ship of war ........ DROMON
" stringed inst. . CLAVICHORD
" trading vessel .......... NEF
" type of short tale ........ LAI
" vessel ................ XEBEC
" viol .................. REBEC
" , Yiddish ............ GOLEM
Medina citizen converted to Islam .....
ANSAL
mediocre ............... MONK, SOSO
meditate ..... MUSE, PORE, PONDER
meditation ............. RUMINATION
Mediterranean fruit ....... AZAROLE
" galley ............. GALIOT
" island; British ........ GOZO
" sea, per. to ......... LEVANT
" ship ........ XEBEC, KEBEC,
SETTEE, ZEBEC
" storm ............. BORASCO
" volcanic is. ........... LIPARI
" wind . LEVANTER, SOLANO,
SIROC(CO)
medium .. MEAN, PSYCHIC, ORACLE
medium line of valve ......... RAPHE
medlar wood ................. MYRTUS
medley FARRAGO, MELANGE, OLIO,
POTPOURRI, SALMAGUNDI
medley; mus. .............. FANTASIA
medley race ................... RELAY
medrick ................. GULL, TERN
medulla ........ MARROW, PITH
medulla oblongata stripe ..... OBLEX
Medusa's sister ............. STHENO
meerschaum . SEAFOAM, SEPIOLITE
meet EQUAL, FIT, MATCH, SEEMLY
meeting ...... RALLY, MALL, SYNOD,
TRYST, JUNCTION, SESSION
meeting of 'Big Three' .... POTSDAM
megapode ................ MALEO
megapode, mound building ... LEIPOA
megalithic chamber ......... DOLMEN
megrim ............ CAPRICE, WHIM
megrims ...... HEADACHE, BLUES
melancholy . TRISTFUL, ATRABILE,
DREAR, DISPIRITED
melancholy, make ............... HYP
Melanesian native ............... FIJI
Melanesian super-being ....... ADARO
melanous ............... BRUNETTE
Meleager .................... KILLER
melicocca ...................... GENIP
Melid's lore ...................... IR
melissa; genus; Old World ...... MINT
melilotus ................... CLOVER

168

melli, comb. form ............. HONEY
mellow ..... MALM, RIPE, OID, SOFT
melodic flourish ............. MELISMA
melodics ....................... MUSIC
melodies . THEMES, ARIAS, STRAINS
melodious ........ ARIOSE, DULCET,
ORPHEAN
melodrama act ............... EMOTE
melody ... CANTILENA, CAVATINA,
CHARM, CHIME, RHYTHM
melody; Anglo-Ind. ............. RAGA
melody in sequence MELOS, ROSALIA
melody, of a ................. PLAGAL
meloid ........................ BEETLE
melon, the ...................... PEPO
melon-pear ................... PEPINO
melt ............ RUN, FUSE, SWALE
melt down ...... RENDER. LIQUEFY
melt ore ....... SMELT, CONVERT
Melville char. .................. ALLEN
Melville novel ................. OMOO
member ....... ORGAN, PART, LIMB
membrane ................. PIA, SKIN
membrane, a fold of ............ PLICA
membrane covering brain MENINGES,
MATER
membrane, web-like ............ TELA
membrane diffusion ......... OSMOSIS
membranous fringe ............. LOMA
memento ........ RELIC, KEEPSAKE
memorabilia ...................... ANA
memorandum . CHIT, NOTE, MINUTE
memorandum book ........ NOTANDO,
TICKLER
memoria ...... RELIQUARY, SHRINE
memorial ...... EBENEZER, RECORD,
TROPHY
memorist ................. PROMPTER
memory .... MIND, REMINISCENCE,
ROTE
memory, loss of .. AMNESIA, LETHE
memory, partial loss of ..... APHASIA
memory, per. to ... CON, MNEMONIC
memory, per. to; var. ........ MNESIC
Memphis god .................... PTAH
Memphite god ...................... RA
men; slang ....... BLOAKS, BLOKES
men speaking same tongue; Fr. ........
LANGUE
mend ...... COBBLE, PATCH, DARN
mendacities ...................... LIES
mendicant ... FAKIR, BEGGAR(MAN)
meniscus ......................... LENS
Mennonite sect. ............... AMISH
meno; mus. ...................... LESS
Menotti ................. GIAN-CARLO
mental defective ............. MORON
mental disorder .......... PARANOIA
mental feeling ... EMOTED, PHRENIC
mental state ... DOLDRUM, MORALE
mentality .......... SENSE, SANITY
menthanol ............ DENATURANT
mention ........ CITE, REFER, MIND
mentum ......................... CHIN
menu ......................... CARTE
merapodite ................... MEROS
mercenary . HESSIAN, HACK, HIRED,
VENAL

merchandise ..... ARTWARE, WARES
merchandise, per. to ... EMPOREUTIC
merchant .......... TRADER, VINTER
merchant guild ................ HANSE
merchant; Hindu ............... SETH
"Merchant of Venice," ..... ANTONIO
"    char. ............... NERISSA
merchant vessel ........... INDIAMAN
mercurious chloride ........ CALOMEL
Mercury .................... HERMES
Mercury, son of ............. ELEUSIS
Mercury, winged cup ....... PETASUS
Mercury, winged shoes ..... TALARIA
Mercury's staff ........... CADUCEUS
mercy ............. BLITHE, GRACE
mere handful ... WISP, FEW, SMALL
mere taste .. SIP, DRAUGHT, GULP,
NIP
merely ............... ONLY, SINGLE,
BARELY
merganser .. HARLE, HERALD, NUN,
SMEE, GOOSANDER, SMEW
merger ...... ABSORPTION, FUSION,
UNION
meridian ..... APEX, ZENITH, NOON
merino ........................ WOOL
merit ........ EARN, MEED, WORTH
Merkel, Miss ..................... UNA
Meropodite ................... MEROS
meros ............ THIGH, SURFACE
merry .. BLYTHE, JOCOSE, JOYFUL
Merry Andrew ....... JOKER, ANTIC,
JESTER, ACROBAT, MIME
merry; Fr. ........................ GAI
merry-go round .......... CAROUSEL
merry-making ...... REVEL, MOMUS,
REEL
merry thought ........... WISHBONE
"Merry wives of Windsor" char. .......
SLENDER
mescal ...................... CACTUS
mescal, liquor-like ............ SOTOL
mesh ........ NET, MITOME, TISSUE
mesial plane, toward ......... MESAD
mesmeric force ...................... OD
Mesopotamia ..................... IRAQ
"    , city .......... EDESSA
"    N. W. wind .... SHAMAL
mesquite ........ ALGAROBA, PACAY,
PROSOPIS
mesquite bean flour .......... PINOLE
message BODE, BREVET, EVANGEL
messenger APOSTLE, NUNCIO, SAND,
TOTY, ENVOY, IRIS, HERALD
messenger, mounted ....... ESTAFET,
REVERE
Messina, rock in the Straits of SCYLLA
met AGREEL, EQUALED, TRYSTED
metal bar on door ................ RISP
"    , bar of ................. INGOT
"    clippings .............. SCISSEL
"    , coarse ............... MATTE
"    coat ................... PATINA
"    containing impurities of the ore .
REGULUS
"    filings ................. LEMEL
"    fissure ................... LODE
"    , heavy ................. LEAD

169

"    ingot ..................... GAD
"    , lightest ............ LITHIUM
"    , lump of ................. PIG
"    plates, thin FOIL, SHIM, LAMES
"    refuse .................... SLAG
"    shaper ................. SWAGE
"    , silver-white ........ CALCIUM
"    slip hold machine .......... GIB
metal, to ornament .... DAMASKEEN
metal-ware ........... REVERE, TOLE
metal worker ................ WELDER
"    zinc blende ........... GALLIUM
metallic alloy ............... SOLDER
metallic chemical element .... COBALT,
                                TERBIUM
metallic content ................. ORY
metallic element .... ORE, LUTECIUM,
                        YTTRIUM, ERBIUM
metallic oxide ................. OCHRE
metamere ...... SOMATOME, SOMITE
metamerism ......... SEGMENTATION
metamorphosis ................... PUPA
metaphor .... SIMILE, TRALATITION,
                                TROPE
metaphor, an extended ........ IMAGE
meteor a ........ BIELID, FIREBALL,
                                LEONID
meteor, exploding ..... BOLIDE, BOLIS
meteorite ................... AEROLITH
meteor's mark ................ CRATER
meteors, shower of ....... ANDROMID
meter ...................... RHYTHM
"    , cubic ................... STERE
"    , gas ...................... WET
"    , millionth of a ........ MICRON
"    unit ....................... MORA
meters, 100 square ............ AR, ARE
methane .................... PARAFFIN
metheglin ...................... MEAD
method ............. SYSTEM, WAY
methylbenzone ............. TOLUENE
methyl ketols ............... ACETOLS
meticulous one ................ PURIST
metier ................. WORK, TRADE
metis ..................... MULATTO
metric measure .. AR, ARE, CENTARE,
                        TONNE, LITRE, STERE
metric measure of surface .... DECARE
metric system, comb. form ..... DECI
metric unit; obs. ......... DECASTERE
metric weight ................ GRAM
metrical ..... ODE, POESY, POETICAL,
                                POEM
"       foot ........ ANAPEST, IAMB,
                        IAMBUS, ARSIS
"       foot of four syllables ...........
                        CHORIAMB IONIC
"       foot of two syllables TROCHEE
"       stress of voice ........ ICTUS
metriculosity .............. PUNCTILIO
metropolitan .......... (ARCH)BISHOP
Metz's river; Fr. ........... MOSELLE
Meuse river .................... MAAS
mew . STABLE, CAGE, DEN, GARAGE
mew, a ......... COB, GULL, SEAGULL
mew, as a cat ........ MIAOW, MIAUL
mew, in the .................... MOLT
mewl ...................... WHIMPER
Mexican agave, species of ...... DATIL

"    beverage ... OCTLI, PULQUE
"    bird .............. TINAMOU
"    blanket ............. SERAPE
"    brigand ........... LADRONE
"    cat, spotted MARGAY, EYRA
"    , Central; anc. ....... OTOMI
"    city ..... JALAPA, OAXACA,
                        ORIZABA, TEPIC
"    clover ................... COCA
"    coin ........... TLAC, TLACO
"    coral drops; genus . BESSERA
"    dish .. TAMALE, TORTILLA
"    distilled liquor ....... SOTOL
"    dollar ................. PESO
"    drug .............. DAMIANA
Mexican early dweller .. AZTEC, MAYA
"    fiber plant ... DATIL, ISTLE,
                        PITA, SISAL, IXTLE
"    food fish ........... SALEMA
"    foot covering .... HUARACHO
"    garment ............. MANGO
"    gopher, pocket ....... TUCAN
"    gruel ................. ATOLE
"    hut ................. JACAL
"    Indian; ...... OTOMI, AZTEC,
                        OPATA, SERI, LIPAN,
                        TOLTEC, MAYAN
"    intoxicating drink .. MESCAL
"    labor union ....... PEONAGE
"    lake ............ CHAPALA
"    landmark ........... SENAL
"    masonry ............. ADOBE
"    mat ............... PETATE
"    money of account ... CUARTO
"    noble ................. TZIN
"    octoroon ........... ALBINO
"    of mixed blood ..... MESTIZO
"    'pancho' ............. VILLA
"    peasant .............. PEON
"    persimmon ....... CHAPOTE
"    pine ................. OCOTE
"    plant; genus ........ AGAVE
"    plant, soap ......... AMOLE
"    plantation ....... HACIENDA
"    policeman .......... RURALE
"    porridge ........... ATOLE
"    priest ............. HDALGO
"    proprietor ...... RANCHERO
"    pyramid ......... TECCALLIS
"    race ................. TOLTEC
"    reed ................ OTATE
"    saloon ........... CANTINA
"    sauce ........... TABASCO
"    scale dove ............. INCA
"    scarf .............. TAPALO
"    seaport .......... ACAPULCO
"    shawl ............... SERAPE
"    spineless cactus .... MESCAL
"    stirrup ........... TAJOADER
"    stirrup cover .... TAPADERA
"    sugar ........... PANOCHA
"    thong ................ ROMAL
"    throwing stick ...... ATLATL
"    town .............. AMECA
"    volcano .. COLIMA, JORULLO
Mexico, State .... SINALOA, HIDALGO
Mexico's ex-pres. ............. ALEMAN
Meuse river ..................... MAAS
Meyerbeer, opera by ...... AFRICAINE

mezereon .................... DAPHNE
mezzanine ................ ENTRESOL
Miami's county ................. DADE
miasma ..................... MALARIA
mica ... BIOTITE, GLIST, ISINGLASS,
TALC
mica lithia ............... LEPIDOLITE
mica-chlorite ............ RIPIDOLITE
mica-trap ................... MINETTE
mice; genus ....................... MUS
mice of India ................. METADS
michael, variety ............. ORANGE
micher ...................... TRUANT
mickle ........ GREAT, LARGE, MUCH
micrastur ...................... HAWK
microbe .......... BACTERIUM, GERM
microcosm ........... WORLD, MONAD
microorganism ................. VIRUS
microscopic algae, order of ... DIATOM
microscopic organism ......... AMOEBA
microspores ................. POLLEN
middle ... CENTRY, MESIAL, MESNE,
MEDIAL
middle Am. linguistic stock ..... YUMA
middle, comb. form ........ MEDI, MES
middling ............ AVERAGE, SOSO
middling stock ............... NANOID
Mid-European ............... SLOVENE
midge .. FLY, GNAT, PUNKIE, STOUT
Midianite prince ................. REBA
mid-lent Sunday ............ LAETARE
midrift ................... DIAPHRAGM
midshipman ................. REEFER
mien .... GUISE, LOOK, AIR, OSTENT
mift ........................ PET, TIFF
mighty ..... POTENT, TIRFUL, VERY
mignonette .................. RESEDA
migratory farm hand ............ OKIE
migration ........... EXODUS, TREK
Mikado, court of ................. DAIRI
mikania ................ WILLUGBAEYA
mike; slang, Eng. ...... LOAF, LOITER
Milan opera house ............... SCALA
mild ..... BLAND, MEEK, BENEDICT,
SOFT
mild offense; law ............... DELIT
mildew .... BLIGHT, MO(U)LD, MUST
mildews ......... DOWNY, POWDERY
Miled's son ........................ IR
milestone ...................... STELE
milfoil ....................... YARROW
milieu ............ ENVIRON, MEDIUM
military ...................... MARTIAL
"        cap ... BUSBY, KEPI, SHAKO
"        cloak ................. SAGUM
"        craft ..................... LST
"        device ................. CROC
"        division ........ UNIT, CORPS
"        engine .. ONAGER, ROBINET
"        force ........ ARMY, LEGION
"        landing pt. ..... BEACHHEAD
"        messenger ......... ESTAFET
"        mine gallery ......... ECOUTE
"        punishment ...... STRAPADO
"        rank BANNER, COLONELCY
"        salue .................. SALVO
"        signal .............. CHAMADE
"        storehouse ETAPE, ARSENAL
"        truck ................ CAMION

"        wind instrument .. ALTHORN
militate .......................... FIGHT
milk ............................... LAC
"        coagulator ............. RENNET
"        crust .................. ECZEMA
"        , curd produced from ... CASEIN,
ZEIGA
"        , curdled .............. CLABBER
"        , fermented ........... KOUMISS
"        fish .....ANGED, AWA, SABALO
"        food ................ LACTICINIA
"        , per. to .............. LACTIC
"        , sour .... CURD, WHEY, WHIG
"        weed fluid ................. LATEX
"        whey ..................... SERA
milk-pail; Eng. ................. ESHIN
milky way ................... GALAXY
mill .................. BOX, QUERN
mill for pulverizing ore .... ARRASTRA
mill, to ........................... NURL
millepore ....................... CORAL
miller ........ BAKER, MOTH, PISTOR
millet ... CENCHRINE, KODA, PEARL
millet, broom-corn ............. HIRSE
millet, Indian .. DURR, DURRA, KODA
millet, Italian ................... MOHA
millet, pearl ................... BAJREE
million, thousand ........... MILLIARD
millimeter, thousandth part ... MICRON
millionth part of an ohm .... MICROHM
mill-pond .......... DAM, DIKE, DITCH
millstone, part of ......... RYND, INK
mill-wheel float ............... LADLE
Milquetoast, Mr. ............. CASPAR
Milton's "Regent of the Sun" ... URIEL
mime ....... ACTOR, IMITATE, COPY
mimic, female .................... MIMA
mimicry .. PARROTRY, APISM, ECHO,
MIMESIS
mince ..... CUT, HASH, SLASH, DICE
minced meat ................. RISSOLE
minced oath .. BEGAD, DRAT, EGAD,
ODS
mincing ...................... MINIKIN
mind ....... NOUS, MOOD, RECK
mind; Lat. ...................... MENS
mind, peace of ............. ATARAXIA
Mindanao language ................ ATA
Mindanao, Phil. I. town .......... DAPA
Mindanao, Phil. I. volcano ......... APO
minds; Scot. ..................... MINS
mine ....... BONANZA, MY, PIT, SAP
"        coal ...................... ROB
"        , deviate from vertical .... HADE
"        entrance ................... ADIT
"        horizontal passage ........ STULM
"        , Lat. ..................... MEUM
"        partition ................. SOLLAR
"        prop .............. STULL, SPRAG
"        rubbish .... ATTLE, GOAF, GOB
"        shaft, place in for water .........
STANDAGE
"        shaft, step in ......... STEMPEL
"        sitter; Eng. .................. LUE
"        stepwise excavation ...... STOPE
"        sweeper ............. PARAVANE
"        tender of air doors .... TRAPPER
"        tub ....................... CORF
"        unsystematically ........ GOPHER

171

" wall or ceiling ............. ASTEL
" ; Welsh ...................... BAL
" worker ................... CAGER
mineral ...... DANALITE, MINE, ORE
"   , amorphous ......... PINITE
"   , black .......... URANINITE,
                            GRAPHITE
"   , carbonate of lime .. CALCITE
"   caoutchouc ...... ELATERITE
"   , crystalline ........ FELSPAR
"   , dark green ....... URALITE
"   deposit ...... LODE, SINTER
"   deposit, (not a vein) . PLACER
"   , gray white .......... TRONA
"   , hard .... ALALITE, SPINEL
"   jelly .............. VASELINE
"   matter, mix .......... MAGMA
"   oil ..................... COLZA
"   , pale yellow ...... EPIDOTE,
                            PYRITE
"   , per. to a ......... GANGUE
"   phosphate of lime ... APATITE
"   pitch .............. ASPHALT
"   plaster of paris ..... GYPSUM
"   pulp ..................... TALC
"   , rare brittle ....... THORITE,
                            EUCLASE
"   salt ..................... ALUM
mineral silicate .................. MICA
"   tar ................... MALTHA
"   water; var. ........ SELTERS
"   , waxlike ........ OZOCERITE
"   , whitish .... BARITE, SPALT
"   , yellow-green ...... EPIDOTE
minerals, per. to a subgroup of .. MITIC
miner's basket .............. DAN, CORF
miner's chisel ....................... GAD
miner's mandrel .................. PICK
miner's pickaxe ......... BEDE, FLANG
miner's safety lamp .............. DAVY
miner's surveying inst. ............ DIAL
Minerva's shield ................. EGIS
mines, guardian of; myth. .... GNOME
mingle ... ADMIX, COALESCE, MELL,
                WEAVE, MERGE, MIX
miniate .................. RUBRICATE
minimum ...... JOT, LEAST, TITTLE
mining excavation ..... SPALE, STOPE
mining passage, corner in .... ARRAGE
mining, to deviate from the vertical in;
                            HADE
mining shack built over a shaft ... COE
mining sleeve ..................... GRID
mining surveyor .............. DIALER
minim ....... SMALLEST, JOT, DROP,
                    TITTLE, WHIT
minion .............. FAVORITE, IDOL
minister .... CURATE, TEND, ANGEL,
                SERVE, DOMINIE, ENVOY
Minn. Center .................... SAUK
minor ...... SMALLER, LESS, YOUTH
minor, in music .................. MOLL
minorate .................. CURTAIL
minoress ...................... CLARE
minority ...... NONAGE, PUPILAGE
Mino's daughter ............. ARIADNE
minstrel .... BARD, GLEEMAN, POET,
        RIMER, HARPER, PIERROT

minstrel, 13th century wandering ......
                            GOLIARD
mint . CHIA, COIN, HYSSOP, RAMONA
"   charge .............. BRASSAGE
"   family ............. CALAMINT
"   ; genus ............... MENTHA
"   , mountain ................ BASIL
"   , rel. to; Span. ........... YERBA
"   sauce; slang, Eng. ....... MONEY
"   seasoned ................... SAGY
minuend ...................... MINISH
minuet, rel. to ............... SCHERZO
minuscule ............ PETTY, CIPHER
minute .... TRIFLING, ITEM, NOTE
minute animals ........ ANIMALCULE
minute organisms SPORES, MONADS
minute orifice ................... STOMA
minx GIRL, JADE, COLLEEN, DOLL,
                            FILLY, MISS
miracle .... ANOMY, MARVEL, PLAY
miracle worker ..... THAUMATURGE
mirage ... SERAB, ILLUSION, VISION
Miranda's father .......... PROSPERO
mioga ......................... GINGER
miolania, extinct .......... TORTOISES
miphkad; Bib. .......... MIR, MYRRH
Miranda; firm star ................. ISA
mire .... GLAR, ADDLE, MOIL, SLUD,
                            OOZE, MUD
mirror ........ CRYSTAL, SPECULUM,
                        REFLECT(OR)
mirror, per. to a .......... CATOPTRIC
mirth ............ FUN, GLEE, SPLEEN
miry . OOZY, SLIMY, BOGGY, LUTOSE
misanthrope .. HATER, TIMON, CYNIC
mischief ............. ILL, ATE, WRACK
misdemeanor CHAMPERTY, OFFENSE,
                SIN, CRIME, FAULT, TORT
misdirect .. PERVERT, LIE, MYSTEFY
miser .... HUNKS, NABAL, NIGGARD
miser Marner ..................... SILAS
miserable ARRANT, WOE, PITIABLE
miserly ...... CLOSE, SORDID, NEAR,
                            TIGHT
misery ............ GRIEF, PANDORA,
                        HEARTACHE
misfortune .............. HARM, ILLS
mish-mash ....................... OLIO
misle ...... MIST, MIZZLE, DRIZZLE
mislead ..... DELUDE, FAIT, ERROR
mismanage ......... BUNGLE, BLUNK
misplay .............. ERR, RENEGE
misprision ......... MISPRIZE, SCORN
mispronunciation .......... CACOLOGY
mis—— ....................... NOMER
"Miss Thompson" play .......... RAIN
missile ... LANCE, ARROW, BULLET,
                OUTCAST, GRENADE
Miss; Lat. ...................... MISSA
missing ... ABSENT, LOST, WANTING
Mississippi county PONTOTIC, LAMAR
Mississippi fish .... CRAPET, CRAPPIE
Mississippi, nickname ......... BAYOU
Mississippi resort .............. BILOXI
Missouri river Indian .............. SAC
misspelling ............ CACOGRAPHY
misspent .... LOST, LOSEL, WASTED
mist .... SMUR, HARR, BRUME, DIM,
                    MISLE, SEREIN

172

mistake ..... BONER, BARNEY, BULL
mistake in date ....... ANACHRONISM
mistake in writing ............ ERRATA
mistake of syntax .......... SOLECISM
mister ........... SIR, DON, GOODMAN
mistress . BEEBEE, DULCINEA, MRS.
mite .. ATOM, MOTE, SPECK, ACARID
miter ..... FILLET, FRANK, GUSSET,
TIARA, CIDARIS
miterworts; genus ........ TIARELLA
mites ............... ACARI, ACARINA
mithridate .................. ANTIDOTE
mitigate QUALIFY, MEAZE, TEMPER
mix ........ STIR, CONSORT, JUMBLE
mix clay for bricks ................ PUG
mix-up, G.I. .................... SNAFU
mix wine ......................... PART
mix with water ................. SLAKE
mix with yeast .................. BARM
mixable .................... MISCIBLE
mixed people ....... DRIZZLE, METIS
mixed type ........................... PI
mixture .. AMALGAM, HASH, SALAD,
MELANGE, OLIO, BONER,
MISCUE
Mizar, small star near .......... ALCOR
mizzle .......... MIST, DRIZZLE, SPIT
moa .............. DINORNIS, RATITE
moa, rel. to the ............. APTERYX
Moab, anc. people of ............ EMIMS
moan . GROAN, SUUM, CRY, LAMENT
moat FOSS, GRAFFE, CANAL, DITCH
mob .... ROUT, THRONG, CANAILLE,
HERD, DROVE, GANG, PRESS
mobster's girls ................. MOLLS
mobster ........ RABBLER, BUTCHER
"Moby Dick" ................... PELEG
"Moby Dick"; author ...... MELVILLE
"Moby Dick," pursuer ........ AHAB
moccasin ...... PAC, MAKAK, SNAKE
mocha stone .................... AGATE
mock ... GIBE, DERIDE, APE, FLOUT,
MIMIC, SCOFF, FLEER, JEER
mock jewelry ...... LOGIE, IMITATION
mockery FARCE, SHAM, TRAVESTY,
DELUSION, RUSE
mockery, evil spirit of ......... MOMUS
mocking .. GAB, FLEERING, JEERING
mocking bird; genus ......... MIMUS
mock-orange .... SERINGA, SYRINGA
mocks ........................ JAPES
mode .. FAD, VOGUE, STYLE, FLAIR
model ...... SITTER, GAUGE, NORM,
SHAPE
model, a kind of ............ MANIKIN
model of a word ......... PARADIGM
model or pattern ........... PARAGON,
ARCHETYPE
moderate ..... BATE, SOME, FRUGAL
moderately in music ........ MODESTO
moderation ...... HOVE, MITIGATION
modern NEO, LATE, NEOTERIC, NEW
modern school of art ............ DADA
modest .. CIVIL, COY, SHY, DEMURE
modified leaf in flower cluster .. BRACT
modify ALTER, ATTEMPER, MASTER
Modjeska; actress ............ HELENA
modulate INFLECT, ADAPT, ATTUNE
moguey ........................ RAFT

mogul .. LORD, NABOB, MONGOLIAN
Mohammed ....... ISLAM, MAHOMET,
MAHOUD
"      , adopted son of .......... ALI
"      , birthplace of ........ MECCA
"      , daughter of ........ FATIMA
"      tomb city ............ MEDINA
"      , wife of .............. AISHA
Mohammed-Malay law .......... ADAT
Mohammed's flight from Mecca HEGIRA
"      successor .............. CALIF
Mohammedan Angel of Death AZRAEL
"      annual fast ........ RAMADAN
"      antenuptial settlement for wife;
MAHR
"      , ascetic .............. FAKIR
"      Bible ..... ALCORAN, KORAN
"      bier or tomb .......... TABUT
"      body of interpreters .. ULEMA
"      calif ..................... OMAR
"      cap ....................... TAJ
"      caravansary ......... IMARET
"      chief ......... SAYID, DATTO
"      court officer ............. AGA
"      creed ................. SUNNAN
"      crusade ............... JIHAD
"      deity ................... ALLAH
"      demon ................. JINNIE
"      devil ....... EBLIS, SHAITAN
"      divorce ............... TALAR
"      drinking cup .......... LOTAH
"      Easter ................... EED
"      fast .............. RAMADAN
"      festival ........ BAIRAM, EED
"      garment .......... ISAR, IZAR
"      guide ..................... PIR
"      hierarchy ............. ULEMA
"      hospice ............. IMARET
"      house ............ SELAMLIK
"      infidel ................ KAFIR
"      judge ............. CADI, RAZI
"      lord .................... SAYID
"      magistrate ............... CADI
"      Malay ............... SASSAK
"      Messiah ............. MAHDI
"      minister of finance ... DIWAN
Mohammedan month JUMADA, RABIA,
RAJAB, RAMADAN, SAFAR,
SHABAN, SHAWWAL
"      mystic .................. SUNI
"      noble ............. AMIR, EMIR
"      , non ................. KAFFIR
"      nymph ................ HOURI
"      , orthodox . HANIF, SUNNITE
"      pantheist ............... SUFI
"      paradise, nymph of .... HOURI
"      platform ........... MASTABA
"      potentate ............ CALIPH
"      prayer ....... SALAT, NAMAZ
"      prayer, hour of ......... AZAN
"      priest ....... IMAM, WAHABI
"      prince .. AMEER, EMIR, SEID
"      religion ................ ISLAM
"      ruler ................ SULTAN
"      sacred book ....... ALCORAN,
KORAN
"      sacred word ............... OM
"      saint ........... PIR, SANTON
"      salutation ............ SALAM

173

" seminary ........... MADRAS
" shirt .................. KAMIS
" slave ............. MAMELUKE
" spirit .... GINN, PIR, GENIE
" stringed instrument .. REBAB
" student ............... SOFTA
" successions ......... CALIPH
" teacher ........ ALIM, IMAM, MOLLAH
" title .... AMIR, CALIF, AGA, NAWAB, NUWAB, SAYID
" unbeliever ........... KAFIR
" veil .............. YASHMAK
" widow, non-marrying, period of IDDAT
" woman's outer wrap .... IZAR
Mohammedans, expected messiah by the MAHDI
moiety ........ HALF, MIDDLE, PART
moil .......... TAINT, TOIL, MEDDLE
Moir, David; pen name ........ DELTA
moist .. DANK, HUMID, WET, DAMP
moist spot ................ DANK, SIPE
moisten .... ANOINT, BEDEW, MOIL, SPARGE
moisten skins ..................... SAM
moisture, exposed to .............. RET
" swollen plant condition ...... EDEMA
moke .................. DOLT, DONKEY
moke; dial. Eng. ........... FOG, MIST
moke, net-like ................. MESH
molar GRINDING, CHOPPER, TEETH
molasses ...... THERIACA, TREACLE
molave ..................... VITEX
mold .. KNEAD, CAST, MUST, PLASM, SOIL, MOULAGE
mold, core of a .......... AME, NOWEL
mold, pouring hole in ........... SPRUE
Moldavia, former capital of ... BALTA, IASI
molded building material ........ PISE
molder's tool ................. FLANGE
molding, convex ............. REEDING
molding, small square ........ LISTEL
molding (see also 'moulding')
moldy ...... FUST, MUCID, MOULDY
mole .... BLES, PIER, TALPA, QUAY, TAUPE, STARNOSE
mole rat; genus ............. NESOKIA
molecule ........ MONAD, PARTICLE
molecule, component ...... ATOM, ION
mole-like animal .... DESMAN, TAPE
molge ..................... TRITURUS
Moliere char. .... DAMIS, DORANTE, SCAPIN
mollifies ...... (A)BATES, SOFTENS
mollify ...... CONCILIATE, PACIFY, SLEEK, APPEASE, RELAX
mollusca MUREX, CHITINS, OCTOPI
mollusca, highest class of ARGONAUT
mollusk .... CLAM, OYSTER, SNAIL
" bivalve .. LEDA, VENERIDA, CHAMA
" , double shell ........ LIMPET
" , edible ........ ASI, MUSSEL
" , eight armed .... OCTOPUS
" , fresh water ...... CHITON, ETHERIA

" , gastropod ABALONE, SLUG
" ; genus .. MUREX, ASTARTE, BUCCINUM
" gills ................. CERATA
" , large part of .... MANTLE
" larval .............. VELIGER
" of Samoa ................ ASI
" , rel. to .... WHELK, CONCH
" , sea ...... ABALONE, SALP
" shell of a univalve; .. COWRY, COWRIE
" teeth ................ RADULA
" , ten armed .......... SQUID
" used for fish bait .... LIMPET
" wrinkled shell ...... COCKLE
" , young ................ SPAT
molt .................... NEW, MUTE
molts .. CASTS, EXUVIATES, SHEDS
Molucca Is. ................... BANDA
moment . SEC, FLASH, POINT, TRICE
monad ............ ATOM, PARTICLE
monadic base, a .......... AMADINE
monarch DYNASTY, TSAR, SACHEM
monarch, greedy .............. MIDAS
monarda .......... HORSEMINT, TEA
monastery FRIARY, ABBEY, HOSPICE
monastic haircut .......... TONSURE
monastic ORDER, MONKLY, OBLATE
monastic visitor .......... DEFINITOR
mondream ........................ JOY
mone .................. CRONE, TELL
monetary .... PECUNIARY, COINAGE
monetary unit (see 'coin' also 'money')
money .. FUNDS, CASH, GRIG, MINA, TALENT, WAD
" , Anglo-Saxon ...... ORE, ORA
" box .............. ARCA, TILL
" changer .. CAMBIST, SARAF, SERAF
" changing ................ AGIO
" coined ................ SPECIE
" found .................. TROVE
" gift ..................... ALMS
" manual .............. CAMBIST
" of greed .............. LUCRE
" 1/60th talent ............ MINA
" premium ................ AGIO
money, roll of .............. ROULEAU
" , Scotch .............. SILLER
" ; slang ..... BOODLE, RHINO, WAMPUM, GILT
" sorter ................ SHROFF
" standard .............. BANCO
" , to coin ................ MINT
" used in a bad sense .... PELF
monger TRADER, VENDER, MERCER
Mongol ............ TARTAR, ASIAN, TAMERLANE
Mongolia, capital of ............ URGA
Mongolia, river of ........ PEI, ONON
Mongolia, silver coin of ...... TUGRIK
Mongolian conjurer .......... SHAMAN
" people of Siberia . YACOOTS
Mongoloid people of Nepal LAPP, RAIS, LAI
mongoose ... ICHNEUMON, LEMUR, URVA
mongrel ...... CUR, HYBRID, MIXED

monial .............. MULLION, NUN
monition ........ ADVICE, WARNING
monitor PREPOSTOR, IBIL, MENTOR
monitor lizard ........ URAN, VARAN
monk .............. ABBATE, PADRE
"   , ascetic ................ FAKIR
"   , community ....... CENOBITE
"   , early English .......... BEDE
"   , Franciscan ....... CAPUCHIN
"   , hermit .......... ANCHORET
"   hood .... AMICE, ATIS, COWL
"   , monastic order ........ FRIAR
"   of the Eastern Church CALOYER
"   , Persian ............ DERVISH
"   , Thibetan .............. LAMA
"   , Turkish ............ DERVISE
monk's hood ATEES, ATIS, ACONITE
monk's title ........................ FRA
monkey; MONA, NISNAS, QUAKARI,
                          VITOE, TOTA
"   , arboreal; W. Afr. ..... POTTO
"   , Asiatic ............. MACAQUE
"   , bearded .......... ENTELLUS
"   , Brazilian ...... TEETER, SAI
"   bread ................. BAOBAB
"   , Capuchin ...... SAPAJOU, SAI
"   , Ceylonese .... MAHA, TOQUE
"   , Diana ............. ROLOWAY
"   flower .............. FIGWORT
"   flower; genus ....... MIMULUS
"   grivet ..................... TOTA
"   house ................... APERY
"   howler ........ ARABA, MONO,
                              STENTOR
"   , long tailed, Asiatic . LANGUR
"   , long tailed, W. Afr., .. PATAS
"   , Malabar ........ WANDEROO
"   proboscis ... KAHA, NOSEAPE
"   puzzle ................... PINON
"   , sacred, of India .... RHESUS
"   , small; So. Am. .. MARMOSET,
                                  TITI
"   , S. Afr.; .... MONA, VERVET,
                      TAMARIN, TEETEE
"   , S. Amer. ALOUATT, ACARI,
                                  SAKI
"   , small, arboreal; ..... GRIVET,
      SIME, TARSIER, TITI, TOTO
monkey spider; genus ........ ATELE
"   squirrel ............. SAMIRI
"   , tufted or bonnet ........ ZATI
monkey-cup; genus ...... NEPENTHE
moneky-like animal NCHEGA, LEMUR
monkeys; genus ............. CEBUS
monkish .................. MONASTIC
mono; prefix ............ ALONE, ONE
monochord ............. SONOMETER
monogram .... CIPHER, CHARACTER
monolith .......... MENHIR, PILLAR
monomachy .................... DUEL
monomaniac ........ CRANK, CRAZY
monopolize ...... ENGROSS, COTROL
monosaccharide .................. OSE
monotonous ....... SAMELY, DRONE,
      DULL, TEDIOUS, THRUM
      HUMDRUM
monster, a ........ HILA, CERBERUS
"   , comb. form ........ TERATO

"   , fabled .............. SPHINX
"   , fabulous ..... BUCENTAUR,
                      HARPY, KRAKEN
"   , female ............. GORGON
"   , fire breathing .... CHIMERA
"   , giant .................. OGRE
"   , in classic myth. . MINOTAUR
"   , medical .............. TERAS
"   serpent ... ELLOPS, DRAGON
monster-like .............. TERATOID
monsters with no hind legs ..... API
monstrous .................... ENORM
Montague Barstow, pen name . ORCZY
Montana, city in ...... KIPP, BUTTE
Montana river ................ TETON
Montgomery's daughter ......... LIZ
month, excess of calendar over lunar;
                                  EPACT
month, of Fr. Rep. .......... NIVOSE
month, per. to .............. ABORAL
month; Span. .................... MES
months ....................... MOONS
monticle ............. HILL, KNOLL
monument TOMB, DOLMEN, RECORD
moo ...... MENHIR, OBELISK, LOW
mood ...... TID, TONE, VEIN, WHIM
moon .. CYNTHIA, LUNA, PHOEBE,
                                  SATEL
"   , area on ................ MARE
"   calf ....... DUNCE, IMBECILE,
                              MONSTER
"   crescent point .... CUSP, HORN
"   goddess; Egypt ............. ISIS
"   goddess; Greek ...... HECATE,
                      ORTHIA, SELENE
"   goddess; Lybian ...... TANITH,
                                  TANIT
"   goddess; Rom. . LUCINA, LUNA,
                                  PHOEBE
"   goddess; Syrian ...... ASTARTE
"   , imaginary inhabitants of; ......
                              SELENITES
"   , inst. for observing ......
                          SELENOSCOPE
"   , of the .............. SELENIC
"   , picture of ... SELENOGRAPH
"   point farthest from earth .......
                                  APOGEE
"   , position of .......... OCTANT
"   , valleys on, (one) ...... RILLE
moon's age at beginning of year EPACT
moon's apogee or perigee ...... APSIS
moonshine ... FLUMMERY, FUSTIAN
moonstone FELDSPAR, HECATOLITE
Moor .......... ALGERINE, BERBER
moor, barren . HEATH, PLAIN, FEN,
                                  LANDE
moor buzzard ................ HARPY
moor, to .. DOCK, FASTEN, ANCHOR
moor-cock .................. GROUSE
Moore, Tho's; book .......... UTOPIA
Moorish garment .............. JUPON
Moorish palace ............. ALCAZAR
Moorish tabor .............. ATABAL
Moor's sailboat .............. SAPIT
moose ........ ALCE, ELAND, ELKE,
                              ORIGINAL
moose; genus ................. ALCES

**175**

moose's pouch ..................... BEL
mop, cannon ........ SWAB, MERKIN
moppet ......... CHILD, DOLL, TOT
mora; law ................... DEFAULT
mora tree ..................... FUSTIC
moral .. ETHICAL, GOOD, EPIMYTH
moral fable .............. APOLOGUE
moral law .............. DECALOGUE
moral poem, short ................ DIT
morally, strengthen ........... EDIFY
morals, description of . ETHOGRAPHY
morass ... BOG, FEN, FLOW, MARSH
Moravia capital ................ BRNO
moray .. CONGEREE, EEL, HAMLET
morays; genus ............ MURAENA
morbid displacement of an organ ......
ECTOPIA
morbid insatiable appetite ADEPHAGIA
mordant .. ACRIL, EROSIVE, BITING
more . AGAIN, MAIR, MAS, PIU, PLUS
more pork of N. Z. ............. RURU
more than this ................. YEA
morello ...................... CHERRY
more-over .... BESIDES, ALSO, AND
ELSE, THERETO
Morgan's raiders ................ REBS
moribund .............. DYING, SICK
moringa seed ................... BEN
morion ...................... HELMET
morion, variety of ......... QUARTZ
Mormon .. DANITE, SMITH, YOUNG,
LAMAN
Mormon officer ................ ELDER
morning ..... EOS, AURORA, MATIN
morning concert, open air ... AUBADE
morning glory ................... NIL
morning; per. to ........ MATUTINAL
morning reception ............ LEVEE
morning star .... JUPITER, LUCIFER,
MARS, SATURN, VENUS
Moro chief ...................... DATO
Moro high priest .............. SARIP
Moro island .............. MINDANAO
Moro tribe ............. ILANO, SULU
Moroccan .................... BERBER
   "    coin .... RIAL, FLOOS, OKIA,
OUNCE
   "    hat ....................... FEZ
   "    infantryman .......... ASKAR
   "    official; Span. ..... CALAPHA
   "    seaport .... AGADIR, CEUTA,
RABAT, TETUAN
   "    town ....... FEZ, TANGIER
   "    tribesman .......... KABYLE
Morocco, district of Spanish .... RIFF
morocco, imitation ............ ROAN
Morocco, ruler of ............ SULTAN
morose ........ GLUM, GRUM, SOUR,
SPLENETIC
morphon, opposed to ............ BION
morro ...... DUNE, MOLE, HILLOCK
Morse code ...................... RUNE
morsel .... SOP, SCRAN, BITE, ORT,
SNACK
morsure ...................... BITING
mort ........ DEAD, DUMMY, FATAL
mortgagee .................... LIENOR
mortal .. DEADLY, FATAL, LETHAL

mortar ................ BOWL, HOBIT
mortar board ............. CAP, HAWK
mortar mixer .................... RAB
mortar, rel. to ....... BRAY, PESTLE
"Morte d'Arthur," author ... MALORY
mortician ............. UNDERTAKER
mortification CHAGRIN, GANGRENE,
SHAME
mortify ABASE, DENY, HUMILIATE
mortise; law .............. AMORTIZE
mortise, machine to ........ SLOTTER
mortuary ............. CINERARIUM
mortuary car ................ HEARSE
mortuary roll ................... OBIT
morvin ................... MALLEIN
mosaic, apply .............. INCRUST
mosaic, gold ................ ORMOLU
Mosaic law .......... TORA, TORAH
mosaic work ................ TESSERA
Moscow, citadel at ........ KREMLIN
Moscow, 3rd International COMINTERN
Moses, elder brother of ...... AARON
Moses, father-in-law of .... JETHRO
Moses, sister of ............. MIRIAM
Moses, wife of ............ ZIPPORAH
Moslem ISLAMIC, SARACEN, MORO
   "    cap ........................ TAJ
   "    capture of Jerusalem .. OMAR
   "    chief ..................... RAIS
   "    devil ................... EBLIS
   "    devotee ............. DERVISH
   "    dignitary ............. SHERIF
   "    doctor of law ............ ULEM
   "    headgear ................... FEZ
   "    in Turkestan .......... SALAR
   "    judge .................... CADI
   "    lawyer ................. MUFTI
   "    leader ..................... AGA
   "    learned teacher .......... ALIM
   "    minister of finance .. DEWAN
   "    , non ................... RAYAN
   "    orthodox .............. HANIF
   "    pilgrimage to Mecca .... HADJ
   "    priest .................. IMAM
   "    religion ............... ISLAM
   "    religious college ...... ULEMA
   "    sage .................... ULEMA
   "    saint .......... PIR, SANTON
   "    school ............ MADRASAH
   "    sect of Alexandria ... SENUSSI
   "    shrine ................. KAABA
   "    state ........ MUSCAT, OMAN
   "    title ..................... SID
   "    tomb dome ............. WELI
   "    tribe, Kartvelian .......... LAZ
   "    viceroy .............. NAWAB
mosque tower ...... JAMI, MINARET
mosquito .. CULICID, GALLINIPPER,
IMAGO
   "    bite preventive .. CULICIFUGE
   "    ; genus ................ CULEX
moss back ...................... FOGY
moss, Ceylon .................. AGAR
moss, like ................... MNIOID
mossbunker ............. MENHADEN
Most Holy Lord; Lat. ............ SSD
most noble ...................... HIRAM
motel ............... STOPOVER, INN

176

moth .. ARRINDA, EGGER, 10, PAGE
moth, genus of clothes ........ TINEA
moth, pearl .................... BOTYS
moth spots; med. ........ CHLOASMA
moth, spotted ............ FORESTER
mother ........ AMMA, DAM, ABBESS
   " , government by METROCRACY
   " of day and light ... NOX, NYX
   " of pearl .. NACRE, ABALONE
   " of presidents ........ VIRGINIA
   " of the gods; CYBELE, FRIGGA,
                          RHEA
   " , related on her side .. ENATIC
   " ; Tag. ..................... INA
Mother Carey's chicken ..... PETREL
"Mother of the Gracchi" .. CORNELIA
moths, sub-order of .. HETEROCERA
moth's wing spot ........ FENESTRA
motion .. AESTUS, GAIT, REQUEST
motion, imparting .......... KINETIC
motion, jerky .............. BOB, LIPE
motion picture ............. CINEMA
motion picture arc light ....... KLIEG
motionless ...... INERT, STAGNANT
motive REASON, PRESS, PRETEXT,
              SAKE, ARIA, MOTIF
motor, speed up .................. REV
mottled .... PIED, PINTO, MARBLED
mottled appearance ROE, CHECKERED
motto ........ ADAGE, GNOME, MOT,
              REASON, POESY
moue; Fr. ................... GRIMACE
mouflon ....................... SHEEP
mould ...... MOLE, KNEAD, MATRIX
moulding .. ASTRAGAL, CYMA, AME
   " , concave ............. COVING
   " , convex .... REEDING, TORUS
   " , curved ............. NEBULE
   " , egg-shaped .......... OVOLO
   " , hollow .............. SCOTIA
   " , narrow ............ REGLET
   " ornamented with disks ........
              BEZANTEE
   " , rel. to a .. ARRIS, CORNICE
   " , small square ........ LISTEL
   " ,wave-like ...... CYMA, OGEE
moult ...... OAOT, CHED, EXUVIATE
mound .... DUNE, HILL, DUN, TEE,
              TUMULUS
mount by ladders ........ ESCALADE
Mount Ranier ................ TACOMA
mountain, African ........ RIF, TSAD
   " , Arctic Zone ........ ALPINE
   " , Babylonian ....... ARARAT
   " , comb. form ............. ORO
   " crest (spur) .......... ARETE
   " formation ......... OROGENY
   " from which Moses saw Canaan;
              NEBO
   " gap .......... GATE, CORRIE
   " , high .................... ALP
   " , highest .......... EVEREST
   " in Asia ............. ALATEAU
   " in Asia Minor ............ IDA
   " in California ........... MUIR
   " in E. Africa ............ PARE
   " in India .............. GHAUT
   " in Thessaly ... OSSA, PELION

   " in Tibet .......... NANSHAN
   " in W. Hemisphere ............
              ACONCAGUA
   " in W. United States . SHASTA
   " lake, small ............. TARN
   " , legendary ..... KAF, MERU
   " , low ................. BUTTE
   " mint ................. BASIL
   " pass ... DEFILE, COL, GHAT
   " peak ................... CONE
   " ridge .. SAWBACK, SIERRA
   " , rocky ............... TETON
   " shelter; Fr. ............. GITE
   " spinach .............. ORACH
   " State .............. MONTANA
   " sunsets, reflection of .........
              ALPENGLOW
mountain, the muses ...... HELICON
   " trail marker .......... KARN
   " under Pelion .......... OSSA
   " , Wyoming .......... MORAN
mountaineer ........ MONTE, AARON
mountaineering peg ........... PITON
mountains, science of ...... OROLOGY
mountains, study of ... OROGRAPHY
mountebank ...... EMPIRIC, QUACK
mourn RUE, SIGH, WAIL, ERME, ERN
mourner .... MOEROLOGIST, MUTE
mournful .......... THRENODIC, SAD
mourning dress .... ALMA, SABLES,
              WEEDS
mouse bird ...................... COLY
mouse, meadow ................. VOLE
mouse, Old World .......... JERBOA
mourse, shrew ................... ERD
mouse, tiny ................ HARVEST
mouse-like ...... MURINE, NUGALE
moutan; Chinese ............. PEONY
mouth ......... LORRIKER, MUN, OS
   " , away from the ...... ABORAL
   " of furnace ............. BOCCA
   " organ .......... CREMBALUM,
           HARMONICA, PANDEAN
   " , part of the ....... PHARYNX
              UVULA
   " , per. to; .. RICTAL, STOMAL,
              STOMATIC
   " , per. to glands of . SALIVARY
   " , river .................... LADE
   " ; Sp. .................... BOCA
   " , thru the ........... PERORAL
   " , toward the .......... ORAD
   " , uttered thru the PAROL, ORAL
   " , wide ................. RICTUS
mouthed, loud ........ THERSITICAL
mouths .......................... ORA
movable parts .............. MOBILES
move .. KELTER, GEE, MOG, SKIRR,
          SNEAK, STIR, BUDGE, SLINK
   " along; slang ......... MOSEY
   " heavily ......... LUG, FIDGET
   " in circles ...... PURL, WRITHE
   " noisily .............. BUSTLE
   " over ...................... JOLL
   " quickly .... BOWZE, HURTLE,
              SPANK
   " rapidly ........ FLIT, CAREER
   " slowly ...... HAG, INCH, PANT

" to and fro ........... SHUTTLE
moved sidewise .... SIDLED, SLUED
moved smoothly ................. SLIP
moved swiftly .......... FLEW, SCUP
movement cure ........ MOTORPATHY
movie comedian ............. COLONNA
movie script ............... SCENARIO
movies; combo. form ............ CINE
movie fare ................. POPCORN
moving .......... NOMADIC, MOTILE
moving picture award ........ OSCAR
mow MATH, MEW, DESS, SHORTEN
mow of hay; Scot. .............. DESS
Mozart; opera by .......... SERAGLIO
much .. MOLTE, SLOSH, FELE, LOT,
                                MANY
mucilage .... ARABIN, GUM, PASTE
mud ...... SLUDGE, GOBBET, MIRE,
                    SILT, SLIME, OOZE
mud bath ............... ILLUTATION
mud eel .......................... SIREN
mud, fix in ................. BEMIRE
mud, living in .......... LIMICOLOUS
mud rake ....................... CLAUT
mud volcano ................... SALSE
mudar fibre ................. YERCUM
muddle ......... ADDLE, MESS, SOSS
muddled ........ SLIMED, BURBLED,
                            MUZZY, REE
muddy ........ GOTE, ROILY SLAKY,
                                MOIST
Muezin's call to prayer ......... AZAN
muffin ..................... COB, GEM
muffle .... MUTE, DEADEN, STIFLE,
                                 WRAP
mug .. NOG, POT, TOBY, CUP, FACE
mugger ............. GOA, CROCODILE
mulberry bark .................. TAPA
mulberry beverage ............ MORAT
mulberry, Indian ... AAL, AWL, ACH,
                            AL, RUBRA
mulberry trees; genus ........ MORUS
mulch ........................ STRAW
mulct ..... AMERCE, FINE, PUNISH,
                            SCOT, STEAL
mule ....... MUTE, HINNY, HYBRID
mules, drove of ................. ATAJO
mull ... PONDER, THINK, SWEETEN
mullet ... LIZA, GOATFISH, SUCKER
mullet, Egypt. .................. BOURI
mullet, Mex. ............ LISITA, BOBO
multitude .... GALAXY, HOST, MOB,
                    SHOAL, CROWD, THRONG
mumble .. CHAVEL, MUMP, MUTTER
mumbo-jumbo ................. FETISH
mummer ............ ACTOR, GUISER
mummy .. CADAVER, RELIC, CORPSE
mummy's spirit .................... KA
mundane ..... TERRENE, SECULAR,
                    TEMPORAL, WORDLY
mungo ...... MUG, SHODDY, WASTE
munia; zool, .................. PADDA
municipal ......... POLITICAL, CIVIC
muniment .. STRONGHOLD, RECORD
munition's center; Ill. ....... PEORIA
muntjac ....................... RATWA
Murad IV ................. AMURATH
murder .. BURKE, HOMICIDE, SLAY

murder of a king .......... REGICIDE
murder of a prophet ....... VATICIDE
murderous .... FELL, GORY, DEADLY
mure ............ IMMURE, IMPRISON
murid ............... DISCIPLE, RAT
murk .......................... GLOOM
murmur ... HUM, COO, CURR, PURL
murmur to .. FRET, REPINE, SOUGH
"Musa Dagh, Days of" ....... FORTY
Murrain ......... ANTHRAX, FEVER
Murray, Mr. ...................... KEN
mus; genus ...................... RAT
Muscat, natives ............... OMANI
muscle . BRAWN, INCISOR, LACERT,
                        TERES, SINEW
muscle, derived from ......... INOSIC
"     , lack of ............... ATAXIA
"     , outward turning .. EVERTOR
"     sugar ................. INOSITE
"     , type of ............ ROTATOR
muscles ........... PSOAS, THEWS
muscovit mieneral ............. MICA
muscular ......... BRAWNY, THEWY
   TOROSE, MIGHTY, STALWART
muscular incapability in walking .....
                                ABASIA
muscular, per. to ............. TONUS
muse ........ PONDER, MULL, RUNE
"  of astronomy ........... URANIA
"  of comedy ............. THALIA
"  of dancing ....... TERPSICHORE
"  of epic poetry ........ CALLIOPE
"  of history ................... CLIO
"  of lyric poetry and love .. ERATO
"  of music ............. EUTERPE
muse of sacred song ..... POLYMNIA
"  of tragedy ........ MELPOMENE
muses, rel. to the ......... PIERIAN
muses, sacred place of AOLEA, PIERA,
                                AONIA
muses, the ................. PIERIDES
mush ...... SAGAMITE, ATOLE, PAP
mushroom . FUNGUS, AGARIC, MISY,
                            TRUFFLE
"     disease ................. FLOCK
"     , part of a ............... GILLS
"     , superior ............... MOREL
"     , umbrella-shaped part of; .....
                                PILEUS
Musial, Mr. ..................... STAN
music, a lead in ................ PRESA
"     , a skip in ............ SALTO
"     aftersong ............. EPODE
"     , Anglo-Ind. melody ... RAGAS
"     bells, set of ............ PEAL
"     canto ................ PASSUS
"     , character in .... KEY, CLEF
"     , grace note in ..... SANGLOT
"     , half major tone SEMITONE
"     hall, low class . ODEUM, GAFF
"     in major ................. DUR
"     , leap in ................ SALTO
"     , major scale in ...... GAMUT
"     , major thirds in, Gr. DITONES
"     , mark in ............... SLUR
"     , measured beat in ..... MOTO,
                                PULSE
"     , melodic phrase in LEITMOTIF

178

"  , melodious in ........ ARIOSO
"  , metrical compo. in .... POEM
"  , nine piece compo. in . NONET
"  , ninth in .............. NONA
"  , non-concerted ........ SOLO
"  , note in Guido's scale; .. ALT,
        ELA, ELAMI, UT
"  , played on a set of bells CHIMB
"  , set of verses in ...... DERRY
"  sextuplet .......... SESTOLET
"  , short song ............. ODE
"  , sign in .............. SEGNO
"  , simple song ..... AIR, TUNE,
        LAY
"  , slowly in . ADAGIO, LARGO,
        LENTO, TARDO
"  , smooth ............. LEGATO
"  , so much ........... TANTO
"  , soprano in .......... CANTO
"  , three, thrice in . TER, TRIAD
"  , time in .... TEMPO, GIUSTO
"  , twice in ................. BIS
musical and rich . OROTUND, TONAL
"  ballad ............ DERRY
"  comedy ............... REVUE
"  compo. ..... FUGUE, MOTET,
        SONATA, CONCERTO
"  direction ........... STA, SOLI
"  direction for silence ... TACET,
        CEASE
"  half globes ........ CYMBALS
"  interlude, short ..... VERSET
"  interval .. TRITONE, OCTAVE
"  medley ..... RONDO, CENTO,
        OLIO
"  nocturne ........ SERENADE
"  note, sharpening of . ECBOLE
musical passage brilliantly executed ...
        CODA, BRAVURA
"  performance .......... REVUE
"  pipe .............. OAT, REED
"  rattle ............... SISTRUM
"  scale, degree of ....... GRADO
"  score ... CELESTA, NOTATOR
"  sign ..................... ISON
"  suite; It. .......... PARTITA
"  theme ........ ETUDE, TEMA
"  third ................. TIERCE
"  work ...... ORATORIO, OPUS,
        OPERA
mus. instrument .. REED, ASOR, OAT,
        ROCTA, KAZOO, BUGLE, UKE
"   "  , African ........... NANGA
"   "  , anc. stringed . BANDORE,
        DULCIMER, PANDURA
"   "  , bass wind ...... SERPENT
"   "  , Biblical SABECA, TABRET
"   "  , brass . CORNET, TROMBA
"   "  , brass three string; ........
        SAMISEN
"   "  ; E. Ind. .... BINA, RUANA,
        VINA
"   "  , flute-like; .. FLAGEOLET,
        THEORBO
"   "  , guitar-like .. LUTE, ROTE,
        UKULELE
"   "  , keyed . CLAVIER, SPINET
"   "  , old ................ REBEC

"   "  , old time ........ CELESTA,
        GITTERN, MARIMBA
"   "  , per. to a ...... PLECTRUM
"   "  , saxhorn family ALTHORN
"   "  , six string ........ GUITAR,
        BANJO
"   "  , small ..... CITOLE, SITOL
"   "  , Spanish ...... CASTANET,
        ATABAL
"   "  , ten string ........... ASOR
"   "  , terra cotta ..... OCARINA
"   "  , trumpet like ... CLARION,
        TUBA, SAX
"   "  , wind .............. FLUTE
musk-cat ...................... CIVET
musket, a kind of ..... HAWK, FUSIL
Musketeer ......... ARAMIS, ATHOS,
        PORTHOS
muskmelon ........ ATIMON, CASABA
muslin . MOSAL, TARLATAN, ADATI,
        SHELA, MULL, NAINSOOK, SEER-
        HAND
muslin bag ................... TILLOT
muslin, E. Ind. .... BAN, JAMLANEE
muslin, Ind. .................. GURRAH
muslin kail ................... BROTH
muslin, striped .............. DORIA
muss .. DISHEVEL, LITTER, CHAOS,
        RUMPLE, MESS, MUDDLE
mussel, fresh water .... NAIAD, UNIO
"  ; genus .............. MYTILUS
"  , large .............. HORSE
"  , part of a ............ BYSSUS
"  , river ................... UNIO
"  , sort of sea .......... NERITA
Mussolini's son-in-law ......... CIANO
Mussulman ..... MOSLEM, SARACEN
must . SAPA, JUICE, MILDEW, STUM
mustaline carnivore ........ MARTEN
mustard . SENVY, WOAD, CHARLOCK
mustard, black .............. NIGRA
mustard gas ................ YPERITE
mustard, per. to . BRASSICA, SINAPIC
mustard plaster .......... SINAPISM,
        CAPSICUM
mustard, white ................ ALBA
muster . GATHER, LEVY, MARSHAL
muster out ................ DISBAND
musty ..... RANCID, FUSTY, HOAR,
        RAFTY, BAD, FETID, RANK
Mut, daughter of ............ CHUNSU
Mut, Egypt. ................. MOTHER
Mut, husband of ................ AMON
mutable FICKLE, ERRATIC, FITFUL
mutate ....... ALTER, SPORT, VARY
mute LENE, MUM, USRD, TACITURN
mutilate .... GARBLE, GELD, MAIM,
        MAR, DEFORM, INJURE
mutiny .......... PUTSCH, REVOLT
mutter ... MUSSITATE, MAUNDER,
        PATTER, MUMBLE, THREATEN
mutton ..... CABOB, SHEEP, KABOB
mutton bird ...................... OII
mutton fish . EELPOT, PORGY, SAMA
mutual ............. JOINT, SYMBION
muzzle ........ NOSE, COPE, SNOUT,
        GAG
muzzy .......... DAZED, CONFUSED

"My Friend Irma;" char. ...... MARIE
my gal—— ........................ SAL
myopic ............... NEARSIGHTED
myriapod ............... CENTIPEDE
myrmicid ...................... ANT
myrtle ....... GUAVA, PERIWINKLE
myrtle; genus ................. VINCI
myrtle; N. Z. ............. RAMARAMA
myrtle-like shrub .......... CAJUPUT
myself; Scot. ................. MASEL
mysterious ....... CRYPTIC, MYSTIC,
                            SECRET
mystery .. RUNE, ESOTERY, CRAFT,
                ARCANUM, ENIGMA
mystic ... EPOPTIC, ORPHIC, RUNIC
"   art ................... CABALA
"   cry ...................... EVOE
"   doctrine ............ ESOTERIC
"   ejaculation ................. OM
"   , initiated .............. EPOPT
"   , pagan ............. GNOSTIC
"   secret sect ............. CABAL
"   word ................ ABRAXAS
mystical ..................... OCCULT
mystical char.; Ger. ..... ECKHARDT
mystical significance ........ ANOGOGE
mystical word ....... ABRACADABRA
mystify ........ BEFOG, OBFUSCATE
myth ............ LEGEND, FIGMENT
mythical flying being HINDU, GARUDA
mythical island in the west ATLANTIS
mythological being ......... CENTAUR
mythological hero .............. AJAX
mythological matricide ...... ORESTES
mythological monster ....... GRIFFIN
mythological serpent ........... APEPI

# N

N, letter ......................... EN
Nabal's wif ................. ABIGAIL
nabob .. DIVES, PLUTOCRAT, MIDAS
nabob depuy ................. NAWAB
nacelle ................ CAR, CHASSIS
nacre, searched for ......... PEARLED
nacrite, variety of ............. MICA
nadir, opposed to ............ ZENITH
naevus .................. FRECKLED
nag ... HENPECK, HECTOR, SCOLD,
     TWIT, PLAGUE, TEASE, HORSE,
     PARAMOUR
Naha, capital of ........... OKINAWA
nahoor ...... BHARAL, SHEEP, SNA
Nahor's wife ................ MILCAH
naiad ............. NYMPH, HYDRIAD
nail .. SPAD, BRAD, GARRON, STUD
"  driven slantingly ........... TOED
"  , headless .................. SPRIG
"  , ingrowing ........... ACRONYX
"  marking on the ......... LUNULE
"  or claw ........ TOE, UNGUIS
"  , shoemaker's ........ SPARABLE
"  size ................. TENPENNY
naive girl ...... INGENUE, ARTLESS,
                         FRANK

naked ..... BARE, EXACT, LITERAL
namaycush .. TOGUE, CREE, TROUT
——Nam ......................... VIET
"Namby-Pamby" ........... PHILIPS
namby pamby INSIPID, SILLY, VAPID
name ..... DUB, TERM, COGNOMEN,
                TITLE, ENUMERATE
"  , assumed .......... ALIAS, PEN
"  , bad ................. CACONYM
"  first ............ PRAENOMEN,
                        FORENAME
"  of a thing ................ NOUN
"  or call ................... CLEPE
"  tablet ..................... FACIA
"  , to ......... NEMEL, NEVEN
"  written backward .... ANANYM
named ........... CITED, YCLEPED
namely; law ............... SILICET
namesake ..... HOMONYM, EPONYM
nanny; Eng. ................... NURSE
Naomi ......................... MARA
maos .............. TEMPLE, CELLA
nap ..... SNOOZE, DOZE, PILE, RAS,
                   SIESTA, WINK
nap, long ...................... SHAG
nape ... SCRUFF, NIDDICK, SCURF,
                       TURNIP
nape of neck . NUQUE, NUCHA, PALL
nape of sheep's neck .......... SCRAG
napery ....................... LINEN
Naphtalite, a .................. ENAN
naphthol, kind of ...... ALPHA, BETA
napkin ......... DIAPER, DOILIE
nap-like woolen cloth ....... DUFFEL
Napoleon at Elba ............. EXILE
Napoleon's (III) mother .. HORTENSE
nappy ........... WOOLLY, DOWNEY
nap-raiser ........ TEASEL, TEAZEL
Naraka; Hindu .................. HELL
narrow opening, having . STENOPAIO
nascency ..... GENESIS, BEGINNING
narcissus ........... EGOIST, NANCY
narcosis ...... DROWSINESS, SLEEP
narcotic HEMP, ANODYNE, BHANG,
         CODEINE, ETHER, COCAINE
narcotic dose COCAINE, DOPE, LOCUS
narcotic plant .. OPIUM, MANDRAKE
nardoo; Austral. ............. CLOVER
nares ...................... NOSTRILS
narghile ..................... HOOKAH
narial ....................... RHINAL
nark; slang ..................... SPY
narrate .. RECITE, RELATE, BRUIT,
                         TELL
narrative .... CONTE, FABLE, TALE
narrative poem ......... EPIC, EPOS
narrow .... CLOSE, ANGUST, LIMIT,
                 SCANT, MEAGER
narrow, comb. form ............ STEN
narrow opening .......... STENOPAIC
narrow staves ................. BUCK
narrow strip of leather ....... THONG
narrowly incised .......... LACINIATE
narrow-mindedness .. BIGOTRY, BIAS
narrows ................. SOUND, STRAIT
narthex ........ PORCH, VESTIBULE
nasal RHINAL, NARINE, OZ(A)ENA
nascency .... BEGINNING, GENESIS

Nash; humorist .............. OGDEN
natal .......... GLUTEAL, INBORN
Nata's wife .................... NANA
nation's history ................ PAST
nation's symbol ............... CREST
native .. INDIGENOUS, ITE, NATAL,
                            SON, TAO
"    agent .......... COMPADORE,
                         COMPRADOR
"    by birth ............ DENIZEN
"    cavalryman of India .. SOWAR
"    chief; India .......... SIRDAR
"    of Asia ................... ARAB
"    of Madagascar ......... HOVA
"    of mineral ............... LIVE
"    , original ......... PRIMEVAL
"    plant ............... INDIGENE
"    salts ............... HALITES
matterjack .............. NEWT, TOAD
natty .. CHIC, NEAT, JAUNTY, TRIM
natural UNFEIGNED, BORN, INNATE
natural condition .............. NORM
natural group ........ ETHNIC, RACE
natural location ............... SITUS
natural philosophy .......... PHYSICS
natural voice; mus. ........ DIPETTO
naturalist .... ANIMIST, BIOLOGIST
naturalization .. DENIZATION, HABIT
naturalize ...... ADAPT, ACCLIMATE
naturals ...................... CRETINS
nature .... ESSENCE, LUND, MOOD
nature, per. to ................ COSMOS
nature worship ....... PHYSIOLATRY
nature's spirit .................... NAT
natus; Lat. ...................... BORN
nausea ................. PALL, QUALM
nauseous .... FULSOME, OFFENSIVE
nautical OCEANIC, MARINE, NAVAL
"    hook ............... BECKET
"    instrument ........ PELORUS,
                         SEXTANT
"    line ... BOBSTAY, MARLINE,
                         EARING
"    nautical mile .......... KNOT
"    term ........ ANEAD, ATRY,
                         ABEAM
"    term for days of poor food ....
                         BANIAN
"    term, "hove clear" ... ATRIP
nautilus .................. ARGONAUT
Nautilus commander ........... NEMO
Navaho hut ................... HOGAN
naval .......... NAUTICAL, MARINE
naval air base; Cal. ........ ALAMEDA
naval depot ............ SCAPA, BASE
naval station; Fr. ............. BREST
nave of a church .......... BODY, NEF
nave of a wheel .......... HUB, HOB
navigate ...... AVIATE, KEEL, SAIL
Navy ship ................... FLATTOP
navigation system ............. LORAN
Navy Task Force ........... ARMADA
nawab ....................... NABOB
Nazi headquarters ............. ZOSSEN
Nazi labor admin. ............... LEY
Nazi symbol .................. FYLFOT
Nazimova; actress ............. ALLA
near ... CLOSE, AT, WITHIN, DEAR

near-hand ........ ALMOST, NEARLY
near sighted .... MYOPIC, PURBLIND
nearby .......... ANENT, GIN, NIGH
neat . ADROIT, NATTY, NICE, TRIG
neat-herd ................... COWHERD
neater ..................... PRIMMER
neb ...................... BEAK, BILL
Nebraskan county ............... OTOE
Nebraskan Ind. ...... RONCA, OTOE,
                    PAWNEE, PONCA
Nebraska's Sen. ........ SEATON, UT
nebulous .............. HAZY, VAGUE
nebulous envelope CHEVELURE, COMA
necessary .. REQUISITE, LIFE, VITAL
necessitate COMPEL, FORCE, OBLIGE,
                         ENTAIL
necessity ........... MISTER, NEED
necessity of life ........... ALIMENT
neck ...... SWIRE, CRANE, CERVIX
"    , a part of the ............ GULA
"    , armor for the ........ GORGET
"    , back of the ... NAPE, NUCHA,
                         SCRUFF
"    , chief artery of ...... CAROTID
"    cloth ... BARCELONA, CRAVAT
"    frill ............. JABOT, RUCHE
"    of land ................. STRAKE
"    part of a coat ......... GEORGE
"    , part of a horse's .... WITHERS
"    , per. to the . PALEA, WATTLE,
                         ..CERVICAL
"    piece .............. BOA, FISCHU
"    scarf ................... ASCOT
"    , thin ................... SCRAG
Necker; Fr. statesman ...... JACQUES
neckerchief, flashy .......... BELCHER
necklace . BEAD, BALDRIC, RIVIERE,
                         TORQUE
necking .................. GORGERIN
necktie CRAVAT, SCARF, TIE, ASCOT
necromancer ... DIVINER, EXORCIST
necromancy .......... GOETY, MAGIC
necropsy ................... AUTOPSY
nectar ............. DRINK, MEGLIO,
                         HONEYDEW
nectar of the gods ........ AMBROSIA
need . LACK, POOR, STRAIT, THARF
needle .......... DODKIN, OBELISK
"    bug ......... NEPA, RANATRA
"    case .......... ETUI, ETWEE
"    finisher ................. EYER
"    gun ................. DREYSE
"    hole under skin ........ SETON
"    in neutral equilibrium .....
                         ASTATIZER
"    , Latin for ............... ACUS
"    , pointed ACERATE, ACEROSE
"    , sea ............... GARFISH
needlefish ................. EARL, GAR
needle-shaped .. ACICULAR, SPICULE
needlework, piece of ......... SAMPLER
negate ... NULLIFY, DENY, REFUTE
negation ....... NE, NULLITY, VETO
negative .... NAE, NOR, DENIAL
negative ion .................. ANION
negative terminal .......... CATHODE
neglect .... SHIRK, OMIT, PREVADE
negligent ....... LASH, LAX, REMISS

181

negotiate .............. DEAL, TREAT
negrito ...................... ATA, ITA
"   , Afr. .... AKKA, BAMBUTE,
                          BATWA
"   , Dutch New Guinea . TAPIRO
"   , Malayan .... ATA, SEMANG
"   of New Guinea ....... KARON
"   , Philippine .... ATTA, AETA
negro EWE, LURI, BINI, ETHIOPIAN,
                          SUK
"   , African DAHOMAN, JUR, VEI
"   , cant name applied to a CUFFEE,
                          QUASHEE
"   dance ................... JUBA
negro, Egyptian ............. NUBIAN
"   from Benin ............... EBOE
"   , gold coast ................. GA
"   Liberian . GREBO, KROO, KRU
"   magico-religious belief ...........
                          FETISHISM
"   , Niger ...... EFIK, IBO, NUPE
"   , offspring of a mulatto and .....
                          SAMBO
"   , offspring of whate and MESTEE,
                          SACATRA
"   people of the Soudan .. HAUSAS
"   Sudan ........... EGBA, JUNJE
"   tribe of Cape Verde ..... SERER
negro-magic ................. VOODOO
negroes of Nigeria ............. BENI
negroes of S. Afr. .......... BASUTOS
negroid, Medit. ............... HAMITE
"   race, Afr. .. BANTU, KAFFIR
"   race of pigmies ........ AKKA
"   S. Kordofan ............ NUBA
"   tribe of Afr. PONDO, TEMBU,
                          XOSA
negus; Ethiopian ............. TITLE
neighborhood; law . PURLIEU, VENUE
neighboring . ACCOLENT, ADJACENT
neither right nor wrong ADIAPHOROUS
nekton .................... SWIMMING
Neleus, son of .............. NESTOR
Nellie Forbush ............... MARTIN
nelumbo; Ceylon ............. LOTUS
nemesis ......... AVENGER, AGENT
nemoral ..................... SYLVAN
neophyte . CONVERT, CATECHUMEN,
                          TYRO, NOVICE
neoplasm ........ BOMBAST, TUMOR
neoteric ............. LATE, MODERN
Nepal, capital of ........ KATMANDU
Nepal, coin of ................ MOHAR
Nepal native ............... GURKHA
Nepal ruler .................... RANA
Nephele, daughter of .......... HELLE
nephew .............. NEPOTE, NEVE
nephrite ...................... JADE
Neptune, Celtic ................ LER
Neptune, discover of ........ GALLE
Neptune's sceptre .......... TRIDENT
Neptune's son .............. TRITON
Neptune's wife ............. MEDUSA
Nereus' wife ................. DORIS
nerflings ................. IDES, IDS
Nero ...................... TYRANT
Nero, successor to ........... GALBA
Nero, victims of .... LUCAN, SENECA

Nero's mother .......... AGRIPPINA
Nero's wife ................. OCTAVIA
nerol ...................... ALCOHOL
nerve blood vessels .......... PLEXUS
"   cell ................... NEURON
"   cell extension ............. AXON
"   , central ................. PUDIC
"   centres ............... CORTEX
"   connective tissue . NEUROGLIA
"   element ............. NEURONE
"   network ............... RETIA
"   passage ................. HILUM
"   , sensory ........... AFFERENT
"   ; sl. .................... CRUST
"   , tumor of the auditory GLIOMA
nerves, found in the ...... LECITHIN
nerves, per. to ................. NEURO
nerves, plexiform arrangement of RETE
nervous ....... JITTERY, TIMOROUS
nervous malady . APHASIA, NEURITIS
nervous seizure ANEURIA, AMOK, TIC
nervous shock; col. .. ONEDGE, TURN
ness ............................ CAPE
nest ............. DEN, NIDE, NIDUS
"   , build a ........ AERIE, NIDIFY
nest of a predatory bird ........ EYRIE
"   of an eagle ................ AERIE
"   of boxes; Jap. .............. INRO
"   , per. to a ............ CUBILOSE
"   , squirrels ................ DRAY
nestle . SNUGGLE, CUDDLE, PETTLE
nestling ................. BIRD, EYAS
nestling place .................... JUG
Nestor ................. SAGE, SOLON
net GIN, TOIL, TRAP, WEIR, SNARE
net, a kind of ...... SAGENE, SNOOD
net, fishing ....... SEINE, TRAMMEL
net, fine silk ................ MALINES
net for catching fry ............. JABB
net of fine threads ......... RETICLE
nether ........... DOWN, INFERNAL
Netherlands ................... DUTCH
"   , city in the ...... UTRECHT
"   coin ................. RYDER
"   commune .......... EDE, EPE
"   measure ........... STREEP
"   , political capital of .. HAGUE
"   possessions . BORNEO, JAVA
"   , province in ...... DRENTE
"   town ........... BREDA, EDE
netted .... INTERWOVEN, RETIARY
nettle; genus URTICA, PARIETARIA
nettle rash .......... HIVES, UREDO,
                          URTICARIA
network .... FRET, MOKE, PLEXUS,
                          RETICULUM, WEB
network, arterial ................. VAS
networks . MESH, SAGENES, RETES,
                          RETIA
neume; mus. ............... PNEUMA
neurad, opposed to ......... HAEMAD
neural ........... NERVAL, DORSAL
neurite, a ................... AXONE
neuro, opposed to ............. HEMAL
neuter ..................... GENDER
neutral body chemical ........ TAURIN
neutral color .................. BEIGE
neutral equilibrium ......... ASTATIC

Nevada city ............ ELKO, RENO
neve .............. ICE, SNOW, FIRN
never ................ NARRA, NARY
nevertheless ........ YET, HOWEVER
nwe .... LATE, NOVA, NEO, FRESH,
NEOTERIC
Newfoundland log house ......... TILT
New Brit. capital ............. BABUL
New Guinea, city in KITBADI, SORON
"       "  , export of ........ COPRA
"       "  gulf ...... HUON, PAPUA
"       "  Is. ........... JOBIE, ARU
"       "  , native of ..... PAPUAN
"       "  , people of .... KARONS,
KEBARS
"       "  port of entry ...... DARU
"       "  river ................. FLY
"       "  victory ............ GONA
"       "  , wild hog of ....... BENE
New Hamp. State flower ...... LILAC
New Mexican county .. OTERO, TAOS
New Mexican river ............. GILA
New Mexican state flower ..... YUCCA
new set ...................... RELAY
new word ......... COIN, NEOLOGISM
New York City ............. GOTHAM
New York County .... ERIE, ONEIDA,
ULSTER
New Zealand, extinct bird of .... MOA
"       "  evergreen tree TARATAH
"       "  fern ........ MAST, TASA
New Zealand fern root ........... ROI
"       "  fuel tree ........ MAPAU
"       "  island ............. OTEA
"       "  lake ............. TAUPA
"       "  , more pork of .... RURU
"       "  mutton bird oil . PETREL
"       "  , native of . MAORI, MORI
"       "  owl ............... RURU
"       "  palm ............. NIKAU
"       "  parrot ...... KAKA, KEA
"       "  premier ......... COATES
"       "  red pine ........... RIMU
"       "  reptile ........ TUATERA
"       "  shrub KARO, RAMARAMA
"       "  tree AKE, KAURI, MIROS,
RATA, PUKA, TARATA,
RIMU, TITOKI, TOTARA,
REDBIRCH, KAIKAKA
"       "  tribe ..... RINGATU, ATI
"       "  volcano ....... RUAPEHU
"       "  wages .............. UTU
"       "  war club ... MERE, MERI
"       "  wingless bird ..... WEKA,
APTERYX
"       "  wren; genus ... XENICUS
news .............. TIDINGS, WORD
news beat .................... SCOOP
newspaper, Falangist ........ ARRIBA
newspaper official ........ REDACTOR
News Service, far East ANETA, TASS
news stand .................... KIOSK
newt ... EFT, EVET, SALAMANDER,
TRITON
newt-like ....... LIZARD, ESK, ASK,
AXOLOTL
next .... NEIST, THEN, IMMEDIATE
next in order .................... EKA

nexus ...................... LINK, TIE
nibble PECK, BROWSE, GNAW, NAB,
BITE, CHAMP, NIP
nice FINE, NEAT, QUEASY, TICKLE
nice discernment ............ ACUMEN
niche ........ RECESS, APSE, NOOK,
TABERNACLE
nick ..... DINT, SCORE, DENT, MAR,
NOTCH
nickel alloy .......... INVAR, KONEL
nickel; sl. ......................... JIT
nickel, symbol for ................... NI
nickname ..... LEN, UGO, MONIKER
nickname for pretender to religion .....
TARTUFFE
nictating ..................... AWINK
nictitae .............. BLINK, TWINK
nidor ........ AROMA, SAVOR, SCENT
nidi ........................... NESTS
nidus ......... NEST, REPOSITORY
niepa bark ..................... NIOTA
nieve; Scot. .................... FIST
Nigeria, capital of ............. LAGOS
"  seaport ............... LAGOS
"  State .................. NUPE
"  town ............ EDE, ISA
Nigerian tribe . EFIK, EBOE, BENIN,
EDO, ARO
niggard .......... MISER, SKINFLINT
nigh ...................... ANEAR, AT
night ....... BELATED, GABE, GABI
night; comb. form .............. NYCTI
night wandering .... NOCTIVIGANT
nightblindness ...... HEMERALOPIA
nightfall, occurring at ... ACRONICAL
night-hawk, Amer. ............. SISK
nightingale ....... PHILOMEL, LIND,
THRUSH
nightjar; S. Am. ............... POTOO
nightmare .... ALP, INCUBUS, MARA
nightshade ..... DATURA, MORELLE,
BELLADONNA
nightsight ............... NYCTALOPIA
nightwatchman ............... SERENO
nihil, or nil; Lat. ........... NOTHING
Nile dam ..................... ASWAN
"  , catfish ................. BAGRE
"  , falls of the .............. RIPON
"  , floating vegetable in ...... SUDD
"  , island in the ............. RODA
"  , rel. to ................. NILOTIC
"  river city ............. ROSETTA
"  ship's captain ........ RAIS, REIS
"  , source of .............. TSANA
"  , tributary of the ........ KAGERA
nimble .... DEFT, FLIT, GLEG, LISH,
AGILE, VOLANT
nimbus ... AUREOLA, GLORIA, HALO
nimiety ...................... EXCESS
nimrod ...................... HUNTER
"Nina Leeds" by ............. O'NEILL
nincompoop ......... DOLT, WITLING
nine days devotion ......... NOVENA
"  headed monster; Gr. ...... HYDRA
"  inches ..................... SPAN
"  number ...... ENNEA, ENNEAD
"  , per. to .............. NONAGON
ninepins .......... KEELS, SKITTLES

183

ninny ... **BLOCKHEAD, DOLT, LOUT, FOOL, SIMPLETON, SAMMY**
ninth ............. **NONUS, ENNEATIC**
ninth day before the Ides ...... **NONES**
ninth day, recurring each ..... **NONAN**
niobe .......................... **FUNKIA**
Niobe's brother ............... **PELOPS**
Niobe's father ............ **TANTALUS**
Niobe's husband ............ **AMPHION**
niobic .................... **COLUMBIC**
nip ...... **BLAST, CHILL, CUT, GIBE, SARCASM**
Nip airbase .................. **MARCUS**
nipa palm ............. **ATAP, ATTAP**
nis .......................... **KOBOLD**
nisus ............. **EFFORT, IMPULSE**
niter .......................... **POTASH**
nitid ............... **GAY, SPRUCE**
nitric acid ............. **AQUAFORTIS**
nitrite .......................... **AZOTITE**
nitrobenzene ................. **MIRBANE**
nitrogen, comb. form .............. **AZO**
nitrogen, old chemistry name ...**AZOTE**
nitroglycerin ............. **GLONOIN**
nitrous acid, salt of ........... **NITRITE**
nitwit .......... **BOOB, DUNCE, FOOL**
niveous ....................... **SNOWY**
nix ........... **SPIRIT, NO, NOTHING**
no ...... **BAAL, NAE, NAW, NE**
no more than .................... **MERE**
no one ...................... **NIX**
Noah's father ................. **LAMECH**
Noah's grandson ............... **ARAM**
Noah's son .. **JAPHETH, SHEM, HAM**
nob .................... **HEAD, NAVE**
nobility ....... **GENTRY, YEOMANRY**
noble **EDEL, EPIC, GRAND, SUPERB**
nobleman ...... **EARL, THANE, LORD, PEER**
nobleness of birth ............ **EUGENY**
nobody ... **JACKSTRAW, NONENTITY**
noctuid .................. **MOTH, WORM**
nocturnal carnivore ............ **RATEL**
nocturnal mammal ............ **LEMUR**
nocturnal signs ............ **ZODIACAL**
nocturne ..... **LULLABY, SERENADE**
nod .......... **NIP, BECK, BOW, WINK**
nodding .... ... **ANNUENT, NUTANT**
node of a poem .................. **PLOT**
node of a stem .................. **JOINT**
nodular bone in a tendon ... **SESAMOID**
nodule .. **KNOT, MASS, LUMP, BUMP**
nodule of stone ........ **AUGE, GEODE**
Noel; Lat. .................... **NATALIS**
noggin ............. **GILL, MUG, PATE**
noise ..... **CLAMOR, BLARE, CHANG, CHORTLE, ROAR, STRIDOR, STREPOR, DIN, ROUT, BOOM**
noise abroad ...... **BRUIT, AIR, PEAL**
noise; dial. Eng. .............. **LEDEN**
noise-ghost ............ **POLTERGEIST**
noisily; go .................... **LARUM**
noisome ............. **FETID, NOXIOUS**
noisy ....... **CREAKY, STREPATANT, BLATANT**
nomad ...... **LURI, ARAB, SARACEN, SCENITE**
nomad magistrate .......... **NOMARCH**
monarchy ...................... **NOME**

nomenclature ....... **ONYMY, NAMING**
nominal ............... **PAR, TITULAR**
nominal recognizance; law ........ **DOE**
nonage ....... **MINORITY, PUPILAGE, NEANT**
nonce .......... **OCCASION, PURPOSE**
nonchalant .... **INSOUCIANT, COOLLY**
nonconformist .. **HERETIC, SECTARY**
nonconformity .......... **RECUSANCE**
none ........... **NARY, NAE, UN, NIN**
nonentity ........ **NOBODY, CIPHER**
nonessential .......... **ADVENTITIOUS**
nonessential in religion **ADIAPHORON**
nonesuch ........ **MODEL, PARAGON**
nonmetallic element **BORON, BROMIN, SILICON, IODIN**
nonmetallic mineral .............. **SPAR**
nonpareil ........... **POPE, SUPREME**
nonpareil, six point .............. **TYPE**
nonplus .. **MYSTIFY, PUZZLE, STUMP**
nonplused ......... **ALL, PERPLEXED**
nonsense .......... **ROT, TOSH, BLAH, FALDERAL, FARRAGO, BLATHER, STITE, AMPHIGORY, BALDERDASH**
nonsense creature ...... **GOOP, SNARK**
noodle dish .................... **RAVIOLI**
nook . **HERNE, CANT, COVE, RECESS**
nooks .... **RETREATS, CORNERS, INS**
noon ............. **MIDDAY, MERIDIAN**
noonday rest ................... **SIESTA**
nootka ........................... **AHT**
nor in ............................... **NIN**
Norbertine ......... **PREMONSTRANT**
norm .................... **MODEL, RULE**
norma .. **PATTERN, SQUARE, GAUGE**
normal **NATURAL, JUST, MEAN, PAR**
Normand; actress ............ **MABEL**
Normandy bagpipe ............. **LOURE**
Normandy, capital ............ **ROUEN**
Normandy cheese .......... **ANGELOT**
Normandy, departments .. **CALVADOS, EURE, MANCHE, ORNE**
Normandy, early conqueror of . **ROLLO**
Norn; myth. ... **SKULD, URTH, WYRD**
Norris; novelist ................ **FRANK**
Norse bard ........ **SAGAMAN, SCALD**
" chieftain ................. **JARL**
" collection of songs; myth. **EDDA**
" deity .. **ODIN, RAN, THOR, VAN**
Norse giant; myth. .. **FAFNIR, JOTUN, MIMIR, LOKI, YMER, YMIR**
" giantess; myth. .. **GROA, NATT, NORN, NOTT**
" god .... **AS, ASA, DONAR, ULL, VALI**
" god, "All Fathers" ........ **ODIN**
" god of discord and evil .... **LOKI**
" god of fruitfulness ........ **FREY**
" god of light ............ **BALDER**
" god of peace .. **FORSETI, FREY**
" god of poetry ..... **BRAGI, ODIN**
" god of sea .... **AEGER, NJORD, YMIR**
" god of sun ............ **BALDER**
" god of thunder ........... **THOR**
" god of war ... **ER, ODIN, THOR, TYR**
" god of watchfulness **HEIMDALL**
" goddess, giant ... **NORN, URTH**

184

" goddess of beauty ...... **FREYA**
" goddess of death ... **HEL, HELA**
" goddess of destiny **MOIRA, NORN**
" goddess of earth .......... **SIF**
" goddess of healing ........ **EIR**
" goddess of history ........ **SAGA**
" goddess of love **FREYA, FREYJA**
" goddess of peace .......... **EIR**
" goddess of the seas **RAN, RANA**
" goddess of the sky ...... **FRIGG**
" gods .. **AESIR, ASA, FORSETI, LOKI, THOR, VANIR, YMIR**
" gods, abode of the ..... **ASGARD**
" gods, king of .......... **WODEN**
" guardian of Asgard **HEIMDALL**
" king; myth. ................ **ATLI**
" lord of the ooze ........ **HOENIR**
" navigator ................. **ERIC**
" nobleman ................. **JARL**
" plateau ................... **FJELD**
" poem ..................... **RUNE**
" poet ...................... **SCALD**
" poetry .......... **RUNE, RUNIC**
" queen of the underworld .. **HEL, HELA**
" saint ...................... **OLAF**
" serpent; myth. ...... **MIDGARD**
" tale ...................... **SAGA**
" viking ................... **ROLLO**
" warrior; myth. ... **BERSERKER**
" watchdog; myth. ........ **GARM**
" wolf; myth. ............. **FENRIR**
" world tree; myth. ... **YGDRASIL**
N. African (see "African")
N. American (see "American")
N. Carolina river ......... **TAR, NEUSE**
N. Dakota city ................. **MINOT**
N. Dakota county ............. **TRAILL**
N. Guinea port .................... **LAE**
N. Pole .............. **RED, POLYNIA**
N. Sea port ................... **EMDEN**
north star ............... **LODESTAR**
North-west highway ........... **ALCAN**
northern **BOREAL, SEPTENTRIONAL, HYPERBOREAN**
northern bear ................. **RUSSIA**
northern constellation . **ANDROMEDAE**
northernmost inhabitable portion of world ..................... **THULE**
Norway ........................ **NORGE**
Norway, coin of ....... **KRONA, ORA**
Norway, early ruler of ........ **HAKON**
Norway, mountain range in .. **KJOLEN**
Norway, patron saint of .. **OLAF, ODES**
Norway river ... **NAMSEN, OI, TANA**
Norway, ter. division ............. **AMT**
Norway's crown prince .......... **OLAF**
Norway's whirlpool ...... **MAELSTROM**
Norwegian counties; collec. ... **AMTER**
" composer ............. **GRIEG**
" county .. **FINMARK, TROMSO**
" eruptive rocks ........ **GABRO, NORITE**
" explorer ... **MOHN, NANSEN, SARS**
" game bird ............. **RYPE**
" governor ......... **AMTMAND**
" inlet of sea ... **FIORD, FJORD**
" land divisions ....... **FYLKIS**

" needlework .... **HARDANGER**
" parliament ....... **LAGTHING, STORTHING**
" town ... **NARVIK, OSLO, NES**
" writer ................. **IBSEN**
nose .... **NASUS, CONK, NEB, SCENT**
" ailment .................. **CORYZA**
" , bee's ...................... **LOR**
" , cartilage of the ....... **SEPTUM**
" , elongated ........... **PROBOSCIS**
" , inflammation of ....... **RHINITIS**
" , long projecting ........ **SNOUT**
" , opening in ................ **NARE**
" , partition in ............. **VOMER**
" , rare .................. **OLFACTOR**
" , snub ................... **SIMOUS**
nosebleeding ............... **EPISTAXIS**
nosegay ................. **ODOR, POSY**
noso; word element .......... **DISEASE**
nostalgia ............ **HOMESICKNESS**
nostology ................. **GERIATRICS**
nostradamus ........ **PROPHET, SEER**
nostril .......... **NARE, NARI, THRILL**
not apt ......................... **INEPT**
not any .......... **NARY, STEAD, NUL**
not divided ................. **UNITARY**
not feral .......................... **TAME**
not, French for ..................... **PAS**
not open, as some seed capsules ...... **INDEHISCENT**
not; prefix ........ **IR, IL, IM, NON, UM**
not so good ...................... **ILLY**
not so much ..................... **LESS**
not to know; Scot. ............. **UNKEN**
not wanted; Fr. ............... **DETROP**
notch **DENT, INDENTURE, JAB, NICK, SCORE, INDENT**
notched ......... **EROSE, CRENATED, SERRATED**
notches ......................... **HILA**
note .. **MINUTE, BILLET, MARGINAL**
" double whole .............. **BREVE**
" , explain by ............... **GLOSS**
" , explanatory ........ **SCHOLIUM**
" , half ...................... **MINIM**
" , marginal ................. **POSTIL**
" musical ................. **PUNCTUS**
" , of ....................... **FAMED**
" , promissory .............. **GOOD**
" , sharpening of; mus. .... **ECBOLE**
" , short ............ **CHIT, CHITTY**
" sounded at kill ............. **MORT**
" , tail of a ................. **FILUM**
" , visible .................... **MARK**
note-book .... **ADVERSARIA, STREET**
notes in Guido scale .... **ALT, ELA, UT**
notes, succession of **STRAIN, TIRALEE**
nothing .. **NICHIL, LUKE, NIHIL, NIL, ZERO**
nothing but ..................... **MERE**
notice .... **GOME, MARK, QUOTE, SEE**
notice for heroic service .... **CITATION**
notice, official ............. **BULLETIN**
notify **APPRISE, CITE, INFORM, TELL**
notion ... **FREIT, OMEN, IDEA, VIEW, WARES, WHIM**
notoriety ...................... **ECLAT**
notwithstanding **NATHLESS, MAUGRE, YET**

185

nougat ............. CONFECTION, NUT
noumenal .................... ONTAL
noun, indeclinable ............ APTOTE
noun, neuter verbal ......... GERUND
noun of common gender ..... EPICENE
noun relation; per. to ........... CASAL
noun suffix .. ERY, ET, IER, ION, FER,
ISE, IST
noun suffix signifying state ...... ENCE
nourice; obs. ................... NURSE
nourish ............... FEED, FOSTER
nourishing ............. ALIBLE, ALMA
nourishment ...... ALIMENT, MANNA,
PABULUM
nous ............. MIND, INTELLECT
nouveau riche .. UPSTART, PARVENU
Nova; astron. .................... STAR
Nova Scotia ........ ACADIA, ACADIE
Nova Scotia cape .............. CANSO
Nova Scotia lake ........... BRAS D'OR
Nova Scotia native ........ BLUENOSE
Novarro; actor .................. RAMON
novel ...... FRESH, RARE, ROMANCE
novice ........ PUNY, TYRO, TYRONE,
YOUNKER, AMATEUR,
NEOPHYTE, TIRO
novitiate .................. PROBATION
Nox; (Rom.) ................. NYX (Gr.)
Nox, brother of .............. EREBUS
Nox, husband of ............... CHAOS
noxious .. EVIL, BANEFUL, NOCENT,
NOISOME
nozzle .................... NOSE, SNOUT
noxious atmos. ............... MALARIA
nozzle, blast furnace ........ TUYERE
nozzle, in mining ................ GIANT
nuance .......... SHADE, VARIATION
nub ................. JAG, KNOB, SNAG
nubia ................. CLOUD, WRAP
Nubian mus. inst. ............. SISTRUM
nubilous ............. CLOUDY, FOGGY
nucha ............................ NAPE
nuclear network fiber ........... LININ
nucleus of regiment ........... CADRE
nucleus, Sun spot ............. UMBRA
nudge ..... PROD, KNUB, POKE, NOG
nudibranch .................... SNAIL
nugae; Lat. .......... JESTS, TRIFLES
nugatory .............. TRIVIAL, VAIN
nugget .......... LUMP, MASS, SLUG
nuisance ................. BANE, PEST
nuisance remover ............. ABATOR
nullah; Hindu ........ RAVINE, GORGE
nullify .. CANCEL, VOID, ABROGATE,
NEGATE, UNDO
numb .......... RIGESCENT, FUNNY,
HEBETATE
number ........ SURD, COUNT, DIGIT,
SCALAR
number, a whole ............. INTEGER
number four ................. TETRAD
number, least whole ............. UNIT
number nine ................. ENNEAD
numbered; Bib. .................. MENE
numbers .... MUSIC, POETRY, VERSE
numbles .................... INWARDS
Numidian city ................. HIPPO

Numidian crane ........ DEMOISELLE
numskull ........... DOLT, LACKWIT,
LOGGERHEAD
nun ...... TERESA, MONIAL, SMEW,
TITMOUSE, SISTER
nun bird; genus .............. MONASA
nun, Franciscan ..... BESTAL, CLARE
nuncio ........ MESSENGER, LEGATE
nuncupative .................... ORAL
nun-moth .................... TUSSOCK
nunnery ..................... CLOISTER
nunnery, founder of first; Eng. EABALD
nunnery ruins ............. MYNCHERY
nunni ........................ BLESBOK
nunting; dial. Eng. ............. SCANT
nuphar .................... NYMPHAEA
nupson ......................... FOOL
nuptial ....... HYMENEAL, BRIDAL
nuque ........................... NAPE
nurse AMAH, AYAH, BONNE, NORICE
nurse, to ........ REAR, TEND, CARE
nurse shark ...................... GATA
nursery, public day ........... CRECHE
nurse's headgear ........... WIMPLES
nut .... BEN, BETEL, BRAZIL, KOLA,
PECAN
nut confection ......... MARCHPANE,
MARZIPAN
nut, per. to ................... NUCAL
Nut, son of ......................... RA
nutation .............. NODDING, NOD
nut-bearing ............ NUCIFEROUS
nuthatch ....... XENOPS, TITMOUSE
nuthatches; genus .............. SITTA
nutlet ........................ PYRENE
nutmeg ................. SEED, SPICE
nutmeg-like fruit ........ CAMARA(N)
nutria producing animal ....... COYPU
nutriment ...... FOOD, ALIMENT
nuts; collec. ..................... MAST
nuts fallen .................... SHACK
nutty; slang ... FLAVOR, ZEST, GAGA
nuzzle ............... BURROW, ROOT
nymph ................... SYLPH
"    abducted by Idas .. MARPESSA
"    beloved by Pan ...... SYRINX
"    changed into laurel tree ........
DAPHNE
"    , fountain .... NAIAD, EGERIA
"    Hesperid ............... AEGLE
"    , mountain ............. OREAD
"    of "Moham. Paradise" .. HOURI
"    , sea NEREID, SCYLLA, SIREN
"    , trees . DRYAD, HAMADRYAD
"    , water .............. UNDINE
"    , wood of Elis; Gr. ARETHUSA
"    , woods ............... DRYAD
nymphaea ................... CASTALIA
nymphs, queen of ................ MAB
nyrosa ...................... AYTHYA
nyssa ....................... TUPELO
nystagmus ........................ TIC
Nyx ............................ NOX
Nyx, personified ............. NIGHT
Nyx's daughter ................. ERIS
Nyx's husband ................. CHAOS
nzambi, rel. to ............. BAKONGO

# O

O, letter .......................... OWE
O; Scot. .......................... OCH
oaf ..... BOOR, DOLT, DUNCE, LOUT,
OUPH(E)
oak .......... CLUB, BRAVE, STRONG
oak bark ........ CRUT, EMORY, MILL
" , California .............. ENCINA
" , European ............. DURMAST
" , fruit of the ...... ACORN, MAST
" , genus of the .......... QUERCUS
" holm ......................... ILEX
" , immature fruit of ...... CAMATA
" , Jerusalem ............. AMBROSE
" of Turkey ............. CERRIS
" , white; Cal. ............... ROBLE
Oakie ......................... MIGRANT
oar ... PADDLE, SPOON, SCULL, PLY
oar blade ............... PEEL, WASH
oar, flat part of ........ PALM, PEEL
oar fulcrum ................... THOLE
oar, part of ............... LOOM, PALM
oars; collec. .................. OARAGE
oars, having one bank of .... UNIREME
oarsman ..................... REMEX
oar-shaped .... REMIPED, REMIFORM
oasis .......................... WADI
oasis in Cen. Asia .............. MERV
oasis in Egypt .............. DAKHLA
oasis in Tunisia ................ GAFSA
oast ...................... KILN, OVEN
oat husks .................... SHUDE
oat thicket ............... CHAPARRAL
oat, wild ..................... CHEAT
oatcake ......................... CAPER
oatear ...................... WAGTAIL
oath VOW, BEDAD, SERMENT, AITH,
DRAT, GOSH
oatmeal cake ........... PONE, SCONE
oats; Fr. ...................... AVOINE
oats; genus ................... AVENA
oats paid in lieu of rent .... AVENAGE
Obadiah ...................... ABDIAS
obdurate ..... HARD, MULISH, STONY
obedient ...... AMENABLE, DUTEOUS
obeisance . HOMAGE, BINGE, FEALTY
obeisance, to make CONGEE, SALAAM,
BOW, CURTSY
obelisk .... GUGLIA, NEEDLE, PYLON
obelisk, reference ............... MARK
Oberon ......................... FAIRY
Oberon, Miss ................... MERLE
Oberon's wife ................ TITANIA
obese ..... FAT, FLESHY, LIPAROUS,
TURGID, PUFFY, PURSY
obey ...... MIND, EAR, HEAR, YIELD
obfuscate ........ CONFUSE, DARKEN
obi ........... CHARM, FETISH, SASH
obit ....... DEATH, RELEASE, REST
object ...... AIM, END, GOAL, THING
object set up to be tilted at . QUINTAIN
object, to .... DEMUR, PROVIDED, IF
objection ..... CAVIL, QUARREL, BAR
objects used by Biblical high priests; ..
URIM
objurgate .... CHIDE, REPROVE, JAW
oblate, opposed to .......... PROLATE

obligation .. TIE, DEBT, BOND, DUTY,
MUST, OWED, ONUS
obliged ........ FAVORED, OBSTRICT
oblique, in mining ............ CLINIC
obliquely ......... AGLEE, ASKANCE
obliterate SPONGE, ERASE, EXPUNGE
obliteration .................. ERASURE
oblivion producer .......... NEPENTHE
oblivion, stream of . SILENCE, LETHE,
NIRVANA
obnoxious ........ LIABLE, HATEFUL,
RANCID, ODIOUS, VILE
oboe, small ......... HAUTBOY, REED,
MUSETTE
obscuration .. NUBLIATION, ECLIPSE
obscure .... NAMELESS, DIM, MIRKY,
ECLIPSE, VAGUE, REMOTE
obscure, to ...... DELUDE, OVERSILE
obscurity CLOUDY, DARKNESS, FOG,
GLOOM
obsecrate ...... BESEECH, ENTREAT
obsequies ... FUNERAL, PYRE, WAKE
obsequious .......... SERVILE, SLICK,
DUTIFUL
observation ...... PROEM, ESPIAL,
ASSERTION, IDEA, REMARK
observatory in Cal. .. LICK, PALOMAR
observe NOTICE, EYE, LO, NARK, SEE
TOUT
observed, matter to be .... NOTANDUM
obsidian ......... LAVA, IZTLE, LAPIS
obsolete .......... DISUSED, ARCHAIC,
EFFETE
obstacle ...... BAR, DAM, LET, SNAG
obstinate DOUR, SET, MULISH, SULK
obstruct ....... DAM, BAR, CLOG, DIT,
IMPEDE, OCCLUDE
obtain ...... EARN, FANG, GET, WIN
obtain with difficulty ...... EKE, SPIN
obtruncate .. LOP, HEW, RETRENCH
obtund ........ BLUNT, DULL, QUELL
obverse .... COUNTERPART, FRONT
obvious .. GROSS, PATENT, EVIDENT
obvolution ................ FOLD, TWIST
oca ................ OXALIS, SORREL
occasion ...... EVENT, NONCE, SELE
occident .............. WEST, SUNSET
occidental ..... HESPERIAN, PONENT
occult ... CRYPTIC, HIDDEN, MYSTIC
occultation ... ECLIPSE, GONE, LOST
occultism ........ CABALA, MYSTERY
occupation ... CALL, NOTE, PURSUIT
occupied ........................ TOOK
occupy ... INTEREST, FILL, OVERSIT
occur ......... BEFALL, COME, LIGHT
occurring at nightfall ... ACRONICAL
occurring at regular intervals ... HORA
occurring, eight day intervals . OCTAN
occurring every fourth year .............
PENTETERIC
ocean .... BRIM, BRINE, DEEP, MAIN,
POND
ocean, deep ..................... JUBE
ocean, on the ................... ASEA
ocean route ..................... LANE
Oceania, part of ........... POLYNESIA
oceanic ........... MARINE, PELAGIC
Oceanus, wife of ............. TETHYS
ocellus .......................... EYE

187

ocelot .......................... CAT
ochre, Indian .............. ALMAGRA
ochre, red .................... TIVER
ochre, yellow .................. SIL
ocilli, one of the ........... STEMMA
octahedrite ................. ANATASE
octave ....................... EIGHT
octave of a feast .......... UTIS, UTAS
Octavia's brother .......... AUGUSTUS
Octavia's husband ........... ANTONY
octopus ........ HEE, POULPE, SQUID
octoroon ..................... METIS
ocular ..... OPTIC, ORBITAL, VISUAL
oculi ......................... EYES
odd ........ AZYGOUS, EXTRA, ORRA
oddity ............... IDIOSYNCRASY
odds and ends ......... BROTT, ORTS,
                        ADVANTAGE
odeon .... HALL, THEATRE, ODEUM
Oder, tributary of ............ NEISSE
odic, electrical force ....... ELOD, OD
Odin ................. WODEN, WOTAN
Odin, brother of ....... VE, VILE, VILI
Odin, son of ..... BALDER, TYR, VALI
Odinic Olympus .............. ASGARD
Odin's horse ............... SLEIPNER
Odin's palace ..................... SYN
Odin's parents .......... BESTLA, BOR
Odin's wife ....... RIND, FRIA, FRIGG
odor; AROMA, FETOR, NIDOR, NOSE,
                            SCENT
odor of cooking meat .......... FUMET
odoriferous principle of violet root .....
                      IRONE, ORRIS
odorous ...... REDOLENT, AROMATIC
odylic ............... ODIC, OD, ODYLE
Odysseus .................... ULYSSES
Odysseus' dog ................ ARGOS
Odysseus' father ............. LAERTES
"Odysseus' Return"; heroine ..........
                          PENELOPE
Odyssey, author of the ......... HOMER
Oedipus' brother-in-law ........ CREON
Oedipus' daughter ........ ANTIGONE
Oedipus' father ................. LAIUS
oestrid fly larva ................... BOT
oeuvre; Fr. ..................... WORK
of a flock ..................... GREGAL
of a reign ..................... REGNAL
of a wife ..................... UXORIAL
of all ............................. AVA
of each ........................... ANA
of like kind ..................... SUCH
of old age ................. GERONTAL
of the age ........................ AET
of the earth ...................... GEAL
of the, French for ................. DU
of the new stone age ....... NEOLITHIC
of the same name ................. ILK
of the summer .............. ESTIVAL
of the third degree ........... CUBICAL
of the tribe of Dan ............ DANITE
of this day ............... HODIERNAL
off .. AGEE, ASIDE, AWAY, BEGONE,
                            DOFF
offchance .................... REMOTE
offend ........ RASP, RASS, CAG, MIF,
                          MORTIFY
offense FELONY, GRIEF, MALUM, SIN

offense against law .......... DELICT
offer HAND, BID, PROPINE, PROFFER
offering, as a vow ........... CORBAN
offering resistance to force RENITENT
offhand .. EXTEMPORE, IMPROMPTU
office ... POST, FUNCTION, STATION,
                            WIKE
office of a datary; Rom. ..... DATARIA
office, relinquish ............... DEMIT
office-holder .............. PLACEMAN
officer ADJUTANT, SHERIFF, TINDAL
officer; abb. .................. SGT, ENS
officer of British royal guard ..... EXON
officer of king's stables ....... AVENER
officer's assistant ................. AIDE
official, an ................... BASHAW
  "    approval .......... VISA, VISE
  "    decree ................... UKASE
  "    , governing .... BUREAUCRAT
  "    order ................ RESCRIPT
  "    sent by king .......... MISSUS
offshoot SPRIG, BRANCH, ISSUE, ROD,
                          SON, SCION
O'Flaherty; novelist .............. LIAM
ogee moulding .. TALON, CYMA, GULA
Ogier ..................... NORSEMAN
"Ogier le Danois," myth. island described
  in ........................... AVALON
ogle ... EYE, LEAR, MARLOCK, LEER
ogre; Fr. ..................... HUGON
Ohio town ... BEREA, XENIA, AKRON
oil .. ASARUM, BEN, GREASE, OLIUM
  "  beetle; genus .............. MELOE
  "  , comb. form ............... OLEO
  "  flask ......................... OLPE
  "  , fragrant .................. ATTAR
  "  lamp ..................... LUCIGEN
  "  made from butter ........... GHEE
  "  market ...................... TELI
  "  obtained from coal ..... PHOTOGEN
  "  of orange ................. NEROLI
  "  ointment .............. OLEAMEN
  "  peculiar smelling ....... ERICINOL
  "  producing ............. OLIFIANT
  "  port ............. ABADAN, HAIFA
  "  producing tree ............... BEN
  "  skin ........................ SEBUM
  "  tree ............. EBOE, MAHWA
  "  tubes, destitute of ....... EVITATE
  "  , unproductive boring for . DUSTER
  "  well gone wrong .......... GASSER
oilbird ..................... GUACHARO
oillet ........................ EYELET
oils, liquid part ......... ELAEOPTENE
oilseed ........ ........ SESAME, TIL
oilstone ........................ HONE
oily ...... FAT, OLEIC, GLIB, OLEOSE
  "  beach tar compound ..... CRESSOL
  "  ketone .......... CARONE, IRONE
  "  liniment ............. OLEANDER
  "  liquid . PICAMAR, TAR, ANILINE,
                            OCTANE
  "  substitute in fats .......... OLEIN
ointment .......... BALSAM, CEROMA,
                   UNGUENT, GREASE
ointment application . EMBROCATION
ointment; Bib. ............ SPIKENARD
ointment, dry .......... XEROMYRUM

188

ointment, healing ....... BALM, LARD, SALVE, NARD
ointment, oil ....... CERATE, CARRON
Oise tributary .................... AISNE
Okinawa capital ................ NAHA
Okinawa commander ...... SPRUANCE
Oklahoma city .................... ENID
Oklahoma county ............. GARVIN
" governor .............. KERR
" Indian; ........ CHEROKEE CREEK, PAWNEE, PONCA
" mountain ............ OZARK
" river ................... RED
" state ............. SOONER
" state flower .... MISTLETOE
okra ..... BENDY, GUMBO, HIBISCUS
old ...... ORRA, NIGHT, SENESCENT, SENILE, GRAY, OGYGIAN, DATED
" age, per. to .. ELDERLY, GERATIC
" Arabian gold coin ........... DINAR
" (archaic) ...................... ELD
" cloth measure ................. ELL
" English coin ............. CAROLU
" English rent ................. TAO
" fashioned ...... QUAINT, FOGRAM
" fashioned word ........ ARCHAISM
" French coin ............. ECU, RIAL
" German coin ............. DUCAT
" hair-do ........................ RAT
" man ... ALTE, GAFFER, GEEZER, NESTOR
" military rank ......... BANNERET
" refrain in songs .............. FALA
old sailor ......................... SALT
" saying ..... ADAGE, MAXIM, SAW
"Old Sod" ........................ ERIN
" , Spanish for ................. VIEJO
" squaw ..................... DUCK
" style war vessel .......... FRIGATE
Old Testament land of riches ... OPHIR
Old Testament writer ......... ELOHIST
old time ............. ELD, QUONDAM
" time object .................... URIM
" woman ... CRONE, GAMMER, HAG
" womanish ..................... ANILE
" world falcon ................. SAKER
" world herb ................. TANSY
Oldcastle, John ............... CODIIAM
olden time; poet. .................. YORE
older .............. SENIOR, STALER
oldest division of Europe ... JURASSIC, LIAS
Oleander; genus .............. NERIUM
oleic acid ...................... OLEATE
oleoresin ....... ANIME, ELEMI, TOLU
olfaction ..................... OSMESIS
Olimpia, husband of .......... BIRENO
Olin; writer ................ STEPHEN
olio ....................... CHOWCHOW
Oliphant; novelist ......... MARGARET
olive ...... OLEASTER, ESCUTCHEON
olive, fruit of the .............. DRUPE
olive, stuffed ................ PIMOLA
olive, wild ................. OLEASTER
olive-oil; comb. form ............ ELAIO
ollapodrida ...................... HASH
olvinic of the rocks ............. OLIC
Olympic cupbearer ....... GANYMEDE
Olympic game site .............. ELIS

Olympic inhab. ................. ATHENA
Olympus of Hindus .............. MERU
Omar Khayyam's country ........ IRAN
omber, card in ................. BASTO
omen PORTENT, ABODANCE, TOKEN
omer's, ten ..................... EPHA
omicron .......................... CETI
omission .... CARET, BALK, ELESION, OVERSIGHT
omit . BATE, IGNORE, LET, DELETE, SKIP
omneity ...................... ALLNESS
omni; a prefix ..................... ALL
omniverous mammal ............. HOG
on dit; Fr. ................... RUMOR
on tap .................... BROACHED
"On the Banks of the Wabash," writer .. DRESSER
on the hither side of the river Po ....... CISPADANE
on the ocean ..................... ASEA
"On The Town"; by ........ LEONARD
on the windward side .... AWEATHER, LEE
on this side; Lat. ................. CIS
onager ............................ ASS
once ..... ANEW, ENE, ERST, YANCE
oncorhynchus ................. SALMON
ondoyant ...................... WAVY
one ........ ITE, UNO, ACE, AN, UNIT
" after the other ........ SERIATIM
" , against ..................... ANTI
" and one hundred ................ CI
" born in a serfdom ............ NEIF
" , comb. form .......... MONO, UNI
" curious to know ........... GOSSIP, QUIDNUNC
" desiring freedom ..................... ELEUTHEROMANIAC
" devoted to a pursuit ........... IST
" engaged in marauding; Ind. LOOTIE
" fond of women .... PHILOGYNIST
" hundred thousand ............. LAC
" instructed in a secret system ...... EPOPT
one next in degree to a knight .......... ARMIGER
" of anc Persian dynasty SASSANID
" of mixed blood ............. METIS
" of the Araceae .............. ARAD
" of the bears ................. URSA
" of the seven wise men of Greece; .. THALES
" ; prefix ..................... MONO
" ; Scot. ........................... AE
" sided ..... ASKEW, UNILATERAL
" spot ......................... ACE
" tenth of a rin .................. MO
" third of an ........ BARLEYCORN
" twelfth inch ................. LINE
" thousand sq. meters ...... DECARE
" weak minded ............... DOLER
" who believes in new things .... NEO
" who feigns illness .. MALINGERER
" who frustrates a plan .. MARPLOT
" who hates argument . MISOLOGIST
" who never laughs ....... AGELAST
" who rules ................ GERENT
" who shoots from ambush .. SNIPER

189

one-footed ...................... UNIPED
one's own; comb. form ............ IDIO
one's self, belief in ......... SOLIPSISM
onion .. BOLL, CEPA, CIBOL, INGRAN
onion bulb .......................... SET
onion; genus .................... ALLIUM
onion, small .. ESCHALOT, SCALLION
onion, young ................... SHALLOT
onion-like herb ................. CHIVE
onion-like plant .................. LEEK
only .............. LONE, MERE, SOLE
onomasticon ............. DICTIONARY
onomatopoeic .... IMITATIVE, ECHOIC
onomato-word ...... BUZZ, CRACKLE
onslaught .......... ATTACK, BRUNT
onus ................. BURDEN, LOAD
onwards in time ................. AKE
onyx ..... NICOLO, ONICOLO, TECALI
oopak ............................... TEA
oorial ............................... SHA
ooze ... EXUDE, SLIME, LEAK, SEEP,
WESE
ooze thru pores ............. TRANSUDE
oozing moisture ................. ADRIP
opah ............................... SOKO
opah, native name ......... KINGFISH
opal ....... HYALITE, PITCH, RESIN
  " , fire .................... GIRASOL
  " reddish ............... HARLEQUIN
  " , precious ................. NOBLE
  " , variety of ......... CACHOLONG,
MENILITE
opalescent .................. IRISATED
opaque ...... DARK, OBSCURE, DULL
open . WAR, OVERT, PATENT, UNDO,
UNSEAL, APERT, PATULOUS
open air ................... ALFRESCO
  " country, an .... WEALD, VELDT
  " for discussion ............. MOOT
  " passage in the woods ..... GLADE
  " shelved cabinet ....... ETAGERE
  " , to gape ............... DEHISCE
  " to scorn ............... DERISIBLE
opening . LOOP, BAY, HIATUS, SINUS,
EVELET, FENESTRA,
FORAMEN
  " , as of mouth ............... OS
  " from the third ventricle PYLAE
  " in a mold ............. INGATE
opening in chess ............... GAMBIT
  " of ear ................. BURR
openings; zool. .............. STOMATA
opera by day ...................... SOAP
opera glass ... BINOCLE, LORGNETTE
opera hat ............. GIBUS, TOPPER
operated ........................... RAN
operatic role ..................... BUFFO
operative, became .......... ENURED
operator .. DEALER, MAKER, AGENT
operculum .................. FLAP, LID
ophidian SNAKE, REPTILE, SERPENT
opiate ...... DOPE, ANADYNE, HEMP
opine ................... DEEM, THINK
opinion .......... DOOM, VIEW, WENE
opinions expressed .............. CREDO
opium alkaloid ................. CODEIA
  " , derivative of ....... MECONIC
  " , Egypt. ............ THEBAINE
  " , extract of .......... CHANDOO

" seed ......................... MAW
" , source of ............... POPPY
oppidan; per. to ...... TOWN, URBAN
oppilate ................... OBSTRUCT
opossum, mouse ......... MARMOUSE
opossum, S. Amer. . QUICA, SARIGUE
opossum, water ............... YAPOK
opponent ....... ENEMY, FOE, RIVAL
opportune ............ APROPOS, PAT
opposed .... ANTI, COPED, FRONTED,
MET
  " against ............... PITTED
  " to entad ............... ECTAD
  " to science ................ ART
  " to stoss ................. LEE
  " to zenith ............... NADIR
opposite OTHER, CONVERSE, POLAR,
CONTRA, HOSTILE
opposition, in ................. WITHER
oppress ...... RACK, SWAY, WEIGHT,
MACERATE
opprobrium .......... INFAMY, ODIUM
oppugn ...................... DISPUTE
Ops, consort of ............... SATURN
Ops, early associate of ........ CONSUS
Ops' festival .................... OPALIA
opt ................. CHOOSE, WISH
optic ............................... EYE
optical apparatus ULTRAMICROSCOPE
optical devices, designating STEOPAIC
optical instrument .......... ALIDADE,
ERIOMETER, LANTERN
optimistic .... HOPEFUL, SANGUINE,
ROSEATE, EXPECTANT, ROSY
opus ......... ETUDE, STUDY, WORK
oquassa ........................ TROUT
oracle ........ SEER, SIBYL, MENTOR
oracle, per. to PYTHONIC, ERUDITE
oracular ......... VATIC, PROPHETIC
oral ............. MOUTH, PAROL, SAY
oral declaration; law .. NUNCUPATIVE
oral pledge, per. to ......... PAROLE
oral region of a radiate, per. to ........
ACTINAL
orange, Chinese ........... MANDARIN
  " flower oil ............. NEROLI
  " ; genus .............. CITRUS
  " , kind of .... HEDGE, MOCK,
OSAGE
  " peel .................... ZEST
  " red .................... CORAL
  " red dyestuff ..... CORALLINE,
ALGA
  " , Spring ............ STYRAX
  " tincture ............. TENNE
'Orange Bowl' site ............. MIAMI
Orange River; S. Afr. ........ GARIEP,
GROOTE
orange seed ........................ PIP
orange, seedless ............... NAVEL
orange-like fruit .. BEL, TANGERINE
orangewood tree ................. OSAGE
orangutan ........ APE, MIAS, PONGO
orator ........ PERORATOR, RHETOR
oratorical .................. ELOQUENT
oratorio, coda in ............. STRETTO
oratorio, Handel's ............. SEMELE
oratorio, Haydn's ............. SEASONS

190

oratory .......... CHAPEL, BETH EL,
CHANTRY, ORIEL
orb bone cavity ................... EYE
orbed ........................... LUNAR
orbit ......... AUGE, ELLIPSE, PATH
orbital point .......... APSIS, APOGEE
orc .............. GRAMPUS, WHALE
orchestra circle ........... PARTERRE
orchid appendage ........... CAUDICLE
"       , Afr. .................... DISA
"       egg ................. OOSPHERE
"       , part of ............. ANTHER
"       plant drugs .......... SALOPS
"       pods, deriv. of ........ VANILLA
orchids, dried tubers of ......... SALEP
orchids; genus ........ DISA, LISTERA
orchids, male ..... PURPLE, CULLION
orchis mascula, roots of ....... SALEB
orcus .......................... HADES
ordain . CALL, SEND, WILL, DECREE,
ENACT
ordained .. PRESCRIPT, LEGAL, DUE
ordeal .... GAFF, CRUCIBLE, TRIAL
order ...... MANDATE, ARRAY, BID,
COMMAND, DIRECT, CLASS, WILL
"       in grammar ............. TAXIS
"       of aquatic mammals . CETACEA
"       of architecture ... DORIC, IONIC
"       of birds, fowl ........ RASORES
"       of tailleurs amphibia ... ANURA
"       of winged insects .... DIPTERA
"Order of — Star" ........ EASTERN
order which includes mites ... ACARID
orders .. GENERA, TUSCAN, DORIC,
IONIC
ordinal ...................... NUMBER
ordinance ...... ASSIZE, LAW. RITE,
STATUTE, DECREE
"       of the 17th century RABINET
ordinances; Lat. .......... DECRETA
ordinary ...... VULGATE, AVERAGE,
NORMAL, NOMIC, RUCK, PROSY
ordinary's court ............ PROBATE
ordnance .. ARMOR, GUNS, PETARDS
ordo; Rom. Cath. .. BOOKLET, MASS
ore ........ IRON, MINERAL, TIN
"       box ....................... FLOSH
"       , earthy-looking ............ PACO
"       fusing establishments SMELTERY
"       , horizontal layer .......... STOPE
"       , impure ................... SPEISS
"       iron, used as a pigment .. OCHER,
OCHRE
"       loading platform ............ PLAT
"       , method of cleansing . VANNING
"       mill roller ......... EDGESTONE
"       , sluiced ............. TRUNKED
"       , small bunches of . NEST, SQUAT
"       trough for washing ...... STRAKE
"       vein ...... STOPE, LODE, SCRIN
"       , worthless .............. MATTE
oread .... NYMPH, PERI, SEAMAID
Oregon, capital of ............ SALEM
Oregon, first explorer of ........ FENO
Oregon mountain . CASCADE, COAST
Oregon, seat of University in EUGENE
orellin, rel. to ................ BIXIN
oreortyx ...................... QUAIL

Orestes, friend of ........... PYLADES
Orestes, sister of ........... ELECTRA
Orestes, wife of ........... HERMIONE
orfe ........................ FISH, ID
organ flutter device ........ TREMOLO
"       interlude ................ VERSET
"       kind of ACCORDION, MELODIAN
"       of speech .. TONGUE, MEMBER
"       , original ................ SYRINX
"       , pipe voicer ............. TONER
"       , pipes of an ...... FLUE, REED
"       , small .................... REGAL
"       stop .... BASSOON, DULCIANA,
OBOE, CELESTA, VIOLA, ORAGE,
PYRAMIDON
organ stops, adjust ..... REGISTRATE
organic .. INHERENT, VITAL, STATE
organic body .................... ZOOID
organic compound ... AMINE, KETOL
organic radical .................. ETHYL
organic remains, without ...... AZOIC
organism AMOEBA, ANIMAL, PLANT
organism in certain plants ..... SPORE
organism, potential ......... IDORGAN
organisms of surface of sea . NEKTON
organization .. UNIT, SETUP, CADRE
"       of Bible classes ... ABACA
"       of World War veterans ....
FIDAC
organize ... ARRANGE, FORM, PLAN
organized body of persons .... CORPS
orgy .................. BINGE, REVEL
oribi ....................... ANTELOPE
oriel ...... BAY, WINDOW, CHAPEL
Orient ........ ASIA, EAST, LEVANT
oriental ....... LEVANTINE, BRIGHT
ORTIVE, EASTERN
"       beverage ............ ARRACK
"       caravansary ........ IMARET
"       carpet .................. KALI
"       cart .................. ARABA
"       Christian .............. UNIAT
"       coin .............. PARA, SEN
"       destiny .............. KISMET
"       dish .......... PILAU, PILAW
"       dulcimer ............ SANTIR
"       dwelling ................. DAR
"       gate; Ind. ................ DAR
"       guitar .................. SITAR
"       hospice .... MARET, IMARET
"       inn ..................... SERAI
"       kettledrum ........ ANACARA
"       laborer .............. COOLIE
"       man servant ........ HAMAL
"       measure; Asiatic . DRA, MAO
"       mendicant priest ...... FAKIR
"       note ................... CHIT
"       nurse .......... AMAH, AYAH
"       palanquin .......... DOOLEE
"       patent .............. BERAT
"       people, anc. .......... SERES
"       , per. to ................ GEM
"       ruler KHAN, SHAH, SULTAN
"       salute .... SAHEB, SALAAM
"       skipper .......... RAIS, REIS
"       tamarisk .............. ATLEE
"       tambourine ............ DAIRA
"       taxi ............ RICKSHA(W)

191

"   vessel ................... SAIC
"   weapon .............. ADAGA
"   weight ..... ABBAS, MISKAL,
                    ROTL, SHI
orifice ...... PORE, OSTIOLE, HOLE,
                  OPENING, MOUTH
orifice, minute PORULE, SPIRACLE,
                  STOMA
orifice, the brain ................. LURA
origan .................... MARJORAM
origin ..... ROOT, BIRTH, GENETIC,
    NATURE, NAS, ALPHA, SEED,
    NEE, PROVENANCE,
    PARENTAGE, RISE
original .......... FONTAL, NATIVE,
             INITIAL, PRISTINE
original design ................... TYPE
originally ............ FIRST, CAUSE
originate .. ARISE, COIN, EMANATE,
        SOURCE, INVENT, STEM
oriole, golden ........ LORIOT, PIROL
orioles, genus .............. ICTERUS
Orion, seen in ......... BETELGEUX
Orion's Hound ............. ARATUS
orison ........ PRAYER, REQUEST
Orkney Islands, capital of the ........
                KIRKWALL
Orkney Is. fishing bank ........ HAAF
Orkney Is. freehold .... ODAL, UDAL
Orkney Islands, largest of the ........
                POMONA
Orkney Islands tower ........ BROCH
Orlando's friend in "As You Like It" ..
                ADAM
ormer; genus .............. HALIOTIS
ormolu; alloy .................. GOLD
ornament . SPANG, AMULET, GUTTA,
        OUCH, DECOR, SEME
ornament, circular ......... ROSETTE
ornament with raised flowers ..........
                BROCADE
ornamental button .............. STUD
ornamental edge on lace ...... PICOT
ornamental vessel ............... VASE
ornamented, as a book-cover . TOOLED
ornaments, set of jeweled .. PARURE
ornate ....... FANCY, FLORID, GAY
ornery ........ COMMON, STUBBORN
orogeny .................. UPHEAVAL
ort ........ END, LEFTOVER, SCRAP
orthorhombic mineral ......... IOLITE
ortolan .................... BUNTING
os .......... BONE, MOUTH, ORA(pl.)
Osaka Bay port ................. KOBE
Osata; dancer .................. SONO
oscillate ........ ROCK, SWAY, WAG,
                WAVER
oscillating ............... LIBRATORY
oscillation transformer ........ TESLA
oscillations ...... SEICHES, PEDESES
oscitate ............ GAPE, YAWN
osculate .................. BUSS, KISS
osier .... SALLOW, WAND, WILLOW
osier band .................. WITHE
Osiris' brother .................... SET
Osiris' father ..................... SEB
Osiris' mother ..................... NUT
Osiris' sister ..................... ISIS

Osiris' son .......... ANUBIS, HORUS
Osiris' wife ........................ ISIS
Osprey ............ FEATHER, HAWK
osseous .......................... BONY
ossicle ............................ BONE
ossuary .................... TOMB, URN
ostensorium ....................... PYX
ostentation . POMP, ECLAT, FLARE,
                PARADE
ostiole ......................... STOMA
osteoma ........................ TUMOR
ostracize .............. EXPATRIATE
ostracoderm, order ........ ANASPIDA
ostracism BAN, EXILE, EXPELLING
ostrich ................ NANDU, RHEA
ostrich tail feathers ............ BOOS
ostriches; genus ................. RHEA
ostrich-like bird ........ EMEU, EMU,
                RATITE
otalgia ...................... EARACHE
Othello's wife .......... DESDEMONA
other; combo. form ............ ALLO
otherness .................. ALTERITY
others ...... ETAL, RESIDUE, REST
otherwise .... ALIAS, ELS, ELSE, OR
otherwise; mus. ................. OSSIA
otidium ...................... OTOCYST
otiose ... FUTILE, INDOLENT, IDLE
Otis; Amer. patriot ............ JAMES
otter ......................... ANNOTTO
otter; genus ................... LUTRA
otter, sea ....................... KALAN
otter, sheep ................... ANCON
ottoman POUF, STOOL, FOOTSTOOL
Ottoman court ................. PORTE
Ottoman Empire, non Moslem subject;
                RAIA
Ottoman Empire, province .. VILAYET
Ottoman, high official ........ PASHA
Ottoman, native ................ TURK
Ottomans, leader of OSMAN, AHMED
ouch .... BROOCH, CLASP, FIBULA
ought ...... BOOD, CIPHER, MOTE,
                NAUGHT
ouija board ........... PLANCHETTE
ounce, ½ of .................... DRAM
oust ..... DEBOUT, EVICT, EXPEL
out . FROM, AWAY, EX, EC, ODDS,
                END
out of; foreign to .......... DEHORS
out of place .................. INEPT
out of sorts .................. NOHOW
out-and-out ...... ARRANT, ERRANT
outbreak .... EMEUTE, RASH, RIOT
outburst ... GERE, ACCESS, FLARE,
          GALE, STORM
outcast .............. LEPER, PARIAH
outcast in federal Japan ...... RONIN
outcome .... DENOUEMENT, ISSUE,
                UPSHOT
outdo .............. EXCEL, SURPASS
outdoor theatre ............ DRIVE IN
outer ............... ECTAL, UTTER
"   coat of grain .. TESTA, EXTINE
"   garment ...... PALETOT, WRAP
"   layer of roots ........ EXODERM
"   Mongolia, capital of ...... URGA
"   , opposed to ............. ENTAL
"   shell of oyster ............ TEST

outfit .............. KIT, EQUIP, RIG
outlandish ...... BIZARRE, STRANGE
outlaw ........ BANDIT, PROSCRIBE
outlet .. ISSUE, EGRESS, OUTCAST,
                            EXIT, VENT
outlet, water ................ BAYOU
outlook FRONTAGE, SCOPE, VIEW,
            PURVIEW, VISTA, WATCH
outlying district ............ PURLIEU
outline ................ ADUMBRATE
outmoded ..................... PASSE
output ............ TURNOUT, YIELD
outrigger .................... PROA
outrival . ECLIPSE, EXCEL, OUTVIE
outspoken .. BLUNT, ROUND, FREE
outstrip ...... BEST, EXCEL, OUTDO
outstripped .......... LED, OUTDONE
outward ...... ECTAD, EXTRINSIC
outward circlings ............ SPIRALS
outward, turn ............... EVERT
outwit EUCHRE, BALK, BEST, FOIL
outwork ......... TENAIL, RAVELIN
ousel ...... RLACKBIRD, PIET,
                            WHISTLER
ovale; Fr. ....................... EGG
ovate inversely ............ OBOVATE
oven; Austral. ................... UMU
oven, drying ............ KILN, OAST
oven for annealing glass ........ LEER
oven mop .................... SCOVEL
over .... ACROSS, ALSO, ATHWART,
                          MAS, TOO
over again .. ENCORE, HAND, ANEW
over and above ........ ATOUR, ATOP
over; prefix ..................... SUR
overact . EXCESS, OUTDO, UNDUE,
                          EMOTE
overawe .... COW, DAUNT, SUBDUE
overbearing CAVALIER, ARROGANT
overcoat BENNY, CAPOTE, ULSTER
    " , close fitting ...... SURTOUT
    " , loose .. RAGLAN, PALETOT
    " , sleeveless ...... INVERNESS
overcome ... BEAT, HURDLE, AWE,
                        BEST, WAR
overdue ................ LATE, TARDY
overfeed ......... AGROTE, PAMPER
overflow .. COME, DELUGE, SPATE,
              TEEM, EBULLIENCE
overflowing, full to ................ BIG
overfull ...................... LUCKY
overhang .......... BEETLE, EAVES
overhead .................... UPKEEP
overjoy .......... ELATE, JUBILANT
overlabored .......... LUCUBRATION
overlapping ............... IMBRICATE
overlay .................... LAP, CEIL
overloaded .............. PLETHORIC
overlook SCAN, IGNORE, MISS, SKIP,
                          SPARE
overmatch .... BEST, CRUSH, ROUT
overplus .............. EXCESS, REST
overpower ... AWE, MASTER, BEAT
overreach .. DUPE, NOBBLE, STRAIN
overrun INFEST, RESPACE, SWARM
over-scrupulous person ....... PRUDE
oversee ........ INSPECT, BLUNDER
overshadow .... ECLIPSE, SHELTER
overshoe .... ARCTIC, GALOSH, GUM

oversight ... LAPSE, CHARGE, CARE
overt .... OPEN, PATENT, PUBLIC
overtake ATAKE, REACH, REJOIN
overthrow DOWN, UNHORSE, WORST
overtop ............... DWARF, EXCEL
overture ........ OFFER, PROPOSAL
overturn ................... SUBVERT
overturned ...... CAPSIZED, UPSET,
                         THREW
Ovid, burial place of ............ TOMI
ovid shape ................... OBOVOID
ovine ......................... SHEEP
ovule ......... EGG, EMBRYO, SEED
ovule; outer integument of . PRIMINE
ovum ...................... OVE, EGG
owe ............ DEBT, DUE, SHALL
owl ..... EAL, LULU, RURU, UTUM,
                 ULLET, WAPACUT
  " , barn ............ MADGE, POUIE
  " , hawk ..................... SURN
  " , parrot, N. Z. KAKAPO, TARAPO
  " short eared ................ MOMO
  " , small ........ HOWLET, AZIOLA,
                           IITIIM
  " , to hoot as an ............ ULULU
  " , wailing of ........ HOOT, ULLET
owl-like .................... STRIGINE
owls; genus ........ SYRNIUM, STRIX
owls, plumed eye-area of ........ DISC
own ..... NAIN, ADMIT, OWE, HAVE
own; Scot. ................. ANE, NAIN
owns ........................... HAS
ox ......................... BEEVE
ox, extinct wild, Caesarean .... URUS
  " , fierce, of India .....TSINE, GAUR,
                           GOUR
  " , forest ...................... ANOA
  " , grunting ..................... YAK
ox, Indian ............ GAYAL, ZEBU
  " , Java .................. BANTENG
  " meat, cured .. BUGLOSS, BILTONG
  " stomach .................... TRIPE
  " , wild horned ................ REEM
  " , working ................... AVER
oxaldehyde ................ GLYOXAL
oxalic acid, salt of ........ OXALITE
oxalis plant ...................... OCA
oxalyl .................... CARBONYL
oxen ...................... BISONS
oxen kind ............ NEAT, NOWT
oxen of the Celebes .......... ANOAS
oxen, Tibetan ........ ZEBUS, YAKS
oxeye ...... BOCE, BOGUE, DUNLIN
oxford ........................ SHOE
Oxford, alumnus of ............ AUNT
Oxford scholar; Eng ............ DEMY
Oxford exams; slang ........ GREATS
Oxford, officer ............... BEDEL
oxide thong ................... RIEM
oxidize ............. CALCINE, RUST
ox-like ...................... BOVINE
oxter ................... ARM, ARMPIT
oxtongue .................... BUGLOSS
oxyacantha ............. HAWTHORN
oxybenzene ................. PHENOL
oxygen, an allotropic form ...... OZONE
  " , binary compound of . OXIDE
  " metal compounds ...... OXIDS
oyez ............... ATTEND, HEAR

oyster ..................... BIVALVE
"    bed ........... LAYER, STEW
"    bed material ........ CULCHES
"    catcher ..... OLIVE, TIRMA
"    , common variety ..... EDULIS
"    farm .. CLAIRE, PARK, PARC
"    gatherer ........... TONGMAN
"    , outer shell of ......... TEST
"    ova ................... SPAWN
"    rake .................... TONG
"    shell ......... HUSK, SHUCK
"    spawn ............... CULTCH
"    , species of ........ MOLLUSCA
"    , young ............ SET, SPAT
oyster-cut .................... TIDBIT
oyster-fish .................. TAUTOG
oyster-grass ................... KELP
oysterloit ................... BISTORT
oyster-plant ................. SALSIFY
ozanna; genus ........... ANTELOPE
Ozark resort ................ IRONTON


# P

P, letter .......................... PEE
P-38's ................... LIGHTNINGS
pabulum .... FUEL, SUPPORT, FOOD
paca ........ LABBA, AGOUTI, CAVY
pace ...... TROT, GAIT, LOPE, STEP,
          TRACE, AMBLE, RACK, RUN
pachyderm .............. ELEPHANT,
                        RHINOCEROS
Pacific island .......... ADMIRALTY
Pacific Is. group ................. TRUK
Pacific timber tree .............. IPIL
pacifier ......... NIPPLE, RING, SOP
pack ........ CRAM, EMBALE, STOW,
       STEEVE, GANG, SHOOK, TRUSS
pack animal ............. BURRO
pack horse . .............. SUMPTER
package ........ BALE, PAD, PARCEL
"    covered with hide ... CEROON
package of pepper, etc. ...... ROBBIN
"    of wool ............... FADGE
packing, clay ................... LUTE
pad MAT, QUILT, TABLET, TRAMP
pad, collar ................. HOUSING
pad, harness ............... TERRET
paddle ... SCULL, SPOON, OAR, ROW
paddock .... GARSTON, FROG, PARK,
                        FIELD, TOAD
Paderewski; comp. ........... IGNACE
Paderewski; opera by ...... MANRU
padre ..... FATHER, MONK, PRIEST
paean ................... HYMN, SONG
pagan ........... ETHNIC, PAYNIM,
                        HEATHEN
pagan, per. to .............. GNOSTIC
page .. BOY, CHILD, LEAF, CAHIER
page, left hand ............... VERSO
page number .................. FOLIO
page, right hand ............. RECTO
Page; songstress ............. PATTI
page, title ................... RUBRIC
pageantry .. PARADE, POMP, SHOW
pages, number the ........ PAGINATE

Paget; actress ............... DEBRA
"Pagliacci," char. ............. TONIO
pagoda TAA, TAE, TEMPLE, PAGOD
pagoda; final on .................. TEE
pagurian ..................... CRAB
Pahlavi's countrymen .... IRANIANS
paid out ..................... SPENT
paillasse ................. MATTRESS
paillette ................. SPANGLE
pain ..... AIL, PANG, ACHE, AGRA
pain, be in ......... THROB, THRAW
painful memories .............. SORES
paint LIMN, ROUGE, STAIN, COLOR
paint face ............ FARD, PARGET
paint spreader .............. SPATULA
paint with vermillion ...... MINIATE
painted pavement used by Romans ....
                        ASAROTUM
painting, method of ...... GRISAILLE
painting on dry plaster ......... SECCO
painting, style of .. GENRE, IMPASTO
painting, technique of ..... TEMPERA
pair .... SPAN, TEAM, YOKE, BRACE
pair of units .......... DYADS, TWO
paired; her ................... GEMEL
pairs; Lat. ..................... PIA
palace . COURT, PRETORIUM, STEAD
Palamon, rival of ............ ARCITE
palanquin bearer .. SIRDAR, HAMAL
palanquin, oriental .. DOOLEE, KAGO
palatable .. TASTY, SAPID, SAVORY
palatal ............ BACK, GUTTERAL
palate, per. to ...... UVULA, VELAR
palate, soft ................... VELUM
palatine .......... PALADIN, ROYAL
palaver .......... CAJOLERY, CHAT,
      DEBATE, FLATTERY, PARLEY
pale .. MEALY, ASHY, BLANCH, DIM,
                        WAN, SALLOW
pale, a ......................... STAKE
pale, become .............. ETIOLATE
pale buck ..................... ORIBI
"Pale Face" ............. CAUCASIAN
pale; Scot. ..................... SCOOP
pale, to ...................... FENCE
pale yellow .................. FLAXEN
palea ...... DEWLAP, FOLD, BRACT
Palestine ................... PHILISTIA
"    , administrative district of ....
                        GAZA, HAIFA
"    battle site ........ ELTEKEH
"    , conquerors of ...... TURKS
"    , lake of .......... MEROM
"    mountain ... EBAL, HERMON,
                        NEBO
Palestine, part of .......... CANAAN
"    , port of ACRE, JAFFA, HAIFA
Palestinian, anc. ........... AMORITE
palestra .............. SCHOOL, GYM
paletot ............ OVERCOAT, COAT
pall ........ CLOAK, MANTLE, SATE
pallet ... BED, PATE, PLACHER, LIP
palisades .............. CLIFF, PALES,
                        IMPALEMENT
palliate ...... COCEAL, EXTENUATE,
                        EXCUSE, TEMPER
pallid ............ PALE, THIN, WAN
pallion ........................... BIT
Pallu's father ............... REUBEN

194

palm .. FANLEAF, ERYTHEA, ENG,
　　　　　　　CYCAD, PRIZE
" , Arabian ................. DOUM
" , areng ................... GOMUTI
" , Asiatic .......... NIPA, NYPA,
　　　　　　　PALMYRA
" betel ............ ARECA, BONGA
" , book ................. TALIERA
" , Brazilian ..... ASSAI, BACABA,
　　　　　　　TUCUM, URUCURI
" , Bussu ................ TROOLIE
" , cabbage ............ PALMETTO
" , Ceylon ............... TALIPOT
" , civet; East Ind. ...... MUSANG
" , cockatoo ............... ARARA
" , cocoanut ................ COCOA
" , drink ............ ASSAI, NIPA
" , dwarf fan; genus ........ SABAL
" , East Indian . TALA, TOKOPAT
" , edible fruit of ............ NIPA
" , fan-leaf .......... PALMETTO,
　　　　　　　TALIPOT
" , farinaceous, deriv. of ..... PITH
" , fern-shaped leaves of . PINNATE
" , fiber ...... BURI, TAL, RAFFIA
" , Florida ................. ROYAL
" , fruit ............... COCOANUT
" , gingerbread ..... DOOM, DOUM
" leaf . OLAY, FROND, OLA, OLLA
" , lily ........................ TOI, TI
" , Malayan ... GEBANG, ARENG,
　　　　　　　GOMUTI
" leaf mat; Span. ........ PETATE
" , nipa ............ ATAP, ATTAP
" of Asia ......... ASSAI, CALAMI
" of the hand ............ THENAR
" of the hand, belonging to . VOLAR
" of the hand, per. to .... PALMAR
" off ......................... FOIST
" , Palmyra ............ BRAB, TAL
" , pith ...................... SAGO
" , reed-like stem of ...... RATTAN
" , sago . ARENG, GOMUTI, IROK
" , South American .. DATIL, ITA,
　　　　　　　NIKAU
" , species of ....... IVORY, WAX
" , starch ................... SAGO
" , stem of ........ CANE, RATAN
" sugar ................. JAGGERY
" tree; genus ................ DOUM
" wine ...................... TODDY
palmate .......... WEBBED, ANTLER
palmetto ....... SERENOA, THRINAX
palmistry ............. CHIROMANCY
palms, genus ..... ARECA, ATTALEA,
　　　　　　　BACABA
palmyra, palm leaf ......... OLA, OLE
palp ..... CAJOLE, FIG, PAT, TOUCH
paludal ........... FENNY, MARSHY
palter ............ HAGGLE, TRIFLE
paltry ......... LACKING, PICAYUNE
pampas ..................... PLAIN
pamper . COSHER, COSSET, POSSET,
　　　　DANDLE, SPOIL, HUMOR, PET
pan, amalgamating ....... YET, TINA
Pan, rel. to; Rom. ........... FAUNUS
Pan, son of ................. SILENUS
pan; sl. ...................... ROAST

panacea ...... ELIXIR, CATHOLICON,
　　　　　　NEPENTHE, SOLACE
panache ............... PLUME, TUFT
Panama canal lake ............ GATUN
Panama currency ............ BALBOA
Panay capital ................. ILOILO
pancake ......... FRITTER, FROISE
panda, Himalayan ......... BEARCAT
panda, the ..................... WAH
pander ........ BAWD, PIMP, CATER
Pandora's box .. RADIO, BLESSINGS,
　　　　　　　JAR
panegyric ....... ELOGE, ENCOMIUM
paneled ....................... PANED
pang . ACHE, RACK, PRONG, THROE
pangolin ................... ANTEATER
pangolin; genus MANIS, PHOLODITUS
panhandles; slang .............. BEGS
panic SCARE, FEAR, FRAY, TERROR
pannier ........... BASKET, DOSSER
Panopolis, chief city of .......... MIN
panorama .... SCENE, VISTA, VIEW
"Pan's Pipes" ................ SYRINX
pant violently ........ GASP, HEAVE,
　　　　　　　THROB
pantarch; obs. ................. OHART
Pantheon, chief gods of Teutonic AESIR
Pantheon, chief Hawaii god ... KANE
panther; COUGAR, LEOPARD, PARD,
　　　　　　　PUMA
panther; dial. .............. PAINTER
panther-like animal JAGUAR, OCELOT
Pantheus' mother ............ AGAVE
pantry AMBRY, SPENCER, CLOSET
pants, leather .......... CHAPARERAS
Papal book of edicts ..... DECRETAL
Papal chancery ............. DATARY
Papal Court ............. SEE, CURIA
Papal envoy, special ..... ABLEGATE
Papal reformer ............ GREGORY
Papal scarf or veil ... FANON, ORALE
Papal sign on letter .......... BULLA
papaya ............. CARICA, PAPAW
paper, broken ................. CASSE
" , cloth-like ............... TAPA
" , crisp thin ........... PELURE
" cutter ............... SLITTER
" , damaged ............ RETREE
" for cutlets ......... PAPILOTE
" for medicinal powders CHARTA
" lighter ................. SPILL
" measure ................ REAM
" nautilus .......... ARGONAUT
" , official ............... TARGE
" once folded ............ FOLIO
" sizes . ATLAS, COPY, CROWN,
DOUBLE, DEMY, IMPERIAL, POTT
" , untrimmed edge ..... DECKLE
papillae ........... CERATA, PIMPLES
Papua, bay in ................ MILNE
papyrus; Egypt. ................. REED
par——; by air .................. AVION
parable .. FABLE, APOLOGUE, TALE,
　　　　　　ALLEGORY, MYTH
parabole ....... CURVE, SIMILITUDE
parade FLAUNT, MARCH, TOP, FILE,
　　　　　　　STRUT, WALK
paradisaic .................... EDENIC

Paradise . UTOPIA, EDEN, ELYSIUM, HEAVEN
paragon ..... TYPE, IDEAL, MODEL, PALADIN, NONPAREIL
paragram ........................ PUN
paragraph ........... SECTION, ITEM
Paraguay city ................. LUQUE
Paraguay tea ......... MATE, YERBA
parakeet ................. BUDGERIGAR
parallelogram ................ RHOMB
paralysis ........... PALSY, PARESIS
paralyze ............... NUMB, SCRAM
paramorphine ............ THEBAINE
paramour ........... LEMAN, LOVER
parapet, dwarf wall .. BERM, PODIUM
parapet, part of .............. CRETE
parapet, V-shaped ........... REDAN
parasite ..... DRONE, SYCOPHANT, TOADY
"    , animal COWBIRD, CUCKOO
"    external ... ECTOPARASITE
"    , marine . REMORA, SPONGE
"    of trout ................. SUG
"    , per. to a ......... FLUNKY
"    plant .......... ENTOPHYTE
parasites, internal ......... ENTOZOA
parasitic fungus ............. LICHEN
parasitic worm ............. TRICHINA
paravane ...................... OTTER
parch . TORREFY, BRISTLE, TORRID
parchment .... DEED, FOREL, PELL, VELLUM, DIPLOMA
parchment manuscript . PALIMPSEST
Pardee; Amer. eng. ............ ARIO
pardi; arc. ......... INDEED, VERILY
pardonable .................... VENIAL
pardon . REMIT, AMNESTY, MERCY, SPARE, REPRIEVE
pare ... RESECT, CURRY, SKIN, SOD
parent DAD, SIRE, GENITOR, PATER
parental affection ........... STORGE
parentage, per to . FREE, GERMANE
parhelion ........................ SUN
pariah ...................... OUTCAST
Paris; coll. ..................... PAREE
Paris, district in ........... AUTEUIL
Paris, Roman name for ..... LUTETIA
Paris, subway in ............. METRO
Parisian ambassador ........ ELCHEE
Parisian designer ............. GRES
Parisian thug ................ APACHE
Parks, of T.V. ................ LARRY
parley ... CONVERSE, TALK, CHAT, TREAT, CONFER
parlor ................. SALON, SALLE
parnassian ...................... POET
parody ........... SATIRE, TAKEOFF
parol ............. ORAL, PLEADINGS
paronomasia ...................... PUN
Paros, native of ............. PARIAN
paroxysm .......... THROE, ANGER, EMOTION
parrot .... LORIE, ARA, COCKATOO, TIRIBA
"    , African ................. JAKO
"    , Aus. ............... CORELLA
"    fashion ................. ARINE
"    fish LABROID, SCAR, SHANNY
"    ; genus .......... PSITTACUS

"    , green ................. CAGIT
"    like ......... ANTHROPOGLOT
"    , long tailed ........... MACAW
"    , monk .................... LORO
"    , New Guinea LORIKEET, LORY
"    , New Zealand .... KARA, KEA
"    , New Zealand; genus NESTOR
"    owl .................... KAPAO
"    , per. to ................. ARINE
"    , psittacoid .............. VAZA
"    , small LORILET, PARAKEET
parry ....... FEND, ELUDE, AVERT, EVADE
parsley; deriv. of ...... APIOL, APIIN
parsley; genus .............. SELINUM
parsnips, water; genus .......... SIUM
parson bird ........................ TUI
parsonage ...... BENEFICE, MANSE, RECTORY
part ROLE, SEGMENT, SHARE, TWIN
"    of a bird's toe .............. LOMA
"    of a flower .............. PETAL
"    of a measure .......... ALIDADE
"    of a step NOSING, RISER, TREAD
"    of a turtle .............. CALIPEE
"    of an ear .............. TRAGUS
"    of animal it cannot scratch ...... ACNESTIC
"    that's kept .............. RETENT
partan; Scot. .................... CRAB
parted .............. CLOVEN, CLEFT
partially burned brick .. BUR(R), BAT, CLINKER
participate ......... SHARE, DIVIDE, PARTAKE
particle .... IOTA, GEN, ATOM, JOT, TITTLE, GRAIN
particle, small ............. GRANULE
parti-colored ......... PIEBALD, PIED
particular ..... SOLE, SINGLE, ITEM
partisan SIDE, ZEALOT, GUERRILLA
partisan groups ............... CAMPS
partition, to ....... SCANTLE, ALLOT
partitions ... SEVERANCES, SEPTA, WALLS, WITHES
partitions, imperfect .... SEPTULATE
partlet HEN, BAND, COLLAR, RUFF
partly illuminated ....... PENUMBRA
partnership ..... CAHOOT, COMATES
partridge CHUKOR, SEESEE, TITAR, YUTU
partridge, a kind of .. GROUSE, QUAIL, TETUR, TINAMOU
partridge food .................. PUPAE
party . SQUAD, DRUM, FAID, SECT, TEA, CLIQUE, SIDE
party, house cleaning ..... WHANG
parvenu .......... ABRIVISTE, SNOB, UPSTART
pasha ........................ DOWLAH
pasquinade ...... LAMPOON, SATIRE
pass SPEND, GHAT, GO, MOVE, SEY
"    a rope thru .............. REEVE
"    , a sudden ................ LUNGE
"    , Alpine .................... COL
"    by ..... ELAPSE, IGNORE, OMIT
"    by, to .................... COTE
"    , dangerous .............. PLIGHT
"    lightly along ... FOIST, SKITTER

" thru cringle ............. REEVE
passage ...... ADIT, ATRIUM, GANG,
TRAVEL, AVENUE, DEFÍLE
passage between two walls ... SLYPE
passage, covered ............... PAWN
passage in a mine ............. STOPE
passage, one end closed .... IMPASSE
passages ........... TRANSIT, ATRIA
passageway .. ALLEY, AISLE, RAMP,
SLIP, ITER
passenger PILGRIM, TOURIST, FARE
passe ........ ANTIQUATED, FADED
passer of bad checks ........... KITER
passing by, a ......... PRETERITION
passion .... PAIN, IRE, YEN, ANGER
passion flower  MAYPOP, MARACOCK
passion for doing grand things .........
MEGALOMANIA
passionate peace ........... NIRVANA
passive ..... QUIET, INERT, STOIC,
passover festival ............... SEDER
passover of "golden fleece" . AEETES
passover, per. to . HALLEL, PASCHAL
passport ......... VISA, VISE, CONGE
passus ........................ CANTO
password ............. COUNTERSIGN
past .... AGONE, DEAD, SINCE, AGO,
YORE, AFTER, OVER
past tense ................ PRETERITE
past tense; Gr. ................. AROIST
paste ..... AME, GLUE, PAP, STICK,
STRASS
pastoral .......... RURAL, COUNTRY
"      cantata ........... SERENATA
"      crook ................ PEDUM
"      god ..................... PAN
"      , per. to ......... AGRESTIC,
SHEPHERD
"      pipe ............. REED, OAT
"      poem .. ECLOGUE, BUCOLIC
pastry . ECLAIR, PIE, SOCK, TART,
TUCK, STRUDEL
pasture ...... AGIST, GRASS, GRAZE
pasture grass ................. GRAMA
pasture land ......... HAM, ING, LEA
pasty mixture ............... MAGMA
pat .. CARESS, FIT, PALP, BUTTER
Patagonian cattle ............ NIATAS
Patagonian deity ............ SETEBOS
Patagonian rodent ..... CAVY, MARA
patch ...... PARCEL, PLOT, TRACT
patch of woods ............... MOTTE
patch, to .... BODGE, CLOUT, VAMP
patcher SARTOR, MENDER, SEWER
patella ............... KNEECAP, PAN
paten ................. DISC, PLATE
paten, filer of notice ..... CAVEATOR
path LANE, ROUTE, TRAIL, BERM,
RODDIN, ORBIT, TRACK
paths, S. W. country ........ COMINOS
patois .... ARGOT, JARGON, SPEECH
patriarch .... FATHER, PATER, SIRE
Patrick, Miss .................... GAIL
patriotism, vainglorious CHAUVINISM
patron saint (female) ....... CECILIA
"      "      of beggars ........ GILES
"      "      of boys ...... NICHOLAS
"      "      of England ........ ANNE,
GEORGE

"      "      of lawyers .......... IVES
"      "      of sailors ......... ELMO
patronage ............... EGIS, FAVOR
patroon's land ................ MANOR
pattern ...... BYSEN, NORM, SEME,
TEMPLATE, PARADIGM, MODEL,
FORMAT, STENCIL
pattern of flower beds .... PARTERRE
Patti; singer ............... ADELINA
patulous .............. GAPING, OPEN
paucity ........ DEARTH, FEWNESS
Paul, companion of SILAS, TYCHICUS
pauldron .................... SPLINTS
Paul's city .................... TARSUS
paunch . BELLY, RUMEN, ABDOMEN
pause ....... STAND, CEASE, SELAH,
STANCE
pave ........... TILE, PATH, COVER
paver's mallet .................... TUP
pavilion .. MARQUEE, TABERNACLE,
TENT
pavilions; Lat. ............... PINNAE
paving stone .......... PAVER, SETT
pavior's hammer ........ REEL, TUP
Pavlova; dancer ............... ANNA
paw ............ GAUM, PATTE, PUD
pawl .... CLICK, DETENT, TONGUE
pawl in a gunlock ............... SEAR
pawl; Ind. ..................... TENT
pawn ...... GAGE, HOCK, PEACOCK,
PLEDGE
pawpaw ........... PAPAW, PAPAYA
pay ............... FEE, REWARD, TIP
pay dirt ........................... ORE
pay the penalty of ............... ABY
paying attention ........... AUDIENT
paymaster ...... PURSER, OFFICER
payment .... KAIN, CRO, MAIL, TAC
paynim .......... HEATHEN, PAGAN
pea, chick ............. CICER, GRAM
pea, health .................. CARMELE
pea, pigeon ....................... DAL
peace .. PAX, SERENITY, NIRVANA
peaceable ........ HENOTIC, IRENIC,
SOLOMON
peaceful ...... HALCYON, IRENICAL
peach ...... CRAWFORD, ELBERTA,
NECTARINE
"      grafted on a quince MELOCOTON
"      , native country of .... PERSIA
"      origin ............... ALMOND
"      ; slang ............... BETRAY
peach-stone ............... PUTAMEN
peacock ........ MAO, PO, POO, SUN
"      blue ................... PAON
"      butterfly .................. IO
"      fan ............. FLABELLUM
"      , female ............. PEAHEN
"      fish .................. WRASSE
"      ; genus ............... PAVO
"      , kind of ............. PAWN
"      , like a ... VAIN, PAVONINE
peage ...................... TAX, TOLL
peak ALP, CONE, CUSP, APEX, SLINK,
CROWN, TOR, TOP
peak ornament .......... EPI, FINIAL
peak, rocky ............... AL, CRAG
peal ............. ECHO, BOOM, CLAP
peanut BUR, GOOBER, MANI, PINDA

197

pear cider ...................... PERRY
pear, late autumn ............... BOSC
pear, prickly .......... NOPAL, TUNA
pear, prickly; genus ........ OPUNTIA
pear-shaped ............... PYRIFORM
pearl .... GEM, ONION, MARGARITE
pearl eye .................. CATARACT
pearlike fruit .............. AVOCADO
pear-like ............ NACRE, OLIVET
pearls of great luster ....... ORIENTS
pearlweed ................. SEALWORT
pearlwort ..................... SAGINA
pearly ......... ROSETAN, OPALINE,
                           PELLUCID
peart ............... BRISK, CLEVER
Peáry; explorer ............. ROBERT
peasant .... COTTAR, HIND, RUSTIC,
             SWAIN, BOOR, CARL(OT)
peasant; E. Ind. ................. RYOT
peasant; Egypt. ............. FELLAH
peasant; Eng. .................. CHURL
peasant; Irish ................ KERN
peasant, farm holding ...... COTLAND
pease; collec. Lat. ............. PISUM
pease crow ...................... TERN
pease, per. to .................. PULSE
peaseweep ........ LAPWING, PEWIT
pea-shaped ................ PISIFORM
peat ............................. GOR
peat bog ................... CESS, MOSS
peat spade ................... SLANE
peavey ................... CANTHOOK
pebble, fig-shaped ............. SYCITE
pebble; Gr. Brit. ............... SCREE
peccary .................... TAGASSU
peck at ............. DAB, NAG, TWIT
peck; Eng. .................. PEGGLE
pectinoid bivalve .......... SCALLOP
peculiar ... ODD, PROPER, UNIQUE,
                      ERRATIC, QUEER
peculiar, comb. form for ......... IDIO
peculiarity .... KINK, QUIRK, TRAT
pedal on piano .............. CELESTE
pedal snow runner .............. SKEE
pedant ...... BLUESTOCKING, PRIG,
                      TUTOR, PURIST
peddler .......... COSTER, HAWKER
peddler's accomplice ........... SHILL
peddler's pack .............. WALLET
pedestal, part of a ......... DADO, DIE
pedicel of umbel ................... RAY
pedometer ................. ODOGRAPH
peduncle .. PEDICEL, STALK, STEM
peduncle, not raised upon a . SESSILE
peduncle, radical .............. SCAPE
peel .... RIND, SKIN, SLIPE, STRIP
peel off DECORTICATE, HARL, PARE
peep .... CHEEP, PRY, PULE, SKEG
peephole ...... APERTURE, EYELET
peepshow ...... RAREE, SPECTACLE
peer .. EARL, EQUAL, FERE, NOBLE
Peer Gynt, mother of ............ ASE
Peer Gynt's lady-friend ...... ANITRA
Peerce ......................... JAN
peer's residence ............. BARONY
peevish ...... PENSY, SULK, TESTY,
                  CROSS, PERVERSE, SOUR
peewee ............. LAPWING, LARK
Pee Wee, baseball ............. REESE

peg .................. HOB, NOB, PIN
peg of wood .......... SPILL, DOWEL
pega ....................... REMORA
Pegasus' rider ....... BELLEROPHON
Peggotty's niece ................ EMILY
Pegu native ...................... MON
pelagic . SEALER, MARINE, OCEANIC
Pelias' (King) son .......... ACASTUS
pellet ... GRANULE, PALLION, PILL
pellicle .................... FILM, SKIN
Pelop's son .... ATREUS, THYESTES
pelota, per. to; Span. ........... CESTA
pelt ........ FELL, HDE, WOOLFELL
pelt, Siberian squirrel ..... CALARER
peltry ...... FURS, HIDES, SKINS
pelvic bone; per. to ............ ILIAC
pen .. QUILL, COOP, COTE, HUTCH,
                          STY, WRITE
penalize ............ PUNISH, MULCT
penalty ...... AMAND, CAIN, RONCE
pencil, belonging to a ........ DESMIC
pencil point ................ APICULA
pendant . TASSEL, TAG, AGLET, BOB
"Pendennis," heroine of ...... LAURA
pendent cone of lime .. STALACTITE
pendent ornament ...... LAVALIERE
pendulous throat skin in animals ......
                              DEWLAP
Penelope GUANS, JACKET, WEAVER
   "     , father of .......... ICARUS
   "     , husband of ..... ODYSSEUS
penetrate .. DELVE, PIERCE, REACH
penetrating ..... INTRANT, SHRILL,
                                DEEP
penguin . JOHNNY, AIRPLANE, AUK
penguin breeding place .... ROOKERY
penguin; genus ............ EUDYPTES
peninsula .... CHERSONESE, NECK,
                      PENILE, IBERIA
penitent .......... CONTRITE, SORRY
penman ............. SCRIBE, WRITER
pennant ... BANNER, ENSIGN, FLAG
pennant, yacht .............. BURGEE
penny ... COPPER, GROAT, SALTEE
penny; Dutch ................ STIVER
penny, New Testament ... DENARIUS
penny-a-liner ................... HACK
pentacle ......... STAR, SYMBOL
Pentateuch ............ TORA, TORAH
Pentheus' grandparent ...... CADMUS
penthouse ...... LEANTO, PENTICE,
                                AERIE
peon ................. SOLDIER, SERF
peon in chess .................. PAWN
peony ........... MOUTAN, PINY
peony; genus .............. PACONIA
people .. FOLK, DEMOS, KIN, LAITY,
                                RACE
people; genus ................. ETHOS
people, lowest order of .... CANAILLE
peopled village ........ HERD, ABADI
pepper . AVA, PIMIENTO, CAPSICUM
   "   and salt ................. GRAY
   "   , mild ............... PAPRIKA
   "   betel ...................... SIRI
   "   beverage ................ KAVA
   "   , Java .................. CUBEB
   "   plant; Borneo .... AVA, KAVA
   "   ; slang .................. PELT

" species of .... BETEL, CAYEN
peppermint camphor ...... MENTHOL
peppermint, synthetic ........ ANISYL
pepper-picker ................. PIPER
peppery ...... CHOLERIC, PUNGENT
perambulator ................... PRAM
perceive . SENSATE, FREDE, NOTICE
perception ........ ACUMEN, SEEING
perch ...... AERIE, ROD, ROOST, SIT
perch, a kind of BARSE, OKOW, POPE
perched ................... LIT, SAT
perchers ................ INSESSORES
percolate MELT, OOZE, SEEP, STRAIN
percolate, to ....... SILT, TRANSUDE
percursor .......... CRIER, HERALD
percussion inst.; mus. .......... TRAP
perdition .. DESTRUCTION, WRECK,
RUIN
peregrine .......... ALIEN, FOREIGN
perennial, hardy; genus ........ GEUM
perennial herbs; genus ....... ARNICA
perfect INVIOLATE, SPHERAL, SOLE
perfect, comb. form ........... TELEO
perfection, standard of . ACME, IDEAL
perfidy ....... APOSTASY, TREASON
perforate .... GRID, DOCK, POUNCE,
PIERCE, RIDDLE, BORE, DRILL,
EAT
perforated block ................. NUT
perforated marker .......... STENCIL
perforated nozzle ............... ROSE
perforated sphere ............... BEAD
perforation ... BORE, EYELET, HOLE
perform again .................. REDO
performer ............ ACTOR, SHINE
performer's style .............. SERIO
perfume .. ATAR, ATTAR, ESSENCE,
ESTER, NOSE, FRANGIPANI
" , aromatic ........ AROMATA,
INCENSE
" , fragant ............... ODOR
" , medicated .......... PASTIL
" , musky ............... CIVET
" , oriental ............ MYRRH
" , strong scented ....... MUSK
" with burning spice ... CENSE
perhaps ..... PERCHANCE, BELIKE,
HAPLY
perhaps; Scot. ............... ABLINS
pericarp .... BERRY, BUR, NUT, POD
peril .... HAZARD, JEOPARDY, RISK
perilously inadequate ........ ICARIAN
perimeter ........... BORDER, AMBIT
period ......... POINT, DOT, TRACK
period of race's apex ........ HEMERA
period of time ..... AEON, AGE, ERA
periodic . ERAL, ANNUAL, ETESIAN
periodical ....... PAPER, JOURNAL,
MAGAZINE, RECURRING
peripatetic ................... WALKER
peripheral ...................... DISTAL
periphery ........ LIP, SPACE, AMBIT
perish ............ DECAY, DIE, ROT
peritoneum, fold of ...... OMENTUM
periwinkle ........ MUSSEL, MYRTLE
Perle of society .............. MESTA
permeate ........ IMBUE, INSINUATE
permission GRACE, LEAVE, LICENSE
permit ALLOW, SUFFER, LET, LEVE

pernicious ...... NOISOME, VICIOUS
Peron, Senora ........... EVA, EVITA
perpendicular ...... VERTICAL, SINE
perpendicular (geom.) .... APOTHEM
perpetuity ....... ETERNITY, SERIAL
perplexes ........ BESETS, CRUXES
perplexing ...... KNOTTY, CARKING
perplexity STALEMATE, FOG, WERE
perquisite APPANAGE, FEE, PROFIT
persecuted ............ MARTYRIZED,
ANNOYED
persecution, flies from .... REFUGEE
Persephone .......... CORA, SPRING
Persephone's mother ...... DEMETER
Perseus, mother of ............ DANAE
Perseus, star of ........ ALGOL, ATIK
Persia .......................... IRAN
Persia, anc. people of .... ELAMITES,
MEDES
Persia, early conqueror of .... CYRUS
Persian ............................ LUR
" book of scriptures .... KORAN
" carpet .... HAMADAN, KALI,
SENNA
" city ......... OMOL, TABRIZ,
TEHERAN, NIR
" civil officer ............. KHAN
" coin ... ASAR, BISTI, DARIC,
DINAR, RIAL, KRAN, STATER
" , comb. form ........... RANO
" copper coin ........ PUL, PAL
" demi-god ............... YIMA
" dyestuff ............... INDIGO
" dynasty, anc. ........ SELJUK
" dynasty, founder of present ...
AGHA
" evergreen ............. OLAX
" evil spirit ARIMAN, AHRIMAN
" fairy ........ ELF, PERI, FAY
" fire worshipper ........ PARSI
" gate ............... BAR, DAR
" gazelle ................. CORA
" gold coin .............. TOMAN
" governor ............. SATRAP
" grass ................. MILLET
" gum .......... TRAGACANTH
" hook money ............ LARI
" language; anc. .......... ZEND,
PAHLAVI, AVESTAN
" lynx ................ CARACAL
" meas. of length .. PARASANG
" mystic .................. SUFI
" myth .................... MAH
" natives .................. TAI
" oil center ............. ABADAN
" pantheist ............. BABIST
" plant .......... OPIUM, POPPY
" poet .... HAFIZ, OMAR, SADI
" port ................ BUSHIRE
" priest ......... MAGI, NADAB
" river .......... KARUN, TAB
" rose ..................... GUL
" ruffian ............... APACHE
" ruler MIR, ATABEK, SHAH,
SULTAN
" salt lake .......... URUMIAH
" salt swamp ............ KAVIR
" sect .......... SHIITE, SUNNI
" screen .............. PURDAH

199

" servant ............... BACHA
" shah .................... ISMAIL
" song bird ............ BULBUL
" spirit of light ....... ORMAZO
" sun god ............. MITHRAS
" tiara ................. CIDARIS
" title .... MIR, MIRZA, SHAH
" town dwellers ... LUR, SART
" trading center ..... ISPAHAN
" tribe ................... NOMAD
" twenty dinars ...... BISTI
" viceroy, anc. ....... SATRAP
" water vessel ........ AFTABA
" water wheel ........ NORIA
" weight . ABBAS, MISKAL, SIR
" writings ............ AVESTA
persiflage ...... BANTER, BADINAGE
persimmon family ............. EBONY
persimmon; Mex. .......... CHAPOTE
persist ....... TORE, LAST, ENDURE
person ..... BEING, ONE, LION, URF,
WIGHT
" accused .......... APPELLEE
" assigned to serve writ . ELISOR
" , dull ...... DORBEL, STOCK
" held as a pledge .... HOSTAGE
" of distinction ...... NOTABLE
" of French descent ... CREOLE
" of mixed blood ...... MESTEE
" , private; law ...... RELATOR
" , small ............... POPPET
" trying to enter a lodge COWAN
" trying to enter a lodge COWAN
personal, comb. form ............ IDIO
personified .............. INCARNATE
perspective .... VIEWS, LANT, VISTA
perspicacious ......... ACUTE, KEEN
perspicacity .................. ACUMEN
persuade ...................... ENTICE
pert .... BRASH, DAPPER, NIMBLE
pert girl .... .. BOLD, SAUCY, MINX
pertain ..... BELONG, RELATE, FIT
pertaining to a river .......... AMNIC
per. to a hypothetical force ..... ODIC
" " a seam ............. SUTURAL
" " ancestral type .... ATARISTIC
" " animals ................ ZOOID
" " antimony ............ STIBIAL
" " debtors' joint obligation .......
CORREAL
" " dissenters' chapel ... PANTILE
" " earth ...... GEAL, TELLURIC,
TERRA
" " fat .................. SEBACIC
" " gambling .......... ALEATORY
" " gulls ................... LARINE
" " heresy ................. ARIAN
" " insects ........ ENTOMOLOGIC
" " meaning in language SEMANTIC
" " medicine ............. IATRIC
" " old age ............. GERATIC
" " oscine birds ....... TIMALINE
" " religious profession ... BABISM
" " room of state ....... CAMERAL
" " sculpture .......... GLYPHIC
" " sea ............. THALASSIC
per. to skin ..................... DERIC
" " skull ..................... INIAL
" " sole of feet .......... PLANTAR

" "the deer .............. CERVINE
" " third thoracic segment of insect
SCUTELLAR
" " tibia .................. CNEMIAL
" " vascular system ........ HEMAL
" " vowel sounds ......... VOCALIC
" " wife .................. UXORIAL
pertinent .. PAT, RELEVANT, ANENT
Peru, drizzling rain ......... GARUA
Peru, early empire of .......... YNCAS
Peru, low hill of ................. LOMA
Peru, low tree of ............ VICHAYA
peruke ......... HAIR, PERIWIG, WIG
peruse .......... SURVEY, CON, READ
Peruvian, ancient ................ INCA
" bark ............ CINCHONA
" city ...................... ICA
" coin ....... DINERO, LIBRA,
PESETA, SOL
" creeper ............... PITO
" deer ..... ALPACA, TARUCO
" department .... CUZCO, ICA,
LIMA, PIURA, TACNA
" fox ..................... ATOC
" goddess .............. MAMA
" hillock .............. MEDANO
" inn .................. TAMBO
" king ................... INCA
" llama ....... ALPACA, PACO
" mark of nobility ... LLAUTU
" partridge ............ YUTU
" plant ... LEARCO, MASSUA,
OCA, TOLA, ULLUCA
" plateau ........... TABLAZO
" relic ................. HUACO
" river .. ACARI, ENE, SANTA,
ILO, RIMAC
" seaport .. CALLAO, ILO, YLO
" shrub .... CHILCA, MATICO,
RATANHIA, RATANY,
RHATANY
" tree ........... ALGARROBO
" tribe ...........INCAS, ANTI
" volcano .............. MISTI
pervade ....... PERMEATE, EXTEND
perverse .... AWK, FROWARD, WOGH
perversely .................... AWRY
perversion of taste .......... MALACIA
pesach ........... PASSOVER, PESAH
peso, silver ...................... DURO
pessimist ............... WORRYCARL
pessimistic ............ FOREBODING,
COWARDLY
pest .......... RAY, BANE, PLAGUE
pester ........ BADGER, RIB, HARASS
pestilence ......... PLAGUE, SCOURGE
pestle .. MASHER, MULLER, BRAYER
pet .............. CODDLE, DANDLE
pet lamb .............. CADE, COSSET
pet, to be in a .. TOUCHY, HUFF, TIFF
petal of an orchid, lower .. LABELLUM
petal, per, to a ....... ALA, COROLLA,
WHORL
petals ...................... ALAE
petals, without .......... APETALOUS
petasus; Gr. ........... CUPALO, HAT
Peter the menace .............. LORRE

200

peter-out; sl. ...... DWINDLE, FADE, WANE
petiole ................... LEAFSTALK
petition ....... ASK, BEG, PRAY, SUE
petrified city; Egypt. ........ ISHMONIE
petrifying ..... PETRESCENT, STONY
Petrograd ................ LENINGRAD
petrol ...................... GASOLINE
petroleum, deriv. of ......... BUTANE, NAPHTHA
petroleum product .......... CANADOL
petticoat ........ BALMORAL, JUPON, KIRTLE
pettish .......... FRETFUL, PEEVISH
petty ...... MINUSCULE, TIN, ORRA, PREGALL, SMALL, TRIVIAL
petty fault .............. PECCADILLO
petulant ............. PERT, WANTON
petulant, more ... SURLIER, TESTIER
pewit ......................... LAPWING
peyote ...................... ..CACTUS
Phaedos school ................. ELIAN
phalanger; Tasmania .......... TAPOA
phanerite ....................... PLAIN
phantasm ........ EIDOLON, IDOLUM
phantom ..................... EIDOLON
Pharoah .................... RAMESES
pharos ...... BEACON, LIGHTHOUSE
phase ...... ASPECT, FACET, STAGE, CHAPTER
pheasant .. CHEER, MONAL, PUKRAS
pheasant, Islan ........... TRAGOPAN
pheasant, brood of ........ NIDE, NYE
pheasant, native ............. LEIPOA
phenol, deriv. ANOL, SALOL, THYMOL, ORCIN, CRESOL
phenomenon .......... EVENT, SIGHT
phenyl ........................... ARYL
philabeg .......................... KILT
philippic .......... SCREED, TIRADE
Philippine aborigine . IFIL, AETA, ATA
"         animal ....... CIVET, LEMUR
"         ant, white ....... ANA, ANAY
"         breadfruit .. CAMANSI, RIMA
"         buffalo ............. TIMARAU
"         canoe ................... BANCO
"         century plant ....... MAGUEY
"         child ................... BATA
"         christianized tribe... BISCOL, TAGALOG, VISAYAN
"         city ........ ALBAY, CAVITE, DAGUPAN, MANILA
"         civil governor .......... TAFT
"         cocoanut deriv. ....... COPRA
"         coin ................... PESO
"         dagger .................. ITAC
"         dialect ..... IBANAG, TAGAL
"         director of health .... HEISER
"         district ............. LEPANTO
"         dogwood tree ............ TUA
"         drink, alcoholic ....... BENO
"         dwarf race .. NEGRITO, AETA
"         evergreen tree ........ KAPOK
"         fabric ........... PINEAPPLE
"         farmer .................. TAO
"         fennel .................. ANISE
"         fern ..................... NITO
"         fetish .. ANITO, IDOL, SPIRIT

"         food staple ..... BAHA, TARO
"         fort ...................... GOTA
"         governor general ......... IDE
"         grass, coarse ......... COGAN
"         hardwood ............. NARRA
"         headman ............. DATTO
"         hemp .................. ABACA
"         house ................. BAHAY
"         idol .................... ANITO
"         Island ........ SAMAR, CEBU, PANAY, TICAO
"         Island; aunt or uncle ... CACA
"         Island forest ............ DITA
"         Island group ........... SULU
"         island, largest ....... LUZON, MINDANAO
"         Island wide stream ..... ILOG
Philippine Islands, discoverer of ........ MAGELLAN
"         knife ............ BOLO, ITAC
"         language TAGALA, TAGALOG
"         lighter ................. CASCO
"         lighthouse .............. FARO
"         limestone ............ EOCENE
"         litter ............. TALABON
"         mountain peak .... APO, IBA, MAYON
"         native ............ ITA, MORO
"         negrito ..... AETA, ATA, ITA
"         oil liquid ........... CEBUR
"         palm ... ANAHAU, CALMUS, NIPA
"         peasant ................... TAO
"         pepper ................. BETEL
"         plum ................ LANSEH
"         port ......... ILOILO, CEBU
"         province .. ILOILO, ISABELA
"         reptile .............. PYTHON
"         rice ..................... PAGA
"         river .......... ABRA, PASIG
"         sarong ........... PATADION
"         sash .................... TAPIS
"         sea ..................... SULU
"         shirt ................... BARO
"         shrub ................. NABO
"         skirt .................... SAYA
"         slave ................. ALIPIN
"         soldier or brigand . LADRONE
"         soldiers' barrack .. CUARTEL
"         springs, hot ............. TIBI
"         summer capital ...... BAGUIO
"         sweetsop ............... ATES
"         thatch .................. NIPA
"         tree ACLE, DAO, DITA, IPIL, TUA
"         tree, large ....... IBA, ANAM, MAMBOG, LIGAS
"         tribe ...... MUNDO, IGALOT, IGORROTE
"         volcano . ALBAY, APO, TAAL
"         water buffalo ...... CARABAO
"         water jar ............. BANGO
"         weapon ................ BOLO
"         wood ....... NARRA, EBONY, SANDAL, TEAK
Phillipine-Malay ............ ITALONE
philomel ............. NIGHTINGALE
Philomela, sister of .......... PROCNE

201

philosopher; French ............ NENAN
" ; German .............. KANT
" ; Greek .... NESTOR, PLATO
" , one of the seven sages ......
SOLON
philosophical .... ERUDITE, SAPIENT
philosophy, anc. ................ STOIC
philosophy, school of . SECT, ELEATIC
phlegmatic ..... COLD, DULL, INERT,
SLOW
phloem ........ TISSUE, BARK, BAST
phlogistic ............ INFLAMMATORY
Phoebad ....PROPHETESS, SEERESS
Phoebe, moon personified .....SELENE
Phoebus ....................... SOL
Phoebus, sun personified ...... APOLLO
Phoenecia, anc. capital .......... TYRE
Phoenician god .................. BAAL
Phoenician goddess of love ... BALTIS,
ASTARTE
Phoenician seaport ............. SIDON
phonetic notation ............. ROMIC
phonetical sound ............ PALATAL
phosphate ................... PALAITE
phosphate of lime ............ APATITE
photo ........................... STAT
photo copy, make ............TINTYPE
photo solution .................. HYPO
photograph ...... HELIOGRAPH, MUE
" developer . ADUROL, ORTOL,
TONER
" powder .... AMIDOL, METOL
" , to ..................... MUG
photographs, color process ............
PINACHROMY
photography, early producer; Fr. .......
NIEPCE
photography, inventor of .... TALBOT
photology ...................... OPTICS
photometric unit .......... PYR, RAD
photo-printing ARTOTYPE, OZOTYPE
phrase .............. EPIGRAM, IDIOM
phrase, style of .... DICTION, SLOGAN
phratry ....... CLAN, CURIA, PHYLE
Phrixo's mother ............ NEPHELE
Phrygian christianizer ... MONTANIST
Phrygian god of vegetation ..... ATTIS
Phrygian king .................. MIDAS
Phrygian river ............. MEANDER
phylactery ......... AMULET, CHARM
phyletic ............ SPECIES, RACIAL
phylloid ..................... LEAFLIKE
physical ........... SOMATIC, BODILY
physician, an ignorant . MEDICASTER
physician; Fr. ..... GALEN, LAVERAN
physicians' group .................. AM
physicians, per. to ............ IATRIC
physicist, famous GALVANI, FARADAY,
MARCONI
physics, branch of ...... PNEUMATICS
physiognomy ............... FACE, MUG
physostigmine ............... ESERINE
pian ........... FRAMBOESIA, YAWS
piano, dumb ................ DIGITORIA
piano, early .................... SPINET
piaster, 120th of ............... ASPER
picaroon .............. ROGUE, THIEF
picatoon . BANDIT, CORSAIR, PIRATE

Piccard, Auguste ......... AERONAUT
picked .... CHOSEN, CULLED, ELITE
picket ..... SENTRY, GUARD, STAKE,
MOOR, POST, TETHER,
PALE
pickle . MESS, ACHAR, ALEC, BRINE,
VITRIOL, MARINADE
pickle salt ...................... SOUSE
pickled pigs feet ................ SOUSE
pickpocket ........ DIP, THIEF, WIRE
picnic ..... GIPSY, JUNKET, OUTING,
PLAY
picoline, rel. to ............ UVITONIC
picture . IMAGE, PASTEL, PORTURE,
TABLEAU, PROFILE,
SCENERY
picture award .................. OSCAR
picture, moving ... CINEMA, FILM, TV
picture viewing inst. .. ALETHOSCOPE
picturesque ........ SCENIC, GRAPHIC
pie dish ........... COBBLER, COFFIN
piebald .. PINTADO, DAPPLED, PIED,
PINTO
piece of armor .... CORSELET, PANE
TACE
piece used to make tight fit ...... SHIM
pieces, split off .............. SPLINTS
piecing out .......... CANTLE, EKING
pieplant .................... RHUBARB
pierbase ....................... SOCLE
pier, kind of ... STILT, SOCLE, ANTA,
MOLE, PILLAR, POST
pierce GORE, STICK, LANCE, ENTER,
STAB, GRIDE
piercer ............ BORER, SPEARER
piercing ...... KEEN, SHRILL, TART,
THORN
Pierre; Fr. .................... LAVAL
pig .......... BACON, DOO, FAR, ELT
" ; African .............. AARDVARK
" deer ................ BABIROUSSA
" dialect ........................ ELT
" , female ...................... SOW
" iron ballast .......... KENTLEDGE
" , male ........................ BOAR
" metal ..................... INGOT
" of lead ................... FOTHER
" , young ........... GRICE, SHOAT,
WHINNOCK
" , young female ....... ELT, GILT
piglike animal .............. PECCARY
pigly ......................... SUINT
pigpen ................ REEVE, STY
pigs, litter of ................ FARROW
pigs, per. to .................. PORCINE
pigsty ....................... FRANK
pigeon ...... ISABEL, PIPER, GOURA,
POUTER, CUSHAT
" , Australian ............ WONGA
" call ......................... COO
" , carrier .... HOMER, HOMING
" , dwarfed ............... RUNT
" , extinct ................ DODO
" , fruit ................... LUPE
" ; genus ............. COLUMBA
" , long tailed; Afr. .. NAMAQUA
" , short beaked .......... BARB

202

pigeon, variety of ........ NUN, RUFF, TUMBLER
pigeon-house ............. COLUMBARY
pigeons, food for ............. SALTCAT
pigeons, per. to ....... PERISTERONIC
pigment, anthracene ....... ALIZARIN
" , arsenical yellow . ORPIMENT
" , black ...................... TAR
" , black, any ........ MELANIN
" , deep blue ............ SMALT
" , board ............. PALETTE
" , brown ..... BISTER, UMBER
" , calico printing .... CANARIN
" , coal tar ............ ANILINE
" , cuttle fish ............ SEPIA
" , deep blue ............. SMALT
" , lake ............... MADDER
" , orange-red ....... REALGAR
" , oxide of lead .... MASSICOT
" , pale yellow ........ ETIOLIN
" , white ............. BARYTA
" , yellow ..... OCHRE, SIENNA
pigmy ...... DWARF, MINIM, SHORT
pignoration .................... PIGNUS
pigtail ........ PLAIT, QUEUE, BRAID
pike ... DORE, GED, PICK, POULANE
pike-like fish ..... ARAPAIMA, LUCE, ROBALO
pilaster molds .................. SPIRA
pilaster, type of ................. ANTA
pilaster-like abutment ....... ALETTE
pilchard .................... SARDINE
pilcher ...... PILCHARD, SCABBARD
pile ..... HEAP, STACK, SHAG, NAP
pile driver ...... RAM, FISTUCA, GIN
piles, defense work of ..... ESTACADE
pilewort .................. FIREWEED
pilewort fiber .................... ADAD
pilgrim ..... WAYFARER, CRUSADER
pilgrim to the Holy Land .... PALMER
pilgrim's garb at Mecca ........ IHRAM
"Pilgrim's Progress," char. in . DEMAS
pill BALL, BOLUS, PELLET, PILULE
pillage FORAY, RIFLE, FLAY, HARRY, SACK, RAPINE
pillar bearing a notice .......... STELE
pillar in buddhist building ........ LAT
pillar with figures ............ OSIRIDE
pillory .... STOCK, TRONE, CANGUE, YOKE
pillow-case ............... BERE, TYE
pilose .......................... HAIRY
pilot AVIATE, FLYER, GUIDE, LEAD, STEER
pilot fish ......... REMORA, ROMERO, WHITEFISH
pilous ...................... HAIRLIKE
Piman Indian ................... OPATA
pimento .................... ALLSPICE
pimp in Gay's "Beggar's Opera"; ...... PEACHUM
pimple ............... PAPULE, QUAT
pin, axle .................. LINCHPIN
" for blocks ......... NOG, DOWEL
" fulcrum for oar ............THOLE
" jackstraw ............ SPILIKIN
" , large tapering wooden ....... FID
" of a dial .................. STYLE

" , small .................. PEG, LILL
" to fasten meat .......... SKEWER
" with a looped head ..... EYEBOLT
pinafore ........... SLIP, APRON, TIER
pince-nez; Fr. ........ EYEGLASS(ES)
pincers ... ORGAN, TONGS, FORCEPS, TEW, PLIERS, FORCIPATE
pinch .. PUGIL, SNAPE, CRAMP, NIP, TWEAK, RUB, GRIPE, STRAIT
pinched .......... ARRESTED, CLEM
pine ... HONE, ARAR, DEAL, KAURI, WARRYN, LANGUISH, FRET, LIN
pine beverage ..................... PINA
pine plant; order ........ BROMELIACI
pine tar extract .............. RETENE
pine, textile screw ............ PANDAN
pineapple ..... PINA, ANANA, NANA
"Pine Tree" State ............. MAINE
pinguid .........ADIPOSE, FAT, OILY
pink ............. CORAL, PAW, STAB
Pinkerton's wife ................. KATE
pinks; genus ................... SILENE
pinkster flower ............... AZALEA
pinna .......... AURICLE, FEATHER
pinnacle .......... CREST, EPI, SPIRE
pinnacle of glacial ice .......... SERAC
pinnacle, rocky .................... TOR
pinochle score ..................... DIX
pinochle, term in .............. MELD
pin-point ............... DOT, TRIFLE
pinquid .................... FAT, OILY
pintado ...... CHINTZ, SIER, CERO
pinto .. SPOTTED, PIEBALD, CALICO
pintons ......................... WINGS
Pinza, Mr. ........................ EZIO
pip .. ACE, HIT, SEED, SPECK, PAIP, SPOT
pipe .. HOOKA, HULVE, REED, TUBE
pipe caking ................... DOTTLE
" , clay ..................... STRAW
" fish ....................... EARL
" fitting ............... CROSS, TEE
" , flanged end of ............. TAFT
" form of ....... TUBULAR, TUBAL
" of peace; Ind. ......... CALUMET
" , oriental .............. NARGILE
pipe player ..................... FIFER
" shepherd's ........ OAT, LARIGOT
" , short ................... DUDEEN
" , small ................... TUBULE
" , smoke ................... TEWEL
pipefish ........................ SNACOT
Piper's son ....................... TOM
pipette ............... TUBE, TASTER
pipit, a ........................ TITLARK
"Pippa ——" ................... PASSES
piquancy ... SPICE, RACINESS, SALT, ZEST, TARTNESS
piquet score ....................... PIC
piquet, winning of all tricks .... CAPOT
pirate .... PICAROON, FREEBOOTER, CORSAIR, LAFITTE
pirate flag ...................... ROGER
pirate's gallows ............ YARDARM
pirate's weapon ................. SNEE
piraya (piranha) .............. CARIBE
piscine propeller ................... FIN

Pisgah's summit ................ NEBO
pismire ........................ ANT
pistol ........ DAG, DERRINGER, POD
pistol case ................... HOLSTER
piston ...................... PLUNGER
pit ...... CAVE, SLUIG, SUMP, BONE,
ENDOCARP
pit in a theatre ............. PARQUET
pit of the peach ............ PUTAMEN
pitch, cobbler's ................. CODE
pitch inst. ............... TONOMETER
pitchard .................... SARDINE
pitchblende deriv. RADIUM, URANIUM
pitcher CROCK, EWER, GORGE, OLLA,
OLPE, TOSSER
pitcher, left-hand ........ SOUTHPAW
pitcher plant ............. NEPENTHE
pitcher, small ale .... BOGGLE, TOBY
pitcher-shaped .......... URCEOLATE
pitcher-shaped vessel ...... AIGUIERE
pitches, as a vessel . PLUNGES, SENDS
pitfall ... TRAP, DECOY, GIN, SNARE
pith .... GIST, JET, PULP, MARROW
pith, full of .. HEATY, FORCE, VIGOR
pith helmet ..................... TOPEE
pith of the Nile .............. AMBASH
pithy .. FORCIBLE, LACONIC, TERSE,
SUTRA(S)
pittance ........ SCANT, SONG, DOLE
pitted ............ FOVIATE, STONED
Pittrich; opera by ............. MARGA
pity .......... MERCY, RUTH, YEARN
pivot pin ...................... PINTLE
pivotal ......................... POLAR
pivoted .......... SWUNG, SWIVELED
pixy .... ELF, GOBLIN, FAIRY, SPRITE
placard .. AFFICHE, POST(ER), BILL
placate ..... CALM, PACIFY, SOOTHE
place . BOUND, STEAD, SPOT, POSIT,
SITUS
"   apart ................... ENISLE
"   beneath ............. INFRAPOSE
"   comb. form ................ TOPO
"   for trade ................. MART
"   frequented ... HAUNT, RESORT
"   from which a jury is taken .......
VENUE
"   , hiding .................... MEW
"   in a row ................ ALINE
"   , in; rare ............... INNEST
"   , intermediate .......... LIMBO
"   , meeting ............... TRYST
"   of ............... LIEU, STEAD
"   of nether darkness .... EREBUS
place, to .................... PUT, SET
"   where an action has occurred ....
VENUE
placed .......... PUT, LAIN, SITUATE
places .................. POSTS, LOCI
placid ...... CALM, SERENE, SUANT
plagiarism ............. CRIB, PIRACY
plagiarist ........ THIEF, BORROWER
plagic ......................... TIDES
plague .... TEASE, HARRY, HECTOR,
TWIT, DUN, PEST
plaid cloth .......... MAUD, TARTAN
plain .. WOLD, MERE, HEATH, MOOR
"   dweller .............. LLANERO

"   elevated ................... MESA
"   , Eur. ................... STEPPE
"   , grassy ... CAMAS, SAVANNAH
"   , Italian ............ CAMPAGNA
"   , Olympic games ........... ELIS
"   , Russian .... STEPPE, TUNDRA
"   , salt-covered .......... SALADA
"   , small prairie ........... CAMAS
"   , So. Afr. ................ VELDT
"   , Span.-Amer. .... LLANO, VEGA
"   , treeless .... SAVANNA, VELDT,
PAMPAS, BARE
plains ...................... DOWNS
plaintiff .. ORATOR, SUER, ACCUSER
plaintive .. SAD, ELEGIAC, WISTFUL
plait ... MILAN, PLEX, HOY, WIMPLE
plaited ....................... KILTED
plaited helmet .... BASINET, BASNET
plaited rope ................... SENNIT
plan .......... DRAFT, ETTLE, PLAT,
SCHEME, STRATEGY
plan, architectural ............. EPURE
plane ........................... AERO
plane chart ................. MECATOR
plane handle ............. TOAT, TOTE
plane, inclined ........ RAMP, SHUTE
plane iron ......................... BIT
plane propulsion .......... JET, ATOM
plane tree ................... CHINAR
plane tree; genus ......... PLATANUS
planet ....... MOON, URANUS, STAR,
WANDERER
"   , most brilliant ......... VENUS
"   , nearest sun ....... MERCURY
"   , recent ................. PLUTO
"   , red ...................... MARS
"   , satellite of ............. MOON
planetarium ................. ORRERY
plange ...................... LAMENT
planisphere ............. ASTROLABE
plank, as a prop ...... SHOLE, SHORE
plank down .......... PAY, ADVANCE
plank of bridge ............... CHESS
planking, breadth of .......... STRAKE
plant (see also 'shrub') .......... SOW
"   ..... ACHE, ALYSSUM, CLOTE,
CLOVER, EXOGEN, FRESIA,
RAPE, SMILAX, TAR, WORT
"   , aconite .................. BIKH
"   adapted to dry climate ...........
XEROPHYTE
"   , African ...... ARGEL, CACOON
"   , agave .................... PITA
"   , algae; genus .......... NOSTOC
"   , alismaceous ......... ALISMAD
"   , Alpine ............ EDELWEISS
"   , ambrosia; genus ... RAGWEED
"   , Amer. ................ CACOON
"   , anise ..................... DILL
"   , any climbing ............. LIANA
"   , apiaceous ............... ANISE
"   , apiaceous-dwarf ........ CUMIN
plant, apoplexy ................. ESCA
"   appendage ............ STIPULE
"   , aralia ................. FATSIA
"   , aromatic ANISE, MINT, NARD,
LAVENDER, TANSY, THYME
"   , aromatic flavoring . TARRAGON

204

"    , aromatic gum ......... ARALIA
"    , aromatic seed .......... ANET
"    , arrow root; Bermuda . ARARAO
"    , arum family .... AROID, TARO
"    , Asiatic fiber .......... RAMIE
"    , Asiatic oil .............. ODAL
"    Assam ..................... TEA
"    , aster family ........... DAISY
"    , astringent, an ....... MATICO
"    , auricula ........... PRIMROSE
"    , Austral. .. CORREA, FUCHSIA,
                    HAKEA, URY
"    , Austral.; genus .... ALSTONIA
"    , bean family ........ LICORICE
"    berry, acid .......... CURRANT
"    , betel pepper, leaf of .... BUYO
"    , bitter ..................... RUE
"    , bitter vetch .............. ERS
"    bodies without stems.... THALLI
"    body in the higher plants ........
                    CARMUS
"    , bog ..................... ABAMA
"    , bone set .............. TEASEL
"    box ..................... BUXUS
"    bramble ................. GORSE
"    , brassica COLE, RAPE, TURNIP
"    , broom ................. CYTISUS
"    , broom; Sp. .. GENISTA, SPART
"    , bud of ..................... CION
"    , burning bush .......... WAHOO
"    , burdock ................ CLITE
"    , cactus ...... CEREUS, DILDO,
                    MESCAL, SAGUARO
"    , cactus kind ...... XEROPHYTE
"    , cactus; Mex. ......... CHAUTE
"    , calyx leaf .............. SEPAL
"    , Canna ................. ACHIRA
"    capsule ..................... POD
"    , calyx leaf .............. SEPAL
"    catchfly ................. SILENE
"    catnip family .... NEP, NEPETA
"    cells .................. GAMETES
"    , cellular flowerless ..... LICHEN
"    , century ....... AGAVE, ALOE,
                    MAGUEY, PITA
"    , chaffy scale ............ PALEA
"    cherry, laurel ........ CERASUS
"    , Chinese ............... RAMIE
"    chlorophyll, lacking ..... ALBINO
"    , climbing ....... LIANA, LIANE
"    clover .................... MEDIC
"    clusters, flat top .......... CYME
"    , cruciferous . ALYSSUM, CRESS
"    , cryptogamous ............ MOSS
"    cuticle .................... CUTIN
"    cutter; S. Am. ............ RARA
"    , cyperaceous ............ SEDGE
"    , dill ...................... ANET
"    , dipsacus; genus ...... TEASEL
"    disease .... BLISTER, ERINOSE,
                    SMUT, APHID
"    , dock-like ............. SORREL
"    , dogwood ............. CORNUS
plant, dye yielding .. MADDER, WOAD
"    dyers medium ........... WELD
"    , E. Ind. .... BENNE, DEUTZIA,
                    MADAR, CREAT, REA,
                    SESAME, SOLA, SUNN

"    , Egypt, aromatic ........ CUMIN
"    embryo of ......... PLANTULE
"    , erica; genus ........... HEATH
"    , euphorbia; genus ..... SPURGE
"    , European .......... AZAROLE,
                    SNEEZEWORT
"    , everlasting ........... ORPINE
"    exudation .............. RESIN
"    fabaceous ................... ERS
"    fern; N. Z. ............... TARA
"    fiber; .... ISTLE, PITA, RAMIE,
                    SISAL, SIDA
"    , flag, sweet ........... CALMUS
"    floating ................ FROGBIT
"    , flower pot ......... CINERARIA
"    , flowering ......... ACANTHUS,
                    BARRETA, CALLA, ORPIN,
                    RHODORA, TAMARIX
"    , flowerless; .... FERN, LICHEN,
                    THALOGEN
"    for tanning .............. SUMAC
"    , fragrant ... ANISE, ANGELICA
"    , fragrant root ........... ORRIS
"    , fruit yielding dye ....... MUSA
"    furze ............ GORGE, ULEX
"    , garden .... ASTER, LETTUCE
"    , garlic, wild ............ MOLY
"    ; genus .... TIA, AGAVE, ARUM,
                    ERINGO
"    , genus isatis ............ WOAD
"    , genus ulex ............. FURZE
"    , grass .................. AVENA
"    , green .................. FECULA
"    , ground ivy ........... NEPETA
"    , growing from inside ENDOGEN
"    growing on sea bottom .. ENALID
"    growing wild ....... AGRESTIAL
"    , growth on a ............. GALL
"    , habitat .......... FORM, ECAD
"    habitat adjustment ..... ECESIS
"    having astringent bark .. ALDER
"    having grape-like leaves . SALAL
"    , haw, black .............. SLOE
"    , Hawaiian .............. OLONA
"    , hawthorn, kind of ... AZAROLE
"    , hay; Tibet ............. KOMAL
"    , healing .............. SANICLE
"    , heath; genus ........... ERICA
"    , holly ................. YAPON
"    , hop vine stem ............ BINE
"    hybridization ............ XENIA
"    , indigo .................... ANIL
"    , interior chaff of PALEA, PALET
"    , ipecac ................... EVEA
"    , Iris family .......... IRID, IXIA
"    , Japanese ....... AUCUBA, TEA
"    , Jap. quince .......... CYDONIA
"    juice ................ MILK, SAP
"    , leguminous .. LENTIL, MEDIC,
                    SENNA
"    lice; genus ............... APHIS
"    , lilac ................. SYRINGA
plant, lilaceous LEEK, ONION, SEGO,
                    TULIP, SOTOL
"    , lily-like ........ ALOE, LOTUS,
                    ASPHODEL, SABADILLA,
                    SQUILL, YUCCA
"    louse ................... APHID

" , lychnis; genus ...... CAMPION
" , main axis of .......... STALK
" , male .................... MAS
" , malvaceous . ALTEA, ESCOBA
" , manioc .. CASSAVA, TAPIOCA
" , marine .............. ENALID
" , marine skeleton ...... CORAL
" , medicinal; ... ARNICA, ALOE,
    BONESET, ANISE, GENTIAN,
    LOBELIA
" menthaceous .......... CATNIP
" , Mexican DATIL, CHIA, SALVIA
" , mignonette-like WELD, WOALD
" , millet, broom corn ..... HIRSE
" , mint; Eur. ........ LAVENDER
" , mint family .. BASIL, CATNIP,
    SAGE
" , modified ............... ECAD
" , monkshood ... ATIS, ACONITE
" , moss-like ......... HEPATIC
" , mulberry; Ind. .......... ACH
" , muscus; Lat. .......... MOSS
" , mushroom .. ACARIC, MOREL
" , mustard family ........ CRESS
" , nep .................. CATNIP
" , nepeta; genus ...... CATMINT
" , N. Amer. ............. GARRYA
" , noxious ................. WEED
" of cabbage family ......... RAPE
" of the heath order ....... LING
" of the lily family .......... IRID
" of vegetable kingdom . EXOGEN
" olacaceae, family ...... OLACAD
" on a heath ...... ERICOPHYTE
" organs ............... STOMATA
" painful to skin ... SMARTWEED
" , pansy .......... HEARTSEASE
" , parsley, annuals of ANISE-DILL
" , parsley, wild; Eng. ... ELTROT
" , part of ........ AXIL, STIPEL
" , pepper .................. ARA
" , perennial .... CAREX, SEDUM
" , Peru ........ OCA, RHATANY
" , Philippine .............. ALEM
" , pitcher ...... DARLINGTONIA
" , poisonous; genus .... DATURA
" poisonous to cattle ........ LOCO
" poisonous to fowls .. HENBANE
" , pore of a .......... LENTICEL
" , prickly ...... BRIER, CACTUS,
    NETTLE, TEASEL
" primrose .......... AURICULA
" rat poison ......... OLEANDER
" receptable ............... TORUS
" , rock .................. LICHEN
" root ................... RADIX
" , rose family ........... AVENS
" , rye fungus .............ERGOT
" , sage, aromatic ........SALVIA
" , sap of certain..........MILK
" , satin flower ........HONESTY
" scales ....PALEAE, RAMENTA
" , sea .........ENALID, ALIMON
" , seaweed, leaf of........FROND
" plant secretion ...................LERP
" , sedge; genus ........... CAREX
" , seed .............. EXOGENAE
" , seed leaf of ...... COTYLEDON
" seed organ .............. PISTIL

" , seedless, per. to ...... AGAMIC
" , sensitive .............. MIMOSA
" shoot ............. CION, STOLO
" shrubbery .............. BETEL
" shrubs; genus ..... ITEA, RIBES
" silene ................. CAMPION
" , snake bite remedy; Mex. GUACO
" , snake root . SENECA, SENEGA
" , snow drop ........... HALESIA
" , S. African ............... ALOE
" , S. American ..... TILLANDSIA
" , soap ..............AMOLE, MO
" , soft wooded ......... FUCHSIA
" , spring ................... GORSE
" stalk .................. HAULM
" , starch yielding .... PIA, TARO
" stem ............. BINE, CAULIS
" stem joint ..... NODE, PAYTON
" , strawberry .......... FRASIER
" , summer .............. SAVORY
" , sun rose ............. CISTUS
" , sweet bay ............LAURUS
" , sweet scented .........YERBA
" , symbol of Ireland..SHAMROCK
" , tansy ............ TANACETUM
" , tapioca ............. CASSAVA
" , taro root .................EDDO
" , taro root, food from........POI
" that bears fruit but once,........
    MONOCARP
" , thorny ..................BRIAR
" tissue; rel. to..........TAPETAL
" , trailing ................. BUYO
" , trifoliate ......... SHAMROCK
" , tropical ... ALTEA, BACCHAR,
    HAMELIA, MANGROVE,
    MUSA, PALM, TARO,
    UDO
" , trumpet ....... BIGNONIA
" used to flavor vinegar
    TARRAGON
" used in perfumery......MYRTLE
" valerian .................. NARD
" vine ...................... VITIS
" , water-side ............. SEDGE
" weed, kind of .....DOCK, WHIN
" W. Ind. climbing..REDWITHE
" , winter flowering ..... EPACRIS
' with bitter leaves........TANSY
" with scale-like leaves.....SAVIN
" yielding a cosmetic dye..HENNA
" yielding an astringent....AVENS
plantation of cacti..........NOPALRIE
planters, government by ..............
    PLANTOCRACY
plants .................SEEDS, FLORA
plants, an order of.........ERICALES
plants bearing bell shaped flowers .....
    GLOXINIAS
plants, per. to growth of....VEGETAL
plaque ...BROOCH, MEDAL, TABLET
plash .....PLEACH, POOL, PUDDLE,
    LIP, PLOP
plasma .............. QUARTZ, WHEY
plaster, coarse ......GROUT, PARGET
plaster-of-paris ....GESSO, STUCCO
plaster, wax .................CERATE
plastic ..............FICTILE, GESSO
plastic clay .....................PUG

plastic repair paste...........SLURRY
plate ..PATERA, URIM, BASE, DISC,
　　　　　　　　　　　　　　　　　GRID
plate-like vessels ...........PATERAE
plate, thin ......LAMELLA, LAMINA,
　　　　　　　　　　　　　　　　　PATEN
plate of a storage battery........GRID
plate of soap frame................SESS
plate shaped like ship ............ NEF
plateau ..........MESA, TABLELAND
plates, wind indicator .............DIAL
platform ROSTRUM, ESTRADE, KANG
platform in a fort ......... BARBETTE
platform, mining .............SOLLAR
platform, nautical .......... MAINTOP
platform, raised...SOLEA, TRIBUNE,
　　　　　　　　　　　　　　　　　DAIS
platinum wire .................. OESE
platoon ........................SQUAD
Plato's school ..............ACADEME
platter; Rom. ................... LANX
platter shaped ........SCUTELLATE
plausible excuse ................ALIBI
play DRAMA, FROLIC, ENACT, ACT,
　　MELODRAMA, ROMP, FEIGN,
　　SPORT
　"　badly ....................STRUM
　"　carelessly ...............TARUM
　"　, exhibiting a ......... STAGING
　"　ground .......... PARC, PARK
　"　mean trick ................. SHAB
　"　, part in a .... EPITASIS, ROLE
　"　silent ............. PANTOMIME
　"　, sportive..JOCULAR, WAGGISH
　"　, to enjoy ...................USE
　"　truant ...................MICHE
playwright ......................INGE
playa ................. BEACH
player .. BARNSTORMER, THESPIAN
plaything .........DIE, BAUBLE, TOY
plea ................ SUIT, ENTREATY
pleachbend .............INTERTWINE
pleasant .........GENIAL, WINSOME
pleasant; Scot. .............LEESOME
pleasantness ...............AMENITY
please ......ARRIDE, ELATE, FANCY
pleased ..................GAME, GLAD
pleasing .....ROSEATE, LIEF, SOOTH
pleasure ....... GREE, WILL, GRACE
pleasure ground .........PLEASANCE
pleasure; per. to ............ HEDONIO
plebiscite .....REFERENDUM, VOTE
pledge SWEAR, BET, GAGE, PLIGHT,
　　　　WAGE, TOAST, VAS, VOW
pledget; med. ...................SWAB
pledgor ......................PAWNER
pleiad ............... MAIA, STEROPE
Pleiades ............... ATLANTIDES
plentiful ....COPIOUS, AMPLE, FULL,
　　　　　　　　　　RIFE, BOUNTIFUL
plenty .....CHEAP, GALORE, MERTH
plenum ............ABUNDANT, FULL
pleon .....................TELSON
Pleven, M. ......................RENE
plexiform .........RETE, NETWORK
plight .......CASE, SITUATION, BAD
plinth, flat ......BASE, BLOCK, ORLO
plod .....DIG, TORE, TRUDGE, SLOG

plot ...CABAL, BREW, PACK, TRICK,
　　　　INTRIGUE, AREA, ACRE
plot of a play ...................NODE
ploughshare ......COLTER, COULTER
plover ...............DROME, SANDY
plover; Am. ......KILLDEER, PIPING
plover, crab ....................DROME
plover; Old World ........DOTTEREL,
　　　　　　　　　　　　　　　　LAPWING
plow ............ ROVE, SCAUT, TILL
　"　blade .................SHARE
plow, crosspiece of...............BUCK
　"　handle ............ HALE, STILT
　"　knife ................... COLTER
　"　, man's first .............STICK
　"　, sole of a ................ SLADE
　"　subsoil ....................MOLE
　"　, type of .................SULKY
　"　, wooden part of ......... CHIP
plowed land ...................ARADO
plowland ................CARUCATE
plowman ................... TILLER
plowshare; dial. ................REEST
plow-wheel, per. to a ......... GANG
pluck off ....ARABLE, AVULSE, PUG
plucky ................. GAME, NERVY
plug ....ESTOP, BUNG, TAP, SPILE,
　　　　　BOTT, SLOG, STOPPER
plug for a cannon's muzzle . TAMPION
plug; med. ........... CLOT, EMBOLUS
plug up ...............CALK, CAULK
plug-ugly; col. ................ROWDY
plum, a kind of......AMRA, DAMSON,
　　　　　　　CHESTON, PERSIMMON
plum, bitter wild................ SLOE
plum cake; Fr. ..................BABA
plum; Eur. ..........GAGE, BULLACE
plum, Java ................JAMBOOL
plum, sapodilla .............LANZON
plumage of bird .................ROBE
plumbago .........GRAPHITE, LEAD
plumber ......................PIPER
plume ...FEATHER, EGRET, CREST,
　　　　　　　　　　　　　　　PANACHE
plump ....FAT, BLUNT, PLOP, TIDY
plunder .... REAVE, RIFLE, BOOTY,
　　　　　　　LOOT, SPOIL, PILLAGE
plunder by stealth ROB, SACK, POACH
plunder by violence ....STRIP, RAPE,
　　　　　　　　RAVAGE, RAVEN
plundered ..........RAPINED, REFT
plunderer ... FREEBOOTER, PREYER,
　　　　　　　PREDOUR, RAIDER
plunge ....................DIP, SOUSE
plunge into a liquid......CLAP, DIVE,
　　　　　　　　LUNGE, (IM)MERSE
plunk ........ BLOW, PLUMP, TWANG
Plutarch's opus ................ LIVES
Pluto .............................DIS
plutocrat .................... CROESUS
Pluto's kingdom ................ HADES
pluvial .........................RAINY
ply ......... FOLD, HANDLE, URGE
pneuma ..BREATHING, SOUL, SPIRIT
pneumonia ........LOBAR, CROUPOUS
poach .......MIX, SHIRR, TRESPASS
poacher ........LURCHER, STALKER
pocket; Fr. .................... POCHE
pocketbook; slang .................LIL

pocketbook, small .......FOB, PURSE
pod ........ ARIL, BOLL, CAROS, KID,
　　　　　　　　　　　　　SHUCK
pod of the red pepper............CHILI
Poe heroine ..................LENORE
Poe's 'Raven'; char. in.......LENORE
poem, anc. Icelandic.............EDDA
　"　, bucolic ............. ECLOGUE
　"　, division of a ......... CANTO
　"　, 8 lines ............... TRIOLET
　"　, epic . EPODE, EPOPEE, EPOS,
　　　　　　　　　　　　　　ODE
　"　, 14 lines .............. SONNET
　"　, French ................... DIT
　"　, irregular, wild .. DITHYRAMB
　"　, mournful .............. ELEGY
poem, narrative ...... EPIC, LAY, LAI
　"　of six stanzas ......SESTINA
　"　, Old Norse ............. RUNE
　"　, pastoral ................ IDYL
　"　, satirical ............... IAMBIC
　"　, 13 line ........... RONDREAU
"Poems of Ossian," hero in; myth. ....
　　　　　　　　　　　　　FINGAL
Poe's bird .................... RAVEN
poesy ......... SONGCRAFT, VERSE
poet IDYLIST, BARD, ODIST, LYRIST,
　　　　　　ELEGIST, METRIST
poet; Ger. .................. HEINE
poetaster ...ASTER, BAVIAN, RIMER,
　　　　RHYMSTER, VERSIFIER
poetic foot ........DACTYL, IAMBUS,
　　　　　　　　　　　SPONDEE
poetry, a line of................ STICH
poetry, muse of;..CALLIOPE, ERATO,
　　　　　　　　　　　THALIA
poets, inspiring to .......... HELICON
poi, source of .................. TARO
poignant .............. KEEN, ACUTE
poinard .................... DAGGER
point . DOT, JIST, JOT, PERIOD, AIM,
　　　　　　　APEX, PRICKLE
　"　, conical ................ UNODE
　"　, geometric, rel. to curve ........
　　　　　　　　　　　ACNODE
　"　, highest .............. ZENITH
　"　in curve of two tangents ........
　　　　　　　　　　　CRUNODE
　"　in law ..................... RES
　"　, lowest .................. NADIR
　"　of compass; Scot. ......... IART
　"　of contact .............. FOCUS
　"　, per. to a central..CIRRI, CRUX
pointed .....CUSP, CONICAL, PIKED,
　　　　　　　AIMED, TERSE
pointed arch, like a ..........OGIVAL
pointed, as a leaf ........ APICULATE
pointed mining tool ............ GAD
pointed, sharp .... APICULA, ACUTE
pointed stick .................... GOAD
pointer in synagogue ............ YAD
pointer, teacher's ............ FESCUE
pointless .............. INANE, SILLY
points .......................... FOCI
points of leaves ............ APICULI
poise .......... BALANCE, LIBRATE
poison ...... TOXIN, ATTER, ETTER,
　　　　　　　　　　FIG, GALL

poison, deadly ......ARSENIC, BANE,
　　　　　　　　　　INEE, UPAS
poison, ivy ...........RHUS, SUMAC
poison, rat ................... SQUILL
poison, snake ............... VENOM
poison with a weed, to .......... LOCO
poisoned arrow ............. SUMPIT
poisoning ................. BOTULISM
poisonous .. LOCO, VENENE, VIROSE,
　　　　　　　　　　VIRULENT
　"　alkaloid ................. CONINE
　"　fish of Japan ............ FUGU
　"　fungus .............. AMANITA
　"　gas ..........STRIBINE, ARSINE
　"　herb; Eur. ........ MANDRAKE,
　　　　　　　　　　　HENBANE
　"　juice ................. HEBENON
　"　lizard ...................... GILA
　"　proteid ..................... ABRIN
　"　protein in castor oil beans RICIN
poisons ......VENIN, VENOM, VIRUS
poke ......BAG, GORE, HOOK, PROD
poker counter ................... CHIP
poker stake ...............ANTE, POT
poker, to call in .................. SEE
pokeweed ..................... POCAN
Poland, anc. king ...............CONTI
Poland, anc. name of.......SARMATIA
Poland, bronze coin of ........ GROSZ
Poland, city of .................. LODZ
Poland, first president of .. PILSUDSKI
Poland monetary unit ......... ZLOTY
Poland, port of .............. GDYNIA
Poland, weight ................. LUT
pole .................... MAST, ROD
　"　, as a symbol .......... TOTEM
　"　, lure for birds .......... STOOL
　"　, memorial; Ind. ............ XAT
　"　of a vehicle ............. THILL
　"　or beam; Gaelic .......... CABER
　"　, positive ................. ANODE
　"　rope dancers .............. POY
　"　Sp.-Amer. .................. PALO
　"　used in handling fish.GAFF, PEW
polecat .. ZORIL, ZORILLA, FERRET,
　　　　　　MARRIPUT, SKUNK
polecat; Eur. .. FITCHEW, FITCHET
polecat; genus ............ PUTORIUS
polecat; S. Afr. ............. MUSANG
poles ................ CABERS, DEMAS
polestar ....... POLARIS, LODESTAR
pole-to-pole ................... AXIAL
police station ........ TANA, THANA
policeman .......... BOBBY, PEELER
policeman's club ...... TRUNCHEON
polish ......... LUSTRE, LEVIGATE,
　　　　　　　PLANISH, ELIMATE
polishing material ............ RABAT
Polish commander .............. BOR
Polish dance .......... KRAKOWIAK
Polish nobleman ............ STAROST
Polish scientist ............... CURIE
polite ....... GENTEEL, DEBONAIR,
　　　　　　　　　　URBANE
polite; Spain ................ CORTES
political division .......... HUNDRED
political division ruled by prince ......
　　　　　　　　　　PALATINATE
political faction ...... BLOC, JUNTA

208

polled ..................... HORNLESS
pollen bearing.STAMINATE, ANTHER
pollen brush of bee .......... SCOPA
pollex ..................... THUMB
Pollyanna spirit .. GLADNESS, GLAD
polloi ........................... HOI
polo stick ................... MALLET
Polonius' daughter ........ OPHELIA
poltroon ...CRAVEN, SCARAMOUCH,
DASTARD
polygon of equal angles ...... ISAGON
polygon of nine sides ..... NONAGON
polygons, certain ........... NGONS
polygraph ................. MYOGRAPH
polymny ......................... SONG
Polynesian article of dress .... MALO
" butterfly ................ .... IO
" chestnut ................. RATA
" divine hero ............. MAUI
" dragon .................... ATI
' god ...... ATUA, PELE, TANE
" Hawaiian ........... KANAKA
" herb ............... TARO, PIA
" island ....... FIJI, PHOENIX,
SAMOA, TOKELAU
" loria .................... TIRIA
" mulberry bark .......... TAPA
" myth ............... AVAIKI
" native ........ MALAY, MAORI
" pine ..................... HALA
" sling ....................... MA
" stock in N. Z. .......... MAORI
Polynesian wages ................. UTU
" yam ............... UBE, UVI
polyp ...... CORAL, HYDRA, TUMOR
polyp, featherlike ........... SEAPEN
polyphonic school, exponent of .. BYRD
pome fruit .. PEAR, APPLE, QUINCE
Pomerania, island of ....... RUGEN,
USEDOM
Pomerania, river of ........... ODER
pommel .......... FLAP, FLAT, KNOB
pommel bag ............... CANTINA
pomp ..... BOBANCE, GALA, STATE
pompano ........ ALEWIFE, SAUREL
pompous .... GRANDIOSE, AUGUST,
PODSNAP, STILTY, BUDGE
Ponce de Leon .................. JUAN
Ponchielli, opera ........... GIOCONDA
pond ........................ LAGOON
pond, small ........POOL, AQUARIUM
pond snail ................... CORET
ponder . TURN, BROOD, MUSE, PORE,
RUMINATE, WEIGH
ponderous .... DULL, ELEPHANTINE
poniard .... STYLET, DIRK, DAGGER
Pons, Miss ....................... LILI
Ponsell, Miss .................... ROSA
pontiff ... BISHOP, POPE, PONTIFEX
pony SHELTY, BRONCO, CAB, NAG,
TATTOO, PIEBALD, PINTO, TAT
poodle ...... BARBET, BEAGLE, PUG
pooh-pooh ............. DERIDE, BAH
pool . CARR, LINN, MERE, PLASHET,
PUDDL, TANK, TARN
pool ball ................... RINGER
pool-ball, black ................ EIGHT
pool, game in ................... PIN
poon tree .......... KEENA, TELUGU

poon tree, Singhalese ........ DOMBA
poor creature ............ PILGARLIC
"Poor John" ............ FISH, HAKE
pop .... CRACK, SNAP, SODA, BURST
pope .................. RUFF, WEEVIL
Pope, family name LEO, PIUS, RATTI,
URBAN, ADRIAN
Pope, the ...................... PAPA
Pope's cathedral .......... LATERAN
Pope's collar .................. ORALE
Pope's court officer .......... DATARY
Pope's crown ................. TIARA
Pope's palace .... VATICAN, PAPACY
Popeye's seetheart ............... OYL
popinjay ............. FOP, PARROT
poplar .... ABELE, ALAMO, ASPEN,
TULIP
poplar; Arab. ................ GARAB
poplar, balsam ................ LIARD
poplar, species of ............ BAHAN
poplar, white ................ ABELE
poppy ........ FOXGLOVE, PAPAVER
poppycock ................. BOSH, ROT
poppy, corn ...... PONOEAU, RHOEAS
poppy, field ................. CANKER
poppy; genus ............... PAPAVER
poppy seed .................... MAW
populace .... DEMOS, MOB, WORLD
popular ........ DEMOTIC, EPIDEMIC
popularity ......... VOGUE, FAME
populus; Lat. .............. POPULAR
porcelain clay ...... CHINA, KAOLIN
porcelain; Eng. ....SPODE, CELADON
porcelain mould ........... RAMEKIN
porch ...... PORTICO, DINGLE, LANI,
STOA, VERANDA(H)
porch toward west; eccl.......GALILEE
porcupine ...... HEDGEHOG, URSON
porcupine grass ................ STIPA
porcupine spine ................ QUILL
pore ...........CON, STUDY, PONDER
pore, minute ......... OSTIOLE, STOMA
pore of plant ............. LENTICEL
pores, without ............. EPOROSE
porgy ............ PAGRUS, SCUP, TAI,
BREAM
pork chop ..................... GRISKIN
pork fish ....................... SISI
porpoise . DOLPHIN, INIA, PELLOCK
porpoise; genus .......... PHOCAENA
porridge ...... BROSE, ATOL, GROUT,
POLENTA
port .. LARBOARD, HAVEN, HARBOR
portable consecrated stone .............
SUPERALTAR
portal, at the ................. ADOOR
portcullis ....... BAR, HERSE, SHUT
portend .... BODE, AUGUR, PRESAGE
portent .. OMEN, OSTENT, MARVEL
porter .... ALE, JANITOR, BERMAN,
BEER, HAMAL
Porter; songwriter .............. COLE
portia tree .................... BENDY
Portia's maid .............. NERISSA
portico .... ARCADE, PORCH, STOA
portico, inclosed space .... PTEROMA
portico, long open VERANDA, XYST,
XYSTUS
portico, Rom. ................ ATRIUM

portico wing; Gr. ............ **PTERON**
portion ...... **DOLE, DUNT, SHARE,**
**PART, SOME**
portoise .................... **GUNWALE**
portrait statue ........... **ICON, IKON**
portraiture, rel. to ............ **ICONIC**
portray .... **DESCRIBE, ACT, FORM,**
**DEPICT, LIMN, PICTURE**
Portsmouth dock .......... **PORTSEA**
Portugal, former gold coin of
**MOIDORE**
Portugal, monetary unit of ... **ESCUDO**
Portugal's Atlan. Is. ......... **AZORES**
Portuguese city ...... **GOA, OPORTO,**
**OVAR**
" coin .. **PECA, DOBRA, PATACA,**
**REI**
" colony; .... **DIU, GOA, MACAO,**
**TIMOR**
" dollar, minor unit .... **PATACA**
" king; anc. ................. **NINIZ**
" lady ........................ **DONA**
" legislature .............. **CORTES**
" measure . **SELAMIN, PE, VARA**
" navigator . **MAGELLAN, GAMA**
" province ....... **TETE, EVORA,**
**ALGARVE**
" river . **DUERO, MINHO, TAGUS**
" title ........................ **DOM**
" weight ........... **LIBRA, ONCA**
posed .............. **MODELED, SAT**
poser .............. **FACER, STICKER**
Poseldon, wife of ....... **AMPHITRITE**
positing .................... **PONENT**
position .... **UBIETY, COIGN, SITUS,**
**LOCAL, STANCE**
positive ... **CONSTAT, PLUS, THETIC**
positive pole .................. **ANODE**
positive saying .............. **DICTA**
positivism . **COMTISM, DOGMATICAL,**
**PLUS**
possessed; poet. ............. **HADST**
possessing feeling .......... **SOULED**
possessing landed property ..... **ACRED**
possession, assume again ... **REVEST**
possum ................. **FEIGN, POGO**
post ..... **DAK, MAIL, NEWEL, XAT,**
**MARKER, PILLAR, STAKE**
post, turning; Rom. ............ **META**
post chaise ............ **JACK, COACH**
poster ...... **BILL, BULLETIN, CARD,**
**PLACARD, STICKER**
posthumous reputation ...... **MEMORY**
postmaster, ex .............. **FARLEY**
postpone ......... **ADJOURN, TABLE**
**PROROGUE**
postponed law case ....... **REMANET**
postscript to a poem .......... **ENVOY**
postulate ...... **POSIT, ASK, DEMAND**
posture ...... **ORANT, POSE, STANCE**
posy boquet ................ **NOSEGAY**
pot, bulging .............. **OLLA, STY**
pot, pear shaped ............. **ALUDEL**
potash, crude ................... **SALIN**
potash feldspar ........ **ORTHOCLASE**
potassium carbonate ......... **POTASH**
potassium compound .......... **ALUM**
potato .... **OCA, IMO, SPUD, TUBER,**
**YAM, YAMP**

potato beetle ............ **HARDBACK**
potato disease ............ **CURL, POX**
potato flour .................... **FLOW**
potato oil ........................ **OTTO**
potato, sweet .............. **PATATA**
pot-boiler, a; slang ....... **LITERARY**
potherbs, rel. to .... **OLITORY, WORT**
pot-walloper ............. **SCULLION**
potency .... **EFFICACY, STRENGTH,**
**POWER, ELAN, VIS**
potent ............ **COGENT, MIGHTY**
potential energy .... **ERGAL, LATENT**
pother .......... **ADD, STIR, WORRY**
pothook .............. **SCRAWL, ROD**
potion ...... **DOSE, DRAM, DRAUGHT**
potpourri .............. **MEDLEY, OLIO**
potsherd ............ **SHARD, TESTE**
potter .......... **MESS, PRY, TRIFLE**
potter's clay .................... **ARGIL**
potter's wheel; **DISK, KICK, JIGGER,**
**LATHE, PALET, THROW**
pottery .. **BLANC, CERAMIC, DELFT,**
**CELADON, UDA**
" , Arezzo ............. **ARETINE**
" clay ................... **KAOLIN**
" decorated .......... **SIGILLATE**
" , enameled, kind of .. **MAJOLICA**
" , fragment of; var. .... **SHARD,**
**SHERD**
" , glass-like ........ **VITREOUS**
" , glazing term ........... **SLIP**
" , Greek for ......... **KERAMOS**
' , mineral ......... **FELDSPAR**
" , vessel for burning ... **SAGGER**
pouce, 1/12th of; Fr. ......... **LIGNE**
pouch ...... **BURSA, POD, SAC, BAG**
pouch girdle .................. **GIPSER**
pouch, highlander's ........ **SPORRAN**
pouched ................. **SACCULATE**
poultry, breed of **ANCONA, DORKING**
poultry disease .......... **PIP, ROUP**
poultry, dish of .......... **GALANTINE**
poultry farm ............... **HENNERY**
Pound; poet ................... **EZRA**
pounding inst. .............. **PESTLE**
pour forth ............. **VENT, WELL**
pour melted glass in water .. **DRAGADE**
pour molten steel ............. **TEEM**
pour off ...................... **DECANT**
pour to the Gods ............ **LIBATE**
pouring hole in a mold ........ **SPRUE**
pourpoint .... **GIPON, JUPON, TUNK**
pout .... **PIQUE, MOUE, MOP, SULK**
poverty .. **DEARTH, ILLTH, LACK,**
**INDIGENCE, PAUCITY, NEED**
powder ........ **TALC, BIR, CORDITE,**
**DUST**
powder, antiseptic .......... **ARISTOL**
powder for skin ... **RACHEL, BORAL**
powder beater ............. **SINTERER**
powder; Ind. .................... **ABIR**
powder, stamping ........... **POUNCE**
powdered; her. ............... **SEME**
power .... **CAN, DINT, GIFT, SWAY,**
**STEAM, JET**
" , degree of .......... **POTENCE**
" device ............ **TELEMOTOR**
" , Latin for ................... **VIS**
" , mighty ........ **ARMIPOTENCE**

"  of attorney .............. AGENT,
PROCURATORY
"  ; theoretical ........ ODYL(E),
ATOM
powerful ....... LEONINE, DRASTIC,
POTENT
practical .... PRAGMATICAL, UTILE
practical joke ...... HOAX, HUMBUG
practice ......... DRILL, COME, USE
practice for specific purpose .. PRAXIS
prae-dial ............ LANDED, REAL
prague ........................ PRAHA
prairie ...... BAY, CAMAS, MEADOW
prairie chicken .............. GROUSE
prairie mud ................... GUMBO
prairie plant ................. CAMASS
prairie wolf ................. COYOTE
praise ...... KUDOS, EXTOL, ACME,
EULOGIZE, EXALT, LAUD
praise of another's facility. MACARISM
praline ................. CONFECTION
prance ..... SPRING, CAVORT, STIR
prandial ... REPAST, DINNER, MEAL
prank .. ANTIC, CAPER, JIG, SHINE
prase ................. CHALCEDONY
prate ............. CHATTER, RANT
prattle .... CLACK, GAB, BLATHER
prayer .. AVE, BENE, ORISON, PLEA,
BEAD, SUIT
prayer bead .......... ROSARY, AVE
prayer book ... BREVIARY, MISSAL,
RITUAL
prayer, hour of, Moham. ...... AZAN
prayer, last of the day .. COMPLIN(E)
prayer rug or carpet; Hindu .... ASAN
prayer, short ................. GRACE
praying figure ................ ORANT
preacher .. HOMOLIST, PULPITEER
preachment ................ SERMON
preceded ........... FORERAN, LED,
PREVENTED
precedence .. LEAD, PAS, PRIORITY
preceding ........ ABOVE, PREVIOUS
precept ........ MAXIM, RULE, WRIT
precept; Heb. SUTRA, TORA, TORAH
precious ..... DEAR, RARE, COSTLY
precious stone; AGATE, NAIF, OPAL,
JEWEL, RUBY, SARD, TOPAZ
precipice ...... BLUFF, CRAG, LINN,
CLIFF, PALI
precipitate . HURRY, FLOC, HEADY,
RASH, HEADLONG
precipitous ......... SHEER, HASTY
precipitous rock ....... SCAR, STEEP
precisely .... FORMAL, EVEN, PRIM
preclude . DEBAR, ESTOP, PREVENT
pre-conceive ................. IDEATE
predatory bird ................. OWL
predicament .... PASS, FIX, PLIGHT
predict ....... BODE, OMEN, WEIRD
predictor ............... SEER, SAGE
predisposed .......... BIAS, PARTIAL
pre-eminent ............. PALMARY
preen ........ PERK, PLUME, DRESS
preface ......... PREAMBLE, FRONT,
PRAYER, HERALD, PROEM
prefecture in China .............. .FU
prefer ............. CHOOSE, ELECT
prefigure .......... AUGUR, IDEATE

prefix ...... BEFORE, AFFIX, TITLE
"  for against ................. ANTI
"  for appearing as if ...... QUASI
"  for before .......... PRAE, PRE
"  for between .............. META
"  for distant ............... TELE
"  for earnest ............... SERIO
"  for false ............... PSEUDO
"  for many ............... MULT
"  for toward .................. OC
"  for twice .................... BI
"  for with ................... COL
"  for wrong .................. MIS
"  used in physics ........... STAT
prejudice ... MISCHIEF, HARM, BIAS
preliminary ........ INTRODUCTORY,
PROEMIAL
prelude .......... PREFACE, PROEM
prelude, short vocal ... RITORNELLE
premises ... GROUNDS, LAND, DATA
premium ..... BONUS, AGIO, STAKE
preoccupied ...... ENGROSSED, LOST
preparation ................... FITTING
prepare ..... FIT, FIX, PAVE, TRAIN
prepare for boiling .......... DECOCT
prepare for the press ............ EDIT
prepare skins for gloves ........ TAW
preposition ...... BY, TIL, TO, IN, AT,
FOR, ON, OUT, OF, WITH
presage ........ BODE, OMEN, OSSE,
DIVINE, PORTEND
prescribe .... ALLOT, ORDAIN, SET
present ........... BESTOW, BOOM,
NOW, LAGNIAPPE
present from pupil to teacher ........
MINERVAL
present time ..... NONCE, CURRENT
presented ...................... AROSE
presently ................. NOW, ANON
preservative ... VINEGAR, MEDICINE
preserve .... CURE, CAN, CORN, TIN
preserve in oil ........... MARINATE
preserved human in the twilight of the
gods ............................. LIF
press ...... WEDGE, CRAM, CROWD,
FORCE, THRONG, IRON, URGE
press, famous ............... ALDINE
press in ranks .............. SERRY
presser ..................... SADIRON
pressing ........ URGENT, EXIGENT
pressure ... INSTANCY, INFLUENCE
pressure unit ...... MESOBAR, ATMO,
BARAD
prestige ......... SWAY, FACE, BIAS
presumptive ... BRASH, ARROGANT,
ICARIAN, DUE
pretend ...... CLAIM, FEIGN, SHAM
pretended omission .... PARALEPSIS
pretender ...... COWAN, IDOL, SNOB
pretense .... ACT, POSTIC, RUSE,
CANT, FEINT, PRETEXT,
SHAM, STUDY, CLAIM
pretermit .......... NEGLECT, OMIT
pretty ................. COMELY, FAIR
pretty; Fr. ...................... JOLI
"Pretty Worm of Nilus" ........ ASP
prevail ... EXIST, DOMINATE, FOLD,
OBTAIN, WIN
prevalent . GENERAL, WIDESPREAD

211

prevaricate .... QUIBBLE, SHUFFLE
prevent ... AVERT, DEBAR, DETER,
FORESTALL, WARN
prevent legally . ESTOP, FORECLOSE
previously ...... ERST, PRIOR, DONE
prey .......... LOOT, SPOIL, VICTIM,
QUARRY, BOOTY, PLUNDER
prey upon .... FEED, RAVIN, RAVEN
Priam's daughter ....... CASSANDRA
Priam's grandfather ............ ILUS
Priam's son ........ HECTOR, PARIS,
TROILUS
Priam's wife ................. HECUBA
price .... CHEAP, RATE, COST, SUM
prick . GAD, PIERCE, QUALM, SPUR
pricket ............... BUCK, CANDLE
prickle . BRIAR, SPICULA, ACULEUS,
SETA, BARB, THORN
prickle, a .. BUR, SPINE, ACANTHA
prickly ...... MURICATE, ECHINATE
prickly heat .................... LICHEN
prickly pear .................... NOPAL
prickly shrub ........ LOASA, BRIAR
pride ............. CONCEIT, VANITY
"Pride and Prejudice"; author ........
AUSTEN
"        "        ", char. in .. DARCY
priest .. CURE, DRUID, ORATORIAN,
OBLATE, PADRE
priest, high . PONTIFF, AARON, ELI,
SHEIK
priest, Tibetan ................. LAMA
priestly ................. SACERDOTAL
priestly cap ................. BIRETTA
priestly vestment ...... ALB, EPHOD
priest's assistant .......... ACOLYTE
"   mantle .................... COPE
"   neckpiece ...... AMICE, STOLE
"   ornament ................. URIM
"   scarf ........ MANIPLE, RABAT
"   surplice ................ EPHOD
"   vestment ........ ORALE, ALB,
SCAPULAR
"   white collar ............. AMICE
"Priests of the Oratory," founder of ....
NERI
prig ................... PRUDE, THIEF
prig; Scot. ................... HAGGLE
prim ...... PRUDISH, SMUG, SMELT
prima-donna ........... DIVA, LEAD,
TRAGEDIAN
primate .. APE, ELDER, PRELATE
prime of life ...... BLOOM, HEYDAY
primer ........... HORNBOOK, TYPE
primitive ........ QUAINT, PRISCAN,
PRISTINE, NAIVE
primordium .... ANLAGE, EMBRYOL
primrose .......... COWSLIP, OXLIP,
PRIMULA
primp ........ DRESS, PREEN, PRINK
prince of darkness ......... AHRIMAN
prince of liars ................... PINTO
prince of poets ............. RONSARD
prince of the sonnet; Fr. .. JOACHIM
prince of Spanish poetry ....... VEGA
prince, petty ................ SATRAP
princess of Argos ............ DANAE
princess of Tyre ................ DIDO
princess or lady; E. Ind....... BEGUM

Princeton's president .......... DODD
principal CAPITAL, ARCH, CAPTAIN
principal meal of the anc. Romans ....
GENA
principality, independent ... MONACO
principle THEOREM, CAUSE, PRANA,
TENET
prink up ............ PRUNE, PRIMP
printed fabric .............. PERCALE
printer's direction, "let it stand" STET
printer's helper ...........AID, DEVIL
printer's ink pad ............ DABBER
printer's mark . SERIF, CARET, STET,
TILDE
printer's measure ........ .. EN, EM
printer's photo-engraving HELIOTYPE
printer's type, mixed ............PI(E)
printing form .................... DIE
"   frame ...... FRISKET, CHASE
"   hand instrument ...... BRAYER
"   mark ....... DELE, ELLIPSE,
DIESIS
"   metal block ............ QUAD
"   mistake ............ ERRATUM
"   plate process ...... CROTYPE
"   press, part of ........ PLATEN
ROUNCE
"   system for the blind . BRAILLE
prior .......... ERE, LEAD, FORMER
Priscilla's husband ............ ALDEN
prisms, pair of ................ PORRO
prison . BRIDEWELL, CLINK, GAOL,
JUG, JAIL, QUOD, CAGE,
PENITENTIARY
"   , federal ........... ALCATRAZ
"   , French ............ BASTILLE
"   in London .......... NEWGATE
"   , Latin for .......... CARCER
"   model by Bantham ...............
PANOPTICON
"   , naval ............ HULK, BRIG
"   , oriental .............. SAGNIO
prissy ........ NICE, PRECISE, PRIM
pristine ......... EARLY, PRIMITIVE
private ........ COVERT, ESOTERIC,
SOLDIER
private, comb. form ............ IDIO
privateer ........ CAP, CAPER, KIDD
privet ............................. IBOTA
privilege under old Eng. law ..... SOC
privileges .......... CHARTER, USES
privy seal .................... SIGNET
prixie ..... BROWNIE, KOBOLD, NIS
prize .... STAKE, ESTEEM, VALUE,
MEED, PALM, TROPHY
probability ........ ODDS, VANTAGE
probation ........... TRIAL, PAROLE
probe ................. SEARCH, TENT
probe or tracer SEEKER, EXPLORER
probe, surgical ...... STYLET, TENT
problem .......... NUT, CRUX, KNOT
proboscide, section .... LORE, LORUM
proboscis .... SNOUT, TRUNK, NOSE
proboscis monkey .......... NOSEAPE
procavia ....................... HYRAX
proceed .. WEND, PLOW, ARISE, GO
proceedings ........... ACTA, DOINGS
proceeds . MARCHES, GOES, INCOME
process in organisms ......... MIOSIS

process in steel making .. BESSEMER
procession .......... CORTEGE, FILE,
LITANY
prochein; law .............. NEAREST
proclaim formally ........ ENOUNCE
proclamation BANDO, BLAZE, EDICT,
NOTICE
Procne, husband of .......... TEREUS
procure ........ FANG, GET, EFFECT
prod ...... GOAD, URGE, POKE, EGG
prodigal .. LAVISH, SPENDER, CLOY
produce ............ CAUSE, CARRY,
ENGENDER, WAGE, GENERATE
produced in a kitchen garden .........
OLITORY
producing cold ................ALGIFIC
product .. CROP, FRUIT, SUM, HEIR
product of cotton fibre used for sizing..
VISCOSE
proem ....... PREAMBLE, PREFACE
profession .................... CAREER
profession; Fr. .............. METIER
proficient .............. ADEPT, APT
profit .... AVALI, BOOT, MEND, NET
profitable . FAT, GAINFUL, PAYING,
UTILE, LUCRATIVE
profits .................... RETURNS
profound ................ RECONDITE,
INTENSE
progenitor of giants; Norse myth. ....
YMIR
progeny .. SEED, ISSUE, OFFSPRING
prognosticate .......... BODE, OMEN,
PREDICT
prognosticator ...... DIVINER, SEER
program . CARD, EDICT, SYLLABUS
progress, planned .. EGRESS, TELESIS
prohibit ... ESTOP, DEBAR, TABOO,
TABU, VETO
prohibited .................... ILLICIT
prohibiting ................ VETITIVE
prohibition .. BAN, DRY, ESTOPPEL
project . PROTRUDE, BEETLE, JET,
JUT, PLAN, SCHEME
projectile . BOMB, MISSILE, ROCKET
projecting pedestal ............ SOCLE
projection .. BULGE, FIN, LEE, LOBE,
NAG, LEDGE
prolific, to be ...... TEEM, FRUITFUL
prolix ........ PLEONASTIC, WORDY
prolocutor ...... ORATOR, CHAIRMAN
prolong ............. SPIN, EXTEND,
STERNIZE
Prome, native of ........ BURMESE
promenade ........ ALAMEDA, MALL,
MARINA, GALLERY, PASEO
prominence ....... SALIENCE, CUSP,
PRESTIGE, CLOUD
prominent .............. PROSILIENT
promised by vow ..... VOTIVE, HOPE
promissory note ...... PLEDGE, IOU
promontory .. CAPE, MOUNT, NESS,
SKAW, LAND
promote . AVAIL, NURSE, INCREASE
promotion . PREFERMENT, BREVET
promotion of Christianity ... IRENICS
prompt .... ANIMATE, EASY, SOON,
YARE, ADVISE, EARLY, TELL

prompter ...... AID, READIER, CUER,
READER
prone, face down FELL, PROSTRATE
prone, face upward .......... SUPINE
prone to take up fads .......... ISMY
prong ..... FORK, NIB, PEG, TANG,
FOLD, TINE
pronoun ....... ...... ME, ITS, YOU
pronounce with hissing sound .........
ASSIBILATE, BURR
pronunciation, correct ... ORTHOEPY
pronunciation mark ........ CEDILLA
proof ...... TRIAL, TEST, EVIDENCE
proofreader's mark . DELE, CARET,
STET
prop .... BRACE, GIB, NOG, STAFF,
SPRAG, STANCHION
prop or support ...... STILT, SHORE
propeller ...... FAN, DRIVER, VANE
propelling device ........... GUN, REV
proper ...... MEET, PRIM, FIT, DUE
property ATTRIBUTE, ASSET, TRAIT
"    , act to regain .... REPLEVIN
"    , bride to husband    CURTESY,
DOS
"    , in law .................. BONA
"    in physics ............ INERTIA
"    , of landed ............ ESTATE,
CADASTRAL
"    , personal ........... CHATTEL
property, receiver of ...... ALIENEE
"    , wanton destruction of ........
SABOTAGE
prophesy, to AUGUR, OSSE, PRESAGE
prophet    ORACLE, MANTIS, SEER
prophet; Bib.    AMOS, HOSEA, SYRUS
prophetess . SEERESS, PYTHANESS,
CASSANDRA, SIBYL
prophetic ................ VATICINAL
prophetical .. PRESCIENT, FATIDIC,
VATIC
propinquity ... NEARNESS, KINSHIP
propitious ........... BENIGN, ROSY,
FAVOR
proportion . END, PRORATE, RATIO
proportional amount RATE, RELATIVE
proposal ....... MOVE, BID, FEELER
proposed international language; . IDO,
OD, RO, ESPERANTO
proposition .. COROLLARY, PORISM,
THESIS
proposition assumed to be true .......
LEMMA
proscribe .. FORBID, BAN, CONDEMN
proscription .... EXILE, OUTLAWRY
prose form ................ ROMANCE
prosecute, in law ...... INTEND, SUE
proselyte to Judaism ............ GER
Proserpina's mother .......... CERES
prosody METER, VERSE, SCANSION
prospect ...... SCENE, VIEW, VISTA
prospectus ................. PROGRAM
prosper ... CHEVE, SPEED, THRIVE
prosperity ......... HAP, UPS, WEAL
prosperity; symb. ....... TURQUOISE
Prospero's sprite .............. ARIEL
prosperous .......... PALMY, SONSY
prostrate ...... ABASE, FELL, FLAT,
NUEL, PRONE, FALLEN

213

prosy .......... DULL, DRY, JEJUNE
protecting influence (A)EGIS, SHIELD
protection ........ APRON, BIB, LEE,
DEFENSE
protector of vineyards ...... PRIAPUS
proteidae, family ......... NECTURUS
proteids ..................... AMINES
protein, granular ........ ALEURONE
" of milk ................. CASEIN
" in seeds ............. PROLAMINS
" of milk ................... CASEIN
" of the blood ........... FIBRIN,
GLOBULIN
" of the egg .......... ALBUMIN
" poisonous ................ RICIN
" source of ................... EGG
proteles; genus ..........AARDWOLF
proteose ................. ELASTOSE
protest ................ ASSERT, AVER
protestant sect ................ AMISH
Proteus ........................... OLM
protoplasm ..................... SPORE
protozoan LOROSA, LOBE, AMOEBA,
MONER
protract ............ SPIN, STRETCH
protuberance . HUNCH, LOBE, SNAG,
NODE
protuberance, occipital ........ INION
protuberance, rounded HUMP, UMBO
prove ......... EVINCE, NURSE, TRY,
TEST
proverb AXIOM, ADAGE, APHORISM,
SAW, SAYING
proverbial saying BYWORD, ARABLE
proverbs, student of PROEMEOLOGIST
provide ... AGREE, SUPPLY, CATER,
LOOK, AFFORD, YIELD
provided ............ BODEN, SOBEIT
providing that .......... PROVISO, IF
province .... BEAT, CIRCUIT, NOME
provincial speech ............. PATOIS
provisional name of plant ADELASTER
provisions .. LARDER, CATES, CHOW
provisions, search for ....... FORAGE
proviso ............ CLAUSE, SALVO
provisory; col. .................. IFFY
provoke ..... BAIT, BOG, SPUR, STIR
prow of a ship ... BOW, NOSE, PROA
proximal; opposed to ......... DISTAL
proxy .. AGENT, DEPUTY, PROCTOR,
VICAR
prude .......................... PRIG
prune .................. FROG, PLUM
prune . SNED, CUT, PRIME, PURGE,
TRIM
prune-like fruit ......... MYROBALAN
pruritus ..................... ITCHING
Prussian city ..... HALLE, AACHEN,
ESSEN
Prussian lancer .... UNKER, UHLAN,
ULAN
Prussian legislature ...... LANDTAG
Prussian seaport .. EMDEN, STETTIN
Prussian village .............. BEECK
Prussian watering place ........ EMS
Prussic acid, discoverer of . SCHEELE
pry ... PEER, LEVER, MOUSE, NOSE
psalm ............................ ODE
psalm, the 98th ............ CANTATE
psalms, aftermatins .......... LAUDS

psalterium ............... MANYPLIES
pseudo ....... BOGUS, SHAM, FALSE,
SPURIOUS
pseudo-morphus ............ EPIGENE
pseudonym ......... ALIAS, ANONYM
pseudonym of Mrs. Humphreys . RITA
pshaw ........................... POOH
psychiatrist ................ ALIENIST
psychic emanation ............ AURAE
psychologist; Fr. ............... BINET
psychotic .......... CAD, PSYCHOSIS
pteric ............................ ALAR
pteris rootstock ................... ROI
pteropod ......... CLIONE, MOLLUSK
ptisan .................. TEA, TISANE
public .............. OVERT, STATE
public council, per. to ..... CAMERAL
public land ..................... AGER
public notices; abbr. .............. ADS
public performer ............ ARTISTE
publication, a preliminary PRODROMUS
publicist ............ WRITER, SOLON
publish ... DELATE, BLAZON, EDIT,
VENT, RADIO, TV
publish of the bans .......... ASKING
published officially .... AIRED, DONE
publisher's announcement .... BLURB
publisher's inscription ... COLOPHON
Puccini; compo. ............ GIACOMO
Puccini; opera by . BOHEME, TOSCA,
BUTTERFLY, LESCAUT, MANON
puce used in decoration of Hindu Pottery
UDA
pucker ...... CREASE, PURSE, FOLD
puckered ................... BULLATE
pudding . SAGO, DICK, DUFF, MUSH,
HOY
"Pudding Jack" ................ ZANY
puddle DUB, PLASHET, PLUD, POOL
Pueblo assembly room .......... KIVA
Pueblo in Luzon ................ IMUS
Pueblo Indian .. HOPI, ACOMA, PIRO
puerile .......... BOYISH, FEEBLE,
INFANTINE
Puerto Principe .......... CAMAGUEY
Puerto Rico beverage .......... MABI
Puerto Rico, conqueror of ..... MILES
Puerto Rico porkfish .............. SISI
Puerto Rico, ter. of ........ CULEBRA,
VIEQUES
puff ... BLOW, FLAM, PANT, WAFF
puff, attached to headdress ..... POUF
puff bird ..................... BARBET
puff up ................ BLUB, ELATE
pug ....... REBUKE, SLIGHT, SNUB
pugil ............ CHAMPION, PINCH
pugalist; sl. ....................... PUG
pugilistic ..... PUGNACIOUS, FISTIC
puisne ............... JUDGE, JUNIOR
pulchritude ................. BEAUTY
pule ............ WHIMPER, WHINE
pulex ............................ FLEA
pull .. PLUCK, TOUSLE, TOW, YANK
pull; Scot. ......................... PU
pulldevil ................... SCRODGILL
pulley-block, per. to ............. ARSE
pulley groove ........ FUSEE, GORGE
pullman ..................... SLEEPER
pulp .......... CHYME, FLESH, PAP

214

pulp, in mining ............... SLIME
pulpit ROSTRUM, AMBO, BEMA, DESK
pulpy dregs ................... MAGMA
pulpy fruit FIG, POME, SIDDOW, UVA
pulpy state .. MASH, FLESHY, SOFT
pulque liquor ................. MESCAL
pulsate .... BEAT, THROB, VIBRATE
pulsatory .... RHYTHMIC, SYSTALIC
pulse, split ...................... DAL
pulverize ......... ATOMIZE, MULL,
                TRITURATE, BRAY
    "    by grinding ........... MEAL,
                COMMINUTE
    "    to a smooth powder LEVIGATE
pulverulent ..... DUSTY, POWDERED
puma ...... COUGAR, FUR, KECHUA
pump .................... FORK, QUIZ
pump, a kind of CHAIN, FORCE, LIFT
pump handle ................... SWIPE
pump plunger .................... RAM
pumpkin .................... PEPO(N)
pumpkin seed ............... SUNFISH
pun EQUIVOQUE, NICK, PARAGRAM
punch PRITCHEL, DOUSE, GAD, JAB,
                PASTE
"Punch and Judy," dog in ...... TOBY
punch, etcher's ............. MATTOIR
punch, spiced ................. NEGUS
puncheon ....... AWL, CASK, POST
punctilious .. EXACT, NICE, STRICT
puncture HOLE, PERFORATE, PRICK
pundit .......... SCHOLAR, NESTOR,
                LEARNED
pung ................. SLED, SLEIGH
pungent PEPPERY, PIQUANT, ACRID
Punic ................ CARTHAGINIAN
Punic warrior ................... SCIPIO
punish ... FRAP, CHASTEN, WREAK
punished ...... SLATED, AMERCED,
                MULCTED, WHIPT
punishment ...... BASTINADO, FINE,
                WRACK, FERULE
punitive ....... PUNISHING, PENAL
Punjab (Ind.), warrior of ........ SIKH
Punjab, State in ............. BAGUL
Punjab town ............ LEIA, SIMLA
punt ............ KENT, POLE, POY
punty, in glass making ..... POINTEL
pupa of an insect ........ CHRYSALIS
pupil .......... NEOPHYTE, TYRO
pupil; Fr. .......... ECOLIER, ELEVE
pupilage ..................... NONAGE
puppet ........ DOLL, MARIONETTE,
                MAUMET, GUY
puppy .. FOP, WHELP, DOG, SHARK
purblind ............ GLAMA, GLAME
purchasable .......... ASALE, VENAL
purchase .......... ACATE, ACHATE
purchase or sale of office . BARRATRY
pure CANDID, CLEAN, MEER, NEAT,
                SIMON, INTEMERATE, MERE,
                INVIOLATE
purfle ............... PURL, BORDER
purgative drug ................ JALAP
purgatory; myth. ... LIMBO, EREBUS
purge .......... PHYSIC, ABSTERGE
purification ............... CATHARSIS
purified woolfat ............. LANOLIN
purify ....... EPURATE, LUSTRATE,
                SPURGE

purifying . DISTILLING, DEPURANT
purl ........ EDDY, FRILL, MURMUR
purloined ........ FINGERED, STOLE
purple dye ................... CASSIUS
purple ragwort .............. JACOBY
purple, shade of ........ LILAC, PUCE,
                TYRIAN, AMARANTH
purpleheart ....... COPAIVA, MEDAL
purport ........ FECK, GIST, TENOR
purpose .... AIM, END, MAIN, SAKE
purpose, a ............... PREDESIGN
purposive ...................... TELIC
purpuraceous ................. TYRIAN
purse ....... CRUMENAL, PUCKER
purser .......... BOUCHER, BURSAR
pursue ..... CHASE, PLOD, FOLLOW
pursue stealthily .............. STALK
pursuit ............... SCENT, QUEST
purvey .......... CATER, PROVISION
push .... GANG, IMPEL, NUB, PING,
                POSSE
push along ............. PROD, TUSH
push-over; sl. ............... SETUP
pursy .... FAT, OBESE, CORPULENT
    "    away ...................... KEEP
put before .................. APPOSED
    "    away ...................... KEEP
    "    in order .......... FARM, MESNE
    "    forth .... APPLY, BUSY, EXERT,
                MOOT, SPROUT
    "    off ................... DOFF, HAFT
    "    on ADORN, STAGE, DON, ENDUE
    "    on the alert; poet. ...... ALARUM
    "    out .... RETIRE, ANGER, EVICT
putrefaction ............ ROT, DECAY
putrid ......... BAD, FOUL, SEPTIC
putterer ........ ROOSER, LOITERER
puttee ...................... GAITER
puzzle ... POSE, CAP, CRUX, GRIPH,
                REBUS, PERPLEX
puzzled ......... MYSTIFIED, POSED
puzzling .... POSING, PARADOXICAL
pygarg ...................... ADDAX
Pygmalion's beloved statue GALATEA
Pygmalion's brother ........... DIDO
pygmy ... DOKO, MANAKIN, ATOMY,
                SHORT, ANT
pygostyle .................... VOMER
pylon ........ MARKER, META, POST
pyramid; Egypt. ............. KHUFU
pyramid, erector of largest .. CHEOPS
pyramid; Mex. ............ CHOLULA
pyramids, Egypt, site near ..... GIZEH
pyramids in ruin, site of ... BENARES
Pyrenees, famous resort of ...... PAU
Pyrenees, highest point of ANETHOU
Pyrenees, 'passes' of the .... PERCHE,
                SOMPORT
pyre ............................ BIER
pyrol ........................... URD
pyromaniac ................. FIREBUG
pyroxene .................... AUCITE
pyroxene mineral ..... SALITE, JADE
Pythagoras, birthplace of ..... SAMOS
Pythagoras, daughter of ....... CAMO
python ....... BOA, DRAGON, SNAKE
python, slayer of the ........ APOLLO
pythonic .................. ORACULAR
pyx .......... BINNACLE, CIBORIUM

215

# Q

Q, letter .......................... CUE
Q.E.D., part of .................. ERAT
qua ................................ AS
quack CHARLATAN, MOUNTEBANK
quack doctor ................. CROCUS
quack grass ................... COUCH
quack, med ... EMPERIC, NOSTRUM
quad ............... QUOD, TYPE
quadragesimal ........ FORTY, LENT
quadrange ..... COURTYARD, QUOD,
TETRAGON
quadrans ..................... CANTON
quadrat ........... EM, EN, SPACER
quadrate .. AGREE, SQUARE, ADAPT,
CONFORM
quadriga ..................... CHARIOT
quadrilateral ............... TESSARA
quadrille ............. CARDS, DANCE
quadroon .................. MULATTO
quadrumane ........... APELET, APE
quadruped .................. MAMMAL
quaere ............ ASK, INQUIRE
quagga-like .................. ZEBRA
quaggy . BOGGY, FENNY, QUEACHY
quagmire ......... BOG, FEN, LAIR
quahog ........... CLAM, QUAHAUG
quail BOBWHITE, COLIN, MASSENA
quail, flock of ........ COVEY, BEVY
quail; genus ............. COTURNIX
quail, to BLENCH, COWER, FLINCH
quails, button ............. TURNIX
quaint ..... PRETTY, PROPER, ODD,
PROUD, SKILLED, WISE
quake ......... DIVER, TREMBLER,
SHUDDER
quaker . CANNON, FRIEND, HERON,
MOTH
quaking ............. ASPEN, TREPID
qualify LIMIT, VARY, TEMPER, ABLE,
FIT, MODIFY, NAME
quality NATURE, ENTITLE, STRAIN,
TRAIT, CALIBER, FEATURE
quality, high STATE, QUALE, TASTE,
FRANK
quality of tone ...... TIMBRE, TONAL
qualm .... NAUSEA, PALL, REGRET
quamash ..................... CAMASS
quandary ........ DILEMMA, STRAIT
quannet ........................ FILE
quant ........ POLE, PUNT, PROPEL
quantity ... DOSE, ANY, KITTY, LOT,
SCAD, SPATE
quantity, irrational ............. SURD
Quapaw Indian ............... OZARK
quarantine ................. ISOLATE
Quarles; poet ............... FRANCIS
quarrel ....... SPAT, BICKER, FLITE,
SCENE, TIFF, MIFF, BOLT,
ARROW, CHISEL
quarrelsome .. CHOLERIC, LITIGIOUS
quarry . CHASE, DELF, GAME, PREY
quarrying term .................. TIRR
quarte ........................ CARTE
quarter note ............... CROTCHET
quarters ......... BILLET, BIVOUAC
quartic curve ............... LIMACON
quartodeciman ............. PASCHITE

quartz .......................... ONYX
quartz, crystalline variety .. RUBASSE
quartz flint .................... SILEX
quartz, green ............... PLASMA
quartz, kind of .. CAIRNGORM, SARD,
SILICA
quartz, leek-green ............ PRASE
quartz, variety . AGATE, AMETHYST,
CITRINE, FLINT, JASPER, TOPAZ
quash . CRUSH, ANNUL, CASS, VOID
quat ........... PIMPLE, PUSTULE
quatch ................... FIAT, SQUAT
quaternion ................... TETRAD
quaternion, turning factor of a VERSOR
quaver .. TREMOLO, TRILL, SHAKE
quay .. LEVEE, WHARF, PIER, KAY
queachy ......... SWAMPY, BOGGY,
FENNY
quean ............... HUSSY, JADE
queasy .. DELICATE, NAUSEA, SICK
quebracho ................. MACAGLIA
quebrith ................. SULPHUR
Queen Anne's lace .......... CARROT
Queen Anne's pocket melon . DUDAIM
Queen Charlotte Is. Ind. ...... HAIDA
Queen Elizabeth, name given to .......
ORIANA
" of Greek gods ........... HERA
" of Hearts ......... ELIZABETH
" of Isles ............... ALBION
" of Roman gods .......... JUNO
" of Sheba .............. BALKIS
" of Spades in Solo ...... BASTA
" of the Antilles .......... CUBA
" of the East ......... ZENOBIA
" of the fairies ... MAB, TITANIA
" of Thebes ............... DIRCE
queened pawn ................... FERS
queenly ............ REGINAL, RANK
queen's camel, Eng. ........ CAMELOT
Queensland's cap. ........ BRISBANE
queer ... FUNNY, FAINT, ODD, RUM
quell ......... ALLAY, END, SUBDUE
quench ...... COOL, SLAKE, STIFLE,
END, SATE
quenelle .................... DUMPLING
quercetin ............. MELETIN, DYE
quercus; genus ................. OAKS
querl ..................... COIL, TWIRL
querulous .................. PEEVISH
quest ................. SEARCH, SEEK
question ... DOUBT, QUERY, CAVIL,
POSE, QUIZ, WAVER
question, mark indicating a EROTEME
questionable . MOOT, ASEA, DUBIOUS
questioning .. GRILLING, HECKLING
questionnaire ....... FORM, FEELER,
STRAW
quetzal ...................... TROGON
queue ......... LINE, CUE, PIGTAIL
quib ................... GIBE, QUIP
quibble .................. CARP, CAVIL
Quichuan Indian .............. INCA
quick APT, YARE, AGILE, DEFT, GAY
quicken .. ANIMATE, ROUSE, SPEED
quickly ..... APACE, LIVE, PRESTO,
PRONTO, DEFTLY, FLIT
quickness, mental . NOUS, DISPATCH
quicksand ............ SYRT, SYRTIS
quickset ......... HEDGE, THICKET

quicksilver ............... MERCURY
quid ......................... CUD, FID
quiddity ............. WHAT, CAVIL
quiddle ........... DAWDLE, TRIFLE
quidnunc ............ GOSSIP, FRUMP
quiescent ....... STATIC, SLEEPING
quiet . EASE, MUM, TUT, HALCYON,
        PEACE, PACIFIC, SILENCE
quiet place ..................... DELL
quietus ......... DEATH, MORT, OBIT
quill feather ................. REMEX
quill feathers ............... REMIGES
quill for playing a spinet ....... SPINA
quill for winding silk ............ COP
quill, porcupine ................... PEN
quillai; Chil. ............. SOAPBARK
quilt .............. CADDOW, DUVET,
        PATCHWORK
quilted silk ............. MATELASSE
quinnat salmon .................. TYEE
quinoline, deriv. ........... ANALGEN
quip ...... JEST, JIBE, TUT, TAUNT
quirt; Mex. ........... ROMAL, WHIP
quisling .......................... RAT
quit ...... CLEAR, FREE, RID, STOP
quits ................... CEASES, EVEN
quiver ....... FLUTTER, SHUDDER,
       TREMOR, SHAKE, CASE
quivering ........ ASPEN, QUAKING
quixotic ..... UTOPIAN, ROMANTIC
quiz ........ CHAFF, POSER, COACH
quod ........ COURT, JUG, JAIL
quodlibet; mus. ............ FANTASIA
quoit ................... DISC, DISCUS
quoit pin ......................... HOB
quoit, stone cover ........ CROMLECH
quoits, mark aimed at ............ TEE
quondam ONETIME, FORMER, ONCE
quota ........... CITE, SHARE, WHO
quotation MOTTO, CITAL, EXCERPT
quotation developed into a short essay
       CHRIA
quotation mark ........ GUILLEMET
quote ...... CITE, ADDUCE, REPEAT
quoth ................... SPOKE, SAID
quota; rare .................... INDEED
quotidian ........ DAILY, ORDINARY
quotient ..................... RESULT
quotity ........ GROUP, COLLECTION


# R

R, letter ......................... ARE
Ra, bull forms of ............... BACIS
Ra, sun god ATEN, CHEPERA, HORUS,
      IOKARIS, SHU, TUM
raad ...................... CATFISH
rabato .......................... RUFF
rabbi, speaking ............... AMORA
rabbit LAPIN, ADAPIS, HARE, BUNNY
  "  burrow ............. CLAPPER
  "  fever ............. TULAREMIA
  "  fur ......... CONEY, CONY
  "  ; genus ................. LEPUS
  "  net ....................... HAY
  "  shelter ............... HUTCH
  "  , swamp ............. TAPETI

"  , young, skin of ........ RACK
rabbit-eared ...... LAGOTIS, OARLOP
rabbit-like animal ...... PERAMELES
rabbit-like rodent ... MARMOT, PIKA
rabbitry .................... WARREN
rabbit's foot ................. CLOVER
rabbit's tail ............... FUD, SCUT
rabble .......... CROWD, MOB, RAFF
rabid .... MAD, RAMPANT, VIOLENT
rabies ......... LYSSA, LYTTA, RAGE
racoon animal ........ PANDA, COON
racoon-like mammal .......... COATI,
      MAPACH
race PEOPLE, CASTE, SORT, STRAIN
"  , an undivided ... HOLETHNOS
"  , channel ............... FLUME
"  , family ......... ILK, STIRPS
"  found in N. France . WALLOONS
"  , gait in a long ......... LOPE
"  mil ....... LADE, CHANNEL,
      CURRENT
"  of dwarfs ......... NIBELUNG
"  , science of the ... ETHNOLOGY
race, short ................... BICKER
"  , to ......................... HIE
"  , water ............... ARROYO
racecourse .... LAP, CIRCUS, HEATS
racecourse marker ............ META
racehorse, inferior ......... PLATER
raceme ............ CLUSTER, SPIKE
racetrack ..... CIRCUS, OVAL, RING,
      ASCOT
racetrack tipster ............... TOUT
Rachel's father ................ LABAN
rachis .. SPINE, BACKBONE, CHINE
Rachmaninoff; compo. ........ SERGEI
racing colors ................ SILKS
racing forecaster TIPSTER, DOPESTER
rack ...... GIN, SKIN, AGONY, PAIN
rack, corn ........................ CRIB
rack, distaff ................... STAFF
rack, floating .................. VAPOR
rack for barrels .................. JIB
rack for plates ................ CREEL
racket .. BAT, CROSSE, DIN, REVEL
racy ...... FRESH, RICH, PIQUANT,
     PEP, PUNGENT, BRISK, STRONG
Radames' love ................. AIDA
raddle ........ FENCE, REED, TWIG
radial ............. QUADRANT, RAY
radial velocity, unit of ........ STROB
radian ............................ ARC
radiance . REFULGENCE, LAMBENT,
      VIVID, BEAUTY, LIGHT
radiant ... AGLOW, BEAMY, NITOR,
      SHEEN, GLORIOUS
radiate BEAM, GLEAM, EMIT, SHED
radiating ...... EMANANT, CASTING
radical ..... EXTREME, LEFT, RED,
      ULTRA, FULL, WHOLE
radicle ..... ETYMON, RADIX, ROOT
radio detector ................. RADAR
radio frequency, of ............ AUDIO
radio gear ................. ANTENNA
radio interference ............ STATIC
radio operator, amateur ......... HAM
radio program rating ........ HOOPER
radio tube ...................... GRID
radioactive dis. ............... RADON

radium, discoverer of .......... CURIE
radium, emanation of .......... NITON
radium, source of ...... CARNOTITE, URANITE
radius .... RADIX, SPOKE, EXTENT
radix .... ETYMON, ROOT, RADICAL
radon; symb. ...................... RN
raffish .. LOW, INFAMOUS, VULGAR
raffle CHANCE, LOTTERY, TANGLE
raft .... CATAMARAN, FLOAT, LOT
raft duck . ...................... SCAUP
raft, or float; Phil. ............ BALSA
rag-baby .. MOPPET, MOPSY, DOLL
rage .. RAVE, FUROR, MODE, RESE, VOGUE, DESIRE, FURY
ragged .......... SCOURY, SHREDDY
ragged piece ................... SHRAG
raging ............. GRIM, RAMPANT
ragout ........... PATOUN, TUCKET
ragout of beef . GOULASH, HARICOT, HASH
ragout of hare ................. CIVET
ragout of salt meat; Fr. ....... SALMI
rag-picker .... CHIFFONIER, TRAMP
ragweed; genus ................... IVA
raid FORAGE, SIEGE, FORAY, TALA
rail . BAR, COOT, COURLAN, CRAKE, SORA
rail, altar ................... SEPTUM
rail at RANT, RATE, SCOFF, ARUNT, JAW
rail, Eur. ................... ORTOLAN
raillery ......... ASTEISM, BANTER, PERSIFLAGE
railroad; col. .......... HURRY, RUSH
railroad flare ................... FUSEE
railroad switch ................. FROG
railroad tie ................. SLEEPER
rails, per. to the ............. RALLINE
rain . BANGE, DAG, MISLE, SEREIN
rainbow ............. ARC, IRIS, ARCH
rainbow, per. to the .......... IRIDAL
rainbow, the; myth. .......... ASGARD
raincoat .......... SLICKER, PONCHO
raincoat; Jap. ................... MINO
rain-gauge .......... HYETOMETER, PLUVIOGRAPH, UDOMETER
rain-spout; Scot. ............... RONE
rain tree ........ SAMAN, GENISARO, ZAMIA
raise EXALT, REAR, TRICE, UPLIFT, BOOST, EXCITE
raised aloft ENLEVE, HEFTED, HOVE
raised to third power .......... CUBED
raised with a bar .......... LEVERED
Rajah's wife ........... RANEE, RANI
Rajmahal creeper ................. JITI
rake LECHER, SATYR, RAFF, ROUE
rake with gunfire ........ ENFILADE
rally ..... COLLECT, JOKE, BANTER
ram CRAM, STUFF, BUCK, PUN, TUP
ram, a kind of ............. WETHER
ram, the ..................... ARIES
ramble .... PROWL, SPROGUE, GAD, ROVE, ROAM, SAUNTER
"Ramblin Wreck" home .. ATLANTA
rame .... BRANCH, CRY, SKELETON
ramentum .......... PALEA, PALET
Rameses, goddess worshipped by ANTA

ram-headed god ............. AMMON
ramification ... BRANCHING, RAMUS
ram-like ................... ARIETINE
rammel ................... CRUMBLE
"Ramona," writer of ...... JACKSON
ramp .......... CRAWL, RAGE, ROMP
rampart . PARAPET, ESCARP, LINE, MOUND
  " , detached ........ RAVELIN
  " , earthen ............... BRAY
  " or raised work ...... AGGER
  " , palisaded ......... VALLUM
  " , part of ............. SPUR
  " , V-shaped ......... REDAN
rampart-like ..... WALL, DEFILADE
rampion ............. CAMPANULA
ram's horn; Heb. .......... SHOPHAR
ramus ..................... BRANCH
ran ................... HARED, SPED
rance, dull red .......... MARBLE
ranch ..... CASA, ESTANCIA, FARM, HACIENDA
rancid ... STALE, FROWZY, MUSTY, RANK
rancor ...... GALL, HATRED, SPITE
rand ...... MARGIN, BORDER, EDGE
range ........ AREA, GAMUT, ORBIT
range finder .......... MEKOMETER
range finder, field ..... TREKOMETER
ranged ......... FORAYED, ROAMED
ranger s goalie .............. RAYNER
Ranier (Mr.) Ind. name .... TACOMA
rank CLASS, GRADE, ESTATE, FILE, ROW, TIER
rankle ......... FESTER, PAINFUL
ransack .............. RAKE RIFLE
ransom RESCUE, REDEEM, RECHACE
rant ........ RAVE, STEVEN, BOAST
rap KNOCK, THWACK, KNAP, TIRL, BOP
rapacious ... AVARICIOUS, LEONINE
rapacious sea worm .............. SAO
rapacity VORACITY, RAVIN, GREED
Rapee, Mr. ...................... ERNO
raphe .............. SEAM, SUTURE
rapid .......... FAST, QUICK, SWIFT
rapids, narrow ........ DALLES, RIFT
rapier .... BILBO, SWORD, VERDUN
rapier-blade heel; It. ....... RICASSO
rapt .. ABSORBED, ECSTATIC, HEED
rare metallic element ..... THORITE, YTTRIUM
Ra's mother ...................... NUT
Ra's wife ...................... MUT
rascal ..... LOON, VARLET, SCAPIN
rascally . MEAN, PAUTENER, FALSE
rash ..... WANTON, ICARIAN, MAD, SCAMP, WILD, GIDDY
rash man ................... HOTSPUR
rash, skin . EXANTHEMA, ERUPTION
rashness ....... TEMERITY, ACRISY
rasp ....... GRATE, FILE, OFFEND
raspberry; genus ............. RUBUS
raspings ..................... SCOBS
rat .. DESERTER, SNOB, APOSTATE
rat; E. Ind. ...................... KOK
rat, kind of ......... MOLE, ROTTAN
rat; slang .......... DRAT, GNAWER
ratafia ............ CURACAO, NOYAU

ratchet ..... CLICK, DETENT, PAWL
rate of exchange ....... AGIO, BATTA
rated .. VALUED, ASSESSED, TAXED
Rathbone, Mr. ................... BASIL
rathe ......... BLOOMING, GROWING
rather .. THAN, ERE, ERER, LIEVER
ratify .......... PASS, AMEN, SEAL,
CONSENT
rational ........ SANE, SOUND, WISE
rations .... DIET, FOOD, QUANTITY
ratite bird ........ MOA, EMEU, EMU
rat-like animal ........... HAMSTER
ratoon ...................... SPROUT
rattan WHIP, LASH, NOOSE, THONG
rattan, per. to .............. CALMUS
ratten STEAL, CRIB, FILCH, POACH
rattle . RALE, CLACK, RICK, SHAIL,
NOISE, PRATTLE, TIRL
rattle, crier's ................ CLAPPER
rattlepate ........................ ASS
rattlesnake plantain ....... NETWORT
rattlesnakes ................ CROTALI
rattletrap; sl. ................. MOUTH
ratwa ..................... MUNTJAC
raucous ...... HARSH, HOARSE, DRY
ravage .......... RAVEN, SACK, EAT
ravaged ...... OVERRUN, RAVENED,
WASTE
rave .......... RAGE, STORM, RANT
ravel ... UNRAVEL, FRAY, SLEAVE
ravelin ..... OUTWORK, DEMILUNE
ravelings, fine .................... LINT
raven; Hawaii ................. ALALA
"Raven God," the ............. ODIN
ravine CLOUGH, GULCH, LIN, DELL,
NULLAH
ravine, narrow ........ STRID, CHINE
ravine, water course in a ...... WADY
raw ............ CRUDE, RUDE, SORE
raw-boned .. GAUNT, SCRAG, LEAN
rawhide whip .... SJAMBOK, KNOUT,
QUIRT, THONG
raw meat, eating of .... OMOPHAGIA
raw sugar ................ CASSONADE
ray .. BEAM, SKATE, DAY, GLEAM
Ray; actor ...................... ALDO
ray, eagle ..................... OBISPO
ray, penetrating ............... GAMMA
ray, thornback ................... DORN
Rayburn; speaker .............. SAM
rayed badge ...................... STAR
rayon fabric ..... ACETATE, VISCOSE
rays, sun's ..................... ACTINIC
raze . DEMOLISH, LEVEL, EFFACE,
ERASE
razee .................... BATTLESHIP
razor-back HOG, FINBACK, WHALE,
RORQUAL
razor .. SCRAPE, SHAVE, RATTLER
razor clam .................... SOLEN
razor, to sharpen ..... HONE, STROP
razor-billed auk ...... FALK, MURRE
razz; sl. ......... DERIDE, RIDICULE
razzle-dazzle ................ CONFUSE
re .. ANENT, ABOUT, CONCERNING
rea ...................... TURMERIC
reach ........ ADVENE, GAIN, SPAN,
ATTAIN
reaching after applause .. CAPTATION

reaction .................... TROPISM
read ..... SKIM, COUNSEL, RELATE
read carefully .......... PERUSE, CON
read metrically ................... SCAN
read publicly ............... PRELECT
reader . LECTOR, LISTER, TEACHER
reader in Eastern Church ANAGNOST
readily ........ CLEAR, LUCID, PAT,
EASILY
readiness .......... ALACRITY, ART,
FACILITY
reading ...... LECTION, VARIATION
reading desk ESCRITOIRE, LECTERN
reading desk, early form of ... AMBO
ready PROMPT, BAIN, HERE, POINT,
YARE, APERT, PRET
real names written backwards .........
ANANYMS
realize .. GAIN, KNOW, SENSE, WIN
really .............. FANCY, INDEED
realm .. DOMAIN, EMPIRE, SPHERE
realm of Jamshid ............. PERIS
reamer WIDENER, BORER, CHERRY
reanimate ... RESUSCITATE, RALLY
rear, toward the ........ ABAFT, AFT,
STERN
reared ..... RAISED, NURSED, BRED
rear-horse ..................... MANTIS
rearing, as a horse . PESADE, STEND
reason ARGUE, CAUSE, RATIOCINATE
reason, higher ......... ADULT, NOUS
reason, want of ............. AMENTIA
reata ....... LARIAT, LASSO, RIATA
reave ........ BREAK, REND, TEAR
rebec ....... LYRE, VIOLIN, FIDDLE,
SAROD
Rebecca's brother ............. LABAN
Rebecca's son ................... ESAU
rebel ..... RED, TURNCOAT, RESIST
rebellion ........ TREASON, MUTINY,
REVOLT
rebound ... RICOCHET, STOT, CAROM
rebounding ... SPRINGY, RECOILING
rebuff CHIDE, LESSON, SLAP, SNUB
rebuke ..... ADMONISH, SLAP, TUT
recalcitrant RENITENT, RESISTANT
recall ... REPEAL, ANNUL, ENCORE
recant .......... ABJURE, RETRACT
recapitulate SUM, REPEAT, REVIEW
recede .. WITHDRAW, EBB, GRANT
receive ...... ADMIT, FANG, RESET,
HOLD
receiver of property in trust . BAILEE
receiver of stolen goods ...... FENCE
recent ....... LATE, NEW, MODERN
receptacle .. HANAPER, CONTAINER
    "    for corporal cloth .... BURSE
    "    for holy water ....... STOUP
    "    for oil in orange vine .. CYST
    "    for sand and water SEBILLA
reception OVATION, INFARE, LEVEE,
SOIREE
recess ... ALA, BAY, CRYPT, NICHE,
SINUS
Rechabite lodge ................ TENT
recidive .................... RELAPSE
recipe .. FORMULA, DISH, REMEDY
recipient ....... COFERREE, DONEE
reciprocate ..... BANDY, EXCHANGE

219

recital .......... NARRATIVE, SAGA, CONCERT, MUSICALE
recitative; mus. ............... SCENA
recite ...... CANTILLATE, REPEAT, SPEAK
reckless MADCAP, HOTSPUR, PERDU
recklessly; dial. ............ RAMSTAM
reckon .. IMPUTE, OPINE, COMPUTE
reckoning . TAB, TALE, DATE, POST, SHOT, COUNT
reckoning table .............. ABACUS
reclaim .. RENEW, TAME, RESTORE
reclaimed land ................ POLDER
recluse ..... ANCHORET, EREMITE, HERMIT, MONK
recoil ....... RESILE, FUNK, WONDE
recollection .............. ANAMNESIS
recompense REPAY, GUERDON, MEED
recompense, a; Irish ............ ERIC
reconcile . ATONE, SETTLE, PACIFY, WEAN, ADJUST
reconnoiter ..................... SCOUT
record ENTRY, ESTREAT, LEGEND, POSTEA, FILE, NOTATE, TAPE
record, formal ...... NOTE, MINUTE, REGISTER
record of events; Lat. .......... FASTI
recorded proceeding .......... ACTUM
recorder .. REGISTRAR, CARTULARY
records ........ ANNALS, ARCHIVES
recount ... RELATE, NARRATE, MIN
recouple ...................... REYOKE
recover . RALLY, RETRIEVE, UPSET, RECOUP, RETOP
recrement ........ REFUSE, SCORIA
rectify .......... AMEND, CORRECT, ADJUST
recuperations ................. LYSES
recurring effect of past experience ..... MNEME
red CERISE, CORAL, ERIC, NACARAT
" cedar .......... JUNIPER, SAVIN
" cherry gum .............. CERASIN
" clay, tropical .......... LATERITE
" corpuscles ............. HEMATID
" cosmetic ................. HENNA
Red Cross Knight, wife of ........ UNA
red dye . AURINE, AL, CHAY, EOSIN, LAC
" , eureka ................... PUCE
" , glowing ............. RUTILANT
" grouse ............. PTARMIGAN
" gum ................ STROPHULUS
" Madeira wine .............. TINTO
" ochre, to mark with ....... TIVER
" paint pigment .... CHICA, LAKE, ROSET
" , pale ................. NACARAT
Red, the ......................... ERIC
Red Sea ................. ERYTHREAN
Red Sea sting ray .......... SEPHEN
red skin preparation . RUBEFACIENT
" stone ................ RUBY, SARD
" translucent mineral .... GARNET
" yellow ............. PEACHBLOW
redact .. REVISE, EDIT, DRAFT, PEN
red-bird ..................... TANAGER
reddish-brown ... AUBURN, RUSSET, SORREL

reddish-brown mineralite .... RULITE
reddish-orange color .......... HENNA
reddish red-yellow ............ AGATE
reddish-yellow ......... OLD GOLD
reddish-yellow dyestuff ... ALAZARIN
rede ....... ADVICE, HAP, LOT, RAD, COUNSEL
Redeemer; Heb. ................ GOEL
redeye ........................ RUDD
redfaced ................... BLOWZED
redmouth fish ................ GRUNT
redness .. ERUBESCENT, BLUSHING
redolent ...... AROMATIC, SCENTED, BALMY
redouble .. .......... ECHO, REPEAT, INGEMINATE
reduce .... DERATE, LOWER, PARE, PULL, THIN
reduce to half ............ DIMIDIATE
redundant PLEONASTIC, PLETHORIC
reduplications .............. JIGAJOGS
ree .................... ARIKARA, DAM
reed-buck .......... BOHOR, NAGOR
reed-loom ...................... SLEY
reed-mace ................. MATREED
reed-pipe ........ KAZOO, MIRLITON
reef ................ CAY, CAYO, KEY
reef a sail . SWIFT, SHORTEN, FURL
reef, mining .... LODE, RIDGE, VEIN
reefer ......... ETON, MIDSHIPMAN, CIGARETTE
reek ...... FUME, SEAWEE, SMOKE
reel ........ TEETER, DANCE, ROCK, STAGGER, SWAY
reel off a story .... SCRIEVE, SCRIBE
reel used in dyeing ............ WINCE
reel, yarn ...................... SWIFT
reem; Bib. ................. UNICORN
reentrant angle in records ...... ACTA
re-expand ................... DEFLATE
Reese; nickname ............ PEEWEE
refectory of a monastery ... FRATER
refer .. ASCRIBE, IMPUTE, ALLUDE, RECUR
refer to ..................... ADVERT
referee ...... MODERATOR, UMPIRE
refined spirit, the ............ ELIXIR
reformer ...... AMENDER, LUTHER
refraction, per. to ..... ANACLASTIC
refractor ....... PRISM, TELESCOPE
refractory ...... INDOCILE, REBEL, RESTIVE, STUBBORN
refrain from the use of .... BOYCOTT
refrain in music DERRY, EPODE, BOB
refuge ......... ROCK, ARK, ASYLA, HAVEN, RETREAT, DOORN
refund ...................... REBATE
refuse .... COOM(B), CULM, DROSS, MARC, ORT, NAYSAY
refuse from coffee beans .... TRIAGE
refute, serving to ELENCTIC, REBUT
regale .... DIVERT, FEAST, TREAT
regard .... DEEM, ESTEEM, HONOR
regards ...... RATES, EYES, HEEDS
Regent diamond ................. PITT
"Regent of the Sun" ......... URIEL
regimen ............. DIET, SYSTEM
regiment, frame work ........ CADRE

region ........ AREA, REALM, BELT, SPACE
region; comb. form ............ NESIA
register .............. ENROLL, LIST, MATRICULATE, ROLL, ROTA, CARTULARY
register, historic .......... ROTULET
register, legal .............. DOCKET
register of deaths ...... NECROLOGY
regret ............ ARUE, REW, RUE, RUTH, SITE, REPENT, DEPLORE, PENITENCE
regulate ........... ADJUST, DIRECT
regulus ........................ MATTE
Rehan, Miss; actress ............ ADA
rehash .................. RECHAUFFE
rehearsal garment ........ LEOTARD
rehearse .... PRACTICE, SAY, TRAIN
reimbue with courage ........ REMAN
Reims, former name ........... REMI
reincarnating principle; Skt. .. MANAS
reins .. HAUNCHES, LEASH, LOINS
reinstate ...... REVEST, ESTABLISH
reiterate .... DRUM, HARP, REPEAT
reject .. ATHETIZE, REPEL, SPURN
rejoicer ...................... ELATER
relate ..... PERTAIN, TELL, RECITE
related      AIM, GERMAN, INHERE, TOLD, AKIN
related by blood AGNATE, COGNATE, SIB
related on the mother's side .. ENATE
related to country .......... PREDIAL
related to Chinese ............ SINITIC
relation .. ACCOUNT, RECITAL, KIN
relational ........ CASAL, NOTIONAL
relative or friend GRANNY, SIB, EME
relatives, favor to ........ NEPOTISM
relax . LOOSEN, EASE, LASK, OPEN, REMIT
relay or post; Ind. ...... DAK, DAWK
release FREE, UNDO, RELET, REST, TRIP, LOOSE
release as claim ............ REMISE
reliance .............. TRUST, HOPE
relic CURIO, HUACA(O), MEMORIAL
relics, cabinet for ............ APSE
relict ............ WIDOW, WIDOWER
relief .. SPELL, BOTE, LAX, SUCCOR
relief, ornamental .. RELIEVO, FRET
religion ...... PIETY, FAITH, TRUST
religious belief ....... DEISM, CREED
"      brotherhood ...... SODALITY
"      devotee .............. FAKIR
"      devotion DEVOUT, NOVENA
"      doctrine, system of .... RITE, CULTUS
"      fair; Ind. .............. MELA
"      hermit ................ MONK
"      jurist ................ GAIUS
"      mendicant ........ SERVITE
"      observance .... FAST, PURIM
"      offering ........ OBLATION, DEODATE
"      order, one of a .. TEMPLAR, MARIST
"      service directories . ORDINES
"      sect ...... AMISH, CENOBY
relinquish ..... LEAVE, YIELD, LET

reliquary ...... APSE, ARCA, CHEST, HUTIA, SHRINE
relish .. CHAW, GUST, ZEST, SAUCE
reluctant .. AVERSE, LOATH, THRO
rely ................. BANK, DEPEND
rely upon ......... DEPEND, LIPPEN
Remagen, river near ........... ROER
remain .... LEAVE, LODGE, THOLE
remainder .......... ARREAR, REST, RESIDUUM
remainder after dividing a number .... UNITATE
remaining in place . LEDGER, LEGER
remains .... ASHES, CORPSE, RUINS
remark .... NOTE, HEED, SAY, SEE
remedy ANTACID, CURE, AID, BOTE, GAIN
remedy, imaginary ELIXIR, PANACEA
remedy, mysterious ....... ARCANUM
remedy, quack ............. NOSTRUM
remedy, soothing .... BALM, BALSAM
remembrance ..... MINNIE, TROPHY
remex ......... FEATHER, OARSMAN
reminder .... MEMENTO, SOUVENIR
remnant ..... RAG, RESIDUE, DREG, REST, SCRAG, ODDMENT, PIECE
remoisten ................... REDAMP
remora, W. Indian ............. PEGA
remorse .... REGRET, PITY, SORROW
remote .......... ELENGE, FORANE, ULTERIOR
remote goal or end ........... THULE
remove .... AVOID, DELE, REMBLE, BAIL, DEBUNK
remove afar off .............. ELOIGN
remove as clothes ...... DOFF, STRIP
remove legally ELOIGN, ELOIN, OUST
remove to another place TRANSLATE
remuneration .......... EMOLUMENT
Remus, brother of ......... ROMULUS
rend ................. CHOP, RIP, RIVE
render ..... CONSTRUE, TRY, YIELD
render harsh .......... HOARSEN
render knotty .................. GNARL
render unstable ............ UNHINGE
rendezvous ........ REFUGE, TRYST, RESORT, BENCH
renegade . APOSTATE, RAT, REBEL
renews of wine ................ STUMS
rennet ........... APPLE, FROG, LAB
rennet, rel. to ............ BEDSTRAW
renounce ......... REJECT, ABJURE, RENEGE, RENAY
renovate RENEW, REPAIR, PHENIX
rent .. RIP, HIRE, TAC, LEASE, LET, TEAR
rent; Eng. law ............ ONSTAND
rental ............ LOAN, KAIN, PORT
repair of buildings .............. BOTE
repand ................. BENT, WAVY
reparation ..... REDRESS, AMENDE, REQUITAL
repartee .......... RETORT, RIPOSTE
repast, a ....... PRANDIAL, LUNCH, TIFFIN, TREAT, MEAL
repast between meals .. COLLATION
repay ... QUIT, ANSWER, AVENGE, MEED

repeal ........ ABROGATE, RESCIND
repeat . RECUR, RETELL, ITERATE,
RAME
repeatedly ............. OFTEN, OFT
repent .............. ATONE, GRIEVE
repeater .... FIREARM, HOLDOVER
repentance .... RUE, RUTH, SHAME
repetition, mechan. ROTE, ANAPHORA
repetition of sound ............ ECHO
repetition of homologous parts ........
MERISM
repetition of idea ...... TAUTOLOGY
replace ..... REPONE, STEAD, STET
replate ........... RETIN, RESILVER
repletion ...... SATIETY, FULLNESS
replica, a ........ COPY, IMAGE, BIS
reply, sharp .... RETORT, ANSWER,
WIT
report .. DILATE, CANARD, BRUIT,
POP, BROADCAST, RUMOR
report, common . NOISE, CRY, GOSSIP
report, legislative ............ CAHIER
report, official .... HANSARD, RADIO
repose ...... SIT, EASE, RELY, REST
reposit ...... DEPOSIT, REPLACE
Repplier; writer ................ AGNES
represent .. ENACT, BISEN, EXHIBIT
representation of the planets and sun..
ORRERY
repress CRUSH, CURB, REIN, STIFLE
repression . INHIBITION, REJECTION
reprimand . SCOLD, SLATE, REBUKE
reproach ..... CHIDE, ODIUM, RACA,
TENCH
reproduction of original ..... ECTYPE
reproof ............ CENSURE, SNUB
reptile ....... LIZARD, TOAD, WORM
reptile, edible .............. TURTLE
reptile, extinct flying .. PTEROSAUR
reptile, extinct land .... DIPLODOCUS
reptile, Nile .................... CROC
reptile, scale of a .............. SCUTE
reptiles, group of ............ SAURIA
"Republic"; author ........... PLATO
repudiate ......... RECANT, REJECT
repugnance ......... DISGUST, HATE,
HOSTILITY
repulsion .. AVERSION, DISGUST. UG
repulsive .... REVOLTING, LOATHLY
reputation ...... NAME, FAME, LOSE
repute ....... ODOR, CREDIT, WORD
reputed ...... DEEMED, SUPPOSED,
PUTATIVE, RENOWNED
request .... ASK, BEG, NURN, SUIT,
PRAY
request, earnest .... INSTANCE, BEG
request, formal ............ ROGATION
requin ........................ SHARK
require ...... LACK, MASTER, NEED
requite .. ATONE, PAY, RETALIATE,
WAR
rescind RECALL, RECANT, REPEAL
rescue .......... RANSOM, SAVE, AID
resemblance, slight . RINGER, BLUSH
resembling a comb ........ PECTINAL
resent ...... MEAN, SAVOR, SMELL,
SNAP
resentment ... DUDGEON, UMBRAGE
reserve .................... BACKLOG

reserved .. ALOOF, DISTANT, KEPT,
UNCO, COY
reservoir .... CAVITY, STORE, BOSS,
SUMP
reside .. BIDE, BIG, DWELL, LODGE
residence DWELLING, ABODE, SEAT
resident of a city ...... CIT, BURGESS
residue .... ORT, REMANET, ASHES,
DREG, DOTTLE, OVER
resignation .... DEMIT, ABDICATION
resiliency ....... TONE, ELASTICITY
resin alkaloid in calabar beans ESERIN
"     as a varnish ............. ANIME
"     balsam gum ........ BDELLIUM
"     , dark brown ...... ELATERITE
"     , fragrant .............. ELEMI
"     , fragrant inflammable;
FRANKINCENSE
"     ; genus ................. MYRRH
"     gum DAMMAR, GUGAL, COPAL,
MASTIC
"     incense ........ SANDARAC(IN)
"     , medicinal ........... ARGEIRA
"     , mineral .......... ELATERITE
"     of So. Amer. tree ...... ACOUCHI
"     of Chian turpentine ...... ALK
"     of the agalloch ........... ALOE
"     substance ................. LAC
"     , synthetic ............. CATALIN
"     , yellowish . GAMBOGE, AMBER
resist ...... STEM, FEND, WITHER,
OPPOSE
resisting . OPPUGNANT, TENACIOUS
resisting power ................. WIRY
resisting pressure ........ RENITENT
resolute ...................... GRITTY
resonant .. SONOROUS, REECHOING
resort ...... PURLIEU, DIVE, GO, SPA
resound ...... ECHO, PEAL, CLANG,
PLANGENT
resource .. MEANS, ASSETS, FUNDS,
MONEY
resourceful ......... FERTILE, SHARP
respiration, normal ......... EUPNOEA
respire .... BREATHE, EX(IN)HALE
respite, give .......... DELAY, FRIST
resplendent ...... AUREATE, GRAND
respond ...................... REACT
response . ANTIPHON, ECHO, REPLY
responsibility ........ CHARGE, ONUS
rest ........ SIT, LEAN, RELY, SEAT,
RECLINE
rest, in reading ............. CESURA
rest, musket ................ GAFFLE
restaurant . CAFETERIA, AUTOMAT
rested ....... LAIRED, SLEPT, SLEP
restless; mus. .............. AGITATO
restorative ..... ACOPON, ANODYNE
restrain ... FETTER, BRIDLE, REIN,
STINT, DETER
restraint .... CURB, BIT, TRAMMEL
restrict .......... LIMIT, TIE, CRAMP
result ........ EFFECT, END, ISSUE,
TOTAL
resume ........ ABSTRACT, RENEW,
REOPEN
ret .............. ROT, SOAK, STEEP
retable ......... GRADIN, PREDELLA
retailer of wine ............. COOPER

222

retained ............... HELD, KEPT
retaliation ...... TALION, REPRISAL
retard .... LATEN, DELAY, IMPEDE, TRASH
retardant ...... OBSTACLE, REMORA
retch .......... HAWK, VOMIT, GAG
rate ....................... NETWORK
retiary . NETLIKE, SPIDER, TELAR
reticule ..... BAG, CABA, ETUI, NET
retinaculum; var. . MITOME, FRENUM
retinue .... CREW, ESCORT, TRAIN, SUITE, CORTEGE
retired . ABED, LONE, WITHDRAWN
retired from service ...... EMERITUS
retort ... REPARTEE, REPLY, QUIP, RIPOSTE, ALEMBIC
retract DISAVOW, RECANT, ABJURE
retreat ....... ROUT, ASYLUM, DEN, HOTTE, LAIR, NOOK, RETIRE, SANCTUM
retreat down to the sea . KATABASIS
retreat, underground ............ ABRI
retrench ...... CURTAIL, DECREASE
retribution .... REQUITAL, NEMESIS
retribution, law of ............ KARMA
retributive ............... VENGEFUL
retrieve ......... RECOVER, AMEND, REGAIN
retrograde .......... RETRAL, SLOW, DECLINE
retund ............................ FIG
return .... RECUR, REGRESS, WIND
return trust ................. RIPOSTE
refuse ..................... ROUNDED
reveal .. EXHIBIT, BID, JAMB, TELL, WRAY, BARE
reveille DIAN, CALL, LEVET, SIGNAL
revel ...... RIOT, CAROUSAL, ORGY, WATCH
revelation .... ORACLE, DISCLOSURE
revenant ................... EIDOLON
revenue . INCOME, YIELD, RENTAL
revenue of bishop, first year .. ANNAT
reverberating . ECHOING, REBOANT, RINGING
reverence .... VENERATE, WORSHIP
reverie .......... DREAM, FANTASY
revers ...................... LAPEL
reversion; law .............. ESCHEAT
reversion to type .......... ATAVISM
reversionary additions ..... ANNUITY
revert: mus. ......... ANTISTROPHE
revile .... ASPERSE, VILIFY, ABUSE, RAIL
revince ...................... REFUTE
reviser .......... AMENDER, EDITOR
revision ...... RECENSION, VERSION
revive ... RALLY, RELIVE, RESPIRE
revoke .. ABJURE, RENEGE, REPEAL
revoke, as a legacy .......... ADEEM
revolution .... CYCLE, GYRE, TURN
Revolution, essayist .......... PAINE
revolutionist ANARCH, MARAT, REB
revolve .... GYRATE, WHEEL, PIRL, SPIN
revolver . PISTOL, REPEATER, GAT
revolving chimney cover ...... COWL
revolving part ... CAM, ORBY, ROTOR

reward ..... GUERDON, MEED, UTU, YIELD, BONUS, OSCAR
reward to a dog ............ HALLOW
rewards ........... REQUITES, PAYS
rhea ........ AVESTRUZ, EMU, OPS, NANDU
rhetoric, repetition in ........ PLOCE
rhetorical ................. ORATORIC
rhetorical figure ............ LITOTES
rheum ............. CATARRH, COLD
rheumatism remedy .... SALACETOL
rhinal ........................ NASAL
rhinoceros ................... ABADA
rhinoceros, black ............ BORELE
rhinoceros, 2 horn ... KEITOLA, REEM
rhizoid ..................... ROOTLIKE
rhoda ........................... ROSE
rhoeadine ................... POPPY
rhomb ...................... LOSANGE
rhombus ................... LOZENGE
rhonchus ............ SNORING, RALE
Rhone tributary ....... ARVE, ISERE, SAONE
rhubarb ................... PIEPLANT
rhubarb; genus ............... RHEUM
rhus, a kind of ............... SUMAC
rhyming scheme ............. TERCET
rhythm MEASURE, LILT, CADENCE, METER
ria .............................. INLET
rialto .. BRIDGE, EXCHANGE, MART
riant ............ AIRY, BLITHE, GAY
ribald ............... ATELLAN, LOW
ribbed ............ COSTATE, RIDGED
ribbon, badge of an order .... CORDON
ribbon binding ............... LISERE
ribbon shaped ............ TAENIOID
ribbon, silk ... TAPE, CORSE, TASTE
ribbon worm ............ NEMERTINE
ribs, per. to the .............. COSTAL
ribwort ................... PLANTAIN
rice boiled with meat .. PILAU, PILAF
rice field ..................... PADDY
rice, inferior; Phil. I. ............ AGA
rice of inferior grade .......... CHITS
rice paste glucose ............... AME
rice refuse .................... SHUDE
rice, wild ....................... REED
rich COPIOUS, FECUND, FAT, OPIME
rich man ...... NABOB, PLUTOCRAT
rich men, very .... CROESUS, DIVES, MIDAS, PLUTO
Richelieu's successor ...... MAZARIN
riches .... EDY, LUCRE, OPULENCE, WEALTH
riches, demon of ........... MAMMON
rickety .................... SENILE
rickshaw ............... JINRIKISHA
riddle . REBUS, ENIGMA, PUN, CRUX
riddle, to ........ PIERCE, SIFT, REE
ridge, anatomical ..... SPINE, RUGA, STRIA
" between two furrows PORCATE
" circular, on shells ......... PILAE
" , low .. PARMA, RAND, CUESTA
" of a drift ..... KAME, OS, OSAR
" of a glacial drift OESAR, ESKER, KAME, ARETE
" of stubble ................. MANE

223

" or mark ........ WALE, WHELK
" , rel. to ................. CARINA
" , sand ............... AAS, OSAR
" , shell ........ VARICES, VARIX
" , to ........................ CHINE
ridicule ROAST, ASTEISM, BANTER,
    PAN, TWIT, MOCKAGE, JEER
ridiculous . ABSURD, FUNNY, IRONY,
    FARCICAL, GROTESQUE
riding breeches ........... JODHPURS
riding school ................. MANEGE
riding whip ................... QUIRT
rifle .... CARBINE, MAUSER, STRIP,
    ROB
rifle ball ........................ MINIE
rifle, convertde breech loading SNIDER
rifle pin .......................... TIGE
rifle, French breech loading ...........
    CHASSEPOT
rift CLEFT, GAP, LAG, RIMA, SPLIT
rig .... EQUIP, LATEEN, BEDIZEN,
    GEAR
Riga, native ........ LATVIAN, LETT
rigging, part of . SPAR, GEAR, ROPES
right .. EMEND, TITLE, DROIT, PAT
right hand ................... DEXTER
right handed page ............ RECTO
right of precedence ................ PAS
right time; Scot. ................... TID
right, turn to ........... GEE, MANO
righteously .......... GODLILY, WELL
rigid ........ STRINGENT, AUSTERE,
    STRICT
rigorous .. DRASTIC, STIFF, STERN
Riis; writer .................... JACOB
rile ... ANGER, OFFEND, ROIL, VEX
rim ...... EDGE, LIP, BRIM, BRINK,
    VERGE
rim of a shield .................. ORLE
rim of a wheel ................ FELLY
rim of a horseshoe ............. WEB
rime ....... ICY, HOAR, HOARFROST
"Rime-cold giant" ...... YMEN, YMIR
rimes, book of ................. EDDA
Rinaldo's steed; Ital. ...... BAJARDO
rind BARK, CRUST, EPICARP, HUSK,
    PEEL, SKIN
ring ... ANNULET, ARENA, BAGUE,
    COTERIE, SET
" , as a bell ..... CLANK, CHIME,
    KNELL, PEAL
" dove ..................... CUSHAT
" finger ...................... JINK
" in a gem setting BEZEL, CHATON
" , metal ...................... BEE
" of a harness pad ....... TERRET
" of rope ............. GROMMET
"Ring of the Nibelung," smith in......
    MIMI
ring, ornamental ............ LEGLET
ring, packing .................. LUTE
ring, small ..... CIRCLET, ANNULET
ringing .......... CLAM, OROTUND
ringlet . CRISP, CURL, LOCK, TRESS
rings, interlocking .......... GIMMAL
ring-shaped ............... ANNULAR
ring-tailed animal .............. COON
ring-worm .................. SERPIGO
ring-worm infection .......... TINEA

rinse .. SLUICE, ABSTERGE, LAVE,
    SIND
Rio de ............................ ORO
Rio de Janeiro native ...... CARIOCA
riot in Russia .............. POGROM
riotous LUXURIANT, WANTON, RAID
riotously ....................... ARIOT
riotously merry ...... SATURNALIAN
rip ............... CUT, REND, TEAR
rip; slang ......... HAG, HARRIDAN
ripe; dial. Eng. .......... RIFLE, ROB
ripen .... MATURE, ADDLE, DIGEST
ripened stalk ................... STRAW
ripening early ............. RARERIPE
ripens ..... MATURATES, MUTURES,
    AGES
ripple EAGRE, PURL, ACKER, FRET,
    RIFF, LAP, WAVE
ris de veau ........... SWEETBREAD
rise ........... GROW, REBEL, SOAR
rise again .. ARISE, REAR, RESURGE
rise from liquid ............. EMERSE
risible ...... ABSURD, LAUGHABLE,
    FUNNY
rising MONTANT, ORTIVE, SURGENT
risk ........ DARE, DANGER, PERIL,
    PLIGHT, HAZARD
rit; Scot. ..................... SCRATCH
ritual . CEREMONY, NOVENA, CULT,
    LITURGY, PRAYER, SALAT
rival EMULATE, EVEN, FOE, MATCH,
    PEER, COMPLETE, VIE
riven .......... CLEFT, RENT, SPLIT
river bank ..... LEVEE, RAND, RIPA
" bank, per. to a ...... RIPARIAN
" , Bavarian ........ EGER, ISAR
" , Belgian .... LYS, DYLE, YZER
" , Bohemian ANGEL, ELBS, ISER
" , Bolivian BENI, IVARI, PIRAY
" bottom land .............. HOLM
" , British-Afr. ............. TANA
" Caesar crossed ....... RUBICON
" channels ................ ALVEI
" , Chilian .......... BIOBIO, LOA
" dragon ............. CROCODILE
" duck ...................... TEAL
" , Dutch ........... EEM, MAAS
" gauge .............. NILOMETER
" horse; abb. ............. HIPPO
" in Arizona ................ GILA
" in Armenia ................ ARAS
" in Austria ACH, DRAVE, ISER,
    SAVE
" in Brazil ...... APA, ACAMEA,
    ACARA, RIO
" in Burma .. IRAWADI, TAPING
" in Chile ................. ITATA
" in China .. HWANG, LAO, WEI
" in Colorado .......... LARAMIE
" in Czech .......... IPOLY, OHRE
" in England .. ALN, ESK, TEES,
    TRENT
" in France .... AIRE, AA, ISERE,
    MEUSE, AISNE, CHER, LYS,
    ORNE, OISE, RHONE, VESLE
" in Germany; ..... ALLE, ELBE,
    ODER, HUNTE, LEK
" in Hades .. ACHERON, LETHE,
    STYX

"	in India ...... GUMTI, KISTNA,
INDES
"	in Indo-China ............. HUE
"	in Italy .. ADDA, ARNO, NERA,
PO, TIBER
"	in Louisiana ............ AMITE
river in Luxemburg ALZETTE, SAUER
"	in Moravia ............... ODER
"	in Nebraska .......... NEMAHA
"	in N. Carolina ............ NEUSE
"	in Peru .... MARANON, ACARI
"	in Portugal .... SABOR, TAGUS
"	in Poland ..... BUG, VISTULA,
SAN, SERET
"	in Rumania .......... SERETH
"	in Russia ...... AA, ABAU, ILI,
NEVA, OREL, OKA
"	in Scotland .... AYR, DEE
"	in Siam ............... MENAM
"	in Siberia . ISET, AMUR, LENA,
OB, OBI
"	in Sicily ............. MAZZARO
"	in South America ... ORINOCO,
APA
"	in S. Carolina SALUDA, PEEDEE
"	in Spain JUGAR, ADAJA, ARGA,
TAGUS, DOURO, RIO
"	in Switzerland .... AAR, REUSS
"	in the Levant .... WADI, WADY
"	in Turkey MESTA, SARUS, ZAB
"	in Tuscany ...... ARNO, ORCIA
"	in Umbria; It. ......... TEVERE
"	in Venezuela ......... CARONI
"	in Yorkshire ............... URE
"	inlet ............ SLEW, SLOUGH
"	, inlet from a ........... BAYOU
"	, isle in ............. HOLM, AIT
"	"Lochinvar" ........... ESKE
"	, mouth of a . BOCA, ESTUARY,
LADE, DELTA
"	near sea ..................... EA
"	nymph ................... NAIS
"	of the underworld ........ STYX
"	passage .................. FORD
"	, per. to a .. AMNIC, RIVERINE
"	siren ................. LORELEI
"	Thames at Oxford ......... ISIS
river to Danube ............ RAAB
"	, winding of a .............. ESS
Rivera; muralist .............. DIEGO
riviere ................... NECKLACE
rivers, fish which ascend .. ANADROM
rivulet ............. BROOK, STREAM
roach; Eur. .............. AZURINE
Roach, Jr. ....................... HAL
road paving ................ TARMAC
road .... ESTRADA, AGGER, DRANG,
ITER, COURSE, (HIGH)WAY
road, cul-de-sac ............. IMPASSE
road runner ......... CUCKOO, COCK
roadster .......... RUNABOUT, AUTO
roam ..... ERR, GAD, RANGE, ROVE
roaming voice ............... VAGANS
roar .. BELL, STEVEN, BROOL, DIN
roar, as a bear ................. FREAM
roar of sea ..................... ROTE
roast .... ASSATE, BANTER, PARCH
roast by fire ................ TORREFY
roast meat; Ind. .............. CABOB

roasting-stick .......... (TURN) SPIT
rob .... FOB, DESPOIL, LOOT, PELF,
TOUCH, RIFLE
Rob Roy, a .................... CANOE
robbed; mus. ................. RUBATO
robber .... RATENER, PAD, REAVE,
YEGG, THIEF, PIRATE
robber class in India ........ DACOIT
robber; Hindu .............. EBONITE
robber privateer ............ CORSAIR
robbery ............. PIRACY, REIF
robe, bishop's ................. CHIMER
robe, camel's hair ................ ABA
robe, light loose ..... CAMIS, CAMUS
robe, light loose ...... CAMIS, CAMUS
robe to ankles ....... TALAR, SYRMA
robe to ankles ........ TALAR, SYRMA
robe, woman's ........ CYMAR, SIMAR
Robert; actor ................... ALDA
"Robin Goodfellow" .... FAIRY, PUCK
Robin Hood ................. BANDIT
Robin Hood's foe ............ SHERIFF
Robin Hood's love ............ MARIAN
Robin Hood's retreat ............ BARN
"Robinson Crusoe"; author of ..DEFOE
"Robinson Crusoe," boy in ...... XURY
Robinson, Mrs. E., pen name ... TALVI
Robinson, Ray ................. SUGAR
roble .................... BEECH, OAK
robot ................... AUTOMATON
robots, play about ................ RUR
robust ....... SOUND, HALE, WALLY
roc, the ............. SIMURG(H), BIRD
rock ....... SHAKE, TEETER, TRASS
rock-candy ............... GIBRALTAR
rock and gravel ............. MORAINE
"	beds, per. to ........... STRATAL
"	, black igneous .......... BASALT
"	boring tool .............. TREPAN
"	cavity ................... DRUSE
"	, cavity in bedded ....... GEODE
"	clay ........ SLATE, GANISTER
"	, comb. form ............. PETO
"	concretions cemented together; ..
OOLITE
"	crystal ingredient ....... SILICA
"	decay ....... GEEST, LATERITE
"	, discarded broken ...... ATTLE
"	, finely broken ............ SAND
"	fish; Cal. .......... REINA, RENA
"	fissile ................... SHALE
"	formed by geyser deposit SINTER
"	, fragmental .......... PSEPHITE
"	, granite-like GNEISS, DIORITE
"	hopper ................. PENGUIN
"	, igneous ... BASALT, PERIDOT
"	, igneous bill of ........... BOSS
"	intrusive ................ DACITE
"	jutting .............. CRAG, TOR
"	laminated; Eng. SHALE, SHAUL
"	of quarts and albite .. ADINOLE
"	oil ........ NAPHTHA, NAPTHA
"	or roll ................ TITUBATE
"	pinnacle ........ NEEDLE, SCAR
"	, porous ......... TUFA, TUFF
"	, schistose ........... EPIDOSITE
"	, siliceous igneous .......... SIAL
"	stratum ............. LENTICLE

225

" , suffix ................. ITE, YTE
" that splits ................. SCHIST
" , volcanic ...... LAVA, DACITE
                                LATITE
" weed ....................... TANG
rocket authority ................. LEY
rockling ........................ GADE
rocks, classific. ............. PAOLASE
rocks, per. to .............. SAXATILE
rocks; slang ................... MONEY
rock-throne; Bib. ............. SENCH
rocky ....... CLIFFY, DIZZY, SHAKY,
                                    WEAK
rocky crag rising above a glacier; ....
                                NUNATAK
rocky decay .... GEEST, SAPROLITE
"Rocky Ford," a .............. MELON
rocky pinnacle ............ SCAR, TOR
rocky seashore plant ........ ACTAEA
rocoa ........................ ANNATO
rod .... EYEBAR, GAT, WAND, BAR
rod, divination ...... RHABDOMANCY
rod, fibrous ................... LYTTA
rod, fishing, reel on .......... TROLL
rod-like ..................... RHABDO
rod or whip .............. GAD, PLET
rod, 16½ feet .......... PERCH POLE
rode goose .................... BRANT
rodent .. HARE, PIKA, UTIA, CAVY,
                                   TUCAN
"   , aquatic . BEAVER, MUSKRAT
"   , Belgian ............ LEPORIDE
"   , bushy tailed ........ MARMOT
"   , European ..... CONEY, CONY,
                                   LEROT
"   ; genus .................... MUS
"   , gnawer ........... MOLE, MUA
"   , jumping; genus ......... DIPUS
"   , large So. Am. ....... CAPYBARA
"   , Mongoloid ..... GOPHER, RAT
"   , mouse-like ...... MICE, VOLE
"   , nocturnal ........... SEWELLEL
"   , rat-like .. VOLE, ABROCOME
"   , S. Am. ........ AGOUTI, DEGU,
                             PACA, MOCA
"   , S. Am. aquatic ........ COYPU
rodents' disease ........ TULAREMIA
rodents; genus ................ LEPUS
rodge ...................... GADWALL
rods, 160 square ................ ACRE
roe ..... CAPRET, OVA, RA, EGG(S),
                                   SPAWN
roentgen rays ........ X, RAES, RAYS
rogation .. SUPPLICATION, LITANY
rogation flower ........... MILKWORT
Rogers, Mr. ...................... ROY
rogue .. HEMP, IMP, KITE, ROGER
                             WAG, KNAVE
rogues, per. to ........ PICARESQUE
roguish  ARCH, ESPIEGLE, PAWKY,
                                      SLY
roisterer; Eng. ................... MUN
role .. CHARACTER, PART, PERSON
roll ..... FURL, LURCH, BUN, LIST,
                             ROTA TROLL
roll along ................... TRUNDLE
roll of army officers ROSTER, CADRE
roll of coins ................ ROULEAU
roll of hair ................ CHIGNON

roller, Chinese ............. SIRGANG
romaine lettuce ................... COS
Roman ........................ LATIN
"   apartment .............. DECUS
"   apostle ................... NERI
"   arch abutment ....... ALETTE
"   assembly .............. FORUM
"   author ................ VARRO
"   awning ............ VELARIUM
"   bars ..................... FESS
"   basilica ............ LATERAN
"   bishop ................. POPE
"   boxing glove .......... CESTUS
"   bronze .................... AES
"   calendar ............. CALENDS
"   Catholic title ............ ABBE
"   chariot ...... ESSED, ESTEDE
"   chest ..................... CIST
"   circus, the barrier ...... SPINA
"   citizen; anc. .......... CASCA,
                                  AERARIAN
"   clan ..................... GENS
"   cloak; anc. .......... ABOLLA,
                                  PLANETA
"   clover ................... OREL
"   coat .................. PAENULA
Roman coin; anc. AUREUS, DINDER,
                                      SEMIS
"   coin, copper .......... AS, AES
"   comic after piece ...... EXODE
"   comic poet .......... TERENCE
"   concert halls ............ ODEA
"   consul ................. SCIPIO
"   court of the pope ...... CURIA
"   court, open ............. ATRIA
"   cupid .................... EROS
"   date ............ NODE, NONES
"   date, calendar in ......... IDES
"   deity ..................... LAR
"   Diana ............... ARTEMIS
"   dictator .............. SULLA
"   dish .................. PATERA
"   divine law;/Lat. .......... FAS
"   diviner .............. AUSPEX
"   domestic god .......... LARES
"   earthwork ............. AGGER
"   emperor ........ OTTO, TITUS
"   empress ............. EUDOCIA
"   entrance ............. ATRIUM
"   fates .................. PARCAE
"   festival days .......... FERIAE
"   festivals of Jupiter ..... FERIA
"   fish sauce ............. GARUM
"   galley ............... BIREME
"   gambling cube ....... TESSERA
"   garment ..... PALLA STOLE,
                             TOGA, TUNIC
"   general ..... MARIUS, SULLA,
                                   TITUS
"   ghosts .... LEMURES, MANES
"   gladiator ......... RETIARIUS,
                                  SAMNITE
"   goal post .............. META
"   god (see also 'God')
"   god, chief .... JOVE, JUPITER
"   god, household LAR, PENATES
"   god of festive joy ...... COMUS
"   god of fire ........... VULCAN

226

"    god of Hades .... DIS, ORCUS,
                               PLUTO
"    god of lightning .... JUPITER
"    god of love ..... AMOR, CUPID
"    god of seas ........ NEPTUNE
"    god of sky .......... JUPITER
"    god of sleep ....... MORPHEUS,
                              SOMNUS
"    god of thieves ...... MERCURY
"    god of underworld . DIS, ORCUS,
                               PLUTO
"    god of woods ..... SYLVANUS
"    god of war . MARS, QUIRINUS
"    goddess (see also 'Goddess')
"    goddess
"    goddess ..................... DEA
"    goddess of agriculture ..... OPS
"    goddess of birth ........ PARCA
"    goddess of childbirth . LUCINA
"    goddess of corpse ... LIBITINA
"    goddess of dawn ..... AURORA
"    goddess of death PROSERPINE
"    goddess of earth LUA, TELLUS
"    goddess of fertility; . ANNONA,
                               FAUNA
"    goddess of fountains FERONIA
"    goddess of harvest ........ OPS
"    goddess of love ........ VENUS
Roman goddess of moon ...... LUNA,
                             PHOEBUS
"    goddess of night .......... NOX
"    goddess of peace .......... PAX,
                             MINERVA
"    goddess of persuasion . SUADA
"    goddess of seas ...... SALACIA
"    goddess of war ..... BELONA,
                      MINERVA, VACUNA
"    goddess of womanhood ... JUNO
"    governor ........ PROCONSUL
"    guard ................. LICTOR
"    hairpin .................. ACUS
"    highway .................. ITER
"    hill .... AVENTINE, CAELIAN,
          PALATINE,      QUIRINAL,
          CAPITOLINE, ESQUILINE,
          VIMINAL
"    historian ..... SALLUST, LIVY,
                               NEPOS
"    holiday .......... IDES, FERIA
"    javelin .......... PILUM, PILE
"    judge ........ AEDILE, EDILE
"    judges, one of three TRIUMVIR
"    jurist ................... GAIUS
"    king .................... ALARIC
"    lands acquired in war ... AGER
"    law ........ CERN, MOS, LEX
"    leader .................... DUX
"    legendary nymph ...... EGERIA
"    legendary king ........ NUMA
"    libation-vessel ........ PATERA
"    libra .......................... AS
"    magistrate; .. CENSOR, EDILE,
          PRETOR, PRAETOR, TRIBUNE
"    maiden who opened the citadel to
          the Sabines ....... TARPEIA
"    malarial plain ....... CAMPANA
"    matron's garment ...... STOLA
"    measure ................. URNA
"    measure, a foot ............ PES

"    midday meal ............ CENA
"    military cloak ......... SAGUM
"    military insignia .... PHALERA
"    money .................. SEMIS
"    month .... MARTIUS, APRILIS,
          MAIUS, JUNIUS, QUINTILIS
"    month, first day of . CALENDS
"    naturalist ............... PLINY
"    official ....... EDILE, LICTOR
"    official in Judea ........ FELIX
"    orator ......... CATO, CICERO
"    ornament .............. BULLA
"    palace .............. LATERAN
"    patriot .......... CINNA, CATO
"    pax; Lat. ............... IRENE
"    people, early ......... SABINES
"    philosopher ......... SENECA
"    poet ...... VERGIL, JUVENAL,
          LUCAN, CINNA, OVID, MACER
"    port; anc. .............. OSTIA
"    pound .............. AS, LIBRA
"    praenomen .............. TITUS
"    priest of pagan deity FLAMEN
"    priestly official ........ AUGUR
"    priests of the cult ... LUPERCI
"    province ................ DACIA
"    road ................ ITER, VIA
"    road, famous .......... APPIAN
"    roads ................ ITINERA
"    room .......... ALA, ATRIUM,
                            TABLINUM
"    rubric ..................... RED
Roman sacrificial plate ...... PATERA
"    seat .................... SELLA
"    senate house ............ CURIA
"    senator .................. CATO
"    serf, female .......... COLONA
"    serf, male ............ COLONUS
"    shields ...... SCUTA, ANCILES
"    shop ................. TABERNA
"    spirits of the dead; LEMURES,
                               MANES
"    sports official ....... ASIARCH
"    street .................. CORSO
"    tax .................... ANNONA
"    term .................... GAINE
"    treasurer .......... QUAESTOR
"    turning post ............ META
"    vessel .............. AMPHORA
"    vestment ................ TOGA
"    virgin warrior ....... CAMILLA
"    war machine; anc. .. TEREBRA
"    weight; anc. ........ AS, BES,
                       DODRANS, LIBRA
"    world of the dead ...... ORCUS
"    writing table ........ DIPTYCH
romance language ......... CATALAN
romance verse, form of ..... SESTINA
Rome, conqueror of .......... ALARIC
"Rome Haul," by .......... EDMONDS
Rome, lake near ................ NEMI
Rome, legendary founder . ROMULUS
Rome, public land in anc. ...... AGER
romp ........ PLAY, SPORT, TOMBOY
romping .......... RAW, RANTIPOLE
Roncesvalles ................ ROLAND
rondure ...... CIRCLE, PLUMPNESS
rone; Scot. . ................. THICKET
ronin; Jap. ..... OUTCAST, OUTLAW

227

rood .............. CROSS, CRUCIFIX
roof CUPOLA, DOME, FIG, GAMBREL
roof angle ........................ HIP
"Roof of the World"; Asia ..... PAMIR
roof of third and fourth ventricles of
  brain; ........................ TELA
roof, overhanging edge of ...... EAVE
roof, raised border ......... COAMING
roof support; Eng. ............. CRUCK
roof; thatched ...... CHOPPER, DAK
roof with thin boards .......... SARK
roofing tile ................. PANTILE
rook ......... CASTLE, CHEAT, CUB,
                       SHARPER
room .. GARDEROOM, SALA, AULA,
       SCOPE, LODGE, QUARTER
room in harem ....... ADA, IDA, ODA
room used for religious rites in Pueblo
  Ind. house ...................... KIVA
roorback ........................... LIE
Roosevelt, Mrs. .... ANNA, ELEANOR
roost ...... SIT, JOUK, PERCH, POLE
root, edible .... POTATO, YAM, TARO
  "   footed .............. RHIZOPOD
  "   form of wood ........ RADICAL,
                       ETYMON
  "   in cough mixture ..... SENEKA
  "   interlacement ...... BOW, KNOT
  "   out ..... EVERSE, ERADICATE
  "   stock, pungent . TARO, GINGER
  "   used in a tonic ............. ATIS
rootlet ...................... RADICEL
rope, dancer's ................... POY
  "   fiber ............. ISTLE, IXTLE
  "   for fastening ship's tackle .......
                    LANYARD
  "   , guiding ................. LONGE
  "   , guy ............ CABLE, VANG
  "   in ship ladder ....... RATLINE
  "   kind of ..... LARIAT, SNOTTER
rope loop; naut. ..... FRAP, PARREL
  "   make a turn with ..... BELAY
  "   of two strands ........ MARLIN
  "   or chain; naut. ............. TYE
  "   , ship's ....... RODE, SHROUD,
                    PAINTER
  "   , slack .................. SLATCH
  "   splicer's tools ............. FIDS
  "   threaded thru block .... REEVE
  "   walker ......... FUNAMBULIST
roped .................... TETHERED
Roper, Mr. ..................... ELMO
roric .......... RORAL, RORY, DEWY
rorqual .......... FINBACK, WHALE
ros, the ........................... RUS
rosary ............ BEADS, CHAPLET
rosary bead ............. AVE, GAUDY
rose ............................ RHODA
rose apple ................. POMAROSA
rose bush, false fruit of ............. HIP
rose, dog ..................... CANKER
rose family .............. ROSACEAE
rose petal oil ........... ATTAR, OTTO
rose-red dye ... EOSIN, RHODAMINE
rose, wild ................. EGLANTINE
roses, honey of ........... RHODOMEL
Rossellini; Mrs. .............. INGRID
rosette-like ................. ROSULAR
rosin; Scot. .................... ROZET

roster .... LIST, ROLL, ROTA, SLATE
rostrum ... DAIS, STAGE, TRIBUNE
rosy . AURORAL, PINK, ROSACEOUS
rot, wet ................. DECAY, RET
rota ................... LIST, COURT
rotate . BIRL, SLUE, GYRATE, ROLL,
        RABATTE, ROTE, WHIZ
rotating piece .................... CAM
rotche ....................... DOVEKIE
rottenstone .................. TRIPOLI
rove ........................... RAKE
rouge, to ................... FUCATE
rough . SCABROUS, HOARSE, RASPY,
        SEAMY, AGRESTIC
rough cloth ..................... TERRY
rough diamond ................. BRAIT
rough hair ..................... SHAG
rough-leaved plant ...... OXTONGUE
rough man ..................... KNUR
roughen ........ FRET, NURL, CHAP,
              FRAY, GNAW
roughshod, go ............. TRAMPLE
roulette, a bet in .................. BAS
Roumania (See Rumania)
round ...................... ORBED
round country dance ............ HAY
round; mus. ................... TROLL
round protuberance ............ UMBO
round timber .................... SPAR
round up ...................... RODEO
roundabout ... INDIRECT, AMBIENT
roundabout, kind of ......... JACKET
rounded and notched ....... RETUSE
rounded projection LOBATE, CRENA,
                TEETH
rouse ..... KINDLE, STEER, WAKE,
        EXCITE, ROUST, HIE
Rousseau hero ................. EMILE
rout .. SCATTER, DEBACLE, CROWD
routine ...... EVERYDAY, REGULAR
rove . RANGE, GAD, PART, SWERVE
rover ..... PILGRIM, WAIF, NOMAD,
               PIRATE
row ....... FILE, BROIL, OAR, TIER
row boat .... CANOE, GIG, RANDAN
row, form in a ......... ALIGN, ALINE
rowan cloak .............. PLANETA
rowanah; E. Ind. .......... PASSPORT
rowdy ...... PLUGUGLY, LARRIKIN
rowel PRICK, URGE, SPUR, WHEEL
rowen . CROP, AFTERMATH, FIELD
rowing match ............... REGATTA
row-lock support ............ POPPET
royal .... AUGUST, KINGLY, BASIL,
        RIAL, IMPERIAL
royal bay .................... LAUREL
royal blue .................... SMALT
Royal crown ................... TIARA
royal court, per. to a ....... ALTMAN
Royal house ...... STEWART, TUDOR
royal mace ................. SCEPTER
Royal Scot. home ....... BALMORAL
royal stars, one of the ..... ANTARES
royal title ............ REGENT, SIRE
Royle; actress ............... SELINA
rub MASSAGE, SMEAR, TRITURATE
rub away .................. ABRADE
rub out ....... OBLITERATE, ERASE,
        EXPUNGE, SCRAPE

rub together ..................... RAKE
"Rubaiyat"; author ............ OMAR
rubber ................. CAOUTCHOUC
"Rubber City" ................. AKRON
rubber compound ERASER, FACTICE,
KERITE
rubber gasket for fruit jars .... LUTE
rubber; genus .................. FICUS
rubber, hard ..... CEARA, EBONITE
rubber, kind of ............ GUAYULE
rubber lining ................. GASKET
rubber sap ..................... LATEX
rubber shoe ................. GALOSH
rubber tree ... PARA, SERINGA, ULE
rubbers, disease in sheep; RAY, SCAB,
SHAB
rubbery .......... ELASTIC, TOUGH
rubbish .............. ATTLE, DROSS
rubbish, mining ............... STENT
rubeola ...................... MEASLES
rubicund .......... FLORID, RUDDY
rubiginously ................. RUSTILY
Rubinstein; opera by ....... DEMONIO
Rubinstein; pianist ............ ARTUR
rubout; Eng. .................... DOUT
rubric ................... TITLE, RED
rubrics, book of ............... ORDO
ruby colored gem ............ SPINEL
ruby, variety ..... RUBASSE, BALAS
rudd, blue variety of ...... AZURINE
rudder ............... HELM, TEMON
ruddle ......................... KEEL
rudeness ......... FERITY, STARING
rudiment ANLAGE, EMBRYO, FIRST
rudiments ......... ABC, ELEMENTS
rue .... DEPLORE, REGRET, GRIEF,
RUTA
rue herb ..................... HARMEL
ruff, female ............. REE, REEVE
ruff, support for a ........... RABATO
ruffer .................... NAPPER
ruffle ......................... DERANGE
ruffle, dust; Fr. ....... BALAYEUSE
Ruffner; radio M.C. ............. TINY
rufous ....................... REDDISH
rug ......... MAT, PETATE, MAUD,
SENNA
Rugby, football ....... GONUM, MAUL
Rugen Is. cape ............... ARKONA
rugged .... ASPER, CRAGGY, HARDY
Ruhr city ...................... HAMM
ruin .. FATE, SPOIL, WRACK, BANE
ruined .......... GONE, DESTROYED,
WRECKED
rule PRECEPT, LEAD, LAW, NORM,
SWAY, MAXIM, REGIMENT
rule for moldings ............ SCREED
ruler . GERENT, EMIR, MIN, PRINCE,
QUEEN
ruler of a religious body . HIERARCH
ruler or governor . DESPOT, DYNAST
ruler's wife ................. EMPRESS
"Rules of Order"; author ... ROBERT
rum distilled from molasses .... TAFIA
Rumanian capital ...... BUCHAREST
Rumanian city . GALAT, LASI, IASI,
JASSY, ARAD
" coin ................ LEU, LEY
" conservative ........... BOYAR

" king .................. CAROL
" king (ex); wife ........ MAGDA
" river .... ALUTA, ARGES, JIU
" river, port ............. GALATZ
" title ...................... DOMN
" unit of currency .. BANI, BAN
rumba king .................. CUGAT
rumen ................. GULLET, CUD
ruminant . ALPACA, GOAT, LLAMA,
YAK, BISON, DEER, SHEEP
ruminant's second stomach ............
RETICULUM
ruminant's third stomach ... OMASUM
ruminants, division of ... UNGULATA
ruminate . CHEW, REFLECT, MUSE
rummy; sl. ............. ODD, QUEER
rumor ... BRUIT, FAMA, HEARSAY,
NOISE, REPORT
rump .......... BREECH, BUTTOCKS
rumple ...... CREASE, MUSS, TOUSE
rumpus ...... FRACAS, NITTY, ROW
run ........ HIE, SCUD, TROT, GAD,
FLOW, LOPE, RACE, SPRINT,
OPERATE
run away .. ELOPE, DECAMP, FLEE
run in haste .... CAREER, ELOPE,
SCUTTLE, FUGITIVE
Runes, inventor of; myth. ... DVALIN
runnel .......... BROOK, CHANNEL,
RIVULET
runner .. TOUTER, COURIER, RACER
running .... EASY, CURSIVE, RAKE
runt .. DWARF, PYGMY, CHIT, ELF
runt of a brood ................. WRIG
runway ..... FILE, RAMP, AIRSTRIP
rupee .. ANNA, CRORE, LAC, LAKH
rupture .. RENT, RHEXIS, QUARREL
rural BUCOLIC, GEORGIC, PASTORAL
rural game ...................... DIBS
rural, per. to . RUSTICAL, AGRESTIC
rural poem .................. ECLOGUE
rush ........ SPATE, PRESS, SURGE
rush, kind of .................. SPROT
Russell, Miss ................. CONNIE
Russia, assembly in RADA, ZEMSTVO
" , city in .. OMSK, OREL, KIEV
" , district in STEPPE, KARELIA
" , former government in west ..
LIVONIA
" , former name for .. MUSCOVY
" , founder of .............. IVAN
" , gulf in ................. AZOV
" holy picture of .......... ICON
" , spirituous liquor of ... VODKA
Russian alcoholic beverage ... KVASS
" carriage TARANTASS, TROIKA
" cathedral .............. SOBOR
" cereal grain .......... EMMER
" chess champion ... ALEKHINE
" clover ................... OREL
" coal area ............. DONETS
" coin . DENGA, LEY, POLTINA,
RUBLE
" community ................ MIR
" composer ................. CUI
" convict shelter ........ ETAPE
" cooperative society .... ARTEL
" cossack ................. TATAR
" council ........ DUMA, SOVIET

" council, political ......... RADA
" dance ................. ZIGANKA
" desert ................. TUNDRA
" dog ................. OWTCHAH
Russian edict ................... UKASE
" empress ............. TSARITZA
" for yes ....................... DA
" fuel oil .............. ASTATKI
" fur .................. KARAKUL
" government ............. TVER
" guild ................... ARTEL
" imperial order ........ UKASE
" inland sea ....... ARAL, AZOF
" instrument; mus. ...... GUSLE
" lake .. NEVA, ARAL, ONEGA,
    ERARA
" landed proprietor ...... BOYAR
" leather . SHAGREEN, BULGAR
" legal assembly .......... RADA
" log hut ............. ISPA, ISBA
" massacre ............. POGROM
" measure ........ LOF, SAGENE
" measure of distance ... VERST
" monetary unit ......... RUBLE
" mountains ....... ALAI, URAL
" musical inst. .... BALALAIKA
" negative ................. NYET
" novelist .............. TOLSTOI
" oil center ............... BAKU
" parliament ............... DUMA
" peasant ........ KULAK, SLAV
" peasant's cap ............. ASKA
" people ................... SLAVS
" plane ..................... MIG
" pound .................... POOD
" prince ......... KNEZ, KNYAZ
" prison or stockade ..... ETAPE
" province ........ AMUR, TULA
" republic .............. KARELIA
" rickets ............... RACHITIS
" river; . NEVA, ONEGA, OREL,
    ROS, LENA, RHA, URAL,
    KARA, VOLGA, DVINA,
    UFA
" ruler; anc. . IVAN, PETER, RO
" sea ...................... ARAL
" secret service .......... CHEKA
" soup .................. BORSCH
" tea urn ............. SAMOVAR
" teacher .............. STARETS
" thatched roof dwelling .. ISBA
" thistle ........ TUMBLEWEED
" town ....... OSA, KOLA, RIGA,
    UMAN, SEREDA
" trade union ............ ARTEL
" tribesman ............. ERGAR
" Ukraine council ......... RADA
" units of measure ... SAGENES
" village community ... MIR, OR
" violinist ............... ELMAN
" wagon, springless ... TELEGA
" watering place ............ EMS
" weight ............. POOD, PUD
" wheat ................. EMMER
" whip .................... PLET
" whip; anc. ............. KNOUT
" wolf hound .... ALAN, BORZOI
russud; Ind. ................. FORAGE

rust ..... CORRODE, EAT, AERUGO,
    ERODE, VERDIGRIS
rust of plants .... BLIGHT, FERRUGO
rust on bronze, etc. .......... PATINA
rust, sport fruit of .......... ACEIUM
Rustam's father ................... ZAL
rustic . GEOPONIC, BUCOLIC, RUBE,
    PLAIN, DORIC, RURAL
rustic . CLOWN, CORYDON, DAMON,
    YOKEL
rustic lover ..... SILVESTER, SWAIN
rustic maiden, any ...... THESTYLIS
rustic peasant .. AGRESTIAN, CLOD,
    BOOR
rustic pipe .............. REED, CORN
rustic, poet ..................... CARL
rustle .. SWISH, FROUFROU, SCROOP,
    STIR
rustling .................. SUSURROUS
Rustrum's son, Persian legend SOHRAB
rutabaga ..................... TURNIP
Ruthenia, county in .............. UNG
Ruth's mother-in-law .......... NAOMI
rutilate ... GLOW, GLITTER, SHINE
Ruy Diaz de Bivar ................ CID
rye; arc. ......................... RIE
rye fungus, also disease ....... ERGOT
rye; genus ................... SECALE
rytina, synonym of HYDRODAMALIS


# S

S, letter ........................... ESS
S-curve ......................... OGEE
S-shaped ....... SIGMATE, SIGMOID
sabbatism ........... REST, ARIANISM
sable ...... BLACK, EBON, PELLET
sable, Alaska ............... SKUNK
sable, Amer. ... MARTEN, LEMMING
sable, species of .. MUSTELA, TATAR
Sabrina river ............... SEVERN
sabulous .. SANDY, DUSTY, FLOURY
sac ............ ASCUS, BURSA, CYST
sacaton ........................ GRASS
saccharine ....... SWEET, HONEYED
saccharine, deriv. of ....... AGAVOSE,
    MALTWORT
Sacco; Ital. ................... NIKOLA
sacerdotal .... PRIESTLY, CLERICAL
sachet .... PAD, SAC, BAG, PERFUME
saclike cavity ....... BURSA, VESICLE
sack . BAG, HAVOC, POUCH, LOOT,
    POKE
sack-but ................. TROMBONE
sacrarium ....... CHANCEL, PISCINA
sacred bean .................... LOTUS
" bull ............... APIS, ZEBU
" cantata ................ MOTET
" casket ............. CIST, PYX
" , comb. form ........... HIERO
" disease ........... EPILEPSY
" Egypt. bird ................ IBIS
" extracts ........... CATENA
" fig tree; India ........... PIPAL
" grove; Gr. ............... ALTIS
" image .... PIETA, ICON, IKON

230

" instrument, Mormon .... URIM
" interdiction ............ TABU
" langauge of Buddhist literature;
PALI
" music ................. MOTET
" , not ................ PROFANE
" scriptures ............ KORAN
" things, traffic in ..... SIMONY
" wine vessel ............. AMA
" word ................... OM
sacrifice ... HOLOCAUST, OBLATION,
LOSS, ATONEMENT, LIBATION
sacrifice of a thosand; Gr. CHILICOMB
sacrificial fire .................... IGNI
sacristy, rel. to a ......... VESTRAL
sad ..... BAD, DIRE, SORRY, WAN
saddle bag; Span. .......... ALFORJA
saddle blanket ..... CORONA, TILPAH
" boot ............... GAMBADO
" bow ....... ARSON, POMMEL
" cloth ..... PANEL, SHABRACK
" corn crusher .......... QUERN
" girth ................. CINCH
" horses . REMUDA, PALFREYS
" , light ...... PILCH, PILLION
" , pack; Sp. Am. ..... APAREJO
" pad ................... PANEL
" , place behind ........ CROUP
" pommel ...... CRUTCH, TORE
" , rear part of ........ CANTLE
" strap ........ GIRTH, LATIGO
saddler .......... COZIER, LORIMER
saddletree cover ............ MOCHILA
sadness PATHOS, DOLENTE, DOLOR
safari; Afr. ................. JOURNEY
safe .. VAULT, CUPBOARD, SECURE
safeblower ............... PETERMAN
safe conduct CONVOY, COWLE, PASS
safekeeping ................ CUSTODY
safety lamp, miner's ........... DAVY
saffron ................... YELLOW
saffron plant ............... CROCUS
sag .... BEND, SINK, WILT, DROOP
sag, in a timber .................. SNY
saga .......... EPIC, TALE, LEGEND
saga; Norse myth. ............. EDDA
sagacious SAPIENT, WITTY, ARGUTE
sagacity .. ACUMEN, KEN, WISDOM
sage ........ SALVIA, WISE, SOLON
sage hen ..................... GROUSE
"Sage of Emporia" .......... WHITE
sage of Pylus ................ NESTOR
sagebrush State ............. NEVADA
sagitta ......... ARRAW, KEYSTONE
saguaro ..................... CACTUS
saiga, Siberian .... AHU, ANTELOPE
sailboat ....... MORO, SAPIT, SKIFF,
YACHT
sail, center of .................... BUNT
sail, corner of a ................ CLEW
sail, edge of a square ........ LEECH
sail, furl a ............. REEF, MAINE
sail, kind of ......... JIB, SPANKER
sail line ........................ EARING
sail, slack part of ............... SLAB
sail, tie a ..................... TRICE
sail, triangular ............. LATEEN
sailboard used to tack ........ RATCH
sailing race term ................. LEG

sailing raft of light logs ...... BALSA
sailing vessel ... BUCKEYE, BUGEYE,
SETEE
sailing vessel of the levant ..... SAIC
sailor . MARINER, MIDDY, SHIPMAN,
TOTY
sailor, cable ................... TIERER
sailor; col. GOB, JACKY, SALT, TAR
sailor; E. Ind. ............... LASCAR
sailor, female ................. WAVE
sailor song ................ CHANTEY
sailor's amusement .... SCRIMSHAW
sailor's baked dish ........... SCOUSE
sailor's choice ..... GRUNT, PINFISH
sailor's furlough ............. LEAVE
sailors' meeting ................. GAM
sailors' mess tub ................. KID
sailors, patron saint of ........ ELMO
sailor's call .................... AHOY
sailor's potion .................. GROG
sailor's quarters ............. FOCSLE
sailor's under .................. ALOW
sailor's wages ............. PORTAGE
sails furled and helm lashed . AHULL
sails laid back .................. ABOX
sails, storm .............. TRYSAILS
saint ..... CANONIZE, HOLY, ANGEL
" , abbreviated ............... STE
saint, inferior worship of a ... DULIA
" , memorial of a .......... RELIC
" , painted .................. ICON
" , patron, of cripples ..... GILES
" , per. to a ... FERETORY, APSE
" , Roman ......... AGNUS, NERI
Saint Andrew's Cross ........ SALTIRE
St. Catherine's home .......... SIENA
Saint Elmo's fire ........ CORPOSANT
Saint John's bread CAROB, ALGAROBA
Saint-Louis is its capital .. SENEGAL
Saint Paul's birthplace ...... TARSUS
Saint Philip; Ital. .............. NERI
Saint-Saens; opera by ........ DALILA
Saint Vitus's dance ......... CHOREA
saints, biographies of HAGIOGRAPHY
saints, catologue of ........ DIPTYCH
saint's tomb ................. SHRINE
sake ... BEHALF, BENEFIT, SCORE
Sakhalin Gulf river .......... AMUR
salaam ... BOW, BEND, CONGE, NOD
salable ...... VENDIBLE, SUITABLE
salad, corn .................... MACHES
salad vegetable ............. ENDIVE
salamander ... OLM, EFT, NEWT,
URODELA, BRASIER, POKER
salamander; Mex. ......... AXOLOTL
salamander, small ....... MORON, BAT
salami ........... SAUSAGE, RAGOUT
salary ............. STIPEND, WAGE
sale ....... AUCTION, DEAL, VEND,
HANDSEL, BARTER
salicylic acid, deriv. ......... ASPIRIN
saliferous ..................... SALINE
Salii, one of the ............. SALIAN
salin ........................... POTASH
saline solution ................. BRINE
saline substances, knowledge of ....
HALOLOGY
saliva PTYALISM, RHEUM, SPITTLE
salivary gland ............ RACEMOSE

231

salivary gland, per. to ..... PAROTID
salix .......... ITEA, OSIER, WILLOW
sallet ........................ HELMUT
sallow ......... PASTY, ADUST, GRAY
sally .. ISSUE, JEST, LEAP, SORTIE,
     START, ESCAPADE
salmagundi ..... HASH, POTPOURRI,
      MEDLEY, OLIO
salmoid fish GWINAID, CHAR, TROUT,
      NELMA, WHITE
salmon, adult ..... NERKA, GILLING
"   , dog .......... CHUM, KETA
"   , female .... BAGGIT, RAUN
"   herring ............ MILKFISH
"   , kind of .... DOG, QUINNAT
"   , landlocked .. QUANANICHE
"   , male .. GIB, KIPPER, COCK
"   net ...................... YARE
"   of Asia .............. TAIMEN
"   , one year old ...... BLUECAP
"   , per. to .............. GRILSE
"   pool .................... STELL
"   , quinnat ................ TYEE
"   shark ........... PORBEAGLE
"   , silver ................ COHO
"   trout-like; Brit. ...... SEWEN
"   third year ....... MORT, PUG
"   , two year old ...... SMOLT,
      HEPPER
"   , young ... ALEVIN, JERKIN,
   PARR, ESSLING, GRILSE,
   PINK, SAMLET, SPRAG
salmonoid fish ................ POWAN
salon ....... PARTY, HALL, LEVEE
saloon BAR, DRAMSHOP, GROGGERY
salt ...... FLAVOR, HUMOR, SAVOR,
    SENSE, TASTE, WIT
salt, a; col. .............. BRINE, TAR
"   , acid ... THALLATE, FORMATE
"   , alkaline ................ BORAX
"   beds ...................... VATS
"   , chemical ... ESTER, LACTATE,
     OXANILATE
"   crystalline ........... ANALGENE
"   , developer .............. AMIDOL
"   , in chemistry .............. SAL
"   lake ...................... CHOTT
"   marsh ................... SALINA
"   mineral astringent ........ ALUM
"   , rock .................... HALITE
"   , soluble ............... ALKALI
"   spring ...... LICK, SALINE
"   , tartaric acid ........ TARTRATE
"   , tax ..................... GABELL
"   , to .......................... KERN
"   tree ...................... ATLE
salt-like ...................... HALOID
salt-works ...... SALTERY, SALINA
salt-works pond ................ SUMP
salt-wort ........................ KALI
saltant ........ LEAPING, DANCING,
      JUMPING
saltation ......... BEATING, SPRING
salted ........... ALAT, MARINATED
saltish concretion on reeds .. ADARCE
saltpeter ...................... NITER
salts ............... CORNS, SEASONS
salty, efflorescence .............. REH

salutary .. HEALTHY, SALUBRIOUS,
    USEFUL, IMMUNE, TONIC
salutation ... ALOHA, AVE, PROSIT,
      SALAM
salute AVE, CURTSY, HAIL, HALSE,
     GREET, KISS, SALVO
salvage ...... SAVE, TRAY, WAITER
salvage .. RESCUE, SAVE, RECLAIM
salve CURE, BALM, PLASTER, TRETE
salver ....... SAVE, TRAY, WAITER
Samara fruit .................... ELM
Sambal language ................ TINO
sambar deer ................... MAHA
same .. ONE, COGNATE, DITTO, ILK
same place, in the; abb. .......... IBID
same, the; Lat. ................. IDEM
sameness .... ANALOGY, IDENTITY,
    PARITY, MONOTONY
samlet ........................ PARR
Samoa, edible mollusk of .......... ASI
Samoan ................ POLYNESIAN
"   barn owl .............. LULU
"   cloth ........... PARA, TAPA
"   clothes ............. PAREUS
"   council ............... FONO
"   food fish ............. SESELE
"   island ............... MANUA
"   mountain ............. VAEA
"   seaport ............... APIA
"   warrior ................. TOA
samovar ............ TEAPOT, URN
sample .... PATERN, SWATCH, SLIP
Samson's city ................. ZORAH
Samson's father ............. MANOAH
Samuel's father ........... ELKANAH
Samuel's mother ........... HANNAH
Samuel's teacher ................ ELI
Sancho Panza, wife of ...... TERESA
San' a is its capital .......... YEMEN
San Antonio in 1836 .......... ALMO
San Francisco resort .... TAMALPAIS
Sanatra, Mrs. .................. AVA
sanction ........ AMEN, FIAT, ABET,
     DUENESS
sanctuary . HAVEN, FANE, TEMPLE,
    ARK, HOME, REFUGE
sanctuary; Heb. ............. BAMAH
sanctuary, inner part ... PENETRALIA
sanctum of a temple ......... ADYTUM
sand, application to body ARENATION
"   bank ...... HURST, SHOAL
"   , dry bed of ......... ESKER
"   dune; Eng. .... DENE, MEDANO
"   eel ............. GRIG, LAUNCE
"   flea ................... CHIGOE
"   grouse ...... ATTAGEN, GANGA
"   launce ............... HORNEL
"   mineral ............... ISERINE
"   particles .................. SILT
"   pear; Chinese ............ PYRUS
"   , quick ............. BOG, SYRT
"   ridge ........ ASAR, KAME, OS,
     OSAR(PI.)
"   spurry; genus ............. TISSA
"   stone .. BEREA, ITACOLUMITE,
     MEDINA, SARSEN
"   sucker ..................... DAB
"   sugar .................... NITER

" tableland; S. Afr. ........ KAROO
" verbena; genus ....... ABRONIA
" with gravel ..... DOBBIN, GARD
sandal ........ BUSKIN, SOCK, SHOE
sandals, winged ............. TILARIA
sandal-wood; order BUCIDA, SANTAL
"       "   , (red), coloring matter from
                                SANTALIN
"       "   , rel. to ....... BARWOOD,
                                CAMWOOD
"       "   ; Skr. ........ CHANDANA
sandarac ................... REALGAR
"       resin ................. TEARS
"       , Sanskrit for ...... SINDURA
"       tree ...... ARAR, CALLITRIS
"       wood ..... ALERCE, ALERSE
sandbar .......................... SPIT
sand-box tree capsule ........ REGMA
sandpiper .. STIB, DUNLIN, TATTLER
"       ; Arctic ............... KNOT
"       ; Eur. .........RUFF, TEREK
"       , female of the . REE, REEVE
"       , genus ............. TRINGA
"       , marsh ......... PECTORAL
"       , small ........ SANDERLING
"       , spotted . TILTUP, TEETER,
                                PEETWEET
Sandwich Islands ...........KANAKA,
                                HAWAIIAN
sandworts; genus ......... ARENARIA
sandy .......... DESERT, ARENOSE,
                    SABULOUS, GRITTY
sandy drift ............ DENE, ESKER
sandy region in S. W. France . LANDE
sanga-like ..................... ZEBU
sang-froid ..... INSOUCIANCE, COOL
sangreal, the ..... GRAIL, SANGRAAL
sanguine ..............RED, CRAYON
sanity .... REASON, LUCID, NORMAL
Sanskrit ........................ VEDIC
"       , analogous phenomena in ....
                                SANDHI
"       college ................... TOL
"       deity ................... ADITI
"       dialect .................. PALI
"       epic character ......... SITA
"       god ADITYA, INDRA, KAMA,
                                VAYU
Sanskrit goddess ......... DEVI, UMA
"       , Indian writer of . KALIDASA
"       language of W. India MARATHI
"       metrical unit ........ MATRA
"       poem ........ RAGHUVANSA
"       vernacular; Hindu . PRAKRIT
Santa Maria tree ............. CALABA
sap .. DRAIN, JUICE, LYMPH, MINE,
                    SAPOR, TRENCH
sap; Fr. ........................ SEVE
sapajou ............ MONKEY, GRISON
saphead; slang ... DOLT, SIMPLETON
sapid .... ZESTFUL, SAVORY, TASTY
sapience ............ SENSE, WISDOM
sapiens homo .................. HOMO
sapiutan .................. ANOA, COW
sapor GOUT, GUSTO, RELISH, TASTE
saporilla, the ...... CHICO, NISPERO,
                                ZAPOTE

Sappho's home ................LESBUS
sappy ... JUICY, SUCCULENT, LUSH
sapwood .......... BLEA, ALBURNUM
Saracen corn .......... BUCKWHEAT
Saracen leader .............. SALADIN
Saracen's comfrey ......... RAGWORT
Saraceny ................. PAGANDOM
Sarah's handmaid ........... HAGAR
sarcastic .. MORDACIOUS, IRONICAL
sarcophagus, roof over .... TEGURIUM
sardine; W. Ind. ................ BANG
Sardinian seaport .............. BOSA
Sardinian structure ..........NURAGHI
sardonic .... MOROSE, CYNICAL, DRY
Sardou, drama by ............ FEDORA
sargasso .................. GULFWEED
sarsaparilla beverage ........... MEAD
sartor ........................ TAILOR
sash .. CUMMERBUND, GIRDLE, OBI
sash weight ................... MOUSE
Saskatchewan capital ........ REGINA
sassafras, oil of .............. SAFROL
sassafras tea ................. SALOOP
Satan LUCIFER, TEMPTER, BELIAL,
                                EBLIS
Satan before his fall .......... AZAZEL
Satan, demon of anger .... ASMODEUS
Satan of the bottomless pit ABADDON,
                    ARCHFIEND, APOLLYON
Satan; Scot. ..................... DEIL
satchel, lady's small .... ETUI, CABAS,
                    ETWEE, BAG, SACK
sate ................. GLUT, SURFEIT
sated .......... ASAD, BLASE, FULL
satellite .. LUNA, MOON, COMPANION
satellite of Uranus .......... TITANIA
satiate .. CLOY, GLUT, GORGE, PALL,
                                SATISFY
satiate, to .............. DAWL, QUAT
satin fabric .. ETOILE, RAYON, SILK
satin sparrow .......... FLYCATCHER
satire .. IRONY, WIT, MEDLEY, SKIT
satirical ............ ABUSIVE, CAUSTIC
satirize .... GRIND, LAMPOON, LASH
satisfaction .... AMENDS, COMFORT,
                    TREAT, DUEL, PAYMENT
satisfaction for a killing; Scot. .... CRO
satisfy .. PAY, SAKE, STAKE, ATONE
satrap ..... MIR, PRELATE, SULTAN,
                    RULER, DESPOT
saturate SEETHE, SOG, STEEP, WET
Saturn satellite ................. DIONE
saturnalia ........... ORGY, RIOTOUS
saturnalian friendship tokens .. XENIA
saturnine .... GLUM, MOROSE, DULL
Saturn's moon .......... IAPETUS
Saturn's rings .... MOONLETS, ANSA
Saturn's wife ..................... OPS
satyr BUTTERFLY, DEITY, SILENUS
Sault Ste. Marie ................. SOO
sauce ............. CURRY, FLAVOR,
                                INSOLENCE
"       for meat .... DAUBE, TABASCO
"       , fish .......... ALEC, TREPOLE
"       , garlic ............... GANSEL
"       , syrupy ............... CREME
"       veloute and onion .... SOUBISE
"       , white vegetable .... VELOUTE

233

saucepan .. POSNET, HORN, SKILLET
saucy . MALAPERT, BRASH, COCKY,
PERT, PIET
sauger .......................... PERCH
Saul's father ..................... KISH
Saul's herdsman ................ DOEG
saunter LOITER, LAG, MOG, POTTER,
STREEL, STROLL
saurel ..... XUREL, SCAD, POMPANO
saurian ............ LIZARD, REPTILE
sausage, kind of . SALAMI, BOLOGNA,
SAVELOY
sausage-shaped ......... ALLANTOID,
BOTULIFORM
saute ........................... FRY
sautoir; Fr. .......... CHAIN, RIBBON
Sava tributary ................ DRINA
savage, a ...................... YAHOO
Savage Is. language ............ NIUE
savin ............. CEDAR, JUNIPER
saving .... CHARY, FRUGAL, RESCUE
savoir-faire .................... TACT
savor ................. SMACK, ODOR
savory ... GUSTABLE, SAPID, TASTY
saw ......... REDE, ADAGE, SPOKE,
MAXIM
saw, a cross cut ................ BRIAR
saw of a sawfish .............. SERRA
saw, surgical ................TREPAN
saw-buck .................... TENSPOT
sawdust ................ COOM, SCOBS
saw-fish ...................... RAY
saw-horse ............. BUCK, JACK
saw-mill gate ................. SASH
saw-palmetto ............... SCRUB
saw-whet ...................... OWL
sax; anc. ................. DAGGER
saxhorn ............ ALTHORN, TUBA
saxifrage ..................... SESELI
Saxon .................... SASSENACH
Saxon coin .................... SCEAT
Saxon swineherd ............. GURTH
Saxon (w) king ............. INE, INA
say ............. AVER, CITE, UTTER
saying ...... ADAGE, SAW, DIT, MOT
sayings of a religious teacher .. LOGIA
scab ......... SCHAB, ESCHAR, RAT
scabbard .. PARA, SHEATH, PILCHER
scabies ......................... ITCH
scad ....... OODLE, SAUREL, SKATE
scale ............... CLIMB, RUSTRE
"    , bony .................. SCUTUM
"    , chaff-like .............. PALEA
"    ; comb. form ............. LEPIS
"    , insect; family ....... COCCIDAE
"    , kind of fish ............ GANOID
"    , measuring ............ VERNIER
"    moss; order ........ HEPATICAE
"    , musical ................ GAMUT
scale of colors .......... TINTOMETER
scale-beetle .................... TIGER
scale-like .................. LEPROSE
scales ...................... RAMENTA
scales on the stems of ferns ... CHAFF
scales, pair of .................. LIBRA
scaling ladder .............. SCALOSE
scallop .... CRENA, QUIN, MOLLUSK
scalloped edge, having a .... CRENATE

scalpel . BISTOURY, LANCET, KNIFE
scaly (low) .... BASE, STINGY, MEAN
scamp .. SCALAWAG, SKIMP, SLIGHT
scamper ...... BRATTLE, HIE, SCUD
scandalize . MALIGN, REVILE, VILIFY
scandalmonger; Eng. ............ CLAT
Scandinavian .... NORSEMAN, LAPP,
DANE
"    goblin .................... NIS
"    god of strife ............ LOKI
"    god of thunder ........ THOR
"    heaven; myth. ...... ASGARD
"    heritable land .. ODAL, ODEL
"    language ............. NORSE
"    legend .......... EDDA, SAGA
"    legendary sea monster ........
KRAKEN
"    musician and poet .... SKALD
"    name ............. NELS, OLE
"    narrator .......... SAGAMAN
"    navigator ............... ERIC
"    ter. division ............. AMT
"    weight ................... LOD
scansores; order ........... TOUCANS
scant .. CHARY, MEET, STINT, FEW
scanty ......... MEAGER, SPARING,
NIGGARDLY, LITTLE,
NARROW
scape bearing .............. SCAPOSE
scar .... BLEMISH, ARR, CICATRICE,
SEAM, CLIFF, SHORE
scarcity ..... WANT, PAUCITY, THIN
scare ...... DAUNT, FRIGHT, PANIC,
COW, ALARM
scare-babe ................... OGRESS
scarecrow ... EFFIGY, GUY, MALKIN,
SHAIL, JACKSTRAW
scaremonger ALARMIST, TERRORIST
scarf .... ASCOT, PENDENT, TIPPET
scarf bird ............... CORMORANT
scarf, clerical ......... RABAT, STOLE
scarf, pope's ......... FANON, ORALE
scarf, woman's ... SASH, BOA, NUBIA
scarf, worn by a priest ...... MANIPLE
scarflike head covering ... RIGOLETTE
scarfskin .... CUTICLE, EPIDERMIS
Scarlett's home ................. TARA
scatter ...... DEAL, LITTER, SPRAY,
(BE)STREW, TED, DISPEL,
DISPERSE, BEGONE
scatter; var. .................. SKAIL
scattered SPARSILE, SETA, SPORADIC
scattered, as fleur-de-lis ........ SEME
scattering .................. DIASPORA
scenario ........................ SCRIPT
scenery ..... DIORAMA, VIEW, SHOW
scenic representation ...... NEORAMA
scent ... FLAIR, NIDOR, NOSE, ODOR,
AURA
scent-bag ...... SACHET, PERFUMER
scented ........... OLENT, SMELLING
schedule ....... CARD, LIST, TABLE
scheme PLAN, AIM, CABAL, COMPLOT
schemer ............ ARTIST, FIGARO
schism .... DISSENT, RENT, SPLIT
schismatic ...... HERETIC, SECTARY
schist, argillaceous ............. SLATE
schizocarp ................... REGMA

Schnozzola .................. DURANTE
scholar PEDANT, SABORA, SAVANT
scholarly .. ACADEMIC, PHILOMATH,
               ERUDITE, LEARNED
scholars ...... APOSTLES, LITERATI
scholarship ......BURSE, ERUDITION,
                     LORE
school; Eng. .................... ETON
school; Fr. .................... ECOLE
school group ...................... PTA
schoolmaster .... PEDANT, SNAPPER
school of fishes ................ SHOAL
school of medicine ............ CLINIC,
                   INFIRMARY
school of philosophers; Gr. .. ELEATIC
school, religious .. SECT, PAROCHIAL
school, riding ............... MANEGE
school, secondary .. LYCEE, ACADEMY
schooner .................... PRAIRIE
schottische .................... POLKA
Schumann-Heink ........ ERNESTINE
science .. ART, PROFICIENCY, SKILL
  "    of character ..... ETHOLOGY
  "    of dining ...... ARISTOLOGY
  "    of healing ....... IATROLOGY
  "    of motion ......... KINETICS
  "    of self-defense ......... JUDO
  "    of virtue ......... ARETAICS
  "    of words ......... SEMANTICS
"Science fiction" locale ........ MARS
sciential .......... CAPABLE, ABLE,
                   COMPETENT
scientific management of land .........
                   AGRONOMY
scientist .......... SAVANT, POLEMIC
scilicet .................... VIDELICET
scimitar ........ SWORD, SAX, TURK
scintilla ... BIT, IOTA, TRACE, WHIT
Scio, inhabitant of ............ SCIOTE
scion .... CLAVE, GRAFT, IMP, SLIP,
                   SON
Scipio .................... AFRICANUS
scoff .. RAIL, FLEER, GIBE, DERIDE
scold . RAIL, RANT, BERATE, CHIDE,
               SHREW, REPROVE
sconce .......... HEAD, TOP, TRICK,
               CANDLESTICK
scoop out ...... GOUGE, CHISEL, DIG
scope ...... TETHER, AREA, RANGE,
               LEEWAY, PLAY, AIM
scopoline .................... OSCINE
scorch . SEAR, CHAR, PARCH, SINGE
scorched .................... ADUST
score .. TALLY, CHALK, SAKE, TICK
scoria ...... AA, SLAG, LAVA
scorify .............. SMELT, REDUCE
scorn ........ GECK, SLIGHT, SPURN,
                   MOCK
scorpine .................... HOGFISH
Scorpio, star in ............. ANTARES
scorpion .. LIZARD, SCOURGE, WHIP
scorpion senna, deriv. of ...... INDIGO
scorpion, water; genus .......... NEPA
scorpion's heart ............. ANTARES
Scot ..... CALEDONIAN, GAEL, PICT
scoter .............. COOT, FULICA
Scots; collec. ................ SAWNEY
Scotland, district of ..... COILA, KYLE

Scotland; Gaelic ................. ALBA
Scotland; Fr. .............,. .... ECOSSE
Scotsman .................. BLUECAP
—— Scott Dec. .................... DRED
Scottish, accent .................. BIRR
  "   , addition ........... EIK, EKE
  "   , arrange in ............. ETTLE
  "   , ask in ................. SPERE
  "   , askew in ............. AGEE
  "    attendant ..... GILLIE, GILLY
  "    awl .................... ELSEN
  "   , awn in ............... OWED
  "    bailiff .................. REEVE
  "    bank .................... BRAE
  "    bism .................... GULF
  "    boundary ............... MEAR
  "    brandy ............. ATHOLE
  "    broadsword ...... CLAYMORE
  "    brook .................... SIKE
  "    brownie .................... NIS
  "    cake .................... SCONE
  "    chack .......... BITE, SNACK
  "    chest .................... KIST
  "    child .................... BAIRN
  "    city .................... AYRS
Scottish clothe ................ CLEAD
  "    cold mist ................ DROW
  "    counsel .......... REDE, REED
  "    court officer ............ MACER
  "    cup ........................ TASS
  "    curlew .................. WHAUP
  "    dagger ................ SKEAN
  "    daisy .................. GOWAN
  "    dance .. FLING, STRATHSPEY
  "   , demure in ............... MIM
  "    dirge ............ CORONACH
  "    dog .............. SEALYHAM
  "    earnest money ........ ARLES
  "   , empty, to .............. TOOM
  "    explorer .................. RAE
  "    eye ........................ EE
  "   , faithful ............... LEAL
  "    farmer .............. CROFTER
  "    fireplace ............... INGLE
  "    for nit; var. ............. NEET
  "    for unit .................. ANE
  "    game .................. SHINTY
  "    glashan ............ CODFISH
  "    godmother CUMMER, KIMMER
  "    goldsmith ................ GED
  "    haul of fish ............. DRAVE
  "    heir .................... TEIND
  "    Highlander ............. GAEL
  "    hillside .................. BRAE
  "    historian ...... HUME, SKENE
  "   , ill-humored ......... CROUSE
  "   , keen in ............... SNELL
  "    kilt .................. FILIBEG
  "    kindred .................... SIB
  "   , lake in . LIN, LOCH, LOUGH
  "    landholder ... LAIRD, THANE
  "    land-tax ................. CESS
  "    list of candidates ....... LEET
  "    low rich river land .... CARSE
  "    lowlander ........ SASSENACH
  "    magistrate ............ BAILIE
  "    marauder .......... CATERAN

" martial music of the bagpipe ... PIBROCH
" , mate in ................ FERE
" mathe ........ GRUB, MAGGOT
" measure ................ CRAN
" , mismanage in ........ BLUNK
" mud rake ............. CLAUT
" , muddled .............. REE
" negative ......... DINNA, NAE
" , nephew in .......... NEPOTE
" , nimble in ............. GLEG
" ox ...................... NOWT
" oxter .......... ARM, ARMPIT
" pay for a killing ......... CRO
" peasant .............. COTTAR
" plaid ................. TARTAN
" plan ................... ETTLE
" poet .... EDINA, MOIR, HOGG
" pole .................... CABER
" porridge .............. BROSE
" pouch .............. SPORRAN
" prefix to names .......... MAC
" pudding .............. HAGGIS
" race ...................... ILK
" river . TEVIOT, AFTON, AYR, DEE, TAY
" rivulet .............. RINDLE
" robbery ................. REIF
" rope ................. WANTY
Scottish rosin ................... ROZET
" scythe handle ......... SNEAD
" self ...................... SEL
" servant ....... GILLY, THANE
" shawl ................. MAUD
" , shivering in .. OORIE, OURIE
" soldier ............ CATERAN
" tartan pattern .... SET, SETT
" , taste in ............... PREE
" tenant ............... CROFT
" tern .................. TARRET
" to; var. .................... TAE
" , toil in ............... DARG
" town ................ BURGH
" tribal payment ............. CRO
" tuyere ................. TEW
" uncle, per. to ............. EME
" , undergo in ............ DREE
" , unroof ............... TIRR
" vigor ................... VIR
" water sprite .......... KELPIE
" weighing machine ...... TRONE
" weight ........ TRONE, DROP
" whimbrel ............. WHAUP
" , whine in ............. YIRN
" , world in ............. WARL
scoundrel ..... CAD, KNAVE, ROGUE, VARLET
scour ...... BURNISH, POLISH, ROVE, SAND
scourge ...... BANE, FLOG, SWINGE, LASH
"Scourge of God" ............. ATTILA
scout .......... FLOUT, SPURN, SPY, FELLOW
scow; Fr. ...................... ACON
scowl .... LOWER, ASPECT, FROWN
scram ...... DECAMP, GET, VAMOSE
scramble .. CLIMBING, MUSS, STRIVE

scrap MORSEL, JUNKRAG, END, ORT, TINT, MELEE, BIT
scrape ....... ABRADE, GIRDE, RUB
scrape the ground in golf .... SCLAFF
scraped linen .................... LINT
scrapings ........ RAMENTA, SOUND
scratch . GRATE, MAR, RIT, SCARIFY
scratch ground for food .... RASORIAL
scrawl, a ...... POTHOOK, SCRIBBLE
screech ........... SCREAK, SHRIEK
screed ........... DIATRIBE, TIRADE
screen ...... BLIND, CLOAK, GRILLE, PAVIS, RIDDLE, SIEVE
" , canvas ........... PAVESADE
" , chancel ..... JUBE, REREDOS
" , ecclesiastical ...... PARCLOSE
" , hall .................... SPIER
" mesh .................... LAUN
" , to ................. HIDE, SIFT
screw pine ...................... ARA
scribble .... SCRAWL, CARD, MARKS
scribe ... SCRIVENER, AMANUENSIS
scrimmage .... FIGHT, ROW, TUSSLE
scrip ...................... BAG, CRIP
script, angular ................ RONDE
scriptural interpreter ...... EXEGETE
scripture ........ TEXT, WRIT, BIBLE
scripture, version of ITALA, VULGATE
scrive ....... SCRIBE, WRITE, SCORE
scrivello ....................... TUSK
scrobiculate .... PITTED, FURROWED
scroll ........ LIST, ROLL, VOLUTE
scromboid fish ................... CERO
scrotum .......... COD, VARICOCELE
scrouge; dial. ..... CROWD, SQUEEZE
scrounge; sl. ................. PILFER
scruff .................. NAPE, SCUFF
scruple (½) .................... OBOLE
scrutinize AUDIT, PROBE, EYE, PRY, SCAN, SIFT, EXAMINE
scryer .............................. SEER
scuffle .. TUSSLE, HOE, FIGHT, FRAY
scull .......... PADDLE, SPOON, OAR
scullion SERVANT, WRETCH, MENIAL
sculptor ........... IMAGER, PHIDIAS, ANGELO
sculptor's chisel ......... EBAUCHOIR
sculptor's tool ............... GRAVER
sculpture in high relief ALTORELIEVO
scup .................. BREAM, FISH
scupper; Brit. sl. .......... MASSACRE
scurry .... HIE, SKELTER, SCUTTLE
scurvy .... SCROBUTUS, LOW, MEAN
scutage ............... ESCUAGE
scuttle .... HOD, SINK, BUSTLE, RUN
scuttlebut ...................... RUMOR
scythe, handle of a ... SNATH, SNEAD
scythe, sweep of a ............ SWATH
Scythian lamb ............ BAROMETZ
sea ............ MAIN, LAKE, OCEAN
" anemone . MAIN, ACTINIA, POLYP
" animal .............. ROSMARINE
" , arm of the SINUS, FIORD, FRITH
" bird ... ERN, CAHOW, KESTREL, ERNE, PUFFIN
" birds; genus ................. SULA
" cow ........ DUGONG, MANATEE
" cow, the Steller's ......... RYTINA

" deity, daughter of a DEINO, ENYO
" demigod ................... TRITON
" dog .................... GOB, TAR
" duck .......... SCOTER, COOT
" Dyak ........................ IBAN
" ear ..................... ABALONE
" , fond of the THALASSOPHILOUS
" ; French for ................. MER
" god; Gaelic ............... LIR, LER
" holly root ................ ERYNGO
" inlet ............. FIORD, FJORD
" lemon ...................... DORIS
" mile ................ KNOT, NAUT
" monster ........ CETE, KRAAKEN
" needle ................... GARFISH
" nettle ....... MEDUSA, ACALEPH
" nymph ..... GALATHEA, NEREID
" nymph who loved Apollo .. CLYTIE
" , per. to the PELAGIC, THALASSIC
" , rise and fall, as the ...... LOOM
" salt producer .......... HALOGEN
" slug .................... TREPANG
" spray ................... SPNDRIFT
" swimming organisms; per. to ......
                              NEKTERIC
" unicorn ................. NARWHAL
" urchin, fossil . ECHINI, ECHINITE
" worm ......................... SAO
sea-green color ............ CELADON
seal .......... OTARY, PINNIGRADE
" bearded ................... URSUK
" fur ....................... URSAL
" jewel ................. BRELOQUE
" , male harp ............. SADDLER
" of a letter ............... CACHET
" on a papal letter ......... BULLA
" signet ......... SIGILLATE, SIGIL
" , young ............ HOPPER, PUP
sealing wax part ................. LAC
seals, flock or herd of ............ POD
seals; genus ......... OTARIA, PHOCA
seals; per. to ............. PHOCINE
seam, lateral .................. RAPHE
seam, per. to ..... SUTURAL, JOINING
seamaid .. SIREN, MERMAID, NYMPH
seaman ... JACKY, NAUTILUS, SALT,
                                 TAR
seamen's chapel .. BETHEL, CHURCH
seamew ........................ GULL
sea-onion .................... SQUILL
seaport; Brazil ...... BELEM, NATAL
sear ..... DEAD, DRY, SERE, BRAISE
search for game; Ang-Ind. .... GHOOM
search minutely COMB, RAKE, SPERE
search out, to ............ EXPISCATE,
                         FERRET, HUNT
searing .......... CAUTER, BURNING
seashore; per. to ........... LITTORAL
seasickness .............. NAUPATHIA
season .......... SPICE, TIME, BEEK,
                         INURE, DEVIL
season; Scot. .................... SELE
seasoning .... GARLIC, FORCE, SALT,
               THYME, CONDIMENT, SPICE
seasons ....... AESTAS, HYEMS, VER
seasons, the ................... HORAE
seat ........ MASTABA, SELLA, SITE,
                             PEWAGE

" cloth ......... DORSAL, DOSSEL
" , coach .................... DICKY
" in a chancel ............... SEDILE
" of honor ................. CURULE
" of justice ................. BANC
" of Ohio N. University ......... ADA
seats, tier of ................... GRADIN
seawan (sewan) ............ WAMPUM
seawater ....................... BRINE
seaweed . WRACK, AGAR, ORE, ALGA,
                     KELP, CARRAGEEN
" , edible ...... DULSE, LAVER
" ; genus .... NOSTIC, ALARIA
" , Japanese .............. NORI
" , leaf of ............. FROND
" , product of .. AGAR, GELOSE
" , variety of ........ OREWEED
seaweeds ................. CONFERVAE
" , calcined ashes of ..... KELP,
                               VAREC
" , deriv. of .......... BARILLA
" , per. to ............ ALGOUS
" , substance found on .. ALGIN
" , tough leathery ...... FUCUS
seaworm, eunicoid ........ SAO, LURG
Seb's children include .... ISIS, OSIRIS
Seb's consort ..................... NUT
sec, opposed to ................. BRUT
secesch ... REB, REBEL, WITHDRAW
secluded .... ISOLATED, CLOISTRAL,
                     COVERT, LONELY
seclusion ... MONASTICAL, PRIVACY,
                   RETIRACY, SOLITUDE
second ............ JIFFY, ASSISTANT
second lieutenants; slang SHAVETAILS
second preparation .............. HASH
second, to ... BACK, SUPPORT, ABET
secondary ........ DERIVATIVE, BYE
secrecy, bind to ................. TILE
secret ...... COVERT, MYSTIC, DERN,
        ESOTERIC, CRYPTIC, RETIRED,
                                  KEY
secret council of state ......... JUNTO
secret, keep ................. ENSEAL
secret place .... ADYTUM, SANCTUM
secret society of Naples .... CAMORRA
secretly ........ SUBROSA, SLY, INLY
secrets ............. ARCANA, BYENDS
sectarian ........ DENOMINATIONAL,
                 HERETIC, HETERODOX
section ....... PART, SEGMENT, FEN,
                        PANEL, AREA
section of 3 folio sheets ..... TERNION
sector .................... ARC, AREA
secular ........ LAIC, LAY, PERIODIC
secund ................ UNILATERAL
secure ........ GET, MOOR, TRICE
security ...... BOND, GAGG, PLEDGE,
             VADIUM, SHELTER, SAFETY
Sec'y of Army ................. PACE
Sec'y of Defense .............. WILSON
Sec'y of State ................. DULLES
sedate ........ QUIET, STAID, STILL,
                                 CALM
sedate; Scot. ................... DOUCE
sedative ........ BROMIDE, NERVINE,
                       ANODYNE, ALDOL
sedge; Chinese ................. MATI

sedge; genus .................... CAREX
sedgelike; genus ................ XYRIS
sedges ..................... CARICES
sediment .. MAGMA, GREAVES, LEES,
SILT, DREGS
seditious FACTIOUS, TREASONABLE,
RIOTOUS
seducer ........ ENTICER, LOTHARIO
see .............. ESPY, VIDE, VIEW,
DISCERN, KNOW, LOOK
see, holy .................... DIOCESE
seed ................. ANISE, SOW, PIT
"  , apple ......................... PIP
"  bearing organ in flower ... PISTIL
"  coating ...... POP, ARIL, TESTA
"  fluid ...................... LATEX
"  , food ............. PEA, LENTIL
"  germ ......... BEGINNING, CHIT
"  , immature ................ OVULE
"  , medicinal .......... FLAXSEED
"  , naked .................. ACHENE
"  of a tropical tree ............ BEN
"  of canary grass .......... ALPIST
"  , one celled .............. CARPEL
"  plant, bitter .............. CUMIN
"  plant, cooking ........ CARAWAY
"  pod, gaping .. DEHISCENCE, KID
"  , primitive ................. SPORE
"  scars ....................... HILA
"  , two valved ....... LEGUME
"  vessel ....... BUR, POD, SILICLE
"  weevil; genus ............. APION
seedcake ........................ WIG
seed-coat, broken .............. BRAN
seedy ...... SHABBY, DINGY, TACKY
seeing ............... SIGHT, ESPIAL
seek ............. EXPLORE, SEARCH
seek after ...... TRY, ENSUE, ASPIRE
seeking ........... SOC, ZETETIC
seeming GUISE, LOOK, QUASI, SHOW
seemly ........ PROPER, COME, MEET
seep ............. PERCOLATE, OOZE
seeress ...... PHOEBAD, SAGA, SIBYL
see-saw ........... CROSSRUFF, TILT
seesaw-like .. BASCULE, BEAT, WAG
seethe ........ BOIL, BULLER, STEW,
COOK, SOB
seething ...... ABOIL, EXCITEMENT
segment .......... TELSON, CANTLE
segment; biol. . LACINIA, METAMERE
segment of an animal ..... SOMATOME
segment shaped ................ TORIC
seine .......... FARE, NET, SAGENE
Seine trib. ................. EURE, OISE
seism ................ EARTHQUAKE
seismic, vertical .......... EPICENTRE
seize CLUTCH, USURP, REAVE, NAB,
YOKE, PREY
seize for debt ........... CONFISCATE
DISTRAIN, EMBARGO
Selassie ....................... HAILE
select .................. CULL, ELITE,
CHOOSE, GOOD, TAKE
selenium, symbol for ............... SE
self ..................... EGO, PERSON
"  , comb. form .......... AUTO, AUT
"  defense ................ JUJUTSU
"  deification ......... AUTOTHEISM

"  denial .............. ASCETICISM
"  derived existence ......... ASEITY
"  fear .................. AUTOPHOBY
"  knowledge ........... AUTOLOGY
"  murderer ............ FELODESE
"  , own ...................... NAIN
self-assertion ...... EGOISM, VANITY
self-centered ... EGOCENTRIC, SMUG
self-confidence ............ APLOMB
self-contradict ........... PARADOX
selfhood, give ............... EGOIZE
self-worship ............. IDOLATRY
sell VEND, BARTER, CANT, MARKET
sell over official rate ........... SCALP
sell; slang ............. CHEAT, TRICK
selvage of cloth .................. LIST
selvedge ................... LISTING
semantic puzzle ......... CROSSWORD
semester ......... BIANNUAL, TERM
semi-circular tart ........ TURNOVER
semi-legendary Greek bard ...... OLEN
Semile's sister .................... INO
Seminole Indian chief ..... OSCEOLA
Semiramis, husband of ........ NINUS
Semite ........ HEBREW, ARAB, JEW
Semitic language ..... GEEZ, HARARI
Semitic (non) people .............. GOG
Semitic weight; anc. ... GERAH, MINA
semolina ........................ SUJI
semper parata ................... SPAR
Senate oratory ............. DEBATE
senatorship ..... TOGA, CHAIR, SEAT
senescent ................. AGED, OLD
senility ........ CADUCITY, DOTAGE,
DECREPIT
senior; Fr. ....................... AINE
seniority ........ ELDER, AGE, DEAN
senoritas' nickname ............. LOLA
sensational ................... LURID
sense .... FLAIR, SAPIENCE, SONCE,
VIEW, INTUIT, SIGHT, SMELL
sense organ ................ SENSILLA
senseless .......... FATUOUS, INEPT,
STUPID
sensitivity, blunted ......HEBETATED
sentence ..... FUTWA, POSY, ADAGE
"  balance .......... PARISON
"  concluding .... EPILOG(UE)
"  construction ....... SYNTAX
"  , latter clause in a APODOSIS
sententious ............ PITHY, TERSE
sentiment ............ MAXIM, TOAST,
OPINION
sentiment, strong .... EMOTION, IRES
sentimental song ..... STREPHONADE
sentinel .... BIDET, GUARD, PICKET,
VIDETTE, SENTRY
sentinel, per. to a ......... PERDUE
sentry ...... KITE, WATCH, SOLDIER
sepal .................. LEAF, PETAL
separate DISCRETE, ISOLATE, REND,
SIDE, PART, SORT
separated ....... FREE, ROULETTED,
SHREDDED, ALONE
separatist ........ PILGRIM, HERETIC
sepia ..................... DUN, INK
sepiolite ............. MEERSCHAUM
sept in Ireland .................. CLAN

septa in corals .............. TABULA
septic poisoning, form of ... PYAEMIA
septuple ................. SEVENFOLD
sepulchral ....... URNAL, CHARNEL
sepulchral chest ............. CIST
sepulchral vault ......... CATACOMB
sepulchre mounds ........... TUMULI
sequence ........ SERIES, STRAIGHT
sequester .................. SOLATE
sequin .............. DISK, SPANGLE
seraglio ............. HAREM, SERAI
sequoia ........... REDWOOD, TREE
serai ................ CARAVANSARY
seraph ............ ANGEL, CHERUB
Serb .............................. SLAV
sere .. SLAW, DRIED, WORN, WRAP,
WAX, WITHERED
serement ........OATH, SACRAMENT
serenade . CALLITHUMP, NOCTURNE,
CHARIVARI
serf .... ESNE, ETA, PEON, THRALL
serf, female .................... NEIF
serf; feudal law ............. VILLEIN
serf, in anc. Sparta ........... HELOT
serf, per. to a .................. BOND
Serian .......................... SERIC
seric ......................... SILKEN
series ......... SET, SEQUENCE
series, graded .................. NEST
series of discussions ..... SYMPOSIUM
series of events ................. EPOS
series of piles ................. DRIFT
series of steps ................ SCALE
series of six ................... HEXAD
serious ...... GRAVE, STAID, SOBER
sermon ........ DISCOURSE, HOMILY
serotine .................... BAT, LATE
serow ........... ANTELOPE, GORAL
serpent ....... ASP, NAGA, BASILISK,
SNAKE
"    , air ............... GREMLIN
"    , Amer. . ABOMA, BOM, BOMA
"    , black ................. RACER
"    , common ............. ADDER
"    , hooded, of India ..... COBRA
"    lizard .................... SEPS
"    of Borneo .............. BOIGA
"    of India ............... KRAIT
"    , Vedic Sky .............. AHI
serpentine SINUOUS, ZIGZAG, SUBTLE
serpent-like ................ ANGUINE
serpigo ........ TETTER, RINGWORM
serrano ........... SQUIRRELFISH
servant BATA, BILDAR, CHELA, GYP
servant, an inferior ........ COISTRIL
servant, liveried ............ FLUNKY
servant of a nobleman ..... EQUERRY
serve ... BESTEAD, DEAL, DO, WAIT
served as escort ............. SQUIRE
service ... RITUAL, AHA, RITE, USE,
WAGE
service for the dead ... DIRGE, SONG,
TUNE
services in R. C. Church .. TENEBRAE
servile ..... SYCOPHANTIC, ABJECT,
BASE
servile agent ................. MINION
servite ................. MENDICANT
sesame grass .................. GAMA

sesame plant ...... TULEMA, BENNE,
TEEL, TIL
sesame seed ................. GINGILI
session SEANCE, COUNCIL, VESTRY
set ........... LAY, PLAT, POST, PIT
set apart ..................... TABOO
set at naught ............. OVERRIDE
set firmly ............. POSIT, PLANT
set in order .............. FILE, POST
set of opinions adhered to ...... CREDO
set of rules ...................... CODE
set on fire .. TIND, KINDLE, ABLAZE
set thickly ...................... STUD
set up ............. RIG, CIRCLE, PUT
seta ...... BRISTLE, HAIRS, SPINES
Seth, father of ................. ADAM
Seth's son ..................... ENOS
Seton .......... ERNEST THOMPSON
setting ................... SCENE, TRAP
settle ... DECIDE, SEAT, NEST, FIX,
SINK
settlings .. FOOTS, LEES, SEDIMENT
set-to ... BOUT, CONTEST, COMBAT,
FIGHT
sets of three hours ........ RANDEMS
Sevareid, Mr. ................... ERIC
seven ....... HEBDOMAD, HEPTADE
"Seven against Thebes," one of the....
TYDEUS
seven, comb. form .............. HEPTA
seven-face solid ..... HEPTAHEDRON
seven gods of happiness ........ EBISU
seven languages ........ HEPTAGLOT
"Seven Year Itch" star ......EWELL
sevenfold ................. SEPTUPLE
severe ..... ACUTE, DRASTIC, DURE
severe critic ................. SLATER
severe critic; Gr. ........ ARISTARCH
sew ....... BASTE, PREEN, SUTURE
sew with gathers ................FULL
sewing machine inventor ...... HOWE,
LESTER
sexagesimal ........ LOGISTIC, SIXTY
sexes, common to both ...... EPICENE
sexivalent, per. to .......... VALENCE
sexton . JANITOR, BEETLE, SACRIST
sextuor; mus. ................. SEXTET
Sforza; Ital. ..................... CARL
shab ...................... SCAB, ITCH
shabby .... SCOURY, SEEDY, TACKY,
RATTY
shack .... COE, TRAMP, CABIN, HUT
shackle . GYVE, TRAMMEL, FETTER
shackler ..................... SLOTTER
shad ........... ALEWIFE, ANTONIO
shad; Eng. ........... ALLICE, ALLIS
shad; Eur. ..................... ALOSE
shaddock ..................... POMELO
shade ...... TINGE, VISOR, NUANCE,
SWAIL, TONE, BLIND, COLOR,
TINT
shade, false ...... GHOST, PHANTOM
shades of the departed ....... MANES,
SPIRIT
shadow DOG, SCUG, SHEPHERD, TAIL
shadow, dark cone of a ....... UMBRA
shadow forth .......... ADUMBRATE
shadow, man without ......... ASCIAN

239

shadow, throwing it opposite ways ..... ANTISCION
shadows, fight with ..... SCIAMACHY
shadows, projecting of .. SCIAGRAPHY
shady .. ADUMBRAL, ELMY, HIDDEN
SHAEF theatre .................. ETO
shaft ..... ARROW, GROOVE, VERGE
shaft; convex swelling of .... ENTASIS
"  handle .................. HELVE
"  , Hindoo ................. LAT
"  of a cart ................ THILL
"  of a column FUST, SCAPE, TIGE
"  of a feather ............. SCAPE
"  of a plant ................ AXIS
"  , steeple ............... SPIRE
shaggy ... HIRSUTE, BUSHY, NAPPY
shake .......... AGITATE, JAR, JOLT
shake off ............... DOFF, SHED
Shakers, founder of ............. LEE
shale .. BAT, SHUCK, FISSILE, ROCK
shall ........... CAN, MUN, MUST, SE
shallot ........... ONION, SCALLION,
ESCHALOT, PLANT
shallow channel ............. LAGUNE
sham .. APE, DUMMY, FAKE, FEIGN
Shamash attendant .......... BUNENE
shamble ........... SHUFFLE, WALK
shameful .. GROSS, VILE, INDECENT
shampoo . MASSAGE, TRIPSIS, WASH
Shan .............................. TAI
shanghai .................. DRUG, SHIP
shank ................... CRUS, GAMB
shank, green legged ............ KNOT
shank, per. to the ............ CRURAL
shank, yellow .............. TATTLER
shanny ....................... BLENNY
shantung ..................... TUSSAH
shanty . HOVEL, HUT, SHACK, SHED
shape ......... MOULD, CUT, MODEL,
DESIGN, FORM, PLAN, GUISE
shapeless ...... AMORPHOUS, CRUDE
shaping core ..................... AME
shaping machine .............. EDGER
shard .. FRAGMENT, SCALE, SHELL
share .... DOLE, LOT, PART, QUOTA
share rent ..... METAYER, METAYGE
shark-eating fish ............... PEGA
shark, nurse .................... GATA
shark, small ........... LAMIA, TOPE
shark, Pacific ......... RHINA, MAKO
sharks adherent ............. RAMORA
sharks; genus .... GALEUS, SELACHII
sharp; Scot. .................. SNELLY
"  , comb. form ... ACET, ACETO
"  , disagreeably ........... EDGY
"  fragments of bone .. SPICULAE
"  sighted ............. LYNCEAN
"  ; Span. ................. AGUDO
"  to the taste ... ACERB, ACRID
sharpen CACUMINATE, KEEN, HONE
sharpened slightly ......... ACUTATE
sharpening of note ........... ECBOLE
sharper ....... CUTER, GYP, CHEAT,
KNAVE
sharp-set .............. EAGER, KEEN
sharpshooter .................. SNIPER
sharter .................... SHREND
shatter ...... DASH, SMASH, SPAND
shave ... CUT, CHEAT, PARE, STRIP

shaveling .... FRIAR, MONK, PRIEST
shavetail ............. ENSIGN, MULE,
LIEUTENANT
Shaw; author ....................IRWIN
shawl; Mex. ........ MANTA, SERAPE
Shawn; dancer ................... TED
sheaf ......... HYPERPENCIL, KERN
sheaf of the wave offering ...... OMER
shear .............. CLIP, NIP, TRIM
shears, cloth .................... LEWIS
sheat-fish .................... WELS
sheath ...... SLEEVE, CASE, OCREA,
THECA, SCABBARD
sheathe .. INCASE, COVER, PLUNGE
Sheba ......................... SABA
shebang; sl. .. SHOP, AFFAIR, THING
Shechem's father ............. HAMOR
shed ..... CAST, COTE, DOFF, MOLT
shed, shelter dugout ............. ABRI
sheen ... GLOSS, LUSTRE, SLENDOR
sheep, brand ......... RUDDLE, SMIT
"  , cry of ........... BAA, BLAT
"  disease .... ANTHRAX, BANE,
BLAST, BRAXY, COE, CORE,
GID, RESP, ROT, SCRAPIE
"  , female ....... EWE, SHEDER
"  fleece ..................... KET
"  fly .......................... FAG
"  ; genus ............. BOS, OVIS
"  , hardy kind of ..... KARAKUL
"  head ..................... JIMMY
"  keeper .................... ABEL
"  laurel ................. KALMIA
"  , kind of ............. MERINO
"  , leader of a flock of .............
BELLWETHER
"  leather ................... ROAN
"  , leg hair of ............. GARE
"  liniment .................... EIK
"  , male .. BUCK, HEDER, RAM,
TUP, WETHER
"  mange ................... SCAB
"  mountain ................. IBEX
"  nahoor .................... SNA
"  of Eng. .. CHEVIOT, DISHLEY
"  of Tibet SHA, SHABO, OORIAL,
URIAL
sheep pen ...................... FANK
"  , per. to ................. ARIES
"  , pet .................. COSSET
"  pox ........ OVINA, WILDFIRE
"  silver .................... MICA
"  skin for tanning BASAN, BASIL,
DONGOLA
"  , species of wild ..... BHARAL,
MOUFFLON
"  , theft of ........... ABIGEAT
"  tic . KEB, KED, MELOPHAGUS
"  , two-year old ...... HOB, TEG
"  , W. Afr. ................. ZENU
"  , wild AOUDAD, ARGAL, URIAL
"  , wool producing ..... MERINO
"  , yearling ...... HOGGET, TAG
"  , young ............. EANLING
sheepfold . COTE, KRAAL, OVIL, PEN,
REEVE, REE
sheephead; W. Ind. .......... SALEMA
sheep-like ...................... OVINE
sheep's-bit ...................... HERB

sheep's eye ..................... LEER
sheep's jacket ................... BRAT
sheep-skin ....... PELT, WOOLFELL,
DIPLOMA
sheer BRANT, PURE, THIN, ABRUPT
sheet, twelve folded ..... DUODECIMO
sheeting ..................... PERCALE
shekel, 1/20th of a ............ GERAH
shelf .. LEDGE, BINK, REEF, SHOAL
shelf, embankment ............. BERM
shell .. CARAPACE, COWRY, SHARD
"    , cast off ........ EXUVIAE (Pl.)
"    cone ................... ADMIRAL
"    , covered with a ..... LORICATE
"    ear ......... ORMER, ABALONE
"    , explosive ......... BOMB, DUD,
GRENADE
"    fish .. BARNACLE, PIPI, NACRE,
COCKLE
"    gastropod ............... CHANK
"    groove ..................... LIRA
"    , marine ................. CONCH
"    mechanism ............ SPALTER
"    mollusk ................. WHELK
"    money . COLCOL, PEAG, SEWAN
"    ridges ................. VARICES
"    shank ................. SANKHA
"    , spiral ............ CARACOL(E)
"    tribal money; Afr. ..... COWRIE
shell-drake ............. MERGANSER
shelly covering of mollusks .... TESTA
Shelly; drama ................. CENCI
shelter .. COVERT, ENSCONCE, ABRI,
DUGOUT, HAVEN
"     , cattle ................. STELL
"     for the aged ........ ASYLUM
"     , movable roof .... MANTELET
"     ; naut. .. ALEE, LEE(WARD)
"     ; prov. Eng. ..... SCUG, SKUG
shelterer ..................... LAIRER
shelyl, kind of ............ SHRAPNEL
Shem, descend. of ............ SEMITE
Shem's son ....... ELAM, ARAM, LUD
shepherd god ..................... PAN
shepherdess ............. AMARYLLIS
shepherd's club ............ MULLEIN
shepherd's pipe ..... LARIGOT, OAT
shepherd's rod ............... TEASEL
shepherd's staff ....... KENT, CROOK
sherbet .......... DRINK, ICE, IMBIBE
Sheridan play ................. RIVALS
sheriff ............. GRIEVE, JAILER
"Sherlock Holmes," author of .. DOYLE
sherry wine ....... OLOROSO, XERES,
SOLERA
Shetland fishing grounds ....... HAAF
shibboleth .. MODE, HABIT, SLOGAN
shield .... ECU, PAVIS, SCU, SCUTE,
TARGE, AVERT, FORBID
"    around base of petiole .. OCREA
"    below dam ............. APRON
"    , as a protection .. AEGIS, EGIS
"    , band across ............. FESS
"    , border in a . BORDURE, ORLE
"    , boss in a ............... UMBO
"    , division of a ............ ENTE
"    , fillet around a .......... ORLE
"    ; heraldry ...... ESCUTCHEON
"    , Roman .. SCUTUM, TESTUDO

"    sacred ................. ANCILE
"    shape ................. PELTATE
shield-shaped .. SCUTATE, THYROID
shift .. FEND, STIR, BAFFLE, VEER,
WEND, DEVIATE, PLEA
shifts .... SHUNTS, CAMISE, SMOCK
shill ..................... ACCOMPLICE
Shillong's cap. ................. ASSAM
shilly-shally HESITATE, VASCILLATE
shin ............... SHANK, CLIMB
shin, per. to .................... TIBIAL
shin plaster ..................... SCRIP
shindy; slang ............. RIOT, ROW
shine ....... BEAM, RADIATE, DIDO,
GLISTEN, AID, GLITTER,
RUTILATE
shiner ............... MINNOW, CHUB
shingle .... CHISEL, GRAVEL, FACIA
shingles ..... HERPES, SIGNBOARDS
shining .... GLARY, AGLOW, LUCID,
NITID, GLOSSY
Shinto ......................... SINTU
Shinto gods ..................... KAMI
Shinto spirits of the dead ....... KAMI
Shinto temple .................... SHA
Shinto temple gateway PAILOU, TORII
Shinto war god .......... HACHIMAN
ship after the cachalot ...... WHALER
"    , ancient ........ NEF, GALLEON
"    , body of ................. HULK
"    , curved timber of ....... APRON,
STEMSON
"    fender ..................... SKID
"    fraud ............... BARRATRY
"    , left side of ................PORT
"    mortgage ............ BOTTOMRY
"    of desert ................. CAMEL
"    , passage from a ............. GAT
"    , square masted ............. BRIG
"    , strengthening timber of a .......
KEELSON
"    table frame ............... FIDDLE
"    , the sheer of a ................SNY
"    timber ..................... BITT
"    , title of captain of a; . RAIS, RAS,
REIS
"    , to stave in bottom of .... BILGE
"    worm ......... BORER, TEREDO
shipjack ......................... SHAD
ship's ballast ............... LASTAGE
ship's beam, top of .... TIMBERHEAD
"    biscuit ................. PATILE
"    bottom, to clean ....... BREAM
"    carpenter ................. CHIPS
"    crew leader ............. BOSUN
"    daily record ................. LOG
"    galley ................. CABOOSE
"    jail ................. HULK, BRIG
"    lifting device .. CAMEL, DAVIT
ships of fame .. MARIA, NINA, PINTA
ship's permit to enter port . PRATIQUE
"    prow ................... PRORE
"    rope ................... SHROUD
"    stern rail ............. TAFFRAIL
shipwreck, goods lost in a .. FLOTSAM
Shirer's journal ................. DIARY
shirker ......... RUNAWAY, TRUANT
shirt ........ CAMISA, SARK, SKIVVY
shirt bosom .............. PLASTRON

shirt front, false .............. DICKY
shirt, long loose ...............KAMIS
shiver .. QUAKE, CHIVEL, SPLINTER
shivering . CREEPY, OORIE, TREMOR
shoal ... CROWD, REEF, BAR, DRAVE
shoat ........ .. ERMINE, PIG, SHOTE
shock ....... JAR, STARTLE, BRUNT
shock, to set up as sheaves .... STOOK
shod ............. CALCED, ENSOLED
shoe ........ BALMORAL, BLUCHER,
      BOOT, CLOG, OXFORD
shoe cleat ........................ CALK
 "  , coarse ....... BROGAN, STOGY
 "  covering .. PRUNELLA, GAITER
 "  , edge of a ................ WELT
 "  , flexible ............. SOLLERET
 "  , gym ................. SNEAKER
 "  , high ......... BUSKIN, MOYLE
 "  , house ....... MULE, SNEAKER
 "  lace ........ LATCHET, WHANG
 "  , low PUMP, SANDAL, SLIPPER
 "  , margin of .............. RAND
 "  part of a .................INSOLE
 "  , rear part of ........ COUNTER
 "  , thick soled .......... CHOPINE
 "  , wooden ... SECQUE, PATTEN,
          SABOT
shoebill; Egypt ................. STORK
shoeholder ........ TREE, SHOEHORN
shoe-lace tag ................... AGLET
shoemaker SOUTER, CRISPIN, SUTOR
shoemaker; Span. ......... ZAPATERO
shoemaker's awl ............... ELSEN
shoemaker's nail .......... SPARABLE
shoemaker's oil stone ............ SLIP
shoemaker's patron saint ..... CRISPIN
shogun ............. TYCOON, CHIEF
shola; Ind. .................... JUNGLE
Sholem; author ...................ASCH
shooi ........................ JAEGER
shoot RATOON, CHIT, TILLER, TWIG
shoot from cover ....... DART, SNIPE
shoot, long flexible ............ VIMEN
shoot of a plant ROD, SCION, STOLON
shooting iron ... PISTOL, REVOLVER
shooting star .....COWSLIP, METEOR
shooting match; Fr. ...... SKEET, TIR
shoots, stripper of small ... BRUTTER
shop ....... MART, ATELIER, BURSE
shopping, mad. for ...... ONIOMANIA
shore COAST, PROP, MARGE, PLAYA,
           SAND
shore bird ........ AVOCET, CURLEW
shore of the sea .... BRINK, STRAND
shore, per. to .............. LITTORAL
short .............. BRIEF, FRIABLE
 "  and fat ................... PODGY
 "  billed rail .................. SORA
 "  essay .................... TRACT
 "  forms ................... ABBRS
 "  legged ............... BREVIPED
 "  lived ............... EPHEMERA
 "  of breath ............ DYSPNEIC
 "  sighted ............... MYOPIC
 "  story; Fr. ................ CONTE
 "  sword ...................... DIRK
 "  tailed water fowl .......... COOT
shortage ......... DEFICIT, ULLAGE
shorten .... DOC, DOCK, LOP, LESSEN

shortened ................... CURTATE
shortening of syllables ...... SYSTOLE
shorthand system ............. GREGG
shortleafed internode ....... ROSETTE
short-napped fabric .............. RAS
Shoshonean ...... OTOE, PIUTE, UTE
shot and shell ................. AMMO
shot one under par ............ BIRDIE
shou, Tibetan .................... DEER
shoulder badge ............. EPAULET
 "  belt ................BALDRIC
 "  blade OMOPLATE, SCAPULA
 "  , gout in the ....... OMAGRA
 "  inflammation ..... OMALGIA,
          OMITIS
 "  muscle ............ DELTOID
 "  of a bastion ........ EPAULE
 "  of a road ............ BERM
 "  , per. to ... ALAR, HUMERAI
 "  , per. to the ..... SCAPULAR
 "  yoke pail ........ COWL, SOE
shovel ....... HAT, SCOOP, SPADE
show ......................... EVINCE
"Show Boat"; authoress .........EDNA
"Show Boat"; by .............. KERN
show off ..................... DISPLAY
showcase, glass ............. VITRINE
showed ........ WORE, EXHIBITED
shower .. SCAT, DROW, MISLE, RASH
shower of meteors ........ ANDROMID
showing desire to fight ........ ANIME
showy .. GARISH, ARTY, GAY, POMP,
     TINSEL, GAUDY, SPORTY,
         CLAPTRAP
shrapnel ..................... SHELL
shred .. RAG, RIP, SNIP, STRIP, TAG
shrew .......... ERD, SCOLD, VIXEN
shrew, a ................... XANTIPPE
shrew; Eur. ..................... ERD
shrew mouse; genus .......... SOREX
shrew mouse; Gr. .. HYRAX, MIGALE
shrew, Sumatrian squirrel ...... TANA
shrewd .... CANNY, CUTE, PRACTIC,
     WILY, ASTUTE, SAPIENT
shrewdness . ACUMEN, ARGUTENESS
shrewish .... TERMAGANT, SNOOTY
shrill creaking noise ........ STRIDOR
shrill tone ... SHARP, PIPY, SHIRLY,
          SKIRL
shrimp of Burma .............. NAPEE
shrimp-like crustacean ....... PRAWN
shrine of a saint .. ALTAR, ADYTUM,
          CHASSE
Shriner; comedian ............. HERB
shrinking ..... COY, SENSITIVE, SHY
shrivel ...... PARCH, WIZEN, CRINE,
          PAUCH
shriveled ...... SERE, SVELTE, THIN
shroff; Ind. ................... BANKER
shroud .. COWL, MASK, CEREMENT,
        KELL, SCREEN
shrouded ............. HID, CLOAKED
shrub (see also 'plant')
 "  ; BUSH, ELDER, HALESIA,
     LAURUS, YEW, LILAC,
     OLEASTER, SALAL
 "  , Adam's needle ......... YUCCA
 "  Arabian, leaves of ...... KAFTA
 "  , Arabian tea ................ KAT

"    , aromatic ARALIA, LAVENDER
"    , Asian ....... BAGO, DEUTZIA,
                    WEIGELA
"    , bean family .... BROOM, ILEX
"    , botany ............. FRUTEX
"    , bushy .... CADE, SAVIN, TOD
"    , California ............. SALAL
"    C. Afr. ................. IBOGA
shrub, cherry ............... CERASUS
"    , climbing ........... BIGNONIA
        CLEMATIS, LIANA, RUBUS,
        VITIS
"    , creeping ................ PYXIE
"    , cytisus ............... BROOM
"    , dogwood ............. CORNUS
"    , E. Ind. medicinal ....... SOMA,
                    MUDAR
"    , elder .................... ELLEN
"    , evergreen; ABELMOSK, AZARA,
        BUXUS, CAMELLIA, CISTUS,
        FATSIA,    HEATH,    ILEX,
        JASMINE,    LAUREL,
        MYRTLE,    OLEANDER,
        SALAL, SAVIN, TITI, PEPINO
"    , evergreen, climbing .. AKEBIA,
                    HEDERA, SMILAX
"    , euphorbiaceous ......... ALEM
"    fence .............. HEDGEROW
"    , flowering; . AZALEA, LILAC,
        OLEASTER, SYRINGA
"    , genus rhus ............ SUMAC
"    , genus rosaceous ...... SPIREA
"    , hardy ... ALTHEA, HEATHER
"    having purple flower .. BARETA
"    , Hawaii rose ........... AKALA
"    , Japan ..... AUCUBA, KERRIA
"    , larch family ........... ALDER
"    , liliaceous .................... TI
"    , maples, the .............. ACER
"    , mint family ....... ROSEMARY
"    , New Zealand ... RAMARAMA,
                    TUTU
"    , of silk fiber ............ ANABO
"    , Old World; genus ... GENISTA
"    , olive .................... OLEA
"    , Oriental ............. HENNA
"    , parisitic ......... MISTLETOE
"    , pepper ................. KAVA
"    , periwinkle ............. VINCA
"    , Peruvian .. SHAMSA, MATICO
"    , pine family ........... SAVIN
"    , prickly ............. BRAMBLE
"    , quince; Jap. ........ CYDONIA
"    , rutaceous ....... JABORANDI
"    , sambucus; genus ..... ELDER
"    , S. Amer. ............. CEIBO
"    , spiny . FURZE, GORSE, ULEX
"    , stunted ................. SCRAB
"    , thick foliage ............. TOD
"    , tropical .... ABELIA, ABRUS,
        ASIS, LANTANA, OLACAD
"    used in tanning ........ SUMAC
"    , W. Ind. .... ANIL, CASSAVA,
                    EBOE
"    , Western U. S. .......... SALAL
shrubs; genus; .... ITEA, LANTANA,
        OLEA, RHUS, OLEARIA,
        RIBES, ROSA, SIDA
shrubs, rel. to .............. BOSCAGE

shudder ... GRUE, QUAKE, TREMOR
shuffle .. RUSE, SCUFF, MIX, TRICK
Shuftu ..................... KASHGAR
shun ...... ESCHEW, EVITE, AVOID,
                    RUN
Shunammite, the .......... ABISHAG
shunt .... BYPASS, FERRY, SWITCH
Shushan; Bib. .................... SUSA
shut out OCCLUDE, BAN, EXCLUDE
shut up . DAM, CAGE, MEWED, END
shuttle .. LOOPER, FLUTE, SLIDING
shy .. COY, SQUAB, TIMID, MODEST
Shylock ...................... USURER
Shylock's daughter .......... JESSICA
Shylock's friend ............... TUBAL
Siamese and Shans, the . TAIS, THAIS
Siamese coin BAHT, LICAR, ATT, BAT,
                    TICAL
"    measure RAI, SOK, NIU, SEN,
                    SESTI
"    river .................. MENAM
"    tongue ............... LAO, TAI
"    Twins, names of . CHANG, ENG
"    weight ... PAI, CHANG, TICAL
sib .... KINSMAN, RELATIVE, AKIN
Siberia, river of .. AMUR, LENA, OB
Siberia, wild sheep of ........ ARGALI
Siberian blizzard ............. BURAN
"    city ................... OMSK
"    commune ................. IDA
"    fish ................... NELMA
"    forest .................. TAIGA
"    gulf ....................... OB
"    ibex ...................... TEX
"    native .... TATAR, YAKOOT,
                YAKUT, YUIT
"    prison sleeping platform NARE
"    redood ........ BUCKTHORN
"    squill ................. SCILLA
"    squirrel ........... CALABER
"    steppes, people of . KIRGIZES
"    swamp ................ URMAN
"    tent ..................... YURT
"    warehouse ............. ETAPE
sibilance mark ... CEDILLA, LEGON
sibilate ............. HISH, SISS, HISS
sibling .............. COMEMBER, SIS
sibyl .... SEERESS, ORACLE, WITCH
Sibyl's cave ................... CUMAE
sicca ......................... SEAL
siccity .......... DRYNESS, ARIDITY,
                    DROUGHT
Sicilian ash ................. MANNA
"    bull ............... PHALARIS
"    evergreen ........... MAQUIS
"    province ............ SUTERA
"    saffron ............. CROCUS
"    secret society ......... MAFIA
"    sumac .............. TANNER
Sicily, capital of .......... PALERMO
Sicily, inhabitants of .......... SICANI
Sicily, river in ................. ACIS
sick a dog on; Aus. .............. SOOL
sick headache ............ MIGRAINE
sick person, a . AEGER, AEGROTANT
sickle .. CROOK, HOOK, RISH, SIVE
sickle-shaped ..... FALCATE, KIMBO
sickness excuse; Eng. univ. ... AEGER
Siculi ......................... SICEL

Sicyon king ............... EPOPEUS
Siddhartha ................. BUDDHA
side .. CHEEK, JAMB, LATUS, SECT,
FLANK
side dish .... ENTREE, ENTREMETS
side kick ..................... PAS
side of canal opposite towpath . BERM
sidero ........................ IRON
sides, unequal .............. SCALENE
sideslip ......................... SKID
sidetrack ....... SHUNT, DISTRACT
sidewise ...... ASKANCE, ATHWART,
LATERAL
sidles ...... EDGES, CANTS, SKEWS
siecle; Fr. CENTURY, GENERATION
siege, of a .............. OBSIDIONAL
Siegfried, slayer of HAGEN, DRAGON
Siegfried's sword .......... BALMUNG
Siegmund's sword ............. GRAM
Siena marble ............. BROCATEL
Sierra Madre peak ........... LOWE
Sierra Nevadas, dense fog . POGONIP
siesta ... NAP, REST, LULL, MIDDAY
sieve .. RIDDLE, BOLT, SILE, TAMIS,
BOLTER, SEARCH
sieve for clay .................... LAUN
sieve-like ...... ETHMOID, CRIBRATE
Sifaka ........................ LEMUR
sift or bolt ............. LUE, SCREEN
sigh .... SITHE, SOB, TWANK, MOAN
sigh, poetic ...... RAY, VISTA, VIEW,
VISION
sigmoid .................. CURVE, ESS
sign ...... OMEN, PARAPH, SYMBOL
sign; mus. ...................... PRESA
sign in magic .................. SIGIL
sign, per. to a .................. SEMIC
signal at night .............. CURFEW
signal, flag ................... ENSIGN
signal, railroad ............... FUSEE
signal, spirit ..................... TAP
signal warning ...... ALARM, ALERT,
CUE, SOS, PHAROS
signaling apparatus ....... TELESME,
HELIO
signature ........ HAND, SEAL, SIGIL
signature, first word of ........ PRIMA
signed .................. ONOMATOUS
significant SEMANTIC, FORCE, SENSE,
TRAIT
silage ........................ FODDER
"Silas Marner"; author of ...... ELIOT
silenaceous herbs; genus .. DIANTHUS
silence ..... OYER, OYEZ, OBLIVION,
LULL, QUIET, STILL, GAG, WHIST
silenced voice of S. Amer. ... PRESNA
silent ... TACE, MUM, MUTE, TACIT
silent, it is ..................... TACET
Silesian town ..................... OELS
silex ........................... SILICA
silica ........................... SILEX
silicate, hydrous MICA, CERITE, OPAL
silicate, pale green .......... EPIDOTE,
EUCLASE
silk, brown ..................... MUGA
" , corded ........... CRIN, FAILLE
" cotton tree ................ CEIBA

" fabric .. TASH, SAMITE, SATIN,
SENDAL, SURAH
" fabric, Moorish ............ TIRAZ
" filling ........................ TRAM
" , gelatin .................. SERICIN
" grass ...................... ISTLE
" , half-mask of; Fr. ......... LOUP
" hat .... CASTOR, TILE, TOPPER
" , India .................... MUGA
" material ........ PANG, SENDAL,
TULLE
" , oak ................. GREVILLEA
" , plain, glossy ......... TAFFETA,
LUTESTRING
" , raw ...................... GREGE
" , reeling ................ FILATURE
" , rustle of ................ SCROOP
" , source of .............. COCOON
" stuff; anc. ................ TARSE
" tester .. DENIERER, SCRIMETER
" , thin .................... ALAMODE
" thread ...................... TRAM
" , twill-woven .... ALMA, TOBINE
" voile ....................... NINON
" waste ....................... NOIL
" , watered ........ MOIRE, TABBY
silken ............................ SERIC
silkweed ................. MILKWEED
silkworm ........ ERI, ERIA, TUSSAH
" , Chin. .. AILANTHUS, TUSSUR
silkworm disease ........... PEBRINE
" eggs .................. GRAINE
" ; genus ............... BOMBYX
" , home of .............. ASSAM
" leaves ...................... ALBA
" , rel. to .... BOMBIC, FILATOR
silky dress material ......... BAREGE
silly .. ASININE, DECIPIENT, DOTE,
APISH, INANE
silver . ARGENT, PLATE, ARGENTUM
" alloy; Ger. .............. ALBATA
" amalgam, cone of .......... PINA
" and gold alloy ........... BILLON
" , ball of .................. POME
" citrate .................... ITROL
" , gilded ............... VERMEIL
" in alchemy ................ LUNA
" in ingots ................ SYCEE
" lace ................... FILIGREE
" , paved space for sorting PATIO
" , symbol for .................. AG
" , uncoined .............. BULLION
silver-fox fur ................. PLATINA
silver-like alloy .. OCCAMY, NEOGEN
silverside .................... SMELT
silversmith, famous ......... REVERE
silybum ......... MARIANA, THISTLE
simian ............... APE, MONKEY
similar .... AKIN, LIKE, RESEMBLE,
SUCH, HOMOGEN, ANALOGOUS
simile ...... METAPHOR, PARABOLE
simmer ..... BOIL, BRAISE, SEETHE
simoon, Cen. Asian .. TEBBAD, WIND
simple ...... OAFISH, MERE, MUTE
simpleton; .... DAW, GEEDE, GUMP,
MORON, NOODLE, GOWK, NINCOM-
POOP, OAF, BOOBY

244

simpleton, synonym for ... ABDERITE
simulacrum ......... UNREAL, IMAGE
simulated ........... FEIGNED, APED
simulation ........ FEINT, PRETENSE
simurgh ......................... ROC
sin .. CRIME, ERR, EVIL, PECCANCY,
VICE
since .. SITH, AGO, AS, FOR, HENCE,
SYNE
sincere .. EARNEST, OPEN, INTENSE
sincerity; symb. ........ AMETHYST
sinecure ......................... SNAP
sind, prince of ................. AMEER
sing cheerfully ...... CHORTLE, LILT
sing with trills .. ROULADE, WARBLE
singer .............. BARD, CAROLER,
DESCANTER
singer, female .......... CANTATRICE
single SPORADIC, ACE, ALONE, ODD,
ONE, CHAR, FRANK, UNAL
single algebraic names ...... NOMIALS
single course in race ............ HEAT
single master vessel ......... TARTAN
single, not one of a pair .... AZYGOUS
singlething ........ UNIT, UNAL, UNE
singly ..... SOLO, APART, KITHLESS
singulf ................... HIC, SIGH
sinister . EVIL, OMINOUS, CAR, LEFT
sink ... FALL, MERGE, SYE, ENGULF
sinker .. DIPSY, PLUMMET, WEIGHT
sinning .................... PECCANT
sinus ............ BAY, BEND, CURVE
sinus in a bone .............. ANTRUM
Siouan Indian .............. OTO, IOWA
Sioux Tribe .................... TETON
sip .... LAP, SUCK, SUP, GULP, PEG
sipper ........................ STRAW
sippet .. CROUTON, BIT, FRAGMENT
sire .. BEGET, MALE, LORD, HORSE
siren .. FOGHORN, CHARMER, LORE-
LEI, ALARM, LURER, ENTICER,
CIRCE
siren of Nile .................... CLEO
Sirius ..................... CANICULA
Sirocco; Madeira Is. ........... LESTE
sisal hemp ................ HENEQUIN
sisera, enemy of .............. BARAK
siskin ......................... FINCH
sissified ......... PRISSY, NICE, PRIM
sister; Lat. ...................... SOROR
sisters .......... NUNS, KIN, NURSES
site ... SEAT, SITUS, STANCE, AREA
site of Taj Mahal .... ASTASIA, AGRA
Sitsang; Chin. .................. TIBET
sitting ...... SEDENT, CONVOCATION
situation CASE, SIEGE, POST, STEAD
Siva; Hindu .............. DESTROYER
Siva's trident ................ TRISULA
Siva's wife ...... DEVI, DURGA, UMA
six footed .................... HEXAPOD
" , group of .................. HEXAD
" in dicing ..................... SICE
" of a kind .............. SEXTUPLET
" , on basis of .............. SENARY
" players ..................... SESTET
" pointed figure ................ STAR
sixth degree, of ............... SEATIC
sixty sixties ............. SAR, SAROS

size of type (see 'type') . AGATE, PICA
skate ......... RAY, GIDE, SKI, SKIM
skedaddle SPILL, BOLT, FLIT, SNEAK
skein ...... HANK, RAP, MESH, WEB
skeleton ..... BONES, RAME, ATOMY,
CAGE
skeleton of ship adjusted ...... RAMED
skeleton organization .......... CADRE
skelp .... SQUALL, STRIKE, THRASH
Skelton, Mr. ...................... RED
skeptic ........ APORETIC, DOUBTER
sketch .... IDEA, MAP, ANA, DRAFT,
DRAW, LIMN, SKIT
skewer TRUSS, PIN, SKIVER, STAPLE
skid ...... SIDESLIP, TRAVOIS, TRIG
skift ............... CAIGUE, SCAPHE
skiing, race, zigzag ......... SLALOM
skilful .... DEFT, DEDAL, APT, FIT,
HABILE
skilful maneuverer ........ TACTICIAN
skill ...... APTITUDE, KNACK, ART,
CRAFT, TECHNIC
skilled in quality ... FINESSE, VERTU
skilled mechanical work ....... SLOYD
skim ..... SCUD, RIND, FLIT, SCOON
skimmed milk, deriv. of ..... LANITAL
skin PARE, BARK, RIND, EPIDERMIS,
PEEL, SUEDE, DERMA
" affection ...... ACNE, PRURITUS
" , beaver .................... PLEW
" , dark .................. MELANIC
" decoration ............. TATTOO
" , destitute of ............ APELLOUS
" disease .... ERYSIPELAS, ACNE,
ECZEMA
" , dryness of ............ XEROSIS
" eruption .. EXANTHEM, MACULA
" finishing .................... TAW
" , fold ...................... PLICA
" , Latin for ................. CUTIS
" , layer of .... TEGUMENT, DERM
" layers ..................... CORIA
" of ......................... DERIC
" of an animal .. PELLAGE, PELL,
PELT
"" of walnut ................. ZEST
" , oil ...................... SEBUM
skin, outer layer of .......... EPICARP
" , redness of .............. RUBOR
" , wine ...................... BOSS
skinflint .. CHEAT, SCREW, PELTER
skink; Egypt .......... ADDA, LIZARD
Skinner, Cornelia ................. OTIS
skins, number of fur .......... TIMBER
skins, rug of ................ KAROSS
skins, season ............. SAM, SAMM
skip ........ FRISK, DAP, HIP, OMIT
skip gleefully ........... CAPER, JUMP
skip, the rebounding of a shot ..........
RICOCHET
skipper; E. Ind. ........ RAS, SERANG
skirl ........ PIPE, SCREAM, SHRIEK
skirmish CLASH, FRAY, VELITATION
skirt attached to coat ........ PEPLUM
skirt, in armor ................ TASSET
skirt, short .. ENGI, BENGI, SKIRTLE,
KILT
skit ...... CAPER, JOKE, PLAY, QUIP

245

skivvy ........................... SHIRT
skittles ............. NINEPINS, GAME
skoal SKAL, SLAINTE, CUP, HEALTH,
TOAST
skulker .... HEDGER, LIAR, LURKER
skull ................ CRANIUM, SCAP
skull, cavity of ................. FOSSA
skull measure ......... CRANIOMETER
skull, part of .............. ASTERION
skull, per. to ..................... INIAL
skull, point of junction in ... BREGMA
skull, protuberance of .......... INION
skullcaps; anc. .... CALOTTES, PILEI
skunk .. ANNA, POLECAT, SEGANKU
skunk; Mex. ................ CONEPATE
skunk-like animal .............. ZORIL
sky blue ........... AZURE, CELESTE
sky, the ....... WELKIN, BLUE, WEK
skylarks; genus .............. ALAUDA
slab of marble ...... TABLET, STELE,
DALLE
slab-like ..................... STELAR
slack ........ CHAFF, FRESE, LOOSE
slacken ....... END, RELAX, REPOSE
slacks ............. DUFFS, TROUSERS
slade ..................... PEAT, GLEN
slag ................. DROSS, SCORIA
slam, to make a ................. VOLE
slander ....... DEFAME, BELIE, HIT,
ASPERSE, CANT, LIBEL
slander, political SMEAR, ROORBACK
slang .......... BLAH, CANT, ARGOT
slant ........ SLOPE, BEVEL, SKEW
slat ........ SLOT, STAVE, TRANSOM
slate .. BLAE, ENROLL, RAG, SCHIST
slate hammer ..................... SAX
slate picker .................... WALER
slater's tool ................. ZAT, ZAX
slattern ........... MOPSY, BUNGLER
Slaughter; baseball .............. ENOS
slaughterer; Eng. .......... KNACKER
Slav ................... CROAT, SERB
slave BULGAR, ESNE, NEIF, SERF,
THRALL, VASSAL, DRUDGE, LASCAR
slave block ................. CATASTA
slave, female ................ ODALISK
slave, female; Gr. .... BAUBO, IAMBE
slave fighting ............. MAMELUKE
slave in anc. Sparta .... ILOT, HELOT
slaver ...... DRIVEL, DROOL, FAWN
slaves, dealer in .............. MANGO
slaw ................. SALAD, RELISH
slay ............ KILL, LYNCH, SLEA
slay by suffocation ............ BURKE
sled .... SLEIGH, TOBOGGAN, TODE,
SLEDGE
sleeky ............. SLY, OBSEQUIOUS
sleep ...... NAP, DOSS, RET, WINK
" , as a deity ............. SOMNUS
" , causing .............. NARCOSE
" , god of; myth. ......... HYPNOS
" , inducing .......... SOPORIFIC
" , insensibility in .. CARUS, COMA
" , midday ................. SIESTA
" , prolonged ............... SOPOR
" , to wander in; Eng. .... DWALE
sleeper DRONE, SUPPORT, BEAM, TIE

sleeping pill ................ SOPORIFIC
sleeping platform in Siberian prison ....
NARE
sleeping sick. source ......... TSETSE
sleepy ........ NARCOTIC, OSCITANT
sleeve .......... ARM, CHEVRON
sleeve, hole for .................. SKYE
sleeveless garment ....... ABA, CADE,
MANTLE
sleigh runner ..................... SHOE
sleigh, box ..................... PUNG
sleigh, sidepiece of a ............ RAVE
slender .. FINE, LANK, PRIN, SVELT,
LEGER
sleuth ............ DECTECTIVE, TEC,
HAWKSHAW
sleuth hound; extinct .......... TALBOT
slice ..... CUT, SLAB, GASH, LAYER,
COAST, GLISSADE
Slichter's forte .......... ECONOMICS
slick, post hole ..................... LOY
slid together ........... TELESCOPED
slide ............. SKID, SLEW, SLUE
slide, a ........................ CHUTE
sliding piece ............. PISTON, CAM
slight .. CUT, LEGER, FAINT, LACHE,
NEGLECT
slight insanity .......... OLIGOMANIA
slightly damaged ............. RETREE
slime GLEET, ICHOR, LIMAN, OOZE
slime deposit ...... SILT, MUCK, MUD
slimsy ................. FLIMSY, FRAIL
slingshot ............. DAVID, SLAPPY,
CATAPULT
slink ........ CRAWL, CREEP, STEAL
slip .. ERR, IMP, PEW, SLIME, SLIVE
slip, leather ..................... REIN
slip secretly ................... CREEM
slip, to ....................... ILLAPSE
slip-knot ................ NOOSE, NOG
slipper ...... SANDAL, NEAP, MULE,
PINSON
slipper, oriental . ROMEO, BABOUCHE
slippery ........ SLY, ELUSIVE, GLIB,
FICKLE, SHIFTY, SHUTTLE
slither ............. SIDLE, SLIDE
Sloan, jockey ..................... TOD
sloe ..................... HAW, PLUM
slogan ... CRY,MOTTO, SHIBBOLETH
sloop, Flemish .................. BOYER
slope SCARP, GLACIS, CANT, RAMP,
SPLAY
sloping bank ..................... BRAE
sloth ........... INDOLENCE, INERTIA
sloth monkey .................. LORIS
sloth, three toed ....................AI
sloth, two toed .................. UNAU
sloughing ................... ECDYSIS
slovenly .. SLIPSHOD, FROWZY, SLOY
slow DELAY, RELAX, LATE, TRAILY,
INERT
slow; mus. .. LARGO, LENTO, TARDO
sludge .......... MIRE, MUD, SLEET
slug ........ DRONE, SNAIL, BULLET
slug, sea .................... TREPANG
sluggish ...... DRONY, FOUL, INERT
slugs; genus .................... LIMAX

246

sluice ...................... GOUT, TOM
slur .... INNUENDO, BLUR, MACKLE
sly ARCH, CAGEY, COVERT, SNAKY,
        FELINE, WARY, WILY, WINK
smack .. KISS, TANG, TASTE, BUSS,
        SNAP, BLOW, PUMP
smack-like .................... SLOOP
small .. WEE, PETITE, MINUSCULE,
        PINK, TOT, LITTLE, LIL
 "   amount ............ TRACE, MITE
 "   anvil ...................... TEEST
 "   area ...................... AREOLA
 "   armadillo ................... PEBA
 "   beadlike process .... ROSTRULUM
 "   bomb .................... PETARD
 "   cube .................. DICE, DIE
 "   flag to mark position ..... FANION
 "   glass of liquor .............. PONY
 "   group ..................... SQUAD
 "   hand bills .............. DODGERS
 "   insect ........................ GNIT
 "   insect pest ................. THRIP
 "   person .................... MIDGE
 "   piece ....... MORCEAU, SNIPPET
 "   rope ..................... MARLINE
 "   saddle horse ................... NAG
 "   ; Scot. .........................SMA
 "   shield ........................ ECU
 "   shields .............. SCUTELLAE
 "   white flower ............. STEVIA
smallage .......... CELERY, MARCH
smaller; comb. form .......... MIO
smallest component of matter .........
        ELECTRON, ATOM
smallness; archaic .......... EXILITY
smallpox, per. to .......... VARIOLAR
smaragd .................. EMERALD
smart ... ACUTE, APT, CHICK, TRIM
smartened up ...... CHIC, TITIVATED
smash .. STAVE, BASH, FALL, RUIN
smatterer ....... SCIOLIST, DABBLER
smear .. DAUB, GAUM, GLAIR, GORM
smell ...... SCENT, FLAIR, ODO(U)R
smell, offensive .. FETOR, OLID, BAD,
        FOUL
smelt ......... SCORIFY, FUSE, PRIM
smelt; N. Z. ................... INANGA
smelting, by-product of .......... SLAG
smile ....... FAVOR, SNEER, LAUGH
smiling ..... MERRY, RIDENT, AGRIN
smirch .. SMUTCH, SULLY, TARNISH,
        BLOT
smirk ......... LEER, SIMPER, GRIN
smite ...... VISIT, AFFLICT, STRIKE
Smith Col., first pres. ......... SEELYE
smithereen .. ATOM, CHIP, FLINDER
smitten .......... ENAMORED, EPRIS
smock ... CAMISE, CHEMISE, TUNIC
smoke AEROSOL, FLOC, CURE, LUNT,
        REEK, SMUDGE
smoke signaler ................ INDIAN
smoking apparatus, oriental NARGILE
smocking, cure by ............. REEST
smolt ...................... SALMON
smooth .. GLAT, LENE, OILY, PAVE,
        SUANT, BLAND, GLIB, URBANE
smooth; comb. form ............. LIO

smooth; mus. ................ LEGATO
smooth over ... GLOSS, GLOZE, CALM
smooth, to ........ DUB, EVEN, IRON
smother .............. BEFOG, STIFLE
smudge ....... SMEAR, SMOKE, SPOT
snaffle ..... BIT, BRIDLE, CURB, GAG
snack ............... CANAPE, SHARE
snafu ............ CHAOTIC, MUDDLE
snail .............. HELICID, HELIX,
        PERIWINKLE, SLUG
snail, marine ................. WHELK
snails; genus ....... NERITA, MITRA,
        TRITON
snake .............. VIPER, REPTILE
 "   , Asian ...... DABOIA, JESSUR,
        BONGAR
 "   , black .................... RACER
 "   , bluish; Ind. ............ KRAIT
 "   charmer's flute ......... PUNGI
 "   , deadly ...... COBRA, MAMBA,
        TAPA
 "   deity ...................... ZOMBI
 "   , Egypt. ...................... ASP
 "   eyes .................. AMBSACE
 "   , Florida ............. MOCCASIN
 "   , harmless Cuban .......... JUBA
 "   , python ............ ANACONDA
 "   , rel. to a .................. LORE
 "   root, black .............. SANICLE
 "   , sand; genus ............. ERYX
 "   , S. Amer. ABOMA, BOM, LORA
 "   wart ............... XENODERM
snake-like .................... APODAL
snakes; genus .................... BOA
snaky ........................ ANGUINE
snapper on whiplash ........ COSAQUE
snap with finger .............. FILLIP
snare ........ NET, GIN, GUM, TRAP,
snare NET, GIN, GUM, TRAP, CATCH,
        NOOSE, TRAPAN, WILE, MESH
snare; Ger. ................... SPRINGE
snark ...................... BOOJUM
snarl .. ARR, TANGLE, GNAR, SNAR,
        YIRR, GROWL, KNOT
snatch TWITCH, WRAP, SEIZE, GRAB
snatched away ............. EREPTED
sneak .... SPY, LURK, SLINK, SNOOP
snee ............................. DIRK
sneer SCOUT, FLEER, GIRD, SCORN
sneeze .. NEESE, SNUFF, CONTEMPT
sneezing ERRHINE, STERNUTATION
sneezewort .............. PATARMICA
snell, a ................... SNOOD, GUT
snib ................. SNUB, REPROOF
snicker .. SNIGGER, TITTER, LAUGH
sniff .......... NOSE, SCENT, SNUFF
snipe eel ..................... THREAD
snipe, flock of .................. WHISP
snipe hawk ................... HARRIER
snivel .. MUCUS, WHINE, CRY, WEEP
snob .. KNOBSTICK, PARVENU, RAT
snobbish UPISH, ARROGANT, PROUD
snood .... FILLET, SNELL, HAIRNET
snoop ...... LURK, PRY, SLY, PROWL
snoot .................... FACE, NOSE
snore ..... RALE, RHONCHUS, SNIFF
snoring ..... STERTOROUS, STERTOR

snout ....... FRONT, NOSE, NOZZLE
snow ..... FIRN, PASH, SLEET, SNA
" , field of .................... NEVE
" fly; genus ............... BOREUS
" grouse .............. PTARMIGAN
" house ................ IGLO, IGLOO
" , Latin for ............NIX, NIVIS
" house; Eur. ................. VOLE
snowflake ...... BUNTING, CRYSTAL,
FINCH
snow-runner ............. SLED, SKEE
snow-shoe ........ PAC, PATTEN, SKI
snowy ............. NIVAL, NIVEOUS
snub; Scot. .................... SNOOL
snuff ... NOSE, MACCABOY, RAPPEE
snuffbox, any ................... MULL
so ....... ERGO, THUS, SAE, SIC, AS,
HENCE
so be it ................ AMEN, STALK
so much; It. .................... TANTO
soak . SATURATE, BATE, RET, SOP
SOUSE, DIP, IMBRUE, SOG, WEEZE
soak in brine ............... MARINATE
soap .. SAPO, SUDS, BRIBERY, RUB
" convert into ......... SAPONIFY
" fish ....................... JABON
" frame bar ................ SESS
" liniment ........... OPODELDOC
" plant .................... AMOLE
soap-like compound ........ SAPONUL
soap-opera ......... DRIVEIN, RADIO
soapstone ....................... TALC
soapsuds ... FOAM, FROTH, LATHER
soaring .. FLYING, HIGH, TOWERING
soar .............. FLIT, SAIL, WING
soaring in spirit .......... ESSORANT
sob ..... SIMPER, YOOP, SAB, SITHE
sobby .................... DAMP, WET
so-be-it ................. ALTERCATE
sober ... CLEANSE, DOUCE, SEDATE
sobriquet AGNAME, ALIAS, HANDLE
social ........ CLAN, TRIBAL, CASTE
" insect ...................... ANT
" outcast ............... PARIAH
" standing .............. ESTATE
" system ................. REGIME
" unit ...................... SEPT
" vacuum ............... ANOMIC
socialism ................ FOURIERISM
society, a .. LODGE, ETHNOS, ORDER
society; Ger. .................. VEREIN
society, Ital. .................... MAFIA
sock; Jap. .......................... TABO
sock of goat's hair .............. UDO
sock, symbol of tragedy ...... BUSKIN
sockdolager ........... FACER, ONER
socker .......................... COE
socket .. MORTISE, ORBIT, PAN, POD
Socrates, disciple of .. PLATO, CERES
Socrates, wife of ........ XANTHIPPE
sod . SWARD, PEAT, TURF, SEETHE
sod, oil like ................. DEGRAS
soda ...................... SALERATUS
soda ash, per. to ........... ALKALINE
soda ash plant .............. BARILLA
soda from seaweeds ........... VAREC
soda niter ............... SALTPETER
sodden SOAKED, SEETHED, BOILED,
DULL, SOGGY

sodium carbonate ......... ANATRON,
NATRON, TRONA
sodium chloride ............ SALT, SAL
sodium oxide .................... SODA
sodium, symbol of .................. NA
sofa SETTEE, CANAPE, CAUSEUSE,
DIVAN
soft flute stop ................. DOLCE
" hair ...................... VILLUS
" material for molding ... FICTILE
" or boggy .............., QUEACHY
" palate, rel. to ............ VELAR
" parts of the body .. SARCOLOGY
" snap .................. SINECURE
" soap; col. BLANDISH, BLARNEY
soften .. MITIGATE, THAW, ALLAY,
TEMPER, MACERATE, RELAX
soften by kneading ............ MALAX
soften leather ..................... SAM
softening, having the quality of .......
LENITIVE
soften skins ..................... TAW
softly; It. ...................... SOAVE
soggy .. HEAVY, WET, DULL, DAMP
soil ... GLEBE, LAND, LOAM, MAUL
soil, barren .. GALL, ARID, LIFELESS
soil, sub .......................... SOLE
solace .. CHEER, CONSOLE, SOOTHE
sol-fa syllables DO or UT . RE, MI, FA,
SOL, LA, SI, TE
solan goose ................. GANNET
solar deity ................. RA, HELIOS
solar disk ........................ ATEN
solar lamp .................... ARGAND
solar over lineal month . SUN, YEAR,
EPACT
solar system, device for describing; ....
ORRERIE
solar-asphyxia .......... SUNSTROKE
soldering ........ BRAZING, UNITING
soldier ... VET, CADET, CHASSEUR,
GUFFY, GI
" bandit .............. LADRONE
" , cavalry .............. UHLAN
" , French ... POILU, ZOUAVE
" , Gaelic ................. KERN
" , Indo-British .......... SEPOY
" , irregular ............. CROAT
" , Moroccan ............. ASKAR
" , Thracian ........ MYRMIDON
soldiers, anc. body of Rom. . COHORT
soldiers, body of ......... MACARONI
soldier's overcoat ........... CAPOTE
"Soldiers Three," char. in . LEAROYD
sole .. MERE, FISH, SLADE, ALONE
sole of the foot .............. PELMA
sole of the foot, rel. to ..... PLANTAR
sole, thin inner .............. RAND
soleated ...................... SHOD
solement ............. ONLY, SOLELY
solemn .... AUGUST, GRAVE, SOBER
solenodon ....... AGOUTA, ALMIQUE
solicit APPLY, SUE, ASK, BEG, COURT
solicitation .. INSTANCE, PETITION
solid, comb. form ... PRISM, STEREO
solidification .... GELATION, UNION
solidified lava ............... COULEE
solitary ..... ALONE, HERMETICAL
solitary; comb. form ......... EREMO

sollar ........ BRATTICE, GALLERY
solmization; mus. ............ SOL, MI
solo .................... ALONE, SELF
solo; mus. ...................... SCENA
Solomon .................... JEDIDIAH
Solomon Is. harbor ............ KIETA
solon LEGISLATOR, SAGE, SENATOR
so-long; It. ............. ARIVEDERCI
soluble crystalline substance ... UREA
solution .... ASSOIL, MELTING, KEY
solution, strength of ........... TITER
solve .... DETECT, EXPLAIN, UNDO
Somaliland, capital of ..... BERBERA
Somaliland desert .............. AROR
sombrerite ...................... OSITE
some .. ANY, ONI, SEVERAL, BODY
somersault ................ FLIP, LEAP
something imagined ...... FIGMENT,
                            STORY
something unfinished ........... QUAB
somewhat ........... PART, RATHER
somite .................... METAMERE
son ....... HEIR, MALE, FITZ, MAC
son-in-law . ATHUM, GENER, ODAM
son of Judah ...................... ER
son of; prefix ...................... AP
son of Ulysses .......... TELEGONUS
son, younger ................. CADET
sonance .............. SOUND, TUNE
sonata, closing measure ........ CODA
song . CAROL, MELOS, DITTY, LEED,
                            RON
song, after .................... EPODE
"   bird ........... TYMOR, VEERIE
"   composition .............. LYRIC
"   , depressing .............. BLUES
"   , erstwhile popular CUCARACHA
"   , French .............. CHANSON
"   , German ....... LIED, LIEDER
"   , Italian .............. CANZONE
"   , merry ..... GLEE, LAY, LILT
"   , mystic .................. RUNE
"   of lamentation ..... THRENODY
"   of Solomon .......... CANTICLE
"   of triumph .............. PAEAN
"   , part ........ FALA, MADRIGAL
"   , per. to ................. MELIC
"   , sacred ........ MOTET, PSALM
"   , short .......... ARIETTA, ODE
"   thrush; Eur. ......... THROSTLE
"   , twin .................... GYMEL
songcraft ...................... POESY
song-like ..................... ARIOSE
sonnet, last six lines ......... SESTET
soon . BETIME, ERELONG, PRONTO,
         TITE, ANON, IMMEDIATE
sooner ........... ERST, FIRST, ERE
soot ... GRIME, STUP, CROCK, SMUT
soot, particle of ........... ISEL, IZLE
soot sawdust ......... COOMB, COOM
sooth .... AUGURY, SWEET, TRUTH
soothe, thing intended to ... PLACEBO
soothing ........ EASING, LENITIVE,
                            ANODINE
soothsayer .... CHALDEAN, AUGUR,
         SEER, WEIRD, TELEMUS
sooty .................... FULIGINOUS
sophism, a ...... ELENCH, FALLACY
sopor .... CARUS, COMA, LETHARGY

soporific ......... ANODYNE, OPIATE
soprano ...... PONS, VOICE, CANTO,
                            TREBLE
sora .................... CRAKE, RAIL
sorcerer CONJURER, WIZARD, MAGI
sorceress ... LAMIA, HELIOS, CIRCE
sorcery, religion of; var. ...... OBEAH
sorcery ...... OBE, ART, OBI, MAGIC
sorcery, negro ................. VOODOO
sorghum; Afr. .............. IMPHEE
sorghum fodder .......... FETERITA
sorghum grain SORGO, CUSH, DURRA,
         IMPHEE, DARI, WHEAT, MOOS,
         MILLET, DOURA(H)
sorites ...... HEAPED, ENTHYMEME
sorocco, dry ................... LESTE
sorrel, wood ...................... OCA
sorrow ... BALE, RUE, RUTH, TEEN,
                  GRIEF, RUING
sorrowful .... DOLENT, SAIRY, WOE
sorry  DICKEY, REGRET, SAD, PITY
sort ... BLEND, CULL, ILK, STRAIN
sortie ........ RAID, FORAY, SALLY
so so ....... AVERAGE, TOLERABLE
sot . DRUNKARD, TIPPLER, BIBBER,
                            TOPER
sough .......... SOB, WHIZ, RUSTLE
soul ... EGO, PNEUMA, SPIRIT, AME
"   , destiny of the ...... THEODICY
"   devastators ............ HARPIES
"   personified ............. PSYCHE
"   , Sanskrit ................. ATMAN
"   symbolized ..................... BA
sound, adventitious ............. RALE
sound, deep ..................... BONG
"   frequencies .............. AUDIO
"   , harsh ........ GRIDE, SCROOP
"   loudly ..................... BLARE
"   , metallic ring .. CLANG, CLINK,
                            TING
"   of a bullet ... PING, ZIP, PRUT
"   of a dove owl ............ CURR
"   of hoof beats ............. CLOP
"   of pouring liquid ... GLUGGLUG
"   , resemblance to .... ASSONATE
sounded ..................... SHILLED
sounding .. SONANT, MELLISONANT
soup ingredient .............. LENTIL
soup, thick .......... PUREE, BISQUE
soup, vegetable ..... OKRA, POTTAGE
sour ..... WRY, ACERB, ACRID, YAR
"   , as of the stomach ....... ACOR
"   cherries ................ EGRIOTS
"   gum tree ................ NYSSA
"   in aspect ........ DOUR, HARD,
                            SULLEN
"   , like vinegar ......... ACETOSE
"   milk ..................... BLEEZE
"   temper ................. MOROSE
"   , turning .... ACESCENT, PRILL
"   voice ............ GRUM, GRUFF
source .... FONS, FOUNTAIN, FONT,
                  CALORIE, SEED
source of ipecac ................. EVEA
source of veratrin ....... SABADILLA
soutache ...................... BRAID
soutane ...................... CASSOCK
South African, (see 'African')
S. Afr. Dutch mistress ............ NOI

249

South American, (see 'American') ....
LATIN
South Dakota Indian ......... BRULE
south; Fr. ........................ SUD
S. Sea Island drink .............. AVA
S. Wales, people of .......... SILURES
S. W. Wind AFFER, AUSTER, NOTUS
"South Wind," author of ... DOUGLAS
southern ..... AUSTRAL, AUSTRINE,
MERIDIONAL
S. constellation ...... DORADO, PAVO
Southern States, col. ........... DIXIE
southwestern ................. SQUAM
sovereign ...... PRINCE, LIEGE, SOV,
CHIEF, RULER
sovereign decree .............. ARRET
sovereign pardon .......... AMNESTY
sovereignties ................. STATES
sovereignty EMPERY, RAJ, SCEPTRE,
DYNASTY, SWAY
Soviet in U. N. ................. MALIK
"    news agency ............... TASS
"    Union founder .......... LENIN
sow SCATTER, SEED, DISSEMINATE
sow bug ...................... SLATER
sow thistle; genus .......... SONCHUS
sow, young ................. ELT, GILT
soybean, enzyme .............. URASE
spa .................... PAX, SPRING
space ... ROOM, CONCOURSE, KIND,
OPEN, EXTENT, WHILE
space between bird's eye and bill LORE
space, per. to .... LACUNAL, AREAL,
SPATIAL
space theory ................. PLENISM
spaces, small .............. AREOLAE
spade .. SHOVEL, LOY, PICK, SPUD,
SLANE
spade, peat ................... SLADE
spado ......................... SWORD
spagyric ................... ALCHEMIC
Spain, famous palace in ... ESCURIAL
"   , Moorish capital of . CORDOVA
Spain, province in .... YESTA, AVILA
"   , river in DUERO, EBRO, ESLA,
TAGUS
"   , seaport of ............. PALOS
"   , ter. div. ........... PARTIDO
spall .... GALLET, CHIP, SPLINTER
span, in inches ................. NINE
spangle .................. PAILLETTE
Spaniard ........... DIEGO, IBERIAN
Spanish Afr. possession ....... ADRAR
"      Am. biscuit .......... PANAL
"      Am. farm HACIENDA, RANCH
"      Am. gruel ............ ATOLE
"      Am. Island ........ ELOBEY
"      Am. knife .......... NAVAJA
"      apron .......... DELANTALE
"      article .............. EL, LAS
"      bay .................. BISCAY
"      belle of lower class .... MAJA
"      blanket ... SERAPE, MANTA
"      bonnet ................. GORRA
"      booth or shop ...... TIENDA
"      'bravo' ................ OLE
"      brigand .......... LADRONE
"      broncho buster ...... GINETE
"      brush .............. CEPILLO

"      calico .............. PERCAL
"      card game ........... OMBRE
"      castle .............. ALCAZAR
"      chief ................. ADALID
"      Christian kingdom .... LEON
"      city ................. RONDA
"      cloak .... CAPA, MANTA
"      cloth, woolen ......... PANO
"      coffee pot ....... CAFETERA
"      coin ... DINERO, CENTAVO,
PESETA
"      coin, old .. CUARTO, DOBLA,
PISTOLE
"      collar .............. CUELLO
"      commander .............. CID
"      council .............. JUNTA
"      court ................. PATIO
"      cowboy ............ GAUCHO
"      cupboard .......... TROSTERA
"      dance ..... JALEO, BOLERO,
CARIOCA, DANZA
"      dance affair .......... BAILE
"      diacritical mark ...... TILDE
"      dish ................. OLLA
"      dollar PIASTER, DURO, PESO
"      dress ................ TRAJE
"      drink ................ PULQUE
"      duty, impost ...... INDULTO
"      dynasty, early ...... OMMIAD
"      epic hero ................ CID
"      fascist .......... FALANGIST
"      feast day ............ FIESTA
"      flat lowland ....... MARISMA
"      fleet .............. CARAVAL
"      for little ............. POCO
"      for pretty ............ LINDO
"      , for river ................ RIO
"      Foreign Min. ......... SUNER
"      for thus .................. ASI
"      gambling game ...... MONTE
"      game ............ PELOTA
"      gentleman GRANDEE, SENOR
"      governess .......... DUENNA
"      government obligation .......
CEDULA
"      gypsy ............... GITANO
"      gypsy dance ............ POLO
"      half-breed .......... LADINO
"      harbor ............. PUERTO
"      hat ..... BOINA, SOMBRERO
Spanish herdsman ....... RANCHERO
"      hero ................... CID
"      holiday .............. FIESTA
"      horse .............. JENNET
"      house ....... CASITA, CASA
"      island . BALEARIC, CANARY
"      inn ........ POSADA, VENTA
"      interjection ............ MANO
"      jar BUCARO, OLLA, TINAJA
"      justice of the peace ENTRADA
"      kettle .............. TETERA
"      kettledrum ......... ATABAL
"      king ................... REY
"      kingdom ........... ARAGON
"      knife ............ CUCHILLO
"      knight ......... CABALLERO
"      lace ................. ENCAJE
"      lady .................... DONA
"      lake ............. ALBUFERA

250

251

speck JOT, WHIT, BIT, GIFT, MOTE
speckled ........ MENALD, MOTTLED
spectacle . PAGEANT, SCENE, SHOW,
        SIGHT, DISPLAY, VIEW
specter .. SHADOW, MANES, MARE,
        WRAITH, GHOST, SHADE,
        SPIRIT, EIDOLON
spectral . EERY, IDOLUM, GHOSTLY
spectroscope ............... ECHELON
specular schist ........... ITABARITE
speculate ..... DOCTRINIZE, THINK
specule, sponge ............... CYMBA
speculum ........ DIOPTER, MIRROR
speech ......... LIP, SONANT, SURD
   " , comb. form for ........ LOGO
   " defect ................. ALOGIA
   " , figurative ... RHESIS, TROPE
   " , figure of . ZEUGMA, LITOTES
   " , loss of ... APHASIA, ALALIA
   " , minor blunders in SOLECISMS
   " , set; Gr. ............... RHESIS
   " , unintelligent ..... CHOCTAW
   " , violent KOMPOLOGY, TIRADE
   " with full breathing ASPIRATE
speechless .............. DUMB, MUTE
speed EXIGENCY, HIE, FAVOR, FLY,
        POST, RUSH
speedy ..... RACING, APACE, RATH
speer ......... SCREEN, PARTITION
spelean ............... TROGLODYTIC
spell ...... ABRACADABRA, HENCE,
        SPEAK, WORD, WRITE
spelling GLOSSIC, NOMIC, HETERIC,
        TALE
spelt ........... ADOR, FAR, WHEAT
spelter ................. ZINC, INGOTS
spend ......... COST, EXERT, WISE
spendthrift ....... WASTREL, DAFT,
        PRODIGAL
Spenserian char. ................. UNA
spent ......... EFFETE, CONSUMED,
        EVANID
sphere .. ORBIT, BALL, GLOBE, ORB
sphere, magnetic steel ..... TERELLA
spherical .. .... GLOBOSE, ROTUND,
        OBICULAR
spherical aberration, free from ........
        APLANATIC
sphery .......... ROUND, STARLIKE
spice ...... MULL, MACE, NUTMEG,
        STACTE, SEASON
spice; Bib. ................... CASSIA
Spice Is. ................... TERNATE
spiced dish .......... CLOVED, SALMI
spices, mill for grinding ...... QUERN
spicule ....... ACTINE, ROD, ASTER,
        SCLERITE
spicule, sponge ....... CYMBA, RHAB
spider ... ACERA, ARACHNID, MITE,
        SCORPION, SKILLET, SNARE
   " appendage ........ PEDIPALPUS
   " fly ........................ TICK
   " garden; per. to ....... ARANEAN
   " , leaping ......... SALTIGRADE
   " monkey; genus .......... ATELES
   " , three legged ........... TRIVET
   " , venomous ....... TARANTULA
   " , web spinning ........ RETIARY,
        TELARIAN

spiders; genus .............. AGALENA
spider's nest ................... NIDUS
spiders, study of ...... ARANEOLOGY
spies .................. PEEKS, PEEPS
spigot .......... DOSSIL, SPILE, TAP
spigot, ale ................... ALETAP
spike .... SPADIX, BROB, EAR, GAD,
        TINE
"spike" team ............... UNICORN
spike-bill .................... GODWIT
spike lavender .................. MINT
spikelet ........ LOCUSTA, SPINULE
spikenard ............. ARALIA, NARD
spill .. SHED, SPLASH, TELL, SPILE
spill over .......... MUD, RUN, SLOP
spin .. PIRL, BIRL, GYRATE, SPURT
spinach, mountain ........... ORACH
spinal ................... RACHIDIAN
spinal affection ............ MYELITIS
spinal chord ... MEDULLA, MYELON
spindle ....... HASP, ARBOR, AXLE,
        MANDREL
spindle, hollow ............. TRIBLET
spindle of a lathe ........... SANDRIL
spindle turning beam ...... TRENDLE
spindle-tree ................... GAITOR
spine .. ACICULA, NEEDLE, THORN
spine, animal ........ CHINE, RACHIS
spinel, ruby .................... BALAS
spineless, make ...... EVENTEBRATE
spinet .................. CLAVICHORD
spinet, rel. to a ........... PLECTRUM
spinet, small .............. VIRGINAL
spinet-like .......... HARPSICHORD,
        AUTOHARP
spinetail ........................ DUCK
spinner ....................... SPIDER
spinner; Eur. .......... GOATSUCKER
spinning .................... AWHIRL
spinning machine .... JENNY, MULE,
        THROSTLE
spinning mite .................. SPIDER
spinning wheel, part of a .... DISTAFF
spinning wheel rod .......... SPINDLE
spiracle .......... BLOWHOLE, PORE
spiraea ................... HARDHACK
spiral ....... COIL, HELICAL, HELIX
spiral canal of cochlea ......... SCALA
spire STEEPLE, CURL, STAG, WHORL
spire, apex of a .................. EPI
spiric body .................... TORE
spirit HEART, METAL, PEP, VERVE,
        VIM, LIFE, MORALE
   " , a good ... NORN, EUDAEMON
   " ; Arabian, myth. ....... AFREET
   " ; Egyptian .............. BA, KA
   " , elemental ............... GENIE
   " , evil ........ AMAIMON, GIMP,
        DEMON
   " , female ... BANSHEE, UNDINE
   " , impish ...................... PO
   " lamp ....................... ETNA
   " , malignant ............... KER
   " of a people ............... ETHOS
   " of censure; Gr. ......... MOMUS
   " of fire ..................... GENIE
   " of nemesis ................. ATE
   " of the air ......... ARIEL, JINNI
   " of venture .......... ERRANTRY

"  , summon ........... EVOCATION
"  , the refined ...... SOUL, ELIXIR
spirited ... RACY, FELL, FERVENT,
                                GAMY
spiritless ............. AMORT, MOPE
spirit-like ...... GHOST, ETHEREAL
spirits; Arab. .................. JINN
spirits; Babylon ................. IGIGI
spirits, guardian ................ GENII
spirits of dead ancestors ...... MANES
spiritual being .................. ENS
spiritual meaning of words . ANOGOGE
spiritual nature, depths of .... ADYTA
spite of, in ................... MAUGER
'spitfire' ...................... NIPPER
spitter ............... BROCK, DEER
spittle insect ......... FROGHOPPER
spittoon; Ind. .................. PIGDAN
splash ....... BLOT, DAUB, LABBER
splashboard ........... FLASHBOARD
splay BEVEL, CARVE, SPREAD, FLAN
spleen .................. MELANCHOLY
spleen, per. to ................. LIENAL
splendid .. AUREATE, RIAL, SUPERB
splendor ........ ECLAT, GITE, POMP,
                                GLORY
splinter SHIVER, SHATTER, FLINDER
split ... CHAP, RIVE, SCHISM, REND
split into two parts .. BIFID, CLOVEN
split pulse ................ DAL, DHAL
split, that may be ............ FISSILE
splotch ................... BLOT, STAIN
Spohr; opera by ........... JESSONDA
spoil ...... PELF, MAR, ROT, IMPAIR
spoil or seize .... LOOT, PREY, SACK
spoilation .. RAPINE, SACK, RAVAGE
spoiled .. WASTED, MOLDED, SHEND
spoilsport ................. MARPLOT
spoke .. RAY, RUNG, BAR, PIN, ROD
spoken IDEOPHONE, ORAL, PAROLE
sponge . ERASE, BADIAGA, ZIMOCCA
sponge, openings in ....... APOPYLE
sponge, orifice of OSCULUM, OSTIOLE
sponge; Scot. .................... SORN
sponge; sl. ...................... MOOCH
sponge spicule TOXA, CYMBA, DESMA,
                        RHAB, TOXON
sponge, vegetable ... LOOFAH, LUFFA
sponger .. CADGER, PARASITE, SORN
sponges, group of ASCONES, SYCONES
spongy ........... BIBULOUS, PITHY,
                                POROUS
spongy substance ........... AMADOU
spooky ... WEIRD, EERIE, GHOSTLY
spool .... BOBBIN, COP, REEL, WIND
spoom .................... RUN, SCUD
spoon ..... LABIS, TROLL, OAR, PEN
spoonbill, roseate ...... AJAJA, AIAIAI
Spoon River poet .......... MASTERS
spore ............... CARPEL, GERM
spore case ..... ASCA, ASCUS, THECA
spores, group of four ........ TETRAD
sport shirt ......... TEE, INFORMAL
Sports Assoc.; abbr. .............. PGA
sports attendance ............. GATE
sporty; slang ....... RORTY, FLASHY
spot ...... MACLE, MACULA, SMIT,
        SPECKLE, BLOT, FLAW, PLACE

spot on playing card ............. PIP
spot, small ......... FLECK, BLOTCH
spotlight ................... ARC, BEAM
spotted beast ......... PARD, CHITAL
spotted fever ..................... TICK
spotted with drop like spots GUTTATE
spousal ...................... NUPTIAL
spout ............ GEAT, JET, SPILE,
                            GARGOYLE
sprang ............... AROSE, LEAPT
spray ...... ATOMIZE, TWIG, STOUR
spread ....... BRUIT, COVER, FEAST,
                    FLARE, DELATE, SET
"  , as a decree ............ EMIT
"  , as plaster ............. TEER
"  for drying .......... THIN, TED
"  in front .............. DEPLOY
"  loosely ................ STREW
"  over ............ BRAY, SMEAR
spreading out ................ RADIAL
spree ........ BENDER, LARK, ORGY,
                WASSAIL, BINGE, FROLIC
sprightliness ............ LILT, LIVELY
sprightly ............ GAY, PERT, TID
spring ........ LEAP, DARTLE, COME,
                    SALTATION, SPA, CEE
spring back ........ RESILE, RECOIL
spring-board ......... RAMP, BATULE
spring-like .................... VERNAL
spring plant ..... CALTROP, THISTLE
spring, small .. GEYSER, SEEP, FONT
spring stay on schooner ...... TRIATIC
springe ........ GIN, NOOSE, SNARE,
                                TRAP
springing back .............. ELASTIC
springing into being .... RENASCENT
springless bullock wagon ...... TONGA
springs .... FONTS, SPAS, THERMAE,
                                BATHS
springtime; Eng. .......... OPENTIDE
sprinkle ...... FLOUR, DEG, SPARGE,
                STREW, BEDROP, BEDEW,
                                SAND
sprinkle; rare ............. SPRENGE
sprinkle with flour .......... DREDGE
sprinkled .......... BEDEWED, SEME
sprinkling ....... ASPERSION, SPRAY
sprite .... DEMON, BROWNIE, ELVE,
                    HOB, IMP, ARIEL
"  , fairy ......... ELF, FAY, PIXY
"  , mischievous ............. PUCK
"  , water .......... NIX, UNDINE
sprocket ......................... TOOTH
sprocket; arch. ... CION, CHANTLATE
sprout ............. BURGEON, CHIT
sprout from a root ............ TILLER
sprout or bud ................... SPRIT
sprout, sugar cane .......... RATOON
spruce ........ DAPPER, GIM, SMUG,
                                TRIM
spruce; genus .................... PICEA
spruce, Jap. ................. ALCOCK
spruce, Norway ................ ABIES
spruce, white ............... EPINETTE
sprue ........... THRUSH, PSILOSIS
spud-like ...................... CHISEL
spume ......... FOAM, FROTH, SCUM
spunk .... AMADOU, TINDER, SPIRIT

spur PRICK, CALCAR, GOAD, ROWEL
spur, having a .............. SPICATE
spur on a gamecock's leg ........ GAFF
spurge .... MILKWEED, EUPHORBIA
spurious . FALSE, IMITATION, SNIDE,
    FAKE, PSEUDO, SHAM
spurt ............ BURST, JET, SPOUT
spy ESPY, PRY, SEE, WORM, SCOUT,
           TOUT
squab .... CRUSH, SLOP, SOFA, FAT
squab, young ................... PIPER
squad of police ................ POSSE
squall .... MEWL, CRY, GALE, GUST
squander .............. SACK, WASTE
square .... QUADRATE, AREA, EVEN
squared circle ................. ARENA
squaring circle ........ CYCLOMETRY,
        CYCLOTOMY
squash .............. PEPO, CYMLING
squeak .... CREAK, CROAK, INFORM
squeeze .... EXTORT, GRIPE, PINCH,
        JAM, NIP
squatter ........ NESTER, NESTLER,
     MULL, PRESS, ZEST
squill; genus ................. SCILLA
squilla ..... ONION, PRAWN, SHRIMP
squinting ........ GOGGLY, STRABISM
squire.... BEAU, ESCORT, GALLANT
squirming ......... EELY, TWISTING
squirrel; Afr. ................... XERUS
 " , burrowing ......... GOPHER
 " , fish .............. SERRANO
 " , flying; Amer. ..... ASSAPAN
 " , flying; E. Ind. ...... TAGUAN
squirrel, ground .... GOPHER, SISEL,
        SUSLIK
 " , ground; genus ...... TAMIAS
 " nest ................... DRAY
 " , pelt of ............. CALABAR
 " shrew ................. TANA
 " shrews; genus ........ TUPAIA
 " , Siberian ........... MINIVER
 " skin ..................... VAIR
squirrel-like; E. Ind. ...... BANXRING
squirrel-like rodents ........ DORMICE
St. Clare ......................... EVA
stab ......... SPIT, GORE, PAUNCH,
       WOUND
stab, in fencing .... PINK, STOCCADO
stabilize ...... POISE, SET, BALLAST
stable ...... BARN, PADDOCK, BYRE,
     MEW, CONSTANT
stable, make .......... FIRM, STEADY,
       SUPPORT
stableman ...... (H)OSTLER, GROOM
staccato, not ................ TENUTO
stack .......... RICK, SCINTLE, PILE
staddle ... CRUTCH, STAFF, SWATH,
     TREE, FRAME
stadium .. COURSE, DROMOS, STADE
staff, bishop's ........ BACULUS, ROD,
       CROSIER
staff carried by the anc. bacchantes ....
       THYRSUS
staff for mountain climbing .... POLE,
  PITON, ALPENSTOCK, BALLOW
staff of an officer ...... BATON, MACE
staff, spiked ................... ANKUS

Stafford, Miss ...................... JO
stag ................... HART, SPADE
stag that has cast its antlers POLLARD
stage ........ PHASE, STEP, APRON,
        LEGIT
stage call on trumpet ........ SENNET
stage scenery ..................... SETS
stage direction ........ EXIT, MANET,
    SENNET, ASIDE, SOLI
stage direction; Bib. .............. IRES
stage extra ..................... SUPE
stage, per. to the .......... SCENICAL
stage remark .................... ASIDE
stage, side scene of the .... COULISSE
stage, slightly raised . DAIS, ESTRADE
stage washout ..................... HAM
stagger .... LURCH, STARTLE, STOT
staggers, the .......... GID, (A)REEL,
      VACILLATE
stagnation .... STASIS, CEASE, DULL
stagy ...... ASSUMED, THEATRICAL
staid ........... DECOROUS, SEDATE
stain .. IMBUE, BLOT, DYE, SMUDGE,
     SMUTCH, TINGE
stair ........... STEP, STILE, STY
staircase, exterior ........... PERRON
staircase, spiral .......... CARACOLE
stairway, moving ........ ESCALATOR
stake ... WAGER, ANTE, BET, PALE,
        PILE
stake used by swordsman ....... PEL
stale . BANAL, FUSTY, TRITE, VAPID
stalemate .......... CHECK, IMPASSE
Stalin's citadel ............. KREMLIN
stalk, dry .. HALM, CAUL, TIGE, KEX
 " for game .................. PREY
 " leaf (footstalk) ........ PETIOLE
 " of a grass ...... STRAW, CULM,
       BENNET
 " of a plant .................. AXIS
 " , short .................... STIPE
 " , small ................. PEDICEL
 " , sugar cane ............. RATOON
stall ..... BOOTH, CRIB, CAVESSON,
     LOGE, SEAT
stamen, summit of .......... ANTHER
stammer ......... HEM, MANT, STUT
stammering .... PSELLISM, APHASIA
stamp ........ BRAND, DIE, PESTLE
stamp out .................... SCOTCH
stamp with a die ..... DINK, IMPRINT
stampede .... DEBACLE, ROUT, RUN
stanch .. STEM, STOP, LOYAL, TRUE
stanchion ..... BRACE, STENT, POST
stand .......... BEAR, HALT, EASEL
stand for casks or vats ..... STILLION
stand it .... BROOK, BEAR, SUFFER
stand, ornamental TEAPOY, ETAGERE,
     ZARF, EPERGNE
stand out ..................... BEETLE
stand, three legged .. TRIPOD, TRIVET
standard ....... GONFALON, CANON,
        FLAG
standard author ................ NORM
standard, per. to a ...... VEXILLARY
standard, Turkish .............. ALEM
standing ........... STATUS, ERECT,
      PRESTIGE

standing out .. SALIENT, AWAY, JUT
standing, with feet on ground STATENT
Standish, Miles; wife of .......... ROSE
stand-offish ...... ALOOF, RESERVED
stannum .......................... TIN
stanza ............ STROPHE, VERSE
stanza, eight line ............ TRIOLET
stanza, ten-line ............ DECALET
stapes .............. STIRRUP, BONES
staple .. FIBER, LOOP, CHIEF, GOODS
star ...... MAE, RIGEL, SADR, SPICA,
WASAT
" apple-tree ................. SHEA
" , brightest ......... SIRIUS, COR
" cluster in Taurus ....... HYADES
" , comb. form .............. ASTRO
" , evening ................ HESPER
" facet ...................... PANE
" , feathered .......... COMATULA
" , fixed . ADIB, ARCTURUS, VEGA
" followers ................... MAGI
" group .................... DIPPER
" , heroic ................ ESTOILE
" in Aquilae ............... DENEB
" in Andromeda ...... ALPHERATZ
" in Argo ..................... NAOS
" in Centauri ............... AGENA
" in Cygnus ................ DENEB
" in Draconis ...... ETAMIN, ADIB,
RASTABAN
" in Lyra .................... VEGA
" in Medusa head .......... ALGOL
" in Orion ......... RIGEL, SAIPH,
BELLATRIX
" in Scorpio .. ANTARES, LESATH
" in Swan ................... SADR
" in Taurus ............... PLEIAD
" in Ursa minor .......... POLARIS
" , morning ............ PHOSPHOR
" , new .............. NOVA, NUVO
" of first magnitude ALPHA, CYGNI
" of five or more points ... MULLET
" , path of .................. ORBIT
" , relating to a ........ ASTREAN,
SIDEREAL
" shaped .... ASTROID, STELLATE
" shaped figure ............ ETOILE
" , shooting ............... LEONID
" , six pointed .......... ESTOILE,
PENTACLE
" thistle ................ CALTRAP
" , variable .................. MIRA
starch, a food ........ FARINA, SAGO
starch grain, nucleus of ........ HILUM
starch, soluble ................ AMIDIN
starch-like ............ ARUM, INULIN
starchy .. AMYLOID, FORMAL, STIFF
starchy root stalk .............. TARO
stare ............ GAPE, GAZE, LOOK,
EXPRESS, GLARE
starfish ...................... ASTERIA
Stark, Adm.; nickname ....... BETTY
star-like ...... PLANETOID, ASTRAL,
STELLAR
starling, thrushlike .............. SALI
stars, covered with ............ SEME
stars, detached SPARSILE, SPORADES
started . ORIGINATED, SPRANG, GAN

starting point ...... DATA, SCRATCH
starwort ........................ ASTER
state ...... ENOUNCE, ESTRE, ETAT,
AVER
State, beehive ................. UTAH
" , buckeye ................... OHIO
" , cotton ............... ALABAMA
" , equality ............. WYOMING
" , gem ..................... IDAHO
" , Green Mountain ..... VERMONT
" , hawkeye .................. IOWA
" , lone star ................ TEXAS
" , mountain ............ MONTANA
" , peninsula ............ FLORIDA
" , treasure ............ MONTANA
"State Fair"; author .......... STONG
state of a benefice when occupied; ......
PLENARTY
" of extremity ................ PASS
" , Swiss federal ......... CANTON
stately .. AUGUST, REGAL, TOGATED
stately woman ...... JUNO, MAJESTIC
statement .... DICTUM, DIXIT, ACCT.
static, opposed to ............ KINETIC
station .... STOP, DEPOT, RANK, SET
stationary .... STATIC, FIXED, STILL
stationary point ............ SPINODE
stationery .. PAPETERIE, PEN, QUILL
statuary, of victors ............ ICONIC
statue ...... ACROLITH, SCULPTURE
statue pedestal projecting member .....
SOCLE
statue, primitive ..............XOANON
statute ........ ACT, DOOM, TREATY
stave ...... LAG, STAP, POLE, VERSE
staves, bundle of .............. SHOOK
stay ..... ABIDE, BRACE, PROP, GUY
staylace ........................ AGLET
stead ........... LIEU, ADVANTAGE,
SERVICE
steady .. GUY, SAD, REGULAR, STAID
steady, not .... ASTATIC, UNSTABLE
steal CRIB, PILFER, SNITCH, FILCH,
NIM, LOOT, RUSTLE, GLOM, ROB
steal, as from a ship's galley MANAVEL
steal feloniously .. RATTEN, PURLOIN
steal game from .. POACH, TRESPASS
stealing ... RAPINE, PIRACY, THEFT
stealthy ..... CATTY, FURTIVE, SLY
steam .. OAM, PUTHER, FUME, REEK
steam, comb. form ............. ATMO
steam, jet of ................. STUFA
steam organ ................ CALLIOPE
stearyl .................... BENZOYL
steatite ......................... TALC
steed CHARGER, COB, NAG, PEGASUS
steel, a kind of .... TOLEDO, DAMASK
steel, armor plate .............. TACE
steel, conversion into .... ACIERATION
steel, metallurgy of ...... SIDERURGY
steel, process of making ............
CEMENTATION
steelyard weight ................. PEA
steep SHEER, SOP, CLIFTY, IMBUTE,
RET, SOAK
steep hillside .......... BRAE, CLEVE
steep slope .................... SCARP
steeper ...................... TEAPOT

255

steeple .. HENNIN, SPIRE, MINARET, FLECHE
steer ... BULLOCK, HELM, CON, PLY, STOT, BOVINE, OX
steer into the wind .............. LUFF
steered wildly ................. YAWED
steeve .......... CRAM, LADE, PACK
stein ................. FLAGON, MUG
Stella ——; star ................ MARIS
stellar-radiated ............. STARLIT
Steller's sea cow .............. RYTINA
stem .... BASE, PROW, BINE, REED, STRAW
stem joints, rel. to ............ NODAL
stem of fungus ................. STIPE
stem, part of ............ HYPOCOTYL
stem, short fleshy .. TUBER, TIGELLA, CORM
stemless .............. ACAULESCENT
stemless evergreen herb ....... GALAX
stench ...... FETOR, PUTOR, STINK
steno; word element ........ LITTLE, NARROW
stenographer of 60 B. C. ......... TIRO
stentorian .......... CLARION, LOUD
step ... GAIT, TRAMPLE, PACE, PAS, TREAD, STAIR, STRIDE
step, arrangement of troops ECHELON
step-ladder, kind of ............. TRAP
step of ladder ........... RIME, RUNG
stepmother, like a ........ NOVERCAL
stepped ................. ACTED, TROD
steps, out of door ............ PERRON
sterile ...... BARREN, EXIGUOUS
stern ................. GRIM, SEVERE
stereotype brush ............. DABBER
stern, toward the . ABAFT, AFT, REAR
sternutation ............... SNEEZING
sternutatory ................ ERRHINE
stertor ......................... SNORE
stevedore ...... UNLOADER, LADER, LOADER, STOWER
Stevens; singer .................... RISE
Stevenson (R. L.), abode in last years .. SAMOA
Stevenson (R. L.) char. ........ HYDE
stew OLLA, HARICOT, POT, RAGOUT
steward .... ERENACH, SENESCHAL, REEVE, ECONOME
steward of royalty .......... DAPIFER
steward or purveyor ....... MANCIPLE
steward to a king ........... DAPIFER
stewardly ........ FRUGAL, SPARING
stibium .................... ANTIMONY
stich ................... LINE, VERSE
stick, as a fishing rod ........... GAD
stick fast .......... ADHERE, STALL, COHERE
stick, jumping ................... POGO
stick or still ........ YET, MOREOVER
sticks, little .... FAGOTS, CHATWOOD
sticky GOO, LIMY, TACKY, TREACLY, VISCID
stiff .............. STARK, STARCHY
stiff joint ............... ANCHYLOSIS
stiffen ........ STARK, STIVE, BRACE
stigma .......... STAIN, BLOT, PORE

stigmatize .... BRAND, TAINT, MARK, NOTE
stiletto ........................ STYLET
still ...... COSH, DRIP, MUM, WHIST, YET, BUT, EVEN
still, cap of a ................. ALEMBIC
stillicide ................. DRIP, DROP
stilt .............. POGO, POLE, POST
stimulate ...... WHET, FAN, PIQUE, URGE, AROUSE
stimulus, threshold of a ........ LIMEN
sting ... SMART, GOAD, PRICK, TANG
sting, as with nettles ....... ACULEUS, URTICATE
stinging ............ CAUSTIC, SHARP
stingy ........ NEAR, SCALY, SORDID
stint .. DUTY, SCANT, SCRIMP, TASK
stinted .......... SCAMPED, LIMITED
stipe ...... PETIOLE, STALK, STEM
stipend .... SALARY, ANN, PREBEND, WAGE, PENSION
stipulate ................. POSTULATE
stir ..... AROUSE, MOVE, ADO, FUSS
stir about .......... ROUST, CAROUSE
stir; sl. ...................... PRISON
stir, tending to ........... AGITATIVE
stir up ......... ROIL, BUZZ, INFLAME
stir up, as colors ................. TEER
stirps ................... RACE, STOCK
stirrup bone ................. STAPES
stirrup leather covering ... TAPADERO
stirrup straps ............. CHAPELET
stitch .... ACHE, CRICK, PAIN, SEW, SUTURE
stitch bird ......................... IHI
stitch in knitting ..... FESTON, PURL
stoa ......... PORTICO, PROMENADE
stoat .............. ERMINE, WEASEL
stock; family ................. STIRPS
stock, N. Am. linguistic ...... UCHEE
stock ticker ...................... STA
stockade ...... BULWARK, REDOUBT, ETAPE, PEN
stocking ............ SHINNER, HOSE
stockjobbing ............... AGIOTAGE
stocky .. PLUMP, STOUT, FAT, STUB
stoker in glass works ........ TEASER
stole .... ORARY, PIRATED, LOOTED
stolen goods, rel. to .......... FENCE
stolen property ................. PELF
stolidity ........ PHLEGM, ADAMANT
stoma ................ OSTIOLE, PORE
stomach ...................... RESENT
stomach, lower opening of .. PYLORUS
stomach of birds ......... CROP, MAW
stomach of ruminants ...... OMASUM, PAUNCH
stomp ........ MASH, TREAD, STAMP
stone PEBBLE, TALUS, FLINT, LAPIS
"      age .............. PALEOLITHIC
"      and wood figure ... ACROLITH
"      , argillaceous ............. SHALE
"      , Biblical ................... EZEL
"      carved in relief .......... CAMEO
"      chip ..................... SPALL
"      chisel ...................... CELT
"      , converting into .... LAPIDIFIC

" crop ........... ORPIN, SEDUM,
ROSEWOOD
" cutter's consumption ............
CHALICOSIS
" cutter's receptacle .... SEBILLA
" dish ..................... COMAL
" , dress roughly ....... SCABBLE
" engraving ............. INTAGLIO
" face ................... ASHLER
" for grinding maize ........ MANO
" , fragments of .......... BRASH
" hammer ................ KEVEL
" heap ..................... CAIRN
stone hollow .................. GEODE
" imitation; Ital. ...... SCAGLIOLA
" implement ............ NEOLITH
" , lustrous ................. OPAL
" made in shape of a pillar HERMA
" nodules ................. GEODES
" of some fruits ............ SEED,
ENDOCARP, PIP
" on which hot glass is rolled ......
MARVER
" paving ........ FLAG, PITCHER,
ROCK
" pestle .................. MULLER
" , philosopher's ......... CARMOT
" , porous .................... LAVA
" , rocking ................ LOGAN
" , semi-precious .. SARD, TOPAZ
" , sharpening ...... HONE, WHET
" slab ............ STELA, STELE
" throwing engine ....... ONAGER
" , trim ...................... NIG
" which served as clue to Egyptian
ROSETTA
stones, conical heap of ........ CAIRN
stones, heap of .................. SCREE
stoneware .......... GRES, POTTERY
stoning, killed by ........ LAPIDATED
stony NIOBEAN, PETROUS, PITILESS
stony concretion .......... CALCULUS
stool ............ CROCK, TABOURET,
STUMP
stool, foot ...... CRICKET, TABORET
stool pigeon; slang .... NARK, DECOY
stool support .................. TRIVET
stop ......... STANCH, CEASE, FOIL,
SURCEASE, DESIST, ARREST,
WHOA
stop fermenting .................. STUM
stopgap ................. MAKESHIFT
stop; naut. ........... AVAST, BELAY
stop up .... OBTURATE, CLOSE, PLUG
stop-watch .................... TIMER
stoppage of debate ......... CLOTURE
stopper .. BUNG, CORK, PLUG, SPILE
storax, early comp. of ....... STYRENE
store BIN, MART, CACHE, HUSBAND
storehouse ............. BARN, ETAPE
PROMPTUARY, LANARY
stork, large .... ADJUTANT, JABIRU,
MARABOU
stork, rel. to the . PELARGIC, HERON,
IBIS
stork's bill; genus .......... ERODIUM
storm .... FUME, RAGE, OUTBREAK
storm recorder ...... BRONTOMETER

Stormovik ...................... PLANE
story ... SAGA, FABLE, TALE, LORE,
JEREMIAD, ANALOGY,
PARABLE, LEGEND
story, absurd . YARN, CANARD, HOAX
story teller .. RELATER, RACONTEUR
stoss, opposed to .................. LEE
stot ......................... BULL, OX
stound ........................ STOP
stout cudgel ............ SHILLALAH
stove ... KILN, ETNA, OVEN, RANGE
stow cargo .................... STEVE
straggler ............ NOMAD, STRAY
straight, comb. form ... LINEAL, RECT
straight lines over algebraic terms; ....
VINCULA
straight out ................. ARTLESS
straight passage ........... ENFILADE
strain . STRESS, TRY, HEAVE, RACE,
BEND, BREED, TAX
strainer ........ SIEVE, SYTH, TAMIS
strait .... ANGUST, KERSEY, NECK,
PHARE, AREA, ISTHMUS
strait near Leyte ............ SURIGAO
Straits Settlement port .......... PRAI
"          "          capital SINGAPORE
strand uniting white and yolk of egg ..
CHALAZA
strange ..... TRAMONTANE, EXOTIC,
UNCO, NOVEL, ODD, RARE
stranger .............. ALIEN, ODDER,
NEWCOMER
strangle . GARROTE, CHOKE, STIFLE
strap LEASH, REIM, STROP, THONG
strap of a bridle ................. REIN
straps, arm-shield ......... ENARMES
strap-shaped .... LIGULATE, LORATE
strass .......................... PASTE
strata, per. to ..... ERIAN, TERRANE
stratagem .. RUSE, FINESSE, TRAP,
TRICK
strategic .. WESEL, ARTIFICE, PLAN
strategus ................... GENERAL
stratified ................ LAMINATED
stratum ........ BED, LAY, DEPOSIT,
SEAM
stratum, rel. to ........ STREW, ZONE
stratum, very thin .. FOLIUM, SHEET
Strauss' comedy . SALOME, ELEKTRA
Stravinsky, Mr. ................... IGOR
straw .. MOTE, CULM, SHIV, STALK
straw coat; Jap. ................. MINO
straw color .......... FLAXY, ISABEL
straw-in-wind .......... OMEN, SIGN
straw, plaited ....... MILAN, SENNIT
straw rope ............ SIME, TETHER
straw to protect plants ........ MULCH
straw-vote man .... GALLUP, ROPER
strawberry-like fruit ........ ETAERIO
strawy ................ STRAMINEOUS
stray ........ ABERR, ERR, GAD, SIN,
EGAR
stray away DIVAGATE, WAIF, LOST
streak in wood .......... FLECK, ROE
streak, narrow ...... STRIA, GROOVE
streaked ................ LINY, LACED
stream .. CREEK, SPRUIT, ARROYA,
RILL, BROOK, FLOW

257

stream, bed of .. CHANNEL, COULEE
stream of forgetfulness ........ LETHE
stream placer, gold washing ...........
                 LAVADERO
stream; Scot. ..................... SIKE
streamlet ....... RUNNEL, RIVULET
streams, meeting of ........ CONFLUX
street; Span. ................... CALLE
street car ........................ TRAM
street-show ............ RAREESHOW
strength .......... SINEW, VIS, MAIN,
               STHENIA, THEW
strengthening .. BRACING, SOBORANT
stress; mus. ..................... ARSIS
stress of voice ................. ICTUS
stretched out .. PROLATE, PORRECT
stretcher .. LITTER, RACKER, STEND
stretcher, fabric ............ STENTER
stretches of intervale beside a river ....
                CARSES
strewing .......... LITTER, SEME
stria .......... FILLET, RIDGE, STRIP
strict .... RIGOROUS, STERN, RIGID,
       STRAIT, PRECISE, EXACT
stride ............................ PACE
strife .. BATE, COMBAT, FEUD, ROG,
          BATTLE, CONTEST
strike gently ...... PUTT, PAT, BUMP
strike out DELETE, EFFACE, ERASE,
                DELE
strike out a vowel ............ ELIDE
strike sharply ...... SMITE, PELTER
strike, to .. CRUNT, WHACK, CLOUT
strike to and fro .............. BANDY
striking, act of .. ILLISION, DASHING
string, hawk ...................... RAN
stringed inst. .. LYRE, ROCTA, ROTA
stringed inst., anc. ........ MANDOLA,
               BANDORE
stringed inst. device .... ELECTRUM
stringent .............. TIGHT, STRICT
strip .. DIVEST, FILLET, PARE, PASS
strip, narrow ...... WELT, LEATHER
stripe .. VITTA, BAR, RIDGE, WALE,
                FILLET
stripe, thread like .............. STRIA
striped antelope .............. BONGO
striped longitudinally ....... BANDY,
               VITTATE
stripes, marked with ...... LINEATE
strobile ........................ CONE
stroke, brilliant ....... COUP, MASSE
stroke, cutting .......... CHOP, SLICE
stroke, short .. FLIP, PUTT, WHISK
stroll ...... PROMENADE, SAUNTER
strolling .................... NOMADIC
strong .. FIRN, FERE, HALE, VIRILE
  "   drink ................... SPIRITS
  "   flavor .......... RACY, ACRID,
                PUNGENT
  "   muscles .... THEWY, BRAWN
  "   point ............ FORTE, LOUD
  "   pressure of a violin bow .........
                SACCADE
  "   S. W., S. Am. wind .. PAMPERO

stronghold ... CITADEL, MUNIMENT,
          FORT, KEEP, FORTRESS
strong-smelling .... FETID, FROWZY
struck .. SMOTE, SMIT, SHUTDOWN
structural order .......... TEXTURE
structural unit ....ID, IDANT, FRAME
struggle ...... COPE, VIE, CONTEST,
               WRESTLE
Stuarts, last of the ............ ANNE
stubble .... EDDISH, BEARD, STUMP
stubble field, unplowed ...... ROWEN
stubble of wheat ............ ARRISH
stubble, tuft of ................ MANE
stubborn ..............., ORNERY, SOT
stud with nails ................ CLOUT
student ...... PLEBE, PORER, PUPIL,
     DISCIPLE, STUDENT, TOSHER
student; Fr. ................... ELEVE
student group ...... CLASS, SEMINAR
  "   of the oceans ...................
         THALASSOGRAPHER
studio ATELIER, ROOM, WORKSHOP
study .............. CON, EYE, PORE,
    CONSIDER, WEIGH, LEER, MUG
study by lamplight ...... LUCUBRATE
study; mus. ................... ETUDE
study of mountains ........ OROLOGY
study of sacred edifices ... NAOLOGY
stuff .. STODGE, CRAM, FILL, RAM,
     SATIATE, FABRIC, PAD, STOW
stuff up .......... BOSS, WAD, STIVE
stuffed and roasted leg of mutton ......
               CABOB
stuffing ...... FORCEMEAT, FARCE,
               PANADA
stulm ........ ADIT, PASSAGE(WAY)
stumble, inclined to .......... PECKY
stumbles; Scot. ............ STEVELS
stump, in drawing ...... TORTILLON
stump of a tree ........ SCRAB, STUB
stun ...... BRUISE, DAUNT, DOZEN
stunning ............. DAZING, FINE
stunt ... ATROPHY, CROWL, DWARF
stunted tree .................... SCRUB
stupefy .... BEMUSE, BESOT, DAZE,
        DRUG, DOPE, PALL, STUN
stupid .... BOEOTIAN, CRASS, DOLD,
    INEPT, DENSE, EMPTY, VOID
stupid, as a goose .......... ANSERINE
stupid, make .......... MOPE, BLANK
stupid person .......... LOON, STIRK,
    FATHEAD, AIRY, ASININE, DULL,
               NOWT
stupidly ..... DOLTISHLY, OAFISHLY
stupor ...... SOPOR, COMA, TORPOR,
    LETHARGY, TRANCE, NARCOMA
sturgeon; genus .......... ACIPENSER
sturgeon, large ...,........ HAUSEN
sturgeon roe .................. CAVIAR
sturgeon, small ............ STERLET
sturgeon, species of ........ OSSETER
sturgeon, white ............ BELUGA
sty ...... PEN, HORDEOLUM, RISING
sty, pustule .... QUAT, BOIL, PIMPLE
style .. DUB, TECHNIC, TON, VOGUE,
    WAY, ENTITLE, FASHION

style, brief reflection ......... GNOME
style of painting .............. GENRE
style of type . RUNIC, IONIC, ITALIC
styled ... YCLEPT, CALLED, NAMED
stylet ........... STILETTO, DAGGER
stylet, surgical ..... PROBE, TROCAR
stylish ...... DRESSY, CHIC, TOPPY,
NIFTY
stylized flower .................... LIS
stylus ............ SCRIBER, SPICULE
styptic, a ...... ALUM, ASTRINGENT
Styx .... STYGIAN, HADES, LETHE
Styx ferryman ............... CHARON
subdue ...... AWE, QUASH, QUELL,
CALM, CENSOR, SOBER, TAME
subject ..... PRONE, THEME, TOPIC,
ENTHRALL, SERVANT, LIEGE
subject to analysis ......... TITRATE
subject to change ...... AMENABLE,
MUTABLE
subject to vassalage ........ ENFEOFF
subjoin ...................... APPEND
subjugate by fear MASTER, OVERAWE
sublime .. EMPYREAL, GLORY, HIGH
submerged ............. AWASH, SUNK
submerged sea plant ...... BENTHOS,
ENALID, ALIMON, SEAWEED
submission .. VAIL, CURTSY, KNEEL
submit .. OBEY, BOW, STAND, YIELD
sub-order of birds..PASSERINE, TODI
subside... SETTLE, RELAPSE, SINK,
EBB, FALL, LANGUISH, WANE
subsist ...... LIVE, FARE, BE, EXIST
substance formed after death .........
ARTIFACT
substantive ..... FIRM, NOUN, SOLID
substitute VICE, COMMUTE, ERSATZ,
SUPPLANT, DEPUTY, MEANS
subterfuge .. BLIND, EVASION, SHIFT
subterranean ..... HIDDEN, SECRET,
PLUTONIC, ABYSMAL, SUNK
subtile ...... TENUOUS, RARE, AIRY
subtle ......... ARTFUL, SLY, WISE,
ASTATIC, DELICATE
subtle emanation .............. AURA,
ATMOSPHERE
subtle variation .. NUANCE, MUANCE
subtlety . FINESSE, GUILE, QUILLET
suburb .... PURLIEU, URBAN, TOWN
subvention .. AID, BLOCK, LEG, REST
subvert ....... RUINATE, CORRUPT,
RUIN
succeed ........ GET, ENSUE, PROVE
success in love; symb. .... EMERALD
successful, be .. LUCKY, ENTER, PASS
successive .. AROW, SERIATE, DAYS
successor; law ......... HERES, HEIR
succinct ...... SHORT, BRIEF, TERSE
succor ........ AID, ASSIST, RELIEF
succulent ...... PULPY, LUSH, PAPPY
succulent fruit ................... UVA
succumb .. DIE, STAND, YIELD, FAIL
suck .... ABSORB, IMBIBE, ENGULF
suction ....................... INTAKE
Sudan, region in ............... SEGU
Sudanese ............ MOSSI, FULAH

sudarium ................. VERONICA,
HANDKERCHIEF
Sudra caste .................... PALLI
suffer .. DREE, LET, SMART, STARVE
suffice CONTENT, SERVE, AVAIL, DO
sufficient ..... BASTANT, ENOW, FIT,
FULL, AMPLE
suffix .. POSTFIX, ATION, INE, OCK,
O'S
"   abounding in ........... ULENT
"   denoting action .......... ENCE
"   denoting equality ......... ENT
"   denoting foot .............. PED
"   denoting full of ............ OSE
"   denoting geological period CENE
"   denoting pertaining to ESE, IC
"   denoting the agent .......... OL
"   from adjectives ............ ENT
"   used in medical terms ..... OMA
"   , verbal .................... ISE
suffocate .. BURKE, ACCLOY, STIFLE
suffocation, partial . APNOEA, SWOON
suffrage BALLOT, VOTE, FRANCHISE
suffuse ...... BATHE, BLUSH, COLOR
sufi disciple ................... MURID
sugar and molasses .......... MELADA
"   , artificial . MANNOSE, ALLOSE,
GULOSE, GLUCOSE
"   , burnt ............... CARAMEL
"   cane .................. SUCROSE
"   cane refuse .......... BAGASSE
"   cane stalk ............. RATOON
"   cleaning ............. ELUTION
"   compound ... TRIOSE, ACROSE,
OSAMINE
"   containing 12 atoms ...... BIOSE
"   , crude ........... GUR, MAPLE
"   crystalline ............ MALTOSE
"   foundation for candy FONDANT
"   fruit ................ LEVULOSE
"   grape ... MALTOSE, DEXTROSE
"   lump ...................... LOAF
"   milk .................. LACTOSE
"   muscle ................ INOSITE
"   , picked up lump ...... TONGED
"   , raw .............. CASSONADE,
MUSCOVADO
"   refining box ... ELUTOR, TIGER
"   sack ..................... BAYON
"   solution .................. SYRUP
"   works; W. Ind. .......... USINE
"   yielding plant ......... XYLOSE,
SORGHUM
sugar-apple .............. SWEETSOP
sugar-berry ............. HACKBERRY
sugars, simple ........ OSES, IDOSES,
KETOSES
suggestion .. CLUE, HINT, WRINKLE
suicidal ..... FIG, DEADLY, LETHAL
suid(ae) .......... HOG, BOAR, SWINE
suit ...... HIT, WOOING, AGREE, FIT
suitable..MEET, IDONEOUS, APT, FIT
suitable for singing ............ MELIC
suitcase ....................... VALISE
suit coat ........................ CLICK
suite ...... RETINUE, STAFF, TRAIN
suitor .. AMOROSO, SWAIN, WOOER

sulcate .......... **CLEFT, FURROWED**
sulfanilamide ............ **DRUG, PARA**
sulk ............... **FANTOD, MOPE**
sulky .. **GLUM, PLOW, SNUFFY, GIG**
sullage ........ **MUD, SEWAGE, SILT**
sullen ...... **MOODY, GRIM, MOROSE,**
     **RUSTY, SATURNINE**
sulpharsenate of copper ... **ENARGITE**
sulphate, double .............. **ALUM**
sulphate of barium . **BARYTA, HEPAR**
sulphate of calcium .......... **GYPSUM**
sulphide compound ...... **ALASKAITE**
 "  of antimony ........ **STIBNITE**
 "  of arsenic .......... **ORPIMENT,**
       **REALGAR**
 "  of iron .............. **TROILITE**
 "  of lead ................ **GALENA**
 "  of zinc ................ **BLENDE**
 "  to darken eyelids; Ind. **SURMA**
sulphite, lead-copper ....... **LINARITE**
sulphur alloy .................. **NIELLO**
sulphur, containing .......... **THIONIC**
sulphuric acid .............. **VITRIOL**
sultanate, Persian Gulf ...... **KOWEIT**
sultry, to make .. **STIVE, HOT, STEW**
Sulu Archipelago, isl. in ...... **JOLO**
Sulu Moslem .................... **MORO**
sum ...... **RECAP, ADD, POT, TOTAL,**
        **FUND**
sumac; genus .................... **RHUS**
Sumatra Island .................. **NIAS**
Sumatran .................. **MALAYAN**
Sumatran, a .... **LAMPONG, REJANG**
Sumatran kingdom ............ **ACHIN**
Sumatran, semi-civilized ..... **BATTAK**
Sumatran squirrel ........... **SHREW**
Sumerian deity ............ **ABU, ANU**
summary . **COMPEND, PRECIS, BRIEF**
summer bird . **CUCKOLD, WRYNECK**
 "  flounder ................ **PLAICE**
 "  , French for .............. **ETE**
 "  house .. **BELVEDERE, GAZEBO**
 "  lilac .............. **DAMEWORT**
 "  , of the .............. **ESTIVAL**
 "  snipe ................ **DUNLIN**
 "  squash . **PATTYPAN, SCALLOP**
summing up ................ **RESUME**
summit .. **ACME, KNAP, APEX, TOP,**
      **VERTEX, SPIRE**
summits ............ **CRESTS, APICES**
summon **EVOCATE, ACCITE, EVOKE,**
   **PAGE, INVITE, (RE)CALL**
summon to court .......... **CITE, SIST**
summoner ...... **APPARITOR, CRIER,**
      **SERVANT**
summons ..... **CALL, SIGNAL, CITAL**
sump ......... **BOG, PIT, POOL, WELL**
sumpter .................. **PACKHORSE**
sun beetle .................... **AMARA**
 "  bittern .................... **HELIAS**
 "  bow .......................... **IRIS**
 "  burn ........... **HELIOSIS, TAN**
 "  , circle of light round ...... **HALO**
 "  , comb. form .............. **HELIO**
 "  crossing equator ........ **EQUINOX**
 "  disk ....................... **ATEN**

 "  fish .......................... **OPAH**
 "  fish; genus .................. **MOLA**
 "  fleck ..................... **LUCULE**
 "  god, Assyr. .................. **NINIB**
 "  " , Babyl. .. **BABBAR, NERGAL,**
     **SHAMASH, UTU, UTUG**
 "  " , Celtic .... **BELENUS, BELI,**
         **LLEU**
sun god, Egypt. ........ **AMEN, AMON,**
  **ATMU, HORUS, KHEPERI,**
   **RA, RHE, SHU, OSIRIS,**
   **TEM, TUM, CHEPERA**
 "  " , Greek **HELIOS, HYPERION,**
      **MENT, PHOEBUS**
 "  " , Hebrew .............. **BAAL**
 "  " , Hindu; .. **ADITYAS, AGNI,**
       **VARUNA**
 "  " , Latin ......... **JANUS, SOL**
 "  " , Norse ............. **BALDER**
 "  " ; Persian .......... **MITHRAS**
 "  " , Sanskrit ........... **ADITYA**
 "  " , Scand. .......... **FREY, ING**
 "  " , Syrian ............. **HADAD**
 "  , greatest distance from .... **APSIS**
 "  , luminous envelope round ........
        **CORONA**
 "  , mock .............. **PARHELION**
 "  pain ............... **HEMICRANIA**
 "  , personified .............. **TITAN**
 "  , per. to the ................ **SOLAL**
 "  rooms ................... **SOLARIA**
 "  spots ......... **FACULA, LUCULE,**
       **MACULA**
 "  , standing still of ...... **SOLSTICE**
 "  worship ............ **HELIOLATRY,**
      **SABIANISM**
sunburst ........................ **ADUST**
Sunda Island ............ **TIMOR, BALI**
Sunday ...... **DOMINICAL, SABBATH**
sunder .... **SEJUGATE, PART, SEVER**
sundial, index of a .......... **GNOMON**
sundog .................... **PARHELION**
sunken fence ............. **HAHA, AHA**
sunn hemp; var. ................ **SANA**
sunrise, **DAWN, DAYBREAK, AURORA**
sun's path .................... **ECLIPTIC**
suns ............................ **STARS**
sunset, toward .............. **WESTER**
sunstroke ...... **CALENTURE, ICTUS,**
    **INSOLATION, SIRIASIS**
sup **DINE, SOPE, DRINK, SIP, SNACK**
supawn ........................ **MUSH**
superabundance .......... **PLETHORA**
superannuated .. **ANILE, AGED, OLD**
superfine ...... **LUXE, EXTRA, NICE**
superfluous ... **REDUNDANT, LUXUS**
superintend ......... **BOSS, OVERSEE**
superior ...... **MISTRESS, PALMARY**
superiority ......... **MASTERY, ODDS**
superlative, the absolute .... **ELATIVE**
superman ............... **NIETZSCHE**
supernatural ...... **HYPERPHYSICAL,**
     **EERIE, ABNORMAL**
supernatural; Arab. .............. **JINN**
supernatural being ...... **GOD, ATUA,**
     **BANSHIE, ANGE**

superscribe ........ **ADDRESS, MARK**
supersede; old law **OMIT, SUPPLANT**
superstitious, rel. to **GOETIC, LEGEND**
supervisor ................. **PROCTOR**
supine .... **INERT, LISTLESS, PRONE**
supping room .. **CENACLE, TEAROOM**
supple ............ **LITHE, LISSOM(E)**
supplement ................. **ADD, EKE**
supplicate ..... **BESEECH, CONJURE,**
      **OBTEST, PLEAD, PRAY**
supplication .... **PETITION, PRAYER,**
     * **LITANY**
supplies ........ **ESTOVERS, STORES**
supplies issued to troops on march ....
      **ETAPE**
supply food ..... **FEED, GRIST, CATER**
support .. **TENON, LEG, LIMB, PEG,**
     **BASE, STELL, SEPIMENT**
support for a statue .......... **SOCLE,**
     **PEDESTAL**
support, slab ........ **PLANCH, TRAY**
support, to ....... **AID, ABET, BUOY,**
     **SHORE, BUTTRESS, PROP**
supported ........ **ABETTED, AIDED,**
     **SECONDED**
supported by two threads .... **BIFILAR**
suppose .. **DEEM, OPINE, WEEN, WIS**
supposed .... **PUTATIVE, SURMISED**
suppress .... **CHECK, QUASH, QUELL**
suppurate ...... **FESTER, MATURATE**
suprarenal ................. **ADRENAL**
supreme **PARAMOUNT, LAST, CHIEF**
surcease .......... **REST, STOP, END**
surcoat .. **CYCLAS, JUPON, GARMENT**
surd ........ **DISC, MAN, VOICELESS**
surd mutes, one of the ...... **TENUIS**
surety .......... **SPONSOR, ENGAGER,**
     **BOND, FACT, PLEDGE**
suretyship; Can. ................. **AVAL**
surf, noise of .......... **ROTE, SURGE**
surf shiner ................. **SPARADA**
surface ...... **NAPPE, PLAT, MEROS**
surface between two flutes of shaft ....
     **ORLO**
surface, growing above .... **EPIGEAN**
surface of water ................. **RYME**
surface, per. to.. **OBVERSE, ACROTIC**
surface, small ...... **AREOLA, FACET**
surfeit ...... **CLOY, JADE, SATIETY**
surfeited with pleasure ........ **BLASE**
surfeiter .......... **SATER, GLUTTON**
surge .. **BILLOW, GURGITATE, TIDE,**
     **WAVE**
surgeon ........ **LEECH, SAWBONES**
surgeon's case of instruments **TWEESE**
  "   hammer .............. **PLESSOR**
  "   instrument; **SCALPEL, SYSTET,**
     **XYSTER**
  "   knife ....... **CATLIN, LANCET**
  "   probe .. **ACUS, STYLET, TENT**
  "   saw .... **TREPAN, TREPHINE**
surgery ..................... **ACIURGY**
surgery, father of modern ...... **PARE**
surgical compress ............ **STUPE**
  "   counter irritant or thread **SETON**
  "   hook, sharp ........ **TENACULA**

"   instrument .......... **TREPAN,**
     **BISTOURY, LEVATOR**
"   machine ................. **SCALA**
"   operation .............. **RESECT**
"   plug ........ **TAMPON, SPLINT**
"   probe, pointed .. **OSTEOCLAST**
"   puncture ............ **CENTESIS**
"   stylet ................. **TROCAR**
"   tow, moist .............. **STUPE**
suricate ...................... **ZENICK**
Surinam capital ........ **PARAMARIBO**
Surinam toad      **PIPA**
Surinam tree, wood of ...... **QUASSIA**
surly ................ **CRUSTY, GRUM,**
     **ARROGANT**
surmise ...... **OPINE, TWANG, GUESS**
surname ....... **AGNOMEN, EPONYM,**
     **PATRONYMIC, FAMILY**
surpass .... **CAP, OUTDO, OUTSHINE**
surpassed ...... **ABOVE, EXCELLED,**
     **TOPPED, BETTERED**
surplice, eccl. ...... **COTTA, PELISSE**
surplus ..... **EPACT, REST, EXCESS,**
     **OVER**
surrealist, modern ............... **DALI**
surrender .. **CESSION, CEDE, REMIT,**
     **YIELD, DEDITION**
surreptitious .. **OCCULT, SLY, SECRET**
surrounding ....... **BESET, AMBIENT**
surroundings **ENTOURAGE, ENVIRON**
surtax .......... **AGIO, EXTRA, LEVY**
survey ...... **POLL, SEEING, VISTA,**
     **PLAN**
surveying ................... **GEODESY**
surveying inst. ......... **THEODOLITE,**
     **YLEVEL**
surveying inst., part of ..... **ALIDADE,**
     **TRANSIT**
surveyor ..... **LINEMAN, OVERSEER**
surveyor's rod ................. **STADIA**
survival .......... **RELIC, OUTLIVING**
susceptible of remedy ...... **SANABLE**
suslik .............. **SISEL, SQUIRREL**
suspended ...... **PENSILE, ASPHYXIA**
suspension .. **HINT, DELAY, RESPITE**
suspension of proceedings ........ **SIST**
suspicion .. **HINT, FEAR, MISTRUST,**
     **SOUPCON**
suspicious ...... **LEERY, SKEPTICAL**
sustained; mus. ............... **TENUTO**
susu-like ................... **DOLPHIN**
susurrus ................... **SOUGHING**
sutlers' shop ............... **CANTEEN**
sutor ............. **COBBLER, SYRUP**
suttee; Hindu ............. **IMMOLATE**
suttle ............... **LIGHT, WEIGHT**
suture .... **PTERION, RAPHE, SEAM,**
     **SEW, JUNCTION**
suzerain .. **LIEGE, NOBLEMAN, LORD**
swab ...... **EPAULET, MOP, MALKIN**
swaddle ...... **BAND, WRAP, MUFFLE**
swag; slang ...... **BOTTY, PLUNDER,**
     **BOODLE**
swage ..... **DOLLY, JUMPER, UPSET**
swagger; prov. Eng. ............ **BOME**
swagger; slang .. **BLUSTER, PRANCE,**
     **SWELL**

swaggering .......... THRASONICAL
swain ....... BEAU, FLAME, DAMON,
      GALLANT, LAD, LOVER
swallow, chimney ............. SWIFT
swallow in again .......... RESORB,
                          ENGORGE
swamp .. BOG, FEN, MARSH, MORASS
  " , boggy ............. QUEACHY
  "  grass ................... SEDGE
  "  in Maryland ......... POCOSON
  " , muddy ............... SLOUGH
  "  plant ..................... SOLA
  " , rel. to ...... DRACO, MIASMA
  " ; Scot. ................. MARLSH
swampland, north of Ganges ... TERAI
swampy .... PALUDAL, ULIGINOUS,
                              UVID
swampy lands ................ SLASH
swampy region . MUSKEOG, TUNDRA,
                             TAIGA
swan, female .................... PEN
swan, male ........................ COB
"Swan of Eternity," Hindu .... HANSA
"Swan of the Meander" ...... HOMER
swan, whistling .... ELKE, HOOPER,
                             OLOR
swan, wild .......... ELKE, HOOPER
swan, young ................. CYGNET
swanky; Brit. slang ............ POSH
"Swann's Way;" by .......... PROUST
swans; genus ................... OLOR
swap .......... TRADE, EXCHANGE
sward ............ SOD, GRASS, LAWN
swarm .... NEST, BIKE, FRY, HERD,
                        HIVE, SNEE
swarming .......... ALIVE, TEEMING
swarthy .... DUN, DUSKY, BISTERED
swastika ..................... FYLFOT
swathe .... WRAP, BANDAGE, BIND
sway .......... RULE, VEER, WAVER
sweat ............ EXUDE, PERSPIRE
Swedish administrative province .. LAN
  "  battle .................... LUND
  "  body guard, one of .. BRABANT
  "  botanist .... BROMEL, FRESIA
  "  coin ............. KRONA, ORE
  "  ell measure ................ ALN
  "  explorer ................ HEDIN
  "  king ...................... ERIC
  "  king and hero ............ WASA
  "  lake .................... MALAR
  "  manual train. ........... SLOYD
  "  measure .. AMAR, STANG, REF
  "  nightingale ................ LIND
  "  philosopher ............... IHRE
  "  territorial division . LAN, LAEN
  "  weight .................... PUND
sweep-stakes ....... LOTTERY, RACE
sweet ..... DOUCE, HONEY, DULCET
sweet cicely; Eur. ............. MYRRH
sweet flag .................. CALAMUS
sweet liqueur ............... RATAFIA
sweet potato .. YAM, BATATA, PATAT
sweet potato; mus. .......... OCARINA
sweetbread ............. RIS, RUSK
sweetbriar, fruit of . EGLANTINE, HIP
sweetheart .... LADYLOVE, LEMAN,
                          VALENTINE
sweetheart, female ...... AMARYLLIS,
                         FLAME, SIS
sweetheart, male BEAU, INAMORATA,
                       SPARK, SWAIN
sweetheart; Scot. .................... JO
sweetsop ................. ATTA, ATES
swell ........ BULB, FOP, NOB, RISE,
              STRUT, BULGE, DISTEND
swell of sea ...... SURF, RISE, WAVE
swelled ............. TUMID, TURGID
swelling .... BLAIN, EDEMA, STYE,
                     BUBO, DROPSY
swelling, per. to ............... NODAL
swelter ............. HASTE, ROAST,
                          LANGUISH
swerve ..... SHIFT, VEER, DEVIATE
swift footed ......... ALIPED, ARIEL,
                          MERCURY
swift; genus ............... HEPIALUS
Swift; pen name ........... DRAPIER
Swift, the ............... BIRD, CRAN
swimming ........ NATANT, VERTIGO
swim, stroke .................. CRAWL
swimmer ................... LEANDER
Swinburne; poet ......... ALGERNON
swindle ..... TREPAN, BAM, BUNCO,
                          GYP, CON
swindler .... BITER, GREEK, SHARK
swindling; Sp. ................ ESTAFA
swine, breed of ...... ESSEX, DUROC,
                          TAMWORTH
swine butcher's shop ....... PORKERY
swine; genus ...................... SUS
swine, male of ............ BOAR, HOG
swineherd in Homer's Odyssey .........
                          EUMAEUS
swineherd; per. to ........... SYBOTIC
swinelike ................... PORCINE
swing music................. JAZZ, JIVE
swings around ................. SLUES
swink; Brit. ............. LABOR, TOIL
swirl ........................... GURGE
Swiss Alps inhab. ............ BRISON
  "  canton ... BERN, GLARUS, URI,
       VAUD, BASEL, NYON, TICINO
  "  capital ................... BASLE
  "  chemist ................ GLASER
  "  coin .. ANGSTER, BATZ, RAPPE
  "  cottage ................ CHALET
  "  house ............ RIEGELHAUS
  "  mathematician .......... EULER
  "  lake ....... BIENNE, LUCERNE
  "  mathematician .......... EULER
  "  measure .......... ELLE, IMMI
Swiss mountain ........ RIGA, SENTIS
  "  mountain pass .. GEMMI, KINZIG
  "  poet ............ AMIEL, USTERI
  "  political division ............ URI
  "  regular army ...... LANDWHER
  "  river; AA, AAR, AARE, REUSS,
                           SAANE
  "  scientist ............... HALLER
  "  theologian ............... VINET
  "  town . CHUR, COIRE, LOCARNO
  "  tunnel ................ SIMPLON
switchman ................. SHUNTER
Switzerland ............... HELVETIA

swivel ........ **PIVOT, TURN, SWING, TRAVERSE**
swollen ............ **BOLLEN, TUMID, BLOATED**
swollen or thick ............ **BLOBBER**
swooping, a ........ **SOUSE, DESCENT**
sword .. **BILBO, BADELAIRE, DIRK, KUKRI**
" , a kind of; **ANDREW, DEGEN, ESTOC, BALDRIC, SPADA, PATA, SAX, TUCK**
" blade heel................ **TALON**
" blade, weakest part of .. **FOIBLE**
" , broad cutting ........ **CUTLASS**
" , dummy .................... **PEL**
" , fencing .................... **EPEE**
" having a curved blade .. **SABER**
" handle ............ **HAFT, HILT**
" , Highland ......... **CLAYMORE**
" lily ................. **GLADIOLUS**
" , long thin .............. **RAPIER**
" , Malayan .............. **CREESE**
" of death ............. **MORGLAY**
" of finest temper ........ **TOLEDO**
" of God ................ **KHALED**
" of mercy ............. **CURTANA**
" of St. George ........ **ASKELON**
" of Siegfried .......... **BALMUNG**
" , oriental ............. **SCIMITAR**
" , pole ................... **GLAIVE**
" , seamen's ............ **HANGER**
" shaped .. **ENSATE, ENSIFORM, XIPHOID, GLADIATE**
" , stronger part .......... **FORTE**
" , two-edged .............. **PATA**
" , two-handed ........ **SPADONE, SPADROON**
swordfish .. **AUS, DORADO, ESPADON**
swordman's stake ................ **PEL**
sworn to secrecy ................ **TILED**
sybarite .......... **EPICURE, LUXURY**
Sycamine ................. **MULBERRY**
sycophant; ...... **FLUNKY, SPANIEL, TOADEATER, PARASITE, TOADY**
sycosis ................... **MENTAGRA**
syllable; Buddhist .................... **OM**
syrup ...................... **TREACLE**
syllable, accented ............ **THESES**
" added to a word ..... **PREFIX**
" , last but one of a word **PENULT**
" , lengthening of a .... **ESTASIS**
" , metrical stress on .... **ICTUS**
" of three morae ...... **TRISEME**
" , omission of last ... **APOCOPE**
" , per. to a ......... **DACTYLIC**
" , short .................. **MORA**
" , shortening of a .... **SYSTOLE**
" used in music ............ **TRA**
syllables, unaccented .......... **ARSES, ATONIC**
syllabus ......... **ABSTRACT, TABLE**
syllogism . **BARBARA, EPICHEIREMA**
syllogisms, series of ......... **SORITES**
sylph ....... **ELF, FAY, PIXY, FAIRY**
sylvan deity ........... **FAUN, SATYR**
symbol **TOKEN, PALM, EMBLEM, OM, SIGN, TOTEM**
symbol, early Christian church **ORANT**

symbol of authority ............ **MACE**
symbolic eye ...................... **UTA**
symbolical ................ **IMAGERIAL**
symmetrical ................ **SPHERAL**
symmetrical anti ......... **ANTIMERE**
sympathy **CONSENT, PITY, CONDOLE**
sympathy, lack of ......... **DYSPATHY**
symptom ..... **NOTE, SIGN, TOKEN, MARK, ALARM, WARNING**
synagogue, anc. founder ........ **EZRA**
synagogue pointer ................ **YAD**
synancioid fish Ind. ............. **LAFF**
syncope ............. **ELISION, FAINT**
synodontoid fish ................ **TIRUS**
synopsis ....... **ABSTRACT, DIGEST, EPITOME, CONSPECTUS**
synthetic silk .. **RAYON, ARTIFICIAL, NYLON**
Syracuse, master of ............. **DION**
Syria, buried city of ............ **DURA**
Syria; Heb. name ................ **ARAM**
Syriac cursive script .......... **SERTA**
Syriac hymn writer .......... **NARSAI**
Syriac script ................ **PESHITO**
Syrian (see 'Assyrian')
Syrian seaport .............. **TRIPOLI**
Syrian tribesman ........... **ANSARIE**
Syro-Phoenician goddess of love ....... **ASTARTE**
Syro-Phoenician sun god ...... **BAAL**
syrup ............ **SORGHUM, MAPLE, TREACLE**
system ... **ISM, METHOD, REGIMEN, ORDER**
system, geological .............. **TRIAS**
system of Gaelic land-holding .......... **RUNDALE**
system of symbols for pitch .. **NEUME**
system of writing for blind .. **BRAILLE**
systematics .............. **TAXONOMY**
syther .......................... **CIDER**
szopelka; Russ. .................. **OBOE**

# T

T, letter ........................... **TEE**
T. N. T. ......... **TRINITROTOLUOL, TROTOL, TOLUENE**
T-shaped ........................ **TAU**
T.V. father ...................... **DESI**
T.V. show ...................... **PANEL**
taa; Jap. ...................... **PAGODA**
tab ............. **FLAP, PAN, STRIP, LABEL, TAG**
tab, shoe ................... **LATCHET, LACE, STRAP**
tabard .............. **CAPE, MANTLE**
tabby cloth ........ **MOIRE, MOREEN**
tabby moth ............... **AGLOOSA**
taberna; Rom. ......... **BOOTH, TENT**
tabernacle .. **HILET, KIRK, TEMPLE**
tabes ..... **ATROPHY, CONSUMPTION**
table, calculating .... **FARE, ABACUS, LIST**

" centerpiece .......... EPERGNE
" , cloth for wiping .......... FILE
" , communion ............ ALTAR
" , companion .... TAPIS, METTE
" linen ................. NAPERY
" philosopher ... DEIPNOSOPHIST
" , three legged .......... TRIVET
" , workman's ............. SIEGE
tableau PICTURE, SCENE, PORTRAIT
table-land .. MERE, MESA, PLATEAU
table-land; Cent. Asian ........ PAMIR
table-land of So. Afr. .......... KAROO
tablet ............ BRED, FACIA, PAD
tablet, medicinal . TROCHE, LOZENGE
tablet of stone ................... STELE
tablet, symbol ................... PAX
taboo .... BAN, INTERDICT, FORBID
tabor, Moorish ............... ATABAL
taciturn ......... SILENT, RETICENT
tack, glazier's .................... BRAD
tack, to GIBE, BEAT, LAVEER, STAY
tack with long stitches ........ BASTE
tackle .. CAT, GARNET, GEAR, YOKE
tacky ...... DOWDY, SEEDY, STICKY
tael, one tenth of ............... MACE
taffeta, kind of ............. SAMITE
taffy; slang .. BLARNEY, FLATTERY
tag ................ FRAZZLE, LABEL
tag, metal ...................... AGLET
Tagalog ..................... MALAYAN
Tagalog child ................... ANAC
Tagalog deity .. BATALA, BATHALA
Tagalog peasant ................... TAO
Tahiti, capital of .......... PAPETEE
Tahiti, native name ........ OTAHEITI
Tahiti; supreme god ........ TAAROA
Tahitian canoe ................... PAHI
Tahitian robe ................... MARO
Tahitian woman ............. VAHINE
Tai race, one of ................... LAO
tail ................... ESCAPE, FLEE
tail, boar's ................. WREATH
tail, having a ................ CAUDATE
tail, kind of short ......... SCUT, BUN
tail of aerial vehicle .... EMPENNAGE
tail-race ......... CHANNEL, FLUME
tailless coat ................ TUX(EDO)
tailless ...... ACAUDAL, ACAUDATE,
                                ANUROUS
tailless amphibian; family .. RANIDAE
tailless animal of Madagascar TENREC
tailor .......... SARTOR, SYNDER
tailor's iron ........ GOOSE, SADIRON
tailor's lapboard ............... PANEL
tain, mirror ...... .... ......... FOIL
tainted ........ BAD, IMBUED, PINDY
Taiwan ..................... FORMOSA
Taj Mahal ................. SHRINE
Taj Mahal, site of ............. AGRA
take .... OCCUPY, TAE, BONE, DOPT,
                    USURP, CATCH, SEIZE
" away .. HEAVE, WREST, ADEEM,
              TOL, DEROGATE, REMOVE
" away from earth .......... EXTER
" off .......... DOFF, BURLESQUE,
                                  FLIGHT

" possession of .. ESCHEAT, SEISES
take; slang .............. GRAB, HOG
take advantage of .. ABUSE, MISUSE
taking, act of ................. RECEIPT
taking out ............ ELISION, DELE
taking place ................... AGATE
talapoin ..........,... GUENON, MONKEY
talc ................. AGALITE, CONTE
talc, impure ................. STEATITE
tale .. GESTE, CONTE, LEED, MYTH,
                            FALSEHOOD, LIE
tale bearer ... QUIDNUNC, BLABBER
" , Chi. ...................... LIANG
" of adventure ................. GEST
" of sorrow ............. JEREMIAD
" , short medieval ............. LAI
" , traditional ................. SAGA
talent, one sixtieth of .......... MINA
talented .... GENIUS, ABLE, GIFTED
Tales, slayer of ........... DAEDALUS
taliera ........................ TARA
talipes ..................... CLUBFOOT
talipot ........................ PALM
talisman  AMULET, CHARM, KARMA,
                                    FETISH
talismanic ......... MAGIC, SORCERY
talk  BLABBER, GAB, CRACK, HARP,
              KNAP, PALAVER, SPEAK
talk foolishly ..    BLATHER, DROOL,
                        DRIVEL, PRATTLE
talk in loud tone ......... GOPE, RANT
talk, rapid ...... PALABRA, PATTER
talk; slang .............. SASS, SPIEL
talker ............ PROSER, MAGPIE
tall ...... HIGH, PROCERE, TAUNT
Tallchief, Maria ......... BALLERINA
tallest race ............ PATAGONIAN
tallow constituent .. SUET, STEARIN
tallow tree; W. Ind. ............. CERA
tally ...... SCORE, SQUARE, NOTCH
Talmud, parts in the ...... GEMARA,
                                    MISHNAH
Talmudic title ................... ABBA
Tamara's domain .......... IMERITIA
talon ............ CLAW, FANG, NAIL
talus ankle .......... DEBRIS, SCREE
tam ............................... CAP
tamarisk salt tree ............. ATLE
tambourine .. TAAR, DAIRA, TABOR,
                        WEIGHT, TIMBREL
tambourine vibrant effect .. TRAVALE
tameness  MANSUETUDE, MILDNESS
"Tamerlane" author ............. POE
tamil yercum ................. MUDAR
Tamiroff, Mr.; actor ........... AKIM
tamper .. TINKER, ALTER, MEDDLE
tan back ................. NAPA, ROSS
tanager; Peruv. ......... LINDO, YENI
tangle ........ SHAG, MAT, SLEAVE,
                                  WEAVE
tangle of dwarf oak shrubs, etc. ........
                                CHAPARRAL
Tanis; Bib. name ................. ZOAN
tank .... GRANT, VAT, POND, POOL
tank stopper ............... BAZOOKA
tankard; anc. ................... HANAP

264

tanker .......................... OILER
tanner's solution .... AMALTAS, BATE
tanning substance ............ SPLATE
Tanoan Indian ................ ISLETA
"Tanqueray, Second Mrs." .... PAULA
tantalize ..... PLAGUE, TEASE, VEX
Tantalus' daughter ............ NIOBE
Tantalus' parent ................ ZEUS
Tantalus' son ................ PELOPS
tantivy ................ RAPID, SWIFT
tantrum ...... ANGER, RAGE, HUFF,
MIFF
tap .... PLUG, SPILE, OPEN, SOUND
tap, a kind .................. BROACH
tape, needle ................. BODKIN
taper ship's timber ........... SNAPE
tapered ...................... TERETE
tapering ...... CONICAL, FUSIFORM,
SPIRED
tapestry .... DOSSER, ARRAS, TAPIS
tapestry, kind of ............ GOBELIN
tapestry-making comb ......... REED
tapestry warp threads ........ LISSES
tapeworm .... CESTODE, ENTOZOON
tapeworm; genus ............. TAENIA
tapioca, source ............. CASSAVA
tapioca-like food .............. SALEP
tapir; Braz. ..................... ANTA
tapir; Ind. ............... SALADANG
tappet ................. LEVER, CAM
Tapuyan tribe APINAGE, BOTOCUDOS,
GES
tar . GOB, JACKY, MARINER, SALT,
SAILOR
tar, mineral ... BREA, MALTHA, TER
Taraf, subdivision of ......... DHER
Taranaki volcano ........... EGMONT
tarboosh ............. TURBAN, FEZ
tardy ......... LATE, BUSTARD, LAG
tare .\.... LEAKAGE, VETCH, WEED
target .... BIRD, MARK, AIM, BUTT
taro dish; Hawai. ................ POI
taro plant ..... GABE, KOKO, COCCO
taro roots ................ EDDOES
taro; W. Ind. .................. TANIA
tarpen .......... MILKFISH, SABALO
tarsus ........................ ANKLE
Tarsus governor; Shak. ...... OLEON
tart .................. SOUR, SUBACID
tartan .................. PLAID, SETT
Tartar .............. TATAR, TURK
  "     horseman .......... COSSACK
  "     king ............. KHANATE
  "     militia, one of ...... UHLAN
  "     nobleman ............ MURZA
tartar, crude ................. ARGOL
Tartarus ...................... HADES
"Tartufe," maid .............. DORINE
task ...... CHORE, PENSUM, STINT
task, took to ............. LECTURED
Tasmania capital ........... HOBART
taste .... PALATE, DEGUST, FREE,
SAPOR, SIP, SAVOR
  "   , a ....................... SMACK
  "   , delighting the ........ FRIAND
  "   , French for .......... SOUPCON
  "   , strong ................... TANG
tasteful ................ NEAT, SAPID

tasteless ... WATERY, FADE, PALL,
VAPID, INAESTHETIC
tasty ... SAPOROUS, SAVORY, NEAT
Tatar (see 'Tartar')
tatouay ................ ARMADILLO
tatter ......... RAG, PATCH, SHRED
tattle DIVULGE, TELL, BLAB, PEACH
tattler .... LAB, QUIDNUNC, GOSSIP
tattoo ................ PINK, POUNCH
tau cross ....... ANKH, CRUX, TACE
taunt .. SNEER, GIBE, QUIP, QUIRK,
TWIT, JEER
taurine ............. BULL, TAURUS
taut .. FIRM, TANGLE, TENSE, TIDY
tauten; naut. ..................... SWIG
tautog .................. CHUB, MOLL
tavern ......... CABARET, INN, PUB,
TABERNA, HOTEL
tavern; Span. .................. TAMBO
taw ........ ALLEY, BEAT, MARBLE
tawny ...... TAN, TIGRENE, DUSKY,
RUBIATE
tawny color ... HUE, SWART, OLIVE,
TENNE
tax . LEVY, SCAT, CESS, SCOT, TAIL,
TOLL, TRIBUTE, EXCISE
  "  assess. on default ...... DOOMAGE
  "  , Chinese provincial ........ LIKIN
  "  , English ................. HIDAGE
  "  from a monopoly ........... REGIE
tax on commodities ... OCTROI, DUTY
  "  or impost .... TAILLE, TAILAGE,
CUSTOM
  "  , Scottish .................. STENT
  "  , Scottish tribal; anc. ........ CRO,
GALNES
taxed a tenth ................ TITHED
taxes, in transit ............. TRET(S)
taxite .......................... LAVA
Taylor, Miss .................... JUNE
tazza ........................... BOWL
tea CAMBRIC, CHA, YERBA, TISANE
  "  , bitter principle of ...... THEINE
  "  box ........................ CADDY
  "  , Braz. holly .............. MATE
  "  , China, third picking ... CONGOU
  "  , Chinese ........ HYSON, PADRA
  "  extract .................. ADENINE
  "  , finely flavored ........... PEKOE
  "  , Formosa ............... OOLONG
  "  , found in ................ TANNIN
  "  , kind of black .. BOHEA, OOPAK
  "  , Labrador ................ LEDUM
  "  plant ................ KAT, THEA
  "  pot ................. TRACK, URN
  "  table ................. TEAPOY
  "  urn; Rus. .............. SAMOVAR
teach ...... EDIFY, COACH, ENDUE,
SCHOOL, CRAM, PRIME,
TUTOR, DRILL, MONITOR
teachable .............. APT, FITTING
teacher .... PEDAGOG(UE), PUNDIT,
SCRIBE
teacher's fee; Eng. ....... MINERVAL
teacher's group .................. NEA
teaching ......... DOCENT, PRECEPT
teacle .......................... SYRUP
teak tree ...................... TECA
teal .................... DUCK, CRICK

team .... JOIN, PAIR, SPAN, BROOD
teamster TOTER, BEARER, CARRIER
tear ................ REND, RIP, RIVE
tear; her ..................... LARME
tear in pieces .. LACERATE, LANIATE
tear up, as trees .... ASSART, ESSART
tear up by roots ..... ARACE, PLUCK
teardrop-like figure; Fr. ....... LARME
tearful ......... MAUDLIN, WEEPING
tears, of ................. LACRIMAL
tease .. BANTER, HECTOR, RAG, RIB
teased ............ FRETTED, VEXED
teasel ............. BONESET, HERB
ted ............... SPREAD, SCATTER
Ted Lewis' follower ......... SHADOW
tedious DREARY, NOXIOUS, ELENGE
tedium ........... BOREDOM, ENNUI
tee-hee .......... TITTER, SNICKER
teenager's party ............... BASH
teeter ............... ROCK, SEESAW
teeth ............ BITERS, INCISORS
"   all alike ............ ISODENT
"   cavity, tissue in .......... PULP
"   , concretion on ......... TARTAR
"   , destitute of ....... EDENTATE
"   , double ... GRINDERS, MOLARS
"   , hard tissue of ....... DENTINE
"   , having .......... MACRODONT
"   , long pointed ........... TUSHES
"   of certain mammals ...... TUSKS
"   , set of ............. DENTURE
"   , sharp ................. FANGS
"   sockets ............... ALVEOLI
"   , upper surface of the molar ......
                              CORONA
"   , without ............... MORNE
teetotaler . RECHABITE, NEPHALIST
teetotum ......................... TOY
tegula ........................ ALULA
tegular ......................... TILE
tegument ...... CORTEX, SKIN, ARIL
tela .......... MEMBRANE, TISSUE
telamon ............... MAN, ATLAS
Telamon's brother .......... PELEUS
Telamon's companion .... HERCULES
Telamon's son ............... AJAX
telegram ......... DESPATCH, WIRE
telegraph code .............. MORSE
telegraph inst., part of a ...... ANVIL
telegraph recorder ........... SIPHON
telegraphy, cable inst. in .... SPACER
telephone inventor ........... BELL
telephotographic lens ......... ADON
telescope site; Cal. ....... PALOMAR
television, name for .......... VIDEO
"   interference .......... SNOW
"   star .... BERLE, SULLIVAN
tell ............. RECITE, SAY, UNLIE
tell against an accomplice .... PEACH
Tell (Wm.), home of ............ URI
telling ........ RELATION, COGENT,
                              POTENT
telluride ....... HESSITE, RADICAL
telopea ................... WARATAH
telpher .............. TELPHERAGE
telson .......... SOMITE, SEGMENT
telson of a king crab ......... PLEON
temblor .... EARTHQUAKE, TREMOR

temon .............. HELM, RUDDER
temper ...... MOOD, METAL, TONE,
                   DANDER, TANTRUM
temper, to ......... ANNEAL, NEAL
temperament ....... CRASIS, ACTION
tempest .... BLAST, ORAGE, SAMIEL
tempest; Cuba ............. BAYAMO
temple, a ...... HUACA, COVIL, FANE
"   , builder of earliest Jewish ......
                              MICAH
"   , chief chamber in a .... CELLA,
                              NAOS
"   , Chinese ............. PAGODA
"   gateway ................. TORII
"   , Hawaii ................ HEIAU
"   , Mexican; anc. ..... TEOCALLI
"   , Moham. ............. MOSQUE
"   , per. to a ........... HIERON
"   , portico of a ....... NARTHEX
"   , rel. to a .............. MARAI
"   vestibule ........... PRONAOS
Templeton; pianist ............ ALEC
tempo, rapid ................ PRESTO
tempo, very slow ............. GRAVE
temporal ...... CIVIL, LAY, WORDLY
temporarily ..... INTERIM, NONCE
tempt ........ DECOY, ENTICE, BAIT
ten decibles ..................... BEL
ten gallon hat ............ SOMBRERO
ten gallons ..................... BATH
ten million rupees ............ CRONIN
ten, prefix ......... DECA, DEKA
ten square chains ............... ACRE
ten, the number .. DENARY, DECAD,
                              DECADE
ten thousand ................ MYRIAD
ten year period ......... DECENNIUM
tenacity rare ................ LENTOR
tenant ............ VILLEIN, RENTER
tenant's neglect to pay ....... CESSER
tenant's tribute; old Fr. law .... CENS
tench-like fish .. CARP, DACE, TINCA
tend ............ CARE, LEAN, MIND
tendency ............... BENT, DRIFT
tender .. HEART, PRESENT, OFFER,
                   SORE, TID, PROFFER
tender style; mus. .......... AMOROSO
tending to assist memory . MNEMONIC
tending to be arid ........ ARESCENT
tending toward an end ...... TELIC
tendon .. SINEW, STIPULE, MUSCLE
tendon, broad flat .... APONEUROSIS
tendril ............. STIPULE, CURL
tendriis ............. CIRRI, SHOOTS
tenebrific ...... GLOOMY, SAD, DARK
tenfold ......... DECUPLE, DENARY
Tennessee, first governor of .. SEVIER
tennis champ. ...... RIGGS, TRABERT
tennis stroke .................... LOB
Tennyson heroine ....... MAUD, ENID
tenon COG, TOOTH, TUSK, MORTISE
tenon-like piece ........ COAK, LEWIS
tenontitis ............... TENONITIS
tenor ... DRIFT, INTENT, PURPORT,
                              EFFECT
tenor violin ..................... ALTO

266

tenrec-like ............... HEDGEHOG
tense ............ RAPT, TAUT, RIGID
tenses, one of the verb; Gr. .... AORIST
tensile ...................... DUCTILE
tent ......... CAMP, TELD, PROBE
tent covering ................... TILT
tent dweller ........ NOMAD, KEDAR
tent; Ind. .. PAWL, TEPEE, WIGWAM
tent, large field .......... MARQUEE
Tent Maker .................... OMAR
tentacle .............. FEELER, HAIR
tentacles, without .......... ACEROUS
tenterhook ............ AGOG, STRAIN
tenth .............................. TITHE
tenuity ...... INDIGENCE, POVERTY,
RARITY
tenuous ...... GASEOUS, RARE, THIN
tenure clauses in deeds .... TENENDA
tenure of land; Eng. .......... SOCAGE
tepee ........ TENT, TIPI, WIGWAM
tequila; Mex. ................. MESCAL
teraph; Bib. .................... IMAGE
teraphim; Bib. ................. IDOLS
terato, comb. form ........ MONSTER
terebinth TEIL, TREE, TURPENTINE
teredo .......... BORER, SHIPWORM
terella ..................... EARTHKIN
tergal .............. BACK, DORSAL
tergiversate ...... EQUIVOCATE, LIE
term ... PERIOD, AGE, ERA, EPOCH,
SEMESTER
term in cricket; col. ............. ROT
term of life .............. SANDS, AGE
termagant . SHREW, VIRAGO, VIXEN
terminal ........ DEPOT, END, YARD
terminal, negative ......... CATHODE
terminal of a leaf ......... APICULUS
terminal, positive ............. ANODE
terminate ..... CLOSE, END, ABATE,
CEASE
termination .. AMEN, BOUND, FINIAL
termination and ten ............ TEEN
termite .... ANAI, ANAY, ANT, KING
tern ... PIRR, SPURRE, THREEFOLD
tern, a .. DAR, KIP, NODDY, STARN
ternary ........................ TRIAD
terns; genus ........ ANOUS, STERNA
terpene .................... NOPINENE
terrace .... DIAS, PLATEAU, BERM
terrace (in marbles) ............ FLAW
terrace, in series ......... PARTERRE
terrapin .......... EMYD, TORTOISE,
CODDLE
terrapin; order ............ CHELONIA
terrapin, red-billed .......... SLIDER
terrestrial .......... EARTHLY, GEAL
terrible ...... DIRE, GAST, FEAREUL
"Terrible, The" ................. IVAN
terrier, Dinmont .............. DANDIE
terrier, kind of .... FOX, SEALYHAM,
SKYE
terrify .... APPALL, ABAST, DAUNT
terse .. CRISP, SUCCINCT, LACONIC,
PITHY
tertiary period ............ PLIOCENE
Tesla; inventor .............. NIKOLA

"Tess and Jude"; by .......... HARDY
tesselate .............. TILE, MOSAIC
test TRIAL, TRYOUT, PROVE, TENT,
TRY
test, as an alloy .............. ASSAY
test orally ................... EXAMINE
test pot .................... CRUCIBLE
testator .................... LEGATOR
tester, or canopy ................. CIEL
testify .............. AVOW, DEPONE
testimonial . TRIBUTE, COMPLIMENT
testor ............ CONNER, CANOPY
testy ........ HEADSTRONG, TOUCHY
tete-a-tete; Fr. .. FACING, OPPOSITE
tether .. BIND, LEASH, TIE, LONGE
tether; Anglo-Sax. .......... TEODOR
Tethys .................... TITANESS
Tethys' brother .............. CRONUS
Tethys' father .............. URANUS
Tethys' husband ........... OCEANUS
tetrachord; mus. . TA, MESON, NETE
tetrad ......................... FOUR
tetter ..... ECZEMA, FRET, HERPES,
LICHEN
Teutonic divinity .............. NORN
    "     dwarf god .......... TROLL
    "     god of chase ............. ULL
    "     god of justice .... FORSETI
    "     god of peace ...... BALDER
    "     god of the sea ........ AEGIR
    "     god of the sky .......... TYR
    "     god of thunder DONAR, THOR
    "     god of war TIU, TIWAZ, TYR
    "     goddess of death ....... RAN
    "     goddess of healing ...... EIR
    "     goddess of peace . NERTHUS
    "     gods ODIN, WODEN, AESIR
tewel .... BORE, FUNNEL, TUYERE
Texa-Leaguer .................... HIT
Texan city ........ ABILENE, ENNIS,
AUSTIN
Texan county ........ SABINE, FRIO,
KNOX
Texan town .... MART, CRANE, ELSA
Texan wild cat ................. EYRA
Texas fever, carrier ............ TICK
Texas, flowering shrub .... BARETTA
Texas itch parasite ............. MITE
Texas shrine ................... ALAMO
textile ........................ ORLON
textile dealer ................. MERCER
textile worker ........... REEDMAN
texture ........ WALE, WEB, WOOF,
WEAVE
Thai ............................ SIAM
Thai native ...................... LAO
Thalia's sister ............... ERATO
Thailand town ................... NAN
Thames estuary sandbank ...... NORE
Thanatos personified ........ DEATH
thanks, great ........... GRAMERCY,
GRATITUDE
that ........... LEST, WICH, WHO
that is ........................ IDEST
thatched .......... HELED, REEDED
thatched roof dwelling .......... ISBA

267

"The Cloister and The Hearth", by .... READE
"the end" .................... THIRTY
"The Egoist," by ........ MEREDITH
"The Flying Dutchman," heroine ...... SENTA
"The Gold Bug," author of ...... POE
"The Immoralist"; author ....... GIDE
"The Just"; Gr. .......... ARISTIDES
"The Kid," by ............... CHAPLIN
"The Light of Asia"; author ARNOLD
"The Literary Fallacy"; author ....... DEVOTO
"The Magic Flute" bell ringer ........ PAPAGENO
"The Maid's Tragedy," heroine in...... ASPATIA
"The Man Without a Country"; author of ........................... HALE
"The Menace" ................. DENNIS
"The Merry Widow"; compo. .. LEHAR
"The Owl and Pussy-Cat," by ... LEAR
"The Pit"; author ............ NORRIS
"The Rivals," char. in .. ABSOLUTE, ACRES, FAG
"The Sails"; constel. ............ VELA
"The Scornful Lady," char. .. ABIGAIL
the same; Lat. .................. IDEM
"The Scorpion's Heart" .... ANTARES
"The Sheriff"; ........ (MARK)CHASE
"The Song of Bernadette"; author .... WERFEL
the, Spanish for ..................... EL
"The Three Musketeers"; author of .. DUMAS
"The Three Wise Men" ........ MAGI
"The Velvet Fog"; by .... MELTORME
"The Virginian"; by .......... WISTER
"The Wandering Jew"; author ... SUE
"The Waters" ..................... SPA
"The Wild Duck"; by ........... IBSEN
theatre .............. STAGE, ARENA
theatre, classic ............... LYCEUM
theatre curtain .............. TEASER
theatre district .............. RIALTO
theatre, Greek ................ ODEON
theatre, low class .............. GAFF
theatre; sl. .................... LEGIT
theatrical INCE, STAGY, ARTIFICIAL, POMPOUS
theatrical entertainment ...... REVUE
theatrical extra ................ SUPER
theatrical representation, art of; ...... HISTRIONIC
theatrical role ............... INGENUE
theatrical tour .................. ROAD
Theban goddess .............. NEITH
Thebes, blind soothsayer of; Gr. ....... TIRESIAS
Thebes, deity of ............... AMON
Thebes, one of the seven against ...... TYDEUS
theca ........ CELL, CAPSULE, CASE
theft-like ........ PIRATIC, LARCENY
theme ........ TEXT, THESIS, TOPIC
then; French for ............... ALORS
then; mus. ........................ POI
theodolite with auxiliary arm ALIDADE
theologian ......... CALVIN, DIVINE, LUTHER
theorbo; mus. .................. LUTE
theoretical ................. ACADEMIC
theoretical power ........... ODYL(E)
theory DOCTRINE, HYPOTHESIS, ISM
theory, proving of a ........ APAGOGE
therapy ......................... CURE
there; Latin for ..................... IBI
there; poet. ...................... YON
therefore .......... THEN, ERGO, SO, HENCE
theriac(a) ...... TREACLE, ANTIDOE
thermic balance ........ BOLOMETER
thersitical .............. SCURRILOUS
thesaurus .................... LEXICON
Theseus' father ............. AEGEUS
thesis .... MONOGRAPH, TREATISE, THETIC, ESSAY
Thespian ............ ACTOR, TRAGIC
Thetis' husband .............. PELEUS
Thetis' son ................ ACHILLES
theurgy ........................ MAGIC
thews ............ MUSCLES, SINEWS
thick .... CRASS, GRUMOUS, ROILY, TURBID
thick, as of the lip ........ BLOBBER
thick place in yarns ............ SLUB
thick, Span. for ............. ESPESO
thicken INSPISSATE, CLOT, CURDLE, LYE, CAKE, SOLIDIFY
thicket .... COPSE, BOSK, COVERT, HEDGE, RONE, BRUSH, COPPICE
thickness ................ LAYER, PLY
thief ..... FAGIN, FILCHER, PIKER, PIRATE
thieves' Latin ................. SLANG
thigh, animal's ................. HAM
thigh bone ............ FEMUR, MEROS
thigh, near the ................ GROIN
thill .................... FILL, SHAFT
thimble ............ SPUT, CAP, RING
thimble rigger .. CHEAT, SWINDLER
thin ...... LATHY, LANK, SCRAGGY, SHEER, BONY, MEAGRE
"   and delicate ......... ARANEOUS
"   , as texture ............. SLEAZY
"   , delicately ............. SUBTILE
"   leather .................... DOLE
"   muslin ..................... MULL
"   out .......... DISBUD, DELETE
"   plate ..... SHIM, TAGGER, TILE
"   scale ................. LAMELLA
"   skinned ......... LEFTODERMIC
thing .. ENTITY, BEING, EXISTENCE
thing found, a ................. TROVE
thing of little value STIVER, TRINKET
thing to be done ........... AGENDUM
things .................... TRAPS, ITS
things done ...................... ACTA
things, exaggerated ....... HOWLERS
things, in law .............. REM, RES
thingumajig .................. GADJET

think .. OPINE, DEEM, MUSE, TROT, WIS, BROOD, MULL
thinly scattered ...... RARE, SPARSE
thinness ........ TENUITY, SLENDER
third degree of scale ...... MEDIANT
third, every ................ TERTIAN
third, in music ................ TIERCE
third power, raise to ............ CUBE
third stage ................ AUTUMN
35 cubic feet ...................... TON
this; Lat. ......................... HOG
Thisbe, paramour of ....... PYRAMUS
thisness ................. HAECCEITY
thistledown ........ EGRET, PAPPUS
thistle family ...... ARNICA, COSMOS
thistle-like plant; genus .... CARLINA
thither ........ THERE, YON(D), TO, TOWARD
thole .. FULGRUM, OARLOCK, BEAR, ENDURE
Thomas; opera by ........... MIGNON
Thompson ......... (ERNEST)SETON
thong KNOUT, STRAP, WHIP, ROMAL
thong, oxide ...................... RIEM
thong; Span. ................... QUIRT
thoom; Scot. ................. THUMB
thorax ......................... CHEST
thorn STUG, SPINE, STOB, PRICKLE
thorn apple ................. DATURA
thorn-back .............. RAY, SKATE
thorn; comb. form .............. SPINI
thornless ...................... INERM
thorn-like .......... SPINATA, SPINE
thoroughwort.. ............ BONESET
thorp ...... HAMLET, VILLA, TOWN
Thor's father .................... ODIN
Thor's magic hammer ..... MJOLLNIR
Thor's stepson ................... ULL
Thor's wife ......................... SIF
those excelling in table philosophy .... DEIPNOSOPHISTS
those in office .................... INS
those interested .............. CARERS
those who give blood ........ DONORS
thought, doctrine of law .... NOETICS
thought, force ............ PHRENISM
thousand years ........ MILLENNIUM, CHILIAD
thousandth .............. MILLESIMAL
thousandth of an inch ............ MIL
Thrace, town in ............. SESTOS
Thracian musician; myth. . ORPHEUS
thrall .......... ESNE, SERF, SLAVE
thralldom ................. BONDAGE, SERVITUDE
thrash TROUNCE, BLESS, BELABOR, CANE, DRUDGE, FLAIL, TAN, FLOG, LAM, URTICATE
thread .... LISLE, REEVE, STAMEN, LINE
"   , ball of ........ CLEW, CLUE
"   , comb. form ............ NEMA
"   fish ...... COBBLER, CUTLASS
"   , shoemaker's ........ LINGEL
"   , silk .................... TRAM
"   , surgical .............. SETON

"   testing device .... SERIMETER
"   worm .. FILARIA, NEMATODE
threadbare .......... TRITE, CORNY, SHABBY
thread-herring ................. SHAD
thread-like FIBROID, FILAR, FILOSE, LINEAR
threads, fine; comb. form ........ BYSS
threads of linen tape .......... INKLES
threads, separate .......... SLEAVES
threap; Scot. ................... ARGUE
three ........ TER, THRIN, TRI, TRIA
three dimensional ............ STEREO
three, group of ......... TERN, TRIAD
three herrings .................. WARP
three in one ................... TRIUNE
three knotted .............. TRINODAL
three of a kind ................ LEASH
three-banded armadillo ......... APAR
three-branched candlestick TRICERION
three-fold TERNAL, TREBLE, TRINE
three-leaved clover .......... TREFOIL
three-legged stand TEAPOY, TREVET
three-mast schooner ............ TERN
three-penny piece; Eng. dial. .. THRIP
three-toed sloth ...... AI, EDENTATE
threnody .... CORONACH, REQUIEM, DIRGE
threshel; obs. ................... FLAIL
threshold . GATE, SILL, DEARN, EVE, LIMEN
threw ......................... TOSSED
thrice; prefix ............... TER, TRI
thrill ........ DINDLE, FLUSH, TIRL
thrilling .................... ELECTRIC
thrive .... ADDLE, BATTEN, PROVE
throat ............... MAW, GULA
throat affection .............. ANGINA
throat, per. to .. ESOPHAGUS, GULAR
throb, to; local .. ACHE, QUOB, QUOP
throbbing .... PALPITANT, PITAPAT
throe .... ACHE, PAIN, PANG, RACK
throne ...... EXALT, SOVEREIGNTY
throng HOST, CREW, SWARM, PRESS
throstle ...................... THRUSH
through ............ DIA, PER, TRUG
throw ... COP, CAST, HEAVE, KEST, YEND
throw carelessly .......... SLAP, SHY
throw obliquely . DEAL, TOSS, SKEW
throw out .. BOUNCE, LADE, ECEST
thrush ...... OUSEL, ROBIN, SPREW, SPRUE, THROSTLE
thrush, Bengal ant .......... NURANG
thrush disease .............. APHTHA
thrush, ground ................ PITTA
thrush, Hawai. .............. OLOMAO
thrush, song .......... MAVIS, VEERY
thrust .... DIG, RETRUDE, DARTLE, ONSET, ALLONGE, LUNGE, POSS
thrust aside .......... SHOVE, DAFF
thrust by pushing .. ENTER, PIERCE
thud ............ BUMP, BEAT, BLOW
thug . GUNMAN, RUFFIAN, CUTTLE, YEGG, GOON, ROUGHNECK

thuja ................... ARBORVITAE
thumb ....................... POLLEX
thumb, per. to ball of ........ THENAR
thump; Scot. PUMMEL, YERK, CLOUR
thunder; myth. ................. THOR
thunderfish ............ LOACH, RAAD
thurify ............. CENSE, SCATTER
thurible ....................... CENSER
thus ................ DYCE, TUS, SUA
thus far .... YET, DEGREE, EXTENT
thus; Lat. ..................... ITA, SIC
thwack CLUB, MAUL, RAP, POMMEL
thwart BAFFLE, BALK, FOIL, SPITE
thymus .... GLAND, SWEETBREAD,
                                    MINT
tiara CROWN, FRONTLET, CORONET
Tibet, capital of ................ LASSA
Tibet, Lama of ................ DALAI
Tibetan antelope ............ GOA, SUS
    "    beer ................... CHANG
    "    city ................... LHASA
    "    ox ....................... YAK
    "    priest ................. LAMA
    "    wild ass .............. KIANG
    "    wild car ............. MANUL
tibia ............ CNEMIS, SHINBONE
Tibur; anc. name ............. TIVOLI
tic; Malay ............. LATA, LATAH
tick ....... ACARID, CREDIT, MITE
tick; genus ........... IXODE, ARGAS
tick, sheep ....................... KED
tick; So. Am. .............. CARAPATO
ticket ........ SLATE, DUCAT, NOTE,
                                    SLIP
tickle ..................... TITILLATE
tidal flow . ESTUARY, SURGE, BORE,
                    EAGRE, EBB, NEAP
tide; Eng. ....................... FAIR
tide, swift; obs. ................. RAT
tidewater ................. SEACOAST
tiding .... ADVICE, NEWS, SLOGAN,
                    REPORT, WORD
tidy ... SPRUCE, TED, NEAT, TRIM,
                                    SNOD
tie a sail ........................ TRICE
tie knot ......................... CAST
tie; Lat. ........................ NEXUS
tie or lash ...................... YERK
tie, universal ................. TACHE
tie up .................. PACK, TRUSS
tier .... RANK, ROW, SERIES, BANK,
                                    CHESS
tiff ................. HUFF, PET, SPAT
tiffin .... LUNCHEON, REPAST, TEA
tiger Amer. ................... JAGUAR
tiger family, of the ........ FELIDAE
tiger in Persia ................. SHEK
tighten .. LACE, STRAITEN, TAUTEN
tighten, as a drum ............. FRAP
tightwad .... FIST, PIKER, STINGY,
                            SKINFLINT
til ........................... SESAME
tile, as of marble ............. DALLE
tile, curved ................. PANTILE
tile, large ............ QUARRY, SLAB

tile pattern ................... MOSAIC
tile, per. to a .............. TEGULAR
tile to ................... TESSELLATE
tiler ...... HELLIER, DOORKEEPER
tilery ........................... KILN
tillage, fit for ................ ARABLE
tilled land: U. S. A. ............ ARADA
tiller ........ FARMER, HARROWER,
            PLOWMAN, SHOOT, SAPLING
tiller naut. ........ HELM, TIMONEER
tillet, the; obs. .............. LINDEN
tilly-vally ...................... BOSH
tilt HEEL, LIST, TIP, JOUST, CAVE,
                        GIUST, ASLANT
timber, convex .............. CAMBER
    "    , decay in ............ DOATY
    "    , down bend in .......... SNY
    "    , half rotten; var. ...... DOTY
    "    , heart wood of .... DURAMEN
    "    , Norway .............. DRAM
    "    of a ship, upright ........ BITT
    "    , squared .............. CANT
    "    support .............. CORBEL
    "    , to taper a ship's ..... SNAPE
    "    tree, (see 'tree')
    "    trees, tropical; genus ..........
                                    SLOANEA
timbre, per. to ........ DRUM, TONAL
timbrel ............ TABOR, SISTRUM
time ... DATE, SPELL, EPOCH, ERA,
                                    TENSE
time, error in order of ANACHRONISM
time fixed for payment of a bill of
    exchange ................... USANCE
time, incalculable period of ...... EON
time; mus. ..................... TEMPO
time of day ..................... NOON
timely ........ EARLY, PAT, PROMPT
timepiece ............ CHRONOSCOPE,
                                    HOROLOGE
timepiece, a kind of .... HOURGLASS
timepiece, per. to a .. GNOMON, DIAL
timepiece, water ........ CLEPSYDRA
times ......................... DATES
times, past; collec. ....... ONST, AGO
timid ...... SCARY, SHEEP, HENNY,
                    MOUSY, SELY, SHY
timon ................. HELM, TILLER
Timor, coin of ..................... AVO
timorous ........ SHRINKING, TIMID
timpano .............. KETTLEDRUM
tin ........................ STANNUM
    "    box ................... TRUMMEL
    "    dinner pail ............ BLICKEY
    "    fish ................... TORPEDO
    "    foil for mirrors ............. TAIN
    "    mine ................ STANNARY
    "    mine, workman in .... SPADIARD
    "    plate, thin ....... FOIL, TAGGER
    "    roofing ................. TERNE
tin sheet ..................... LATTEN
    "    smelting, slag from .... QUITTER
    "    , symbol for ................. SN
tinamon; So. Am. .. YUTU, TATAUPA
tinct; arc. ..................... IMBUE
tincture .... DASH, IMBRUE, TRACE

270

tind; Scot. .................... KINDLE
tinder, artificial ..... AMADOU, PUNK
tine ............. BIT, PRONG, TYND
tinea ..................... RINGWORM
tined, three ............ TRIDENTATE
tinge .. CAST, COLOR, DYE, IMBUE,
TINT
tinge; Scot. ............... SOO, THIRL
tint ... HUE, NUANCE, TONE, STAIN
tint; dial. ................. BIT, SCRAP
tintinnabula ................... BELLS
tiny MINUTE, PETITE, TEENY, WEE
tiny creature ...... ATOMY, MINIMUS
tip ...... LIST, CANT, HEEL, POINT,
TILT, TOE, COCK, POURBOIRE
tippet ............. ALMUCE, SCARF,
MUFFLER
tipple NIP, BIB, GILL, LIQUOR, POT
tippler .. TOPER, PIGEON, TUMBLER,
WINER
tipster ......... TOUT, SPECULATOR
tipsy ........ REE, DRUNK, GROGGY,
MERRY
tirade ............. SCREED, SPEECH
tire ... BORE, TUCKER, SHOE, FAG,
IRK, JADE
tire saver ........ RECAP, RETREAD
tire shoe ..................... CASING
tisane ........................ PTISAN
tissue .. BAST, FAT, FABRIC, FIBER,
WEB
"      connecting . TENDON, STROMA
"      decay, of .............. CARIES
"      , hardening of a .. SCLEROSIS
"      , nerve ................... ALBA
"      , weblike ................ TELA
tissues, substance in ........ SARCINE
titailleur ............... SKIRMISHER
Titan, a ......... OCEANUS, ATLAS,
HYPERION
Titan, female .......... DIONE, RHEA
Titan; Hindu myth. .............. BANA
titanate ............ ISERITE, RUTILE
titanic ...... ENORMOUS, GIGANTIC
titanite ...... LEDERITE, SPHENE
Titania's husband ........... OBERON
titanic iron ore sand ........ ISERINE
titanium, principal ore of .... ILEMITE
Titans, one of the . IAPETUS, CRONOS
Titan's parents ...... GAEA, URANUS
tithe .......... TEIND, TENTH, TAX,
DECIMAL
tithing ........ DIME, TEN, DENARY
titi ........................... MONKEY
titivate, to .... SPRUCE, CULTIVATE
titlark ........................... PIPIT
title .. MUNIMENT, NAME, CAPTION
title of dignity ........ ESQUIRE, SIR
title of respect; Eastern .. AGA, BABA
titled member of Stock Ex. Eng. .......
ORCHID
titmice, family BLUECAPS, PARIDAE
titmouse ... GOOSANDER, TAT, MAG,
PARUS, JACKSAW, OXEYE,
BLUECAP
titmouse, blue .. TOMTIT, NUN, YAUP

Tito (Josip) .................... BROZ
Tito, followers of ............ CROATS
titter ...... TEHEE, GIGGLE, LAUGH
tittle ..... GOSSIP, IOTA, JOT, WHIT
tittup ............... CAPER, PRANCE
title, diacritical mark .... TILDE, DOT
titular ................. COG)NOMINAL
"Titus Andronicus," queen .. TAMORA
Tivoli, anc. Roman name ...... TIBUR
Tlingit Ind. .................... TONGA
Emesis ...................... DIACOPE
toastmaster ................... EMCEE
to .... AT, FORWARD, ON, THITHER
" another place; Lat. ............ ALIO
" be; Fr. ....................... ETRE
" be; Lat. ...................... ESSE
" bend .......................... FLEX
" bring forth .................. HATCH
" condense and hold ........ ABSORB
" go ............................ FARE
" knight ......................... DUB
" to love; Fr. .................. AIMES
" make blunt ............... OBTUND
" pack ........................... TIN
" paint .......................... LIMN
" paint, comb. form; Lat. ...... PICTO
" pieces ...................... APART
" plot ..................... MACHINATE
" sail, wind abeam .............. LASK
" that ...................... THERETO
" wit .......... NAMELY, SCILICET,
VIDELICET, VIZ
toad .. AGUA, PIPA, LIZARD, THING
toadflax ..................... RAMSTED
toast .. BREDE, LEEP, SOAKER, TAN
toast; pledge .................. SKOAL
tobacco ...... CAPORAL, UPPOWOC,
LATAKIA, CAPA, KNASTER,
VUELTA, CUBAN
tobacco left in pipe .......... DOTTEL
tobacco pipe ................ CHIBOUK
tobacco plant, heart leaf .... RATOON
tobacco pouch .................. DOSS
toby ........ CIGAR, HIGHWAY, MUG
tode .............................. SLED
toe ................ DACTYL, DIGIT, TAE
toe, the great ................. HALUX
toga .......................... TRABEA
together ...... SAMEN, UNION, MASS
together; prefix ................... COM
toggery ............. CLOTHES, GARB
toggle .... COTTER, KEY, BOLT, ROD
toil ........... DARG, SNARE, NET
toilet case ............ ETUI, ETWEE
Tojo Jap. general ............ HIDEKI
token .... SCRIP, AMULET, BADGE,
EARNEST, INDEX, SIGN
token of respect .......... ACCOLADE
tolerate ...... STAND, ABIDE, BEAR,
BROOK
toll RING, KNELL, PEAGE, TAILAGE
Tolstoy ........................... LEO
Toltecs, anc. capital ............ TULA
tolypeutine ...... APAR, ARMADILLO
Tom Tulliver's river ............ FLOSS

271

tomb ...... MASTABA, CRYPT, LAIR, VAULT
tomb, empty ............. CENOTAPH
tomb for bones of dead ...... OSSUARY
tomboy ... HOYDEN, ROMP, TOMRIG
tommy .............. FOOL, PODGER
Tom-O'-Bedlam ............. MADMAN
Tom-of-Lincoln ................. BELL
tomorrow; Span. ............ MANANA
toncan ...... ARACARI, TEAN, TOCO
tone ................ ENERGY, VIGOR
tone of character; mus. ...... TIMBRE
tone, rhythmical ............ CADENCE
tone, variation in; Fr. ...... NUANCE
toneless ...................... ATONY
Tonga Is. district ............ VAVAU
tongs; slang .............. OVERALLS
tongue LORRIKER, DIALECT, PRATE, TAB
tongue, a ...................... PALE
tongue bird ................ WRYNECK
tongue bone ................. HYOID
tongue fish ..................... SOLE
tongue, small projections on PAPILLAE
tongue, tip of the ............ CORONA
tongueless toads; genus ..... AGLOSSA
tongue-like processes ....... LIGULAE
tongues, the ................. GLOSSA
Tonkin; Indo-Chin. cap. ....... HANOI
tonneau ....................... TONNE
tonsil ........... AMYGDALA, TISSUE
too ........ ALSO, AND, ELSE, OVER
too much ... NIMIETY, EXTREMELY
too much; Fr. .................... TROP
tool .. REBEL, CONER, PUPPET, RAT
 " , bookbinder's ............. GOUGE
 " , cutting .................. ADZE
 " , engraver's ............... BURIN
 " , flat spreading ........ SPATULA
 " for cames ............... LADKIN
 " for cleaving shingles ...... FROW
 " , garden ..... SEEDER, DIBBLE, HOE, RAKE, SPADE
 " , marble workers ......... FRAISE
 " , metal workers . DOLLY, SWAGE
 " , steel, for lossening ore ..... GAD
 " , trimming .................. ZAX
tools ....... DOLLY, KIT, MATTOCKS
tools, theft of ................ RATTEN
toomly ................ EMPTY, IDLY
toot; Scot. ............. DRAFT, SHOR
toot plant ....................... TUTU
tooth ................. GAM, INCISOR
 " , comb. form for ....... ODONTO
 " decay .................... CARIES
 " gear wheel .................. COG
 " grinding surface ......... MENSA
 " , having but one .... MONODONT
 " , lower part of ........... FANG
 " molar ..................... WANG
 " or spike ................... TINE
 " , part of ............. DENTINE
 " , projecting ............... SNAG
 " sockets ............... ALVEOLI
 " sprocket wheel ............ GUB
toothache ..... WORM, ODONTALGIA
toothless .. DENTALGIA, EDENTATE
top .. APEX, CAP, COP, VERTEX, LID
top, a child's .................... NUN
top of a stand for making tiles .. CRISS
top or ridge . CREST, SUMMIT, ACME, APEX
top, "put-or-take" ....... TEETOTUM
tope ............ RIG, STUPA, SHARK
Topeka Governor ................. ARN
toper .. BOOZER, DRUNK, TOSSPOT, SOT
Topi, Ind. ................... HELMET
topiary ......... CLIPPED, TRIMMED
topic .......... THEME, TEXT, HEAD
topical ........ THEMATIC, LOCAL
topical heading ................ TROPE
topics ...................... THEMATA
topknot on the tragic mask ... ONKOS
topmast square crossbar .......... FID
topnotch ................. CREST, ACE
top-shaped ............. TURBINATED
topsy-turvy ..... ASKEW, INVERTED
tor ................................ CRAG
tora ........................... TETEL
torbernite ................... URANITE
torch .......... LANTERN, CRESSET
torchman ................... LINKMAN
tore, per. to ................ TOROIDAL
torero ............... BULLFIGHTER
torment RACK, TEASE, BAIT, DEVIL, PLAGUE, BADGER
tormenter .......... BAITER, STRIGIL
torn ........... RIVEN, RENT, SPLIT
torpedo ...... DETONATOR, MISSILE
torpedo fish ...................... RAY
torpedo, front end of ............ NOSE
torpedo, inventor of the . WHITEHEAD
torpor ............. COMA, STUPOR
torque .... STRAIN, TWIST, COLLAR
torrent .... FLOOD, FLOW, STREAM, SPATE, DOWNPOUR
torrid .. TROPICAL, HOT, PARCHING
tortilla cooking dishes .... COMMALES
tortoise ........................ EMYD
 " , Cen. Amer. ........ HICATEE
 " , marsh; genus ......... EMYS
 " ; order ............ CHELONIA
 " shell ............. CARAPACE
 " , South Amer. ... MATAMATA
 " , species of .......... GOPHER
torture ...... MARTYR, PAIN, RACK, FLAY
tocsin ................ ALARM, BELL
toss about .... BANDY, TAVE, FLING
tosspot .... DRUNKARD, SOT, TOPER
tot .... ADD, CHILD, COUNT, DRINK
total ...... UTTER, ENTIRE, WHOLE
total development of a particular vegetation ................ EOSERE
totem post ..... XAT, FIGURE, POLE
totipalmatae ........ STEGANOPODES
totter .. BRANDLE, ROCK, SHAKE
toucan .............. ARACARI, TOCO
toucan; Fr. ................. GUARANI
touch ...... SHAVE, PALP, IMPINGE, MEET, TIG, TWIDDLE
touch, as a medium .... TRIAL, TENT, TEST
touch; comb. form ................ TAC
touch, examine by .... TRY, PALPATE
touch; Fr. ................. SOUPCON

touch; inst. for measuring ............. HAPTOMETER
touch, perceptible by ........ TACTILE
touch up, as a motor ............. REV
touch-down ...................... GOAL
touch-hole ...................... VENT
touch-me-not; Lat. ...................... NOLI-ME-TANGERE
touching .... ATTINGENT, TANGENT
touchstone ......... TEST, BASANITE
touchwood; AMADOU, PUNK, SPUNK, TINDER
touchwood, per. to ............ AGARIC
tough .... WIRY, COHESIVE, WITHY, LEATHERY
tough; col. ... ROWDY, DISORDERLY
tough pitch ................... COPPER
toughen .................... TAW, TOR
Toulouse, magistrate of ... CAPITOUL
tourists' lodge ................. MOTEL
tourmaline, black ............ SCHORL
tourmaline, colorless ...... ACHROITE
tourmaline, green and blue INDICOLITE
tourmaline, red .......... RUBELLITE
tournament CONTEST, JOUST, MATCH
tourniquet ...... GARROT, BANDAGE
tow ....................... HALE PULL
tow, of flax hemp .... HARDS, HURDS, CODILLA
tow rope .......................... TEW
toward .......... GAIN, TO, LATERAD
toward; prefix ...................... AD
toward the center ............. ENTAD
toward the exterior ........... ECTAD
toward the mouth .............. ORAD
toward the red corpuscle side . HEMAD
towards .................... YNESCHE
towel .......... CLEAN, DRY, WIPER
towel fabric ................... TERRY
tower ..... MINARET, TURRET, TOR, TORRION
"     , as a marker ............ PYLON
"     , Buddhist ................. TOPE
"     , circular ................. DOME
"     , circular fort ...... MARTELLO
"     , Indian ................... MINAR
"     , mediaeval ............ DONJON
"     of glacial ice ............ SERAC
"     , pyramidal ..... SIKHRA, SIKRA
"     , small ............... TOURELLE
"     , small round .......... RONDEL
"     , Spanish ............. ATALAYA
"     , spirical .. STEEPLE, CUPOLA
towhee ............ CHEWINK, FINCH
town by ocean; abbr. ............. SPT
townsman ..... RESIDENT, CIT, CAD, SELECTMAN
townsman at Eton College .. OPPIDAN
toxic in snake poison ......... VENOM
toxine ............. POISON, VENENE
toy .......... DALLY, TOP, BAUBLE TEETOTUM
toy bear ........................ TEDDY
trabea ........................... TOGA
trace ...... CLEW, VESTIGE, TRACK, TRAIL
trachite .................... DOMITE
track, a .......... RUT, FOOTPRINT
track of a deer ................. SLOT

track of a wild animal ........ SPOOR
tractate .................... TREATISE
tract, level ................... STEEPE
Tracy (Dick) Mrs. .............. TESS
trade ......................... CRAFT
trade; Fr. ..................... METIER
trademark .................... BRAND
trader ............... (FELL)MONGER
tradesman ............. ARTISAN, CIT
trading .......... MONGERY, VENAL
trading post .. MART, STATION, FORT
tradition ......... FOLKLORE, MYTH
traffic, per. to ............. PERMUTE, SIMONIACAL
trafficking ...... BROKING, TRADING
tragacanth; Persian ............. GUM
tragopan ................. PHEASANT
trail SPOOR, ABATURE, DRAG, FOIL, SLOT
trail along ......... TRAPE, TRUDGE, FOLLOW
trail, per. to a . VENT, ODOUR, SCENT
trail; Sp. ...................... COMINO
trailleur; Algerian ............. TURCO
train .. CORTEGE, RETINUE, BREED, DRESS, CHAIN, NURTURE
train hawk .................... AFAITE
tramp . HOBO, LANDLOPER, NOMAD, BUM, PAD
tramp, kind of ......... WALLETEER, SUNDOWNER
tramp, to ...... HIKE, TRAPE, VAMP
tranquil ..... SERENE, EASY, LOWN, STILL
transact .......... DEAL, DO, TREAT
transaction ........ ACTUM, TRAFFIC
transcend ...... EXCEL, OUTDO, CAP
transcript ................. APOGRAPH
transept ............ PLAGE, ARMS
transfer ... CEDE, DEPUTE, GRANT, LET, CONVEY, PASS, REMOVE
transfer design ................. DECAL
transfer legally ........ ALIENATION, ATTORN, ABALIENATE
transfix .. NAIL, IMPALE, PIN, STAB
transform ...... TRANSMUTE, TURN
transgress .. VIOLATE, INFRACT, SIN
transition ............... KATABOLISM
translated ... RENDERED, DECODED
translation .... PONY, PARAPHRASE
transmitting device .. MIKE, SENDER
transparent .... DIAPHANOUS, LAKY
transparent mineral ............. MICA
transport ... SHIP, RAPT, RAPTURE, CARRY
transportation ....... RAILAGE, DAK, LATION
transpos. of sounds and letters ........ SPOONERISM
Transvaal gold region .......... RAND
Transvaal legislature ........... RAAD
trap . NAIL, NET, PIT, GIN, SPRINGE, TOIL
trapper . SNARER, DECOYER, LURER
trapshooting, form of .......... SKEET
trash ............. JADE, JOG, TRAMP
trashy . TRUMPERY, WASTE, TOSHY
travel . TOUR, MUSH, PEREGRINATE
travel about ................. BEROLL

traveler ....... VIATOR, WAYFARER
traveler, commercial AGENT, BAGMAN
travelers, company of ...... CARAVAN
traveling ................. VIATORIAL
traveling; Ger. ............... REISEND
traveling, of .................... VIATIC
traverse for watching ........ PATROL
traverse in rear ........... PARADOS
travesty ........ PARODY, LAMPOON
trawl ................. DRAGNET, FISH
treacherous person ........... JUDAS
treacle ........ MOLASSES, THERIAC
tread .......... STEP, VOLT, WALK,
TRAMPLE
tread, circular .................... VOLT
treasure ... STORE, CHERISH, PRIZE
treasure trove ....... MONEY, PLATE
treasury ...... EXCHEQUER, BURSE,
CHEST, FISC
treat REGALE, MANIPULATE, SHOUT
treat badly .......... FRAME, ILLUSE
treatise ..... THESIS, TRACT, ESSAY
treatise, elementary .......... DONAT,
GRAMMAR
treatise on fruit trees ....... POMONA
treatise on trees ................. SILVA
treatise, preface to a ......... ISAGOGE
treaty ...... MISE, PROTOCOL, PACT
treble ........... LATTEN, SOPRANO
tree, Abys. (dried flower of) ... CUSSO
 " , acacia, Austral. ........ MYALL
 " , acacia family ... BABUL, SIRIS
 " , Afr. .. AKEE, BAOBAB, COLA,
BITO, COPAIVA, SAMANDURA
 " , Afr. prickly ash ........ ARTAR
 " , alder ...................... ARN
 " , allspice .............. PIMENTO
 " antidote for snake bite . CEDRON
 " , apple ..................... SHEA
 " , apple; genus ........... MALUS
 " , ash, mountain . ROWAN, SORB
 " , Asian . OLAX, TI, ACLE, DITA,
MEDLAR
 " , Asian (scrubby) .. ASAK, BITO
 " , aspen ...................... APS
 " , Austral. .... TODART, BOREE,
GMELINA, MARARA
 " , balsam ......... WILGA, TOLU
tree, balsam poplar ............ LIARD
 " , baobab .......... SOURGOURD
 " bark ......... TAN. CRUT, ROSS
 " , beech ........ BUCK, MYRTLE
 " , beech, Chile ............ ROBLE
 " , betel nut ............... ARECA
 " , birch; genus ......... BETULA
 " , birch, small .......... ANSU, TI
 " branches ............... RAMAGE
 " , Brazilian ................ ANDA
 " , buckwheat ............... TITI
 " , bully .................. BALATA
 " , candle nut ...... KUKU, AMAS
 " , carica .... PAWPAW, PAPAYA
 " , Cen. Amer. ............. AMATE
 " , Cen. Amer. oil ..... EBO, EBOE
 " , chicory ................. BUNK
 " , Chilean timber MUERMO, ULMO
 " , Chinese cultivated; var. ........
KINKAN
 " , coffee ................. CHICOT

 " , cottonwood ............ ALAMO
 " , custard-apple (family) .........
SWEETSOP
 " cutting ...................... LOT
 " , cyrillaceous .............. TITI
 " , dead ............... RAMPIKE
 " , devil; Ind. ................ DITA
 " , devil's cotton ........ ABROMA
 " , dogbane, (species) . APOCYNUM
 " , dogwood .... NYSSA, TUPELO
 " , dogwood; genus ...... CORNUS
 " , drupe bearing ............ BITO
 " , dwarf ............. ARBUSCLE
 " , dyewood; Phil. I. .......... TUA
 " , E. Afr. .................... MOLI
 " , E. Ind. .......... ACH, ASOKA,
BANYAN, DEODAR, PINEY,
POON, SAJ, SAL, TEAK,
TOON, MEE, SIRIS, NEEM,
PRESS, ACANA, FIG
 " ; E. Ind., genus ....... ABROMA
 " , emblem of Hawaii ..... LEHUA
 " , eucalyptus ........ GUM, YATE
 " , evergreen . FIR, HOLM, OLIVE,
YEW
 " , evergreen; N. Z. ..... TARATA
 " exudarion .......... RESIN, SAP
 " , fabaceous ............... AGATI
 " , fir .................... BALSAM
 " , firs; genus ........... ABIES
 " , flowering; U. S. ........... TITI
 " , forest ............. DITA, TUA
 " fraxinus .................... ASH
 " fustic .................... MORA
 " , gamboge family ...... CALABA
 " , genip, wood from ........ LANA
 " genus .................... ACER
 " , glasswort ............... JUME
 " ; Guiana ................... MORA
 " , guinea food ............ AKEE
 " , gum . BABUL, BALALA, ICICA,
XYLAN
 " , Hawaiian . KOA, LEHUA, OHIA
 " , hickory, species of ..... PECAN
 " , holly .................... HOLM
 " , holly, species of .......YAPON
 " , honeyberry ............. GENIP
 " ; India . AMRA, BANYAN, BEYR,
SAL
tree, Indian silk cotton ........ SIMAL
 " , iron ............. ACLE, IXORA
 " , Japanese ....... HINOKI, SUGI
 " , Javanese ................. UPAS
 " juneberry ............. SERVICE
 " , lacebark ............ LAGETTA
 " , large, madder family .. BANCAL
 " , laurel .................... BAY
 " , linden LIN, LIME, LINN, TEIL,
TILE
 " , locust ................. ACACIA
 " , locust, pod of .......... CAROB
 " , lotus ................... SADR
 " , low evergreen ........ ABROMA
 " , Malay apple .............. OHIA
 " , margosa .......... NEEM, NIM
 " , marmalade .. MAMEY, CHICO,
SAPOTE
 " , Mediterranean ......... CAROB
 " , Mexican rubber ........... ULE

274

"  , Mexican, wood of ...... FUSTIC
"  , mimosaceous ............ SIRIS
"  mosses .................. USNEA
.  "  moth .................... EGGER
"  , mulberry; Ind. .. AAL, ACH, AL
"  , myrtaceous ......... EUGENIA
"  , ngalo ..................... KIO
"  , oak, Cal. live ......... ENCINA
"  , oak, Cal. white ........ ROBLE
"  oak, holm .............. HOLLY
"  oak, Jerusalem ... AMBROSE
"  , olive; genus ............. OLEA
"  , palm; (see 'palm')
"  , Palmyra; Ind. ............. TAL
"  , papaya ...... CARICA, PAPAW
"  , pea ..................... AGATI
"  , pear ......... PERRY, PYRUS
"  , pear, prickly ........... NOPAL
"  , pepperidge ........... TUPELO
"  ; Philippine .. ANAGAP, BETIS,
                          TUA, YATE
"  , pinaceous .. KAURI, SEQUOIA
"  , pine ......... OCOTE, SABINE
"  , pine, China and Japan . MATSU
"  , pine family . CEDAR, CONIFER
"  , plum; genus .......... PRUNUS
"  , plum, wild .............. SLOE
"  , poisonous SASSY, BUNK, UPAS
"  ; Polynesia ............. IPIL, TI
"  , poon .................. KENNA
"  , poplar ABELE, ALAMO, ASPEN
"  , quercus; genus ........... OAK
"  quillai .............. SOAPBARK
"  , rose-family; Eur. .... MEDLAR
"  , rowan .. ASH, SERVICE, SORB
"  , rubber ......... CAUCHO, ULE
"  , salt ............ ATLE, ATLEE
"  , sandalwood; N. Z. ...... MAIRE
"  , sandarac ..... ALERSE, ARAR,
                          MOROCCO
"  , sapodilla .............. SAPOTA
"  , sassafras ................ AGUE
"  , shade ..................... ASH
"  shoot ........................ LOT
"  , snake ......... GIMP, LORA
"  , soapbark ............. QUILLAI
"  , sourgourd ........... BAOBAB
tree, S. American ...... EBO, CACAO,
                          JUME
"  , S. Am.; genus ....... COPAIUA
"  , S. Am. evergreen ... PAPAYA
"  , spruce; white ..... EPINETTE,
                          LARCH
"  , strawberry ........... ARBUTE
"  , tallow .................. CERA
"  , tamarack; Am. ........ LARCH
"  , tamarisk; Ind. ........... ATLE
"  , taxus; genus ............. YEW
"  , tecoma, species of ..... ROBLE
"  , terebinth LIME, LINDEN, TEIL
"  , thorn, Jerusalem ..... RETAMA
"  , thorny .................... BEL
"  , timber; Asia ...... RASAMALA
"  , timber; Chin. .......... KAYA
"  , timber, forest . ASH, IHI, RATA
"  , timber; Hawaii ........... KOA
"  , timber; India .. OAK, DAR, SAL
"  , timber, inferior ......... ANAM

"  , timber; N. Z. .. RIMU, KAURI,
                          RATA
"  , timber, of Pacific ......... IPIL
"  , timber, Phil. Is. ..... LANETE,
                          AMAGA
"  , timber; S. Am. .. TALA, PEKEA
"  , timber; W. Ind. ....... ACANA
"  , traveler's ......... RAVENALA
"  , tropical .... ANUBING, COLA,
                    DAGAME, INGA, NEPAL
"  , trop. Am. BALSA, DALI, OLAX,
                    PAWPAW, SAPOTA
"  trunk ............ BOLE, CABER
"  , tupelo .................. NYSSA
"  varnish; Jap. ............. RHUS
"  , wattle; Austral. ........ BOREE,
                          COOBA, COOBAH
"  , W. African .... AKEE, BUMBO
"  , W. Ind. .... ACANA, BALATA,
                    GENIP, LOBLOLLY
"  , W. Ind. cabbage .... ANGELIN
"  , willow .................. OSIER
"  , willow; genus ............. ITEA
"  yielding cocoa bean ....... CACO
"  yielding gum .............. ICICA
"  yielding oil ................ TUNG
"  yielding quinine ..... CINCHONA
treeless plain ..... PAMPAS, LLANOS,
                    TUNDRA, STEPPE
treenail ........ NOG, EG, PIN, SPIKE
trees ..................... FOREST
"  , genus ...... OWENIA, CITRUS,
                    ULMUS, ACER
"  , grove of ... DENDRITE, TOPE
"  , maple; genus ............ ACER
"  , mulberry; genus ....... MORUS
"  , olive; genus ............. OLEA
"  , per. to ............ ARBOREAL,
                          CACUMINAL
"  , pine grove of ....... PINETUM
"  , rain ...... GENISARO, SAMAN
"  , rows of ............... STICH
"  , science of life of ...... SILVICS
tree-toad; genus ................ HYLA
trefoil ................ CLOVER, ARCH
trellis ARBOR, ESPALIER, PERGOLA
tremble ..... DODDER, JAR, QUAKE,
                    SHAKE, THRILL
tremulous ........... ASPEN, QUAKY,
                          TREMANDO
trench GAW, FOSS, LEAT, MOAT, SAP
trencher PLATTER, VIANDS, SAPPER
trend .. SWING, TENDENCY, TENOR
trespass DEBT, ENCROACH, TRIPET,
                          POACH
tress ...... LOCK, RINGLET, BRAID,
                          PLAIT
trews; Scot. ............... TROUSERS
triad ......................... TRINARY
trial ........... DOOM, ESSAY, TEST
trial perform. ............. PROLUSION
trial, per. to ............... EMPIRIC
trial, scene of a famous ........ RIOM
triangle ...................... TRIGON
triangle, draw circle within . ESCRIBE
triangle, side of a ............... LEG
triangle, the ................ TRINITY
triangular decoration ..... PEDIMENT
"  piece in a sail .......... GORE

275

" sail ... LATEEN, SPINNAKER
" shaped .. DELTOID, OXYGEN, SCALENE
tribe . CLAN, RACE, FAMILY, HORDE
tribe, Belgian-Gaul ............. REMI
tribunal ...... FORUM, BAR, COURT, SEAT
tribute .... OVATION, TAX, HOMAGE
trick .. GULL, FLAM, JAPE, TREPAN, WILE, GAG, RUSE, DOES
trick or deception ..... DIDO, FRAUD, GLEEK
tricked, one easily ...... DUPE, GULL, CULLY
trickery ....... ART, LEGERDEMAIN
trickle .. DRILL, SEEP, DROP, FLOW
tricks, play mean ............... SHAB
tricky .... QUIRKY, CRAFTY, SNIDE
trident ......... SPEAR, LEISTER
tried .. RELIABLE, CHOICE, ETTLED
Trieste measure ................. ORNA
trifle ....... DALLY, MONKEY, DOIT, PINHEAD, TOY, FRIVOL, POTTER
trifle, insignificant ......... ACE, FICO
trifles . STIVERS, AMBSACES, NUGAE
trifling .. PALTRY, PIFFLE, URCHIN
trifoliate ................... TERNATE
trifoliate plant .......... SHAMROCK
trig ............ NEAT, SMART, TRIM
triglyphs, space between .. METOCHE
trigo ........................ WHEAT
trigon .......... TRINE, HARP, LYRE
trigonometric figure ... COSINE, SINE
trill ........ ROLL, TWIRL, WARBLE
trilling, by ................. UVULAR
trillion; comb. form .......... TREGA
trim ..... PREEN, CLIP, LOP, NEAT, SHRAG, SNED, NIFTY, PERK
trim a coin ........................ NIG
trimming of lace ...... GARD, JABOT
trine ................. TRIPLE, TRIO
trinity ................. THREE, TRIAD
trinket ..... BIJOU, BIBELOT, GAUD, TAHLI
triode ..... CATHODE, GRID, PLATE
triphthong ................ TRIGRAPH
triple .......... THRIN, THREEFOLD
triple crown .................. TIARA
triple grass ... CLOVER, SHAMROCK
triplet ............. TERCET, TRINE
triplet lily; genus .......... HOOKERA
tripod ..... EASEL, SPIDER, TRIVET
tripod, double ..................... CAT
Tripoli, ruler of ................. DEY
triptych ...................... TABLET
trisaccharide .................. TRIOSE
trismus ....... LOCKJAW, TETANUS
Tristram's beloved ............ISEULT, ISOLDE, ISOLT
tristful ......................... SAD
trite ... BETIDE, BANAL, PERCOCT, ........ STALE
trite expression ..... CLICHE, CORNY
triton ................... EFT, NEWT
triturate ............. GRIND, BRAY, PULVERIZE
triumph .......... EXULT, VICTORY
trivet ............... KNIFE, TRIPOD
trivial . DOGGEREL, NICE, NOMINAL

trivial action ............... FRIBBLE
troche .......... LOZENGE, TABLET
trochee ....... CHOREUS, TROCHAIC
trochilus; arch. ................ SCOTIA
trochlea; obs. ................ PULLEY
trogon ...................... QUETZAL
Troilus' father ................. PRIAM
Trojan .......................... ILIAN
Trojan horse, builder of ....... EPEUS
Trojan slave ................... SINON
Trojan warrior .............. AGENOR
troll; Teut. folklore ........... GNOME
trolley ...... BARROW, LACE, TRAM
trombone ...... SACKBUT, SAMBUKE
trombone mouthpiece .......... BOCAL
trome; obs. .................... ARRAY
trommel .. BUDDLE, SIEVE, SCREEN
trona ................... NITRUM, URAO
troop; Anglo-Ind. .......... RESSALA
troops .... ARMY, BATTERY, SQUAD
troops in reserve ........... ECHELON
troops, quarters for .......... ETAPE
trop; Fr. .................. MANY, TOO
trope, any ................... EUOUAE
trophy ..... AWARD, OSCAR, PRIZE, SPOILS
tropic ............... CIRCLE, SOLAR
tropical bird .... MOTMOT, MANAKIN, TODY
" cetacean ................. INIA
" clay ................ LATERITE
" cuckoo ..................... ANI
" disease ................. SPRUE
" dolphin ................... INIA
" fish, family ......... SCARIDAE
" fruit . INGA, MANGO, PAPAYA
" monkey ................ ARABA
" palm .......... ASSAI, CYCAD
" plant ........ AGAVE, TRIURID
" root stock ............... TARO
" tree, (see 'tree') silk .... SIRIS
" wild cat ................. EYRA
Tros, son of ....................... ILUS
Trotsky; writer ................. LEON
troubadour ........ JONGLEUR, POET
trouble SORE, SUSSY, ADO, AIL, IRK
trough ...... DALE, HOD, MANGER, STRAKE, TOM
trough between waves ...... VALLEY
trough inclined ................ CHUTE
trousers ................... PEGTOP
trout CHARR, SEWEN, GULL, KELT, LONGE, TOGUE
trout parasite .... NAMAYCUSH, SUG
trout, per. to a ...... TRUTTACEOUS
trowel ................ DARBY, FLOAT
Troy, defender of ............. ENEAS
Troy, founder of ................. ILUS
Troy, last king of ............. PRIAM
Troy, mountain of ................. IDA
Troy, name of anc. .... ILION, ILIUM
Troy, per. to anc. ............ ILIAC
Troy, region of; anc. .......... TROAD
truant ......... TRIVANT, VAGRANT
truce; Fr. ..................... TREVE
truck .......... VAN, LORRY, WYNN

276

truckle . CRINGE, KNUCKLE, YIELD
trucks with trailers ............. SEMIS
trudge .......... PLOD, PACE, WALK
true ...... LEAL, VERY, GERMANE,
STANCH, ALINE, FAC(T)
true skin ..................... DERMA
truffle .... EARTHNUT, MISY, FUNGI
truism .. PLATITUDE, POSTULATE,
AXIOM
truly .. AMEN, YEA, DULY, RIGHTLY
Truman, Mrs. Harry ............ BESS
Truman; playwright ........... CAPOTE
Truman's, Mr., birthplace .... LAMAR
Trumbull; painter .............. JOHN
trumpet .. BUCINA, LURE, CLARION,
TUBA
trumpet, blare of .......... TANTARA
trumpet blast .. BLARE, DIAN, LEVIT
trumpet creeper ............ TECOMA
trumpeter ............ AGAMI, TROUT
trumpeter perch ........ MABO, MADO
trumpet-shell ................. TRITON
truncheon .... CLUB, STAFF, BATON
trundle ...... WHEEL, ROLL, TRUCK
trunk ...... BOLE, COFFER, STOCK,
BOX, CHEST
trunk of an animal .... TORSO, SOMA
trust .. REPOSE, RELY, FIE, HOPE,
TRIG
trusty .......... STAUNCH, CONVICT
truth .... UNA, DEED, FEALTY, TAO
truth; Chin. philos. .............. TAO
truth, personification of .......... UNA
truthful ....... INGENUOUS, VERDIC
try .... ESSAY, TRIAL, ETTLE, PUT,
SAY
try again ........ RETEST, RETASTE
try for luck ................. HANDSEL
tsetse fly ...... KIVU, MAU, MUSCID
tsetse fly, allied to .............. ZIMB
tsetse fly disease ............ NAGANA
tsetse fly; genus .......... GLOSSINA
tsine ....................... BANTENG
tub ........ HOD, TUN, PIGGIN, VAT
tub for water .............. DAN, VAT
tub, small wooden ....... KID, FIRKIN
tuba's mouthpiece ............. BOCAL
tube .... DUCT, BOUCH, PIPE, HOSE
tube for concrete under water TREMIE
tube; mus. ................... SALPINX
tube on which silk is wound ...... COP
tube, priming ................. AUGET
tube, tapering . BURETTE, STENOSIS
tuber EDDOE, JALAP, OCA, POTATO,
TARO, YAM
tubiform ..................... TUBATE
tubular cavity ................... ITER
Tuchin's house ............. YAMEN
tuck ......... FOOD, RAPIER, PLEAT
tuck up ................. KILT, COVER
tuckahoe ...................... PORIA
tucker ........ BORE, FAG, IRK, TIRE
Tuesday French for .......... MARDI
tufa ..................... LIMESTONE
tuff ........................ DETRITUS
tuft ..... CREST, GOATEE, TUSSOCK

tuft of feathers .............. ALULA
tuft on a bird's head ............ COP
tufted .......... COMOSE, CRESTED
tufts ........... SCOPULAS, COMAE
tug .. EFFORT, PULL, TRACE, TOIL
tule ............ BULRUSH, SCIRPUS
tule root .................. WAPATOO
tulle; Fr. ................. LACE, NET
tumble about FLOP, SAULT, WALTER
tumble-weed ............. AMARANTH
tumbler ............ ACROBAT, DOVE
tumbrel .................. DUMPCART
tumeric .......................... REA
tumor ................. EDEMA, YAW
tumor, fleshy .............. SARCOMA
tumor, glandular .......... ADENOMA
tumor, small ...... WEN, MORO, PAP
tumult .... BABEL, DIN, FRAY, RIOT
tumult; Fr. ................... EMEUTE
tumulus ........... BARROW, MOUND
tun, half a ...................... PIPE
tun shell, fossil of ............ DOLITE
tunalike ................... ALBACORE
tune ........ SONANCE, LEED, LILT,
SPRING, TOY
tung oil; prod. of ........... VARNISH
tungsten mineral ........ SCHEELITE
tungsten, source of .. CAL, WOLFRAM
tunic ...... ACTON, CHITON, STOLA,
TOGA, BLOUSE
tunic, medieval ...... GIPTON, JUPON
tunicate ........ SALP, SALPA, BULB
tunicle ................... TEGUMENT
tunics .............. CAMISE, SMOCK
tuning of strings to lower pitch ANESIS
Tunis, ruler in ............. BEY, DEY
Tunisian town ...... BIZERTA, SFAX,
SOUSSE
tunny-roe .............. BOTARGA(O)
tup ............................. RAM
tupelo gums ................... NYSSA
Tupian tribe, one of .... ANTA, MURA
Turania, a people of .......... AKKAD
turban PATTA, MUDIL, SEERBAND,
TURF
turbid ......... FECULENT, ROILED,
MUDDY, ROILY
turbot ...................... FLATFISH
turbulent ........... VIOLENT, WILD
turdine-like .................. THRUSH
turf ...... SOD, PEAT, CESS, DIVOT,
SWARD, VAG, GRASS
turgent ................... SWELLING
Turk . OSMANLI, OTTOMAN, TATAR
Turk, the Grand ............. SULTAN
Turk man-o-war ............ CARVEL
Turkestan district ............. PAMIR
Turkestan Moslem ............. SALAR
Turkestan, mountain in .......... ALAI
Turkestan, native of ............ SART
Turkestan river ................... ILI
Turkestan tribe ... KIRGHIZ, USBEGS
turkey buzzard ............ VULTURE
Turkey, capital of ANKARA, ANGORA
"    , city of; ... ADANA, EDESSA,
SCUTARI
"    , float used in .......... KALAK
"    , governor of a province in WALI

| | |
|---|---|
| " , in Asia ........... ANATOLIA | " religious war . CRESCENTADE |
| " , president of .......... INONU | " reservist ............... REDIF |
| " , sea in ................. ARAL | " royal grant ........... FIRMAN |
| " , town of ............. ADANA | " saber .. OBOLUS, YATAGHAN |
| turkey, wild ........ TOM, BUSTARD | " sailing vessel . CARAVEL, SAIC |
| turkey, young .. POULT, CURASSOW | " seaport ........ ADALIA, ENOS |
| Turkish ambassador ......... ELCHEE | " Simoon ............... SAMIEL |
| " army corps .............. ORDU | " soldier ........ NIZAM, REDIF |
| " army officer ............... AGA | " standard ................. ALEM |
| " caliph ...................... ALI | " standard, former ........ TOUG |
| " cap ............ FEZ, CALPAC | " statesman ............... AALI |
| " cavalryman ............. SPAHI | " subject (non-Moslem) ... RAIA |
| " coin, copper .............. PARA | " summer house .. KIOSK, YALI |
| " coin, gold ................. LIRA | " sultan .................. CALIF |
| " coin, old silver ....... ALTILIK | " sword ............. YATAGHAN |
| " coin, silver .. PIATER, ONLUK | " tambourine ............. DAIRA |
| " college ................. ULEMA | " tax ................... AVANIA |
| " commander .... AGA, SIRDAR | ".. title of honor .. GHAZI, AGHA |
| " court ................... PORTE | " title of respect .... BABA, BEY, |
| " decree ................... IRADE | AGA |
| " district ........ ORDU, CILICIA | " veil, (women's) .... YASHMAK |
| " dollar ............... PIASTER | " vilayet ............... KISSABA |
| " fermented drink ........ BOZA, | " village ................. ADANA |
| MASTIC | " weight .... BATMAN, CHEKE, |
| " flag ..................... ALEM | KERAT, ROTL, OKA, OKE |
| " garment ............... GAFTAN | " zither .......... ARIA, CANUN |
| " general ............... KAMAL | "Turk's Cap, lily ......... MARTAGON |
| Turkish government ANGARIA, GATE, | Turks of India ............... AFRIDI |
| PORTE | Turku Is. .................... ALAND |
| " governor .. BEY, DEY, MUDIR | Turku; Swed. name ............... ABO |
| " grandee .............. BASHAW | turmeric ... CURCUMA, OLENA, REA |
| " high official .. PACHA, PASHA | turn .. REVERT, GYRATE, ROTATE, |
| " hospice ................ IMARET | VERT |
| " imperial harem, lady of ........ | " , act in ................ ALTERN |
| KADEIN | " aside ....... SWERVE, DETOUR, |
| " imperial standard ALEM, TOUG | SHUNT, WRY |
| " infidel ................. GIAOUR | " comb. form .............. TROPO |
| " inn .......... IMARET, SERAI | " frontward .............. OBVERT |
| " javelin ..... JEREED, JERRID | " out to others .............. FARM |
| " judge .................... CADI | " outward ................. EVERT |
| " leader ......... AGA, KEMAL | " rapidly ..................... TIRL |
| " linear measure .............. PIC | " , revolving ......... GYRE, REV |
| " magistrate . CADI, AGA, CABI | " right ......... GEE, STARBOARD |
| " measure ALMUD, DJERIB, DRA, | " to left ............. HAW, PORT |
| DRAH, KILE, KILO, OKA, PIK | turncoat ... RENEGADE, RUNAGATE |
| " measure (new) .......... KHAT | turned back ........... EVOLUTE |
| " minister ............... VIZIER | turned in any direc. .......... CREEN |
| " money of account ..... ASPER | turned outward ........... EVERTED, |
| " mountain ............. ARARAT | EXTRORSE |
| " mountain ranger .......... ALAI | turned over ................. KEELED |
| " musical inst. .......... KUSSIR | turned, the one side ...... ..SPLAYED |
| " name ............... ALI, AALI | turning spirally ........ SINISTRORSE |
| " officer .... ATABEG, ATABEK, | turned up ...................... ACOCK |
| AGA | Turner, Miss .................... LANA |
| " official ........ EMEER, EMIR, | turnip ... NAVE, NEEP, RUTABAGA |
| OSMANLI, MIR, PASHA | turnip formed ............. NAPIFORM |
| " open pavilion ........... KIOSK | turnip, order .......... CRUCIFERAE |
| " palace ................. SERAI | turnip, wild .......... NAVEW, RAPE |
| " patent ................. BERAT | turns about ................... SLUES |
| " peasant ................. RAYA | turnsole ................. HELIOTROPE |
| " people ............. OSMANLIS | turnstone ................. REDLEG |
| " pipe ................ CHIBOUK | turn-table, gun ............... RACER |
| " prayer rug ............. MELAS | turpentine distillate ....... GALLPOT, |
| " prefect ................... WALI | RESIN |
| " president, first ........ KEMAL | turpentine tree ............. TARATA, |
| " province ............. VILAYET | TEREBINTH |
| " race, Eur. branch .. OSMANLI | turret ..... BUTTE, TOREL, TOWER |
| " regiment .......... ARNI, ALAI | turret, revolving armored ... CUPOLA |
| | turtle COOTER, JURARA, TERRAPIN |

" back .................. CELT
" , fresh-water ............. EMYD
" giant .................... ARRAU
" , hawksbill ............... CARET
" , part of a CALIPASH, CALIPEE
" , per. to ........... CHELONIAN
" shell ................. CARAPACE
" , snapping .. SNAPPER, TORUP
" , S. America ....... MATAMATA
turtles; genus . CHELONE, TESTUDO
Tuscan wine .............. CHIANTI
tusk ......... RAZOR, FANG, IVORY
tussah .................. SHANTUNG
tussis ...................... COUGH
tussock .... BRUSHWOOD, THICKET
tutelary deities . LARES, LAR, GENII,
                  DAEMONS, PENATES
tutor DOCENT, GOVERNOR, MENTOR
tutto; mus. ........... ALL, WHOLE
tuyere ...... NOZZLE, TEW, TEWEL
twaddle .... FLAPDOODLE, DRIVEL,
                              FUSTIAN
twaddle; slang .................... ROT
twang .......... PLUNK, SURMISE
tweak .......................... PINCH
tweeg .............. HELLBENDER
tweezers .................... MULLET
"Twelfth Night" char. ORSINO, VIOLA
twelfth part ................ UNCIA
twenty ........... CORGE, SCORE
twenty one pounds; Bengal ...... SER
twenty, per. to .............. ICOSIAN
twenty quires ................ REAM
twenty years ........... VICENNIAL
twenty-fourth part . KARAT, CARAT
twibill .................. MATTOCK
twice; prefix .................. BI, DI
twig ........ ROD, SWITCH, WITHE
twig, flexible .................. OSIER
twig used for grafting ......... SCION
twigs, full of ................ RODDY
twigs, made of . VIRGAL, WATTLED
twilight ...... CREPUSCULAR, DUSK
twilight; Norse myth. ... RAGNAROK
twill ................................. RIB
twin ........ COUPLE, TWO, GEMEL,
              DUPLICATE, SIAMESE
twin crystal MACLE, AKIN, SIMILAR
twine ...... COIL, CORD, WREATHE
twine, hank of .................. RAN
twinge ......... PAIN, PANG, QUALM
twink .................... NICTITATE
twinkle .............. BLINK, WINK
twins, zodiacal .............. GEMINI
twirl .............. SPIN, WHIRL
twist ... QUIRK, SNAKE, COIL, TIRL,
    TURN, SQUIRM, TWEAK, OLIVER
twist around ....... CURL, ENLACE,
                      GAUCHE, SLUE
twist in rope .................. GRIND
twist inward .............. INTORT
twist of horsehairs ........... SETON
twist to and fro WRENCH, WRIGGLE
twisted TORC, AWRY, TORTILE, WRY
twisted cord .............. TORSADE
twisted roll of cotton .......... SLUB
twisting ........ SPIRAL, WRESTING
twistings .................. TORSIONS

twit ........ JOSH, TAUNT, BANTER
twitch . JERK, TWEAK, VELLICATE,
                                YANK
twitching ...................... TIC
twitter .... GARRE, GIGGLE, TITTER
two ............................. BRACE
" and ½ inches .............. NAIL
" celled .............. BILOCULAR
" colors ............... DICHROMIC
" , consisting of ............ DYAD
" edged and sharp ... ANCIPITAL
" fingers ............. BIDIGITATE
" forked ............... BIFURCATE
" handed ....... AMBIDEXTROUS,
                  MANUS, BIMANAL
" handed animals ....... BIMANA
" headed .............. ANCIPITAL
" herring ,oysters, etc. ...... WARP
" toed sloth ................. UNAU
" wheeled carriage ..... VOLANTE
" wheeled chariot ......... ESSEDA
twofold BINAL, DIDYMOUS, DUPLE,
          BINARY, DOUBLE, TWIN
"Two Years Before the Mast"; author .
                                DANA
Tyche .................... FORTUNE
tycoon ............. BARON, SHOGUN
tylopod ........................ CAMEL
Tyndareus' step-child ........ HELEN
Tyndareus' wife .................. LEDA
type ........................... TOKEN
" , assortment of ............ FONT
" , blank ............ QUAD, QUAT
" collection ................. FONT
" face, part of a ............ KERN
" frame ................... CHASE
" , kind of ...... IONIC, ELZEVIR,
                      PICA, RONDE
" measure ................. EM, EN
" mold .................... MATRIX
type of bridge .............. BASCULE
" of ode ................. PINDARIC
" , part of a ................... NICK
" , sizes of; .. AGATE, BOURGEOIS,
              BREVIER, BRILLIANT,
        COLUMBIAN, DIAMOND, ENG-
          LISH, MINION, NONPAREIL,
        NORM, PEARL, PICA, PRIMER,
          ROMAN, PARAGON
" style .. CASLON, IONIC, ALDINE
" term .................... CASE, PI
" tray .................... GALLEY
typewriter roller ... SPACER, PLATEN
type-writer type .............. ELITE
typhoid fever; Sp. ...... TABARDILLO
typical example ............... NORM
Tyr ................. ER, SAXNOT, TIU
tyrant ....................... DESPOT
Tyrant of Syracuse ..... GELO, HIERO
tyre ............................. WINE
Tyre, destroyers of ......... MOSLEMS
Tyre, king of .................. HIRAM
Tyre, modern town .............. SUR
Tyre, princess of ................ DIDO
tyro ........ ABECEDARIAN, NOVICE
Tyrol district; Ital. ........ TRENTINO

# U

U-boat, base ...................... KIEL
U, letter ........................... EU
U.N. agency ................... UNESCO
U.N. confer. (woods) ....... BRETTON
uberous ..... FRUITFUL, ABUNDANT
ubiquitous ............ OMNIPRESENT
Uchean Indian .................. YUCHI
ugliness; symb. .................. TOAD
ugly ............... SURLY, VICIOUS
ugly; Sp. ........................... FEO
uhlan ................ SOLDIER, ULAN
Ukraine, money of account ... GRIVNA
Ukraine's Holy City ............. KIEV
Ukrainian legislature PODOLIA, RADA
ulcer in cow's foot ................ FOUL
ule, deriv. of .. LATEX, CAOUTCHOUC
ulema, leader of ................. IMAM
ulex; genus .................... FURZE
ullage ...... DEFICIENCY, WANTAGE
ulmacae family .................... ELM
ulna .......................... CUBITUS
Ulrica in "Ivanhoe" ............ CRONE
Ultima Thule; anc. ........... ICELAND
ultimate ................ LAST, FINAL
ultimatum ......... DEMAND, ORDER
ultimate atom ................ MONAD
ultimo, opposed to .......... PROXIMO
ultra .. RADICAL, EXTREME, GROSS
ululant ......... HOWLING, WAILING
ululate ........ PULE, BELLOW, CRY,
ROAR
Ulysses, antagonist of ............ IRUS
Ulysses' faithful hound ........ ARGUS
Ulysses' father ............... LAERTES
Ulysses' wife ............. PENELOPE
umbellifer-like ................ CELERY
umber ............ GRAYLING, DUSKY
umberbird ................ UMBRETTE
umbo ............ BEAK, BOSS, KNOB
umbrage ............ OFFENSE, SHADE
umbrella grass; Aus. ........... MILLET
umbrella, large ................. GAMP
umbrella tree; Am. ........ MAGNOLIA
umbrella tree; Austral. ..... GINSENG
umbrette, the ................. UMBER
umpire ............. ARBITER, JUDGE
unaccented .................... ATONIC
unaccented, opposed to ........ THESIS
unaccented part of bar; mus. .... ARSIS
unadorned .... STARK, BALD, FORM,
GRACE
unadulterated .. FRANK, NEAT, PURE
unadvised ....... INDISCREET, RASH
unaffected ........ NAIVE, GENUINE,
SINCERE
Unalaska native ............... ALEUT
unanimous .......... SOLID, AGREED,
MUTUAL
unappropriated ..... OPEN, ORPHAN,
WAIF
unaspirated .................... LENE
unau ........................... SLOTH
unavowed .................. ULTERIOR
unbeliever ...... HERETIC, SKEPTIC,
KAFIR, INFIDEL, PAGAN

unbend ................. FRESE, REST
unbleached ............ ECRU, MUSLIN
unblenched ............. UNDAUNTED
unbranched antler ................ DAG
unbroken .... CONTINUATE, INTACT
unburden .. DISLOAD, EASE, REVEAL
unbury ...................... EXHUME
uncanny ...... WEIRD, EERIE, UNCO
unceremoniously ...... SLAP, ABRUPT
uncertain ... WAUGH, WAW, VAGUE
unchecked .......... RAMPANT, FIFE
uncle ....... NUNCLE, NUNKS, OOM,
PAWNBROKER, SAM
uncle, per. to ............. AVUNCULAR
uncle; Scot. ........ EAM, EME, YEME
unclean ........ IMMUND, TREF, VILE
unclose ......... OPE, OPEN, SPREAD
unclothe ...... TIRL, DIVEST, STRIP
unco ........... UNCANNY, STRANGE
uncommon .... SPECIAL, NICE, RARE
uncompromising .............. ULTRA
unconcerned .... INSOUCIANT, FREE
unconscious .............. NAIVE, OUT
unconsciousness ............. NARCOSIS
unconventional ...... EASY, DEGAGE
unconventional; Fr. ............ OUTRE
uncouth one .......... GALOOT, LOUT
uncover; Scot. ..................... TIRL
uncritical ...................... NAIVE
unction ....... UNGUENT, SOOTHING
unction, administer ............ ANELE
unctuous .. GREASY, OILY, PINGUID,
SALVY
unctuous waxy mixture .... LANQLIN,
CERATE
uncultivated .. FALLOW, WILD, ARID
uncultured ....... BRUT, PHILISTINE
undaunted .... SPARTAN, FEARLESS
undecided . ACRISY, PEND, DILEMMA
under ...... INFERIOR, NEATH, SUB
underbrush beaten by a stag ABATURE
underdone .. RARE, REAR, PARTIAL
undergird ................ FRAP, BIND
undergo cell destruction ......... LYSE
undergo; Scot. .................. DREE
underground fungus ............. ROOT
underground stem ............. TUBER
underhand . COVERT, DERN, SECRET
underlined in red ............. RUBRIC
undermine ......................... SAP
undersea ........................... SUB
understanding .... BRAIN, ENTENTE,
DIG, INWIT
understatement .............. LITOTES
understood ..... ASSUMED, IMPLIED,
TACIT
undertake .. FANG, POSTULATE, TRY
undertaker ...... CERER, MORTICIAN
undertaking ...... ACT, AVAL, MOOD
undertaking, zealous ....... CRUSADE
undertow .................... RIPTIDE
under-water mass of cement .... PAAR
underwear .... LINGERIE, BVD, SLIP
underworld ........ EREBUS, SHEOL
underwrite ........ FINANCE, INSURE
undeserving .... INDIGN, UNWORTHY
undeveloped ................ EMBRYO,
RUDIMENTARY

undine ..... NYMPH, GNOME, SYLPH
undo .......... COOK, LOOSE, RUIN,
DESTROY
undomesticated ........ FERAL, WILD
undone ........ DISHED, RARE, RUIN
undraped ................ NUDE, BARE
undressed fur .................... PELT
undulating .......... ARIPPLE, WAVY
undulation ............ HEAVE, SURGE
undyed ............... CORAH, PLAIN
undying ............ AMARANTHINE,
IMMORTAL
unearth .... DETECT, ROOT, SEARCH
unearthly ............. EERIE, WEIRD
uneasiness ........ MALAISE, UNREST
uneducated .......... BENIGHT(ED),
UNLEARNED
unemployed .... IDLE, OTIOSE, LAZY
unending .. TERMLESS, BOUNDLESS
unequal, comb. form .... DISPARATE,
ANISO
unequal side and angle ...... SCALENE
uneven ........ EROSE, ODD, ROUGH
unexpected .... INOPINATE, SUDDEN
unfading flower .......... AMARANTH
unfair ............... PARTIAL, FOUL
unfamed .......... HUMBLE, LOWLY
unfeathered .................... SQUAB
unfeeling ............. BRUTAL, STOIC
unfilled cavity in a lode ........ VUGG
unfit ............. INEPT, DISQUALIFY
unflattering .......... FRANK, BLUNT
unfold EVOLUTE, DEPLOY, EVOLVE,
DEVELOP, UNFURL
unforeseen .................... CHANCE
unfragrant ............... OLID, FETID
unfrequented ............... SOLITARY
unfriendly .... ACARPOUS, INIMICAL,
MALIGN, HOSTILE
unfurl ............... SLACK, UNFOLD
ungainly .......... NUNTING, WEEDY
ungirt ............... LOOSE, UNKNOT
ungrateful person ........... INGRATE
unguent ... NARD, CHRISM, ALIPTIC,
SALVE, OINTMENT, POMADE
ungula . CLAW, HOOF, NAIL, TALON
ungulate ........................ TAPIR
unhappiness .... UNSEL, WOE, GRIEF
unhealable ........ INSANABLE, RAW
unheard ........... SURD, UNKNOWN
unhorse ................. OVERTHROW
unicellular animals ............. OOZOA
unicellular plant ............... SPORE
unicorn .......... MONOCEROS, REEM
unicorn fish ........ NARWHAL, UNIE
uniform ...... EQUAL, EVEN, LEVEL
uniform slope, bring to ..... AGGRADE
uniformly; poet. .................. EEN
uninflected .................. APTOTIC
unintelligent .......... BRUTE, DULL
union .. FUSION, LEAGUE, MERGER,
LIAISON
union of different things ... AMALGAM
union, trade .................... GUILD
uniplanar point, a ............. UNODE
unique ....... ALONE, SINGLE, SOLE
unique person ........... LONE, ONER
unit .......... ACE, ONE, SYLLABLE

" , caloric .................... THERM
" , electric ... AMPERE, COULOMB,
MHO, OHM, PROTON, VOLT,
WATT
" , English gold coin ....... LAUREL
" , heat .................... CALORIE
" , hypothetical ............. ID, IDIC
" , magnetic ......... GAUSS, KAPP,
OERSTED, WEBER
" , mathematical .............. RADIX
unit of resistance ................. OHM
" , social ..................... SEPT
" of angular velocity ........ STROB
" of electrical capacity ...... FARAD
" of electrical conductivity .... MHO
" of electrical pressure ...... BARAD
" of electrical resistance ...... OHM
" of energy .......... QUANTA, ERG
" of flux density ............. GAUSS
" of force DYNE, OD, TONAL, VOLT
" of inductance ............... HENRY
" of kinetic energy ............ ERG
" of light ....... LUMEN, LUX, PYR
" of magnetic flux ....... MAXWELL
" of magnetic potential ...... GILBERT
" of measure PARSEC, REL, CRITH
" of measure of angular velocity .....
STROB
" of meter .......... MORA, STERE
" of power .................... WATT
" of pressure ...... BARAD, BARIE
" of reluctance ..... REL, OERSTED
" of saturation ............ SATRON
" of speed .................... VELO
" of velocity ................... KIN
" of weight MAUND, CARAT, CRITH
" of work ... ERG, ERGON, KILERG
" of work energy ............. JOULE
" , ultimate ................. MONAD
" , wire ......................... MIL
unite .. FAY, LINK, CONJOIN, FUSE,
YOKE, ALLY
U.N. Gen. Ass. Pres. ........ ENTEZAM
" problem ...... FORMOSA, KOREA
" Sec'y General .................. LIE
" Sir Benegal ................... RAU
United States general ......... MEADE
united with . FEDERATED, WELDED,
IMP, ONED
universal lang. ......... ESPERANTO
universal successor of deceased HERES
universal writing ....... PASIGRAPHY
universe ...... COSMOS, MACROCOSM
university group ............ SEMINAR
university governor .......... REGENT
University, growing body of a SENATUS
unjudged ...................... ACRISY
unjust ............ PARTIAL, UNFAIR
unkeeled ...................... RATITE
unkempt . ROUGH, SHAGGY, UNTIDY
unkind .... BRUTAL, CRUEL, HARSH
unknown; Lat. ..................... IGN
unknown person .. INCONNU, IGNOTE
unknown quantity in an equation COSS
unlawful .... CONTRABAND, ILLICIT
unlearn ...................... FORGET
unleavened ................. AZYMOUS
unleavened bread ............... AZYM

281

unless ........ NISI, WARN, EXCEPT
unlike ............ DIVERSE, SUNDRY
unload .... REMOVE, RELIABLE, RID
unlooked for .... CHANCE, HAP(PEN)
unlucky .......... FEY, ILL, INFAUST
unmarried .......... CELIBATE, SOLE
unmetrical composition ........ PROSE
unmixable ............... IMMISCIBLE
unmoral ...................... AMORAL
unmoved .... DEAD, INERT, SERENE
unorganized .... ACOSMIC, ENZYM(E)
unpeople ................ DEPOPULATE
unplowed UNTILLED, FALLOW, LEA
unqualified ........ SHEER, PLENARY
unravel ................ FEAZE, SOLVE
unreal ........ ARTIFICIAL, CHAOTIC
unrefined .... CRUDE, GROSS, CRASS
unroll ........... EVOLUTE, UNFURL
unruffled .. SERENE, STILL, SEDATE
unruly ........ LAWLESS, TURBULENT
unseasoned ...... UNTIMELY, GREEN
unsheathe ...................... DRAW
unshorn sheep ..................... TEG
unskilful .. MALADROIT, AWKWARD
unskilled ............ INAPT, PUISNE
unsociability ................... FROST
unsorted wheaten meal ........... ATA
unspeakable ............... VILE, BAD
unspoken . INEFFABLE, ORAL, TACIT
unstable ...... LABILE, INCONSTANT
unsuitable ..................... INEPT
unswear ........ ABJURE, RECANT
untamed ............ FERINE, FERAL
untanned skin ...................... KIP
untanned skins of certain animals ......
                             SHAGREEN
untheode ................... UNLEDE
unthinking .... PUERILE, HEEDLESS
untidiness ............ MESSY, LITTER
untie ................ LOOSE, UNKNOT
until ....... HENT, TO, TWILL, TILL
untold ......... VAST, COUNTLESS
untouched .......... PURE, PRISTINE
untwine ........................ FRESE
untwist .................. FAG, FEAZE
Unungun ..................... ALEUT
unusual ...... RARE, EPIGENE, SELD
unvitiated ......................... PURE
unvoiced ....................... SURD
unwilling ... LOATH, ESCHEW, NILL,
                          LOTH, AVERSE
unwise ...... INSIPIENT, IMPOLITIC
unwonted ............ RARE, UNUSED
unworthy .... INDIGN, UNDESERVED
unwrinkled ...... BRENT, SMOOTH
unwritten ............ PAROL, BLANK
unyielding .... ADAMANTINE, STIFF
up to ..................... TILL, UNTIL
upas tree poison .............. ANTIAR
upholstery fabric VALANCE, TOURNAY
upholstery silk ............. TABARET
uplander ........ RUSTIC, SANDPIPER
upon ................... ABOVE, ATOP
upon; prefix ................. EPI, SUR
upper ................... VAMP, BUNK
upper; Ger. ..................... OBER

uppish .. DRUNK, ASSUMING, PROUD
upright support ................. STUD
uproar .. DIN, HUBBUB, NOISE, RIOT
upsilon shaped ................. HYOID
upstart .......... PARVENU, SNOB
upward bend in lumber ............ SNY
upward; prefix .................... ANO
uraeus .............................. ASP
uranium ................... CARNOTITE
Uranus, daughter of ............ RHEA
Uranus, wife of ............. GAEA, GE
urban district in Cheshire, Eng. HOOLE
urban division ................... WARD
urban inhabitant ................... CIT
urban life ....................... TOWN
urbane ..... BLAND, POLITE, SUAVE
urchin ..... HEDGEHOG, IMP, ELFIN
urd .............................. PYROL
Urd, var. of ..................... URTH
urde ........................... CLECHE
uredo ............ HIVES, URTICARIA
urge . INCITE, PLYDUN, EGG, GOAD,
            HIE, ABET, DUN, SPUR
urgent .......... APPEALS, EXIGENT
urial ................... OORIAL, SHA
Uriel .................... ARCHANGEL
urn .............. PIG, KIST, STEEN
urn, copper ................. SAMOVAR
urn-shaped ............... URCEOLATE
Uroxanthin ................. INDICAN
Ursa ............................. BEAR
ursine howler ............ ARAGUATO
Urth ............................ NORN
urus ................... AUROCHS, TUR
us ........................ WEUNS, WE
usance .. USAGE, USE, USARY, TIME
use .... AVAIL, EMPLOY, EXHAUST,
        TREAT, URE, WONT, CONSUME
use of a divining rod ........... DOWSE
use of one part of speech for another ..
                             ENALLAGE
useful ........................... UTILE
useless ...... IDLE, INUTILE, NULL,
                             OTIOSE
usher .. SEAT, DOORKEEPER, SHOW
Usnach, son of ................ NOISE
Uspallata Pass ................ ANDES
U.S. Budget direc. ............ DODGE
U.S. Treasurer ................ PRIEST
ustulate .................... SCORCHED
U.S.S.R. news agency ............ TASS
usurp ........ ASSUME, SEIZE, TAKE
Utah, appellation of ........ BEEHIVE
Utah mountain ........ UINTA, PEALE
Utah state flower ................ SEGO
utmost EXTREME, MAXIMUM, LAST
"Utopia," author of ........... MOORE
utopian .... IDEALISTIC, VISIONARY
utricle ..................... BAG, SAC
utter .. SHEER, BRAY, EMIT, MOOT,
            STARK, DRAWL, INTONATE,
            PERFECT
utter; poet. ................. SYLLABLE
utter publicly .... SAY, TELL, VOICE,
            ENOUNCE, INTONATE

# V

V, letter .......................... VEE
V-shaped piece .............. WEDGE
vacancy ..... BLANK, GAP, OPENING
vacant, be .... INANE, VOID, EMPTY,
WAKE, IDLE
vacation ............ RECESS, SPELL,
RESPITE
vaccine, per, to ....... LYMPH, VIRUS
vaccinia ..................... COWPOX
vacillated ... SEESAWED, WAVERED,
TEETERED
vacuities ...................... INANES
vacuum, opposite of ........ PLENUM
vacuum tube ...... DIODE, TETRODE,
ELECTRODE
vadium; law ...................... BAIL
vagabond .. BUM, WASTREL, LOREL,
RODNEY, HOBO, VAGRANT
vagabond; Irish ........... RAPPAREE
vagans; mus. ................ QUINTUS
vagrant TRAMP, NOMAD, OTIOSLER,
PIKER, PROWLER, PICARO
vague DIM, HAZY, OBSCURE, LOOSE
vain ...... BOOTLESS, EMPTY, IDLE,
WASTE, FUTILE
vain boasting ....... FANFARONADE
vain fellow; Bib. ................. RACA
vainglory GASCONADE, POMP, SHOW
vale BACHE, DALE, DELL, DINGLE,
GLEN
Val's father .................... AGUAR
valediction ...... ADIEU, FAREWELL
valedictory .. APOPEMPTIC, ORATION
valentine ....... GIFT, LOVE, TOKEN
valet .............. CRISPIN, SQUIRE
Valetta, native of ......... MALTESE
valid mood of third figure .... FERISON
valid, not ................. NULL, VOID
validate ..... ATTEST, RATIFY, SEAL
validity .......... FORCE, COGENCY
valise, small vanity .... ETUI, ETWEE
valley . DALE, VALE, COMBE, GLEN,
SWALE, DINGLE, DELL
" bet. volcanic cones ...... ATRIO
" ; Bib. .................... HELA
" , English ........ DEAN, DENE
" in Argolis; Gr. ......... NEMEA
" in the Levant .... WADI, WADY
" Indian .................. DHOON
" of Hinnom .......... GEHENNA
" of misery; Bib. ........... BACA
" of S. Africa .............. VAAL
" of the moon ............. RILLE
" of the Sahara .......... SAMEN
" , stream ..... CREEK, COULEE
valorous man ....... HERO, GALLANT
value .... ADMIRE, ESTEEM, CARAT,
STERLING, PAR, WORTH
value, assay ...................... LEY
value, of least possible ........ PLACK
valueless ...... BAFF, THREEPENNY
vamose .. GO, LAM, SCRAM, DECAMP
vamp ........ RECOCT, SOCK, UPPER
vampire ......... BAT, LAMIA, FLIRT
vandal ............ HUN, CONOCLAST

Van Gogh town ................ ARLES
vane .............. FAN, PHANEKILL
vang; naut. ...................... ROPE
vanish FLY, FADE, PASS, EVANESCE,
WEDE, RECEDE
vanity ........ ABEL, BREATH, SHAM
vanity box; Fr. ........ DORINE, ETUI
"Vanity Fair;" char. .......... SHARP
vapid .. POINTLESS, STALE, FLAT,
INSIPID
vapor ....... RACK, REEK, FOG, GAS,
MIST
vapor, comb. form .............. ATMO
vapor pressure indicator TONOMETER
vaporous ...... STEAMY, HALITUOUS
Varangian ....................... ROS
variable ......... PROTEAN, MOBILE,
MUTABLE
variation in text of author ... LECTION
variegate ............ ENAMEL, FRET
variegated .. PAINTED, PIED, PINTO,
SHOT, DIVERSE
variola ................... SMALLPOX
various ......... DIVERSE, SEVERAL
varnish .... JAPAN, ADORN, EXCUSE
varnish and oil mixture ...... MEGILP
varnish ingredient LAC, COPAL, ELEMI
varnish oleoresin .............. DAMAR
vas ................... DUCT, VESSEL
vascular, per. to .... HAEMAL, HEMIC
vase ................ DIOTA, JAR, URN
" , a kind of .. DRUM, ECHEA(pl.),
TAMBOUR, ETUI
" , Egyptian .............. CANOPIC
" , Greek .......... DEINOS, DINOS
" handle ..................... ANSA
" , jasper; Rom., ver. ... MURRINE
" , ornamental ........... EPERGNE
" used as a cinerary urn ... DEINOS
" used as an oil vessel ...... ASKOS
" with separate cover .... POTICHE
vassal ... SLAVE, LIEGE, MAN, SERF
vassalage, subject to ...... ENFEOFF
vast .. HUGE, SEA, UNTOLD, GREAT
vat ........ BAC, GYLE, KEEL, TANK
vat for mash ......... KEEVE, KIEVE
vat, large ................. KIER, TUN
Vatican Chapel .............. SISTINE
vaticanism ................ CURIALISM
vaticinator ................... ORACLE
vault FORNIX, CRYPT, LEAP, TOMB
vault, charnel house ..... OSSUARIUM
vault, niche .............. CATACOMB
vaulted ........... CONCAVE, DOMED
vaulted roof ................. CAMERA
vaults ........ EMBOWS, ENSPHERES
vaunt.. ........ CROW, BOAST, VAPOR
veal ................ RACK, VITULINE
vector ... FORCE, ROTOR, VELOCITY
vector, opposite of ............ SCALAR
vedantic philosophy ........ VEDANTA
Vedas, divinity of the ......... DYAUS
Vedic-Aryan dialect ............. PALI
Vedic god ............ SAVITAR, AGNI
"Veep"; the ................... ALBEN
veer ............ WEAR, YAW, SWAY
Vega's constellation ............. LYRA
vegetable UDO, PEASCOD, RUTABAGA

283

"   bath sponge **LOOFAH, LUFFA**
"   mold ................. **HUMUS**
"   , onion-like **LEEK, SHALLOT**
"   oyster .............. **SALSIFY**
"   rubbish .............. **WRACK**
"   tracing paper ........... **ECU**
vegetables .................... **TRUCK**
vegetables; Fr. . **LEGUMES, LOMENTS**
vegetate ........ **HIBERNATE, GROW**
vegetation, floating .............. **SUDD**
vehemence .... **HEAT, ZEAL, ARDOR,
FIRE**
vehement .......... **ARDENT, EAGER**
vehemently .................... **AMAIN**
vehicle ..... **DEVICE, SLEDGE, TAXI,
CALECHE, CAR, GOCART, VAN**
vehicle; Ind. ................... **TONGA**
Veidt, Mr. .................... **CONRAD**
veil ...... **CLOAK, MASK, PRETENSE**
"   , head, for women .......... **CAUL**
"   in fungi ................... **VELUM**
"   in mosses ............. **CALYPTRA**
"   , papal .................... **ORALE**
veiled ........ **VELATE, CURTAINED,
INCOGNITO**
vein ................ **TENOR, RENAL**
vein; Lat. ........... **VENULA, VENA**
vein, metal bearing ............ **LODE**
vein of ore .......... **LENS, BONANZA**
vein, small ore .................... **HILO**
vein-stone ................... **GANGUE**
veinless ..................... **AVENOUS**
veiny ...................... **VENOSE**
Velez, Miss ...................... **LUPE**
velo, acceleration of one per second ....
**CELO**
velocity unit ...................... **KIN**
velvetleaf .................... **PAREIRA**
venal ......... **HIRELING, CORRUPT**
vender; law .................. **ALIENOR**
vendetta ........................ **FEUD**
veneer ......... **ENAMEL, FACE, LAC**
venerable .. **OLDEN, AUGUST, HOAR,
PROTEAN**
venerate .. **REVERE, LOVE, RESPECT**
veneration ............... **AWE, DULIA**
Venetian church .............. **FRARI**
"   district ............. **RIALTO**
"   formal barge ... **BUCENTAUR**
"   medal; Ital. **OSELLA, OSELA**
"   pleasure boat ..... **GONDOLA**
"   ruler ...... **DOGE, PODESTA**
"   song ........... **BARCAROLE**
"   traveler ................. **POLO**
"   water street .............. **RIO**
"   watering place .......... **LIDO**
Venezuela, grassy plains ...... **LLANOS**
"   , Indian of .. **CARIB, TIMOTE**
"   river ......... **PAO, ORINOCO**
"   state .................... **LARA**
"   town ................... **AROA**
"   , tree of .............. **BALATA**
Venezuelan god ................ **TSUMA**
"Veni vidi ——" ................... **VICI**
Venice, Is. near .............. **BURANO**
venom ........ **GALL, MALICE, VIRUS**
vent ...... **OUTAWE, SAY, AIRHOLE**
venthole ............ **BUNG, SPIRACLE**

ventilated ............ **AIRED, WINDY**
ventral ...... **STERNAL, ABDOMINAL**
ventricles, roof of .............. **TELA**
ventriloquism ............ **HARIOLATE**
venture ........ **DARE, WAGE, BOLD,
BRAVE**
Venus ...... **VESPER, APHRONDITE,
ASTARTE**
Venus, boy beloved by ........ **ADONIS**
Venus, epithet of ......... **CYTHEREA**
Venus' fly trap .............. **DIONAEA**
Venus' girdle ................. **CESTUS**
Venus planet .. **LUCIFER, PHOSPHOR**
Venus, son of ................... **CUPID**
Vera, of Hope's show .......... **VAGUE**
veracious ............. **TRUE, VERITY**
veranda . **LANAI, PYAL, STOA, STOEP**
verb, a ........................ **RHEMA**
verb; obs. ................... **VOCABLE**
verbal noun, the .............. **GERUND**
verbal quibble **PUN, SHIFT, SOPHISM,
WORDINESS**
verbal suffix ..................... **ESCE**
verbenaceae ... **LANTANA, TECTONA**
verbiage .................. **PROLIXITY**
verbose ............. **PROLIX, WORDY**
verbs, derived from ....... **RHEMATIC**
verd ............................. **GREEN**
verd antique, banded ....... **RICOLITE**
Verdi; opera by ..... **AIDA, OTHELLO**
Verdi opera char. .......... **AMNERIS,
RADAMES**
Verdugo; actress .............. **ELENA**
Verdi's first opera ............ **OBERTO**
verdigris ...... **RUST, FILM, PATINA**
verecund ..................... **MODEST**
verge ... **BRINK, EDGE, MARGE, TOP**
verge of authority ............. **WAND**
Vergil's "Aeneid," queen in ...... **DIDO**
Vergil's family name ......... **MARO**
verify to ............ **ATTEST, PROVE**
verily ........ **AMEN, AVER, INDEED**
verisimilitude **TRUTH, PROBABILITY**
verity ................... **FACT, REAL**
veriform ............ **LONG, SLENDER**
vermifuge .. **ANTHELMINTIC AGENT**
vermilion ............. **RED, PIGMENT**
Vermont, city of .... **BARRE, LYNDON**
vernal, per. to ................ **SPRING**
versation ................... **WINDING**
verse . **ALBA, CONSIDER, FIT, POEM,
STICH**
"   , a **RONDEL, STROPHE, STAVE**
"   , form in .............. **TROCHEE**
"   group................. **STROPHE**
"   group, per. to **IONIC, PALINODIC**
"   having eight feet .. **OCTAMETER**
"   having three feet ...... **TRIPODY**
"   , musical ................. **STAFF**
"   , nonsensical ........ **DOGGEREL,
LIMERICK**
"   of four meters .... **TETRAMETER**
"   of three feet ......... **TRIMETER**
"   of two measures ...... **DIMETER**
"   , pause in ................ **CESURA**
"   , romance form ......... **SESTINA**
"   stress, per. to ............. **ICTIC**
"   with hidden motto .... **ACROSTIC**

versed .............. ADEPT, SKILLED
versification .......... ORTHOMETRY
versifier .... POETASTER, RIMESTER
version .... EDITION, TRANSLATION
version of Bible ............ VULGATE
version of Bible; Latin ....... ITALA
verso .............. BACK, REVERSE
vertebra .................... SPONDYL
vertebrate axis ........... AXON, RAY
vertebrates, warm blooded ...... AVES
vertent ...... REVOLVING, TURNING
vertex ........... APEX, TOP, ZENITH
vertical .......... PLUMB, UPRIGHT
verticillate ................ WHORLED
vertigoes; Latin .................. DINI
Vertumnus' beloved ......... POMONA
verve ............ ELAN, PEP, SPIRIT
verve, act with ................. EMOTE
very ...... REAL, TRUE, TOO, MUCH,
     SAME, WELL, GENUINE, TRES
very light ................. FIREWORK
very much, comb. form ............ ERI
vesicle ..................... CYST, SAC
vespa; Lat. ..................... WASP
vesper ............. STAR, EVENING
Vespucci; Ital. .............. AMERIGO
vessel . DIOTA, CASK, DUBBER, VAS,
     VAT, MUG, BOWL, CRAFT
   " , amount lacking of full in a ....
     ULLAGE
   " , any round sailing .. CORACLE
   " , assaying .............. CUPEL
   " , beer .................. POURIE
   " , broad shallow ............ PAN
   " , Chinese .................. JUNK
   " , coal trade; Eng. .......... CAT
   " , coaling .............. COLLIER
   " , coasting .. BILANDER, DONI,
     HOY, LUGGER, PATAMAR,
     TARTAN
   " , combining form for ..... VASO
   " , cooking (airtight) AUTOCLAVE
   " , cylindrical glass ....... BOCAL
   " , deep table ......... TUREEN
   " , drinking .... GOURD, JORUM,
     STEIN, TANKARD, AMPULLA,
     STOUP
   " , Dutch GALIOT, KOFF, YANKY
   " , earthen .... CROCK, PANKIN
   " , E. Indian BALLOON, MANCHE
   " , Ecclesiastical ...... AMA, PYX
   " , filter glass ........... ALUDEL
   " , fishing, sailing ...... SEALER,
     SMACK
   " for ale or wine ........ JUBBE
   " for holding illuminant CRESSET
   " for napkins, salt, etc. ...... NEF
   " for oil ... CUP, CRUSE, DUBBA,
     FONT
   " for refining ............. CUPEL
   " for separating liquids ...........
     TRITORIUM
   " for sugar refining ....... ELUTOR
   " , goods cast overboard to lighten
     a ..................... JETSAM
   " (house boat) of the Nile ........
     DAHABEAH

   " , Indian coasting ...... SHIBAR
   " , large rowing; Scot. .. BIRLINN
   " , lateen rigged; Medit. FELUCCA
   " , Levantine ... SETEE, KETCH,
     SAIC
   " , (log) raft .............. BRAIL
   " , Malay .......... PRAU, PROA
   " , merchant ............ ARGOSY
   " , narrow sterned .......... PINK
vessel, one masted oriental ..... DHOW
   " , part of .. SKEG, PROW, DECK,
     KEEL
   " , per. to a ................ VASAL
   " , sailing ........... BARK, DONI,
     PINNACE, BUGEYE
   " , saucer-like ........... PATERA
   " , single masted ... SLOOP, HOY
   " , small drinking . NOG, NOGGIN
   " , small wooden COGUE, PIGGIN,
     SKEEL
   " , square rigged .... BRIG, SNOW
   " , steering of a ............ COND
   " , stern of a .......... STEERAGE
   " , stone or clay . STEAN, STEEN
   " , Thames; Eng. ...... BAWLEY
   " , three masted .. BARK, TERN,
     XEBEC, ZEBEC
   " , toward stern of ........... AFT
   " , trading .............. BAGGALA
   " , twin hull ........ CATAMARAN
   " , war; Flemish ....... FRIGATE,
     BOYER
   " , wicker .................... POT
   " , wine service .............. AMA
   " , with three banks of oars .......
     TRIREME
   " , with two banks of oars BIREME
   " , Venetian state .. BUCENTAUR
vessels fitted into each other .. ALUDEL
vessel's keel, after-part of ...... SKEG
vest as a right ................ ACCRUE
vest, stuffed .................. ACTON
vest, woolen .... GILET, WAISTCOAT,
     LINDER
Vesta; Gr. .................... HESTIA
vestal ..... VIRGINAL, CHASTE, NUN
vestal virgin ................... TUCCIA
vestibule ..... HALL, LOBBY, FOYER,
     NARTHEX
vestige RELIC, SIGN, TRACE, TRACK,
     TINCTURE, SHRED
vestment ........ CHASUBLE, EPHOD,
     SCAPULAR
   " , alb-like ............ SACCOS
   " , Arabian ................ ABA
   " , clerical ....... ALB, AMICE,
     CASSOCK
   " , eucharistic ....... MANIPLE
   " , liturgical .............. COPE
   " , outer ........... CHASUBLE
   " , priest's ... SURPLICE, ALB,
     STOLE
vestry ........... SACRISTY, CHAPEL
vesuvianite ................ IDOCRASE
vetch ................... AKRA, FITCH
vetch, bitter ..................... ERS

vetch, common ................ SATIVA
vetches ....................... TARES
veterinarian ........ FARRIER, LEECH
vex ... HARASS, CARK, FRET, RILE,
        ROIL, YEARN, IRK, NETTLE
vexation .. CHAFE, CHAGRIN, TEEN,
        THORN, TRAY, IRRITATION
vexatious ...................... PESKY
vexed ................ GRAME, SPITED
vexed explicative ................ DRAT
vial CRUET, AMPUL, PHIAL, BOTTLE
viand .................... CATE, FARE
viatic ....................... JOURNEY
viator ...................... TRAVELER
Viaud's pseudonym .............. LOTI
vibrant .......... TRAVALE, VOICED
vibrate ... JAR, DINDLE, RESONATE,
        TIRL, CLIMPSE, QUAVER,
        THROB, VIEW
vibration measuring inst. TONOMETER
vicar ... PASTOR, CURATE, DEPUTY
vice .. LEHTER, PLACE, SIN, STEAD
vice cap ...................... CHUCK
vice jaw ....................... CHAP
vice king .................... VICEROY
vice-president .................. VEEP
victim .. GULL, DUPE, PREY, CULLY
victor ........ CONQUERER, MASTER
victorine ............ PEACH, TIPPET
victory .......... NIKE, PALM, SIGHE
victory, celebrating ........ EPINICIAN
victory, hymn of .......... EPINICION
victory, memorial of .......... TROPHY
victual .............. EAT, FEED, KAI
vie ...... COMPETE, EMULATE, FAY,
        CONTEND, LIFE
Vienna ........................... WIEN
Viet ............................. NAM
view VISTA, SEE, SCAUPE, EYE, KEN,
        SPECE, GLIMPSE
vigil PATROL, WATCH, ARGUS, EVE
vigilant ...... ALERT, AWAKE, WARY
vigilantes; col. ................. POSSE
vigor, .. FORCE, STAMINA, STHENIA,
        SEVE, VIR, ENERGY,
        LIFE, VIM
vigorous .......... FETTLE, COGENT
viking ............... PIRATE, ROVER
Viking poet .................... SKALD
vilayet ....................... EYALET
vile .......... ABJECT, MEAN, WILE
vilify .. MALIGN, REVILE, TRADUCE
village TOWN, HAMLET, DORP, KAIK,
        THORPE
village, Afr. ...................... STAD
village, fortified ................. BURG
village, stockaded; S. Afr. ...... KRALL
villain ........ KNAVE, WICK, GIANT
villain, low ..... BEZONIAN, CAITIFF
villain of "Othello" ............... IAGO
villatic ................. RURAL, FARM
villein CEORL, CHURL, CARL, ESNE,
        SERF
Villon; poet: Fr. ............ FRANCOIS
vim . PEP, ZIP, ELAN, ESPRIT, GIMP,
        FORCE, SPIRIT

vindicate ASSERT, JUSTIFY, AVENGE
vine, climbing .................... LIANA
vine, fruit bearing . GRAPE, CUPSEED
vine parasite ................... APHIS
vine, part of a ..... CIRRUS, TENDRIL
vine support .................... RISEL
vine, twining ................... BINE
vinegar . ACETATE, ACETUM, EISEL
vinegar and wine ................ PUSK
vinegar; comb. form .......... ACETO
vinegar, dregs of ............ MOTHER
vinegar, made of ale .......... ALEGAR
vinegar, preserve in ....... MARINATE
vines, covered with .......... LIANAED
vinous aroma .................... WINY
vinous grosbeak ................. MORO
viol ........ ROPE, RUANA, SARINDA
viola ............................. ALTO
Viola's brother, Shak. .... SEBASTIAN
violations of sentence structure ........
        ANACOLUTHA
violent people Norse folklore ..........
        BERSERKERS
violently ....................... AMAIN
violet .......................... MAUVE
violet dye ..................... ARCHIL
violet root glucoside ........... IRIDIN
violet leaves, oil in ............. IRONE
violin, barritone ............... CELLO
violin bow ...................... ARCO
violin, famous AMATI, ROCTA, STRAD,
        CREMONA
violin, first .......... REBEC, REBAB
violin, part of a ............... NECK
violin, per. to ...................... KIT
violin player .. BULL, NERO, MORINI
violin-shaped ............... WAISTED
violin, tenor .................... ALTO
violinist ....................... STERN
viper ...... ADDER, ASP, CERASTES
viper; E. Ind. ................. KUPPER
viper's bugloss ............ BUGWEED
virago .............. FURY, RULLION,
        TERMAGANT, VIXEN
vireo ..................... GREENLET
Virgil, birthplace of ............ GAUL
Virgil, patron of ......... MAECENAS
virgin ......................... VESTAL
Virgin Is. discoverer of .. COLUMBUS
Virgin Is.; sec'y of .......... LOVETT
Virgin Mary's flower ...... MARIGOLD
virgin warrior in the "Aeneid" ........
        CAMILLA
Virginia ......................... DARE
Virginia creeper .. IVY, AMPELOPSIS
    "    juniper ............... CEDAR
    "    pine ............. LOBLOLLY
    "    poke ............ HELLEBORE
    "    wake-robin ............ ARUM
    "    willow ................. ITEA
Virginia woodcock .......... PEWEE
virgularian ................. SEAROD
virtu, article of ................ CURIO
virulence ...... . MALIGNITY, HATE
virulent ............. RABID, BITTER
virus ............... POISON, VENOM
virus ailment .................... FLU

286

viscous ..... (S)LIMY, ROPY, STICKY, GLUEY, SIZY
vise ................ CLAMP, WINCH
Vishinski, Mr. ............... ANDREI
Vishnu, incarnation of ..... KRISHNA, RAMA
visible .. PATENT, OBVIOUS, OPEN
visible to naked eye .. MACROSCOPIC
Visigoth .................... TEUTON
Visigoths, king of the ........ ALARIC
vision; comb. form ............. OPTO
vision, double ............ DIPLOPIA
vision, poor ............ SIGHT, MOLE
vision, science of ........ OPTOMETRY
visionary .. FEY, IDEAL, DREAMER, UTOPIAN, AERY
visit between whale ships ....... GAM
visiting, a .................... SOKEN
Vistula tributary ................. SAN
visual disorder ......... STRABISMUS
vita; Lat. ......................... LIFE
"Vita Nuova"; author ........ DANTE
vital INHERENT, SOULED, MORTAL, ORGANIC
" affinity ............. METABOLIC
" air ...................... OXYGEN
" fluid ..................... LATEX
" force .................. NEURISM
" growth force ....... BATHMISM
" juice ........................ SAP
" , per. to .............. VIABLE
" strength ............. STAMINA
" thought force ....... PHRENISM
vitality .................... LIFE, SAP
vitellus ...................... YOLK
vitiated DEBASED, PICAL, SPOILED
vitreous sodium carbonate .... TRONA
vitreous stone .............. APATITE
vitriform mineral ............... APAR
vitrine .................. SHOWCASE
vitriol .............. CAUSTIC, SORY
vituperation .................... ABUSE
vivacity ....... DASH, ELAN, VERVE
vivandier .................... SUTLER
vivarium ............... PARK, STEW
vivary ........................... POND
vixen ................ SHEW, VIRAGO
Vladimir Ilich Ulianov .......... LENIN
vocal ................... SONAT, ORAL
vocal composition .............. MOTET
vocal flourish .............. ROULADE
vocally, utter ............. PHONATE
voe ............ BAY, CREEK, INLET
voice ALTO, BASS, EMIT, SOPRANO
voice; Lat. .................... VESTA
voice, loss of .............. APHONIA
Voice of Abilene ................. IKE
voice, powerful ............ STENTOR
voice sound .................... MEDIA
voice, roaming .............. VAGANS
voiceless ANAUDIA, SPIRATE, SURD
voiceless sound ............... TENUIS
voices, for all .................. TUTTI
void ABOLISH, NULL, ANNUL, EGEST
void of space .................. INANE
volatile .......... ESSENCE, FITFUL, FLIGHTY, MERCURIAL
volatile flux .................... SMEAR
volatilize .................... EXHALE

volcanic ejection ............. BELCH
" fragments of lava .. LAPILLI
" glass .. PERLITE, OBSIDIAN
" glass froth .......... PUMICE
" lava .... LATITE, LAPILLI
" mud ........ MOYA, SALSE
" rock .. PERLITE, RHYOLITE
" saucer .............. CRATER
" tufa ....... TERRAS, TRASS
" vent ................. CRATER
volcano, extinct; Jap. ........ ASOSAN
" , fluid rock of a ........ LAVA
" in Iceland ............ ASKJA
" goddess; Hawai. ....... PELE
" in Japan . ASAMA, ASO, FUJI
" in Mindanao, P. I. ....... APO
" in United States .... SHASTA
" ; Ital. .... ETNA, VESUVIUS
" , Martinique ......... PELEE
" , mouth of ..... FUMAROLE
" of Guatemala ..... ATITLAN, FUEGO
" of Java ....... GEDE, RAUN
" of the Andes .... COTOPAXI
" of the U. S. ........ LASSEN
" , slaggy eruption of . SCORIA
" , Sumatra .......... MERAPI
Volga, anc. name ................. RHA
Volga, city on ............. SAMARA
volley ............. PLATOON, SALVO
volplane ................... GLIDE
"Volpone," char. in ........... MOSCA
Volsunga Saga, king in .......... ATLI
volt, or demi-volt ......... REPOLON
Voltaire; novel by ......... CANDIDE
Voltaire's name ............. AROUET
volti; mus. .................... TURN
voluble ........ FLUENT, GLIB, OILY
volume . BULK, CUBAGE, MO, TOME
volume in ten parts .... DECAMERON
volume of statutes ............. CODEX
volumetric analysis, determine by; ..... TITRATE
Volund, brother of ............... EGIL
volute .. CILERY, MOLLUSK, SCROOL
volva; Lat. ................. COVERING
voodooism .................... OBEAH
voracious .................. EDACIOUS
voracity ........ EDACITY, RAPACITY
vortex ........... EDDY, APEX, GYRE
Vosges m't'n pass ........... BELFORT
votary .................... DEVOTEE
vote .... STRAW, LOGROLL, BALLOT
vote of assent .... PLACET, AYE, NOD
votes, receptacle for .......... SITULA
Votipka, Miss ............... THELMA
vouch for ........ ATTEST, SPONSOR
vouchsafe ...... BESTOW, CONCEDE, DEIGN
vow .. VOTARY, PLEDGE, PROMISE, SWEAR
vow, dedicated by a .......... VOTIVE
vow; dial ........................ VUM
vowel change in German ..... UMLAUT
" gradation .......... ABLAUT
" , mark placed over ... MACRON
" point; Heb. ............. TSERE
" , short ................. BREVE

287

" sign .................. DIERESIS
" sound, per. to ........ VOCALIC
vowels, contraction of two .... CRASIS
vowels, group of two ........ DIGRAM,
DIGRAPH
Vulcan .................. HEPHAESTUS
Vulcan, brass made by ........ MALOS
vulcanite ................. EBONITE
Vulcan's son .................... CACUS
Vulcan's wife ................... VENUS
vulgar ................ LEWD, RIBALD
vulgar looking ..... DOWDY, FRUMPY
vulgate .......................... ITALA
vulpine .................... ALOPECOID
vulture ............... CONDOR, PAPA
vulture, bearded ..... HAMMERGEIER
vulture, black; Cen. Am. .... ATRATA,
URUBU
vulture, Old World .......... GRIFFIN

# W

waag; Afr. ........ GRIVET, MONKEY
wabayo, deriv. of ............. OUABAIO
wabble ............ TITTER, WOBBLE,
VACILLATE
wachna ........................ CODFISH
wacker; Eng. ................. QUAKER
wacky; sl. .................... ERRATIC
wad ........ MASS, BAT, PLUMBAGO,
LUMP, PAD, STUFF
waddle ............. PODDLE, WAMBLE
wade ................. FORD, PLODGE
wadi; Afr. ...... CHANNEL, STREAM
wad-set; Scot ............ MORTGAGE
wading bird So. Am. ...... FLAMINGO,
JACANA, HERON
wading birds (see also "Bird") .........
GRALLAE
wafer box .......................... PYX
waff ..................... BLAST, PUFF
waff; Scot. .............. WORTHLESS
waffle ................. GOPHER, CAKE
waft ............. BEAR, CARRY, SEAL
wag FARCEUR, ROGUE, WIT, MOMUS
wage .......... HIRE, PAY, STIPEND
wager ........ BET, PLEDGE, STAKE,
HAZARD
wages in N. Z. ................... UTU
waggish .. ARCH, JOCULAR, ROGUISH
Wagner; comp. .............. RICHARD
Wagnerian Hero ............. TRISTAN
Wagnerian opera .. RIENZI, PARSIFAL
wagon .. TRAM, TONGA, VAN, WAIN,
CART, CAR, CAISSON,
CHARIOT, COACH
wagon, oriental covered ........ ARABA
wagon pin ..................... CLEVIS
wagon shaft .................... THILL
wagon, springless; Rus. ...... TELEGA
wagon thill .................... BLADE
wagon tongue ........... NEAP, POLE
wahoo fishes ..................... PETOS
waif ....... GAMIN, STRAFE, STRAY,
WASTREL

wail .......... SOB, WOW, ULULATE
wailing ........................ SCREAM
wainscot ................. CEIL, PANEL
waist . BODICE, BASQUE, GARIBALDI
waist in dress making ........ CARPEL
waistband ................. BELT, SASH
waistcoat ... DOUBLET, VEST, GILET
waistcoat unlined ............ SINGLET
wait .......... LINGER, STAY, TARRY
wait; Sp. ..................... ESPERE
waiter; Fr. .................... GARCON
waiter, large ................ SALVER
waive .......... FORGO, RELINQUISH
Wake Is., temporary name ...... OTORI
wake-robin; ... ARUM, CUCKOOPINT,
TRILLIUM
Waldensian .................. LEONIST
wale ................ BLOW, RIB, WELT
Wales, anc. name .......... CAMBRIA
Wales, floral emblem of .......... LEEK
Wales, legendary prince ...... MADOC
Wales, people of .............. WELSH
walk STRAM, DADDLE, GAD, TRAMP,
TREAD, MUSH, PLOD
walk aimlessly MINCE, LURCH, PAUP
walk, shaded ....... ALAMEDA, MALL
walked softly .................. STOLE
walking about .............. PASSANT,
PERIPATETIC
walking like a bear .... PLANTIGRADE
walking meter .......... PEDOMETER
wall, inclose in .................. MURE
wall, inner .................... ESCARP
wall lizard ...................... GECKO
wall, of a .................... PARIETAL
wall, outer face of ........ PARAMENT
wall, turf .................. FEALDIKE
wallaba .......... ⟨... APA, ARAWAK
wallaroo ................... KANGAROO
waller; piano, jazz ................ FATS
walls, dividing ................... SEPTA
walls of cavity ................. PARIES
walnut skin ....................... ZEST
walrus . BRUT, MORSE, ROSEMARINE
walrus herd ....................... POD
walruses .................. PINNIPEDIA
Walter; actor .................... ABEL
wampee; China ................ GRAPE
wampum; Ind. .... BEADS, SEAWANT
wampum, kind of ..... PEAG, PEAGE,
ROANOKE
wan ............ FADE, HAW, PALLID
wand ...... CADUCEUS, ROD, VERGE
wand, a kind of ..... BATON, BAGUET
wand, interwoven ........... WATTLE
wand, royal ........ MACE, SCEPTER
wand, short .. CUDGEL, TRUNCHEON
wander .. EGAR, GAD, MOON, RANGE,
ROVE, TRAPE
wander aimlessly . STRAY, DIVAGATE
wander widely ROAM, PEREGRINATE
wander in a winding course ............
SCAMANDER, MEANDER
wanderer .. ARAB, NOMAD, TRUANT,
VAG
wandering ...... ODYSSEY, ERRANT,
VAGRANT, NOMADIC, ASTRAY

wandering, a kind of .... ABERRANT, DELIRIUM
wandering religious votary .. PALMER
wanderoo ................... MACAQUE
wane ........... ABATE, EBB, FADE
wane, opposed to ............... WAX
wangle ............. FINAGLE, WAG
wanigan ......................... ARK
want ....... ABSENCE, LACK, MISS
want of appetite ............. ASITIA
want of desire ........ INAPPETENCE
wantage ..................... ULLAGE
wanted ............. LACKED, NEED
wanton .... FREE, RAMPANT, WILD, RANK
wapiti .................... DEER, ELK
war agency ............... OSS, OWI
"War and Peace"; author of TOLSTOY
war, an agreement in ........ CARTEL
" bird .......................... ACE
" machine .................... TANK
" scare; British ............. FLAP
" trophy; Ind. ............... SCALP
" vessel ............... CORVETTE
warble SING, CAROL, TRILL, YODEL
warbler; Eur. ............ BECCAFICO
warbling ........... CHIRM, CHIRP
ward off ..... FEND, FENCE, PARRY
warden, forest ............. RANGER
warder .................... TURNKEY
wardrobe ....... ALMIRAH, AMBRY, CABINET
warehouse ......... GODOWN, DEPOT
warehouse; Fr. .......... ENTREPOT
warehouse; Siberian ........ ETAPE
warfare CRUSADE, STRIFE, POLEMY
warlike native of Brit. Ind. ..... SIKH
warm ...... CALID, HUMID, MUGGY
" , growing ......... CALESCENT
" inner sole ............... SOCK
" , keep .................... STOVE
" , moderately ......... TEPEFY
" , per. to ........... THERMAL
" room; Rom. ...... TEPIDARIUM
" , Span. for ............ CALIENTE
warmed over; Fr. ........ RECHAUFFE
warmth ...... ARDOR, ELAN, ZEAL
warmth, moderate ............ TEPOR
warn ...... ADVISE, FLAG, SIGNAL, PREVISE
warner ..................... MENTOR
warning ... ALERT, OMEN, SEMATIC
warning; law ............... CAVEAT
warning signal; . ALARUM, BEACON, TOCSIN, BLINKER, SIREN
warp ........ BIAS, DISTORT, SWAY
" in weaving ............... CRAM
" thread (loom) ......... STAMEN
" threads in tapestry weaving ..... LEASE
" , to ........... DEFLECT, CAST
" yarn ....................... ABB
warrant ... ENSURE, ABLE, PLEVIN
warren .................... RABBITRY
warrigal ...................... DINGO
warrior, Am. Ind. ............. SANNUP
warrior; Bib. ................. EHUD
warrior, fabled female ..... ASLAUGA, AMAZON

warrior, professional; Rom. ................. GLADIATOR
wars; ancient ......... PUNIC, ROSES
warship, inferior ............. RAZEE
warship; Sp. ............... GALLEON
warship, three bank ........ TRIREME
warship, two bank .......... BIREME
wart ............. TUMOR, ECPHYMA
wart hog; Afr. ................ SWINE
wary . CANNY, WISE, ALERT, MIND
wash . RENCH, LEACH, LAVE, NET, TYE
wash, a kind of .............. LOTION
wash for a still ............. SPERGE
wash lightly .......... RINSE, LAVE
wash out, to ... ELUTRIATE, ELUTE
washing ... BATH, LAVAGE, SLUICE
washings from elution ...... ELUATE
Washington city ............ YAKIMA
wasps' nests ............ VESUIARIES
wasp ...... HORNET, JIGA, WHAMP
wasp, Lat. ................. VESPID
waste ..... IDLE, FRITTER, BANGLE, CHAFF, SPILL, RAVAGE
waste fiber ...................... NOIL
waste, to ......... LOSE, TABID, EAT
waste, to lay .......... HAVOC, SACK
wasted GAUNT, POOR, SPARE, LANK
wasteful ........ PRODIGAL, LAVISH
wasting away ...... TABETIC, TABID
wasting away, a EATEN, MARASMUS
wasting time ................... IDLING
wastrel ... ARAB, VAGABOND, WAIF, LOSEL, SPENDTHRIFT
wat ....... DROUGHTY, HARE, HOT
watch ..................... EYE, TEND
" , as a soldier PERDUE, SENTRY
" chain ................. ALBERT
" , mounted ........... VEDETTE
" pin ...................... STUD
" time ............... HOROLOGE
" tower ..... BEACON, MIRADOR
" tower; Sp. ........... ATALAYA
watchful . ALERT, WARY, VIGILANT
watchful guardian ............ ARGUS
watching ............. VIGIL, SEEING
watching, secret ....... ESPIONAGE
watchman; Gr. myth. .... CERBERUS
watchman; Norse ......... HEIMDAL
watch-pocket .................... FOB
watch-word .. SHIBBOLETH, SIGNAL
watch-works, device in ESCAPEMENT
water ..................... RAIN, SEA
" bag ................... CHAGEN
" bettle's leg ......... SATIREME
" bottle ............... CARAFE
" brain in sheep ............. GID
" brash ................. PYROSIS
" channel ............... FLUME
" channel below a mill race ....... TAILRACE
" clock ............. CLEPSYDRA
" cocks ................... KORAS
" color ............ AQUARELLE
" course . FLUX, RACE, TINKLE, WADY, CANAL, YORA
" course ............. NULLAH
" , French for ............. EAU
" gauge ............ UDOMETER

289

" hen ...................... COOT
" jar ............ BANGA, LOTA
" lifting engine; ... NORIA, RAM,
　　　　　　　　　　　SHADOOF
" lilies; genus ....... NELUMBO
" lily .......... WOCAS, WOKAS
" lily; Lat. ......... NYMPHAEA
" mill ..................... CLOW
" nymph ................. NAIAD
" nymph, soulless ..... UNDINE
" opening ................... GAT
water opossum ................. YAPOK
" ousel ................... DIPPER
" passage ................ SLUICE
" plants genus ............ TRAPA
" rat ....................... VOLE
" rat slang ................ THIEF
" receptable eccl. .......... FONT
" , resembling ........ HYDATOID
" sapphire ................ IOLITE
" , sheet of .............. NAPPE
" spirit ... ARIEL, NIX, UNDINE
" , Spanish for ............. AGUA
" spout ..... SPATE, GARGOYLE
" sprite ............ KELPIE, NIS
" sprite, female ........... NIXIE
" substance . BAREGIN, GLAIRIN
" thrush .................. OUZEL
" , to .................. IRRIGATE
" , to search for ......... DOWSE
" trench, artificial ......... LEAT
" vessel orient. .. AFTABA, LOTA
" wheel ..... DANIADE, NORIA,
　　　　　　　TURBINE, TYMPANUM
" wheel, Egypt.; var. ...... SAKIA
water-bearer .............. AQUARIUS
water-boatman .... CORIXA, SKIPPER
water-bottle; Brit. .......... CANTEEN
water-cress ............ EKER, PERRO
waterfall .... CASCADE, FOSS, LINN
water-fowl .................. PELICAN
wateriness ................. AQUOSITY
watering place ............ OASIS, SPA
waterless ................ ANHYDROUS
water-like culture ............. LYMPH
watered; Fr. ..................... MOIRE
waters; Hindu ................ AP, APAS
water-shed ................... DIVIDE
waterwort ................... ELATINE
watery AQUEOUS, TEARFUL, SOGGY,
　　　　　　　　　　　　　　VAPID
watery eye ...... EPIPHORA, RHEUM
watery portion of animal fluid SEROUS,
　　　　　　　　　　　　　　　SERUM
wattle ............ DEWLAP, LAPPET
wattle of a fowl .................. GILL
wattle of certain birds ..... CARUNCLE
wattle tree ...................... BOREE
wave .......... RIPPLE, BLESS, FLAP
wave; comb. form ............... ONDO
wave, large .. DECUMAN, SURGE, SEA
wave, ship a .................... POOP
wave, tidal ..................... EAGRE
wave, top of .................... CREST
wave-train ................. ANTENNA
wave, violent ................... BORE
wave-like moulding ............. CYMA

waver .. LISP, TEETER, VEER, SWAY
waves lift ...................... SCEND
wavy ......... UNDE, ONDY, UNDATE
wavy, as of leaves ........... REPAND
wax .............. CERE, GROW, PELA
" , bees, fatty acid of .... CEROTIC
" , candle ................. CIERGE
" , cobbler's ................. CODE
" , cover with ................ CERE
" figure ............... CEROPLAST
" , grave ............. ADIPOCERE
" match .................... VESTA
" ointment ................ CERATE
" unguent, compo. of ..... CEROMA
" , yellow ................ CERESIN
waxlike mineral used in candle making;
　　　　　　　　　　　　　OZOCERITE
waxy ................ CERAL, FICTILE
waxy substance, basis of cork SUBERIN
way ....... PATH, VIA, WONT, MODE
way, on the ..................... AGATE
way out ................ EGRESS, EXIT
wayfarer ....... VIATOR, TRAVELER
waylay ........ AMBUSH, ROB, SEIZE
waywiser ................. ODOMETER
we; Lat. ......................... NOS
weak .... DEBILE, FADE, PECCABLE,
　　　　　　　　　　　　　　　WAN
weak minded ........... DAFT, DOTOR
weaken PETER, CRAZE, SAP, UNMAN
weakening .................. DILUENT
weakfish ... TOTUAVA, SQUETEAGUE
weakling ...................... PULER
Weakness ASTHENIA, FAULT, SOFT
weakness in character . FOIBLE, FRAIL
weakness of any organ ........ ATONY
weal .. SUCCESS, WELFARE, STATE,
　　　　　　　STRIPE, WALE, WELT
wealth ............. CAPITAL, RICHES
wealth, mad pursuit of . PLUTOMANIA
wealth, person of .......... OPULENT,
　　　　　　　　　MAGNATE, MONIED
wealth, worship of ...... PLUTOLATRY
wean; Scot. ...................... CHILD
weapon ....... CLUB, SWIRD, ADAGA,
　　　　　　VOULGE, GAT, TOMAHAWK
" , long-handled; anc. HALBERD
" , medieval ........ CROSSBOW,
　　　　　　　　　　　　　　GISARME
" , prehistoric ............. CELT
" , single edged ........... BOLO
" , war; early ........ POLEAXE
" , wooden; Ind. BOW, MACANA
wear ............ CHAFE, FRAY, FRET
wear away ..... ABRADE, CONTRIVE,
　　　　　　　　　　　　　　　ERODE
wearied .... IRKED, FAGGED, JADED
weariness ............. ENNUI, SLEME
wearing away . EROSION, DETRITION
wearisome TEDIOUS, DREE, OPEROSE
weary .... TIRE, BORE, JADE, SPENT
wea-sand ...... TRACHEA, WINDPIPE
weasel .... MUSTELLE, STOAT, VARE
weasel, family ......... OTTER, STOT
weasel, white; N. Am. ........ ERMINE
weasel-like .. MINK, FERRET, TAYRA,
　　　　　　　　　　　　MUSTELLINE

290

weather cock ............ FANE, VANE
weather map line ............. ISOBAR
weathers ............. SKIES, BRAVES
weave ENTWINE, MAT, PLAIT, REEL
weave together ............. PLEXURE
weave twigs ................. WATTLE
weaver; stage name .............. PAT
weaver bird .......... BAYA, TAHA
weaver's reed .................... SLEY
weaving, art of .................. LOOM
weaving batten ................ LATHE
weaving cylinder ................ BEAM
weaving, formed by ......... TEXTILE
weaving straw ................ RAFFIA
weaving term .................... LISSE
weaving tool                 SHUTTLE
web ... WEET, CAUL, TELA, TISSUE
web, per. to a ..... RETIARY, TELARY
Webb, Jack; prod. .......... DRAGNET
webbed ............. KELD, PALMATE
webbing on a bird's foot; .... LOBATE,
                             PALAMA
web-footed .... OARY, TOTIPALMATE
wed ...... ESPOUSE, MARRY, MATED
wedding snow .................... RICE
wedge ...... CAM, COTTER, GIB, KEY
wedge for a wheel ............. SCOTCH
wedge or lock .................. QUOIN
wedge, to ........ STOW, CHOCK, JAM
wedge-like contrivance ........ CLEAT
wedge-like piece ........... EMBOLUS
wedge-shaped  CUNEATE, SPHENOID
wedge-shaped timber tree ....... TENON
wee ........... LITTLE, SMALL, TINY
weed .......... DOCK, JUNK, TARE,
                KNAWEL, PLANTAIN
weed, poisonous ................. LOCO
weed, prickly .................... BUR
weed, to ............... EXTIRPATE
weed, wiry grass ............. DARNEL
weeder ......................... SPUD
weeding machine .... ABERUNCATOR
week day, per. to a .......... FERIAL
week, having intervals of .... OCTAN
weekly ................. HEBDOMADAL
ween ..... EXPECT, FANCY, THINK
weep ... LAMENT, SOB, LERM, ORP,
                SOIN, BLUBBER, CRY
weevil ....... BOUD, CURCULIO, KIS
weevil, bean; genus ........... LARIA
weevil, cotton .................... BOLL
weevil, plum .................... TURK
weevils; genus ................. APION
weft, crossed ...... BALANCE, BEAM,
                              WOOFED
weighing ..................... TARING
weighing machine .... TRONE, SCALE
weight . ROTL, HECTOGRAM, HEFT,
                TON, POISE, STRESS
"     , allowance ............. TRET
"     , Anglo-Ind. ..... SER, TOLA
"     , apothecaries; anc. ... OBOLE
"     , as a load .............. CLOG
"     , balance ............. RIDER
"     , Burmese ........... KYAT
"     , Chinese; CATTY, FAN, HAO,
            KIN, LI, PICUL, TAN, TAEL
"     , clock ................ PEISE

"     deducting fare ...... SUTTLE
"     , Denmark ........ LOD, ORT
"     down ................ BALLAST
"     , Egyptian; anc. ......... KAT
"     , English; obs. ......... MAST
"     , equal ............. ISOBARIC
"     , estimated in terms of .......
                            PONDERAL
"     , Hindu ........... SER, TAEL
"     , hundred; Eur. ..... CENTAL,
                          CENTNER
"     , Madras ............. POLLAM
"     measure ........ MINIM, TON,
                          METAGE
"     , metric unit of ......... KILO
"     , minute portion .... MOMENT
"     nightmare .......... INCUBUS
"     of Arabia ........... DIRHEM
"     of France; .. GRAMME, KILO,
            LIVRE, ONCE, SOL;
"     of gold in Br. Ind. ...... TOLA
"     of Great Britain for coal KEEL
"     of Greece .............. MINA
"     of India ............ PICE, SER
"     of Japan ....... MO, FUN, RIN
"     of Java ............... AMAT
"     of lead ................. CHAR
"     of Mongolia ............. LAN
"     of Netherlands WIGT, WIGTJE
"     of 100 pounds ........ CENTAL
"     of Persia ................... SIR
"     of Russia ........ DOLA, LOT
"     of Siam .. BAT, CATTY, KATI
"     of Spain .... ARROBA, MARCO
"     of Syria ............... COLA
"     on a purse net ........... TOM
"     , pharmaceutical OBOL, OBOLE
weight, precious stones ....... CARAT
"     , relating to .......... BARIC
"     , Roman; anc. ........ AS, BES
"     sash cord ............. MOUSE
"     , Straits Settlement .... CHEE
"     , system of ............ TROY
"     , Turkish .......... OKA, OKE
"     , wool, cheese, etc.; ... CLOVE,
                          NAIL, TOD
weights of Germany ............ LOTE
weighty .......... ONEROUS, SOLID
weir .... BARRIER, BURROCK, DAM,
                GARTH, NET, SEINE
weird ..... ELDRITCH, EERIE, EERY
weka; N. Zeal. .................... RAIL
welding ................. ARC, FUSING
welfare ...... SUCCESS, SELE, WEAL
welkin ................ HEAVEN, SKY
well .. GAY, HALE, TRIG, AIN, BIEN
"     boring drill ................... JAR
"     born ................... EUGENIC
"     done ............. BRAVO, GOOD
"     , feeling ............. EUPHORIA
"     , lining of a ..... STEAN, STEEN
"     pit ......................... SUMP
"     up ......................... WALL
Welland ...................... CANAL
wellaway ...... ALAS, REGRET, WOE
Welles, Miss .............. BARBARA
Welles; actor ................. ORSON
Welles; diplomat ............ SUMNER
Welsh ..................... CYMRIC

Welsh author .......... LLEWELLYN
Welsh boat ................. CORACLE
Welsh dialect ................ CYMRY
Welsh dog ...................... CORGI
Welsh hamlet ................... TREF
Welsh mus. assembly .. EISTEDDFOD
Welsh Prince ................... IDRIS
Welsh rabbit .............. RAMEKIN
Welsh, the; col. .............. TAFFY
Welshman ............... CAMBRIAN
welt ... FRINGE, HEM, LASH, WALE
welter ................. BURL, ROLL
Welzy; novelist ............... EUDORA
wen .................. MOLE, TALPA
wend .............. GO, PASS, SHIFT
wergild ............. ERIC, FINE, CRO
W. African .............. ASHANTEE
W. African baboon .... DRILL, WOOD
"        "     Gold Coast city .... ACCRA
"        "     monkey ............. MONO
"        "     plant .............. ESERE
"        "     reedbuck ......... NAGOR
"        "     tree ............... AKEE
W. Indian coral is. ........... CAICOS
"        "     fish; ... BACALAO, CERO,
                              SESI, TANG
"        "     fish, basslike ........ BOGA
"        "     flea .... CHIGOE, CHIGRE
"        "     island ........... ARUBA
"        "     liquor ............ MOBBY
"        "     locust .......... ALGAROBA
"        "     native ............ CARIB
"        "     negro ........ EBO, EBOE
"        "     remora ............ PEGA
"        "     rodent ........... HUTIA
"        "     shark .............. GATA
"        "     snapper, black-fin .... SESI
"        "     sorcery ............. OBI
"        "     tallow tree ......... CERA
"        "     tree .. CALABA, BONACE,
                              ARALIE
West Indies, one of the ........ NEVIS
West Indies, sugar works of .... USINE
West, Miss ..................... MAE
W. Point, second year .... YEARLING
West Saxon earl; Eng. ..... GODWIN
western ................. HESPERIAN
"Westward Ho," char. in ...... LEIGH
wet .......... SOPPING, DANK, SOAK
wet, as flax ........................ RET
wether ................... CALF, SHEEP
Weyland's men ............. AVIATORS
whack .................. BEAT, EXCEL
whacky .............. MADCAP, WILD
whale .............. CETE, CALF
"     , Arctic ........ NARWHAL, ORC
"     , carcass of ............. KRENG
"     fat ........................ CETIN
"     , female ................. COW
"     killer ......... GRAMPUS, ORCA
"     morbid secretion in . AMBERGRIS
"     oil cask .................... RIER
"     , sperm ............. CACHALOT
"     , strip blubber from .... FLENSE
"     , white .................. BELUGA
whale-bone .......... BALEEN, BAYA
whales' food BRIT, HERRING, SPRAT
whales, school of ........... GAM, POD

whales, skin ................. SCULP
whang ...... CHUNK, BANG, STRIKE
whangee; genus .............. BAMBOO
wharf .... DOCK, JETTY, KEY, QUAY
wharf, elevated staging upon a STAITH
wharf space ................. QUAYAGE
Wharton, Edith; hero .......... FROME
what; dial. ............... ANAN, EH
whatnot CABINET, ETAGERE, STAND
whaup ...................... CURLEW
wheal ........ WALE, STRIPE, WELT
wheat .......... DURRA, DURUM
"    , beards of ................ AWNS
"    , cracked ................ CROAT
"    , disease of ...... AECIA, BUNT,
                              SMUT, ERGOT
"    , gritty part of ...... SEMOLINA
"    , head of .................. EAR
"    , Indian ................... SUJI
"    , kind of; Ger. ............ SPELT
"    , outer coat of ............ BRAN
"    , repository for ... MATTAMORE
"    , substance of .......... GLUTEN
"    , trade; abb. .................... AT
wheatear .................... CHACK
wheedle BAM, BLANDISH, INVEIGLE,
                              COAX
wheel check .................... SPRAG
"    , grooved .............. SHEAVE
"    , iron tire of ............ STRAKE
"    , little .......... ROO, ROTELLA
"    of a spur ................. ROWEL
"    part ................... HUB(CAP)
"    , projecting part of a ...... CAM
"    , resembling a HELM, TROCHAL
"    , rim, part of ............ FELLY
"    shaped .... ROTATE, ROTIFORM
"    spokes .................... RADII
"    , swivel ................... CASTER
"    , toothed .................... COG
"    turbine ........ ROTOR, NORIA
wheeze ................. GAG, TRITE
whelk .... PIMPLE, PUSTULE, SNAIL
whelp .......... CHIT, PUPPY, TOOTH
when .. AS, WHEREAS, WHILE, THO
whenever ..................... ONCE
where; Fr. ......................... OU
where; Lat. ........................ UBI
wherefore ........... WHY, BECAUSE
whereness .................... UBIETY
wherry ...................... ROWBOAT
whet ...... GRIND, HONE, SHARPEN
whether .................. EITHER, IF
whey of milk .................. SERUM
whickered ...... BLEATED, NEIGHED
whiffle ........... SHIFT, VACILLATE
Whig poet ........................... OG
while .......... AS, UNTIL, DURING
whilom; arc. ................. FORMER
whim .. CAPRICE, FREAK, MAGGOT,
        TOY, DRUM, CHIMERA, VAGARY
whim, having a ......... VAGATONIC
whimper ........ MEWL, PULE, SNIFF
whimsical .... FANTASIA, NOTIONAL
whimsicality .... GROTESQUERY, ACT
whimsy CROTCHET, HUMOR, FANCY

whim-wham .. TRINKET, GIMCRACK
whin .. ...... FURZE, GORSE, ROCK
whine PULE, SNIVEL, YAUP, GROWL
whinny ................ HINNY, NEIGH
whip .... LASH, CAT, FLAGELLATE,
            WALE, FROTH, LASH
whip; Afr. .................. KOORBASH
whiplash, snapper on ........ COSAQUE
whip, rawhide ...... QUIRT, SJAMBOK
whip; slang .................... WHISK
whip with three lashes .......... PLET
whipping mark .................. WEAL
whirl ................. GYRATE, REEL
whirling ..... PIROUETTE, GYRALLY
whirlpool ... GORCE, EDDY, VORTEX
whirlwind in Atlantic .............. OE
whirred ........ BIRRED, REVOLVED
whisk broom .................... RINGE
whiskers of a cat ............. VIBRISSA
whiskey ...... MOONSHINE, POTEEN
whist dummy .................... MORT
whistling sound .............. STRIDOR
whit ... DOIT, ATOM, BIT, IOTA, JOT
white ............ HOAR, ALABASTER
  "   ant ............. ANAY, TERMITE
  "   comp. in soap ........ STEARINE
  "   crystalline alkaloid .... ACONITE
  "   filmy clouds ............... CIRRI
  "   fish ...................... ATINGA
  "   , growing .......... CANESCENT
  "   lead ..................... CERUSE
  "   of egg ..................... GLAIR
  "   substance used as gum DEXTRIN
  "   thorn .............. MAYFLOWER
  "   , very ................... SNOWY
white-collar girls ............. STENOS
white-fish ......... LAVARET, CISCO,
                            VENDACE
white-friars in London ...... ALSATIA
White House, designer of ..... HOBAN
White House V.I.P. ............ ADAMS
whiten ...................... ETIOLATE
whither ...................... WHERE
whitish .. ALBESCENT, MOONSTONE
whitlow ..... AGNAIL, FELON, FLAW
Whitman; poet ................. WALT
Whitsunday .............. PENTECOST
whittle ............ PARE, CUT, TRIM
whiz ..................... HUM, WHIRR
who ........................ THAT, WA
whoa; Scot. ...................... PRUH
whole PURE, TOT, UNCUT, ALL, SUM
whole; comb. form ................ TOTI
whole note; mus. ........ SEMIBREVE
wholeness ... ENTIRETY, INTEGRITY
wholly ..................... ALL, QUITE
whoop ........ CALL, PURSUE, URGE
whooping cough .......... PERTUSSIS
whop .......... DASH, PITCH, STRIKE
whorl of floweret ..... RAY, VERTICIL
whorls, having ................. SPIRED
whydah ............... BIRD, WHIDAH
wicked, the; Bib. .............. BELIAL
wicker basket .................... KISH
wicker cradle .............. BASSINET
wicket ........... ARCH, GATE, HOOP

widen .... SPREAD, FLUE, BROADEN
widgeon ....... GOOSE, SMEE, WHIM,
                            BALDPATE
widgeon; Amer. ... POACHER, ZUISIN
widgeon; genus .............. MARECA
widower or widow ............ RELICT
widowhood .................. VIDUAGE
widow's dower right .......... TERCE
widow's mites ................. LEPTA
wife ... FRAU, RIB, BRIDE, SPOUSE
  "   , bequest to ........... DOS, DOT
  "   , French for ............. FEMME
  "   killer ................. UXORICIDE
  "   , Lat. ..................... UXOR
  "   , of a ................... UXORIAL
  "   of rajah ................... RANI
  "   of Tristan; var. ........... ISOLT
  "   , one ............... MONOGAMY
  "   sacrifice; Hindu ........ SUTTEE
wig ........... PERUKE, TOP, TUFT
wig; French ......... TETE, TOUPEE
wig, worsted ................... JASEY
wigwam ...................... TEPEE
wild UNEXPLORED, FERAL, FERINE,
                                REE
  "   beast ............ GNU, ONAGER
  "   beasts .................... ZIIM
  "   boar, per. to ............ APRINE
  "   buffalo of India ........ ARNEE
  "   cat; Cent. Am. ............ EYRA
  "   cat; Sumatra .............. BALU
  "   desolate region ........... WASTE
  "   goat of Caucasus ........... TUR
  "   , growing, in the fields AGRARIAN
  "   hog ....................... BOAR
  "   hog of E. Ind. .,... BABIROUSSA
  "   hog of New Guinea ........ BENE
  "   honey bee ............. DINGAR
  "   horse; Asia ............. TARPAN
  "   sheep ................... ARGALI
  "   sheep of India ..... OORIAL, SHA
  "   swan ...................... ELKE
wilde-beeste ...................... GNU
wilderness FOREST, PARAN, WASTE,
                            ZIN, WILDS
wildly .......... MADLY, SAVAGELY
wile ....... ART, RUSE, TOY, TRICK
Wilhelmina's child .............. MINA
will ..... BEHEST, MUN, VOLITION
will, convey by .............. DEMISE
will, having made .......... TESTATE
Willard, fighter .................. JESS
Williams, of Boston .............. TED
willing ........ BAIN, FAIN, PRONE,
                            MINDED
willingly ..... GLADLY, LIEF, LIEVE
willow ......... SALIX, ITEA, OSIER,
                            TEASER, WOLF
  "   basket .............. PRICKLE
  "   catkin .................... RAG
  "   hat ................... SALACOT
  "   plaited ............... WICKER
  "   twig ........ WITHE, SALLOW
willows ......... HOLT, SALICETUM
willowy . SVELT, SLENDER, SUPPLE
willy-nilly; local Eng. ..... WAGTAIL
wily . ASTUTE, CRAFTY, FOXY, SLY
wince ...... RECOIL, REEL, FLINCH
wind, Afr. .......... SIMOON, SAMIEL

" , Alpine .......... BORA, FOEHN
" , any ........... NOSER, NOTUS
" cloud ..................... SCUD
" , coastal, of Chile and Peru SURES
" , cold ........ MISTRAL, PUNA
" , cold (myth.) SANSAR, SARSAR
" , desert ............... SIROCCO
" , dry; N. East ...... BISE, BORA
" , dry, of Madeira Is. ...... LESTE
wind, east ..................... EURUS
" , Egyptian .. KAMSIN, KHAMSIN
" , equatorial ............. TRADE
" , gentle ........ AURA, ZEPHYR
" gauge ........... ANEMOMETER
" instrument ...... HORN, BUGLE,
                HELICON, OCARINA
" , Medit. . MISTRAL, LEVANTER,
                SOLANO, PTESIAN
" , north ........ AQUILD, BOREAS
" , north-east .... CAECIAS, GALE
" , north-west .......... ETESIAN
" , per. to .. ANEMONAL, VENTAL
" , Peruvian ....... PUNA, SURES
" rope ............. COIL, WOOLD
" , science of the .... ANEMOLOGY
" , sheltered from the .......... LEE
" , soughing of the ............ SOB
" , south .................. AUSTER
" , south; Eur. ............... BISE
" , south-east ........... EURUS
" , south-west ...... AFER, NOTUS
" , south-west, strong ... PAMPERO
" storm, Asiatic MONSOON, BURAN
" , strong . TEMPEST, BIRR, PUNA
" , summer ............... AESTAS
" , to ................... SINUATE
" tower ................. BADGIR
" , warm, moist ........ CHINOOK
" , west .. FAVONIUS, ZEPHYRUS
" yarn .................... WINDLE
windfall ..... BOON, VAIL, FORTUNE
windflower ................. ANEMONE
winding ... SNAKY, AMBAGE, SPIRAL
windlass .... CRAB, CAPSTAN, REEL,
                WINCH
windmill pump ..................... GIN
windmill sail ............... AWE, FAN
window, bay ...... FENESTRA, ORIEL
window in roof .. SKYLIGHT, DORMER
window, oval dormer .......... OXEYE
windpipe ... THROPPLE, WEASAND
windpipe, sub-division of . BRONCHUS
windrow ........... SWATH, TRENCH
winds, father of ........... ASTRAEUS
winds, God of ........ ADAD, AEOLUS,
                BOREAS, ERUS, KAARE,
                NJORD, RAMMAN, VAYU
winds; myth. .......... SASARS, VENTI
windshake ................. ANEMOSIS
Windward Is. ...... GRENADA, LUCIA
wine .... VIN, ASTI, GRAVE, NEGUS,
                VINO, MEDOC, MOSELLE
" , Bordeaux type .... MARGEAUX,
                COSNE
" bottle ................. MAGNUM
" , Burgundy, white ...... CHABLIS
" cask .... BOSS, BUTT, LEAGUER
" , deposit from new ...... GRIFFE

" dipper ..................... OLPE
" dregs .............. MARC, SALIN
" , dry; Fr. ..................... SEC
" , ecclesiastical ............. TENT
" ; Eur. .................. MUSCAT
" evaporation ............. ULLAGE
" , flavoring of ........... DOSAGE
" , French .... MADEIRA, MEDOC,
                HERMITAGE
" glass .................. RUMMER
" , Hungarian ... RUSTER, TOKAY
" , India .................... SHRAB
wine jug ....................... OLPE
" , light ................. CANARY
" , Madeira ................. TINTA
" making, per. to .... OENOPOETIC
" measure .................. PIPE
" measure, Rus. ...... BOUTYLKA
" merchant ............. VINTNER
" pitcher .......... OLLA, OLLE
" receptacle .................. AMA
" , red .................. CLARET
" renews ................. STUMS
" sampler ................. TASTER
" , sherry ..... OLOROSO, XERES
" shop; Fr. .......... ESTAMINET
" skin .................... ASKOS
" , Sp. .............. CHARNECO
" , spiced .. NECTAR, SANGAREE
" , strength of ............. SEVE
" , Tagalog for ............. ALAC
" , to make ................. VINT
" , unfermented ............. MUST
" vaults .................. SHADES
" vessel AMA, CRATER, AMPHORE
" , white . SACK, HOCK, MALAGA
" with honey ............. MULSE
wines, study of ENOLOGY, OENOLOGY
wing . ALULA, ALA, PENNA, PINION
" , a; Gr. ................. PTERON
" cover ............. ELYTRUM
" cover of a beetle ........ SHARD
" , equip with ............. IMP
" of a building ...... ELL, ALETTE
" , part of a ... AILERON, FLANK
wing-footed ................. ALIPED
winged ....... FLEW, AILE, ALATE,
                PENNATE
" boots ............... TALARIA
" cap of Mercury ...... PETASUS
" elm ................. WAHOO
" fruit .................. SAMARA
" horse .............. PEGASUS
" manikin .................. KER
" , two .............. DIPTERAL
" , two; her. ................ VOL
" warrior; Gr. ........... ZETES
wingless ...... DEALATE, APTERAL,
                EXALATE
wingless bird ............. APTERYX
wing-like ..... ALA, ALAR, PTEROID
wing-like; Gr. ... PTERIC, PTEROTIC
wings of insects, nerve arrangement ...
                NEURATION
wink ... BAT, NICTATE, NICTITATE
winner ............... ACE, EARNER
winner of the Golden Fleece ... JASON
"Winnie the Poo"; by ........ MILNE
winning members, the ........ TERNS

294

winnow ....... SIFT, WIM, FAN, STIR
Winslow; Brit. .............. EDWARD
winsome .......... BONNY, MAGICAL
winter; Fr. ....................... HIVER
wintergreen, false ............ PYROLA
winter-like .................. BRUMAL
winter, of .................... HIEMAL
winter, per. to .............. BRUMAL
winter, to .............. HIBERNATE
"Winter's Tale," char. in ... PERDITA,
EMILIA
"Winter's Tale," rogue in AUTOLYCUS
wipe . EFFACE, GIBE, TAUNT, SWAB
wire brush ........................ CARD
wire, foil of ................. LAMETTA
wire measure ............. MIL, STONE
wire, platinum looped ............ OESE
wire worm ................. MYRIAPOD
wireless ................ PHONE, RADIO
wireless detector ............ PERIKON
wires, cross ................... RETICLES
wirra; Irish ...... LAMENT, SORROW
Wisconsin Indian .................... SAC
wisdom ... GNOSIS, LORE, SAPIENCE
wisdom tooth .................. MOLAR
wise ..... SAPIENT, SANE, ERUDITE,
SAGE, SAGACIOUS
wise man NESTOR, ORACLE, SAVANT,
SAGE, SOLOMON, SOLON, WITAN
wise men of the east ............. MAGI
wise saying ............ ADAGE, REDE
wiseacre ......... GOTHAM, SCIOLIST
wish WUSS, ASPIRE, INVOKE, VOTE
wish, tense expressing ..... OPTATIVE
wishbone .................. FURCULUM
wishy-washy ............. FORCELESS
wisp .......... RUMPLE, TAIT, WASE
wisp of straw ..................... WAP
wit ...... HUMOR, SENSE, TID, WAG
wit, feeblest form of ............. PUN
witch ..... HAG, LAMIA, SIREN, HEX
witch, famous ........... LILIS, CIRCE
witch, male .............. WARLOCK
witchcraft BROOM, SORCERY, MAGIC
witchery .............. HEXER, SPELL
witch-hazel ...... HAMAMELIS, OPLE
with; prefix ........................ COM
with speed; obs. .................. TIVY
with the bow; abb. ................. CA
withdraw ... AVOID, DISAVOW, QUIT,
RETRACT, SECEDE
wither .......... FADE, SERE, DECAY
Withers, Mr. .................... GRANT
with-hold .. CHECK, ABSTAIN, DENY
within .............. INNER, INTO, ON
within, comb. form . END, ENDO, ESO
without, comb. form ............. ECTO
"   fever .............. APYRETIC
"   fluid ................. ANEROID
"   , French for ............. SANS
"   inclination ........... ACLINIC
"   , Latin for ............... SINE
"   limitation of time ...... AORIST
"   polarity .............. ASTATIC
"   purpose .......... IDLY, MINUS
"   ribs .............. DECOSTATE
"   side columns ........ APTERAL

withstand ...... LAST, OPPOSE, BIDE
witness .. TESTIFY, ATTEST, TESTE
wits ............................. HEAD
witticism ....... MOT, SALLY, SLENT
Witt's planetoid ................. EROS
witty ........ DROLL, GASH, SHARP
wivern ...................... DRAGON
wizard SHAMAN, FIEND, SORCERER,
PELLAR
wizen ...... DRY, WITHER, SHRIVEL
woad ................. GLASTUM, DYE
woe ..... BANE, GRIEF, AFFLICTION
wold; Eng. .................... DOWNS
wolf .................. COYOTE, LOBO
wolf, head of a ................. HURE
wolf; myth. .............. WEREWOLF
Wolfe; Irish, poet .......... CHARLES
Wolfe, Thomas; hero .......... GANT
Wolfert; writer .................... IRA
wolfhound; Rus. ....... BORZOI, ALAN
wolfish ........................ LUPINE
wolf-like ........................ THOOID
wolframite ......................... CAL
wolfsbane .. ACONITE, MONKSHOOD
Wolsey's birthplace ......... IPSWICH
wolverine .............. CARCAJOU
woman .... BURD, DISTAFF, MULIER
woman adviser ................. EGERIA
woman, beautiful ....... HOURI, PERI,
BELLE, VENUS
woman, beloved ......... INAMORATA
woman; comb. form .............. GYN
woman explorer ................... OSA
woman, frenzied ............. MAENAD
woman-hater ............ MISOGYNIST
woman, killing ............. FEMICIDE
woman, noble .............. DUCHESS
woman, old .. CRONE, GAMMER, HAG,
VECK
woman, old; Scot. ........... CARLINE
woman ruler ............. MATRIARCH
woman's club ................. SOROSIS
woman's garment ............. BODICE
wombat; Aus. .......... GROUNDHOG
women's apartments; Gr. ... THALAMI
wonder ..... AWE, RARITY, MUSE
wonder, world ................. PHAROS
wonderful ......... MIRIFIC, UNIQUE
woo .............. COUNT, SPARK, SUE
wont .. HABIT, HAUNT, USE, DESIRE
wood, a large collection of ...... TREES
"   , billet of ................. SPRAG
"   , block, small ........ DOOK, NOG
"   , comb. form ............ LIGN(O)
"   demon ........................ NAT
"   drug, bitter ............. QUASSIA
"   dust .............. COOM, COOMB
"   , East Indian KOKRA, ENG, SAL,
SATIN
"   engraving ........ XYLOGLYPHY
"   , flexible; obs. ............ EDDER
"   gum ...................... XYLAN
"   , hard ..... NARRA, COCOBOLO,
EBONY
"   hen; N. Z. ................ WEKAS
"   hoopee ................. IRRISOR
"   horse .................. TRESTLE

295

" hyacinth ................. SQUILL
" , Ind. ..................... SISSOO
" , ironwood of Pegu ......... ACLE
" louse .................... SLATER
" , mottled streak in .......... ROE
" or grove; per. to ...... NEMORAL
" overlaying ............... VENEER
" partly charred ............. BRAY
" peg in boat .............. THOLE
" pin .............. NOG, FID, SPILE
" pores, one of the cortical ..........
                              LENTICEL
" sage .............. .. AMBROSE
" screen (war) ......... BLINDAGE
" shoe .................... PATTEN
" sorrel .............. OXALIS, OCA
" stand, top of ............... CRISS
" stork .................... IBIS
" , strip of BATTEN, LATH, LATT,
                              SPLINE
" support, in a mine ..... COG, NOG
" tar oil ................ CREOSOTE
" used for cabinet work ....... YEW
" wheel ................... GLAZER
" wheel brake .............. SPRAG
woodbine CREEPER, HONEYSUCKLE
woodchat ................... SHRIKE
woodchuck ................. MARMOT
woodcock-like ................. SNIPE
wooded landscape .......... BOSCAGE
wooden ................... TREEN
wooden brick ..................... NOG
wooden bowl ......... KITTY, MAZER
wooden hanger for carcasses .. STANG
wooden pin ....... FID, SPILE, THOLE
wooden shoe ............ CLOG, SABOT
wooden tub; dial. Eng. ............ SOE
wooden vessel ............... PIGGIN
woodland deity .......... PAN, SATYR,
             SILENIUS, FAUN, SILVANUS
woodpecker ... YAFFLE, AWL, CHAB,
             ...... ...... FLICKER
woodpecker-like; Brazil .... JACAMAR
woodpeckers; genus ............ PICUS
wood-sorrel; genus ........... OXALIS
woods ....... GROVE, SYLVA, MOTTE
woods, love of ........... HEMOPHILY
woodwind ........... OBOE, BASSOON
woody ........... LIGNEOUS, XYLOID
woody tissue.. ................. XYLEM
woody vines; genus .......... HEDERA
woof ........... ABB, WEFT, FABRIC,
                              TEXTURE
wool ................... HAIR, ANGORA
" , a small knot in ............ BURL
" blemish ..................... MOTE
" , comb ........................ CARD
" , combing of ................. NOIL
" fabric, soft ..... SERGE, TRICOT,
                              BEIGE
" fabric, thin.. DELAINE, HERNANI
" fat ...................... LANOLIN
" , fatty substance from sheep SUINT
" , inferior ...... CLEAMER, HEAD
" , knot of .............. NEP, NOIL
" , old weight for .............. TOD
" on sheep's leg .............. GARE

" , remove foreign substance from ..
                              GARNETT
" , short .................... BROKE
" , to tease out ......... TUM, TOSY
" , twisted roll of ............. SLUB
" , undyed .................. BEIGE
" , unravel .................. TEASE
woolen cloth .. (E)TAMINE, DOESKIN,
                    SARCILIS, KERSEY
woolen cloth strainer . TAMIS, TAMMY
woolen, coarse .................. COTTA
woolen fabric ... ARMURE, ETAMINE,
                    TARTAN, CASHA
woolen goods ...... MOREEN, YERGA,
                              SATARA
woolen goods, remade ........ SHODDY
woolen twilled stuff .. RATINE, SERGE
woolen vest ................ LINDER
woolen waste ..................... FUD
woolens ........................ YARNS
wooly ....... LANOSE, FLOCCULENT,
                              LANATE
wooly covering ............... FLEECE
woozy ...................... MUDDLED
word blindness ................ ALEXIA
" book ...................... LEXICON
" , deletion of last letter of a ......
                              APOCOPE
" derived from another .. PARONYM
" , figurative use of a ...... TROPE
" , Gypsy ...................... LAV
" having same sound but different
      meaning ........ HOMOMORPH
" , imitative ......... ONOMATOPE
" , last syllable of ......... ULTIMA
" , magical ................ SESAME
" , misuse of .......... MALAPROP
" of honor ...... PLEDGE, PAROLE
" of sanction ........... AMEN, YEA
" , omission of a middle letter of a ..
                              SYNCOPE
" opposite to another in meaning ....
                              ANTONYM
" put for another ........ METONYM
word puzzle ..... ANAGRAM, REBUS,
                    ACROSTIC, CHARADE
" , repetition of a ........... PLOCE
" , root form of ........... ETYMON
" sign .................. LOGOGRAM
" square, a .......... PALINDROME
" that unites .............. COPULA
" , unknown meaning ...... SELAH
" used for another ...... METONYM
" , vowel omission ........ APHESIS
wordiness .. PLEONISM, PROLIXITY,
                              VERBIAGE
words, doctrine of ........... NEOLOGY
words, legislates about .. LOGOGOGUE
words, loss of appropriate .. APHASIA
words, per. to shortening of . APHETIC
words, play upon .................. PUN
words spelled alike but pronounced
      differently .......... HETERONYMS
words, spiritual meaning ... ANAGOGE
wordy ........................ PROLIX
work ......... EFFORT, ERGON, JOB,
                    (CO)ACT, RUN

296

work by the day ............. CHARE
work, disposition toward .... ERGASIA
work hard ...... MINE, MOIL, MUCK,
        OPERATE
work perseveringly ... TOIL, PEG, PLY
work, unit of ............... OPUS, ERG
work unskilfully .... FUNGE, PINGLE
work with black inlay ........ NIELLO
work-bag .................. RETICULE
work-horse ...................... CAPO
workman ........ ARTISAN, FLOATER
workman who replaces striker .... RAT
workshop .... LAB, ATELIER, PLANT
world .... REALM, COSMOS, EARTH,
         GLOBE
world, end of; Hindu ............. KALI
world; Fr. ..................... MONDE
world; Scot. .................... WARL
world, the great ......... MACROCOSM
World-War II reporter ........... PILE
world wide .. ECUMENIC, PANDEMIC,
        PLANETARY
worldly ....... MUNDANE, TERRENE
world's largest land mass .... EURASIA
world's oldest city ........ DAMASCUS
worm ..... NAID, LURG, ESS, LEECH,
      NEMATODE, TERMITE
 "  , earth ..................... MAD
 "  , edible ................. PALOLO
 "  , fluke ................. PLAICE
 "  , mud .................. IPO, LOA
 "  , round, (any) ......... ASCARID
 "  , ship ........ BORER, TEREDO
 "  , silk ...................... ERIA
 "  , snail-like ................ SLUG
 "  that infects eye ............. LOA
 "  , thread ............... FILARIA
 "  track ................. NEREITE
worm-eating mammal ......... MOLE
worms, class of ........ NEMERTINEA
worms, larval stage ........ CERCARIA
wormwood ...................... MOXA
worn ...... SERE, TATTERED, TRITE
worn away .... ABRADED, ATTRITE,
       EATEN, EROSE
worn out .. JADED, SPENT, EFFETE,
       PASSE, SEEDY
worried ........... FAZED, ANNOYED
worry BAIT, FRET, CADDLE, HARRY,
        VEX, STEW
worrying ................... CARKING
worship ... SERVE, HONOR, REVERE,
        ADORE
worship of angels and saints ... DULIA
worship, place of ............... ALTAR
worship, system of ... FETISH, CULT,
        RITUAL
worst ..... ACE, ROUT, BAD, DEFEAT
worsts ................ BESTS, BEATS
worth ...... CARAT, MERIT, VALOR,
        VALUE
worth, thing of little ......... STIVER
worthless ........ PUTID, RACA, RAP,
    FUTILE, PALTRY, SCURVY
worthless fellow BUM, JAVEL, LOSEL
worthless leaving ....... CHAFF, ORT,
        TRASH

worthy of .......... BESEEM, MERIT
wound ...... LESION, RIST, SCATHE,
        TRAUMA
wound, discharge from a ...... ICHOR,
        SANIES
wound, lint to dilate a ......... TENT
woven with variegated color DAMASSE
wrack ........ SEAWARE, SEAWEED
wraith APPARITION, FOOD, SPECTRE
wrangle ....... BRAWL, MELL, SPAR,
      BICKER, DISPUTE
wrap . CADE, CAPE, CERE, SWATHE
wrap fishing line with wire .... GANGE
wrap, long loose .............. PELISSE
wrap up .................. ENROL, MOB
wrapper for fabrics ............ TILLOT
 "  , Japanese ........... KIMONO
 "  , morning; Fr. ...... PEIGNOIR
wrapping machine .............. BALER
wrapping, parchment ........ CHARTA
wrasse ............. CUNNER, FISHES
wrath ..... ANGER, RAGE, GRIM, IRE
wreath ............ ANADEM, CROWN
wreath; her. .................... TORSE
wreath; Hawai. .................... LEI
wreath of laurel .............. IRESINE
wreck .. RUIN, SMASH, RAZE, UNDO
wreckage ........ FLOTSAM, JETSAM
wren KINGLET, REED, SEDGE, STAG
wrench ............. SPRAIN, WRAMP
wrench, a kind of .......... SPANNER
wrest ...... ELICIT, REND, GARBLE,
        WRING
wrestling hold ........ HALF NELSON
wrestling, place for ....... PALESTRA
wrestling, throw in .............. HIPE
wrestling trick .................... CHIP
wretch, despicable ............ CAITIFF
wretch; Hindu ................ PARIAH
wretch, mean ................ CULLION
wretch, scabby ............... RONION
wretched ..... PALTRY, SAD, YEMER
wriggling ........................ EELY
wrinkle ...... RIMPLE, RUCK, SEAM,
        RUGA
wrinkled RUGATE, RUGOSE, RUGOUS,
       CORRUGATED
wrinkles, free from ......... ERUGATE
wrist .......................... CARPUS
wrist-bone ................... CARPAL
writ ........ PONE, TESTE, PROCESS,
        VENIRE
writ, judicial .. CAPE, ELICIT, TALES
writ of execution .............. ELEGIT
writ, order for ..... BREVE, PRECIPE
writ to serve in court ...... SUBPOENA
write .......... TOOTLE, INDITE, PEN
writer, Amer. ..................... POE
writer, French ................. RENAN
writer, Norwegian .............. IBSEN
writer of poems .............. ELEGIST
writing, cipher ...... CRYPTOGRAPHY
writing inst., like a .......... STYLAR
writing used in anc. manuscript UNCIAL
writing-desk ............ ESCRITOIRE
written above ......... SUPRASCRIPT
written, not ...................... ORAL

written, under ............ SUBSCRIPT
wrong ..... EVIL, SIN, WRY, CHEAT,
HAY WIRE, VICE
wrong, civil ............. TORT, MALA
wroth ............... ANGER, IREFUL
wryneck ...... LOXIA, TORTICOLLIS,
WEET, SNAKEBIRD
wryneck; genus ................. IYNX
Wyclif, disciple of ... HUSS, LOLLARD
Wyoming, city in ........... LARAMIE
Wyoming Rockies ............. TETON
Wyoming mountain ........... GENIE
wytch in Shakespeare's "Tempest" ....
CYCORAX


# X

X ................................... TEN
X, letter ............................ EX
xanthic acid, salt of ...... XANTHATE
xanthine; rel. to ............... BLOOD
Xanthippi's husband ....... SOCRATES
xanthous ..... YELLOW, MONGOLIAN
Xavier; Span. Jesuit ......... FRANCIS
xenium; Gr. ................. PRESENT
xenodochy ............. HOSPITALITY
xenon; symb. ........................ XE
xenos .............. ALIEN, STRANGE
xeres ................ JEREZ, SHERRY
xerophyte .................... CACTUS
xerotic ............................. DRY
Xingu river; India .............. ANETO
xiphoid . ENSIFORM, XIPHISTERNUM
Xnty .................... CHRISTIANITY
xylem ...................... HADROME
xylite, rel. to .............. ASBESTOS
xylo; word elem. ............... WOOD
xyloid-like ....... LIGNEOUS, WOODY
xylonite .................. CELLULOID
xylophone ..... MARIMBA, GIGELIRA,
SARON
xyst; Gr. ..................... PORTICO
xyster ..................... SCRAPER


# Y

Y, letter .......................... WYE
y-clepped CALLED, NAMED, YCLEPT
yabbi; Austral. ............. DASYURE
yacare; S. Am. ........... CROCODILE
yacht pennant ............... BURGEE
yaffle ................. WOODPECKER
yahoo .... SAVAGE, COARSE, ROUGH
yak ................ SARLAK, SARLYK
yak of Cent. Asia .................... OX
yakin; genus .............. BUDORCAS
yaksha; Hindu ................ GNOME
Yalta palace ................. LIVADIA
Yalta, sea near ... MARMORA, BLACK
Yale ............................... ELI
yam bean .......... BONIATA, KAMA
yam; Hawai. ..................... HOI

yam; Malay ....................... UVI
yam; Phil. I. ..................... UBI
Yangtse river ................. KIANG
Yank; Mickey ............. MANTLE
Yankee from Olympus . ...... NINNY
Yankee pitcher ...... LCPAT, RASCHI
yap .......... .. BARK, YELP, NOISY
yard ...................... GARTH
yard; law ............... CURTILAGE
yard, 1/16 ...................... NAIL
yard; sail tackle ................. TYE
yard measure .................. VERGE
yards ....................... SPARS
yards (1¼) ...................... ELL
yarn ......... STORY, TALE, THREAD
  "    ball ..................... CLEW
  "    , bleached ............ SPINEL
  "    , conical roll of ............ COP
  "    for the warp ............... ABB
  "    measure .... CLUE, CLEW, LEA
  "    , skein of .......... HANK, RAP
  "    spindle .................. HASP
  "    , to wind ............... WARP
  "    , twisted ....... CREWEL, FOX
  "    waste ................. THRUM
  "    winder ............... PIRNER
yarrow .... MILFOIL, SNEEZEWORT
Yasmin's daddy ................ ALY
yaud; Scot. var. ............... YADE
yaupon ............ CASSINE, HOLLY
yaw ............. DEVIATE, TUMOR
yawl; var. .................... DRANE
yawn ... GAPE, OSCITATE, CHASM
yawn; Scot. ...................... GANT
yawning ......... OSCITANT, AGAPE
yaws ................... FRAMBESIA
yclept .. STYLED, CALLED, NAMED
ye ......... THEE, THE, THOU, YOU
yea .......... PRO, AFFIRM, FOR
year, ¼ of ....... RAITH, TRIMESTER
yearly meeting of Highland association;
MOD
yearly payment; Can. .......... CENS
yearn .... HANKER, WISH, CRAVE,
HO, PINE, LONG
years, 1000 ................. CHILIAD
years; Lat. ...................... ANNI
yeast .. BARM, LEAVEN, FERMENT
yeh .......................... SCREAM
yell director . CHEERLEADER, CRIER
yellow ...... CHROME, ECRU, GULL,
JAUNE
  "    alloy AICH, BRASS, SEMILOR
  "    , as butter ............ BLAKE
  "    bugle ................ EVE, IVA
  "    calla .................... AROID
  "    , canary ............. MELINE
  "    color ...... XANTHIC, ALOMA,
AMBER
  "    color, of a pale BUFF, FLAXEN
  "    coloration .......... ICTERINE
  "    , deep ............ SAFFRON
  "    dye stuff ... MORIN, MARTIUS
  "    iris .................... SEDGE
  "    , kings ............ ORPIMENT
  "    ochre ...................... SIL
  "    , pale, pigment ....... ETIOLIN
  "    pome-like fruit ..... AZAROLE

" pond lily ................. KELP
" race ................... MONGOL
" river .............. HWANGHO
yellow-bird ............... GOLDFINCH
yellow-hammer ........ SKITE, YITE,
FLICKER, FINCH
yellow-hammer State ...... ALABAMA
yellowish ............... LUTESCENT
yellowish brown ................. TAN
yellowish catechu .......... GAMBIER
yellowish crystal substance ... MORIN
yellowish green .............. OLIVE
yellowish-green mineral .... EPIDOTE
yellowish powder ......... TANNOGEN
yellowish red ................. SANDY
yellows ..................... JETERUS
yelp .. BARK, YIP, YAP, YAUP, CRY
yelp; col. ......................... KIYI
Yemen capital .................. SANA
Yemen seaport ............... MOCHA
Yemen, town ........ DAHHI, DAMAR
Yemen's ruler .................. IMAM
yen .... DESIRE, HANKER, YEARN
yenite ....................... LIVAITE
yercum, bark yielding ........ MUDAR
yes, French for .................... OUI
yes, Russian for ................... DA
yes, Spanish for ................... SI
yet .............. AGAIN, BUT, STILL
yew .......... CONIFER, HEMLOCK
yew; genus .................... TAXUS
yield . CEDE, LOSE, RELENT, CROP,
VAIL, SOFTEN
yield gold ........................ PAN
yoke ............. CANGUE, PILLORY
yokel ...... BOOR, BUMPKIN, HICK,
RUSTIC
yolk of egg ................. YELLOW
yore; poet. ........................ ELD
young fox ........................ CUB
young hare ................. LEVERET
young herring .................... BRIT
young oyster .................... SPAT
young person ................. YONKE
young squab ................... PIPER
younger son .................... CADET
youngster .. BABY, BIRD, LAD, TAD,
TOT
youth ........ LAD, TEEN, ALADDIN
yow; sl. ........................ OUCHE
Yuan ........................... TAEL
Yucatan gentleman ............ SENOR
Yucatan Indian ................. MAYA
yucca fibre ..................... ISOTE
yucca-like plant .............. SOTOL
Yugoslav ............ SERB, SLOVENE
Yugoslav seaport ............... POLA
Yugoslav silver coin ........... DINAR
Yugoslav town ................. PIROT
Yugoslavia, city in .......... SENTA,
SKOPLJE
Yugoslavia commune .......... STIP
Yugoslavia Is. .................. PAGO
Yugoslavia, native of .......... CROAT
Yugoslavia, province in ..... BANATE
Yugoslavia, river in .... UNA, DRINA,
SAVA
Yutang ......................... LIN

# Z

Z, letter ................ IZZARD, ZED
zac; Caucasian .................. IBEX
zacate ................... GRASS, HAY
Zagreus; Gr. .............. DIONYSUS
Zambal ....................... MALAY
Zambal, language of the ........ TINO
Zambales, P. I. capital ............. IBA
zanja ........................... CANAL
zany ..... FOOL, BUFFOON, CLOWN,
SAWNEY, BADAUD, GABY, POOP
Zanzibar Sultan, titled ........ SAYID
zarf ................... CUP, HOLDER
zeal ........ ARDOR, MOOD, FERVOR
Zealand Island fiord .............. ISSE
zealot ......... DEVOTEE, PARTISAN
zealot, religious .............. FANATIC
zebra, extinct variety of ..... QUAGGA
zebra wood ..... ARAROBA, MYRTLE
zebuder, Caucasian ........ IBEX, ZAC
zenana .......... HAREM, SERAGLIO
zenith ................... ACME, APEX
zenith, point opposite ......... NADIR
Zeno, daughter of ...... PROSERPINA
Zeno, follower .............. STOIC
zero ........ CIPHER, NAUGHT, NIL,
NOTHING, BLANK, HOUR
Zerulah's son ................. ABISHAI
zest ...... FLAVOR, RELISH, TASTE,
GUSTO, GLEE, RAPTURE
zestful ................. SAVOR, SAPID
Zeus' attendant ................. NIKE
Zeus, attribute of .............. AEGIS
"     , avenger ............ ALASTOR
"     , brother of ............. HADES
"     , connected with ... TIR, TIRR,
TIU, TIW
"     , consort of ............. HERA
"     , epithet of ............. SOTER
"     , festival in honor of . NEMEAN
"     , messenger of .............. IRIS
"     , mother of ............. RHEA
"     , oracle seat .......... DODONA
"     , princess beloved by .. EUROPA
"     , sister of ............... HERA
"     , son of .... AEACUS, APOLLO,
ARES, ARTEMIS, PERSEUS,
HERMES
"     , surname of ........ ALASTOR
"     , wife of . DIONE, HERA, LETO,
MAIA, METIS, THEMES
Zidon, goddess of ...... ASHTAROTE
zigzag ....... CHEVRON, CRANKLE,
AWRY, TACK
zinc .......... TUTENAG, SPELTER
zinc alloy ......... BIDRI, PAKTONG
zinc and copper alloy ........ OROIDE
zinc arsenite, hydrous ..... ADAMINE
zinc silicate ............... CALAMINE
zinc sulphate ............ GOSTARITE
zingel; Eur. .................... PERCH
Zionist clergyman ............ VOLIVO
zip .................. HISS, SIBILATE
Zipangi Is. ................. CIPANGO
zither, lyre-like ............... ROTA

zizany ........... COCKLE, TARES
Zobeide, half sister of ........ AMINA
zodiac sign ...... CRAB, LEO, LIBRA,
PISCES, GEMINI, ARIES,
RAM, VIRGO
zodiac 10° division ........... DECAN
Zola; novelist ................ EMILE
zone .... ISLE, BELT, CLIME, GIRTH
zoogeographic division ..... EOGAEA
zoographies ............ BESTIARIES
zooid of a coral growth .... POLYPITE
zoological vessel ................ ARK
zoril .......... POLECAT, ZORILLA,
MARIPUT
Zoroaster commentator ........ ZEND
Zoroastrian ......... PARSEE, YEMA
"         scripture ........ AVESTA

zounds .......................... OONS
zuche .......................... STUMP
Zuider .......................... ZEE
zuisin ...................... WIDGEON
zule; her. ...................... ROOK
Zulu army ..................... IMPI
"    king .............. CETEWAYO
"    marauder ................. VITI
"    meeting .............. INDABA
"    spear ................ ASSAGAI
Zululand capital ........... ESHOWE
zylophone ................ MARIMBA
zymogen, substance actuating a ......
KINASE
zymone .................... GLUTEN
zythepsary ................ BREWER

300

# A

Abominable Snowman ·········· YETI
Acheson, Mr. ················· DEAN
acrobat's net ········· TRAMPOLINE
actor Brynner ················· YUL
  " Coward ················ NOEL
actor's aid ········ TELEPROMPTER
actress Andrews ············· JULIE
  " Brigitte ············ BARDOT
"A Death in the Family" author AGEE
adman ·················· HUCKSTER
administrative order ···· DIRECTIVE
"Advise and Consent" author DRURY
aerial bomb .. BLOCKBUSTER, ROC
African kingdom ·········· BURUNDI
  " republic .... CHAD, CONGO,
  DAHOMEY, GABON, GHANA,
  MALI, GUINEA, MAURITANIA,
  NIGER, RWANDA, SOMALIA,
  SENEGAL, TOGO
aimless sketch ·············· DOODLE
air bends ·········· AEROEMBOLISM
air boundary ················ FRONT
aircraft, air discharged by prop ·····
  SLIPSTREAM
  " , angle made by wing ········
  DIHEDRAL
  carrier ·········· FLATTOP
  " , control surfaces .. ELEVONS
  designer ········ SIKORSKY
  " , fairing over propeller hub ···
  SPINNER
  " , fairing over radar aerial ····
  RADOME
  " , flapping of aerofoil ··········
  FLUTTER
  " , flapping wing ··············
  ORNITHOPTER
  " , high efficiency glider ········
  SAILPLANE
  " instrument ... BAROGRAPH
  " , landing overstalled ··········
  PANCAKING
  " , main member of fuselage ···
  LONGERON
  " , movable flaps ········ GILLS
  " , navigational aid ······ GEE
  " , notice to airmen .. NOTAM
  " , radar navigational aid ······
  LORAN
  " , rate of climb indicator ······
  VARIOMETER
  " , rearward aerodynamic force.
  DRAG
  " , recovery from a dive ········
  PULLOUT
  " , simple form of parachute ···
  PARASHEET

  " , small airscrew .. WINDMILL
  " , structure for nacelles ······
  MONOCOQUE
  " , towed target ······ DROGUE
  " , trainer ················ LINK
  " , tube with open end . PITOT
  " , twisting force ····· TORQUE
  " , unit of pressure . MILLEBAR
Air Force girl ················· WASP
air maneuvers ········ AEROBATICS
air navigation system ····· SHORAN,
  TACAN, TELERAN
airplane, bombing ······ SUPERFORT
  " dome ······· ASTRODOME,
  BLISTER
  " engine ············ RAMJET
  " engine covering .. COWLING
  " formation ······ ECHELON
  " , high pressured ········ JET
  " instrument .... BOMBSIGHT
  " propeller ······· AIRSCREW
  " wing section ········· FLAP
air-raid shelter ·········· BUNKER
Alaskan highway ············ ALCAN
  " artist ·········· AH GU PUK,
  LAURENCE, MAYOKOK
  " peninsula ··········· KENAI
  " town ·········· FAIRBANKS
alcohol effective against poisoning BAL
alkaloid, colorless .... NORNICOTINE
American admiral ·········· HALSEY
  " anthologist UNTERMEYER
  " archeologist ... ANDREWS
  " artist ... CADMUS, FLAGG
  " astronomer .... SHAPLEY
  " authoress ········ FERBER
  " baritone ········ ROBESON
  " cartoonist ·········· CAPP
  " composer ······ COPLAND
  " diplomat ········ BOWLES
  " dramatist CROUSE, ODETS
  " editor ·········· MENCKEN
  " educator ····· HUTCHINS,
  KIRK, TRILLING
  " entertainer .HILDEGARDE
  " evangelist ······ GRAHAM
  " financier ········ BARUCH
  " illustrator .... ROCKWELL
  " industrialist ········ FORD
  " journalist ········ ADAMS,
  GUNTHER
  " lecturer ········· THOMAS
  " librettist ········ LERNER
  " musician ········ CONDON
  " novelist ······· FARRELL,
  FAULKNER

" painter ......... BENTON, CURRY, WYETH
" pediatrician ....... SPOCK
" physician ............ SALK
" physicist .......... SABINE
" pianist .. (VAN) CLIBURN
" playwright .... KAUFMAN
" poet ...... ELIOT, FROST, NASH, SANDBURG
" publisher ....... COWLES, HEARST, HOWARD, KNOPF, LUCE
" sculptor ....... BORGLUM
" singer .. DARIN, FABIAN
" song writer ..... BERLIN, LOEWE, RODGERS, PORTER
" soprano .......... CALLAS, KIRSTEN, MUNSEL
" statesman .... ACHESON, BARUCH, DULLES, LODGE, NIXON, RUSK, STEVENSON
" surgeon ............ MAYO
" writer CALDWELL, MEAD
amphibian tank ........ ALLIGATOR
" tractor .. AMTRAC, DUCK
"Andersonville" author .... KANTOR
anesthetic, local ..... NUPERCAINE PROCAINE, TETRACAINE
" quick-acting .............. PENTOTHAL, PHENACAINE
animated cartoon producer . DISNEY
ant, dwarfed male ....... MICRANER
" , large male ......... MACRANER
Antarctic sea ............. WEDDEL
antiaircraft missile ............ GAPA
" weapon .. SKYSWEEPER
" weapon emplacement .... FLAKSHIP
antibiotic .......... ACTINOMYCIN, AUREOMYCIN, CAPREOMYCIN, CHLORAMPHENICOL, STREPTOMYCIN
antimalarial drug .......... ATEBRIN
antimissile missile .............. ABM
aquatic organisms ........ NEUSTON
arable soil ............... AGROTYPE
Argentine workman .. DECAMISADO
argument .................... HASSLE
arid ........................... XERIC
Army proving ground .... ABERDEEN
arrange a ballet .... CHOREOGRAPH
art of space travel .. ASTRONAUTICS
artificial feeding .. GASTROGAVAGE
Asian bird ............ MYNA, PITTA
" cow .......... ZO, ZOBO, ZOH
" evergreen .............. BAGO
" gangster ............. DACOIT
" mountains ............. ALAI
" official ................... IMAM
" plain .................. CHOL
" sardine ................ LOUR
" shrub ...... TCHE, TEA, THEA
" tableland .............. PAMIR
" tree ...... AŠOK(A), BANYAN, NARRA
Asiatic plant .............. TAMPALA

" republic .... TADJIK, TAJIK, TADZHIK
astronaut Gagarin .............. YURI
atomic nucleus ........... NUCLIDE
" particle LEPTON, HYPERON, MUMESON, NEUTRINO
atom-smashing machine .............. SYNCHROTRON
atrophy ............. PANATROPHY
attack by slugging ........ MUGGING
auditory hallucination .... PHONEME
Australian ..................... AUSSIE
" bee ................ KARBI
" bird ...... COOEY, KOEL, LOWAN, MALLEE
" boomerang ........ KILEY
" cape ....... HONE, YORK
" city ..... MANLY, PERTH
" cockatoo .......... GALAH
" hut ...... MIAMIA, MIMI
" marsupial ...... WOMBAT
" parrot .............. LORY
" peninsula .......... EYRE
" pepper ............ KAVA
" prime minister .. MENZIES
" shield ............ MULGA
" tribal group ........ KOKO
Austrian biographer .......... ZWEIG
" novelist ............ KAFKA
" physicist ..... MACH, RABI
" psychiatrist ........ FREUD
" weight .............. UNZE
author Caldwell ............ ERSKINE
authoress Ferber .............. EDNA
auto shelter ............. CARPORT
automatic laundry .. LAUNDROMAT
" pilot ......... GYROPILOT
Azores island .... FAYAL, FLORES, PICO
" volcano .................. PICO
Aztec hero's wife .............. NANO

# B

Babylonian ancient city .... AKKAD, CUNAXA
" Bacchus ............ SIRIS
" chaos .............. APSU
" priestess ......... ENTUM
Bahama island ... ABACO, ANDROS, ELEUTHERA
Balaam's beast ................... ASS
Balearic island .......... MAJORCA
ballerina FONTEYN, (NORA) KAYE, MARKOVA, SHEARER, TALLCHIEF
ballet director ........ BALANCHINE
" scenario ........... LIBRETTO
Baltimore stove .......... LATROBE
bamboo, tough ............ TONKIN
band leader . LOMBARDO, VALLEE, WARING, WELK
Barbados native ................ BIM
"Barnes Dance" ...... METAKINESIS

302

Barstow, Mrs. Montagu ...... ORCZY
base: slang ...... COTTON-PICKING
baseball coach . DUROCHER, DYKES
"    executive ........ HUBBELL
"    field dispute .... RHUBARB
"    manager LOPEZ, STENGEL
"    player ...... MARIS, MAYS
baseballer Koufax .. LEFTY, SANDY
baseball's Pee Wee .......... REESE
"    southpaw ........ KOUFAX
Bashkiv capital ................ UFA
Basque game ................ PELOTA
bathing suit ................ BIKINI
Bavarian city ................... HOF
"    lake ................ WURM
"    weight .............. GRAN
Behan, Mr. .............. BRENDAN
Belgian commune .... BOOM, JETTE,
MOL(L), NAMUR,
VORST, ZELE
"    river .,.... DYLE, LEIE, LYS
SAMBRE, SCHELDE
"    statesman ........... SPAAK
Bengal singer ................ BAUL
Berber tribe .. DAZA, TIB(B)U, RIFF
Bermuda arrowroot ARAROA, ARARU
Bhutan pine ................... KAIL
Biblical charioteer ............. JEHU
"    country ........... CANAAN,
CHALDEA, PUL, SEIR
"    desert .............. PARAN
"    garment CESUTH, SEMLAH,
TSAIPH
"    giant ........ ANAK, ENIM,
GOLIATH
"    hunter ............. NIMROD
"    language ............ ARAMIC
"    measure .... BEKA, CUBIT,
EPHAH, GERAH, SHEKEL
"    queen .... ESTHER, SHEBA,
VASHTI
"    river ...... ABANA, ARNON,
JORDAN, KISHON,
NILE, ZAB
"    shepherd ............. ABEL
"    valley ........ BACA, ELAH,
SHAVEH, SIDDIM
biographical sketch ........ PROFILE
birds' air route ............. FLYWAY
Biscay island ............. RE, YEU
blackberry .......... YOUNGBERRY
Black Muslim's leader .. MUHAMMAD
Blake's symbol ................ ZOAS
Bland, pen name ............ NESBIT
Boeotian capital ............ THEBES
"    region .............. IONIA
Bohemian pianist ........... SERKIN
bomb, thermonuclear ..... NEUTRON
Bombay city ................. SURAT
"    mountain .............. ABU
book of reprints ............ OMNIBUS
Borneo, island near .... ALOR, BALI,
CELEBES, JAVA, JOLO,
MOA, OBI
"    measure ....... GANTA (NG)
"    port ................... MIRI
bosc ........................... PEAR
bowler ...................... KEELER

boxer Liston ................. SONNY
"    champions .... CLAY, LISTON,
MARCIANO
brain wave .......... ALPHA, BETA
branch line of railroad ........ JERK
"    of electronics ....... BIONICS
Brazilian cape .................. FRIO
"    dance .............. SAMBA
"    fiber ................ IMBE
"    forest .............. MATTA
"    lagoon .............. PATOS
"    pianist ............ NOVAES
"    soprano ............ SAYAO
"    tree .............. MURURE
"    wood .............. EMBUIA
breed of terrier .............. LHASA
bridge expert ................. GOREN
bright star ...... SUPERNOVA
British baby carriage .......... PRAM
"    diplomat .............. LLOYD
"    field marshal MONTGOMERY
"    guitarist ............. BREAM
"    machine gun .......... BREN
"    philosopher ........ RUSSELL
"    prime minister ....... HOME
"    prime minister, ex ............
MACMILLAN
"    prince . ANDREW, CHARLES
"    princess ................ ANNE
"    submarine detector .... ASDIE
broadcasting system ........ AM, FM
Buddhist, Chinese ................ FO
"    delusion ............ MOHA
"    form ................ RUPA
"    novice ............. GOYIN
Burmese Buddhist .............. MON
"    chief .............. BO, BOH
"    gate ................ TORAN
"    governor .... WOON, WUN
"    knife .. DAH, DHAO, DOW
"    language . CHIN, KACHIN,
KUKI, LAI, PEGU, WA
"    monk .................... BO
"    tree .................. ACLE
Burundi, capital of ...... USUMBURA
"    , king of ......... BAGAYA
"    , natives of ......... BATWA,
BAHUTU, WATUSI
Byzantine coin .............. BEZANT
"    empress ............ IRENE
"    mosaic .............. ICON

# C

Caesar, conspirator against ... CASCA
"    robe of ................. TOGA
"    site of famous message ZELA
California ............... ELDORADO
"    college or university MILLS,
UCLA, U.S.C.
"    county ..... INYO, KERN,
LAKE, MONO, NAPA,
YOLO, YUBA
"    lake .... BUENA, CLEAR,
EAGLE, GOOSE, HONEY,
MONO, OWENS, TAHOE

"     motto ............ EUREKA
"     mountain ...... PALOMAR
"     pass ........... DONNER
"     port ................ ORD
"     sea ............. SALTON
"     wine area ......... NAPA
callus ..................... TYLOMA
Cambodia .. CAMBODGE, CAMBOJA
camera .................. POLAROID
Cameroon tribe ................ ABO
Camorra ..................... MAFIA
Canadian bay ............... HECLA
"       cape ............... CANSO
"       highest peak ....... LOGAN
"       island ............. HARE
"       lake . CREE, GRAS, SEUL,
                          TESLIN
"       scientist ....... BANTING
"       statesman ........ MASSEY
Canal Zone city .... ANCON, COLON
Canary Island ............. PALMA
canvas for ski ............ CREEPER
care of the aged ........ MEDICARE
Caroline island .. PALU, TRUK, YAP
Charpentier opera .......... LOUISE
carried in space ...... SPACEBORNE
Carroll character ........ DUCHESS,
                   HATTER, RABBIT
cartoonist Low's colonel ...... BLIMP
Caspian Sea, river to . ARAS, EMBA,
             KUMA, KURA, TEREK,
                     URAL, VOLGA
Castro, Mr. .................. FIDEL
Caucasian ........ IRANIAN, OSSET,
          SEMITE, SLAV, SVAN(E),
                   TATAR, TURK
"       carpet .............. KUBA
"       ibex ................. ZAC
"       moslem .......... LAZ(I)
"       rug ....... BAKU, CHILA,
          DERBEND, KAZAK, SUMAK
"Cavalleria Rusticana" character ....
                   ALFIO, LOLA
cave enthusiast ........ SPELUNKER
Celtic dart ................... COLP
"      language ....... BRYTHONIC,
          CELTIC, CYMRIC, MANY
"      pasture ...... COLLOP, COLP
"      priest .................. DRUID
Ceylon ape ........ LANGUR, MAHA
"      bay .................. PALK
"      governor ............ DISAWA
"      hill dweller ............ TODA
"      soldier .............. PEON
"      strait ................. PALK
"      tree ................... TALA
Channel island ...... JERSEY, SARK
Charisse, dancer ................ CYD
Chatham ...................... PITT
Chaucer's inn ............. TABARD
cheese .. CAMEMBERT, CHEDDAR,
          COTTAGE, EDAM, MYSOST,
              ROQUEFORT, SWISS
"      , Belgian ........ LIMBURGER
"      dish ....... CAKE, RAREBIT,
                       SOUFFLE
"      , Dutch .... COTTAGE, EDAM
"      , French .. BRIE, ROQUEFORT

"      , green ............. SAPSAGO
"      , Italian ........ GORGONZOLA
"      lover .......... TUROPHILE
"      , Scotch ............. DUNLOP
"      , soft .................... BRIE
chemical compound ........ TRIMER
Cheshire district .... HALE, HOOLE,
                          MARPLE
Chilean city or town .. ANGOL, LOTA,
                          TALCA
"      desert .......... ATACAMA
"      island ............... HOSTE
"      mountain ... MAIPU, PULAR
"      volcano . CALBUCO, LASCAR,
                          LLAIMA
Chinese aborigine .. MANS, MANTZU
"      arch ................ PAILOU
"      blue ............... NIKKO
"      Caucasian ..... LOLO, NOSU
"      chestnut ............. LING
"      dialect ........ CANTON, WU
"      diplomat ............... KOO
"      factory .............. HONG
"      feudal state ........... WEI
"      island ...... AMOY, QUEMOY
"      laborer ............ COOLIE
"      musical instrument SAMISEN
"      negative principle ...... YIN
"      philosopher ....... LAOTSE,
          LAOTZU, MOTI, MOTZU,
                   YUTANG (LIN)
"      positive principle .... YANG
"      silk . PONGEE, SHANTUNG,
                          TUSSAH
"      sky .................... TIEN
"      sleeping platform .... KANG
"      wormwood ........... MOXA
choreographer .... (ANTON) DOLIN
Christian feast ............. AGAPE
Cipango .......... JAPAN, NIPPON
Circe's father .............. HELIOS
clarinetist Artie ............. SHAW
clay, burned piece of ........ TESTA
"      , mineral ............. NACRITE
clay mold ....................... DOD
clergyman and author ........ SHEEN
"Cloister and Hearth" author READE
cloth, camel's hair ........ CAMLET
"      , homespun .............. KELT
"      , metallic ............... LAME
"      , modern ... DACRON, NYLON,
                          RAYON
"      , wrapping .. BURLAP, TILLOT
cloud formation ........ MAMMATUS
coal, heat-treated ............ COKE
"      , size of . CHESTNUT, EGG, PEA
coat, double-breasted .. REDINGOTE,
                          REEFER
"      , monk's ............. MELOTE
coercive indoctrination ...............
                   BRAINWASHING
coffee brewer ................ SILEX
cold front .......... KATAPHALANX
Coleridge's "sacred river" .... ALPH
collapsible boat .......... FLATBOAT
collar, papal ........ FANON, ORALE
collector of phonograph discs ........
                   DISCOPHILE

304

college barracks .............. DORM  
" building ................. LAB  
" group .... FRAT, SORORITY  
" in Georgia ............. EMORY  
" in Iowa ................. COE  
" in Kentucky .......... BEREA  
colorless gas ............ BUTADENE  
Comedian Bert ................ LAHR  
"Comedy of Errors" character .......  
ADRIANA, ANGELO, LUCE,  
LUCIANA, PINCH, SOLINUS  
comet ......... BIELA'S, HALLEY'S,  
HOLMES', OLBERS, SWIFT'S  
comic strip .............. CARTOONS  
commander of NATO .... NORSTAD  
comminute into particles MICRONIZE  
communications satellite .. SYNCOM,  
TELSTAR  
Communist curtain ........ BAMBOO  
complain .................... GRIPE  
composer Bartok .............. BELA  
" Carmichael ...... HOAGY  
compound used for arthritis . ACTH,  
CORTISONE  
compressor ........ SUPERCHARGER  
computing device ........... ANALOG  
" machine .......... ENIAC  
conducive to peace of mind ...........  
ATARACTIC  
cone of silence ................. NULL  
Congo, capital ...... LEOPOLDVILLE  
" , province .......... LULUABA  
conservative .............. RIGHTIST  
Constantine's birthplace ...... NIS(H)  
constellation, altar ............. ARA  
" , balance ........ LIBRA  
" , bull .......... TAURUS  
" , crab .......... CANCER  
" , crane ............ GRUS  
" , cross ............ CRUX  
" , dipper ........... URSA  
" , dog ............. CANIS  
" , dragon ........ DRACO  
" , eagle ......... AQUILA  
" , fish ............ PISCES  
" , herdsman .... BOOTES  
" , hunter ......... ORION  
" , lion .............. LEO  
" , ram ............ ARIES  
" , sails ............ VELA  
" , water bearer AQUARIUS  
" , whale ......... CETUS  
contraption ............... GISMO  
Copperfield, Mrs. ............... DORA  
Corinth king .............. POLYBUS  
Cornish town prefix . TRE, POL, PEN  
Cossack ..... CAVALRYMAN, TURK  
" captain ......... SOTNIK  
" regiment ..... POLK, PULK  
Cote d'Azur .............. RIVIERA  
crank; col. .............. CRACKPOT  
Crete ...................... CANDIA  
" , capital of ............. CANEA  
" , mountain in .............. IDA  
Crimea ...................... KYRM  
Crimean city ................ KERCH,  
SEVASTOPOL, YALTA  
" seaport ............. YALTA  

Croatian capital ............ ZAGREB  
Cromwell, Oliver ............. NOLL  
" , Oliver, site of victory .....  
NASEBY  
crossed beet and carrot .... WOBBLE  
crystalline compound .... BORAZON,  
PABA, TEPHROSIN,  
TYRAMINE  
" substance .... ROTENONE  
Cuban bird ... TOCORORO, TROGON  
" castle ................ MORRO  
" dance ................ CONGA  
" fish .................. DIABLO  
" musical instrument . MARACA  
" premier ............. CASTRO  
" rodent ....... HUTIA, PILORI  
" tree .................... CUYA  
Cugat, Mr. .................. XAVIER  
Cush's father .................. HAM  
" son .......... NIMROD, SEBA  
Czech composer ............. FRIML  
" county .................. UNG  
" mountain ............. TATRA  
Czigany ..................... GYPSY  

# D

Dahomey tribe ........ EWE, FON(G)  
dam, Arizona—Nevada ...... DAVIS,  
HOOVER  
" , Australia ................. HUME  
" , California ............ SHASTA  
" , Canal Zone ............ GATUN  
" , Egypt .................. ASWAN  
" , Missouri ................ OSAGE  
" , South Carolina ....... SALUDA  
" , South Dakota ............ OAHE  
" , Tennessee ............ NORRIS  
" , Virginia ................ KERR  
dancer Amaya .............. CARMEN  
dangerous drug ...... THALIDOMIDE  
Danish chief .......... JARL, YARL  
" county ............... SORO  
" island .... AERO, FALSTER,  
FAROE, FYN  
" peninsula ........ JUTLAND  
" physicist .............. BOHR  
" pianist ............... BORGE  
" prince .... HAMLET, OGIER  
" sand ridge .... SCAW, SKAGI  
" seaport .............. VEJLE  
" speech ................ STOD  
" trading post .......... THULE  
" trumpet ............ LUR(E)  
Darwin's boat .............. BEAGLE  
daylight vision .......... PHOTOPIA  
"Dead End" playwright .. KINGSLEY  
Dead Sea, river to ARNON, JORDAN  
deficiency of oxygen in tissues .......  
ANOXIA  
Defoe character ... CRUSOE, MOLL,  
XURY  
Delaware county .... KENT, SUSSEX  
delayed reaction .... DOUBLE-TAKE

delay of progress .... BOTTLENECK
dentist .......... PROSTHODONTIST
deported civilian .................. DP
destructive ocean wave .... TSUNAMI
detecting device ............. SONAR
developed by radioactivity ............
    RADIOGENIC
device for amplifying sound .. MASER
"   device for taking soundings ...
    MIARIMETER
"   to determine height of clouds .
    CEILOMETER
Dickens character ............ GAMP,
  MICAWBER, OLIVER (TWIST),
    URIAH (HEEP)
Dione's consort ................. ZEUS
Dioscuri ........ ANACES, CASTOR,
    POLLUX, TWINS
disease germ killer ...... ANTIBIOTIC
dismissal; col. .......... BRUSH-OFF
displaced person ...... DP, EVACUEE
District of Columbia flower ..........
  (AMERICAN BEAUTY) ROSE
divective, opposite of .. ADVECTIVE
divergent ............... DIVECTIVE
diving sphere ...... BATHYSCAPHE
Dnieper tributary ..... BUG, DESNA,
    PSEL, SULA
Dodecanese island .. COO, COS, KOS,
    PATMO(S), RHODES
dog, Arctic ............. KEESHOND
" , French working ........ BRIARD
" , Hungarian ................. PULI
" , Welsh .................... CORGI
Dorsetshire borough ......... POOLE
drama critic .'... ATKINSON, BROWN
drive-in waitress .......... CARHOP
drug addict, slang ......... JUNKIE
drug, ataractic .......... RESERPINE
drummer Gene .............. KRUPA
drunkenness detector . ALCOMETER,
    DRUNKOMETER
dry region ............ XEROCHORE
Dumas character ARAMIS, PORTHOS


# E

E ......................... EPSILON
ea ... DEITY, EACH, INLET, RIVER
eaglewood ...... AGALLOCH, ALOES
earth satellite, U.S. .... EXPLORER,
  VANGUARD, ATLAS,
    DISCOVERER,
  PIONEER, MIDAS,
  ECHO, COURIER,
  TIROS, SAMOS,
  RANGER, MERCURY,
  ARIEL, MARINER
"   "   , U.S.S.R. .. SPUTNIK,
  LUNIK, VOSTOK,
  COSMOS, MARS
East African cedar ........ DEODAR
"   "   discoverer ...... GAMA
Ecuador city or town ...... AMATO,

CUENCA, IBARRA, LOJA,
  MANTO, NAPO
"   seaport ............. MANTA
Ecuadorian tennis player .. SEGURA
Egyptian bird .. BENU, IBIS, SICSAC
"   boat .... BARIS, CANGIA,
  FELUCCA, SANDAL
Egypt, body, mortal .......... KHET
Egyptian cape ................ SUDR
"   captain ........ RAIS, REIS
"   catfish .. BAGRE, DOCMAC
"   chaos .................. NU
"   cobra ................ HAJE
"   cotton ............... PIMA
"   cross of life ........ ANKH
"   fertile land ...... GOSHEN
"   gate .............. PYLON
"   guard ............. GHAFIR
"   headdress of ruler URAEUS
"   heaven .............. AARU
"   intelligence .......... CHU
"   lute ................. NABLE
"   month ... APAP, HATHOR,
  MECHIR, MESORE,
  PAYNI, TOTH, TYBI
"   mouse .............. JERBOA
"   oasis ...... KHARGA, SIWA
"   party ............... WAFD
"   peninsula ........ PHAROS
"   physician ....... IMHOTEP
"   plant .............. CUMIN
"   plateau .............. TIH
"   policeman ........ GHAFIR
"   port .................. SAID
electrical scanning device ............
    ICONOSCOPE
electromagnet ............ GROWLER
electron tube ........ STROBOTRON
eliminate segregation DESEGREGATE
Elizabeth I ................. ORIANA
Emile Herzog .. (ANDRE) MAUROIS
energy of the mind .... PSYCHURGY
English actor .............. COWARD
"   actress .......... ANDREWS
"   architect ... ADAM, SCOTT,
    WREN
"   author .............. POWYS
"   cathedral city ......... ELY
"   Channel, river to EXE, ORNE,
  RANCE, SEINE, SOMME
"   college ... BALLIOL, ETON,
    HARROW
"   comedienne ...... GINGOLD
"   county ............... SHIRE
"   emblem ................ ROSE
"   essayist . ADDISON, LAMB,
    RALEIGH
"   explorer . CABOT, HUDSON,
    RALEIGH
"   forest .......... SHERWOOD
"   headland ............. NAZE
"   hills ......... CLEE, WOLDS
"   historian ........ TOYNBEE
"   humorist ............. LEAR
"   noble . DUKE, EARL, LORD,
    PRINCE, SIR
"   novelist . CRONIN, HUXLEY
"   order ............. GARTER

" , down ..................... BAS
" dramatist ........ COCTEAU
" , dream ................. REVE
" , dry ..................... SEC
" , duke ................... DUC
" , dungeon .......... CACHOT
" , egg ................... OEUF
" , equal(ity) ...... EGAL(ITE)
" , eye ..................... OEIL
" exclamation .......... HEIN
" explorer .......... CARTIER
" , extravagant ....... OUTRE,
                           PRODIGUE
" , father ................ PERE
" , finally ................. ENFIN
" , five .................... CINQ
" , friend ............. AMI(E)
" , game ................... JEU
" , gift ................. CADEAU
" , God ................... DIEU
" , good .................... BON
" , goodbye ............. ADIEU
" guerrilla fighters .. MAQUIS
" , gravy .................... JUS
" , gray ................... GRIS
" , grimace ............. MOUE
" hat designer (LILY) DACHE
" , head ................... TETE
" , here ...................... ICI
" , honeysuckle ........ SULLA
" , house .............. MAISON
" , illustrator ............ DORE
" , impressionist ........ MONET
" inventor .......... BAUDOT
" , lace .............. ALENCON
" , leather ................ CUIR
" , leave ................ CONGE
" , milk .................. LAIT
" mime ........... MARCEAU
" , month .. MOIS, MAI, MARS,
                             JUIN
" movie director ........ CLAIR
" , museum ............ MUSEE
" , nail .................... CLOU
" , nobleman ..... COMTE, DUC
" , noon .................. MIDI
" , nothing ............. RIEN
" , novelist .......... MAURIAC,
                          MAUROIS
" painter ............ DERAIN
" patron saint .......... DENIS
" , permission ........... CONGE
" philosopher ........ SARTRE
" pianist ........ CASADESUS
" , pocket .............. POCHE
" , poem ................. VERS
" poet BAIF, MAROT, VILLON
" , priest ................. ABBE
" , pupil ............... ELEVE
" , railway station ........ GARE
" ridge ................ VIMY
" , roast .................. ROTI
" royal family CAPET, VALOIS
" savant .............. AMYOT
" , saying .................. DIT
" , sea .................... MER
" , shelter .... ABRI, COUVERT
" , shield .. BOUCLIER, EGIDE

" , silk ..................... SOIE
" , sister ................. SOEUR
" , son ..................... FILS
" , soul ................... AME
" soprano .............. PONS
" , south .......... MIDI. SUD
" , spirit . AME, ELAN, ESPRIT
" , star ............. ETOILE
" , style .................... TON
" , summer ............. ETE
" , sweetbreads ........... RIS
" , then .......... ALORS, DONC
" , true ................. VRAI
" , Tuesday ............ MARDI
" underground troops .........
                           MAQUIS
" , vineyard ...... CRU, VIGNE
" , wall .................... MUR
" , water ................. EAU
" , where .................... OU
" , wood .................. BOIS
" writer ......... MAUROIS
" , yellow ............. JAUNE
Freya's wife .................. GERTH
Friendly island .............. TONGA
fylfot CROSS, EMBLEM, SWASTIKA


# G

Galilee, town in . CANA, NAZARETH,
                            TIBERIUS
Gandhi ................... MAHATMA
Ganges vessel .. PUTELEE, PUTFLI.
Gath, king of .............. ACHISH
gasoline thickener .......... NAPALM
Gawain's father ................. LOT
Geb's consort .............. NU, NUT
" offspring ......... ISIS, OSIRIS
Genoese family .............. DORIA
Gerar king ............ ABIMELECH
German ................... BOCHE
" , about ................. ETWA
" , air ................... LUFT
" , airplane ............. STUKA
" , already ............. SCHON
" , angry ................. BOSE
" , animal ............... TIER
" armament works .. SKODA
" , away .................. WEG
" bacteriologist ........ KOCH
" , bank .................. UFER
" , beautiful ............. SCHON
" , because ............. WEIL
" , bed ................... BETT
" , bench .............. BANK
" , blue ................. BLAU
" , boat ................. BOOT
" , bread ................ BROT
" , breeze ............. LUFTIG
" , bright .............. HELL
" , but .................. ABER
" , cake ............. KUCHEN
" cathedral city ... COLOGNE
" , chap ................. KERL

308

| " | , cheese ............... KASE | " | inventor .......... DIESEL |
|---|---|---|---|

" , cheese ............... KASE  
" , chemist .......... BUNSEN  
" , chicken ............. HUHN  
" , child ................. KIND  
" , clean ............... REIN  
" , clever .............. KLUG  
" , clock ................. UHR  
" coal region ..... AACHEN, KREFELD, RUHR  
" , coat .................. ROCK  
" , cold ................. KALT  
" , commune ............ MARL  
" , complete ............ GANZ  
" composer ...... ABT, BACH, WAGNER, WEBER  
" , corner .............. ECKE  
" , courage .............. MUT  
" , cow .................... KUH  
" , day .................... TAG  
" , dead .................. TOT  
" , dear .................. LIEB  
" , deep .................. TIEF  
" , distant .............. WEIT  
" , district .............. GAU  
" , doctor .............. ARZT  
" , dog .................. HUND  
" , door .................. TUR  
" , dumpling ........ KNODEL  
" , earl .................. GRAF  
" , early .............. FRUH  
" , east .............. OST(EN)  
" , eight .............. ACHT  
" , eleven .............. ELF  
" , empty .............. LEER  
" , entire .............. GANZ  
" , evening ............ ABEND  
" , eye .................. AUGE  
" , far .................. WEIT  
" , fat .................. DICK  
" , fellow .............. KERL  
" , field .............. FELD  
" field marshal .... ROMMEL  
" , firm .................. FEST  
" , five .................. FUNF  
" , foot .................. FUSS  
" , forest .............. WALD  
" , four .................. VIER  
" , fruit .................. OBST  
" , full .................. VOLL  
" , glad .................. FROH  
" , good .................. GUT  
" , gray .................. GRAU  
" , green .............. GRUN  
" , guest .............. GAST  
" , hair .................. HAAR  
" , half .................. HALB  
" , hall . AULA, DIELE, SAAL  
" , hat .................. HUT  
" , head .................. KOPF  
" , heart .............. HERZ  
" , high .................. HOCH  
" , hill .................. BERG  
" , holiday ......... FEIERTAG  
" , home ...... HAUS, HEIM  
" , honor .............. EHRE  
" , host .............. WIRT  
" , hot .............. HEISS  
" , ice .................... EIS  

" inventor .......... DIESEL  
" island ...... FOHR, INSEL  
" , joke ................ SPASS  
" , lake . CHIEM, SEE, WURM  
" , late .................. SPAT  
" , lazy .................. FAUL  
" , leaf .................. BLATT  
" , league .............. BUND  
" , left .................. LINK  
" , leg .................... BEIN  
" , measles .......... MASERN  
" metaphysician ...... KANT  
" military highway ............ AUTOBAHN  
" , mind ................ SINN  
" , moon ................ MOND  
" , mouth .............. MUND  
" , narrow ................ ENG  
" , nation .............. VOLK  
" , near .................. NAHE  
" , neat .................. NETT  
" , neck .................. HALS  
" , never .................. NIE  
" , new .................... NEU  
" , nine ................ NEUN  
" , no .................... NEIN  
" , noise .............. LARM  
" , nose ................ NASE  
" novelist .............. MANN  
" , number .............. ZAHL  
" , ocean .............. MEER  
" , old .................... ALT  
" , only .................. NUR  
" , or .................... ODER  
" painter ............ GROSZ  
" , part .................. TEIL  
" , path .................. WEG  
" , picture .............. BILD  
" , poor .................. ARM  
" , prison ............ STALAG  
" pronoun . DU, ICH, SIE, UNS  
" , proud .............. STOLZ  
" psychologist ...... KOHLER  
" , red .................... ROT  
" , roof .................. DACH  
" scientist ............ MACH  
" , seat .................. BANK  
" , sentence .............. SATZ  
" , shoe .............. SCHUH  
" , shore .............. UFER  
" , short .............. KURZ  
" , six .................. SECHS  
" , skirt ..... FRAUEN, ROCK  
" , small ................ KLEIN  
" , solid .................. FEST  
" , son .................. SOHN  
" , star .............. STERN  
" , steel .............. STAHL  
" steel center ........ ESSEN  
" , steeple ............ TURM  
" , still .................. NOCH  
" , sun .................. SONNE  
" , superior ............ OBER  
" , sweet .............. SUSS  
" , table .............. TISCH  
" , ten .................. ZEHN  
" , there .............. DORT  
" , thick .............. DICK

"		, thin .................. DUNN
"		, thing ............... DING
"		, three ............... DREI
"		, time ............ MAL, ZEIT
"		, tired .............. MUDE
"		, today ............. HEUTE
"		, train ................. ZUG
"		, trousers ............ HOSE
"		, true ................ WAHR
"		, two ................. ZWEI
"		, valley ................ TAL
"		, very ............... SEHR
"		, village .............. DORF
"		, watch ................ UHR
"		, wet ................. NASS
"		, where ................. WO
"		, white ............. WEISS
"		, whole ............... GANZ
"		, world .............. WELT
"		, worth .............. WERT
"		, year ................ JAHR
"		, yellow ............. GELB
"		, young .............. JUNG
Germany ..................... REICH
Geronimo .................. APACHE
Ghana capital ............... ACCRA
Ghent's river ........ LYS, SCHELDE
giant plant .................. KRUBI
Gibraltar, legendary founder of GEBIR
"		, point opposite .... CEUTA
Gilbert island .... MAKIN, TARAWA
Gingold, Miss .......... HERMIONE
given to informality ..... TWEEDY
glands, having large MACRADENOUS
gliderlike bomb .................. BAT
G-man ........................ FRED
"Gold Bug" author ............. POE
Goya subject ...... ALBA, DUCHESS
grail .. AMA, BOWL, CHALICE, CUP
Grail, knight of . BORS, GALAHAD,
			PERCIVALE
Great Commoner ................ PITT
"Great Expectations" hero ...... PIP
Greek assembly ...... AGORA, PNYX
"		, bay or inlet ........... SUDA
"		, bondman ......... PENEST
"		, cape ....ARAXOS, ARAXUS,
			MALEA, PAPAS
"		Catholic .......... UNIAT(E)
"		church .......... ORTHODOX
"		column ....... DORIC, IONIC
"		, contest ................ AGON
"		, courtesan .......... ASPASIA
"		, dance .. HORMOS, STROPHE
"		, division ..... IPIROS, KRITI,
			THRAKI
"		drama ................. MIME
"		, earth .............. GE, GEOS
"		eparchy ............. DORIS
"		galley .. BIREME, TRIREME,
			UNIREME
"		, garment CHITON, CHLAMYS
"		geographer .......... STRABO
"		, group dancing and singing ....
			BOUZOUKEE
"		gulf ....... ARGOLIS, ARTA,
	CORINTH, ENOS, LACONIA,
		PATRAS, SALONIKA

"		, headband .......... TAENIA
"		, leather flask ............ OLPE
"		, marriage ............ GAMOS
"		marsh district ....... LERNA
"		mathematician ...... EUCLID
"		movie director CACOYANNIS
"		organization.... EAM, EDES,
			ELAS
"		, people ................ DEMOS
"		, pitcher ................ OLPE
"		resistance group .. EAM, ELAS
"		river ...... LERNA, PENEUS
"		, sacred place ........ ABATON
"		, star ........ ASTER, ASTRON
"		, subdivision .......... PHYLE
"		time .............. CHRONOS
"		tribal division .... PHRATRY
"		village .................. OBE
"		, voting place ........... PNYX
"		, word ................. LOGOS
Gromyko, Mr. .............. ANDREI
group of modeled figures .. DIORAMA
"		singing ........ HOOTENANNY


# H

Haggard novel ................... SHE
Haitian bandit ................. CACO
"		coin ................ GOURDE
"		evil spirit .... BAKA, BOKO
halftone picture ....... DUOGRAPH,
			DUOTONE
Hamath king .............. TOI, TOU
Hamilton's birthplace ........ NEVIS
Hampshire borough ....... ROMSEY
"		district .......... FLEET
Haran's brother ......... ABRAHAM
"		son ..................... LOT
Hawaiian ............. POLYNESIAN
"		, angry .............. HUHU
"		, apple ............. MAILE
"		city ......... HONOLULU
"		, cliff .................. PALI
"		, cloak .............. MAMO
"		, common or profane .. NOA
"		, cord .................. AEA
"		, feast .............. LUAU
"		, fiber ............ WAUKE
"		, firm .................. HUI
"		, fish poison .... AUHUHU
"		game ................ HEI
"		god ................ KANE
"		gooseberry ......... POHA
"		king ......... KALAKUA
"		, loincloth ........... PAU
"		mountain ...... WAIANAE
"		mountain apple ... MAILE
"		mountain range KOOLAU
"		, newcomer ...... MALHINI
"		nut ................. LITCHI
"		paper cloth KAPA, OLONA
"		pepper .............. AVA
"		pine .................. IE
"		root ........... AWA, TI

310

```
"       temple ........... HEIAU        Hungarian composer ...... BARTOK,
"       tern ................ NOIO                                 KODALY
"       timber tree ........ OHIA        "        conductor ...... DORATI,
"       windstorm .......... KONA                                  REINER, SZELL
"       wood ..... KAMINI, KOU,          "        legislature ... FELSOHAZ
                          MILO           "        measure ............. AKO
hawk, blind ................... SEEL     "        physicist ........ TELLER
hawk cage ..................... MEW      "        violinist ........ SZIGETI
hawk-headed god ............. HORUS      hut, portable ................ NISSEN
Hawkeye State ................. IOWA     hybrid bovine .................. ZHO
Hazor king .................... JABIN    hydrocarbon wax .......... MONTAN
heat-insulating board .... CELOTEX
heat-resistant alloy ...... CERAMAL,
                          CERMET
Heber's wife ................... JAEL
Hebrew acrostic .............. AGLA
helicopter landing place .. HELIPORT
Helios' sister .............. ARTEMIS                 I
"Henry VI" character BONA, CADE,
                       HUME, VAUX        ice performer ................ HENIE
Hera's son .................... ARES     Iceland bay ................... FAXA
herat ....................... CARPET     "      city or town ............ VIK
Hesperides ..... AEGLE, HESPERA,         "      legislature ........ ALTHING
                          HESTIA         "      volcano .... ASKJA, HEKLA
Hesperus' father ........ ASTRAEUS       idealistic ............... LONGHAIR
"       mother .............. EOS        Illinois county . BOND, CASS, CLAY,
Hestia's father ............ CRONOS               COOK, FORD, KNOX,
hi-fi enthusiast ........ AUDIOPHILE              LAKE, LEE, OGLE, PIKE,
"   loudspeaker ......... MONITOR                 POLK, WILL
high blood pressure HYPERTENSION         "      river .................. SPOON
Himavat s daughter ......... DIVA        "      town ..................... ZION
Hindu, alkali plains ........... USAR    incendiary bomb ........ ELECTRON
"   , ancestor of man ...... MANU        impish gnome ............ GREMLIN
"     betel nut ............. SUPARI      India ................... IND. TAMIL
"   , charitable gift ........ ENAM      Indian, abuse ......... GALI, GALEE
"   , cottage ................ BARI       "   , acrobat ................. NAT
"     disciple ............... SIKH       "     animal ........ DHOLE, ZEBU
"   , essence ..... AMRITA, RASA          "     antelope .... CHIRU, NILGAI
"   , estate ............... TALUK        "     army officer ...... JEMADAR
"   , exchange rate ........ BATTA        "     astrologer ............. JOSHI
"     foot dye .............. ALTA        "   , bail ................... ANDI
"     magic ........ JADU, MAYA           "   , banker ............. SHROFF
"     mantra .................. OM        "   , bear .......... BALOO, BALU
"     mountaineer .......... BHIL         "     bearer ............. SIRDAR
"     poet ................. TAGORE       "   , bison .......... GAUR, TSINE
"   , poison from aconite .... BIKH       "     black wood ............. BITI
"     pundit ............... SWAMI        "     boat ....... DONGA, DUNGA
"   , rice .................... BORO      "     bodice ................ CHOLI
"     rite .................. ACHAR       "     bond ................... ANDI
"     silversmith ........... SONAR       "   , British rule ............ RAJ
"   , summer residence ... MAHAL          "     calico ...... SALOO, SALLOO
hinterland ............ GRASSROOTS        "     canoe ................ TANEE
Hippocrates, drug of MECON (OPIUM)        "     cape .................. DIVI
Hittites ancestor .............. HETH     "     capital ............... DELHI
"       capital ............. PTERIR      "     capital, summer ...... SIMLA
Hollywood columnist ...... HOPPER         "     cashmere .......... ULWAN
"Home Sweet Home" composer ......         "     cavalryman ......... SOWAR
                          PAYNE           "     cedar .............. DEODAR
Hong Kong bay ............... MIRS        "     ceremonial chamber ... KIVA
hood tying under chin .. BABUSHKA         "     chamois ............. SARAU
Hophni's brother .......... PHINEAS       "     church .............. SAMAJ
"       father ................. ELI      "     cloak ............... CHOGA
Horae .. DIKE, EIRENE, EUNOMIA            "     cloth ..... SALU, SAL(L)OO,
horizontal rudder ...... HYDROFOIL                SURAT, TAT, ULWAN
hormone . CORTISONE, ESTROGEN,            "     cloth strip ........... PATA
                ESTRONE, PROLACTIN        "     coconut ........... NARGIL
hostess Mesta .............. PERLE        "     crocodile ........... GAVIAL
Huguenot leader ........... ADRETS        "     custom ............. DASTUR
```

| | | | |
|---|---|---|---|
| " | desert ................. THAR | " | vehicle ... EKKA, GHARRY, |
| " | disease .............. AGROM | | RATH, TONGA |
| " | district ......... DAYA, GYA, | " | veranda ............... PYAL |
| | MALABAR, SIMLA | " | vessel . LOTA(H), PATAMAR |
| " | dog, wild ............. DHOLE | " | vine .... GILO, ODAL, SOMA |
| " | epic ............ RAMAYANA | " | viol .................. RUANA |
| " | falcon . BES(A)RA. DHOTI, | " | violin ....... SAROD, SAROH |
| | SHAHEEN, SHAHIN | " | watchman ............. MINA |
| " | fish ........ CHENAS, DORAB | " | , wayside step ........ PARADO |
| " | flute ............ BIN, PUNGI | " | whaler .... HOH, QUILEUTE |
| " | footstool .............. MORA | " | wine ............... SHRAB |
| " | goat, wild MARKHOR, TAHR | " | wood ... ENG, KOKRA, SAL, |
| " | gorge ................. TANGI | | TOON |
| " | granary GOLA, GUNGE, GUNJ | " | xylophone ............ SARON |
| " | grant ................. ENAM | Indiana county ... CASS, CLAY, JAY, |
| " | grass .... DOORBA, GLAGA, | | KNOX, LAKE, OHIO, |
| | KUSHA, MANO, RAGI | | OWEN, PIKE, RUSH, |
| " | handkerchief .... MALABAR | | VIGO, WELLS |
| " | hawk ................. SHIKRA | Indic language .................. PALI |
| " | helmet .................... TOPI | Indo-Aryan ...... KHATRI, RAJPUT |
| " | herb .... PIA, SESAME, SOLA | Indonesian ........ BATTAK, DYAK, |
| " | hill dweller ........... DOGRA | | IGOROT, LAMPONG |
| " | hills .................... GARO | " | island .. BALI, BORNEO, |
| " | holy man .... FAKIR, SADHU | | CERAM, CELEBES, |
| " | horse disease ........ SURRA | | SUMATRA. TIMOR |
| " | hut .................... TOLDO | " | lake ............... TOBA |
| " | invader .............. SACAE | " | president ..... SUKARNO |
| " | lace .................... GOTA | informal gathering ................... |
| " | lady .......... BEGUM, BIBI | | KAFFEEKLATSCH |
| " | , land between two rivers DOAB | informed (slang) ............... HEP |
| " | landing place ........... GHAT | insecticide ..................... DDT |
| " | merchant SETH, SOUDAGUR | insulin co-discoverer .......... BEST, |
| " | midwife ................ DHAI | | BANTING |
| " | minstrel .............. BHAT | intellectual ............... EGGHEAD |
| " | musket ball ............ GOLI | inventor of escape-lung .... MOMSEN |
| " | musical instrument .... BINA, | " | " gadgets .... GADGETEER |
| | RUANA, SAROD, SARON, | " | " training airplane ... LINK |
| | VINA | involved language GOBBLEDYGOOK |
| " | nut ...................... NUT | Ionian city or town .... MYUS, TEOS |
| " | Ocean island ...... CEYLON, | " | gulf ................ PATRAS |
| | MALDIVE, MAURITIUS, | " | island . KAI, LAUT, LET(T)I, |
| | MINICOY | | PAXOS, ZANTE |
| " | ox ..................... GAUR | Iowa county .... CASS, CLAY, IDA, |
| " | pageant .......... TAMASHA | | LEE, LINN, LYON, PAGE, |
| " | palm ................... NIPA | | POLK, SAC, TAMA |
| " | panda .................. WAH | " | society ............... AMANA |
| " | partridge ............. KYAH | Iranian, angel .................. MAH |
| " | , people of N.W. ........ JATS | " | bird ............. BULBUL |
| " | physicist ............ RAMAN | " | carpet .... HAMADAN, KALI |
| " | pigeon .............. TRERON | " | civil officer .......... KHAN |
| " | plum .................. AMRA | " | dyestuff ............ INDIGO |
| " | property .............. DHAN | " | evil spirit ........ AHRIMAN |
| " | reception .......... DURBAR | " | fairy ................. PERI |
| " | road .................. PRAYA | " | fire worshipper ... PARSEE, |
| " | root ..................... ATIS | | PARSI |
| " | savant ...... BHAT, PUNDIT | " | , gate ..................... DAR |
| " | score ................. CORGE | " | gazelle ............... CORA |
| " | shrub ..... ARUSA, MADAR, | " | governor .......... SATRAP |
| | MUDAR, ODAL | " | grass .............. MILLET |
| " | sorghum ............... CUSH | " | hero ....... RUSTAM, YIMA |
| " | spinning wheel .. CHARK(H)A | " | , moon ................. MAHI |
| " | surety .................. ANDI | " | mystic ............... SUFI |
| " | teacher ................ GURU | " | oil center .......... ABADAN |
| " | tower ................ MINAR | " | river ... KARUN, TAB, ZAB |
| " | tracker .............. PUGGI | " | rug .................. SENNA |
| " | umbrella ............ CHATTA | " | sacred cord .......... KUSTI |
| " | vegetable, any green .. SABZI | " | screen ............. PURDAH |
| | | " | seaport .............. BASRA |

"        , sir .................... AZAM
"        tiara .............. CIDARIS
"        tile ................ KAS(H)I
"        trading center ..... ISPAHA
"        water vessel ...... AFTABA
"        water wheel ......... NORIA
"        writings .......... AVESTA
Irish   accent ....... BLAS, BROGUE
"        ancient capital ......... TARA
"        bay .......... CLEW, GALWAY
"        , borrowed stock ......... DAER
"        cape ................... CLEAR
"        chisel .................... CELT
"        county CAVAN, CORK, KERRY,
                MAYO, MEATH, SLIGO
"        district .................. BIRR
"        dramatist .... BEHAN, SHAW,
                SYNGE, YEATS
"        garment ......... INAR, LENN
"        lake .. CONN, CORRIB, DERG,
                ERNE, LOUGH, MASK,
                NEAGH, REE
"        landholding system  RUNDALE
"        legislature ......... EIREANN
"        luck .................... CESS
"        mountain ........ COMERAGH,
                DONEGAL, SPERRIN,
                WICKLOW
"        refugee .................. SAER
"        river . BOYNE, CAVAN, ERNE,
                FOYLE, SHANNON, SUIR
"        seaport ... DUBLIN, TRALEE
"        statesman ........... BRISCOE
"        sweetheart ................ GRA
"        , white .................. BAWN
Iroquois demon ............... OTKON
Isaac's son ................... JACOB
Iseult's husband .............. MARK
"        love .............. TRISTRAM
Isis' mother ..................... NUT
Isle of Wight borough ......... RYDE
isomeric compound ......... PYRAN
Israel ................... SION, ZION
"        , ancient city ........ BETHEL,
                SAMARIA, TIRZAH
"        , camp ................ ETHAM
"        , city or town .......... RAMLE
Israeli port .. ACRE, HAIFA, JAFFA
Istanbul caravansary IMARET, SERAI
Italian actress ... ANGELI, LOREN,
                MAGNANI
"        art center ............ SIENA
"        bandit .......... BRIGANTE
"        basso .......... BACCALONI
"        canal(s) .. CANALE, CANALI
"        Celtic tribe ........ SENONES
"        chest ............. CASSONE
"        coastal region ..... LIGURIA
"        composer  GUIDO, MENOTTI,
                VERDI
"        conductor ..... MANTOVANI
"        dance ............. CALATA,
                COURANTE, VOLTA
"        , dear .................. CARO
"        , dome ................. CIMA
"        dynasty, former .... SAVOY
"        , flower ................ FIORE
"        game ............... BOCCE

"        gulf .... GENOA, SALERNO,
                TARANTO, VENICE
"        , hand ................. MANO
"        harp .................. ARPA
"        headland .........„... SCILLA
"        island  CAPRI, ISCHIA, LIDO,
                LIPARI, SARDINIA, SICILY
"        millet ........ BUDA, MOHA
"        movie director . ROSSELLINI
"        , nothing .............. NULLA
"        painter . CANALE, GIOTTO,
                LIPPI, LUINI, ROSSI,
                SARTO, SPADA
"        , peak .................. CIMA
"        pie ................... PIZZA
"        , plateau ................ SILA
"        political party .... BIANCHI,
                NERI
"        region .......... CALABRIA,
                CAMPANIA, LAZIO, LIGURIA,
                MARCHE, PIEMONTE,
                PUGLIE, SARDEGNA,
                SICILIA, TOSCANA, VENETO
"        resort ........ CAPRI, COMO
"        restaurant ........ PIZZERIA
"        secret police .......... OVRA
"        singer ..... CARUSO, GIGLI,
                PINZA
"        soprano ........ ALBANESE,
                TEBALDI
"        tenor ........... CORFLLI,
                MARTINELLI, SCHIPA
"        verse ................. RANN
"        violin maker ........ AMATI
"        volcano  ETNA, STROMBOLI,
                VESUVIUS
ivories ...... DICE, KEYS (PIANO),
                TEETH
Ivory Coast capital ........ ABIDJAN


# J

Japan, Japanese . CIPANGO, NIPPON
Japanese administrative division .FU
"        admiral ............... ITO
"        American .......... NISEI
"        army reserve ........ HOJU
"        art with paper .. ORIGAMI
"        baron ............... HAN
"        bay ...... AMORT, MIKU,
                OSAKA, TOSO
"        Buddhism ............. ZEN
"        cape .... DAIO, IRO, JIZO,
                MELA, MINO, NOMO, OKI,
                OMA, SADA, SAWA, SUZU,
                TOI, YA
"        carp .................. KOI
"        cedar ................ SUGI
"        cherry .............. FUJI
"        class, lowest ...... HEIMIN
"        clogs .............. GETA
"        clover ............. HAGI
"        combat plane ........ ZERO
"        composition ...... HAIKAI

313

"     confection ........... AME
"     crash pilot .... KAMIKAZE
"     drama .......... NOGAKU
"     garment  HAORI, KIMONO,
                             OBI
"     harp ............... KOTO
"     immigrant ... ISSEI, NISEI
"     island . HONDO, HONSHU,
             IZU, KURIL, KYUSHO,
                            SADO
"     , Jodo deity  AMIDA, AMITA
"     mountain ............ FUJI
"     nobility . DAIMIO, KUGE,
                          SAMURAI
"     peninsula .............. IZU
"     persimmon .......... KAKI
"     plant ..... AUCUBA, TEA
"     plum ........... KELSEY
"     porgy ................ TAI
"     premier .. KISHI, KONOYE
"     quince .......... JAPONICA
"     salmon .......... MASU
"     school of painting .. KANO
"     seaport ..... KOBE, MOJI,
                        OITA, UBE
"     sliding door ...... FUSUMA
"     storm ......... MONSOON,
                         TYPHOON
"     sword .. CATAN, CATTAN
"     title ................ KAMI
"     verse .... HOKKU, TANKA
"     wasp genus ........ TIPUIA
"     wisteria ............. FUJI
Japheth's father ............. NOAH
Java capital .............. JAKARTA
" , Javanese ........... COFFEE,
             MADURESE, SUNDANESE
"     language ........ KAVI, KAWI
"     port ................... TEGAL
"     volcano .... SEMERU, SLAMET
Jayhawk state .............. KANSAS
jazz musician ................ MONK
"     pianist .............. BRUBECK
Jehiel's son ..................... NER
Jesse's father .................. OBED
"     son ................... DAVID
Jesuit founder ............ LOYOLA
Jezebel's husband ............. AHAB
"     victim ............ NABOTH
jinx ................. HEX, WHAMMY
Job's comforter ..... BILDAD, BOIL,
                             ELIHU
"     hometown .................. UZ
jockey ...... ARCARO, SHOEMAKER
John, Gaelic ..................... IAN
"     , Irish .............. EOIN, SEAN
"     , Russian ................. IVAN
Jocktan's father ............... EBER
"     son .................. OPHIR
Jonathan's father ............. SAUL
Juliet's betrothed ............. PARIS
"Julius Caesar" character . BRUTUS,
                      CASCA, CICERO,
                      CINNA, PORTIA
juvenile killings ........ TEENICIDE

# K

Kashmir, alphabet ......... SARADA
"     town ................... LEH
Katanga official .......... TSHOMBE
Kazan, Mr. ..................... ELIA
kegler ......................BOWLER
Kelly, circus clown ........ EMMETT
Kentish freeman .............. LAET
Kentucky college ............ BEREA
"     county ..... BATH, BELL,
                   BOYD, CLAY, HART,
               KNOX, LEE, LYON, OWEN,
                           PIKE, TODD
Kenya district ............ KAJIADE
"     reserve ................. MASAI
Khedive's estate ........... DAIRA
Khrushchev's birthplace KALINOVKA
Khrushchev, Mr. ............ NIKITA
Kilimanjaro peak ............. KIBO
Kill en masse ................ PURGE
King Ferdinand ............. BOMBA
"King Henry IV" character . BLUNT,
                   HAL, PERCY, POINS,
                             SCROOP
King of Bath ................... NASH
"     " Belgium .......... BAUDOIN
"     " Dwarfs .......... ALBERICH
"     " Fomorians ......... BALOR
"     " Golden Touch ........ MIDAS
Kish's father .................... NER
"     son .................... SAUL
Kol dialect .......... HO, MUNDARI
Korzeniowski ............. CONRAD
Kronos' wife ................. RHEA

# L

Laban's daughter .. LEAH, RACHEL
labor leader ...... HOFFA, LEWIS,
                   MEANY, PETRILLO,
                    QUILL, REUTHER
"     union ...................... CIO
Labrador tea ............... LEDUM
Laconian capital ............ SPARTA
Lady Churchill ...... CLEMENTINE
lake, Asia ... BAIKAL, URMIA, VAN
"     , Australia ...... EYRE, FROME
"     , California ..... GOOSE, MONO,
                             SODA
"     , Ethiopia . DEMBEA, T(S)ANA
"     , Europe, largest ....... LADOGA
"     , Finland ............ SAIMA(A)
"     , Gobi Desert .............. HARA
"     , Great .......... ERIE, HURON,
                    MICHIGAN, ONTARIO,
                             SUPERIOR
"     , Hoover Dam ............ MEAD
"     , Iran .................... URMIA
"     , Italy .... ALBANO, BOLSENA,
                     COMO, GARDA, NEMI
"     , New York . GEORGE, ONEIDA,
                      OTSEGO, PLACID

314

" , Russia ........ ARAL, BAIKAL,
BALKASH, ILMEN,
LACHA, LADOGA, ONEGA,
SEG, TOPO, VIGO, VOZHE
" , state ................ MICHIGAN
" , Switzerland . BIENNE, LEMAN,
LUCERNE, MORAT,
THUN, ZUG
" , third largest ............. ARAL
Lama, chief ................. DALAI
Land east of Eden ............. NOD
Land of midnight sun .... NORWAY
"    " Nod ................. SLEEP
"    " promise ......... CANAAN,
PALESTINE
"    " rising sun .......... JAPAN
"    " the rose ....... ENGLAND
"    " the shamrock . EIRE, ERIN,
IRELAND
"    " the thistle ...... SCOTLAND
Landolphia fruit .............. ABOLI
Langobard king ............. ALBOIN
Lao Tse concept ................ TAO
Lapetus' son ........ PROMETHEUS
"    wife ............ GAEA, GE
Lapland city or town .......... KOLA
"    sled ............. PULK(A)
Latin .......... CUBAN, ITALIAN,
SPANIARD
" , alas ..................... VAE
" , another ........ ALIO, ALIUS
" , born ................... NATUS
" , both .................... AMBI
" , brother ............. FRATER
" , bug ................... CIMEX
" , but, yet ................ SED
" , copper ............. CUPRUM
" , custom ................ RITUS
" , day ............ DIEM, DIES
" , deny .................... NEGO
" , divination .............. SORS
" , dog ................... CANIS
" , door .................. JANUA
" , earth ................. TERRA
" , equal .................... PAR
" , eternity ...... AEVO, AEVUM
" , evil ......... MALA, MALUM
" , field .................... AGER
" , force or power ........... VIS
" , from ..................... DE
" , gentle ................. LENIS
" , go ............... IRE, VADO
" , himself .................. IPSE
" , hope .................... SPES
" , lamb ................ AGNUS
" , law ................ JUS, LEX
" , learned ............. DOCTUS
" , man ................... HOMO
" , mind .................. MENS
" , mine .................. MEUM
" , mountain .............. MONS
" , needle ................. ACUS
" , nobody ................ NEMO
" , observe ............... NOTA
" , old ................... VETUS
" , order ................. ORDO
" , other(s) ALIA, ALIUS, ALTER
" , our .................. NOSTER

" , prison ............. CARCER
" , same ................... IDEM
" , ship .................. NAVIS
" , side ................. LATUS
" , sister ............... SOROR
" , skin .................. CUTIS
" , stone ................ LAPIS
" , there ..................... IBI
" , this ..................... HOC
" , thus ............... ITA, SIC
" , toad .................. BUFO
" , total ........ OMNIS, SUMMA
" , unless ................. NISI
" , water ................. AQUA
" , where .................... UBI
" , wool .................. LANA
Lawrence, T. E. ............. SHAW
layer of granitic rocks .......... SIAL
Leander's love ............... HERO
leatherlike cloth .......... KERATOL
Lebanon capital ........... BEIRUT
"    city or town ..... HERMEL,
SAIDA, SUR, ZAHLE
lecturer Thomas ............ LOWELL
Leda's lover ................. SWAN
"    son ...... CASTOR, POLLUX
Liberian coast ................. KRU
"    native ............ VAI, VEI
"    town ................. SINO
Libyan gulf ................. SIDRA
"    measure .......... DRA, PIK
"    oasis ................ SEBHA
"    town ................ DERNA
Liechtenstein capital ........ VADUZ
lighter-than-air craft .. AEROSTAT
liquid for cooling cylinders  COOLANT
"    soap ................ NAPALM
literary critic . BROOKS, FADIMAN
Little Russia ... POLAND, UKRAINE
Livonian .......... ESTH, LETT, LIV
Locrine's father ............. BRUT
Lohengrin's bride ............. ELSA
Lollobrigida ................... GINA
Lolo .................... NOSU
Lombardy king ............. ALBOIN
Louisiana county .......... PARISH
"    parish . ACADIA, ALLEN,
CADDO, GRANT, SABINE,
TENSAS, WINN
Louis XVI nickname .......... VETO
"Love's Labor Lost" character .......
BIRON, BOYET, DULL,
DUMAIN, MARIA
lower frequencies loudspeaker ........
WOOFER
Loyalty island ......... LIFU, UVEA
Lucius Domitius Ahenobarbus ..NERO
lunar mission ............. APOLLO
luxurious .................... PLUSH
Lynette's knight ............ GARETH

# M

"Macbeth" character ....... ANGUS,
BANQUO, DUFF, HECATE,
LENNOX, MACDUFF, ROSS

315

Macedonia, ancient capital ... PELLA
"         city or town ... DRAMA,
                EDESSA, PYDNA
"         king ............. ABGAR
Madeira island capital .... FUNCHAL
Madrileno ................... SENOR
mahua butter .... FULWA, PHULWA
Maine bay ................... CASCO
"     college ...... BATES, COLBY
"     county KNOX, WALDO, YORK
"     island .................. ORRS
"     motto ............... DIRIGO
Majorca city ............... PALMA
"     island ........ IBIZA, IVIZA
Malabar canoe ............. TONEE
"         measure ............... ADY
"         people ................ NAIR
Malay boat ................... TOUP
"     canoe .......... PRAH, PROA
"     chief ............ DATO, DATU
"     city or town ........... IPOH
"     cloth .................. BATIK
"     , condition ............ LATA
"     island . BALI, JAVA, PENANG,
                SUMATRA, TIMOR
"     isthmus .................. KRA
"     , mental aberration ...... LATA
"     mountain ............ TAHAN
"     palm ......... ARENG, TARA
Maldive Island capital ....... MALE
Malta island ........ GOZO, MELITA
"     wind GREGALE, LEVANTER
Man, Isle of, capital ...... DOUGLAS
"Man Without a Country" .. NOLAN
Manchu tribe ........ DAUR, DAURI
Manchurian town .... AIGUN, PENKI
Manu, laws of ................ SUTRA
Marceau, Mr. .............. MARCEL
Mariana Island ............... ROTA
marihuana cigarette ....... REEFER
Mark Twain ................... SAM
Marquand's detective .......... MOTO
Marshall island EBON, MILI, NAMUR,
                RALIK, RATIK
Martinique volcano .......... PELEE
Maryland county . CECIL, HOWARD,
                KENT, TALBOT
Massachusetts city or town .. LYNN,
                SALEM, WARE
"         county .... BRISTOL,
                DUKES, ESSEX, SUFFOLK
Mayan year ................... HAAB
"     , year-end day of calendar ....
                UAYEB
means of spreading propaganda ......
                AGITPROP
"Measure for Measure" character ....
                ANGELO, ELBOW,
                FROTH, JULIET
mechanical game . PINBALL,
                COCKAMAROO
Mediterranean grass .......... DISS
"             gulf .......... TUNIS
"             herb genus .... AMMI
"             island ....... CAPRI,
                CRETE, ELBA,
                MALTA, SICILY
"             resort .. COMO, NICE

"         , river to AUDE, EBRO,
                JUCAR, NILE, RHONE
"         tree .. CAROB, OLEA
Medusa ................... GORGON
Medusa's sister .......... EURYALE
Medusa, slain by .......... PERSEUS
Mehitabel ...................... CAT
"Mein Kampf" author ...... HITLER
Melville character .... AHAB, MOBY
"         novel ................. TYPEE
member of swing band ...... HEPCAT
men's underwear .......... SKIVVIES
Menuhin, Mr. ............... YEHUDI
"Merchant of Venice" character .....
                JESSICA, LORENZO,
                PORTIA, SHYLOCK, TUBAL
mercy killing ......... EUTHANASIA
"Merry Widow" composer .... LEHAR
"Merry Wives of Windsor" character.
                CAIUS, FENTON, FORD,
                NYM, PAGE, PISTOL,
                ROBIN, RUGBY
method of aircraft navigation NAVAR
Mexican American .......... GRINGO
"         basket grass ........ OTATE
"         cactus ............ MESCAL
"         composer .......... CHAVEZ
"         dove .................. INCA
"         drug ................ JALAP
"         painter . OROZCO, RIVERA,
                SIQUEIROS
"         resort ........... ACAPULCO
"         river . CONCHOS, FUERTE,
                SALADO, TONTO, YAQUI
"         state . COLIMA, DURANGO,
                JALISCO, SONORA,
                TABASCO, YUCATAN
"         volcano ........ PARTICUTIN
Michigan county ..... ALGER, BAY,
                CASS, CLARE, DELTA,
                IONIA, IOSCO, IRON, KENT,
                LAKE, LUCE, WAYNE
"         river ................. CASS
middle-class ......... MIDDLEBROW
Midianite king ... EVI, HUR, REBA,
                ZUR
"Midsummer-Night's Dream"
    character ....... EGEUS, HERMIA,
                OBERON, PUCK, QUINCE,
                SNOUT, SNUG, THESEUS,
                THISBE
migratory worker .............. JOAD
mile runner ................. LANDY
military store .................... PX
million deaths ........ MEGADEATH
"         tons .............. MEGATON
Minerva ........ ATHENA, AZALEA
miniature projection apparatus ......
                MOVIOLA
Minnesota county ...... CASS, CLAY,
                COOK, LAKE, LYON,
                PINE, POLK, POPE, RICE,
                ROCK, SCOTT, TODD
Mishna(h) festivals .......... MOED
"         section .......... ABOT(H)
Mississippi county ... CLAY, HINDS,
                LEE, PIKE, TATE, YAZOO
miss a cue ........ BUNGLE, FLUFF

Missouri county ...... ADAIR, CASS, CLAY, COLE, DADE, DENT, HOLT, IRON, KNOX, LINN, PIKE, POLK, RALLS, RAY, OZARK
Mitchell, Helen Porter ..... MELBA
"mobile" sculptor .......... CALDER
moccasin ................... LOAFER
Mohammedan, ablution before prayer. WUDU
"    blacksmith .. LOHAR
"    blood relationship .... NASAB
"    capturer of Jerusalem. OMAR
"    convert, early ANSAR
"    shrine ....... KAABA
Mohicans, last of ........... UNCAS
Moldavia ................. ROMANIA
Moldavia town ...... IASI, JASSY
Molotov cocktail .............. BOMB
Molucca island .. CERAM, MALUKU
Mongol ..... BURIAT, ELEUT, HU, KALMUCK, KHALKHA, SHARRA
"    , dynasty .............. YUAN
"    , Siberian ............. TATAR
"    tribe ................. SHAN
Montana city ............. HELENA
"    county . BLAINE, CARTER, HILL, LAKE, PARK, TETON, TOOLE
"Monte Cristo" author ....... DUMAS
"    "    hero ........ DANTES
More's land ................. UTOPIA
"    work ................. UTOPIA
Moro prince ................. CACHIL
Moroccan .............. MOOR, RIFF
"    general .............. KAID
"    land ................. GISH
"    region ............ ER, RIF
moron ...................... AMENT
Morro castle site .......... HAVANA
Mossi language .......... MO, MOLE
Mount of Olives ............. OLIVET
mountaineering ring .. KARABINER
"    shoes ................
KLETTERSCHUHE
movie director .............. KAZAN
"    process ...... TECHNICOLOR
"    producer ........ PREMINGER
Mozambique native ............. YAO
Mrs. Montagu Barstow ...... ORCZY
"Much Ado About Nothing" character.
ANTONIO, CLAUDIO, HERO, LEONATO, URSULA
Muhammad ................. ELIJAH
Munro, H. H. ................. SAKI
musical group ................ COMBO
"    instrument .... NOVACHORD
mystery story .......... WHODUNIT

# N

Naples ..................... NAPOLI
"    king ................. MURAT
"    secret society ..... CAMORRA

Napoleon's battle ..... ACRE, JENA, ULM, WATERLOO
"    brother-in-law .. MURAT
"    island . CORSICA, ELBA, HELENA
Nash, Richard ................. BEAU
Naval Reserve girl ........... WAVE
"    safe-conduct pass .. NAVCERT
navigation system .. LORAN, SONAR
Nazi concentration camp .. DACHAU
"    guards .. SCHUTZSTAFFEL. SS
Near East .................. LEVANT
"    East native .... ARAB, TURK
Nebraska city ............... OMAHA
"    county ..... BOYD, BURT, CASS, CLAY, GAGE, HALL, HOLT, KNOX, LOUP, POLK, ROCK, YORK
Nepal district ................ TERAI
"    mongoloid ............. RAIS
"    mountain EVEREST, LHOTSE
"    native ................... KHA
"    peak ..................... API
"    tribesman ............. AOUL
"    warrior ............. GURKHA
Nereid chief ............... THETIS
Netherlands ......... FRIESLAND, HOLLAND
"    aborigine ......... CELT
"    anatomist ......... RAU
"    badger ............. DAS
"    botanist .... (DE)VRIES
"    capital .. AMSTERDAM
"    colonist ........... BOER
"    cupboard .......... KAS
"    dialect ........... TAAL
"    island .......... ARUBA, CELEBES, TEXEL
"    merchant's league .......
HANSE
"    painter ... BOSCH, DOU, EYCK, HALS, HOET, LELY, LIS
"    poet ......... DECKER
"    political party . GEUZEN
"    river . EMS, LEK, MAAS, SCHELDT, WAAL
"    scholar ...... ERASMUS
"    ship .. GALLIOT, KOFF
"    uncle .............. EME
"    woman .......... FROW
Nevada county . ELKO, LYON, NYE, STOREY, WASHOE
New Caledonia bird .......... KAGU
New Deal agency . CCC, NRA, NYA, TVA
New Englander ................ YANK
newfangled .................. NOVEL
Newfoundland cape ............ RACE
New Hampshire county ........ COOS
"    "    mountain ... FLUME
New Hebrides island ... EFATE, EPI, TANA
"    port .............. VILA
New Jersey county BERGEN, ESSEX, HUDSON, MERCER, MORRIS, OCEAN, PASSAIC, SALEM, SUSSEX, UNION

" " river .............. TOMS
New Mexico county ..... EDDY, LEA,
LUNA, MORA
" " region, old name COBOLA
" " town ............ RATON
" " turpentine tree TARATA
news commentator ...... BRINKLEY,
CRONKITE, HUNTLEY
New York baseball team ...... METS
" " city ............... OLEAN
" " county . ESSEX, GREENE,
LEWIS, TIOGA, YATES
" " mountain .. BEAR, SLIDE
" " subway .... BMT, IND, IRT
" " university or college .......
ALFRED, COLGATE, CORNELL,
ELMIRA, HOBART, VASSAR
New Zealand bell bird ....... MAKO
" " caterpillar ... AWETO,
WERI
" " cattail ........ RAUPO
" " , compensation .... UTU
" " corn .......... KANGA
" " fish ........ HIKU, IHI
" " fort .......... PA, PAH
" " harbor ........ OTAGO
" " island .......... NIUE
" " pigeon .......... KUKU
" " plant .......... KARO
" " raft ............. MOKI
" " rail bird KOKO, WEKA
" " shark .......... MAKO
" " vine .............. AKA
" " wood robin ...... MIRO
Nicaragua city or town ....... LEON,
MANAGUA
Nicotinic acid ................. NIACIN
Niger, mouth of ............... NUN
Nigerian region .............. BENIN
" river ...... BENUE, NIGER
Nile River deified .............. HAPI
" " bird ................. IBIS
" " boat .... BARIS, CANGIA
" " city or town ABRI, ARGO,
ASYUT, IDFU, ISNA,
QINA, QUS
" " native ............ NILOT
" " Negro .... JUR, LUO, SUK
" " region ............. NUBIA
" " , source of ......... TSANA
" " valley depression .. KORE
Nobel Prize scientist .......... LIBBY
noninflammable gas .......... FREON
Norse Adam . ASK(R), BURE, BURI
" dialect ................... NORN
" epic .................... EDDA
" explorer .......... ERIC, LEIF
" hero ................. EGIL(L)
" letter ................... RUNE
" night ............ NATT, NOTT
" poem .................... RUNE
North Carolina cape ......... FEAR,
HATTERAS
" " county . ASHE, CLAY,
DARE, HOKE, HYDE,
LEE, NASH, PIT,
POLK, WAKE
" " river ...... PEE DEE

" " sound ......... CORE
" " university .... DUKE
North Dakota city ............ FARGO
" " county . CASS, DUNN,
EDDY
North Pole discoverer ........ PERRY
" sea port . BERGEN, BREMEN,
HULL
" " , river to ... ALLER, DEE,
EIDER, ELBE, EMS,
MEUSE, RHINE, TEES,
TYNE
Norwegian soprano ...... FLAGSTAD
" statesman ........... LIE
nostalgia ............. NOSTOMANIA
Nova Scotia bay ............. FUNDY
" " cape BRETON, GEORGE,
SABLE
novelist Huxley ............. ALDOUS
" Vidal ................... GORE
nuclear chemist ........... SEABORG
" physics ....... NUCLEONICS
" pile .............. REACTOR
nursery furniture ........ PLAYPEN
Nyasaland prime minister .... BANDA


# O

oil-bearing seed ............. JABOTY
oil, lubricating ................. LUBE
olive-shaped ............... OLIVARY
one careless with trash .. LITTERBUG
one of beat generation .... BEATNIK
opera executive ................ BING
optical lens ............... CONTACT
orchestra conductor .... STOKOWSKI
" leader ............. CUGAT
ornamental belt ........... CINCHER


# P

paper bonded under heat .... PAPREG
parachute strap .............. RISER
" surface .......... CANOPY
parade of cars .......... AUTOCADE,
MOTORCADE
part of hearing aid ...... EARMOLD
personality test ....... RORSCHACH
pertaining to heat energy ............
THERMONUCLEAR
" " old age diseases ........
GERIATRIC
Peruvian singer ............. SUMAC
Philippine statesman ....... ROMULO
phonograph record ........ PLATTER
photograph featuring legs; col. .......
CHEESECAKE
physician and philosopher ............
SCHWEITZER
pianist Henderson .......... SKITCH

# S

"	loudspeaker ........ TWEETER
smoke and fog ................. SMOG
"	"	haze .............. SMAZE
snake, poisonous .............. HABU
soapless soap ......... DETERGENT
soften meat fibers .... TENDERIZE
sound-absorbing pane .......... GOBO
soup, curried ........ SENEGALESE
"	, South American ... GAZPACHO
Soviet statesman ........ GROMYKO,
	MIKOYAN, MO' OTOV
space dog .................. STREIKA
space for refueling APRON, TARMAC
Space monkey ................. ENOS
"	traveler ........ ASTRONAUT,
	COSMONAUT, COSMONETTE
"	vehicle ........ SPACECRAFT,
	SPACEMANSHIP,
	SPACESHIP
Spanish cellist .............. CASALS
"	composer ............ FALLA
"	guitarist .......... SEGOVIA
"	painter .... PICASSO, SERT
"	pianist .............. ITURBI
speed of sound ............... MACH
spiritual healing ........ PSYCHIASIS
splitting of an atom ........ FISSION
Stan, the Man .............. MUSIAL
starvation ............. LIMOCTONIA
State flower, Alabama .. CAMELLIA
"	"	, Alaska .................
	FORGET-ME-NOT
"	"	, Arizona ...... (GIANT)
	CACTUS, SAGUARO
"	"	, Arkansas ...... APPLE
	BLOSSOM
"	"	, California .. (GOLDEN)
	POPPY
"	"	, Colorado . COLUMBINE
"	"	, Connecticut ............
	(MOUNTAIN) LAUREL
"	"	, Delaware ...... PEACH
	BLOSSOM
"	"	, Florida ...... ORANGE
	BLOSSOM
"	"	, Georgia	(CHEROKEE)
	ROSE
"	"	, Hawaii ...... HIBISCUS
"	"	, Idaho ....... SYRINGA,
	(LEWIS)
	MOCK-ORANGE
"	"	, Illinois . (BUTTERFLY)
	VIOLET
"	"	, Indiana ........ PEONY
"	"	, Iowa ... (WILD) ROSE
"	"	, Kansas .. SUNFLOWER
"	"	, Kentucky GOLDENROD
"	"	, Louisiana .. MAGNOLIA
	(GRANDIFLORA)
"	"	, Maine ... (PINE CONE
	AND) TASSEL
"	"	, Maryland ..... BLACK-
	EYED SUSAN
"	"	, Massachusetts ..........
	MAYFLOWER
	(TRAILING) ARBUTUS

"	"	, Michigan ....... APPLE
	BLOSSOM
"	"	, Minnesota .. (SHOWY)
	LADY'S-SLIPPER
"	"	, Mississippi . MAGNOLIA
"	"	, Missouri . HAWTHORN
"	"	, Montana	BITTERROOT
	(LEWISIA)
"	"	, Nebraska GOLDENROD
"	"	, Nevada .. SAGEBRUSH
"	"	, New England . BLUETS,
	RUE
"	"	, New Hampshire ........
	(PURPLE) LILAC
"	"	, New Jersey ; (PURPLE)
	VIOLET
"	"	, New Mexico .... YUCCA
"	"	, New York ....... ROSE
"	"	, North Carolina ........
	DOGWOOD
"	"	, North Dakota .. (WILD
	PRAIRIE) ROSE
"	"	, Ohio ...... (SCARLET)
	CARNATION
"	"	, Oklahoma	MISTLETOE
"	"	, Oregon ..... (OREGON)
	GRAPE
"	"	, Pennsylvania ..........
	(MOUNTAIN) LAUREL
"	"	, Rhode Island .. VIOLET
"	"	, South Carolina ........
	(YELLOW) JESSAMINE
"	"	, South Dakota .PASQUE
"	"	, Tennessee ........ IRIS
"	"	, Texas .. BLUEBONNET
"	"	, Utah ...... SEGO LILY
"	"	, Vermont ........ (RED)
	CLOVER
"	"	, Virginia . (AMERICAN)
	DOGWOOD
"	"	, Washington .. (COAST)
	RHODODENDRON
"	"	, West Virginia ..........
	(ROSEBAY)
	RHODODENDRON
"	"	, Wisconsin .... (WOOD)
	VIOLET
"	"	, Wyoming ... (INDIAN)
	PAINTBRUSH
Stengel, Mr. ................... CASEY
Stevenson, Mr. ................ ADLAI
stratified deposit ............. VARVE
strikebreaker ........... FINK, SCAB
strip of public land .... GREEN BELT
stripteaser .............. ECDYSIAST
style of jazz .................. BEBOP
submarine mountain ........ GUYOT
summer theater circuit .. STRAWHAT
superhighway ....... EXPRESSWAY,
	FREEWAY
supplies by aircraft ......... AIRLIFT
suppression of ideas . BOOKBURNING
Swedish soprano .......... NILSSON
Swiss psychiatrist ..... RORSCHACH
synthetic fiber .............. SARAN
"	material .......... DYNEL
"	rubber . AMERIPOL, BUNA

# T

Taiwan, capital of .......... TAIPEH
tank farming ....... HYDROPONICS
tear gas .............. LACRIMATOR
Tebaldi, soprano ............ RENATA
television ad ........ COMMERCIAL
ten amperes ............ ABAMPERE
Tennessee Ernie .............. FORD
terrier, kind of ..... MANCHESTER
theatrical producer . LEVIN, SCHARY
"The Edge of Sadness" author .......
                                  O'CONNOR
"The Good Earth" author .... BUCK
thermionic tube ........ KENOTRON
timorous person .... MILQUETOAST
tiny embroidery beads .... SOUFFLE
"To Kill a Mockingbird" author ..LEE
tooth extraction ....... EXODONTIA
tractor ................. BULLDOZER
tranquilizer ... LIBRIUM, MILTOWN
transparent plastic .......... LUCITE
treat against shrinkage . SANFORIZE
treatment of drinking water ..........
                                 FLUORIDATION
trick or scheme ............ GIMMICK
trousers .................... SLACKS
truth serum ............ PENTOTHAL
Tse-tung ....................... MAO
TV broadcast, (col.) ...... TELECAST
TV camera tube .......... ORTHICON
TV screen coating ...... PHOSPHOR
typewriter, form of ...... TELETYPE

# U

"Ulysses" author ............. JOYCE
underwater apparatus ........ SCUBA
    "     swimmer ..... FROGMAN
unit of acceleration ............. GAL
  "  "  circuit power ........... VAR
  "  "  conductance ..... ABHENRY,
                                    ABMHO
  "  "  force .............. NEWTON
  "  "  illumination ............ PHOT
  "  "  mass .... GEEPOUND, SLUG
  "  "  radiation ......... RAD, REP
  "  "  sound absorption ..... SABIN
  "  "  telegraphic speed ..... BAUD
  "  "  TNT power ........ KILOTON
Unprincipled politician ................
                             SNOLLYGOSTER
U.S. overseas corps .......... PEACE
USSR premier ....... KHRUSHCHEV
U Thant, Mr. ................. SITHU

# V

vacuum tube ............ HEPTODE,
    KLYSTRON, MAGNETRON,
                       MEGATRON
ventriloquist ..... (EDGAR) BERGEN
Vietnam, South, former president ....
                                   DIEM
  "  ,  "  , premier ... KHANH
  "  ,  "  , principal city .......
                                  SAIGON
violinist ......... ELMAN, HEIFETZ,
      MENUHIN, OISTRAKH
  "    Bull .................... OLE
vitamin(e) B ............. ANEURIN,
                      THIAMIN(E)
  "    G .......... RIBOFLAVIN

# W

warfare, nonaggressive .. SITZKRIEG
war gas ................... ADAMSITE
water exhibition ........ AQUACADE
weather-resistant plywood .. IMPREG
weed killer WEEDICIDE, HERBICIDE
welfare organization .......... CARE
West Indies music ........ CALYPSO
wipe out . ELIMINATE, LIQUIDATE
work shift ... GRAVEYARD, SWING
  "  while on relief ... MOONLIGHT
worship of machines ...................
                     MECHANOLATRY
writer Huxley .... ALDOUS, JULIAN
  "  Maurois ................ ANDRE
  "  of gags ............ GAGSTER

# X

X-ray photography . PLANIGRAPHY,
                     TOMOGRAPHY

# Y

yellow pigment ...... ZEAXANTHIN

# Z

Zweig, Mr. .................. STEFAN